Contemporary
Literary Criticism

Yearbook 1988

Guide to Gale Literary Criticism Series

When you need to review criticism of literary works, these are the Gale series to use:

If the author's death date is: **You should turn to:**

After Dec. 31, 1959
(or author is still living)

CONTEMPORARY LITERARY CRITICISM

for example: Jorge Luis Borges, Anthony Burgess,
William Faulkner, Mary Gordon,
Ernest Hemingway, Iris Murdoch

1900 through 1959

TWENTIETH-CENTURY LITERARY CRITICISM

for example: Willa Cather, F. Scott Fitzgerald,
Henry James, Mark Twain, Virginia Woolf

1800 through 1899

NINETEENTH-CENTURY LITERATURE CRITICISM

for example: Fedor Dostoevski, Nathaniel Hawthorne,
George Sand, William Wordsworth

1400 through 1799

LITERATURE CRITICISM FROM 1400 TO 1800
(excluding Shakespeare)

for example: Anne Bradstreet, Daniel Defoe,
Alexander Pope, François Rabelais,
Jonathan Swift, Phillis Wheatley

SHAKESPEAREAN CRITICISM

Shakespeare's plays and poetry

Antiquity through 1399

CLASSICAL AND MEDIEVAL LITERATURE CRITICISM

for example: Dante, Homer, Plato, Sophocles, Vergil,
the Beowulf Poet

Gale also publishes related criticism series:

CHILDREN'S LITERATURE REVIEW

This series covers authors of all eras who have written for the
preschool through high school audience.

SHORT STORY CRITICISM

This series covers the major short fiction writers of all nationalities
and periods of literary history.

ISSN 0091-3421

Volume 55

Contemporary Literary Criticism

Yearbook 1988

The Year in Fiction, Poetry, Drama,
and World Literature and the Year's
New Authors, Prizewinners, Obituaries,
and Outstanding Literary Events

Roger Matuz
EDITOR

Mary K. Gillis
ASSISTANT EDITOR,
CLC YEARBOOK

Gale Research Inc.

DETROIT • NEW YORK • FORT LAUDERDALE • LONDON

STAFF

Roger Matuz, *Editor*

Sheila Fitzgerald, Sean R. Pollock, David Segal, Robyn V. Young, *Associate Editors*

Mary K. Gillis, *Assistant Editor,* CLC Yearbook

Cathy Falk, Ruth P. Feingold, Susan Miller Harig, Anne Sharp, Susanne Skubik,
Bridget Travers, Debra A. Wells, *Assistant Editors*

Jeanne A. Gough, *Production & Permissions Manager*
Linda M. Pugliese, *Production Supervisor*
Jennifer Gale, Suzanne Powers, Maureen A. Puhl, Lee Ann Welsh, *Editorial Associates*
Donna Craft, Christine A. Galbraith, David G. Oblender, Linda M. Ross,
Editorial Assistants

Victoria B. Cariappa, *Research Supervisor*
Karen D. Kaus, Eric Priehs, Maureen R. Richards, Mary D. Wise, *Editorial Associates*
Heidi N. Fields, Judy L. Gale, Filomena Sgambati, *Editorial Assistants*

Sandra C. Davis, *Permissions Supervisor (Text)*
H. Diane Cooper, Kathy Grell, Josephine M. Keene, Kimberly F. Smilay,
Permissions Associates
Lisa M. Lantz, Camille P. Robinson, Shalice Shah, Denise M. Singleton,
Permissions Assistants

Patricia A. Seefelt, *Permissions Supervisor (Pictures)*
Margaret A. Chamberlain, *Permissions Associate*
Pamela A. Hayes, Lillian Quickley, *Permissions Assistants*

Mary Beth Trimper, *Production Manager*
Anthony J. Scolaro, *Production Assistant*

Arthur Chartow, *Art Director*
C. J. Jonik, *Keyliner*

Laura Bryant, *Production Supervisor*
Louise Gagné, *Internal Production Associate*
Shelly Andrews, Sharana Wier, *Internal Production Assistants*

Contents

Preface   vii

Acknowledgments   xi

Authors Forthcoming in *CLC*   xvii

The Year in Review

The Year in Fiction. 3
Robert Wilson

The Year in Poetry 7
Sidney Burris

The Year in Drama. 13
Robert Cohen

The Year in World Literature. 23
William Riggan

New Authors

John Ed Bradley   1959- 31
American novelist

Ethan Canin   1960- 35
American short story writer

Michael Chabon   1965?- 41
American novelist

Elizabeth Cooke   1948- 46
American novelist

Trey Ellis   1962- 50
American novelist

Judith Freeman   1946- 55
American short story writer

Alan Hollinghurst   1954- 59
English novelist

Barbara Kingsolver   1955- 64
American novelist

Eric Larsen   1941- 69
American novelist

Patrick McGrath   1950- 73
English short story writer

I. Allan Sealy   1951- 78
Indian novelist

Anton Shammas   1951- 85
Arabian-born Israeli novelist

Paul Watkins   1964- 92
American novelist

Prizewinners

**Literary Prizes and Honors Announced in
1988**. 99

T. Coraghessan Boyle   1948- 105
PEN/Faulkner Award: Fiction

Peter Carey   1943- 112
Booker Prize

Caryl Churchill   1938- 120
Obie Award

Pete Dexter   1943- 128
National Book Award: Fiction

Gabriel García Márquez   1928- 133
Los Angeles Times Book Award: Fiction

David Henry Hwang   1957- 150
Tony Award

M. T. Kelly   1947- 156
Governor General's Award: Fiction

Gwendolyn MacEwen   1941-1987 162
Governor General's Award: Poetry

Najib Mahfuz   1912- 170
Nobel Prize

William Meredith   1919- 190
Pulitzer Prize: Poetry

Toni Morrison   1931- 194
Pulitzer Prize: Fiction

Salman Rushdie   1947- 214
Whitbread Award: Fiction

Alfred Uhry   1937?- 264
Pulitzer Prize: Drama

Obituaries

Necrology 271

Raymond Carver 1938-1988. 273
   American short story writer

René Char 1907-1988 285
   French poet

Robert Duncan 1919-1988. 290
   American poet

Robert Heinlein 1907-1988 300
   American novelist

Louis L'Amour 1908?-1988 306
   American novelist

Alan Paton 1903-1988. 310
   South African novelist and nonfiction writer

Miguel Piñero 1946-1988. 316
   Puerto Rican-born American dramatist

Clifford Simak 1904-1988 319
   American novelist and short story writer

Topics in Literature: 1988

The Controversy Surrounding
   In Search of J. D. Salinger 325

T. S. Eliot Centenary 345

The Seventh Annual
   Young Playwrights Festival 376

The Wartime Journalism of Paul de Man . . 382

Literary Criticism Series Cumulative Author Index 427

CLC Cumulative Nationality Index 475

CLC-55 Title Index 489

Preface

Every year, an overwhelming number of significant new publications and literary events confront readers interested in contemporary literature. Who are the year's notable new authors? What important dramas have been introduced in theaters? Who are the recipients of the literary world's most prestigious awards? What literary events stimulated public interest and received substantial media attention? Finally, who among our best-known writers died during the year, and where can one find memorial tributes, reminiscences, and retrospective essays covering their careers?

To answer such questions and assist students, teachers, librarians, researchers, and general readers in maintaining awareness of current literary activities and trends, *Contemporary Literary Criticism Yearbook* is published as part of the ongoing *Contemporary Literary Criticism (CLC)* series.

The *CLC* series provides readers with a comprehensive survey of modern literature by presenting excerpted criticism on the works of novelists, poets, playwrights, short story writers, scriptwriters, and other creative authors who are now living or who died after December 31, 1959. A strong emphasis is placed on including criticism of works by established authors who frequently appear on syllabuses of high school and college literature courses.

To complement this broad coverage, the *Yearbook* focuses more specifically on a given year's literary activities and highlights a larger number of currently noteworthy authors than is possible in standard *CLC* volumes. The present *Yearbook,* for example, contains entries on such internationally acclaimed novelists as Toni Morrison *(Beloved)* and Gabriel García Márquez *(Love in the Time of Cholera),* whose recent award-winning works appeared on the *New York Times* best-sellers list and were the top two fiction publications noted in a survey compiled by *Rolling Stone* magazine ("What the Kids Who Really Read Are Really Reading") of books purchased by college students in the United States during the 1988-1989 academic year. In general, the *Yearbook* provides critical overviews of the past year's works in various genres, supplies up-to-date critical commentary on new authors and prizewinning writers, and notes the deaths of major literary figures. In addition, the *Yearbook* expands the scope of regular *CLC* volumes by focusing upon outstanding and controversial topics that serve to remind us of literature's influence on culture and society. Since the majority of authors covered in *Yearbook* and regular *CLC* volumes are living writers who continue to publish, an author frequently appears more than once in the series. There is, of course, no duplication of reprinted criticism.

Scope of the Work

CLC, Volume 55: Yearbook 1988 includes excerpted criticism on over 40 authors and provides comprehensive coverage of the year's significant literary events, including the unprecedented international controversy surrounding Salman Rushdie's novel *The Satanic Verses* and the numerous events and writings occasioned by the observance of the centenary of T. S. Eliot's birth. The *Yearbook* is divided into five sections: "The Year in Review," "New Authors," "Prizewinners," "Obituaries," and "Topics in Literature."

The Year in Review—This section consists of specially commissioned essays by prominent writers who survey the year's new works in their respective literary fields. In *CLC Yearbook 1988* "The Year in Fiction" is viewed from the perspective of Robert Wilson, book critic for *USA Today* and former member of the National Book Critics Circle Board of Directors. "The Year in Poetry" overview is presented by Sidney Burris, poet *(A Day at the Races),* critic (a study of Irish poet Seamus Heaney—*The Poetry of Resistance: Seamus Heaney and the Pastoral Tradition*—is in press), and assistant professor of English at the University of Arkansas. "The Year in Drama" is reviewed by Robert Cohen, who has authored such well-known theater texts as *Theatre, Giraudoux: Three Faces of Destiny, Acting Power, Acting One, Acting Professionally,* and *Creative Play Direction* and has contributed articles to major theater journals. Mr. Cohen has directed plays for the Colorado Shakespeare Festival, the Utah Shakespeare Festival, and the Focused Research Program in Medieval Drama at the University of California, Irvine, where he is Chair and Professor of Drama. "The Year in World Literature" is discussed by William Riggan, Associate Editor of *World Literature Today,* an international quarterly published at the University of Oklahoma, for which he regularly reviews new foreign fiction, poetry, and criticism and contributes essays. Mr. Riggan is the author of *Picaros, Madmen, Naïfs and Clowns: The Unreliable First-Person Narrator.*

New Authors—*CLC Yearbook 1988* introduces thirteen writers who published their first book or first work in English translation during 1988. Authors were selected for inclusion if their work was reviewed in several prominent literary periodicals. Although regular *CLC* volumes often cover new writers, the *Yearbook* is intended to provide more extensive and timely coverage of initial publications.

Prizewinners—This section of the *Yearbook* commences with a list of literary prizes and honors announced in 1988, citing the award, award criteria, the recipient, and the title of the prizewinning work. The list has been redesigned for the present volume to include a greater amount of information in a more accessible format. Following the listing of prizewinners is a presentation of thirteen entries on individual award winners, representing a mixture of genres and nationalities as well as established prizes and those more recently introduced. In addition to winners of major American awards for fiction, poetry, and drama, recipients of several outstanding international prizes are featured. Thus, we include the Nobel Prize, bestowed upon Egyptian novelist Najib Mahfuz, Great Britain's distinguished Booker Prize, awarded in 1988 to Australian novelist Peter Carey, and Canada's Governor General's Literary Awards, represented in the present *Yearbook* by entries on M. T. Kelly and Gwendolyn MacEwen.

Obituaries—This section begins with a necrology, briefly identifying eight prominent authors who died in 1988, followed by entries on eight other recently deceased writers. The entries consist of reminiscences, tributes, retrospective articles, and obituaries, as well as excerpts from significant articles or books that were not included in previous *CLC* entries on these writers.

Topics in Literature—This new section of the *Yearbook* focuses on literary issues and events of wide public interest, as evidenced in extensive multimedia coverage. For example, three teenage playwrights whose works were performed during a month-long run in a major New York theater as part of the Seventh Annual Young Playwrights Festival are featured in an entry that includes reviews by several leading drama critics. In addition, this section of the *Yearbook* contains entries on the controversies surrounding the biography *In Search of J. D. Salinger* and the discovery that eminent Yale scholar Paul de Man contributed articles to collaborationist publications in his native Belgium during World War II. These entries are intended to serve as forums wherein diverse opinions and insights are presented, allowing the reader to better understand the various implications concerning the controversies.

Format of the Book

With the exception of the essays in "The Year in Review" section, which are written specifically for this publication, the *Yearbook* is composed of excerpted criticism. There are approximately 400 individual excerpts in *CLC Yearbook 1988,* drawn from hundreds of literary reviews, general magazines, distinguished newspapers, books, and scholarly journals. *Yearbook* entries generally follow the same format as regular *CLC* volumes with some variations and additional features. *Yearbook* entries variously contain the following elements:

- The **author heading,** which is included in entries in the "New Authors," "Prizewinners," and "Obituaries" sections, cites the author's full name. The portion of the name outside the parentheses denotes the form under which the author has most commonly published. If an author has written consistently under a pseudonym, the pseudonym will be listed in the author heading and the real name given on the first line of the author entry. Also located at the beginning of the author entry are any important name variations under which an author has written. For new authors and obituaries, the author's name is followed by the birth date and, in the case of an obituary, the death date. Uncertainty as to a birth or death date is indicated by question marks. For prizewinners, the author's name is followed by the title of the prizewinning work and the award received.

- The **subject heading,** which is included in entries in the "Topics in Literature" section, defines the theme of each entry.

- A brief **biographical and critical introduction** to the author and his or her work precedes the excerpted criticism in entries in the "New Authors" and "Prizewinners" sections; the subjects, authors, and works in the "Topics in Literature" section are introduced in a similar manner.

- **Cross-references** have been included in all sections, except "The Year in Review," to direct the reader to other useful sources published by Gale Research: *Contemporary Authors,* which includes detailed biographical and bibliographical sketches on more than 92,000 authors; *Children's Literature Review,* which presents excerpted criticism on the works of authors of children's books; *Something about the Author,* which contains heavily illustrated biographical sketches on writers and illustrators who create books for children and young adults; *Dictionary of Literary Biography,* which provides original evaluations of authors important to literary history; *Contemporary Authors Autobiography Series,* which offers autobiographical essays by prominent writers; and *Something about the Author Autobiography Series,* which presents autobiographical essays by authors of interest to young readers. Previous volumes of *CLC* in which the author has been featured are also listed in the introduction.

• A **portrait** of the author is included, when available, in entries in the "New Authors," "Prizewinners," "Obituaries," and "Topics in Literature" sections.

• An **excerpt** from the author's work is included, when available, in entries in the "New Authors" and "Prizewinners" sections, in order to provide the reader with a sampling of the author's style and thematic approach.

• The **excerpted criticism,** included in all entries except those in "The Year in Review" section, represents essays selected by editors to reflect the spectrum of opinion about a specific work or about an author's writing in general. The excerpts are presented chronologically, adding a useful perspective to the entry. All titles by the author featured in the entry are printed in boldface type, which enables the reader to easily identify the works being discussed.

• A complete **bibliographical citation**, designed to help the user find the original essay or book, follows each excerpt.

Other Features

• A list of **Authors Forthcoming in *CLC*** previews the authors to be researched for future volumes.

• An **Appendix** lists the sources from which material in the volume has been reprinted. Many other sources have also been consulted during the preparation of the volume.

• A **Cumulative Index to Authors** lists all the authors who have appeared in *CLC, Twentieth-Century Literary Criticism, Nineteenth-Century Literature Criticism, Literature Criticism from 1400 to 1800,* and *Classical and Medieval Literature Criticism* along with cross-references to these Gale series: *Short Story Criticism, Children's Literature Review, Authors in the News, Contemporary Authors, Contemporary Authors Autobiography Series, Contemporary Authors Bibliographical Series, Dictionary of Literary Biography, Something about the Author, Something about the Author Autobiography Series,* and *Yesterday's Authors of Books for Children.* Users will welcome this cumulated author index as a useful tool for locating an author within the various series. The index, which lists birth and death dates when available, will be particularly valuable for those authors who are identified with a certain period but whose death date causes them to be placed in another, or for those authors whose careers span two periods. For example, Ernest Hemingway is found in *CLC,* yet a writer often associated with him, F. Scott Fitzgerald, is found in *Twentieth-Century Literary Criticism.*

• A **Cumulative Nationality Index** alphabetically lists all authors featured in *CLC* by nationality, followed by numbers corresponding to the volumes in which they appear.

• A **Title Index** alphabetically lists all titles reviewed in the current volume of *CLC.* A title is followed by the author's surname in parentheses and the corresponding page numbers where commentary on the work may be located. Titles of novels, novellas, dramas, films, record albums, and poetry, short story, essay collections are printed in italics, while all individual poems, short stories, and essays are printed in roman type within quotation marks; when published separately (e.g., T. S. Eliot's poem *The Waste Land*), the title will also be printed in italics.

• In response to numerous suggestions from librarians, Gale has also produced a **special paperbound edition** of the *CLC* title index. This annual cumulation, which alphabetically lists all titles reviewed in the series, is available to all customers and will be published with the first volume of *CLC* issued in each calendar year. Additional copies of the index are available upon request. Librarians and patrons will welcome this separate index: it saves shelf space, is easily disposable upon receipt of the following year's cumulation, and is more portable and thus easier to use than was previously possible.

Suggestions Are Welcome

The editors welcome the comments and suggestions of readers to expand the coverage and enhance the usefulness of the series. Please feel free to contact us through Gale's toll-free number: 1-800-347-GALE.

Acknowledgments

The editors wish to thank the copyright holders of the excerpted criticism included in this volume, the permissions managers of many book and magazine publishing companies for assisting us in securing reprint rights, and Anthony Bogucki for assistance with copyright research. We are also grateful to the staffs of the Detroit Public Library, the University of Michigan Library, and the Wayne State University Library for making their resources available to us. Following is a list of the copyright holders who have granted us permission to reprint material in this volume of *CLC*. Every effort has been made to trace copyright, but if omissions have been made, please let us know.

COPYRIGHTED EXCERPTS IN *CLC*, VOLUME 55, WERE REPRINTED FROM THE FOLLOWING PERIODICALS:

The American Book Review, v. 10, November-December, 1988. © 1988 by *The American Book Review.* Reprinted by permission of the publisher.—*The American Poetry Review,* v. 18, March-April, 1989 for "Raymond Carver: Going through the Pain" by Ted Solotaroff. Copyright © 1989 by Theodore Solotaroff. Reprinted by permission of Georges Borchardt, Inc. for the author./ v. 17, May-June, 1988 for " 'Slow Pace of the Future' " by René Char, translated by Charles Guenther; v. 17, May-June, 1988 for "René Char: Twelve Poems" by Charles Guenther. Copyright © 1988 by World Poetry, Inc. Both reprinted by permission of the respective authors.—*Asian and African Studies,* v. 11, Autumn, 1976. © 1976 by the Institute of Middle Eastern Studies, University of Haifa. Reprinted by permission of the publisher.—*The Bloomsbury Review,* v. 8, January-February, 1988 for "Matters of Life & Death: An Interview with Raymond Carver" by William L. Stull. Copyright © by Owaissa Communications Company, Inc. 1988. Reprinted by permission of the author.—*Book World—The Washington Post,* November 1, 1987; April 3, 1988; April 24, 1988; July 10, 1988; September 25, 1988; October 9, 1988; December 18, 1988; January 29, 1989. © 1987, 1988, 1989, *The Washington Post.* All reprinted by permission of the publisher.—*Booklist,* v. 84, January 15, 1988. Copyright © 1988 by the American Library Association. Reprinted by permission of the publisher.—*Books in Canada,* v. 16, June-July, 1987 for "Anarchy and Afterthoughts" by Susan Glickman; v. 16, November, 1987 for "The Impossible Dream" by Terry Goldie; v. 17, April, 1988 for "Stories and Hauntings" by M. T. Kelly. All reprinted by permission of the respective authors.—*Boston Review,* v. XIII, April, 1988 for a review of "Emperor of the Air" by Sven Birkerts. Copyright © 1988 by the Boston Critic, Inc. Reprinted by permission of the author.—*Canadian Literature,* n. 118, Autumn, 1988 for "Long Light" by Patricia Keeney. Reprinted by permission of the author.—*Canadian Woman Studies/les cahiers de la femme,* v. 9, Summer, 1988 for "Dedication: Gwendolyn MacEwen (1941-1987)" by Jan Bartley. Reprinted by permission of the publisher and the author.—*Chicago Tribune,* February 17, 1989. © copyrighted 1989, Chicago Tribune Company. All rights reserved. Used with permission.—*Chicago Tribune—Books,* March 6, 1988 for "Witty Novel Chronicles Family's Fall" by James Idema; May 1, 1988 for "Fleeing the Past: Resolving Three Generations of Miscarried Hope" by Douglas Seibold; June 19, 1988 for " 'Oscar & Lucinda': Victorian Adventure Offers Thrills, Heartbreak, Comedy" by Frederick Busch; August 7, 1988 for "The Graphic Horrors of a Moral-Less Man" by Dean Faulkner Wells. © copyrighted 1988, Chicago Tribune Company. All rights reserved. All reprinted by permission of the respective authors./ February 28, 1988; March 20, 1988. © copyrighted 1988, Chicago Tribune Company. All rights reserved. Both used with permission.—*The Christian Science Monitor,* March 16, 1988 for a review of "Family Attractions" by Diane Manuel; April 22, 1988 for "A Roundup of First Novels about Coming of Age" by Diane Manuel. © 1988 the respective authors. All rights reserved. Both reprinted by permission of the respective authors./ March 23, 1988; March 2, 1989. © 1988, 1989 The Christian Science Publishing Society. All rights reserved. Both reprinted by permission from *The Christian Science Monitor.*—*The Chronicle of Higher Education* b. XXXIV, July 13, 1988 for "It's Time to Set the Record Straight About Paul de Man and His Wartime Articles For a Pro-Fascist Newspaper" by Jonathan Culler. Copyright © 1988 *The Chronicle of Higher Education.* Reprinted with permission of the publisher and the author.—*Commentary,* v. 84, December, 1987 for "Toni Morrison's Career" by Carol Iannone. Copyright © 1987 by the American Jewish Committee. All rights reserved. Reprinted by permission of the publisher and the author.—*Commonweal,* v. CXV, May 20, 1988; v. CXV, July 15, 1988. Copyright © 1988 Commonweal Foundation. Both reprinted by permission of Commonweal Foundation.—*The Courier,* v. 41, June, 1988.—*Cross-Canada Writers' Quarterly,* v. 8, 1986 for "A Poet's Journey into the Interior" by Gwendolyn MacEwen. Copyright 1986 by the author. Reprinted by permission of the Literary Estate of Gwendolyn MacEwen./ v. 10, 1988 for a review of "Afterworlds" by Martin Singleton. Copyright 1988 by the author. Reprinted by permission of the Literary Estate of Martin Singleton.—*Daily News,* **New York,** February 19, 1988. © 1988 New York News Inc. Reprinted with permission.—*The Daily Telegraph,* March 30, 1987. Reprinted by permission of the publisher.—*The Dallas Morning News,* July 17, 1988. © *The Dallas Morning News,* 1988. Reprinted by permission of the publisher.—*Event,* v. 17, Spring, 1988. Reprinted by permission of the publisher.—*The Fiddlehead,* n. 156, Summer, 1988 for "Dreams, Reality, and Oral Tradition" by Andrea Bear Nicholas. Copyright by the author. Reprinted by permission of the author.—*Financial Times,* March 30, 1987. Reprinted by permission of the publisher.—**Fort Worth**

Authors Forthcoming in *CLC*

To Be Included in Volume 56

Steven Berkoff (English dramatist)—Berkoff has gained notoriety for his satirical portrayals of British society and his innovative modernizations of classical dramas. Among his most recent productions is a controversial adaptation of Shakespeare's *Coriolanus.*

Edmund Blunden (English poet, critic, and biographer)—Greatly influenced by the English Romantic movement of the nineteenth century, Blunden evokes the beauty of nature in his predominantly pastoral poetry. Reflections on his experiences as a military officer during World War I temper the idyllic qualities of such collections as *The Shepherd* and *The Waggoner.*

Bruce Jay Friedman (American novelist, short story writer, dramatist, and scriptwriter)—Friedman's fiction focuses on the serious and comic aspects of Jewish assimilation into American society. In such novels as *Stern* and *A Mother's Kisses,* he examines the guilt and repression felt by his luckless protagonists and their families.

John Clellon Holmes (American novelist, essayist, poet, and short story writer)—Holmes is best remembered for his objective portrayals of the rebellious lifestyles of writers who were involved in the Beat movement of the 1950s. His novel *Go* is generally credited as the first authentic chronicle of the Beat phenomenon.

Ivan Klima (Czechoslovakian short story writer, novelist, dramatist, and essayist)—A dissident writer whose fiction has been banned in his native country since 1970, Klima portrays the lives of ordinary individuals living under communist rule. Among his works to be translated into English are *A Summer Affair* and *My Merry Mornings: Stories from Prague.*

Rhoda Lerman (American novelist)—Best known for such metaphorical novels as *Call Me Ishtar* and *The Book of the Night,* Lerman uses elements of fantasy to comment on contemporary sexual relationships and the role of women in society.

François Mauriac (French novelist, nonfiction writer, critic, dramatist, and poet)—Winner of the 1952 Nobel Prize in Literature, Mauriac is considered one of the most important Roman Catholic authors of the twentieth century. Both his fiction and nonfiction writings reflect his concern with sin, redemption, and other religious issues. Such novels as *Thérèse* and *Vipers' Tangle* also offer vivid depictions of life in the Bordeaux region of southwestern France.

Raja Rao (Indian novelist and short story writer)—Recipient of the 1988 Neustadt International Prize for Literature, Rao is best known for his metaphysical novels in which he frequently juxtaposes Indian and Western intellectual and spiritual approaches to the problems of existence.

William Saroyan (American dramatist, short story writer, and novelist)—A prolific author of works in several genres, Saroyan was praised for his romantic and nostalgic celebrations of American innocence and idealism. Critical commentary in Saroyan's entry will focus on his Pulitzer Prize-winning drama, *The Time of Your Life.*

Arno Schmidt (German novelist, short story writer, translator, critic, biographer, and essayist)—An important figure in German literature, Schmidt is renowned for bold innovations with prose structure and typography and for satirical novels that present a dystopian vision.

Isabel Allende (Chilean novelist)—In her novels *The House of Spirits, Of Love and Shadows,* and the recent *Eva Luna,* Allende combines elements of realism and fantasy to examine the tumultuous social and political history of South America.

Samuel Beckett (Irish-born dramatist and novelist)—A recipient of the Nobel Prize in Literature, Beckett often combines humor and tragedy in his works to create an existential view of the human condition in which life is regarded as meaningless. Beckett's entry will focus on his seminal absurdist drama, *Waiting for Godot.*

T. S. Eliot (English poet, critic, and dramatist)—A principal founder of modernism, Eliot greatly influenced modern letters with his innovative and distinctively erudite verse and criticism. Eliot's entry will focus on *The Waste Land,* an epic widely considered among the major works of twentieth-century poetry.

Percival Everett (American novelist and short story writer)—An author of tragicomic fiction, Everett often focuses upon characters who transcend destructive personal relationships to achieve a sense of self-worth. His novels include *Suder* and *Walk Me to the Distance.*

Richard Greenberg (American dramatist and scriptwriter)—In his plays *The Moderati,* a satire of self-absorbed literary society, and *Eastern Standard,* a critique of young middle-class professionals, Greenberg uses sympathy and humor to explore the American obsession with wealth and materialism.

Danilo Kis (Yugoslavian novelist and short story writer)—Kis first attracted critical acclaim in Western countries for his novels *Garden, Ashes* and *A Tomb for Boris Davidovich,* both of which focus upon the persecution of European Jews during World War II. Kis's recently translated short story collection, *The Encyclopedia of the Dead,* has further enhanced his international reputation.

Peter Klappert (American poet)—Klappert garnered praise for the wit and technical innovations of his first poetry collection, *Lugging Vegetables to Nantucket,* for which he received the Yale Series of Younger Poets Award. His sequence *The Idiot Princess of the Last Dynasty* has been compared to such celebrated works as Ezra Pound's *Cantos* and John Berryman's *The Dream Songs.*

Cormac McCarthy (American novelist)—McCarthy is regarded as an important contributor to the Southern Gothic tradition as exemplified by such authors as William Faulkner, Carson McCullers, and Flannery O'Connor. McCarthy's novels, which are often set in his native Tennessee, are praised for their inventive dialect and powerful examinations of evil.

Mbongeni Ngema (South African dramatist)—Ngema's plays illustrate the consequences of apartheid and humanity's capacity for injustice. His recent musical drama, *Sarafina!,* inspired by the Soweto uprising of 1976, chronicles the efforts of South African high school students to fashion a play from their country's tragic history.

Andrei Voznesensky (Russian poet)—A protaagaa of Boris Pasternak, Voznesensky is one of the Soviet Union's most prestigious contemporary poets. His complex experimental verse reveals a profound love for his country and often explores the alienation of youth in industrial society.

The Year in Review

The Year in Fiction

by Robert Wilson

Even while I was reading my way through it, 1988 seemed a quiet year for American fiction. Writing careers were launched and, perhaps, sunk, but few among those already afloat seemed to pick up much momentum, and no single novel or book of stories seemed certain to loom down the years, retrospectively making this a year to remember. The publication in the United States in early 1989 of Salman Rushdie's *The Satanic Verses,* and the subsequent furor that the novel caused, made 1988 recede even more quickly than it might otherwise have done. But then the Rushdie affair is truly unprecedented; never before has a work of fiction attracted so much of the world's attention all at once. One of the sad lessons of this ugly business might be that we should welcome quiet years like 1988. Fiction writers, many of them, at least, really are what Rushdie's wife Marianne Wiggins said they are—subversives. Although the reasons why Rushdie's particular book received this particular recognition are many and complicated, I don't doubt that more than a few of the books described below, if read by large numbers of people in this country who do not normally read serious fiction, would be met with a hue and cry. Perhaps it is better that literary fiction is written and read in relative obscurity. Perhaps we should be grateful that more people don't read more books.

WHAT FAMILIARITY MOSTLY BREEDS

That said, let's those of us who do read books turn first to the writers we know well who were published in 1988. Of the dozen books by such writers listed below, only three were met with universal praise and no trace of disappointment.

Thomas Flanagan's *The Year of the French* won the National Book Critics Circle Award. His new book, **The Tenants of Time,** is another large historical novel about Ireland's Troubles, this time set in the nineteenth century and centering on four men who participate in an uprising against a British police barracks. **The Tenants of Time** has been nominated for the PEN/Faulkner award.

Wheat That Springeth Green was written by J.F. Powers, who won the National Book Award a quarter century ago for his only other novel, *Morte d'urban,* and who is a short story master. This novel tells the story of an ordinary Minnesota priest trying to retain his sanctity in the modern world.

Raymond Carver, whose influence on other writers has grown by leaps and bounds in the last five years, died in August, shortly after **Where I'm Calling From: New and Selected Stories** appeared. This collection by the master chronicler of working-class lives includes seven new and thirty reprinted stories.

These nine other well-known writers were received with varying degrees of ardor:

Larry McMurtry's **Anything for Billy** is a novel set on a much smaller stage than his Pulitzer-winning *Lonesome*

Dust jacket of Where I'm Calling From: New and Selected Stories, *by Raymond Carver. Jacket design by Lorraine Louie. Jacket illustration by Trent Burleson.*

Dove. This book concerns a hack novelist who goes West for material for his fiction.

Although **Breathing Lessons** is not Anne Tyler's best novel, this story of a day in the life of a meddlesome Baltimore woman and her grumpy husband is filled with her shy humor and careful observations of contemporary life.

The Death of Methuselah and Other Stories by Nobel Laureate I. B. Singer, deals with love and woman's betrayal of man. The ground that this book covers is not new for Singer, but there is a humorlessness and an acrimoniousness here that *is* new for him.

Rosacoke Mustian, the heroine of Reynolds Price's affecting first novel, *A Long and Happy Life,* is called Rosa in his new work, **Good Hearts.** Rosa lives in Raleigh with Wesley Beavers, formerly her boyfriend, now her husband of twenty-five years. Closely resembling the plot of the earlier book, **Good Hearts** follows Wesley to Nashville and, later, traces his reconciliatory return to Raleigh.

Nothing that Joseph Heller has written has compared with

3

Catch-22, but **Picture This** is a stunningly bad novel that plays off the Rembrandt painting *Aristotle Contemplating the Bust of Homer* and features Heller's forgettable theories about history.

S., one of John Updike's minor novelistic efforts, is an epistolary novel flowing from the pen of a sexy North Shore woman who has left her husband for the spirituality and (need I say it?) sexuality of an Arizona ashram.

Some say that Harold Brodkey has been at work for the last three decades on the great novel of our era. **Stories in an Almost Classical Mode,** published this year, is not that novel, but some of the twenty-five stories may be fragments of it. Although Brodkey's language can be precious or pompous, the best of these stories, often about childhood, have a brilliance that makes the claims made for him seem possible.

In **The Truth about Lorin Jones,** a weak, predictable novel by Alison Lurie, who won the Pulitzer Prize for her novel *Foreign Affairs,* a woman leaves her husband and job and begins a feminist biography of an artist whose career and life, she believes, were sabotaged by men.

With **The Western Lands,** William Burroughs, who wrote *Naked Lunch,* completes a trilogy that includes *Cities of the Red Night* and *The Place of Dead Roads.* The kaleidoscopic narrative of **The Western Lands** combines various meditations on immortality with a firm belief that our society richly deserves the annihilation towards which it is heading.

WHAT LESS FAMILIARITY BREEDS LESS OF

Rather like that of the person who processes these words, the body of fiction writers in this country is far broader in the middle than it is at the extremes. There are countless novelists whom the publishers cruelly designate as "midlist"—that is, who are neither unknown nor terribly well known and who deserve to be published but probably won't make any money. The selection below from these multitudes is not too arbitrary, I hope. Several of them, notably Don DeLillo and William Kennedy, do not really belong in the middle, but I couldn't bring myself to class them with the writers above, although many more charitable readers would.

The Beautiful Room Is Empty, by Edmund White. A sequel to his autobiographical novel *A Boy's Own Story* this book deals with the mental anguish of being gay in the days before gay liberation.

The Beginner's Book of Dreams, by Elizabeth Benedict. By the author of *Slow Dancing,* this is the story of a young woman growing up in Manhattan who begins to understand herself through her growing power as a photographer.

Born Brothers, by Larry Woiwode. A ponderous look at the Neumiller family, who appeared in his wonderful earlier novel, *Beyond the Bedroom Wall,* this work is narrated from the viewpoint and memory of the elder son, Charles.

Breaking Gentle, by Beverly Lowry. Her fifth novel is a witty and affectionate look at a family that raises quarter-horses near Austin, Texas.

Can't Quit You, Baby, by Ellen Douglas. The story of a white Southern woman who learns the deepest meaning of racism and the effects it has had on her black maid's difficult life. I thought that this was one of the best American novels of the year.

The Corner of Rife and Pacific, by Thomas Savage. A nominee for the PEN/Faulkner award, his thirteenth novel tells of a Montana family from 1890 to 1920.

Dalva, by Jim Harrison. The title character of this novel by the author of *Legends of the Fall* returns to the rural Nebraska farmhouse built by her great-grandfather.

Fair and Tender Ladies, by Lee Smith. A sweet and affecting novel by the author of *Oral History* which takes the form of letters written over a period of sixty-five years, by a mountain girl from Virginia.

Kick the Can, by television newsman Jim H. Lehrer. A comic tale of a one-eyed college graduate who goes searching for adventure in the Southwest.

Krazy Kat: A Novel in Five Panels, by Jay Cantor. Cantor, who also wrote *The Death of Che Guevara,* here composes a sort of sequel to the famous comic strip in which Krazy, after the death of her creator, tries with a vengeance to fit into contemporary life.

The Greenlanders, by Jane Smiley. From the author of *The Age of Grief,* a novel in the form of a Norse saga about the extinction of a five-hundred-year-old settlement of Norse peoples in Greenland.

The Houseguest, by Thomas Berger. A funny, Kafkaesque novel from the author of *Neighbors* about an uninvited houseguest who terrorizes a family in its summer home.

Last Notes from Home, by Frederick Exley. The final book in a trilogy that began with *A Fan's Notes* has flashes of that first book's brilliance, but it is maddeningly digressive as it follows the fictional Fred Exley in his further pursuit of heroism.

Libra, by Don DeLillo. Nominated for the National Book Award and the National Book Critics Circle Award, this novel by the author of *White Noise* reimagines the Kennedy assassination as the work of the CIA.

Palm Latitudes, by Kate Braverman. Three women from the barrio of east Los Angeles relate their life stories.

Paris Trout, by Pete Dexter. Winner of the National Book Award, this novel depicts the trial of a small-town Georgia racist who believes that he can get away with murder as long as the victim is black.

The Place in Flowers Where Pollen Rests, by Paul West. Despite its awkward title, this is a "remarkably ambitious and troubling work," according to Thomas R. Edwards, that tells of a Hopi Indian who finally takes refuge in his native culture after horrifying experiences in contemporary society.

Prisoner's Dilemma, by Richard Powers. From the author of *Three Farmers on Their Way to a Dance,* this book about a family trying to cope with their father's retreat into fantasy is "an intellectual tour de force, alive with movingly human characters," in the opinion of Bruce Allen.

Quinn's Book, by William Kennedy. A novel by the author of *Ironweed* that erratically and unsatisfyingly mixes a story of nineteenth-century upstate New York (including Kennedy's native Albany) with magic realism and a kaleidoscopic

Cover of Libra, *by Don DeLillo. Cover photograph (c) Tony Spina.*

structure that leaves out many of what would have been the narrative's most dramatic moments.

The Risk Pool, by Richard Russo. This is the second novel by this talented younger writer (his first was *Mohawk*) about a dying, blue-collar town in upstate New York.

Sailing, by Susan Kenney. A sequel to her novel *In Another Country,* this book continues the story of a couple faced with the husband's cancer who turn to sailing to distract them from his inevitable end.

Second Chances, by Alice Adams. By the author of *Listening to Billie,* this novel examines a year in the life of a group of friends in their sixties who look back on moments they have shared.

Silver, by Hilma Wolitzer. The story of an on-again, off-again marriage facing the hazards of middle age.

Spence + Lila, by Bobbie Ann Mason. From the author of *In Country,* this short novel explores the love of two simple country people in late middle age who must face Lila's hospitalization for breast cancer.

Tracks, by Louise Erdrich. The third of four novels set on or around a North Dakota Indian reservation, this is the earliest

in time, opening in 1912, with members of the Chippewa tribe facing the extinction of their reservation and their culture.

WHAT THE SOUL OF WIT IS

The popularity of the short story with writers, readers, and critics does not seem to have diminished in 1988. This is perhaps reflected in the National Book Critics Circle choice [in 1989] of *The Middleman and Other Stories* by Bharati Mukherjee as the best book of fiction of the year. This collection features immigrants from all over, but especially from Mukherjee's native India, who energetically embrace their new lives in America. Other interesting and admired collections from 1988:

Blood Line: Stories of Fathers and Sons, by David Quammen. In two of the three long stories in this collection, Quammen, a respected author of essays on nature and science, deals with fathers who die more or less accidentally at the hands of their sons. The third, actually a short novel, uses techniques and a style reminiscent of Faulkner's *Absalom, Absalom.*

The Coming Triumph of the Free World, by Rick DeMarinis. Fourteen stories about lower middle-class people who face their difficult lives with pluck and humor.

Dusk and Other Stories, by James Salter. Nominated for a PEN/Faulkner award, this volume contains stories that have a tendency towards brittleness, but the title piece, about a woman of a certain age whose erstwhile lover has returned

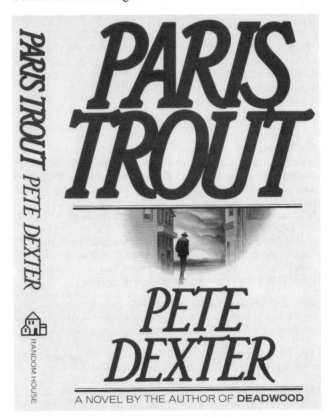

Dust jacket of Paris Trout, *by Pete Dexter. Jacket design by Paul Bacon.*

to his wife, is as good as Salter's excellent novels, *A Sport and a Pastime* and *Light Years.*

Emperor of the Air, by Ethan Canin. An ambitious if uneven collection of stories about family relationships told by narrators young, old, and in between.

The Hidden Side of the Moon, by Joanna Russ. Stories from throughout her career by a writer of science fiction with strong feminist concerns.

Jack of Diamonds and Other Stories, by Elizabeth Spencer. Of the five stories in this, her eleventh book, the two best, according to Robb Forman Dew, are "The Business Venture," about a white Southern woman who goes into business with a black Vietnam veteran, and "The Cousins," about five young cousins who spend a summer in Europe before assuming adult responsibilities.

Margaret of the Imperfections, by Linda Sexson. A first collection of stories in which country people accept the variety of religious experiences that touch their lives.

Safety Patrol, by Michael Martone. Hilma Wolitzer wrote that this collection, by the author of *Alive and Dead in Indiana,* "resounds with intelligence and honest emotion, and it makes for very satisfying reading."

Selected Stories, by André Dubus. Bleak, often violent stories about unremarkable characters from the Merrimack Valley north of Boston.

Sunburn Lake, by Tom De Haven. By the author of *Funny Pagers,* three stories each about a female singer, told in the first person—one set in the past, one in the present, one in the future.

Women and Children First, by Francine Prose. By the author of *Bigfoot Dreams,* stories about people in their thirties and forties facing middle age with a combination of shrewdness and resignation.

AND THE FIRST SHALL BE LAST

Did I imagine it, or is it possible that some reaction set in during 1988 against the first novel by a college sophomore who managed to get a six-figure advance from an editor destined to lose his shirt—and his job? Perhaps that is only wishful thinking. One first novel that did fit the big-advance bill was Michael Chabon's ***The Mysteries of Pittsburgh,*** about the son of a Jewish gangster who comes of age and falls in love in Pittsburgh. Another novel that drew wide review attention was Jonathan Franzen's ***The Twenty-Seventh City,*** a verbally inventive novel set in St. Louis in some not-too-distant future time. Other first novels that were well-received:

Arts and Sciences: A Seventies Seduction, by Thomas Mallon. A comic but thoughtful novel about an insecure graduate student who badly needs to lighten up.

The Bean Trees, by Barbara Kingsolver. The vivid story of a young Kentucky woman who travels West.

Her Own Times, by Judith Grossman. Traces the life of a woman from a lower-middle-class family in wartime London to her undergraduate days at Oxford.

Soft Water, by Robert Olmstead. The story of a reclusive

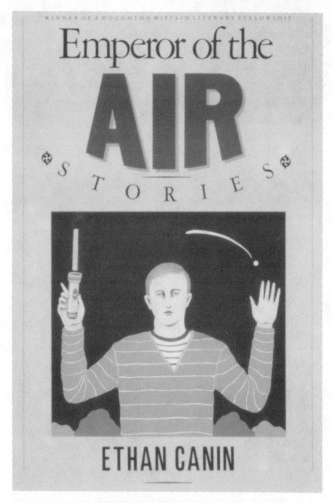

Dust jacket of Emperor of the Air, *by Ethan Canin. Jacket design by Ronn Campisi. Jacket illustration by Dagmar Frinta.*

woodsman who gets in trouble when he reenters society in search of a mate.

Vanished, by Mary McGarry Morris. Nominated both for the National Book Award and the PEN/Faulkner award, this novel looks unflinchingly at parricide and the kidnapping of a baby.

These, then, are a few of the books of American fiction published in 1988. It was, as I have said, a middling year for such books, falling somewhere in the vast middle between memorable and forgettable.

The Year in Poetry

by Sidney Burris

In a London home near Picadilly, Ernest and Gilbert, the principal characters of Oscar Wilde's dialogue, *The Critic as Artist* (1890), discuss the vicarious pleasures of art and the authentic joys of criticism. For Gilbert, the two activities invigorate, elucidate, and strengthen one another. Ernest, the prosaic, methodical thinker, continually sharpens the foil of Gilbert's wit, and Ernest deserves much of the credit for the success of the conversation. Without Ernest's humble submission to Gilbert's opinion that the Greeks were a nation of art critics, the twentieth century would have been denied one of Gilbert's most famous and prophetic formulations—uttered as a riposte to Ernest's pointed lament for the Greeks, who were snared, in his view, by a critical temperament, that is inferior to the creative genius. Gilbert's reply collapses the distinction between the two faculties:

> The antithesis between them is entirely arbitrary. Without the critical faculty there is no artistic creation at all worthy of the name. You spoke a little while ago of that fine spirit of choice and delicate instinct of selection by which the artist realizes life for us, and gives to it a momentary perfection. Well, that spirit of choice, that subtle tact of omission, is really the critical faculty in one of its most characteristic moods. . . .

Ernest naively responds that all great artists work unconsciously and are often far wiser than they know. Gilbert takes the opportunity—Ernest's opinions are always, for Gilbert, opportunities—to correct Ernest and to complete his own argument. "It is not really so," Gilbert chortles. He continues:

> All fine imaginative work is self-conscious and deliberate. . . . Every century that produces poetry is, so far, an artificial century, and the work that seems to us to be the most natural and simple product of its time is always the result of the most self-conscious effort. Believe me, Ernest, there is no fine art without self-consciousness, and self-consciousness and the critical spirit are one.

"That spirit of choice, that subtle tact of omission"—these are the important phrases of the earlier passage, and they represent for Wilde the foundations of the critical "self-consciousness" that quickens the best writing of any century. Although Wilde is far ahead of his time in toying with the notion that the criticism of art is itself an artistic production worthy of aesthetic design *and* appreciation, his insistence on "self-consciousness" and "omission" aligns him with the traditional practice of speculating on the nature of the poetic genius or character—the coherent sensibility, evident within each poem, that mysteriously severs, modifies, or accepts the varied elements of English and American literary practice.

These severings, modifications, and acceptances reveal the intimate maneuvers of the poetic character or genius as it creates the personality that survives within the poem. The verse of young poets often falls prey either to the dominant idiom of its generation or to the characteristic inflection of a chosen master, and just as often these two powerful influences are joined in a suffocating union—the master often creates the sound of the generation. Confronted with the stern instruction of a literary heritage, the young writer begins on familiar ground and recreates familiar sounds, and the attentive reader must learn to hear old melodies put to new tasks and to recognize in these poems the unruly moment when the poetic character first asserts itself with cacophony, surprise, and resistance.

Younger American Poets

Often the early unnoticed accomplishments of a writer's career lie in aesthetic decision—"I *will* write a sonnet sequence," one poet decides, or "I will *not* write a sonnet sequence," another decides—and haphazard experimentation accounts for many of the failed poems that eventually are excluded from the selected edition. But occasionally these private decisions so luminously manifest themselves in the structure of the poem that the reader gradually becomes aware of a methodical, unflinching integrity, a "self-consciousness," as Wilde would have it. In the case of Garrett Hongo's **The River of Heaven** (Knopf, The Lamont Poetry Selection for 1988), this "self-consciousness" accounts for the singular accomplishment of the volume. Hongo, born in Hawaii of Japanese ancestry, relies heavily on the traditional narrative line, the storyteller's art, but he softens its typical linearity with regular excursions into simple and joyful description. "Mendocino Rose," the prefatory poem of the volume, represents a California pastoral, as the poet listens on his car stereo to a favorite Hawaiian tenor who, while singing the line, "*Ipo lei manu /* . . . I send these garlands," presses the poet to resolve his own song. For Hongo, the resolution is visually oriented, ecstatically rendered: "the roses seemed everywhere around me then, / profuse and luxurious / as the rain in its grey robes, / undulant processionals over the land, / echoes in snarls of extravagant color, / of the music / and the collapsing shapes / they seemed to triumph over." Repeatedly, Hongo balances an appropriately profane narrative with his own sacred rhetoric of description. Only a fine critical intelligence—in Wilde's sense of the term—could fashion a verse, a poetic style, that so efficiently recognizes and celebrates its special gifts. Hongo's talents are extravagantly displayed in this collection.

Both extravagance and parsimony can found a poetic style; while the sins of the former involve overabundance and volume, those of the latter often assume that subtlety must always replace the full and comprehensible intonations of the public voice. In **Faith** (Wesleyan), Lynne McMahon writes quietly of the isolated incidents that often resist description yet insistently intrude on our lives. The title poem begins, "Although what shimmers / in this white corridor / is only a short / in the fluorescent / tubes, and what sounds / like a celestial chorus / only pneumatic doors / sucking the air, / some- / thing of the light / and music of this place / is beautiful." This "something" that is "beautiful" commands her attention from poem to poem, and in "Patois," while walking in a Parisian cemetery in search of Proust's and Colette's sepulchres, she neatly rebuffs the clichés that would have muffled most poets who attempted such a typical project, and she does it simply by describing the wind: " . . . a sound like sea-surge, a moan of surf, / Began. It was the wind, we thought, which / Having no trees to claw, or water or grasses / To record its passing, had devised a keening / Against the corner monuments." Although the analogy is skillfully developed throughout the poem, this simple moment of invention, the wind insistent on recording its passing by brushing against the gravestones, reveals the subtle tact of omission that Wilde found so necessary to the critical faculty, to the artistic intelligence that ultimately shapes the literary work. By viewing the wind from this skewed perspective, McMahon forces the reader to forget—or omit—the traditional associations that often cluster around such a funereal, windy scenery. Invention, in fact, is McMahon's quiet, dependable talent, and when the situations of her poetry allow her gift to flourish, she deploys a language that moves suddenly beyond the contemporary idiom and into the realm of authentic stylistic development.

Poetic style is more easily described than analyzed, and one of the signal accomplishments of *Town Life* (Henry Holt) lies in Jay Parini's ability to align his verse with a tradition of writing that never existed—the American Grand Style. Wallace Stevens was often capable of a similar illusion, investing his radically original language with a feeling of antiquity, and although he shares nothing else with Stevens, Parini in this respect plies a similar trade and is provided with enviable benefits. The antiquated character of Pan, for example, fits seamlessly into the narrative of "Syrinx," and still, by the poem's end, appears in the reinterpreted guise that characterizes the mythological revision of the late twentieth century: "That day / he lay as if / unmade against / a mossbank, trying / to recall a note / more overheard / than heard, a sleight / of wind, a sudden / rightness passing." Hopkins spoke of the Parnassian tradition in English writing, particularly as embodied in Tennyson's work, and Parini's debt to this sonorous line is a deep one. But most American poets have benefited from similar genealogies. Parini, by hook or by crook—and again, poetic style is far more difficult to analyze than describe—has concocted a poetry that seems not only to break new ground in its handling of old themes but, more mystifyingly, invokes the authority of a literary tradition that it busily creates line by line—a stylistic accomplishment of the first order.

Judith Baumel's *The Weight of Numbers* (Wesleyan, winner of The Walt Whitman Award) moves fluently in and out of various dictions and rhythms, one often providing an implicit commentary on the other. An early stanza of "Speaking in Blizzards" recreates the declarational tonality of unadorned prose: "A character in a current magazine / story says that a man's only female friend / is his sister. His was long dead." The following stanza adopts the effortless elegance of a Lowellian formality:

> So I phone you, the noise on the line
> a fuzz, like snow on a TV screen
> and believe I hear the wires under snow,
> and see their imaginary criss-crosses
> dipping a bit, between the lakes, at Buffalo.

Baumel seems suited to proceed in a number of directions, and her athletic intellect, a quality often obscured in first books by the rigors of composition, should lead her to profitable subject matters.

Paul Lake's first full-length collection is entitled *Another*

Kind of Travel (University of Chicago), and its formal diversity alone—rhyming couplets, starched and mannerly quatrains, lanky free verse, the tumbling short line that continually resets the left margin—qualifies the volume as a compendium of poetics vessels. But Lake's vessels are fully loaded, and he has much to say. In the poem "Hog Killing Christmas," he skillfully revises the hunter's tradition—engraved in the literary tradition by Faulkner—of swabbing the young man's forehead with the blood of his first deer by domesticating the entire mythology and substituting for the deer's blood the blood of Doreen, the sow he ultimately slaughters. Macabre, perhaps Gothic, the poem accurately depicts the rigid moralities that often govern what seem to be innocuous situations, and in this sense Lake's meditations never avoid the discipline of evaluation. Even in "Apparition," a poem of classical sublimity, Lake constructs the image of a woman stooping over a drawer with an interplay of shadow and light that is carefully imprecise. Her body is one that

> . . . embraced takes on such substance
> as a body fully nine-tenths water
> might take—
> moon pale, with a taste of ocean.

The gently erotic overtones unite the senses, and the poem, which had begun by stimulating the reader's visual curiosity, ends, as all subliminal meditations must, by implicating and finally transcending physical desire.

Ron Smith's *Running Again in Hollywood Cemetery* (University of Central Florida) often deploys a descriptive scheme that is similar to Lake's, but where Lake trusts the rhythms of his narrative to resolve a succession of images, plots, and structural tensions, Smith turns resolutely toward moral analysis. The eloquent, hard-won laurels of his poems often lie midway through them because it is there, in the fray, that morality is most useful. In "Wood," Smith begins with the apt description, "My wood is split and stacked / in angular perfection." And two lines later, he records that "Black ants came out / like guilt when / my ax broke those barrelshapes." Throughout this coherent, well plotted collection, Smith ponders without affectation, without excessive intellection, the difficulties that attend the formation of a secular ethics, and it is the courage of his engagement that provides the cohesion of his poems.

Although *Lucky Seven* (Wesleyan) would fit nicely in any discussion of narrative poetry, Jordan Smith's accomplishments, like Hongo's, often lie in those areas where he attempts to modify his narrative line. For Smith, modification involves transcendence, wherever he may find it—in his characters, in his landscapes, in his revelatory eye for detail. His stories often return at the end to the objects or sceneries that began them, but these objects and sceneries are typically viewed from a refurbished perspective. In "The Hudson at Mechanicville," Smith begins, "Below the Chesapeake & Ohio's / Tanker cars stalled mid- / Span on an iron trestle, / The sun has joined a barge / To glory on the water." By the poem's end, he has returned to the same scene, and although he never lifted his gaze from the river and its surroundings, Smith had not until now seen this particular river:

> The river a dark blue drift
> Of smoke, where two scows
> Were moored, and the shadows
> Of the loading crew bent
> And lifted, weighted with the grace

Of presence in such transience.

The first-person pronoun—used lustily by many poets—is used sparingly by Smith, but the presence of the poetical character, the refining sensibility that actively exercises Wilde's "subtle tact of omission," extends throughout the poem. The pronoun appears once, midway through his narrative, when Smith pauses and confesses that "I have kept my devotions / To the second-floor window / Of a duplex. . . ." Smith's devotional sympathies need no imposing subject to utter them; they inform his landscape and his people, and at the precise moment when they turn his stories from narration to celebration, his essentially religious imagination finds its felicitous and distinctive form.

Nowadays, the domain of extended narrative writing seems most obviously to fall within the novel's purview, but, happily, many poets are unruffled by the conquering genre. Kate Daniels's *The Niobe Poems* (Pittsburgh) and Andrew Hudgins's *The Lost War* (Houghton Mifflin)—the former seeking historical wisdom from mythology, the latter mythological significance from history—constitute book-length meditations on a clearly announced and carefully annotated subject. Divided into short lyrics of varying intention, both collections accept the twentieth-century solution to the long poem as they construct a poetic sequence that depends for its structural integrity on an accumulated meaning.

Although *The Niobe Poems* concerns the myth of the boastful Niobe, whose seven sons and seven daughters were murdered by Artemis and Apollo as the result of Niobe's maternal pride, the reader learns nothing of importance about the myth itself, and that is to Daniels's credit. As she continually weaves in and out of the mythological framework, the emotional provenance of the myth emerges, and herein lies the poet's dominant concern. The wisdom gained from sacrifice and tragedy, the ennobling values of simple survival, and the indomitable will to rewrite the terms of that survival according to one woman's hard-won self-knowledge—these are the conceptual categories, the "gifts," that Niobe glorifies in the last sentence of Daniels's formidable book: "From her hands and skirts / as she walks away, gifts are falling, / glistening and trembling in the wet, dark grass."

Sidney Lanier—the Civil War soldier, the poet, the flautist—provides Andrew Hudgins his subject. The title of his collection, *The Lost War* (Houghton Mifflin), acknowledges far more than the Confederate forces's defeat at the hands of the Union Army; it also recognizes that from Lanier's perspective—and Lanier occasionally assumes the role of an Everyman—the war as an abstract, nationalistic rallying cry is regularly *lost* to the divisive, concrete horrors that daily assault the soldier. Hudgins's ability to sustain a plain but plaintive style of writing from poem to poem allows him to depict with honesty and precision the myriad of fears and doubts that attend the individual when confronted with the enormity of war and its aftermath. In "A Christian on the Marsh," the opening poem of the book's final section, Lanier gives voice to the poignant, essentially elegiac combination of love and death: "I know the earth desires me back, / desires the part of me that's earth— / and I'm not sure how much that is, / despite the mud-suck at my ankles / that's luscious, sexual. . . ." Hudgins finds in Lanier a kind of saint's relic, a sacred, archaeological discovery that stimulates the autumnal, purgative meditations on Lanier's life. Like the saint's relic, however, this portrayal of Lanier's life speaks of a redemptive survival, and it is the singular accomplishment of

Dust jacket of After the Lost War, *by Andrew Hudgins. Jacket design by Sara Eisenman (c) 1987. Jacket illustration by Barry Moser (c) 1987.*

this collection that Hudgins consistently trains his eye on the ascending, saintly aspects of our fallen lives.

RECOMMENDED: Peter Balakian, *Reply from Wilderness Island* (Sheep Meadow); Elton Glaser, *Tropical Depressions* (University of Iowa); Marie Howe, *The Good Thief* (Persea); Brigit Pegeen Kelly, *To the Place of Trumpets* (Yale); Richard Lyons, *These Modern Nights* (University of Missouri); Elizabeth Seydel Morgan, *Parties* (Louisiana State University); Eric Pankey, *Heartwood* (Atheneum); Donald Revell, *The Gaza of Winter* (University of Georgia); Jeffrey Skinner, *A Guide to Forgetting* (Graywolf).

Contemporaries

Richard Wilbur's *New and Collected Poems* (Harcourt Brace Jovanovich) and W. S. Merwin's *Selected Poems* (Atheneum) were the two most important books published during 1988 by living American poets. Wilbur's first volume, *The Beautiful Changes and Other Poems,* appeared in 1947, and now, some forty years later, those early poems are surprising in their new context. Wilbur is neither the versifier his detractors have indicted nor the classical formalist his advocates have defended. His best poems swiftly and effortlessly fulfill the technical requirements of his chosen form, but his real subjects often lie below the gleaming surface of his prosody. Wilbur's verse never tolerates willful mystification, although it amply accommodates, for example, the mysterious, destructive powers of the natural world. In "Fern-Beds in Hampshire County," Wilbur sees the waving ferns as a green ocean, and then, without warning, he pauses to remark,

> Whatever at the heart / Of creatures makes them branch and burst apart, / Or at the core of star or tree may burn / At last to turn / And make an end of time, / These airy plants, tenacious of their prime, / Dwell in the swept recurrence of / An ancient conquest. . . .

Wilbur unflinchingly turns his mannerly couplets to an examination of the unnamed aggression that lies "at the heart / Of creatures" and that somehow defines "their"—for which we read, "our"—existence. Such moments are not rare in Wilbur's poetry, and they bring with them the pain and joy of honesty, paying homage to the ordered forms and ratiocinations of high culture while acknowledging—often confronting—those disruptive forces that render such culture precious and necessary. With the publication of this volume, Wilbur's niche in American literature is even deeper than before, and its depth will surprise those who thought they knew him intimately, as well as those who claimed to know him too well.

Merwin's career has been driven by the anxious energies of experimentation. From the earliest ballads of *A Mask for Janus,* which caught Auden's ear for the Yale Series of Younger Poets Award, to the latest ones, which scorn punctuation, Merwin's verse bears an eloquent testimony to his refusal to linger long with any single style, and the appearance of his **Selected Poems** will allow his readers to observe the seismic shifts in his poetic method. Perhaps his translations, which number over fifteen volumes, account for his flexibilities—

transforming the semantic event, as George Steiner has phrased it, of one poem in one language into another poem in another language—and encourages the sort of conceptual fluidity that might account for Merwin's evolving stylistics. The art of translation involves more than a sense of dueling grammars, and when Merwin's accomplishment receives a comprehensive consideration, his obvious devotion to other languages will figure significantly in the evaluation. He has never been one to worry over the anxieties of writing because his ceaseless devotion to the task has left him little time to develop such anxieties, yet in one of the last poems of this collection he recalls speaking to John Berryman:

> I had hardly begun to read
> I asked how can you ever be sure
> that what you write is really
> any good at all and he said you can't
>
> you can't you can never be sure
> you die without knowing
> whether anything you wrote was any good
> if you have to be sure don't write

And so the poem ends, an unpunctuated poem that fears the punctuation of the poetic talent. Merwin is at it again, inventing, reshaping, and ransacking the tradition with a creative idiosyncrasy unparalleled by any other American writer.

Donald Hall's newest collection, **The One Day** (Ticknor and Fields), is a tripartite, book-length narration. The perspectives of a male, a female, and an omniscient narrator structure the first section, "Shrubs Burnt Away," and through their voices and the thirty-six ten-line stanzas that provide them their vehicle arises a simple story of a complex nostalgia. Hall attempts a broad, historical critique, but the breadth of the volume remains credible because it issues from a deeply personal perspective—"we enter and explore this house," Hall writes in the only note to the poem, "moving from room to room, surprised by the decor, always remaining within the single structure." Avoiding the characteristic boredom that often arises from a schematic work requires aesthetic maturity and formal control, and these qualities are in abundant evidence in **The One Day.** Michael Heffernan's newest collection, **The Man at Home** (University of Arkansas), begins with a two-part poem in terza rima that is remarkable for the way in which the more traditional diction of the first section yields, gaining momentum, to the jazzy diction of the second section, essentially effecting a renovation of the form. This collection ends with a blank verse piece that finds ample room for Bobby's Creole Restaurant, Stan Musial, Howard Nemerov, Julio Iglesias, and Diurnia, "goddess of the everyday." Heffernan is fundamentally a poet of wit, and poets of wit have typically considered detachment and exclusion to be both poetic and intellectual *desiderata.* But Heffernan's most impressive talent is that of accommodation—he cultivates the illusion that his carefully made lyrics are joyful exercises in indiscrimination. He has the saint's awareness of the body's sundry physical processes because they are the clearest, most constant reminders of our mortality; he shares the lay reader's secular concern for preserving a sacred, but public language; and he enjoys the heretic's liberty to find the transcendent moment wherever he pleases. Heffernan's book bristles with the kinds of invention, both conceptual and formal, that only a keen sense of tradition allows.

Philosophical poetry has few authentic practitioners today because didactic poetry, its original arena, is no longer written. Kelly Cherry's new book, **Natural Theology** (Louisiana

Dust jacket of Richard Wilbur: New and Collected Poems. *Jacket design by Vaughn Andrews.*

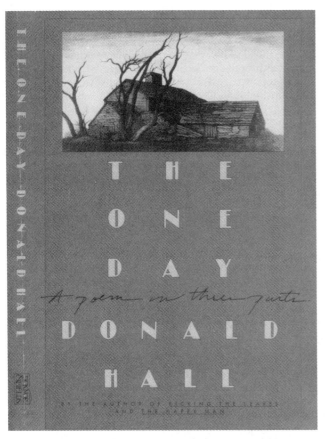

Dust jacket of The One Day: A Poem in Three Parts, *by Donald Hall. Jacket design by Sara Eisenman. Jacket illustration by Thomas W. Nason.*

State University), while it does not revive didacticism, accomplishes a far more useful task as it demonstrates the ways in which the short lyric might develop a philosophical argument. In "Hunting: A Story," Cherry details the expedition of a party of ancient hunters, and while the poem attempts to recover the origins of human consciousness and sexuality—no small task—it indicates the civilizing process these forces must ultimately undergo by deploying the couplet to describe the sexual union of two of the hunters: "I warm my hands in the hollow space / between your neck and the ground's hard face, / or in the hair on your back / like a mane, and the black / night erupts into flame in our brilliant tent: / your flesh igniting mine like a flint." The civilized couplet and the sexual animal—these are indicative of the congresses often achieved by Cherry's lyric philosophy. Linda Pastan's newest collection, **The Imperfect Paradise** (Norton)—the title is taken from Stevens's "The Poems of Our Climate"—relishes a Stevensian aestheticism, but couches it, in the title poem, within a Judeo-Christian context. The six sonnets that make up this sequence marshal a moving argument for the validity of "geographies of what we only feel," and as she watches someone at work in the garden, "planting the shadblow and the peonies, / making azaleas, hollies, dogwoods grow," she imagines the anonymous character in the closing line of the book, "digging up Eden with a single hoe." Pastan's imagination, revisionary in its most fundamental persuasion, consistently gives a fresh and credible expression to the varied subjects it confronts.

Philip Church's ten-part, book-length poem, **Furnace Harbor: A Rhapsody of the North Country** (University of Illinois), frustrates accurate description. The poem concerns the small town of Fayette—now a ghost town—which is located on a peninsula that extends off the southern shore of Michigan's Upper Peninsula. The poem records local history and lore, personal reminiscences, and the poet's deep debt to the complex phenomena of the North American Lake Country with an arresting array of symbols, rhythmic phrases, and narrative perspectives. Equally expansive but covering a life's work, Thomas McGrath's **Selected Poems, 1938-1988** (Copper Canyon) epitomizes the rambunctiously expansive writing that Whitman has forced us to label Whitmanesque. Even in McGrath's most minimal efforts—in "Poem," for example—he sounds at once the note of interrogation and blessing that characterized Whitman's relation to the "mass" he created. "How could I have come so far?" McGrath asks, continuing, "And always on such dark trails! / I must have travelled by the light / Shining from the faces of all those I have loved." McGrath is one of the last practitioners of the old American optimism, and his poetry, always benevolent and adventuresome, never loses sight of the old American vitality.

RECOMMENDED: David Bromage, **Desire** (Black Sparrow); Michael Burkard, **Fictions from the Self** (Norton); Jane Flanders, **Timepiece** (University of Pittsburgh); James Baker Hall, **Stopping on the Edge to Wave** (Wesleyan); Daniel Hoffman, **Hang-Gliding from Helicon: New and Selected Poems** (Louisiana State University); Ursula K. LeGuin, **Wild Oats and Fireweed** (Harper and Row); Walter McDonald, **After the Noise of Saigon** (University of Massachusetts); Heather McHugh, **Shades** (Wesleyan); Paul Nelson, **The Hard Shapes of Paradise** (University of Alabama); Diana O'Hehir, **Home Free** (Atheneum); Frederick Turner, **Genesis: An Epic Poem** (Saybrook); Diane Wakoski, **Emerald Ice: Selected Poems, 1967-1987** (Black Sparrow).

International

New Directions published Octavio Paz's magisterial *Collected Poems* last year, and in 1988 they offered the final section of the collection, *A Tree Within,* as a separate volume. Now, as then, Eliot Weinberger's English versions seem gracefully rendered, and because both volumes are bilingual, those who know Spanish well are able to make their own judgments concerning the various strengths of Weinberger's work. Paz's poetry has always been highly respected both in Mexico and abroad, but these two volumes will provide the general reader and the critic with the evidence, handsomely packaged, to begin a serious assessment of his accomplishment.

Roberto Juarroz, an Argentine writer greatly admired by Paz, has also found an able translator in W. S. Merwin. *Vertical Poetry* (North Point), which gathers together thirty years of writing, represents the first English translation of this poet, and his work clearly merits the superlatives that the Spanish-speaking community has bestowed on him. Like Paz, Juarroz shares a dogged belief in the transcendental qualities of seeing, of creatively visualizing the world around him—the book begins with the lines, "A net of looking / holds the world together." But unlike Paz's work, Juarroz's poetry depends more loudly on the imagination to lend integrity and value to mundane experience, and when read in conjunction, the two poets exemplify the extraordinary range and depth of contemporary verse written in Spanish.

Because of the rising interest in Latin American authors, and perhaps because of our proximity to the countries concerned, many American readers of poetry have become more familiar with translations of contemporary verse than with the verse currently being written in our native tongue in Great Britain and Ireland. *The Poetry Book Society Anthology* (Hutchinson) appears annually and provides for the American reader an accessible and inexpensive introduction to contemporary English and Irish poetry. Familiar names grace the table of contents (Adcock, Heaney, Jennings, Stevenson), but David Constantine, the editor, has also included a generous sampling of writers largely unknown in this country, and the collection, although not designed as a textbook, would serve admirably in any class devoted to contemporary poetry.

Stevie Smith, an English writer whose work many Americans know, died in 1971, and her work has been climbing, however erratically, in stature ever since. Most critics classify her verse with the ambiguous label "original," and certainly no other writer *sounds* precisely like her. In the manner of a regionalist writer, her verse records a local inflection unrecognizable to those who live beyond the region. *New Selected Poems of Stevie Smith* (New Directions), which includes her sophisticated and whimsical drawings, provides the fullest gathering of her work to date. She strove hard to avoid pretension, convolution, and stylistic contortion, and if that is the goal of all writers, then certainly she succeeded more than most.

Song of the West: Selected Poems of George Trakl (North Point Press) offers for American readers the best introduction currently available to the Austrian poet whose reputation has heretofore grown by generous and destructive measures of infamy and rumor. At last, the poetry will speak for itself. Born in 1887, Trakl was a contemporary of T. S. Eliot, who was born a year later, and many of the narrative experiments associated with the precocious author of "The Love Song of J. Alfred Prufrock" were being carried on by the equally talented author of "Helian," a long poem magnificently rendered by Robert Firmage, the translator of this collection. When considered as a European phenomenon, Modernism must now make ample room for Trakl's work, and although he died in 1914, he left behind, as this collection eloquently demonstrates, a substantial and sophisticated poetry.

Italian poets have recently received the translator's attention as well—Eugenio Montale's *The Storm and Other Things* and Cesare Pavese's *Hard Labor* are examples from the past two years—and in 1988 Ruth Feldman and Brian Swann have made available, for the first time, Primo Levi's *Collected Poems* (Faber). Levi is well known as a writer of prose, but because much of his verse bears eloquent witness to the German atrocities of the Second World War—Levi was sent to Buna-Monowitz, a subsidiary of Auschwitz, in 1944—this collection will find its place among the classics of the period. The singularly most distinctive characteristic of Levi's writing, and one that abounds in his last poems, concerns the deep lyricism of his vision, even when confronted with the enormity of the prison camp. Levi's prison poetry does not deal in atrocity and horror; as if tacitly confessing that an accurate portrayal of these events approaches the impossible, he resorts to the analogy, the verbal correspondence that will render his experience more accessible to the rest of the world. "Monday" is typical, beginning with the quiet question, "Is anything sadder than a train / That leaves when it's supposed to, / That has only one voice, / Only one route?" Answering simply that "there's nothing sadder," Levi continues, this time resorting to the analogy:

> Except perhaps a cart horse
> Shut between two shafts
> And unable even to look sideways.
> Its whole life walking.

The pastoral image of the "cart horse" conjures a spoiled innocence as the word "unable" pleads for forgiveness, for the willingness to remove the burden of responsibility from the individual participant and transfer it to the larger human condition of moral weakness and blind obedience. This is Levi's lyrical, benevolent gift, and as it dignifies, through forgiveness, the human spirit residing in these poems, his verse pays homage to the Italian language that it nobly deploys.

RECOMMENDED: Yehuda Amichai, *Poems of Jerusalem* (Harper and Row); Eugenio de Andrade, *Memory of Another River* (New Rivers); Sophia Mello Breyner, *Marine Rose* (Black Swan Books); Odysseus Elytis, *The Little Mariner* (Copper Canyon); Lars Gustafsson, *The Stillness of the World before Bach: New Selected Poems* (New Directions); Miroslav Holub, *The Fly* (Bloodaxe); Vicente Huidobro, *Altazor* (Graywolf); Jean Joubert, *Black Iris* (Copper Canyon); Ivan V. Lalic, *Roll Call of Mirrors* (Wesleyan); Alastair Reid, *Weathering: Poems and Translations* (University of Georgia).

The Year in Drama

by Robert Cohen

There really is a lake under the Paris Opera House. It was initially created by seepage from the unexpectedly high water table encountered during the building's deep excavations—and was then pragmatically adapted into a permanent feature of the House to provide water for the original scenery-shifting machines. The machines are gone, but the lake is still there, storing water against the threat of fire; you can actually ride a boat on it, and inspectors do so once a year when checking the foundation. But what's a subterranean lake without a ghost or two? The legend of a phantom haunting the Opera House arose shortly after the House opened in 1875, and since then the legend has led to a French horror novel (by Gaston Leroux), an American film (with Lon Chaney), and a British musical play (by Andrew Lloyd Webber)—a play which has now led to American ticket sales of over $500,000 a week at the Majestic Theatre on Broadway. Indeed, it now appears that Mr. Webber's American royalties will be significantly impacting the U.S. international trade balance well into the next century.

The musical play is, of course, *The Phantom of the Opera,* which, in addition to setting new box office records, also dominated this year's Tony Awards as well as the New York sweatshirt and poster market. Indeed, *Phantom* has moved into wholly new para-theatrical commercial fields, and Phantom perfume has worked its way into pricey scent boutiques all around the country. The white Phantom half-mask has, in fact, become one of the best-known corporate logos in America.

Phantom is also first-class music theater, replete with spectacular stage effects, eye-popping costumes, extravagant scenes, and well-tempered, ear-filling sounds, of the sort for which Webber is justly famous. It's not without affect, either, and while it has aspects you don't want to think about overly much (what horror story doesn't?), *Phantom* can leave you emotionally wrung out by the final curtain.

It's a triangular affair, as always with the French, with the *liaisons dangereuses* intact from Leroux: Christine, a ballet girl turned prima-diva at the Paris Opera, is at the vertex, her affections torn between Raoul, the Vicompte De Chagny, and the Phantom, who signs his name O. G. ("Opera Ghost") and haunts the stage from his watery subterranean refuge. Raoul—rich, handsome, undaunted, and a childhood friend of Christine's to boot—has his undoubted appeal, but it's the mystery of the half-masked, deformed, underworldly Phantom that inspires Christine's darker passions. And ours, too. (No one is trying to market a "Vicompte De Chagny" perfume at Bloomingdale's these days, I've noticed.) The structure is simple, as triangles tend to be, and archetypal—it is prefigured by Giraudoux's *Intermezzo,* in which a pretty French girl is also torn between a handsome young suitor and a lake-dwelling ghost. In both plays (perhaps Giraudoux was influenced by Leroux?), the French girl ends up with the suit-

Playbill for The Phantom of the Opera.

or, but not without tearing off a corner of her heart forever. We all have our phantoms, as the French know only too well.

Who is this Phantom? He's many things. He's the Angel of Music who has secretly been teaching Christine to sing, shepherding her elevation from the *corps de ballet* to a soprano soloist. ("Somehow I know he's always with me. . . . He—the unseen genius," she sings, ". . . I find the Phantom of the Opera is there—inside my mind.") He's both a deformed carnival freak and a onetime prodigy composer/magician who escaped from a traveling fair and now hides in the bowels of the Opera House. He's also the ghost of Christine's father, lurking in the graveyard of her memory. And, finally, of course, he's Andrew Lloyd Webber, the musical Svengali of

13

modern romanticism. (Webber's wife, Sarah Brightman, created the role of Christine—which Webber wrote for her—in both the London and New York productions.) Do these separate spectral identities ever come together? In the music, yes. Webber's score is braided like a rope; it's as sinewy and supple as anything ever seen on the New York stage. It's almost one very long song with multiple verses, and its appeal is steadily, relentlessly hypnotic. It's enrapturing, or at least it's enwrapping, and you just sit back and let it all wash over you: there's almost nothing to think about. What punctuation is needed to keep you in focus is mainly provided by stage effects: a popping and falling chandelier, the Phantom's entrance atop gilded proscenium putti, Styx-like gondola boat rides amidst a stage full of rising (and apparently floating) candles, a pack of sewer rats, through-the-scenery disappearing acts, a free-hanging noose (the "Punjab lasso") that does a few folks in, half a dozen fireballs spewed out of a skull, and the Phantom's public de-masking at the grand opera premiere. Director Hal Prince and production designer Maria Bjornson brilliantly dazzle our eyes and keep us from falling into a Phantomic reverie.

Do we care? The show delivers solid entertainment; it's a wonderful visual oratorio; but our caring about the characters requires an utterly compelling performance in the title role, which Timothy Nolen—in the second company, which I'm afraid I saw—did not in the least deliver. Nolen had the unenviable task of taking over for Michael Crawford, who had received extraordinary acclaim in the part. In an interview, Nolen said, "Michael's performance was beautiful. Ethereal. Not of this world. . . . Literally, a Phantom. . . . My character isn't as beautiful. My Phantom is *not* ethereal. He's very much of this world." But then he's simply a criminal. Why should Christine fall in love with him? And why should we want her to? After all, *Raoul* is very much of this world, and better at it: he's rich and handsome (and artistic and vulnerable) besides, so Nolen's approach (or his inadequacy) left the second-cast Broadway production sadly unbalanced, and the audience was left rooting for the Vicompte. And for the chandelier. See this one when you can (my tickets, purchased for a Monday night eight months in advance, were in the back row), but see it with a "literal Phantom" if you can.

Les Miserables last year, and **Phantom** this year, have fully reinstated the "Big Broadway Musical," so it was no surprise that **Legs Diamond** would try to join the genre, which it did, billing itself precisely that way ("A Big Broadway Musical") on posters slapped on buildings and buses throughout the city. It was only a Big Broadway Disaster, however, and was fun to watch if only to see how many things are needed in a Broadway musical and how a small fortune can be expended without getting *any* of them onto the stage.

Legs was easily the most embarrassing show in recent Broadway history. The show was written (music *and* lyrics) by Peter Allen, until now a popular Radio City Music Hall star; Allen also played the title role of Legs—though without ever deciding, as actor or writer, who Legs was or what he was supposed to do. Or what anybody else was supposed to do. A show-bizzy gangster musical is as far as I can go. During the many weeks of previews—at which full price was charged to the largely tourist audience—most of the principal characters were written out of the show, and by the time it opened there was nothing much in front of the fast-moving tracer-lighted scenery but the amazingly square-faced Mr. Allen,

grinning manically and, in the absence of anything that could be called supporting characters, narrating the story (such as it was) between his own ineffably immemorable songs. The show—one of whose producers was George Steinbrenner, owner of the New York Yankees—got a truly gleeful pounding from the critics, almost as raucous as Dan Quayle received earlier in the year ("bring along your crossword puzzles," said the *Times*), and closed at a total loss reckoned at about $6 or $7 million. Mr. Allen's curtain call, in which the whole cast lines up to chant "Here comes Legs! Here comes Legs!," was as depressing a moment as the American theater has had since Mr. Lincoln was assassinated.

The most prized play of the year was David Henry Hwang's very curious, very exciting **M. Butterfly,** which was honored with four of the top five annual playwriting awards: the Tony (best play), the Drama Desk (best new play), the Outer Critics Circle (best Broadway play), and the John Gassner (best American play). It is certainly a slam-bang piece of theater, the kind of Broadway performance that rarely fails to generate the big stamping, whistling, standing ovations that make theatergoing an engulfing experience.

The title is an ambiguity: it's not "Mme. Butterfly," but it's not exactly "Monsieur," either—though there's a period after the initial initial, the author pronounces the title as "emm butterfly," which provides no precise semantic clues as to the gender of his fascinating insect. This proves significant, of course, for as you may have learned by now, the play concerns a French (male) diplomat whose lover of twenty years, a Chinese opera singer, astonishingly proves, after the fact, to be a man rather than a woman, and an international spy in the bargain. This much, Mr. (not M.) Hwang assures us, is based on a true story, although the rest of the play is presumably created afresh.

This has been called a play of ideas, and, indeed, ideas here fly (or at least flutter) about the theater as densely as monarchs in May. Song Liling, the opera star, first appears singing an aria of Cio Cio San's (from *Madame Butterfly*) at a recital at the German Ambassador's in Beijing. There she captivates one René Gallimard, a married functionary in the French embassy. But Gallimard's admiration of the Puccini opera earns him only a rebuke from the singer: "Consider it this way," says Song,

> "What would you say if a blonde homecoming queen fell in love with a short Japanese businessman? He treats her cruelly, then goes home for three years, during which time she prays to his picture and turns down marriage from a young Kennedy. Then, when she learns he has remarried, she kills herself. Now, I believe you would consider this girl to be a deranged idiot, correct? But because it's an Oriental who kills herself for a Westerner—ah!—you find it beautiful."

Gallimard finds the argument, and the singer, extraordinarily fetching; he takes up with her, and for twenty years she "pleasures" him in what appear to his mind as mysterious Oriental ways. That Gallimard never discovers his mistress is male is passed over lightly: "He never saw me completely naked," Song tells a judge, "I did all the work. He just laid back." But who dominates whom? East or West—or the West's version of the East? Man or Woman—or Man's version of Woman? The Red Guards send Gallimard back to Paris (where he finds "better Chinese food than I'd eaten in China"), and, shortly afterwards, Gallimard's Butterfly comes after him as

Playbill for M. Butterfly.

a foreign spy. An undressing scene (for Song) and a cross-dressing one (for Gallimard) seem to get to the bottom of things—but does it? "As soon as a Western man comes into contact with the East," says Song, "he's already confused." Well, we're all pretty confused. Does Gallimard love the fantasy of the Butterfly or the reality of the man pretending to be the Butterfly? Does the Butterfly love the man's adoration or his confusion? Or does Comrade Chin have the inside story: "Yeah, I knew what was going on! You two . . . homos! Homos! Homos!" Are we wading again in the waters of homosexual fantasy, in one of the great traditions of mid-century American drama? Is this *Tiny Alice Named Desire?*

I'm not going to be foolish enough to proffer answers to these questions. Hwang doesn't, and I think we're all quite happy that he doesn't even try. ("I'm a man who loved a woman created by a man. Everything else simply falls short," Gallimard concludes.) What Hwang does provide (and what director John Dexter intensifies) is a marvelous theatricality: two black-suited could-be Kabuki dancers/stage assistants; a gaggle of energetic Chinese Opera instrumentalists, peeking through scrims and shogi screens; an enormous red spiraling ramp, serving as set and vortex; several breathless and high-energy flashes of (dorsal) male and female nudity; and lots of heavy-hollering angst and agonizing in the central performance by John Lithgow as the duped diplomatist. B.D.

Wong (a male) is fine in both his/her guises as Monsieur/Madame Butterfly, but when we are asked to sympathize with his character at play's end—when Lithgow rejects him—Wong doesn't quite deliver the goods. The play ends in a great bath of sound and fury, but the ambiguity of the title is never fully escaped or transcended, and the issues that remain come to a halt rather than a conclusion. Who dominates? The spectacle does, for one. The director, for another. John Dexter has always been superb at generating apparent climaxes to plays that don't actually have them, and I think the leaping ovation that greets *M. Butterfly*'s final blackout (yes, it's leaping; a standing ovation would seem pedestrian next to this one) belongs at least as much to him as to the prize-winning actors or author.

My own "best play" award goes to August Wilson's ***Joe Turner's Come and Gone,*** which, unfortunately, came and went (at the Ethel Barrymore Theatre) before many in the New York audience had the chance to sample its many merits, not the least of which was the most gripping reunion scene in recent stage memory. The reunion is of a mother and daughter, and what makes the scene (and the play) particularly remarkable is that neither are principal characters; the mother has only just arrived on the scene, and the daughter is all but nonspeaking throughout most of the action. What Wilson has accomplished is some sort of stage miracle: he has created an entire world of characters so real, so bursting with potential, so thrilling in their mix of wisdom and naiveté, that we care deeply for the whole lot of them, even when we know only a shred of their stories. And Wilson has shaped the content and context of their lives with the depth of a true master. This is a play we should be reading and seeing for the rest of our lives—an American classic of the highest order.

It's not, strictly speaking, a piece of realism, although, as there is a lake under the Paris Opera, so there was a real Joe Turner (brother of a nineteenth-century Tennessee governor, Turner lured freed slaves into roadside crap games, then abducted them for seven years of involuntary plantation servitude). Wilson's play is set, plainly enough, in a Pittsburgh boarding house in the summer of 1911. Seth and Bertha are the fiftyish resident owner/managers; he moonlights by making metal pots and pans out back (selling them to a retailer for twenty cents apiece), she cooks the two meals a day, with fried chicken on Sunday. Bynum, a conjurer and "binding man" ("just like glue I sticks people together"), and Selig, a "first-class People Finder," regularly pass through the house, in a sort of Chekhovian way, and Mattie and Molly, independent ladies (one desiring to stay so), become upstairs tenants during the course of the play's events. Into this home that's kind of a house comes an ex-deacon, Herald Loomis, and his daughter, Zonia; they are looking for Zonia's mother, lost these seven years—since Herald was "catched" and bound by Joe Turner. It is the reconciliation of Zonia and her mama that provides 1988s most indelible theatrical moment, but the rich human environment that Wilson creates is equally masterful and unforgettable.

We have, in ***Joe Turner,*** a lyrical, visionary, and undogmatic survey of the effects of slavery (the characters, with the exception of Selig, the People Finder, are black), the roots of which still nourish so much of American economics, morality, and culture. Joe Turner is not himself in the play (like slavery, he's "come and gone"), and Herald Loomis never even saw him in the flesh, but it's Turner who drives the action. Turner's era was post-Reconstruction, but the destructive spirit (and its attendant recklessness and prideful abandon) of the slave trader lived wantonly within him. Loomis remembers these slavers from the old days, and he draws the requisite conclusions: "[All] I seen was a bunch of niggers dazed out of their wooly heads. And Mr. Jesus Christ standing there in the middle of them, grinning. . . . Great big old white man . . . your Mr. Jesus Christ. Standing there with a whip in one hand and tote board in another, and them niggers swimming in a sea of cotton." Reconstruction could free the slaves but could not release their minds. That release would have to come from deeper wellsprings than the ex-deacon Loomis possesses.

It's a characteristic of Wilson's work that the play's coda, Bertha's astonishing "all you need in the world is love and laughter" speech, is in no sense a sentimentalized homily, as it would be in a poorer play (such as *Italian American Reconciliation*—see below): here, it is a direct expression of the full life of free people. It is itself love and laughter. "It is a dance and demonstration of her own magic, her own remedy that is centuries old and to which she is connected by the muscles of her heart and the blood's memory," says Wilson in his published stage direction, and, most happily, actress L. Scott Caldwell, who played the role, made Bertha's dance as palpable to the stage audience as it is to the reader of the play's text. This is certainly one of the best produced and best performed plays I have ever seen. The drama is directed by Lloyd Richards (first at the Yale Repertory Theatre, then at the Old Globe Theatre in San Diego, where I saw it, then on Broadway), and the improvised Juba song—"reminiscent of the Ring Shouts of the African slaves"—that the cast creates at the close of the first act is an astonishing piece of brilliant ensemble performance. The life of this work is so vivid, so engaging, so enrapturing, that one wants *Joe Turner* to have an audience for the next ten generations, and it was a deep disappointment that this work had such limited exposure in the theater capital. This time, anyway.

The verdict has to remain out for *Speed-the-Plow,* David Mamet's scathing satire on the Hollywood film producers with whom he now deals fairly regularly. (Since receiving the 1984 Pulitzer Prize in Drama for *Glengarry Glen Ross,* Mamet has become a celebrated screenwriter and director, with *The Untouchables* and *House of Games* to his growing credits.) This is a wickedly funny and spellbinding play which in production simply collapsed in the final scene, owing to a wholly inadequate performance in the play's sole female role. Mamet has never been known as a woman's writer anyway (his best known plays, *Glengarry, A Life in the Theatre,* and *American Buffalo,* feature all-male casts), so the fault may perhaps lie with the writing, but at this point who can tell? All that can be said for sure, from this end, is that a brilliantly witty and engaging situation dissolved in fake hysterics and bathos at the Royale Theatre, and Ron Silver (who won the best actor Tony for his performance) and Joe Mantegna could only stand there and watch the blood run out of their veins.

I was not one who bemoaned the announcement that Madonna would be playing a lead role in *Speed-the-Plow;* I had heard very good things about her workshop performance at Lincoln Center two years ago, and I very much enjoyed her performance in *Desperately Seeking Susan* on the screen. In the first half of *Speed-the-Plow,* where she plays a functional role, she is fine: attractive, believable, quick-witted, and completely non-distracting as she feeds cues into the brilliantly

dynamic battle waged by Silver and Mantegna—she a temporary clerk-typist, they two small-time producers headed for the big bucks with some extraordinary trash. But in Act II the temp typist turns semi-perm lover (to Mantegna) and persuades him to dump the trash—and Silver with it—in favor of a worthy, world-saving scientific treatise in which he believes. ("Hey, I believe in the Yellow Pages," cries the panicking Silver, "but I don't want to film it!")

Maneuvering between these two Mametesque giants, Madonna quivers, shrieks, and blubbers; suddenly we're out of Mamet-land and back in acting class. And the problem is that acting is all that Mamet and director Greg Mosher are offering us: three actors (two of them outstanding); no set other than the house drapes and four pieces of office furniture (two covered by paint drops); the furious pace of these two rasping rascals fighting for their business lives; and a secretary hungry for . . . what: love? power? We're asked, but we can't care. As Silver says as his world is collapsing around him, "I wouldn't believe this shit if it was true!"

Mamet deserves a big stage success—a play that not only wins some awards but brings in the customers night after night, which by themselves the Tony, the Pulitzer, and the Critic's Circle awards cannot guarantee. It is understandable that the management of *Speed-the-Plow* looked to a name above the title other than the author's this time, and the name was a good one, but it just didn't work out. We need to see this play with a full cast, and see what it's really like.

The monster musicals were not the only tuners in town, and two separate four-performer musicals (one a double-feature) garnered considerable acclaim and a handful of awards in New York during 1988, proving that at least sometimes less is more. I particularly enjoyed the double feature, which is double-titled *Romance/Romance* in honor, I presume, of its bifurcated structure.

Romance/Romance begins with Arthur Schnitzler's short story "The Little Comedy," and it's as elegantly debauched—and detached—as anything in the Schnitzler canon. Alfred Von Wilmers is a bored, turn-of-the-century Viennese count: Josefine Weninger a beautiful, rich, and abandoned mistress: each, seeking an affair on the other side of the Danube, feigns a raffish poverty at their first encounter. I'm a starving poet, he boasts; I a country milliner, she maintains. Thusly, together, they drink cheap city wine and take long strolls in the Vienna woods. But the sham stales and the rusticity palls; each privately decides to drop the pretense and show their true colors (black and gilt) at a subsequent meeting. "How operatic!," Josefine cries wickedly, as they meet in their *fin de siècle* finery and immediately begin planning their subsequent affairs. It is a highly acidulous and symmetrical conclusion.

This first half of *Romance/Romance* is virtually perfect, and perfectly performed by Scott Bakula and Alison Fraser, who sing all twelve musical numbers (two other actors perform in peripheral roles). It is a dramaturgical novelty—an epistolary musical—in that most of the text, spoken and sung, takes the form of letters to confidants, and the continuous reporting of the relationship, providing a running commentary/prophecy on both past and future, together with the deliberate symmetry and obvious contrivance of the plot, keeps the story supercooled. Schnitzler would love this adaptation. There's a conscious Sondheimian influence; the work is anti-sentimental and anti-romantic, making the title not a redundancy but a reflection, as though the slash dividing the two words of the title were a divisor—romance divided by romance, equaling . . . ?

The second half of the evening is not perfect; the same actors play a modern (Southampton, Long Island) husband and wife—though not each other's—skirting adultery. The other two actors are more involved this time (they play the would-be-cheated-ons) and there's no letter-writing; the play takes place in the present time, and it is a bit less interesting, possibly for that reason—for there's little we can care about whether or not Sam and Monica do or don't. The Sondheimian influence remains (part one looks back to *A Little Night Music,* part two to *Company*), but influence does not mean "as good as," and part two completes the evening without capping it. Still, **Romance/Romance** is a clever and extremely lively theater piece, with fine music by Keith Herrmann and wonderful directing by Barry Harman, who also contrived the book and lyrics.

I can only have a little to say about **Oil City Symphony** in this essay, since the work only marginally qualifies as drama (and that, mainly, because it is performed in a distinguished New York theater, the downtown Circle in the Square). Actually, **Oil City** is an extended nightclub routine in which four entertaining performers parody a concert—of their own devising—as if performed by former students of "Oil City High School." The Bleeker Street theater has been reconfigured for the occasion as an Ohio high school gymnasium (the performers enter through doors marked "Home" and "Visitor"), and the high school music teacher, "Miss Reeves," is selected nightly from the audience. The satire is gentle and low-key; we all do the Hokey Pokey and we turn ourselves about, and we laugh at our innocent and possibly provincial beginnings. It's all pleasant, but it wears thin well before it's over. The show is framed with religious songs—"Count Your Blessings" at the beginning, "In the Sweet By and By" at the end—and it indulges in both shamelessly, taking off what edges of satire could be considered deliberately meaningful. One is left with wistful but somewhat declining amusement, which is not substantially turned around by the distribution of punch and cookies at the end.

I don't know if there's ever been a play more serious and well-intentioned than Athol Fugard's **The Road to Mecca,** which won the New York Critics' Circle foreign play award in 1988. **Mecca** concerns a depressed and eccentric elderly sculptress, "Miss Helen," who has taken to knocking over lit candles in her little village house and to scaring the local children with her odd, Mecca-facing statues that are placed in the front yard. Two very devoted friends visit Miss Helen during the play; the village pastor, Marius Byleveld, who is urging her to move into the "Sunshine Home for the Aged," and Elsa Barlow, a "serious young woman" from distant Capetown, who is urging her to stay home. Both have Miss Helen's interests at heart—but they are different interests. What's at stake, in addition to the usual nursing-home dialectic between freedom and security, is a weighing of the need to protect an eccentric artist from the imposed conformity of village society. The theme is somewhat Giralducien (think *Madwoman of Chaillot*), but the action transpires in a bleaker Ibsenist setting. This is not an entirely felicitous combination.

Fugard directed the New York premiere and also played the role of Marius; Yvonne Bryceland, who we are given to understand is South Africa's leading actress, played Miss Helen, reprising the role from the London production where she re-

ceived the Olivier Award for her efforts. She and he are both dutifully applauded here—there is intelligence and sensitivity at every turn, and enough fireworks to move things cogently along—but the play, which takes a long time getting started, never takes us very far. The relationship of the two women, who are the sole characters of the first act, seems arbitrary and accidental (Fugard admitted he wrote the play in part as a response to a challenge that he had never written a major scene for two women), and the central character of Miss Helen is believable without being particularly interesting—not to mention charming, exciting, unique, inspiring, or even artistic. (The character is based on a real Helen Martins, who, after her suicide, became recognized as a major South African artist; perhaps the South African audience can read Martins's real qualities back into the play and visualize biographical and historical values that the drama itself does not contain.) There's good intellectual energy here, and clear storytelling, but none of the fascination and dramatic action of *A Lesson for Aloes,* or *Master Harold . . . and the Boys,* or *Sizwe Banzi Is Dead.* The characters in the second act are three very lonely and unhappy people, and the anguish of their loneliness is not ameliorated by anything said or accomplished during the play—indeed, the drama ends with Marius departing in defeat, and Helen and Elsa taking Valiums in victory. But if chemicals are the solution, who needs the play? What works in **Mecca** above all else is the set (John Lee Beatty), which Miss Helen has decorated with dozens of candles and thousands of pieces of colored glass, hung from strands, that twinkle in the candlelight like so many stars. This stage set represents the glory of freedom and art, if funkily, which the play otherwise only discusses in the most sober tones.

I enjoyed **Woman in Mind** immensely and was sad to see it close before its time, although Stockard Channing was memorialized afterward with a Drama Desk award for best actress in her role of Susan—the woman so astonishingly in mind. The title is a pun; Susan is indeed in her own mind most of the time. She also lives, however, in the mind of others—including those others who exist only in her mind. This is a play filled with cognitive and epistemological paradoxes, and a writer less skilled than Alan Ayckbourn would get haplessly lost in it, but Ayckbourn provides us with an inside look at organic mental disorder better than any playwright thus far (the competitors are Arthur Kopit, in *Wings;*, Jean-Claude von Itallie, in *The Traveller;* and Simon Gray, in *Melon;* plus, perhaps, William Shakespeare, in *King Lear*). And the inside look is both wildly funny and devastatingly sad.

Susan, like many schizophrenics, lives in two worlds: a bountiful fantasy world of tennisy young Etonians, and a far more dismal "real" world of her drearily solemn husband, Reverend Gerald, and his tiresome sister, Muriel. "I cope with the sheer boring slog of tidying up after both of you," says Susan, but she copes mainly by copping out—to her imaginary lover-husband, in his dashing long whites, and to their infinitely precious and adoring children. Were that the sum of Ayckbourn's vision, we would have a satisfactory and fascinating diversion, but midway through this wonderful journey Susan's worlds collide; the fantasy family starts appearing in her real world, and her mundane family penetrates her reveries. Susan is not merely a victim of hallucinatory illness, and she is no prize patient or helpless victim. Ayckbourn has given her refreshingly human characteristics, some sufficiently unpleasant, which underlie her mental torment. I am happy to say that the dreary characters do not turn out merely to be the villains of this piece, and schizophrenia does not appear, in the style of some sentimental pop psychologists, as a right and charming response to the nuclear world.

Woman in Mind has curious parallels to **The Road to Mecca:** both plays concern eccentric provincial women looked after by well-meaning pastors, both women almost burn down their own houses in questionable accidents, both plays deal with the conflict between individual creative vision and social conformity. **Mind** is the superior work, in my opinion, because the character is neither solemnized nor sentimentalized; we root for Susan not because we're good people, but because she fascinates and amuses us. The opening scenes of **Woman in Mind** are attractive and hilarious, and they redouble rather than restrict the serious, probing power of the play's conclusion.

I had the odd feeling at Neil Simon's **Rumors** that the actors were writing the play—or at least making up its plot—even as the dramatic events transpired. Yet while such improvisational giddiness (or the appearance of such) may create theatrical vivacity in a satiric work, it has an enervating effect here, for Simon has intended **Rumors,** his twenty-seventh Broadway show (including musicals and revues) in twenty-eight years, to be a farce, and in farce the characters must be driven by the plot—they can't be seen to manipulate it arbitrarily to serve their own interests. That's not to say, however, that the play is without its screamingly comic moments, and the $2 million Broadway advance, together with Simon's unflagging talent to amuse, guarantees barrels of laughter on 44th Street throughout the end of the 1980s. The less-than-compelling plot details a formal, Manhattan apartment anniversary dinner, to which the guests arrive seriatim—finding somewhat less than they expected. Apparently, the hosting couple (whom we never meet) have celebrated their anniversary in a less-than-romantic fashion, leaving the host upstairs bleeding from a gunshot wound, the hostess locked in the basement, and the "help" fled to saner quarters elsewhere in town. The purported farce essentially consists of each guest hiding this information from the next ("generally speaking," Simon explains in an interview, "in a farce, people are trying to withhold information from other people"). There's a rationale given to explain the various hidings, but it's not remotely compelling, and there seems to be no penalty for the inevitable failure that concludes each of these attempted deceptions—the withholder just gives in, reveals the hidden facts, and tries again on the next arriving guest. Nothing even keeps these characters onstage, much less urges them to cook their own dinner—which, ludicrously, they proceed to do. Nothing except the need to have a cast hang around to do a play. What we have in **Rumors** is not a plot but a pretext, and the evening cannot sustain itself for two acts, any more than could a Sid Caesar skit on *Your Show of Shows,* the kind of piece that Simon wrote so brilliantly thirty years ago.

Simon withholds information without the corresponding element of terror which information cures. Without the terror, there's no need for information; without the need for information, the withholding is merely arbitrary. What is farcical about my withholding from you the population of Nepal? When Molière withholds information from Arnolphe in *The School for Wives,* the poor man is shaken to the depths of his prostate; when Michael Frayn's playactors hurl themselves backstage in *Noises Off,* they are only inches from the humiliating panic of going back on without their pants on. The anxious moments of **Rumors** are nothing but mild character neu-

roses of well-off socialites; we don't share them at all (even well-off socialites don't share them—even Simon doesn't share them, I hazard), and we certainly don't get *scared* on these characters' behalfs, even for a moment. Yet fear propels us into farce and makes us willing to buy all its improbabilities. Here we have only nervous tics. The minor traumas of the play—a pinched nerve, a nicotine fit, a nervous bladder—are, like the main plot, simply forgotten when the laughs are wrung out of them (the young wife so urgently trying to get to the bathroom seems to have absorbed her problem by play's end), and the increasing histrionics of Simon's wonderful cast (Ron Liebman, in particular, as the pinched nerve) seem to be intended only to keep the play alive, not to escape the dread of farce's (essential) motivating humiliation. One can still applaud Simon's superbly crafted undercuts, his brilliant comic aggression, his impeccable architecture of the wild tale wildly spun out. And one can laugh real tears, which is worth the price of admission any day in winter. But there's something missing in **Rumors.**

And there's a lot missing from **1000 Airplanes on the Roof,** which is by David Hwang (see **M. Butterfly**) and Philip Glass, with designs and projections by Jerome Sirlin. This is a touring show for one actor (Patrick O'Connell), a live orchestra, and Mr. Sirlin's projections against a series of intermediate proscenia, somewhat magically slit for Mr. O'Connell's occasional exits and re-emergences. What it's all about is anybody's guess, apart from the delusions of the main and only character ("M" - without the butterfly?), who, as we gather, wanders out with a young girl on a casual date and then wanders out of his mind for much of the rest of the week—either spilling into hallucinations, as he fears, or, perhaps, picked up by alien beings (who make the sound of one thousand airplanes on the roof, he thinks). The work is ideal for touring (performances range from a Vienna airport, an Australian performing arts complex, the Music Hall Center in Detroit, dozens of college theaters and auditoriums, and the Beacon Theatre in New York, where I saw it somewhat off to the side and out of the preferred angle for viewing Sirlin's apparently more spectacular perspectives). It all seemed rather collegiate to me, as there was nothing about this particular young man's experience that seemed in the least compelling, his hallucinations being no more original or interesting than my own, and the Glass score does little to expand the Glassian (or modern) repertoire. College writers often get charged up with the discovery that there's more to life than meets the eye, and there is, but the more lasting (and mature) discoveries give us more of the shape of what's out there in the great beyond (or the great beneath) than **1000 Airplanes** does.

A. R. Gurney has been one of America's most prolific playwrights during this decade, and both his **Another Antigone** and **The Cocktail Hour** opened in New York this year. **Another Antigone,** which I was only able to read—it having played an abbreviated run—is perhaps an excessively academic exercise (it's about a college student who submits a play on the theme of Antigone—"another *Antigone,*" the professor groans—in lieu of a term paper), but **The Cocktail Hour** is a wonderfully literate, amusing, and, at the right moments, touching family comedy.

Family comedy is not a common genre in the United States. It has some play in England, where Simon Gray and Alan Ayckbourn have a go at it every year or so, but our family plays tend to be quasi-tragedies (*Long Day's Journey into*

Night, Death of a Salesman) or at least solemn (*The Subject Was Roses, Fences*), and the wit and whimsy of a desperately and comically collapsing familial affection is rare on American stages. *Cocktail Hour* has the added fillip of metadrama; it is an autobiographical play about a playwright who has written an autobiographical play (also entitled *The Cocktail Hour*), and he's brought it home to show mom and dad. "It's about you, Pop," John says, as he plops his manuscript on the cocktail table amidst the drinks Pop is stirring up for the cocktail hour. From then on, the past commingles with the present; memories, rivalries, resentments, and cross-generational conflicts of opinion (several about the drama) are lubricated with increasing amounts of gin and vermouth. There's nothing terribly surprising here: John never felt as loved as he wanted, it turns out; his father aches with his lack of respect; Mom broods over lost opportunities, romantic and professional; and sister Nina (who drops in for her share of the libations) feels utterly abandoned when she discovers how small a part she has been given in John's play. As in *Rumors,* dinner is being burned offstage all the while. Nothing surprising, but nothing clichéd, either. *The Cocktail Hour* is pretty much what it says it is: an overextended drinking session (it's more like two hours, and that's part of the point; dinner is burned by the smoldering of buried family antagonisms) with some *veritas* with the vino and bonhomie with the booze. A splendid production, too, from the Old Globe Theatre in San Diego (which also previewed *Rumors* and *Joe Turner* this year), with an outstanding performance by Nancy Marchand as the mother—a popped bubble of failed effervescence.

Larry Shue died in an airplane crash in 1985; he was already well known as the author of a popular dramatic comedy, *The Foreigner,* and became better known, posthumously, with the production of *The Nerd,* which I quickly dismissed ("shallow comedy") in these pages last year. But *Wenceslas Square,* though a slight work which played at the Public Theatre under Jerry Zaks's terrific direction early in 1988, is not shallow at all, and it can only make us lament Shue's early death all the more. The production, which was dedicated to the memory of its author, seems to have been assembled out of a partially completed manuscript, and its fragmentation goes well with its memorial and (again, like *The Cocktail Hour*) metadramatic character. Shue is here represented by Dooley, a scenery designer, who flashes back (for us) on his 1974 visit to Czechoslovakia in the company of one Professor Corey, who had gone to Prague to update an earlier work on the Prague Spring of 1968. Victor Garber plays the mature Dooley in the Zaks production, and when Bruce Norris assumes Dooley's younger self in the flashbacks, Garber moves over to play all the male Czechs that Dooley meets. Dana Ivey, another inspired choice, plays all the females. Young Dooley and old Corey, then, become our semi-innocents abroad in Eastern Europe, with an interchangeable cast of post-Dubcekian Czechs to mix and meddle with. Shue is perhaps at his wittiest in this, his last play; he shines linguistically, and gives Zaks a broad field for sprightly business and caricaturistic imagination. Nothing in *Wenceslas Square* confronts the deeper mendacities of political terror and oppression, though these are skirted repeatedly, but the play makes you laugh and think at the same time, which is still a rare quality. Shue's intelligence and theatrical authority can't be dismissed this time, which makes his earthly removal all the more dismal.

I cannot give a complete review to John Shanley's *Italian-American Reconciliation* because it simply does not appear to be a complete play. The first act is wonderful; it's sort of a modern *commedia dell'arte* sketch in New York's Little Italy, with two boys in and out of love with two girls. Aldo, the Arlecchino character, is in charge of manipulating the overall situation (Aldo's best friend, Huey, is in despair: he wants to break up with his girl, Theresa, and reconcile with his wife, whom Aldo loves), but Aldo can't control himself; he can't grow up, and his manipulatory efforts become comic misadventures. John Turturro made for a most rascally appealing Aldo, and, as with Shanley's Oscar-winning *Moonstruck,* there's some wonderfully exalted dialogue in the text ("you're like a cut-off thumb in a glass of water," Theresa tells Aldo), but the play completely dissolves after the intermission. Huey's reconciliation is forced, his wife is a sterile non-character (she's too bitterly neurotic to be interesting, except clinically), and Aldo's problems (my-father-doesn't-love-me, etc.) and his puerile moralizing ("leave room for love") are unworthy of modern theater, much less of Arlecchino. Shanley has his work cut out for him here, but there's a shot at a lasting work in the American dramatic repertory if he can (and does) put a second act on this that matches and completes the first.

A play with greater strengths, and perhaps deeper problems, is Wendy Wasserstein's *The Heidi Chronicles,* which opened with great success (and a subsequent Pulitzer Prize) at the Playwright's Horizons at the end of the year. It was such a success, indeed, that I couldn't get a ticket to see it until the play reopened on Broadway the following March, where, I suspect, the problems became more evident than they appeared in the significantly smaller off-Broadway playhouse. A chronicle—the word means a historical record, chronologically arranged—is by nature episodic rather than dramatic in structure: Shakespeare for example, took Holinshed's Chronicles and dramatized them, making them into what came to be called history plays. Wasserstein simply presents us with some raw historical (though presumably fictional) data: twelve episodes—at approximately two-year intervals between 1965 and 1989—in the life of one Heidi Holland, academic art historian, and her unfulfilled (and unfulfilling) relationships with Peter, a bright, kind, homosexual pediatrician, and Scoop, a philandering, overweening, occasionally charismatic Jewish businessman. Heidi's character is well drawn and, by Joan Allen, beautifully played. She is intelligent, affectionate, perceptive, and retiring: she doesn't drive the chronicle as much as she watches helplessly while it more or less happens to her. "I feel stranded," she reports, and we can only agree, equally helpless. While the play takes its typical topical turns, something like a TV movie (the high school dance, the "clean for Gene" rally, the protest march, the women's consciousness-raising group, the retrospective television talk show, the obligatory—for a gay-themed contemporary play—AIDS crisis scene), it is never merely programmatic; the characters are unique, interesting, and affecting, and from time to time we root for them. But the play has no momentum; the episodes are fragmentary and sporadic rather than compelling. We see characters break up before we've really seen them get together, and we don't share at all in their developmental processes. And Wasserstein's characters are simply too passive with each other for us to get very involved with them. They seem to want nothing from each other besides passing time agreeably and reporting on their affairs, ruing wryly for what is not. We want to root, but we end up having nothing to root *for.* Heidi becomes more and more opaque as the play goes on: not only is she passive and stranded, she leaves *us* passive and stranded. She ends the play pretty much in a daze, which we gather she will pass on

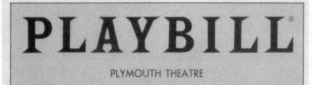

Playbill for The Heidi Chronicles.

to her newly-adopted child, whom we pity, which I am certain Ms. Wasserstein does not wish us to do.

I wanted to like this play more. Its scenes are terrific, and we'll be seeing lots of them in acting classes and auditions over the next few years. There's enough genuine wit and touching affection for two plays, and the action moves adequately. Wasserstein's dialogue is never labored nor trite, her subject is compelling, and the play's performances, under Daniel Sullivan's expert direction, are clean, imaginative, and energetic. **The Heidi Chronicles** lacks a dramatic focus, however, that would create sustained audience empathy for the characters and a growing involvement in their situation. It also lacks ambition; when the going gets tough, the play, I'm afraid, gets lazy. If I did not root for the characters, I'm still rooting for Wasserstein.

I found far less to root for in Richard Greenberg's **Eastern Standard,** although it had a very promising response from the critics both off-Broadway, where it began at the Manhattan Theatre Club, and on Broadway, where I saw it. This seems to me a completely synthetic work, like *Coastal Disturbances* (reviewed in this space last year), which comes from playwriting classes or workshops rather than from human experience or observation, not to mention creative imagination or literary genius. **Eastern Standard** is—if this can be imagined—a

silly play about AIDS and the homeless. Two couples—one gay, one not—pair off after a meeting at a restaurant, and they, together with the restaurant's waitress and a homeless madwoman who is found muttering there, end up in a Fire Island summer house for the play's second act. There they hammer out their many disappointments: an architect is depressed because he is forced to build sterile buildings rather than prettier, old-fashioned ones; an artist can't paint because he's being rejected by an attractive man with AIDS who, by trying to keep his illness secret, makes the artist doubly rejected; an actress can't get theater work, the homeless madwoman woman can't get home nor medicine, and no one is successful in finding love or permanence. All this goes into the summer home blender, where it is mixed with large doses of alcohol and a scattershot of caustic witticisms, resulting in jejune conclusions. The whole package is mildly entertaining, but no more so than a well-designed adult situation comedy, and I found distinctly unpleasant the cruel edge of presumed superiority in these apparently rich young people who smugly dispense with unemployed actresses and the psychotic homeless. The acting is quite weak (one has no sense that these people could in any way be in love, or have any passion, or even be successful in the professions they presume to profess; when the architect quits his job, we find it ludicrous, and when his girlfriend comes back and proposes to him—because he's "there"—we are appalled). Even the scenery and costumes barely meet a professional—much less a Broadway—standard. This play will probably be better served (if that's the word for it) by a good community theater than it is here.

I would like to have reported on more plays outside of New York this year, but most of those I saw had come into New York by year's end and are reviewed above. One exception: Marlane Meyer's surprising **Kingfish** commanded a great deal of critical attention at its Los Angeles Theatre Center premiere this fall, and the LATC production was at the least very skillfully contrived. Kingfish is a black wooden box on four legs with illuminated green teeth, a rope tail, and a chain around its front; the box is treated as a dog, and a black-suited actor suspended above the stage barks and pants doggy-fashion into a microphone, providing Kingfish with a semblance of dialogue. The (relatively) more human characters are somewhat barked for as well; they are moved about by the equally suspended play director, who intones the script's stage directions from above, sometimes with a great deal of urgency. A black scrim box set contains much of the action—Kingfish is a black box housed within a black box—and a hellish red glow illuminates the surrounding LATC stagehouse—fly ropes, fire exits, and all. To further the *No Exit* theme, lighting and sound board operators are elevated in front of (and flanking) the stage, and occasionally all of the surrounding "characters" (the "para-characters?")—the board operators, the director, and the barker—react with alarm to what's going on with the seeming humans (and the boxy canine) below. And what is going on? Wylie (played impishly by scriptwriter Buck Henry) is an aging queen; he's been mugged on the street by Hal, a young hustler, who he subsequently "adopts," along with Hal's CIA patron, Finney. Round and round they go; hell is other people—with a barking box. Neither as intellectually provocative as Sartre's equilaterally triangulated model nor as theatrically gripping as any of Pinter's variations (*The Caretaker,* for example), Meyer's play is often amusing and once in a while cynically poignant. "He has been treated like meat," says Wylie of the hustler. "He *is* meat," responds Finney.

Kingfish doesn't fall apart at the end because it isn't that well put together to start with, but the deconstructive moment in the second act, when Hal disassembles the dramatic fiction of Kingfish's reality ("I am telling you from experience that that is not a dog. It's a box!"), can be nothing more than a gag, no matter what the program notes say. I would hope the time will come when playwrights finally understand that to switch the audience's level of perception is a totally *meaningless*—even if theatrical—dramaturgical act. It can be funny, it can be surprising, it can even be thrilling, but it cannot convey meaning, simply because it has no context: it destroys the very context in which meaning—any meaning—exists. (Destroy the ground under your feet and you cannot jump; remove the water and you cannot swim.) ***Kingfish*** is playing with theatrical convention, sometimes very cleverly. One has no feeling that the author knows (or cares) much about the characters, however, except as they are integers in her often-surprising stage picture.

The Year in World Literature

by William Riggan

It seems only fitting that the literary year 1988, which saw the Egyptian novelist Najīb Mahfūz honored with the Nobel Prize and the Indian novelist Raja Rao named the winner of the Neustadt International Prize, was dominated by writers from the Third World, primarily Africa and Asia. European and Latin American letters experienced a comparatively weaker year, though producing a number of notable new works by established authors and relative newcomers alike, particularly in the Slavic and Germanic countries.

Asia and the Pacific

Japan's only Nobel Prize winner, Yasunari Kawabata, loved the short-story form above all others, and **Palm-of-the-Hand Stories** presents the reader of English with seventy of them, just over half of the author's total output; ranging in length from a few paragraphs to six pages, they exhibit a dazzling variety of styles and moods but focus on many of the same concerns which mark his famous novels: time's passage, love, loneliness, and the conflict between tradition and modernity. A much earlier classic of Japanese literature, Natsume Sōseki's compellingly squalid and self-conscious 1908 "antinovel" **The Miner,** an exercise in philosophy and subversive narrative irony more than in the storytelling art and often compared by Japanese scholars to Sartre's *Nausea,* also made its first appearance in English. The noted 75-year-old Yoshiko Shibaki was accorded a major Japanese literary award for the richly detailed but slightly melodramatic **Yukimai** (Snow Dance), set among practitioners of traditional Japanese dance and refined entertainment. Japan's perennial Nobel nominee Yasushi Inoue continued in the historical vein that has characterized his work for the last two decades with **Wind and Waves,** which recounts the dramatic story of the Mongol invasions of Korea and Japan during the thirteenth century. Shūsaku Endō, the current president of the Japan PEN Club and a practicing Catholic in predominantly Buddhist and Shinto Japan, brought out **Sukyandaru (Scandal),** a "psycho-philosophical mystery" which relies on a doppelgänger motif to explore the darker side of human nature, particularly sin, redemption, and death. The noted dramatist and novelist Kōbō Abé brought out **The Ark Sakura,** an audacious and savagely humorous novel set in a mazelike underground quarry populated by a cast of miscreants and misfits who have stocked it to the hilt in anticipation of an imminent nuclear holocaust. The younger generation of Japanese writers was ably represented by Yuko Tsushima (daughter of the famed late novelist Osamu Dazai), a selection of whose stories from 1973-1984 reached a worldwide audience in English in early 1988 as **The Shooting Gallery** and revealed a talented, sensitive author possessing a particular affinity for society's abandoned and exploited elements.

From China, new prose collections by Lu Wenfu (**The Gourmet and Other Stories, Vie et passion d'un gastronome**

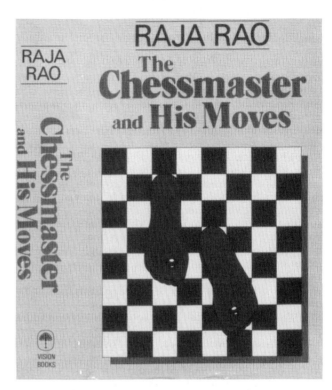

Dust jacket of The Chessmaster and His Moves, *by Raja Rao.*

chinois [Life and Passion of a Chinese Gastronome], and **Le puits** [The Well]), Feng Jicai (**The Miraculous Pigtail**), and A Cheng (**Les trois rois** [The Three Kings], **Le remontée vers le jour** [Preparing Again for the Day]) brought readers in Europe and the Americas an excellent sampling of the range of recent Chinese short fiction, from the personal to the political to the lyric to the humorous. Lu Wenfu's diverse talents, encompassing lyricism and an exquisite irony as well as sociohistorical realism and sharp satire, were particularly impressive. A more unusual view of contemporary China was conveyed by the anthology **The Chinese Western,** in which stories focus on farmers, truck drivers, artisans, and adventurers in the Gobi wastes, or on an occasional educated youth sent there from an eastern metropolis for reeducation. The short tales in **Lapse of Time** by the young woman writer Wang Anyi center on the problems of her coevals, a generation whose lives were disrupted by the Cultural Revolution and who must now deal with the new practical realities of Deng Xiaoping's China. The year's biggest sensation among readers and critics alike, however, was doubtless **Blood-Red Sunset** by the former Red Guard writer Lao Gui (literally "Old Ghost," pen name of Ma Bo); the novel chronicles the experiences of the author and his confederates in Inner Mongolia during the tumultuous Cultural Revolution and, in the words of the eminent Chinese writer and critic Liu Binyan, "is a tale of resistance, struggle, betrayal and, ultimately, the protagonist's awakening to the tragic consequences of his deeds. . . . This may indeed be the first example of a work steeped in honesty and candor since as far back as 1949, or even earlier."

India's esteemed novelist Raja Rao marked the fiftieth anniversary of his literary debut and his receipt of the 1988 Neustadt Prize by publishing **The Chessmaster and His Moves,** the massive first volume of a projected trilogy covering an enormous range of themes philosophical, religious, and historical. As in *The Serpent and the the Rope* of a quarter-century before, the work's primary movement is toward an integration of East and West, both within the divided protagonist and authorial alter ego and in the larger thematic context, as seen especially in the lengthy final section, "The Brahmin and the Rabbi." Anita Desai's new novel **Baumgartner's Daughter** also spans two very different worlds (in this case Indian and German) and attempts some kind of understanding or reconciliation between them, although with a somewhat lighter touch and less cosmic concern than Rao's work. Nirmal Verma's award-winning Hindi stories of Indian alienation at home and in Central European exile became available in English in 1988 as **The World Elsewhere.** From Pakistan, meanwhile, emerged **The True Subject,** a beautiful selection of famed Urdu poet Faiz Ahmed Faiz's finest work. By far the year's most controversial work, however, was Salman Rushdie's **The Satanic Verses,** a daringly imaginative tale of survival, reincarnation, metamorphosis, and migration that has offended several constituencies, particularly the Muslim world, for its perceived sacrilege against Mohammed. This novel has prompted book-burnings in both East and West as well as death threats against the author and his publishers in Great Britain and the United States; the uproar has unfortunately overshadowed the book's many virtues, including its comic and satiric force, its sheer verbal brilliance, and its thoughtful probing into the questions of faith and disbelief and also of racial identity and discrimination in Thatcher's England.

In a year when much world attention was focused on Korea for events both athletic and sociopolitical, the journalist and novelist Ahn Junghyo brought out **White Badge,** cleverly subtitled "A Novel of Korea." Vitally concerned with matters of conscience, memory, and morality of conduct, it tells the story of a modern-day Korean intellectual and publishing executive whose increasing alienation and repressed guilt over his cowardice during military service in Vietnam—both personified in the form of an erstwhile comrade-in-arms who has now ominously rematerialized in Seoul—now threaten to destroy both his personal life and his career.

Africa and the West Indies

The Nigerian novelist Chinua Achebe, whose work many critics place on a par with that of 1986 Nobel laureate (and Achebe's countryman) Wole Soyinka, brought out in 1988 **Anthills of the Savannah,** his first full-fledged novel in twenty years. The story follows three principal characters through a series of epochal changes in their nation's government and society that test the nature of power, ambition, courage, conscience, and love, but the novel's schematic quality and pervasive use of Nigerian pidgin have thus far evoked more negative comment than praise. Cyprian Ekwensi—colorfully

dubbed "the Nigerian Defoe" some time ago—continued his prolific career with two new books: **Jagua Nana's Daughter,** the sequel to 1960's bawdy and (at that time) scandalously sensual *Jagua Nana,* and **For a Roll of Parchment,** a text first written in the 1950s but now adapted for contemporary tastes and first publication, about the widespread African veneration for a foreign university degree. **Memory of Departure,** an extraordinary first novel by Tanzanian-born Abdurazak Gurnah, is a lyric coming-of-age story set in a squalid seaport town and described by one critic as "a compelling study of one man's struggle to find a purpose for his life and a haunting portrait of a traditional society collapsing under the weight of poverty and rapid change." Es'kia Mphahlele, frequently called the "elder statesman of black South African writers," brought out a new volume of short fiction, **Renewal Time,** late in 1988. The stories in this volume date from his twenty-year exile period (which ended with his return home in the mid-1980s) and are marked by a continuing concern for the tragedy of apartheid. The white South African author Breyten Breytenbach collected the best of his prison poems in his own English reworkings (from the Afrikaans) as **Judas Eye and Self-Portrait/Deathwatch.** Breytenbach is an acquired taste as a poet, but his linguistic brilliance and his importance as a symbol of Afrikaner resistance to apartheid's abuses make his new works significant and worthy of attention. The poetry of Ghana's Kofi Awoonor also bears a strong sociopolitical strain but without the wild excesses of Breytenbach, as is clearly evident in **Until the Morning After,** which gathers the best of his verse from the years 1963-1985.

From non-English-speaking Africa in 1988 came two works by Sony Labou Tansi of the Congo: **Les yeux du volcan** (The Volcano's Eyes) is an exuberant exercise in magical realism, full of crimes and wars and revolutions and freely merging fantasy with fiction in its condemnatory tale of governmental corruption and general ignorance, while **The Antipeople** takes a smaller target—the sanctimonious headmaster of a small teachers' college in Zaire—and works far more successfully as a morality tale about a world of banal evil. **The World of "Mestre" Tamoda,** written in an Angolan prison during the 1960s by the soldier-poet-novelist-diplomat Uanhenga Xitu, gathers three loosely related novellas depicting life in prerevolutionary Angola of the 1940s, including a cross-racial and interclass love affair and a comic nod to oral tradition in the persona of the garrulous bush-lawyer Tamoda. The noted Afrikaans novelist and critic André Brink, in a departure from his usual contemporary settings and themes, turned to the world of legend and myth in **Die eerste lewe van Adamastor** (Adamastor's First Life), recasting in an African context the tale of the fabled giant who was denied the love of Thetis and was transformed by Jupiter into a rugged cliff, whereupon he took out his anger on any and all ships that ventured past him off the Cape of Storms. An undercurrent of commentary on the unsuccessful mixing of disparate cultures is readily discernible but unobtrusive.

The most noteworthy new works from the Caribbean in 1988 were the lushly lyric and threateningly mysterious novel **Hadriana dans tous mes rêves** (Hadriana in All My Dreams) by the Haitian-born René Depestre, and **Ton beau capitaine** (Your Handsome Captain), a one-character play by Guadeloupe's Simone Schwarz-Bart dramatizing the sufferings of the "wretched of the earth," in particular the loss of culture and community through forced labor and the resulting separation of peoples and individuals. Trinidad's Earl Lovelace weighed in with **A Brief Conversation and Other Stories,**

Dust jacket of The Antipeople, *by Sony Labou Tansi.*

which features a wide range of characters—a young dandy, a struggling businessman, a group of impoverished carnival-goers, a lowly shoemaker, an itinerant barber—whose stories together add up to a richly textured rendering of contemporary social history on the island as well as a persuasive moral comedy.

Middle East

The monumental anthology *The Literature of Modern Arabia,* produced under the general editorship of Salma Khadra Jayyusi, offered English readers a truly first-rate gathering of recent texts from Saudi Arabia, Kuwait, Yemen, and the Emirates, among others, with an emphasis on writings of crisis and protest, identity quests, and attempts to return to an ancient heritage or adapt it in some meaningful way to the present. In addition to his Nobel selection, Najīb Mahfūz saw three more of his novels rendered into English in 1988: *Respected Sir,* a slim 1975 work about overreaching ambition in pre-1950s Egypt; *The Search,* an allegorical quest tale with dark Jungian undercurrents and a rich—perhaps excessively rich—lode of Arabic-Islamic cultural symbolism that will doubtless thwart most Western readers' ready enjoyment or understanding; and *Fountain and Tomb,* a collection of short, interrelated, impressionistic, first-person stories that combine to present a picture of a particular Cairene "quarter" as a microcosm of Egyptian life during the earlier decades of this century. Mahfūz's talented countryman Yusuf Idris also saw another of his short prose works brought to the attention of a worldwide audience with the publication (in a bilingual format) of the novella *A Leader of Men,* an intense psychologi-

cal study of a "tough" protagonist's struggle to come to terms with his homosexual inclinations. Egyptian-born Andrée Chedid's *Mondes Miroirs Magies* (Worlds Mirrors Magics) offered twenty-one stories, sketches, and reflections spanning three thousand years, from biblical times to the present, and ranging in mood from tragedy to poignant romance to warm affection to light irony. The novel *Cities of Salt* by the relatively unknown 'Abd al-Rahman Munif, a Saudi with Jordanian nationality, and the imaginary biography *Leo the African* by the Lebanese author Amin Maalouf, were two other noteworthy works to emerge from the Arab world in 1988.

Israel's Aharon Appelfeld departed somewhat from his basically autobiographical theme of Holocaust horror to examine post-Holocaust trauma in *The Immortal Bartfuss,* a typically spare and rather Kafkaesque tale of taciturn survivors of World War II whose moral outrage and linguistic minimalism serve only to eliminate the consolation of friendship and companionship in their new lives abroad. The famed Israeli novelist and playwright A. B. Yehoshua weighed in with the moving and psychologically penetrating novel *Molcho* (translated as *The Continuing Silence of a Poet*), in which the eponymous hero attempts to come to terms with his wife's death and to rebuild his life while staying faithful to her dear memory. Jalal Al-e Ahmad, perhaps the best-known Iranian exile currently publishing, came to public attention in the West through the translation of his prescient 1961 novel *By the Pen.* The story of a revolution and of two writers who question whether the new ruling powers are able to govern in accordance with their professed ideals or must soon resort to methods not unlike those of their deposed predecessors, this work will doubtless evoke in the minds of most readers Iran's 1978 upheavals and the establishment of the Islamic Republic.

German

New novels by West Germany's Martin Walser and Gert Hofmann and by Austria's Friederike Mayröcker topped the list of creative works in German for 1988. Walser's *Jagd* (Hunt) extends its central metaphor of pursuit into several arenas, including business competition and the chase for sexual and political dominance, in the story of a complex triangle involving real-estate agent Gottlieb Zürn, who will be familiar to Walser's readers from his previous novel, *Schwanenhaus* (Swan House). With *Vor der Regenzeit* (Before the Rainy Season) Hofmann spins an exotic, panoramic tale of intrigue and danger in the lush setting of a South American rain forest. Mayröcker's *Mein Herz mein Zimmer mein Name* (My Heart My Room My Name) offers a startling 350-page monologue cast as a single unending sentence, an alternately compulsive and confessional tirade spoken as much to fend off loneliness and silence and fear as to convey either meaning or message. Critics are feasting on the work, but readers are likely to be few.

Elsewhere in the German-speaking realm, *Meduse,* by Switzerland's Gertrud Leutenegger and *Seltsamer Abschied* (Strange Farewell), by Hermann Lenz proved somewhat disappointing, given the quality and popularity of their earlier work. The former is a dense, complex chain of lyric associations sparked by a near-mythic seaside encounter with huge medusa, or jellyfish; the latter is the seventh in a sequence of semiautobiographical narratives centered on the writer Eugen Rapp, a lachrymose figure whose numerous misfortunes now generate only self-pity and blinkered sentimentality. The Czech émigré Ota Filip solidified his metamorphosis into a German writer with *Die Sehnsucht nach Procida* (Yearning for Procida), which covers forty years in the serio-comic, adventure-filled life of a picaresque Schweikian refugee from Central Europe now uneasily resettled in the West. Günter Grass weighed in with *Zunge zeigen* (Stick Out Your Tongue), the written and pictorial record of his six-month stay in India. The primary emotion left at visit's end is shame—hence the title, since the gesture it describes indicates precisely that in Bengali and is represented in many tales of the goddess Kali in particular.

Other Germanic

Leading Dutch prose writer Harry Mulisch published the highly autobiographical novel *De pupil,* recounting essentially his own youthful wartime experiences and the start of his novelistic career soon thereafter. The Swedish novelist Sven Delblanc showed that he can write adroitly for the stage as well, presenting in *Damiens* the intricate and deadly eighteenth-century power struggle between the idealistic title character and that past master of realpolitik, Cardinal Richelieu. Kerstin Ekman of the Swedish Academy weighed in with *Rövarna i Skuleskogen* (Robbers of Skule Forest), a striking and idiosyncratic panorama of Swedish history from medieval times to the present day that is recounted from the perspective of a troll who lives among humans for over five centuries. The superb Finland-Swedish poet and prose writer Bo Carpelan was brought once again to the attention of English readers with the publication of *Voices at the Late Hour,* nominally a novel but more accurately characterized as a stirring series of vignettes of and reflections on and by several family members who have survived the first wave of a nuclear attack.

Russian

The prominent Soviet author (and deputy to the Supreme Soviet from his native Kirghizia) Chinghiz Aitmatov led the way for Russian-language literature in late 1987 and early 1988 with the publication of his novel *Plakha* (The Block), an unprecedented exposé of narcotics trafficking and abuse in the USSR and, more importantly, a philosophical reflection upon such matters as religion in an atheist state and the intolerance and inhumanity of the Stalinist legacy. This book is a must for anyone interested in contemporary Soviet culture and society and is sure to appear soon in most major Western languages. Anatoli Rybakov's *Children of the Arbat* made its English-language appearance in early 1988, several months after its original Russian publication and two decades after its composition. Compared to Aitmatov's new book—not to mention Pasternak, Solzhenitsyn, Grossman, et alia—its revelations about the Stalinist years seem rather tame stuff, presenting no real challenge to current or recent ideological orthodoxy. From another era entirely but in a similar vein to Aitmatov came the first-ever English version of *A Godforsaken Hole,* by Evgeny Zamyatin. The setting of *A Godforsaken Hole* is czarist Russia, but its concern with a corrupt, brutal, and hypocritical closed world is very much in the spirit of his later masterpiece on the nascent Soviet society, the 1924 dystopian classic *We.*

The Queue, by Anatoly Sorokin, consists entirely of dialogue: from the intellectual patter of a self-professed writer, to the rhythms and colloquialisms of ordinary Russian speech, to the grunts and silences (rendered as blank spaces and pages) of the subliterate as they all wait in modern-day Russia's interminable queues to purchase foodstuffs and other necessities—a wonderful conceit executed (and translated) at a level of near perfection. Abroad, two of the best-known Russian exiles brought out English editions of their most recent work. 1987 Nobel winner Joseph Brodsky's three-act play *Marbles* presents a classical dialogue (the setting is ancient Rome "two centuries after our era") between two prisoners debating such subjects as freedom, reality versus illusion, and literature's permanence versus politics' transience. Vassily Aksyonov brought out *Quest for an Island,* which contains the title story and other short fiction as well as several dramatic works, mostly in the satiric tradition of Bulgakov and Mayakovsky. The émigré author Nina Berberova's 1936 novella *The Accompanist* made its first appearance in English and received solid reviews for its controlled account of a potentially melodramatic story of a homely young pianist's growing distrust and envy of her employer, a beautiful and famous diva who enjoys a life of privilege amid the hardships of post-World War I St. Petersburg.

Other Slavic

The septuagenarian Czech prose writer Bohumil Hrabal, best known in the West for the 1960s film based on his novel *Closely Watched Trains,* brings off a risky experiment in his new novel, *Svatby v domě* (Wedding in the House), by telling this entire story of courtship, betrothal, betrayal, and recovery through a timid young woman's point of view. *Indecent Dreams* assembled translations of three novellas from the 1960s by the fine Czech émigré writer Arnošt Lustig. All of these pieces are set in the Nazi-occupied wartime Czechoslovakia that figures in virtually all of Lustig's fiction. Poland's multi-talented Tadeusz Różewicz was honored with the publication of a deluxe two-volume edition of his collected plays and theatrical sketches, including *The Card File,* a classic work of the European repertory. The fiction of the late Polish writer Alexander Wat was presented to Western readers in the collection *Lucifer Unemployed,* which is prefaced by Nobel laureate Czesław Miłosz. The high esteem accorded the work of the stylish Serbian prose writer Danilo Kiš was enhanced by the appearance of the story collection *The Encyclopedia of the Dead* in a quality English translation. Kiš's countryman, Milorad Pavic, still enjoying the enormous success of various translations of his inventive and engaging *Dictionary of the Khazars,* brought out a new novel, *Predeo slikan čajem* (Landscape Painted with Tea). Once again, Pavic is playing with the very nature of reading, for the book is designed to be "solved" as much as perused, to be approached like a crossword or an acrostic, and even includes the requisite "instructions" on how to go about the task. Outside the Slavic orbit, the prolific Ismail Kadare, Albania's sole writer of international repute, brought out one new novel and two more translations of recent works: *Koncert në fund të dimrit* (Concert at the End of Winter), a 700-page fictional account of Albania's dramatic break with Mao's China in the late 1970s; *Die Schleierkarawane* (The Caravan of Veils), a gathering of three historical tales all focusing on Albania under the yoke of the Ottoman Empire; and *Eschyle ou l'éternel perdant* (Aeschylus or the Eternal Loser), a literary manifesto couched in the form of an invocation to Aeschylus, Homer, and Shakespeare to justify his chosen vocation and literature in general.

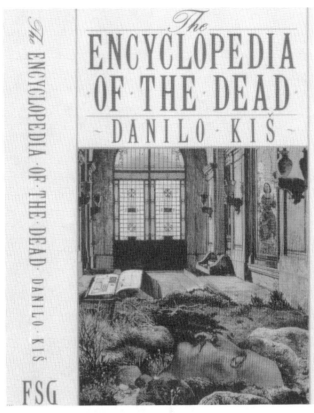

Dust jacket of The Encyclopedia of the Dead, *by Danilo Kis. Jacket design (c) 1989 by Cathy Saksa.*

Spanish and Portuguese

The outstanding Peruvian novelist Mario Vargas Llosa issued two important new books over the last twelve months, topping the year's literary news in Spanish America. *El hablador* (The Storyteller) employs a double narrative thread typical of Vargas Llosa's best early work, interweaving a personal history of growing up in Lima and an itinerant storyteller's folkloric oral history of the Peruvian Amazon Indians to achieve a remarkable and surprisingly effective narrative synthesis. *Elogio de la madrasta* (Stepmother's Pet) presents an erotic tale of incest and corruptive innocence that is noteworthy for both its sensuality and its sensitivity. *Ifigenia y otros cuentos* (Iphigenia and Other Stories) gathered a number of recent and older prose selections by Gonzalo Torrente Ballester, one of Spain's most honored authors. *Constancia and Other Stories for Virgins* brought the best of Mexican writer Carlos Fuentes's recent short fiction to the English-reading public. These stories all convey a certain mystery, magicality, and linguistic experimentation. In *Myself with Others,* meanwhile, Fuentes the essayist stepped to the fore, expounding on subjects ranging from the personal (e.g., the background to the writing of such works as the early novella *Aura*) to the more generally literary (Borges, Kundera, Diderot, García Márquez) to the public or political (U.S. policy in Central America). A play by García Márquez, *Diatriba de amor contra un hombre sentido* (Diatribe of Love against a Seated Man), premiered in Buenos Aires, but the universally bad reviews ("a superficial, repetitive and tedious melodrama" was a typical report) would seem to indicate that the au-

thor's marvelous novelistic talents do not necessarily carry over to the stage.

The prolific Brazilian novelist Jorge Amado's sprawling frontier novel *Showdown* was splendidly rendered into English in 1988 by the peerless Gregory Rabassa for the delectation of readers to the north. The novel *The Strange Nation of Rafael Mendes* by Amado's compatriot Moacyr Scliar offered that same audience a more subtle and less spectacular—but still wonderfully comic—account of financial and sexual schemings in modern-day Brazil. Three of the most important *new* Portuguese works to appear in Brazil during 1988 were Nélida Piñon's vividly entertaining novel *A doce canço de Caetana* (Caetana's Sweet Song), about a mediocre actress's return to her hometown for a production of *La Traviata; No fundo das águas* (In Deep Waters), Oswaldo França Junior's sweeping epic of rural modernization; and Darcy Ribeiro's *Migo* (Self), a Rabelaisian satire of today's self-absorbed Brazilian intelligentsia, which the author sees as largely responsible for the current chaotic state of affairs in that country.

French and Italian

Robert Pinget produced *L'ennemi* (The Enemy), a disturbingly ambiguous tale exploring the very nature of the writer's craft and his "exorcistic struggle against chaos" that is one of the year's most readable French novels. Patrick Modiano stylishly covered familiar ground in *Remise de peine* (Remission of Pain), a fragmentary reminiscence of a flawed childhood and adolescence in a provincial town. Claude Mauriac at last brought his autobiographical "Time Immobile" series to a conclusion after thirty years with volume Ten, *Oncle Marcel* (Uncle Marcel; the title notes his relationship to Proust by marriage), and his octogenarian coeval Julien Green brought his much-praised sixty-two-year *Journal* up to the present with a new installment covering the years 1981-1984.

The most notable new title to emerge from Italy in 1988 was *Quando Dio uscì di chiesa* (When God Left the Church) by the talented Triestine author Fulvio Tomizza. This work features a set of historically based accounts of the Inquisition's cruelties and abuses in the Istrian peninsula during the sixteenth century. A new work by Umberto Eco, *Il pendolo de Foucault* (Foucault's Pendulum), was announced for the end of the year.

Other European

The 1979 Nobel laureate, Odysseus Elytis of Greece, saw *The Little Mariner,* his recent collection of verse and lyric prose, reach a worldwide audience with the publication of an English translation by Olga Broumas. The award-winning poet and playwright Paavo Haavikko of Finland issued *Viisi sarjaa nopeasti virtaavasta elämästä* (Five Series about Rapidly Fleeting Life), his first new collection of verse in a decade. The five divisions in this work alternately engage the themes of death and the relationship between money and power throughout human history. The anthology *On Our Own Behalf* did readers and feminists everywhere a great service by providing a first-rate anthology of women's fiction from Catalonia, a region long rich in cultural endeavors but suppressed for nearly four decades under Franco and now at last flourishing once more. And finally, the late Salvador Espriu, rated by many as the finest contemporary Catalan poet, was memorialized in *Per a la bona gent* (For Good People), which gathered all of his previously unpublished verse, much of which is rooted in the sociopolitical realities underlying publication in the author's once-banned native tongue.

New Authors

John Ed Bradley

1959-

American novelist and journalist.

Tupelo Nights centers on John Girlie, who, like Bradley, was a star football player at Louisiana State University. Pressured by his domineering mother, Girlie decides against pursuing a professional football career and returns to his backwater hometown in Louisiana. Faced with no opportunities for meaningful employment and haunted by his family's troubled history, Girlie lapses into an aimless and degenerate lifestyle. His relationship with an older woman eventually exacerbates the conflicts in his life, with dire and tragic consequences. Several commentators linked *Tupelo Nights* with the Southern Gothic mode of fiction, noting the novel's decadent elements and its emphasis on how individuals are profoundly affected by family and social environments. While some critics disapprovingly cited melodramatic effects, most praised Bradley's recreation of local color and dialect and his skill at maintaining a grim tone. Miranda Seymour stated: "*Tupelo Nights* has a bitter, fated sadness in it which eats into you like acid, but it only just escapes being sentimental. . . . [Bradley] succeeds in bypassing monotony to achieve the hypnotic, grief-laden tone he wants. It is a long time since I read a first novel that troubled and stirred me so much as this."

MICHIKO KAKUTANI

Old Field, La., is one of those small backwater towns that's seen better days. Though its residents once liked to boast that the town was "the yam capital of the world," soybeans— which a local politician mocks as "pretend food"—are the money crop now, and farmers worry that they will lose the land inherited from their fathers. Dozens of people have moved away in search of work, and to outsiders, Old Field remains "another stop on your way south to the Coast or east to the statehouse or west to Texas," a place to stop "for gas and to use the bathroom and get directions."

John Girlie, the narrator of John Ed Bradley's first novel [*Tupelo Nights*], has grown up in Old Field, and he says he knows the town so well that he can drive it blindfolded and "overcome every hard curve and pothole." . . .

Like so many novels of small town life, *Tupelo Nights* seems to have been modeled on Sherwood Anderson's *Winesburg, Ohio*. Both novels focus on a youthful narrator who's struggling to come to terms with his hometown. Both take place largely at night, during those hours that throw the shadowy underside of village life into relief. And both feature a cast of grotesques—people whose isolation and loneliness have warped their spirits, turning them into emotional cripples, frustrated and incomplete. Marriages in Old Field tend to be short, nasty and brutish, ending in divorce or abandonment, and other relationships are often infected by a perverse sexuality. The narrator's mother, for one, tries to seduce him while he's taking a bath; and his best friend, Charley, spends his free time watching porno movies and boasting obscenely about his sexual prowess.

Just as disturbing is the proliferation of suicides in Old Field. John Girlie's grandfather has put "the busy end of a .16-gauge automatic shotgun into his mouth and pulled the trigger;" one of his girlfriends thrusts a carving knife into her belly, and his mother threatens to starve herself to death unless her sons capitulate to her incestuous demands. Charley, who works as a gravedigger, repeatedly announces that he's ready to bury himself; in fact, the cemetery where he works slowly becomes a metaphor for the entire town—a moribund place, populated by angry shades and lost dreams.

Although John was born and raised in Old Field, he became a football star at Louisiana State University and is offered a chance to turn pro. His mother, however, insists that he come back home, and out of guilt or cowardice or hope, he returns to Old Field. "I moved back," he says, "believing I could start all over again." This desire to start over—a vestigial manifestation, Mr. Bradley implies, of the old frontier ethic—apparently runs strong in John's family: years ago, his father walked out, abandoning his wife and sons in favor of a new life; and his brother abruptly announces that he's changing his name—he can't stand being called Sam Girlie anymore.

Unfortunately, John's hopes of starting over in Old Field quickly founder—an indication not only of his own weaknesses but also of the attenuation of possibility in this small town. For a while he works at a stultifying job, hanging out with Charley and passing the time playing pinball, shooting pool and getting drunk. Neighbors remind him of his former days of glory, and like Brick in *Cat on a Hot Tin Roof,* John is soon reliving his athletic feats of the past—late at night, he goes out for long runs, "carrying an invisible football tight against my body, stiff-arming invisible opponents who stumbled and fell trying to defend against my many moves."

In time, John meets one Emma Groves, an older woman who's lost her husband to insanity and her only child to crib death, and their torrid romance quickly enrages his possessive mother. As delineated by Mr. Bradley, neither of these relationships is the least bit convincing. John's mother comes across as a deranged nymphomaniac bent on manipulating and seducing her son, while Emma emerges as a needy and demanding mistress intent on bullying her lover into marriage by insulting his masculinity. In fact, both women are portrayed as such harridans that it's hard to sympathize with John's plight; instead we wonder how he can be so stupid and passive as to want to participate in their transparent games. As a result, the main story line in *Tupelo Nights* feels flimsy and contrived.

When Mr. Bradley moves away from the melodramatics of this triangle, however, he is considerably more persuasive. He has a good ear for the quirky, down-home vernacular of his characters, and his descriptions of the town itself reverberate with a sad lyricism that captures his hero's nostalgia and bitterness for a vanished time and place.

> *Michiko Kakutani, "Fresh Starts and Repeated Failure," in* The New York Times, *April 9, 1988, p. 19.*

MIRANDA SEYMOUR

Tupelo Nights is a strong, sad and wonderfully imaginative first novel from a Louisiana writer. Its setting, naturally, is the American South. John Girlie is a gentle, decent young man living at home with a devoted and semi-demented mother, whose maternal feelings are tinged with a desire she is not ashamed to show. In one of the more bizarre scenes, she sits by her son's bath, slowly ladling milk over her naked body while he looks away. John has two other problems, a surname which invites derision and his family history.

"I come from a long line of quitters," he tells his friend Charley, to which Charley can only answer: "You surely do." John has already quit a career in football, but he is not yet ready to join Charley on the lowest level of defeat, digging artistic graves and sniffing cocaine under the tupelo trees in the cemetery.

Underneath the tupelo trees, John meets Emma Groves,

mourning her dead baby. They fall in love and John falls into the old trap of having to choose between doting mother and possessive lover. Emma mocks him as a mama's boy. Mama is ready to starve herself to death (or at least, into better shape) to woo him away from "that horrible, promiscuous little piece of trash". Justifying himself every step of the way, John lives up to the Girlie history and quits, exchanging guilt-ridden love for the knowledge that "there was far too much behind me to think I could ever simply drive away from where I'd been".

Tupelo Nights has a bitter, fated sadness in it which eats into you like acid, but it only just escapes being sentimental. Bradley takes risks all the time. He uses most of the clichés of Southern novels, not least the time-honoured soft dialogue of repetitions: "They'll run me down for an autograph." "They'll run you down?" "For an autograph." But he succeeds in bypassing monotony to achieve the hypnotic, grief-laden tone he wants. It is a long time since I read a first novel that troubled and stirred me so much as this.

> *Miranda Seymour, "Maternal Love's Destructive Nature," in* The Sunday Times, *London, May 15, 1988, p. G6.*

JAYNE ANNE PHILLIPS

It's been said that Americans have the longest childhoods in the world. John Girlie, the protagonist of *Tupelo Nights,* is living, at 23, a haunted, Southern male version of the maxim. *Tupelo Nights* is the first novel of John Ed Bradley, who, like John Girlie, grew up in a small Louisiana town and was a high school sports star who played football at Louisiana State University. Mr. Bradley, a former reporter and sportswriter for The Washington Post, brings clarity and a measured lyricism to the writing of fiction, attempting to break through the stereotypes associated with novels about small-town Southern life. In the case of several of the male characters in *Tupelo Nights,* he succeeds memorably. And the town of Old Field, the former yam capital of the world and the old homeplace of the Alamo hero Jim Bowie, comes vividly alive.

John Girlie, the elder son of a locally famous family, knows something about heroes—and the lack of them. His grandfather, Jason Girlie, a politician and defiant scalawag, loses his money gambling on oil deposits and ends by living alone above his men's clothing store. John's father, Jay, a handsome lawyer and amateur boxer, disappears when John is 9, taking nothing but a pickup truck later found in a nearby village. Jason reports his son missing and, running for a re-election he will lose by a landslide; increases his press coverage by insisting that Jay has been kidnapped. But no ransom is ever demanded, no clues ever found.

John and his younger brother, Sam, are left to grow up in the shadow of a small-town scandal. Jealously, John guards every remembered moment with his father and, even as a teen-ager, thinks he glimpses Jay in the town's cafes. He takes as his legacy the belief that "in this world it is possible to leave at any moment and never return, to go away and begin again, and dying is not the only way."

The further tragedy of Jay's disappearance lies in the fact that his sons are left in the manipulative control of their mother, who seems to know more about the desertion than she ever tells. Janie Maines Girlie, a former beauty queen, married young and gave birth to John at 20. . . .

At 10, [John] is emotionally responsible for his mother, and her possessive refrains echo through his childhood. . . . Sam, younger than John by four years, does not take up the role of man of the house as gallantly as his brother. He has the sense to build a safe retreat for himself, a tent of blankets and sheets arranged over chairs, wherein he can neither hear nor respond. Long before his mother can bring herself to do so, Sam dares to declare his father dead.

John escapes by going to L.S.U. to play football, becoming a hometown hero in his turn. But after his last game Janie persuades him rather easily to give up a shot at the pros. . . . So John comes home to live with his mother, hoping to make everything "right and simple." But his grandfather has committed suicide and his old friend Charley Harwood, a kindred soul who was raised by his charismatic father to be a Jesuit priest, has quit the seminary and returned to town, bent on self-destruction. Charley, who works as a gravedigger in order to pay off his college loans, decides that he feels God's presence among the tombstones. He insists that he sees the town's ghosts while hitting lines of cocaine and sitting in a newly dug grave.

John and Charley have been a likable high school and college duo, hunting together, taking girls to a funky motel and using a well-rehearsed version of John's childhood abandonment to elicit sexual sympathy. But they are not so attractive in their new incarnations, even to themselves. Butch and Sundance with a pathetic contemporary twist, they're grown men living with their parents, unable to plan or move on, unable to love, sealing their friendship with drunken, doping escapades through the graveyards of the sleeping town. . . .

One sleepless night, John cuts through the St. Jude graveyard as "snow started to fall through the wintry cathedral of black tupelo trees" and watches "something dark in a cape or a long coat or blanket stopping at the foot of a grave," unable to stop crying. He falls in love with this mysterious figure, a woman named Emma Groves, a nurse 10 years older than he and 10 years younger than his mother. . . . When John's affair with her begins in earnest, he quits his job but maintains the pretense of working, unable to confess the relationship to his mother, who has already pronounced Emma "older and she's had more men than you could count."

John continues a double life worthy of any responsible, straying married man, taking care to dirty his work clothes, promising Emma the situation will change. Meanwhile, Charley's general dissolution worsens. . . . Sam, having escaped to L.S.U., seals his separation from his family by notifying them that he has changed his name. Devastated, John's mother takes to her bed and pledges to fast until Sam recants. She makes obvious sexual advances toward John and provokes a confrontation that ends in blows. But when John finally leaves her, he finds that he is alone. Charley, camping out in the generous grave he has dug for himself on his father's farm, is talked out of dying but won't leave town. Emma is unable to be physically distant from her son's grave. Ironically, John finds himself repeating aspects of his father's unknown odyssey.

Tupelo Nights is alternately comic and horrendous, and Mr. Bradley shows courage in exploring the difficult topics of heroism and desertion, manipulative love and loyalty, mother love and incest. Strengthened by a graceful, direct prose and a masterly depiction of a childhood stunted by unacknowledged grief, the novel is weakened by important characterizations that remain one-dimensional.

John's mother is pampered, grasping, a clear and present villain. When she tries to make love to her son she is, finally, monstrous; any disguise as an understandably clinging mother is dropped. The reader looks in vain for the subtle complexity of, say, *Murmur of the Heart,* Louis Malle's disturbing film about incest, or Gina Berriault's little-known novel *The Son.* And although Emma is a likable, sympathetic character, she doesn't inhabit the book fully, as do John and Sam. She seems a too-perfect invention, mother to the child and man in John, an attractive, willing, inevitable but finally unavailable mirror image of Janie Girlie. Emma's dramatic crisis, told as a postscript, seems out of character for a woman so modest that she even conceals the sound of her urination from her lover. But John Girlie is a memorable antihero, a man who can't grow up until he walks away from women. His precise, evocative voice skillfully fuels this story of what happens to a boy when the men in his life desert him.

Jayne Anne Phillips, "'Talk to Me, Tell Mommy Something'," in The New York Times Book Review, *June 19, 1988, p. 10.*

An excerpt from *Tupelo Nights*

Exactly three months and a day after my father left, my mother decided it was time to clear the smell of her husband from her bedroom. She poured his cologne down the toilet and flushed it again and again until the handle stuck and Mr. Happy Leoswane, the plumber, was called on to fix it. She and Sylvie stored some of my father's clothes in two oversized cedar chests in the outdoor kitchen, then after a few days a pickup truck arrived, and two silent young men loaded the chests onto the bed of the truck, secured them with long pieces of hay-baling twine and drove off as my mother and my brother and me watched from the living room window. A few days later, my mother and Sylvie sent every article of bed linen to the cleaners to be laundered, along with the rest of the clothes he had kept hanging in his dressing closet, including his best suits and hats and the fine Oxford dress shirts with his initials, JBG, sewn on the cuffs.

When the laundry came back in white cardboard boxes and clear plastic wrappers, my mother had Sam and me add it to the top of a great pile of his private things she had made on the back lawn. If we spent too much time looking over the heap of my father's private letters and papers and favorite books, photographs and record albums, she made a terrific fuss and threatened to punish us both. When we asked her what she was doing—why the pile—she said she was doing what she must and told us to please try to understand. "It may seem like a silly grown-up thing to you now, but one day it won't," she said. "One day it will seem very simple and the right thing to do."

CARTER COLEMAN

So " 'You talk about football and what a big hero you were. You tell me you were such a big man out there. Why can't you be a big man out here? You're a mama's boy, Johnny.' " Charged by his lover two-thirds of the way through [*Tupelo Nights*], the accusation cuts to the core of Johnny's character. An all-American LSU linebacker, John Girlie forsook a pro career, returned to the stagnant confines of Old Field, La., all on behalf of his mother. *Tupelo Nights* is the coming-of-age story of a mama's boy.

The atmosphere is baleful, a sort of Southern Gothic reminiscent of Truman Capote's *Other Voices, Other Rooms*. A graveyard beneath tupelo trees is a predominant backdrop. There, Johnny visits his oldest pal, Charlie, an ex-seminarian who abuses whiskey and weed while cutting out graves with a backhoe. Charlie is an archetypal angry, aimless young man. . . . It is also in the cemetery that Johnny falls in love from afar; nightly he watches the beautiful red-haired Emma come to the unmarked grave of her infant son. . . .

His intense devotion to his mother runs back to his ninth year when she told him, " 'You're the man, you're the boss around here now, John.' "

Now, with her second son Sam vowing from Baton Rouge never to return home, even changing his name, John is all she has left. . . .

[Janie Girlie], of course, abhors the idea of Emma—generating a crescendo of tension: Will Johnny inform his mother of what has grown into a passionate affair with the lonely, older beauty?

The tension snaps with Janie's last-ditch efforts to hold on to her son. (p. 3)

Tupelo Nights is a convincing tale of a young man torn between the lure of first love and the duty toward his bereft mother. The churchyard, the marsh, the farms and Cajun dives are painted with almost photorealistic clarity. The supporting cast of Old Field folk are all vividly portrayed. Although Emma remains something of a cipher, beyond the complete comprehension of her 23-year-old lover, Johnny's inner life is evoked with verity. Some moments—such as when he masturbates in the cemetery while longing for Emma—are excruciatingly honest.

It is refreshing to read a first novel with a reflective hero rather than a numb denizen of a *Less Than Zero*. The notion that setting shapes character, a tenet of the Fugitive and Agrarian literary movements, has deep roots in the Southern psyche. Old Field itself seems responsible for the ethical bent of its native son. Johnny has not set out on a search for sensual gratification like so many of his fictional contemporaries; instead he grasps for small-town virtues.

In the opening pages, he says that he came home to make everything "right and simple"—a refrain that is echoed throughout the book. In the postscript, he tells of a recurring dream in which he announces to his mother, father, brother, and Emma, all the souls he has lost, " 'I just want to make everything right and simple.' " Impossible, they reply. But it is a dream that he will always cherish, a vision of what could never be. (pp. 3, 10)

[*Tupelo Nights*] is a moving work, tender, heartfelt and as lonesome as the bayou on a misty night. (p. 10)

Carter Coleman, "Mama's Big Boy Walks Out," in Los Angeles Times Book Review, *July 10, 1988, pp. 3, 10.*

ANDREW ROSENHEIM

The chief legacy of the American Civil War may well be the South's own sense of exclusion. Themes such as racial division, rural poverty, domestic violence and the prominence of religion in daily life recur in the fiction of the region and have usually made it readily distinguishable from other American writing. These themes are still evident in the work of younger Southern writers. Although the unique traditions of the South have been a rich source for its literature, they have also sometimes proved fairly predictable, and the line between familiarity and monotony is easy to cross. . . .

[Influence seems a more oppressive problem for male Southern authors than for their female counterparts], and it is of course Faulkner who has loomed over later Southern literary ambitions, his voiceprint audible in writers as diverse as Robert Penn Warren and Reynolds Price. Others, such as Walker Percy, have come to suggest alternatives, and it seems characteristic of this new sense of liberation from Faulkner that the narrative in John Ed Bradley's *Tupelo Nights* should be more suggestive of Hemingway. John Girlie, a young football player recently graduated from college, returns to his home town in search of his roots and what is left of his family. The shakiness of Girlie's ties is unsettling enough, but his deepest friendship is infused as much with hate as with affection; his relationship with the erratic Charley Paul Harwood superficially resembles the male "bonding" of Hemingway's Nick Adams stories, but here friendship is twisted by Harwood's instability and violence.

What emerges most clearly from this account of a young man's unremitting unhappiness is the cool, arresting cleanness of the writing. Bradley writes a simple, visually vivid prose; occasionally, as with Hemingway himself, the simplicity sounds strained:

> None of it was easy and all of it was hard. I thought I was going to miss it, but how good it was to have done it. Not everyone had.

The "it" here is, unmomentously, American football. Some readers may be glad that John Girlie's playing days are over; but for the most part the language of the novel quite delicately reflects the emotional vagaries of its hero.

Andrew Rosenheim, "Voices of the New South," in The Times Literary Supplement, *No. 4469, November 25-December 1, 1988, p. 1306.*

Ethan Canin

1960-

American short story writer.

Most of the stories in Canin's acclaimed collection *Emperor of the Air* feature sensitive and meditative characters who confront personal or familial crises. Employing a graceful prose style replete with precise descriptions, well-developed metaphors, and poignant recollections, Canin presents characters attempting to come to terms with death, old age, superficial relationships, or unfulfilled ideals and ambitions. Ron Givens described Canin's method of storytelling: "A situation is introduced, a character is revealed, and we think we know what this particular fictional world holds. Then something unexpected happens. . . . Call these moments epiphanies. It's a measure of Canin's talent and sensitivity that we gain . . . insights only as his characters do. He writes his way into their hearts—and takes us with him."

Several pieces in *Emperor of the Air* originally appeared in magazines and anthologies, and many were composed while Canin attended the University of Iowa Writing Workshop and Medical School at Harvard University. Canin is a recipient of the Houghton Mifflin Literary Fellowship, which was established in 1935 to recognize new authors for works of outstanding literary merit.

JONATHAN YARDLEY

The phrase "auspicious debut" has for so long been used so casually and frequently by reviewers that it no longer means anything; this is a pity, for Canin's debut is indeed auspicious. Though the nine stories in *Emperor of the Air* are uneven, and though their sameness of voice has a somewhat numbing effect, these slight and occasional shortcomings are more than compensated for by the sureness of Canin's prose and the maturity of his intelligence; in a culture that encourages the perpetuation of adolescence well into one's third decade, he is that increasingly rare young person whose outlook on life is genuinely adult.

This is reflected in two of the collection's most successful stories, **"Emperor of the Air"** and **"We Are Nighttime Travelers."** Each is narrated by a man in his late sixties, who has come to a moment of quiet but intense crisis. In the first, the narrator, a teacher of biology and astronomy, is being pestered by his neighbor, a man whom he does not like, to cut down a 200-year-old elm that is infested with insects. "The elm was ancient and exquisite: we could not let it die," he tells himself, and maps out retaliation against his enemy. But then he sees the man in a moment of private affection with his son and undergoes an epiphany:

"I wanted to run, or kick a ball, or shout a soliloquy

into the night . . . How could one not hope here? At three weeks the human embryo has gill arches on its neck, like a fish; at six weeks, amphibians' webs still connect its blunt fingers. Miracles . . . . What it is to study life! Anybody who had seen a cell divide could have invented religion."

A miracle of a different sort occurs in **"We Are Nighttime Travelers,"** but it is a miracle all the same. Frank and Francine have been married 46 years, "and I would be a bamboozler to say that I have loved her for more than half of these." In retirement they are apart; she stays in the house, he flees it so as to be alone. A salesman all his life, he has unexpectedly discovered poetry: "It's made me melancholy in old age, sad when if I'd stuck with motor homes and the National League standings I don't think I would have been rooting around in regret and doubt at this point." Yet the poetry connects him to the old lover within himself, and in the story's lovely conclusion he and Francine find each other once again.

If these are perhaps the two most successful stories in the collection, the others are not much less accomplished. Like most young male writers, Canin is strongly interested in relationships between fathers and sons, but unlike most such writers, he does not see these relationships in simplistic or self-pitying terms. In **"The Year of Getting to Know Us"** an aloof father resists his wife's effort to bring the family closer together; "You don't have to get to know me," he tells his 16-year-old son, "because one day you're going to grow up and then you're going to *be* me"—an observation of telling acuity, but one it is not given to many young writers to understand.

Over and again, Canin produces similar evidence of unusual maturity; several stories, for example, are about how rapidly life proceeds—"no man makes truly proper use of his time"—and yet how "we learn so slowly" the lessons it teaches. He knows too that we are "alone in the world" and that it is terribly hard to maintain one's decency when one's psychological territory is encroached upon.

> *Jonathan Yardley, "Canin's Mature Miracles," in*
> The Washington Post, *January 20, 1988, p. C2.*

CHRISTOPHER LEHMANN-HAUPT

It ought really to be of merely biographical interest that Ethan Canin—the author of this strong collection of short stories [*Emperor of the Air*], and a winner of the Houghton Mifflin Literary Fellowship—is in his final year of medical school.

Still, reading *Emperor of the Air,* one can't help noting gratefully how much these remarkable stories are preoccupied with matters of ultimate concern—of life and death, of youth and aging, of wealth and poverty and of the heart not only as the seat of human emotions but also as the organ that pumps lifeblood through the system.

In the technically accomplished title story, an old man describes his contest with a younger, somewhat brutish neighbor who wants to cut down an ancient elm infested with vermin, to protect the three saplings in his yard. The narrator, who has recently suffered a myocardial infarction, schemes to save his tree. "I lay in bed thinking of the insects, of their miniature jaws carrying away heartwood."

In other stories in the volume, people die of heart disease, a young woman is afflicted with epilepsy, a young man struggles to overcome the birth defect of a crippled hand. If there is a spokesman for the author in these stories, it is the narrator of **"The Carnival Dog, the Buyer of Diamonds,"** one Myron Lufkin, a student at Albert Einstein College of Medicine, who finds learning the myriad facts of the body "like trying to drink water from a fire hose."

It wasn't death that bothered Myron;

> it was the downhill plunge of the living body—the muscles that stretched off the bones into folds, the powdery flesh odors of middle-aged men. He longed for some octogenarian to stand up suddenly from a wheelchair and run the length of a corridor. . . . He hated the demise of the spirit.

How then do these stories seek to resurrect the spirit? By conquering a domain that transcends the flesh, or, in the metaphor of the book's title, by establishing emperors of the air. The narrator of **"We Are Nighttime Travelers,"** a salesman for 40 years, takes up writing poetry in his old age and with it tries to rekindle a love affair with his wife. In **"Star Food,"**

the son of people who run a grocery store spends his time up on the roof studying the sky, "looking for things that no one else saw." . . .

In the best of these nine stories, the contest between flesh and spirit is a standoff, whether defined in terms of the earth versus the sky, or of machines versus art, or of male versus female, or of knowledge versus feeling. In [**"Emperor of the Air"**], the old man who defends the dying elm is a high school biology and astronomy teacher for whom the stars, though he sometimes tries to see them "as milky dots or pearls," are "forever arranged in my eye according to the astronomic charts." His rival, "small and afraid," is ignorant of the heavens, and must lie to his son by identifying "Cygnus's bright tail and the outstretched neck of Pegasus" as "the sword that belongs to the Emperor of the Air."

But unlike the childless narrator, the neighbor has a son to whom he can lie about the heavens. For all his shortsightedness, he has provided for the future, and, as the narrator concedes, "How could one not hope here?"

In **"American Beauty,"** the collection's masterpiece, an epileptic young woman named Darienne cultivates her talent for painting and music, while her hostile brothers conspire at renovating a motorcycle. The brothers call her crazy because of her eccentric ways, while she insists they are incapable of feeling. At the climax, she kicks over a tray containing parts of the machine they are working on. The older brother knocks her down. . . .

It is only after this outburst that the three can discover one another.

In **"Star Food,"** the boy on the roof of the grocery store finally admits to himself that he won't fulfill his mother's hopes that he discover something new in the air and achieve a special kind of fame. But coming down off the roof is like giving up another kind of star food. It is like coming out of the movies.

> I liked the movies because I imagined myself doing everything the heroes did—deciding to invade at daybreak, swimming half the night against the seaward current—but whenever we left the theater I was disappointed. From the front row, life seemed like a clear set of decisions, but on the street afterward I realized that the world existed all around me and I didn't know what I wanted. The quiet of evening and the ordinariness of human voices startled me.

The way these stories transcend the ordinariness of human voices is also startling.

> *Christopher Lehmann-Haupt, in a review of "Emperor of the Air," in* The New York Times, *January 25, 1988, p. C24.*

RICHARD EDER

Emperor of the Air, Ethan Canin's first collection of short stories, is a series of shots that find their target with devastating accuracy and frequent grace. It is target-shooting, to be sure, with pauses to reposition and set up. It is not quite the same as pursuing a live and recalcitrant quarry through swampland, and having to take the shots that the chase allows.

An excerpt from "Emperor of the Air"

When I was a boy in this town, the summers were hot and the forest to the north and east often dried to the point where the undergrowth, not fit to compete with the deciduous trees for groundwater, turned crackling brown. The shrubbery became as fragile as straw, and the summer I was sixteen the forest ignited. A sheet of flame raced and bellowed day and night as loud as a fleet of propeller planes.

Whole families gathered in the street and evacuation plans were made, street routes drawn out beneath the night sky, which, despite the ten miles' distance to the fire, shone with orange light. My father had a wireless with which he communicated to the fire lines. He stayed up all night and promised that he would wake the neighbors if the wind changed or the fire otherwise turned toward town. That night the wind held, and by morning a firebreak the width of a street had been cut. My father took me down to see it the next day, a ribbon of cleared land as bare as if it had been drawn with a razor. Trees had been felled, the underbrush sickled down and removed. We stood at the edge of the cleared land, the town behind us, and watched the fire. Then we got into my father's Plymouth and drove as close as we were allowed. A fireman near the flames had been asphyxiated, someone said, when the cone of fire had turned abruptly and sucked up all the oxygen in the air. My father explained to me how a flame breathed oxygen like a man. We got out of the car. The heat curled the hair on our arms and turned the ends of our eyelashes white.

My father was a pharmacist and had taken me to the fire out of curiosity. Anything scientific interested him. He kept tide tables and collected the details of nature—butterflies and moths, seeds, wildflowers—and stored them in glass-fronted cases, which he leaned against the stone wall of our cellar. One summer he taught me the constellations of the Northern Hemisphere. We went outside at night, and as the summer progressed he showed me how to find Perseus and Boötes and Andromeda, how some of the brightest stars illuminated Lyra and Aquila, how, though the constellations proceed with the seasons, Polaris remains most fixed and is thus the set point of a mariner's navigation. He taught me the night sky, and I find now that this is rare knowledge. Later, when I taught astronomy, my students rarely cared about the silicon or iron on the sun, but when I spoke of Cepheus or Lacerta, they were silent and attended my words. At a party now I can always find a drinking husband who will come outside with me and sip cognac while I point out the stars and say their names.

Emperor consists in large part of close variations on a few themes. They tend to come in sets. Four are about the warfare between fathers and growing sons. In two of these, the father is absent, literally or by self-absorption; the result is what a Roman historian described as making a desert and calling it peace. In the other two, the father is close and demanding; after the rebellion, comes reconciliation and rebuilding.

Two stories have old men coming to terms with the prospect of death. Two others, less closely linked, touch upon the en-circlement that lack of privilege places around American lives. . . .

Canin's images are highly charged, closely packed and worked out with care and meticulousness. They are neatly anchored in whatever realistic setting Canin has selected; there is hardly a break between their prosaic roots and their mythical tops. . . .

[In **"Star Food,"** the] son of a grocery store owner is torn between his father's gentle insistence that he must be practical and help out, and his mother's urging that he must be impractical and dream. He lies on the store roof and looks at the stars; he avoids confronting a shoplifter because she intrigues him.

And then, looking skyward again, he sees four jet fighters hurtle by. Human industry also makes stars, and it must be fed. The boy helps his father catch the shoplifter. Then he lets her go. The balance between father and mother, between the world as work and the world as dream, is maintained.

It is maintained altogether perfectly and with an altogether excessive administration of symbols. There is a bloodlessness in Canin's stories and, above all, a sense that he is using life to illustrate his patterns, rather than discerning patterns in the life he invents.

Even in the other father-son stories, where there is more a sense of passion and unpredictability, each encounter and transaction are attached with significance. There are no half-loaded wagons in Canin's train.

His epiphanies are first-rate, and they are also everywhere. They do not transform the stories; they virtually are the stories. Their schooling is flawless but they don't seem able to take recess, which is where, at any school and in stories, as well, the mud, the bruises and the glory are inflicted.

Richard Eder, "'Emperor': Variations on Few Themes," in Los Angeles Times, *February 3, 1988.*

DAVID LEAVITT

As in most first collections, some of the nine stories brought together in Ethan Canin's *Emperor of the Air* work better than others, and some of them don't work at all—yet one comes away from reading the best of them with the refreshing sense of having encountered a writer earnestly devoted to his craft. . . .

In **"Pitch Memory,"** the best story in the collection, a young woman must rescue her widowed mother, an inveterate shoplifter, when she is caught stealing a blouse at J. C. Penney's. "In our family," the young woman tells us, "violence has always been glancing and reflected"; so, too, is her narration, which moves restlessly, fixing on certain key scenes, then going on to others. With the exception of the narrator, we learn, everyone in the family has perfect pitch, so perfect, in fact, that for fun they vie with one another to identify the makes of cars by the sounds of their horns. What the story seems to urge is the value of a different way of listening, less precise yet more acute, which allows the narrator, unlike her mother, "to understand the sadness of certain notes." . . .

The narrator of **"Star Food"** is a boy trapped between the pragmatic ambitions of his father, who is a grocer, and his mother's hope that he will become, as she puts it, a person of "limited fame." The boy is dreamy, and likes to sit on the roof of the grocery looking at the sky. "My mother felt that men like Leonardo da Vinci and Thomas Edison had simply stared long enough at regular objects until they saw new things," he tells us, "and thus my looking into the sky might someday make me a great man. She believed I had a worldly curiosity. My father believed I wanted to avoid stock work." What is impressive about **"Star Food"** is the way Mr. Canin avoids the potential sentimentality of his subject, offering instead a surprisingly mature coming-of-age story in which what the boy "discovers" is compromise and solitude.

"American Beauty," a longer story, starts off clumsily, but ends up reflecting the range of Mr. Canin's capacities. Told in a curt, almost uninflected prose style, the story revolves around the 16-year-old narrator's ambivalent relationship with his 27-year-old brother, Lawrence, an almost demonic figure who alternately repels and compels his siblings. One of Lawrence's hands has only two fingers—his mother calls it "cloven"—and when his sister remarks that he will never get a job because of it, Lawrence reacts with a violence that isn't surprising—as in **"Pitch Memory,"** violence has been "glancing and reflected" all along.

At the end, Lawrence implicates his brother in his own brutality, claiming it to be an inviolable aspect of masculinity. " 'You're going to turn into a son of a bitch, just like me.' He smiled slightly. 'Just like every guy in the world.' " It is the young narrator's troubled response to this coldly deterministic attitude that gives the story its pathos and its power.

What [**"Pitch Memory," "Star Food,"** and **"American Beauty"**] have in common is a youthful narrator; when Mr. Canin speaks through the voices of older or middle-aged men, he does less well. **"Emperor of the Air"** and **"We Are Nighttime Travelers,"** both of which are narrated by old men, recall John Cheever's bite, his dark underside; for all their eeriness, the stories are at heart sentimental. . . .

If the old-man stories recall Cheever (and, perhaps, Peter Taylor), those narrated by middle-aged men also tread familiar territory—that particularly American, particularly male anomie. As in **"American Beauty,"** Mr. Canin's prose in these stories is intentionally uninflected, but the writing is sloppier, less controlled. Describing the inside of a car trunk, one narrator observes, "it was dense black inside the trunk, colorless, without light." . . .

[These narrators] tell their stories simply and forthrightly, as if to describe anything too artfully would somehow obscure the truth or call their masculinity into question. All this has worked well with other writers, but as with the relentlessly goodhearted **"Emperor of the Air,"** the approach in this case is never fully convincing, nor does it seem particularly to belong to Mr. Canin, whose prose is generally so much richer. One senses, again, the insertion of received ideas in lieu of real feeling. It isn't surprising that the best part of **"The Year of Getting to Know Us"** is a flashback, in which the narrator recalls hiding in the trunk of that family car, then listening while his father has sex with his mistress in the back seat; once again, the perspective of children proves to be Mr. Canin's strong point. And if **"Where We Are Now,"** in which a husband and wife pretend to be wealthier than they are while taking tours of houses for sale, necessarily brings to mind the similar scene in Mona Simpson's novel *Anywhere but Here,* it's probably because the desperation and earthy

humor with which Ms. Simpson describes her house-touring mother and daughter results in something so much more lively and affecting, so much more *felt,* than what Mr. Canin has given us. . . .

Too often in many of these stories an excess of artfulness surrounds a core of false sentiment, or mix-and-match alienation. Near the middle of the otherwise sure-footed **"Pitch Memory,"** the narrator recalls her father's death in the following way: "I remember coming into the kitchen on the evening after he died. My drawing, scissored from the school calendar, hung by banana magnets on the refrigerator." That's the entire recollection, and what's disturbing about it is that it really has nothing to do with the father. There's no memory of him at all here, only of the narrator's drawing, and so that lovely, emotionally powerful "I remember" doesn't take us anywhere; it only seems to.

Unfortunately, I had that sense about a lot of Mr. Canin's stories. His talent is prodigious, but too often he uses it merely to set off special effects; the story that calls out urgently to be told is the rare one here. I admire Mr. Canin for his skill and imaginativeness, and I have no doubt that he will produce very good books; but in *Emperor of the Air,* to borrow a phrase from Henry James, he seems to have studied the architecture of the house of fiction at the expense of the life inside its walls.

David Leavitt, "As Children and Others See It," in The New York Times Book Review, *February 14, 1988, p. 7.*

RON GIVENS

Because Ethan Canin writes very well, the stories in *Emperor of the Air* are full of surprises. A situation is introduced, a character is revealed, and we think we know what this particular fictional world holds. Then something unexpected happens: an old man suddenly understands what he's missed by not having children, a young man visualizes the nasty adult he is becoming, a young woman comprehends the incomprehensibility of her mentally disturbed mother. Call these moments epiphanies. It's a measure of Canin's talent and sensitivity that we gain these insights only as his characters do. He writes his way into their hearts—and takes us with him.

Canin is a graceful stylist, and his metaphors work on many levels. One story, **"Pitch Memory,"** is about a young woman who has come home for Thanksgiving, only to be confronted by her increasingly eccentric mother. At an earlier time, the narrator and her mother and sister would sing together. Even though the narrator lacked the perfect pitch of her mother and sister—literal disharmony—this tradition would bring them together after her father died. It's this musical blind spot—and the inability to truly know some things—that the narrator ponders when the Thanksgiving visit is wrenched toward chaos. . . .

Such tenderness and melancholy run through all the nine stories in *Emperor of the Air,* Canin's first collection. His characters learn about life as they live it, and the lessons don't come easy. . . . Canin's people, like most of us, don't muse on what it all means until they have to. And they pay the price.

Ron Givens, "Epiphanies and Sad Surprises," in Newsweek on Campus, *March, 1988, p. 43.*

DAVID GUREWICH

Considering the ripe wisdom that suffuses [the] often meticulously wrought stories [in *Emperor of the Air*], it is surprising to find out that their author is only 27 years old. Canin is no brat-packer. Existential driving around, rebelling without a cause, running away from home to stroll endlessly through K-Marts—these fashionable motifs do not interest him. His characters aren't the type to break out into mindless group sex, nor do they constantly see their faces reflected in mirrors between geometrically perfect lines of cocaine.

Rather, they are decent, hard-working, middle-class people, without social pretensions. ("I am an average man," says the protagonist of **"We Are Nighttime Travelers."**) They are self-effacing and likable and, well, *nice*. "I think most people will respond to honesty," says an assistant high school coach in his mid-30s. "I think that's where people like us have to lead the way." (A sensitive coach—after decades of brutes? Hasn't the author ever seen *The Last Picture Show?*) . . .

Canin's characters do have their moral lapses, but they are unfailingly sensitive, intelligent and reflective.

As *Emperor of the Air* depicts it, the American family is troubled and unsettled, yet each member goes to extraordinary lengths to appreciate the concerns of the others. Too many writers slash at the Norman Rockwell picture with savagery—Canin maps out the minute cracks in the paint with careful, surgical precision.

In **"The Year of Getting to Know Us"**—not the best story in the collection, but clearly one of the most ambitious—the teenaged narrator is arrested for smashing the school counselor's windows and is brought home. At dinner his mother declares that "next year, starting tonight, is going to be the year of getting to know us better." Although the determination is touching, unease lingers: What are the rending forces assailing this ordinary family?

The boy's father is a successful businessman who made a fortune by "being able to see the truth in any situation." He is also a golf addict and a philanderer. "You don't have to get to know me," he says to his son, "because one day you're going to grow up and then you're going to *be* me." If the proof of this is worked into the story somewhat awkwardly, the maturity of the notion itself is nevertheless impressive.

My personal favorite is **"Where We Are Now."** The aforesaid coach is dragged by his wife to shop for a house the couple has no money to buy. You can't help feeling the lost ambition (he wanted to be a pro ballplayer), the quiet despair of an honest man caught in the midst of Southern California's real estate-money-drugs insanity. And the ending is a clincher.

As in any collection, the quality of the stories varies (**"Lies"** should have been discarded after the creative-writing workshop for which it might have been written), and there is some duplication of themes. In **"American Beauty,"** a 16-year-old's elder brother almost smashes their sister's head with a hammer and then tells him: " 'You would have hit her too. You just don't know it yet. . . . If something ever goes wrong, you're going to turn into a son of a bitch, just like me. . . . You can't get away from it.' He tapped his chest.

'It's in your blood.' " The stab at familial determinism is not bad, it was better done in **"The Year of Getting to Know Us."**

Reading through these stories, you start to recognize that the narrators—the male ones, at any rate—are essentially the same person at various stages of life. And if you are not utterly beguiled by the smoothness of it all, you may also notice how confidently Canin switches from one age perspective to another.

The author is no trailblazer. His stalwart suburbanites are easily traceable to early Cheever; his first-person, present tense style has been tempered in the crucible of Raymond Carver's minimalism (perhaps he qualifies as a post-minimalist, since his characters open up *in* the lines rather than between them). . . .

Canin's talent is beyond dispute. His stories are keenly intelligent, and at his best his control seems absolute. In fact, that bothers me a little. Is it possible that he has become too technically proficient too soon? Much as that might delight his old instructors at the University of Iowa writing program, I hope it is not the case. Maybe in his next book Canin will leave a button or two undone. Like his "nighttime travelers" do. (p. 22)

David Gurewich, "Breaking Away from the Brat Pack," in The New Leader, *Vol. LXXI, No. 5, March 21, 1988, pp. 21-2.*

SVEN BIRKERTS

Canin has a highly-honed, if cumulatively predictable, narrative procedure [in his stories collected in *Emperor of the Air*]. Most of his stories begin, following Aristotle's advice, *in media res*. They plant the hook straightaway with some beguilingly mysterious statement. **"Pitch Memory,"** for instance, starts: "The day after Thanksgiving my mother was arrested outside the doors of J.C. Penney's, Los Angeles, and when I went to get her I considered leaving her at the security desk."

Once he has the reader on the line, Canin backtracks, introducing vignettes of character history, directing them toward the present, toward the crisis or mystery promised in the opening. When that point has been reached, he lets the narrative loose to find what is, invariably, an unexpected resolution. Indeed, I can't believe that Canin thinks out his endings; they have the rightness of something felt for and risked by the heart. The final revelations redeem what occasionally feels like a programmatic way of setting things up.

Canin works with contemporary settings and age-old dilemmas. His main subject is the American family. Nearly all of his characters are caught in the toils of some family dependancy—daughters meshed with mothers, sons with fathers, siblings with one another. Canin calibrates degrees of entrapment and freedom. His special gift is for exposing tensions, rendering them volatile, and then slipping a slender lit filament into their midst. He is open-eyed and tender in his essential disposition, but he is not afraid of the harsher truths.

"The Year of Getting to Know Us," one of the shrewdest of the stories, begins with a grown-up son, Lenny, visiting his father in the hospital. There follow several scenes where Lenny remembers moments from childhood and adolescence, from the time before his parents divorced. A sub-narrative unfolds. Lenny recounts how he once hid himself in the trunk of his father's Lincoln, beside his golf bag; how he trapped himself into hearing a backseat tryst with a mistress. Lenny cried out, bringing about this confrontation:

> His steps kicked up gravel. I heard jingling metal, the sound of his key in the trunk lock. He was standing over me in an explosion of light.
>
> He said, "Put back the club socks."
>
> I did and got out of the car to stand next to him. He rubbed his hands down the front of his shirt.
>
> "What the hell," he said.
>
> "I was in the trunk."
>
> "I know," he said. "What the goddam."

The episode is a triumph of minimalism. But Canin is not really a minimalist—he is after deeper, more varied resonances. Against these memories, therefore, he plays a counter-memory. Lenny is led to recall the time that he discovered that his wife, Anne, was having an affair. The parallelism may seem too obvious at first, but it's not. For Canin is not interested in the dynamics of betrayal so much as in his evolving portrait of a man with strange kinds of distance in his heart. When Anne finally confesses, Lenny is unusually passive; there is even a hint of masochistic relish.

Everything is in place for the final twist. . . . [One] night, unable to sleep, he eases the old Lincoln (the very same car) out from his father's garage. He drives through the night. At dawn, as he heads home in a drizzle, another memory surfaces. A family vacation, the year his mother designated as "The Year of Getting to Know Us." Lenny and his father stand overlooking the ocean; his father speaks.

> "Listen," he said. "We're here on this trip so we can get to know each other a little bit." A hundred yards below us waves broke on the rocks. He lowered his voice. "But I'm not sure about that. Anyway, you don't *have* to get to know me. You know why?"
>
> "Why?" I asked.
>
> "You don't have to get to know me," he said, "because one day you're going to grow up and then you're going to *be* me."

I got the old authentic chill when I read that. And it was by no means the only recognition in this superlative collection. (pp. 29-30)

Sven Birkerts, in a review of "Emperor of the Air," in Boston Review, *Vol. XIII, No. 2, April, 1988, pp. 29-30.*

Michael Chabon

1965?-

American novelist and short story writer.

In *The Mysteries of Pittsburgh,* a coming-of-age novel, Art Bechstein encounters a dizzying series of people and events during the summer following his graduation from college. Through these experiences Art gains insight on the nature of love, friendship, and sexuality and examines his conflicting feelings toward his father, a powerful gangster. While some critics contend the novel has several plot contrivances, most praised Chabon's lyrical descriptions of sensual pleasures, his well-paced story development, and his ability to capture eccentricities of character. Many likened the style and concerns of Chabon's novel with works by F. Scott Fitzgerald. Mac-Donald Harris stated that *The Mysteries of Pittsburgh* is "full of youthful power and energy that's as refreshing as spring rain." Hardcover rights to the novel sold for $155,000, one of the highest figures ever paid for a first work of fiction.

ALICE McDERMOTT

[*The Mysteries of Pittsburgh*] is a first novel by a talented young writer that is full of all the delights, and not a few of the disappointments, inherent in any early work of serious fiction. There is the pleasure of a fresh voice and a keen eye, of watching a writer clearly in love with language and literature, youth and wit, expound and embellish upon the world as he sees it, balanced by a scarcity of well-developed characters and a voice so willing to please that it seldom goes beyond the story's surface.

As is the case in so many first novels, **The Mysteries of Pittsburgh** is a coming-of-age story, the chronicle of a single summer in which a young man confronts both his family and his sexuality and thus finds them forever changed.

This is the summer Art Bechstein has finished college, the last summer of his youth, as he sees it. . . .

Art is the son of a gangster, the Jewish moneyman for a Washington crime family who conducts his paternal business at lunch and dinner meetings during periodic trips to Pittsburgh and can reduce his grown son to public, sputtering tears with a delicately applied harsh word. Art learned the true nature of his father's profession on the day of his bar mitzvah, six months after his mother's accidental death, and has sought ever since to separate himself from it. "I saw that it inspired in him an angry shame, so I came to associate it with shame. . . . I never afterward had the slightest desire to tell his secret to any of my friends; indeed, I ardently concealed it."

This summer those friends materialize in a single day, during Art's final trip to the university library. (Despite his four years in Pittsburgh, he seems utterly alone in the city until then.) There, as he stands before the elevator, his eyes meet those of a lovely young woman behind a kind of bank-teller grille. Moments later, he receives much the same look from a fair-haired boy reading a Spanish potboiler. Outside, he meets the boy, Arthur Lecomte—a droll, charming homosexual who knows Phlox, "the Girl Behind Bars," and introduces Art to the "splendid" Jane Bellwether, whose splendor seems to be derived chiefly from her status as girlfriend to the legendary Cleveland, Arthur's best friend.

After the recent spate of novels that seem to begin and end arbitrarily, with resolutions no more satisfying than a shrug, it is both refreshing and encouraging to find a writer who so skillfully sets down the elements of his plot, diligently sets them spinning and then carefully attempts to bring about both a climax and a resolution. Michael Chabon, whose short stories have appeared in *The New Yorker,* has learned well from the writers he appears to admire—F. Scott Fitzgerald especially—and his control over his story, the wonderful use he makes of each description, of Pittsburgh itself, are often astonishing.

Soon enough, Art and Phlox are lovers, Arthur's appeal begins to have its effect on Art, and Cleveland arrives, bringing with him the link to Art's father's shadowy business. Cleveland, at 25, is an aging prankster, a big-bellied, long-haired, motorcycle-driving alcoholic full of violence and literature. He aspires to be "big." . . .

Working for a loan shark in the lower echelons of the same crime family, Cleveland knows that Art's father is *big,* and eventually forces Art into introducing them. Their meeting takes place in a Pittsburgh hotel room full of thugs. Cleveland comes away from it with a new mentor, the city's biggest jewel fence, and Art with both his father's full and devastating disapproval and "the barrier that stood between my family and my life" forever breached. In reaction, he becomes Arthur's lover. There follows some homosexual bliss and some heterosexual confusion. . . . Then Cleveland, pursued by police helicopters and clutching a doll filled with stolen jewels, calls on Art to save him from what both recognize as Art's father's wrath. Art cannot, and Cleveland meets a lyrical and neatly foreshadowed demise. . . .

Cleveland's "big" exit illustrates the book's greatest flaw: throughout, events and images seem to emerge not from the novel itself but from the author's desire to make his story neat. As a result, exploration of character and emotion is often sacrificed for the sake of an image or a symbol or a turn in the plot; the carefully controlled pace of the novel's action leaves the author and the narrator little time for insight or introspection. We are told, for instance, that Art never speaks of his "singing mother" or her mysterious death, but given that he is the eye and the mind through which the story is told we must also conclude that he never thinks about her either, which seems impossible. She remains a denial of the plot rather than a fact of Art's life.

The other characters don't fare much better: Jane is splendid but insubstantial and Phlox, though physically, vividly substantial, is emotionally flat. Even Cleveland remains a vehicle, and only the sad and charming Arthur manages at times to exceed the limitations of the novel's structure. The book's conclusion—Cleveland's death, Art and Arthur's forced flight—seems to arise more out of an adolescent fantasy of the power of a parent scorned than from anything the novel has revealed about the complex and difficult relationship between a powerful man and his sensitive son.

Nevertheless, there is much to admire here, and what the novel lacks in insight it compensates for in language, wit and ambition, in the sheer exuberance of its voice: the voice of a young writer with tremendous skill as he discovers, joyously, just what his words can do.

Alice McDermott, "Gangsters and Pranksters," in
The New York Times Book Review, *April 3, 1988,*
p. 7.

BRETT LOTT

Early on in Michael Chabon's remarkable, if flawed, first novel, [*The Mysteries of Pittsburgh*], the recently de-girlfriended narrator, Art Bechstein, is standing on a street corner one evening in the company of his new-found friend, the suspiciously good-looking and convivial Arthur Lecomte.

Suddenly, Abdullah, one of Lecomte's cohorts pulls up in a convertible Fiat, and Art finds himself sitting on the trunk, wind in his hair, as they whip through the night streets of Pittsburgh.

> "The people in the cars that managed to pull alongside the Fiat," Art muses, "gave me the same shake of the head and roll of the eyes that I myself had often given other young drunks in fast cars. I decided not to think about them, which proved to be a simple thing, and stared into the wind, and into the steady flow of street-lights."

Much of the tone of *The Mysteries of Pittsburgh* is taken from this one scene: Bechstein's simply choosing not to notice, not to think of how he spends his summer after graduation, the months of June, July and August swimming past in sweltering heat and cool nights while he watches lights and lives fast.

That tone might make one think of *Pittsburgh* as just another in the increasingly long line of Bret/Tama/Jay books being put out by the publishing world's corral of jaded young writers, and in many ways it is. There is the obligatory coolness to all things, exemplified by Lecomte and "all the hip places he had been, the perfect manner of the life he lived, his sarcastic brilliance, his hard amusement." There are the long nights at parties coupled with the intense nostalgia for a time when we were all just kids in sneakers talking on porch steps while the sun failed in the West. There is even the repressed memory of Bechstein's dead mother, a fact which, astonishingly like [Jay] McInerney's first book [*Bright Lights, Big City*], seems to give impetus to Bechstein's lost-boy attitude.

There is, too, the unbridled booze, the unbridled family structure, and, of course, the unbridled sex. But it's the issue of sex here that makes Chabon's book different. Not that the sex per se is different—his renderings, in fact, are rather tame—but the manner in which sex becomes Bechstein's reference point, his identity through a summer spent first in a few rather sex-filled weeks with the quasi-beautiful Phlox. . . . (p. 1)

Then comes August, and sex with Lecomte: " 'Are you in full capacity of your faculties?' " Lecomte asks of Art, who has been ducking and evading the feelings he's been having for him all summer. " 'I can't be certain; no,' " says Bechstein. Lecomte's reply: " 'Well, it's about time,' he said. He pinched my earlobe. 'Let's go exhaust all the possibilities.' "

Exhaust they do, but Bechstein still seesaws between Phlox and Arthur, never quite sure which to choose over the other, both wanting him with enough unspent energy as to "make love" to him anytime, anywhere: on doorsteps, in study carrels. Even in bed.

But what keeps this book from falling into the abyss of the Lost Young Americans oeuvre is Chabon's willingness to delve deeper, his ambition to find out precisely what love is, whether homosexual or heterosexual. . . .

The flaws [in *The Mysteries of Pittsburgh*] are many: superfluous characters like Jane Bellwether, who is given so much attention in the early pages of the book that we suppose she might be Art's love interest, only to have her summarily dropped half-way through; Cleveland, Jane's paramour and Art's terminally straight rich-boy-turned-biker friend, a perpetual jokester and tough guy with a golden heart; Abdullah and Lurch and Feldman and Riri, even the unnecessary if hilarious diversion of three pit bulls named Manny, Moe and Jack thrown in for some doggy-sex fun.

In one of the more puzzling twists here, Bechstein realizes he must accompany Cleveland, a lowly grunt in the Pittsburgh underworld, on a whirlwind tour of his collection route, Bechstein's father being, quite coincidentally, a high-level, low-profile accountant for the Mafia.

And in the climactic scene of the book, a Cagney-esque "top o' the world, Ma" denouement in which Cleveland is chased by police until he looms larger than life atop a factory building, we see the author's hand guiding us along, leading us toward some armchair psychologist's point: Cleveland is at once everything his dad never was and everything his dad is right now—only a gangster. There is, too, that nagging, an-

noying my-mother-is-dead-don't-talk-to-me undercurrent that seems to want to take on more presence in the book, but doesn't.

But what makes this book—and Chabon—worth our attention is the intent. Contrary to the tone set by that ride on the trunk of the Fiat, Chabon has chosen not merely to record all the ills of an oversexed, overindulged generation with nowhere to go but to bed or to a bar; he has chosen to explore, to enter this world and try to find what makes it work, why love and friendship choose to visit some, deny others. This first novel's flaws pale when one looks past them to the heart here, the compassion for characters simply trying to wade through a world too filled with itself to let real love surface, breathe, and take us in. (p. 11)

> Brett Lott, *"Lover in a World too Full for Love,"* in Los Angeles Times Book Review, *April 17, 1988, pp. 1, 11.*

M. GEORGE STEVENSON

[Interest in] yuppie picaresques tends to peak during politically conservative, economically expansive times. The '20s, '50s, and '80s all contributed waves of fingers-on-the-pulse-of-a-generation novels. *This Side of Paradise* revealed the mating habits of Ivy Leaguers and their debs, helping to define the '20s roar; Holden Caulfield's 1951 discomfiture at his gray-flannel future turned him into a misunderstood JD; the 1984-5 one-two punch of *Bright Lights, Big City / Less Than Zero* signaled the beginning of the current cycle. But as readers of *This Side of Paradise* know, the book that sets a generational style isn't necessarily the best. *The Sun Also Rises* is a much better novel than *TSOP*, Frederick Exley's 1968 *A Fan's Notes* is the genre's finest '50s chronicle, and Michael Chabon's *Mysteries of Pittsburgh* may well be the high point of the current batch.

Unlike its contemporaries, *Mysteries* suggests Scott rather than Ernest. The chronicle of one Art Bechstein's summer-after-college-graduation, it opens:

> At the beginning of the summer I had lunch with my father, the gangster, who was in town for the weekend to transact some of his vague business. We'd just come to the end of a period of silence and ill will—a year I'd spent in love with and in the same apartment as an odd, fragile girl whom he had loathed, on sight, with a frankness not at all like him. But Claire had moved out the month before. Neither my father nor I knew what to do with our new freedom.

Bechstein's voice has an immediacy as bluff and confidential as a well-matched freshman roommate and is filled with the surety peculiar to those who have yet to discover stylistic doubt.

It's lucky the voice is so persuasive, because *The Mysteries of Pittsburgh* consists almost entirely of the potentially mundane musings, details, and events of Bechstein's summer, during which he works at a stupid job, drinks heavily, has affairs with a slightly unbalanced but lovely girl and a less obviously unsuitable, even more beautiful boy, all while getting involved in a major subplot with his gangster father and his self-consciously legendary friend Cleveland Arning. Yet Chabon/Bechstein communicates the personal importance of every thought and action (and the youthful energy with

---

An excerpt from *The Mysteries of Pittsburgh*

Perhaps five seconds after I realized that we were standing on a loud street corner, surrounded by Mohawks and black men with frankfurters, and were no longer in the bar with a strangling ashtray and a voided pitcher between us, a white Fiat convertible with an Arab in it pulled up and honked at us.

"Abdullah, right?"

"Hey, Abdullah!" Arthur shouted, running around to the passenger's seat and diving into the red splash of interior.

"Hey, Abdullah," I said. I still stood on the sidewalk. I had drunk very much very quickly and wasn't following the action of the film too well. Everything seemed impossibly fast and lit and noisy.

"Come on!" shouted the blond head and the black head. I remembered that we were going to a party.

"Go on, asshole," someone behind me said.

"Arthur!" I said. "Did I have a backpack at some earlier point this evening?"

"What?" he shouted.

"My backpack!" I was already on my way back into the bar. Everything was darker, quieter; glancing at the Pirates game flashing silently, in awful color, over the bald head of the bartender, I ran to our booth and grabbed my sack. It was better, there in the ill light, and I stopped; I felt as though I had forgotten to breathe for several minutes.

"My backpack," I said to the ganged-up waitresses who chewed gum and drank coffee at a table by the dead jukebox.

"Uh huh," they said. "Ha ha." In Pittsburgh, perhaps more than anywhere else in our languid nation, a barmaid does not care.

On the way out again, I suddenly saw everything clearly: Sigmund Freud painting cocaine onto his septum, the rising uproar of the past hour and a half, the idling Fiat full of rash behavior that lay ahead, the detonating summer; and because it was a drunken perception, it was perfect, entire, and lasted about half a second.

---

which they are conceived or accomplished) so expressively that something as commonplace (and significant) as a first kiss becomes:

> with my ridiculous heart beating as though I were that first German laborer, ignorant of engineering and about to remove that first wooden support from that first lacy thousand-ton dome of poured concrete, I made a fractional movement toward her lips with mine; then I drew her slightly into the shadow of a little tree and kissed her . . .

The quiet lushness of both the conceit and the language are typical of Chabon's fresh, convincing style. What makes the novel extraordinary, however, is the exactness and care with which he manipulates such images and patterns of images. For example, a seemingly offhand allusion to Blanche Du-Bois (when Arthur, who eventually becomes Art's lover, calls Art's girlfriend on her exaggerated behavior) is both part of a larger pattern of movie references and an unobtrusive omen of the serious self-destructiveness and delusional acting-out to come.

In the acting-out, however, Chabon's stylistic superiority can't completely make up for his first novelist's misjudgments in the plot. Though it stands to Chekhovian reason that a gangster in the first paragraph demands some mob action before the final page (and that the father-son relationship so begun requires resolution for better or worse), Chabon's decision to link the two worlds is problematic. . . . Everything comes together in a way that feels manipulated and at odds with the fluid naturalness of the prose. It is telling that the sections dealing with this subplot are the only ones narrated at a remove.

Still, *The Mysteries of Pittsburgh* is the best book about being romantic, not completely formed, and emotionally 21 I have read since Ron Carlson's *Betrayed by F. Scott Fitzgerald* (1977). Making a reader experience again a sense of endless possibility is one of the most satisfying and quintessentially American things an American bildungsroman can do. Chabon's *The Mysteries of Pittsburgh* adds to the canon one of the rare novels actually able to do it.

> M. George Stevenson, "Couth Youth," in The Village Voice, *Vol. XXXIII, No. 16, April 19, 1988, p. 60.*

CAROLYN BANKS

There's a lot of talk about [*The Mysteries of Pittsburgh*]. It's almost as if there's going to be a great big literary bash. The guys who will be on the guest list are a cinch: Tom Sawyer and Huck Finn and Holden Caulfield and a more recent entry, *Less Than Zero's* Clay. And now, from *The Mysteries of Pittsburgh,* Art Bechstein. The joke is, all the other guys will bring a girl. Bechstein won't be able to make up his mind.

But that's way too flip, Bechstein's struggle with his dual attraction to a girl named Phlox and a guy named Arthur LeComte is what endears him to us. That and his at once humorous and poignant perceptions.

Bechstein has just graduated from college, winding down his final term with "a week-long fusillade of examinations and sentimental alcoholic conferences with professors whom I knew I would not miss. . . ." On the first day of his summer vacation, he dines with his father, an inordinately literate

gangster. He also sees Phlox for the very first time, and, while observing a street brawl ("I never understand how people can be perfectly frank all over the sidewalk like that, in public.") meets Arthur LeComte. . . .

And so it—not just the book, with its wonderful quirks and puzzles and flirtations, but our bond with Art Bechstein—begins.

We are swept, as Art Bechstein is, into an enormously attractive circle of characters. Like Bechstein, we're taken with the ease of their youthful eccentricity, with their idle but witty talk. There is Jane, with kooky parents and a perfect golf swing; Cleveland, whose appeal is his self-created sense of doom, and of course Phlox and Arthur. . . .

These two at once divine that they are rivals and are therefore always at odds. To Arthur, Phlox is "the evil love nurse." Phlox retaliates with pity and scorn: "I just think it's disgusting and a shame. Men who sleep with men are just big cowards." Still, we share Bechstein's observation that the two are "like an advertisement for summer and beauty and healthy American sex." Bechstein's ambisexuality is a given.

The adventures that ensue are sometimes rollicking (as when, house sitting for Jane's parents, they breed the family's overprotected bitch to a trio of Pit Bulls) as are the conversations or even fragments. . . .

But there's also—lest this novel be categorized as a romp—the plot's downside. Bechstein's affiliation with Cleveland enters here. Cleveland is the Bad Boy who wants to be badder still. His plan includes Bechstein's gangster dad. The elder Bechstein had seemed harried and comic, sort of like Everyfather, as he said things to his son like, "My God . . . your hair—you look terrible. Do you want me to give you the money to buy a comb?" Now he assumes the menace that his occupation always implied.

And so, though we laugh our way through much of it. *The Mysteries of Pittsburgh* is a sad book at heart. Its message, plainly stated, is voiced by Arthur LeComte: "You turn into whoever you've supposed to turn into." What this book does so nicely is to chart the fits and starts and lurches along the way. It's a chronicle of the "lovely, dire summer" when Bechstein "lusted with greater faith, hoped with greater abandon."

> Carolyn Banks, "Bright Lights, Steel City," in Book World—The Washington Post, *April 24, 1988, p. 5.*

ROZ KAVENEY

In first novels, writers have to make the most dramatic decisions about voice; what they decide will determine how people categorise them thereafter.

It would be nice to believe that no one writes a novel thinking of it as a Fitzgeraldian celebration of doomed youthful pleasure, or a terse examination of women's oppression, or a piece of pawky Southern realism, but this is not that sort of world. It is almost impossible to write without knowing at some point how what you are writing will be described when it gets out into the wide and wicked world, and self-consciousness is, if not a fault, then at least a fact in [the first novels of Michael Chabon, Marica Quedneau, Kaye Gibbon, and Glenn Savan]. Even when a novelist is not working in a defined commercial genre, a sense of category, no matter how loose, makes it impossible to be innocent.

The Mysteries of Pittsburgh is shameless about the whole thing: Michael Chabon has decided to be the Golden Boy, and pretty much gets away with it. The Bildungsroman is always a novel about writing a novel; the choices which young Art Bechstein makes are not only between lovers and companions but also between the sort of novel he is going to inhabit, between a sort of non-aristocratic *Brideshead,* a combination of Kerouac and George V. Higgins, and some kind of "Have them meet cute" Hollywoodish romance. Like most novels about bisexuality, this has an implied copy-book heading about not having your cake and eating it, but crass moralising is not what Chabon's about.

It is probably not the case that the respectable echelons of the Mafia, or the staff of down-market bookstores, look or act like this, but Chabon has the capacity to convince us that they do and to make the very fact magical, an opening of doors onto rich variety of which we had not dreamed. His underlining of the realities which, through Art Bechstein's infatuated perception, he romanticises—the biker rebel Cleveland is developing a beergut; the elegantly camp Arthur housesits the sort of house his mother cleans—can get crudish, but at least there is a sense of the need to control lushness. Chabon knows how to get from A to B in his scarlet convolvulus of a plot; he can drop the level of pose in his style to describe a burglary or a beating, and elevate it to the point of rhetoric for his knowing elegiac coda. (pp. 34-5)

> *Roz Kaveney, "As They Mean to Go On," in* New Statesman, *Vol. 116, No. 2981, May 13, 1988, pp. 34-5.*

JONATHAN KEATES

At the heart of [the very title of *The Mysteries of Pittsburgh*] lies a defiant paradox. Almost since its foundation, Pennsylvania's "Iron City" has been a byword for industrial hideousness at its most irredeemably banal. . . .

Mystery, for Michael Chabon, dwells less in the city's fuliginous allure than in its evident capacity for making things happen. Art Bechstein's graduation term has no obvious highlights in view beyond a last essay on Freud's preoccupation with the nose as the nexus of human desire. A half-hearted saunter through the university library produces Phlox Lombardi and Arthur Lecomte, both of whom take up positions at either pole of Art's ambiguous sexuality and fur-

nish the inconclusive lines of erotic counterpoint underpinning the narrative.

Ex-punk Phlox, however edgy and impassioned, is made to seem less vital to Art than hard, waspish, elegant Arthur, who leads him to Cleveland, glamorous biker and demon king, periodically flinging open the trapdoor to let out sulphurous whiffs of the Pittsburgh underworld which finally claims him. The traditional formula of the socially callow Jewish boy whoring after strange gods is neatly fragmented by the introduction of the hero's father, a gangland operator surrounded by a retinue of "friends" and "uncles" with suspect bulges under their jackets. . . .

Hype of the most shameless kind has attended this novel since its publication, and the twenty-four-year-old author has been assigned his niche in the dubious pantheon of quality brat fiction. In fairness to Chabon it should be said immediately that *The Mysteries of Pittsburgh* reveals a far wealthier, more varied talent than those of writers such as Bret Easton Ellis and Jay McInerney, whose range is largely confined to a series of elegant tricks and postures. His style has an enviable suppleness and fluency which offers the perfect vehicle for the moral feints and shifts of the cool crowd he portrays. In essence, the central trio (and Cleveland himself for all his 1500cc glitz) are without much in the way of charm, originality or purpose, yet Chabon sustains our interest through a positively anthropological scrutiny of their improvised rituals of courtship and hostility.

The trouble arises, as nearly always in this newest generation of American novelists, as soon as the author starts admiringly contemplating the glassy surface of his own verbal sophistication. When we read that the library is "the dead core of my education, the white, silent kernel of every empty Sunday I had spent trying to ravish the faint charms of the study of economics, my sad and cynical major", we can hear Scott and Zelda spinning penitently in their graves.

Chabon needs to spend more time on structure, and on avoiding the type of sudden jerk into lachrymose solemnity which rushes this book to its close. He is not yet the master his publishers wish us to suppose him, but if he can keep off the hemlock and nepenthe of premature celebrity he should do very well indeed.

> *Jonathan Keates, "The Boy Can't Help It," in* The Times Literary Supplement, *No. 4446, June 17-23, 1988, p. 680.*

Elizabeth Cooke

1948-

American novelist.

In *Complicity,* Cooke focuses upon the troubled lives of two remaining members of the Rhoades family, middle-aged Amanda and her daughter Maggie. Following the death of her mother, Amanda journeys with Maggie to the family's long-neglected cabin in the remote Maine woods. While Amanda explores her dark family history and uncovers truths surrounding the odd behavior of her parents and the mysterious deaths of her father and her son, Maggie attempts to ease her strained relationship with her mother. Reviewers noted Cooke's vivid evocation of the emotions of her characters, which are reflected in their responses to the sublime natural environment where most of the story is set.

KIRKUS REVIEWS

How many sorrowful mysteries can be enacted and revealed from a summer house on top of a lakeside mountain in Maine? Here [in *Complicity*], in first-novelist Cooke's Rhoades family, the deaths and disappearances and strategic silences keep coming—until the summer house is in flames and every member of the family but one is dead.

First to go is Amanda Rhoades' mother Eleanor, a stern-faced matriarch who's had a stroke and whispers a secret as she dies: 50 years ago, she punished her husband's single infidelity by forbidding him to "touch," or love, his daughter Amanda. Learning this, tortured Amanda decides to pay a final visit to the summer house where most of the crucial events of her life took place and where her father, victim of a drowning "accident," lies buried. Amanda's daughter, Maggie, who has always felt unloved by Amanda, insists on accompanying her, and the result is a series of revelations: how the drowning "accident" was suicide; how the inheritance from that suicide was Amanda's envy of her daughter, whom Amanda's father loved; how another "accident"—the shooting of Amanda's son in the woods eight years before—was also suicide; how the disappearance of a silver pocket watch once belonging to Amanda's father's lover was thievery and the disappearance of a pet canary named after a girl with whom Maggie's brother fell in love was murder; and how, for Amanda, as these grim memories rush upon her, the only answer is to wipe out the family. . . .

This is a dense book—it suffers from too much enchantment with its characters' tormented lives, and is repetitive and sometimes vague. But it is also shapely; and by the end. . . . it has accumulated real—and promising—power.

A review of "Complicity," in Kirkus Reviews, *Vol. VI, No. 23, December 1, 1987, p. 1637.*

PUBLISHERS WEEKLY

From the alternating viewpoints of mother and daughter Amanda and Maggie, this quietly eloquent first novel [*Complicity*] records a family's terse transactions as they complicitously hide behind lies. They share violent memories: the shooting deaths of Amanda's father and son Evan; Amanda's cold denial of her husband; her rejection of the women Evan loved. The family plays out its tight drama in a wooded, mountainous New England setting, where they own a rough lakeside cabin built by a great-grandfather. The heady beauty of the place seems over-hung with menace; Amanda remarks, "You must always be prepared for death on this lake." Time shuttles seamlessly back and forth from Amanda's repressed girlhood to a here-and-now in which affectionate Maggie struggles to break through her mother's brittleness and fear for her "weak" heart. The narrative surface, often made up of echoing repetitions and bleakly vacant comments, contrasts with a tumultuous inner world, where feelings can only be experienced through the sufferings of natural creatures—notably swallows, owls and loons. These moments account for Cooke's strongest writing, although the novel's contrived wrap-up may disappoint. (pp. 63-4)

A review of "Complicity," in Publishers Weekly, *Vol. 232, No. 23, December 4, 1987, pp. 63-4.*

SUSAN J. HEEGER

One kind word, one smile. That's all Amanda wanted from her father. Instead, he doted on her daughter, Maggie, dooming the girl to Amanda's hatred. Poor Maggie, in turn, mysteriously dotes on her mother, swallowing Amanda's lies about the past and submitting to her endless bullying.

So misery is passed from generation to generation in Elizabeth Cooke's first novel, **Complicity.** So too is an individual's bargain with the family group presented as a matter of survival. Where Cooke goes wrong with her rich—if familiar—theme, is in her failure to grasp that between reader and writer, complicity is a far more voluntary proposition.

The novel opens compellingly, with a deathbed confession. After 58 years of silence, Eleanor Elliott finally explains her late husband's coldness to their Amanda: "I told him he was not to touch you, not to speak to you, ever."

Behind this astonishing command lies a dark secret only hinted at ("He didn't even know I was carrying you. . . . You were five months old when he came home"). But the scene sets the tone for the entire book—heavy foreboding. The implication is that after Eleanor's death—with only two family members living—all the dirty little family secrets will explode.

Indeed, as soon as possible, Amanda bolts off on a sort of truth mission to her father's grave near the family summerhouse in Maine. Maggie, the other survivor, insists on going along, raising the probability that mother and grown daughter will at least square off and come to new terms or die trying.

We are disappointed on two counts. First, Cooke's narrative method subverts present drama by sandbagging the novel in the past. The two women exist almost wholly on memories—so much so that they can't talk or eat or take a walk without dreaming of other talks, other meals, other moments more fully developed than the ones present.

The second problem lies with the characters themselves. Amanda is an utter harridan, with superhuman reserves of cruelty. If she isn't scorning Maggie's plain looks, she's repeating her daughter's comments as if awe-struck by their stupidity. Maggie rolls over and takes it. Wallowing in self-pity, she never challenges the blows dealt her, or the lies told her, until truth smacks her on the head.

It's hard to root for these people, let alone expect them to change. They're too devoted to a clannish misery unleavened by humor and overloaded with symbols—mangled loons, fire-charred animals, etc.

The novel's forward momentum is further hobbled by Cooke's language. Given to wordiness ("Maggie's arm rises and she waves a hand"), Cooke is also jarringly inexact in her

---

An excerpt from *Complicity*

These mountains, Amanda thinks. These are my mountains.

The black Peugeot wheels through the mountain roads on an early October morning. Amanda narrows her grey eyes, taps her black onyx ring against the rim of the steering wheel, presses her foot firmly against the accelerator.

These are my mountains, she thinks again, but the land is dying, growing ancient. She runs her eyes over the slopes of mountains, colors dusty as dusk in the early morning sun.

"Did you say something, Mother?" Maggie asks, her china blue eyes warm, as she widens them to look at Amanda.

"Did I say something? Oh, just about the mountains, how it's like coming home to be on this road."

"It's been too long, for both of us," Maggie offers. "After all these years—"

"All these years?" Amanda repeats. "It's hardly 'all these years,' dear, just eight, and there are reasons, you know there are reasons."

Maggie closes her eyes, hears her own voice when she told her mother that she wanted to come to Land's End. Inside her pockets her fingers play, making lines through the material against her thighs, tiny circles and perfectly shaped hearts.

"I hope we're doing the right thing, Mother," Maggie says, sitting upright.

"Margaret, I told you I wanted to see my father's grave once more before I see my own, and—"

"Mother, you've got to stop this, you're only fifty-eight, you're in good health." Maggie wonders why her mother insists upon such words.

Amanda hunches further over the wheel. The black onyx ring twirls around her finger, rubs against the steering wheel. From beneath her black beret bits of silver hair curl out like tiny fingers. "Dr. Wescott reminded me only last week that the swelling in these joints will last as long as I do. When I ask him what's wrong, he says it's my old age. Old age, Margaret, that's what is wrong with me. And my heart, it has always been weak."

"I don't think he means 'old age' as in 'about to die,' Mother. He's known you for so long. I'll bet he's teasing." Maggie smiles, to hide her irritation.

Amanda ignores her words. "The land looks lonely this time of year," she muses.

"Lonely?" Maggie looks out the window. "It's anything but lonely, Mother, it's warm and safe, it's—"

"It looks lonely to me, Margaret. And at your age, I probably couldn't see it any better than you." Amanda pauses, slows the car. "But we're here, aren't we, and we shall make the best of it."

descriptions ("His blue eyes folded in on themselves," "The lake's rounded bulging surface was black as a moonstone").

As the book winds down, the waters get muddier, with statements like, "She finally knew the truth," coming out of nowhere.

By this time, however, the reader will be long gone, all patience and complicity exhausted by the wait for drama, humor, wisdom and the feel for life deeply lived that good writing delivers.

> Susan J. Heeger, "Bargains of a Family's Survival," in Los Angeles Times Book Review, February 7, 1988, p. 12.

VALERIE SAYERS

In *Complicity,* Elizabeth Cooke's carefully constructed first novel, a mother smooths an afghan on her son's bed and tells him of making it for her father: "I couldn't decide whether to have three colors or two. Mother said two is always better because it's purer. Cleaner, she used to say."

Complicity, like the afghan passed from generation to generation, is a two-color work; the story's colors are past and present, and both are described purely and cleanly, indeed. In alternating tenses, Ms. Cooke . . . unfolds the story of three generations of women in a style so austere—so lean, so dependent on simple declarative sentences—that it could almost be a satire of the dominant style in American fiction today.

I must admit right off that I am one of those readers ready to run screaming from the bookshop at the sight of another present-tense narrative told in the flat, affectless voice of the 80's. But Ms. Cooke, I am glad to report, is not merely following a fashion. Though there are a few instances of awkwardness in this unmusical prose, for the most part Ms. Cooke knows exactly what she is doing. Her characters—who could also, for the first half of the book, be satires of repressed New England WASP's—are as well suited as characters could be to a repressed style; and as they come to know more of themselves, the language describing them unwinds and expands, and the novel becomes more and more engaging.

Maggie Rhoades, the story's protagonist, is a young artist whose maternal grandmother dies of a stroke in the opening pages. The first line of the book—"Eleanor had two faces"—prepares us for the legacy of dishonesty and hypocrisy Maggie and her mother will inherit from the old woman. Maggie is an easy target for the hurtful slings her mother aims in her direction: she is forever defending those who have wounded her, much to the dismay of her brother and her lover.

Maggie's mother, Amanda, drives a black Peugeot, twists a black onyx ring round her finger and wears a black beret. Relentlessly black soul that she is, she is a far more compelling character than her remote, passive daughter. Though we learn in the opening scene that her own mother forbade her father ever to touch her; though we know that her mother's sexual instruction included the advice that breasts are "just fatty tissue" and that a husband's admiration is something she "needn't enjoy"; though we watch her secretly witness her father deciding whether to pull the trigger on himself, still we feel little pity for Amanda. Her own cruelty to Maggie is on a grand scale, operatic in scope if not in style. "My, but

you are vain, Margaret," she tells her daughter. "And for one so plain."

The present-tense action of *Complicity* follows Amanda and Margaret as they make an autumn journey to Land's End, the family's old summer retreat, after an absence of eight years. . . . As mother and daughter entangle themselves in their memories and grievances, the flashbacks of *Complicity* give us glimpses into the two women's sadly parallel childhoods.

From her biblical epigraph—a reference to the resurrection of the dead—to her fiery conclusion, Ms. Cooke makes it clear that Maggie must assume moral responsibility for confronting the past. Part of this confrontation will be with the natural world to which her family has so often retreated; both present- and past-tense scenes accumulate imagery of earth, fire, water, air. There are some lovely variations on these elemental themes throughout: in the first scene, Maggie's grandmother is described as having lashes "like bits of ash."

But Ms. Cooke's metaphorical pattern becomes too ornate when she crowds images of birds into both Amanda's and Maggie's scenes; the loon's first call is evocative, and the metaphor of the swallows trapped in the chimney is apt, but by the end of the novel the beating of the birds' wings on every other page has become as oppressive as the attention Amanda pays to the beating of her heart.

Occasionally, the narrator's voice is as humorless and heavy-handed as the bird imagery; we are told—after a scene giving us the same information—that Maggie is, for her mother, "a reminder, however dim and unrecognized, of a love submerged." But statements of the obvious are the exception, not the rule; for the most part, Ms. Cooke wisely relies on action, past and present, to demonstrate complicity in the family traditions of deceit and denial.

Though *Complicity* opens with an 80's voice, it concludes with some old truths; its climax is constructed with elements as basic as fire and water, salvation and damnation. I have not, after reading it, developed a taste for flat-voiced present-tense narrative, but I am grateful to read a book by a first novelist who so painstakingly weaves the colors of past and present into a moral pattern.

> Valerie Sayers, "The Sins of the Mothers," in The New York Times Book Review, February 28, 1988, p. 11.

ELIZABETH COOKE

"The inspiration for [*Complicity*] lay in the feelings that the setting evoked in me—of beauty versus ugliness, life versus death, honesty versus deceit. Out of this setting came a character who would discover herself through the setting and the action that would take place there.

"It also began with two images—that of a woman kicking the grave of her father who had commited suicide, and a fire that raged in a lakefront summer home."

Asked about what motivates her to write and what she hopes to accomplish through her writing, Cooke replied: "I am driven to write. It is how I live. The desire to find and discover my characters and their situations intrigues and fascinates me. I am completely free when I write; there are no censors, no expectations, no other voices but my own. . . .

"What I hope to accomplish is the communication of my beliefs and ideas about life to anyone who will read what I write.

"Since the reading of literature is what has taught me about people, about history, about the physical and spiritual world, I want to be part of that in any way I can, that recording of life."

Ms. Cooke commented about authors who have influenced her: "Henry James. From him I learned about the writer's eye and how I see. Reynolds Price. From him I learned how to write about characters that I love."

> *Elizabeth Cooke, in correspondence with* CLC Yearbook.

Trey Ellis

1962-

American novelist, essayist, and journalist.

A comic novel set in New York City, *Platitudes* revolves around the efforts of Dewayne Wellington to complete a post-modernist romance novel featuring two middle-class black teenagers. Experiencing writer's block, Dewayne grudgingly seeks advice from Isshee Ayam, a celebrated feminist novelist and critic who promptly condemns his work as sexist and trendy. Isshee offers her own version of the novel, written in the more conventional form in which she established her reputation. Thus, Ellis's work parodies and comments upon differing styles within the African-American literary tradition, including realism and experimentalism and male versus female approaches to similar subject matter. Marcellus Blount commented: "If Alice Walker and Ishmael Reed got together to write a novel, it might read a bit like *Platitudes*. . . . Ellis wreaks havoc with two sets of conventions: the male protagonist vs. the world, and the degradation of black womanhood. . . . He manages to insulate himself from thematic censure by manipulating his point of view to make his characters bear the brunt of his criticisms, instead of the real contemporary black writers and white audience whom they represent." While Ellis's inclusion of surveys, charts, menus, song lyrics, and dialogue from films and television programs drew a mixed critical response, most reviewers were impressed with his use of adolescent vernacular and his acerbic examination of contemporary sexual and literary politics.

PUBLISHERS WEEKLY

Earle Tyner, [the] 16-year-old black bourgeois [protagonist of *Platitudes*], falls in love with Dorothy LaMont, a young waitress at her mother's down-home Harlem diner. As Earle plots encounters with Dorothy, taking an after-school job near the restaurant, the teenagers' friendship weathers upsets but eventually deepens and strengthens. Earle and Dorothy are characters in a novel-within-a-novel here, ostensibly creations of newly divorced, depressed black writer Dewayne Wellington. Dewayne appears mainly in his letters to Isshee Ayam, successful black feminist author and critic of Dewayne's work-in-progress called "Platitudes." Isshee, whose own novels bear such titles as *Chillun' o' de Lawd* and *My Big O' Feets Gonna Stomp Dat Evil Down,* offers in letters to Dewayne her revisions of "Platitudes," with Earle and Dorothy cast as poor schoolchildren in 1930s rural Georgia. As the writers reconcile their differences over Dewayne's rapidly developing story, the two relationships—that of Dewayne and Isshee and that of the doubly fictional Earle and Dorothy—parallel each other, both closing with pat endings. Ellis demonstrates an ear for adolescent lingo and a sharp

grasp of teenage pursuits and pleasures; at its best, his book is entertaining and the young protagonists sweetly appealing. But too often, *Platitudes* degenerates into tedious attempts at wit and humor, as in Isshee's plodding literary contributions or Ellis's version of Earle's PSAT exam, an annoying joke. This aptly named first novel is, finally, predictable and self-indulgent.

A review of "Platitudes," in Publishers Weekly, *Vol. 234, No. 1, July 1, 1988, p. 72.*

KIRKUS REVIEWS

[*Platitudes* is an experimental] first novel that has two black writers (one male, one female) jousting to provide a more definitive version of black life.

First: Earle and Dorothy are middle-class black teen-agers in New York City. Earle lives with his mother (the alcoholic father is dead); he is a "fatso nerd" and a computer buff who hangs out with two like-minded buddies. Dorothy goes to a

Catholic school, works part-time in her mother's Harlem restaurant, enjoys hot discos and an interesting sex life; she is a whole lot more hip than Earle. These kids are the creation of Dewayne Wellington, a middle-aged writer whose former wife ("a well-connected matriarch of the black New York bourgeoisie") has bad-mouthed him around town and prevented him getting work. Second: a feminist writer, Isshee Ayam, intervenes with her own version of Earle and Dorothy, moving them back into the long-ago rural South. . . . Wellington's handling of his teens is less consistent, ranging from straight-forward realism through stream-of-consciousness to the broadly satirical ("she holds his raven penis, insinuates it into her snowy self"). Neither Wellington's nor Ayam's storyline has much energy behind it, so Ellis pads out their work with a spoof on PSATs, lists (a waiter reels off a page-long list of desserts), snatches of dialogue heard while channel-switching, and references to politicking in the black literary community. At the end, the two writers meet for a night of romance and (once Dewayne has aroused himself at the typewriter) passion.

Self-conscious doodling. (pp. 995-96)

A review of "Platitudes," in Kirkus Reviews, *Vol. LVI, No. 14, July 15, 1988, pp. 995-96.*

MAURICE J. BENNETT

Although [**Platitudes**] can be identified as a kind of *Bildungsroman* or portrait of the artist as a young man, Trey Ellis's first novel is more than just another story of adolescent initiation (the loss of virginity, the discovery of love), more than another picture of the writer writing (how to tell the tale?). It addresses a conflict percolating in the black literary community that concerns perceived disparities in the reception of black male and female authors. For some, the publishing and critical attention awarded a galaxy of prominent women—Toni Morrison, Alice Walker and Gloria Naylor—has been accompanied by the slighting of their black male colleagues. The conflict surfaces here in **Platitudes** as two competing narratives—one by the struggling male artist, Dewayne Wellington, the other by the equally fictional but award-winning female author, Isshee Ayam.

At issue is how to tell the story of Earle Tyner, a young man struggling with being 16 years old. In Wellington's story, Earle is a middle-class black (a rare species in contemporary black fiction) attending private school in New York and hanging out with his buddies Andy and Donald. Wellington portrays them through a loose combination of dialogue, stream of consciousness writing and soliloquy, with frequent radical shifts in point of view. Interspersed are lists of things: a sex survey; television shows and commercials; questions from the Preliminary Scholastic Aptitude Test. In this last, the student is asked to choose the pairs of words that most closely resemble "miscegenation: crime." The choices include "black: beige" and "zebra: ape," but the correct answer is "Jane Russell: a sexy woman," "because just as miscegenation used to be a crime, Jane Russell used to be a sexy woman," "because just as miscegenation used to be a crime, Jane Russell used to be a sexy woman." All these devices are cleverly used to convey the serio-comic confusion of adolescent consciousness and its predilection for obsession, fixations on public image and sex. The heart of the plot is Earle's

quest for the lovely Dorothy (who attends an upper-class Catholic school).

Except for rather incidental references to racial considerations, such as Earle's Harlem voter registration job, he and his friends are indistinguishable from their white counterparts. Nerds in both their own and others' eyes, they are the new generation of the computer-literate, who worry about girls and think about college.

Isshee Ayam's tale is a response to Wellington's advertisement for aid in completing his own story. Her version moves South to a rural black community where Earle is protected by a bevy of strong, proud black women. He still pursues a black maiden, but, in so doing, rejects a set of ignorant sexist buddies for the uplifting companionship of a higher social, moral and intellectual ideal. . . .

Ayam begins one chapter titled, "Sunday Go To Meetin' ":

> Mama leaned over the makeshift stove, frying a spoonful of cornmeal mush and reboiling last week's coffee for her and her grown daughters. But for Earle, their seed carrier, their hope, Mama squeezed the last drops of milk from the shriveled and near-spent teats of their wizened goat, Sojourner.

Through Ayam, Ellis parodies those celebrations of the autochthonous black female now ubiquitous in the literature, with her creative, prelogical, essentially uterine defiance of masculine insensitivity and oppression. Ayam disapproves of what she considers Wellington's pornographic focus and his post-modern stylistic excesses, and she wraps her story in hyperbolic, pseudo-mythopoeic diction completely devoid of irony. For those familiar with the fiction that Ellis is satirizing, there is the pleasure of recognition; his point is well made.

Behind the comedy, however, lies the serious issue of the literary representation of black experience. The Rev. Jesse Jackson's strong presidential campaign this year was built largely on a rhetoric addressing itself almost exclusively to the concerns of the poor and downtrodden. But there has long been some version of a black middle class that has expanded and diversified since the Civil Rights revolution of the 1960s. Who speaks for these people? Which is the more accurate portrait of black adolescence—Wellington's self-referent mumblings of the urban bourgeoisie, or Ayam's up-from-slavery saga of the folk? And implicitly (inevitably?), which is the more ideologically correct?

That the two visions might be reconciled is suggested by the fact that both narratives end with the union of Earle and Dorothy, and it is difficult to tell which is the more sentimental. Wellington's stylistic experimentalism and Ayam's mythic hyperbole take different routes to the same conclusion. And although she remains proud to be the author of such masterpieces as *Hog Jowl Junction* and *My Big O' Feets Gonna Stomp Dat Evil Down*, Ayam gradually softens her opposition to Wellington's work.

Despite all its serious implications, Ellis' novel *reads* like an amusing *jeu d'esprit:* it is an auspicious beginning.

Maurice J. Bennett, "The Black Preppie and the Sharecropper's Son," in Book World—The Washington Post, *October 9, 1988, p. 9.*

MARCELLUS BLOUNT

If Alice Walker and Ishmael Reed got together to write a novel, it might read a bit like *Platitudes,* Trey Ellis's story about the secret lives of two talented black writers, Dewayne Wellington and Isshee Ayam, and their teenage protagonists. Wellington is full of "reckless eyeballing" and self-admiration; Ayam is an ardent womanist whose faith in "living by the word" lights her way to the bank. Inevitably, these opposites attract. Their story lines merge. Our two novelists fall in love.

Wellington, the struggling postmodernist, lives off his ex-wife's alimony check in an Upper West Side apartment and spends much of his time, when not working as a proofreader at Klein, Klein and Feldman, trying to write a new book about Earle, a nerdish, overweight black teenager whose greatest ambitions in life end with Cal Tech and M.I.T. and begin with getting laid. . . . Wellington and Earle become obsessed with Dorothy, the daughter of "one of those fundamentalist, tough-as-nails black women who, underneath, are pussycats."

Wellington hardly gets into his plot before he realizes that his only clear memory of adolescence is what it felt like to pop boners all the time. When he tells his readers to write to him with suggestions, he gets from Ayam no ordinary "Dear Dewayne." She begins tentatively:

> What genus of disturbed, DT-ridden Muse rattles through the chambers of your vacant head? What oh what can evoke such a perverse perversion of pen and ink? Is it that you were encouraged to lick squids as a child? Told it was all right to play with yourself at the school assembly?

Throughout *Platitudes,* Ellis reveals his fondness for Ayam's expertise in parody, disdain, and the well-aimed metaphor, even when he turns them against her. If Ayam is justified in dismissing Wellington's novel-in-progress as "postmodernist, semiological sophism," then what might he say about her distinguished oeuvre: *Chillun o' de Lawd, Good Lord, Gimme a Good Man!, Heben, Hog Jowl Junction* (the novel and the major motion picture), and *My Big Ol' Feets Gon' Stomp Dat Evil Down* (for which she received the Rockefeller Book Award)?

In Ayam's letters to Wellington, she turns his novel inside out. While Wellington locates his tale amid the apartment buildings, schools, nightclubs, and restaurants of Manhattan, Ayam puts Earle and Dorothy in Lowndes County, Georgia, off Route 49, where black women, abandoned by their husbands, deceived and abused by other black men, are forced to prostitute themselves for their children's sake. Ellis wreaks havoc with two sets of conventions: the male protagonist vs. the world, and the degradation of black womanhood. Or, as Wellington writes to Ayam: "How can I thank you for dragging my meagre tale back to its roots in Afro-American glory-stories?" If this is what sells, no wonder his first novel, *Hackneyed,* is available only in manuscript form.

Fortunately, neither of their stories has any particular moral, except perhaps "all's well that ends well, especially if it begins with satire." *Platitudes* is serious fun. Ellis remembers the social antics of teenagers: the sex and romance, anxiety and confusion, trials and frequent tribulations. He manages to insulate himself from thematic censure by manipulating his point of view to make his characters bear the brunt of his criticisms, instead of the real contemporary black writers and white audiences whom they represent. He gracefully straddles the boundaries of contemporary sexual and racial literary politics. His style and sentiments are outrageous, and the brother gets away with it.

Marcellus Blount, "Double Vision," in The Village Voice, *Vol. XXXIII, No. 48, November 29, 1988, p. 66.*

ERIC LOTT

In the annals of the so-called New Black Aesthetic—what one critic has described as a Harlem Renaissance on floppy disk—Trey Ellis's first novel [*Platitudes*] will go down as a young writer's call for a truce in the black literary world. Folding into the novel itself recent disputes between feminists and their detractors over how blacks are to be represented in fiction, *Platitudes* casts a plague on both the Alice Walkers and the Ishmael Reeds. Reed's several attacks on Walker's *The Color Purple* (book and movie), and his polyphonic fictional diatribe *Reckless Eyeballing,* which alleges a widespread conspiracy against black men, have earned him righteous retribution from many quarters. Neither author is named in *Platitudes* but the satirical resemblances are close enough to count. Ellis's strategy unfortunately only partially succeeds; the Reeds come out relatively unscathed. But despite its shortcomings, the book marks the emergence of a talent equal in wit to the best of the "postnationalist" generation Ellis belongs to: filmmakers Warrington and Reggie Hudlin, performance artist Alva Rogers, hip-hop deejays and rappers, novelist Terry McMillan. Most of these artists rely on a recombinant irony no less politically earnest for its ritual dismemberment of the elders.

In an essay forthcoming in the journal *Callaloo,* Ellis playfully describes the impulse behind these new developments as "neobarocco"—an "open-ended, New Black Aesthetic [inherited] from a few Seventies pioneers that shamelessly borrows and reassembles across both race and class lines." This produces, in Ellis's novel, a mutant assemblage of love story, postmodern narrative techniques and postliberation political intentions whose effect is something like crossing Spike Lee with Gilbert Sorrentino. Ellis is a kind of hip-hop novelist, flinging bits of TV, sociobabble, charts and quizzes onto pages already cluttered with a mix of styles and multiple tales. *Platitudes* is staged as competing versions of a story by two black authors who are politically at odds: a celebrated feminist, Isshee Ayam, and a frustrated, aging former nationalist, Dewayne Wellington. . . . Their alternating installments narrate the progress of Earle, a naif, and Dorothy, his elusive object of desire.

Platitudes means to make explicit, through its warring authors, the more or less hidden motives Ellis sees fueling much recent black fiction. Part of the point is that Wellington's novel stalls until Ayam provokes a sense of embattled urgency over the characters of Earle and Dorothy: then it goes, and with a bullet. . . . The more misogynist the Wellington chapters become, often out of jealousy of Ayam and other successful writers, the more the Ayam chapters conjure changes of heart out of benighted males. The installments tussle until Wellington and Ayam somehow realize a sense of solidarity and consummate their stories, and then their relationship. The present impasse between black men and women has deformed the writing that might take them beyond it, goes the conceit; now they must write themselves into some kind of harmony.

But a real sense of resolution eludes this allegory of black literary politics. For one thing, Ellis is clearly more invested in Wellington's Earle, saving his most savage attacks for Ayam's sentimental prose and politics. Though **Platitudes** means to distance the stories of both authors by its main device, Wellington's tale is the one finally endorsed; the various jokes on Ayam go unanswered. The problem is authors on both sides of the gender divide are guilty of Ayam's *Green Pastures* excesses. She is the author of the best-selling books *Chillun o' de Lawd, Hog Jowl Junction* and *My Big Ol'Feets Gon' Stomp Dat Evil Down;* her prose recalls the more tiresome writing of racial uplift. . . . Those rightly suspicious of the impulse to lampoon black women's writing in this age of backlash will find ample cause for alarm in **Platitudes.** To be sure, Wellington is nailed for the way his envy of successful male and female writers infects his novel in progress, but it is finally only Wellington's personal progress, his involvement with Ayam, that is resolved, and not the political mess he has instigated.

This flawed satire is overshadowed in any case by Ellis's preoccupation with the inner drives and desires of a historically new (and underrepresented) character, the black M.I.T.-bound adolescent. Ellis has a fine ear for adolescent inner monologue. Near the beginning, Earle, the buppie boy brought up between the white and black worlds, goes uptown:

> Where's my food? I don't want to be killed up here. . . . Stop fooling around and just look mean so they won't know you're not from uptown. Yeah, iss cool whussup yeah. Shit Earle they spotted you a half hour ago. Yeah there he is the black Howdy Doody face, I bet he's got lots of bread on hisself—bread? Do they still say that?

There is a welcome absence of sociological talk about being in a difficult racial and class position, and much good writing about how it feels to be there. Ellis also coaxes a bemused interiority out of Dorothy's Valley-girl jargon, the kind of feat most young novelists are still reaching for. (pp. 691-92)

Ellis hedges his bet by having Ayam speak overpreciously about this story's "dialectic between class struggle and cultural assimilation," but that's pretty much the tale he has to tell. "Yeah, this class shit is crazy," says Dorothy; and while consoling herself that after business school it's Morgan Stanley and five figures, she reflects that it's cool to have an absent father and a mother who runs a Harlem diner: "And just once I want some Graham or Brett or Ethan to say, You're joking, but they never do 'cause they think I'll rip their dick out." As with this highly conflicted bit of self-consciousness, Ellis lets his characters' contradictions stand, and by doing so engages the politics of representation much more daringly than he can in the allegorical frame. If literary conventions like Ayam's don't do justice to the people they hope to represent—as Ralph Ellison put it, "Watch out there, Jack, there's people living under here"—the point would seem less to punish the presumed offenders than to invent some characters that break the molds. Ellis has gone some way toward doing that.

This itself is no mean political act, as I have hinted. And it doesn't by any means preclude technical self-consciousness; the New Black Aesthetic is full of self-reflexive moves. But

---

An Excerpt from *Platitudes*

What a black foxy babe! She's only the prettiest black chick I've ever seen and the last time up there I didn't even see a one that grabbed me. Wow I bet she dances, the way she stands so straight and she's no dummy or junkie or nothing you could tell by the way she talked, her mom was right she is wild just the way I like em (heh heh). Talked? What a goombah stu-nod you are talking over her like a parrot and besides running into her like Ray Charles or something she probably hates you for that but what if she doesn't? Earle stop it, don't get your hopes up because something always happens remember Janey (Oh I'm sure she wants me guys 'cause once at assembly she took off her shoes and crossed her legs so her foot was leaning right into my pants and she didn't move it for at least a minute) and you thought you'd go off like Old Faithful right there while Mister Wyte was introducing the renowned Joe Schmoe Wind Ensemble but no more of that, but what if Dorothy—what if she wants you? Who knows why but love is blind I hope to God because then I've got a chance, geez it's been so long since I've seen some pretty girl I didn't want to just bone right there in the downtown train and man, Dorothy, I'd die just to kiss her wouldn't even stick it in even if she paid me, even if she begged like those Hustler douchebags but she wouldn't that's for sure. And another thing, even though she's Ay number-one fantasy fuel I'll never schwang the wonker over her picture. Bad luck, and Janey proves it, and to tell you the truth I didn't even notice her breasts or butt or nothing I couldn't tell you what her bod's like if you paid me, but I bet it's fanfuckintastic that's for sure and that's another thing, Operation Dorothy, I'm going up there all the time and dress well and not even do it at all until at least after our first date or for this whole month, whichever comes first. Crap! You passed the fuckin stop Mr. Potatohead, geez . . .

November 30, 1984

To Whom It May Concern:

   Are you so blindly enthralled with that postmodernist, semiological sophism (that incidentally *nobody* believes in anymore) that the words "narrative" and "continuity" mean nothing to you? Have you never read Baldwin?

   Your transparent jealousy of my oft-praised literary successes is truly pathetic to behold. I receive so many vitriolic letters from countless other underachieving middle-aged black male "artists" who cannot bear to watch a sister trade in *your* feeble slaps and drunken sexual abuse for American Book Awards and tenured chairs at Princeton. I feel for you, sir, but only enough to beg you to heed my heartfelt advice: For God's sake . . . LEARN A TRADE!!!!!!

Isshee Ayam

P.S. Don't think I didn't catch that childish barb about the (multi) award-winning, San Francisco-based writer and her mother's frying pan. Grow up.

there do seem to be stories at loggerheads in *Platitudes.* Not those of Ayam and Wellington, but Ellis's amusingly ironic one of buppie adolescents in Harlem set against his earnest tale of disaffected authors in a paradise regained—the "new" aesthetic, strangely, versus an old story of insurmountable differences overcome by love. In a way the literary-political allegory could deepen the rift it would heal. As moving as the reunion of Ayam and Wellington is, sexual consummation is not the richest image of resolution for a political situation of longstanding inequity. Heterosexual romance too often reiterates precisely this inequity. And it is the work that Ellis parodies, that of Walker and others, that has done something to clarify this matter. The emergent aesthetic Ellis and his cohort are producing should avoid such ties to the politics of the past. (p. 692)

Eric Lott, "Hip-Hop Fiction," in The Nation, *New York, Vol. 247, No. 19, December 19, 1988, pp. 691-92.*

DORIS JEAN AUSTIN

Trey Ellis's *Platitudes* is a jazzy scatting around the traditional novel—and when it works, it works very, very well. . . . Reader, be warned: the sophomoric quality of the prose at the beginning of the book is intentional. We meet Dewayne Wellington, author of the first 13 pages, on page 14—in what turns out to be a letter to the public asking for help. "It's embarrassing to stumble so obviously in so public a forum," Dewayne confesses, admitting that he doesn't know what to write next. But help comes on the very next page in a letter from Isshee Ayam, whose own simpering prose is a caricature of some of the more mythologically oriented feminist writers. In the first of many rewrites of Dewayne's experimental and sexist story, Isshee shows him what she thinks he ought to have done—and the hysterical roller coaster ride has begun . . . But in spite of Trey Ellis's wonderfully tongue-in-cheek depiction of the flaws in Dewayne's work, as a satire *Platitudes* threatens to collapse under the weight of so much stylistic posturing. Mr. Ellis is most successful when he's being irreverent about sacred subjects, social and political, American and un-American. There are more than a few laugh-out-loud and shake-your-head-at-the-awful-truth scenes in this insightful first novel—if only you can persevere.

Doris Jean Austin, in a review of "Platitudes," in The New York Times Book Review, *February 19, 1989, p. 20.*

Judith Freeman

1946-

American short story writer.

Many of the stories in *Family Attractions* involve characters attempting to find contentment after having experienced changes and disruptions in their lives. The title story, for example, focuses on a sixty-three-year-old bachelor who marries a younger woman and gradually assimilates with her family and friends, and "The Botanic Gardens" concerns a middle-aged woman seeking companionship while on vacation shortly after her fiancé's death. Freeman draws upon her Mormon heritage in "Clearfield," "Going Out to Sea," and "Death of a Mormon Elder" to develop themes regarding relationships, religious belief, and personal identity. Michiko Kakutani noted that Freeman's characters "may suffer the aftereffects of divorce, death and dislocation, and yet they still hunger after the idea of a home, something that will give them a sense of their 'place in the world.' " Kakutani added: "Ms. Freeman has a clear, unpretentious prose style and an ability to weave the small comic and tragic occurrences of domestic life into pleasingly organic narratives."

MARY ELLEN QUINN

"Family" in various manifestations is the focus of [*Family Attractions*], which shows people trying to connect, looking for an emotional center, yet remaining essentially alone. There is George, in the title story, who finds himself trying to father two adolescent girls when he marries a younger woman after years of bachelorhood. There is Beatrice, a widow in **"The Botanic Gardens,"** whose need for companionship throws her in with the wrong man in a foreign city. In the poignant but never sentimental **"Going Out to Sea,"** teenage Marva is thrust into maturity by an early marriage and a sick baby. . . . These stories are not confined to a single perspective but embrace the point of view of male and female, young and old. Several are set in Utah and reflect the author's Mormon heritage. This is a strong collection that, in common with the best fiction, shows instead of tells. (pp. 827-28)

> *Mary Ellen Quinn, in a review of "Family Attractions," in Booklist, Vol. 84, No. 10, January 15, 1988, pp. 827-28.*

MERRILL JOAN GERBER

In her first published collection of short stories, *Family Attractions,* Judith Freeman tells her tales in passionate voices strong with the authority of deeply felt experience, folk wisdom, and close observation of life.

The most important and affecting stories in the book are the final two [**"Going Out to Sea"** and **"Clearfield"**], both about a young Mormon woman from Utah whose overwhelming responsibility in life is to care for her sick son. . . . The power of the stories comes from the accretion of detail, not from Freeman's prose, which is often bluntly, at times excessively, prosaic. Her ingenuousness of tone, however, protects the reader from characters who boast an easy irony or trendy cynicism.

In **"The Botanic Gardens,"** Beatrice, a 48-year-old woman on vacation alone in Australia after her fiance has died suddenly, says: "It was terrible to be alone in a foreign city. Every day you had to think of things to do, create everything from scratch, as though you were an artist confronted with an empty canvas or a writer peering at blank paper." Beatrice's confession expresses an unfashionable truth about travel that we may have thought but kept to ourselves. Little truths like these appear, often unexpectedly, throughout the stories.

An excerpt from "The Botanic Gardens"

Just as the music began, the man with the Joycean looks appeared and sat just in front of her, next to a thick pillar against which he leaned during most of the concert, assuming a posture of relaxed and evident blissfulness.

And again, when the concert was over, he came out and stood next to her, as before, on the front steps. She was having difficulty finding the sleeve of her coat and he attempted to help, though in truth, she felt more awkward than if she'd been left to manage alone.

Once her coat was on he said, "There, I think we've got it."

She thanked him. A soft rain had begun to fall, although it had yet to make anything really wet.

"Goodness," she said, "I'd planned on taking a walk in the Gardens, but with this rain, I don't know. Do you think it's really going to come down, or is this a bluff?"

They both looked up at the sky, and then across at the gates of the Botanic Gardens.

"It could," he said. "It certainly could come down. Perhaps I could walk with you through the Gardens? I've an umbrella, you see."

"Fine," she said, "yes, that would be fine."

His name was Kevin McDonald, and when he pronounced it in his jaunty Australian accent, Beatrice found it very appealing. They walked along the narrow pathways, stopping occasionally to read the names of plants written on small plaques placed in the ground. The Gardens were immense, covering acres of ground. In the Gardens was evidence of man's will to explore, Beatrice said. When the world was still hardly circumnavigated, small as your village and otherwise terrifyingly abstract, botanists had gone forth in search of plants from other continents and had brought back evidence of the diversity of life on earth. In various sections of the Gardens, bits of growing things from Uruguay, Borneo, the Baltic coast, Ceylon—all the farthest reaches of the globe—had all taken root, lovingly placed in the new soil by the plant hunters. The world had been gathered together in the Gardens, and now, she herself was a witness not only to the multifarious forms of vegetation, but to the very spirit of conquest and acquisition that had sent the botanists forth. On such themes she expounded before Kevin McDonald, until they reached the restaurant in the gazebo at the center of the Gardens and he suggested they get something to eat.

Standing next to him in the cafeteria line, she was struck by the absolute blueness of his eyes. She had once heard a lecture on iridology. The woman who spoke said the irises in people's eyes become mottled out of evil and confusion, or sickness, and that for every organ in the body, there is a corresponding point in the eye. Corruption shows up as dark flecks, irregularity, discoloration. All babies are born with either blue or brown eyes. Hazel comes later, the lecturer said, as a result of confusion and evil. Could it be that Kevin McDonald was so free from evil and confusion that his eyes had retained the clear blue color of a baby's eyes?

Though not extraordinary when taken one at a time, they seem to build overall to an admirable wisdom.

A man Beatrice meets at a concert has a face in which "she discovered shades of James Joyce." She later discovers the man drives a McDonald's Roasted Nuts truck. "She looked out at the sea, which had a farther-reaching feeling than the ocean in California did. She thought, It's always going to be like this. There would only be a series of wrong things, primary events turned sour." . . .

Freeman attempts to use symbols in her stories the way Flannery O'Connor used them in hers: They're meant to work on a literal level even as they produce deeper and resonanting levels of meaning. Some, . . . seem a bit heavy-handed, while others work quite effectively. In **"Camp Rose,"** a not-so-young woman has just told her married lover goodby, and has come to visit with her family in her brother's mountain cabin. When she finds her mother writing out a formula for homemade window cleaner, she "imagines making a gallon of window cleaner. She knows she'd never use it. In the three years she's lived in her present apartment, she's cleaned the windows once." This detail seems unimportant until the end of the story when Ann's dream of buying an old cottage next to her brother's property is dashed. Back in Los Angeles, she thinks, "Like most ideas, it was just an idea, it wasn't ever really there." Depressed and catching cold, she "thinks of getting into bed and being really, truly sick." But instead she goes to the market and buys the ingredients for the window cleaner:

> It's like alchemy. She expects something remarkable, like a genie, to rise up out of the fumes. By the time the sun sets behind a row of billboards, the panes of glass are so transparent it's very hard to believe there is anything between herself and the shapes of things out in the world.

In the best moments of these stories, we lose our awareness of reading a story and move through Freeman's fictional transparency directly into the world she wishes to reveal to us.

> *Merrill Joan Gerber, "The World through a Washed Window," in* Los Angeles Times Book Review, *February 14, 1988, p. 13.*

MICHIKO KAKUTANI

The backdrop of many of these stories [in *Family Attractions*] seems familiar: trailer camps named "Camelot Mobile Home Park," condominiums done up as mock Italian villas, split-level apartment units with cheap carpeting and chipped formica. We meet a woman who sits on her fire escape in Los Angeles, watching the activity in the local supermarket's parking lot below, and another who talks about how she's drifted away from the Mormon beliefs of her parents, how she no longer believes "in anything anymore." . . .

The people Judith Freeman has delineated in these strong, plain-spoken tales, however, are not the rootless, deracinated Americans who have become so familiar in recent fiction, rather, they're individuals who continue to try to define themselves in terms of family and tradition. They may not always succeed. They may suffer the aftereffects of divorce, death and dislocation, and yet they still hunger after the idea of a home, something that will give them a sense of their "place in the world." The girls and women frequently speak of wanting to marry and have children—one calls it "the highest calling in life"; and they spend much of their time looking for the right man, a man with whom they can share "a future of companionship and gaiety and mutual enlightenment."

In fact, the need for partnership seems to keep many of Ms. Freeman's people together, sustaining them in the face of marital discord and changing values. As a result, how a marriage or familial relationship endures and evolves is a recurrent theme in these stories. **"The Death of a Mormon Elder,"** a neatly orchestrated tale of love and faith and doubt, shows how a Mexican couple who have moved to the States and become Mormon converts relate to the new community around them, and how those new relationships, in turn, affect their perception of each other. . . .

The woman who's living with a Vietnam veteran in **"It Sure Is Cold Here at Night"** has come to feel similarly alienated from her boyfriend: she cannot comprehend what he went through in the war and no longer shares his enthusiasm for hunting and violent movies. . . . And the heroine's father in **"Camp Rose"** has spent the better part of his life politely distancing himself from his family. "His garden," Ms. Freeman writes, "was his buffer between the world of the copper mine, which he came to hate, and the eight children and wife who waited at the table, about whom he had the most complicated feelings. 'I never should have had eight children,' he said to Ann when she was older. 'I didn't have the temperament for it.' . . .

In the face of such emotions, why do these characters cling to the rules and rituals of domesticity? For some, it's a pledge of faith—in family and continuity; for others, an escape from loneliness; and for still others, a hedge against the perils of the world that are continually threatening to overtake them. In story after story, these perils are symbolized by an animal, a kind of representative of the dangers that lurk just beyond the flimsy fences of civilization: "a bat, moving out at dusk from some dank and darkened dwelling"; coyotes, howling in the canyons beyond Beverly Hills; turkeys gobbling wildly in their pens; sharks swimming offshore, just beyond the pretty tourist beaches.

A list of images like this tends to make Ms. Freeman's writing sound a lot more schematic than it is. Although this volume includes one notably weak story—**"What Is This Movie?"** is a cutesy, predictable portrait of three generations of women, including an irritatingly spunky grandmother who has recently discovered the joys of sex—and several that are unexceptional, if well crafted. *Family Attractions* marks the debut of a talented writer. Ms. Freeman has a clear, unpretentious prose style and an ability to weave the small comic and tragic occurences of domestic life into pleasingly organic narratives. Her voice—low-key, unsentimental and accented with the sounds of California and the West—is distinctively her own, and it allows her instinctive storytelling powers to shine through.

Michiko Kakutani, in a review of "Family Attrac-

tions," in The New York Times, February 17, 1988, p. C21.

BEVERLY LYON CLARK

We may witness death in Judith Freeman's first collection of short stories, as well as illness, painful memories and bickering, yet *Family Attractions* nonetheless celebrates moments of feeling and connection. . . . Although Ms. Freeman tends to overstate her points by telling what she has already shown—sometimes making her metaphors and endings strain too obviously for significance—she is superb at capturing dialogue, especially the dialogue of cross-purposes. Thus, in the story **"What Is This Movie?"** a young girl itemizes the attractions of two boyfriends, her mother discourses on cats and her grandmother's boyfriend comments on the food he is cooking in a scene featuring "as many conversations . . . as there were people." Still later, the grandmother and granddaughter discuss their preferences in men, dissolving the years. And, finally, all three generations agree, instantaneously, on how to deal with the mother's dissolute boyfriend. As this story demonstrates, the episodes in Ms. Freeman's book portray the disconnections of modern life, but they also manage to achieve a refreshing warmth.

Beverly Lyon Clark, in a review of "Family Attractions," in The New York Times Book Review, March 6, 1988, p. 20.

DIANE MANUEL

Judith Freeman makes an appealing publishing debut with *Family Attractions,* a collection of 11 short stories that generally affirm the small, unheralded acts that hold families together in a fast-changing world.

An inviting tone is set in the title story in which a 63-year-old bachelor marries and becomes father, overnight, to two teenage daughters.

In succeeding stories, the point of view shifts from an adolescent who's having her first brush with sensuality in **"Pretend We're French,"** to a spinsterish traveler whose wariness of men takes center stage in **"The Botanic Gardens."**

The author's Mormon upbringing figures in two of the most effective tales: Faith is found and abandoned in **"The Death of a Mormon Elder,"** and in **"Clearfield"** a single mother, no longer active in the church, discovers how far she has come in finding her own self-worth.

Freeman's writing is warmly intuitive, and many of her stories are braced with sardonic humor.

Diane Manuel, in a review of "Family Attractions," in The Christian Science Monitor, March 16, 1988, p. 20.

JUDITH FREEMAN

Concerning autobiographical elements in *Family Attractions,* Freeman replied: "All writers are good at remembering. I partook of my experiences. I had the idea of *truth in memory.* That's what I called the process of simply trying to remember something in accurate detail—not embellishing or judging it. Quite a faithful record can evolve. . . . Some of the stories—the Mormon tales for instance—relied on memory this way. These are what you could call the autobiographical stories (**"Death of a Mormon Elder," "Going out to Sea," "Clearfield"**). I think I relied on a sense of magic in these stories a little more so these elements would be even lighter. Truth can sometimes feel like a burden; I wanted to make it lighter."

Asked about what motivates her to write and what she hopes to accomplish through her writing, Freeman responded: "All writers must want to know more about themselves, but I hope my investigation extends beyond that. I look at the world partly like a photographer does. In other words, I'm recording some things, and reporting on more than the state of my own life."

Freeman discussed an author who influenced her work: "When I read the short story 'Death in the Woods,' I thought Sherwood Anderson was a wonderful storyteller. I thought it was a story told in such a straight and simple way. It was a monumental story based on a small event—an old woman with a heavy bundle struggling through snowy woods. I saw the power of landscape in his work, and I wanted some of that power for myself."

> *Judith Freeman, in correspondence with* CLC Yearbook.

Alan Hollinghurst

1954-

English novelist, editor, and critic.

Through the unlikely friendship that develops between Hollinghurst's two protagonists, William Beckwith and Lord Charles Nantwich, *The Swimming-Pool Library* compares the experiences of homosexuals in England during the early 1980s with those of previous eras of the twentieth century, when homosexuality was unlawful. Beckwith, a wealthy and handsome young man, saves the life of elderly Lord Nantwich and later agrees to edit his biography. Hollinghurst juxtaposes scenes of Beckwith's sexual adventures with excerpts from Nantwich's diaries, revealing the effects on Britain's homosexuals of hostile social attitudes and laws. While some critics were discomfited by the novel's numerous sexually explicit scenes, most praised *The Swimming-Pool Library* as an accurate portrayal of the promiscuous lifestyle of some homosexuals prior to the initial illnesses and deaths in England caused by Acquired Immune Deficiency Syndrome (AIDS). Vince Aletti described the book as "at once an elegy for and a celebration of hedonism past."

MICHAEL WOOD

When we say the world is small we mean it isn't much of a world: more of a village or a club, lacking the profusion and unpredictability that worlds are supposed to have. The world Alan Hollinghurst evokes in this remarkable first novel [*The Swimming-Pool Library*] is not at all small. Almost anything can happen in it, it has many inhabitants and plenty of new recruits. But it is cruelly, brilliantly specialized, haunted by repetitions, by a relentless sense of what its narrator, William Beckwith, might call *déjà eu*. Beckwith is gay in both senses, homosexual and reckless, and his promiscuity is nothing short of heroic. . . . Beckwith is terribly conscious of his mostly overwhelming appeal, and a friend suggests his last words are likely to be "How do I look?". Beckwith himself rather disarmingly speaks of his vanity having become "so constitutional that it had virtually ceased to be vanity". He is recently down from Oxford, in London now, the confident, leisured grandson of a distinguished peer. Beckwith cruises clubs, hotels, Soho cinemas, parks, swimming pools; falls in love with teenagers, gets roughed up, toys with the idea of writing the biography of a lord whose life he happens to have saved, and who. . . . There are surprises in the plot and they shouldn't be spilled in a review. The year of the narrative is 1983, and Beckwith remembers it as "the last summer of its kind there was ever to be". . . .

The novel is described on the dust-jacket as "an elegy for ways of life which, since AIDS, can no longer be lived". It

is true that the book lucidly memorializes the world AIDS must have depopulated, and that what we are likely to remember of it most vividly are its scenes, rather than its plot or its people. . . . Beckwith recalls this world fondly but also with an astringent and undeceived precision. Indeed his writing (Hollinghurst's writing) is so sure-footed and sharp that even the most disagreeable moments in the book are entirely compelling. Beckwith is too vain to be ironic, but he is quick and aware and funny, and a perfect guide to these murky, volatile regions. Hollinghurst's gamble—and it comes off—is to get us to feel the charm of this disreputable and self-absorbed young man; to like him without approving of him. . . .

But to say this is to remember that AIDS is not mentioned in the book. The disease casts a horrific shadow, but only a shadow, and there are dooms which *have* arrived in the novel's pages and are its commanding subjects. . . . The chief dooms are ageing and the risk of violence. The beautiful Beckwith knows he is not like the old blokes in the loo in the park, but also knows he may not always be so different: "I felt a faint revulsion—not disapproval, but a fear of one day

59

being like that." Ronald Firbank becomes a sort of mannered patron saint of the book, and is glimpsed in a film taken shortly before his death, "a bona fide queen", coughing, laughing, enjoying an "impromptu kind of triumph". The triumph is real but also pathetic, because it is pure style and parody, bereft of all the hectic physical attractions Beckwith lives by and can't think of living without. The biography Beckwith is thinking of writing is a "fore-echo" of his own story, since the now eighty-three-year-old lord, too, was Winchester and Oxford and gay. Beckwith will have screwed a lot more, but otherwise done much less. Can this be all liberation means? It is at this point that the dooms of age and violence meet up. Looking for a black boyfriend who has disappeared, Beckwith is beaten up by a group of skinheads, and understands (not before time, we may feel) the ridiculous physical (and other) risks he has long been taking. . . . And he grasps for the first time the "vulnerability of the old, unfortified by good luck or inexperience".

Hollinghurst's mysterious title points to the repeating patterns. Both Beckwith and the old lord like to swim, and in the basement of the lord's house is a mosaic fragment, the floor of a Roman swimming pool. This is an ancient anticipation, far more than eighty-three years back, of the image under which Beckwith figures his life. He was a prefect in a school where prefects were called librarians, and the swimming pool changing house, scene of his "earliest excesses", became in schoolboy slang the Swimming Pool Library. . . . The changing house is a lost utopia, a paradise of unquestioned sexual pleasure, a time before scorn and complication, an innocent world before the underworlds this book so memorably depicts. . . . We may find it hard to grasp the sort of innocence he has in mind, and Beckwith himself finds it harder and harder. But the swimming Romans would have understood.

There are occasional awkwardnesses in this book. In order to get a good run of gay history, Hollinghurst has the old lord born with the century, and Beckwith dipping into the chap's notebooks and diaries for 1920, 1926, 1943 and so on. This is plausibly done, although it doesn't have the campy panache and exactness of Beckwith's prose, but there is something slightly comic about Beckwith's reading the things whenever his author needs a flashback. "There was a section of Charles's diary I had been reading . . ."; "I sat up . . . with a bottle of Scotch and Charles's Oxford diary . . ."; "I settled down to read about Charles's doings long ago . . .". These narrative excuses are a touch too diligent. I found the sexual detail a bit merciless too. However this is clearly a deeply imagined, much thought on, elegantly composed work. Few novels in recent years have been better written, and none I know of has been more intelligent.

Michael Wood, "A Bathing Beauty's 'Belle Époque'," in The Times Literary Supplement, *No. 4429, February 19-25, 1988, p. 185.*

JOHN LANCHESTER

Writing about sex tends to go wrong in one of two related ways. The first is through embarrassment or over-excitement on the part of the author: overly rhapsodic descriptions of sex, in particular, tend to cause feelings of unease (Lawrence, Mailer). The other, subtler way is through the failure to show sex as a function of character: to depict sex in fiction as a holiday from personality is to make sex, in fictional terms, merely

digressive. One of the triumphs of *The Swimming-Pool Library*—a startlingly accomplished first novel—is the tonal control it achieves in writing graphically and explicitly about homosexual sex while never seeming flustered or prurient, and never wavering in the amused, ironic control of the narrating voice. . . . The measured, formal movement of the prose, its hints of scholarly fastidiousness, give a flavour of comedy of manners to 'acts in which', the architecture-loving narrator remarks, 'the influence of the orders, the dome, the portico, could scarcely be discerned.' However Dionysian the events depicted—fellatio, sodomy, an erection passing along a line of men in the shower 'with the domino effect of a Busby Berkeley routine'—the narrator's tone remains, in keeping with his personality, resolutely Apollonian.

The novel is William Beckwith's account of summer 1983. . . . [He] is handsome, rich, homosexual, talented, narcissistic, promiscuous and lazy—as lazy and as cultured as the 'superfluous man' of the 19th-century Russian novel. Cruising in a public lavatory in Kensington Park, Will saves the life of Charles Nantwich, an 83-year-old gay peer of the realm, 'the sort of chap who turns up in the lives of other people'. Nantwich is physically frail and prone to 'blanking'—sudden mental absences—but he is more purposeful and manipulative than is immediately apparent, and he is adroit at tactical use of the 'egocentric discontinuities' of his conversational style. He wants Will to write his biography and to that end hands over his diaries, extracts from which form a considerable part of *The Swimming-Pool Library.* The diaries chronicle Nantwich's education (Winchester and Oxford—just like Will) and his time as a District Commissioner in the Sudan, as well as his holiday and wartime experiences in London. The contrast between Nantwich's life and Will's is one of the main themes of the novel: Nantwich's life has been shaped by the criminalisation of his sexuality, and by the way in which that impelled him towards a life of 'philanthropic sublimation'.

The theme is emphasised and its general applicability is tested by passages in the novel which deal with the work of the generation of artists who did their work in the closeted pre-Wolfenden climate. If the idea of 'homosexual writing' is useful, it probably applies best to the period when homosexuality was criminal, and hence when the fictional treatment of same-sex love had to be implicit, indirect, deflected, latent. Hollinghurst's unpublished M. Litt thesis, which I stumbled across as a graduate student, made a forceful case for this idea as applied to the work of Firbank, Hartley and Forster. His novel takes up the idea in asides: 'It's the whole gay thing, isn't it,' Will remarks to a boyfriend reading [Hartley's] *The Go-Between,* 'the unvoiced longing, the cloistered heart.' The most extended and moving treatment of the theme comes with Will's visit to the opera in the company of his grandfather: the opera is Britten's *Billy Budd.* Interval discussion of the work's 'deflected' sexuality is interrupted by the appearance of Peter Pears, who arrives as a living witness from a kind of heroic era for homosexual artists.

The Swimming-Pool Library is a rich and clever and funny novel. The richness is in large part a matter of the density of detail the book manages to accumulate. . . . Will's architectural enthusiasms provide a starting-point for his distinctive but absolutely compelling vision of London, which is always under the careful tonal control already mentioned. The meticulous realism of the novel is accompanied by a careful use of imagistic and symbolic parallelings. A typical piece of simultaneous realism and symbolism is the fact that Will's best friend James keeps his diaries (which are secret-but-not-secret: Will reads them with James's tacit consent) on the same shelf as he keeps his treasured collection of Firbank novels (which embody, more than any other novelist's work, a technique relying on secrecy and implication). The most important current of images relates to swimming-pools and subterranean places. The two main pools in the novel are the one at the Corinthian Club (site of the Busby Berkeley shower-scenes) and the archaeological remains of Roman baths which are preserved under Lord Nantwich's house. . . . The images parallel the contrast on which the novel is built, but Hollinghurst is careful to avoid too straightforward a correspondence between the symbolic and the explicit levels of the book, and other underground images are plentiful: the 'sub-aqueous' atmosphere of Firbank's Café Royal (also a kind of sexual marketplace), the 'subterraneous' back parts of the hotel where Phil works, the underground night-club called The Shaft, and the Underground itself, where the novel opens with Will contemplating two night-shift maintenance men 'with a kind of swimming, drunken wonder, amazed at the thought of their inverted lives'.

But if the richness of the book is a matter of detail and specificity, its cleverness has a lot to do with one bold technical stroke, which is summarisable by the fact that there are no women characters in *The Swimming-Pool Library.* The novel adheres rigidly to Will's point of view, and that point of view is strictly circumscribed. His absolute immersion in London gay life has the effect of excluding women and heterosexuals from his consciousness. . . . The effect of this circumscription is enhanced by the temporal location of the novel in 1983, before the first UK deaths from Aids occurred. . . . Will's ignorance about Aids gives a flavour of the summer of 1914 to the summer of 1983, and the limited nature of his *Weltanschauung* makes him not especially likeable but at the same time curiously prelapsarian and innocent. His hedonistic self-confidence, his sense that 'I was both of the world and beyond its power,' has a historical poignancy of which he is unaware.

This effect is local and verbal as well as structural: much of what Will says seems to be darkened by the pressure of another possible reading, a reading which has a deeper vision of life than the narrator's. 'It was all very clean,' he remarks of the lavatory where he saves Nantwich's life, 'and at several of the stalls under the burnished copper pipes (to which someone must attach all their pride), men were standing, raincoats shrouding from the innocent visitor or the suspicious policeman their hour-long footlings.' The observation about the pipes is a typical piece of Beckwithian aestheticism, an instance of the 'camp, exploitative, ironical control' of his expression: how amusing, that some troglodyte should spend his days cleaning the Gents. But there is, at the same time, a kind of latent compassion and humanity about realising that lavatory fittings don't get that clean just by accident, and in realising that someone's life must therefore be entirely bound up in keeping them that way. You are fleetingly led to wonder, as Beckwith clearly does not, what that would be like if it were your life.

The double focus—operating in that moment of an observation which is both Will's and more than Will's—becomes increasingly important as the novel progresses. Where there is a darkening and enriching of the words Will speaks, it usually derives from the sense that those words have an ethical di-

mension of which he is not fully aware. As the story moves along and the various forms of idealism it depicts (emotional, aesthetic, erotic, familial) turn sour, the ethical dimension presses on the reader more and more. . . . It isn't quite clear how far the events of *The Swimming-Pool Library* lead Will to realise the limitations of his own behaviour and world-view. For the reader, those limitations could not be made clearer (though it is a novel that is bound to attract galumphing misreadings and denunciation). (pp. 11-12)

John Lanchester, "Catch 28," in London Review of Books, *Vol. 10, No. 5, March 3, 1988, pp. 11-12.*

An excerpt from *The Swimming-Pool Library*

As a child, on visits to Marden, my grandfather's house, days had been marked by walks along the great beech ride which ran unswervingly for miles over hilly country and gave out at a ha-ha and a high empty field. Away to the left you could make out in winter the chicken-coops and outside privies of a village that had once been part of the estate. Then we turned round, and came home, my sister and I, spoilt by my grandparents, feeling decidedly noble and aloof. It was not until years later that I came to understand how recent and synthetic this nobility was—the house itself bought up cheap after the war, half ruined by use as an officers' training school, and then as a military hospital.

Today was one of those April days, still and overcast, that felt pregnant with some immense idea, and suggested, as I roamed across from one perspective to another, that this was merely a doldrums, and would last only until something else was ready to happen. Perhaps it was simply summer, and the certainty of warmth, the world all out of doors, drinking in the open air. The trees were budding, and that odd inside-out logic was evolving whereby the Park, just at the time it becomes hot and popular, shuts itself off from the outside world of buildings and traffic with the shady density of its foliage. But I felt the threat too of some realisation about life, something obscurely disagreeable and perhaps deserved.

Though I didn't believe in such things, I was a perfect Gemini, a child of the ambiguous early summer, tugged between two versions of myself, one of them the hedonist and the other—a little in the background these days—an almost scholarly figure with a faintly puritanical set to the mouth. And there were deeper dichotomies, differing stories—one the 'account of myself', the sex-sharp little circuits of discos and pubs and cottages, the sheer crammed, single-minded repetition of my empty months; the other the 'romance of myself', which transformed all these mundanities with a protective glow, as if from my earliest days my destiny indeed been charmed, so that I was both of the world and beyond its power, like the pantomime character Wordsworth describes, with 'Invisible' written on his chest.

JON SAVAGE

The Swimming Pool Library is set in an enclosed corner of

the gay world, 1983. Within two pages we are reading that the summer of that year was "the last of its kind there ever was to be". 1983 was the year that Aids fully entered the consciousness, lives or bodies of English gay men and this event gives Hollinghurst's five-year-old narrative—as is deliberate—the sense of an age almost further in the past than the pastiche early 20th-century diaries that punctuate the book.

In fiction, the fundamental break presented by Aids—and its wider ramifications of oppression and suffering—has given rise to a quest for gay identity, humanity and continuity comparable to the self- and external analyses undergone since the early '80s by many gay people. Despite the fact that the oversignifying initials are not mentioned, *The Swimming Pool Library* is a part of this response, being a serious, critical yet partisan examination of one aspect of English gay life: its sex, its milieu, its sensibility and its history. (pp. 26-7)

This is a closed world, both of class and sex. No women appear in Beckwith's round of pleasure as he plunges head first into the almost unlimited delights available to his privilege. Some of the book is very sexy—in that the graphically described acts occur between recognisable, complex characters—but there are qualification clauses. Beckwith himself is revealed as shallow, shiftless and selfish: a narcissist capable of exploitation but not affection. Despite his intelligence, he is incapable of seeing the consequences of his actions or in thinking through the implications of his position, raised in "power and compromise". . . .

The book's apparent snobbery masks a sharp look at the English class system. The gay world's codes, its infinite subtleties, instant alliances and cruelties—the racist and ageist tendencies here described—are also part of the hostile world outside, just as gays aren't "separate" from society. This is made clear in a sequence where Beckwith is taken to Covent Garden by his grandfather: his gayness, although unstated between them, is both acknowledged and squashed by one single adjective. This is the subtle side of the oppression which Beckwith discovers is part of his own life as external reality begins to intrude. . . .

Within these layers, Hollinghurst loops discussions on Firbank, the psychogeography of London and gay history. He writes with a trace of Orton—that "irresistible combination of elegance and crudity"—and with a sure eye on his own manipulations: he warns us against finding, like those who hark back to the days before liberalising legislation, the past "unbelievably sexy". *The Swimming Pool Library* is a pertinent, provocative book which, if anything, errs on the side of too much structure; at its curiously rushed conclusion, nothing is resolved. Despite "having that most oppressive of feelings—that some test was looming", Beckwith returns to his question mark of cruising. Does he, like that psychological pattern he embodies, pass through adolescence into maturity? (p. 27)

Jon Savage, "Last Summer," in New Statesman, *Vol. 115, No. 2971, March 4, 1988, pp. 26-7.*

PETER PARKER

[The sensibility of Hollinghurst's novel *The Swimming-Pool Library*] is English Literary Homosexual: the camp here is of the highest. The protagonists . . . , may spend their time grovelling around the damp floors of urinals, but goodness they're cultured. Will Beckwith, Hollinghurst's decoratively parasitic Wykehamist narrator, describes sexual longing in terms of 'a Straussian phrase sweeping from the top to the bottom of the orchestra'. The urgent, rutting rhythms of *Le sacre du printemps* might have been a more appropriate reference, but then Will is self-deluded, so bound up in his workout narcissism that he imagines himself to be in love when he is simply in lust, 'riding high on sex and self-esteem'. A telling number of mirrors reflect Will's gilded image as he sails through the book, including, chillingly, 'the glossy, speckled darkness' of his lover's pupils. When he is beaten up and steels himself to face the looking-glass, he resembles nothing so much as Dorian Gray trembling before the Picture.

It was Wilde who memorably described the long road to homosexual reform as 'red with monstrous martyrdoms' and a martyr theme runs through the book, from the fate of Lord Nantwich, whose biography Will might write, to the kitsch Gilbert-and-George-ish work of a photographer who snaps butchers' boys in the poses of dying saints. However, it is Wilde's disciple, that specialist in fictional martyrology, Ronald Firbank, who is the most pervasive literary presence. Quite apart from the two touching appearances he makes in the story, Firbank provides a number of sly echoes . . . , and the novel's epigraph. . . .

This is a marvellously *knowing* book, crammed with spot-on observations of its homosexual milieu. The infamous and innumerable scenes of sexual gorging are perhaps necessary to mirror Will's relentless appetite. Food imagery abounds, and in one encounter Will is tenderised and (in every sense) forced on a kitchen chopping-board. There may also be another sly literary joke, at Betjeman's expense, for when Hollinghurst's Wykehamist anti-hero is 'satisfying fleshy wants' he tends to nibble at rather more than a petit beurre.

The publishers warily describe this highly literate, witty and energetic novel as an 'elegy' for the pre-AIDS era. For all its vitality and good-humour, one is inescapably reminded, as Will goes on his promiscuous way, of Conrad's anarchist Professor in *The Secret Agent:* 'He passed on unsuspected and deadly, like a pest in the street full of men.'

Peter Parker, "Beautiful Uptown Firbank," in The Listener, *Vol. 119, No. 3054, March 17, 1988, p. 21.*

VINCE ALETTI

The Swimming-Pool Library, a first novel by the deputy editor of the *TLS,* arrives trailing extravagant praise from British reviewers and impressive best-seller stats. Edmund White's notice, excerpted on the back cover, compares the book to *Vile Bodies, Love in a Cold Climate, Our Lady of the Flowers,* and—if that weren't enough—*Lolita.* It's a bit much for the skeptical reader, ever wary of well-connected writers and their jazzy jacket copy, especially the fragrant bouquets heaped on first fiction. Too often, the publicity is more inventive, more persuasive than the prose. But *The Swimming-Pool Library* isn't another of those bright hot-air balloons; it's a buoyant, smart, irrepressibly sexy book that is easily one of the year's most important debuts. If Alan Hollinghurst is not yet a Waugh or a Nabokov, his language, his wit, his audacity, and the ambition of his design suggest he'd be more comfortable in the company of these modern giants than with the miniaturists, cartoonists, and crass entertainers who are his contemporaries. Taking as his subject not just gay life but gay history—the shaping, suppression, and persistence of a sensibility—Hollinghurst serves up an intricately plotted fiction that has the heft and resonance of a classic modernist novel, the sprawl and surprise of an intimate memoir. Call Hollinghurst a savvy new traditionalist—Edith Wharton with a twist. . . .

[The narrator, William Beckwith,] in his mid twenties, is wealthy, privileged, deliberately out of work. He's a character who, had he appeared some decades earlier, might have spent country-house weekends with Sebastian Marchmain or exchanged tipsy repartee at Brat's with Tony Last. But the year is 1983. . . . By locating Beckwith's sunny *belle époque* in the last year before AIDS destroyed the notion of untroubled sex, Hollinghurst gives his novel a charged, last-gasp mood of rue and excitement. *The Swimming-Pool Library* becomes at once an elegy for and a celebration of hedonism past.

Beckwith's busy sex life threads the novel with flushed romanticism and explosive bursts of vividly graphic fucking around. Intoxicated by the possibilities, Will seems bent on satisfying an appetite whose full range he's only just discovered, and he describes his encounters with a breathless immediacy that's never too hurried to pin down the sensual details or slip in a few keen psychological asides. Even when there's no willing flesh nearby, sex is always in the air, and Beckwith is helplessly, often hilariously alert. . . . Through Will, Hollinghurst takes possession of London—from the opera house to the public toilet, the plush men's club to the trashed towerblock—and plunges us into a city bristling with social and sexual signifiers (many of them so frightfully British they're likely to elude us Yanks). It's like cruising with Joe Orton and Ronald Firbank. . . .

Will's more immediate gay (grand)father figure, and the novel's other key character, is Charles Nantwich, who is exactly as old as the century. Lord Nantwich stumbles into the story early on when Beckwith, nosing around in a park lavatory, sees the old party mutter "Oh deary me" and collapse at a urinal—"a substantial, tweed-clad figure sprawled across

the damp tile floor." Will performs mouth-to-mouth, revives the stranger, and leaves, only to encounter him weeks later in the pool at the Corinthian Club. Although Nantwich doesn't seem to recognize him as the young man who saved his life, he takes a fancy to Beckwith and seizes on him as the person to help organize and publish his memoirs.

With this unlikely, fortuitous pairing, Hollinghurst bridges gay generations and sets his dense design in motion. If his plot turns on rather too many parallels and coincidences, his deliberate juxtaposition of past and present is an unexpectedly rich device. Dropping in large chunks of Nantwich's diaries alongside Beckwith's equally obsessive but at times rather oblivious chronicles puts them both in perspective. . . .

Hollinghurst, who begins by diverting us with sex and sophistication, is up to something quite a bit more serious as well. No matter how charmed the lives of his gay aristocrats, violence and oppression are close at hand. Hollinghurst lavishes Beckwith with the ripe fruits of liberation but gradually wakes him to the unchanging perils of gay life—betrayal, police entrapment, fag bashing—and balances the comfort of history with its chastening lessons. In the end, Will's easy assumptions have been blasted and his love life is in temporary disarray, but Hollinghurst knows him too well to paint him much wiser or more subdued. The last line finds Beckwith back at the Corinthian, in the social swim, eyeing "a suntanned young lad in pale blue trunks that I rather liked the look of." As for Hollinghurst, who carries all this off with consummate grace, wit, and intelligence, I imagine him like the gossip columnist in [Firbank's] *The Flower Beneath the Foot* who "only closed her notebook towards dawn, when the nib of her pen caught fire."

Vince Aletti, "Lust Horizons: Alan Hollinghurst's Remembrances of Things Past," in VLS, No. 68, October, 1988, p. 32.

Barbara Kingsolver

1955-

American novelist, short story writer, poet, and nonfiction writer.

The Bean Trees concerns Taylor Greer, a young woman who leaves her small hometown in Kentucky to search for a more fulfilling life. While driving west across the United States, Taylor becomes the guardian of an abused child whom she names Turtle. Taylor and the child eventually settle in Tucson, Arizona, where they share the home of Lou Ann Ruiz, an abandoned young mother. Through her relationships with Turtle, Lou Ann, and Mattie, an energetic woman who runs an auto repair shop and houses Central American political refugees, Taylor gains a greater sense of self-identity, community, political conscience, and responsibility. Although some critics found Taylor too noble-minded to be entirely realistic, most praised Kingsolver's wit and her ability to capture the nuances of the Southern dialect. Margaret Randall described *The Bean Trees* as "a story propelled by a marvelous ear, a fast-moving humor and the powerful undercurrent of human struggle."

PUBLISHERS WEEKLY

Feisty Marietta Greer changes her name to "Taylor" when her car runs out of gas in Taylorville, Ill. By the time she reaches Oklahoma, this strong-willed young Kentucky native with a quick tongue and an open mind is catapulted into a surprising new life. . . . *The Bean Trees* is an overwhelming delight, as random and unexpected as real life. The unmistakable voice of its irresistible heroine is whimsical, yet deeply insightful. Taylor playfully names [an abandoned child] "Turtle," because she clings with an unrelenting, reptilian grip; at the same time, Taylor aches at the thought of the silent, staring child's past suffering. With Turtle in tow, Taylor lands in Tucson, Ariz., with two flat tires and decides to stay. The desert climate, landscape and vegetation are completely foreign to Taylor, and in learning to love Arizona, she also comes face to face with its rattlesnakes and tarantulas. Similarly, Taylor finds that motherhood, responsibility and independence are thorny, if welcome, gifts. This funny, inspiring book is a marvelous affirmation of risk-taking, commitment and everyday miracles.

> *A review of "The Bean Trees," in* Publishers Weekly, *Vol. 233, No. 2, January 15, 1988, p. 78.*

KAREN FITZGERALD

The Bean Trees covers expansive territory—literally and figuratively. Yet, despite the large sweep of the canvas, the char-

acters remain firmly at the novel's center. Taylor Greer, a poor, young woman, flees her Kentucky home and heads west. Like other heroes, real and imagined, in American literature and history, she goes off in search of opportunity and excitement. While passing through Oklahoma, she becomes responsible for a two-year-old Cherokee girl. The two continue on the road. When they roll off the highway in Tucson, Taylor and the child (whom she has named Turtle, for the way she tenaciously grips anything she gets her hands on) meet Mattie, a widow who runs Jesus Is Lord Used Tires and is active in the sanctuary movement on the side. Mattie befriends Taylor, gives her a job, and dispenses TLC as generously as Lou Ann, Taylor's new roommate, deprecates herself. Lou Ann, whose husband has just left her and their newborn son, rents a room in her house to Taylor and Turtle, and the foursome go on to build a chosen family that includes Guatemalan refugees and elderly neighbors.

Given such ostensible contrivances of plot and character, *The Bean Trees* would seem to be on a collision course with its own political correctness. But Barbara Kingsolver has resisted turning her characters into mouthpieces for the party line. Instead, she has written a vivid and engaging novel that is concerned more with love and friendship than with the perils of single motherhood and the politics of the sanctuary movement. It is refreshingly free of cant and the self-absorption of such overrated, urbane young novelists as Tama Janowitz and Jay McInerney.

From the very first page, Kingsolver's characters tug at the heart and soul. It is the growing strength of their relationships, rather than any virtuoso literary pyrotechnics, that gives the novel its energy and appeal. . . .

The give-and-take, the love and affection and support, allows, *encourages,* the women to flourish. This human chain operates in much the same way as rhizobia function with wisteria vines. Rhizobia are microscopic bugs that live in the roots of such leguminous plants, turning nitrogen gas into fertilizer, allowing the vines to thrive in poor soil, and ultimately to metamorphose into long green pods—the "bean trees" that so fascinate the horticulturally minded Turtle.

Friendship is not new literary terrain for women novelists; Doris Lessing staked out the territory in 1962 with *The Golden Notebook,* and others have followed suit. But the topic has become of consuming interest for contemporary feminist writers. . . . The surge in theoretical dissections of friendship underscores the importance that these relationships play in women's lives, but it is the fictional treatments that capture their spiritual and emotional texture. Barbara Kingsolver has rhapsodized the everydayness of such havens in a hard world, and in doing so, she has written an entertaining and inspiring first novel.

Karen FitzGerald, "A Major New Talent," in Ms., *Vol. XVI, No. 10, April, 1988, p. 28.*

JACK BUTLER

Barbara Kingsolver can write. On any page of this accomplished first novel [*The Bean Trees*], you can find a striking image or fine dialogue or a telling bit of drama. This, for example . . . : "Her old hand pawed the air for a few seconds before Ivy silently caught it and corralled it in the heavy black sleeve." Even when the line is quoted out of context, we can see in it the clumsy animal intransigence of a stubborn old woman in those verbs, and the darkness of fate and motive in that heavy black sleeve. When you know that the old woman is the paternal grandmother, visiting from Kentucky, of one Lou Ann Ruiz, and that this grandmother has spent her entire stay in Arizona finding fault with Tucson for being so dry, with Lou Ann for moving so far away and marrying a "heathern" Mexican and with the heathern for working on Sundays, and that the old woman is insisting on wearing her coat, regardless of the 80-degree weather, because it's January, the tiny moment gains tremendous resonance.

It is one thing to create a vivid and realistic scene, and it is quite another to handle the harmonics of many such scenes, to cause all the images and implications to work together. And it is extremely rare to find the two gifts in one writer. How can I say it? Barbara Kingsolver doesn't waste a single overtone. From the title of her novel to its ending, every little scrap of event or observation is used, reused, revivified with sympathetic vibrations. *The Bean Trees* is as richly connected as a fine poem, but reads like realism. Its author is a poet, a Kentuckian who, like her main character, Taylor Greer,

has transplanted herself to Tucson, and her book is a strange new combination: branchy and dense, each of its stories packed with microstories, and yet the whole as clear as air. It is the Southern novel taken west, its colors as translucent and polished as one of those slices of rose agate from a desert rock shop. . . .

Taylor's given name is Marietta, but as soon as she leaves, she changes it. This move is completely indicative of her character. Taylor is a sort of down-home superwoman—bright, articulate, innately fair and decent, tough as they come and yet country to the bone. Here she is on the road, in a bar in Oklahoma, facing down a troublemaker:

> "You got anything to eat that costs less than a dollar?" I asked the old guy behind the counter. . . .
>
> "Ketchup," the gray-hat cowboy said. "Earl serves up a mean bottle of ketchup, don't you, Earl?" He slid the ketchup bottle down the counter so hard it rammed my cup and spilled out probably five cents' worth of coffee.
>
> "You think being busted is a joke?" I asked him. I slid the bottle back and hit his beer mug dead center, although it did not spill.

That line about the 5 cents' worth of spilled coffee is typical Taylor Greer, both in acuteness and in dialect. So is her comment, a page earlier, about this same gray-hatted cowboy and the brown-hatted Indian sitting next to him: "I guess now Indians can be cowboys too, though probably not vice versa."

The question of speech is not merely a matter of style. When Taylor and Lou Ann Ruiz meet, they feel at home with each other because they talk alike. This busy story also eventually involves a pair of Guatemalan refugees, Estevan and Esperanza. Back home, Estevan taught English; now he will teach Taylor to see her own words from the viewpoint of an outsider, and thus show her how subtly language is linked to political reality. Another of the major subplots of the book, also associated with language, is the gradual development of a child called Turtle, for whom Taylor becomes responsible. Turtle has been brutalized and does not, for a long time, talk. When she does begin, her first words are the names of vegetables, including, most prominently, beans. There is a stark fine poetry in this talking by naming, and when Ms. Kingsolver ties it in with the book's name and the fate of Turtle's mother, the echoes are sonorous indeed. . . .

I must describe the one fault I found with *The Bean Trees.* After [the personalities and relationships of the characters] were in place, after the story posed its two central problems and began bringing it all home, it lost its immediacy for me. In the first third of the book, Taylor is vividly real; in the rest of it, her observations are as shrewd, her speech as salty, her heart as true, but she seems to have lost that passionate *presence.* I simply quit caring so deeply.

In part, I can explain my reaction as small-mindedness. Taylor becomes too perfect, too right. She confronts prejudice, trauma, self-abnegation, chauvinism, and always, always has the right attitude. Well, I've known people like that. Still. . . . The other characters are purified to types as well. . . .

Who can be against the things this book is against? Who can help admiring the things this book is for? But reality suffers, though the author's precision remains. At one point late in

An excerpt from *The Bean Trees*

When I drove over the Pittman line I made two promises to myself. One I kept, the other I did not.

The first was that I would get myself a new name. I wasn't crazy about anything I had been called up to that point in life, and this seemed like the time to make a clean break. I didn't have any special name in mind, but just wanted a change. The more I thought about it, the more it seemed to me that a name is not something a person really has the right to pick out, but is something you're provided with more or less by chance. I decided to let the gas tank decide. Wherever it ran out, I'd look for a sign.

I came pretty close to being named after Homer, Illinois, but kept pushing it. I kept my fingers crossed through Sidney, Sadorus, Cerro Gordo, Decatur, and Blue Mound, and coasted into Taylorville on the fumes. And so I am Taylor Greer. I suppose you could say I had some part in choosing this name, but there was enough of destiny in it to satisfy me.

The second promise, the one that I broke, had to do with where I would end up. I had looked at some maps, but since I had never in my own memory been outside of Kentucky (I was evidently born across the river in Cincinnati, but that is beside the point), I had no way of knowing why or how any particular place might be preferable to any other. That is, apart from the pictures on the gas station brochures: Tennessee claimed to be the Volunteer State, and Missouri the Show-Me State, whatever that might mean, and nearly everyplace appeared to have plenty of ladies in fifties hairdos standing near waterfalls. These brochures I naturally did not trust as far as I could throw them out the window. Even Pittman, after all, had once been chosen an All-Kentucky City, on the basis of what I do not know. Its abundance of potato bugs and gossip, perhaps. I knew how people could toot their own horn without any earthly cause.

And so what I promised myself is that I would drive west until my car stopped running, and there I would stay. But there were some things I hadn't considered. Mama taught me well about tires, and many other things besides, but I knew nothing of rocker arms. And I did not know about the Great Plain.

The sight of it filled me with despair. I turned south from Wichita, Kansas, thinking I might find a way around it, but I didn't. There was central Oklahoma. I had never imagined that any part of a round earth could be so flat. In Kentucky you could never see too far, since there were always mountains blocking the other side of your view, and it left you the chance to think something good might be just over the next hill. But out there on the plain it was all laid out right in front of you, and no matter how far you looked it didn't get any better. Oklahoma made me feel there was nothing left to hope for.

the book, Turtle experiences a frightening reminder of her early horrors, and much is made of the damage this sort of reoccurrence can do—but then the subject is dismissed. Turtle sails on, basically unperturbed. Taylor is selectively naïve, which is real enough; but eventually her areas of ignorance and savvy begin to seem chosen for effect. When, for example, she volunteers for a risky mission near the end of the story, we are given a passage of blatant false modesty. The intent appears to be to portray her as not only heroic but also humble, and it simply isn't credible. The Taylor we have met so far would know very well that she was doing a brave thing.

Perhaps the problem is one of overmanipulation. At the same time the characters faded on me, I started to see the images and the plot coming. And the story began to feel a bit like an upbeat novel for teen-agers—because, although it considers true and terrible realities, only certain resolutions are permitted.

On the other hand, *The Bean Trees* is still a remarkable, enjoyable book, one that contains more good writing than most successful careers. I'd definitely urge you to read it—if only to prove to yourself that it has one less flaw than a certain reviewer might think.

Jack Butler, "She Hung the Moon and Plugged in All the Stars," in The New York Times Book Review, *April 10, 1988, p. 15.*

DIANE MANUEL

This refreshingly perceptive first novel [*The Bean Trees*] celebrates a young woman's coming of age in an unusual setting peopled by wonderfully outrageous characters. In a neatly constructed tale, Barbara Kingsolver gives readers something that's increasingly hard to find today—a character to believe in and laugh with and admire. . . .

The scenario has a familiar ring, as does its independent and irreverent '80s heroine. But Kingsolver delivers enough original dialogue and wry one-liners to put this novel on a shelf of its own: Taylor disparages the traffic out West as "moving about the speed of a government check" and recalls that when she crossed into Rocky Mountain time, "I had set my watch back two hours and got thrown into the future."

That's not to say this is merely laugh-a-minute fluff, however. The tire-repair shop where Taylor works is also a safe house for Central American refugees, and as she gradually learns about the suffering some of her newfound friends have endured, she begins to make her own significant commitment to protecting their hard-won freedom. This is character development at its richest, with Taylor growing from happy-go-lucky hillbilly to caring friend and parent.

Diane Manuel, "A Roundup of First Novels about Coming of Age," in The Christian Science Monitor, *April 22, 1988, p. 20.*

MARGARET RANDALL

[*The Bean Trees* is] a first novel that's fast reading but long-staying. It starts off with the narrator's first-person childhood memories. You think this is great: something for light consumption on the daily commuter train or to be absorbed in the pleasure of a steaming tub. And this is certainly a book that can be read in just those places. But it's not simply another trashy (read: delicious) piece of fiction. You are thoroughly hooked by the time you realize Barbara Kingsolver is addressing and connecting two of our most important issues.

The Bean Trees is about invasion. Invasion, not as it is probed and theorized about by political thinkers, psychologists, or academics. Invasion as it is experienced by middle America. And not middle-*class* America, but real middle America, the unemployed and underemployed, the people working in fast-food joints or patching tires, Oklahoma Indians, young mothers left by wandering husbands or mothers who never had husbands. In this novel you travel from Kentucky to Arizona and never even have to consider the sophisticated complexities of New York, San Francisco, or Chicago.

The Bean Trees is hilariously funny. You laugh out loud. I literally fell off my chair. You turn the pages and wheeze, empathetically amazed and delighted by the characters who people these pages; by their perceptions of themselves and the world and by the decisions they make for their moral as well as physical survival. . . . (p. 1)

Pace-wise, or in some of its rhythms, *The Bean Trees* has something in common with Jack Kerouac's classic *On the Road.* But its meaning is exactly the opposite. Kingsolver's characters don't opt for dropping out of society; they are desperately trying to survive within its confines. For unexpected yet believable humor, made from the more painful observations of our culture, it takes me back to William Eastlake's *Portrait of the Artist with Twenty-Four Horses.*

But it would be misleading to compare Kingsolver with either of these male authors. In style and vision, she has written a book all her own, and with a deep female consciousness that feels like bedrock when put up against some of the preachier, more explicitly feminist works. Attempting to define this published-yet-new author, Georgia Cotrell's name comes to mind; Kingsolver's prose style has something in common with Cotrell's use of language in *Shoulders.* She also shares Cotrell's curiosity about a given (although different) social group, her integrity in shying away from surface judgments when looking at complexities and contradictions, and her explorations of non-traditional families.

Two lines of narrative eventually converge in Kingsolver's novel. There is our heroine, telling her story with the quiet unsophisticated irony of a tough and travelin' Kentucky woman. She leaves home bent on getting herself a new name and decides she'll take the cue from wherever she runs out of gas. "I came pretty close to being named after Homer, Illinois, but kept pushing it. I kept my fingers crossed through Sidney, Sadorus, Cerro Gordo, Decatur, and Blue Mound, and coasted into Taylorville on the fumes. And so I am Taylor Greer," she announces early in the story.

And there is an alternating-chapter third-person narrative: Lou Ann, also from Kentucky but already a sometime Tucson resident, whose rodeo-riding husband Angel Ruiz loses what sense of self he may once have had when an accident takes one of his legs below the knee. Irritable and dissatisfied, he leaves Lou Ann before their child is born. . . .

The Bean Trees, on one well-fashioned plane, is the story of how these two poverty-level women find one another through want ads and mutual need, how they aid one another by pooling their meager resources and sharing a house, how they help one another go on learning about life and what it means.

The end of the scene in which Taylor and Lou Ann join fortunes is worth repeating. The former has answered a house-to-share ad placed by the latter. "Lou Ann hid her mouth with her hand. 'What?' I said. 'Nothing.' I could see perfectly well that she was smiling. 'Come on, what is it?' 'It's been so long,' she said. 'You talk just like me.' "

These two apparently different women are immensely compatible. . . .

This is also the story of Mattie, Mattie of Jesus Is Lord Used Tires, and the occupants of her labyrinth second floor: people like the nervous young priest on the motorcycle, and Estevan and Esperanza, who come and go in the night. After a short stint frying up fast food at Burger Derby, Taylor rebels and goes to work for Mattie, a knowledgeable woman who drinks coffee from a white mug on which hundreds of tiny rabbits are having sex in hundreds of different positions. . . .

There are endless delightful moments in this book. A typical Kingsolver scene happens when Taylor is introduced to Lou Ann's cat:

> "You wouldn't believe what your cat is doing," I said. "Oh yes, I would," Lou Ann said. "He's acting like he just went potty, right?" "Right. But he didn't as far as I can see." "Oh no, he never does. I think he has a split personality. The good cat wakes up and thinks the bad cat has just pooped on the rug."

As is necessary to any decent novel about ordinary America, fundamentalism as a *leitmotif* surfaces every once in a while. Taylor hits Oral Roberts country on her trip West, and the knowledge that she can always call 1-800-THE LORD keeps her going through many a near-desperate time. . . .

Taylor doesn't read about the brutal sexual abuse of children in a book. She discovers it the first time she bathes Turtle. Her knowledge is confirmed months later when she takes the child to a pediatrician and listens to him tell her the terrified little girl she has imagined is perhaps a year and a half is probably closer to three. Sometimes they just stop growing, he says.

Taylor knows nothing about the wars in Central America, and how the US government promotes those wars and then rejects their victims, until she becomes friends with Estevan and Esperanza and accepts the fact that some people work fast-food or assembly lines, others have used tire shops and sanctuaries.

Two related versions of invasion, the sexual invasion of a child's body and the political invasion of a nation's sovereignty, come together and unfold in this story of ordinary people who understand both realities as they touch their own lives. This is also a story about racism, sexism and dignity. It's a story propelled by a marvelous ear, a fast-moving humor and the powerful undercurrent of human struggle.

Something happens in *The Bean Trees.* It's one of those old-fashioned stories, thankfully coming back onto our literary scene, in which there are heroines and anti-heroines, heroes and anti-heroes, ordinary humans all. They go places and do things and where they go and what they do makes sense for them . . . and for us. There are surprises in this book. There is adventure. And there is resolution, as believable as it is gratifying.

Barbara Kingsolver, herself a Kentuckian living in Arizona,

clearly knows whereof she writes. Her prose is effortless and lovely, her structure easy, her evolutions warm and deeply satisfying. Invasion as metaphor is not new with this novel. It has surfaced over the past several years in poetry and prose by some of our most important women writers. Here it occupies a new territory, that of the commonplace, mostly undramatic, story, told and lived by commonplace people, most of them women.

Trite as it may sound, reading **The Bean Trees** bolsters my belief in an isolated but essentially generous American people. The system will continue to hype us with words and images that systematically distort our sense of world and self. But as long as we retain the capacity to see and feel, as long as the connections are made in our lives and as long as books like this one are written to help us recreate our common memory, we will be able to leave worthy lives to those coming along behind us. (p. 3)

> *Margaret Randall, "Human Comedy," in* The Women's Review of Books, *Vol. V, No. 8, May, 1988, pp. 1, 3.*

BARBARA KINGSOLVER

Kingsolver described the extent of autobiographical detail in her novel: "It is set in places I have lived, concerned with the issues I think about most, and peopled with characters who are like me, or people I've known. They make the decisions I would make if I lived inside this particular plot.

"The two principal characters, both women, are very different: one is adventurous and the other is terrified of life. They were drawn from disparate aspects of my personality that have long been at war. As I wrote the novel, the characters grew to be close friends, and I realized how much these two sides of myself depend on one another for survival."

When asked what she hopes to accomplish through her writing, Kingsolver replied: "I am horribly out-of-fashion: I want to change the world. I write because I have a passion for storytelling, but also because I believe fiction is an extraordinary tool for creating empathy and compassion. . . .

"I want my fiction to pull readers into the troubles and joys of people they might not otherwise know, and afterward, I want them to look at life a little differently. And I write to promote hopes; resolution in fiction is easier than in life, but it can resonate in ways that make life seem full of the *possibility* of wondrous solutions."

> *Barbara Kingsolver, in correspondence with* CLC Yearbook.

Eric Larsen

1941-

American novelist, short story writer, and critic.

Set against the stark landscape of the Minnesota plains, *An American Memory* explores the lives of three generations of a family plagued by emotional rigidity. Central to the narrative are Malcolm Reiner's attempts to overcome his deep sense of isolation by recreating his family history, particularly the lives of his father and paternal grandfather. Shifting between present and past and utilizing multiple perspectives, Larsen's fragmented, imagistic narrative blends recollections, dreams, and diary entries as well as Malcolm's impressions as he rummages through old clothing and photographs. Douglas Seibold noted: "Malcolm Reiner's narrative becomes his attempt at reclamation and recovery, the means of discovering the substance of both his ancestors' lives and his own, and resolving their three generations of miscarried hope." Larsen's expressive imagery, which connects emotional states of his characters with the landscape surrounding them, was praised by reviewers, some of whom compared *An American Memory* with the early works of Wright Morris. Ronald Reed added: "Larsen has managed no easy feat. He has written a rich, multilayered drama that is as abstract as memory and as concrete as perception."

DOUGLAS SEIBOLD

An American Memory is about the grip of the past and the great cost of the struggle to be free of it: here, that cost entails grief, paralysis, and madness. It covers a time roughly approximating the last century. Eric Larsen's narrative is composed of short, discrete passages, sometimes a page long, sometimes less. These are arranged into a series of twelve self-contained episodes told mostly by Malcolm Reiner, a young man of Norwegian heritage who grows up in a town called West Tree, Minn. He relates the history of his family, beginning with his grandparents and continuing into the present of his own life.

Malcolm's paternal grandfather was a Lutheran pastor and missionary of national consequence. His eldest son and namesake, Harold (Malcolm's father), rebels inwardly against everything his father represents, especially his faith. The pastor dies of pneumonia brought on by a strenuous mission to eastern Europe, and the teenaged Harold returns with his family to the midwest, to West Tree (the pastor had led an important congregation in New York). Young Harold sees the move as his final liberation from his father's oppressive ghost. Larsen suggests a little of that burden in noting that the family is still dressed in mourning at the time of their trip—three years after the pastor's death.

Harold marries the prettiest girl in town and they settle down in West Tree. Malcolm's mother is the only child of two thwarted actors who run West Tree's movie theater. She is a sheltered girl brought up to fear almost everything, not least the histrionic passions of her own parents. . . .

But Harold's vision of freedom from the past dissolves, as does his promise. He takes up photography, writing, and innumerable hobbies, but all are eventually discarded. Malcolm interprets his father's life as dedicated to nothing less than surpassing time, to finding some way to escape his own suppressed personal history. . . .

Distinguished by its clarity, gravity, and elegance, Larsen's prose style is the book's greatest virtue. Two chapters are written in the voices of Malcolm's sisters, Ingie and Hannah, and they feature that style at its best—particularly Hannah's, an account of the family on summer holiday at Lake Superior that achieves a hallucinatory beauty. These chapters come as something of a relief from Malcolm's voice, which at times seems almost too self-involved, too precious, as in the passages from his "notebook" that divide some of the chapters.

The book's flaws stem from the same source as its strengths— the author's obsessive preoccupation with his subject. . . .

Malcolm Reiner's narrative becomes his attempt at reclamation and recovery, the means of discovering the substance of both his ancestors' lives and his own, and resolving their three generations of miscarried hope. It is an essay at overcoming what's lost to time and silence, and it is not an unsuccessful one.

[*An American Memory*] is a serious, worthy novel, and of how many among the countless put out each year can that be truly said? It is Larsen's first book. Judging from the copyright dates of sections that previously appeared in periodicals, he has been assembling it for at least the last eight years. With its publication he exhibits a weight and accomplishment uncommon to first novelists.

> *Douglas Seibold, "Fleeing the Past: Resolving Three Generations of Miscarried Hope," in* Chicago Tribune—Books, *May 1, 1988, p. 5.*

DINITIA SMITH

Eric Larsen's [*An American Memory*] takes us by surprise. Initially, it appears to be simply a memoir of a Midwestern family, written in the plain, spare language of, say, Wright Morris's early work, with its images of small-town life, of faded clapboard barns, of individuals cast against the great space of the plains. But as the novel unfolds, Mr. Larsen's true agenda becomes apparent—to describe the descent into madness of a man engaged in an obsessive search for the meaning of his father's life. . . .

An American Memory is as much a prose poem as a novel, with 12 chapters, each divided into stanza-like sections, each a haunting and exactly rendered word picture, an image of the past that survives to torment and preoccupy Malcolm. "In spite of our better judgment and without hope of success," he says, "we find ourselves attempting to imagine, recapture, seize again the exact moment in abandoned, echoless, irretrievably lost time when the eye of the doomed photographer saw precisely what we now see."

As the book proceeds, we hear, successively, the stories of Malcolm's grandparents, parents and siblings, each story moving back and forth in time. Slowly, the form of the novel evolves, from a relatively straightforward description of events at the beginning, to mere fragments of interspersed episodes, bits of a religious pamphlet, passages that begin or end in midsentence, parodies of psychological cant.

There are many Joycean echoes in the novel—for example, of the catechism section in *Ulysses*. Describing his father's journey westward after the death of his own father, Malcolm asks: "What, during his journey into the heart of the continent, had my father seen from the windows of the train? He had seen the remarkable and exhilarating absence of his father, translated into the openness, freedom, and grandeur of the country. Crystalline sunlight."

Family stories, moments of violence, stay in Malcolm's mind forever, sometimes take on a dangerous intensity—a story about his maternal grandfather threatening his grandmother with a pistol during a jealous fight; his father in the barn kicking the animals in a fit of rage. Malcolm is one of those children who are unusually affected by the events of life, a child whom shadows threaten to drown. . . .

The novel ends with the narrator walking his children in New York City, far from the plains, the swirling and tapering snow, the sun on a lake—yet he is content. "My daughter's arms are raised above her head. Her face is thrown back in laughter. Her small legs, having pushed her upward, have not yet returned to the earth." These redemptive passages are not so powerful as those depicting Malcolm's pain; the characters of his mother and sisters and wife not so vividly drawn as those of Malcolm and his father.

On the whole, *An American Memory* is a beautiful work. Mr. Larsen . . . has written this novel in language as sparse and wind-riven as the Midwest of his imagination, "a frozen wilderness that reached outward to the low circle of the horizons," in which only the very strong, capable of bearing great loneliness, can endure.

> *Dinitia Smith, "Into the Heart of the Continent," in* The New York Times Book Review, *May 29, 1988, p. 7.*

JAMES MARSHALL

[*An American Memory* is] the work of a fresh and powerful new talent. Larsen's narrative focuses on a father-son relationship, on an attempt by the son to understand the father in order to understand himself. The son—Malcolm Reiner— becomes a victim of the encroaching darkness of psychosis; when he is cured of his illness he becomes liberated from his family and from forces of American history—forces that have crippled the fathers and sons of four generations of the Reiner family.

When Malcolm's father takes over a farm, within a few years it grows rank and fallow. . . . The farm becomes a symbol of the course of history: The American West as the region of freedom has become an illusion that obstructs the growth of the individual and his society.

Larsen also uses other voices, including the writings of Malcolm's stern Victorian-American great grandfather, a sequestered, culturally abandoned Norwegian immigrant. His writings make for an ironic, comic contrast with Malcolm's own notebooks.

Larsen's narrative technique may at first seem a puzzling barrier to understanding. The conventional devices of dialogue and progressive scenes have been replaced by the postmodernist method of multiple perspectives. This may be analogous to Picasso's cubist figures who appear monstrous at first, but who on study ultimately assume a form and shape as a result of the unusual and various perspectives. Larsen's "silences" offer moments that hold time in suspension while Malcolm finds a greater but still incomplete understanding of his father.

At one point the mirror on an old bureau, a symbol of the Reiner family past, falls and shatters into fragments and we recognize that all perspectives, however varied, will not provide the one magic key to the past, or to Malcolm's thwarted but seeking self. The past, family history and perhaps history itself, cannot be whole and complete. Fragments, or perspectives, are all the mind can grasp.

> *James Marshall, "Powerful Novel Explodes Myth of*

the American West," in The Providence Sunday Journal, *June 5, 1988.*

An excerpt from *An American Memory*

Few people, I imagine, could succeed in living their lives with such a degree of emotional rigidity as my father succeeded in living his; it seems to me now, looking back from the vantage point of my own adulthood, that my father was a nearly perfected master of guardedness and repression. Throughout his life, he kept major parts of his emotional life securely buried and deeply in hiding—from his children, from others outside the family, perhaps from himself as well.

The years of his childhood, for example: My father made a largely successful effort to live as though no childhood had preceded his adult life. For as long as I knew him, he discouraged or denied questions about his early years; with scorn, aloofness, and impatience, he stifled the asking. When questions did arise, as happened seldom, my father showed lack of interest, then claimed to have no memory of what was being asked, and, finally, turned away with an impatient scorn, showing an abrupt disdain for those who had asked him.

My father's repudiation of those early years, I realize now, was highly disciplined and very nearly total; he had committed the years of his childhood and youth to an eternity of death through silence. His desire, I suppose, was nothing less than to eliminate history.

RONALD REED

Here is a well-named book. The title, *An American Memory,* describes, eloquently and succinctly, both the subject matter and the method of Eric Larsen's first novel. A man remembers the boy he was as that boy tries to reconstruct his family using the clues offered in an attic trunk. The boy delves back into his family's past, discovers the blind spots of history, the actions that seem unexplainable, and finds that memory is a mirror that invents as much as it reflects.

At the heart of the story, surrounded by memorabilia, sits Malcolm. It is sometime in the 1950s, someplace in the Midwest, and Malcolm, though he is not fully aware of it, is becoming overwhelmed by coldness and silence and fear. His father dominates the life of the family, standing apart, barely concealing a seething anger. Malcolm's mother, as one would expect, is timid, but that timidity is fueled by a fear that comes as much from the rest of her environment as it does from her husband. . . .

[She] was raised in an environment that seemed devised to nurture fear in children. The focal point of that childhood was an incident where Malcolm's maternal grandfather pulled a gun on his wife and threatened her with death. Malcolm's mother, being not without sense, married as much to escape terror as she did because she loved her husband-to-be. Unfortunately for her, that husband-to-be would provide only more of the same frightening intimidation. . . .

The father was raised in a strict, religious family. Malcolm's grandfather was a missionary, and when he died, the father was free to forge his own identity. Freedom does not guarantee success, and as Malcolm enters his adolescence, it is clear that the high point of the father's life was reached during his service in World War II. As that war recedes further and further into the past, the father's bitterness and anger grow. It is too facile to say that the father's bitterness is caused by the simple failure of great dreams. There is more here, and it tears at Malcolm as he struggles to understand the man he fears and hates.

American Memory is that rarity among first novels. It is a mature work that is emotionally compelling and intellectually satisfying. . . . Along with [Malcolm], the reader becomes a sort of emotional detective, foraging among clues, attempting to distinguish the significant from the trivial. At the same time, what rescues *An American Memory* from being a simple coming-of-age tale is the fact that the boy's reconstructive attempt is seen through the eyes of the mature man that he has become. And that man is at least as complex as his father.

Larsen has managed no easy feat. He has written a rich, multilayered drama that is as abstract as memory and as concrete as perception. *An American Memory* is an excellent novel.

> *Ronald Reed, "Family Ties—Fear and Failure," in* The Dallas Morning News, *July 17, 1988.*

ALAN DAVIS

In his book *Healing Fiction,* the psychiatrist James Hillman recounts how C. J. Jung, spiritually alone at a crucial juncture, survives his isolation: "he turned to his images. When there was nothing else to hold to, Jung turned to the personified images of interior vision." This way of the image—entered into, imaginatively reconstructed—is the way of much contemporary fiction, including *An American Memory,* Eric Larsen's successful first novel. . . . Because the way of the image is usually episodic, a kind of literary pointillism, it's an appropriate method for a story about emotional isolation. . . .

How to stitch together images when they lack emotional coherence becomes the narrator's central problem. If all history, finally, is *interested* history, put together according to a subsumed emotional or ideological slant, then Malcolm is trapped in the flattened quotidian, able to tell us what happened but not what it means. He usually sees the migration of his father to the plains of the Midwest, for example, as "purely historical, possessing only those limited meanings that can continue to reside in a single moment long abandoned in time."

It is to Larsen's credit that he chose to tell his story in a lyric voice rather than in the voice of minimalism, that genre of flattened emotional horizons; family history is tacked into place sentence by sentence until we come to feel the severely repressed emotion (i.e., madness) that causes Malcolm's eventual collapse. On the northern plains people go mad quietly. . . . The narrative's early attention to Malcolm's paternal grandfather, a revered Lutheran minister, makes clear how much the old Northern European forms of religion are to blame for such unhappiness. Larsen's chronicle lets us understand how much madness has been institutionalized through generations, so that a father, especially, must be reserved, formal, and emotionally aloof from his children, especially his boys. . . .

The narration itself, for all its luminous prose, can be overly earnest, overly distant. In some ways, until near the end, the book is a family's dour swan song. Everywhere there are skulls, the imagery of decay and dissolution. We tire of such people in fiction just as we avoid them in life. To hell with these jerks! we want to say. Let them stew in their own juices. But that's the point, of course. We can cast off religion, but we can't cast off its guilt, nor can we leave our fathers behind. Perhaps, Malcolm speculates, his father migrated westward "to meet with me in the unsought and gratuitous encounter of my own birth." It's a narcissistic thought, but a primal one, and one that is always true.

An American Memory finally succeeds on those terms. It's a moving meditation on time and history, with many passages worth quoting for their poetic precision. Malcolm's father, a dilettante, lives through a "long drama of beginnings"—a photographer, for example, who took "an ambitious series of photographs of the surface, from various angles, of his own desk," His hopes, ambitions, and daydreams quietly deteriorate to bitterness, particularly after the birth of his children, who "made time move." An American Adam, he becomes archetypal, more than a genealogical study: he's pure possibility, content only in the Navy during World War II, or on relentless vacations in a fast car in "carefully staged rituals of escape," covering lots of ground and never staying in a place more than a night. "Careful never to visit the same place twice, he could be free from memory."

Early reviewers have compared the novel to Marilynne Robinson's *Housekeeping,* and it's true that Larsen's narrator breaks under the emotional isolation of his past. But *An American Memory* is finally more hopeful, and less relentlessly poetic, than Robinson's book. The finish is powerful, an instance of descent into and return from psychosis, and the summarizing image, a family image, no longer isolates but rings with emotional resonance. The iniquity of the fathers, however, *is* visited upon the children unto the third and fourth generation, and there is no getting around the suffering involved: every family history becomes personal history. In a world where values have been either inflated or flattened out—two processes amounting to much the same thing—family history, with all its baggage, can still carry meaning, found in the images we hold to, the ones we create our day-to-day fictions from.

Alan Davis, "Literary Pointillism," in The American Book Review, *Vol. 10, No. 5, November-December, 1988, p. 19.*

ERIC LARSEN

Larsen remarked on the difficulties involved in the writing and publishing of *An American Memory:* "I think that writing itself is always an obstacle: various conventions of storytelling constantly tend to take over, or try to, pulling the narrative toward conventional truths and away from real ones, or toward aspects and attitudes and voices of narratives that already exist and away from what's—in subtle but important ways—independent from what's gone before. All this makes for a hard struggle, and often a slow one. . . .

"*An American Memory* is made up of twelve chapters; six of these appeared in literary quarterlies as short stories. The book itself, in whole or in part, went to thirty-two publishers before being taken on by Algonquin Books of Chapel Hill. It went also to five agents, one of whom handled it for two submissions, then discontinued it."

When questioned about what he hopes to accomplish through his writing, Larsen answered: "To get at a truth that's real and not false, I suppose, one that's not just inherited or ready made (since that kind tends no longer to be the truth but only a copy); to do this without affectation or mannerism, and yet somehow in a way that's captivating. And of course all this must have to do with a truth that's of clear importance in some way, worth devoting one's efforts to (and a reader's efforts)."

Larsen discussed his literary influences: "In studying English prose, in whatever ways I have or did, I thought a line could be drawn from the 18th century—Defoe and Addison and Swift—to Jane Austen and on to George Eliot, then, in a big jump, to the Joyce of *Dubliners,* the early work of Hemingway, and things like the Molloy novels of Beckett. This may all be untrue, and there are lots of omissions in between, but in any case these are some of my great favorites, and in one way or another—like anyone's great favorites—they've had secret and tricky influences. I think that all influences are things that have to be in some ways subdued and controlled (Faulkner is the towering example of an influence that can just consume writers), but I also think I may be a writer who is hyper-conscious of echoes, for better and for worse. People sometimes don't believe me when I tell them how much I've loved reading in the eighteenth century, but it's been an important thing for me. This long answer (if it is an answer) leaves out Virginia Woolf. I often think that *To the Lighthouse* is the finest book ever written."

Eric Larsen, in correspondence with CLC Yearbook.

Patrick McGrath

1950-

English short story writer.

The pieces in *Blood and Water and Other Tales* are written in a postmodern Gothic style wherein stock elements of the horror genre—including lush descriptions of grotesque or bizarre incidents and settings—are rendered with a comic twist. Describing this method, Stephen Schiff noted: "[McGrath] appropriates like mad, regurgitating outmoded styles and formulas with a heavily ironic wink." Several of McGrath's stories develop an allegorical expiation of sin, featuring a character guilty of a sexual transgression who consequently suffers death or disfigurement. In "The Angel," for example, a decadent man gains everlasting life in a slowly decomposing body, and "Blood Disease" concerns an adulterous woman beset by vampire-like people. Other stories contain vivid descriptions of innocent or demented characters encountering brutality or supernatural phenomena. Greg Johnson remarked: "McGrath clearly relishes . . . grisly scenes, and he incorporates them inventively into tales that collectively offer a brilliant pastiche not only of the conventional Gothic but of such modern obsessions as sexuality, psychoanalysis, and the nature of storytelling."

PUBLISHERS WEEKLY

Mixing the macabre, the fantastical, the gruesome and the illusionary with a lush and word-loving style, McGrath [in *Blood and Water and Other Tales*] conjures up an extravagant selection of worlds in which to set his modern, psychological stories. In **"The Lost Explorer,"** a little girl finds an anthropologist from Africa dying of malaria in the garden behind her London home and manages to keep his existence, his death and burial a secret from her parents. **"Blood Disease"** describes the subterranean methods by which a group of English villagers afflicted with pernicious anemia alleviate the symptoms of their affliction. . . . With elegance, humor and respect for the dark side of human nature, McGrath also offers an angel, an hermaphrodite and the ghosts of the world's great psychoanalysts in the polished and entertaining, eminently readable stories in his first collection.

A review of "Blood and Water and Other Tales," in Publishers Weekly, Vol. 232, No. 26, December 25, 1987, p. 61.

FAREN MILLER

The publicity copy describes Patrick McGrath as "a Poe for the '80s, the first postmodern-gothic storyteller." Such blatant disregard of Clive Barker . . . might make the whole

statement suspect, yet there's some truth to that label, "postmodern-gothic." In *Blood and Water and Other Tales,* McGrath explores outre themes with an elegant economy, less blatantly outrageous than Barker (or the purple prose of Poe), but far removed from the gritty bleakness of much current horror writing. . . . McGrath moves easily between scenes of late-imperial Britain and modern Manhattan. Some of the tales deal in the un-supernatural compulsions of murderers (**"Blood and Water"**] manages to make the subject powerfully eerie all the same). Others introduce such time-honored chillers as East Indian curses (**"The Black Hand of the Raj"**) and vampirism (**"Blood Disease"**), deftly understated and tinged with elegy or irony.

"Hand of a Wanker" comes closest to Barker, as the severed organ in question infests a trendily decadent Manhattan nightclub; and the fly's-eye view in **"The E(Rot)ic Potato"** is cheerily gruesome. McGrath ventures into regions all his own in other stories, most notably **"The Angel"** (marvelously appalling) and **"The Skewer"** (in which an elderly aesthete is bedeviled by miniature, winged psychoanalysts). There's even a bit of sf in the bloodthirsty post-apocalyptic humor of **"The Boot's Tale"**, shifting into pure eloquence at the end.

Blood and Water takes violence and madness out of the realm of splatter films, granting them the cool, lyric dignity of the best English ghost stories.

Faren Miller, in a review of "Blood and Water and Other Tales," in Locus, Vol. 21, No. 1, January, 1988, p. 15.

MICHIKO KAKUTANI

Consider these scenarios: A prim Victorian maiden travels to Bombay to marry her fiancé, who's in the Indian Civil Service, only to discover that her beloved is suffering from a horrible affliction known as "The Black Hand of the Raj"—a hand has literally sprouted from the top of his head and eventually strangles him. A demented English gentleman, whose wife is suffering from a bizarre sexual malady, takes offense when her doctor declares his intention to write about her in a medical journal and abruptly murders the medical man while he's taking a bath. An elderly art critic goes out for an evening walk with his dog and meets with three miniature psychiatrists—Freud, Otto Rank and Ernest Jones—who proceed to drive him crazy.

Clearly there's nothing mundane about [***Blood and Water and Other Tales***] by the English-born writer Patrick McGrath. Severed hands, dead monkeys, swarming insects, pickled body parts and menacing pigmies proliferate in ***Blood and Water.*** The backdrops tend to be fairly standard-issue gothic sets: ancient Southern plantations, isolated manor houses, places where ghosts like to lurk; and everywhere spiritual and physical decay presides. In **"Ambrose Syme,"** Lancashire schoolboys are drawn to "a damp pocket of the moors" known as Blackburn's Bog, the sinister setting of terrible crime, and in **"Marmilion,"** a photographer ventures into the Louisiana bayous, where she becomes obsessed with a crumbling mansion that's "foul with the smell of nesting rodents and rotting plaster." Other settings may appear more pleasant—bucolic, even—but for Mr. McGrath, they, too, conceal dreadful secrets. . . .

Echoes of other writers . . . reverberate throughout this volume. **"Marmilion,"** which focuses on a haunted house and the possible live entombing of a man, obviously recalls Poe's "Fall of the House of Usher," and **"The Angel,"** which portrays a man condemned to eternal life despite a body that's collapsing from the excesses of a long and decadent life, owes something of a debt to Oscar Wilde's *Picture of Dorian Gray.* In terms of their sensibility and their bravura style, however, Mr. McGrath's tales perhaps most insistently recall the horror films of Brian DePalma. Not only do they share those movies' baroque romanticism and their tendency to mix up narrative conventions in an expressionistic, post-modern stew, but they also share a similar preoccupation with sex and guilt, violence and death.

A Roman Catholic preoccupation with sin and guilt hangs heavily over these stories, and in many of them sex—or even thoughts of sex—lead to illness, dismemberment or death. A priest who has successfully, repressed his sexual urges for years suddenly succumbs to a fit of passion, resulting in a murder as well as his own death. . . .

In other cases, the loss of innocence is less overt. A little girl's encounter—imaginary or not—with a dying explorer who mysteriously appears in her parents' backyard symbolizes her first steps into adolescent awareness, and a young journalist's interview with a mass murderer marks her own initiation into the brutalities of real life. Indeed, such narrative setups—involving an innocent observer who becomes privy to some sort of horrible knowledge—are used repeatedly by the author to underline the omnipresence of evil and the insistent fact of death.

The most consistent aspect of Mr. McGrath's writing is his nearly magnetic attraction to the morbid, and there are moments when this imp of the perverse leads him to sprinkle his narratives with gratuitously weird or disgusting details. . . .

"The E(rot)ic Potato," a tale narrated by a fly named Gilbert, seems like little but a willful display of grotesque humor, culminating in an unpalatable description of rotting flesh and insect sex. [**"Blood and Water"**], too, often reads like a flashy exercise in sensationalism. The reader also wonders why Mr. McGrath insists on using words like estivate (to pass the summer in a state of torpor) and umbrelliferous (umbrella-bearing) when simpler words or phrases might do, and why he feels the need to insert dead monkeys and disease-carrying insects in stories where they are superfluous, even intrusive.

Such complaints, however, should not detract from Mr. McGrath's genuine achievement. This young English writer possesses a natural storytelling gift (that shines, at its best, when he leaves off imitating other writers and trusts his own instincts) and an ability to invest his narratives with a disturbing psychological subtext. Combined with his gothic imagi-

---

An excerpt from "The Black Hand of the Raj"

In India, the appearance of a certain sort of plump and blustery raincloud is a sure sign that the monsoons are at hand. One such cloud drifted now across the moon and threw the swaying compartment into deep shadow. So it was that when Cecil slowly removed the pith helmet, Lucy was at first uncertain what exactly she was looking at. Her first thought was of a dark brown lily splayed limply from a short thick stem attached somehow to Cecil's skull; but how could that be? And then the raincloud drifted on and in the sudden glow of moonlight she realized that the brown stem was in fact a *wrist;* that it was *growing* out of Cecil's head; and that the dark limp lily atop it was a *hand!*

For a dreadful moment all sympathy fled Lucy's heart, and she knew only horror. She stared aghast at the gruesome sprout, and her own hands flew to her mouth. Cecil watched her from hooded and anguished eyes. "Now you see why I wear my pith helmet," he said, and covered the alien extremity.

There was little left to tell. Once the hand had come through, it proved to be rather active, constantly pulling his hair and sticking its fingers in his ears. Dr. Crumbler had refused to amputate, saying it was connected to the brainstem, and instead prescribed a heavy sedative. Twice a day Cecil would have to inject a few cc. into the thing's wrist to keep it quiet. "In fact," he said, glancing at his watch, "it's about time. Darling, would you mind?"

---

nation and dark, splenetic humor, the result is fiction that can be as powerful as it is strange.

Michiko Kakutani, in a review of "Blood and Water and Other Tales," in The New York Times, *February 24, 1988, p. C25.*

JOHN BLADES

In their inexhaustible zeal to promote new and unknown authors, publishers are fond of invoking the name of some past or present master, as the basis (usually shaky) of comparison. By this process of instant immortalization, Patrick McGrath arrives as a "Poe for the '80s," according to the jacket for his ***Blood and Water and Other Tales,*** which then goes on to describe him as the "first postmodern gothic storyteller." In this case, however, McGrath's publishers have demonstrated unusual discrimination in the search for antecedents. If the task had been left to me, I would have raised the ancestral ghosts not just of Poe but of H. P. Lovecraft, Roald Dahl, Oscar Wilde, Hieronymus Bosch, Ivan Albright, Rod Serling, Thomas Tryon, Tennessee Williams, Truman Capote, Ingmar Bergman and Mel Brooks, to name but a few of those who seem to have cast their spell over McGrath's 13 stories. As for McGrath being our first gothic "postmodernist," well, if that means a writer who is out to mock and satirize, to draw and quarter his predecessors, with a prose style that has more wicked edges than a medieval mace, then his publisher's description is right on the money.

To judge by his abattoir humor and his ravenous obsession with physical decay, McGrath is surely the most consciously visceral of modern writers, post or otherwise. The book's first story, **"The Angel,"** describes an encounter on New York's Bowery between a writer named Bernard Finnegan and an aristocratic derelict, Anson Havershaw, whose "beautiful" decadence embodies the contradictions of hedonism and spirituality, demonism and saintliness. In the final scene, Havershaw ritually disrobes before the aghast Finnegan, revealing beneath his "bizarre corset" not only rotting outer flesh but the decomposition within, the "faint gleam of his spine, and . . . the forms of shadowy organs."

"The Angel" sets both the scene and the tone for McGrath's other satanic tales, most of which are littered with body parts, reek of putrefaction and teem with Garbage Pail grownups. Jack, the artist in **"Lush Triumphant,"** lives above Dorian's restaurant in New York's meat district, an area whose most noteworthy sights are the "headless carcasses of skinned hogs hung from hooks" and a huge garbage can stuffed with "kidneys, heads, chunks of fat, pieces of feet, and . . . a single unblinking eyeball."

Let these examples serve as fair warning to the reader with a sensitive stomach and a polite sense of humor. Having neither, I'm forced to admit not only an affectionate weakness but an unholy admiration for a number of McGrath's weirder stories. At their grotesque best, they are diabolically funny parables about the bestial excesses of modern life, which stalk the narrow border dividing man from animal, civilization from savagery. At their weakest, they are anemic and pointless parodies, as in **"Hand of a Wanker,"** which exhumes that old myth about the severed, murderous hand. Here and elsewhere, McGrath aims for magic surrealism, but misses. For all their gothic virtues, these tales fall into the category of

vampire fiction, drawing their considerable comic energy from the lifeblood of their many ancestors.

John Blades, "Bloody Humorist Catches Spirit of Modern Times," in Chicago Tribune—Books, *February 28, 1988, p. 3.*

STEPHEN SCHIFF

The Gothic strain in American literature has suffered a gloomy fate. Its very popularity has ghettoized it, walled it up in a horror chamber bordered on one side by the grand viziers of the best-seller list (Stephen King, Peter Straub, et al.), on another by the raven-haired virgins and saturnine seducers of the romance novels, on yet another by pulp magazines and comic books and finally by the movies, whose efficiency in the manufacture of nightmares is unsurpassed. Fear sells. And yet the Gothic short story, which possesses one of the proudest bloodlines in American letters (Irving, Hawthorne, Poe, James, Faulkner, Flannery O'Connor and so on), has almost vanished from the realm of literary fiction. Serious people don't take it seriously anymore.

Patrick McGrath is trying to change all that. . . . Most of the [stories in ***Blood and Water and Other Tales***] long palpably for a gentler age, an age when the world's wildernesses still harbored unimaginable sights and sounds, an age when science had not yet explained away so much of the inexplicable and, especially, an age in which word-spinners could fashion filigrees of ornately layered prose without sounding arch or uppity or out-of-date.

Mr. McGrath has been called a post-modernist, but no one could accuse him of jumping on the minimalist bandwagon. His prose gushes and twirls, winding around itself in thick, wordy coils. . . . [In] **"The Skewer,"** an admittedly demented art critic complains, "It is precisely this atmosphere of tenebrous deliquescence which sounds within me the 'thanatoptic chord.' " Tenebrous deliquescence is, in fact, Mr. McGrath's reigning mode, and while his publishers insist that he's "a Poe for the '80s," his deliriously Latinate locutions sound more often like an H. P. Lovecraft satire, with pinches of Ambrose Bierce sprinkled about like pepper. In fact, Mr. McGrath may be a true post-modernist in the sense that Philip Johnson and David Salle are post-modernists—he appropriates like mad, regurgitating outmoded styles and formulas with a heavily ironic wink. . . .

The finest story in this volume, **"Blood Disease,"** is a virtuosic vampire yarn that begins with a cell's-eye view of a mosquito imparting malaria to a hapless anthropologist and winds up in sunny Berkshire, with a tableau of sanguinary horror that would do Bram Stoker proud. Along the way, Mr. McGrath paints a grimly funny portrait of a parasitic planet, of lovers feeding upon lovers the way a flea feeds upon the arm of a small boy—of ordinary biological appetites run amok.

But Mr. McGrath isn't always that good. Although his gallows humor works wonderfully in patches, the general tone of elaborate facetiousness can, like any other brand of insincerity, grow annoying. And the lesser tales are little more than inflated one-liners—Charles Addams cartoons gussied up in rhetorical finery. They typically begin with a lot of gaudily pedantic throat-clearing, only to give way, for instance, to a yarn about a forlorn British sahib who one day finds a hand growing from the top of his head. It's as if the curlicued prose were an apology for gruesome subject matter.

There is a clue in all this to what killed the serious Gothic short story. When the form grew popular enough to become a mainstay of schlock culture, the single, concentrated effect (which Poe prescribed as the short story's goal) came to overpower the subtleties of syntax and tone that created it. How could the dry-ice nuances of James or O'Connor compete with the noisy horrors in any Stephen King chapter, let alone the google-eyed fiends that makeup technicians like Rick Baker or Rob Bottin devise for the screen? If serious Gothic fiction is to survive, it clearly can't rely on plot twists and shockeroo endings alone. It has to haunt and tantalize by weaving webs of suggestion and symbolism, by digging into the psychologies of enmeshed characters, by joking with us about the language of terror—in short, by doing what only well-wrought prose can do. At his worst, Patrick McGrath exemplifies the trap that Gothic literature has fallen into. At his best, he points the way out.

Stephen Schiff, "Vampires and the Landed Gentry," in The New York Times Book Review, *March 6, 1988, p. 6.*

GREG JOHNSON

In his first collection, ***Blood and Water and Other Tales,*** Patrick McGrath succeeds brilliantly in adapting the Gothic fantasy to a postmodernist aesthetic program. Like [Joyce Carol Oates], he favors extreme psychological situations and characters victimized by violence and isolation, but his work is more akin to her parodic versions of Gothic, such as *Bellefleur,* than to the grim contemporary stories in *The Assignation.* McGrath's tales are deliberate sendups of the stereotypical Gothic fantasy; he cheerfully delivers gloomy mansions, tales within tales, physical grotesques, psychotic isolates, and numberless murders and suicides. Sigmund Freud is depicted on the dust jacket and presented comically in one of the finest tales, **"The Skewer,"** as a fifteen-inch-high gremlin tormenting one of McGrath's typically repressed protagonists. The other major figure haunting this collection is Poe, especially in accounts of psychotic brother-sister attachments recalling the Ushers, and in **"Marmilion,"** where a man is bricked up alive inside a fireplace. Or is he? Many of McGrath's tales are told in a deliberately ambiguous, conjectural manner, their narrators often detached, uncertain, or otherwise unreliable. Thus the volume suggests a running commentary on the generally unreliable texture of narrative art, the cunning interpenetration of imagination and reality, even as it immerses the reader in a humorous, quirky, no-holds-barred Gothic world in which the most fearsome and violent of human fantasies are brought to vibrant and dramatic life.

In **"Ambrose Syme,"** the hero is a classicist at an English public school called Ravengloom. A repressed homosexual whose impulses drive him to murder a young boy, Syme is presented as a victim of his own carnal appetites but also as a figure of fun, as when McGrath explains how Syme learned as a young man to sublimate his erotic longings:

> Ambrose Syme was first terrorized with visions of eternal damnation, and then taught how to displace energy from the lower part of his body to the upper. The technique employed in his case was somewhat analogous to the operation of the common refrigerator, in which liquid is pumped up through tubes

to the evaporator at the head, being turned in the process into *gas.* . . . Ambrose Syme did not turn his sexual urges into gas, exactly; rather, he learned to convert them into long, ponderous sentences of a verbose and bombastic turgidity which he then translated into Latin verse.

[**"Blood and Water"**] likewise combines horrific events with an arch narrative manner, and it offers another isolated English setting, this time a country house called Phlange, "a stately Georgian pile." Another decaying mansion recalling the house of Usher, Phlange is presented wittily as being threatened not by supernatural turbulence but by plumbing problems, so that the unbalanced master of the house, Sir Norman, spends much of his time "deep in the cellars of Phlange, those drear crypts which still bear the malodorous and fungoid scars of the floods of '28." Entering "deep psychotic territory," Sir Norman ultimately murders and beheads the family doctor and causes the suicide of his wife, Lady Percy. Carrying the doctor's head into the bathroom where his wife lies in her bloody bath water, "Sir Norman drops his head and presses his lips to the wound on the wrist of the corpse. And thus we leave him, as the gloom of twilight steals upon the chamber and the flies begin to gather on the doctor's eyes."

McGrath clearly relishes such grisly scenes, and he incorporates them inventively into tales that collectively offer a brilliant pastiche not only of the conventional Gothic but of such modern obsessions as sexuality, psychoanalysis, and the nature of storytelling. Perhaps the most brilliant example is **"The Arnold Crombeck Story,"** narrated by a woman journalist who seeks to advance her reputation by interviewing a notorious serial killer in the days just before his execution. To her surprise and mounting horror, she finds a perfectly intelligent, charming, sprightly man who apparently feels no remorse for his crimes and no fear of his impending fate. In fact, he cheerfully discusses the efficacy of English methods of execution as opposed to American. After one such encounter, the narrator writes: "Time spent in Arnold's company allowed for no relaxation, no ease. He *engaged* one, at every moment. It was extraordinarily stimulating; it was also extraordinarily debilitating. I went back to my hotel and took a hot bath, feeling weak and somewhat queasy. That night I vomited violently for the first time since I was a little girl." Arnold Crombeck's vivid disquisitions on murder and execution begin to suggest that he is a stand-in for McGrath himself ("Like a preacher, Arnold proceeded to develop his text") in that his storytelling mode is chiefly humorous, direct and matter-of-fact, yet seems designed to unsettle his audience. To say more would reveal a brilliant surprise ending—another stock convention of Gothic mysteries that McGrath exploits often and skillfully—but it should be apparent that the narrator's "objective" relationship to her story and protagonist gradually breaks down. Clearly delineating writer and subject, narrator and narrative, sanity and insanity, **"The Arnold Crombeck Story,"** like others in this collection, finally shows that such dichotomies are false and thus becomes an allegory of storytelling itself. (pp. 848-49)

Greg Johnson, "Isn't It Gothic?" in The Georgia Review, *Vol. XLII, No. 4, Winter, 1988, pp. 840-49.*

PATRICK McGRATH

McGrath discussed the inspiration for the pieces in ***Blood*** *and Water and Other Tales:* "Each story had a separate inspiration, generally an image or an idea that fascinated me without my knowing quite why. Writing the story was a means of exploring and 'solving' that fascination, e.g. with a twentieth century angel: a man haunted by a tiny Freud; 'vampires' who suffer from pernicious anemia; a disembodied hand."

Asked to describe the creative process of his work, McGrath replied: "This is a book of tales, and I was in each case faced with the problem of uncovering, or exhuming, the story I knew to lie buried within the images, ideas and characters that sprang up in my imagination. Discovering what particular story was trying to get itself told demanded much trial and error, much going down of blind alleys."

The author commented on his literary influences: "I detect in my work touches of Poe, Wilde, Saki, Waugh, Conrad, Firbank. Conrad for what he can do with light and shadow, both atmospheric and moral; Firbank for his unfailing elegance; Waugh for his mordant wit; Poe for his recognition of the unconscious forces of the mind, and of the fictional potential of psychopathological states; Saki for showing what can be done with manners and horror against a backdrop of polite English society."

　　　　Patrick McGrath, in correspondence with CLC Yearbook.

I. Allan Sealy
1951-

Indian novelist.

Set in India and spanning two centuries, Sealy's mock epic *The Trotter-Nama* chronicles the fortunes of seven generations of an Anglo-Indian family named Trotter. Between requests for drinks and numerous other narrative digressions, the unreliable narrator, Eugene Trotter, recounts the decadence and odd antics of his once-illustrious family. Frequently compared to Salman Rushdie's novel *Midnight's Children*, Sealy's ambitious, self-reflexive narrative emphasizes humorous, informative, and colorful digressions over linear plot development. A factual plot summary, wrote Timothy Mo, "would bring a wry grin to the face of anyone who has sampled the novel—it affords no clue whatever to what it is like." While the numerous characters represent the foibles of their class and time, they also demonstrate the plight of the Anglo-Indian minority before, during, and after British dominion over India. Rita Joshi commented: "[*The Trotter-Nama*] is at once a comical peep into history and a highly inventive work of fiction."

PUBLISHERS WEEKLY

A *nama* is an epic or chronicle; the *Akbar-Nama* is one of the great medieval histories of India. **The Trotter-Nama,** a fictional chronicle of seven generations of the Anglo-Indian Trotter family is nothing if not ambitious. This first novel by an Anglo-Indian writer sets out to be a Great Big Book, and in more than 600 pages steeped in raj atmosphere, it succeeds admirably . . . Narrated by Eugene, the Seventh Trotter, the chronicle goes back to the original and splendid Great Trotter of the 18th century whose successes begin the tale. His good fortunes are diluted by subsequent generations of lesser talents, including those who fail to make a go of peddling rain gauges. The present finds the Trotter palace turned into a crumbling hotel and improvidence replacing excesses of the past. Despite his impecunious state, Eugene has inherited the family sybaritic genes and is adept at taking small pleasures where he can. This Seventh Trotter, who forges miniatures for a living, is deeply attuned to the minutiae around which Indian life revolves. The narrative possesses a droll and authentic quality in its immensity. While not consistently ironic enough to be deemed an outright satire, it's often funny. Sealy's literary feat should be especially welcomed by those with a big appetite for tales of India under the British.

A review of "The Trotter-Nama," in Publishers Weekly, *Vol. 233, No. 7, February 19, 1988, p. 69.*

TIMOTHY MO

There's been a coup in the sleepy little kingdom of British fiction. The Subcontinental Fabulists rose up and slaughtered the Kitchen Realists in a Night of Long Pens. Once, the majority of English novels were parochial, petty and technically unadventurous to the point of blandness. They were also overwhelmingly by Anglo-Saxon writers. They still are, but now yeasty foreign organisms pullulate in all that dough, making the loaf rise into exotic shapes.

Writers like Kazuo Ishiguro from Japan, Caryl Phillips from St. Kitts, Hanif Kureishi from Pakistan, Peter Carey from Australia and Amitav Ghosh from India have enormously enriched the form. As Salman Rushdie wittily put it, parodying the Star Wars saga: "The Empire strikes back." The latest probationer to aspire to add his voice to this motley-hued choir is I. Allan Sealy. As an Anglo-Indian from Allahabad, now settled in New Zealand after an education in Michigan and British Columbia, he is about as extreme an example of the new diaspora of Commonwealth fiction as you could ask for. In fact, to use on the author the terms of his relentlessly cerebral, self-reflective work, if Mr. Sealy didn't exist it would be necessary to invent him.

The Trotter-Nama would have seemed more impressive seven years ago. In following in the steps of Salman Rushdie, Mr. Sealy has the advantage of a context and a recognizable tradition. The blank incomprehension that was the fate of *Midnight's Children* in many critical quarters when it appeared will not befall *The Trotter-Nama*—quite so often, anyway. On the other hand, this large novel is also as debt-ridden as the third world that is its subject. You can have an instructive time playing "spot the influences," chiefly those of Gabriel García Márquez and Mr. Rushdie. A rather self-defensive little passage on literary echoes (which, typically, Mr. Sealy takes literally—"BOUM," echoing the sound of the Malabar caves in *A Passage to India* doesn't minimize the derivativeness. It is quite possible to compose a modish, "experimental" work that is as deeply unoriginal, unreflective and convention-bound as the basic product of the most pedestrian Kitchen Realist. . . .

[A factual plot] summary would bring a wry grin to the face of anyone who has sampled the novel—it affords no clue whatever to what it is like.

The construction is fairly simple: Eugene indulging in eccentric, italicized monologue at start and finish; the main narrative, interrupted frequently by small interpolations (on Indian sweetmeats, the monsoon, nonexistent instruments like the gypsonometer, the correct method of mining curry powder and such like); and doggerel, with the resumption of the main narrative indicated by headlines: "(CHRONICLE RESUMED)." At times it looks like a set of gambits in search of a novel. The provision of a contents list of whimsical headings ("Mango-fool," "How the smoked glass is made," "Etc e.g.", "How Immaculate Bleach is made") is something of a give-away in fancy modern novels. It means the author is striving to give an appearance of sophistication of construction. Such devices are purely cosmetic and always redundant. The form of such books has been won easily. True shape consists of balancing of themes and narrative, and is gained hard. They come from the inside. Complexity is not sought; it is imposed.

Mr. Sealy's cast is vast, and though he can often write prose supremely well, he's less good at that most fundamental task of the novelist, making people live on the page. It's the Achilles' heel of the cleverest Subcontinental Fabulists. The Great Trotter ("not much above four feet tall") is vivid. (He dies when he falls out of his balloon's gondola). Fonseca, the demi-Portuguese barber, is good and so is the Second Trotter, the military or gypsy Trotter, Mik. Mr. Sealy has an admirably confident way of dropping them just as names or parts into the early narrative and only much later supplying detail about them. But after these early personalities the standard drops. It becomes, to be honest, hard keeping track of who is who. Worse, you don't care. . . .

The Trotter-Nama depends heavily on wit and words, but this is a desperately hard act to bring off, and talented though Mr. Sealy is, he often stumbles. The touch has to be faultless, the jokes exactly right. The puns are dire, execrable, and stay in the mind instead of the piercingly good sentences. . . .

The criticism is harsh. I. Allan Sealy, at 37, should not receive the indulgence customarily extended to first-timers. It would insult his gifts. At a time when the glittering, high-tech, state-of-the-art novels come from Latin and Indian writers of the third world rather than their more insular American contemporaries, Sealy can be saluted. But in retrospect, there was an awful lot about the Kitchen Realists that one misses.

*Timothy Mo, "From the Mines of Curry Powder,"
in* The New York Times Book Review, *February
28, 1988, p. 14.*

JAMES IDEMA

One June morning in the last year of the 18th Century, Justin Aloysius Trotter, originally Trottoire, also known as the Great Trotter, Tartar Sahib to his servants and, most significantly, the First Trotter, tumbled into a canal from his balloon some 2,000 feet above *Sans Souci,* the estate he had created in north central India.

No one witnessed the accident, and Justin's body, swept quickly into the Ganges and eventually into the Bay of Bengal, was never found. But in the few seconds it took him to fall to his death he was able not only to survey in all their detail the vast buildings and grounds that were rising rapidly to meet him but also to solve complex philosophical and mathematical conundrums and to picture "all that happened next before it came to pass."

Such phenomena are useful in this prolix and confusing but richly inventive and often very funny chronicle of a fictional Anglo-Indian family. . . .

At least *The Trotter-Nama* is not a dull family history. *Nama* means roughly book or chronicle in Hindi, not history, a distinction the narrator takes pains to point out.

No conventional chapters ease the way and no single plot draws the reader toward any sort of resolution. Instead, the chronicle spills forth pell-mell, irregularly interrupted by entertaining digressions; recipes, instructions, verses, hymns, journal entries, commentaries—some of them obviously germane, some containing sly hints, some mere airy afterthoughts.

The scope of this first novel is immense—seven generations, more than two and a half centuries, a cast of, well, hundreds, and in the background the rumble of the real events that swept India from the days before the British raj into the modern age of post-independence. At the center is this family of Anglo-Indians, a minority group whose political and social status changed as imperialism faded from the scene. In the end they were stranded by history, divided and confused as to whether to call India or England home. . . .

The Trotter-Nama is a unique, imaginative and challenging book that will reward the patient and the attentive reader.

*James Idema, "Witty Novel Chronicles Family's
Fall," in* Chicago Tribune—Books, *March 6, 1988,
p. 7.*

BHARATI MUKHERJEE

The Trotter-Nama is a clever book. Occasionally it is a hilarious book. Mostly, however, it is a tiresome, show-offy, obese book.

Inside this obese book, awaiting liposuction, is a small, lithe novel about the loyalty crises of Anglo-Indians in colonial and postcolonial India, where both British settlers and local Indians abhor racial adulteration. . . .

Sealy's chronicler is Eugene, a painter and forger of miniatures and a seventh-generation Trotter. Eugene's physical appearance has obvious symbolic implications. His complexion is neither black nor white but gray, so gray that he disappears altogether in black-and-white photographs. And he has one brown eye and one blue eye.

The strongest sections of the book are those in which Sealy addresses, with charm, with wit, the survivalist maneuvers of Anglo-Indians. "A strange sad monadic people," explains Peter Jonquil, a Manchester journalist writing a piece on the community. "They live in a kind of bubble—or many bubbles. They speak a kind of English . . . They fantasize about the past. They improvise grand pedigrees."

Sealy's Trotters are aware of their not-quite-pukka sahibness. They remember that when Thomas Henry, the Fourth Trotter, had been looking for a governess for his daughter, Victoria, English applicants had "lasted no longer than the interview; they had not supposed they were to teach a black child." Their tragedy is that, though the British look down on them for being "black" and openly discriminate against them in the Indian Civil Service, they regard themselves as "white" and therefore superior to the Indians. They mimic British English as well as they can (Sealy satirizes their speech with great effect); they talk of England as "home" and argue against a Bill that would allow Indians to try Europeans in court; when Independence finally comes, the lighter-skinned among them scatter to Britain, Canada and Australia. . . .

In the last few pages of the chronicle, Sealy's Anglo-Indians share something of the tragedy of Naipaul's Trinidad Indians. "I was saying, not too many of us left and half of those waiting to leave . . . But what to do? . . . Where to go? I don't know. Here, you look into my eyes. See? Tell me now. *Where* to go?"

For Sealy's characters, the solution, playfully offered, is to sign up as flight attendants and "remain forever suspended in the air over Constantinople," that bicontinental, bicultural city.

Unfortunately, the story of the Trotter family gets lost as Sealy indulges in bombastic parodies and tired literary mannerisms. He never quite frees himself from the choke-holds of E.M. Forster, Gabriel Garcia Márquez and Salman Rushdie. What's even more disappointing is that Sealy fails to do what Rushdie did in *Midnight's Children*—quicken history with a novelist's passion. His historical references (for instance, to The Blotting Paper Scandal in the sweetmeats industry) and his digressions (on clarified butter, on wholesomeness, on the recipe for Trotter Curry and many, many more), unlike Rushdie's, too often seem pointless and exhibitionistic rather than brilliant.

In the end, all we have to admire in *The Trotter-Nama* is the author's self-conscious virtuosity.

> *Bharati Mukherjee, "An Anglo-Indian Family Caught Between Two Worlds," in* Book World— The Washington Post, *April 3, 1988, p. 4.*

GYDE MARTIN

Behind the somewhat enigmatic title of I. Allan Sealy's first novel hides a very popular type of fiction—the family chronicle. But don't let this familiar label suggest that you are about to enter familiar terrain. In the hands of such writers as Gabriel Garcia Marquez (*One Hundred Years of Solitude*) and Isabel Allende (*The House of Spirits*), the family saga has come a long way since Galsworthy's *Forsyte Saga*. Sealy's *The Trotter-Nama* may well be the beginning of the next generation.

Unrivaled in its scope, "the epic of the Trotters" is a fast-paced romp through seven generations of an Anglo-Indian family, related by Eugene, the last of the Trotters or, as he prefers, "the chosen Trotter." By profession a forger of antique miniatures. Eugene spins his yarn the way he paints: never imitating slavishly but always intent on improving the original. His family history is consequently no dull list of "begats" but a portrait gallery of eccentric Trotters, whose individual tragedies, with a little touching up, become hilarious and often fantastic episodes.

There is, foremost, the Great Trotter, (a.k.a. Justin Trottoire), the French mercenary turned Englishman. . . . There is Mik, the next Trotter, who managed to prove his identity in the last minute with his . . . let's call it a birthmark. There are the matriarch Victoria, who swoons at the sight of all unclothed limbs, table legs no exception; Alec, the turn-of-the-century dandy who gatecrashes British tea parties as a photographer; Queenie, the greatly envied owner of the only Sears catalog on the banks of the Ganges; and many other Trotters, all caricatures of their particular periods, from the late 18th century to the present.

Eugene is no bore either. With booze as his muse, he is a high-spirited narrator indeed. . . . In the hands of Eugene, the inspired forger, the Trotter saga becomes thus an exhilarating parody of 200 years of English literature in a tone reminiscent of *Tristram Shandy*.

But this novel isn't all fun and literary games. Along with the entertaining antics of the Trotters, we get a glimpse of what it meant, and means, to be an Anglo-Indian. Through the fates of several Trotters, Sealy, himself an Anglo-Indian, subtly sketches the plight of those who might have bridged the gulf between East and West but instead were disowned by rulers and ruled alike. . . .

Yet despite its serious theme, this is not a polemical novel— no outcry against history's injustices, no cry for restitution. It is rather an attempt to freeze the past before it melts away like Trotter ice, to give the last of the Anglo-Indians, to whom this novel is dedicated, a cultural identity. As such *The Trotter-Nama* is a deeply moving reflection of the need for a history in all of us and on the ways we create our histories.

> *Gyde Martin, "Pageant of Anglo-Indian Family that Transcends Literary Parody," in* Fort Worth Star-Telegram, *May 8, 1988.*

MUKUL KESAVAN

The Trotter-Nama like the *Babur-Nama* or the *Akbar-Nama*, is an epic chronicle, not scrupulous historical fiction, nor a novel of manners. This allows its chronicler or narrator (who makes regular appearances in italics throughout the book) liberties unavailable to the grave, responsible novelist. This saga of the clan Trotter over many generations is continuous-

An excerpt from *The Trotter-Nama*

Some remarks on the monsoon of Hindoostan

The rains of Hindoostan come after the summer and before the winter (just in between). In the south they come in winter too, but that is another matter.

The main rains come in between and that is the point. To us of the north they are brought by winds from the southeast, but geographers call it the southwest monsoon. It is most perplexing, but even in new bottles a little old wine is worth all the tea in China. *Monsoon* means simply, season; thus is the confusion confounded. The rainy monsoon, then, is my theme; blame the Arabs: it is their word. Gentle breezes come skipping over the Arabian Sea, gathering moisture, the little poppets. Arabs in dhows sigh and set their faces homeward. Dolphins grin and flying fish frolic, but the clam he will scruple. Clouds are massing, the southwest wind blows and the curtains go up. Now the Malabar rice paddies are glinting bosom-jewels. On the Konkani coast a shapely mother tumbles into the church of St Francis Xavier, warm fat drops falling around her. Goans are clapping, Bombay is buoyant, but here in the northern plain is still no rain. From the Arabian Sea the cloud messenger mounts the Western Ghats; Mandakranta (slow-stepping) is his pace. Lovers' hearts quicken, breaths hasten, lips fasten, and pulses are firm. But that is the south and it is all very well. Here the ground is still cracked and wineskins are crazed. The monsoon advances to the Vindhya range, weeps over Ujjain, darkens Bengal. But here in the north mouths are dry, throats parched, and beaks kept open. Assam is awash, Cherra Punji afloat, Darjeeling soaking: but Nakhlau is a desert, Sans Souci an empty cup.

When, up stand the Himalayas, beside which the Western Ghats are footling stools, and the clouds are deflected up the Gangetic plain. Kites, circling at two thousand feet, spy them first. Next a joyous peal sounds from the elephant stables. The Turcoman master-gelder's nostrils flare. In the library a sheaf of paper stirs, stroked by a thumb of wind, but the bard is not alarmed, for the monsoon is a second-order wind. It is not like the yellow storm, which upsets wine jugs onto precious manuscripts and keeps the epic poet up till shoot of dawn drying folios under towels and blankets. Lightning flickers, thunder growls—fie, pi-dog: do not crouch under the desk!—and the skies are a delicious grey. The first patter comes, of pearls, then a drumming of diamonds. Earth's cracks heal, wineskins mend, and lovers put tiffs away. All is made green and lovely. The chambermaid looks with longing eyes at the poet, but he will not. Pearls ground up with wine are said to help; he stands his cup outside the Water Door. The lotus pond is filling up, the water hyacinth blushes, the water chestnut pales. The Tank swells, the Kirani babbles, toads tattle, urchins ululate; but the camels are smiling formally. Green are the fields, the lawn, the maze; purple the jamun, rose the eyes of my beloved. We are all in love with her: is she not as pretty as a boy? Has she not brought the rain from the south after long drouth?

ly interrupted by information on, speculation about and celebration of ice, indigo, mangoes, ballooning, silent movies, miniatures, lineages, cannon, gulab jamuns and the snake in a chronicler's Eden: History. . . .

This is the sort of narrative promiscuity that prompts protagonists of concision, transparent form and the clean, uncluttered, narrative, to propose a set of related amendments. Sooner or later, I. Allan Sealy will be told that perfect novels are streamlined, sinewy, taut, tight and lean, and ***The Trotter-Nama*** is, by this measure, slack, self-indulgent, flabby and could do with being half its size. The difficulty, of course, is that a critical vocabulary borrowed from the idiom of body-building or aerobics is musclebound when it is used to describe a novel that makes no attempt to look like Mr Universe.

So what sort of novel is it? It is formally a chronicle of an Anglo-Indian family, which begins with the founder, Justin Aloysius Trottoire, an 18th century mercenary born of a marriage between a Franco-Swiss and an Egyptian Copt (called Joseph and Miriam) and ends with a Trotter of the seventh generation, our contemporary Eugene: forger of miniature paintings, failed castrato and the narrator of this chronicle.

Therefore, if one pillar of the chronicle is lineage or pedigree, the other is geography, the geography of Sans Souci, the huge Trotter estate consolidated by the founder, just off the city of Nakhlau, on which he built the most majestic folly. The fortunes of the family and those of Sans Souci, on which the clan's main and cadet branches live and die till the post-Independence diaspora, are inseparable.

Is this, then, the great Anglo-Indian novel? It is written by one and he has dedicated it to the others. It has characters who say 'men' and 'and all'. It has references to prominent Anglo-Indians worked into the narrative: Henry Derozio, James Skinner and more contemporary figures, who, given the law of libel, appear under invented names. It talks about railway colonies and explores the difficulty Anglo-Indians have in assigning a satisfactory meaning to 'Home'. It sketches the dilemma of the Anglo-Indian community after the Raj is dismantled. So it is certainly a novel where Anglo-Indians are the focus of the action. But to pigeonhole ***The Trotter-Nama*** as an Anglo-Indian novel would be like classifying Salman Rushdie's *Midnight's Children* as the great Indian Muslum epic. . . .

This novel celebrates with marvelous sensuality and precision things untranslatably Indian: *gur, ghee, kbas-ki-tak mat-ki-rani, mango-fool* and the *Dussehri* aara. And it does this with the disarmingly simple device, mentioned earlier, of stopping the narrative dead and explaining 'How jaggery is made'.

The familiarity of the world conjured up by Sealy shows us that the category Anglo-Indian transcends ethnic affiliation. Given our colonial past we are all part of the Anglo-Indian world and this is particularly true of metropolitan Anglophones. Coffee tables, rocking chairs, trousers, hybrid food, puddings eaten with teaspoons, fantasies about gabled roofs covered with snow are a long way from being a monopoly of the Trotters or the Anglo-Indian community that they epitomise. In fact, if the novel in English, written by resident or diasporic Indians, must be labeled, much better that it be called Anglo-Indian, a legitimate term, born of a great historical encounter, instead of the puling Indo-Anglian, born of prejudice, whose only purpose is to distance Indian writers in English from a community made by the same colonial encounter that gave them the language they write in.

I. Allan Sealy is too prodigiously talented a novelist to be contained in such labels. *The Trotter-Nama* is the best novel in English you are likely to read this year. He writes prose so wonderfully and in so many registers—magical, comic, enigmatic, playful that he could dispense with plot and still mesmerise his audience. He can turn his hand to anything, from a glitteringly period description of Nakhlau (after Firdausi) to an inverted retelling of Kipling's *Kim* where the main character is Michael Trotter, Mik for short. Or there is this wonderful passage where he sends up empire fiction from Kipling to M. M. Kaye. It is a recipe called 'How the Raj is done':

> I wish to shew how the Raj is done. This is the play of children, good adept, rest easy. You must have the following ingredients. (It matters little if one or another be wanting, nor is the order of essence. Introduce them as you please, and as often.) Let the pot boil of its own.
>
> An elephant, a polo club, a snake, a length of rope, a rajah or a pearl of price (some use both), a silver moon, a dropped glove, a railway junction, some pavilions in the distance, a *chota peg,* a tent peg, a learned brahmin, a cruel king, a *chapati* (or *chaprasi*), a measure of justice, gunpowder, equal portions of law and order, a greased cartridge, a tamarind seed or else a cavalry regiment, a moist eye, some high intentions, two pax of Britannica Glucose biscuits, an ounce of valour, something in the middle, a Victoria Cross, a soupcon of suspense, a bearer, a *dhobi* (or *dhoti*), *achee-chee,* a *dekchi* (or deck-chair), a pinch of dust, a trickle of perspiration, a backdrop with temples or mosques (some use both), a church pew, a little fair play, a boar, some tall grass, a tiger, a rain cloud, a second snake or a mongoose, a flutter of the heart, a sharp sword, a bared ankle, walnut juice or burnt cork (some use both), a boy of British blood unsullied, a locket.
>
> The sharp adept will notice that all the above ingredients are present in my book—except the last but one. Some will quibble that this last (but one) lack is sufficient of itself to disqualify my book and I admit the lack is grave. I begin to wonder, but it is too late. The fault is mine alone.

A final word. Ignore carpers who claim *The Trotter-Nama* is derivative by invoking the shades of Gabriel Garcia Marquez and Rushdie. Yes, this is magical realism if you like, and true, Marquez did mention ice in *One Hundred Years of Solitude* and of course, *Midnight's Children* features a family saga as well. But then, consider two novels of another time and place: *The Brothers Karamazov* and *Fathers and Sons.* Both novels feature relatives in their titles; both were written by contemporaries (Dostoevsky 1821-81 and Turgenev 1818-83) who were both, broadly, realist. I haven't heard anyone cry foul yet.

> *Mukul Kesavan, "A Glittering Anglo-Indian Odyssey," in* Overseas Hindustan Times, *June 19, 1988.*

TONY JESUDASAN

Indo-Anglian novelists have traditionally subsisted by writing with forked pens. More often than not, their works have been a rutting of their semantic sophistry, elegant empty

tomes, winning prizes for works forgotten the following year; justifying their self-imposed exiles by taking refuge in the white skin of their minds. Thus we have the case in point of Mr Salman Rushdie winning the Booker prize for a highly overrated novel, which did not even bother to acknowledge its unabashed beating of an Indian march on Gunter Grass's German *Tin Drum.* Allan Sealy's *The Trotter-Nama* quietly entered this depressing literary landscape and just about got lost in the wake of the controversy generated by another overstated Rushdie mediocrity, *The Satanic Verses.* Sealy's novel heralds a turning point in Indo-Anglian literature. At a time when fiction of the fabulist genre is fashionable, *The Trotter-Nama* stands out as an original. Sealy's quirky humor is bizarre and exuberant, his prose intense and eclectic. The novel is the closest thing we have to a backwoods coup in contemporary Indian fiction.

The Trotter-Nama is a Rabelaisian extravaganza spanning two hundred years, seven generations and two cultures. It tells the story of an Anglo-Indian clan, from its founding in the eighteenth century by a French mercenary officer, through its heydays in the nineteenth century, to its sad decline. The significance of the novel lies not just in its inventive portrayal of Anglo-Indians and their motley contributions to the making of India, but also in its description of life and times in Nakhlau, the connoisseur's name for the city of Oudh.

Sealy spent most of his childhood in Lucknow, studying at La Martiniere, and the influences are apparent in the Imam Bara-like structure of his epic storytelling. Once you get in, the fun is in not knowing if you will get out.

The uninhibited chronicler of the *Trotter-Nama* is the seventh of his line, a plump painter of forged miniatures who delights in weaving a gossamer web of legend over his shifting transient needs. Other Trotters include the great Trotter (born Trottoire), who started it all amassing a fortune through gunpowder, ice and indigo, only to die an outrageous death by falling from the gondola of his balloon; a clerk migrating through the great Indian Mutiny; a drunken piano tuner; and the Victorian materfamilias Philippa, who manages self-impregnation just by thinking about England.

As times change, so do the Trotters, their grandeur dying a slow death, their ancestral palace, Sans Souci, reduced in contemporary times to a run down hotel. Sealy's handling of the Anglo-Indian theme is emotive and herculean. He has done for his community what in a sense Joyce did for the Irish, illuminating its soul through sheer poetry and imagination. In his myopic review in the *New York Times* [see excerpt above] Timothy Mo criticizes the novel for its frequent digressive interpolations on Indian sweetmeats, the monsoon, the current method of mining curry powder, unaware that this stylistic embodiment owes its origin to the *Akbar-Nama,* a work that greatly influenced Sealy's own form of narrative.

Why a novel about Anglo-Indians? Sealy, himself an Anglo-Indian, says he wanted to set the record straight and that the book was a quest. The community at best got a gratuitous acknowledgement of its existence in the works of English or Indo-Anglian authors before and after Independence. . . .

Post Independence, the community got depleted in India, with most members migrating to Britain and Australia in "search of a better life". . . .

Sealy's second novel, currently in the works, will not make

V. P. Singh or for that matter Rajiv Gandhi happy. . . . If the novel is anything like the **Trotter-Nama** it's time to give . . . Mr. Sealy a standing ovation and to announce the emergence of a major Indian writer.

> Tony Jesudasan, *"An Anglo-Indian Odyssey," in* Indian Express, *January 1, 1989.*

RITA JOSHI

The Trotter-Nama is as unusual as its name suggests. Chronicling the seven generations of an Anglo Indian family, the book is at once a comical peep into history and a highly inventive work of fiction. The book is dedicated by the author who, we are told, is himself an Anglo Indian, to other Anglo Indians. The Anglo Indian community in India is perhaps more divided between Western and Indian cultures than other communities. This book, in a way, reflects that uncertain sense of identity in its broken form of narrative, with back and forth motions in time and a number of interpolations. In writing the novel, the narrator, the seventh generation Trotter, is out to prove himself by recalling the grand vicissitudes through which his family fortunes have been. Sealy provides us with a family tree of the Trotters, which establishes their close interlinks with Indian historical processes for over 200 years. Sealy's more serious aim in the book seems to be to illustrate the fact that the Anglo Indian community in India is itself the direct result of a historical process. The form of the novel, with an increasing number of interpolations, illustrates the sense of fragmentation within this community over the years. . . .

The most memorable parts of the book include perhaps its initial chapters dealing with the fortunes of the great Trotter, Justin Aloysius Trotter. His eccentric inventions and his death caused by a balloon crash, the comic-eccentric behaviour of his relatives and underlings are delineated with the comic genius of a Hogarth. . . .

Perhaps what is more striking about this novel, than the story itself, is the style. The narrative is full of deliberate breaks achieved by epic-like comments in verse and several interpolations, which include recipes, descriptions of *khus-khus,* horses, salamanders and other seemingly irrelevant details, like the following 'Literary Echoes'.

> I wish to introduce literary echoes. For a long time I have wished to introduce literary echoes. I have yearned and yearned to introduce literary echoes but have held back for fear of ridicule or misunderstanding. Now I have found courage but I will do it quickly and limit myself to three. They follow:
> DA!
> DA!
> DA!
> (*The Waste-Land*)
> Boum
> Bou-oum
> Ou-Boum
> (*A Passage to India*)
> Sunya!
> Nya!
> Nya!
> (*The Titar Nama*)
> This is what I wished to do. Now it is done and my heart is eased. The echoes swell my chronicle and

immensely increase its prestige. Praise Him. Praise Him. Praise Him.

If **The Trotter-Nama** is a spoof on history, it is also a spoof on the novel form. It is a novel written in violation of the novel form, moving back and forth in time and deliberately introducing breaks in the continuity of the narrative. The aim is not just comical—the effect is to emphasise that the world of art and fiction have their own rules. Thus while **The Trotter-Nama,** by virtue of its title, pretends to be a historical account of facts, its form highlights its invented fictional component. The effect is to bemuse the reader and to startle him into taking fresh notice again and again of the narrative as he reads it.

We are reminded of the fictional techniques of the eighteenth century English novelist, Henry Fielding, in his novels including *Joseph Andrews* and *Tom Jones.* Fielding called his novels biographies and then went on to include interpolatory chapters discussing the function of art and the role of realism in it. The inside jacket of the book states that **The Trotter-Nama** falls in the same tradition as Marquez—however Fielding and his mentor, Cervantes, seem to have been a stronger influence on Sealy.

In a touching bit of assertiveness, one of the Trotters sums up the question of Anglo Indian identity, the central thrust of the book:

> 'I will have my people called by their proper name which is Anglo Indians. The descendants of the Saxons and the British were called Anglo Saxons, their descendants with the Normans were called Anglo Normans, and we are the Anglo Indians.'

> 'And the descendants of the French and Indians are they Franco-Indians?' jeered Dr. Hall. He had heard of the Great Trotter. 'And are there not then,' he continued, 'Luso-Indians, and Hispano-Indians?'

> Alex thought for a while before replying. Afterwards, because he was not a man of ideas, and knew it, he was always proud of his untutored reply:

> 'No,' he said, 'because they no longer speak French or Portuguese or Spanish, but English.' He had summed up his people.

The success of Sealy's novel lies not just in the authentic sounding strange tale but in the way the artificial style has been so magnificently sustained. Unfortunately, all Indian novels in English today are judged by the yardstick of Rushdie's *Midnight's Children* so that they all begin to sound like variations of Rushdie's archetype. In fact Sealy's book is very different in its aim and its scope from Rushdie's book—his approach to the novel form itself illustrates this.

> Rita Joshi, *"A Spoof on History," in* Sunday Observer, *India, February 19, 1989.*

I. ALLAN SEALY

Sealy discussed the inspiration for **The Trotter-Nama:** "I wanted to write a fictive history, that of the Anglo-Indians, in a form that was not alien (as is the novel) to India. The *nama,* or chronicle, used by court historians to the Mughal emperors, seemed quite the right blend of narrative and whimsy for my purposes. Nevertheless, the European novel tradition, especially that strand from Laurence Sterne down to Günter Grass, was meat and drink to an apprentice writer. The result was a hybrid form which matched its subject, a people formed by the overlap of Europe and India."

Sealy commented on the process of writing this work: "The writing took two years, the rewriting another year. Earlier there'd been a year with an abandoned draft, and before that three years' research. A dissertation came in between the two hauls and may have helped me stay the distance in the final 1000-page manuscript. The publication of another Indian novel, *Midnight's Children,* stole some of my thunder and occasioned some rewriting. For instance, my hero was originally born at midnight with India's independence. Such notions were in the air."

Sealy described his motivation for writing and his intended audience: "I write for satisfaction, respect, a living, in that order. Novels are my public speech, poetry my private. I hope to entertain and instruct, ancient ideals, but also to understand myself and exorcise a few private ghosts.

"I write for an international audience, but there is a residual nationalist in me who especially values the attention of the Indian reader."

> *I. Allan Sealy, in correspondence with* CLC *Year-book.*

Anton Shammas

1951-

Israeli novelist, poet, and nonfiction writer.

A Christian Arab who is a citizen of Israel, Shammas draws upon his heritage and cultural distinctions in *Arabeskot* (1986; *Arabesques*), his first work to be translated into English. As related from the perspective of the fictional character Anton Shammas, this intricately structured novel begins in the remote Israeli village of Fassuta and moves to Paris and Iowa City to chronicle the protagonist's search for personal identity. *Arabesques* explores Israeli history by interweaving actual political events with significant incidents in the lives of Shammas's family and other Fassuta villagers. Originally written in Hebrew, *Arabesques* generated positive reviews in Israel while prompting debate concerning the legitimacy of Arab authors in Israeli literature. Some Western critics concluded that the episodes set outside Fassuta lack the impact of his lyrical rendering of the town and its inhabitants. Nevertheless most commentaters responded enthusiastically to the novel's English translation and compared Shammas's richly textured narrative style to those of Gabriel García Márquez and William Faulkner.

YAEL LOTAN

Something momentous has happened in Hebrew literature.

Even before discussing [**Arabesques**] and its literary merits, one cannot avoid discussing, firstly and primarily, the fact that an Israeli Arab has broken into Hebrew literature. Moreover, he has achieved this not from the side, but rather through the front door, the main entrance of literature, with a big, solid and rich novel which is entirely based on Israeli experience. The use of the word Israeli is no mistake, for the life of an Israeli Arab from the Galilee, born in this state, is decidedly Israeli, closer to Tel Aviv than to Amman or Damascus.

This is an Israeli Hebrew work in every respect. The average Israeli reader will feel close to the book and its characters. Certainly he will feel far closer to this novel and its author than to Jewish novels written in the United States.

The richness of Anton Shammas' literature comes first of all from his family, from the village where he grew up, and from the associations he brings with him from then and there. In this respect he is similar to Marcel Proust on the one hand, and to David Shahar on the other. Like these writers he too weaves the texture of his story from tiny threads, too numerous to count, which he draws from his raw materials. He draws on scenes of his childhood and from the family and social ties bound up with them which no longer exist, having been swallowed up by changing reality. . . . In Shammas'

book the threads extend far back into the past before the narrator's birth and forward to the present, extending over various countries but coming back to focus on the northern Galilee.

The physical, geographical nexus is the village of Fassuta. . . . The village bears marks from every period, including the long generations of Turkish rule, the period of English rule, and the Jewish rule which followed. Under all these, the small Christian population maintained itself modestly and quietly, trying to preserve its identity and to avoid suffering at the hands of authorities unsympathetic to their ways and beliefs.

> In this village, "which lies at the end of the road," collective family memories are woven into a rich and complex fabric over the generations, and one need pull on only one thread, for it is impossible to know what it will draw after it.

> I . . . grasp the end of that thread which he (Abdullah el-Asbah) carded and wove into the warp and woof of my life, and, like that weaver, I snap the

thread by tugging on it hastily and find myself reflecting on a possibility that has come my way by virtue of the new reality, and before I have a chance to fortify my actions with intelligence, I beat the ravelled thread and card it again, trying to give it an absolutely different colour and work it back into the damaged pattern and tie up what had been sundered.

Thus all of time lies before Shammas like a carpet, and he examines the twists of its weave: "Before me I see the future, and before me I see the past." People who are unconnected with Fassuta are unwittingly woven into these arabesques. . . . However these threads also have a dangerous power, and their combination can lead to acts of destruction and ruin, as we see at the end of the book. (pp. 41-2)

The feeling of split and duality [for the Israeli Arab involved with Hebrew culture] has characterised Shammas' writing for several years. In his first book of poetry, *No-man's Land* (and the title speaks for itself) there is a powerful poem, **"Yeletov"** (i.e. "yeled tov," the Hebrew for "good boy"). In the poem the main image comes from the judgement of Solomon—the dead child and the living one; the sword which is meant to slice the living child in two is suspended over him, "and to tell the truth, at this moment I view the play with a smidgen of concern. I'm worried about the wholeness of my limbs."

In this novel the dead child and the living one again appear. The dead child is the first Anton Shammas, after whom the author is named. He is also a mysterious infant who died, supposedly in a hospital in Beirut. But perhaps he did not die but was put up for adoption and is today known as Michael Abbid. However, this duality becomes a symbol of the dual identity of the Israeli Arab. A Jewish author, Yehoshua Ber-On, with whom the narrator goes to Iowa, is trying to create the figure of an Arab intellectual. In the course of his relations with the narrator, he discovers again and again that the figure he is trying to create keeps slipping away from him. . . .

However, political apprehensions of this kind are not the lot of the Israeli Jew alone. The narrator meets a cousin who fled to Lebanon years ago. In the wake of the war which Israel recently waged there, the cousin visits his native village. The way he talks is deeply oppressive to the narrator, for he has become a dedicated Phalangist. In contrast, another relative, Hanneh, the granddaughter of his Aunt Mari, who is married to Sabri Jiris, is killed in the bombardment of the Centre for Palestine Research in Beirut. The threads lead in every direction, cross every line, are exposed to all the convulsions that wrack the Middle East, and conjoin with the personalities and eccentricities of the characters.

Only a *true writer* could create the complex net in which all these fish are caught, each flopping in his own way, where what first seems to be coincidence turns out, upon closer examination, to be the product of history and character. Shammas is such a true writer.

Another element in this book which gives it a unique quality, not only in our literature, but in modern literature in general, is the presence of nature as part of the total fabric. This is not the nature of the poets, whose task is to give an objective dimension to the movements of their hearts, nor is it the nature of the kibbutz, which contains a good deal of self-awareness based as it is on an ideology of conquering the land, the con-

crete meaning of which is producing crops for the market. This is nature in its most organic sense, the world in which the villager lives, imposing itself on his way of life from morning to night. . . .

The immediacy of nature in which the events are anchored in Anton Shammas' book, the seasons of the year, the weather, the changes in climate, give the characters and the events affecting them an almost palpable authenticity. Another highly successful thing here is the way he uses the language to transmit that feeling. The sections connected with the earth and the climate are written in a language anchored in those ancient strata of Hebrew which are still rooted to the soil. In the urban passages the language becomes "modern," elliptical, and sophisticated—as befits the world in which it lives and acts. The most powerful demonstration is in the chapter describing the old olive press, something which has disappeared in the years since the narrator's childhood. Every word here is marvellously accurate, and if anyone wishes to recreate a primitive, preindustrial olive press, he may use this chapter as an instruction manual. The language in which it is written gives one a feeling of distance in time, the feeling of *temps perdu*.

If this book were not an excellent one from every point of view, one might think it was a one-time event rather than harbinger of future developments. However, since it is an excellent novel, I have no doubt that it marks an important turning point in our cultural life. (p. 43)

> Yael Lotan, "Towards an Israeli Literature," in
> Modern Hebrew Literature, Vol. 13, Nos. 1-2, Fall-
> Winter, 1987, pp. 41-4.

DOV VARDI

Although we cannot judge the works [Shammas] may have written in his mother tongue, his mastery of Hebrew matches that of most writers in Hebrew today. His first novel [*Arabesques*] was preceded by two small volumes of poetry (*Hardcover*, 1974, *No–Man's Land*, 1979), which already foretold his talent. The language he uses is intellectual and firmly rooted in the sources of modern Hebrew. Perhaps it is Arabic, with its strict literary traditions and its determined avoidance of the common and colloquial, that underlies the Hebrew, acting as a counterpoint, that creates his distinct prose.

Shammas also has an unusual ability to make the reader visualize in all its realistic detail the world of his village. Like the Flemish masters of the seventeenth century, he too uses his brush to represent every sort of texture and light, thus creating an illuminated and vivid background for a dramatic situation. . . . (pp. 175-76)

What gives the novel its name is the arabesque of the family saga and the memories that take one from a village near Beirut at the beginning of the past century during the days of the British Mandate, to Fassuta, a village located on the southern side of the Lebanese border. The stories intermingle with each other, creating an intricate pattern from which we learn to know the various members of the Shammas family and others in the villages and towns that formed their world. Of particular interest to the reader are the references to the Great Arab Uprising in the late thirties and to "Forty-Eight," Israel's War of Independence, which turned many Arabs into refugees. Shammas is not writing a political novel, however, even when he speaks of the anemones blooming in spring: "They are red like the blood of those who died in the name of Falestin. But in my veins there is blood of another color, diluted with defeat and acquiescence. . . . Falestin is lost forever."

Interwoven with the Oriental, timeless, and formless part of the work are several chapters written on an entirely different plane. The narrator takes us to Paris and then to Iowa City, where he attends the Writers Workshop. We follow the development of a complex relationship between him as a Pales-

tinian Arab Israeli and the Israeli writer Yehoshua Bar-On . . . , who sees him in the light of a "Jew's Jew" upon whom to model his coming novel, then drops him for a "genuine" Palestinian Arab who supports the PLO. *Arabesques* is a challenge to Hebrew writers on their own grounds and in their own tongue, as well as a breakthrough for the Palestinian Arab in his striving to resolve his identity within the framework of the State of Israel. (p. 176)

> *Dov Vardi, in a review of "Arabesques," in* World Literature Today, *Vol. 62, No. 1, Winter, 1988, pp. 175-76.*

An excerpt from *Arabesques*

Elaine had seen other things before that day with her brother Elias, but she didn't dare allow them across the threshold of her lips or even the threshold of her heart. She buried them inside herself and guarded them as fiercely as she later would guard the cookie dish behind the locked mirror. Until she was about seventeen, she did not even allow herself to think about them. And when she finally did, she could not grasp their meaning. She would see images alternately rising and sinking into the oil slick that writhed and flickered on the surface of the saucer. She once saw a child dying. The child is her own son and also the son of another woman who is her kin, who comes to find out whether all is well with him. He changes shape and grows within her, a dead child grows within her, a corpse twines inside and passions try to root it out until they concede, placated. Then, twenty years later, she sees . . .

"Breathe deeply, Elaine, and look at the oil slick, look hard and concentrate on the slick," her brother says to her now. She does as he bids her, and tries once again to penetrate the sealed world behind the tiny oil slick. But she sees nothing except the saucer set on the embroidered tablecloth, nothing except the oil slick on the surface of the water, nothing except her obstinate brother, who several months earlier had invited a delegation from the Hareesa monastery overlooking Junia in the north to come to their house in Tyre and observe the wonders of the nine-year-old girl who can see into the *mandal*. The delegation observed the wonders and subsequently published in the journal of the order, which my mother now proudly hands me, a skeptical and detailed article about the little girl who could describe minutely whole shelves of books in the monastery's library. But even then she tells them nothing more. She does not tell them that she also sees an olive-colored bookcase, embedded in a thick wall, or that she sees that dying boy removing the books from it, spreading them on the sofa, and selecting from among them the journal in which the article would appear, thanks to her brother, the angry and disappointed brother who now grabbed the saucer and flung it out the door, where it twirled over the railing at the top of the seven steps leading up to the entrance and landed with a crash and shattered on the white limestone paving. The water trickled through the pores in the stone, but the oil stain on one of the paving stones did not fade and will appear nine years later in one of the pictures in the family album that I so loved to look at when I was a child.

IRVING HOWE

Anton Shammas is a Christian Arab born in the Galilee who has written his first novel in Hebrew. Defining himself not just legally but also culturally as an Israeli, he has said that the book is his "real identity card"—though a careful reading of *Arabesques* may persuade one that this identity card is not so readily decipherable: it contains a good share of ambiguities. . . .

Shammas evokes traditional Arab life as well as, more uneasily and obliquely, the political sensibilities of contemporary Arab intellectuals. The strongest parts of the novel, the beginning and the end, are set in the Catholic Arab village of Fassuta in the Galilee, a place that is laden with historical associations: "Our village is built on the ruins of the Crusader castle of Fassove, which was built on the ruins of Mifshata, the Jewish village that had been settled after the destruction of the Second Temple by the Harim, a group of deviant priests." This seemingly innocent sentence introduces what will be one of Shammas's subthemes, modestly and calmly suggested: the deep entanglement of Jewish and Arab claims and traditions in his homeland.

The novel's title, apart from its possible pun, is also apt, with its evocations of brevity and decorativeness, both of which are features of Shammas's storytelling. Quick "takes" or narrative segments cut across time and place to create the kinds of juxtapositions Faulkner has made familiar, while common objects—a key, a cookie jar, a barber's chair—serve as emblematic links between narrative segments in a faintly Proustian way. Still another possible influence is Marquez, who seems visible in Shammas's effort to lift village detail above the ordinary, endowing it with a historical, sometimes a "magical" dimension. But if Shammas has borrowed, he has made such devices his own, for he is a canny writer, mixing oral storytelling with modernist sophistication, or at least placing them in close relation. And he has the considerable advantage that the life he portrays is unfamiliar to most American readers, including those who may have read a few Israeli novels in which Arabs appear as shadowy "others." *Arabesques* really brings, as novels were once supposed to bring, "news" from elsewhere.

There are bright, sometimes glittering little portraits of the customs and manners of Fassuta's inhabitants over the past seventy-five years, quick and at times deliberately "torn" snapshots of family and clan. Shammas seems entirely aware of the dangers of "local color," the irritating possibility that his book might move Israeli Jewish and American liberal readers to a kindly condescension. But this danger is largely, if not entirely, avoided through Shammas's narrative voice. He is blessed with a good supply of charm; he uses humor to keep events at a distance; and he launches occasional thrusts against the dominant Israeli power. The thrusts seem only natural in an Arab writer, and Shammas's seldom are tainted by standard ideology; the humor is easy to take and to like; but the charm can make one a bit nervous, since modern readers, trained to suspect charm, may wonder whether a writer endowed with it is trying to slip something past them. But after a while, say the first ten pages, I found myself happily yielding to Shammas's charm, first because it is so genuinely good-spirited and affectionate and second because it serves him as a way not only to approach but also to put himself apart from the communal life he remembers. Behind the charm lie the Arab Revolt of 1936 and the Palestinian movement of today, not as slogans but as felt actualities. On Shammas's roof there are no fiddlers.

The opening chapters introduce a series of neatly sketched people who neither require nor receive sustained characterization. Shammas evokes them by showing their typical gestures and concerns and the patterns of their relationships. With very little description he is able to suggest how Grandmother Alia, a tough old bird, copes with the wanderlust (due, she says, to "a wrinkle in the mind") of her husband, who leaves for Brazil, and her son. . . .

Such figures are quickly drawn, through vignettes and anecdotes. Here Shammas is at his best: he is secure in his knowledge of Fassuta, at ease with memories, luring us to savor the past. Though he is also working toward a larger thematic end, I found myself reading these early chapters for the sheer pleasure of encountering the people in his village. . . .

In its entirety *Arabesques* seems to follow the pattern of the *Bildungsroman*—and here there are problems. The pattern is familiar enough: a young man, educated into discomfort with his origins, leaves his town or village, comes to the metropolis to experience money, women, and dissoluteness, and then, sadder, perhaps wiser, returns home. . . . But it does not quite work in *Arabesques* as Shammas moves his central character, also named Anton Shammas, from Fassuta to Paris and Iowa City. It does not work for two reasons.

First, the hero of *Arabesques* finds Paris disabling; he feels lost and confused there, as if all the problems of his life in Israel were still besetting him. Paris cannot be for him the glorious temptation it was for characters in Balzac and James, so that the city as place and idea fails to become the expected strong contrast to Fassuta. Once the fictional Anton Shammas arrives in Iowa City to join an international writer's conference, the prose turns soft: we hear rather too much about the cordiality of director Paul Engel and the togetherness, if also the tensions, of the participants. What the scheme of the novel seems to require as a moment of drama turns out to be rather flat.

But suppose the idea that *Arabesques* is a *Bildungsroman* is false, too hastily picked up by this reader; suppose that Shammas means to suggest that, given his background and origins, his protagonist cannot easily manage the journey. Then, presumably, we should dispense with the kind of expectations raised by the scheme of the *Bildungsroman*. But that, alas, doesn't help the book very much, since at least for me, the segments dealing with Paris and Iowa City continue to be weak, certainly inferior to those set in the Galilee and the West Bank.

Because of these thematic and structural problems, Shammas's effort to build a complex narrative of suspense—one

that leads to the discovery of Laylah Khoury in the West Bank and an encounter in Iowa City with a lost cousin who has become a spokesman for the Palestinian movement—doesn't have quite the impact it should have. I take it that the encounter with Anton's cousin, a more militant Arab double, is meant to carry some political implications, filling out, so to say, the author's "identity card." But it lacks the ease and persuasiveness of the chapters in which Shammas writes about his village; indeed, it seems willed. At least in literature, militancy can rarely compete with memory.

Shammas excels with the vignette and the anecdote. As in the fiction of writers as different as Leskov, Sholom Aleichem, and Silone, the anecdote serves as a basic unit of narrative. It becomes for Shammas a kernel of received wisdom, a stripped essence of collective memory, a last gesture of the downtrodden. Quick and intuitive, fixed on particulars, sly and sometimes wise, the anecdote can bring everything together, an entire way of life.

When Uncle Jiryes decides to leave Fassuta and travel to South America, his mother, Grandmother Alia (who had failed while nursing him "to infuse his body with that serenity which comes from staying home"), grows desperate. She tells him "of how much she had suffered when she nursed him, only to have given him of her milk in vain." At this point the anecdote takes on a deadpan literalism:

> My uncle then calculated that the quantity of milk he had suckled from my grandmother was the equivalent of two dairy cans. About a week before his departure, he got up very early one morning, untied Uncle Yusef's donkey and set out with it for the village. An hour later, the donkey came back alone, bearing two dairy cans of milk. My grandmother covered her face with her head scarf and said nothing.

This lovely little story could only be spoiled by exegesis. But let me note a prelude and postlude to it. Three pages before the anecdote we learn that many years later Grandmother Alia "preserved [her son Jiryes] in her mind by telling a story about two dairy cans of milk he had once brought her, which always made her laugh so that she would have to hide her face behind her head scarf." If the head scarf implies sadness in the anecdote, the earlier passage shows time turning sadness into amusement. But then, to give things still another turn, we read a bit after the anecdote that forty years later Jiryes's younger sister would say: "My dear brother Jiryes, as you lay on your deathbed [in a distant land], was there no one near you to give you a glass of water?" . . .

Where Anton Shammas will go from here as a writer, whether in Hebrew or Arabic, it is hard to know. But his book has already added something notable to Israeli literature.

Irving Howe, "News from Elsewhere," in The New York Review of Books, *Vol. XXV, No. 6, April 14, 1988, p. 5.*

WILLIAM H. GASS

[*Arabesques*] is a history of its author's youth, although its immediacy reaches farther back in time than the life it is rendering, and becomes the memoir of a family and a fabled region—Galilee. *Arabesques* is a search for origins, and there are secrets, but I shall keep those secrets and allow the text to reach them in its own way. The path of its plot, like the layers and loops named by its punning title, winds through a maze of characters, times, motives and meanings, as Anton Shammas hunts for Anton Shammas in one of the more confused and confusing regions of the world. Despite its autobiographical qualities, it calls itself a fiction, perhaps because it tumbles chronology about and suddenly shifts its point of view, adapting to its purposes methods of narration more frequently found in fiction; perhaps because it might have seemed presumptuous in one still so young, to compose a life; but I prefer to believe the real aim of this impressively beautiful piece of prose is the discovery and definition, even the creation, of a self, not merely an account of a self already made. (p. 1)

The book is divided into "Tale" and "Teller," two voices that are given alternate, if not equal, opportunities. The Tale concerns itself with origins, with "who I was," and recreates the village life of the author's family, sorting out aunts, uncles, brothers and cousins like clothes to be washed, and evoking the odors of bread and earth, the colors of sky and walls. Like many conquered and crisscrossed countries, the Holy Land is an active producer of orphans and the hunt here for a heritage among doubles and substitutes rivals anything in Dickens, who also specialized in displaced persons. The Teller (who has several points of view but only one voice) returns to the Tale the way Mr. Shammas himself returns from Iowa and Paris to the splintered Palestine of his past. The Teller and the Tale are one, an epigraph from John Barth intimates, but the division of the narrative into the Teller's now, and the Tale's then suggests a sundering which the search is attempting to heal. How is the "what I am" to be reconciled with "what I was"?

In one sense, this is accomplished by shaking the family tree until the fruit falls; but in another, profounder sense, it is reached simply by rendering, recreating, celebrating "what is" and "what was" together, like camel and car on the same road. We might call it being faithful to the phenomenological facts. Readers will be reminded of Gabriel García Márquez's magical Macondo more than once, not only because, for us, this novel's local color is equally exotic, but because the mythological, the primitive, the superstitious are weighed in the same tray with the scientifically real. The commonplace life of the village of Fassuta is suffused with the supernatural. Here, the uncommon is common, too. Divine coincidence is one strand of the fabric of existence. People foresee the future as often as they misplace the past. Anton Shammas does not allow the magical to move beyond metaphor into myth, however, the way Mr. García Márquez does. He is a reconciler, not an exploiter. He does not, that is to say, "poetize" these peasant peculiarities for the pleasure of big city tourists.

One scene can stand for many that function in a similar way. A 9-year-old girl (whose lineage is immediately and painstakingly traced, just as everyone else's is, as if it scissored their silhouettes) has the ability to read the *mandal,* a saucer of water on the surface of which a slick of olive oil is spread; in its slightly iridescent clouds certain gifted eyes can see things frequently far away in place and time. At the behest of her brother, a delegation from a local monastery observes the girl and writes an account of her powers, among them an ability to describe entire shelves of books in the monastery library. (This report, itself, eats its way through the text like a worm at home.)

She does not tell the delegation all she sees, however. Some things she can scarcely tell herself; she hides them away, like

every future, in the past, and refuses to think of them again till they arrive like a fist on the door or a shot in the street. . . . (p. 48)

Now, at her brother's urging, she is gazing at the surface of the oil and at first she perceives there three horses, a tree by the monastery, a place to dig for treasure (each of these is a recurrent element in the story); then, abruptly, she sees nothing—only the oil, the saucer, a tablecloth. Annoyed, her brother flings the saucer out the door and over a railing where it shatters on the paving of the courtyard below. The spilled oil stains the stone, and the stain "will appear nine years later in one of the pictures in the family album" which the narrator loved to look at as a boy. The little girl in the center of the photo is his mother at the age of 3, and the text slides immediately into her image, recalling the occasion, but also what the child was thinking, feeling, smelling: a pair of white doves, a Patriarch's rough, perfumed beard. A similar shift in a writer like Jorge Luis Borges would be used to produce a kind of metaphysical wonder, but here the *mandal* serves as a symbol of the writer's task and as a reminder of how intermittent revelations are, how tenuous the connection between things is and how much imagination must surround facts to make them live.

The author as a little boy studies a photograph of his mother as a little girl. On the stones at her feet is a stain made earlier when the saucer, into which another young girl gazed, was flung from the house by her brother. Thus the present looks back at the past to see the past peering forward toward the future. And thus we also learn how we are bound together as much by forgotten gestures as by historic ones, bound by modes of feeling and perception, bound by the shared sting of an ambiant dust. (pp. 48-9)

Arabesques is set in a time of troubles as continuous and vengeful and stubborn and fanatical as Ireland's—in which security, economics and religion practice death; rebellion, suspicion, bravery, conquest and betrayal occupy as many houses as the soldiers; and destruction and disruption are like winds and rainstorms, as common as climate. The arrest of a husband, the failure of a crop, the disappearance of a son, illness or theft, are all equally part of the hardness of a life that goes on anyway, persisting in spite of daily pain and disappointment, a life that can still take quiet pleasure from a mouthful of oil-dipped bread, the oil soaking the grain the way it once stained a stone in a photo. In such grim and desperate circumstances we might expect the author to blow a trumpet or a whistle, to blame and expose and champion this side or that, to wear away one hardness beneath the heel of another. But here is one more reason—in addition to his technical skills, his empathy and generous powers of observation—to regard Anton Shammas as an artist, for he sustains an even-handed, rational, responsive tone throughout, keeping his eye clear and his heart clean, so that these complex and contradictory and acrimonious conditions rise around us, as we read, with their own independence and integrity.

To get to the bottom of an artist, to get to the bottom of a book or, in this case, a life is paradoxically to concentrate on surface. For if the texture of the prose is not rich and subtle, moving and observant, energetic and peaceful by turns, nothing—whether political, sexual, theological or esthetic—will have been accomplished by all that ingenious plotting. Arabesques wind, right enough, but so does a scribble. Secrets are turned up here by the narrator's spade, only to melt away, as if the secrets were made of snow, snow grown underground like inverted grass. . . .

[In *Arabesques,* ten-year-old] Anton Shammas is sent into the depths of the family cistern to clean it and scoop out its accumulation of muck, for he is now the right size; and just as the author will lower himself later through the increasing dimness of his history, so the boy is roped at the waist (ropes at waist and neck are also recurrent elements) and sent down between the wet cold mossy stones into the silt and its silence like a bullet backed into its barrel, or the self returning to its source. Every action of the boy, every quality of feeling, is richly symbolic, but Mr. Shammas never loses sight of the situation itself, which is rendered with calm and perfect poetry, redolent with both odor and wonder, and primeval sensuality.

An 11-year-old girl is sent down to help him, a decision he suffers with great chagrin and "the feeling that this whole enchanted world, which I alone inhabited, a world in which I imagined no one but myself had trod, would come to an end once I, against my will, had to share it with someone else." However, the girl is the occasion, as he steadies her in the slime, for his first great erotic response, one which will be repeated at the conclusion of the book.

The sharing unexpectedly transforms his shame into excitement, and now all of us descend into the well with him. If the sections of the book which describe events in Paris or in Iowa are markedly less rich, they should be, because the narrator's life in those places is necessarily more superficial—a condition which allows us a final esthetic note, namely that surfaces tend to be wealthier when they cover correspondingly wealthy depths.

No search for a self can end with a simple "that's it!" But for the reader, Anton Shammas now has a most definite description and a straightforward identity. He is quite simply the author of *Arabesques.* (p. 49)

William H. Gass, *"Family and Fable in Galilee,"* in The New York Times Book Review, *April 17, 1988, pp. 1, 48-9.*

HILLEL HALKIN

By the strictest standards of disinterestedness, I should not be reviewing Anton Shammas's *Arabesques,* for I played a role in its publication, though a small and not entirely successful one. In the summer of 1985, I was asked by a Tel Aviv literary agent if I would write a report for Harper & Row on a Hebrew novel by Shammas that was still in manuscript. I agreed. I had never read anything of his before and knew only that he was a young Israeli Arab poet who wrote in both Arabic and Hebrew; but Arab authors writing in Hebrew are not a commonplace even in Israel, and I looked forward to the book with curiosity.

It arrived, I began to read, and I was captivated. Or at least I was for the better part of it, an intricate and original saga of a Christian Arab family in the Galilee. Of course, our sense of originality tends to be something of an illusion. What produces it is a writer's ability to stand between us and certain authors he has loved—and in his deft joining of the historical and the fabulous, of careful detail and spun fantasy, Shammas called such authors to mind. What if he did, though? So perfectly suited was his style to his subject, and so superbly

did he handle the complexities of both, that even if, say, *One Hundred Years of Solitude* and its epigones had never existed, one felt that *Arabesques* would be the same.

Not that it was an easy book to read. On the contrary: with its huge cast of grandparents, uncles, aunts, nephews, nieces, and cousins, its time frames that leapt back and forth among numerous points between the 1830s and the 1980s, and its mazelike plot whose destination kept one guessing, it rather resembled a puzzle that had to be pieced painstakingly together. Often I found myself turning back for enlightenment to some previous chapter or passage whose full import became apparent pages later. And yet the picture that emerged as the pieces slipped into place was drawn in exact perspective.

In the foreground, the Shammases, a mixed clan of peasants, craftsmen, smugglers, wanderers, storytellers, believers, bethedgers, and survivors, struggling to steer their modest lives past the hidden shoals of history and genetics. In the middle ground, the village of Fassuta, a remote spot in the Upper Galilee whose residents, unlike their Muslim neighbors . . . , do not first fight the Jews and then flee to the refugee camps of Lebanon during Israel's War of Independence, but rather stay quietly put and become citizens of a Jewish state. In the background, the Arabs of Palestine and the terrible traumas of 1948 and 1967 that have pursued them relentlessly since. And finally, glimpsed yet further back where the receding lines converged (for, if in nothing else than our habitual unpreparedness for fate's blows, are we not all Palestinians?), the human condition.

And the Hebrew: a rich, lyrical, sinuous prose, double-jointedly defying the syntactical knots into which its long sentences kept threatening to tie it. Not the least surprising thing about it, moreover, was its "Jewishness," its allusive sounding of biblical and rabbinic texts to make complex, unstated statements in a manner typical of Hebrew literary tradition, though not especially of Israeli writing today. For example, when at one point I was told how, in the autumn of 1948, the local commander of the victorious Haganah issued an order for the Fassutians to be expelled to Lebanon and then rescinded it upon receipt of a bribe from the village priest, the text read:

> The priest went forth and came before the commander. He laid an envelope on the table and said to him, "This is all there is." The heart of the commander was sufficiently softened by the twenty pounds that he did not banish the inhabitants from their village. A message was sent to those in Rmaïch [a village across the Lebanese border] that the decree was annulled.

The Hebrew, however, did not say that the commander's heart was "softened." It said that it was "hardened" (*vayehezak lev ha-mefaked ba-kesef*), using the same archaic verb form as the Book of Exodus when it tells us, "And Pharaoh's heart was hardened. . . . Then the Lord said to Moses, Pharaoh's heart is hardened, he refuses to let the people go." The irony was multiple: the commander is not being obdurate—rather, *vayehezak* here has the sense of "was firmed up"—but he too decides that the people will not go and he too has become a little Pharaoh, crowned by the sudden turn of events over his Christian subjects, who until recently would not have dreamed in their worst nightmares of being ruled by a Jew. . . . And who was playing on the Hebrew Bible in a time-honored Jewish way to tell me this? A Christian Arab narrator named Anton Shammas! He had written, I thought, a splendid book.

Until, that is, I reached the last third of it, at which point the enchantment went awry. Suddenly Fassuta and its inhabitants vanished. The scene shifted to Paris, where the narrator of *Arabesques* was stopping on his way to an international writers workshop in Iowa, and then to the workshop itself. Did I say narrator? But he too had partly vanished—or rather there was now a second narrator beside him, a Hebrew novelist named Yehoshua Bar-On, plus two new major female characters who were introduced by an unidentified voice.

And as if that were not confusing enough, it soon transpired that the original Anton Shammas might not have written *Arabesques* at all. Two other candidates for authorship were put forth. One was Bar-On, who confides that he is planning to write a novel based on material to be gotten from Shammas, with whom he is attending the workshop. The other was Michael Abyad, a cousin of Shammas's, falsely believed to have died in infancy, who works for the PLO in Beirut and travels to Iowa with a manuscript of a book he has written about Fassuta. Michael Abyad, however, is not the name given him at birth. What is? Why, Anton Shammas, of course.

The quality of the fantasy had also changed. Part One, for instance, ended hauntingly with the dynamiting (for construction purposes) of a legendary cave that the villagers, in more gullible times, once believed to contain buried treasure and to be guarded by a mythical rooster:

> The sound of a dull explosion shook the earth under our feet. . . . Tiny fragments of rock from the spill of detritus hovered in the air and drifted down on our heads. A cloud of dust rose from the place where the rock had sat ever since the day the *djinnis* had put it there to seal their cave.

> And now the dust disperses in the cold February wind, revealing a gaping white mouth and clods of earth. Relieved laughter escapes the lips of the witnesses to the scene, and even Hilweh [a cousin of the narrator's who still believes in the rooster's existence] smiles in embarrassed disappointment. But very quickly the smile freezes on her lips, her eyes are fixed on the sky, her hand points upward, and a sharp scream escapes from her:

> "Look! Over there!"

> And a feather, a crimson feather, turns round and round, dizzily descending in slow circles over the gaping white mouth, and lands caressingly upon the clods of earth.

When this same feather mysteriously reappeared in Part Two, however, clutched by a small boy (the son of yet another of the narrator's many cousins) who has tripped and fallen in Paris—

> He was lying there frightened, his face smeared with dust and his body trembling like a feather in the wind. And in his hand he was holding an astonishingly beautiful feather, crimson in color [which inexplicably disappears a moment later]

—the hocus-pocus was merely arch. It was, in fact, pure Mary Poppins.

I felt cheated. No longer was I reading a magical novel about an ordinary yet wondrous Palestinian village, but rather a flat exercise in literary modernism, with its airplane flights and cocktail parties, its self-conscious artifice and look-at-meness, its multiple narrators, split identities, and writers writing about writers writing about writing. No doubt Shammas had his reasons for it all, and I supposed that I could guess what some might be, but were any of them worth the price of spoiling a little masterpiece?

Fortunately, the situation seemed remediable. The first part of *Arabesques* was quite complete in itself. Why not, I thought, publish it independently, leaving the material from Part Two for another book? Shammas's agent, when I put the idea to her, thought it had merit. In fact, she said, she would like me to suggest it to Shammas. And so the three of us met for lunch one day in a Jewish section of Jerusalem, not far from the street where he lived. But it did not prove to be a meeting of minds. Shammas, though conceding that he too was unsatisfied with the relationship between the book's two parts, was not disposed to jettison one of them, and his somewhat ironically distant manner made it clear that I was not the person to convince him to do so.

We parted amicably, I wrote my report, and eventually *Arabesques* came out in Hebrew. Curious to see its final form, I bought a copy. As I had expected, Shammas had not taken my advice. Yet neither had he left Parts One and Two alone. He had done, in my opinion, something far worse: he had shuffled them together like two decks of cards. Several chapters about Fassuta and a chapter about Paris. Another chapter about Fassuta and a chapter about Iowa City. Fassuta once more and back to Iowa City again, etc. It was definitely the modernistic solution.

Looking back today on that lunch, I suspect Shammas may have felt patronized. He had put a great deal of himself into *Arabesques,* and Yehoshua Bar-On, Michael Abyad, and the rest of Part Two belonged to something he wished to say about the ambiguities of being a Hebrew-writing Palestinian in Israel. Here was I, a Jew he had never met before, telling him to stay away from the complications of the modern novel and to stick to being the village storyteller, which was obviously all an Arab author was good for.

Of course, nothing could have been further from my mind. But I was not acquainted with Shammas's views or with his feelings of non-acceptance by the Jewish society in whose language he so brilliantly wrote. . . . (pp. 28-30)

"I feel an exile in Arabic," [Shammus] writes, "which is the tongue of my blood. And I feel an exile in Hebrew, which is my stepmother tongue, in no small measure because Hebrew writers [like Yehoshua] consider it to be a Jewish language." Yet Hebrew *is* a Jewish language, and homelessness, as has often been observed, is not the worst address for a writer. The original Part Two of *Arabesques* was about this sense of homelessness, as Part One was about the sense of home. Faced with the radical incongruity between them, Shammas vexedly broke them and scrambled them together, when he should have sundered them. But *Arabesques* is an important Hebrew novel, and one hopes that it will not be his last. (p. 32)

Hillel Halkin, "One Hundred Years of Multitude," in The New Republic, *Vol. 198, No. 18, May 2, 1988, pp. 28-32.*

Paul Watkins

1964-

American novelist.

Set during the last days of the Third Reich, *Night over Day over Night* centers upon Sebastian Westland, a German teenager who joins the Nazi SS. The novel follows Sebastian and his fellow recruits, most of whom have enlisted under pressure or with vague ideals of duty and heroism, as they endure boredom and humiliation in basic training and experience the horrors of combat during the Nazi defeat in the Ardennes campaign. Watkins's impressionistic, first-person narrative vividly portrays the effects of battle on his increasingly benumbed protagonist. Michiko Kakutani noted: "Mr. Watkins's orchestration of the combat scenes attests to a remarkably assured command of narrative and a journalistic instinct for the telling detail. He succeeds in communicating not only a visceral sense of blood, noise and horror of the battlefield but also an understanding of the consequences these conditions of violence can have on young, unformed minds."

KIRKUS REVIEWS

Watkins re-creates a narrow slice of WW II in [*Night Over Day Over Night,* a] conventional but painstakingly detailed story of a German boy who joins the S. S. in the final and increasingly desperate year of the Third Reich. (p. 157)

Sebastian Westland is 17 (and caught up in a dalliance with a married woman of 32) when he leaves his school-friends and family and goes off for military training. . . . After a home-leave, Sebastian and his fellow boy-soldiers are sent to the western front, where bit by bit they are immersed into the absoluteness of the horrors of the last-ditch war—in which orders have been given that the badly wounded be killed. As a small part of the Ardennes offensive, most of the young soldiers are indeed killed—in battle scenes that are astonishing for their feel of authenticity and flawless expertise of detail, and that rivet the reader to the page. Forced at one point to shoot unarmed American prisoners in the field, and himself later wounded—although not gravely enough that he will be shot—Sebastian finds opportunity to murder his own S. S. training-commander (he uses a ceremonial dagger given only to members of the S. S.) but then, helpless in the maelstrom, returns to battle as his world seems to explode and crumble about him.

Troubled now and then by fleeting anachronisms and flat notes ("I haven't been off with other girls, all right?" "I was pissed off beyond words"), and susceptible occasionally to the artificiality of a hand-me-down lyricism, Watkins' effort remains on balance a gripping tour-de-force of battle fiction, however well-travelled the road it follows, providing an awesome glimpse of the self-destructive desperation of the end of the Reich. (pp. 157-58)

A review of "Night over Day over Night," in Kirkus Reviews, *Vol. LVI, No. 3, February 1, 1988, pp. 157-58.*

PUBLISHERS WEEKLY

This remarkably accomplished first novel [*Night over Day over Night*] comes at World War II from an unusual angle. Its protagonist is the wry, embittered 17-year-old, Sebastian Westland, who lives in a small German town and, during the last year of the war, enlists in the SS. It is essentially a coming-of-age-in-battle story, in a tradition dating to Stephen Crane and beyond, but is fresh, moving and horrifying partly because of the solidity of the writing, partly out of the palpable sense of doom and terror that enfolds these crippled young lives. Watkins, a young Anglo-American who has apparently made a hobby out of European wars, has an astonishing eye for detail in people, weather, light, landscape. Sebastian is more than just fashionably disaffected; the very soul seems to have been chilled out of him, so that everything that happens to him—his aimless drinking with his buddies, his involvement with an obsessive married woman, the rigors of his manic training, the final overwhelming horror of the Ardennes campaign—is starkly objectified. Only in the scenes with women does Watkins's touch falter slightly and betray his comparative youth; in every other respect the book is a dark triumph, with the grip of nightmare.

A review of "Night over Day over Night," in Publishers Weekly, *Vol. 233, No. 6, February 12, 1988, p. 72.*

JOHN BLADES

With the chief exceptions of Tolstoy and Stephen Crane, the classic war novelists have salvaged their raw materials directly from experience. For obvious reasons, a noncombatant writer has to be either supremely confident or extremely foolish to attempt a book about combat. Well, Paul Watkins is nobody's fool, as he proves with great assurance in his first novel, **Night Over Day Over Night.** Still in his early 20s, Watkins could scarcely have chosen a subject, or a protagonist, further removed from his own experience. . . .

To make his task even more hazardous, Watkins, an American writer, approaches his subject from the "wrong" side. The story is told by Sebastian Westland, a German teenager, who joins the Waffen SS at the end of 1944. Hitler's Navy and Luftwaffe have already been crushed, and along with them, all hopes of a German victory. But Sebastian doesn't know this, and the news that his father has been killed on the Russian front prompts him to enlist, the day after his 17th birthday. Before Sebastian leaves for basic training, a friend warns him: "You are part of it now. You are part of Total War. You've signed youself up for a war to the end. You can't surrender. If you did, they would shoot you anyway."

Before his ritual baptism by fire, Sebastian, like soldiers in every army (and almost every war novel), must undergo the ritual basic training, not only the rigorous combat exercises but the drunken, sexual escapades. Assigned to *Bad Tölz,* an ancient castle that has been transformed into an SS camp, Sebastian finds himself in a company of familiar military types, most of whom are also in their teens. . . .

In many ways, Sebastian himself comes to represent a more banal form of Naziism. When he is finally immersed in Total War, in the Ardennes forest around a site known as "Heartbreak Crossroads," his narration is so clipped and matter of fact that he doesn't seem to recognize what an aggressive automation he has become. With great clarity but almost no emotion or introspection, Sebastian describes the battlefield atrocities. . . .

Though Sebastian is still alive at the end, his soul is as dead as those corpses that litter the charred pine forests around him. He does perform one dubious act of charity by leaving a pistol with a wounded comrade, so he can shoot himself. Otherwise, his only concern is survival. He kills another German soldier to get his motorcycle. He never directly confronts the morality of the Nazi cause, expressing only a hollow cynicism rather than remorse. "I knew it had failed," he says. "Operation Autumn Fog just another bogus campaign at the end of a war. Soon forgotten. The dead put away in

mass graves. Soon far in the past. The woods full of caved-in foxholes and rusted metal."

"Night Over Day Over Night" refers to the impressionistic impact made by an artillery barrage in darkness, but it also carries unmistakable intimations of mortality, allusions to the brevity of life, especially in a combat zone. Watkins' book is certain to bring him comparisons not only with Stephen Crane but with Hemingway, for its crystalline prose, and with Remarque, for its parallels with his World War I classic, *All Quiet on the Western Front.* The similarities are real, but Watkins has a style and angle of vision that are distinctly his own, and unlike Sebastian's decimated comrades in arms, his virtuosic first novel won't easily be forgotten.

John Blades, "Novelist Looks at War through German Eyes," in Chicago Tribune—Books, *March 20, 1988, p. 3.*

An excerpt from *Night over Day over Night*

Mother applied to be the town air-raid warden. They gave her a black greatcoat, a nickel-plated whistle, and a strange helmet with a long, flared front and back and two semi-circles cut out around the ears. It had a decal on it that said "AIR DEFENSE."

She made an oath to Adolf Hitler down at the post office and took a course in rifle shooting but gave up after the second day because she knocked out one of her front teeth. On the first day at the shooting range, she had only aimed through the front sight when she pulled the trigger, which made a ricochet off the back wall that sent the instructor running for cover. She gave up her pay to the Winter Relief Fund and borrowed a bicycle from Mrs. Müller down at the bakery.

Every night after sunset she cycled around town making sure all the blackout curtains were drawn so that none of the RAF bombers could use the town lights to guide themselves into Cologne. If someone's curtains weren't drawn, she wouldn't knock on the door and remind them. She'd stand in the street and blow a whistle until people started coming out of their houses to see what the matter was. Then when the offending family opened their door, usually having drawn their curtains and now faking innocence, Mother would say in a loud voice, "If Your Curtains Aren't Drawn The War Will Go On!" That was the slogan on the posters she was given to stick up, showing a giant black bomb heading toward a house with one window lit up.

She became the most unpopular woman in town after about a week of riding around town blowing her whistle. She came home at midnight, the greatcoat down to her ankles and torn from the times when she got the tail caught in the chain that locked the wheel and sent her off into a pasture or the ditch. And from wearing the helmet, her hair would be its normal curly self around the edges but molded like an egg on top where the helmet had been.

She started going out again after midnight and sometimes didn't come back until ten o'clock the next day. Then she'd sleep all afternoon and go out again after dark. She looked like a vampire, pale with purple blotches under her eyes.

I found out later that she used to catch a ride over to Remagen, flag down some car in her "AIR DEFENSE" helmet and say it was official business. She went to the antiaircraft battery, which had its guns set up on each of the black towers of the bridge over the Rhine. They let her sit in the control room and stare out the window at the tracers thrashing red lines across the sky. She liked the *pom-pom* sound of the guns when they fired for the half hour that the planes were overhead, fifteen minutes going one way and fifteen the other. Afterward she'd stand around with the gun crew, learning to smoke cigars, drinking apple schnapps, and eating cucumber sandwiches. They played Mozart on a Gramophone to the whole of Remagen through a bullhorn. They never shot down a plane. Mother said they just pointed the gun barrels up in the air and fired off all the shells they had because no one could see the aircraft.

Walther and I used to sit at the breakfast table before school, while she was still over in Remagen, eating uncooked porridge and firing spoonloads of flour mixed with water at each other across the room. I told him that if we ate lots of uncooked porridge and then drank hot water, we'd pop.

When we came home late in the afternoon, she'd have cleaned up the mess and Walther would bounce on her bed until she woke up. Then she'd tell us about the firing the night before, fists clenched over her head like she was shooting the gun, loading the shells, shouting orders for better trajectory into an invisible telephone held to her ear. Sometimes she took her helmet off the bedpost and put it on her head to liven up the story.

MICHIKO KAKUTANI

In many respects, the narrator of Paul Watkins's daring first novel [*Night over Day over Night*] is already familiar to us from a host of earlier war novels—from *The Red Badge of Courage* to *All Quiet on the Western Front* to *The Naked and the Dead.* Like so many other protagonists, Sebastian is summoned by his country to go to war. He joins a regiment, makes friends and rivals within the group, survives the rigors of training, sees combat, experiences fear, exhilaration and frustration. He kills people, he's wounded and he watches his comrades die. In the process, he loses his boyish innocence and emerges a changed man. . . .

Sebastian tells us his story directly from some vague point in the future, speaking in the alternately casual and poetic tones of the perpetual adolescent. His creator, Paul Watkins, is a 23-year-old American educated at Eton and Yale University, and he seems to have deliberately given Sebastian a thoroughly recognizable, contemporary voice—a voice whose very familiarity forces us to confront the banality of evil. In fact, through much of the book, we forget that Sebastian is fighting for Hitler; he seems like a generic soldier, obeying orders and hoping the war will end so he can return home, return to his carefree consumption of girls and beer and food.

Sebastian is not a particularly sensitive or introspective individual, but like the hero of Louis Malle's film *Lacombe, Lu-*

cien, he's a kind of empty vessel, someone whose innocence and ignorance make him an adequate soldier and an incomplete human being. He and his fellow recruits don't think about politics or morality, they are quite possibly ignorant of the Third Reich's policies and certainly blind to its implications. Their concerns are day-to-day ones—will they get in trouble with a superior officer, will they manage to get enough to eat, will they survive the next offensive, the next battle.

Sebastian does make a couple references to the SS's emphasis on blind loyalty and obedience, but *Night over Day over Night* contains only one scene overtly involving Nazi ideology, and it is used to underscore the apolitical nature of enlisted men like Sebastian. While in training camp, the recruits are shown wax molds of German, Jewish and Anglo-Saxon noses and lectured on "the racial barriers that separated our different cultures." After class they respond by melting the wax molds—a prank motivated not by moral outrage but by simple schoolboy boredom with a pompous instructor.

Like Lucien Lacombe, Sebastian chooses his fate casually, almost unthinkingly. Boys over the age of 17 are asked to sign up, and Sebastian chooses the SS more or less on impulse. He, like many other recruits, isn't particularly eager to join, most are afraid of dying, some already feel the German war effort is doomed. One bunkmate points out that he never had any real choice in the matter: his father threw him a surprise party, pulled out the enlistment papers and made him sign in front of family and friends. Another recruit named Breder talks about "not wanting to shirk responsibility," but Sebastian observes, "He probably couldn't remember why he joined." "There weren't always concrete reasons to give," he adds. "Breder probably took one look at the enlistment poster that said, 'Your Comrades Are Waiting for You in the Waffen SS,' and joined because he figured he needed a few comrades."

Using handfuls of briskly orchestrated details, Mr. Watkins fills in Sebastian's pre-SS life and his life in boot camp with scenes that have the offhand immediacy of snapshots in a photo album. . . .

Although two melodramatic incidents (one involves a woman's murder of her husband, the second, another murder within the ranks of the SS) are not fully assimilated into the storyline, Mr. Watkins's orchestration of the combat scenes attests to a remarkably assured command of narrative and a journalistic instinct for the telling detail. He succeeds in communicating not only a visceral sense of the blood, noise and horror of the battlefield but also an understanding of the consequences these conditions of violence can have on young, unformed minds.

In relating Sebastian's adventures, Mr. Watkins has bent over backward not to portray him as a hateful Nazi mouthing racial obscenities, but instead tries to show him as a simple soldier caught up in a historical maelstrom he cannot comprehend. Sebastian never participates in the rounding up of prisoners, never hears about the death camps. As a result, the full horror of his story happens not in the pages of this provocative novel but offstage in our memories and minds.

Michiko Kakutani, "First Novel Sketches Evil with What's Not Said," in The New York Times, *March 26, 1988, p. 18.*

PAUL WEST

Paul Watkins is 23 years old, born of English parents but educated at Yale, and currently a graduate fellow in creative writing at Syracuse University. When he was 15 he walked his way across the battlefields of World War I: Holland, Belgium, the Rhineland, and he lived in Germany at the same age as his hero. Anyone who has not read [*Night over Day over Night*] will wonder if the tour paid off (it did: he sucked the tang of carnage from those ancient bloodbaths, and his action writing, like his work with landscape, is throughly convincing). Psychologically the novel is less engrossing, not least because Watkins lets Sebastian tell things in his own right, and Sebastian is a 17-year-old Hun less analytical than wowed by the scurvy trade of death, as he would be. The parts of his mind that don't deal with SS rigors and the Ardennes carnage don't exist, which is to say the book lacks contrast and counterpoint such as a third-person narrator might have delivered. (p. 5)

The best writing in the novel comes not at the gory climax, when Sebastian behaves like the genuine SS he aspired to be, but during the long phony war of SS training. He goes from a town near Remagen on the Rhine, where his Nazi zealot of a mother plays Mozart on a gramophone through a bullhorn, to camp in Bavaria where they tattoo his blood group in his armpit and life becomes subject to the whims of Sergeant Voss, who seems once to have been taller than he is and rages about with spit flying from his mouth: an insane survivor whom Sebastian in the end knifes to death.

With von Schwerin the snob, and prosaic Handschumacher from the Austrian-Swiss border, Sebastian huddles under his cape watching water come to the boil, learns how SS camouflage differs from the army's (round-edged not hard-edged), and discovers "the randomness of pain, the great fragility of the flesh." With his fellow recruits, for a prank, he melts down the pink wax noses used by the racist lecturer on Teutonic and Jewish physiognomy. He listens to Hitler's rantings and can remember nothing of what was said. Seated in the cockpit of a shot-down Allied fighter plane, he presses a red button and machineguns cows a couple of fields away. After they graduate, Voss cons them all into tossing their ceremonial daggers into a deep well. Away they go, lethal cannonfodder, to a world in which helmets shine like wet eggs, one way up, or fill like birdbaths the other, and explosions smell like pigs, and you touch your lips along the jawbone of someone wounded, to feel what pulse there is. (pp. 5, 14)

The novel's physicality is imposing, and almost makes up for its lack of depth. Watkins has done his homework well, although I cannot believe that Sebastian, alive and aware during July 1944, didn't hear about the bomb plot against Hitler (who crowed survival and vowed revenge on the radio) or that there was enough balsa wood around in that year for German boys to make gliders with. There was virtually none in England and the substitute was called obechi. (p. 14)

Paul West, "Blood and Iron: Coming of Age in Hitler's SS," in Book World—The Washington Post, *April 24, 1988, pp. 5, 14.*

PAUL WATKINS

Watkins discussed the inspiration for *Night over Day over Night:* "I was a student in Germany at age sixteen, the same age as the character in the book, and I stayed with a family of old Prussian aristocrats, who fled the Russians at the end of [World War II]. The father of the family found himself, in the closing stages of the war, in a similar situation to the book's main character. Along with several anecdotes from veterans of both sides, inspiration for the work came mainly from my time in Germany and the father of the family I stayed with."

In preparation for writing the novel, Watkins performed extensive research: "I spent months reading long-out-of-print volumes, both in German and English, on the Ardennes Campaign. I walked through the battle area and slept in the woods near Rockerath. I studied German equipment at the Imperial War Museum, the Arnhem Museum, and in various flea markets, where much of the clothing, weapons and medals seem to show up. I also spent many hours talking with both American and German veterans before I felt confident enough to begin the novel."

Questioned about his motivation for writing, the author replied: "I am motivated to write because, for some time now, I have been under the impression that I'm not much good at anything else."

Paul Watkins, in correspondence with CLC Yearbook.

Prizewinners

Literary Prizes and Honors

Announced in 1988

•Academy of American Poets Awards•

Fellowship of the Academy of American Poets

Awarded semi-annually to recognize distinguished achievement by an American poet.

Alfred Corn
Donald Justice

The Lamont Poetry Selection

Established in 1952 to reward and encourage promising writers by supporting the publication of an American poet's second book.

Mary Jo Salter
Unfinished Painting

Lavan Younger Poets Award

Established in 1983 to annually recognize three accomplished American poets under the age of forty.

Marie Howe
Naomi Shihab Nye
John Yau

Walt Whitman Award

Secures the publication of the first book of a living American poet.

April Bernard
Blackbird Bye Bye

•American Academy and Institute of Arts and Letters Awards•

Academy-Institute Awards

Awards are given annually to encourage creative achievement in art, music, and literature.

William Barrett, David Bottoms
Rosellen Brown, David Cope
John Clellon Holmes, John McCormick
James Seay, William Weaver
Norman Williams
(awards in literature)

Witter Bynner Foundation Prize for Poetry

Established in 1979 and awarded annually to recognize an outstanding younger poet.

Andrew Hudgins

E. M. Forster Award

Established in 1972, a monetary award is presented annually to a young English writer toward financing a stay in the United States.

Blake Morrison

Sue Kaufman Prize for First Fiction

Awarded annually to the best first fiction published during the preceding year.

Kaye Gibbons
Ellen Foster

Rome Fellowship in Literature

Established in 1951 to recognize young writers of promise, a year's residence at the American Academy in Rome is awarded annually.

Edward Hirsch

Richard and Hinda Rosenthal Foundation Award

Awards given annually for accomplishment in art and literature. The literature award recognizes a work of fiction published in the preceding year which, while not a "commercial success," is considered a literary achievement.

Thomas McMahon
Loving Little Egypt

Jean Stein Award

An award is presented annually to recognize a writer of either fiction, nonfiction, or poetry, in alternating years.

André Dubus
(fiction)

Harold D. Vursell Memorial Award

Awarded annually to a recent work for the quality of its prose style.

Jonathan E. Maslow
Bird of Life, Bird of Death

Morton Dauwen Zabel Award

Presented in alternating years to poets, fiction writers, and critics, to encourage progressive, original, and experimental tendencies in American literature.

Clement Greenberg
(critic)

•James Tait Black Memorial Book Prize•

Sponsored by the University of Edinburgh and awarded annually for the best work of fiction and the best biography published during the previous year.

George MacKay Brown
The Golden Bird: Two Orkney Stories
(fiction)

•Booker Prize for Fiction•

Britain's major literary prize is awarded annually in recognition of a full-length novel.

Peter Carey
Oscar and Lucinda
(see entry below)

•Georg Buchner Preis•

Awarded annually by the German Academy of Language and Poetry to recognize writers whose works further the cultural heritage of Germany.

Albert Drach

•Goncourt Prize•

Awarded annually in France by the Academie Goncourt to recognize a prose work published during the preceding year.

Erik Orsenna
L'exposition coloniale

•Governor General's Literary Awards•

To honor writing that achieves literary excellence without sacrificing popular appeal, awards are given annually in the categories of prose fiction, prose nonfiction, poetry, and drama. Officially known as the Canadian Authors Association (CAA) Literary Awards.

Gwendolyn MacEwen
Afterworlds (poetry)
(see entry below)

M. T. Kelly,
A Dream like Mine (fiction)
(see entry below)

John Krizanc,
Prague (drama)

•Drue Heinz Literature Prize•

Established in 1980 to recognize and encourage the writing of short fiction, this annual award is given by the University of Pittsburgh Press.

Reginald McKnight
Moustapha's Eclipse

•Hugo Awards•

Established in 1953 to recognize notable science fiction works in several categories.

David Brin
The Uplift War
(novel)

Orson Scott Card
Eye for Eye
(novella)

Ursula K. LeGuin
"Buffalo Gals, Won't You Come out Tonight"
(novelette)

•Lenore Marshall/*Nation* Poetry Prize•

Established in 1974 to honor the author of the year's outstanding collection of poems published in the United States.

Josephine Jacobsen
The Sisters: New and Selected Poems

•Los Angeles Times Book Awards•

Awards are given to authors in various categories to honor outstanding craftsmanship and vision.

Gabriel García Márquez
Love in the Time of Cholera
(fiction)
(see entry below)

Richard Wilbur
New and Collected Poems
(poetry)

•National Book Awards•

Established in 1950 to honor and promote American books of literary distinction in the categories of fiction and nonfiction.

Pete Dexter
Paris Trout
(fiction)
(see entry below)

•National Book Critics Circle Awards•

Founded in 1974, this American award recognizes superior literary quality in several categories.

Philip Roth
The Counterlife
(fiction)

C. K. Williams
Flesh and Blood
(poetry)

•Nebula Awards•

Established in 1965 to honor significant works in several categories of science fiction published in the United States.

Pat Murphy
The Falling Woman
(novel)

Kim Stanley Robinson
The Blind Geometer
(novella)

Pat Murphy
"Rachel in Love"
(novelette)

102

Kate Wilhelm
"Forever Yours, Anna"
(short story)

Alfred Bester
(grand master award)

•Neustadt International Prize for Literature•

Established in 1970 and awarded biennially, this prize honors a living author who has made significant and continuing contributions in poetry, fiction, or drama.

Raja Rao

•New York Drama Critics Circle Award•

Awards are presented annually in several categories to encourage excellence in playwriting.

August Wilson
Joe Turner's Come and Gone
(best play)

•Nobel Prize in Literature•

Awarded annually to recognize the most distinguished body of literary work of an idealistic nature.

Najīb Mafūz
(see entry below)

•Obie Award•

Awards in various categories are given annually to recognize excellence in off-Broadway and off-off-Broadway theater productions.

Caryl Churchill
Serious Money
(best new play)
(see entry below)

•PEN American Center Awards•

Ernest Hemingway Foundation Award

Awarded annually to encourage the publication of first fiction by young American authors.

Lawrence Thornton
Imagining Argentina

PEN/Faulkner Award for Fiction

Annually recognizes the most distinguished book-length work of fiction by an American writer published during the calendar year.

T. Coraghessan Boyle
World's End
(see entry below)

•Pulitzer Prizes•

Awarded in recognition of outstanding accomplishments by American authors in various categories within the fields of journalism, literature, music, and drama. Literary awards usually recognize excellence in works that concern American life.

Toni Morrison
Beloved
(fiction)
(see entry below)

William Meredith
Partial Accounts: New and Selected Poems
(poetry)
(see entry below)

Alfred Uhry
Driving Miss Daisy
(drama)
(see entry below)

•Tony Awards•

Officially entitled the American Theatre Wing's Antoinette Perry Awards, this award is presented in recognition of outstanding achievement in the Broadway theater.

David Henry Hwang
M. Butterfly
(best play)
(see entry below)

•United States Poet Laureate•

Created in 1986 by an act of Congress to honor the career achievement of an American poet.

Howard Nemerov

•Whitbread Literary Awards•

Awarded annually in several categories to encourage and promote English literature.

Salman Rushdie
The Satanic Verses
(novel)
(see entry below)

Yale Series of Younger Poets

Awarded annually to honor the outstanding verse of a promising young American poet who has not yet secured wide public recognition.

Thomas Bolt
Out of the Woods

T(homas) Coraghessan Boyle

World's End

The PEN/Faulkner Award: Fiction

American short story writer, novelist, and editor.

An author of irreverent comic fiction replete with satiric and ironic twists, Boyle is often linked with such absurdist and experimental authors as Thomas Pynchon and John Barth for his use of black humor and stylistic blend of formal language and modern argot. Like all of Boyle's work, *World's End* (1987) juxtaposes everyday contemporary concerns with fictionalized historical commentary to reveal ludicrousness in human behavior, past and present. Boyle commented: "I like to use history as part of the myth that informs what we are now, rather than reproducing factually what might have happened. . . . [What] I want to end up with is a story that uses the history, the characters and the place as elements in a satisfactory, artistic whole."

World's End examines the cyclical, intertwined fates of three families living in the fictional Hudson River Valley community of Peterskill, which is based upon Boyle's hometown of Peekskill, New York. Written in part, according to Boyle, "as a way of imagining my own family's roots, which are very uncertain," *World's End* compares recurring patterns in the region during the seventeenth and twentieth centuries, centering on such themes as rivalry, betrayal, revenge, and the extinction of family lines. Episodes set in the seventeenth century describe conflicts between three clans: the Van Brunts, a Dutch family of tenant farmers led by their rebellious but ignorant father, Jeremias; the Van Warts, a domineering family of Dutch landlords who own the Van Brunt farm and attempt to exploit the household; and the Kitchawank Indians, a tribe cheated of their lands, who are led by Mohonk, a brave who has an illegitimate child, Jeremy, by Jeremias's sister. The Van Brunt tradition of rebellion and betrayal is established in *World's End* when Wouter, Jeremias's son, allows his cousin Jeremy to be unjustly executed by the Van Warts. This event results from Wouter's loss of respect for his father, who hypocritically begged forgiveness of the Van Warts after refusing orders to help build a road.

The main protagonist of *World's End* in the 1960s is Walter Van Brunt, the abandoned and alienated son of a political activist. Walter's estrangement stems from the knowledge that his father may have betrayed his family, friends, and communist ideals during a brutal incident reminiscent of the actual Peekskill riots of 1949. Walter's father is said to have helped conservative mobs attack blacks, women, and communists at a summer concert that was to feature black activist and performer Paul Robeson. Following a symbolic motorcycle collision with a historical marker that results in the amputation of his foot, Walter is prompted to investigate and eventually embrace his family history. Walter's traitorous alliance with Depeyster Van Wart, heir to the dwindling fortune of the Van Wart estate, ends in disaster for both himself and his former friends. Depeyster's most obsessive desire—to obtain a male heir—is ironically defeated by a descendant of Jeremy Mo-

honk, who impregnates Depeyster's spiteful wife and convinces her to tell her husband that he fathered the infant. Although the novel received mixed reviews, Boyle attained a widespread popularity that had eluded his earlier works despite their critical acclaim. Benjamin DeMott lauded *World's End* as "a smashing good book, the peak achievement thus far in a career that seems now to have no clear limits."

Boyle initially attracted critical attention for his first volume of short fiction, *The Descent of Man and Other Stories* (1979). Many pieces in this collection lampoon such political and literary figures as Idi Amin and Norman Mailer, while others address the triumph of natural forces over civilization. In the title story, a man whose lover works at a primate research center loses her to a chimpanzee who is translating a work by Friedrich Nietzsche into Yerkish; in another tale, "Quetzalcoatl Lite," an explorer roams the Amazon in search of the elusive "brew of the ancient Aztecs." The stories in Boyle's second collection, *Greasy Lake and Other Stories* (1985), proceed from similarly imaginative premises; "Ike and Nina," for example, depicts a love affair between Dwight Eisenhower and Nina Krushchev. Placing Boyle among "the select cadre of American humorists," Peter Ross hailed *Greasy Lake* as "a triumphantly funny assembly, incredibly diverse in its inspirations and foundations, and crafted with a technical skill and lexicon that reminds one of Terry Southern and S. J. Perelman."

Boyle's first novel, *Water Music* (1981), unites past and present in its fictionalized account of nineteenth-century Scottish explorer Mungo Park and his ill-fated second mission into Africa. Juxtaposing the tone and format of the Victorian picaresque novel with vibrant modern vernacular and black humor, Boyle satirizes Park's travels and exaggerates the physical hardships suffered during his expedition. In *Budding Prospects: A Pastoral* (1984), a novel with a more realistic and contemporary setting, a teacher who is disillusioned with never having completed anything is lured into growing marijuana for profit. Despite numerous obstacles, he learns responsibility through his struggle to harvest the crop.

(See also *CLC,* Vol. 36; *Contemporary Authors,* Vol. 120; and *Dictionary of Literary Biography Yearbook: 1986.*)

MICHIKO KAKUTANI

T. Coraghessan Boyle has emerged as one of the most inventive and verbally exuberant writers of his generation. Rather than using his gifts to create polite mirrors of contemporary reality, he has chosen, like Robert Coover and Donald Barthelme, to mix up naturalism with large doses of hyperbole and metaphor to create storybook collages that comment on older forms of literature even as they reinvent essential American myths. In his latest novel [*World's End*], a vast and wordy epic that spans four centuries and more than 400 pages, he attempts not only to examine the implications of the American Dream, as he's done in earlier works, but also to tackle the complicated issues of freedom, class and race involved in the founding of our nation. . . .

Mr. Boyle has taken as his setting the lovely countryside of the Hudson River Valley, and he's selected the works of Washington Irving as a literary antecedent. In addition to bearing a family name familiar to readers of "The Legend of Sleepy Hollow," his hero, one Walter Van Brunt, will undergo a series of adventures that recall those of famous Irving characters. Like Ichabod Crane, Walter (as well as his ancestors) suffers from an eating disorder. Like Crane, he has a mysterious encounter with a specter that results in a terrible accident. And like Rip Van Winkle, he becomes an unwitting time traveler—though instead of journeying into the future like Rip, he will meet up with ghosts from his past, ghosts that will drag him back into the muck and confusion of ancient family history.

Walter's motorcycle accident, which is described in terms reminiscent of Ichabod Crane's run-in with the headless horseman, results in the loss of his foot; and while recuperating in the hospital, he has a visit from his long-lost father, Truman—or so he imagines. In the ensuing weeks and months he becomes increasingly obsessed with his father's bizarre disappearance and the elusive truth of his life.

Is it true, as Walter's adoptive parents have always told him, that Truman was a traitor—an informer, who sold out his family and Socialist friends during the violent, anti-left Peterskill riots of 1949? Is it true he cold-bloodedly abandoned Walter and his mother, driving off in a car owned by the right-wing tyrant Depeyster Van Wart? What role in all this was played by Truman's secret manuscript titled "Colonial Shame: Betrayal and Death in Van Wartville, the First Revolt"? And how were the fates of Walter and Truman prefigured by the destinies of their ancestors?

As Walter sets off in search of answers to these questions, his daily life begins to unravel: a few days after his wedding, he finds himself tumbling into a messy affair with Mardi Van Wart, the disaffected daughter of his boss, Depeyster; he discovers that his wife, Jessica, is having an affair with his hippie friend, Tom Crane; he loses his remaining foot in another accident; and he has a disturbing talk with a dwarf who alledgedly knows his father's secret. These events take place sometime in the late 60's, and as he did in *Budding Prospects,* Mr. Boyle uses his quick, ironic command of sociological detail to both evoke and satirize a disturbed America in which, as he once wrote, "rape, murder, cannibalism, political upheaval in the Third World, rock-and-roll, unemployment, puppies, mothers, Jackie, Michael, Liza" are incapable of inducing a reaction.

Interspersed in alternating chapters with these recent events is Mr. Boyle's account of what happened to Walter's ancestors—an account, set down in the same noisy, colloquial prose used in the contemporary portions of the book. . . .

Certainly this historical echo chamber gives Mr. Boyle plenty of opportunity to explore his interests in propagation and the development of the species, . . . as well as a chance to score various points about the problematic evolution of American democracy. Unfortunately, many of those points—that white men stole the Indians'-land, that the upper classes have always distrusted the left—are simplistic and poorly delineated. Worse, there's something mechanical and cumbersome about Mr. Boyle's orchestration of time past and time present: his subsidiary characters (in both the 17th and 20th centuries) proliferate in such profusion that we never really get a chance to know them as recognizable individuals, and even Walter's tale begins to sound increasingly contrived. Instead of feeling that he's living out some inexorable family destiny, we end up suspecting that he is just another pawn in the author's elaborate chess game.

Still, there's much to enjoy in this volume. *World's End* gives Mr. Boyle lots of room to display his manic gift for language, his love of exaggeration and Grand Guignol effects, his ability to work all sorts of magical variations on literature and history. It's just that, in this case, the end product doesn't do full justice to those talents.

Michiko Kakutani, in a review of "World's End," in The New York Times, *September 23, 1987, p. C27.*

BENJAMIN DeMOTT

In the beginning the world of *World's End,* T. Coraghessan Boyle's third novel, seems *déjà vu.* A workday peters out. An unpromising 22-year-old named Walter Van Brunt is discovered sharing joints and beer in a bar called the Throbbing Elbow. His companions are Hector Mantequilla ("ragged wild hair") and Mardi, who's wearing a hand-dyed paper miniskirt with matching panties—a dress "so short as to expose the nether curve of her buttocks." "I got something for you, man—something special," says Hector, taking Walter's arm. "In the men's room, you know?"

Certainly we know, or at least we assume that we know. Following Hector will admit us to the confines of a familiar school of contemporary fiction (c. 1965-85). In this quarter weed and literary allusion proliferate, narrators and characters alike speak sardonically, plot is minimal and the backward reach of time stops at the Vietnam War. Lead on, Hector, we think without zest. Explore the drug culture. Meet the need for views of whacked-out layabouts "doing lines" in the men's room.

But within moments we're turned around—surprised and genuinely engaged. Widening his angle of vision, the writer shows us that drink, dope and sex are merely incidental influences on the party night in progress. Walter and his mates are in Peterskill, N.Y., an hour up the Taconic from Manhattan, not on the Coast or Mexico-bound. When midnight deviltry dumps them into the Hudson, swimming for the moorings of a fleet of mothballed merchantmen, the sounds of their roistering commingle with eerie murmurs. On the deck of the U.S.S. *Anima*, a rusted hulk, Walter Van Brunt catches sight of the ghost of a vanished elder amidst a crowd of "ragged, red-eyed, drooling" bums. . . .

A minute later, the novelist directs our attention away from the roisterers, sending us back three centuries to a "five-morgen farm" close to a Hudson River trading post, the turf on which Walter's ancestors (a father, a mother, three children) began their American life. Hollanders indentured "for all their days on earth," the family is obligated to pay the patroon, within six months of their landing, "five hundred guilders in rent, two fathoms of firewood (split, delivered and reverently stacked in the cavernous woodshed at the upper manor house), two bushels of wheat, two pair of fowl, and twenty-five pounds of butter."

During the first 30 pages of *World's End* we watch these settlers thrive and endure catastrophe. In the same stretch of writing we also see a battle in a modern-day Peterskill kitchen between Walter's father and those he charges with kidnapping his son; we leave the Throbbing Elbow for good and listen to a Kitchawank medicine woman chanting against *pukwidjinnies*—ghost spirits and devils; we witness loss of limb by gangrene (1663) and by motorcycle crash (1968); we hear a patroon's agent coldly evict a helpless child (the only survivor of the indentured family) for defaulting "the conditions of your agreement"; we learn how a portion of the ancient Mohawk and Kitchawank tribal cultures entered the blood of Walter Van Brunt; we come to know a descendant of the original patroon—an ancestor-obsessed, mid-20th-century factory owner named Depeyster Van Wart, father of the miniskirted Mardi (in time he will become Walter's employer and surrogate-father).

The narrator who speaks to us of these matters seems concerned not alone with registering the hum and buzz of another age—the terror of Lowlanders transported to a "barbaric new world" teeming with trees, demons, savages, strange animals—but with such problems as that of rendering correctly the thunder, in our own day, of revved-up Norton Commando motorbikes. His apparent assumptions are that it's still feasible for a fiction writer to shape helpful historical and social perspectives on more or less contemporary lives, and that there are continuities within change.

And his world has scale, levels, density. In these pages fathers struggle for their sons' respect, lose it, and live to see their sons caught in the same cycle. Farm girls gather eggs at peaceful dawns, tomahawks are hurled in fury, people quarrel at checkout counters. Oppressors oppress. Guests drink and dance at weddings (the drinks are " 'Sopus ale, cider and Hollands out of a stone jug," and the music comes from penny whistles, overturned kettles and "a *bombas* that made use of a pig's bladder for a sound box"). Fearful punishments are meted out to the unlucky—from a week in the stocks to solitary at Sing Sing (originally Sint Sinks); fearful political frustration explodes on the right and left. . . . (pp. 1, 52)

Yesterday the label "wit writer" seemed apt for the creator of this world. In four works of fiction published between 1979 and 1985 T. Coraghessan Boyle showed himself to be lively and language-intoxicated—but determinedly disengaged. (p. 52)

Writers of stature—Robert Coover and William Gass among them—praised Mr. Boyle's work. Here and there a story that began as a comic bit would seem to grow restive, as though assailed momentarily by a hunger for seriousness. . . . But caprice and mugging were the norms, and the career seemed to point in the direction of superior literary horseplay, not heft.

World's End totally transforms that outlook. It isn't a pontificating work, and the wit writer hasn't disappeared. He has, however, powerfully challenged his own disengagement—the constraints of automatic knowingness and habitual irony. And this movement of mind creates space for moral and emotional as well as esthetic reality, producing a narrative in which passion, need and belief breathe with striking force and freedom.

The book's pivotal 20th-century events—one actual, the other imaginary—are the Peekskill riots of 1949, wherein locals attacked "kikes and niggers" up from the city to hear a Paul Robeson concert, and a late-60's act of sabotage against the Arcadia, an invented countercultural peace and ecology ship moored in the Hudson. Key roles in each event are played by representatives of the Van Brunts and Van Warts, Dutch immigrants whose ambitions first became entangled when the doomed, indentured Van Brunts commenced scratching a living for their almighty patroon. A major concern throughout is power and its mutations, and a behavioral phenomenon under frequent scrutiny is treachery.

Links exist, as I said, between this book and the author's earlier work. Black comedy and literary allusion erupt occasionally in the presentation of Van Brunt, who in 1968 is an accident-prone college dropout with a 4-F deferment. (Walter's first collision with history—he bangs into a historical marker while cavorting on his Norton—costs him half a leg; we're told often that his avowed hero is Meursault, Camus's famous nihilist.) Traces of the ungenerosity toward bottom dog dreamers and others that blemishes some of the author's shorter fiction also surface in *World's End.* (pp. 52-3)

But belief in human range and possibility is stronger here than in any of Mr. Boyle's previous books, and it generates a dozen or more characters—Indians, merchants, hippie idealists, others—sufficiently various to experience complex reactions and stimulate them in readers. Even young Walter himself—undisciplined, half-educated—has a grainy nature. He can distinguish "mindless, brick-throwing racist[s]" from people mildly infected with Bircherism, and he possesses, in addition, a strong imagination of guilt. He's tormented by the version of his father as traitor that's come down to him, through his mother and other relatives—partisans of the Socialist Left who are convinced that his father colluded with the moneyed Van Warts to set them at the mercy of the anti-Communist mob during the riots. (A substantial portion of the narrative follows Walter's struggle to find his father and to penetrate the mystery of his behavior.)

It's not primarily the sense of character, though, that lies at the root of this book's distinction; it's the ceaseless reaching for broader contexts, more comprehensive views—the push for a vision of interrelationships, the obvious impatience with self-preoccupation. As *World's End* interweaves, fugally, the lives of long-gone peasants, slaves, landholders and displaced Indians with those of last season's activists, wantons, *rentiers* and factory hands, we're conscious of recurrences and echoes. Past and present, sharply separated by the chapter structure, are fused in motifs and unstressed parallels. The themes that emerge aren't riveting when stated abstractly. We knew before *World's End* that, in many ages, the powerful have done poorly at conjoining power with remorse, have been incapable either of seeing their opposition as other than rude, crude and lawless or of remembering the rude, crude, lawless acts by which their own ascendancy was gained. Neither is it news that, in many ages, the powerless, blinded by rage and uneducated into the complexity of things, have settled for stereotypes of their masters, asked impossible heroism of themselves and failed their best hopes.

But themes like these are deepened and freshened when they are developed in a narrative that shuttles between epochs usually understood as discontinuous. We grasp in new terms their connection with the American social and political experiment. We see their pertinence to the succession of conflicts involving flimflammed Indians, manorial lords, spies, patriots, Stalinist *provocateurs,* enemies of "the Communist-inspired, anti-American, long-haired hippie outrage." The continual summons is toward unaccustomed speculation—thoughts about permanence and change, forces and processes that seem independent of persons. The ultimate effect is to move us beyond ourselves.

And it is, of course, history—that "peculiar call of the spirit," as G. M. Trevelyan termed it—that holds the key to the accomplishment. When religious commitments collapse, science deflates itself, and political illusions are universally seen through, history may well be the only call anybody's spirit can heed, the only resource left for slaking our hunger for seriousness. But what an immense resource! This is what one feels, engrossed in Mr. Boyle's evocations of riot, insurrection and the days between. *World's End* is a smashing good book, the peak achievement thus far in a career that seems now to have no clear limits. (p. 53)

Benjamin DeMott, *"Ghost Ships on the Hudson," in* The New York Times Book Review, *September 27, 1987, pp. 1, 52-3.*

An excerpt from *World's End*

Next thing Walter knew he was on his bike (bike: it was a horse, a fire-breathing, shit-kicking terror,

a big top-of-the-line Norton Commando that could jerk the fillings out of your molars), the washed-out, bird-bedeviled dawn flashing by on either side of him like the picture on a black-and-white portable with a bad horizontal hold. He was invincible, immortal, impervious to the hurts and surprises of the universe, coming out of Peterskill at ninety-five. The road cut left, and he cut with it; there was a dip, a rise—he clung to the machine like a new coat of paint. One hundred. One-oh-five. One-ten. He was heading home, the night a blur—had he passed out in the back of Hector's car on the way back from Dunderberg?—heading home to the bed of an existential hero above the kitchen in his adoptive parents' clapboard bungalow. There was dew on the road. It wasn't quite light yet.

And then all at once, as if a switch had been thrown inside his head, he was slowing down—whatever it was that had got him up to a hundred and ten had suddenly left him. He let off on the throttle, took it down—ninety, eighty, seventy—only mortal after all. Up ahead on the right (he barely noticed it, had been by it a thousand times, ten thousand) was a historical marker, blue and yellow, a rectangle cut out of the gloom. What was it—iron? Raised letters, yellow—or gold—against the blue background. Poor suckers probably made them down at Sing Sing or something. There was a lot of history in the area, he supposed, George Washington and Benedict Arnold and all of that, but history really didn't do much for him. Fact is, he'd never even read the inscription on the thing.

Never even read it. For all he knew, it could have commemorated one of Lafayette's bowel movements or the discovery of the onion; it was nothing to him. Something along the side of the road, that's all: Slow Down, Bad Curve, oak tree, billboard, historical marker, driveway. Even now he wouldn't have given it a second glance if it weren't for the shadow that suddenly shot across the road in front of him. That shadow (it was nothing recognizable—no rabbit, opossum, coon or skunk—just a shadow) caused him to jerk the handlebars. And that jerk caused him to lose control. Yes. And that loss of control put him down for an instant on the right side, down on the new Dingo boot with the imitation spur strap, put him down before he could straighten up and made him hit that blue-and-yellow sign with a jolt that was worthy of a major god.

Next afternoon, when he woke to the avocado walls, crackling intercom and astringent reek of the Peterskill Hospital's East Wing, he was feeling no pain. It was a puzzle: he should have been. He examined his forearms, wrapped in gauze, felt something tugging at his ribs. For a moment he panicked—Hesh and Lola were there, murmuring blandishments and words of amelioration, and Jessica too, tears in her eyes. Was he dead? Was that it? But then the drugs took over and his eyelids fell to of their own accord.

"Walter," Lola was whispering as if from a great distance. "Walter—are you all right?"

He tried to pin it down, put it all together again. Mardi. Hector. Pompey. The ghost ships. Had he climbed the anchor chain? Had he actually done that? He remembered the car, Pompey's wasted face, the way Mardi's paper dress had begun to dissolve from contact with her wet skin. He had his hands on her breasts and Hector's were moving between her legs. She was giggling. And then it was dawn. Birds going at it. The parking lot out back of the Elbow. "Yeah," he croaked, opening his eyes again, "I'm all right."

Lola was biting her lip. Hesh wouldn't look him in the eye. And Jessica—soft, powdered, sweet-smelling Jessica—looked as if she'd just run back-to-back marathons and finished last. Both times.

"What happened?" Walter asked, stirring his legs.

"It's okay," Hesh said.

"It's okay," Lola said. "It's okay."

It was then that he looked down at the base of the bed, looked down at the sheet where his left foot poked up like the centerpole of a tent, and at the sad collapsed puddle of linen where his right foot should have been.

RICHARD EDER

With his exhilarating sprinter's gait and a serious ability to surprise us at 200 and 500 yards, T. Coraghessan Boyle has run a five-miler with mixed results.

World's End is a complex historical cycle, flavored with an original pungency, set in the old Dutch country of New York's Hudson Valley. Three families, going back respectively to a powerful patroon, to one of the patroon's tenant farmers, and to the displaced Kitchawank Indians, play out their bitter and ironic entanglements over 300 years.

The characters—oppressors and oppressed, betrayers and betrayed, seducers, rebels and holy fools—appear and reappear, cast in roles that repeat themselves over the generations. When young Walter Van Brunt turns his back on his family's leftist traditions in the 1960s and goes to work for a wealthy descendant of the Van Wart patroons, he re-enacts a betrayal by Wouter Van Brunt in the 1720s. The half-Indian Jeremy Mohonk, whom Wouter denounced for defying the Van Warts, was hanged; in 1931, another Jeremy Mohonk begins 15 hellish years in Sing Sing after attacking another Van Wart. Wouter smolders when he catches sight of the smoldering Saskia Van Wart; Walter ignites when he meets the pyromaniac Mardi Van Wart 10 generations later.

A sweeping historical saga? Not at all. Boyle is attempting something more ambitious and more difficult. The present of his story is the more or less recognizable present: suburban adultery and real estate, counterculture kids, sex, drugs and an instance or two of growing up. It is invaded by the past; by ghosts, first of all—more or less literal ones—and then by stories. Telling what happened among the Van Warts, the Van Brunts and the Mohonks in the 1680s, the 1720s and then—skipping way forward—in the 1920s and 1940s, these stories are conveyed directly to the reader, largely over the heads of the present-day characters. But all this recurring and ghost-ridden past aims to give them a darkling and often comical dimension of fatality.

Boyle is a joyful and sinuous storyteller who revels in his own momentum and makes us revel in it as well. His fatality is an intriguing device that gives an edge to the stories for a while, but eventually proves cumbersome and unwieldy.

The stories go backward, forward and sideways. . . .

Boyle writes with energy and wit. His passion for the history, geography and legends of the New York Dutch is infectious. He has an ability, rare nowadays, to convey the beauty and magic of a mountain, a river, a forest. Place names and odd phrases exhilarate him. A lively account of a fight between Jeremias Van Brunt and his father-in-law is further lit up by the Dutch-Indian term for the young man's ball-and-chain weapon. It is a Weckquaesgeek Pogamoggin.

The writer uses language with color and precision. Of the blighted Katrinchee, he writes that her mind was "a butterfly touched with frost." Truman Van Brunt, estranged in his heart from his family, would "come to bed like a man with an arrow in his back." An 18th-Century Van Wart retainer, getting off his horse, "smoothes the seat of his sweat-soaked and tumultuous pantaloons."

The historical cross sections come alive with their detail and tensions. Boyle is particularly good at his eccentrics: an old Indian messenger, a present-day hippie who lives in the woods and emerges as something of a hero. He has more difficulty with the larger characters who bear the burden of his theme.

[Depeyster Van Wart] has one striking foible—he eats dirt that he carries around with him in an envelope—but he is an abstract and essentially uninteresting villain. So are his Van Wart forebears. His daughter, Mardi, is a routine temptress. Villainy aside, Walter's father is unfocused; there seems to be very little concealed in his murkiness. His confrontation scene with Walter comes out anticlimactically; his revelations have been foreshadowed. Walter himself, whose initial indeterminacy is alluring, gets thinner and less plausible as he goes along.

In truth, he and most of the other present-day characters are not only invaded by the past but flattened by it. Or rather, they are flattened by the awkwardness of having three centuries of fatality come to a point in them. They are not developed with sufficient strength and profundity to bear it. Fate rarely seems like something of their own; it works upon them with gear-clashing and lever-strain.

> *Richard Eder, "Kismet Comedy from New Holland to New York," in* Los Angeles Times Book Review, *October 11, 1987, p. 3.*

CYNTHIA COTTS

T. Coraghessan Boyle has always impressed me: he's erudite, wicked, hip, and funny as hell. In *World's End,* his fifth book of fiction, he pulls the act off again, juggling a thousand gems with kaleidoscopic control. So what if he drops a few on the floor? . . .

[*World's End*] is ambitious, maybe too much so. By choosing to write historical fiction, Boyle gets to show off his prowess as storyteller and narrative engineer. He sends his haunted main character on a search, opening the possibilities of a mystery story à la Poe or Borges, and toys with political comment, invoking a real riot between Communist and fascist forces in 1949. But his long suit, and the one he should stick with, is comic, contemporary realism. The best scenes take place in the '60s, when he gets down to lampooning lifestyles of the left and right.

The '60s cast includes Walter Van Brunt, a fatherless 22-year-old given to grisly hallucinations; his wife, Jessica, a tall, angular, well-bred biologist; and his friend, Tom Crane, a glorious eccentric who drops out to live in a secluded shack. Walter's mind is twisted by Mardi Van Wart—a crazy, luscious hippie who lures him to the shipwrecks on the Hudson at midnight—but it's twisted worse by her father, Depeyster. (The old man is CEO of the local foundry and a John Bircher from way back.)

Boyle has such fondness for these folks that he can both make fun of them and make them likable. In a typical scene, Van Wart has opened his house to visitors and is showing them the wall built by his ancestors in 1650, when his family shows up: a lithe wife in deerskin and leggings, a nubile daughter in leopard print bikini. The embarrassment of the patrician is priceless.

As is the druggie's zeal. Tom has just fixed Jessica a scrumptious tofu dinner in his shack when Mardi bursts in with a gift. "It was, she assured them, the best, the purest, the most potent, unrefined, mind-numbing, groovy and auspicious hash they'd ever partake in the glory of."

Boyle writes exquisite sentences, as always, mixing the soaring arcs of high diction with chilled-out patois. The facility of his tone and pacing is evident throughout, as when, ensconced in his study, Depeyster Van Wart is taken by surprise. He "caught a glimpse of scarves and feathers and headbands, hair matted like a dog's, the stuporous troglodytic expression of the dropout, burnout, and drug abuser: his daughter was home."

But it's the metaphors that steal the show, always tailored to context. An Indian medicine man looks "like a dandelion gone to seed," and a hippie's hands flutter "like flushed quail." The river lies "flat and still as hammered pewter" while the sky looks "dead, caught up on the mountains like a skin stretched out to dry." A woman's lips have the "faintest taste of wild onion and rose hips."

Boyle is hot on ornament. Episodes devoted to Dutch settlers tap into the culture of the Netherlands; his descriptions recall 17th century Dutch painting—dramatically lit tableaux of daily life, tinged with comedy and pathos—and he sprinkles the text with Dutch words. He sends up types—the burgher, the maiden, and the fop—who, he suggests, haven't changed much since Renaissance ferment first produced the middle class.

As chapters alternate between the 17th and 20th centuries, certain characters and events repeat themselves. The rosy-cheeked young *huis vrouw* becomes an angelic career woman, the miscegenating wench a mischievous hippie chick. Over the generations, two young Walters think of their fathers as heroes, two fathers turn their sons into cowards. Betrayal of trust becomes as much a genetic trait for the Van Brunts as revenge is for the Mohonks and abuse of power is for the Van Warts.

Boyle's main theme seems to be cyclical history. That would explain why Walter, a self-appointed existentialist hero, falls into a role imposed on him by fate. Fate brings the ghosts and goblins of the Hudson Valley round and round through the generations. But the apparitions that tail Walter don't lead him from nihilism to a more transcendental worldview, they merely spur on his search for a father. As with the existentialism and cyclical history in this novel, the magical elements often stand in where motivation is lacking.

Boyle's leading ladies tend to be predictable, either good wives or spacy sexpots. This isn't just the sexism bred in male academics. The women are symptomatic of a more central cop-out: when Boyle constructs such tricky narratives as the one in *World's End,* he ends up having to manipulate characters, so their behavior conforms with the intended outcome. If he hadn't been torn between the conventions of the mock-epic and the realist chronicle, Boyle might have written a more revealing ending. He might have called Tom Crane back for an encore. As it is, Walter's search for a lost father leads only to flat, unenlightened despair. That despair could have had real tragic resonance, instead of the joky kind old Van Wart imagines for Walter: "It was a tragedy. It really was. It was Sophocles. It was Shakespeare." In the next book, I hope Boyle will either isolate the perfect pitch of his burlesque, or train his voice not to crack on high drama.

Cynthia Cotts, in a review of "World's End," in VLS, *No. 60, November, 1987, p. 3.*

JOHN CALVIN BATCHELOR

T. Coraghessan Boyle has the gift of gab, and in [*World's End*] he displays a talent so effortlessly satirical and fluid that it suggests an image of the author at a crowded inn of wicked wits in a tale-telling fight for best space at the hearth.

World's End is a rollicking and dark fable of the Hudson River valley stretching from its Dutch foundation to the American contretemps during the Vietnam war. It is written with a voice that can compete with Swift, Byron, Irving, Twain and all those anonymous Irish liars.

The story begins in the summer of 1968 in the make-believe village of Peterskill, N.Y. (Boyle is a native of Peekskill), deep within the haunted fens where the mountains find the Hudson. Walter Truman Van Brunt, a Cornell graduate who is awaiting the draft at the local foundry, is celebrating his 22nd birthday with drink, drugs and contrariness. Rather than go straight home to his foster family and his beloved Jessica, he lingers at a tavern with rascals. Soon, in a haze, he is swimming into the Hudson along with the luscious Mardi Van Wart, the wealthy daughter of local gentry. Mardi dares him to climb aboard one of the ghost fleet of freighters anchored since the Second World War near West Point. . . . Walter complies, only to encounter his grandmother's ghost and other demiurges; he also suffers what he calls "an attack of history."

Panicky Walter flees to his motorcycle, presently missing a curve and rudely finding one of those roadside historical markers. . . .

[As it turns out] Walter has been attacked by history and lost a foot. What follows is a literary dig into the mysterious rise and ruin of Peterskill. There are no accidents in Boyle's tales; fate is a smirking arbiter.

In alternating chapters, sewn together by the author's jocular tongue and not a little of what could be called love of the Lilliputian in characters, Boyle investigates what has laid footloose Walter low. The trail begins with the Kitchawanks, the

Native American tribe who first thrived thereabouts. They are . . . introduced to capitalism by the poltroonish Dutch, who matter-of-factly steal everything.

Enter the patroonish Van Warts in the mid-17th century, reaching out from their roost in Haarlem to lay claim to the land and to subcontract to tenant farmers. Thereupon come the strong-backed and weak–minded Van Brunts, who plow land suspected of being cursed; and the Cranes, who lurch toward pedagogy and school-making.

The Kitchawanks are not absent, just disowned. They circle the white slaves gingerly until one of their number, Mohonk, is called upon by the luckless Van Warts to rid them of a strange mind affliction that would have delighted Washington Irving. Planting the land has made Harmanus Van Brunt ravenous and he is eating himself and his family to death. Kitchawank magic prevails for a moment, but finally the Van Brunts are shattered: the daughter has run away to produce a vengeful half-breed named Jeremias Mohonk, and the son is left footless and Van Wart-hating.

Three centuries later, the same players occupy the same cursed ground and inescapable stations. Depeyster Van Wart is a modish, 51-year-old, right-wing Yalie who would dine with the devil for a male heir. The Van Brunts are a shattered family, with father runaway and suspect as having betrayed the town during a riot in 1949 and mother dead of grief. The Cranes are represented by the draft-dodging and ecology-minded Tom Crane. And the Kitchawanks are reduced to one unrepentant, fiftyish convict named Jeremy, who has sexual appetites that include the mistress Van Wart.

At the close all is hilarious and cruel. One is left in that crowded inn waiting for this great banshee of a liar to begin again.

John Calvin Batchelor, "Hudson River Frolic," in Book World—The Washington Post, *November 1, 1987, p. 4.*

JOHN CLUTE

There has always been iron in the soul of T. Coraghessan Boyle, a punitive grimness that deformed much of his early work. Novels like ***Budding Prospects*** . . . bore messages of determinism and spiritual penury that sorted ill with the outgoing, rambunctious inflation of the tales they told. Only in some of his excellent short stories did he seem capable of expressing the harsh Calvinism of his underlying vision without arbitrary jerks of the rein. The publication of ***World's End,*** his third novel, has therefore been awaited with some apprehension.

It must be admitted that a manic bonelessness does mar some few pages of this enormous book, and that Boyle does at times insist too stridently on his feckless protagonists' lack of any

genuine autonomy; but these are trivial blemishes. As a whole, ***World's End*** is an integrated piece of storytelling, balanced and poised and dire. For its characters, it is a crushing machine, which limns a world without exit; nowhere in the small town of Peterskill on the Hudson River, where the action is set, does any moment of hilarity or joy or love do more than strengthen the grip of the past.

In 1968, haunted by the ghosts of his mangled family and dizzy with drink, young Walter Van Brunt crashes his motorcycle into a historical marker next to the home of the Van Warts, who have dominated the Peterskill stretch of the Hudson since the time of the first Dutch settlers. He loses his right foot (and his bearings) in the accident, but fails to recognize any significance in the first amputation, for he conceives of himself as utterly free, a latter-day Meursault from Camus's *L'Etranger.* By the end of the novel, however, young Walter will have been almost literally drawn and quartered in a series of revelations and betrayals which eerily replicate the events commemorated on the marker that, in taking his foot, hogties him to the bitter ground.

Beneath his foot lies an intricate history. In 1663, the first Van Brunt in America arrives in what is not yet Peterskill, and becomes a tenant farmer on lands owned by the Dutch patroon, the first Van Wart. This indenture of the Van Brunts becomes a servitude so deeply ingrained as to seem almost genetic. One Van Brunt after another comes grotesquely to grief against the cold realities of a world based on ownership; and it seems inevitable that, thirty years on, a third-generation Van Brunt will bungle a useless revolt and betray his collaborators to the gallows, and that a historical marker will eventually be erected at the point where character became destiny.

The two strands of story occupy alternate chapters throughout ***World's End,*** but it is the seventeenth-century Peterskill that Boyle brings most vividly to life, so surefootedly that at points the book seems almost nonchalant. . . .

By tying the fate of his hippie-like protagonist to a dark reading of the real shape of American history, Boyle has freed himself from the chill spite of his early work, the sense that he tended to create characters on whom he could wreak revenge for behaving in ways he could not himself explain. However seriously one takes the predestination that shapes his new novel, there can be no doubting its power and grievous urgency as a principle. For all the sweep and clatter of the tale, for all the *grand guignol* exuberance which undercuts its doctrinal base, a grave compassionate calm resides in the telling of ***World's End,*** the sense of a creator finally at home in his work.

John Clute, "Van Warts and All," in The Times Literary Supplement, *No. 4456, August 26- September 1, 1988, p. 927.*

Peter Carey
Oscar and Lucinda
Booker Prize: Fiction

Australian novelist and short story writer.

Oscar and Lucinda (1987) delineates the odd romance between Carey's eccentric title characters, who are drawn together by their passion for gambling. The novel begins with Oscar's childhood in rural nineteenth-century Devon, England, where he lives with his father, a renowned naturalist and a preacher in the fundamentalist Plymouth Brethren sect. Critics noted similarities between this strained father-son relationship and that recounted by Edmund Gosse in his spiritual autobiography, *Father and Son* (1907). Gambling on what he believes is a sign from God, the adolescent Oscar reluctantly rebels against the teachings of his father and joins the Anglican Church. Later, at Oxford University, Oscar relies on earnings from wagering on horseraces to pay for his living expenses and tuition. The narrative also relates events in Lucinda's sheltered childhood in rural Australia, which ends at age eighteen with her mother's death. She uses her inheritance to purchase a glass factory and relocate to Sydney. Lucinda's brusque country manners and active management of her factory make her an outcast in Sydney, and gambling provides her only social outlet. After failing to engage in a more active social life during a stay in England, Lucinda meets Oscar on her return by boat to Australia, where he plans to begin a ministry. Oscar and Lucinda become involved in a strange, tragicomic love affair beset by frequent farcical misunderstandings, culminating with Oscar undertaking a horrific river journey through the Australian outback with materials for building an elaborate glass church.

Carey's expansive narrative is composed of more than one-hundred short chapters gradually unfolding plot details, odd bits of information, direct addresses to the reader, and frequent use of glass and water imagery. The narrative also features a plethora of well-developed minor characters and authentic descriptions of nineteenth-century London, Sydney, Oxford, and rural New South Wales. Hermione Lee commented: "Like Carey's contemporary historical fabulists of the post-colonial world—Salman Rushdie, Timothy Mo, and Michael Ondaatje—he can plunge in freely and make new shapes out of a great mass of rich material."

Carey's first three works display some of the same features for which *Oscar and Lucinda* received praise. *The Fat Man in History* (1974), a collection of short stories, and the novels *Bliss* (1981) and *Illywhacker* (1985) are inventive mixtures of the fantastic and the ordinary rendered in an exuberant yet controlled prose style. In these works, Carey satirizes bourgeois social values and explores through comedic devices the illusory nature of reality. As in *Bliss* and *Illywhacker,* Carey endeavors in *Oscar and Lucinda* to reimagine Australian history. Thus, these works explore gaps between the "official" history of Australia, which recounts the heroic efforts made by white settlers to civilize the outback, and the aboriginal history which was subsumed and virtually obliterated. With

Oscar and Lucinda, according to Francis King, Carey "confirms his position as the finest of Australian novelists to appear since Patrick White."

(See also *CLC,* Vol. 40 and *Contemporary Authors,* Vol. 123.)

PETER CAREY [INTERVIEW WITH **EDMUND WHITE**]

[Edmund White]: *At this point I don't think any American writer would feel he or she could be or should be the national novelist. Do you feel the obligation to forge the conscience of your race?*

[Peter Carey]: I certainly felt that obligation in ***Illywhacker.*** I felt the country still had to be invented—even seen. We Australians haven't been invented yet. But this situation irritates me. Who has to worry about what it means to be English, or Chinese? But it's also an advantage. We don't have the dead weight of history pressing down on us. We're free and stupid enough to think we can do almost anything. It's only 200 years since the invasion, after all.

In your last two books, **Illywhacker** *and* **Oscar and Lucinda,** *you manage to touch on key questions, such as the domination of the Aboriginal people, the violence of the outback, the national cringe before European culture, the strength of Australian women and so on. How programmatic are your books?*

Certainly in *Oscar and Lucinda* I began that process of day-dreaming, producing a book by thinking about the soon-to-be-discarded Christian culture coming in and destroying the Aboriginal landscape—that was my starting point. . . .

Your books are full of a curiosity about how things work—how glass is made, how buildings are constructed, about how wheat was harvested in the 19th century. What I like is how the factuality of your fiction is juxtaposed with the fairy-tale atmosphere. Is that a conscious strategy?

I've always been interested in how the physical world of the story changes in order to reflect a change in a character. For instance, I have a short story in which someone becomes a tow truck. If you want such a transformation to take place, then the reader must be able to believe in the reality of the physical world.

But more important, if I investigate how things might really be, or have been, this pursuit can lead to great richness. For instance, *Oscar and Lucinda* was really born because I had the idea of a church floating down a river. I needed a prefabricated church. I knew there was a Victorian technology of cast iron. I asked a friend who's an architect how it was done and he said most such buildings at the time were made of glass. He asked me, "Why not have a glass church?"—and that led to the central image of the novel, a glass church floating on water. By pursuing how things really work I was handed this wonderful gift. How things really work is always more interesting than something one might invent. . . .

How do you research your books?

Well, I try to find corners for the action, because life does take place in corners. For instance, to write a scene in *Oscar and Lucinda* I went to Devon for a day. I found a pebble. I saw a stream in which Oscar could wash out his milk pail. I took notes about the colours. Of course the function of these details is often to slow down the gallop of the headlong narrative. I also read a lot. For that section I read Edmund Gosse's *Father and Son* and Philip Gosse's *A Naturalist's Rambles on the Devonshire Coast*. But I'm such a bad scholar, I feel like a man with a white cane knocking into knowledge. (p. 8)

Peter Carey, in an interview with Edmund White in The Sunday Times, *London, March 20, 1988, pp. 8-9.*

HERMIONE LEE

A glass church, constructed out of segments, held together by a cast-iron frame, measuring 50 feet long and 22 feet six inches wide, and weighing 12 tons, floats on a barge down a river in New South Wales in 1865. It is watched from the jungly banks, with amazement, by hidden aborigines and drunken colonials. Sitting inside it is a red-headed clergyman from Devon, overcome by aquaphobia. He has reached this point, after a horrifying journey through the interior, because of a

bet made with the woman he loves, whom he has completely misunderstood and will never see again.

The glass church is like [*Oscar and Lucinda*], a prodigious and enchanting invention, a gamble, a spectacular 'folly', a most unlikely *tour de force*. Like the church, the novel is built of segments—short chapters, bits of lives—which at long last interlock. Like the church, it is heavy—a great, fat, slow book, freighted down with the cast-iron of fact and history—but also light: fantastical, playful, buoyant.

The lives built of this fictional glass are, appropriately, both frail and tough. *Oscar and Lucinda* involves a national history and a family legacy—Oscar is the narrator's great-grandfather—and is much concerned with inheritance. But it is also a very peculiar love story, between two fanatical, unaccommodating misfits. Lucinda Leplastrier is the daughter of a strong-willed English feminist, a friend of George Eliot (not very convincingly characterised) who has turned herself, after her gentle, curious husband's death, into an Australian farmer. The mother has given Lucinda 'one substantial gift—that she did not expect anything small from her life.' Orphaned at 18 [Lucinda] invests her inheritance in a glassworks, and shocks the narrow society of Victorian Sydney by consorting indiscriminately with clergymen and gamblers, and refusing to act like an unprotected girl.

Coming towards her along an unlikely trajectory is an equally passionate gambler, the Rev. Oscar Hopkins, whom the Church Missionary Society has sent out to bring the word of Christ to New South Wales. Oscar, pale, nervy, eloquent, odd, is the son of a famous naturalist, a member of the fundamentalist Plymouth Brethren. (The painful comedy of his childhood is lifted, with ingenuity and acknowledgments, from Edmund Gosse's marvellous autobiography *Father and Son*.) Oscar has rejected his father's fanaticism for the dismal training of Anglican foster parents, but, at Oriel, led astray by a day at the races, he has discovered his ruling vice. His deadly serious, absurd attempt to reconcile his addiction with his vocation ('Our whole faith is a wager . . . We must gamble every instant of our allotted span') sends him to the colonies, and thus to the coincidence of his meeting with Lucinda.

Their strange affinity develops through a series of marvellously extravagant, intense, tragi-comic scenes. . . . Milling around them, with lavish vigour, are clergymen, businessmen, explorers, landladies, gamblers, glassblowers, all vertiginously detailed and emphatic.

The novel's virtue is to make us mind, tenderly, about this awkward and ill-starred pair, even though they are brought so artificially together, and made to speak ('on my behalf it would be best if we did not discuss the matter') in stiff Victorian phrases. At the same time *Oscar and Lucinda* makes a ferocious caricature of Australian history, doing for nineteenth-century British Colonial influence what *Illywhacker* did for the country's twentieth-century dependence on America and Japan. Like Carey's contemporary historical fabulists of the post-colonial world—Salman Rushdie, Timothy Mo, Michael Ondaatje—he can plunge in freely and make new shapes out of a great mass of rich material.

But, like them, he must also find a way of treating terrible horror and violence. The attempt to Christianise what is 'not a Christian landscape at all' begins as a comedy, but ends in bitter outrage, as the white story is at last rewritten from the point of view (noticeably missing in *Illywhacker*) of the 'blacks'. The two narratives are irreconcilable. . . . Carey's passion for detail makes itself felt. . . . He has a wonderful curiosity about things and their workings: phosphorescence, glass, celluloid, betting systems, ocean liners, clay pots, ink-mixing. . . . But, like glass, things seem not to be solid: they metamorphose as you look at them. . . . So the novel, improbably triumphant, keeps floating off from dense realities to airy play.

Hermione Lee, "Duo Down Under," in The Observer, *March 27, 1988, p. 42.*

D. J. ENRIGHT

Peter Carey's [*Oscar and Lucinda*] is in the traditional, Victorian manner, long and densely populated, rich in description and detail, somewhat Dickensian in characterisation or, in its ecclesiastical passages, not remote from Trollope (though cast in Australian paths rougher than those of Barsetshire). Compared with Carey's last novel, *Illywhacker,* it is a sober book, blessedly so perhaps, but spiritedly sober, and—if I may risk damning with strong praise—it makes solid and enjoyable reading.

Oscar Hopkins is a weird young cleric, a refugee from Devon and the Plymouth Brethren . . . , seen variously as 'a queer bird, a stork, a mantis, a gawk' and as the possessor of a heart-shaped face, 'like an angel by Dante Gabriel Rossetti', Lucinda Leplastrier is an orphan with a modest inheritance; her mother was something of a bluestocking, a friend of George Eliot ('It would chill you, Marian, to walk down a street in Parramatta'), and her father a farmer in New South Wales.

Both of them give offence; Lucinda by her wilful, unladylike behaviour (she hates crinolines and silly hats, favouring bloomers—a rational but not a respectable costume), and Oscar, a Myshkin-like figure, because of the unpredictable mixture of feebleness and fervency in him. He bets on the horses to make money for the greater glory of God, and to pay for his passage to Australia, in the year 1865. Lucinda gambles too, but in her case it's for the sheer excitement of it. . . .

Neither is made for amorous tricks, and their love, hemmed about by shyness, misunderstanding and hurt, is 'edgy, anxious, sometimes angry'. A rare kiss carries a stronger charge than a dozen contorted copulations in today's currency. What could well be the atmosphere of New South Wales in the mid-19th century is rendered adroitly: the nervous snobbishness, the pressure to conform outwardly, the hardheaded business bustle, the casual contempt for 'the blacks'. . . .

The book is firm yet uncensorious in its characterisation, the good never improbably good, the bad less than vile. Despite the fears aroused in us for the two outsiders, a quiet and largely affable humour is ubiquitous. Lucinda's visits to the Prince Rupert's Glassworks are unwelcome, for the gob-gatherer gets the gob wrong and the second blower's walls come out uneven. 'They are poor ignorant lads, and easily distracted by a lady,' the foreman tells her. When she reminds him that she is the proprietor, that it is her business, he answers: 'I know, mum, but it be our craft, mum, you see. It be our *craft.*'

There is a degree of what has been termed 'data overload' in *Oscar and Lucinda,* but Carey's informativeness is never positively dull, and one theme running through the novel is the thirst for knowledge, especially invigorating in these days of professionalism and the feeling that whatever remains to be discovered or invented is likely to work to our detriment. Only at the end does overt violence erupt. We could hardly expect a happy outcome to the story of Oscar and Lucinda, but we might have hoped for a more peaceable one. Oscar cannot endure water, and hence [a] glass church must be transported, in crates and by bullock carts, through unmapped territory, the party led by a crazed clerk who aspires to fame as an explorer. Yet the phantasmagoric trek has an unearthly power, suggestive of a farcically conducted quest or pilgrimage. Like any honourable gambler, Oscar must pay his debts. 'Give me a hard journey, dear God.'

D. J. Enright, "People in Glass Churches," in The Listener, *Vol. 119, No. 3056, March 31, 1988, p. 29.*

GEOFF DYER

One of Peter Carey's best stories, **"The Chance",** tells of a disintegrating society dominated by the Genetic Lottery. For 2,000 Inter-Galactic dollars, anyone can enter the lottery and emerge with a new body and age but with memories more or less intact.

The outcome is random: the narrator of the story has ended up with the big, broken body of an ageing street-fighter. . . . Something similar has happened to Peter Carey.

He built his reputation in Australia in the '70s with his masterly short stories and consolidated it with a first novel *Bliss* (1981). He made it big—in every sense—in 1985 with the 600 pages of *Illywhacker,* which was shortlisted for the Booker [Prize]. *Oscar and Lucinda* is almost as long. The great strength of a story like **"The Chance"** was the way Carey packed 20 pages with as much inventiveness as you find in the average novel. In a sense, then, he was always bursting at the seams. His stories felt like glimpses of a much larger imaginative world and, in the last two novels, aided by some agile softwear, he has thrown the doors wide open. It is as if he has gone through a *generic* lottery and ended up with the intimidating bulk of a Victorian novelist.

For the first 400 pages *Oscar and Lucinda* reads like a cross between Dickens and Edmund Gosse, between *Father and Son* and *Dombey and Son;* for the last hundred it is like [Patrick White's] *Voss* in the style of a quietly benign illywhacker (White and son?). Oscar's father is a member of the Plymouth brethren and, like Edmund, the growing boy is overwhelmed by the sinfulness of virtually everything. He defects to the Anglican church and goes up to Oxford where he becomes a priest and a compulsive gambler. In 1865, after Oxford, he takes a boat to Australia and *en route* meets Lucinda, a lonely strong-willed young woman who shares Oscar's passion for gambling and has just acquired a glassworks in Sydney. Their friendship is choked both by their own shyness and by the scandal it provokes. . . .

These are the bare bones of a story which takes pride in its limitless powers of incidental accumulation. Typically the short chapters begin midway through a scene and gradually, like someone walking back up a downward escalator, make their way back to the beginning. Alternatively we begin in the wings and watch new characters . . . make their way towards the centre stage where they will participate briefly in the main action before it is suspended once again. The characters are halted in mid-stride, mid-gesture; scenes are suspended in mid-crisis as everything makes its way jerkily towards everything else.

While this makes the book frustrating to read, it does ensure that every sentence is animated by the rhythm of Lucinda's exasperated passion and Oscar's stick-limbed awkwardness. . . .

An artist is usually someone who develops material in such a way that it generates a principle of self-ordering that is also, simultaneously, an active agent of self-editing. In Carey's case, however, as he has matured as an artist so the potential for self-ordering in his material has become increasingly identified with its capacity for endless self-expansion. With **Illywhacker** he hit upon an idea and a form that enabled him to wander at whim across Australian geography and history. In **Oscar and Lucinda** he has all but abolished the distinction between narrative progression and sideways expansion.

Lucinda is both touched and infuriated by Oscar; likewise Carey's novel tries the reader's patience as much as it entertains. Appropriately, then, you leave this book with feelings similar to those experienced at the end of a long and not entirely successful love affair: for the last year it might have been more trouble than it was worth but, once the end is in sight, you look back on all the good things and almost wish it could go on longer. But, mostly, you wish things had turned out differently.

Geoff Dyer, "The Long, Long Love Affair," in New Statesman, *Vol. 115, No. 2975, April 1, 1988, p. 28.*

An excerpt from *Oscar and Lucinda*

There was a small roofed section on Mr Myer's boat, but it seemed that this was more intended for the shelter of the engine than the driver and, in any case, it was decorated with so many oily cans and rags that [Lucinda] thought it better to pretend an affection for the bracing air beside the cauliflowers.

A thin sheet of cloud began to materialize in the sky—the smoke from burning hedgerows on farms along the banks—and it was soon so general that the river, in response, assumed a pearly yellow sheen. She had never been on a boat before. She had never been to Sydney. She sat on a rough packing case in the bow, her hands in her lap, shivering. . . .

The river journey was picturesque, with so many pretty farms along its banks. Lucinda could not look at them without feeling angry. She looked straight ahead, shivering. It was cold, of course, but not only cold that caused this agitation. There was a jitteriness, a sort of stage fright about her future which was not totally unpleasant. She dramatized herself. And even while she felt real pain, real grief, real loneliness, she also looked at herself from what she imagined was Sol Myer's perspective, and then she was a heroine at the beginning of an adventure.

She did not know that she was about to see the glassworks and that she would, within the month, have purchased them. And yet she would not have been surprised. This was within the range of her expectations, for whatever harm Elizabeth had done her daughter, she had given her this one substantial gift—that she did not expect anything small from her life.

It would be easy to see this purchase—half her inheritance splurged—on the first thing with a FOR SALE sign tacked to it—as nothing more than the desire to unburden herself of all this money, and this may be partly true. But the opposite is true as well, i.e., she knew she would need the money to have any sort of freedom. It is better to think about the purchase as a piano manoeuvred up a staircase by ten different circumstances and you cannot say it was one or the other that finally got it there—even the weakest may have been indispensable at that tricky turn on the landing. But of all the shifting forces, there is this one burly factor, this strong and handsome beast, i.e., her previous experience of glass via the phenomenon known as *larmes bataviques* or Prince Rupert's drops.

You need not ask me who is Prince Rupert or what is a *batavique* because I do not know. I have, though, right here beside me as I write (I hold it in the palm of my left hand while the right hand moves to and fro across the page) a Prince Rupert drop—a solid teardrop of glass no more than two inches from head to tail. And do not worry that this oddity, this rarity, was the basis for de la Bastie's technique for toughening glass, or that it led to the invention of safety glass—these are practical matters and shed no light on the incredible attractiveness of the drop itself which you will understand faster if you take a fourteen-pound sledgehammer and try to smash it on a forge. You cannot. This is glass of the most phenomenal strength and would seem, for a moment, to be the fabled unbreakable glass described by the alchemical author of *Mappae Clavicula*. And yet if you put down your hammer and take down your pliers instead—I say "if," I am not recommending it—you will soon see that this is not the fabled glass stone of the alchemists, but something almost as magical. For although it is strong enough to withstand the sledgehammer, the tail can be nipped with a pair of blunt-nosed pliers. It takes a little effort. And once it is done it is as if you have taken out the keystone, removed the linchpin, kicked out the foundations. The whole thing explodes. And where, a moment before, you had unbreakable glass, now you have grains of glass in every corner of the workshop—in your eyes if you are not careful—and what is left in your hand you can crumble—it feels like sugar—without danger.

It is not unusual to see a glass blower or a gatherer scrabbling around in a kibble, arm deep in the oily water, sorting through the little gobs of cast-off cullet, fossicking for Prince Rupert's drop. The drops are made by accident, when a tear of molten glass falls a certain distance and is cooled rapidly.

You will find grown men in the glass business, blowers amongst them, who have handled molten metal all their life, and if you put a Prince Rupert's drop before them, they are like children. I have this one here, in my hands. If you were here beside me in the room, I would find it almost impossible not to demonstrate it to you, to take my pliers and—in a second—destroy it.

So it was a Prince Rupert's drop, shaped like a tear,

but also like a seed, that had a powerful effect on Lucinda Leplastrier. It is the nature of these things.

FRANCIS KING

The narrator of this remarkable novel [*Oscar and Lucinda*]—as it were, Peter Carey himself—is a present-day Australian who looks back on the life, brief in its span but long in its telling, of his great-grandfather. Whether Carey's Oscar Hopkins is intended to be a fictional portrait of Edmund Gosse is a question which one inevitably asks oneself for the first 50 or so pages. . . .

Like Gosse's *Father and Son,* the opening narrative fulfils Gosse's ambition of being 'the record of a struggle between two temperaments, two consciences and almost two epochs'. Written in extremely short paragraphs made up of extremely short sentences, it suggests that already, at the outset of his marathon, the author is short of breath. 'The path was almost at the sea. He did not like that part of the path. . . . He took a new path. It went down through a dark coppice.' As in the case of Ernest Hemingway, one wonders if the author has ever heard of subordinate clauses. But once Oscar has left the narrow coombs of Devon and the crowded streets of Oxford and London for the wide, parched vistas of Australia, Carey's stride lengthens. . . .

Both physically and intellectually Oscar is an unimpressive creature. Nor spiritually is he all that impressive. Lucinda and others see goodness in him, but this is not the positive goodness of a man valiant for truth but the negative goodness of a man who shrinks from falsehood. Herein lies the novel's one fault. One would guess that Carey sees his protagonist as one of fiction's holy fools—best exemplified by Prince Myshkin, Dostoevsky's 'Idiot'. But this man, innocent to the extreme of inanity, so much terrified of the sea that on the voyage out to Australia he cannot bear to look at it, and incapable of declaring his love for Lucinda even though he shares her home and everyone assumes them to be living in adultery, often seems too feeble a mainspring for so complex a fictional mechanism. His intentions are always worthy; and yet, like so many people with worthy intentions, he brings disaster to those around him. . . . (p. 32)

Lucinda, left a rich orphan on the death of her intellectual father and mother (the latter, a feminist convinced that women's emancipation will be achieved through a proliferation of factories, has enjoyed George Eliot's friendship), is a far stronger and more interesting character, used by Carey to demonstrate the difficulties encountered by a woman in what, in the 19th century far more than today, was essentially a man's world. Unlike Oscar's, Lucinda's passion for gambling can be fulfilled only with difficulty. Male gamblers, whether on board the ship out to Australia or in the Chinese-owned dives of Sydney, resent the presence of a woman among them. When Lucinda buys her glass factory, her workmen feel uncomfortable and even resentful if she appears there. Inevitably, her final destiny is to become a champion of women's rights.

United by their passion for gambling and their unavowed passion for each other, Oscar and Lucinda are also united by their obsession with the idea of erecting a glass church—totally impractical in a country so torrid—in a remote corner of Australia. It is the transport of this glass church across previously unsurveyed country, with the constant threat of death from the hostile aborigines, which provides a powerful climax in which the book takes off from realism into symbolic fantasy. This glass church represents a dream at once seductive, useless and dangerous. It destroys many people, among them Oscar himself, and it leaves Lucinda a pauper.

As a piece of historic reconstruction the novel is impressive. Here is a 19th-century Devon even more remote from Oxford, Cambridge and London than Sydney is today; here are the Cremorne Gardens, as Whistler knew them when he painted his Nocturnes; here, above all, is an Australia in which (as Carey cruelly shows in the scenes involving his pretentious Jimmy d'Abbs, born in England as Ditcher Dabbs' boy) high life suggests a group of servants dressing up in their masters' clothes and then aping them in their absence.

As a piece of writing, the novel is no less impressive. It has a Dickensian amplitude; and the energy of its writing—similes and metaphors jostle one another, giving off a baleful phosphorescence, like the medusas of the Indian Ocean about the ship on its way to Australia—is also Dickensian. As in Dickens there are improbabilities, sentimentalities and coincidences of a kind that writers more fastidious but less gifted would avoid. But Carey here confirms his position as the finest of Australian novelists to appear since Patrick White. (pp. 32-3)

Francis King, "Edmund Gosse Goes to Australia," in The Spectator, Vol. 260, No. 8334, April 2, 1988, pp. 32-3.

MARGARET WALTERS

Peter Carey's *Oscar and Lucinda* is a tall story, as elaborate and fantastical as any of the yarns spun by the trickster hero of his last novel *Illywhacker.* For one thing, it's a family history, and we're all of us secretly stunned by the coincidences which have resulted, against the odds, in our existence. And the narrator's account of his great-grandfather, the Reverend Oscar Hopkins, is, by any standards, a weird one. It begins in Devon, with a Christmas pudding snatched from the child's lips by his harsh Plymouth Brethren father. It ends—as a direct consequence of that pudding—half a world away in 1866, as Oscar sits, ill and miserable, in a glass church drifting on barges down a remote Australian river. . . .

Carey, like his two main characters, is a gambler: he has a bet on with the reader. He lays his plots in exuberantly meticulous detail, each segment carefully slotted into its proper place in the slowly emerging pattern, until we're led to that silly, beautiful conceit, the glass church, and find it, like the novel, plausible, irresistible.

Oscar and Lucinda is a long novel, and—like the 19th-century writers Carey is challenging—it's ambitious. Love, death, religion, sin, personal and national identity—they're all in there somewhere. But it's his feeling for physical detail and process that makes Carey's prose sing. Devon lanes, the seedy streets of Notting Hill, race tracks, dog fights, an ocean liner, a glass factory, a Chinese gambling den, a stuffy clerk's room—they're all conjured up in brilliant, solid detail. And even minor characters emerge with hallucinatory clarity. . . .

But at the core of the novel there's an odd, off-beat love story, between a pair of gamblers—the obsessive Oscar and the compulsive Lucinda. Oscar gambles for God; desperately worried that his much-loved but sternly Fundamentalist father was wrong about that Christmas pudding, he starts looking for signs of God's will, throwing stones in a kind of mystic hopscotch. The message from God seems to be that he must leave home (he and his father are both heart-broken) and dump himself and his agonised conscience on the Anglican priest. (This part of the story is adapted, very movingly, from Edmund Gosse's *Father and Son.*) At Oxford, and desperately poor, Oscar is serenely confident God will provide, and so he does, at the race track and dog fights and the card table. A toss of a coin convinced him that God needs him as a missionary to New South Wales: he embraces the notion fervently because he doesn't want to go, being terrified of water.

Carey takes chances with Oscar. He's feeble, febrile, usually filthy; on the last dreadful expedition with the church he suffers agonies because he's too prim to bathe naked with the other men. He's self-absorbed and selfless at the same time, accident-prone, masochistic: a kind of holy fool. But just as he grates intolerably on our nerves, nothing but an 'Odd Bod', as his fellow students claim, 'a queer bird, a stork, a mantis, a gawk', we glimpse him through the loving eyes of his father, his one Oxford friend, or Lucinda, and suddenly, with his heart-shaped face and red hair and green eyes he's a Dante Gabriel Rossetti angel. . . .

Lucinda is one of the novel's triumphs, a complex, difficult, convincingly intelligent woman. . . . Unladylike, childishly impatient of convention, she's as blind, in her way, as Oscar is, and as selfish. But she's a survivor—the end of the book leaves her with nothing at all, but we believe the narrator's claim that her real life is just beginning. Her strength is her adaptability. Refusing to live according to set patterns, contemptuous of pious hypocrisies, she's vulnerable, confused and often unhappy. But she's learned from her mother not to settle for anything small, and she sets out to invent her own life. The instinct that attracts her to glass is sure: she knows

> that glass is a thing in disguise, an actor, is not solid at all, but a liquid, that an old sheet of glass will not only take on a royal and purplish tinge but will reveal its true liquid nature by having grown fatter at the bottom and thinner at the top, that even while it is as fragile as the ice on a Paramatta puddle, it is stronger under compression than Sydney sandstone, that it is invisible, solid, in short, a joyous and paradoxical thing, as good a material as any to build a life from.

Carey is both funny and precise about the difficulties of an independent-minded woman in the crude, prim, pretentious world of Victorian Sydney. . . . [Lucinda] complains bitterly to her mentor, the Reverend Dennis Hasset, about the power of men; when he understandably looks puzzled—he's quite unable to cope with her energy, and her innocent defiance of convention helps to ruin him—she explains impatiently that it's the power 'of *men,* men in a group, men in their certainty, men on a street corner or in a hall. It is like a voodoo.' She finds freedom from that male voodoo in the underworld of gambling, where class and sex count for very little. Guilty about her unearned fortune, she's more excited by losing than by winning: but the real pull is that she feels free of the 'corsets of convention' at the tables, she is 'not compelled to pretend, could be silent without being thought dull, could frown without people being overly solicitous

about one's happiness, could triumph over a man and not have to giggle and simper.'

The love that grows between the pair—on the ocean liner, in a Chinese gambling hell, at Lucinda's glass works—is extravagantly comic, desperately intense, and based on ignorance and misunderstanding. . . . Gamblers to the core, they cut through their uncertainties and pledge their love with an elaborate wager: Oscar sets out, the church he's dreamed packed into boxes dragged by oxen, into the bleak interior.

The ridiculous and terrible journey calls out some of Carey's best writing. His novels, increasingly, seem to be attempts to come to grips with that harsh, intractable land, so resistant to literary vocabulary, its brief history so scarred with violent paradoxes. In *Bliss,* the hero escaped from the corrupt city to the bush, where a man can still build and plant and live idyllically free. In *Illywhacker,* Carey's vision is darker; one of the characters, Leah, earns her living by writing, and though she loves the vivid colours of the townships and small dusty roads, she recognises that they are 'raw optimistic tracks that cut the arteries of an ancient culture before a new one had been born'. She admits sadly that 'it is a black man's country, sharp stones, rocks, sticks, bull ants, flies. We can only move around it like tourists.' In ***Oscar and Lucinda,*** the well-meaning religious tourists are killers. Lucinda recognises the truth when one of her gambling friends, making polite conversation, remarks that they're living in a 'non-Christian landscape'. She's suddenly overwhelmed by childhood memories of the blacks—already being exterminated—she'd once glimpsed by the back creek. 'She was frightened, not that they would hurt her, it was a bigger fear than that. She turned and ran. . . . She felt ghosts here, but not Christian ghosts.' Oscar, of course, is oblivious to the harsh bright country Lucinda sees so clearly. Ill, drugged, fearing that the wager was prompted by the devil, he notices nothing. . . .

Locked in the labyrinth of his European theology, caught between God and the devil, Oscar hardly begins to understand what the 'christianising' of that 'non-Christian landscape' involves. It's left to Kumbaingiri Billy, an old black man the narrator had met as a child, to tell the nasty bloody story of the coming of the white men and their strange glass church. And there's a further irony that the novel leaves hanging. Oscar gives his life for love, for the bright beautiful church that is, surely, godly, and a triumph of the human imagination. But 'after only one hundred and twenty years this church, the one in which my mother sang "Holy, Holy, Holy" . . . the one my great-grandfather assembled, shining clear, like heaven itself, on the Bellingen River, this church has been carted away. It was not of any use.'

Margaret Walters, "You Bet Your Life," in London Review of Books, *Vol. 10, No. 8, April 21, 1988, p. 20.*

FREDERICK BUSCH

Peter Carey's long adventure is as fine a love story and as fascinating an exploration—of the South of England, the wilds and primitive cities of Australia, the intensities and psychic densities of the Victorian Age in both countries—as any reader could wish. [*Oscar and Lucinda* is] as good a lesson in how to work with clean, powerful prose as any writer could wish. I make the novel sound like the answer to prayers. Perhaps it is. Surely it is about prayers, and their answers, as much as it is about fate and the sadness of families and that time when science, faith and the industrial revolution collided.

The novel feels "old-fashioned" in that its narrative persona knows everything, including what his characters don't. The novel unfolds over generations, and it spans oceans. And it remains a thoroughly contemporary novel, as intelligent and moving as anything I've read in years.

Carey's narrator is the great-grandson of the Oscar of the title. As the narrator introduces us to his eccentric family, and then its history, we learn that, like all authors, the narrator, while referring to himself in the first person as he narrates a third-person novel, is composing himself as well as his story: If certain events hadn't transpired, he says, "I would not have been born. There would be no story to tell." For him the story is a matter of life and death.

The story that's told is magnificent. Young Oscar Hopkins lives on the Devon coast with his dissenting naturalist father, a widower. They spend much time wading into the sea, collecting specimens of marine life about which the father writes. Oscar sees the ocean as the embodiment of death—a perception central to the novel—and when his father walks into it, "The sea was an amoeba, a protoplasm. It opened its salt-sticky arms and closed around the man." This is the sort of description Carey writes . . . : controlled, yet remarkably evocative of the mind perceiving what is observed as well as of the phenomenon itself. The prose is like glass; the 111 short chapters are like panes of it, assembled to afford not only vision, but structure.

While Oscar learns to gamble as a way of praying, of attempting to discern God's will, and thus achieves the only moments of peace he knows, Lucinda, early-orphaned daughter of a widowed Englishwoman in Australia, is finding her sole solace in the jam jars her mother used to organize an increasingly desperate life. (Both title characters live in terms of organization of chaotic events.) (p. 1)

They will start to love each other. We will start, then, to applaud Peter Carey for the way he maneuvers his characters toward one another, and a powerful love, and a gamble—based on each moment of their history we've observed, and on the pressures of bourgeois Victorian society—that yields a thrilling Victorian adventure story, and a loss that is heartbreaking and comical at once.

The plot must remain yours to discover, though this much can be disclosed: The gamble and adventure involve the manufacture in Lucinda's factory of a glass-and-iron church in the style of the Crystal Palace, . . . a journey by Oscar (some of it over dreaded water) to bring the church to a man of God whom Oscar does not wish to serve, but whom he thinks Lucinda does, while she wants him to stay home and wed her. It is a steely reader who does not demand of Oscar that he stay, and who does not gape or groan at the flood of the final paragraphs, when past and present, story and language all perfectly slide into place.

The novel is made of particularities—animal, vegetable, geographical, historical. We experience a living world in which a man does not press directly at a point, "but came at it, like a mouse around a skirting board, all stops and starts and quick gray scurries"; a landscape lies "bleeding from the stabbing and hacking of the cedar cutters." The people who observe Carey's world, and the world they observe, exchange properties; everything is alive with what sees it or what it sees.

Carey's sentences are informed by his fervent attention to his characters, to their world. I think that everything matters to Carey, who might cry out with Lucinda, about the gamble that is central to the book, " 'We are wagering everything. We place ourselves at risk.' "

Carey writes the way a novelist should: as if the world he has created, and his own private life, are at stake. Carey wins the throw, and—if there is any justice—the profound admiration of many, many readers. (pp. 1, 11)

Frederick Busch, " 'Oscar & Lucinda': Victorian Adventure Offers Thrills, Heartbreak, Comedy," in Chicago Tribune—Books, *June 19, 1988, pp. 1, 11.*

CAROLYN SEE

We have a great novelist living on the planet with us, and his name is Peter Carey. To be "great," to be "major," Dame Helen Gardner reminds us in an essay on T. S. Eliot, the writer's work

> must have bulk; he must attempt with success one or the other of the greater . . . forms, which tests his gifts of invention and variation . . . his subject matter must have universally recognized importance, and he must treat it with that imaginative authority we call originality; he must have something at once personal and of general relevance to say on important aspects of human experience.

To these lofty criteria, let me add—with perfect certainty—a great novelist must open up the reader's heart, allow the reader to remember the vastness and glory—and shame and shabbiness—of what it is to be human. . . .

But the purest, safest, surest mark of greatness in a novelist is ease. Stendahl danced. Melville danced. Carey dances.

Oscar & Lucinda is Carey's third novel. His first, **Bliss,** unfolded silken bolts of lustrous prose, took man and the land as its theme, was set in the present, and made you heartsick when you finished, because you could never read it again for the first time. **Illywhacker** grandly summed up the history of Australia through generations of scalawags; it dealt with romantic love, obsession, racism, the twin urges to build and to destroy. . . .

Oscar & Lucinda exponentially expands Carey's material across oceans and continents to England. His hero and heroine—like John Donne's "Stiffe Twin Compasses"—are destined to be together, even as they are apart. Carey doesn't set his envisioned "England" in competition with "Australia"; he merely takes a look and sets in motion an extraordinary dance that involves splendid, layered swirls of image and metaphor, and amazing feats of prose style. (Since this begins in Victorian England, the first sections are written—as by a master forger—in the purest Victorian-novel form. Then, in the second half, as coarse, vital, bright, sinful Australia impinges on events, the prose coarsens but becomes, itself, more vital. . . .) Finally, Carey dances with the very greatest issues of now or any other time; our relationship with the divine.

Does all this sound too pretentious to tackle? Too profound to read? No, it is easy, easy, beautiful beyond words. Young

Oscar Hopkins grows up in 19th-Century Devon. He's a pinched, motherless boy whose father is a preacher of the Plymouth Brethren—and yet a great, sweet, meticulous lover of nature. The elder Hopkins is so close to his God, and yet so debased in his beliefs, that he nearly strangles his son when he takes a bite of forbidden Christmas pudding. That Christianity which forbids all pleasure—is that what we are meant to follow? Young Oscar, having tested that fruit, becomes an Anglican, then a clergyman, and we are with him, *deep* in the concerns of Victorian England.

Across oceans and continents, in rural Australia, Lucinda grows up fatherless; her mother, an intellectual, and friend of Marian Evans/George Eliot, broods over her lot. Lucinda's mother loathes farming, but stays after her husband's death, despite the condescending farmers around her. When she dies, she has sold off her land and leaves Lucinda a fortune. (Stolen money, of course, since the land belongs to the blacks, and Lucinda knows her fortune is filthy lucre.)

The plot? Oscar and Lucinda are secret, compulsive gamblers. They meet on shipboard in a cunning, lovely set-piece, where she confesses to this incredibly lovable clergyman all the times, places and ways in which she has had occasion to commit the sin of gambling, to which he answers:

> Our whole faith is a wager . . . we bet that there is a God. We bet our life on it. We calculate the odds, the return, that we shall sit with the saints in paradise . . . we must gamble every *instant* of our allotted span. We must stake *everything* on the unprovable fact of His existence.

From then on, this pair of soul mates devote themselves, together, to poker, to fan-tan, to horse racing, to dice—and to the bringing of Christianity and civilization to a land where the country is "thick with sacred stories more ancient than the ones he carried in his sweat-slippery leather Bible." Through heroism, idealism and murder, Oscar brings Christian stories that an aborigine will later (not unkindly) remember: "My aunty . . . saw Jesus, Mary, Joseph, Paul and Jonah—all that mob she never knew before."

Oscar and Lucinda's great enterprise is based on misunderstanding, and some of that "vaulting" ambition. Lucinda has acquired a glassworks (and the passages on the properties of glass rival Melville's reflections on the whiteness of the whale). Her whole thought is to build a monument, a *structure,* something different. She has constructed a model of a glass church. Oscar, believing his beloved to love another clergyman upcountry, offers to deliver it to that Godforsaken outpost.

But outside their idealism and self-absorption, great, growing Australia exists, humming its own tune. And the men who must guide Oscar are murderous brutes. His idealistic quest or errand becomes an excursion into hell. . . . "He had bet there was a God. He had bet on Goodness. He had bet he would be rewarded in paradise. He had bet he would carry this jewel of a church through the horrid bush and have it in Boat Harbor by Easter. . . . Then he saw, in the corner of his mind, the possibility that the glass church was just the devil's trick." Oscar knows, horribly, that his life is "riddled with sin and compromise."

There's so much richness here. The sweetness of the star-crossed lovers. The goodness within the stifled English clergyman. The perfect irrationality of human behavior as it plays itself out in minor characters. The splendid narrative strategy, in which the Victorian device of the author speaking over the heads of the reader, turns, by the end, into something entirely different and surprising. . . .

But, mostly, if you liked Julien Sorel climbing that ladder, if you liked Ishmael clinging to the wreckage and understanding human friendship, if you wish that you too, along with Proust, could conjure up the taste of a madeleine as it melts, deliciously in your mouth, you're going to read ***Oscar & Lucinda,*** you're going to love it; you're going to remember it forever.

Great novelists, like the saints, don't all live in the past. They're here, now, and they're smiling.

Carolyn See, *"A Dance to the Music of Eternity,"* in Los Angeles Times Book Review, *June 19, 1988, p. 2.*

Caryl Churchill
Serious Money
Obie Award

English dramatist and scriptwriter.

A leading contemporary English playwright, Churchill employs unconventional dramatic methods to examine social and political values from historical and contemporary perspectives. She is often linked with writers of the "Fringe Theater," a group of British dramatists who rose to prominence during the 1970s with experimental plays informed by socialist ideals. Although they reflect left-wing and feminist sentiments, Churchill's works offer various viewpoints on social issues. In her Obie-winning play *Serious Money* (1987), for example, Churchill captures the challenge and excitement of the stock market while also exposing greed, materialism, and corruption as qualities that assure success in that business. In *Serious Money,* as in most of her works, Churchill utilizes poetically resonant language and explores some of the deep rooted values of Western society.

Serious Money is set in the financial district of London after the "Big Bang," a term that describes the surge in stock acquistion and trading following the 1986 deregulation of the London stock market. The play opens with references to Thomas Shadwell's *The Volunteers, or The Stockjobbers,* a late seventeenth-century drama that portrayed frenzied speculating in London during that era. Like Shadwell's play, *Serious Money* is rendered in verse replete with assonance, rhyme, and the jargon of high finance. Depicting a group of characters who have dedicated their lives to making money by exploiting the economic structure of society, Churchill examines such topical issues as takeover bids, payoffs, corruption, international finance, and drug smuggling. Robert Brustein noted: "*Serious Money* is a prodigiously researched examination of the workings of the world's money markets, where virtually all recognizable human feeling is subordinated to a passion for acquisition." The play centers on a wealthy young female stock trader investigating the suicide of her brother. She discovers that he might have been murdered because he had information concerning a takeover bid, and her inquiry uncovers various unsavory business practices. While critics agreed that Churchill successfully evoked the hectic lifestyle of people associated with stock trading, several commentators debated whether the play served to glamorize or critique this profession.

Churchill began her theatrical career while an undergraduate at Oxford University, where her first two plays, *Downstairs* (1958) and *Having a Wonderful Time* (1960), were produced. During the mid-1960s, she wrote plays for radio and television. With the rise of the Fringe Theater in the late 1960s, Churchill found outlets for theatrical performance of her work. Many of her plays were produced at the Royal Court, a subsidized alternative theater, where Churchill became the first female resident playwright. She initially drew critical attention with *Owners* (1972), a realistic work that explores sexual roles and social injustice. In this play, a female real estate

agent's ruthless drive for success causes hardships in her marriage and among residents of a working-class neighborhood. In *Objections to Sex and Violence* (1975), Churchill pursues her interest in feminist ideology by depicting a female terrorist and examining the relationship between sexuality, violence, and power. Churchill's next play, *Light Shining in Buckinghamshire* (1976), explores the combination of religious and revolutionary fervor that contributed to rebellion during the Cromwellian era of English history. *Vinegar Time* (1976), also set in the seventeenth century, focuses on the persecution of witches to suggest that women often serve as scapegoats for social problems.

Churchill received an Obie Award for *Cloud Nine* (1979), which enjoyed extended runs in London and New York. A farce in which rampant sexual activity underlies genteel manners, this play is alternately set in colonial Africa during the Victorian era and present-day London. The characters age only twenty-five years, however, reflecting Churchill's view of the slow progress of social change. With actors portraying several characters, among other theatrical devices, Churchill underscores what she perceives as the artificiality of conventional sex roles. Churchill stated that in *Cloud Nine* she sought to reveal how sexual oppression, like colonial repression, is dehumanizing to all individuals. She added: "I brought together two preoccupations of mine—people's internal states of being and the external structures which affect them, which make them insane."

Churchill also employed a disjointed time structure in *Top Girls* (1982), a satire which implies that women can attain professional success only by adopting the worst traits of men. This play begins with a dinner party at which a group of prominent female historical figures congratulate a present-day businesswoman on her success, while subsequent scenes relate the tensions of the woman's daily life. In *Fen* (1983), which portrays lower-class women who have failed to benefit from recent efforts toward equality of the sexes, Churchill blends an exploration of economically exploited farm workers with particular problems of her female protagonists, including one woman's dilemma of choosing between her lover and her children. *Softcops* (1984), a seriocomic examination of themes relating to crime, punishment, and social responsibility, relies heavily on Michel Foucault's sociological study *Surveiller et Punir* (*Discipline and Punishment*). The characters in this play represent various social approaches to the deterrence of crime.

(See also *CLC*, Vol. 31; *Contemporary Authors*, Vol. 102; *Contemporary Authors New Revision Series*, Vol. 22; and *Dictionary of Literary Biography*, Vol. 13.)

MICHAEL RATCLIFFE

[*Serious Money* is] a vigorous, aggressive, funny and much-needed attack on British values. . . .

Churchill has stood at the heart of the Big Bang [a term used to describe the effect of the 1986 deregulation of the London Stock Market], and defined a world living off high-speed stealth, champagne and air, in which a white knight is a young woman in a scarlet blouse, and the start of Chicago trading at lunchtime attracts a crowd of *arrivistes* in red and yellow blazers like the hosts and hostesses in 'Hi-De-Hi.' The rich get rich by staying in debt, the smart take a risk instead of a fee.

This London bazaar of speculation goes back at least to Thomas Shadwell's *The Volunteers, or The Stockjobbers* (1692), an apt and witty extract from which forms a brief overture to Churchill's play. Shadwell's speculators trade futures in a putative company of Chinese rope-dancers which will probably never leave China; Churchill's trade in, among many commodities, money which does not exist.

Serious Money is an unruly piece, much of it written in a loose, springy, assonant, and semi-rhyming verse. A plot of defiant convolutedness is narrated by a ruthless American softy, Zack, and includes an illegal takeover bid, a split to the Department of Trade and Industry and the suicide or murder of one Jake, the only public schoolboy who can keep up with the unscrupulousness of a Thatcherised working class. The rage of Jake's sister Scilla is less for his death than for the concealment of his great wealth while still alive.

This is not a feminist critique of a male world. Men, women, blacks, Latin Americans and Jews are all on the money game, and join in the chilling rap of mindless obscenities which explodes at the end of the first act. The women, indeed, are crucially powerful. . . . [The] whole thing, though not quite free from romanticisation and still bearing the signs of homework insufficiently subsumed, is very bracing indeed.

Michael Ratcliffe, in a review of "Serious Money," in The Observer, *March 29, 1987.*

NEIL COLLINS

Serious money is pure genius. . . . [It is] the first play about the City [the financial district of London] to capture the authentic atmosphere of the place.

The action is based on a takeover battle which bears some curious similarities to the Guinness bid for Distillers last year. . . . It is not about how Guinness won, of course, and the characters keep referring to the Guinness case lest anyone sees their lawyers portrayed rather too accurately. . . .

The technical detail is terrific. The authentic atmosphere of the bizarre, which bursts out at the start of the play from the floor of the pompously named London International Financial Futures Exchange, contrasts with the sedate scene later at the London Metal Exchange.

Both rituals are incomprehensible to the outsider, but Caryl Churchill has caught the difference between LIFFE, trading in ever more obscure forms of money and flourishing, and the LME, trading in real commodities and dying. Just when you are hopelessly lost, a character steps out of the ruck to explain what the markets are doing. It is far more entertaining, and far more informative, than a dozen text books.

Scilla Todd, a LIFFE dealer, is the daughter of a conventionally rich stockbroker who is appalled that his expensively educated daughter should opt for life among the barrow boys, even if they are all earning more than they can drink or drive. She explains, "It's a cross between roulette and space invaders".

Her brother Jake is found dead, and she sets out to investigate, first out of curiosity, then out of greed when she senses a large illicit income she knew nothing about. . . .

[Jake had] been helping an American arbitrageur, conveniently female to avoid looking too much like America's insider trader, Ivan Boesky. Jake's leaked information [about the attempted takeover of Albion by Corman, a much smaller business] had put Albion into play. Billy Corman is frighteningly effective as the megalomaniac who tramples on the doubts of his advisers by reminding them of the size of their fees.

In the course of trying to win support from any quarter, Corman enlists a Peruvian businesswoman aptly named Jacqinta Condor, whose knowledge of cocaine, copper prices and the LME far exceeds her interest in the boring old mines she owns back home. Her lesson in the economics of Third World Aid, where the rich get Eurobond and the poor country gets debt, ends with a double–cross. Under intense political pressure, Corman abandons his bid.

There is, of course, no happy ending, except the biting song by Ian Dury ("Five More Glorious Years") and the confidence that money and greed conquer all. It is not necessary to follow the plot too closely, nor to believe that everyone in the City is as young, unpleasant and uncouth as the main characters. It's just that the good guys have been out of the limelight recently.

The script, written in verse, fairly cracks along and the pace never flags. . . . Love the City or hate it, but see this.

Neil Collins, in a review of "Serious Money," in The Daily Telegraph, *March 30, 1987.*

MICHAEL COVENEY

Caryl Churchill's expositive comedy [*Serious Money*] is a hectic "hot off the presses" look at the City of London after Big Bang. The production is prefaced with a scene from Thomas Shadwell's *The Volunteers* (1692), a premonitory flash of a nation on the rampage for shares in public enterprises and leisure markets (for performing monkeys and rope acts). We cross-fade to a babble of dealing and forecasting in a trading pit. . . .

The cast of eight . . . switch roles and locations with dizzying speed. The play is as much about the City as about Wall Street and, indeed, the explosion in international dealing that has put paid to the clubbiness and cartel of the City. . . .

It sounds exhilarating and some of it is. . . . There are good moments of explanation, and even better ones of musical explosion at the end of each half—both songs have words by Ian Dury, the first an obscenity scat chant for gaudily-jacketed trading oiks, the second a pulsating pub rock hymn to five more glorious years of a Tory Government, concupiscence and ratified pillage.

But Ms Churchill has spun a thriller narrative through the middle of the dealings and betrayals that is both feeble and muddling. There is a hovering air of what it is that has driven the public schoolboy Jake to suicide, but the details are buried in such awkwardly affixed second act developments as the copper mine sales of a Peruvian heiress and the cocaine market manoeuvrings of an Eton-educated Nigerian potentate. And even readers of [the *Financial Times*] may wonder what has Jake actually *done* and what is the connection between the DTI [Department of Trade and Industry] investigation and the little Yorkshire businessman whose go-getting secretary has, without his approval, put his name to an artistic mural.

There are pleasurable echoes, you will have noted, of the Guinness affair, the Boesky business and the Halpern hype, although the extraordinary sight of Mr. Ralph Halpern and his loyal wife being cheered to the echo by shareholders shortly after the revelations about his private life is never really improved upon by Ms Churchill. I believe this is something to do with her dogged, graffiti-like approach. No question, she and the cast have done their homework. But there is more theatrical juice and conviction in a public play like *Brassneck*, David Hare's and Howard Brenton's panoramic view of finance and the family in the Britain of a decade or so ago . . . ; or in the same pair's recent *Pravda*.

Neither was probably as earnestly researched as *Serious Money*, but in yielding stronger theatrical resonance they caught a spirit of the times more successfully. Ms Churchill's technique of wrapping the text up in a versifying mélange of

Victorian pantomime couplets and second-rate doggerel after the style of Steven Berkoff is another great drawback. Where iambics are used, the scansion is erratic and annoying. And the rhyming of four-letter crudities becomes predictable and uninventive. The idea is to catch the desperate furore and noisiness of the dealers' world, but the text needs much more highlighting and pointing—the overlapping dialogue passages and ensemble "blah-blahs" are just messy.

The play is certain to be successful, as the topic is so hot and the subject itself an excitingly new one for the theatre. But it marks no great development in Ms Churchill's compositional methods, no advance on *Top Girls* or *Cloud Nine.*

Michael Coveney, in a review of "Serious Money," in Financial Times, *March 30, 1987.*

MICHAEL BILLINGTON

[*Serious Money*] is a play for fresh businessmen. It assumes the audience either knows or will quickly deduce the roles of a fan club, a concert party, a white knight or an arbitrageur and is up to date in dirty take-over tactics. But even if your knowledge of the City is pretty shaky, it is hard to resist the show's satirical exuberance and ensemble attack.

There are many reasons why the show works. The most basic is that you feel Ms Churchill, the director . . . , and the cast are as fascinated by the City's frenzied energy as they are appalled by its moral unscrupulousness.

The story they tell is a complicated one. . . .

But its main thrust is that the new, post-Big Bang City is merely the old writ crude and that the Square Mile is a place where no bad deed goes wholly unrewarded.

What Ms Churchill captures superbly is the restless dynamic of the modern City. 'I work on the floor of LIFFE," proclaims [a] . . . supercharged Sloane referring, of course, to the London International Financial Futures Exchange, where the basic commodity is money. But the rancid joke at the heart of the play is that, for a whole new generation of dealers and traders, making money breed has become life itself.

It is clearly a world where class is subordinate to acumen and where a Cockney with a CSE in metalwork can get ahead as fast as a girl from the shires. Sex, Ms Churchill suggests, is also an after-thought: one very funny scene shows an American banker and a Peruvian tycoon comparing Filofaxes as they unavailingly try to make a simple date.

The form of the play is also the key to its energy since Ms Churchill has cast much of it in a rhyming verse that suggests a weird mix of Hilaire Belloc, Cyril Fletcher and provincial panto. Sometimes it is just doggerel: at others it trimly encapsulates a point. "If it was just insider-dealing," a City apologist points out, "It's not a proper crime like stealing."

Michael Billington, in a review of "Serious Money," in The Guardian, *March 30, 1987, p. 13.*

ANDREW RISSIK

Caryl Churchill's *Serious Money* is a wicked, glitterball comedy about high finance and low cunning which is kept buoyant by the sheer momentum of evil. It gets some of its mad licence from the only prominent genre of Jacobean drama to survive the Restoration, the "city comedy" or moral satire whose target was urban avarice.

We begin with a periwigged scene from Thomas Shadwell's 1692 play, *The Volunteers,* and then the front curtain rises on the City of London in the late 1980s, a sleek, designer-built interior where heavily stocked cocktail cabinets sit side by side with bright computer screens.

What follows is a suavely complex financial horror cartoon, in which the pursuit of money lends life a savage, aphrodisiac energy, and where characters thrive or die according to their fitness for this gangster pace. The plot runs at breakneck speed, like a strenuous few hours on the Stock Exchange, and although, to a layman, it is often impossibly intricate, the emotional essentials are clear enough.

We are in the world of corrupt takeover bids, where cash is sloshing about like bilge water, and where failure provokes one well connected character, an Old Etonian commercial paper dealer called Jake Todd, to commit suicide. His sister, Scilla, attempts to uncover the circumstances of his death, but finds she has a taste for wheeler-dealer chicanery, and ends the play as a sort of moral defector, seduced by the raffish impetus of diamond-hard capitalism.

Ms Churchill's concerns have something in common with the collaborative Tory epics of [Howard] Brenton and [David] Hare, those huge, sulphurous tales of villainy and intrigue like *Brass Neck* and *Pravda.* And, for a while, Scilla looks as if she is following the path of Curly in David Hare's *Knuckle,* searching for truth and talking tough.

But *Serious Money* is never a moral mystery, and its helter-skelter satire is too urbanely facetious to convey any authentic tone of outraged morality. The writing lacks the dark impassioned insolence which created Lambert Le Roux and *Pravda,* or that insight into the amoral beauty of absolute mercantile power which lay beneath the comic-strip riot of its dialogue.

Here, the characters talk in aphoristic rhyming verse whose technical polish lends the play an elegant doggerel fluency: we are reminded of Betjeman or Clive James, not the mordant comedies of Ben Jonson, Massinger and Congreve.

The success of the play is a success of communicated theatrical bravado. . . . The boldness and detail . . . the juggling of naturalism and cartoon turn the City's fiscal squalor into a high-spirited bacchanal.

Andrew Rissik, in a review of "Serious Money," in The Independent, *March 30, 1987.*

VICTORIA RADIN

Coming into the Royal Court to see *Serious Money* I was crushed against a wall by a large gentleman who evidently saw no reason why my presence should impede his progress towards his chosen destination. The episode served as a fitting introduction to Caryl Churchill's new comedy, whose subject is the Big Bang in the City but whose real theme is the naked ruthlessness and greed that characterises much of life in Britain in the late 1980s. The 20 characters (played by eight actors) steal, cheat, lie and vigorously trample down anyone who stands in their way. 'Greed has been good to me,' enthuses a young whizzkid. The tone is hectic and exuberant,

and the audience responds in kind. At the end of the first half, when the cast hissed out a rapping song whose words, written by Ian Dury, were largely a list of expletives, we all reacted as if we'd heard music from paradise.

Churchill is not out to instruct. The terms 'corporate raider' 'leveraged buy-out' and 'junk bond', despite the fact that I've now watched people being, doing or buying these things for two hours, remain as gnomic as ever; and I wouldn't be able to explain the finer points of such plot as there is. Basically there are two of them. One concerns the death of Jake who has been amassing a fortune, or what I do now understand to be 'serious' money, by shopping inside information to a very hard lady in New York called Mary-Lou. His sister embarks on a mission to discover the real facts behind his death—though much more from desire to lay hands on his money than out of feelings of family piety, which the play reveals to be universally extinct. At the same time, this Scilla, daughter of a stockbroker, is involved in a conspiracy to buy up a 'good, old-fashioned' Northern firm called Albion, no less. This scam is masterminded by Billy Corman, a drop-out from a CSE metalwork course whom Scilla's father describes as an 'Oik', or 'one of those barrow boys you expect to see on a street corner selling cheap watches'. . . .

Churchill doesn't make the mistake of thinking Corman is any worse than the representatives of older money, whom she shows to be every bit as ruthless; nor of believing that integrity ruled before the Bang released naked greed in its most incontrovertible forms. Her curtain-raising scene lifted from Thomas Shadwell shows Restoration pillars of the establishment merrily dreaming up trading chicaneries and a playwright rejoicing in it. Churchill rejoices in it too; and has a good time at peppering her play with awful puns, rhyming couplets and theatrical in-jokes. I could have done without some of these sallies, and with more of the rhyming, which tends, like the dynamic of the piece, to die out in the second half. And the couplets, which seemed so marvellous when they were flying at one like the bubbles in a glass of champagne (a drink that Corman calls 'poo', as in 'a glass of poo') look fairly dismal when one reads over one's notes the next day. I don't think this is a lasting work, but its quality of cheap immediacy, an inky newness like this morning's tabloid, gives it a freshness one rarely sees in the theatre: it feels as if it had been written today. (p. 25)

Victoria Radin, "Cash, Bang, Wallop," in New Statesman, *Vol. 113, No. 2923, April 3, 1987, pp. 25-6.*

CLIVE BARNES

The trouble with Caryl Churchill's *Serious Money* is that it is not particularly serious. It is certainly about money, but at times its arcane technical lingo sounds to the uninitiated about as comprehensible as The Wall Street Journal in a Sanskrit edition.

This play . . . is fundamentally a vitriolic revue sketch.

It is carelessly written in bile and rhyming couplets and dangerously extended in ideas and length. Yet for all this, it is distinguished by a fantastic energy that fuels its gifted performers, sending them into orbit with wonderfully manic antics.

An excerpt from *Serious Money*

ZAC.
It would be great to see you while you're over here.

JACINTA.
Maybe we could drink some English beer.
I have a meeting at eight,
It won't go on late.
Maybe at half-past nine?

ZAC.
No, I don't think . . .
I'll be stuck with Corman, I can't get out for a drink.
Eleven's probably fine.

JACINTA.
I'm having late supper
With terribly upper-
class people who buy my plantation.

ZAC.
And after that?

JACINTA.
Unfortunately they live in Edinburgh.

ZAC.
How you getting there?

JACINTA.
By helicopter.

ZAC.
I'm beginning to run out of inspiration.

JACINTA.
Breakfast?

ZAC.
Would be great except I have to have breakfast/
with Corman till this deal goes through.
I suppose I might get away for a minute or two.

JACINTA.
That would be heaven.

ZAC.
Maybe eleven?

JACINTA.
Eleven I see my lawyer.
At twelve–

ZAC.
No, please.

JACINTA.
I see some Japanese,
Just briefly in the hotel foyer.
So we meet for lunch?

ZAC.
I have to be in Paris for lunch. I'll be back by four.

JACINTA.
That's good!

ZAC.
But I have to go straight to Corman.

JACINTA.
What a bore.

ZAC.
Maybe we could . . .

JACINTA.
Dinner tomorrow
Much to my sorrow
I have with some eurobond dealers.

ZAC.
Cancel it.

JACINTA.
Business.

ZAC.
Shit.

JACINTA.
Afterward?

ZAC.
Bliss.
No, hang on a minute.
I have as a guest a
Major investor,
I have to put out some feelers.
(The only time he can meet me is after a show.)
I guess I might be through by 1 a.m.

JACINTA.
Zac, I could cry,
There's a nightclub I buy,
And really I must talk to them.
So maybe next morning
You give me a ring?

ZAC.
Maybe I can get out of breakfast with Corman,/
I'll call you first thing.

JACINTA.
Which day?

ZAC.
Tomorrow.

Serious Money is intended as a picture of the London Exchange Market—and, by connection and inference, the International Exchange Market—since the deregulation of the London Stock Exchange a couple of years ago, apparently known to its participants as the "Big Bang."

This deregulation has, it seems, changed the entire pattern of London finance, permitting British versions of yuppies to ride high on easy money, champagne, cocaine and Porsches.

The class system in the City—London's name for its financial district—has broken down, although it has left picturesque ruins. Now the law of the jungle has been imposed, very successfully, upon the playing fields of Eton.

Takeovers, insider trading, the entire financial mystique as well as the actual horse-track techniques of the financial market, are displayed with a savage good humor.

There is a kind of story—a young man who knew too much has died a violent death, and his sister, who wants money rather than revenge, sets about finding out whether his abrupt demise was suicide or murder.

Confusion is rampant as the play flickers between past, present and future like a berserk time machine, while the Protean actors all take many roles, adding to the mix-up. Such narrative as there is has far less impact than the atmosphere, the characters and, of course, their lack of character.

These people are animals—they use stupidly insensate gutter language that would make David Mamet's realtors blush with envy and never use five or six letters when four letters will do, and their ferocious quest for money as a symbol of power is sickening.

Or should be. The curious thing is that Churchill has fallen in love with these very same objects of her political scorn. She admires their buccaneering spirit—she may deplore the bloodshed, the drinking and the language, but she has a yen for the pirates.

No wonder that in London—where *Serious Money* is a serious West End hit—the play has become the darling of the shirking classes, and the Sloane Rangers have made it a home away from home, exulting in the Churchillian glamorization of their sordid realities.

Sloane Rangers? Ah yes, this may be a difficulty for non-English-speaking Americans. There are many, many phrases and references—watch out for the one about Sid!—that might fall on deaf Yankee ears.

Yet everyone will—flatteringly if falteringly—get some of the references, both the Anglicisms and the money talk, and as for the rest, you can take it as authenticating the atmosphere.

I must say I understood the play much more the second time around—I first saw it in London last summer—and, perhaps as a consequence, at least enjoyed the performances more.

The play itself I still find trivial, self-indulgent and somewhat toadying to its audience. I have come to expect more from Churchill and her director, Max Stafford-Clark, on an intellectual and moral level for both of them, and also on a technical level for Churchill. . . .

The play is an unintentional fake. In the interstices of its scabrous hysteria there are some slicky-witty lines, but what is one to make of a play that tries to preach to the unconverted and ends up glorifying their ethical bankruptcy?

And turning a neat profit on the moral failure. Perhaps Brecht—that most pragmatic of political playwrights—would have found it funny. Somehow, I didn't. Call me square.

> *Clive Barnes, "After the 'Big Bang'," in* New York Post, *December 4, 1987.*

FRANK RICH

When the antiquated London stock market finally cast off tradition and plugged into the deregulated frenzy of modern Wall Street in 1986, the phenomenon was heralded as the Big Bang. In *Serious Money,* a ferocious new satire about the financial wheeler-dealers born in the ensuing boom, Caryl Churchill takes the term literally.

The play . . . travels to the trading pits and board rooms of London's financial district, the City, to find the precise pitch of the arena of arbitrage, inside trading, greenmail, corporate raiding and leveraged buyouts. *Serious Money* wants us to hear the very sound of megascale greed as it is practiced on that circuit of telephone wires and computer screens blinking 24 hours a day from Tokyo to New York.

That sound is not the sound of music. It is not the polite ringing of a cash register. It is not even the insistent chatter of a ticker tape. The noise, emanating from the brokers and bankers and dealers in *Serious Money* is a cacophonous, feverish screech of numbers and obscenities that builds into a mad roar. It is, indeed, a big bang, and it rivals other apocalyptic explosions of our nuclear age in its potential for devastation. As Ms. Churchill and the recent crash both demonstrate, the bursting financial bubble can leave small investors, large corporations, third world countries and Western economies shattered in its wake.

Yet in the theater, the noise creates a strange, if chilling, exhilaration. If *Serious Money* is an angry, leftist political work about ruthlessness and venality, about plundering and piggishness, it is also vivid entertainment. The fun comes in part from the vicarious pleasure always to be had in watching the flimflams of others. Ms. Churchill opens her play with an excerpt from a 1692 Thomas Shadwell comedy about stock jobbers—and a bit of *The Solid Gold Cadillac* could have made the same plus ça change point. But even more of the evening's lift can be attributed to Ms. Churchill's own inventive approach to her enduring subject. As her characters have rewritten the rules of the marketplace to create a new order of Darwinist capitalism, so she rewrites the rules of the theater expressly to capture that bizarre world on stage.

Such daring is typical of this playwright, who in her previous *Cloud Nine* and *Top Girls* has sent characters floating between historical periods and genders to make trenchant points about sexual and economic oppression. While *Serious Money* is well aware of Ben Jonson, Restoration comedy and Brecht, it has been written in its own outrageous style. The script is almost entirely composed of rhymed couplets, many of them juvenile and scatological, some of them clever ("If it was just inside dealing/It's not a proper crime like stealing.") The action is fast and confusing—intentionally so, given all the overlapping dialogue—and the people are no more than cartoons. The closest thing *Serious Money* has to a plot—the mysterious death of a commercial paper dealer—is never even resolved.

The overall result, repetitive and unruly as it sometimes may be, is wholly theatrical. Though based on up-to-the-minute research and clearly inspired in part by the actual Guinness and Boesky scandals in London and New York, *Serious Money* is not a "Nightline"-style documentary. Nor is it a work of satirical narrative fiction, like *The Bonfire of the Vanities,* Tom Wolfe's thematically related novel about a high-rolling Wall Street bond trader. Ms. Churchill valiantly makes the case, as so very few playwrights do these days, that the stage can still play its own unique role, distinct from that of journalism or television or movies, in dramatizing the big, immediate stories of our day.

Only in a theater could we watch a Peruvian businesswoman deliver a long, rhymed soliloquy that captures the fashions, ethos and economic basis of a cocaine-fueled branch of the OPEC jet set. Or watch the traders on the floor of Liffe—the London International Financial Futures Exchange, and pronounced like "life"—transform their hand signals and brokerage jargon into a rap number (with lyrics by Ian Dury) that really makes their business seem, as one character describes it, "a cross between roulette and Space Invaders." While Ms. Churchill does periodically send her players forward to explain terminology and history, one need not be able to define "junk bonds" or know the real-life basis of a scene inspired by the fall of Lehman Brothers to grasp her polemical drift. Visceral theater, not didactic sermonizing, is the medium of her message.

Nor is that message as simplistic as one might think. To be sure, Ms. Churchill is tough on red-suspendered, champagne-guzzling hustlers who speed down the fast lane in BMW's and Lamborghinis on their way to the scrap heap at age 35. She is also tough on the paternalistic, old-style businessmen overturned (and often taken over) by the new deal-makers and on African and black American entrepreneurs who sell out their own for a share of the spoils. But **Serious Money** is more an indictment of a system than of specific sharks and crooks. When money—not even land or widgets or pork bellies—is the main commodity traded on the floor of Liffe, the game loses all connection to life. Real lives are soon cold-bloodedly crunched along with the fast-flying abstract numbers.

When **Serious Money** falters—and it does, notably after intermission—the problem is only partly Ms. Churchill's refusal to engineer her story as niftily as Mr. Wolfe or a Restoration playwright might. . . . In **Serious Money,** the heartlessness of the late 80's finds its raucous voice in comedy that is, as it must be, hilariously, gravely sick.

> Frank Rich, "Rewriting the Rules," in The New York Times, *December 4, 1987, p. C3.*

MIMI KRAMER

It's easy to see why [**Serious Money**] was such a big hit in London. (It broke box-office records at the Royal Court, then moved to the West End, and it is running still.) It combines the spectacle of actors misbehaving (using bad language, pulling down one another's trousers, pretending to vomit, or simulating defecating horses) with a confirmation of many of the British intelligentsia's most dearly held beliefs: that privatization and free enterprise are bad things, that "the British Empire was a cartel," that foreigners buy Burberrys, that money is somehow something that one is better off yearning for than having, and that while various hidden vices may be permitted in good society, open ambition is unpleasant and impolite. I don't think American audiences are so likely to be snowed by Miss Churchill's play. I think it will be pretty clear to everyone that the satire is rather tame and serves to glamorize rather than to ridicule the world of high finance, by making money look sexy and exciting—which, of course, it is. In fact, I think it will be pretty clear to most people that Caryl Churchill and the Royal Court Theatre (and, by extension, the Public Theatre) are cashing in on eighties ethics and yuppie fashion. (Your average Wall Street whiz kid is far more likely to be amused than chastened by Jake's cynical "Greed's been good to me!")

A number of aspects of the production seem to look wistfully back to a more gracious past. The evening begins with a snatch of Handel's "Water Music" and a brief scene from Thomas Shadwell's 1692 comedy *The Volunteers; or, The*

Stock Jobbers, played before the curtain, at the end of which trumpets blare, the curtain opens to reveal . . . [a] technology-laden set (three clocks, eight computer terminals, forty-nine wall phones), and the actors march ceremoniously upstage. This all makes for quite beautiful and impressive theatre, but it has little purpose other than to establish that high finance has been around for a long time and once had charm. (The inept post-punk pop songs, which end both acts, and in which actors rhythmically shout jargon mixed with obscenities at the audience, pushing and jostling each other out of the way, likewise seem to cast a cold eye on the ugly modern world.) The most vivid and moving speech in the play is a description of what London's financial district used to be like before deregulation:

> The stock exchange was a village street.
> You strolled about and met your friends.
> Now we never seem to meet.
> I don't get asked much at weekends.
>
> Everyone had a special name.
> We really had a sense of humour.
> And everybody played the game . . .

Nicknames, houseparties, playing the game—these are the graces and accoutrements of the old-boy network.

The fact is that, for all the hipness and topicality of **Serious Money,** the whole production reeks of nostalgia. But that's the irony of so much British left-wing theatre: it's such a funny mixture of groping radicalism and Old World values. One sees this in Miss Churchill's earlier work. **Cloud 9**—a play about how women have feelings, too—used elaborate cast-doubling and time-warp tricks to make the point that the British Empire was a very bad thing. **Top Girls** discovered that careerist feminism is not compatible with good socialist principles. These are conflicts that could absorb only an audience of Englishmen lost in the ideological mists of time. (p. 120)

> Mimi Kramer, "Business as Usual," in The New Yorker, *Vol. LXIII, No. 43, December 14, 1987, pp. 119-20.*

ROBERT BRUSTEIN

Caryl Churchill writes hard-boiled, unpredictable, untidy plays, and with **Serious Money,** . . . she is at the top of her disheveled form. I was first exposed to the left hook of this unusual English dramatist when her early work **Owners** opened at a London fringe theater in 1972. It was a play about rack-renting in the East End, a terse treatment of social injustice in a style of episodic realism—ironic, cold, and detached enough to disguise a subterranean fury. The arresting thing about **Owners** was not its relatively conventional form so much as its disinterested radical posture. A product of a fiercely independent mind, it offered a negative Marxist critique unblemished by Marxist ideology. Since that time, in such plays as **Cloud Nine, Fen,** and **Top Girls,** Churchill has been experimenting with more fantastical techniques, but her remorseless inquest into the English social system continues unabated. **Serious Money** may be the most incisive autopsy she has yet attempted.

It is also an extremely difficult, sometimes even repellent play. **Serious Money** is a prodigiously researched examination of the workings of the world's money markets, where virtually all recognizable human feeling is subordinated to a passion for acquisition. American drama is often faulted for lacking public dimension. What's missing from *Serious Money* is any sign of private emotion other than covetousness. This, I gather, is precisely Churchill's point. In the world of money, all vestiges of softer virtues—love, loyalty, friendship, family feeling, the aesthetic sense—must be ruthlessly eliminated as obstacles in the path of profit; venality is the foundation stone of political and financial empire. In *Serious Money*, Plutus and Hobbes are reincarnated in the shape of Ivan Boesky (his spirit also informs the recently released movie *Wall Street*), whose much-quoted tribute to greed as the basis for the health and wealth of nations is the theme of the play.

The result is a dramatis personae of ruthless robots whose behavior seems as automated as the computer systems they use to conduct their corporate raids, mergers, takeovers, deals, and arbitrages. The setting for *Serious Money* might be a Pac-Man game: a maze of squeaking mouths devouring other mouths and getting gobbled up in turn. These hungry mouths are filled not only with corporate corpses but with venal epigrams: "You don't make money out of land, you make money out of money." "Being in debt is the best way to be rich." "Anyone who can buy oranges for ten and sell at eleven in a souk or bazaar has the same human nature and can go equally far." One character would like to own "a big cube of sea, right down to the bottom, all the fish, weeds, the lot, there'd be takers for that." Another prefers a square meter of space "and a section of God at the top." Corporations are in business not to produce products but to produce money, and governments (also moneymaking machines) exist to facilitate the process through deregulation. (p. 27)

Churchill is a feminist, but one of her theatrical virtues (also displayed in *Top Girls*) is a capacity to create female characters as covetous and corruptible as her males. (She is equally democratic toward black American dealers and African plutocrats.) Perhaps the most cunning figure in the play is a Peruvian businesswoman named Jacinta Condor who, when not speculating on the London metal exchange, is selling cocaine and paying off the *contras*. And perhaps the most chilling scene concerns Jacinta's unsuccessful effort to make a date with a young American banker, when both are too busy arranging deals to find an hour for lunch or dinner. . . .

None of Churchill's rapacious birds and beasts of prey has a recognizably human moment, but then neither do the cormorants of Ben Jonson's *Volpone* or Henri Becque's *The Vultures* or Bertolt Brecht's *Saint Joan of the Stockyards*, the satiric tradition to which *Serious Money* belongs. Like her mordant predecessors, Churchill seems to have a sneaking admiration for the foibles of cheats and charlatans. Underneath her ferocious irony lies an understanding that the worst excesses of capitalism can be exciting and engrossing, which is why so many intelligent, dynamic people today are attracted to business. But she is also conscious of how debilitating such practices can be to the brain and spirit—of how "when the trading stops, you don't know what to do with your mind." . . .

[The] absence of a human dimension in the writing prevents the acting from becoming truly distinguished, and the plot is too complicated to be absorbed in a single sitting. As a result, *Serious Money* is not a truly successful work of theater. But it is something considerably more important—a scathing social anatomy of the greedy scavengers feeding on the rotting economic flesh of the West. (p. 28)

> *Robert Brustein, "Birds and Beasts of the West," in* The New Republic, *Vol. 198, No. 3, January 18, 1988, pp. 27-8.*

DOUG WATT

Serious Money, Caryl Churchill's hard-edged, brilliantly cynical depiction of the stock market, is as scorchingly effective with its new and almost exclusively American Broadway cast as it was with the British one that introduced it here last fall. . . . Rest assured, the play seems to tell us, that in a world of uncertainties there exist certain constants—greed, self-interest, deceit, ruthlessness and corruption—that transcend national borders to achieve universality. *Serious Money* is positively gleeful in dealing with these absolutes. Shockingly, it must end its brief Broadway run tomorrow night for lack of business.

Serious Money is almost totally in rhyme, as you have doubtless heard, with much of it raunchy (even sophomorically so). . . .

The fact that there is really no plot hardly matters. The headlong, dizzying pace is as intoxicating as a roller coaster ride as this unscrupulous lot (there is much doubling and even tripling in the cast of eight) spins backward and forward in time and place.

The thread of a plot is about the possible murder or suicide of a young inside trader who keeps reappearing in flashbacks, along with the attempts of his sister, another trader, to get to the bottom of it. But the case is never solved, the search dropped, for it turns out that the sister was more interested in her late brother's potentially profitable inside knowledge than in the circumstances of his death. Churchill's unwavering eye on rapaciousness never slips into sentiment or any trace of genuine feeling. So ends the short Broadway life of possibly the season's most fascinating play. . . . Churchill, who obviously spent a good deal of time studying The City, lets this wildly energetic society of winners and losers speak for itself, without the slightest trace of didactism.

Serious Money is fast, furious and funny, a sight for soreheads who recently guessed wrong in the market, as well as one for sore eyes.

> *Doug Watt, " 'Serious Money' Runs Out," in* Daily News, *New York, February 19, 1988.*

Pete Dexter
Paris Trout
National Book Award: Fiction

American novelist and journalist.

Written in colloquial prose that details violence and tension with subtle wit, *Paris Trout* (1988) chronicles a ruthless murder and its effects on the small Southern town of Cotton Point, Georgia. The title character of this novel is a brutal and intimidating white grocer and loan shark. Unable to collect a debt from a black man, Trout shoots two innocent black females and remains indifferent to the moral and legal repercussions of his action. After a perfunctory trial before a bigoted jury and judge, Trout receives a light sentence for his crime and is soon released. As Trout rapidly descends into a hostile state of paranoia and madness with further tragic consequences, the frightened townspeople are forced to confront their own hypocrisies, prejudices, and complicity. While Dexter was faulted by some commentators for creating a predictable plot, he was lauded for his solid characterizations, and critics observed that the reactions of the characters to Trout's actions illuminate their attitudes toward racism and injustice while underscoring his dominating personality. Dexter has written two other novels, *God's Pocket* (1984) and *Deadwood* (1987).

(See also *CLC*, Vol. 34.)

JUDITH PATERSON

Pete Dexter's *Paris Trout* begins in the 1950s as the first tremblings of the civil rights movement start to shake the status quo in the Deep South.

Dexter, author of two well-received previous novels, chooses a community very much like his hometown of Milledgeville, Ga., as the setting for a novel that carries violence and evil to the kind of extreme that Southern writers and their readers love. Cotton Point, as he calls it, is a small city with lots of nice people, a college, a military academy and a healthy business community.

Into that stable world where everyone plays by long-prescribed rules, comes Paris Trout, a personification of evil rivaled only by William Faulkner's Popeye and a few of Faulkner's other bloodless drifters. Even before Trout shoots a 14-year-old black girl in the senseless killing that sets the action rolling, we know there is something wrong with him.

He cannot make even the simplest moral distinctions. Before it is over, his unyielding conviction that everything he does is right has thrown the whole town off its moral center and exposed the link between Trout's depravity and the town's si-

lent endorsement of all kinds of inhumanities—including racism, sexism and economic exploitation. . . .

[*Paris Trout*] is a psychological spellbinder. Watching this grim antihero spoil everything he touches will take your breath away and probably interfere with your sleep for a night or two.

Judith Paterson, "Southern Discomforts," in Book World—The Washington Post, *July 10, 1988, p. 8.*

DEBORAH MASON

[The title character of *Paris Trout*] was only taking care of business, trying to collect on Henry Ray Boxer's debt. That little black girl, Rosie Sayers, who got shot and killed in the scuffle, shouldn't have got in his way, or the woman with Rosie, who still walks around with Trout's bullet in her chest.

"I did what was right as rain," Trout tells his lawyer, and believes it. When the eye-for-an-eye rule is mentioned, Trout says, "Those ain't the same kind of eyes and they ain't the same kind of rules."

Mr. Dexter has created a character whose racism is a blunt, unregenerate fact, as primitive and willful as an earthquake or a rainstorm—and just as sealed off from argument, examination or questions of mercy. What the town's polite society takes care to disguise in Sunday-go-to-meeting euphemisms, Paris sets in defiant, ugly relief; he makes it easy for them to believe they are innocent of racism.

Trout's stubborn assumption that what he calls "the real rules" will eventually free him is, at first, simply an embarrassment to Cotton Point, an ostensibly enlightened Eisenhower-era Southern town. As Trout presses his claim more ominously, the townspeople come to fear him: he is dragging out into the air and light their own elaborately camouflaged prejudices. And still they excuse him because they have to excuse themselves.

Three years after a jury has found Trout guilty of second-degree murder, he remains free—but his inner corrosion has brought paranoia and derangement. When Mr. Dexter describes Trout's increasingly erratic behavior, he often comes perilously close to losing his bearing and turning the book into a thriller, using Trout's outcroppings of brutality and growing arsenal of guns to titillate rather than to advance the plot. It's as if he has to sell us on Trout's total depravity: being a racist killer isn't enough.

Mr. Dexter's strongest suit is his exquisite understanding of the finely meshed engines of greed, appetite and self-interest that drive a small town. . . . Mr. Dexter draws [Cotton Point's inhabitants] with precise and detailed conviction—their giddily adolescent parties and casual infidelities, their utterly utilitarian disparagement of blacks. When Trout's lawyer, Harry Seagraves, tells his wife that Trout has shot two black women, her first question is, "Did they work for anyone we know?"

Mr. Dexter's characterization of Seagraves is particularly persuasive—no glib paraphrase of the all-purpose, rumpled, hard-drinking, conscience-torn Southern lawyer. True, Seagraves is rumpled and hard-drinking, but his steely assessment of his own interests when he takes on the case makes his slow, agonizing waking to the horror of Trout's actions and his own complicity all the more affecting.

The primary agent of Seagraves' conversion is Hanna Trout, Paris's wife, a plain-spoken, bluntly sensual middle-aged woman—a former schoolteacher. You sense that Mr. Dexter, who writes regularly for *Playboy* and *Esquire,* is at pains to show that he can create a strong, resonant female character. For the most part he succeeds, although Hanna's assigned role of primal woman and conscience of Cotton Point occasionally gets on your nerves.

Trout's private victimization of Hanna by sexual abuse and corrosive disregard is analogous to his public victimization of Rosie Sayers, and there are lingering suggestions that each woman asked for what she got from Trout. Rosie never gets the chance to defend herself against this accusation. But Hanna, as it turns out, is one of the few people in Cotton Point who refuses to yield to Trout. She is the only white person to go to Rosie's funeral; she later refuses to appear at her husband's trial. And Hanna is the only character to escape

the grotesque outcome of Cotton Point's three-year collaboration with the killer of a 14-year-old child.

At a time when virulent racial incidents can no longer be conveniently fenced off in small Southern towns, Mr. Dexter's great accomplishment is to remind us, with lucidity and stinging frankness, the lengths to which we will go to deny our own racism and to reassure ourselves that we are innocent. (pp. 7-8)

> *Deborah Mason, "Unexamined Lives in Cotton Point," in* The New York Times Book Review, *July 24, 1988, pp. 7-8*

DEAN FAULKNER WELLS

"In the spring of that year," begins Pete Dexter's finely crafted new novel [*Paris Trout*], which takes place just after World War II,

> an epidemic of rabies broke out in Ether County, Georgia. The disease was carried principally by foxes and was reported first by farmers, who, in the months of April and May, shot more than seventy of the animals and turned them in to the county health officer.
>
> (p. 3)

Within Ether County, however, the town of Cotton Point is about to be assaulted by Paris Trout, a man as potentially lethal to those whose lives he touches as any rabid animal.

Brilliantly and frighteningly characterized, Trout is a sociopath who sees himself not only as beyond the reach of the law but also as far beyond all morality.

For him, right and wrong do not exist. He believes that he has the right to do anything, even commit murder. And ultimately the citizens of Cotton Point must come to terms with Trout and all that he stands for.

Rosie Sayers, a 14-year-old illiterate black child is Trout's first victim. Trout and an ex-cop who was dismissed from the police force for "excessive" brutality to blacks enter the house where Rosie lives. They have come to collect a debt. Both are armed. Without provocation, the two men open fire. Rosie dies from gunshot wounds from Trout's .45 pistol. Another black woman is seriously injured. (pp. 3, 9)

With that murder, Dexter sets the stage for a penetrating examination of the rest of his cast of characters—as their reactions to Trout reveal their attitudes about racism, law and society, violence and, finally, good and evil.

Harry Seagraves is a successful smalltown lawyer, a sophisticated, self-assured man who ironically agrees to defend Trout out of a sense of social obligation.

Because Trout runs a general store and serves as a banker for black people, he is a powerful man locally. Seagraves thus sets out to defend the status quo—and the inequities—of Cotton Point.

"We are all flawed people," Seagraves rationalizes, "some more than others."

Ward Townes is the prosecuting attorney, a practical man of

courage and conviction who is not ruled by the inbred mores of Cotton Point.

Then there is Carl Bonner, the divorce lawyer hired by Trout's estranged wife, Hanna. The town's perennial Eagle Scout, Bonner is an obsessive over-achiever who feels alienated from all around him. And he also is intricately involved in Trout's life. . . .

Hanna is the only person Trout fears; he thinks she plans to poison him. His paranoia becomes rampant: He covers his bedroom floor with panes of glass to warn him if anyone is coming. He puts a sheet of lead under his mattress to keep anyone from shooting him through it. His hotel room becomes an arsenal.

Perfectly offsetting graphic horror and comedy, Dexter brings all these characters together in an explosive conclusion.

Cotton Point's sesquicentennial celebration culminates in a parade. The police are drunk, as are most of the town's leading citizens. The town's only ambulance is being used in the parade. And from a second-story window of the courthouse, Paris Trout looks on, armed and dangerous.

"Even if we're all on the same road," Seagraves says, "Paris Trout doesn't have any brakes."

Pete Dexter's powerfully emotional novel doesn't have any brakes either. Hang on, because you won't be able to stop until the finish. (p. 9)

> *Dean Faulkner Wells, "The Graphic Horrors of a Moral-Less Man," in* Chicago Tribune—Books, *August 7, 1988, pp. 3, 9.*

PETE AXTHELM

The well-traveled columnist Pete Dexter has produced his big novel. In Paris Trout, shopkeeper, moneylender and murderer, he has created not only a cold, gaunt villain but a force that challenges the morals of an entire Georgia town. With a touch of the mastery that graces the best fiction about the South, Dexter has conjured up characters stroked broadly, voices that ring true—and vignettes crafted in miniature in a way that haunts.

Take an early walk to the store with a wise and doomed 14-year-old black child named Rosie. Near her tar-roofed slum home, she notices that the town sawmill stands in ugly solitude: "It made sense to her that trees wouldn't dare grow near a sawmill." Amid an epidemic of rabies, she encounters a fox and figures that it seems to recognize her. Bitten and terrified, Rosie returns home to face one of her mother's "visitors" at their shack. "He was holding a knife in his teeth. It resembled a smile."

Standing on their own, such images would be a dark delight worthy of Flannery O'Connor. But Dexter is going for the home run here. As the plot expands, there are numerous echoes of Faulkner. Paris Trout's horribly debasing rape of his wife with a water bottle recalls Popeye's savagery against Temple Drake in *Sanctuary*. The town's vaguely noble lawyer is spiritual kin to Gavin Stevens in *Intruder in the Dust*. Trout surely descends from Flem Snopes in *The Hamlet*.

Perhaps these references will lead some to dismiss *Paris Trout* as derivative. But Dexter has chosen the best of all to

derive from, then gone about building his own world. While Trout personifies a peculiar regional brand of evil, his wife, Hanna, achieves a fierce and stoic nobility. And the lawyer caught in the maelstrom, Harry Seagraves, abandons his safe Kiwanis Club good fellowship for bravery and ethics that he never knew were within him.

Although Trout, unrepentant killer of the black child Rosie, is his client, Seagraves is increasingly obsessed with the dead girl. He is also drawn, almost inevitably, to Hanna Trout. He succumbs to temptation with an uneasy control somewhere between Kiwanis and chaos: "He was reckless now, he had taken it too far and delivered himself into her hands. But part of being reckless was knowing you were reckless, and he was."

This is a reckless novel. A very fine writer knows he has taken large gambles and aimed at the highest level of Southern fiction. He has made a score.

> *Pete Axthelm, in a review of "Paris Trout," in* Newsweek, *Vol. CXII, No. 13, September 26, 1988, p. 74.*

GEORGE MELLY

Pete Dexter's *Paris Trout* is a good read. It's set in Faulkner country and examines the dark psychopathic undercurrents in a small town in the 1950s, leading up to a horrific and convincing climax, but it is free of Faulkner's convoluted style. The prose is taut, the feeling for time and place exact. Paris Trout himself—the name is certainly Faulkneresque—is a small shopkeeper and usurer, a sadist who has married above himself, an eccentric teetering on the edge of madness. He acts as the catalyst of a tragedy which draws in the whole community.

Predictably enough, given the setting, this involves black people and their vulnerability in a racist context, but there is nothing stereotyped in the way [Dexter] handles his characters. Not all the blacks are saints, nor all the whites fiends— on the contrary. Trout himself is as much a tragic figure as he is, both physically and mentally, a repulsive one. Nor does the author cheat through the use of hindsight. Nobody of either race much questions the status quo. They live within it, behaving well or badly according to their natures. There is plenty of tension, and the ability to set the characters within a landscape of cinematic credibility. Without being particularly original, it's a solid achievement heightened by wit and a flawless ear and eye. (p. 38)

> *George Melly, "Southern Talent," in* New Statesman & Society, *Vol. 1, No. 18, October 7, 1988, pp. 38-9.*

MAUREEN FREELY

It is hard to read *Paris Trout* without thinking of *To Kill a Mockingbird*. It is set in the 1950s in the small Georgia town of Cotton Point. The eponymous villain runs the general store and gives loans to blacks. Fat, foul, smelly, psychotic and greatly feared, he is a law unto himself. But when he shoots an innocent black girl and her foster mother while chasing down a debt, the townspeople decide he has gone too far and see to it that he is prosecuted.

Much of the story concerns the trial, the appeal, the light sentence and the ease with which it is avoided. Because the author assumes an audience that does not need to be educated about this particular brand of social injustice, he is able to step back and give a dispassionate view of a town in thrall to a bigot. Pete Dexter writes with a comfortable drawl that nevertheless avoids Southern excess. His tone is that of the enabling gossip.

Rather than pinning his characters down, he treats them as curiosities that might at any moment reveal hidden depths or unsuspected strengths. And they do—he gives complex portraits not just of Paris Trout, but also of his lawyer and of Hanna, his abused wife, who comes to understand her husband better than anyone else.

> *Maureen Freely, "M for Massacre," in* The Observer, *November 6, 1988, p. 44.*

An excerpt from *Paris Trout*

Seagraves and Trout walked through the courtroom's main entrance. Ward Townes was already sitting at the prosecution table, the spectator seats were close to empty. People had gone home.

The room had a hollow sound without spectators. Whispers carried, words spoken out loud seemed to hang in the air.

Judge Taylor came in buttoning his robe. There was grease on his chin, and he was sweating. When he settled, he checked the papers on the desk in front of him and then instructed the court officer to bring in the jury. Trout stared at them as they filed into their seats. Seagraves could see a pulse in his forehead. Only two of them glanced back, the foreman and a woman from Homewood.

The judge asked the foreman if the jury had reached a verdict. The air in the room smelled a hundred years old. "Yessir," he said.

Trout slowly stood up, his eyes still fixed on the jury box.

The foreman did not see him rise, he stared at the paper in his hands. " 'We find the defendant guilty of second-degree murder,' " he read. Then he looked up and found Paris Trout staring at him. A look passed over the foreman's face, and when it was gone, so was his color.

Seagraves stood up too. "We request a poll of the jury," he said.

One by one the jurors stood and pronounced the same verdict. Only one—the woman he recognized from Homewood—dared to look Trout in the eye. Seagraves wondered if she cared anymore who it was that had got her city water.

"Mr. Trout," the judge said when the last juror had spoken, "you have been found guilty of second-degree murder in the death of Rosie Sayers. Do you have anything further to say at this time?"

Trout turned his look on the judge but did not answer.

ANDREW ROSENHEIM

Paris Trout bluntly recalls the harsh, institutionalized racism of the segregationist South; the subsequent racial vicissitudes of the nation as a whole, however, mean that the non-Southern reader can no longer look upon this prejudice as a form of regional exoticism. Paris Trout, the eponymous figure in Pete Dexter's disturbing novel, is a solitary, violent businessman who exploits the black community of his small Southern town by lending money at extortionate rates. He shoots and kills a young black woman, is arrested and tried, and, though local justice is predisposed in his favour, is at last convicted, to face a minor jail sentence. He soon discovers that he can buy his way out of even this mockery.

An act of violence, a subsequent trial, racialism at the tense core—the parallels with *To Kill A Mockingbird* are manifest, and like the earlier novel, ***Paris Trout*** casts an extraordinarily strong narrative spell. Yet Dexter resolutely avoids Harper Lee's sentimentality; the "decent" lawyer of his novel is also the defence attorney for racist Trout. He (and everyone else) is scared of Trout, sensing a psychopathology that, at the end of the novel, runs homicidally amok. There are no heroes here, not even a guileless narrator; the movement of the novel's point of view among its characters undermines what tentative attachment we might otherwise form to any of them.

> *Andrew Rosenheim, "Voices of the New South," in* The Times Literary Supplement, *No. 4469, November 25-December 31, 1988, p. 1306.*

ROBERT TOWERS

Although he was born in Michigan and has subsequently lived in—and written about—other parts of the country, Pete Dexter spent part of his boyhood in Georgia and has been able to re-create convincingly [in ***Paris Trout***] the mores of an era when blacks were still referred to (formally) as Negroes and when the notion that they deserved equal justice with whites in a court of law had barely begun to take root in the rural South.

We meet first a severely deprived and possibly retarded fourteen-year-old black girl, Rosie Sayers, who, in the opening pages, is bitten on the leg by a rabid fox. We also meet a harsh-mannered white man in his sixties, Paris Trout, who keeps a general store and lends money to the local blacks in the small, central Georgia town of Cotton Point. . . .

The novel moves back and forth between the major characters—poor Rosie, whose story is soon told; Seagraves, whose behavior and attitudes reflect the prevailing ethos of the town's establishment; Trout's pathetically abused wife, Hanna, who had once befriended Rosie; and the eager young lawyer, Carl Bonner, whom Hanna hires to help her get a divorce from Trout. It is through their eyes and the eyes of a great many minor characters that we see Trout as he pursues his obsessed and threatening course through the novel.

We watch with revulsion as he sodomizes Hanna with a bottle of mineral water, as he forces unwanted food into her mouth, as he holds her head under water in the bathtub. We follow him through his trial, hear his self-justifications (which never include a moment's remorse for the murder of Rosie) and his lies. To the surprise of nearly everyone, he is convicted and given a ridiculously short sentence. Then, three years later, after all his appeals have failed, we accompany Trout (still flagrantly carrying a pistol) and the wary sheriff to the state prison farm where he is supposed to begin serving his sentence—only to watch him bribe a local judge to free him on a writ of *habeas corpus.* By this time he has so intimidated Cotton Point that nothing is done to bring him back to jail—and the novel plunges ahead to an apocalyptic shoot-out involving most of the main characters that the reader will have anticipated many pages beforehand.

Only rarely are we told directly what Trout is thinking. The picture we get from Dexter's description of him is that of a full-blown paranoid case, a shabby, unkempt, violent man reeking of urine who thinks that his wife is poisoning him. . . . By making his central character an out-and-out psychotic, Pete Dexter has, I think, run afoul of what seems to approach being a literary axiom: that while neurosis may lend itself to fictional treatment, psychosis generally does not. A character wholly given over to mad obsessions and thus entirely cut off from other people tends to arouse in the reader only a clinical curiosity or—if the madman's deeds are horrific enough—a sensationalist thrill. The descent of a person into madness may be fascinating, moving—even tragic; but madness itself is essentially dull once all possibilities of interesting conflict with others or any sense of conscience have been removed.

The effect of madness upon others can of course be made interesting, and Dexter attempts to do so in the case of Seagraves and Hanna. The experienced, rather jaded lawyer who must defend a repellent client while nursing pity for his victim is a nicely conceived character. Similarly, one can respond with sympathy to the plight of the wife, who married late to escape spinsterhood only to find herself captive of a brute determined to terrorize, humiliate, and possibly murder her. When the lawyer and the abused wife are brought togeth-er, Seagraves urges Hanna to keep up the appearance of a normal marriage with Trout in order not to prejudice his coming trial. Hanna refuses, saying that her husband is an "aberration" and that she will not be a party to the shooting of children. . . .

[A] love affair soon develops between the two in the ominous shadow of Paris Trout, with much closely described activity in bed.

These characters and this relationship are convincing—up to a point. Unfortunately, Pete Dexter never takes his material beyond what is journalistically plausible. His characters stay on the surface, lacking distinctive voices or personalities. Where he is most successful is in evoking a southern community of that period, ranging from the blacks who live in such places as Damp Bottoms and Indian Heights to the substantial folk like Seagraves and his wife who live on Draft Street. There is a wonderfully funny account of the town's celebration of its sesquicentennial—in which every man in town is required to grow a beard and stocks are put up to punish those still beardless after a certain date.

Mr. Dexter's prose is lucid and efficient, but without much color or individuality. The story gets swiftly told; it is an interesting story, though not one that I found engrossing or of much moral weight. *Paris Trout,* . . . will, I expect, fade rather quickly in the memory of most of its readers. (p. 18)

Robert Towers, "Intruders in the Dust," in The New York Review of Books, *Vol. XXXVI, No. 2, February 16, 1989, pp. 18-19.*

Gabriel (José) García Márquez
Love in the Time of Cholera
Los Angeles Times Book Awards: Fiction

Colombian novelist, short story writer, journalist, critic, scriptwriter, and dramatist.

Spanning from the late nineteenth century to the 1930s, *Love in the Time of Cholera* (originally published in 1985 as *El amor en los tiempos del colera*) explores various manifestations of love and examines themes relating to aging, death, and decay. Set in a South American community plagued by recurring civil wars and cholera epidemics, this novel vividly details the local environment as well as the emotional states of the three principal characters. The nonlinear narrative delineates poignant events in ordinary life and the history of the region, blending social realism with elements of sentimental literature and soap operas. Conflict is initiated when Florentino Ariza, a telegraph operator whose interests include music and literature, falls passionately in love with Fermina Daza, the daughter of a wealthy man, and woos her clandestinely through letters and serenades. Disapproving of this teenage romance, Fermina's father takes his daughter on a long, arduous journey. Upon her return, Fermina loses interest in Florentino and eventually marries Dr. Juvenal Urbino, a wealthy and distinguished gentleman whom many critics likened to the "ideal man" in popular romance fiction. After being rejected, Florentino silently maintains his unrequited affection for Fermina for fifty-one years, nine months, and four days, until they meet again at her husband's wake and he renews his vow of eternal love.

García Márquez intertwines the experiences and personalities of Florentino, Fermina, and Dr. Urbino to meditate upon love as well as social and cultural issues. The doctor, for example, becomes an outstanding figure in the community by advocating methods to combat cholera, and he represents positive qualities associated with wealth, high culture, and education. Fermina reflects the values and options of women in Latin American society. The couple's long and ultimately mysterious relationship provides a context for exploring various aspects of marriage. Themes relating to devotion, romance, and eroticism are addressed through Florentino, who enjoys numerous sexual adventures while sustaining his emotional attachment to Fermina. Critics praised García Márquez's witty epigrams and observations, playful associations between the physical symptoms of cholera and the intense emotions of anger and love, and his exploration of motivation and interpretation of human behavior. Thomas Pynchon stated: "[García Márquez] writes with impassioned control, out of maniacal serenity: the Garcimarquesian voice we have come to recognize from [his earlier] fiction has matured, found and developed new resources, been brought to a level where it can at once be classical and familiar, opalescent and pure, able to praise and curse, laugh and cry, fabulate and sing."

García Márquez was born in Aracataca, Colombia, where he lived with his grandparents for the first eight years of his life.

The storytelling of his grandmother, the long decline of Aracataca, and the myths and superstitions of the townspeople all played major roles in shaping García Márquez's imagination. Awarded the Nobel Prize in Literature in 1982, García Márquez is among the group of Latin American writers who rose to international prominence during the 1960s, a period of fruition often referred to as the "boom." The immense international success of García Márquez's novel *Cien años de soledad* (1967; *One Hundred Years of Solitude*), which Pablo Neruda described as "the greatest revelation in the Spanish language since the *Don Quixote* of Cervantes," the acknowledged importance of such writers as Jorge Luis Borges, Neruda, and Octavio Paz, and the appearance of translated works by Carlos Fuentes and Mario Vargas Llosa, among others, led to affirmation of Latin American letters as a potent force in contemporary literature. The enthusiastic critical reception of García Márquez's work is usually attributed to his imaginative blending of history, politics, social realism, and fantasy. Although not widely evidenced in *Love in the Time of Cholera*, García Márquez often makes use of the technique of magic realism, embellishing his work with surreal events and fantastic imagery to obscure the distinctions between illusion and reality. In addition to *One Hundred Years of Solitude* and *Love in the Time of Cholera*, Garcia Marquez has published numerous short stories and such acclaimed novels as *La mala hora* (1961; *In Evil Hour*), *El otoño del patriarca* (1975; *The Autumn of the Patriarch*), and *Crónica de una muerte anunciada* (1982; *Chronicle of a Death Foretold*).

(See also *CLC*, Vols. 2, 3, 8, 10, 15, 27, 47; *Contemporary Authors*, Vols. 33-36, rev. ed.; and *Contemporary Authors New Revision Series*, Vol. 10.)

GABRIEL GARCÍA MÁRQUEZ [INTERVIEW WITH MARLISE SIMONS]

[Simons]: *You have just finished a play and are writing film scripts and directing a film institute. Are you changing your life?*

[García Márquez]: No, because I am writing a novel [*Bolivar*]. And I am finishing this one so I can start another. But I have never had so many things going on at the same time. I think I have never before felt so fulfilled, so much in the prime of my life.

I'm writing. Six different stories are being filmed. I'm at the cinema foundation. And the play [*Diatribe of Love Against a Seated Man*] will be opening this year in Argentina and Brazil.

For a long time, of course, things did not work out for me—almost the first 40 years of my life. I had financial problems; I had work problems. I had not made it as a writer or as anything else. It was a difficult time emotionally and psychologically; I had the idea that I was like an extra, that I did not count anywhere. And then, with *One Hundred Years of Solitude,* things turned. Now all this is going on without my being dependent on anyone. Still, I have to do all sorts of things. I have to sit on a bicycle in the morning. I am on an eternal diet. Half my life I couldn't eat what I wanted because I couldn't afford to, the other half because I have to diet.

And now, in your latest book, Love in the Time of Cholera, the theme and style seem very different. Why did you write a love story?

I think aging has made me realize that feelings and sentiments, what happens in the heart, are ultimately the most important. But in some way, all my books are about love. In *One Hundred Years* there is one love story after another. *Chronicle of a Death Foretold* is a terrible drama of love. I think there is love everywhere. This time love is more ardent. Because two loves join and go on.

I think, though, that I could not have written *Love in the Time of Cholera* when I was younger. It has practically a lifetime's experience in it. And it includes many experiences, my own and other peoples'. Above all, there are points of view I didn't have before. I'll be 60 this year. At that age, one becomes more serene in everything.

Also more generous, perhaps. Because this is a tremendously generous book.

A Chilean priest told me it was the most Christian book he'd ever read.

And the style? Do you see this as a departure from your earlier work?

In every book I try to take a different path and I think I did here. One doesn't choose the style. You can investigate and try to discover what the best style would be for a theme. But the style is determined by the subject, by the mood of the times. If you try to use something that is not suitable, it just won't work. Then the critics build theories around that and they see things I hadn't seen. I only respond to our way of life, the life of the Caribbean. You can take my books and I can tell you line for line what part of reality or what episode it came from.

There was an insomnia plague in One Hundred Years of Solitude, and in one of your stories a plague killed all the birds. Now there is the Time of Cholera. What is it that intrigues you so about plagues?

Cartagena really had a great plague at the end of the last century. And I've always been interested in plagues, beginning with *Oedipus Rex.* I've read a lot about them. *A Journal of the Plague Year* by Daniel Defoe is one of my favorite books. Plagues are like imponderable dangers that surprise people. They seem to have a quality of destiny. It's the phenomenon of death on a mass scale. What I find curious is that the great plagues have always produced great excesses. They make people want to live more. It's that almost metaphysical dimension that interests me.

I have used other literary references. *The Plague* of Camus. There is a plague in *The Betrothed* of Alessandro Manzoni. I'm always looking up books that deal with a theme I'm dealing with. I do it to make sure that mine is not alike. Not precisely to copy from them but to have the use of them somehow. I think all writers do that. Behind every idea there is a thousand years of literature. I think you have to know as much as possible of that to know where you are and how you are taking it further.

What was the genesis of Love in the Time of Cholera?

It really sprang from two sources that came together. One was the love affair of my parents, which was identical to that of Fermina Daza and Florentino Ariza in their youth. My father was the telegraph operator of Aracataca [Colombia]. He played the violin. She was the pretty girl from a well-to-do family. Her father was opposed because the boy was poor and he was a liberal. All that part of the story was my parents'. . . . When she went to school, the letters, the poems, the violin serenades, her trip to the interior when her father tried to make her forget him, the way they communicated by telegram—all that is authentic. And when she returns, everyone thinks she has forgotten him. That too. It's exactly the way my parents told it. The only difference is they married. And, as soon as they were married, they were no longer interesting as literary figures.

And the other source?

Many years ago, in Mexico, I read a story in a newspaper about the death of two old Americans—a man and a woman—who would meet every year in Acapulco, always going to the same hotel, the same restaurants, following the same routine as they had done for 40 years. They were almost 80 years old and kept coming. Then one day they went out in a boat and, in order to rob them, the boatman murdered them with his oars. Through their death, the story of their secret romance became known. I was fascinated by them. They were each married to other people.

I always thought I would write my parents' story, but I didn't know how. One day, through one of those absolutely incomprehensible things that happen in literary creation, the two stories came together in my mind. I had all the love of the young people from my parents and from the old couple I took the love of old people.

You have said that your stories often come from a single image that strikes you.

Yes. In fact, I'm so fascinated by how to detect the birth of a story that I have a workshop at the cinema foundation called "How to Tell a Story." I bring together 10 students from different Latin American countries and we sit at a round table without interruption for four hours a day for six weeks and try to write a story from scratch. We start by going round and round. At first there are only differences. . . . The Venezuelan wants one thing, the Argentine another. Then suddenly an idea appears that grabs everyone and the story can be developed. We've done three so far. But, you know, we still don't know how the idea is born. It always catches us by surprise.

In my case, it always begins with an image, not an idea or a concept. With **Love in the Time of Cholera,** the image was of two old people dancing on the deck of a boat, dancing a bolero.

Once you have the image, then what happens?

The image grows in my head until the whole story takes shape as it might in real life. The problem is that life isn't the same as literature, so then I have to ask myself the big question: How do I adapt this, what is the most appropriate structure for this book? I have always aspired to finding the perfect structure. One perfect structure in literature is that of Sophocles' *Oedipus Rex.* Another is a short story, "Monkey's Paw," by an English writer, William Jacobs.

When I have the story and the structure completely worked out, I can start—but only on condition that I find the right name for each character. If I don't have the name that exactly suits the character, it doesn't come alive. I don't see it.

Once I sit down to write, usually I no longer have any hesitations. I may take a few notes, a word or a phrase or something to help me the following morning, but I never work with a lot of notes. That's what I learned when I was young. I know writers who have books full of notes and they wind up thinking about their notes and never write their books.

You've always said you still feel as much a journalist as a writer of fiction. Some writers think that in journalism the pleasure of discovery comes in the research, while in fiction the pleasure of discovery comes in the writing. Would you agree?

Certainly there are pleasures in both. To begin with, I consider journalism to be a literary genre. Intellectuals would not agree, but I believe it is. Without being fiction, it is a form, an instrument, for expressing reality.

The timing may be different but the experience is the same in literature and journalism. In fiction, if you feel you get a scoop, a scoop about life that fits into your writing, it's the same emotion as a journalist when he gets to the heart of a

story. Those moments occur when you least expect them and they bring extraordinary happiness. Just as a journalist knows when he's got the story, a writer has a similar revelation. Of course, he still has to illustrate and enrich it, but he knows he's got it. It's almost an instinct. The journalist knows if he has news or not. The writer knows if it's literature or not, if it's poetry or not. After that, the writing is very much the same. Both use many of the same techniques. (pp. 1, 23)

What are you trying to achieve at the cinema foundation?

I'd like to see film-making as an artistic expression in Latin America valued the same way as our literature is now. We have very fine literature, but it has taken a long time to be recognized. It has been a very hard struggle. And sometimes it is still difficult.

The literature now seems to have a life of its own.

You know, this really started to happen when we conquered our own readers at home. When they started to read us in Latin America. We had always thought the opposite was important. When we published a book, we didn't care if it was sold here as long as we could get it translated. And yet we knew what would happen. It would be translated and get a few obligatory critical notes from the specialists. The book would stay within the Spanish Studies ghettos of the universities and never get out. When we started to be read in Latin America, everything opened up.

The same is beginning to happen with film. There are now good films being made in Latin America. And this is being done not through great productions with a lot of capital. It is done within our own means and with our own methods. And the films are appearing at the international festivals and are being nominated for prizes. But they still have to conquer their own audience here. The problem lies with the big distributors. They need to spend a lot of money to promote unknown films and then they get no returns. The day our films make money, the whole focus will change. We saw it in literature; we will see it in films in the years ahead.

Politics is so important to you. But you don't use your books to promote your political ideas.

I don't think literature should be used as a firearm. But, even against your own will, your ideological positions are inevitably reflected in your writing and they influence readers. I think my books have had political impact in Latin America because they help to create a Latin American identity; they help Latin Americans to become more aware of their own culture.

An American asked me the other day what was the real political intention behind the cinema foundation. I said the issue is not what is behind it but what lies ahead of it. The idea is to stimulate awareness of the Latin American cinema, and that is fundamentally a political objective. Of course, the project is strictly about film-making but the results will be political. People often think that politics are elections, that politics are what governments do. But literature, cinema, painting and music are all essential to forging Latin America's identity. And that's what I mean by politics.

Would you say that is different from placing artistic talent at the service of politics?

I would never do that. Well, let me be clearer. The arts are always at the service of politics, of some ideology, of the vision the writer or the artist has of the world. But the arts should never be at the service of a government. (p. 24)

What was it like to write the play? Did that give you any trouble?

Well, it's really a monologue that I wrote for Graciela Duffau, the Argentine actress. It's called *Diatribe of Love Against a Seated Man.* An angry woman is telling her husband everything that passes through her head. It goes on for two hours. He is sitting in a chair reading a newspaper and doesn't react at all. But a monologue isn't entirely a play. That is, there are many rules and laws of the theater that don't apply here.

And what is your next writing project?

I'm going to finish *Bolivar.* I need a few more months. And I'm going to write my memoirs. Usually authors write their memoirs when they can no longer remember anything. I'm going to start slowly and write and write. They won't be normal memoirs. Every time I have 400 pages ready, I'll publish a volume and see. I could go up to six. (p. 25)

> Marlise Simons, *"García Márquez on Love, Plagues and Politics,"* in The New York Times Book Review, *February 21, 1988, pp. 1, 23-5.*

PAUL GRAY

Because of the time warp of translation, it took three years for Gabriel García Márquez's novel *Cien Años de Soledad* to reach and astound the English-speaking world as *One Hundred Years of Solitude* (1970). That rousing chronicle of a mythical South American town and a family doomed to heroism and folly established its author's international reputation. Among the book's magical properties was the power to transform a once obscure Colombian journalist into the recipient of the 1982 Nobel Prize for Literature. García Márquez, of course, published other works along the way to Stockholm, including three novels, several collections of stories and dusted-off samples of old newspaper reporting. But none of these achieved the glitter and scope of his most triumphant narrative, which concluded, after all, with a warning that the lightning of inspiration does not strike twice: "Races condemned to one hundred years of solitude did not have a second opportunity on earth."

Perhaps countless readers' hopes for another *Solitude* have been misguided. Rumors have been building, though, of something big in progress. Another long, ambitious García Márquez novel has been wending its way toward English translation, accumulating impressive numbers in the process: sales of more than 1 million in the original Spanish version, hundreds of thousands of copies snapped up in West Germany, Italy and France. The U.S. debut of *Love in the Time of Cholera* comes preceded by considerable thunder.

The noise is justified. This book will not make anyone forget *One Hundred Years of Solitude,* and thank goodness for that. Instead, García Márquez, 60, offers a spacious mirror image of the novel that made him famous. This time out, surface events largely conform to the dictates of plausibility. No one ascends bodily into heaven; the famous plague of insomnia that swept through *Solitude* here becomes literal, recurrent ravages of cholera morbus. The bizarre and outlandish are relegated to the domain of private lives, to characters who must construct for themselves elaborate fictions to follow in order to stand the shocks and tedium of being alive.

The setting is an imagined "sleepy provincial capital" on the South American shores of the Caribbean, where on one Pentecost Sunday Dr. Juvenal Urbino, 81, falls to his death while trying to retrieve a pet parrot from a mango tree. This calamity sets church bells tolling and mourners swarming to the Urbino household, for the deceased physician had been one of the most honored and distinguished residents of the city. Among the visitors is Florentino Ariza, 76, president of the River Co. of the Caribbean, who approaches the bereaved widow, Fermina Daza, 72, and says, "I have waited for this opportunity for more than half a century, to repeat to you once again my vow of eternal fidelity and everlasting love." Fermina furiously shows him the door.

This contretemps calls for a bit of explaining, and García Márquez flashes backward to tell all. . . .

Will Florentino and Fermina find happiness at the long, bitter end? García Márquez answers this question eventually, but the success of his novel does not depend on the outcome. The genius of *Love in the Time of Cholera* is the filling-in of the gaps of ordinary life, the munificence of detail that can be exacted from a place where, as Dr. Urbino muses, "nothing had happened for four centuries." Nonetheless, the torpid scenery provides a beguiling background. . . .

History may have abandoned this backwater metropolis, once heralded as "the gateway to America," but life goes on in stunning profusion. García Márquez generously populates a place "where everything was known, and where many things were known even before they happened, above all if they concerned the rich." But the constant gossip actually pays little heed to class distinctions. Whatever their status, the author's characters energetically play their parts in the human comedy. They are born to die. Hearts are enchanted, broken and sometimes put back together again. Wisdom accrues to those who have grown too old to profit by its possession. This novel is filled with surprises, but not those of the amazing variety. The constant, throbbing fascination here is the shock of recognition.

> Paul Gray, *"A Half-Century of Solitude,"* in Time, *New York, Vol. 131, No. 13, March 28, 1988, p. 77.*

THOMAS PYNCHON

Love, as Mickey and Sylvia, in their 1956 hit single, remind us, love is strange. As we grow older it gets stranger, until at some point mortality has come well within the frame of our attention, and there we are, suddenly caught between terminal dates while still talking a game of eternity. It's about then that we may begin to regard love songs, romance novels, soap operas and any live teen-age pronouncements at all on the subject of love with an increasingly impatient, not to mention intolerant, ear.

At the same time, where would any of us be without all that romantic infrastructure, without, in fact, just that degree of adolescent, premortal hope? Pretty far out on life's limb, at least. Suppose, then, it were possible, not only to swear love "forever," but actually to follow through on it—to live a long, full and authentic life based on such a vow, to put one's alloted stake of precious time where one's heart is? This is the extraordinary premise of Gabriel García Márquez's new novel *Love in the Time of Cholera,* one on which he delivers, and triumphantly.

In the postromantic ebb of the 70's and 80's, with everybody now so wised up and even growing paranoid about love, once the magical buzzword of a generation, it is a daring step for any writer to decide to work in love's vernacular, to take it, with all its folly, imprecision and lapses in taste, at all seriously—that is, as well worth those higher forms of play that we value in fiction. For García Márquez the step may also be revolutionary. "I think that a novel about love is as valid as any other," he once remarked in a conversation with his friend, the journalist Plinio Apuleyo Mendoza (published as "El Olor de la Guayaba," 1982). "In reality the duty of a writer—the revolutionary duty, if you like—is that of writing well."

And—oh boy—does he write well. He writes with impassioned control, out of a maniacal serenity: the Garcimarquesian voice we have come to recognize from the other fiction has matured, found and developed new resources, been brought to a level where it can at once be classical and familiar, opalescent and pure, able to praise and curse, laugh and cry, fabulate and sing and when called upon, take off and soar, as in [the description in *Love in the Time of Cholera*] of a turn-of-the-century balloon trip. . . . (pp. 1, 47)

This novel is also revolutionary in daring to suggest that vows of love made under a presumption of immortality—youthful idiocy, to some—may yet be honored, much later in life when we ought to know better, in the face of the undeniable. This is, effectively, to assert the resurrection of the body, today as throughout history an unavoidably revolutionary idea. Through the ever-subversive medium of fiction, García Márquez shows us how it could all plausibly come about, even—wild hope—for somebody out here, outside a book, even as inevitably beaten at, bought and resold as we all must have become if only through years of simple residence in the injuring and corruptive world.

Here's what happens. The story takes place between about 1880 and 1930, in a Caribbean seaport city, unnamed but said to be a composite of Cartagena and Barranquilla—as well, perhaps, as cities of the spirit less officially mapped. Three major characters form a triangle whose hypotenuse is Florentino Ariza, a poet dedicated to love both carnal and transcendent, though his secular fate is with the River Company of the Caribbean and its small fleet of paddle-wheel steamboats. As a young apprentice telegrapher he meets and falls forever in love with Fermina Daza, a "beautiful adolescent with . . . almond-shaped eyes," who walks with a "natural haughtiness . . . her doe's gait making her seem immune to gravity." Though they exchange hardly a hundred words face to face, they carry on a passionate and secret affair entirely by way of letters and telegrams, even after the girl's father has found out and taken her away on an extended "journey of forgetting." But when she returns, Fermina rejects the lovesick young man after all, and eventually meets and marries instead Dr. Juvenal Urbino who, like the hero of a 19th-century novel, is well born, a sharp dresser, somewhat stuck on himself but a terrific catch nonetheless.

For Florentino, love's creature, this is an agonizing setback, though nothing fatal. Having sworn to love Fermina Daza forever, he settles in to wait for as long as he has to until she's free again. (p. 47)

The heart's eternal vow [runs] up against the world's finite terms. The confrontation occurs near the end of the first chapter, which recounts Dr. Urbino's last day on earth and Fermina's first night as a widow. We then flash back 50 years, into the time of cholera. The middle chapters follow the lives of the three characters through the years of the Urbinos' marriage and Florentino Ariza's rise at the River Company, as one century ticks over into the next. The last chapter takes up again where the first left off, with Florentino, now, in the face of what many men would consider major rejection, resolutely setting about courting Fermina Daza all over again, doing what he must to win her love.

In their city, throughout a turbulent half-century, death has proliferated everywhere, both as *el cólera,* the fatal disease that sweeps through in terrible intermittent epidemics, and as *la cólera,* defined as choler or anger, which taken to its extreme becomes warfare. Victims of one, in this book, are more than once mistaken for victims of the other. War, "always the same war," is presented here not as the continuation by other means of any politics that can possibly matter, but as a negative force, a plague, whose only meaning is death on a massive scale. Against this dark ground, lives, so precarious, are often more and less conscious projects of resistance, even of sworn opposition, to death. Dr. Urbino, like his father before him, becomes a leader in the battle against the cholera, promoting public health measures obsessively, heroically. Fermina, more conventionally but with as much courage, soldiers on in her chosen role of wife, mother and household manager, maintaining a safe perimeter for her family. Florentino embraces Eros, death's well-known long-time enemy, setting off on a career of seductions that eventually add up to 622 "long-term liaisons, apart from . . . countless fleeting adventures," while maintaining, impervious to time, his deeper fidelity, his unquenchable hope for a life with Fermina. At the end he can tell her truthfully—though she doesn't believe it for a minute—that he has remained a virgin for her.

So far as this is Florentino's story, in a way his *Bildungsroman,* we find ourselves, as he earns the suspension of our disbelief, cheering him on, wishing for the success of this stubborn warrior against age and death, and in the name of love. But like the best fictional characters, he insists on his autonomy, refusing to be anything less ambiguous than human. We must take him as he is, pursuing his tomcat destiny out among the streets and lovers' refuges of this city with which he lives on terms of such easy intimacy, carrying with him a potential for disasters from which he remains safe, immunized by a comical but dangerous indifference to consequences that often borders on criminal neglect. (pp. 47, 49)

[Dumb] luck has as much to do with getting Florentino through as the intensity or purity of his dream. The author's great affection for this character does not entirely overcome a sly concurrent subversion of the ethic of *machismo,* of which García Márquez is not especially fond, having described it elsewhere simply as usurpation of the rights of others. Indeed, as we've come to expect from his fiction, it's the women in this story who are stronger, more attuned to reality. When Florentino goes crazy with love, developing symptoms like those of cholera, it is his mother, Tránsito Ariza, who pulls him out of it. His innumerable lecheries are rewarded not so much for any traditional masculine selling points as for his obvious and aching need to be loved. Women go for it. "He is ugly and sad," Fermina Daza's cousin Hildebranda tells her, "but he is all love."

And García Márquez, straight-faced teller of tall tales, is his biographer. At the age of 19, as he has reported, the young writer underwent a literary epiphany on reading the famous opening lines of Kafka's "Metamorphosis," in which a man wakes to find himself transformed into a giant insect. "Gosh," exclaimed García Márquez, using in Spanish a word we in English may not, "that's just the way my grandmother used to talk!" And that, he adds, is when novels began to interest him. Much of what come in his work to be called "magic realism" was, as he tells it, simply the presence of that grandmotherly voice.

Nevertheless, in this novel we have come a meaningful distance from Macondo, the magical village in *One Hundred Years of Solitude* where folks routinely sail through the air and the dead remain in everyday conversation with the living: we have descended, perhaps in some way down the same river, all the way downstream, into war and pestilence and urban confusions to the edge of a Caribbean haunted less by individual dead than by a history which has brought so appallingly many down, without ever having spoken, or having spoken gone unheard, or having been heard, left unrecorded. As revolutionary as writing well is the duty to redeem these silences, a duty García Márquez has here fulfilled with honor and compassion. It would be presumptuous to speak of moving "beyond" *One Hundred Years of Solitude* but clearly García Márquez has moved somewhere else, not least into deeper awareness of the ways in which, as Florentino comes to learn, "nobody teaches life anything." There are still delightful and stunning moments contrary to fact, still told with the same unblinking humor—presences at the foot of the bed, an anonymously delivered doll with a curse on it, the sinister parrot, almost a minor character, whose pursuit ends with the death of Dr. Juvenal Urbino. But the predominant claim on the author's attention and energies comes from what is not so contrary to fact, a human consensus about "reality" in which love and the possibility of love's extinction are the indispensable driving forces, and varieties of magic have become, if not quite peripheral then at least more thoughtfully deployed in the service of an expanded vision, matured, darker than before but no less clement.

It could be argued that this is the only honest way to write about love, that without the darkness and the finitude there might be romance, erotica, social comedy, soap opera—all genres, by the way, that are well represented in this novel—but not the Big L. What that seems to require, along with a certain vantage point, a certain level of understanding, is an author's ability to control his own love for his characters, to withhold from the reader the full extent of his caring, in other words not to lapse into drivel. . . .

There comes a moment, early in his career at the River Company of the Caribbean when Florentino Ariza, unable to write even a simple commercial letter without some kind of romantic poetry creeping in, is discussing the problem with his uncle Leo XII, who owns the company. It's no use, the young man protests—"Love is the only thing that interests me."

"The trouble," his uncle replies, "is that without river navigation, there is no love." For Florentino this happens to be literally true: the shape of his life is defined by two momentous river voyages, half a century apart. On the first he made his decision to return and live forever in the city of Fermina Daza, to persevere in his love for as long as it might take. On the second, through a desolate landscape, he journeys into love and against time, with Fermina, at last, by his side. There is nothing I have read quite like this astonishing final chapter, symphonic, sure in its dynamics and tempo, moving like a riverboat too, its author and pilot, with a lifetime's experience steering us unerringly among hazards of skepticism and mercy, on this river we all know, without whose navigation there is no love and against whose flow the effort to return is never worth a less honorable name than remembrance—at the very best it results in works that can even return our worn souls to us, among which most certainly belongs *Love in the Time of Cholera,* this shining and heartbreaking novel. (p. 49)

Thomas Pynchon, "The Heart's Eternal Vow," in The New York Times Book Review, *April 10, 1988, pp. 1, 47, 49.*

JEAN FRANCO

Set in a stagnant tropical port at the turn of the century, *Love in the Time of Cholera* tells the story of Florentino Ariza's prolonged passion for Fermina Daza, a passion that is finally consummated after fifty years, nine months and four days, when they are both over 70 years old. The consummation takes place on a riverboat that flies the cholera flag in order to protect their privacy. When Fermina undresses, Florentino finds her "just as he imagined her. Her shoulders were wrinkled, her breasts sagged, her ribs were covered by a flabby skin as pale and cold as a frog's"—which does not prevent him from exploring "her withered neck with his fingertips, her bosom armored in metal stays, her hips with their decaying bones, her thighs with their aging veins." The boat cannot land because of the cholera flag, so the couple, enjoying "the tranquil, wholesome love of experienced grandparents," are destined to live out their lives perpetually journeying up and down the river through a calamitous and ruined landscape, clinging hopefully to the last vestiges of life.

The humor of this autumnal romance cannot, however, dispel the odor of mortality. On the very first page, the reader is greeted "with the aromatic fumes of gold cyanide" and the suicide of the Caribbean refugee Jeremiah de Saint-Amour. The doctor who writes the death certificate is Fermina Daza's 81-year-old husband, Juvenal Urbino, who hours later is killed falling from a ladder as he tries to coax a parrot from a tree. It is at the funeral that Florentino renews a courtship he had begun half a century earlier.

The novel retraces the story of their love and separation: Fermina's adolescence under the jealous guardianship of a father who had made his money in contraband and wanted her to be a great lady; her brief engagement to the illegitimate and lowly Florentino; her marriage to the brilliant European-educated doctor Juvenal Urbino; and her then exemplary life (marred only by a two-year separation caused by her husband's infidelity). Meanwhile, Florentino has a brilliant career with the riverboat company and becomes an impenitent and bizarre womanizer who, when he is over 60, is capable of assaulting a maid "in less time than a Philippino rooster" and leaving her in the family way. His lovers include a 50-year-old widow who receives him stark naked with an organdy bow in her hair, an escapee from the lunatic asylum and, when he is over 70, a schoolgirl "with braces on her teeth and the scrapes of elementary school on her knees."

The humor and pathos of aging and death are subjects that have obsessed García Márquez from his earliest writings. His first novel, *Leafstorm,* was about a funeral. In *One Hundred*

Years of Solitude, there are dozens of tiny vignettes of death—Amaranta Úrsula preparing her own shroud, José Arcadio Buendía's dying dream of walking through room after room until he meets the man he has killed, and the matriarch, Úrsula, concealing her blindness from her children before lucidly dying. In *Love in the Time of Cholera* bodies fail long before passions are spent. . . .

Decay is part of the landscape. The colonial Caribbean port where Fermina and Florentino pass most of their lives is familiar García Márquez territory. It was in towns such as this that he wrote his first sketches for a novel in the late 1940s and which he chronicled as a journalist in Barranquilla and Cartagena. It was here that he collected the repertoire of legend, anecdote, small-town boredom and eccentricity that he has drawn on ever since. Not that there is any nostalgia in *Love in the Time of Cholera,* which moves from the stagnation of colonialism to the devastation of modernity in the time it takes to turn a page. Although the cobbled streets of the city recall "surprise attacks and buccaneer landings," "nothing had happened for four centuries except a slow aging among withered laurels and putrefying swamps." On the edge of the town are the old slave quarters, where buzzards fight over the offal from the slaughterhouse. Cadavers are everywhere, some dead of cholera and others in the wars. (p. 573)

By the end of the novel and its "happy ending," the mood is paradoxically apocalyptic. Fermina and Florentino's love boat, which once had steamed through an idyllic landscape, now passes "calcinated flatlands stripped of entire forests." The manatees "with their great breasts that had nursed their young and wept on the banks in a forlorn woman's voice were an extinct species, annihilated by the armored bullets of hunters for sport." Natural life has almost disappeared, "the parrots, the monkeys, the villages were gone, everything was gone."

For this is the irony of García Márquez's novel—that the genial good humor disguises apocalyptic foreboding. The same civilization that idealizes lovers produces a global wasteland, and the private fantasies of romance are rafts on a sea of public devastation. Fermina and Florentino salvage their own idyll but are themselves part of the destruction, a last nineteenth-century romance that can only find a heart of darkness (not for nothing is Joseph Conrad a character in the novel; he is accused of cheating Fermina Daza's father in a shady arms deal). Fermina and Florentino's love boat, indeed, adds to the devastation, since it has polluted the river waters and consumes the last of the forests on the riverbanks. It is this ambiguous relationship of private felicity and mass destruction that provides the novel with its disturbing undertow.

In his novels, García Márquez constantly returns to one particular historical period—from independence to the first decades of the twentieth century. It is the hundred years of Macondo in *One Hundred Years of Solitude* and of the dictatorship in *The Autumn of the Patriarch.* What fascinates him, evidently, is the meeting of fierce Latin idiosyncrasy with rationalism and modernity. Yet *Love in the Time of Cholera* is not only about the past but also about the anachronistic life forms that still survive in the ruins left by nineteenth-century progress. In this respect, the novel shares the *fin de siècle* mood of much contemporary Latin American writing. (pp. 573-74)

Jean Franco, "Mementos Mori," in The Nation,

New York, Vol. 246, No. 16, April 23, 1988, pp. 573-74.

ANGELA CARTER

Love in the Time of Cholera begins with a whiff of bitter almonds; a man whose very name speaks of the holiness of the heart's emotions, Jeremiah de Saint-Amour, has "escaped the torments of memory with the aromatic fumes of gold cyanide." It is the first suicide by cyanide his doctor, Juvenal Urbino, has attended that was *not* provoked by unrequited love. The septuagenarian Saint-Amour has killed himself simply because he decided to do so, in order to escape those indignities the passing years have already heaped upon Doctor Urbino. (p. 1)

The death of Jeremiah Saint-Amour and the devotion of his surviving mistress are dealt with in a few pages, but they provide a succinct overture for the rest of the novel, rehearsing its major themes of love, death, the torments of memory, the inexorability of old age. Dr. Juvenal Urbino, himself in his eighties, won't survive the day of his patient's death, in spite of the solicitude with which his wife, Fermina Daza, tends his geriatric decline.

After Dr. Urbino takes a tumble from a ladder whilst in pursuit of an escaped parrot, who should come to vow undying love to the widow but the very same man she once brutally jilted exactly 51 years, nine months and four days before.

The bulk of the novel directs us back to the past. We learn how, once upon a time, the beautiful young Fermina Daza was courted by the somewhat lugubrious yet nevertheless attractive Florentino Ariza, she the daughter of a kind of gangster, he the illegitimate son of a woman who dabbled in pawnbroking. The affair, passionate yet entirely chaste, was conducted mostly by letters and Fermina Daza put an abrupt stop to it as soon as she realized she was in love, not with the unfortunate young man, but with the idea of love itself.

Shortly thereafter, she married the entirely eligible Dr. Urbino, far above her station, and became a great lady, spending a good deal of time in Europe in the manner of rich Latin Americans at the turn of the last century, bearing two fine children, undergoing the customary vicissitudes of marriage and finding at last a glorious contentment. And yet; "She always felt as if her life had been lent to her by her husband." García Márquez does not pursue the theme of Fermina Daza's contingency but there it always is, an unacknowledged irritation, like the pea in the bed of the princess. (pp. 1, 14)

As for Florentino Ariza, in spite of his lifelong fidelity of the heart, he becomes a great lecher, always providing he doesn't have to pay for it. (He turns out to be something of a miser, too.) His affairs often turn out disastrously. One of his mistresses is murdered by her cuckolded husband. A casual pickup turns out to be a homicidal maniac. When he is in his sixties, he seduces the 14-year-old girl who will later kill herself when he finally persuades Fermina Daza to go on a river trip with him.

Love is a word that occurs frequently throughout the novel; sometimes it jars. For example, Florentino Ariza's secretary spends her life looking for a man who once raped her, not in order to wreak appropriate vengeance but because: "Lying there on the rocks, her body covered with cuts and bruises, she had wanted that man to stay forever so that she could die of love in his arms." This seems implausible, in however magical a context of realism, and "love" scarcely an appropriate word here.

The novel ends with Fermina Daza and Florentino Ariza together at last, taking a trip up river on a boat called *New Fidelity,* into the interior, only to discover that the magical jungle of memory, imagination and the past has been laid waste, the trees chopped down to fuel the steamers, the river clogged with swollen corpses floating down to sea. "All that was left was the vast silence of the ravaged land." This is the hideous backdrop to the ancient couple's honeymoon and it throws into question much of the glamour of the cozy, cocooned, indulged lives that have gone before. . . .

At the novel's end, [Florentino Ariza] and Fermina Daza sustain the privacy of their curious idyll by hoisting the yellow quarantine flag and claiming there is cholera aboard. This strategy ensures they will never touch on the shore again. The captain of the vessel is immediately "overwhelmed by the belated suspicion that it is life, more than death, that has no limits." In spite of this affirmative flourish, *Love in the Time of Cholera* seems to deal more with libido and self-deceit than with desire and mortality, although it is such a sumptuous book that I am left with the idea that perhaps García Márquez was intending some kind of radical soap opera in the manner of Bertolucci's movie *1900.* (p. 14)

> *Angela Carter, "Garcia Marquez; Sick with Love and Longing," in* Book World—The Washington Post, *April 24, 1988, pp. 1, 14.*

MICHAEL WOOD

The most casual reader of García Márquez notes his fondness for numbers. There are one hundred years of solitude, and in the novel of that name the rain pours down on Macondo for exactly four years, eleven months, and two days. A traveler circles the earth sixty-five times. Gargantuan eaters consume for breakfast eight quarts of coffee, thirty raw eggs, and the juice of forty oranges. The numbers call up an air of legend, a precision that mildly mocks the idea of precision. But numbers can also suggest patience, an intimacy with the slow seepage of time. Closer to the numerical flavor of his new novel [*Love in the Time of Cholera*] (published in Spanish in 1985), the sad and long-suffering hero of *No One Writes to the Colonel* needs, we are told, every counted minute of the seventy-five years of his life to arrive at the simple word that summarizes both his defeats and his dignity, his refusal to accept the unacceptable. He is a courteous, old-fashioned man, and has earlier rebuked a group of local youths for swearing. At last, however, nothing short of rude anger will do. "*Mierda,*" the colonel says.

Love in the Time of Cholera ends on a milder phrase, but one that has been similarly stored, one that similarly reflects an arithmetic of obstinacy and concentration. A captain asks how long he can be expected to keep his boat going up and down a tropical river, and the answer he receives has been brewing for "fifty-three years, seven months, and eleven days and nights." It is an answer that looks forward as well as backward: "Forever."

It takes the reader some time to get here too, and I found myself counting pages occasionally, the way the characters count years and months. Good stories are best told slowly,

Thomas Mann says, but it is possible to have too much of a good thing, and Mann may not be the ideal witness in such a cause. García Márquez really needs the snail's pace he sets, I think, but we are probably going to need some patience to understand his need.

The book begins with a corpse, and the scent of almonds, which indicates death by cyanide. "It was inevitable," the doctor thinks who is examining the body, "the scent of bitter almonds always reminded him of the fate of unrequited love." Inevitable, fate, love: we are reading the opening sentence of the book, and we seem already to be deep in an old-fashioned romantic novel. So we are, but we are also caught in the first of García Márquez's narrative lures. What is inevitable is not that deaths by cyanide should be those of lovers, but that the doctor should think of such deaths. This one in fact is the first cyanide death he can recall that has nothing to do with love, unrequited or requited. It is not an exception that proves the rule but an unruly event that makes us wonder whether we know what the game is.

The doctor himself unfortunately doesn't have much time to wonder, since he dies later the same day in a ridiculous accident, trying to recapture an escaped parrot. And this is the second narrative lure we have already stumbled into. The story we hear at length in the first part of the book is not that of the corpse, as the initial plot moves seem to promise, but that of the doctor and his city and his day. In the rest of the book we hear little more of the corpse or of its earlier life, but a great deal more about the doctor, and his wife/widow, and the indefatigable, obsessive fellow who has been in love with her for the amount of time so carefully detailed above.

The corpse is that of Jeremiah de Saint-Amour, an escaped convict turned photographer, who killed himself at the age of sixty (not seventy, as the translation says, anxious perhaps to stick to the traditional human span) because he had decided long ago that he did not want to live beyond that age. Sadly, at the end he found himself regretting his resolve, but couldn't think of changing it—"as the date approached he had gradually succumbed to despair as if his death had been not his own decision but an inexorable destiny." This is an important phrase. *Love in the Time of Cholera,* like García Márquez's other novels, is an exploration of destiny, but of *this* kind of destiny: the kind we invent and displace and fear and desperately live up to or die for. (p. 6)

The book has been compared to a naturalist novel and to a photograph album. It's a lot more like the second than like the first, but we might like to pause over the idea of a sophisticated, *affectionate* naturalist novel, an evocation of an old, grubby, rigid world for its own sad and charming sake, and not for any grim Zolaesque demonstration it might permit. This is a place where an old-fashioned mother can castigate even the contents of her daughter-in-law's sleep: "A decent woman cannot have that kind of dream." The doctor, returning to the city from a long stay in Europe, can hate its filth and its rats and its disease and its backwardness, but still love it enough to look at it straight:

> "How noble this city must be," he would say, "for we have spent four hundred years trying to finish it off and we still have not succeeded."

From the paupers' cemetery, one can look down on

> the entire historic city, the broken roofs and the decaying walls, the rubble of fortresses among the brambles, the trail of islands in the bay, the hovels

of the poor around the swamps, the immense Caribbean.

This is not a romantic vision, but it is a way one might talk of home, and the English prose, incidentally, is a good example of the effectiveness and fluency of this translation.

There is much discussion of reading in the book, of the doctor's European culture (he is a fan of Loti and Anatole France), of poetry competitions, and above all of the sentimental romances and poems through which so many people conduct so much of their imaginative lives—what García Márquez calls *versos y folletins de lágrimas,* sensibly rendered by [translator] Edith Grossman as "verses and tearful serialized love stories." A central character immerses himself in books, reads everything from Homer to the lousiest local poets. . . . García Márquez's implication, I take it, is not exactly that this is an ideal reader, but that there are many worse, and that serious, critical readers are often the worst of all. The language of the book itself, as I have suggested, is that of fate and broken hearts and eternal passions, of "mists of grief" and "delirious spring"; of "private hell" and "the desert of insomnia"; of blood pounding in the veins and "eternal night on a dark sea." Yet the effect, finally, is neither pastiche nor straight imitation but a form of homage to popular literature, an acknowledgement of the truths of feeling it catches in its often soupy prose. And the prose here is not soupy, in spite of the phrases I've just quoted; stately rather, a graceful orchestration of old verbal tunes.

What distinguishes this novel from the sentimental work it continuously alludes to is not irony or distance but a certain persistent lucidity. This is not a tearful text; just scrupulously loyal to tearful stories, only occasionally murmuring words like "fallacy" and "illusion." If it moved faster it would have to judge summarily, settle issues, could hardly avoid the recourse to irony. As it is, time and our patience situate the events and the characters. A girl, for example, is suddenly sure that what she thought was love is nothing of the kind. She looks at the suitor she has not seen for some time and feels not the passion she has been diligently nurturing but only an "abyss of disenchantment," *desencanto,* one of those wonderfully mournful Spanish words we find both in Baroque poems and lingering as the names of modern streets and lanes. Is she right, or is her great disenchantment just ordinary disappointment, of the kind lovers often feel after absences? She is probably wrong, and the text, much later, hints that she is. For the moment, though, she is sure she is right, acts on her feeling, condemns her suitor to a lifetime's despair; moreover, since she is not a person who can admit mistakes, she will in her own terms always have been right, whatever shifts of feeling may take place in what this novel calls her heart.

When García Márquez writes of her "discovery," and of the "correctness" of her decision, the words are simple and clear, but several meanings have piled up in them. They point, among other things, to a conviction that alters reality and then takes that alteration as proof of the conviction's justice. A form of destiny. Conversely, the suitor thinks of himself as someone who has "loved in silence for a much longer time than anyone else in this world ever had"; in spite of the fact that he has slept with hundreds of other women (he has a list of 622, but there are other affairs too casual to be registered), and even loved some of them. His fidelity is like her certainty, clear to its possessor, questionable to others. By fidelity he means being unable to forget or replace his first love, and

being able to ensure that news of his apparent infidelities doesn't reach her. And the great romantic moment of the book is also a great climax of hypocrisy. The old boy has kept his antics so quiet that he is able to say, casually and with a steady voice, like a character in a truly terrible novel, "I've remained a virgin for you." His partner, as it happens, doesn't believe him for an instant, even though she knows nothing of his six hundred plus adventures, but she too is fond of romance and likes "the spirited way in which he said it."

García Márquez has very much made one kind of suspense his own. It consists in giving away conclusions, and leaving the reader to guess at how they are reached. The moves are often surprising, and I won't spill all the beans, but only say that the trick characteristically involves removing most of the plausible narrative props, making us dizzily wonder whether already reached conclusions actually can be reached. It is another way of playing with destiny. Liberty creeps into unlikely human spaces, even what has happened seems doubtful, and hindsight, surely the safest of all forms of prophecy, turns risky.

Thus we know in this novel that the couple I have just evoked do not marry when young, since we first meet them at the ludicrous death of her husband, the doctor. The suitor is now seventy-six, she is seventy-two. He has been waiting, since she first turned him down, for "fifty-one years, nine months, and four days"—a little less than two years short of the final count we have already seen. We learn of their courtship, his numerous affairs, her marriage to the doctor, the doctor's single, scared infidelity, the lovers' happy, belated, foolish reconciliation, old skeletons still able to dance and get frightened at their feelings—though then we are told, in a fine phrase, that they wonder what they are doing "so far from their youth," and that their relation is "beyond love," because it is "beyond the pitfalls of passion, beyond the brutal mockery of hope and the phantoms of disillusion"—*desengaño,* another of those great Spanish words for cheated desire, caught up again in an ancient rhetoric of suspicion of the world.

What we can't picture, what we must follow page by page, is how any of this can actually come about, how obstacles are removed, how people can bring themselves to say and act as they must to ensure the named developments. García Márquez's formality is impeccable here, a slow joke in its own right. He almost always refers to the doctor by his full name and title, for example: Dr. Juvenal Urbino. His wife invariably appears under her Christian name and maiden name, Fermina Daza; her stubborn lover under his Christian name and family name, Florentino Ariza. No modern intimacies of appellation. The text is not solemn. There are sly gags, fantastic images, and abrupt violences; a group of brothers called after popes (Leo XII, Pius V, and so on); a baby carried around in a bird cage; a woman discovered in adultery and murdered by her husband without a word; a ghost who waves from the river bank; a black doll that silently, eerily grows, becoming too big for its dress and its shoes; a suicide for love (with laudanum, though, another blow to the doctor's theory). But the prose is unruffled, affects not to notice anything untoward. This is a stylistic act, of course, but the chief feature of the act is its discretion. Irony would be too strong a word for the almost invisible humor, the scent of skepticism in the following sentence: "He was a perfect husband: he never picked up anything from the floor, or turned out a light, or closed a door." Such a husband *is* perfect in one respect: not a chink between him and the myth.

The time of cholera, which is over and not over, is the time of romantic love. Love is like cholera, we are told several times in the book, even its physical symptoms, dizziness, nausea, fever, and the rest, can be the same. Like cholera, love is mortal, exclusive (because it separates us from our world), and undiscriminating (because it doesn't care what kind of victims it gets). García Márquez is fond of telling interviewers that the book he took with him when he first left Colombia for Europe was Defoe's *Journal of the Plague Year*—an anecdote which apart from doubtless being true suggests an interest in communities doomed to clinical isolation. The community here is the teeming Caribbean city, not the backland of Macondo, but it is also the community of all those, in Latin America and elsewhere, who are perhaps too keen on morbid metaphors of love. Love is a disease in this book, and this is a romantic novel; but the disease is one of the self-deluding, stubborn will, a fruit of mythology and obstinacy rather than any fate beyond ourselves.

Indeed the word itself becomes subject to a kind of creative disintegration or dissemination. At first and most prominently used to evoke the unique, histrionic, weepy passion, the endless topic of soap operas and *folletíns,* the kind of thing that drives people to death through cyanide, it gradually attaches itself to quite various human activities and affections: a long marriage, for example, begun without love, and then finding it and losing it and finding it; the "emergency love," the "hurried love" peddled in brothels; the "loveless love" of desperate people; love for a city, as we have seen; the love of children, love of food, love for life. The first of Florentino Ariza's many mistresses teaches him that "nothing one does in bed is immoral if it helps to perpetuate love." Florentino Ariza himself thinks at one point, "The heart has more rooms than a whorehouse," a secular twist on the rumored many mansions of heaven.

The heart: home of sentiment and dream and nostalgia, but also of more erratic, unpredictable emotions, the place where life itself can always turn up and surprise us. Love is the name for attractive and disreputable impulses as well as for all the noble enchantments and illusions, the *encantos* and *engaños,* with which we garnish our insufficiently romantic times. If love were always and only a disease, it could only be because life is. Writers have suggested this, but García Márquez is not one of those writers. (pp. 6, 8-9)

> Michael Wood, *"Heartsick," in* The New York Review of Books, *Vol. XXXV, No. 7, April 28, 1988, pp. 6, 8-9.*

PAUL BAILEY

'Love no med'cine can appease' wrote the 17th-century clergyman-poet Giles Fletcher, who died young of malaria. The line comes from the undivine Wooing Song he inserted into his devotional poem "Christ's Victorie and Triumph". This otherwise high-minded cleric understood passion: 'Not all the sea his fire can quench.'

I was frequently reminded of Fletcher's isolated outburst of feeling while reading Gabriel García Márquez's resonant novel [*Love in the Time of Cholera*]. No medicine can appease the love Florentino Ariza cherishes for Fermina Daza. It sustains and possesses and often torments him over a peri-

od of 'fifty-three years, seven months, and eleven days and nights.' . . .

Florentino Ariza's long exile from his beloved is not a virginal one. The old-looking young man, who carries a black umbrella on the hottest day, is the vulnerable object of several women's affections. His need for physical satisfaction is patent behind his prim exterior. Before he is reunited with Fermina Daza, he chalks up 622 conquests—and that number doesn't include the ones he has no wish to record. Widows are especially partial to him, being similarly desperate for sexual consolation. His relationship with the Widow Nazaret lasts 30 years, 'thanks to their musketeers' motto: *Unfaithful but not disloyal.'* She is the only one of his hundreds of lovers who shows him tenderness, and when she dies he pays for her grave in a respectable cemetery and is the sole mourner at her funeral. On their first night of love-making, she says of the husband she has recently buried: 'I am happy because only now do I know for certain where he is when he is not at home.'

'I adore you because you made me a whore,' she tells him more than once. And with that statement comes the realisation that, 'He had taught her that nothing one does in bed is immoral if it helps to perpetuate love.' The perpetuation of love is an important theme in the book, and not just for Florentino Ariza. It slowly becomes clear—for the pace of the narrative is deliberately slow—that Fermina Daza's love for her husband is profound, through all the vicissitudes of their marriage. . . .

Love in all its varied manifestations is celebrated and lamented in this eventful novel: platonic love; loveless love; the love that suddenly grows between two people who have lived together without it; maniacal love, and that love which—as the title indicates—is like a sickness unto death. No one describes the morbid condition of unrequited love with more authority than Márquez: the fever, the cramps, the heartburn. And he does so with no recourse to romanticism, despite the fact that many scenes seem to have strayed in from the pages of romantic, as well as Romantic, fiction. He informs us that Florentino Ariza reads novelettes and great poetry, and is incapable of distinguishing the two—it's only the message that matters. Márquez, like Joyce, is a great respecter of the tripe the lovelorn read for comfort, although he is incapable of writing it.

The background to this novel is one of constant ferment. Cholera epidemics wipe out huge numbers of the population, and a state of permanent civil war seems to be taking place. European culture comes to the city through the efforts of Juvenal Urbino, who has the latest books sent from France and who tries to persuade the authorities to invite Cortot, Thibaud and Casals to play in the Dramatic Theatre. Joseph Conrad is slyly introduced into the narrative, and Oscar Wilde puts in a more conventional appearance. Time is made to pass slowly, if not sluggishly.

The fact that Márquez has the Loayza brothers named after popes—Pius V, Leo XII—causes me no worry at all, but I was taken aback when I read that a woman has 'astonished breasts'. My astonishment persists. Edith Grossman has translated Márquez's often circuitous prose very well, with only a few really jarring Americanisms, such as the beastly 'overly'. She has caught the sombre and subtle tone of a deeply considered and satisfyingly ambiguous novel—the best, in my view, that Márquez has written.

Paul Bailey, "The Loved One," in The Listener, *Vol. 119, No. 3069, June 30, 1988, p. 29.*

An excerpt from *Love in the Time of Cholera*

Florentino Ariza was one of the few who stayed until the funeral was over. He was soaked to the skin and returned home terrified that he would catch pneumonia after so many years of meticulous care and excessive precautions. He prepared hot lemonade with a shot of brandy, drank it in bed with two aspirin tablets, and, wrapped in a wool blanket, sweated by the bucketful until the proper equilibrium had been reestablished in his body. When he returned to the wake he felt his vitality completely restored. Fermina Daza had once again assumed command of the house, which was cleaned and ready to receive visitors, and on the altar in the library she had placed a portrait in pastels of her dead husband, with a black border around the frame. By eight o'clock there were as many people and as intense a heat as the night before, but after the rosary someone circulated the request that everyone leave early so that the widow could rest for the first time since Sunday afternoon.

Fermina Daza said goodbye to most of them at the altar, but she accompanied the last group of intimate friends to the street door so that she could lock it herself, as she had always done, as she was prepared to do with her final breath, when she saw Florentino Ariza, dressed in mourning and standing in the middle of the deserted drawing room. She was pleased, because for many years she had erased him from her life, and this was the first time she saw him clearly, purified by forgetfulness. But before she could thank him for the visit, he placed his hat over his heart, tremulous and dignified, and the abscess that had sustained his life finally burst.

"Fermina," he said, "I have waited for this opportunity for more than half a century, to repeat to you once again my vow of eternal fidelity and everlasting love."

Fermina Daza would have thought she was facing a madman if she had not had reason to believe that at that moment Florentino Ariza was inspired by the grace of the Holy Spirit. Her first impulse was to curse him for profaning the house when the body of her husband was still warm in the grave. But the dignity of her fury held her back. "Get out of here," she said. "And don't show your face again for the years of life that are left to you." She opened the street door, which she had begun to close, and concluded:

"And I hope there are very few of them."

When she heard his steps fade away in the deserted street she closed the door very slowly with the crossbar and the locks, and faced her destiny alone. Until that moment she had never been fully conscious of the weight and size of the drama that she had provoked when she was not yet eighteen, and that would pursue her until her death. She wept for the first time since the afternoon of the disaster, without witnesses, which was the only way she wept. She wept for the death of her husband, for

her solitude and rage, and when she went into the empty bedroom she wept for herself because she had rarely slept alone in that bed since the loss of her virginity. Everything that belonged to her husband made her weep again: his tasseled slippers, his pajamas under the pillow, the space of his absence in the dressing table mirror, his own odor on her skin. A vague thought made her shudder: "The people one loves should take all their things with them when they die." She did not want anyone's help to get ready for bed, she did not want to eat anything before she went to sleep. Crushed by grief, she prayed to God to send her death that night while she slept, and with that hope she lay down, barefoot but fully dressed, and fell asleep on the spot. She slept without realizing it, but she knew in her sleep that she was still alive, and that she had half a bed to spare, that she was lying on her left side on the left-hand side of the bed as she always did, but that she missed the weight of the other body on the other side. Thinking as she slept, she thought that she would never again be able to sleep this way, and she began to sob in her sleep, and she slept, sobbing, without changing position on her side of the bed, until long after the roosters crowed and she was awakened by the despised sun of the morning without him. Only then did she realize that she had slept a long time without dying, sobbing in her sleep, and that while she slept, sobbing, she had thought more about Florentino Ariza than about her dead husband.

S. M. J. MINTA

Love in the Time of Cholera, García Márquez's longest novel to date, is set in a small town in Colombia between the late 1870s and the early 1930s. It is a novel about commitment and fidelity under circumstances which seem to render such virtues absurd, about a refusal to grow old gracefully and respectably, about the triumph sentiment can still win over reason, and above all, perhaps, about Latin America, about keeping faith with where, for better or worse, you started out from.

This long novel has a tiny cast. There are only three characters of substance: a woman, Fermina Daza, and the two men who share her life, Juvenal Urbino, her husband for half a century, and Florentino Ariza, her devoted admirer, who, after a lifetime of waiting, becomes her lover. . . .

All this might make the reader fear a novel of cloying sentimentality and gross improbabilities, and, indeed, García Márquez has recognized that his book is a mixture of the twentieth-century television soap opera and its nineteenth-century equivalents. Florentino can say "there is no greater glory than to die for love", and he can tell Fermina, after his thousand and one nights of infidelity, "I kept my virginity for you." And we shake our heads in disbelief. But the triumph of the novel is that it uncovers the massive, submerged strength of the popular, the clichéd and the sentimental, while the too solid world of Urbino, so reasonable, so lucid, so commendably progressive, is a world that is dying with him.

Urbino is a great man and a good one. He is one of those nineteenth-century Latin Americans who went to Europe, came under the influence of contemporary Liberalism, and were enchanted by the promises which an age of unfettered optimism and competition seemed to hold. Here was the final solution to the problems of the backward South American economies. Urbino studies medicine in France, and then returns to spread the benefits of all he has learned. He comes back to a town where the legs of patients' beds are still placed in water in the hope of preventing infection. He heroically opposes such superstition, and works, with complete dedication, to improve standards of hygiene. When a cholera outbreak threatens to overwhelm the town, as had once happened in his father's time, Urbino knows what to do and tragedy is averted. Yet he remains a man who will never know his own country, a man who needs to subscribe to *Le Figaro* "so as not to lose the thread of reality", a man blinded by the promise of a dream that is forever future. His town remains resolutely the way it has always been: arid, lying "at the margin of time", suffocating in the heat and growing old "amidst fading laurels and rotting marshes". In the end, it is Urbino who appears ridiculous, one who dies, not for science, not for love, but for a parrot.

Love in the Time of Cholera is a vast celebration of all that Urbino is not: it is a novel in praise of spontaneity, sexual passion, disorder and vitality, a triumph of the uncertain, sprawling confusion of life over the comforting, dull precision of authority, a victory of the indigenous over the imported, old age over death, the popular over the learned. Wittily, the novel also celebrates the sheer joy of reading: for where Florentino can indulge indiscriminately in the volumes of the Biblioteca Popular, Urbino is condemned by his superiority to read only the best books in the world, all identically bound in monogrammed calfskin.

In *One Hundred Years of Solitude*, the elusive gypsy sage, Melquíades, comes to take refuge in Macondo, "bereft of all his supernatural faculties as a punishment for his fidelity to life". Such fidelity lies at the heart of *Love in the Time of Cholera*. The times may, indeed, be less propitious, but the continuity seems no less exemplary for that.

S. M. J. Minta, "In Praise of the Popular," in The Times Literary Supplement, No. 4448, July 1-7, 1988, p. 730.

GALEN STRAWSON

Widely acclaimed and compared, books like Gabriel García Márquez's *One Hundred Years of Solitude* and Salman Rushdie's *Midnight's Children* are more often owned than read. There is a high drop-out rate—at page 20, page 50, page 70. It's something to do with the choking particulars, the factual luxuriance, the sheer *data*—the 72 chamberpots, the dozen batiste handkerchiefs, the empty pickle jars, the suicidal hiccoughs and pepperpots, the 16 defeats and the bright orange bird-droppings.

Life is full of such stuff (look at any normal room), but we learn to override the blast of detail. With books like these, so clamorous with things, we are easily put out. We find no peace; no measured construction of character; a lack of narrative grip; something inhuman about the stacking of the human facts. These books need time, if they are to be rewarding.

Love in the Time of Cholera is worth a lot of time. It is set on the Caribbean coast of Colombia in an unnamed and sewerless city (presumably some more or less magical version

of Barranquilla) in the period from the late 1870s to the late 1930s. Slight and bespectacled, Florentino Ariza waits for the greater part of a century to consummate his love for Fermina Daza. After a long and secret courtship in their youth (he writes every day, 'his hair in an uproar of love'), he loses her to the esteemed Dr Juvenal Urbino, a man of great public works and European education.

He then has to wait for more than half a century for the good doctor to die; and it takes more than two years to win Fermina Daza. . . .

The fact remains that for most of the book—and for most of their lives—they are apart. . . .

[Fermina Daza] pursues her successful marriage with Dr Juvenal Urbino. These two do not love each other at first, but they 'invent true love'—quite a lot of it. Their most serious argument is about a bar of soap. She forgets to replace the soap in the bathroom, and refuses to admit it. So he moves out for three months, and they don't speak for another four. Finally he capitulates. 'There was soap', he says, and regains his bed. . . .

They are happiest in old age, when 'together they had overcome the daily incomprehension, the instantaneous hatred, the reciprocal nastiness and fabulous flashes of glory in the conjugal conspiracy.'

From time to time *Love in the Time of Cholera* bogs down in unnecessary descriptive agglutinations—it wanders off course. The sentimentality about the girls who sell 'emergency love' in the 'transient hotel' is winning, but threatens to overshoot. And there are moments of verbal excess— Florentino Ariza is 'shaken by a thunderbolt of panic that death, that son of a bitch, would win an irreparable victory in his fierce war of love'.

It may also be objected that García Márquez seriously lacks an account of human wickedness—that although his people are vividly imperfect, they are always impossibly innocent. Should we accept this just because it is part of the magic in García Márquez's 'magic realism'? I don't think so. It is something less contrived. It is rather that García Márquez's insight into human turpitude and pettiness is inseparable from amusement and forgiveness, and from intense affection. Hence his particular fictional intelligence, and the deep charm of his art.

This charm is nowhere more clear than in *Love in the Time of Cholera*. The book is rich and brilliant with emotion—an extraordinary poeticisation of old age. It brings everything close: the disabling heat, the presence of the sea, the storms, the smell of shit on the wind, the great coastal swamps behind which García Márquez was born in 1928, the civil wars in the background as regular as the seasons. It suggests that true love is not blind, but sees all the faults and does not mind.

Galen Strawson, "Sixty Years of Celibacy," in The Observer, July 3, 1988, p. 42.

ELIZABETH A. BEVERLY

I am tempted to proclaim that no one else writes like Gabriel García Márquez, but what I mean more precisely is that no one else has invited me to read the way he has. For if *One Hundred Years of Solitude* is in some way about the fictional village of Macondo, and *The Autumn of the Patriarch* (1976) about the illusory potency of a Caribbean dictator (to cite only two of his previous fictions), then these novels are equally about the delight of finding within myself the ability to read with generosity, compassion, and no small degree of surprise. I know I'm not alone in my pleasure. . . .

[*Love in the Time of Cholera*] has already logged several months on the *New York Times'* bestseller list. This suggests that people want not only to read about a kind of love which both defies and redeems time, anger, and contagion, but to spend time reading about it. People understand that to García Márquez our literacy matters. And in this novel . . . García Márquez dazzles with wit and command. His stylistic flourishes: precise numbers, careful but random catalogues, extravagant cadenced prose, slightly syrupy diction, phantasms glimmering in the margins (a perceptibly growing doll, a ghost waving from the shore), are all present.

In *Love in the Time of Cholera,* these devices do not dominate, but serve the bold, circling narrative. Whether we read to find out how remarkably well the book is written, or to find out just what happens to the elderly Florentino and Fermina, the point is that we read. And if García Márquez's narrative dazzle and our curiosity get us to read in the first place, then we'll learn something. For although this author can never be accused of being didactic, he does want to teach us.

The lesson begins with the title. It is both a tease and a stunner. Great Russian novels come to mind. Here we encounter two massive Western abstractions undercut by disease, and a disease which sounds a lot like a human emotion. There is humor in this title; there is significance.

As we begin reading we know we are in the right book; we hear about love, about time and its passage, even about "the great cholera epidemic." But how the title directly concerns the story we have little idea. In this opening section we follow a man through a day. He is elderly, fastidious. He has had a friend, a man friend, and on this day, finds out that his friend is not the person he seemed to be. Not at all. This revelation comes from the friend's own hand, and for the rest of the day, this revelation spreads through our man's life. It unsettles him; he cannot keep his footing, literally cannot keep his footing. And so he falls.

I have risked revealing a glimpse of the plot because it seems important to assert that, in this section, García Márquez is teaching us one way to read his novel. We are like his man, believing that we know certain facts about these kinds of big books, believing even that we are being invited to read the lives of one set of characters. Then, astonishingly, we find out that this novel isn't what it seems to be at all; we must readjust. We feel unsettled; we lose our footing, and fall through time into the dense narrative of early love. The second section suggests that we start over.

The loss of footing is a sure touch, because we can lose footing only if we have feet. And that, surely, is García Márquez's absolute knowledge. He understands and writes about embodiment, not The Incarnation, but *our* incarnation, the simple fact that we play out our lives stranded inside of bodies. Bodies trap us in time, in disease and, if not in love itself, then at least in our need for love. (p. 410)

García Márquez knows one way to bridge the distance between bodies, one way to meet. He knows the power of the right word at the right time. This novel is about the desperate attempt to communicate. Hundreds of letters exchange

hands, missives are slipped under doors, telegraph wires hum, even a telephone is installed. What passes for dialogue reads more like the significant aphorism set off by colons, for, over the course of time, only the powerful words are remembered.

Over the course of time, Florentino, the love-letter-writer, learns how to write better; Fermina, the recipient, learns to read more generously. Florentino learns that longing can never be satisfied, but it can be shared; Fermina learns what longing really is. They are able to learn at all because of their patience. And, of course, it is the virtue of patience and the suffering of patients that allows us to recognize and accept love, time, and even cholera.

If the narrative is not direct, if it requires *our* patience at times, this is primarily because García Márquez reminds us continually that authorial whim is the only reason that the two main characters have been singled out to star in this novel. Their lives are no more privileged than those of other people who haunt the prose of this book. . . . García Márquez's generous embrace of these lives encourages us to recognize the rich riot of our own lives. It seems merely accidental that we too cannot be included in this novel.

But in a way we are. For just as Florentino knows that in order for love to exist it must be proclaimed and heard, so does García Márquez know that the only way for *Love in the Time of Cholera* to exist is for us to read it. I am reminded of Charlotte Brontë who, through Jane Eyre's voice, calls to us through the years: "Reader, I married him." She needed, still needs, for us to bear witness. García Márquez requires the same act. He asks us to attend to the matters raised by the title: love, age, disease/death. . . .

This book is a big thing, and the sheer heft of it can comfort a body. The lesson lies not only in *what* the book says (that love through time may actually exist) or *how* it says (with technical virtuosity, humor, and pathos), but *that* it says at all. When night comes, some of us flip on the light, nestle under the covers with a book, and begin to read. If the book is good, and we hope it's good, we may learn how to dream our way into the next full-bodied day. I suspect that García Márquez knows about our hope; I suspect that that is the reason he writes like no one else. (pp. 410-11)

> *Elizabeth A. Beverly, "The Distance between Bodies," in* Commonweal, *Vol. CXV, No. 13, July 15, 1988, pp. 410-11.*

MONA SIMPSON

It is hard now to recover the thrill of underground discovery, the hand-to-hand ardour, the feeling of claim engendered by *One Hundred Years of Solitude.* But *Love in the Time of Cholera,* like *Autumn of the Patriarch* before it, gives us something altogether new. With gorgeous, lucent writing, full of brilliant stops and starts, majestic whirls, thrilling endings, splendour and humour, the magician of our century takes on psychological realism.

Gabriel Garcia Marquez tells his stories with a strange omniscience. He is as capable of seeing the dignity in homeliness and poverty as the hidden jokes and rituals of opulence, as comfortable with science, magic, voodoo, ghosts, as with the riddles of Catholicism. The sources of his omniscience seem to be lodged not in any moral or political system, but rather in time—his voice holds the perspective any sensible person would have, given an easy sliderule to the future. And if Time and History are impartial, or impartial to the fate of individuals, so is Garcia Marquez. He loves his characters, but with a full knowledge of their limitations, which he blames less on them than on their position in history and in the Earth's geography. In his propensity to write passionately, and even beautifully, about the inner life of a character he ultimately dislikes, his insistence on never sentimentalising his protagonists in such a way as to exceed their place in history, he is a Marxist, but he is also a Catholic in his conception of what is universal and inherent in character, in his belief in the soul. These two visions fight it out through the narration, and like everything else in Garcia Marquez, they fight strongly, giving the characters' public and interior lives a deeply-coloured, taut, specific brilliance.

The narrator in *Love in the Time of Cholera* (as in earlier stories, such as **"Big Mama's Funeral"**—in some ways a preliminary sketch for *Autumn of the Patriarch*) sometimes slips into plural pronouns, creating a sense of a communal voice. At a formal party, overturned by weather, 'name cards were in confusion and people sat where they could in an obligatory promiscuity that defied our social superstitions on at least one occasion.' But though this voice—this sense of a community, this implication that communal progress and communal decline (rather than glamorous or special individuals) are the heroes and villains—remains constant from Garcia Marquez's early novels and stories through *Love in the Time of Cholera,* it tells a very different story.

We are not back in Macondo. We are not (really) in the 19th century. Though set twenty or so years before the calendar turns over into our century, *Love in the Time of Cholera* shows a decidedly modern sensibility, an urban rather than a rural society, and shows it with less mysticism and more social detail than was deployed in the earlier works. We are in an unnamed Caribbean city, said to be a composite of Cartagena and Baranquilla, and the fictional leap from imaginary village to unnamed port city cannot be underestimated. One can make up a village, starting from the very beginning, as Garcia Marquez did in Macondo, with his prehistoric eggs and things so new they had no names and his community where no one was past thirty and no one had ever died. Macondo, fully-created, can stand for much larger universes, but it is mostly, fundamentally, stubbornly itself. The unnamed coastal Caribbean city of this novel can never truly be held in the palm of the author's hand. It seems too real. Too big. It holds the resonance and reality of many deaths before our story even begins. It is a city with a history that matches the world's. . . .

[The] pace, [the] level of realism, tends towards metaphor rather than allegory. We never quite lose life, life in our world, the way we could in Macondo. This is, of course, a loss and a gain. The intrusion of reality, however, allows for majestic psychological revelations which would have been completely impossible in Macondo. When the young doctor comes home from Europe, he feels a mixture of loyalty and revulsion. 'He was still too young to know that the heart's memory eliminates the bad and magnifies the good, and that thanks to this artifice we manage to endure the burden of the past. But when he stood at the railing of the ship and saw the white promontory of the colonial district again, the motionless buzzards on the roofs, the washing of the poor hung out to dry on the balconies, only then did he understand to what extent he had been an easy victim to the charitable deceptions of nostalgia. The ship made its way across the bay through a floating blanket of drowned animals.'

The narration is full of worldliness. The community with whose voice this narrator speaks is a full century older than Melquiades's timeless agrarian voice in *One Hundred Years of Solitude.* This narrator knows, for example, when 'only the most sophisticated' wore their ordinary clothes and that rich, high-born ladies from the District of the Viceroys won't wear a particular European-designed shoe because it is too much like the slippers 'black women bought in the market to wear in the house'. This narrator uses references far beyond the Caribbean city of the novel, describing 'the way Arabs cry for their dead' and 'the pubic hair of a Japanese'. At the same time, one feels an intimacy with contemporary Latin America, its jumble of contradictions, its settled air of mixed heritage, decay. (p. 22)

Spanning the half-century roughly between 1880 and 1930, the novel is about love, in all its ages. Garcia Marquez is said to have modelled the romantic triangle on the courtship of his parents, though the years correspond more to the lives of his grandparents. No matter. On the first page, we see Dr Juvenal Urbino, a dapper and illustrious octogenarian, presiding over the examination of a recent suicide by gold cyanide. The opening is a kind of joke. *'Era inevitable,'* the narration begins, 'that the scent of bitter almonds reminded him of the fate of unrequited love.' We learn that the victims of unrequited love often have crystals in their hearts. But the suicide here was the victim not of unrequited love, but of a resolution against old age, of the eternal battle against mortality. Nor is suicide the fate of any of the loves, requited or not, in this book. Much has been written about Faulkner and Kafka as the mentors of Garcia Marquez, but in this thorough and intricate exploration of time and desire, he is an heir to Proust. (Proust's father, Professor Adrien Proust, is playfully mentioned as the famous epidemiologist Juvenal Urbino studied with in Paris.)

'The heart changes,' Proust wrote, 'and that is our greatest tragedy.' Like a sensible grandmother, Proust admonished the unrequited lover not to suffer so much, promising that long after the lover becomes indifferent, the object of so many pains will desire him, futilely. You get what you want only after you want it. Garcia Marquez takes this riddle to its extravagant conclusion. What if you tricked fate and the heart didn't change? Garcia Marquez has always written about magic, the art of legitimate deception. Now, he takes on nothing less in need of sleights-of-hand than the human heart, replete with its 20th-century doubts and woes. But a constant heart is the destiny of Florentino Ariza.

Only Garcia Marquez would dare to write for nearly a hundred pages about extravagant, pink, innocent, high-pitched, romantic love. Florentino Ariza falls irrevocably in love with Fermina Daza one day in the last century: he is delivering a telegram to her father and comes upon her teaching her spinster aunt to read. He woos her with letters. His letters were 'a dictionary of compliments, inspired by books he had learned by heart because he had read them so often'. Reading and writing are integers in the accumulating arithmetic of their adolescent love and it is no accident that it is the children who teach their parents to read. Fermina Daza 'would lock herself in the bathroom at odd hours and for no reason other than to reread the letter, attempting to discover a secret code, a magic formula hidden in one of the 314 letters of its

58 words, in the hope that they would tell her more than they said.' He sends her a lock of his own hair. She sends him the veins of leaves dried in dictionaries, the wings of butterflies, the feathers of magic birds. It is the stuff of sighs and violets and valentines. Florentino, sick with love, eats roses until he shows symptoms of cholera. They are both half-orphans, he the illegitimate son of a scandalous liaison, she the daughter of a reputed horse thief. Their epistolary romance, aided by the kind and now-literate spinster aunt, culminates after years of secret serenades from the paupers' cemetery in a proposal that rings of an ultimatum. The response arrives 'torn from the margin of a school notebook, on which a one-line answer was written in pencil' and reminds us that we are still in the kingdom of childhood, where love lives in a pure and eternal air, devoid of the earthiness and torment of the body, before any intimations of mortality. 'Very well, I will marry you if you promise not to make me eat eggplant.'

In *Love in the Time of Cholera,* the proportion of Marquesian plot to character has radically changed. He still introduces thousands of plots, traditional and idiosyncratic, from the most predictable to the sublime, but they only hover around the central characters. In a cartoon gesture, Lorenzo Daza, Fermina's shady father, stalls the wedding. He has other plans for his Fermina. 'When his wife died he had set only one goal for himself: to turn his daughter into a great lady.' Surprise, surprise. 'The road was long and uncertain for a mule trader who did not know how to read or write and whose reputation as a horse thief was not so much proven as widespread.' He turns out, in fact, to be no mere horse thief but an arms-dealer, having dealings with Joseph Conrad, but that is slipping the sliderule ahead. (pp. 22-3)

For a while, action seems to take over. The pace of the narrative speeds up, as Lorenzo takes Fermina on a journey to 'make her forget'. They travel the ridges of the Sierra Nevada, amid Aruac Indians. On this frontier, Fermina and her cousin Hildebranda feel the exhilarations of girlhood, learning to masturbate and going daily to the regional telegraph office, where messages from Florentino wait. During her absence Florentino, too, lives the last of his boyhood. Diving in search of sunken galleons, he enters the 'interior still waters of the archipelago in whose coral depths they could pick up sleeping lobsters with their hands'. Except for these brief scenes, there are no childhoods in this book.

It is not Lorenzo Daza, after all, who prevents Fermina from marrying Florentino. That kind of plot only goes so far in this novel. Garcia Marquez sets up the predictable plot only to get a little fun out of it before twisting it around or letting it fall away softly. The real obstacle is much more internal and thus, finally, modern. When Florentino sees the returned Fermino walking through the market, he recognises her maturity—her 'braid had grown in, but instead of letting it hang down her back she wore it twisted over her left shoulder, and that simple change had erased all girlish traces'—and follows 'the gold of her laughter'. She, on the other hand, seeing him, recognises only a mistake. 'No please,' she says to him. 'Forget it.' Sweet, innocent high-childhood romance does not end in marriage. Letters, veins of leaves, locks of hair tumble back to their originators and thus begin the 51 years, nine months and four days of Florentino's vigil. For it is Florentino's fate to wait for love and to make the most out of waiting.

Meanwhile, Peggy Sue gets married. We're never sure why, but then neither is she. Many crucial questions of motivation, though hovered over, are left, as they are in life, mysterious.

Many suggest—a jealous lover of Florentino Ariza blatantly says it—that Fermina Daza married for money a man she didn't love. She does not see it that way. No. 'She was stunned by the fear of an opportunity slipping away, and by the imminence of her 21st birthday.' What, exactly, is true? It is true that before she accepted the Doctor's proposal her father arrived home drunk one night and said: 'We are ruined. Totally ruined.' It is true that Fermina Daza was alone in the world. 'Her former schoolmates were in a heaven that was closed to her.' Here as elsewhere, it is and isn't so simple. Garcia Marquez has succeeded in making a character the product of her history, of her place in a social system, but also independent of it.

For his part, Dr Juvenal Urbino, though wooing a girl beneath his class, is not motivated by a great passion. This would seem to defy the arithmetic of Marxist prediction.

> The truth was that Juvenal Urbino's suit had never been undertaken in the name of love, and it was curious, to say the least, that a militant Catholic like him would offer her only worldly goods: security, order, happiness, contiguous numbers that, once they were added together, might resemble love: almost be love. But they were not love and these doubts increased her confusion, because she was also convinced that love was really what she most needed to live.

And so they marry, for better or worse. Garcia Marquez leaves it at that and moves on, because, of course, as we all know in the 20th century, marriage belongs at the beginning, not the end of a novel.

While *One Hundred Years of Solitude* and *Autumn of the Patriarch* are full of first and last things, in this novel, Garcia Marquez's spirit of invention turns inward to the intimate discoveries of one marriage. 'He was the first man that Fermina Daza heard urinate . . . That memory often returned to her as the years weakened the stream, for she never could resign herself to his wetting the rim of the toilet bowl each time he used it.' Dr Juvenal Urbino would say: 'The toilet must have been invented by someone who knew nothing about men.' On their honeymoon, Fermina says: 'How ugly it is, even uglier than a woman's thing.' Whatever else it is, marriage is not romance. It doesn't resemble what Fermina Daza embroidered with Florentino Ariza, whom she has deliberately forgotten and who lingers in her imagination only as a field of poppies.

Garcia Marquez writes brilliantly about the daily bonds and tensile strength of a marriage. And throughout, the question 'but is it love?' hovers, floats, skirts the tankard that is marriage. . . .

Dr Urbino, a self-satisfied husband, is given to pronouncements on the matter. He told his medical students: 'After ten years of marriage women had their periods as often as three times a week.' To himself he mused: 'The problem with marriage is that it ends every night after making love, and it must be rebuilt every morning before breakfast.' . . . Garcia Marquez has a diabolical knack for the drama of domestic arrangements. 'If anything vexed her, it was the perpetual chain of daily meals . . . He was a perfect husband: he never picked up anything from the floor, or turned out a light or closed a door.' Dr Juvenal Urbino makes statements worthy of Desi Arnaz. He's an old-style husband charming enough to make the reader almost nostalgic for chauvinism. 'This stuff tastes of window,' he rants. 'This meal has been prepared without love.'

For her part, Fermina Daza, the lonely girl of the forlorn mansion, becomes a woman of the world. She turns into the bourgeois great lady her father wanted her to be. . . . Fermina becomes the kind of Latin American woman who, as the saying goes, has more in common with a woman in Miami than with another Latin American woman two miles away in the *pueblos jovenes.*

While Fermina Daza is shopping and running a household, moving through the satisfactions of a settled family life, Florentino Ariza waits with a 'mineral patience' for her husband to die. 'She and her husband made an admirable couple, and both of them negotiated the world with so much fluidity that they seemed to float above the pitfalls of reality. Florentino Ariza did not feel either jealousy or rage—only a great contempt for himself. He felt poor, ugly, inferior and unworthy.'

Garcia Marquez has written before about poverty and about riches—a brilliant early story, **"Tuesday Siesta"**, about the dignity of the poor in the face of sleepy convention comes to mind—but he has never before taken on the psychology of yearning, the thwarting character of the desire for more. Here he writes, ruefully and comically: 'In those days, being rich had many advantages, and many disadvantages as well, of course, but half the world longed for it as the most probable way to live for ever.' In Macondo, people did live for ever. In **Love in the Time of Cholera,** their wistful collective desire tells us a great deal about the internalised longings born of class inequality.

Florentino Ariza, poet and rose-eater, turns Horatio Alger, in order to live up to the imagined demands of his increasingly bourgeois—and elusive—love. He rises in the ranks of the River Company of the Caribbean, working at business by day, moonlighting in the Arcade of the Scribes, writing love letters for the sick at heart, the disenfranchised. 'Love is the only thing that interests me,' he says to his uncle, president of the River Company. 'The trouble,' his uncle says to him, 'is that without river navigation there is no love.' And in all his years as a businessman (he eventually becomes president of the company), Florentino Ariza never manages to write 'just one acceptable business letter'. He works his way up the ladder to prove equal to the task of wooing Fermina Daza (should her husband ever die), but he never develops a passion for river navigation. The fleet of paddle-wheel steamboats seems not to exist for him, except on paper. In fact, his rise in the world of work is largely engineered by a faithful (and female) assistant, who learns the political machinery of the company on Florentino's behalf. (p. 23)

With the kind of magical absurdity which has taken the place of the more extravagantly coloured miracles of Garcia Marquez's earlier books, Florentino Ariza gets his long-awaited second chance. Dr Juvenal Urbino dies in a cartoon pageant of indignity, trouserless, suspendered, chasing an errant parrot down from a mango tree.

The Paramaribo parrot himself emerges as a character, an agent of perversity, aiding Florentino Ariza's cause. 'On rainy afternoons, his tongue loosened by the pleasure of having his feathers drenched, he uttered phrases from another time which he could not have learned in the house and which led one to think that he was much older than he appeared.' Like Melquiades, who was also as old as the world, he has

magical powers but still, he is only a parrot. His role is much smaller and more comic than that of Melquiades who functions as the master of ceremonies in **One Hundred Years of Solitude.** In that book we had a magician gypsy authoring the world: we now have a universe in which our lives are determined by absurd events caused by a mad parrot. Magic here is subsumed into the human, colouring human emotion rather than flourishing tricks of its own.

Florentino Ariza, now rich, still poetic, after his setback of 51 years, nine months and four days, resumes his wooing the first night of Fermina Daza's widowhood. He is told, in no uncertain terms, to go away. Foiled but undaunted, Florentino Ariza starts his suit the way he did the first time: through the mail, though with a very different kind of letter. This time there are no skeletons of butterflies, no wings of flowers, no symptoms of cholera. Florentino Ariza types his letters. 'In a certain sense it was his closest approximation to the business letters he had never been able to write.' Love letters become Florentino Ariza's most profound business, and the inversion is telling in a novel infused and obsessed with correspondence, with the sense of magic that is the written word. Earlier on, Fermina had been 'captivated on the spot by a paper seller who was demonstrating magic inks'. When the new century is celebrated by an inaugural journey in a balloon (another civic project of Dr Juvenal Urbino's), it was used to deliver a letter, the first 'mail transported through the air'. The magic ink—writing and reading—works: it can win love and recover love. If a childhood romance, hand-made with epistolary ardour and laced with phrases learned from the Spanish romantic classics, couldn't survive in the face of aristocracy, money, adulthood, the barge of bourgeois life, it can at least resurrect itself by the end, with the help of a typewriter.

This is not a story of boy meets girl, boy loses girl, boy gets her back. Garcia Marquez, as ever, remains stubbornly committed to the voice of the community: individual happiness is not considered an absolute good. So although Florentino Ariza gets Fermina Daza back, his life of devotion was not lived without cost. And Garcia Marquez does not spare us the details of these costs, however much we may be cheering Ariza on. 'For her sake he had won fame and fortune without too much concern for his methods,' we are told. When Florentino Ariza and Fermina Daza embark on what is to be a dazzling river trip at the book's end, we see what cost the earth has borne for Florentino's inability to write a proper business letter, for his concentration on love and not on river navigation.

> Fifty years of uncontrolled deforestation had destroyed the river: the boilers of the riverboats had consumed the thick forest of colossal trees . . . the alligators ate the last butterfly and the maternal manatees were gone, the parrots, the monkeys, the villages were gone: everything was gone . . . At night they were awakened not by the siren songs of the manatees on the sandy beaches but by the nauseating stench of corpses floating down to the sea.'

Garcia Marquez and his communal voice judge the single-minded pursuit of love harshly, and his judgment extends to a literature which is only about love, never about the business of the world. . . . Not that anyone else fares very much better. Even Dr Juvenal Urbino's virile, civic-minded undertakings seem dubious. 'The restoration of the Dramatic Theatre . . . was the culmination of a spectacular civic campaign that involved every sector of the city in a multitudinous mobilisation that many thought worthy of a better cause.'

There seem to be no real politics, no real politicians. . . . The nine civil wars which rage during the half-century of the book seem to be only a human plague, not fought for any discernible cause other than raw destruction. (pp. 23-4)

As for Fermina Daza and Florentino Ariza, they, too, live in the world. As friends in old age, they are immune neither to local class prejudice and snobbery (when Fermina Daza's son invites Florentino Ariza to the social club, he is turned away because of his illegitimate birth) nor to the fate of the river, which they share, when they take a final trip on a River Company of the Caribbean steamboat. . . . Much of the time they suffer from heat and pestilence, from the stench of death on the river, as the boat seems to plough through islands of sand.

They are not immune to history. And they are old. Florentino Ariza is bald. The first night of romance, Fermina Daza sends him away, saying: 'Not now, I smell like an old woman.' But they are not merely products of personal and public history. 'Both were lucid enough to realise, at the same fleeting instant, that the hands made of old bones were not the hands they imagined before touching. In the next moment, however, they were.' Garcia Marquez has brought a new depth to the meaning of the word 'magic'. (p. 24)

Mona Simpson, "Love Letters," in London Review of Books, *Vol. 10, No. 15, September 1, 1988, pp. 22-4.*

David Henry Hwang
M. Butterfly
Tony Award: Best Play

American dramatist.

Based on an actual incident, *M. Butterfly* (1987) concerns the bizarre twenty-year love affair between a French diplomat stationed in China and a diva of the Beijing Opera. In Hwang's play, the singer, a male who plays female soprano roles, conceals his sexual identity from the diplomat during their affair in order to obtain information for the Chinese government. Through flashbacks, Hwang's fictive diplomat, Rene Gallimard, relates the story from his prison cell in France, where he is incarcerated on charges of conspiracy. Critics interpreted *M. Butterfly* as an allegorical exploration of gender, illusion versus reality, and East-West relations. Gallimard's improbable deception by the spy with whom he was intimate for twenty years is depicted as representative of the Western world's willful misperception of the East as feminine and inferior. These themes are further expiated through the parallel Hwang creates between his story and Giacomo Puccini's opera, *Madame Butterfly*. Hwang inverts the plot of Puccini's opera by presenting a Western male, rather than an Oriental female, as the gullible victim of romantic love.

Hwang's blending of diverse theatrical styles and techniques places *M. Butterfly* within the postmodern movement in art. For example, Hwang makes use of *kurogo,* the "invisible" stagehands of Asian theater who make scenery changes during the action of the play; elements of character, plot, and theme are developed through musical motifs, a device of European opera; and Hwang's extensive use of flashback and flashforward rather than linear chronological progression is a common feature of modern drama. While some critics questioned the effectiveness of Hwang's social observations, most applauded his inventive manipulation of factual material. Clive Barnes stated: "*M. Butterfly* sizzles with the immediacy of theater at its most challenging and entertaining."

Prior to *M. Butterfly,* Hwang wrote two plays that explore the experiences of Asian-Americans from several perspectives. *FOB* (1979), his first work, details the struggles of Chinese-Americans to maintain their cultural identity while assimilating into American society. *FOB,* which stands for "Fresh Off the Boat," was awarded an Obie for best new play of the 1980-1981 season. *The Dance and the Railroad* (1981) is set in California in 1867 at the time of a strike by railroad workers. The play draws upon folklore, history, and myth to celebrate Chinese culture. Hwang's use of gymnastics and an improvised Chinese-style opera foreshadows the technical bravura of his award-winning *M. Butterfly.*

CLIVE BARNES

It has as many layers as a chrysanthemum bulb, or a Kabuki make-up, and it unfolds as leisurely as a Chinese banquet, or a fake geisha girl doing a striptease in a San Francisco tourist joint. It enriches, it fascinates, it offers thought to feed on.

It starts by saying East is East and West is West, that woman needs man and man must have his mate, and very often, and on many levels, lips can say no and eyes can say yes.

It wonders why Giacomo Puccini's little opera *Madama Butterfly*—based on David Belasco's instant Yankee folk-legend—is so popular with the white devils who frequent opera and its emotional suburbs.

Then it turns everything upside down—sexism, racism, and man's infinite ability for self-delusion—in a whole bouncing series of acrobatic theatrical somersaults.

It is David Henry Hwang's play *M. Butterfly,* based loosely on fact, or at least the headlines of fact. . . .

I heartily recommend it to you. It will move you, it will thrill you, it may even surprise you. It is a play not to be missed, and it is a play once caught that will never be forgotten.

Layers! Titillating, bed-time kimono, silk-rich layers! *M. Butterfly* started with an actual news story in the *New York Times.* A Paris espionage trial. Transvestite agent lures French diplomat—after 20 years liaison and "fathering of child," victim expresses shock that prima-donna spy was man. . . .

I personally took the whole thing with a pinch of salt as simply bad or sensationalist reporting. How could even the most naive diplomat posted to China not be aware that China's major performing art, the Peking Opera, like much of the Oriental theater, was an exclusively male preserve, just as is major-league baseball in the United States?

American playwright Hwang saw more in the story, took a quantum leap into art, and ran with it.

Obviously the "opera" aspect of it appealed to him, and he came up with the *Madam Butterfly* idea. From then on in, all the playwright-lepidopterist had to do was pin his idea, or ideas, down on to the stage. And this . . . he has managed magnificently.

Remarkably Hwang and [director] Dexter have made a supercharged Broadway vehicle out of what could have been a very rickety rickshaw.

There are two vital aspects to Hwang's vision. The first is that racism and sexism are curiously related in the mind of Western man. The second is that the reality of fantasy has no meaning in the self-deluding focus of true love. . . .

Hwang is suggesting that the whole concept of a wilting, submissive Oriental girl to a white cad, not only represents a rape-concept lurking in many Occidental masculine hearts, but also mirrors politically the West's imperialist attitude to Eastern culture.

It is the kind of idea—forget, as does the playwright, that Oriental society traditionally is itself macho-sexist and male-oriented and concentrate on the politico-sexual metaphor—that is the ripe kernel of drama.

Add to this the concept of love's self-delusion—taken to its ultimate degree of trust and folly—and you have a play, or at least its makings.

M. Butterfly never cheats—well, perhaps a little in its massively effective grandstand, grandslam ending involving sex transference—in making Hwang's point, beyond sex and politics, that "happiness is so rare, and our hearts will turn somersaults to protect it."

And we must believe . . . with our diplomat toward the end, when he says with utter sincerity, and seeming truth: "In China I once loved and was loved by the perfect woman." Who has fooled whom? . . .

The play has its faults. The writing can embrace such pedestrian exchanges as "She eats out of my hand / She was probably very hungry," and the minor characters . . . remain resolutely ciphers of dramatic convenience.

But the diplomat and his lover—these are creatures of substance and beauty. . . .

All in all, *M. Butterfly* sizzles with the immediacy of theater at its most challenging and entertaining.

Clive Barnes, "Sex and Silk When East Meets West," in New York Post, *March 21, 1988.*

FRANK RICH

It didn't require genius for David Henry Hwang to see that there were the makings of a compelling play in the 1986 newspaper story that prompted him to write *M. Butterfly.* Here was the incredible true-life tale of a career French foreign service officer brought to ruin—conviction for espionage—by a bizarre 20-year affair with a Beijing Opera diva. Not only had the French diplomat failed to recognize that his lover was a spy; he'd also failed to figure out that "she" was a he in drag. "It was dark, and she was very modest," says Gallimard, Mr. Hwang's fictionalized protagonist, by half-joking way of explanation. When we meet him in the prison cell where he reviews his life, Gallimard has become, according to own understatement, "the patron saint of the socially inept."

But if this story is a corker, what is it about, exactly? That's where Mr. Hwang's imagination, one of the most striking to emerge in the American theater in this decade, comes in, and his answer has nothing to do with journalism. This playwright, the author of **The Dance and the Railroad** and **Family Devotions,** does not tease us with obvious questions such as is she or isn't she?, or does he know or doesn't he? Mr. Hwang isn't overly concerned with how the opera singer, named Song Liling, pulled his hocus-pocus in the boudoir, and he refuses to explain away Gallimard by making him a closeted, self-denying homosexual. An inversion of Puccini's *Madama Butterfly, M. Butterfly* is also the inverse of most American plays. Instead of reducing the world to an easily digested cluster of sexual or familial relationships, Mr. Hwang cracks open a liaison to reveal a sweeping, universal meditation on two of the most heated conflicts—men versus women, East versus West—of this or any other time.

As a piece of playwriting that manages to encompass phenomena as diverse as the origins of the Vietnam War and the socio-economic code embedded in Giorgio Armani fashions, *M. Butterfly* is so singular that one hates to report that . . . [one] must overcome a number of obstacles to savor it. . . . The production only rises to full power in its final act. . . . Until then, one must settle for being grateful that a play of this ambition has made it to Broadway, and that the director, John Dexter, has realized as much of Mr. Hwang's far-ranging theatricality as he has.

As usual, Mr. Hwang demands a lot from directors, actors and theatergoers. A 30-year-old Chinese-American writer from Los Angeles, he has always blended Oriental and Western theater in his work, and *M. Butterfly* does so on an epic scale beyond his previous plays, let alone such similarly minded Western hybrids as *Pacific Overtures* or *Nixon in China.* While ostensibly constructed as a series of Peter Shafferesque flashbacks narrated by Gallimard from prison, the play is as intricate as an infinity of Chinese boxes. Even as we follow the narrative of the lovers' affair, it is being refracted through both overt and disguised burlesque deconstructions of *Madama Butterfly.* As Puccini's music collides throughout with a percussive Eastern score by Lucia Hwong, so Western storytelling and sassy humor intermingle with flourishes of martial-arts ritual, Chinese opera (Cultural Revolution Maoist agitprop included) and Kabuki. Now and then, the entire mix is turned inside out, Genet and Pirandello style, to remind us that fantasy isn't always distinguishable from reality and that actors are not to be confused with their roles.

The play's form—whether the clashing and blending of Western and Eastern cultures or of male and female characters—is wedded to its content. It's Mr. Hwang's starting-off point that a cultural icon like *Madama Butterfly* bequeaths the sexist and racist roles that burden Western men: Gallimard believes he can become "a real man" only if he can exercise power over a beautiful and submissive woman, which is why he's so ripe to be duped by Song Liling's impersonation of a shrinking butterfly. Mr. Hwang broadens his message by making Gallimard an architect of the Western foreign policy in Vietnam. The diplomat disastrously reasons that a manly display of American might can bring the Viet Cong to submission as easily as he or Puccini's Pinkerton can overpower a Madama Butterfly.

Lest that ideological leap seem too didactic, the playwright shuffles the deck still more, suggesting that the roles played by Gallimard and Song Liling run so deep that they cross the boundaries of nations, cultures, revolutions and sexual orientations. That Gallimard was fated to love "a woman created by a man" proves to be figuratively as well as literally true: we see that the male culture that inspired his "perfect woman" is so entrenched that the attitudes of *Madama Butterfly* survive in his cherished present-day porno magazines. Nor is the third world, in Mr. Hwang's view, immune from adopting the roles it condemns in foreign devils. We're sarcastically told that men continue to play women in Chinese opera because "only a man knows how a woman is supposed to act." When Song Liling reassumes his male "true self," he still must play a submissive Butterfly to Gallimard—whatever his or Gallimard's actual sexual persuasions—unless he chooses to play the role of aggressor to a Butterfly of his own.

Mr. Hwang's play is not without its repetitions and its overly explicit bouts of thesis mongering. When the playwright stops trusting his own instinct for the mysterious, the staging often helps out. . . .

Though *M. Butterfly* presents us with a visionary work that bridges the history and culture of two worlds, the production stops crushingly short of finding the gripping human drama that merges Mr. Hwang's story with his brilliant play of ideas.

Frank Rich, " 'M. Butterfly,' a Story of a Strange Love, Conflict and Betrayal," in The New York Times, *March 21, 1988, p. C13.*

JOHN BEAUFORT

Dazzling theatricalism dominates the scene and ultimately wins the day for *M. Butterfly,* the mock tragedy by David Henry Hwang. . . .

Drawing on Noh and Kabuki traditions, using incidental music that contrasts fragmented Puccini with Oriental pizzicato and percussion, *M. Butterfly* tells the forlornly comic tale of an East-West affair that ended in a spy scandal. For his own purposes of irony and interpretation, Mr. Hwang fictionalizes an actual espionage case that shocked French diplomatic and political circles in 1986. The action consists of a long flashback in which imprisoned ex-emissary René Gallimard recalls his doomed romance with Song Liling, a star of the Peking Opera whom he met and fell in love with back in the 1960s.

In the course of over-leisurely background reminiscences, Gallimard remembers the events that led to the awakening illicit passions of a young married government careerist. The French naif's preconceptions about the Orient and particularly its women—the latter inspired by *Madama Butterfly*—provide Hwang with a ready target for satire and ridicule.

Yet the playwright preserves a modicum of sympathy for his smitten adventurer. . . . He is an all too easy foil for the beautiful, subtly demure Song Liling, whether she is gradually submitting to his advances or exploiting their relationship to meet the new intelligence-gathering demands of Chairman Mao. Among the more amusing scenes in *M. Butterfly* are the confrontations between the opera star and Comrade Chin.

The dizzying course of Gallimard's love life is matched by the ups and downs of his diplomatic career. Elevated, to his own surprise, to first consul, he is subsequently sent home after having guessed wrong both about the French in Indochina and the Americans in Vietnam. Meanwhile, in one of the play's more explicit scenes, Gallimard extends his philandering. As satirical observer, Hwang likes nothing better than to range across the East-West horizon for targets of opportunity. Whether in terms of Chinese acrobatics or antic Western behavior, *M. Butterfly* is seldom without distractions and diversions. . . .

The author and director mingle fantasy, stylization, and vernacular realism. The final transformation scenes are master strokes of theatrical invention. . . .

M. Butterfly is not a play for all tastes. But as the latest satire on East-West relations by the Chinese-American author of such plays as *F.O.B., The Dance and the Railroad,* and *Family Devotions,* it finds Hwang in lively form.

John Beaufort, "Puccini Wouldn't Recognize It: 'M. Butterfly' Brings a Chinese Spy Tale to Stage," in The Christian Science Monitor, *March 23, 1988.*

JACK KROLL

In *M. Butterfly,* Hwang has clearly aimed to create a Broadway sensation. And in terms of theatricality, a truly bizarre plot and an air of almost impudent self-confidence, he may well have succeeded. But looked at closely, this butterfly is a paper lepidopteran. Hwang has concocted a play that consumes itself in its own cleverness, that takes so many twists and turns that it spins itself into a brilliant blur.

The play is based on the incredible true story of a 20-year sexual liaison between a French diplomat in Peking and a star of the Chinese Opera who turned out to be a man in drag. Not only that, but the devious diva was also a spy who was pressing the diplomat for information about the Vietnam War and other matters. Not only *that,* but the transvestite-singer-spy had pretended to have a baby, which was provided by the Chinese government. At this moment the foggy Frenchman is in prison in Paris for espionage, still insisting, according to Hwang, that his paramour was a woman.

Well, as Confucius would say, what a megillah. And to it Hwang has added many fillips of his own, chiefly the use of Puccini's *Madama Butterfly* as a metaphor for the racism that informs Western attitudes toward the East. . . . Through the various turns of the story the *Butterfly* metaphor is mined for every conceivable implication: the macho West thinks of the East as passively female; a chap like Gallimard can feel like a man only with an all-compliant woman; even the Vietnam War can be explained as another outbreak of the "Butterfly" syndrome.

But in 1988 it's hard to accept the 1904 *Madama Butterfly* as a relevant symbol of East-West relationships. And would that work really be in the repertoire of a member of the Peking Opera in the People's Republic? And, even though the play is based on a true story, we expect a playwright to help us understand why after 20 years a man hasn't figured out that his lover is another man. For besmirching the legend of French sexual sophistication alone, Gallimard should have been sent to Devil's Island.

At every level the play defies belief. We are asked to accept that this bumbling embassy official is a crucial figure in the French intelligence network. The Vietnam stuff is pure malarkey, with dialogue like "So, the Americans plan to begin bombing," which sounds like something out of Fu Manchu. There's a big revelation scene in which we watch six minutes (an eternity) of Song Liling removing her makeup to reveal she's a man. In the age of *La Cage aux Folles* this scene holds no shocks for an audience—not to mention the fact that anyone can see from the start that she's a he.

Hwang is a natural playwright whose desire to astonish has subverted the intellectual legitimacy of his play.

> *Jack Kroll, "The Diplomat and the Diva," in* Newsweek, *Vol. CXI, No. 14, April 4, 1988, p. 75.*

EDITH OLIVER

Of all the young dramatists at work in America today, none is more audacious, imaginative, or gifted than David Henry Hwang. . . . [His new play, *M. Butterfly*], is based on an actual episode in 1964, a French diplomat stationed in Beijing took as his mistress a star of the Beijing Opera, and only after they had been together for many years—when both of them were arrested in Paris and charged with being spies for Communist China—did he find out that "she" was actually a man. The story broke in the newspapers in 1986, and Mr. Hwang knew at once that it was made to order for his own ironic cast of mind. From the beginning of his career, the underlying theme of his plays has been the elusive, enduring power of the Asian spirit vis-à-vis the West, and so it is here. When his first play, *FOB,* opened Off Broadway in 1980, I described it as "funny, mysterious, and often beautiful;" **M. Butterfly** is funny, mysterious, and often beautiful in its arresting production on Broadway. . . . [Gallimard, the diplomat], tells us of his awkwardness as a schoolboy at his lycée and of his difficulties with women as a young man, and we then see scenes of his marriage and scenes with his boss at the consulate in Beijing. He also tells the story of Puccini's *Madama Butterfly,* as Cio-Cio-San moves down a ramp that curves from upstage to downstage center, and, in time, they lip-synch a duet from the opera. Puccini's score pervades the play. The diplomat and the singer meet, and the progress to the affair begins, with the playwright discoursing on the subtleties of Oriental

sexuality and of transvestism, and we find out exactly how the hoax was perpetrated. . . . The action throughout combines, sometimes blends, realism and ritual. I note—and not for the first time in reviewing Mr. Hwang—that it is almost impossible to indicate in synopsis the richness and resourcefulness of his plays and the steadiness of his complex plots. He seems as familiar with his ancestral customs and sensibilities as he is with his Western ones, but his satiric eye and his glorious humor are all his own. And he inspires confidence in the audience every step of the way.

> *Edith Oliver, "Poor Butterfly," in* The New Yorker, *Vol. LXIV, No. 7, April 4, 1988, p. 72.*

JOHN SIMON

There is a marvelous play in the true story underlying David Henry Hwang's **M. Butterfly,** but Hwang lets it slip through his fingers. A French diplomat in Peking conducted a twenty-year affair with a star of the Peking Opera specializing in female roles. Without leaving his wife, he set up clandestine housekeeping with the actor, a Maoist spy, who gleaned some confidential materials about the Vietnam War. The actor even produced a blond baby he claimed to have borne the diplomat. The Frenchman was eventually transferred back home; the actor, during the Cultural Revolution, spent four years in a labor camp. Then, however, he was sent to Paris to continue his love affair-cum-spying. The diplomat took him back and divorced his wife. Discovered and tried, he was sent to prison. Through all this, he insisted that he never realized his lover was a man.

Can love be *that* blind? Can wish-fulfillment fantasy be *that* strong? Can a diplomat stationed in Peking not know that all roles in the Peking Opera are taken by men? Could the French, who were au courant, not have known that the Chinese would not have allowed a lesser foreign diplomat two apartments? Why was there no suspicion of espionage until much later? What really went through the French wife's head? What became eventually of the actor and the Eurasian child? And if it was all just to mask a homosexual affair, exactly how did that work? No real answers.

Hwang is rightly interested in both the sexual and political implications, both the private and public problems. He is curious about the borderline between sexualities and the games people play in that no-man's- or no-woman's-land. Also about the lies one lives because of social, moral, religious, and political pressures. The troubled relationship of East and West obsesses him. The son of affluent Chinese Americans, he has scores to settle with both America and the new China, the former for making him embarrassed about his ethnicity, the latter for repudiating his bourgeois status and Armani suits. Not quite in tune with either culture, he lets loose genuine indignation, which gives the play what life it has.

But Hwang is unwilling or unable to explore the deeper workings of the central relationship. For psychology, he often substitutes one-liners and posturing; for tormented poetry, angry rhetoric. On the political side, he tries to squeeze far too much mileage out of *Madama Butterfly* to convey male fantasies at the expense of submissive women, Occidental fantasies at the expense of a conquered Orient. But it doesn't really work, because René Gallimard and Song Liling keep reversing roles, with the passive Song often in active ascendance, exploiting Gallimard, yet in the end affirming his lasting love. It barely works on the personal level, much less the symbolic.

Unfortunately, potshots, sarcasms, double entendres (e.g., the comical female commissar, out of some kind of *Stinkweed Drum Song,* admonishing Liling, "You represent our great Chairman Mao in every position you take!") are no substitutes for making us care and leave with more understanding than we came in with. This has much to do with authorial laziness. Anyone willing to name his French hero after the best-known Parisian publisher, and the chief French diplomat after one of France's main military ports (M. Toulon, indeed!), has scant respect for the sensuous quiddity of details. But the real rub is that Hwang brings in too many schematic issues and underdeveloped secondary characters, and the principals are not alive enough to excuse all this blurring at the margins. When the commissar, later, says, "You go to France and be a pervert for Chairman Mao," this is not only crude and preposterous in the light of Maoist policy toward homosexuality, but also the same joke milked.

Another bad sign is that the five minutes during which Song wordlessly removes his female makeup and garb and changes back into a man are among the most theatrically effective; I mistrust a play in which so long an absence of dialogue comes as a relief. Nevertheless, Hwang does have some good lines, as when Gallimard tries to explain his alleged blindness with "Happiness is so rare that our minds can turn somersaults to protect it." That, to me, would have been a play: two creatures artfully and desperately deluding each other and themselves to maintain a consuming illusion; the sexual and international politics could have arisen organically out of that folie à deux, of which Hwang gives us too little. We could have been spared such cardboard characters as a Danish girl and Marc, a sort of jock and frat brother of René's, who says things like "One night can we just drink and throw up without conversation?" How un-French can you get? No talk? (p. 117)

John Simon, "Finding Your Song," in New York Magazine, *Vol. 21, No. 15, April 11, 1988, pp. 117-19.*

MOIRA HODGSON

[*M. Butterfly*] is a series of flashbacks from the cell of Rene Gallimard, the French diplomat who has been sent to prison for treason. He is a shy fellow who calls himself the "patron saint of the socially inept" and whose slablike face is etched with the sufferings of the gangling, awkward boy with whom none of the girls wanted to dance. But when he came across some girlie magazines as an adolescent, his body "shook not with lust but with power." Gallimard believes that he can become a complete man only if he can control a shrinking butterfly of a woman, which is why he is so easily duped by the diva Song Liling.

False notes creep into the play from the start. It is written in a hearty old-fashioned American slang, as if the author were aiming to please coachloads of matinee patrons. The actors, whether they are supposed to be French or Chinese, buttonhole the audience with clichés, like a group of back-slapping traveling salesmen over a round of drinks. No effort is made to establish a hint of French colonial decadence. Hwang's Gallimard talks with a childhood friend about school popu-

larity contests—in France?—and is given to such expressions as "Phooey on my job."

It is not hard to believe that Gallimard might be smitten when he first sees Song Liling as Madame Butterfly (despite her lamentable singing voice). But would this naïve wimp actually be capable of behaving with the premeditated cruelty of a Viscomte de Valmont until she surrendered? Early on it becomes apparent that their relationship is an inversion of that between Pinkerton and Madame Butterfly in the opera. Song Liling laughs at Gallimard's response to the work in which he has found her so moving: "What would you say if a blond homecoming queen fell in love with a short Japanese businessman? . . . Because it's an Oriental who kills herself for an American you find it beautiful."

Hwang never gets to the bottom of Gallimard's character. He doesn't question whether the Foreign Service officer knew that Song Liling was in fact a man ("It was dark and she was very modest"), nor does he make him into a self-deluded homosexual. But by skipping this element of the diplomat/diva relationship (in fact, making a joke of it) and moving on to the wider issues of East versus West and the origins of the Vietnam War (Gallimard is involved in the making of Western foreign policy in Vietnam), Hwang misses an important key to Gallimard's character and fails to make him convincing. (p. 577)

With *M. Butterfly* Hwang has cottoned on to a fascinating story, but it is beyond his powers. The play has a brilliant and clever structure and is filled with fascinating ideas and insights, yet half-way through it topples over on itself. In the long run it is middlebrow Broadway entertainment—as shallow and glib as a Hollywood film script. (p. 578)

Moira Hodgson, in a review of "M. Butterfly," in The Nation, *New York, Vol. 246, No. 16, April 23, 1988, pp. 577-78.*

ROBERT BRUSTEIN

David Henry Hwang's *M. Butterfly* . . . is an effort not so much to mix cultures as to demonstrate how and why they clash. Played on a modified Kabuki stage—a large red surround equipped with travelers and screens and circular walkways—it is the story of a French vice consul who falls in love with a performer from the Peking opera and ends up in prison for revealing diplomatic secrets. Although based on an actual espionage trial, the spy story interests Hwang a good deal less than the love affair (p. 28)

The playwright seems as bemused by the diplomat's obtuseness as we are, and accounts for it only by suggesting, through his characters, that darkness and feigned modesty obscure the fact that humans have more than one orifice for sexual pleasure. Considering that Rene Gallimard (as this would-be Pinkerton is called) also photographed sensitive documents for his lover without asking why, he must be considered excessively stupid even by Western diplomatic standards. As for Song Liling (the name of his Chinese Butterfly), he seems unusually cunning even by standards of inscrutable Oriental shrewdness. Since it is hardly a secret that women in Peking opera are played by men, the most convincing explanation is that Gallimard was unconsciously aware of his beloved's sex from the start.

Using Puccini's opera as a parallel reinforcing plot, Hwang

exploits the story for its political, cultural, and sexual implications, his theme being that Western treatment of the East—Vietnam included—is motivated by myths of male domination and female passivity, in short by the same relationships one finds in *Madama Butterfly*. According to Gallimard, who adores playing Pinkerton ("very few of us would pass up the opportunity," he smirks at the audience), "Orientals will always submit to a greater force." But, as another character suggests, the Western use of "greater force" stems from a fear of sexual impotence; "the whole world is being run by men with pricks the size of pins."

The danger of such large cultural generalizations is to replace one form of stereotype with another. Hwang's sexual-racial explanation of Western imperialism leaves unexplained Margaret Thatcher's policies, not to mention any number of atrocities committed by the more feminine East (though he does identify Red China as a macho society that refuses to recognize homosexuality). Gallimard nevertheless atones for his sexist stupidity by putting on Butterfly's kimono and makeup and committing hari-kari, as Song Liling, in a Western business suit, is given Pinkerton's final cry of "Butterfly" over the corpse. (pp. 28-9)

[*M. Butterfly*] is notable more for its intentions than its execution. Hwang has an excellent subject, and he has obviously thought a lot, if not very originally, about the origins of racism and imperialism. But the work has no subtext and lacks the gift of language. These are serious flaws in a piece so full of direct address, for without subtleties of language, the oratory grows tiresome, the characters lack depth, and the romantic story loses its pathos. T. S. Eliot once complained about another playwright of ideas, Bernard Shaw, that the poet in him was stillborn. Hwang's poetic ovum hasn't even been fertilized yet, and his prose could use some ripening too. He's got an eye for a good story; when he develops a better ear, we may have another good playwright. (p. 29)

Robert Brustein, "Transcultural Blends," in The New Republic, *Vol. 198, No. 17, April 25, 1988, pp. 28-29.*

M(ilton) T(errence) Kelly
A Dream like Mine
Governor General's Literary Award: Fiction

Canadian novelist, short story writer, poet, dramatist, and journalist.

A well-known champion of Native American rights, Kelly creates a dramatic forum for his concern with the destruction of Native culture in his award-winning novel *A Dream like Mine* (1987). In this work, an unnamed journalist travels to an Ojibway reserve in northwestern Ontario to research an article on alcoholism among Native Americans. Arthur, a Métis Indian, abducts the protagonist and forces him to witness the kidnapping and torture of the manager of a paper company that is polluting the water on the reserve. These three characters, along with an elder of the tribe, make a dark journey of discovery across rural Canada that critics have likened to the plot of James Dickey's novel *Deliverance*.

The structure of *A Dream like Mine* is typical of the "Indian novel," a sub-genre which usually features a white protagonist on a spiritual quest in a Native culture. The form of these narratives is often conceived as a journey during which alienation from the land is identified as the source of the white culture's anomie. Andrea Bear Nicholas observed: "What makes *A Dream like Mine* so powerful and so unlike most other novels and descriptions of Native People is the clear and direct connection it makes between Arthur's seemingly irrational violence and the deliberate and calculated violence of colonialism." Critics commended the clarity and immediacy of Kelly's first-person prose. Norman Sigurdson maintained: "The action is vivid and shocking, and the author has a sure handle on the native lore involved. *A Dream like Mine* is an impressive piece of work."

(See also *Contemporary Authors,* Vols. 97-100 and *Contemporary Authors New Revision Series,* Vol. 19.)

dramatic without being melodramatic while writing of kidnappings, torture and killings.

A Dream Like Mine—the title is from the Ojibway saying "You cannot harm me, you cannot harm one who has dreamed a dream like mine"—takes place in late September in the Ojibway country around Kenora. An unnamed newspaperman-narrator travels to Heron Portage Reserve to develop an idea on traditional native healers and their success in treating alcoholics, He has been told to make it into "a mini-feature; serious, but light, tight and bright."

It turns out, however, that the elders of the Ojibway tribe are astonishingly political and that no story about them can ever be light, tight and bright. In return for the reporter dropping a story that could never come out the right way, a story that would merely "interview a bunch of Indians, balance them by quoting a bunch of experts, and do another chronicle about drunks and child abuse and suicide and jails that explained nothing and led nowhere," Wilf Redwing, one of the

T. F. RIGELHOF

[*A Dream Like Mine* is a] short, compact, compelling novel of racial violence in northwestern Ontario [that] deserves an illustrious fate. It ought to be reviewed widely, sold by the thousands, translated into several foreign languages, scrutinized closely by literary critics and made into a movie.

That is to say, it ought to make the same sort of impact on consciousness and culture as James Dickey's *Deliverance* did nearly two decades ago. Like Dickey, M. T. Kelly is a poet with a searing concern for the violences endemic to his time and place, and the ability to personify these violences within characters without lessening their individual realities. Unlike Dickey, however, Kelly does not require a closet full of stock-in-trade Hemingwayisms to support his enterprise. Kelly is, among other things, a playwright, and he knows how to be elders, promises him a sweat ceremony and other introductions to traditional beliefs.

And it is in the depths and darkness of the sweat tent that the narrator finds the real story and beliefs that didn't seem part of his original bargain. He finds himself at the centre of a tale from which he cannot easily extricate himself, and one which places Wilf Redwing and himself in strange and strained relationships to two other men, a Métis shaman named Arthur and Tunslow "Bud" Rickets, the manager of the paper company that has been polluting Ojibway waters and injecting lethal levels of mercury into their traditional food chain. To say more of what happens would be to say too much: the plotting is tight and meticulous, and it unfolds in ways that both thrill and horrify. . . .

Kelly—and this is his brilliance in this piece of writing—makes his audience's sympathies and antipathies for his characters flow and recoil in shockingly violent ways. On the surface, less gets done in this story by way of murder, mayhem and torture than happens in a Ted Woods thriller. But Kelly's violences make for intellectual clarity and a more civilized consciousness. He doesn't try to sate the human appetite for melodrama. He is involved with that much larger artistic concern, the awakening of possibilities for self-affirmation and self-denial.

Kelly clearly sees many of the interconnections between sadism, masochism, success worship, power worship and nationalism that George Orwell dwelled upon in his classic analysis of *No Orchids For Miss Blandish,* interconnections that too few novelists are willing to explore to the necessary depths when confronting the politics of Canada, past and present. By viewing them unflinchingly in the context of one small episode within a continuing tragedy of race relations, he does between the covers of a novel what Antonin Artaud sought to do within the contours of theatre—that is, he "causes the masks to fall, reveals the lie, the slackness, baseness, and hypocrisy of our world . . . and in revealing to collectivities of men their dark power, their hidden force . . . invites them to take, in the face of destiny, a superior and heroic attitude they would never have assumed without it."

To do this is to do something much more than to craft a convincing docudrama. To do this is to bring to new life the old assertion that "literature is news that stays news." To do this is to create an art that a good society can never adequately reward and one that a bad society cannot afford to ignore.

> T. F. Rigelhof, *"The Real Story behind the Story,"* in The Globe and Mail, *Toronto, October 24, 1987, p. C19.*

TERRY GOLDIE

Some time ago, M. T. Kelly's name began to appear on reviews of various books about Indians. His persona was quite consistent: someone of liberal sympathies concerned with accuracy. Often the review was accompanied by the comment that Kelly was working on a novel about native people. *A Dream Like Mine* provides an interesting example of what happens when a white author obsessed with "getting it right" tries to write right himself. Can it be done?

Judging from this work, it can't, but not for want of trying. *A Dream Like Mine* exhibits signs of being the most ardent attempt ever in white Canadian fiction at defeating both the

---

An excerpt from *A Dream like Mine*

I had come to this place to attend a sweat ceremony. I'm a reporter, and I'd had an idea for a story on traditional native healers. These shamen had apparently had success in treating alcoholics in Kenora, a town blighted with the effects of Indian drinking. A story about drunken Indians and a new treatment was familiar enough not to challenge anyone and I easily got two days to fly to Kenora and interview some of the medicine men. "It's a heavy enough subject," I was told. "Make it a mini-feature; serious, but light, tight and bright."

The medicine men, it turned out, were funded by the Ontario Government, Ministry of Health. An ex-girlfriend who worked in the ministry put me on to the funding. Maybe there'd be a story in that, I'd thought. Yet when I met the elders whose names I'd been given I found them sympathetic and legitimate. No story about them would ever be light tight and bright. They were also astonishingly political. Wilf said he could see the headlines: *Government Funds Witchdoctors.* "It doesn't get out the right way," he said and asked me not to write about them and their religion.

Maybe I have a soft spot for old men because my dad died when I was a kid and he would have been around Wilf's age if he'd lived; or maybe I was tired and just didn't want to interview a bunch of Indians, balance them by quoting a bunch of "experts," and do another chronicle about drunks and child abuse and suicide and jails that explained nothing and led nowhere. What I did want was to find out more about traditional beliefs and Wilf promised me this sweat ceremony for my cooperation. I also think he liked me.

"Do you know about the spider?" Wilf asked.

"No. Yes, I think I've heard. . . ."

"The spider is sacred to the Sioux, enemies of our people from away back, from the West. The 'Mighty Sioux.' " He shrugged with good natured contempt. "You can still see the rivalry when we play hockey."

The word hockey was familiar enough that I tuned out for a moment, staring at the fire, feeling again where I was, not listening, enjoying my nervousness, and the fire did make me nervous. The rocks in it were white hot. Split slabs of wood burned, bark out, around this white hot core. The burning wood came up in a cone like a tipi, and there was something touching about the fire's neatness amongst the, well, squalor was too strong a word, but amongst the mess I could see around me: the house off to my left lit with bare light bulbs, the broken chairs, the barren ground. Above the aurora suddenly began, and Wilf stopped talking. At first I thought spotlights in town were sweeping up to announce the opening of a new car dealership. But the town didn't throw up the lights of a city, and town was far away. A huge moon, an hysterical shamen moon, framed by spruce trees, seemed too big. The night again felt cold.

racist and the romantic, those tendencies that cloud all of us when we try to come to terms with native peoples.

The plot of the novel is very simple. A journalist with a long-standing interest in natives goes north to participate in a sweat ceremony. He is kidnapped by Arthur, a visiting Métis, and taken on a journey with the real focus of Arthur's attack, Bud, a polluting industrialist.

The essential statement of the book is about the liberal concerns of the journalist and the violence of Arthur. The journalist constantly recites the past iniquities by whites throughout the Americas to see if justification can be found for the apparently psychopathic revenge inflicted by Arthur.

It seems like a worthy consideration, of the sort posed by Che Guevara when he said, "There are no innocent bystanders in a war of revolution." But in the process of exploring the unanswerableness of the problem, Kelly falls into the same traps that seem to ensnare all narratives about Indians.

The basic pattern of the "Indian novel" follows a white in search of personal or national identity who turns to native peoples for assistance, whether because of some holistic mysticism that is attributed to them or because they are the truly indigenous peoples. His/her interaction with them takes the form of a journey into the wilderness, often with a subplot that emphasizes Indian association with and white alienation from the land.

In this process, certain qualities and abilities are shown to be intrinsic parts of native peoples. Sexuality and violence are often in the foreground, as is mysticism, which usually is presented in connection with a deep understanding gained through oral tradition, acclaimed as far superior to the superficialities provided by writing. (p. 30)

Kelly's *Dream* might be read as a comment on how the inadequacy of the narrator's nativist desires leads him into a nightmare, but the verdict can't be so simple. The journalist reflects on the absurdity of many of these romantic concepts and then the novel uses them, apparently unself-consciously. On encountering Wilf, an old Ojibway, the narrator laments the stereotype of the wise old man of the tribe, fount of oral tradition. Guess what Wilf turns out to be?

The novel avoids the sexual stereotype—no Indian maidens floating through—but Arthur's violence is as forceful, if not as graphic, as that in Thomas Keneally's Australian novel, *The Chant of Jimmie Blacksmith.* Like Keneally, Kelly shows native violence to be a response to white genocide.

Another element the Canadian novel shares with the Australian is the representation of the native as remnant of the past. Wilf seems to be a "true" Indian, but even he decries the inadequacy of his life in comparison with that of his father. Arthur, a former alcoholic, sees himself as an avenger, but as a Métis he also could be a psychotic mutant of miscegenation, not an extension of the heroic Indian of past warpaths but an example of the decadent present. Neither he nor the narrator reflects on this, however. . . . (pp. 30-1)

In any case, the narrator, having entered the wilderness of the native and communed with his violence, eventually returns to civilization. Like the similarly unnamed narrator of Margaret Atwood's *Surfacing,* who taps the essence through the aura of Indian rock paintings, he is by no means completely

whole but is much closer than the blindly unreceptive hunters encountered in both novels.

A Dream Like Mine has the feeling of autobiography. Not that Kelly shares the experiences of his narrator, but that he shares his confusion at how to recognize the evils of white history and yet not turn to absurd romanticism. At how to support native claims for redress and yet not accept the possible corollary of violent attacks on individual whites. At how to create a story in which the characters represent Indianness and yet reject the usual representations of Indians.

A worthy fight, which Kelly fails to win, though I suspect victory will elude other battlers as well. Keneally's novel is no doubt a much deeper version of the struggle, but Kelly's compares well with most other works, such as Philip Kreiner's *A People Like Us in a Place Like This,* and is far superior to many, such as Susan Musgrave's *The Charcoal Burners.* But the final word is still very far away. . . .

The title of *A Dream Like Mine* seems to hope for a mystical insight, like Wilf's dreams in the novel. Perhaps such claims need to recall some history. Our ancestors thought they had taken over the Indian land, and now we find they didn't quite make it. Our novelists show that a friendly expropriation of the Indian spirit isn't that easy either. (p. 31)

Terry Goldie, "The Impossible Dream," in Books in Canada, *Vol. 16, No. 8, November, 1987, pp. 30-1.*

JUDITH FITZGERALD

M. T. Kelly writes novels with a kind of passionate intensity not often found in contemporary literature. In *A Dream Like Mine,* for example, he handles highly explosive materials with a kind of grace under pressure. The result? Spontaneous combustion.

A Dream Like Mine travels a traditional narrative route. A journalist heads north to discover and report on sacred Indian rites at the Heron Portage Reserve near Kenora, Ontario. Under orders to make his article "light, tight and bright," the journalist attends a sweat ceremony, an Ojibway cleansing ritual which renews body and spirit. . . .

Revenge, an ugly scar of a word, dominates the emotional and physical landscapes of this novel. On one side of the gulf stand Native Canadians intent on forcing "the white man" to see the extent of the destruction of a way of life; on the other side stand journalists and pulp-and-paper mill bosses intent on exploiting the process of destruction. Neither side, as Kelly vividly demonstrates, can lay claim to absolute correctness.

Violence becomes the operative word. The narrator attempts to maintain a typical *laissez-faire* attitude towards the entire issue and discovers he cannot, primarily because he becomes a victim of the violence so often romanticized in cowboy and Indian conflicts. Here, in the heart of the land, in the still of the starless night, violence erupts and shatters both violators and violated.

The carnage defeats itself almost in spite of itself. Questions of right and rights do not exist in the final pages of this novel.

Arthur takes Bud, the pulp-and-paper mill boss, as a hostage. He takes the journalist as insurance. Narrative tension builds until it becomes a series of peaks on a roller-coaster ride to hell. Solutions twist and turn on themselves; answers do not emerge. "There can be no revenge, I thought. What good is revenge? Massacre societies, sacrifice societies, history. It happened somewhere else."

Kelly's storytelling strengths derive from his ability to create unforgettable characters. Arthur, Wilf, Bud and the narrator all act and react consistently in spite of the incoherence of the chaos unfolding within and around them. Kelly also draws heavily on his poet's way with words. The taut and grim narrative adds new meaning to the idea of playing with fire.

Judith Fitzgerald, "Kelly's Taut, Grim Narrative," in The Sunday Star, *Toronto, November 22, 1987, p. C9.*

NORMAN SIGURDSON

A Dream Like Mine is a gripping and powerful short novel that explores themes one might have thought had already been exhausted. M. T. Kelly, a Toronto-based playwright, novelist, and poet (*I Do Remember the Fall, Country You Can't Walk In*), manages to wring new life out of the old subjects of the clash between white technology and native culture and the poor city boy in over his head in the woodsman's world.

The story is narrated by a Toronto *Globe and Mail* reporter obsessed with native culture, who ventures out to a reserve near Kenora, Ontario to learn more about Ojibway traditions. Little by little he becomes drawn into the world of a strange, psychopathic Métis named Arthur, who is, symbolically, from "out west". Arthur, along with a gentle and enigmatic elder named Wilf Redwing, embarks on a journey of terrorist theatrics, with the unnamed narrator as both spectator and participant.

Arthur turns the narrator's foggy, liberal opinions into concrete action by kidnapping and torturing Tunslow "Bud" Rickets, the manager of a paper mill that is pouring lethal pollutants into the Rainy River. The exhausting, horrific trek through the northern bush with the violent and unpredictable Arthur, the arrogant and pathetic Bud, and the narrator—suspended between the roles of kidnap victim and co-conspirator—is reminiscent of another powerful short novel by a poet, James Dickey's *Deliverance*.

The narrator's sympathy alternates between captive and captor. Some readers may find it difficult to sympathize with the narrator, who is more a caricature of the naive liberal than a realistically drawn character. Nonetheless, the action is vivid and shocking, and the author has a sure handle on the native lore involved. *A Dream Like Mine* is an impressive piece of work. (pp. 24-5)

Norman Sigurdson, in a review of "A Dream like Mine," in Quill and Quire, *Vol. 53, No. 12, December, 1987, pp. 24-5.*

M. T. KELLY

[*The remarks below are excerpted from a transcript of M. T. Kelly's acceptance speech at the Governor General's Awards ceremony in Calgary, Alberta, in February, 1988.*]

We put up at the foot of a great chain of mountains . . . all the snowy cliffs to the southward were bright with the beams of the sun, while the most northern were darkened by tempest . . . (When we reached the heights) our view was vast and unbounded . . . the eye had not the strength to discriminate its termination.

If anyone had a sense of place, of Canada, it was David Thompson, and the wonder he felt pervading this part of the country in 1798 has not diminished for a visitor today. That's why I'm so pleased to receive this Governor General's Award here in Calgary. It seems no one can come to this part of the country and be unaffected, as evidenced by the great body of literature that has come out of the West. To me, this is a place of very ancient history, of impersonal, brilliant light, of echoes and stories and hauntings.

I'm also pleased that these Governor General's Awards are associated with the Olympic Arts Festival and the Olympics. I believe that it matters that the arts be declared officially important, and we have had our troubles with the place of the arts in Canada—writers feeling so marginal that they become half mad with bitterness. . . .

I would also hope that awards like this will encourage the larger publishers to publish more serious literature. There are problems with Canadian publishing, as everyone in this room knows, and if the literary presses remain the spirit of the country, in one sense a whole generation of writers has been rendered mute. They can't get to their audience.

Because of the themes of *A Dream Like Mine* I cannot conclude without speaking of the land claims of the Lubicon Lake Indians. They also have to do with a sense of place, but with much more than that. I am not one of those for whom literature or poetry—in W. H. Auden's words—"makes nothing happen," flowing "on south / from ranches of isolation." I believe that to change people's minds—and governments are people—we must not rely solely on economic or other arguments, but must create a sense of imagination. The Lubicon Lake Indians—all Native peoples and their cultures—are not simply artifacts to be displayed in museums or societies that are part of our multiculturalism and are interesting from an ethnological point of view. They are people and cultures from whom we can learn another way of looking at the world. This is not misplaced pantheism or aesthetic luxury; it is essential if we are going to continue on this planet, if we are going to leave our children *anything* that is wild, *anything* that is beautiful. Listen to these Indian voices, harken; they seem to me the very breath of the Americas.

M. T. Kelly, "Stories and Hauntings," in Books in Canada, *Vol. 17, No. 3, April, 1988, p. 7.*

ANDREA BEAR NICHOLAS

For the Native People of the Americas the story told by M. T. Kelly in *A Dream Like Mine* is not only fiction, but truth—not only a dream, but reality. At the beginning readers are invited along with the narrator/journalist to join in a sweat-lodge ceremony, at once the heart and the womb of Native American culture. From thence they are drawn to embark on a journey into another reality, the reality of the world looking out from the sweat-lodge. Slowly and by shocking blows of physical pain the reader and narrator come to see beyond the romanticisms, distortions, and omissions of historians and anthropologists. For a few moments the pain and grotesque reality of the Indian world is experienced direct-ly—and no longer "as if through a membrane."

Like the web of a spider, this story is as finely woven and symbolic as the stories of Wisekedjak of the Ojibways and Guluwuskub (Glooskap) of the Wabanakis (including Micmacs and Maliseets). Each of its characters is a symbol of a modern reality of Indian existence. Two of the characters represent different sources of death for Native People, and ironically, both sources are generally referred to as "the West." In traditional Native cultures the Land of the Dead is in the West; and to all Native cultures the source of unimaginable death has been, and continues to be, the western world, its diseases, its philosophies and technologies. In *A Dream Like Mine* the strange and psychotic Indian, Arthur, symbolizes death in the traditional sense. He is from the West (Land of the Dead), and is the embodiment of living death. He does not know his culture, but he knows what has been done to it, and he has experienced the legacy of its destruction in a shattered life, in hunger, disease, alcoholism, and squalor. Like a character in a Greek tragedy he is driven by the pain of his experience. The other source of death for Indian people, western technological culture, is symbolized by the middle-aged manager of a paper company that is killing the waters, destroying the Native culture, and dehumanizing the Native People. Even his name, Bud Rickets, conjures up images of deficiency, deformation, and living death. Wilf, the wise but lonely elder, symbolizes Native traditional culture and its teachings, all that Arthur has missed. Wilf quietly suffers the degradation of police beatings, broken treaties, and outlawed traditions, and he knows the futility of trying to interfere with either of the two sources of death. The narrator/journalist symbolizes all that is good in non-native society, but he is equally powerless to alter the course of events, not that he does not try. In many ways he typifies the open-minded liberal, but he displays more than the usual share of sympathy arising from knowledge of the genocidal history of the Americas.

The drama of the novel lies in the bringing together of the four characters/symbols; and its gripping suspense arises from the unpredictability of reversed power relationships. Early in the book Arthur, the ordinarily powerless Indian, overpowers Rickets and exults in his newfound power. "I'll wear a robe," he says, and referring to Rickets says, "He's a Maya, and I'm a priest." It is the realization of the dream of the colonized man everywhere. (pp. 98-9)

What makes *A Dream Like Mine* so powerful and so unlike most other novels and descriptions of Native People is the clear and direct connection it makes between Arthur's seemingly irrational violence and the deliberate and calculated violence of colonialism. One of Kelly's techniques for making the connection is to have the narrator dwell on the powerful historical images of genocide in the Americas at the very moment he is suffering enormous pain inflicted by Arthur. The images are graphic, of seventy million deaths, of mutilation, and of soldiers playing ball with the breasts of Native women. (p. 99)

Kelly reinforces the connection between Arthur's violence and historic violence in a conversation between Wilf and Arthur. Normally patient and understanding, Wilf suddenly lectures Arthur angrily by comparing the folly of his ways to the folly of Wisekedjak, the Ojibway deceiver-trickster who stained the earth with the blood of both men and animals. Clearly, Arthur is disconnected from his own culture and the instructions of its rich oral traditions. The violence in this case is the violence of colonialism, which continues to destroy a people by masquerading as democracy and destroying the oral traditions of their history. It is a violence symbolized by the sudden and intrusive nightmarish vision of a heron goring a powerful bear in the gut with its beak, a vision so real as to be seen by all except Bud Rickets, but felt as a physical injury to the gut only by Arthur. Is it dream, is it reality, or is it just a spectacular oral tradition turned bloody prophecy? Suddenly it seems not necessary to know.

The merging of dreams, reality, and oral traditions is unique to non-western cultures. As an instructive technique its effectiveness has been tested by time and ages. What more potent way to convey a message of such profound importance to the survival of Native cultures and people—nay, to the survival of humanity itself? Just as Arthur had to face the prophecy, the vision of his own hatred and destruction, so must the creators of all death. (p. 100)

Andrea Bear Nicholas, "Dreams, Reality, and Oral Tradition," in The Fiddlehead, No. 156, Summer, 1988, pp. 98-100.

MARK ABLEY

The richer, bigger, and glossier our cities become, the more our writers seem to concentrate on the physical wilderness and on the spiritual victims of power. One reason may be simply that many authors, feeling themselves marginal to contemporary society, are better equipped to write about characters on the fringe than about the sluices of wealth and authority. The modern literature of many countries, indeed, is full of eloquent voices doubting the joys of progress and expressing a kind of solidarity with those wounded by change. Literature can also act as a disturbing alternative to the confident shallowness that is embodied in so many TV programmes and in so much newsprint. As D. H. Lawrence angrily observed in an article called "Enslaved by Civilization":

> Certainly you mustn't have an emotion to call your own. You must be good, and feel exactly what is expected of you, which is just what other people feel. Which means that in the end you feel nothing at all, all your feeling has been killed out of you. And all that is left is the artificial stock emotion which comes out with the morning papers.

The resurrection of raw emotion has been a prime goal of a whole generation of male Canadian poets, notably John Newlove, Patrick Lane, Gary Geddes, and Michael Ondaatje. These writers, all of whom were small boys during the Second World War, have sustained a fierce tension between their cool control of language and their savagery of subject matter. It's as if they can't bring themselves to trust peace—as if violence alone were real. A similar tension exists in three recent works of fiction by men who are also in their forties: Seán Virgo, David Carpenter, and M. T. Kelly. In each case, the novel or collection of short stories represents a turning away from the central obsessions of our society and a search for value elsewhere.

The rejection of urban society is most explicit in Kelly's novel *A Dream Like Mine,* which earned him the governor general's award for fiction. . . . The book is narrated by an unnamed journalist from Toronto, who has flown up to northwestern Ontario in order to research a feature about traditional Indian healers. His curiosity soon enmeshes him in a web of environmental terrorism: the journalist is kidnapped by an unbalanced, violent Indian called Arthur who is desperate to avenge the degradation of his people's lives and land. Intellectually, the journalist knows all about Indian pain—he has read that American soldiers used to play catch with the hacked-off breasts of Navaho girls, and he understands that the settlement of parts of this continent followed the distribution of smallpox-infected blankets among its native peoples. He *knows* too much; he doesn't *feel* enough.

A Dream Like Mine is a prolonged effort to initiate the reader into Indian suffering. It's an attempt to shock us out of our bored acceptance of "the Indian problem." Kelly is effective at using ancient Ojibway stories . . . to offset present-day events. The cleverness of the novel's structure, though, arises from its main character, Arthur. Far from being some passive recipient of the white man's iniquity, he behaves like an unpredictable criminal. Acting out of a thirst for revenge, Arthur cannot be appeased by reason. He's a complex and stunning character. As the American novelist and naturalist Peter Matthiessen wrote in a letter to Kelly last year, "All the work you have done with Indians and Indian matters over the years has not been wasted, it is justified by this figure alone."

Matthiessen's remark rightly implies that *A Dream Like Mine* grows from a great deal of passionate learning. The narrator's rage at a wasteful industrial society and his grief at our rape of the natural world are also M. T. Kelly's, and one of the novel's strengths is the way it provides an unforced space for a sort of public grief:

Finally I saw my own home, then the great flat sil-

ver plain of Lake Ontario, near which I grew up. Ontario, the Beautiful Lake of the Iroquois. That lake had been dead so long, all my life, flat and shining and empty and grey . . . I knew clearly how the lake had been killed, how the life in it, the water, was changed into something inert, sterile. So much emptiness.

Like his narrator, Kelly has worked extensively in Toronto journalism. His own fantasies of violence, it seems clear, form part of the fabric of Arthur's vengeful bitterness, just as the author's helplessness to alter the onrushing course of history enters into the passive, bewildered consciousness of the book's narrator. Out of his personal divisions, Kelly has forged a tough, sour, unified novel.

His narrator feels betrayed not so much by Arthur as by the old shaman Wilf Redwing, who cooperates in the kidnapping. By implicating a traditional healer—master of the sweat lodge, wellspring of moral authority, dreamer of visions—in violent crime, Kelly avoids easy responses in the reader. His novel is a deeply felt lament for the natural world and the old ways, but it's not sentimental. It tries to get beyond our stock emotion of helpless outrage to ask: "After such knowledge, what forgiveness?" (pp. 66-7)

Mark Abley, "Wild Men," in Saturday Night, *Vol. 103, No. 8, August, 1988, pp. 66-8.*

Gwendolyn (Margaret) MacEwen

Afterworlds

Governor General's Literary Award: Poetry

Canadian poet, novelist, dramatist, author of children's books, short story writer, and travel writer.

Afterworlds (1987) incorporates elements found throughout MacEwen's work, including her continuing exploration of the psyche and its connection to the physical world. Many of the poems in this volume feature a speaker who addresses a figure that MacEwen's critics have called her "Male Muse." References to "preworlds," "afterworlds," and "inner worlds" allude to the areas in which MacEwen's mystical poems are typically set. In such poems as "Genesis 2" and "You Can Study It if You Want," MacEwen exhibits humor as well as a sense of the sacred. Jan Bartley noted: "In *Afterworlds*, MacEwen's words are mature and startling, hurled at us with energy, wisdom, love and good humour."

Born and educated in Toronto, MacEwen left school at an early age to devote herself to a literary career. At the time of her death in late 1987, she had published eleven volumes of verse, three children's books, two collections of short stories, and two novels, as well as numerous radio plays for the Canadian Broadcasting Company and various works of nonfiction. She received a Governor General's Award for *The Shadow-Maker* (1969), a surreal verse exploration of the dream world and the unconscious. In *Magic Animals: Selected Poems Old and New* (1974), a transitional volume in her career, MacEwen demonstrated a new economy of language focusing on the violent nature of humankind. MacEwen's ventures into fiction allowed a more extensive examination of her interest in the writer as myth-maker. In *Julian the Magician* (1963), deceptively simple prose transforms the life and death of a Christ figure into a modern fable that tells of divinity in all humans.

MacEwen is perhaps best known, in the words of Mary Di Michele, as a poet of "mystic intensity." Her work is widely praised for its sensual imagery and plangent phrasings. She depicts the physical realm as being integral to the abstract, sacred world, and her poems are often perceived as incantatory. MacEwen has experimented with a variety of forms in pursuit of her poetic interests. *Afterworlds*, for example, contains free-verse lyrics, prose poems, a radio play in verse, and a sequence of poems in the form of letters. The first poem, "The Grand Dance," names each of the sections into which *Afterworlds* is formally divided and shares imagery and phrasings with "The Tao of Physics," the final piece, giving unity to a diversity of styles and themes. Robin Skelton remarked that with *Afterworlds*, "MacEwen has moved from being a poet of consequence to being a poet of greatness."

(See also *CLC*, Vol. 13; *Contemporary Authors*, Vols. 9-12, rev. ed., Vol. 124 [obituary]; *Contemporary Authors New Revision Series*, Vols. 7, 22; *Something about the Author*, Vol. 50;

and *Dictionary of Literary Biography*, Vol. 53.)

GWENDOLYN MacEWEN

I write, first of all, in order to make sense of the chaotic nature of experience, of reality. But—and this is more important—I also write in order to construct a bridge between the 'inner' world of the *psyche* and the 'outer' world of things. For me, language has enormous, almost magical power, and I tend to regard poetry in much the same way as the ancients regarded the chants or hymns used in holy festivals—as a means of invoking the mysterious forces which move the world, inform our deepest and most secret thoughts, and often visit us in sleep.

I am drawn to ancient religions and symbols as surely as a

thirsty animal is drawn to a deep dark pool of water on a hot afternoon. . . .

An awful lot gets said about what poems are supposed to be about, what certain poets are *trying* to say, and so on. The truth is of course that poems mean exactly what they mean—in the same way that dolphins leaping above the waves mean that they are leaping about the waves. And poets are never *trying* to say something; they've either said it in the poem or the poem doesn't get written. Nor is there, as we're often tempted to think, some secret hidden meaning in the poem that we're supposed to uncover after a lot of struggle. It's true that some poets are more complex than others, but poets have better things to do than to be deliberately difficult and play hide and seek with the reader.

Poetry stems from the Here and Now, but it can dive into the Past and the Future with blinding speed. In the trilogy of *Star Wars,* the wisdom of the Past is used to deal with the situations of the Future. In these films, when the hero is completing his dangerous missions, he decides to trust in 'the Force'—his sixth sense or intuition or the universal mystery itself—to direct him towards his target. It's that kind of trust which is needed in reading and understanding poetry, because nearly all poetry deals one way or another with the great mystery which is all around us.

Both the poet and the reader of poetry must listen to that inner voice which instructs them to drop their defenses and trust in the 'force'. We are citizens of the Past and of the Future. We are also inhabitants of the Present, and as such we must have a very acute awareness of the reality in which we find ourselves in order to survive. Poetry is not an escape, in the way in which some books and films are escapes. It is not a tip which transports us out of ourselves; on the contrary, it is a journey into the *interior,* an exploration which never ends.

Poetry travels between the 'inner' world of the *psyche* and the 'outer' world of things, and between Past and Future. In a way the poet resembles a magician or a time-traveller with so much freedom of movement in his mind. The wonderful thing about poetry is that it gives you absolute freedom of thought, and that freedom should be with you whether you are writing a poem or reading one.

I made a statement some years ago about my reasons for writing, and that statement still holds true today:

I write in order to communicate joy, mystery, passion . . . not the joy that naively exists without knowledge of pain, but that joy which arises out of and conquers pain. I want to construct a myth.

> *Gwendolyn MacEwen, "A Poet's Journey into the Interior," in* Cross-Canada Writers' Quarterly, *Vol. 8, No. 3-4, 1986, p. 19.*

ROBIN SKELTON

It is five years since Gwendolyn MacEwen dazzled us with her *T. E. Lawrence Poems* and *Earthlight.* Her new collection, *Afterworlds,* is equally radiant with perception and passion, and the wit and sensuality rarely have been equalled. The radio verse play **"Terror and Erebus"** suffers somewhat from having a texture particularly appropriate to radio: less intense than the lyrical poetry. But the long prose-poem narrative **"Letters to Josef in Jerusalem"** has enormous power,

as do the other prose poems; indeed, in the section **"Afterthoughts"** the prose poem becomes, perhaps for the first time in Canada, a superbly delicate and passionate medium for meditation and memory. MacEwen has, moreover, a truly poetic vision. Her every line and phrase explore the territory in which poetry alone can walk. If one were to define "pure poetry", one would have to refer to this poet as its most effortless and magical Canadian practitioner. MacEwen has moved from being a poet of consequence to being a poet of greatness.

> *Robin Skelton, "Poetry: Packing All the Power into Two of Seven Titles," in* Quill and Quire, *Vol. 53, No. 5, May, 1987, p. 24.*

SUSAN GLICKMAN

> A moment in a small hotel with an old man who was a sheriff in the Wild East, talking of Lawrence and Palestine, and the radio tells us a new satellite has been launched at Cape Canaveral. He is almost deaf, so I point to the dark skies above Galilee and make circles with my hand. All the wars he has fought
>
> Retreat into the silence of space.
>
> **"Letters to Josef in Jerusalem"**

Readers familiar with Gwendolyn MacEwen's work will remember this old man, his stories and photographs of Lawrence of Arabia. We met him in an earlier avatar of **"Letters to Josef,"** the suite of Middle-Eastern poems called **"One Arab Flute"** published in *The Shadowmaker* (1969), and he was also recalled in the foreword to *The T. E. Lawrence Poems* (1982). But in his first incarnation he was simply local colour; in his second, a guide to the private imagination. Here, in keeping with the cosmology of MacEwen's new book [*Afterworlds*], he is a frail survivor of a time when war, however muddled and ineffectual, involved courage and afforded dignity—implied *some* dimension of humanity. MacEwen followed him into that past in her last volume; this one points "to the dark skies" and "the silence of space."

But it does so without vaporizing social reality and political history; comparison of **"Letters to Josef"** with **"One Arab Flute"** reveals how much more thoughtfully MacEwen has explored her 1962 trip to Israel as the years have passed; how much more meaningful a symbol—globally and personally—the besieged and divided holy city has become over those years. For *Afterworlds,* MacEwen's most polemical book since *The Armies of the Moon* (1972), insists on the collective nature of the human experiment. Whatever ardours or miseries the individual experiences—and a whole section of love poems to MacEwen's "Male Muse" attests to them—no one acts alone, no couple acts alone, against history.

Comparison with *The Armies of the Moon* is suggested most strongly by the schematic organization of *Afterworlds:* like the earlier book, this one is framed by a pair of cyclical poems, the first of which provides contextual definitions for the titles of the book's internal divisions. Here they are **"Ancient Slang," "Anarchy," "Apocalypse," "Afterimages," "After-Thoughts,"** and **"Avatars."** The first section sets up the cosmology of the book: "Being means breaking the symmetry of the void / So life is not a fearful but a broken symmetry" (**"Vacuum Genesis"**). The second section defines the relationship of poetry to the world and suggests that poetry ought to be "as ruthless and beautiful and amoral as the world is" (**"But"**). Section three consists of two long works, the **"Letters to Josef"** and **"Terror and Erebus,"** her verse drama about the Franklin expedition to discover the Northwest passage. Both of these poems are dialogic; Rasmussen searches for the remains of the Franklin expedition to discern its meaning, as the letter-writer tries to reconstruct the meaning of Jerusalem for Joseph. Thematically and aesthetically we are at the centre of the book in this section, **"Apocalypse."**

The fourth and fifth sections, **"Afterimages"** and **"After-Thoughts"** form a kind of pair also; first elegiac lyrics and then prose poems about the author's childhood. The prose poems here are more carefully crafted than those in *The Fire-Eaters,* but except for the wonderful **"The Man with Three Violins,"** MacEwen hasn't yet mastered the stylistic possibilities of the form, although it's clear what she *wants* from it: a play of narrative against epiphany. Another exception: **"Me and the Runner,"** which, careering through 18 commas with bravado and grace, provides a link to section six, **"Avatars,"** the love poems. Here cosmology is redefined in terms of the body:

> The sound we made when we came, love,
> Will sound the same and is the same
> As the cry we will make when we go.
>
> **("Daynights")**

And yes, it is a female cosmology. . . . This is serious poetry; it never forgets "the holiness of the heart's affections" in its terror of and respect for "the silence of space." But to understand this book, don't start with the deliberately "thematic" poems that frame it. Start with **"Polaris,"** the meditation of a prisoner of the Gulag, which concludes . . . :

> If you consult the polestar for the truth
> of your present position, you will learn that
>   you have no
>   position, position is illusion (consider
>   this
> endlessly still self, endlessly turning);
>
> this prison is actually your freedom, and
>   it is you, it is you, you
> are the only thing in this frozen night
>   which is really moving

> Susan Glickman, "Anarchy and Afterthoughts," in
> Books in Canada, Vol. 16, No. 5, June-July, 1987,
> p. 26.

PHYLLIS WEBB

Gwen, I didn't know it had been so bad, such a long way down these past months to the Afterworlds, or that the door and the blue wings opened and closed in that sound of death you said you knew the tune of. Your last poems so big with cosmos & semen & gold—and I'm afraid adjectives that came too easily over the years: *terrible, beautiful, splendid, fabulous, wonderful, remarkable, dark, exquisite, mighty*—all of which you were as your cat waited to take over the typewriter and get on with its sublime works while you were out colliding with Barker Fairley in a metaphysical blizzard or handing a coin to the ferryman for the last ride. . . . As you lay there dying in seizure was it your lord Life or your lord Death who came to collect a last poem as you careened into *the beautiful darkness?*

> **An excerpt from "Letters to Josef in Jerusalem"**
>
> Do you still write your angry avant-garde plays?
>
> I have the photo you sent me, of actors with mime-white faces all dying in different ways. Some go all limp and funny, they give up their hold on reality; others just die like clocks, they wind down. You always loved irony; there was that play about the man in the British army fighting the Nazis, then in the Irgun fighting the British.
>
> It was the folly, you wrote me, the *foolness* of it all.
>
> We sat all night long and listened to your friends play jazz on the roof of the theatre where you lived; we discussed how modern drama differed in the East and West. You said an old writer had called you a beatnik and tried to rough you up. Kids down in the streets below us screamed in the lost dialects of Babylon. I had just seen Kirk Douglas in *Spartacus* speaking Hebrew. You said—Look at the children, why
>
> Do we keep making the beautiful children?
>
> There was a beggar you tried to befriend, but he screamed "God will burn you!" when you offered him money or cigarettes. He had seen his family consumed in a village in Iraq and they had never stopped burning. In the West, you said, you hunger for violence; you flirt with it. In the East we have it;
>
> That is the difference.
>
> And years later you write to tell me politics does not matter, only theatre. Night falls like a dead bird or a dusty curtain. Are the kids still screaming in the streets below you? Tell them to stop, tell them all to stop and watch your mime-white clowns dancing down the foolish night, playing live, playing dead, playing everything that is allowed in the theatres of war.
>
> The folly, Josef, the foolness of it all.

And was it really beautiful? Tell me. Was it dark? Or did the cat get your last fabulous word?

> *Phyllis Webb, "Gwendolyn MacEwen 1941-1987,"*
> *in* The Malahat Review, *No. 81, Winter, 1987, p. i.*

M. T. KELLY

Poet Gwendolyn MacEwen, who died . . . at the age of 46, met the world with such emotional intensity that when you talked casually with her she would often turn her feelings aside with a joke, a stream of conversation as she turned her head away, an evasive twinkling gleam in her eye. She readily acknowledged the passion and mysticism of her poetry, but her role as a writer, as a feeling person, seemed to tire her at times. . . .

Her world was a haunted one. She is on record as saying that at times she found it difficult to distinguish between realities except when she was writing, but she wrote all her life, and all those who are interested in "the real, unexplored country which lies *within* the country we think we have conquered" will always be grateful for her perceptions of reality. . . .

Perhaps her way of seeing was too intense. In *Afterworlds* she writes, "Let me make this perfectly clear. I have never written anything because it is a Poem . . ." She concludes, "What matters is what is out there in the large dark / And in the long light, / Breathing." In retrospect *Afterworlds* seems an ominous book. There is the title, and the cover, a photograph of four children looking out over a darkening Lake Huron, entitled "Vigil." Gwendolyn is the child seated on the far right. The epigraph to the book talks about "the eternal moods of the bleak wind" not the gaiety of flowers, and ends with the words "Remember Thee."

It would be impossible to forget her. She was perhaps the best reader of poetry in Canada, and her shimmering, magical images could possess the mind like spirits.

> M. T. Kelly, "MacEwen Possessed a Talent That Was Fragile, Precocious," in The Globe and Mail, Toronto, December 2, 1987, p. C5.

MARTIN SINGLETON

There are many images of light and music [in *Afterworlds*]. In spite of deeply-felt, carefully-articulated sorrow and anger at injustice, MacEwen's world-view remains optimistic. Part V of her long sequence **"Letters to Josef in Jerusalem"**, where "death stutters its idiotic message in the throats of the guns", ends with the realization that "it is just a few minutes to the end of the world". Part VII, however, opens "but there are moments when we dare to believe Peace"; this occurs "when the passionate light shines on purple grapes, yellow beer, the green and violet slopes of Mount Miron".

MacEwen writes "I promise you these lines / Are as real as your name"; although much of *Afterworlds* deals with magic in her lyrical, passionate way, the magic is always centered in the commonplace. The external world and its connections with one's reality may and often do change; the self abides. In **"Polaris, Or Gulag Nightscapes"**, the protagonist shifts from observer of slowly turning constellations to "the only thing in this frozen night which is really moving". There is constant focus on self-discovery; paradoxically this is often achieved through self-acceptance: "and we who are left behind you / struggling to become what we already are".

Much of the poetry deals with the past, whether mythical, historical or personal. . . . MacEwen is *engaged,* and both dark and light, good and evil, dream and cold reality are served well by her long fluid lines, her repetition and the essential music of her rhythms. . . . [Her] images illuminate, but never obfuscate, her thought.

One of *Afterworlds'* basic concerns is language, especially the power of the Poem; the caps are the author's, and deliberate. Although she can write, perfectly honestly and with an insight which is enviable, that "all you should ever care about / is what happens when you lift your eyes from the page", she is also aware of the awful power of, and the destruction wrought by, poetry. In **"But"**, the Poem warns,

> Do not hate me
> Because I peeled the veil from your eyes
> and tore your world
> To shreds, and brought

The darkness down upon your head.

Moving smoothly between prose-poem and pure lyric, love poems and poems of anger and regret, between past and future and the shifting interface between inner and outer reality, *Afterworlds* is the latest superb book from one of Canada's real national assets. (pp. 22-3)

> *Martin Singleton, in a review of "Afterworlds," in* Cross-Canada Writers' Quarterly, *Vol. 10, No. 1, 1988, pp. 22-3.*

GILLIAN HARDING-RUSSELL

Although Anne Szumigalski and Gwendolyn MacEwen are highly individual poets, their poetry shares certain traits. Poetic constructs to present ideas graphically or stories to dramatize a psychological dimension are found in both *Dogstones* (a selected work with a new title section) and *Afterworlds.* Perhaps a little self-centred in their visions, each poet develops a pattern of images bearing private meanings the reader must pick up: stones, angels, elephants, dogs, cats, beetles, days of the week (with proverbial connotations) appear in both poets' worlds. In post-modern metapoetical style, the two books are preoccupied with the nature of art and with an association of art with religion. (p. 95)

[Cryptic] in her method and individual in her vision, MacEwen in the opening poem **"The Grand Dance"** suggests the significance of the title *Afterworlds*. As in Szumigalski's "A House with a Tower," the poet-speaker refers to herself as a 'liar' and further develops the concept of the male-lover muse who informs her early poetry, notably the Governor General Award-winning *The Shadow-Maker.* Reflecting the middle-aged poet's shifting preoccupations, lord Death dances in night skies of the universe, and the poet-speaker, against her promise, attempts to express the ineffable through poetry:

> I promised you I would never turn you into poetry,
>   but
> Allow this liar these wilful, wicked lines.
>
> I am simply trying to track you down
> In preworlds and afterworlds
> And the present myriad inner worlds
> Which whirl around in the carousel of space.
>
> I hurl breathless poems against my lord Death,
> Send these words, these words
> Careening into the beautiful darkness.

That the muse, lord Death, exists in 'preworlds and afterworlds' suggests his timelessness and the cyclical nature of beginnings and endings. . . . MacEwen gives us a marvellous sense of a multifaceted reality outside the poem and, perhaps, impenetrable by the poem.

Just as the woman becomes the voice of inspiration when the wind alters her voice to something strange and otherworldly in Szumigalski's "The Question," so the poet-speaker is the medium for the muse's expression in MacEwen's **"Stones and Angels."** She has tried to find a stone for Yanni (a figure for the 'king' or superior everyman, the latent poet) to paint on; but stones are 'lost sheep in the golden dust,' 'blind eyes of lost gods,' 'stars that failed and fell here' and 'faces of watches without hands.' The poet-speaker aspires to be 'master of time' by recreating 'the great loneliness which is God' 'in the mad dynamic silence' of poems.

> We would paint the universe the colours of our
>   minds
>   and flirt with death, but
> Whether we dance or faint or kneel we fall
> On stones.

However, man is limited by the 'colours' or the constitution of his mind in the same way that the man and woman in Szumigalski's poem are forced to reproduce images from the tangible world to represent the intangible 'question.' (pp. 97-8)

MacEwen borrows from history the story of the Franklin expedition in the long poem **"Terror and Erebus."** In the opening stanzas, the poet looks back from the perspective of a century and, with the security of 'comfortable maps,' wonders about the expedition and its cost in human lives:

> How could they know what I now know,
> A century later . . .
>
> That the ice can camouflage the straits
> And drive men into false channels,
> Drive men into white, sliding traps . . . ?

Answering her own question, the poet-speaker sympathizes with the ideal that drove these men. She exclaims that he, Franklin, 'created the Passage / By *willing* it to be,' and that to follow his idealistic impulse 'one does not need geography.'

Both *Dogstones* and **Afterworlds** are spiritually-oriented books of poetry. The difficult style using esoteric images and poetic constructs that align the secular and colloquial with the sacred and incantatory represents a distinctly postmodern impulse to discover meaning in a chaotic, richly diverse reality. Here are two poets who require the reader to meet them more than half way; but then readers today might themselves be considered latent poets. We admire Szumigalski's and MacEwen's attempt to construct superimposed structures of reality without the modernist's rage for a too simplified order. As post-moderns, these poets indulge in the fertile complexity of a reality that allows for infinite possibilities of meaning and unmeaning. (pp. 98-9)

> *Gillian Harding-Russell, "Chinese Boxes of Reality:*
> *Structures and Amalgams," in* Event, *Vol. 17, No.*
> *1, Spring, 1988, pp. 95-100.*

JAN BARTLEY

Is it possible to read Gwendolyn MacEwen's **Afterworlds** without the knowledge that this is her last gift to us, her last open secret? Probably not, not yet. Irresistibly, meanings shift; the bold exotic vision, the outrageous images—sometimes seductively vague, sometimes sharp and knife-edged—become at once more transparent, more profound. Consider, for example, how the photograph included in *Afterworlds* becomes one of its poems: taken by MacEwen's father, it shows mostly sky streaked by clouds, sunlight spilling over water, a clearly defined horizon, and, in the foreground the silhouette of a tree, the silhouettes of four children sitting on a bench looking out over the water. "Gwendolyn MacEwen," we are told, "is the child seated on the far right." She is the small, vulnerable shadow on the far right, and the very angle of her head makes one wonder what she sees in the twilight. "The eye *creates* the horizon," says MacEwen, "the

ear *invents* the wind." We are free and obliged to invest her words with meaning, and to allow those meanings fluidity. MacEwen would approve of this wondering, this re-reading and re-seeing. Her poetry has always been a balancing act between convictions and questions, pulling us to "where the passage lies / Between conjecture and reality."

Yet, **Afterworlds,** even reread in the knowledge of our loss, is not a mournful book. It is tough-minded, sometimes tender, courageous and often humorous. Like other poetry collections, most notably **The Armies of the Moon,** its six sections . . . suggest a linear pattern, a rational mode of linking ideas and images. However, MacEwen has always been a superb craftswoman of the curve, mistrusting the simplicity of straightlines. In **Afterworlds,** once again, the straightline curves into a circle; the past and future intersect in the intensity of a single "breathing" moment; the images of one poem are echoed in another; the last poem mirrors the first, the simple notion of progression is complicated by the more marvellous notion of multi-faceted interrelationship. We are left with, and gain: "Words, these words / Careening into the beautiful darkness." In **Afterworlds,** words do not stand still. In **"Let Me Make This Perfectly Clear,"** MacEwen warns us of their elusiveness:

> All I have ever cared about
> And all you should ever care about
> Is what happens when you lift your eyes from this
>   page.
>
> Do not think for one minute it is the Poem that
>   matters.
> It is not the Poem that matters.
> You can shove the Poem.
> What matters is what is out there in the large dark
> And in the long light,
> Breathing.

What is out there in the large dark? The next poem, **"But,"** tells us:

> Out there in the night between two trees is the
>   Poem saying:
> Do not hate me
> Because I peeled the veil from your eyes and tore
>   your world
> To shreds, and brought
>
> The darkness down upon your head.

Circles. Words, especially MacEwen's words, can create a glittering appearance of reality, invested with form and meaning. Or they can destroy that illusion, suggesting instead the profound silence of a question mark. (pp. 87-8)

[In] the long poem **"Terror and Erebus,"** wherein the ghost of our past informs our present and wherein MacEwen becomes our poetic conscience, challenging us to reinterpret our past, we are again warned of the relative worth of words. The explorer Rasmussen, who searches for meaning in the doomed Franklin expedition to find the Northwest Passage, asks the Eskimo Qaqortingneq what happened to Franklin's papers, logs and reports, but receives this answer:

> *Papers,* oh yes!
> The little children found papers
> In the great ship
> But they did not understand papers.
> They played with them
> They ripped them up

> They threw them into the wind
> Like birds . . .

This specific reply to a specific question becomes *the* answer to the poem's larger epistemological question: how can we know our past, how can we know anything? Rasmussen says, "Nobody needs to read." We need to see instead the "real journals" of people's lives, what lies beyond the words and beyond the pages. We need not just rationality, but passion and imagination. In the poem's last stanza, Rasmussen talks of the Northwest Passage and glimpses also the mythic passage still waiting to be explored:

> Now the great passage is open,
> The one you dreamed of, Franklin,
> And great white ships plough through it
> Over and over again,
> Packed with cargo and carefree men.
> It is as though no one had to prove it
> Because the passage was always there.
> Or . . . is it that the way was *invented,*
> Franklin?
>   That you cracked the passage open
> With the forces of your sheer certainty?
>   Or is it that you cannot know,
> Can never know,
> Where the passage lies
> Between conjecture and reality . . . ?

MacEwen's poetry has always occupied this passage. She has always inhabited the two worlds of fantasy and reality and married them in her vision and her crazy, beautiful words. In the disturbing **"Letters to Josef in Jerusalem,"** she can capture love and shame in a single moment:

> In Beersheba your wicked black camera aims itself
>   at an
> Arab woman and her child. She demands money
>   for
> whatever part of their souls you intend to steal. She
>   suckles
> her child, her magnificent dark breast exposed; it
>   is as
> though the child is suckling the night. She turns
>   away from
> the camera;
>
> It is her face she wishes to hide. . . .

In *Afterworlds,* MacEwen's words are mature, and startling, hurled at us with energy, wisdom, love and good humour. Read them again and again, but lift your eyes from the pages too, to see what MacEwen has always promised and warned us would be there. (p. 88)

Jan Bartley, "Dedication: Gwendolyn MacEwen (1941-1987)," in Canadian Woman Studies/les cahiers de la femme, *Vol. 9, No. 2, Summer, 1988, pp. 87-8.*

PATRICIA KEENEY

The poetry of Gwendolyn MacEwen is pure. Like water. You can see so clearly through it. It quenches your thirst. It also ponders the universe, a spectacle both grand and intimate; it contemplates the world with its festering sores of racial paranoia and xenophobia. At the centre of all this clean high running is MacEwen herself probing, invoking, remembering, suffering, smiling.

In a first section of *Afterworlds* called **"Ancient Slang"** she

speaks like an oracle—personal to everyone, wondering where all the words go. They become afterthoughts, "lethal gossip of the spheres." She gives us also **"The White Horse"** of wisdom and innocence, "the first horse to come into the world," who looks at you wondering why you are here when all your countries are broken. We meet the Loch Ness monster, "this swan of Hell," "this ugly slug" in a brilliant tour de force that has the lugubrious legendary beast dying of loneliness "In his mind's dark land, / where he dreamed up his luminous myths, the last of which was man." MacEwen is best when writing from her breathless cosmic imagination but falters a little in poems such as **"Genesis 2,"** where she is simply playing Rubik's Cube with God or where she is foisting little poetry jokes on us. Even here, however, there are exceptions. In **"Let Me Make This Perfectly Clear,"** she tells us to shove the poem qua poem and concentrate on what matters—"out there in the large dark / And in the long light, Breathing."

MacEwen makes unexpected identification with curious figures from recent history. In her poems they tell our story—the Niagara Daredevil who discovers what truth is by flinging himself into the canyons of his soul; Eva Braun reflecting on Hitler as a lover, with the voice of sardonic decadence: "Marlene Dietrich told some guy who wanted her: 'I'll sleep with you when Hitler's dead.' Then after the war the guy confronted her with her promise and Marlene said: 'Hitler's alive and well and living in Argentina. Goodbye.' " In a cold, spare section called **"Apocalypse,"** where Rasmussen searches for the remains of the Franklin expedition, various voices image the splendid but merciless aesthetic of death by freezing in a land that is "the white teeth / Of a giant saw." The snow is a ruined vault where he reads traces of pain. The other long poem in this section called **"Letters to Josef in Jerusalem"** is a lyric indictment of contemporary political madness. Deftly, MacEwen turns a personal attack into the leitmotif that blends lyricism with social vision producing such chilling insights as "Things do not fall apart; it is worse: everything is fused in an awful centre."

"After-Thoughts," MacEwen's prose section, is not as startling or disturbing but then these are after-thoughts. The delightful exception is **"1958,"** a nostalgic revel in batwing sweaters and ducktails that is wholly sustained. The book ends with **"Avatars,"** breathless, quivering love poems delivered by a full female voice documenting the stunning disaster of ecstasy. . . . (pp. 150-51)

Patricia Keeney, "Long Light," in Canadian Literature, *No. 118, Autumn, 1988, pp. 150-52.*

CYNTHIA MESSENGER

[In *Afterworlds*] we find the variety of forms and many of the persistent and compelling themes which are the trademarks of MacEwen's work. One has the sense in *Afterworlds,* perhaps more so than in MacEwen's other volumes, of a single, small "I" trying to discover its place in the cosmos. This "I" witnesses suffering and injustice, contemplates death, and enjoys sex, expressing all through the strange good humour of the persona's despair. MacEwen's amused, slightly bored voice saves this collection from the dark vision of life that subtly infuses and, because of its cumulative effect, almost overwhelms the poems.

MacEwen's voice in *Afterworlds* is self-consciously the voice of the "poet." In several poems she draws attention to the "poem" and to the act of writing, only to isolate and discard them because they cannot recreate experience. MacEwen's exploration of "poetry" and her simultaneous denial of poetry are fascinating and also problematic in *Afterworlds.* When MacEwen attempts to define her art in terms of concrete experience, she founders. Her weakest poems are in fact those that address "poetry." But what is she trying to say? The sentimental metaphors and the italicization of "poetry" convey MacEwen's attempt to express the "essence" of poetry (which is possibly her most serious mistake). Art is not, after all, the equivalent of experience, no matter how profound the experience may be for the poet; nor can a definition of art be contained in a metaphorical abstraction of heightened experience.

MacEwen's sensual/sexual response to life dominates the poet's imagination in *Afterworlds.* "The Anonymous Caller," "The Letter," "You Know Me," "Absences," and "Niagara Daredevil" are several examples of poems which feature unattainable lovers who are, in many cases, outcasts, anti-heroes, or strangers. The poet's attraction to the unattainable is part of the aestheticizing of failure that is intrinsic to MacEwen's art. (pp. 754-55)

The "you" of many of MacEwen's poems is the elusive lover whose love is fragile and temporary, or non-existent. MacEwen both celebrates and mourns this figure in her poems, mourns partly because the act of writing poetry is a frustration. The poet's most profound experiences of love are apocalyptic—they end even as they occur.

Afterworlds is an extended consideration of "apocalypse," but the apocalyptic imagery cannot sustain, with any seriousness, its overuse to convey MacEwen's sensual contact with the world. Even when apocalypse points in the poems to political strife, the suffering of children, the end of the world, its effect is weakened because it is asked to carry too much meaning. The profundity of the image of annihilation must be expressed through an equally profound art. MacEwen's poetry fails too often as poetry, so that any significance in the imagery or the sentiments expressed is lost.

Happily, MacEwen's prose poems are more effective than her lyric poems. I suspect her talent lay in narrative and in the delineation of character. **"Letters to Josef in Jerusalem"** are probably the best poems in *Afterworlds.* In **"Letters to Josef in Jerusalem"** we have a sense of the sensitive and perceptive "I" that has sustained much of Gwendolyn MacEwen's work. (p. 755)

Cynthia Messenger, in a review of "Afterworlds," in Queen's Quarterly, *Vol. 95, No. 3, Autumn, 1988, pp. 754-55.*

RONALD B. HATCH

From Aristotle onwards, virtually all the major aestheticians have assumed that the artist has a special responsibility to reveal the world's hidden patterns. For his sixteenth-century English audience, Sir Philip Sidney offered the definitive restatement of Aristotle, Horace, and Philostratus when he said that the poet should range into the 'divine consideration of what may be, and should be.' Even when the Romantic revolution in epistemology overturned the earlier conception of mind and world, poets and critics continued to expect the artist to explore hidden dimensions, especially those within the

mind itself. 'Sublimity,' Kant claimed in his *Critique of Judgment,* 'does not reside in anything of nature, but only in our mind, insofar as we can become conscious that we are superior to nature within, and therefore also to nature without us.' This Romantic belief in a hidden world of ultimate beauty and value, which somehow remains dependent upon the poet's inner vision, has exerted an enormous influence on Canadian poetry from the nineteenth century to the present. In reading through the collection of Canadian poetry for this past year, one is struck repeatedly by the way in which our finest poets push beyond the diurnal world of everyday life to disclose hidden realms of force and significance.

The very title of Gwendolyn MacEwen's new volume *Afterworlds* alerts readers that they will not be entering *this world* of space and time, at least not as it is usually perceived. In MacEwen's world we hear humanity's continuous dialogue with creation down through the ages. People do not exist merely as individuals, but as all mankind over time. MacEwen evokes the sense of a world force dancing through the ages in which 'the particles of light cast off from your hair / Illumine you for this moment only.' Her project, which resembles that of Schopenhauer in *The World as Will and Idea,* leads her reader behind the momentary illumination of the present to the dancer himself.

In order to bring her audience to accept the new vision, MacEwen proceeds first to disorient her reader with frequent addresses to a mysterious 'you.' While this 'you' might be a friend or lover, he obviously represents much more, since MacEwen says that she is 'trying to track you down / in preworlds and afterworlds.' Only in the volume's final poem, which repeats many of the phrases and lines of the introductory poem, do we learn that 'you' is Lord Siva. As Creator and Destroyer, Siva dances within the darkness to create the world as a ring of fire.

After disorienting the reader as to the nature of the dark force propelling both man and the universe, MacEwen leads the reader through a section entitled **"Anarchy,"** in which we see our everyday surface world in all its seeming chaos: people pay lip service to the sacred, but continually allow it to be undermined by the banal strictures of everyday life. For example, MacEwen describes women buying ingredients for the feast of Easter, especially the paschal lamb: 'Before the Eastern Orthodox Easter, women / carrying red eggs / Fret and haggle over a pound of Christ.' Turning from the Old World to our own situation in the New, MacEwen indicates that perhaps our way of finding truth lies in the feats of the Niagara Daredevil, Karel Soucek: 'The only way to find out / Who you are / Is to fling yourself into the canyons of your soul / Or walk a thousand miles over rock and snow.'

Much in the volume celebrates the violence associated with being: 'Being means breaking the symmetry of the void / So life is not a fearful but a broken symmetry.' The sense of movement is everywhere, and acknowledged as necessary, but it also brings a price terrifying in its beauty: 'I dream of tiny ancient horses / The bird insane in the jaws of the cat / The world, delirious with dawn.' Throughout, one senses the primeval desire for a vision which goes beyond the multifarious small pleasures of the surface to a unified reality of experience.

MacEwen's sense of the circularity of time emerges from her placement of the section entitled **"Apocalypse"** in the middle of the volume, and not at the end, which allows **"Apoca-**

lypse" to assume its secondary meaning of rebirth. This section comprises two long narrative poems: **"Terror and Erebus"** was originally a radio script from the 1960s, telling the story of Franklin lost in the Arctic on his search for the Northwest Passage and of Rasmussen's search for Franklin; the second poem, **"Letters to Josef in Jerusalem,"** narrates the present-day division of the ancient city of religions. Taken together, the two poems reveal how mankind forever loses its unity, on personal, social, and even imaginative terms.

Moving beyond **"Apocalypse"** to **"Afterimages"** and **"After-Thoughts,"** MacEwen describes her attempts to re-enter the original reality. **"The Yellow House,"** in particular, provides an elegiac description of childhood's visionary existence. These parts of the volume also contain a kind of quirky humour. She mocks her own anagogic representation of the world in a poem which takes the form of a letter. 'Hello,' she begins, explaining in a few brief lines the entire Dante-Frye theory that the world takes the shape of the imagination of the universal man, and then breaks off with the breezy line, 'I'll write you again tomorrow'—as if tomorrow had not already been swallowed up in the theory.

In the final section, **"Avatars,"** MacEwen succeeds in fusing the personal with the mythic. In reading lines such as 'How I long to return to you, / to enter the dark world of your mouth,' one cannot help thinking of MacEwen's untimely death this year. Yet these final poems contain no sadness. Instead, they breathe ecstasy, for here MacEwen experiences the god-lover so intimately that he proves more alive, more 'real,' than the world around. In **"A Coin for the Ferryman,"** MacEwen speaks of embracing 'a loneliness like no other,' of living with it till it becomes my friend.' The poem in this context becomes the coin, and although MacEwen recognizes that the 'currency is long since cancelled,' she affirms that Charon will take it, knowing 'all too well / Of our coming and going, our swimming, our drowning.' MacEwen ends with the certainty that these poems 'will lead us both across the final waters.' (pp. 32-34)

Afterworlds represents a remarkable achievement and repays many rereadings. So intensely rendered is the vision that the reader may join with MacEwen in finding the darkness of the dancing god more captivating than the light of the physical world. (p. 34)

Ronald B. Hatch, in a review of "Afterworlds," in University of Toronto Quarterly, *Vol. LVIII, No. 1, Fall, 1988, pp. 32-49.*

Najīb Mahfūz

Nobel Prize in Literature

(Also transliterated as Naguib Mahfouz) Egyptian novelist, short story writer, dramatist, scriptwriter, and journalist.

Generally regarded as modern Egypt's leading literary figure, Mahfūz is the first Arabic-language author awarded the Nobel Prize in literature. Mahfūz is best known for novels in which he creates psychological portraits of characters whose personal struggles mirror the social, political, religious, and cultural concerns confronting his homeland. He first won respect during the mid-1940s for a series of novels set among the impoverished districts of Cairo. These works depict futility and tragedy in the lives of lower-class characters who contend with social injustices and the ineluctablity of fate. Mahfūz secured his reputation during the mid-1950s with a trilogy of novels chronicling significant experiences in the lives of a middle-class Cairo family as well as Egypt's changing social and political milieus from 1917 to 1944. In later works Mahfūz makes extensive use of such literary devices as allegory, symbolism, and experimental narrative techniques to explore political issues, social and cultural malaise, spiritual crises, alienation, and decadence in contemporary Egypt. Discussing his career achievement, the Nobel Committee noted: "[Through] works rich in nuance—now clear-sightedly realistic, now evocatively ambiguous—[Mahfūz] has formed an Arabian narrative that applies to all mankind."

The stories in *Hams al junūn* (1938), his first publication, reflect Mahfūz's abiding interest for characters striving to endure in oppressive social environments. Many of these pieces explore themes relating to deviance and conformity. Mahfūz's first three novels, *'Abath al aqdār* (1939), *Rādūbīs* (1943), and *Kifāh Tība* (1944), are historical narratives set in ancient Egypt that contain allusions to modern society. Most critics agree that Mahfūz's talent matured with *Khān al-Khalīlī* (1945), his first novel set in contemporary Cairo. M. M. Badawi commented: "[*Khān al-Khalīlī*] began a series of eight novels in which [Mahfūz] emerged as the master *par excellence* of the Egyptian realistic novel, the chronicler of twentieth-century Egypt, and its most vocal social and political conscience. With titles taken from the names of streets of old Cairo, the novels offer a panoramic vista of the Egyptian lower and lower-middle classes, with the minute details of their daily lives vividly and lovingly portrayed. . . . [Mahfūz's Cairo] is a recognizable physical presence; its powerful impact upon the lives of characters is as memorable as that of Dickens's London, Dostoevsky's St. Petersburg or Zola's Paris." In *Khān al-Khalīlī* and two other acclaimed works from this period, *Zuqāq al-Midaqq* (1947; *Midaq Alley*) and *Bidāya wa-nihāya* (1951; *The Beginning and the End*), Mahfūz evokes authentic detail and blends formal language with colloquialisms while depicting the struggles of individuals in repressive environments.

Mahfūz's trilogy of novels, *Bayn al-Qasrayn* (1956), *Qasr al-*

Shawq (1957), and *al-Sukkariyya* (1957), collectively referred to in Arabic as *al-thulathiyya* and in English as *The Cairo Trilogy,* is considered a masterpiece of Middle Eastern literature. Fusing colorful evocations of ordinary events in the lives of several generations of a middle-class Cairo family with detailed descriptions of the transforming patterns of Egyptian society, these works encompass such topics as the Egyptian Revolution of 1919, the effects of modernization on cultural and religious values, and changing social attitudes towards women, education, and science. Sasson Somekh stated: "No future student of Egyptian politics, society or folklore will be able to overlook the material embodied in Mahfūz's Trilogy."

In his later work, Mahfūz shifts from his characteristic style of objective realism to make more extensive use of symbolism and various unconventional narrative techniques. *Awlād Hāratinā* (1959; *The Children of Gebelawi*), for example, is an allegory in which Egypt's present-day social concerns are linked with those of the past. Mahfūz explores broad themes, including the nature of evil and the meaning of life, by modeling his characters on such figures as Adam, Satan, Moses,

Jesus Christ, and Mohammed, and he ambivalently personifies science and technology as the modern prophets of humanity. This controversial work was first serialized in a newspaper in 1959 but not published until 1967. Menahem Milson commented: "On approaching the modern era, [*Awlād Hāratinā*] deals with the question of science and the scientific approach as opposed to religion and the traditional world view. The religious circles in Egypt felt that the novel did not treat the sanctities of Islam with appropriate reverence, and publication of this work in book form was therefore prohibited." The novel was eventually published in Lebanon.

al-Liss wal-kilāb (1961; *The Thief and the Dogs*) evinces Mahfūz's experiments with unconventional techniques, as he employs a stream-of-consciousness narrative to create a psychological portrait of a wrongly imprisoned man who wreaks revenge on his betrayers upon his release. This is one of several works in which Mahfūz portrays a criminal as a rebel against narrow and oppressive values that are frequently represented by unscrupulous policemen. *al-Summān wal-kharif* (1962; *Autumn Quail*) concerns a corrupt bureaucrat who loses his pension following the revolution of 1952, when Egypt's wealthy King Faruk was forced to abdicate. Refusing to work under the new regime, the man gradually sinks into decadence and despair. *al-Tarīq* (1964; *The Search*), which is often interpreted as a parable of a religious quest, centers on a young man seeking his father, who abandoned him at birth. *Tharthara fawq al-Nīl* (1966) documents the cynicism and superficial lifestyles of young professionals in Egypt. Most of the scenes in this novel take place on a houseboat, where a group of bureaucrats and artists congregate to share drugs and sex. *Mīrāmār* (1967), one of Mahfūz's most acclaimed later works, examines the behavior of several male residents of an Alexandrian boarding-house when a beautiful and naive young rural woman is hired as a maid. The novel extends from a particular focus on the jealousies, rivalries, and dubious values of the men and the woman's attempts to assert her identity and self-reliance to a general critique of Egyptian society. *Hob taht al-Matar* (1973) and *al-Karnak* (1974) contrast the repressive actions of authorities during the regime of Gamal Abdel Nasser with the idealism of young people hoping for political and social reform. Reflecting the content of much of Mahfūz's later work, these novels also examine the disillusionment and malaise that affected Egypt following the country's military defeat in the Six-Day War of 1967.

In addition to his fiction, Mahfūz's influence on Egyptian literature expands to several other areas. He contributes columns on a wide range of topics to *al-Ahram,* a leading Egyptian newspaper, and as a dramatist and scriptwriter Mahfūz has endeavored to elevate the intellectual content of theater and film in Egypt. He has also published several collections of short stories, including *Khammarat al qitt al-aswad* (1968; *The Black Cat Tavern and Other Stories*), *Taht al-mizalla* (1969), and *Hikāya bilā bidāya walā nihāya* (1971). *God's World* (1973) offers English translations of stories from several phases of Mahfūz's career.

(See also *CLC,* Vol. 52.)

MENAHEM MILSON

Najīb Mahfūz is undoubtedly the most famous Egyptian writer today; his popularity in Egypt and the rest of the Arab world is complemented by the wide interest in his work shown by Western students of Arabic literature and of Egyptian society. Mahfūz, who first achieved fame in the 1950's as a realistic writer, has since the early 1960's become known for his symbolical or allegorical writing. He appears to have lost nothing of his appeal. Although the precise meaning and intention of his symbols may not be fully understood, their relevance to the current problems of Egypt is generally recognized by Egyptian readers. Mahfūz's images and dramatic plots are powerful enough to evoke their sympathetic response, even if the underlying conceptual scheme is not exactly clear to them. (p. 157)

At the outset of his literary career [Mahfūz] published a number of novels with plots taken from the history of ancient Egypt. Subsequently, in the mid-1940's, a series of novels set against the background of contemporary Egypt began to appear. The crowning achievement of his work in the realm of the realistic novel is his trilogy of the history of a Cairo family, which was published in the years 1956-7 [**Bayna 'l-qasrayn** (1956), **Qasr al-shawq** (1957), and **al-Sukkariyya** (1957), known collectively as the **Cairo Trilogy**]. According to Mahfūz himself, he had completed this work before the 1952 revolution but delayed its publication for several years. With the publication of the trilogy, Mahfūz won great acclaim in Egypt and in other Arab countries, and was recognized as the greatest of the Egyptian novelists.

In 1959 Mahfūz published the allegorical novel **Awlād hāretnā** (**Children of our neighbourhood**) in instalments in the newspaper *al-Ahrām*. In **Awlād hāretnā** he grapples with the problems of civilization, as it has evolved under the guidance of the three great monotheistic religions until the modern age. This novel deals allegorically with the place of religion in society and with the relations between religion and political power. On approaching the modern era, the story deals with the question of science and the scientific approach as opposed to religion and the traditional world-view. The religious circles in Egypt felt that the novel did not treat the sanctities of Islam with the appropriate reverence, and publication of this work in book form was therefore prohibited in Egypt. It was published in Lebanon in 1967.

From 1961 onwards, Mahfūz has published several novels, considerably different from the realistic works on which he had gained his reputation during the 1950's. These novels differ from those of the 1940's and 1950's in structure, style and thematic focus. Like the earlier works, these novels are set in Egypt (and for the most part in Cairo), but unlike the former novels they are basically concerned with the alienated individual. Social reality is described sparingly and only when necessary as a background for the problem of the individual. The problems of the individual as represented in these novels are not social problems (poverty, oppression, etc.), but existential problems: anxiety, loneliness, the worthlessness and purposelessness of life. These novels could be called 'the novels of the alienated hero'.

The change in form and style seems to be correlated with the change in thematic focus; with attention directed essentially to the inner world of the individual, the use of internal monologues becomes more prominent. The amount of dialogue increases while the language becomes more terse and loaded with hints and symbols.

[Since 1960] Mahfūz has also published numerous short stories of which many are symbolical or allegorical. Their themes are similar mostly to those which we find in his larger works, namely, the existential problems of the individual and the larger problems of the very foundations of civilization. Another characteristic of these stories is that the ideational content is often more strongly pronounced than in the novels he published in the 1960's. In the short stories as in the novels, these universal problems are perceived in a particularly Egyptian setting.

It should be emphasized that, despite the obvious differences between Mahfūz's novels of the 1960's and those he wrote in the 1940's and 1950's, there was no sudden revolution in his writing. The third volume of the trilogy (*al-Sukkariyya*) points both thematically (the problem of alienation) and stylistically in the direction which Mahfūz was to take in the 1960's. (pp. 157-59)

Let us begin our excursion into the world of Najīb Mahfūz by way of one of his short stories: **"The other face"** (**"al-Wajh al-ākhar"**), published in the collection *Taht al-mizalla,* which was written in 1967. The narrator is a famous educator telling the story of his long friendship with two brothers, one a police officer, the other a criminal. He has known both of them since childhood. His sympathies are, quite understandably, with the policeman and not with the criminal. The struggle between the brothers reaches its climax when the police officer has been appointed as chief of police in the city where his gangster brother is operating. The narrator tries in vain to arrange some reconciliation between the two. Eventually the police kills the gangster, and when the narrator hears of the criminal's death he is deeply distressed and falls into a state of emotional and moral confusion. His value system has been shaken by this event and he realizes that, whereas in the past he regarded the police officer as the ideal hero, he has now come to regard the slain criminal as his ideal. As his whole value system has now been inverted, the narrator announces his decision to leave the field of education and become an artist. The subject of his first painting is to be a nude girl. He says that reason failed him, and he now prefers to act madly and destructively.

Now let us consider more closely the characters and motifs of this story. It is in fact an essay in a fictional mode on the conflict between human passions on the one hand and social order on the other. In the fictional structure of the story the narrator, *qua* educator, is presented as having attempted to act as arbiter. Mahfūz hints a number of times that the clash between the two brothers is really a conflict between two tendencies which may both be inherent in one and the same person, drawing him in divergent directions. The very name of the story, **"The other face"**, also suggests this notion of inner ambivalence. Speaking about the gangster brother, the narrator says to the policeman: 'He is not a creature of another species. He is a captive of those passions which we have undertaken to repress.' The policeman answers: 'That is the difference between civilization and barbarity'. The conflict between the brothers represents a problem of universal dimensions, it is concerned with the very foundations of civilization. The policeman describes his brother in the following terms: 'a mad storm, an uncontrollable eruption, a furious bull.' On the other hand, the policeman is referred to as a man who is characterized by rationality (*'aql*). However, when uttered by the gangster brother, 'rationality' sounds like a vice rather than a virtue. (pp. 160-61)

The unbridled passions are often referred to as 'madness'. This attribute . . . is ascribed a number of times to the criminal brother. Once the narrator has shifted his preference to the criminal, he declares also that he chooses to abandon the company of rational people and become a madman. He says, 'I shall turn away from those who are rational and respectable, and let the whirlpool sweep me away. Let them be happy and useful, and let me be mad and destructive and may Satan accept me'.

The sexual instinct ranks first and foremost among the elements which defy rationality in Mahfūz's work. Some of the crimes ascribed to the gangster are connected with sex (pimping, sexual assault, etc.). In the final scene, which dramatically demonstrates the conversion of the narrator, we see him stepping towards his model, the nude woman, a gesture with strong sexual overtones.

On the day the gangster is killed, the narrator is struck by some inflammation in one of his legs which leaves him limping. This infirmity seems to suggest that with the killing of the gangster, the very person of the narrator has been injured. Hinting that the struggle between the two brothers may have actually taken place in the mind of the narrator, Mahfūz has him say: 'We were three and we were one'.

In this dramatic story of ideas we are faced with a system of concepts and symbols aligned in two contrasting sets: civilization, rationality and the police, and on the other side, primeval instincts and passions, crime, madness and nudity. Satan, too, appears to be among the elements which are in opposition to civilization; in the final scene of the story the narrator exclaims: 'Let Satan accept me!' This, as we shall presently see, is a point of great significance in the symbolical language of Mahfūz.

Let us now pursue our investigation by examining the central motifs and symbols of the story as they occur in other, both earlier and later, works of Mahfūz. First we shall consider the great allegorical romance *Awlād hāretnā*. This work, which treats the development of civilization from Adam's time to the modern age, is divided into five parts, each of which deals with one stage of that history. The story of the patriarchal lord, Jabalāwī and his sons Adham and Idrīs is used allegorically to describe the beginning of civilization. The name Adham is a close approximation of Adam, and Idrīs is a name similar phonetically and morphologically to Iblīs, the Qur'ānic name of Satan. When choosing a superintendent for his estate, the father passes over Idrīs, his eldest son, and picks Adham for the job. Idrīs, arrogant and violent by nature, bursts out in anger against the father's decision, and in retribution he is banished from his father's house with the order never to return. Adham and his wife too are soon to be banished by his father. Adham's offence is that, following the request of his brother, he attempts to discover what is written in the patriarch's will, which presumably specifies the fortunes of his descendants. The meek Adham did not want to do this, but he was unable to resist temptation because his wife coaxed him into it. This and numerous other details remind us repeatedly of the Biblical story of the Fall, but we cannot dwell here on the parallels between Mahfūz's story and the Biblical one. We should rather consider further the characterization of the brothers. The violent conduct of Idrīs is described in some instances, by the attribute of 'madness'.

Adham, for his part, asks his brother to come back to his senses, in Arabic 'to return to reason or rationality'. When his wife is tempting him to look at the father's will, Adham prays, 'O God, give back to her her reason'. By contrast with the violent Idrīs, Adham is described as humble, patient, obedient and self-restrained. When Adham is asked by his father what caused him to act as he did against his better judgment, he answers, 'The Devil'. Idrīs is described also as a drunkard (sikkīr), or as one who gets 'drunk and boisterous', and speaking of himself he says, 'Wine has ruined my dignity.' It should be recalled that in the story **"al-Wajh al-ākhar"**, the criminal brother is accused, among other things, of 'boisterousness' ('arbada), a term used mostly to describe the behaviour of drunks.

We may better understand the significance of these images of Satan and drunkenness if we bear in mind their Islamic connotations. According to Islamic tradition (based on the Qur'ān) Iblīs (Satan) was banished by God in punishment for his arrogance and disobedience, for he alone refused God's order to the angels to prostrate themselves before Adam. Arrogance and disobedience are the very same qualities for which Idrīs also is condemned in **Awlād hāretnā.**

The drinking of wine and all alcoholic drinks is strictly forbidden in Islam. Many Muslims may disregard this prohibition, but the consciousness that wine is a forbidden thing is always present. Hence, for Muslims, drunkenness suggests not only the expectable implication of impropriety, but also that of disobedience. There is, however, another significance of wine which is also part of Islamic tradition, though, admittedly, reflecting a very particular strand within Islam, namely Sūfism or Islamic mysticism. In Islamic mysticism wine symbolizes the yearning for God, and drunkenness the state of mystical trance or ecstasy. Mahfūz is well acquainted with the concepts of Sūfism, and indeed we find that in his works wine and drunkenness appear to suggest both rebelliousness and ecstatic joy.

Various types of crime become inextricably intertwined in the lives of Idrīs and Adham: Idrīs makes his living as a thief and a highwayman, one of Adham's sons kills the other; Idrīs's daughter has secret amorous relations with Adham's son and is thus considered guilty of dishonouring her family. Summing up the situation, Idrīs says in bitter irony: 'The illustrious Jabalāwī now has a granddaughter who is a whore and a grandson who is a murderer'. As it turns out, the descendants of the great patriarch are the issue of the union between whore and murderer. This is Mahfūz's way of declaring that sexual delinquency and brutal aggressiveness are hereditary traits of mankind.

To continue our excursion into the world of Najīb Mahfūz, we shall go further back chronologically to his novel **Bidāya wa-nihāya (Beginning and end)**, published in 1949. **Bidāya wa-nihāya** is a story about a Cairene family of the lower middle-class. The novel begins when the head of the family, a minor government official, dies leaving behind him a wife and four children—three sons and a daughter. The eldest son is a handsome youth with exceptional physical strength; a dropout from school, he drifts into underworld life to become a bouncer in a café in the brothel district, a drug dealer and the lover and protector of a prostitute. We last encounter him when, wounded by rival gangsters and on the run from the police, he seeks temporary asylum at his mother's house.

The sister, who has had no education, must work as a seam-

stress in private homes to support her mother and two younger brothers, who are still in high-school. A rather plain-looking girl with no dowry, she does not have bright prospects for a suitable match. She lets herself be seduced by a young grocer who secretly promises marriage to her, but he does not keep his word. Driven by poverty as well as by loneliness, despair and the need to assert her femininity, she begins to prostitute herself. This is of course unknown to her family; she finds occasion for her brief escapades when she goes to work as a seamstress.

When the older of the two brothers finishes high-school, he accepts an appointment as a secretary in a school outside Cairo in order to help his family. The youngest brother is selfish, ambitious and vain. He is completely obsessed with the social conventions of the upper class which he would like to join. He is therefore all the more agonized by the poverty of his family. He takes care to conceal his family's humble circumstances from his classmates. When he finishes high-school, he refuses to continue his studies in a teachers' college, which is free, and chooses to go instead into the military academy, which requires tuition fees but is socially more prestigious. He is able to follow and eventually complete his studies in the military school at the cost of considerable hardship to his family and not without some financial help from his criminal brother.

One day the sister is arrested while she is with one of her clients. The police notifies her brother, the military officer, discretely in order to spare his reputation. For his sake she is released without charges. After she has been released, her brother pressures her into committing suicide for the sake of 'the family's honour'. Having watched his sister drown herself, he is gripped by remorse, and realizes for the first time how ruinous his vanity has been. At the very end of the book we leave him when he too is about to commit suicide. (pp. 161-65)

I tend to think that the story of these two brothers in **Bidāya wa-nihāya** offered Mahfūz a realistic illustration of the ideational clash which is allegorized in **"al-Wajh al-ākhar"**. The possibility of such a clash seems to be envisaged by the gangster when his young brother (who still does not know of his criminal occupation) is coming to seek his financial help for joining the military academy. (p. 166)

The sister is guilty of the offence for which her sex and situation determine her. It is noteworthy that in addition to her poverty, one of the motives which lead her to sexual delinquency is the need to satisfy her erotic instincts.

I shall quote here part of the conversation between the sister and her brother, taking place after she has been released from the police station; this part of the conversation comes after she has told her brother that she will kill herself. The brother asks her about her sinful escapade:

> 'How could you do this? You? Who would imagine this?'
> She sighed and said in submission and despair,
> 'It was God's decree'.
> Angrily he shouted,
> 'No, the Devil's decree'.
> She answered in the same rueful voice,
> 'Yes'.

When again he asks her how she has fallen into sin, she answers: 'It was the Devil's decree'. To this the brother retorts: 'You are the Devil, you have ruined us all'.

Just as the allegorical representation of various human inclinations in *Awlād hāretnā* and **"al-Wajh al-ākhar"** can be seen as derived from the realistic example of the brothers and sister in *Bidāya wa-nihāya,* so we can find in Mahfūz's earlier works what could be termed the realistic model of the patriarchal lord, Jabalāwī. I have in mind here the figure of al-Sayyid Ahmad 'Abd al-Jawād, the head of the family in [the *Cairo Trilogy*]. Al-Sayyid Ahmad 'Abd al-Jawād is the autocratic lord of his family, his word is an order that must be implicitly obeyed by his wife and children. The title *al-Sayyid* (Arabic: 'master', 'chief' or 'lord') introducing his name is the common honorific of a respectable merchant; however, the insistence with which the author uses it in referring to Ahmad 'Abd al-Jawād, and the fact that many of the other characters of the story refer to him or address him as al-Sayyid certainly emphasize his status. While imposing on his family strict observance of the traditional standards concerning the seclusion of women from all male company, except that of the nearest kin, al-Sayyid regularly satisfies his own hedonistic inclination outside his house. In the company of his friends he frequents the houses of famous singers who cater for the pleasures of well-to-do merchants; there he indulges in wine, music and licentious relations. Indeed, in that company he, the stern patriarch, is known as a *bon vivant* and is distinguished for his prowess as a lover.

We are reminded of the figure of al-Sayyid Ahmad by the figure of the father in the novel *al-Tarīq* (*The way,* published in 1964). In this novel the hero sets out to find his father, whom he has never met, and, as it eventually turns out, his quest is doomed to failure. The attributes of the elusive father in *al-Tarīq* are power, wealth, generosity and insatiable appetite for women. It has been more or less generally recognized that the novel *al-Tarīq* is a parable on a religious quest. The name of the father, Sayyid Sayyid al-Rahīmī (which in approximate translation can be tendered as 'Lord Lord Merciful'), seems to underline this religious meaning. The parallelism between the picture of the father in the trilogy and the great patriarch Jabalāwī in *Awlād hāretnā,* is admittedly only partial. Although the majestic Jabalāwī is no ascetic (he has many wives and children), there is certainly no frivolous aspect in his personality.

Still, just as Yāsīn, the debauched son of al-Sayyid Ahmad in the trilogy, claims [in *Qasr al-shawq*] to have taken after his father in his lechery, so does Idrīs claim to have acquired his ruthlessness from his father. When Adham rebukes his brother Idrīs for treating people rudely, the latter retorts: 'It is your father who taught me to treat people rudely and mercilessly'. Yāsīn and Idrīs both seem to consider their perverse conduct as derived by heredity or imitation from their fathers, or they at least attempt to make them somehow responsible for their transgressions. The excesses of which these two recalcitrant sons are guilty (sexual indulgence in the one case and violent aggressiveness in the other) result indeed from innate inclinations; hence their imputations could not be wholly groundless. The parallelism between the case of Yāsīn and his father and that of Idrīs and his may illustrate the analogy between the realistic and the mythical in the mind of Mahfūz.

The figure of the law-breaker as a rebel against the established order can be found already in some of Mahfūz's earliest works. In the story **"Yaqzat al-mūmyā'"** ("The awakening of the mummy") [published in *Hams al-junūn* (1938)] we are told of a hungry fellah who attempted to steal some of the meat that was given to the dog of a rich Pasha. The poor fellah is caught by the servants of the Pasha, is beaten and taken to the village police. The poor fellah is called a thief by his oppressors. **"Yaqzat al-mūmyā'"** is very heavily loaded with social and political messages, some of which fall outside the range of this article, but from the particular viewpoint of this study, the juxtaposition of 'thief' and 'dog' is noteworthy, for we encounter it again in the novel *The thief and the dogs* (*al-Liss wa'l-kilāb*).

The thief and the dogs (published in 1961) is an exquisitely accomplished short novel; it is a complex parable in which the thief is a rebel against social injustice, as well as an individual trapped in the existential problems of loneliness and anxiety. 'Dogs' in the title of that story literally signifies the police hounds which in the end surround the thief, but this is also the term used by the thief for the police themselves, and in a broader sense it signifies all of those who betrayed him. In a conversation between the thief and his lover, the prostitute, he says 'The majority of our people are not afraid of thieves nor do they hate them; but they instinctively hate dogs'. In the end of the story the thief is shot dead by the police; his fate is similar to that of the gangster in **"The other face"**.

The thematic connection between various forms of law-breaking (theft, prostitution and all sorts of sexual misbehaviour), madness or irrationality and the Devil is suggested time and again by linguistic forms. We have seen some of these suggestive usages in the story **"al-Wajh al-ākhar"** and in *Awlād hāretnā;* however, these forms can be seen in most of Mahfūz's works. (pp. 166-69)

In the story **"al-Wajh al-ākhar"** the outcome of the struggle between order (the policeman) and rebellion (the criminal) is that the rebellious hero is destroyed. The conflict, however, is not settled, for, as we have seen, the sedate educator (the narrator) now declares himself to be a destructive madman; he who formerly was one of the props of the established morality has now come to denounce the values which he once upheld. This conclusion of the story may be seen as a kind of 'poetic justice': the narrator, who first seemed to side with the policeman, now assumes the role of the vanquished gangster. To be sure, the way in which the narrator challenges the established order differs from that of the gangster. His challenge is manifested in madness, not in crime, but, as has already been observed, madness and law-breaking are intertwined in many of Mahfūz's works.

In order to grasp more fully the significance of the final scene of this story (the narrator *qua* mad artist turning toward his model, a woman in the nude), we should examine further what is suggested by madness and nudity in Mahfūz's works.

The problem of madness is the subject of one of Mahfūz's earliest stories, **"The whisper of madness"** [the title story of *Hams al-junūn*]. The madness of the hero in this story reportedly is not a permanent mental illness; it is a passing phase in his life which is almost totally forgotten. It was a short spell lasting a day or so; following that he was confined for a while in an asylum. The story is an attempt to understand what madness is by recalling what happened in this short period in the life of the hero.

The hero one day begins to question all social conventions and habits and, what is worse, he also begins to behave in a manner defying those conventions. Getting ready to go out in the morning, he asks himself: 'Why don't we strip these clothes off ourselves and throw them to the ground? Why don't we appear as God created us?' Without carrying out this thought he sets out for a walk.

Passing near a sidewalk restaurant, he is grieved by the sight of people dining there while hungry children in rags are sitting nearby. He snatches a chicken from one of the tables and throws it to the ground near the hungry children. Following this incident, in his favourite café, he attacks a distinguished looking gentleman and hits him on the back of his neck. This he does for no good reason, except that he feels like doing it. Outraged, the victim of the attack retaliates with slaps and kicks, and our hero barely escapes and leaves the café.

On his way he notices a lovely young woman walking with a male escort, and he feels an urge to touch her breast. He cannot see why he should desist from following this urge and does just that, which of course brings upon him the angry reaction of the people around in the form of curses, insults and beating. This does not exhaust his desire for more adventures, and he remembers his thoughts from the morning about the absurdity of wearing clothes. He removes his clothes and 'appears naked as God created him'.

We should now return to the question with which the author opens this story: 'What is madness?' Under the heading of madness, we encounter an unexplained outburst of aggressiveness. In the incident with the young woman, madness is a defiance of the norms controlling the relations between the sexes. Nudity, the climactic manifestation of the spell of madness in this story, is seen by the hero as the natural free state of man, 'as God created him'. We also have here a protest against the socio-economic order when the 'madman' feeds the hungry children.

The various incidents described by Mahfūz in this story are too disparate to be considered symptoms of one particular mental illness; they seem to be concocted to fit an allegorical scheme. Madness here is the name for a rebellion against the social and cultural shackles which limit human freedom. (pp. 169-71)

Mahfūz's interest is not primarily psychological but rather cultural and moral. Admittedly, mental disorder may actually result from the individual's inability to sustain the tension between natural impulses and the restraints imposed on him by society. However, Mahfūz is not really concerned with individual mental pathology. The pathological state of the individual is seen by him as an extreme form of a universal human predicament: the conflict between social order and freedom, between civilization—the creation of homo sapiens—and the instincts of man, the animal.

In one of his most recent works, **Qalb al-layl,** published in 1975, Mahfūz spells out this intrinsic contradiction bedevilling man individually and civilization as a whole. **Qalb al-layl** (*The middle of the night*) is ostensibly a confession of an aging man reviewing his childhood, education, loves and political views. It is, in fact, a philosophical essay in a fictional garb.

The protagonist recalls his clash with his grandfather (who brought him up in his house). The grandfather (a powerful patriarch, quite similar to Jabalāwī in **Awlād haretnā**), would like his grandson to marry the girl he has chosen for him, whereas the hero wants to follow his own passions. The grandfather considers this behavior a manifestation of dis-

obedience (he says to the young man: 'You are recalcitrant') whereas the young man declares that this is freedom. The old man says: 'This is madness which would cause the insane to leave my old house'. To which his grandson answers: 'Real paradise is in madness'.

The protagonist of **Qalb al-layl** further explains his views on this inner conflict between rationality and irrationality:

> There is a private tragedy, but I would like first to present to you my views on a universal tragedy, namely, the tragedy of *homo sapiens* (*al-insān al-'āqil*). Before reason was created, man had been in harmony with himself and with his life. It was a harsh life of struggle which he was unable to control; he was like any other animal. But when he was given reason and began to create civilization, he undertook the burden of a new trust, a responsibility which he could not possibly escape and, at the same time, was not suited to carry . . . What is taught by reason is opposed by the natural instincts. To this day the instincts have had the upper hand, at least in public life. Reason has not achieved absolute dominance except in science. In everything else it yields to the instincts; even the products of science itself are consumed by the instincts. While reason retains its own language in the sphere of scientific research, the language to which the millions respond is still the language of emotions and instincts: songs of nationalism and patriotism and racism, stupid dreams and delusions. This is the universal tragedy. Its red clouds will not dissolve until the voice of reason rises high and instincts subside toward withering and extinction.

According to this opinion (which is that of the author as much as of Ja'far al-Rāwī, the protagonist), the irrational impulses (*gharā'iz*) affect man not only individually but collectively as well. In fact, it is emphasized here that the dominance of the irrational impulses over the collective behaviour of social groups is almost absolute. The remark about the products of science being consumed by the instincts seems to refer to the fact that those in power manage to enlist the scientists in their service; consequently, politics, which is dominated by irrational factors, may be said to have subordinated science, which is the accomplishment of reason.

Kamāl, the pensive hero of the third part of the trilogy, **al-Sukkariyya,** (who [as Mahfūz stated in an interview in *Hiwār,* Vol. 3, 1963] represents the author's intellectual quandries), is fascinated by the sight of the enthusiastic masses in a nationalist rally: In the midst of the masses he feels that 'reason is locked in a bottle for a while and the repressed forces of the soul break loose . . . and the instincts (*gharā'iz*) spring forth'. Tired of his thoughts and doubts, he feels like joining those masses 'to revive his blood stream and derive warmth and youth'. The masses appear to him as acting without reason (*bilā 'uqūl*), yet he perceives in their gathering 'the dignity of conscious instincts'.

The recognition that collective behaviour is dominated by irrational impulses is not new, then, with Mahfūz; his attitude towards this phenomenon, however, appears to have changed. In **al-Sukkariyya** (which was completed before the 1952 revolution) Mahfūz speaks with admiration and envy about the masses who act without being held back by reason. Twenty-three years later, in the passage quoted from **Qalb al-layl,** horror and revulsion seem to have replaced admiration and envy: Mahfūz now speaks of 'stupid dreams and delusions' which the masses cherish, and he mentions in this connection the ominous 'red clouds'.

This more recent attitude of Mahfūz is already reflected in the short story **"al-Majnūna"** (**"The mad one"**), published [in the collection **Khammārat al-qitt al-aswad,** (**The Black Cat Tavern,** 1968)]. 'The mad one' in this story is the senseless war between two neighbouring quarters. It would seem that Mahfūz has become frightfully aware of the dangers inherent in the irrationality affecting the relations between national or religious groups. (pp. 172-74)

Mahfūz's attitude to the phenomena which he brings under the name 'madness' is wrought with ambivalence. He seems to recognize the danger of anarchy, but cannot help sympathizing with those who 'go mad' under the pressure of inborn impulses. (p. 175)

I shall now like to come to a question I have so far suspended, namely, how the development of Mahfūz's art affected the significance (allegorical or non allegorical) of the images discussed above. However, before proceeding, let me put forward some conceptual assumptions.

In the following analysis I am using the familiar distinction between three modes of fiction: allegory, mimesis and myth. I regard each of these modes as standing in a particular relation to one of three levels of reference. Allegory corresponds to, or, we should better say, is preoccupied with the level of abstractions. Mimesis endeavours to represent the phenomenal concrete reality. Myth is meant to represent the archetypal, which is believed to be, as its name indicates, more fundamental and more constant than the phenomenal. To be sure, one hardly finds any one of these three modes in a pure form. Nevertheless, this tripartite distinction is important as an analytical tool. It may help us in determining which mode is predominant in a given work, or, as the case more frequently is, in understanding the various forms of convergence and mixture of different modes.

When we read the stories of **Hams al-junūn,** Mahfūz's first collection, we cannot help the impression that these stories reflect theoretical ideas about human society and mentality more than direct observation of reality. This is not to say that Mahfūz was not familiar with or interested in the contemporary social scene. On the contrary, Mahfūz was then, as he has been ever since, deeply concerned with Egyptian society. According to his own testimony [in an interview in the Egyptian periodical *al-Kātib,* January 1963], before the 1952 revolution his impulse to write was essentially that of a social critic.

We should recall here some facts concerning the intellectual formation of Mahfūz, which may help us understand his literary approach when he wrote the stories of **Hams al-junūn.** In that early stage of his literary career he seems to have been very much under the influence of Salāma Mūsā (in whose journal, *al-Majalla al-Jadīda,* he published his articles in the early thirties). Mahfūz appears to have subscribed to the socialistic beliefs of Salāma Mūsā (Fabian socialism) and to have absorbed some of his views on the proper role of literature. Salāma Mūsā, a sworn rationalist, believed that science (understood to include both the natural and social sciences) would bring salvation to humanity. Literature can be beneficial only if it is put at the service of society. This the conscientious writer should do by deriving his ideas from science and making his literary works the vehicle of the 'correct' ideas. Already as a highschool student Mahfūz became interested

in philosophy, sociology and psychology, which interests he was to pursue as a student of philosophy in the university. Influenced by the theories which he learned and by the above mentioned instrumentalist view of literature, Mahfūz must have felt that, as a writer of fiction, he could only offer illustrations of those truths which were presumably contained, in a fuller and more exact form, in the level of abstraction. The pre-eminence of ideas above the world of experience and the perception of the senses is the hallmark of allegory. Mahfūz's fictional writing in the collection **Hams al-junūn** is the outcome of his desire to reform society, and his primary purpose throughout it is to convey ideas. Not every story in this volume is allegorical, but the literary approach of the writer is, on the whole, didactic. This stage in Mahfūz's literary development was fortunately short, and mimetic art soon prevailed over social ideology and speculative theory.

In his Cairene novels, from **al-Qāhira al-jadīda** (published in 1945) to **al-Sukkariyya** (published in 1957), Mahfūz endeavours to grasp social reality as observed directly by him. These stories need not be explained by and cannot be reduced to a set of theoretical ideas and moral precepts; they have an artistic existence of their own. Admittedly, many of the characters of these novels represent something beyond their fictional role. Stern patriarch, submissive wife, obedient and dutiful son, rich merchant and other such persons are individual characters as well as social types. Mahfūz has certainly retained the impulse of a social critic and the pathos of a moralist; however, the novelist in him has come into his own.

In **Awlād hāretnā** and specifically in its first part, which is relevant to our discussion, we encounter a new approach to reality on the part of Mahfūz. It has already been mentioned that **Awlād hāretnā** is an allegorical book. However, saying that its first part, 'Adham', is an allegory of the beginning of human civilization takes us only so far toward understanding the unique nature of this work. In 'Adham' Mahfūz retells the stories of Satan's rebellion and of the Fall in close parallelism to the Biblical and Qur'ānic traditions. But when we examine Mahfūz's version, we find that the protagonists of the mythical story, as recreated by our author, are modelled on the characters of his Cairene novels (which, in their turn, represent social types). By combining the plots of familiar legends and the human types which he had long studied in their social context, Mahfūz produced, in the first part of **Awlād hāretnā,** something essentially new, a Mahfūzian mythology. Its characters are archetypes, and the relations between them are construed as archetypal patterns.

When **Awlād hāretnā** is viewed in this fashion, its significance as a turning-point in Mahfūz's literary development becomes manifest. It has established a mythical level beside the other two (the phenomenal and the ideational) in reference to which Mahfūz's works should be understood. Since the publication of **Awlād hāretnā,** Mahfūz has not produced any work in which the mythical mode is as predominant as in it. However, in all of his subsequent works one must postulate the mythical level of reference. Mahfūz's language now carries the connotations of his mythology. (pp. 176-79)

Menahem Milson, "Reality, Allegory and Myth in the Work of Najīb Mahfūz," in Asian and African Studies, *Vol. 11, No. 2, Autumn, 1976, pp. 157-79.*

JOHN FOWLES

Open cities are the mothers of open societies, and their existence is especially essential to literature—which is why, I suppose, we cherish our illusions about them, and forgive them so many of their sins. In the case of Alexandria, that prototype cosmopolis and melter of antitheses, we can hardly be blamed. *Antony and Cleopatra,* Cavafy, E. M. Forster, Lawrence Durrell . . . there is a formidably distinguished list of foreign celebrants and from them we have taken an indelible image of the place. It is languorous, subtle, perverse, eternally *fin de siècle;* failure haunts it, yet a failure of such richness that it is a kind of victory. What we have conspicuously lacked, in this comfortable pigeon-holing, is a view from the inside, from modern Egypt herself. The one we are now granted may come as something of a shock to those who still see Alexandria through European eyes. Only the sense of failure remains . . . and perhaps not least in the announcement of the death of the old city of our communal literary dream.

Though Naguib Mahfouz—now in his sixties—is his country's most distinguished novelist, with a formidable body of work behind him, it would be idle to pretend his name is familiar in the West. I am very sure it is not because he is not worth reading; but nor is it quite a case of mere insularity on our side. Cairo may be only a few hours' flight from London or Paris, but the cultural journey is much more complex and hazardous. Of all the world's considerable contemporary literature, that in Arabic must be easily the least known, which is one very good reason why the Arab mind remains something of a mystery to Westerners—and the more mysterious as it becomes more urban and sophisticated. In one way it is a misfortune that so many great English writers, such as Doughty and T. E. Lawrence, have concentrated on the Bedouin side of the story; very few of us have any clear picture at all of how twentieth century educated Islam lives, feels and thinks.

One obvious hurdle is the Arabic language itself. With its sharp distinction between spoken and literary forms, it is far from easy to translate into a pragmatic, almost purely vernacular language like English—with all its own time-honoured notions of the 'right' style and method in fiction. The differences among the spoken dialects of Arabic are much greater than among those in English; yet an Algerian and an Iraqi writer, because of the literary *lingua franca,* have no difficulty in reading each other's work. This much wider potential readership helps explain why serious writers in Arabic have resisted all attempts to evolve a demotic written form; but in addition the 'vulgar' forms of Arabic are principally languages of transaction, lacking the finesse and richness a novelist requires of his basic clay; and there are in any case purely technical problems, due to the nature of cursive script, in notating the vernacular. That does not mean a modern Arab writer cannot employ colloquial usages in certain areas. A translator has to allow for that—and then jump to the other historical extreme with all the echoes of *al 'arabiyyat al fusha,* the classical form fundamentally derived—despite a greatly enriched vocabulary—from the language of the Koran and the eighth century founding fathers of Arabic philology, al-Khalil and Sibawaih. These resonances are obviously nearly impossible to render in another tongue without descending to fustian and the mock-biblical.

Then stylistically Arabic has an odd conjunction of paucity of rhetorical device but great subtlety of syntax and grammar. A translator into English is faced with the constant problem of staying true to his text on the one hand and making some accommodation to English stylistic conventions on the other. To take two small examples, both ellipsis and repetition of words are favourite devices in Arabic . . . and in general the very reverse in English. Perhaps the problem is best grasped by analogy with other arts; by recalling the difficulty of transcribing Arabic music, or of 'translating' the visual ellipsis and repetition characteristic of Islamic decorative technique into a European pictorial style.

This linguistic Iron Curtain has kept us miserably short of firsthand information about the very considerable changes that Egypt has undergone in this century; and that alone, quite apart from the novel's intrinsic merits, makes the publication of **Miramar** in English a most welcome thing. Though the book is set in Alexandria, it is essentially about Egypt itself and the normal conflicts—both public and personal—that have arisen during the successive revolutions of these last sixty years.

It is not for nothing that the better educated male characters in the story all revolve around the shrewd-naïve figure of the peasant-girl, Zohra. The fellaheen (from *falaha,* to till) are the heart of Egypt, and the heart of all its problems of social progress and national identity. Their age-old exploitation haunts every Egyptian conscience, just as their frequently mulish adherence to tradition is the despair of every Egyptian liberal—though it must be added that very little in the last five millennia has shown the fellaheen to be wrong in suspecting the motives of would-be world-changers descending on the Nile Valley. Their character was once described to me thus:

> Among the women the sole interest is sex, which is related to food and money; among the men the major interest is money, which is related to sex and food. Their lives are brutal; they live on an eternal frontier, where each year makes its own tradition, and strength is all that counts, so far beyond the reach of what we regard as civilization as to seem surreal, though we have all met their tough sweetness before, in the Russian novelists.

That is clearly not quite the case with the heroine of **Miramar.** It is precisely her determination to emancipate herself that the men about her admire . . . or resent; and why they are perhaps best defined by their varying reactions to her, since she stands for Egypt itself. To Western readers the miseries of her situation may seem exaggerated, a shade 'Victorian' and melodramatic. I can say only that the peasant nursemaid in the house where I stayed in Cairo in 1972 had had very closely similar experiences to those of Zohra. She too was trying to educate herself, against intense family opposition—and in spite of the fact that they appropriated all her wages for their own upkeep. Only a month before I met her she had been publicly beaten in the street by her brother for refusing an old man her father had ordered her to marry for flagrant reasons of self-profit. Wahiba knew just enough English to have the story of my novel *The French Lieutenant's Woman* explained to her; and I count it as one of the most touching compliments I have ever been paid that this unhappy and courageous girl exclaimed, when she had understood the main theme, 'Oh it is my story, it is me.'

The symbolic overtones of this kind of exploitation, so skilfully used by Naguib Mahfouz, do not need elaborating. But a brief reminder . . . must be given of the political and historical background to *Miramar.*

The driving spirit behind modern Egyptian nationalism was Sa'ad Zaghloul (1860-1927). His long opposition to both the Sultanate and the British Protectorate led eventually to his being deported to Malta in 1919, along with his leading supporters. The whole of Egypt rose in protest, and the exiles were finally allowed to send a *wafd,* or delegation, to the Versailles Peace Conference. Though they failed there, containing Wafdist agitation forced the Milner Commission to recommend termination of the Protectorate (though not a British 'presence', which lasted until 1954) in 1922. The first elections in 1924 gave the Wafd Party, which on this occasion had massive support from otherwise very disparate sections of society, a huge majority. Sa'ad Zaghloul became prime minister.

The history of the next three decades was one of continual political seesawing, with the much-needed internal social and economic reforms largely sacrificed to the land-owning interest, the enduring problem of Anglo-Egyptian relations, and party squabbles. The once solid Wafd Party itself split into factions. The 1952 arson and riots in Cairo helped bring about the *coup d'état* of July 23, carried out by a military junta headed (or more accurately, figureheaded) by General Mohammed Neguib. Both the monarchy and parliamentary government were abolished. Neguib gave way in 1954 to Colonel Nasser, who initiated the famous programme of social, educational and land reform—the Revolution, whose consequences are to be seen on every page of *Miramar.* The Revolution is now regarded in Egypt as an almost total failure; but then so was the French Revolution in France, at the same remove.

It must be remembered that politically the novel (published in 1967) is already dealing with past history. In the last decade Egypt has become far less of a socialist country than it appears in [*Miramar*] Effective power now resides with a new urban bourgeoisie—the 'New Class', of whom President Sadat himself is an example. Statistically the top twentieth of the nation, this class had been quick to exploit, in a thoroughly capitalist way, the inherent weaknesses of Nasserist socialism—the population explosion, the growth of consumer demand, the switch from a shortlived national to a much deeper-rooted personal aspiration. (pp. vii-x)

Appearing just before the disastrous 1967 war with Israel, the novel was a courageous anticipation of a subsequent 'loosening of tongues' or release of steam after the thirteen years of tight control of the press and the arts practised by the Nasser regime. Mahfouz had already, in 1959, incurred the wrath of El-Azhar University, the bastion of Moslem traditionalism, with a religious and social allegory *Awlad haratina,* . . . in which one of the characters is God, and Moses, Jesus and Mohammed also appear. Despite his very considerable prestige ('approaching pharaohdom' in the tart phrase of one Cairo critic), he was obliged to publish in Lebanon. In 1967 *Miramar,* with its far from kind view of the 'centres of power' (*scilicet* the Arab Socialist Union), reflected perfectly the feelings many Egyptian intellectuals had held in private towards the political excesses and mistakes of the past decade.

However, Mahfouz is most certainly not some Egyptian equivalent of an English Tory. His disillusionment was far less with specific policies and theories of the Egyptian left than with the moral failure (best represented in his novel by

the figure of Sarhan) of the Revolution in practice. What haunts his novel, indeed, is something deeper than disillusion: despair at the eternal and cruel dilemma of his country. Western concepts like 'social equality' and 'freedom of the individual' have little meaning in Egypt, where the legal system is exiguous and the judiciary have no power over the executive. In any case, the country allows exceptional social mobility. It has to, when almost everyone is engaged in a no-holds-barred struggle for personal economic survival. Mahfouz's view is therefore more akin to the stoical, pessimistic side of humanism, both European and Islamic. History and geography are the fundamental villains; or the nature of things. We are perhaps not too far removed from the spirit of the most famous of Cavafy's poems.

> Now what's going to happen to us without barbarians?
> Those people were a kind of solution.

Two classes suffered, the one economically, the other morally, during the attempt to found a Moslem socialism—the rich and the ambitious. The first, the hereditary landlords, are represented in the novel by Tolba Bey and Hosni Allam, the blind reaction of one generation turned into the feckless nihilism of the next; and the second class, the ambitious, by Sarhan and Mansour—the one sunk in an amoral hypocrisy, a blend of Tartuffe and Uriah Heep, the other retreated into a sort of narcissistic no-man's land. This latter pair may, I think, be seen as inevitable victims of a world locked in battle over the frontier between social good and personal survival.

An excellent . . . study of Egypt's economic problems [*The Egyptian Economy, 1952-1972* by Robert Mabro] makes it clear why the country feels this conflict with peculiar acuteness. Egypt is poor in natural resources and consequently short of white-collar jobs, a situation not helped by the great expansion, admirable in itself, in educational facilities since 1954. On top of that, population growth has been steadily accelerating (it now stands at some 2.5% *per annum*) and combines politically 'difficult' features of high density and youthful composition. Almost all major Egyptian institutions in both private and public sectors are painfully overstaffed, with lamentable effects on managerial efficiency and productivity. Qualifications mean very little; and influence, very nearly all, which explains the importance given to the marriage theme in *Miramar.* All that really happened in the Revolution was that wealth and influence were redistributed among a new elite; the detritus of the old was despatched to the Pension Miramar.

It is against this background that the predicament of the three young men in *Miramar* should be read, and their egocentricity, their lostness, their duplicity, understood. But, of course, such victims of greater circumstance, torn between self-interest and self-contempt, exist everywhere today, both East and West; and although some of the outward signs of tension—the outbursts of inappropriate laughter, the sudden plunges into sincere respect and emotion—may be specifically Egyptian, the basic type is surely universal. If we set aside moral judgements, perhaps the most attractive of the younger men is the playboy, Hosni. At least he is going down in style. His strange and memorable slogan, *ferekeeko,* is explained in the notes; and again, in one form or another, some very similar word or phrase has crept into almost every language in recent years. Again the keynote is despair—young blood defeated by the irremediable faults of a very old world.

One other fickle element, quite literally element, in **Miramar** requires a brief comment: that is the weather. The repeatedly evoked clouds, storms and rain certainly reflect a society in painful evolution, but one may guess that they are also emblematic of the unpredictability of history, of forces beyond human control. Rain may suggest hope and fertility in the West, but we are in a grimmer, more fatalistic world here. So is it with the remnants of the old cosmopolitan Alexandria; Egypt is beyond help from that direction, too, now. (pp. xi-xiii)

[Mahfouz's] work can be broadly divided into three periods. He began with three historical (the so-called 'pharaonic') novels, but then wrote a series on social themes, the masterpiece of which was the **Trilogy** (completed in 1957). This huge and partly autobiographical work revealed the struggles and convolutions of Egyptian society with a Balzacian breadth and degree of technical innovation unparalleled in any other writer of his time. Some critics have complained of over-richness and plot proliferation, but the achievement was considerable.

His second period, beginning in 1959, forsook social realism for metaphysical allegory, or man in society for man in time, and showed a much increased use of symbolism and the stream-of-consciousness technique, sometimes resulting in a language nearer to poetry than to prose. The third period, dating from **Miramar** in 1967, shows a synthesis of these two rather different previous stages in his growth. Mahfouz has also published seven collections of short stories—there have been four since 1969—whose themes and styles echo the development in his novels. In general the tendency on this side of his writing has been to abandon conventional realism.

Mahfouz is not without his critics in his own country, as I have already suggested. He may be something of a literary pharaoh; but at least he appears to be a refreshingly modest one. Philip Stewart records the following of a conversation with him:

> Mahfouz's reticence comes from a deep-seated humility which can be illustrated by his view of his own work. He is glad that his books are read and agrees that he is amongst Egypt's leading authors; but, when asked how he would rate his own books in relation to European literature, he said they were "probably, like the rest of modern Arabic literature, fourth or fifth rate". He suggested tentatively Shakespeare, James Joyce and Tolstoy as examples of first-rate writing, and Wells, Dickens, Thackeray, Shaw, Galsworthy, Huxley and D. H. Lawrence as second or third-rate European writers. Asked for examples of even lesser European writers, he said he had never read any and was not interested to do so, adding that he did not suppose many Europeans would be interested in modern Arabic literature as it has produced only such writing. He supposes that the reason for this is that literature is formed by its social context and by the attitudes of its readers, and that, since Egypt is still undergoing the industrial and social revolution which Europe passed through a hundred and fifty years ago, Arabic literature must use the technique and subject-matter of the nineteenth century. While there is nothing startling about this view, it is remarkable that it should be held by Egypt's best-selling novelist.

Clearly it is not easy for Westerners to place a writer so adamantly self-disparaging (even if one suspects Koranic precept plays a part in the judgement), and the greater part of whose work remains untranslated and therefore unknown. But I think few will disagree that we are with **Miramar** in the hands of a considerable novelist, and one who knows his country's complex problems, and complex soul, profoundly. Work of this quality also explains why Egypt was long seen by other Arabs as the literary leader of their world.

Like all novels worth their salt, **Miramar** allows us the rare privilege of entering a national psychology, in a way that a thousand journalistic articles or television documentaries could not achieve; and perhaps more importantly, beyond that, we can encounter in it a racial temperament that has been widely misunderstood in the West. The sometimes bizarre emotional mobility of the younger characters, their disorientation, their sensibility, their strikingly Romantic (shades of Chateaubriand) addiction to despair and *Weltschmerz* . . . these things may seem rather remote from our general picture of the Egyptian character, at any rate as formed by our image of their more recent political leaders. But this is an active, and unimpeachably witnessed, view of what we too often see as a passive—or impassive—culture.

If it cannot dispel every illusion or ignorance we hold about Egypt, it represents a very considerable first step. I sincerely hope that the reader will share the pleasure and interest I have got from this very revealing, and very human, novel. (pp. xiv-xv)

John Fowles, in an introduction to Miramar *by Naguib Mahfouz, edited by Maged el Kommos and John Rodenbeck, translated by Fatma Moussa-Mahmoud, revised edition, Heinemann, 1978, pp. vii-xv.*

An excerpt from *Miramar*

I liked the weather in Alexandria. It suited me. Not just the days of clear blue and golden sun; I also liked the occasional spells of storm, when the clouds thickened, making dark mountains in the sky, the face of morning glooming into dusk. The roads of the sky would be suddenly hushed into ominous silence. A gust of wind would circulate, like a warning cry or an orator clearing his throat; a branch would start dancing, a skirt would lift— and then it would pounce wildly, thundering as far as the horizon. The sea would rage high, foam breaking on the very curbs of the streets. Thunder would bellow its ecstasies out of an unknown world; lightning would coruscate, dazzling eyesight, electrifying the heart. The rain pouring down would hug earth and sky in a wet embrace, elements mixing their warring natures to grapple and heave as if a new world were about to be born.

Only after that would sweet peace fall on the city. The darkness would lift and Alexandria would show a face made serene by her ablutions— sparkling roads, spots of fresh dark green, a clean breeze, warm sunshine—in a tranquil awakening.

I watched the storm from behind the glass of my window panes until it finally cleared. This drama of the elements touched a sympathetic cord in my inmost heart. I had a premonition that forecast, in terms still incomprehensible to me, my personal destiny.

When the clock had moved round to strike the hour
I stopped my ears against any further sense of time.

But strange sounds invaded the quiet of the room.
An argument? A fight? (There's enough going on
in this *pension* to keep a whole continent amused.)
Something told me that as usual it concerned
Zohra. A door opened noisily and the voices were
now clear: Zohra and Sarhan. I leaped to my door.
Face to face, with Madame in the middle, they were
standing in the hall.

'That's none of your business,' Sarhan was shouting. 'I'll marry as I like. I'll marry Aleya.'

Zohra was fuming with anger, furious at the way
she'd been used, at the collapse of her hopes. So the
bastard had had what he'd been after and wanted
to run away. I went up to him, took him by the
hand and led him into my room. His pyjamas were
torn and his lips were bleeding.

'She's a wild beast!'

I tried to calm him down, but he wouldn't stop.

'Can you imagine? Her Highness wants to marry
me!' I tried to quiet him, but he still went on. 'The
crazy bitch!'

I'd had enough of his shouting. 'Why does she want
to marry you?'

'Ask her! Ask her!'

'I'm asking you.'

He looked at me, listening for the first time.

'Why? There must be some reason behind such a
request.' Then he asked guardedly, 'What are you
getting at?'

I shouted, 'I'm getting at the fact that you're a bastard.'

'What did you say?'

I spat in his face. 'There,' I shouted. 'I spit on you
and the like of you. Traitors!'

We crashed together, pounding each other until
Madame ran in to separate us. 'Please, please,' she
pleaded, 'I'm fed up with all this. Settle your quar-
rels outside, not in my house. Please.' She took him
out of the room.

ROGER ALLEN

The reception of Arabic literature in the West has . . . always been set within a complicated array of cultural attitudes. The intricate questions of "influence" and cultural exchange between the two remain the subject of much controversy. While research on the implications of the presence of
Arabic lyric poetry and picaresque narrative in ninth-century
al-Andalus (as Spain was termed) continues to tantalize some
scholars and antagonize others, the influence of Sir William
Jones's translations of Eastern poetry and of Galland's translation of *The Thousand and One Nights* on the history of European literature is scarcely open to debate. More recently,
and particularly following the colonization of many countries

in the Arab world by Europe in the nineteenth century, the
process has been predominantly unidirectional. The genres of
the novel and drama were to a large degree transplanted into
modern Arabic literature direct from the Western tradition,
rapidly superseding any attempts at reviving older genres. It
was in the realm of poetry, the most vigorous of the classical
genres, that the neoclassical tendency persisted longest, but
it too came under the influence of Western "schools" of poetry. (p. 201)

It is within the context of this confusing set of influences and
attitudes that modern Arabic literature and the West confront each other. That there should be misunderstanding and
"anxiety" on both sides is hardly surprising. It would also
seem unreasonable to expect that any exercise in transcultural evaluation such as that essayed by the Nobel Prize Committee should not be a reflection of the general situation.
With that in mind, I will address some of the issues raised
within the framework of the prize and its selection committee
under three headings: access to Arabic literature in the West;
the Nobel Prize criteria; and finally, a short segment concerning those Arab authors whose candidacy seems plausible
within the current terms of reference.

Many Western readers are exposed to a monument of Arabic
literature at a relatively early age in the form of *The Thousand and One Nights,* a work which has for a long time provided a rich source of entertainment for children. I myself
can vividly remember being taken to see pantomime versions
of both "Aladdin" and "Ali Baba" as a child. Ironically, this
huge collection of tales was never regarded as literature by
the Arabs themselves, and current scholarly interest is largely
the result of Western attention, initially to the sources and,
more recently, to narrative structure and techniques. The
popularity and exoticism of these tales within Western culture seems to have produced two major results. In the first
place, it fostered a fantastic view of Middle Eastern culture,
something which has been documented by a large number of
sources and which finds what is perhaps its extreme representation in such media as the cinema (from the Sinbad films of
Douglas Fairbanks Sr. to more recent examples such as *The
Jewel of the Nile*). Second, the almost automatic selection of
tales from this collection for anthologies of "world literature"
succeeded to a large degree in blocking any further interest
in searching for other examples of literature written in Arabic. The wealth of classical Arabic poetry remained essentially a closed book except to a few scholars, and even they were
not of any great assistance: the German scholar-poet Nöldeke
gave his opinion (in the introduction to a collection of Arabic
poetry) that the esthetic pleasure gained from a reading of the
poems hardly justified the pain involved. Thus, the general
Western readership, endeavoring to evaluate examples of literature produced in today's Arab world, may perhaps be considered to be at a double disadvantage: not only are they presented with works which seem to show a strong reliance on
Western models with which they are already familiar; but
also the history of the Arabic literary tradition, available to
them through their own general education and the more direct avenue of translation of the "classics," is incomplete and
distorted. There is thus an unsettling lack of context.

If we turn now to a consideration of the criteria under which
the Swedish Academy's Nobel Committee operates, some of
the issues which need to be raised in connection with the
above survey become clear. One of the members of the jury
itself, the Swedish physician-novelist Lars Gyllensten, readily

acknowledges a point which has already been made: "Literary works are more or less bound to the literary environment in which they are created, and the farther away from it one is, the harder it is to do them justice." I might observe that, on the basis of my comments above, the epithet *far* in this instance needs to be interpreted within the context of cultural attitudes rather than pure geographic distance. The same writer then goes on to make what is, for the purposes of Arabic literature, a statement of major importance.

> The task of awarding the Nobel Prize in Literature involves the obligation of trying to find methods for keeping oneself *au fait* with what is happening in literature all over the world and for appraising it, either on one's own or with the aid of specialists. Finally, the prize awarders must try to familiarize themselves with the works of most value, directly or via translations, and to make a careful assessment of their quality with all the viewpoints conceivably necessary for a reasonable evaluation.

Two issues emerge here: first, the question of evaluation; and second, that of translation. On the matter of translation, one has to state fairly bluntly that, as far as English is concerned, modern Arab *littérateurs* have not been particularly well served by translation (although the situation seems at least marginally better in French). (pp. 201-02)

The second issue raised by Gyllensten's statement involves evaluation, and most particularly the phrase "with the aid of specialists." If we assume the phrase "Arabic literature" to incorporate literary works written in the Arabic language throughout the Arabic-speaking world, then we have to acknowledge that the Nobel Committee is presented with an enormous and probably impossible task; for few indeed are the critics and scholars, whether Arab or non-Arab, whose knowledge of the field is sufficiently broad to encompass the entire region and the variety of genres involved and to present the committee with a list of nominees which will transcend political, religious, and cultural boundaries. Here we must refer to the documentation regarding the nomination procedure itself.

> The right to nominate candidates for the Prize in Literature is granted to members of the Swedish Academy; and of the French Academies which are similar to it in character and objectives; to members of the humanistic sections of other academies, as well as to members of the humanistic institutions and societies as enjoy the same rank as academies and to university professors of aesthetics, literature and history.

In view of the extremely small number of "specialists" in Arabic literature to whom the members of the Nobel Committee might have access and indeed of the relatively few contacts between Western scholars in the field and Arab *littérateurs* and literary critics, it is hardly surprising that this nominating procedure has not worked in favor of nominations from the field of Arabic literature.

Another feature of the criteria for nominations which has been much debated concerns the stipulation in Alfred Nobel's will that the prize honor someone whose writings have been "of an ideal tendency," a phrase which is interpreted by Gyllensten to mean "a striving for the good of mankind, for humaneness, common sense, progress and happiness . . . literary achievements with constructive aims." While this rubric has been liberally interpreted, several critics

have suggested dropping it altogether. Those who have any familiarity with the history of the Arab world during the course of this century, and most particularly in the decades since World War II, will perhaps realize that "common sense, progress and happiness" have not been attributes which have provided the driving force for the majority of Arab authors. Alienation, rebellion, confrontation, rejection, revolution, self-sacrifice, struggle—these have been far more characteristic of the literature of the last several decades.

All this said, it will perhaps not be a surprise if I eschew the opportunity to compare recent prizewinners with potential nominees from the Arab world. No Arab has as yet won the prize; whether one will (or can) under the current criteria seems open to doubt. That is not to say, of course, that there are not Arab *littérateurs* who are worthy of nomination. I would like to devote just a few lines to a consideration of my own short list: Najib Mahfuz (sometimes written as Naguib Mahfouz) of Egypt and Adunis (or Adonis) of Lebanon. Both manage to combine two considerations: in the first place, they are preeminently great writers; second, translations of many of their works are available in at least English and French. However, this availability in English translation itself presents us with a problem. In the case of Mahfuz, the novels which are now available in translation are, in the main, part of a series being published by the American University in Cairo Press. Because of the order in which the translations were completed, the novels have appeared in essentially random sequence; most especially, Mahfuz's major monument and contribution to modern literature as a whole, *Al-Thulathiyya* (*The Trilogy;* 1956-57), has yet to appear. The slightly earlier *Al-Bidaya wa-al-Nihaya* (1951; Eng. *The Beginning and the End*) is now available, along with *Zuqaq al-Midaqq* (1947; Eng. *Midaq Alley*), but the bulk of the published translations are from novels which were written in the 1960s; though all are of extreme interest within the perspective of the recent history of Egyptian society, they are of varying literary quality in both the original and in translation. (pp. 202-03)

Najib Mahfuz is acknowledged throughout the entire Arab world as the great pioneer in the mature Arabic novel, and he has achieved that distinction by dint of sheer hard work, tenacity, patience in adversity (both political and medical), and a disarming humility. He is recognized as the Arab world's leading writer of fiction because he has not only produced a whole stream of excellent novels over a period of four decades, but also turned the novel, as a means of societal comment and criticism, into an accessible and accomplished medium. His is a nomination which, the normalities of Arab politics aside, would be welcomed throughout the Arab world. (p. 203)

Roger Allen, "Arabic Literature and the Nobel Prize," in World Literature Today, *Vol. 62, No. 2, Spring, 1988, pp. 201-03.*

ROGER ALLEN

Like *The Thief and the Dogs, Autumn Quail, The Beggar,* and *Miramar* . . . , *The Search* belongs to the series of relatively short novels—by comparison at least with some of [Mahfouz's] earlier works of social realism—which were originally published during the troubled decade of the 1960s, a period when the initial euphoria with which the majority of Egyptians had greeted the revolution of 1952 had been replaced by a realization of the challenges involved in adapting to and living with the changes which new societal and political priorities had brought about.

Each one of these novels concentrates on the circumstances and fate of a single character, in the process making use of many of the psychological and symbolic devices available to the modern novelist. In *The Search* this technique is seen in a concentrated form. Sābir, the child of a union between a famous Alexandrian "madame" and a father who then disappeared, is given the task of finding his long-lost father. All his mother can provide by way of information shortly before her own death is the man's name: Sayyid Sayyid al-Rahīmī. Sābir's "search" takes him to Cairo and into the arms of Karīma, the licentious young wife of the owner of the boardinghouse where he stays during his fruitless quest. An advertisement which he places in the "missing persons" columns of a newspaper also brings him into contact with Ilhām, a charming and cultivated girl with whom he genuinely falls in love. However, his passion for Karīma leads him to fall into her trap and to kill her aged husband. Gradually but inexorably the net tightens; the police eventually catch up with him at the house of Karīma's mother, and he is condemned to death. All is lost, including the pure love of Ilhām.

The novel emerges, then, as a quest or rather a journey, and like many such tales, its use of symbols rises to a level redolent of allegory. In the process of interpretation a resort to the names used is almost inevitable, and it is in that context that I would suggest that the adopted English title over- or even misinterprets. The Arabic title of the work is *Al-Tarīq,* which means "The Way/Path/Road." Not only does any one of these alternatives suggest the idea of a *journey* better than the actual English title (which tends to give some emphasis to the detective aspect of the work), but each also underlines the clearly mystical undertones of the original title word. When we also realize that *Sābir* is an Arabic adjective meaning "patient, dogged," that *Ilhām* means "inspiration," that *Sayyid* implies "Lord, master, Sir," and that *Rahīmī* is a derivative of *Rahīm* or "merciful" (one of the epithets used with reference to God), then we are only beginning to explore the rich symbolic possibilities presented by Mahfouz's novel. As to whether this "road" is in quest of religious fundamentals, political identity, or family roots, the potential polyvalence of the symbols in the novel renders many interpretations possible, as Mahmūd al-Rabī'ī notes on the back cover. In this context I should register a certain disappointment that, unlike many other works in the Mahfouz series, *The Search* has no introduction to acquaint the Western reader with either the novelist or the work itself. Even in an age when one is encouraged to begin by reading the text itself, such aids to the adventurous transcultural reader are surely still almost essential. (pp. 328-29)

Roger Allen, in a review of "The Search," in World Literature Today, *Vol. 62, No. 2, Spring, 1988, pp. 328-29.*

ROGER ALLEN

Al-Bidaya wa-al-Nihaya, [translated] as *The Beginning and the End,* occupies an interesting place within the sequence of works which Naguib Mahfouz (or Najīb Mahfūz) published during the 1940s and early 1950s. These are the so-called "quarter" novels in which he draws heavily on his intimate acquaintance with the older quarters of the capital city to produce a set of portraits of urban Egyptians in their struggle with the inexorable laws of poverty and with the effects of political turmoil, both internal and external. *The Beginning and the End,* with its concentration on the life and fate of the various members of a single family and its attention to details of location and history, may be seen as something akin to a preparation for the much larger, massive project which was to become *The Trilogy (Al-thulathiyya,* completed in 1952 but not published until 1956 and 1957). Mahfouz tells us in fact that the research which led up to the composition of *The Trilogy* occupied his attention for some five years, making it seem more than likely that *The Beginning and the End* was being written while its author's characteristically meticulous preparations for the larger work were under way.

The novel is a typical piece of social realism. The setting in both time and place is authentically portrayed and serves as a backdrop for the story of a Cairene family whose members respond to the pressures and demands of life in their own unique, separate ways. As each member tries to cope with the consequences of the death of the family wage earner (the event with which the novel begins), the emotional makeup of each individual—the selfishness and depravity of Hasan, the humility and loyalty of Husayn, the driving social ambition of Hasanayn (who becomes an army officer), and the irrepressible sexual appetite of Nafisa—are all drawn together into a series of events which lead to a tragic conclusion.

It has to be admitted that, although the novel does not match *The Trilogy* in its close attention to local detail and in the integration of the lives and careers of the various family members into the intellectual and political currents of the time, it does manage to probe some of the complexities of Egyptian youth in the 1940s through carefully drawn portraits of Husayn . . ., Hasanayn . . . and, to a lesser extent, Nafisa. . . . [*The Beginning and the End* is] an important new addition to the corpus of novels by Mahfouz available in English, providing further evidence of his tremendous skill as a novelist and also of the remarkable way in which he has developed his craft so that topic and vehicle are well matched.

Roger Allen, in a review of "The Beginning and the End," in World Literature Today, *Vol. 62, No. 3, Summer, 1988, p. 504.*

SHEILA RULE

Naguib Mahfouz, an Egyptian novelist, playwright and screenwriter, won the Nobel Prize in Literature . . . , becoming the first Arabic writer to win literature's highest award.

The Swedish Academy of Letters said in its announcement that Mr. Mahfouz, "through works rich in nuance—now clear-sightedly realistic, now evocatively ambiguous—has formed an Arabian narrative art that applies to all mankind." Mr. Mahfouz's body of writing "speaks to us all," the academy said.

Mr. Mahfouz, who once described himself as "a fourth- or fifth-rate writer," is the author of 40 novels and collections of short stories, several plays and more than 30 screenplays. About a dozen of his books have been translated into English, although not all are still in print. (p. A1)

Lotti el-Kholi, a friend of the writer, said Mr. Mahfouz's books had at one time or another upset both religious and political leaders. Mr. Kholi said three of Mr. Mafouz's novels—

The Thief and the Dogs (1961), *Chatting on the Nile* (1966) and *Miramar* (1967)—had attacked the military coup that brought Gamal Abdel Nasser to power in Egypt in 1952. "The books spoke of the shortcomings of dictatorship at a time when no voice dared to speak out against Nasser's regime," Mr. Kholi said.

One novel, *Children of Gabalawi,* published in 1959 with the theme of man's everlasting search for spiritual values, was barred in Egypt because of its controversial treatment of religion. The book included characters based on Adam and Eve, Moses, Jesus and Mohammed, as well as a modern scientist. . . .

Mr. Mahfouz, who lives in Cairo, was born in 1911, the son of a civil servant. The academy noted that little was known about his personal life because he gives few interviews. But it quoted him as saying that he "learned to believe in science, socialism and tolerance" at an early age. He worked in the cultural section of the Egyptian civil service from 1934 until his retirement in 1971.

The new laureate made his name as a novelist with a broadly conceived trilogy, published in 1956 and 1957, which centers on a Cairene family. Parts bear names from Cairo's oldest streets and quarters. His depiction of the city has been compared by critics with Dickens's London, Dostoyevsky's St. Petersburg and Zola's Paris.

[*Chatting on the Nile*], published in 1966 but not translated into English, is considered a prime example of Mr. Mahfouz's novellas. *God's World,* published in 1973, is viewed as an example of his achievement as a short-story writer. "If the urge to write should ever leave me," Mr. Mahfouz said in a recent interview, "I want that day to be my last." (p. C32)

> *Sheila Rule, "Nobel Prize in Literature Awarded To an Arabic Writer for First Time," in* The New York Times, *October 14, 1988, pp. A1, C32.*

WILLIAM H. HONAN

Critics sometimes call Naguib Mahfouz the Balzac of Egypt because of the way his works express the pulsating energy of city life and because of their psychologically nuanced characters and broad social concern.

Mr. Mahfouz's work is largely unknown in the United States and Europe, although several of his shorter novels have been translated into English. . . . *The Cairo Trilogy,* which he wrote in the late 1950's and which is generally regarded as his most important work, was translated into Hebrew and published in a limited edition in Israel.

Each of the three books in *The Cairo Trilogy* is named for a street in the old section of the city and each chronicles three generations of a Cairene family before, during and after the 1952 military coup that overthrew King Farouk and eventually brought Gamal Abdel Nasser to power.

"It is a masterwork," said Sasson Somekh, a professor of Arab studies at Tel Aviv University and a visiting research fellow in the Department of Near East Studies at Princeton, "because it is not just a social portrayal but penetrates the psyche, the intellect and the soul of the Egyptian people."

"The trilogy is a monumental work," added Roger Allen, a professor of Arabic and Comparative Literature at the University of Pennsylvania who has translated three of Mr. Mahfouz's novels and a collection of short stories. "He spent five years researching it before he started to write. Then it filled three volumes, with over 1,500 pages. Nothing like it before had been written in Arabic."

"It is also a symbolic work," Mr. Somekh said in an interview [on Thursday, October 13, 1988], "because through the development of its characters you can see the development of modern Egypt. Kamal, the main character in the last two volumes, becomes estranged from the Islamic religion of his parents. He reads Darwin and Nietzsche, and his faith becomes shaky and eventually he rejects religion. There are also a great many women in the novel. At the beginning, they are not even allowed to look out a window for fear of being seen and are very much under the domination of men. The transition is seen when a modern woman enters the family through marriage. She is not home-ridden and—almost a feminist—she demands equal rights and seeks to help build a new society."

"Women play an important role in all of his work," Mr. Somekh said. "They are active, not passive characters, and they are frequently used to symbolize the changes in Egypt today. For example, in *Miramar,* a novel written in 1967, Mahfouz tells the story of a village girl who comes to work in a hotel in Alexandria. She is exploited by many men, but she resolves to fight back, and by the end she has resolved not to be a passive victim any longer but to take her fate in her own hands. She symbolizes the changes in Egyptian society."

Mr. Allen also cited one of Mr. Mahfouz's novels that got the author in trouble with the Nasser Government. In the novel *The Thief of Dogs* (1961), Mr. Mahfouz told the allegorical story of a man who searches for those who have wrongly caused him to be imprisoned, Mr. Allen said. When he finds his enemies, he shoots at them but misses and kills an innocent bystander. The novel ends with the police having cornered him in a cemetery. "This was taken to mean that things were not going well in the Egyptian revolution," Mr. Allen said.

Another book, *The Children of Gabalawi,* a novel he wrote in 1959, was immediately found offensive because it contains an allegorical representation of Mohammed as an all-too human, simple and womanizing man.

Because of his support for President Anwar el-Sadat's peace treaty with Israel, Mr. Mahfouz's works were banned in many Arab countries, although those restrictions have been lifted.

> *William H. Honan, "From 'Balzac of Egypt,' Energy and Nuance," in* The New York Times, *October 14, 1988, p. C32.*

JOHN RODENBECK

Like Pushkin, Mahfouz is the fountainhead of whatever native tradition he belongs to, not its product. Though his Arabic teachers quickly noted the schoolboy's stylistic precocity—he published his first serious article when he was only 17—the Cairo University undergraduate read philosophy, not literature, and was recognised as something of an expert on Bergson. By 1936, though, it was clear to him that he could only be a writer, a recognition that he characteristically transformed into a conscious choice, 'not unlike,' he has said, 'a marriage'. To support himself and his vocation—no writer in the Arab world can live by writing alone—he took a job at Cairo University. Three years later, in 1939, he published his first novel, then entered the Egyptian civil service, where he remained until he reached the compulsory retirement age of 60 in 1971.

'None of my books,' he has said, 'is without a political dimension.' The secular liberalism in which he was educated has been hard-pressed in Egypt throughout his lifetime and is now remembered mainly by intellectuals of Mahfouz's own generation. Mahfouz shares with Marxists the belief that politics shapes the inner life of individuals; and a sense of political frustration resides at the core of all his characters and situations. This sense is not always very obvious in his writing, however, and he was spared the unpleasant experiences that some of his generation went through for the sake of their political convictions. He had already achieved a considerable reputation, in any case, as early as 1944; and the publication of the last volume of the **Cairo Trilogy** in 1957 made him—as some of his more spiteful critics complained—almost a sacred cow. Only one of his later books has been banned in Egypt, a rather remarkable fact, given the bitter sense of alienation they invariably reflect.

Though political frustration and alienation are his characteristic themes, Mahfouz claims that as an artist he feels himself fulfilled. 'I have achieved,' he says, 'everything I set out to do'. And certainly, though he claims that in Egypt only the rich and uncaring can afford not to be sad, he has always seemed a happy man. Now he is rich, too. Jubilant crowds gathered in the street in front of his house on the night of the Nobel announcement and it will obviously take several months for all the furore to die down. After that he can resume his daily walks and the stints with his cronies at the coffee house in the centre of town, where the talk and the thinking that are necessary to his work can begin again.

John Rodenbeck, "Old Man of Cairo," in The Observer, *October 16, 1988, p. 43.*

R. Z. SHEPPARD

Recognized as the father of the modern Arab novel, Mahfouz is frequently compared with such 19th century social realists as Dickens and Balzac. In nearly 40 novels and a dozen story collections, he has dealt with the social and political upheavals Egypt has experienced during his lifetime. His main contribution, says Sasson Somekh, a visiting professor of Arabic literature at Princeton, is the "creation of a new Egyptian style" that combines the narrative manner of classic texts such as *The Thousand and One Nights* with contemporary subject matter.

The author has lavished an accumulation of vivid detail on re-creating his special part of the world. "He's immensely attached, in the most loving way, to Cairo," says Edward Said, a professor of English and comparative literature at Columbia University. Indeed, Mafouz seldom leaves the city, where he lives in a modest apartment with his wife and two daughters. Retired in 1971 from his post as an adviser to the Minister of Culture, he spends most of his time in cafés, drinking coffee and exchanging gossip. He is also known as one of the best joke tellers in Cairo, no small compliment in a land noted for its wit.

Mahfouz's untranslated trilogy **Al-Thulathiyya** (1957) is a

1,500-page family saga that spans 27 years and both World Wars and is read as a microcosm of Cairene society. He supported Gamal Abdel Nasser's 1952 coup d'état but gradually grew disillusioned with the colonel's policies. "It is true that the revolution liberated the Egyptian people and pushed them into modern life," says Mahfouz, "but it led to many wars that tired us out." Mahfouz found himself at the center of controversy in 1979 when he publicly backed Anwar Sadat's peace treaty with Israel. As a result, he was denounced by Islamic fundamentalists, and his works were banned in many Arab countries. . . .

The author . . . is in demand, but he is unlikely to stray far from his favorite cafés, not even to accept his Nobel and its $390,000 cash prize in December. He is pleading frail health, although Ahmed Bahaa-Eldin, columnist for the newspaper *al-Ahram* and a close friend, says that he chuckles at the excuse. The Arab world's best-known novelist is, Bahaa-Eldin notes, famous among his friends for his fear of flying.

R. Z. Sheppard, "A Dickens of the Cairo Cafés," in Time, *New York, Vol. 132, No. 17, October 24, 1988, p. 75.*

EDWARD SAID

Naguib Mahfouz's achievement as the greatest living Arab novelist and first Arab winner of the Nobel Prize has in small but significant measure now retrospectively vindicated his unmatched regional reputation, and belatedly given him recognition in the West. For of all the major literatures and languages, Arabic is by far the least known and the most grudgingly regarded by Europeans and Americans, a huge irony given that all Arabs regard the immense literary and cultural worth of their language as one of their principal contributions to the world. Arabic is of course the language of the Koran, and is therefore central to Islam, in which it has a hieratic, historical and everyday use that is almost without parallel in other world cultures. Because of that role, and because it has always been associated with resistance to the imperialist incursions that have characterised Arab history since the late 18th century, Arabic has also acquired a uniquely contested position in modern culture, defended and extolled by its native speakers and writers, belittled, attacked or ignored by foreigners for whom it has represented a last defended bastion of Arabism and Islam.

During the 130 years of French colonialism in Algeria, for example, Arabic was effectively proscribed as a quotidian language: to a lesser degree, the same was roughly true in Tunisia and Morocco, in which an uneasy bilingualism arose because the French language was politically imposed on the native Arabs. Elsewhere in the Arab *mashriq* Arabic became the focus of hopes for reform and renaissance. As Benedict Anderson has shown, the spread of literacy has spurred the rise of modern nationalism, in the midst of which narrative prose fiction played a crucial role in creating a national consciousness. By providing readers not only with a sense of their common past—for example, in the historical romances of the early 20th-century novelist and historian Jurji Zaydan—but also with a sense of an abiding communal continuity, Arabic novelists stood squarely wherever issues of destiny, society and direction were being debated or investigated.

We should not forget, however, that the novel as it is known in the West is a relatively new form in the rich Arabic literary tradition. And along with that we should keep in mind that the Arabic novel is an engaged form, involved through its readers and authors in the great social and historical upheavals of our century, sharing in its triumphs as well as its failures. Thus, to return to Mahfouz, his work from the late Thirties on compresses the history of the European novel into a relatively short span of time. He is not only a Hugo and a Dickens, but also a Galsworthy, a Mann, a Zola and a Jules Romain.

Surrounded therefore by politics, and to a very great degree caught up in the contests of the native as well as the international environment, the Arabic novel is truly an embattled form. Mahfouz's allegorical novel, **Awlad Haritna** (1959), takes on Islam, and was banned in Egypt when it was about to be published. His earlier **Cairo Trilogy** (1956-7) traversed the phases of Egyptian nationalism, culminating in the 1952 Revolution, and did so critically and yet intimately as a participant in the remaking of Egyptian society. **Miramar** (1967), his *Rashomon*-style novel about Alexandria, puts a sour face on Nasser's socialism, its abuses, anomalies and human cost. During the late Sixties, his short stories and novels addressed the aftermath of the 1967 war, sympathetically in the case of an emergent Palestinian resistance, critically in the case of the Egyptian military intervention in Yemen. Mahfouz was the most celebrated writer and cultural figure to greet the Egyptian-Israeli peace treaty in 1979, and although his books were banned in Arab countries for a time after that, his reputation as a great writer was too well established to be diminished for long. Even in Egypt the position he took was apparently unpopular, yet he has not only survived the temporary opprobrium but has emerged (if anything) more august and admired.

Mahfouz's career is of course distinguished in the Arab world not only because of the extraordinary length of his writing life, but because his work is so thoroughly Egyptian (and Cairene), based as it is on a territorial and imaginative vision of a society unique in the Middle East. The thing about Mahfouz is that he has always been able to depend on the vital integrity and even cultural compactness of Egypt. For all its tremendous age, the variety of its components and the influences on it—the merest listing of these is inhibitingly impressive: Pharonic, Arab, Muslim, Hellenistic, European, Christian, Judaic etc—the country has a stability and identity which have not disappeared in this century. Or, to put it differently, the Arabic novel has flourished especially well in 20th-century Egypt because throughout all the turbulence of the country's wars, revolutions and social upheavals, civil society was never eclipsed, its identity was never in doubt, was never completely absorbed into the state. Novelists like Mahfouz had it always there for them, and accordingly developed an abiding institutional connection with the society through their fiction.

Moreover the main historical and geographical features of the Cairo mapped by Mahfouz have been handed down to the generation of writers who came to maturity in the post-1952 period. Gamal al-Ghitani is like Mahfouz, in that several of his works—for example, his recently translated *Zayni Barakat*—are set in districts like Gamaliyia, which is where Mahfouz's realistic novel, **Midaq Alley,** is also set. Ghitani considers himself one of Mahfouz's heirs, and the overlap in setting and treatment confirms the generational relationship between the older and the younger man, made more explicit through the city of Cairo and Egyptian identity. For later generations of Egyptian writers Mahfouz offers the assurance of a point of departure.

Yet Mahfouz as, so to speak, patron and progenitor of subsequent Egyptian fiction is not by any means a provincial writer, nor simply a local influence. Here another discrepancy is worth noting. Because of its size and power, Egypt has always been a locus of Arab ideas and movements; in addition, Cairo has functioned as a distribution centre for print publishing, films, radio and television. Arabs in Morocco, on the one hand, Iraq, on the other, who may have very little in common, are likely to have had a lifetime of watching Egyptian films (or television serials) to connect them. Similarly, modern Arabic literature has spread out from Cairo since the beginning of the century; for years Mahfouz was a resident writer at *al-Ahram,* Egypt's leading daily paper. Mahfouz's novels, his characters and concerns, have been the privileged, if not always emulated, norm for most other Arab novelists, at a time when Arabic literature as a whole has remained marginal to Western readers for whom Fuentes, Garcia Marquez, Soyinka and Rushdie have acquired vital cultural authority.

What I have sketched so schematically is something of the background assumed when a contemporary, non-Egyptian writer of substantial gifts wishes to write fiction in Arabic. To speak of an 'anxiety of influence', so far as the precedence of Mahfouz, Egypt and Europe (which is where, in effect, the Arabic novel before Mahfouz came from) is concerned, is to speak of something socially and politically actual. Anxiety is at work not only in determining what was possible for a Mahfouz in a fundamentally settled and integrated society such as Egypt, but also in determining what, in a fractured, decentred and openly insurrectionary place, is maddeningly, frustratingly *not* possible. In some Arab countries you cannot leave your house and suppose that when and if you return it will be as you left it. You can no longer take for granted that such places as hospitals, schools and government buildings will function as they do elsewhere, or if they do for a while, that they will continue to do so next week. Nor can you be certain that birth, marriage and death—recorded, certified and registered in all societies—will in fact be noted or in any way commemorated. Rather, most aspects of life are negotiable, not just with money and social intercourse, but also with guns and rocket-propelled grenades.

The extreme cases in which such eventualities are daily occurrences are Palestine and Lebanon, the first of which simply stopped existing in 1948, and was reborn on 15 November 1988, the second a country that began its public self-destruction in April 1975, and has not stopped. In both polities there are and have been people whose national identity is threatened with extinction (the former) or with daily dissolution (the latter). In such societies the novel is both a risky and a highly problematic form. Typically its subjects are urgently political, and its concerns radically existential. Literature in stable societies (Egypt's, for instance) is only replicable by Palestinian and Lebanese writers by means of parody and exaggeration, since on a minute-by-minute basis social life for Lebanese and Palestinian writers is an enterprise with highly unpredictable results. And above all, form is an adventure, narrative both uncertain and meandering, character less a stable collection of traits than a linguistic device, as self-conscious as it is provisional and ironic.

Take first two Palestinian novelists, Ghassan Kanafani and Emile Habibi. . . .

Whereas Kanafani's occasional, but affecting melodramatic touches put him within reach of Mahfouz's novels in their disciplined and situated action, Habibi's world is Rabelais and even Joyce to the Egyptian's Balzac and Galsworthy. It is as if the Palestinian situation, now in its fifth decade without definitive resolution, produces a wildly erratic and freewheeling version of the picaresque novel, which, in its flaunting of its carelessness and spite, is in Arabic prose fiction about as far as one can get from Mahfouz's stateliness.

Lebanon, the other eccentric and resistant society, has been rendered most typically, not in novels or even stories, but in far more ephemeral forms—journalism, popular songs, cabaret, parody, essays. The Civil War, which officially began in April 1975, has been so powerful in its disintegrating effects that readers of Lebanese writing need an occasional reminder that this, after all, is (or was) an Arabic country, whose language and heritage have a great deal in common with those of writers like Mahfouz. Indeed, in Lebanon the novel exists largely as a form recording its own impossibility, shading off or breaking into autobiography (as in the remarkable proliferation of Lebanese women's writing), reportage, pastiche, or apparently authorless discourse.

Thus at the other limit from Mahfouz is the politically committed and, in his own highly mobile modes, brilliant figure of Elias Khoury, whose earliest important work of fiction, *The Little Mountain* (1977), now appears in English for the first time. Khoury is a mass of paradoxes, especially when compared with other Arab novelists of his generation. Like Ghitany, he is, and has been for at least twelve years, a practising journalist. Unlike Ghitany—whose gifts for invention and verbal bravura he shares—Khoury has been a political militant from his early days, having grown up as a Sixties schoolboy in the turbulent world of Lebanese and Palestinian street politics. . . .

Also unlike Ghitany, Khoury is a publishing-house editor, having worked for a leading Beirut publisher for a decade, during which he established an impressive list of Arabic translations of major Post-Modern Third World classics (Fuentes, Marquez, Asturias).

In addition, Khoury is a highly perceptive critic, associated with the avant-garde poet Adonis, and his Beirut quarterly *Mawaqif*. Between them, the members of the *Mawaqif* group were responsible during the Seventies for some of the most searching investigations of modernity and Modernism. It is out of this work, along with his engaged journalism—almost alone among Christian Lebanese writers, he espoused, from the heart of West Beirut and at great personal risk, the cause of resistance to the Israeli occupation of South Lebanon—that Khoury has forged (in the Joycean sense) a national and novel, unconventional, Post-Modern literary career.

This is in stark contrast to Mahfouz, whose Flaubertian dedication to letters has followed a more or less Modernist trajectory. (p. 10)

Khoury's work embodies the actuality of Lebanon's predicament, so unlike Egypt's majestic stability as delivered in Mahfouz's fiction. I suspect, however, that Khoury's is actually a more typical version of reality, at least as far as the present course of the Middle East is concerned. Novels have always been tied to national states, but in the Arab world the modern state has been derived from the experience of colonialism, imposed from above and handed down, rather than earned through the travails of independence. It is no indict-

ment of Mahfouz's enormous achievement to say that of the opportunities offered the Arab writer during the 20th century his has been conventional in the honourable sense: he took the novel from Europe and fashioned it according to Egypt's Muslim and Arab identity, quarrelling and arguing with the Egyptian state, but always its citizen. Khoury's achievement is at the other end of the scale. Orphaned by history, he is the minority Christian whose fate has become nomadic because it cannot accommodate itself to the exclusionism which the Christians share with other minorities in the region. The underlying aesthetic form of his experience is assimilation—since he remains an Arab, very much part of the culture—inflected by rejection, drift, errance, uncertainty. Khoury's writing represents the difficult days of search and experiment now expressed in the Arab East by the Palestinian *intifadah,* as new energies push through the repositories of habit and national life and burst into terrible civil disturbance. Khoury, along with Mahmoud Darwish, is an artist who gives voice to rooted exiles and the plight of the trapped refugees, to dissolving boundaries and changing identities, to radical demands and new languages. From this perspective Khoury's work bids Mahfouz an inevitable and yet profoundly respectful farewell. (p. 11)

Edward Said, "Goodbye to Mahfouz," in London Review of Books, *Vol. 10, No. 22, December 8, 1988, pp. 10-11.*

ANTON SHAMMAS

In the acceptance speech he sent to the Nobel Prize committee to substitute for his presence, Naguib Mahfouz asked the permission of his far-off audience to present himself as the son of two civilizations "that at a certain time in history have formed a happy marriage"—the civilization of the Pharaohs and that of Islam. Then he told an abrupt little story about each. After a victorious battle against Byzantium, he said, the Muslims gave back prisoners of war in return for a number of books of the ancient Greek heritage in philosophy, medicine, and mathematics. "This was a testimony of value for the human spirit in its demand for knowledge," Mahfouz said, "even though the demander was a believer in God and the demanded a fruit of pagan civilization."

Jorge Luis Borges, who might have envied this Egyptian descendant of Averroës the honor that had befallen him, would also have detected in this cryptic anecdote the whimsical tricks of repetition that history often plays in his own writings. Was Aristotle's *Poetics,* that wonderful "fruit of pagan civilization," among these ransomed books? That would have probably been the first question to come to Borges's mind. Averroës, known to the Arabs as Ibn Rushd, was the philosopher and physician who, in the twelfth century in Islamic Spain, saved the *Poetics* from oblivion in his commentary on Aristotle—a book that would "justify him in the eyes of mankind," as Borges says.

In the charming tale entitled "Averroës' Search," Borges describes the failure of Ibn Rushd to translate into Arabic the two words mentioned at the beginning of the *Poetics:* "comedy" and "tragedy." Circumscribed by Islam, where the word "theater" did not exist, Averroës could never have known the meaning of these two arcane words that pervaded the *Poetics.* Loitering over the riddle, he is distracted by "a kind of melody"—the noise of some children who are playing in the courtyard of his house in Cordoba. One is playing the part of the muezzin, the other is crouched motionlessly beneath him as if he is a minaret, and the third, abject in the dust, is the faithful worshiper. The "melody" of their noise does not connect with anything else in Averroës's mind. Later, at a friend's house, he listens to an Arab traveler who has been to China, where he attended a theatrical performance of sorts, without knowing what it was. The other guests do not seem to understand why such a large number of people would be needed in order to tell just one story—"a single speaker can relate anything, however complex it may be." Averroës goes back to his house and writes:

> Aristu [Aristotle for the Arabs] calls panegyrics by the name of tragedy, and satires and anathemas he calls comedies. The Koran abounds in remarkable tragedies and comedies.

"History," Borges adds, "records few acts more beautiful and more pathetic than this Arabic physician's consecration to the thoughts of a man from whom he was separated by fourteen centuries."

Averroës died on December 10, 1198. Naguib Mahfouz, 790 years later, celebrated his seventy-seventh birthday on the morning after the Nobel Prize ceremony of December 10, 1988. Mahfouz was born in 1911, the year that the first Arabic novel, *Zainab* (a name he also would use later), was being written in Paris, by another Egyptian writer, Muhammad Hussein Haikal. Forty years before, the first Arabic play had made its debut in Cairo.

Mahfouz published his own first novel in 1939, at the age of twenty-eight. Seven years later, when he started writing his masterpiece, **The Cairene Trilogy,** the Arabic novel was still far from having emerged as a mature form. In the twelfth century of Averroës's Spain, and simultaneously in Egypt, Arab culture was grappling with the texts of ancient Greece and was refining the art of storytelling of *The Arabian Nights.* Eight hundred years later, by the end of the nineteenth century, this literary tradition had already deteriorated and was not able to provide the "single speakers" with voices of their own. The storyteller of *The Arabian Nights,* in his Second Coming to the Orient, had to learn it all anew, from scratch, through Western eyes. And he came back singlehanded—that is, one could say, without his left arm. *The Arabian Nights* has a polyphonic style of storytelling in which, as in a piano piece, the left hand provides a framing accompaniment that fills out the harmonic texture, a basic story, and lets the right hand carry out the melody of a subsidiary tale and then return to the bass and leave it again with another melody.

The "ground" is not always a framing story; it is often the evoked cultural and historical setting that gives a sense of local validity to a novel. Such a ubiquitous yet elusive cultural presence underlies *Don Quixote,* the presence of the lofty, yet impractical and vanishing world of chivalry in Spain at the turn of the seventeenth century. This world is conveyed, as it were, by Cervantes's left hand—a world of popular, knightly romances that he is drawing on and mocking at the same time. What makes the works of Gabriel García Márquez so different from those of his contemporaries in Arabic literature is, among other things, his ability to squeeze into Macondo the qualities that give the place both a local validity through its mastery of the Colombian "ground" (imagined as that might be) and the fictional validity of the stories he tells. This polyphonic style became homophonic in Arabic litera-

ture. Márquez, whose literary origins go back to Andalusia, can be seen as a more privileged Mahfouz: his storyteller came to him intact, with two hands, via *Don Quixote.* Mahfouz—and all other modern Arabic writers for that matter—are the bereft ones: their storyteller came back to them with an amputated left hand. A perfect Western revenge.

Why couldn't Averroës understand the meaning of tragedy and comedy; why couldn't he relate to the "melody" played in his courtyard by those children? Douglas R. Hofstadter, who in *Gödel, Escher, Bach* discusses the concepts of "figure" and "ground" in various contexts (mathematics, art, and music), could have given us a different, less Borgesian, answer. Hofstadter would contend that the same could have happened to Averroës had he lived until 1720 and listened to one of Bach's unaccompanied sonatas for violin. In music, especially in Baroque music, there is often a distinction between figure and ground, between melody and accompaniment—the melody is usually in the forefront of our attention, while the accompaniment (the harmony) is subsidiary in some sense. In a Bach sonata for unaccompanied violin, the accompaniment, or the ground, is not even there; it exists only in the cultural mind of the listener, who implicitly "plays" it while listening to the melody. How could Averroës, then, listen to the melody of "comedy" and "tragedy" if he had not known what the ground for these two figures is all about?

In a gesture that recalls Hemingway's in 1954, Mahfouz, who has left Egypt only twice in his life, did not show up at the Nobel Prize ceremony last December in Stockholm. He sent his two daughters to collect the award. Ian Wooldridge, who introduced the recent TV program on the 1988 Nobel Prizes (a TV special, produced by Turner Broadcasting for cable television), told the viewers from his chair at the Thousand-And-One-Guest-Banquet that followed the ceremony: "It's a great shame that our literature laureate, Naguib Mahfouz, can't be here tonight, but in his honor we have some music from his country, a taste of Egypt." What followed were three seated Egyptians, in traditional dress, entertaining the white-tie audience with "some music." (p. 19)

The history of the Nobel Prize "records few acts more beautiful and more pathetic" than these folk Egyptian singers, trying to "represent" their country's cultural spirit, especially if their music is juxtaposed with an "Orientalist" piece for cello played earlier during the ceremony—"Arab Village," by Gunther Schuller. The flat, straightforward song of the Egyptian trio, performed during the banquet while everybody was being served the royal hors d'oeuvres, set the right note for the evening. What sounds like a nice piece of Egyptian folk music when played in a Cairene nightclub can only be kitsch when taken out of its setting and made to "represent" modern Arabic literature in a celebration that has been long overdue.

The same embarrassing reaction might occur when one reads Mahfouz's acceptance speech in its English translation. A virtuoso of multilayered, highly orchestrated storytelling, Mahfouz might have written another Faulknerian speech if he had wanted to ("I decline to accept the end of man"). Instead, he sent a rather trite speech, in which, at one point, he says to his listeners, Mahfouzian tongue in Egyptian cheek: "But what do you expect from one coming from the third world?" . . . [The speech] reads exactly like most of the novels and short stories that the copious Mahfouz has published after 1975 (at the rate of almost three books every two years). These are sketchy texts that sound as if they were written at random, desperately in need of a meticulous, compassionate editor.

The year 1975 marks also an important phase in Mahfouz's political involvement. In his weekly column in the daily *Al-Ahram,* he wrote that the Arabs must seek for peaceful ways to live with Israel. This was the first time that any Arab intellectual of his standing had broken the circle of consensus in Arab politics. Consequently, his books and the films whose scripts he had written or which were adapted from his works were banned in many Arab countries. And when in 1977 he was one of the few Egyptian intellectuals to adamantly support Sadat's initiative for peace with Israel, and later to endorse the Camp David accords, many Arab, and especially Palestinian, intellectuals felt that their god had failed. However, his reputation as the leading Arab writer hardly suffered.

It must have been *The Cairene Trilogy* particularly, published in 1956-1957, and the other works written before 1975, that the Swedish Academy had in mind when it said in its citation that Mahfouz won the award for "works rich in nuance, now clearsightedly realistic, now evocatively ambiguous." (pp. 19-20)

Mahfouz's fame as the leading Arab writer was acquired with the publication of his *Cairene Trilogy.* This work, fortunately, is not among the fourteen books by Mahfouz translated into English; it came out in a quite good Hebrew translation, though, some years ago. Even now, thirty years later, the *Trilogy* is seen by young Arab writers as a wall of China that stands in their way. Most of what has been translated from Mahfouz (except for the novel *Midaq Alley* perhaps) are works limited to the "figure": it takes a great deal of charity on the part of the reader to enjoy these superb, albeit unaccompanied, melodies in their English translation. In the *Trilogy,* however, the ground bass also is abundantly present. Three generations of a Cairene family come to life through 1,500 pages. . . . Kamal Abd al-Gawad, of the second generation, and the central character especially in the second part of the trilogy, is Mahfouz himself in disguise, who creates the history of modern Egypt through the lives of three generations of the Abd al-Gawad family.

The first volume opens in November 1917 and covers a period of seventeen months, culminating in the rebellion of 1919 against the British. The effects of the Great War, the fraying of the old system of political control, and demonstrations against it by the supporters of the Wafd party, are part of the background for the slow-moving story of life in the house of a well-to-do Cairene family. The father, Al-Sayyid, is a Janus figure, the master of the double standard: every night he returns in the small hours from wild evenings of wine and women, expecting his submissive, worried wife, Amina, to be waiting for him at the top of the stairs, holding the lantern to light his way.

Amina is the prisoner of such expectations and of the huge house itself. She is confined within a shadowy world of spirits and later by the burdens of motherhood. Yaseen, her stepchild, a clerk in a school, is a rougher and more vulgar version of his father, and at times his rival in pursuing women. Her son Fahmi is a law student who, after a frustrating love affair, turns to politics, and eventually, at the end of the first volume, is shot dead in a demonstration. The second son, Kamal, a vigorous, imaginative child in the first volume, turns in the next volumes into a passive intellectual. To a cer-

tain extent he is not only Mahfouz in disguise but also seems meant to suggest the collective situation of Arab intellectuals toward the end of 1944; having left, or having wanted to leave, the old house of tradition, he now faces the modern Western forces and values that are both tempting and seem to require him to take determined action to change his world. The sudden exposure to new kinds of choice makes him retreat, a victim of his own inaction. A graduate of a teacher's college, he teaches English and contributes hackneyed articles on modern philosophy to literary magazines. He can no longer reconcile his inherited faith with his acquired knowledge, and finds himself drifting to atheism, much to his father's chagrin.

Kamal is juxtaposed, especially in the third volume of the *Trilogy,* with the third generation of the family, each of whose members wants to try out his own answers to the predicaments of the fathers. Two of his nephews—his sister's sons—choose separate, contradictory political careers: one finds refuge in the Muslim Brotherhood, the other in Communism. Yaseen's son opportunistically uses his homosexuality to develop relationships with high political figures, and so helps his relatives get better jobs. Though published in 1956-1957, the *Trilogy* ends in 1944, eight years before the revolution led by Naguib and Nasser. (p. 20)

It so happened that on the same day that Mahfouz's Nobel Prize was announced in October, the Roman Catholic Church announced that the Shroud of Turin, venerated by millions of Christians over the centuries as the burial cloth of Jesus, turned out to be a fake. It occurred to me, without for a moment implying that Mahfouz is a fake, that most Arab novels written after the *Trilogy* bear, in some way or another, the negative image of Mahfouz—an image, one might say, that inexorably filters through the shrouds used to cover the face of the Cairene Christ as part of a rebellion against him. Only three Arab writers have achieved the nearly impossible task of escaping Mahfouz's imprint, to my mind: the Sudanese Tayeb Salih in his *Season of Migration to the North* (1966), which was written in London (English translation published in the UK in 1970); the Palestinian Emile Habiby in his *Pessoptimist* (1974; the English translation was published in the US in 1982); and the Syrian Salim Barakat in his *Fuqaha' al-Zalam* (*Sages of Darkness,* to be published by PROTA, the Project of the Translation from Arabic), which was written in Cyprus and published in 1985. (pp. 20-1)

I browsed through the translations of Mahfouz into English, and came across one of my favorite short stories, **"Al Khala' "** translated into English as **"The Wilderness"** (in *God's World,* translated by Akef Abadir and Roger Allen, 1973), from his collection *The Black Cat Tavern,* published in Arabic in 1968.

It is the story of a minor tragedy about betrayal and revenge, one of Borges's favorite themes. Sharshara, who was banished from his Cairene neighborhood to Alexandria on the night of his wedding, after he had been forced by one Lahluba to divorce his bride, Zainab, is coming back now after twenty years, driven by the vengeance that has given him a reason to live. Surrounded by his thugs, he is heading for a showdown with Lahluba, the gang leader who robbed him of his Zainab, as well as his dignity and freedom. . . .

[Why was the title **"Al-Khala' "** translated as] **"The Wilderness"?** The Arabic word, which occurs elsewhere in the story, according to my *Hans Wehr Arabic-English Dictionary,* means, among other things: emptiness; empty space, vacancy; open country; (and in certain phrases) under the open sky; outdoors, in the open air. In Mahfouz's story, and in my village in the Galilee, *khala'* means where the village houses end and the vacant lands begin, where human beings no longer have dominion. "The Wilderness" of the English translation adds, perhaps inadvertently (which is worse), a Christian touch to the original Arabic ("The voice of one crying in the wilderness. . . . / And immediately the Spirit driveth him into the wilderness. / And he was there in the wilderness forty days, tempted of Satan." Mark 1:3, 12-13). So the vengeful Sharshara, returning from his "wilderness," his exile in Alexandria, to the scene of his humiliation, may become for some readers an inverted Christ figure of sorts, a man with a blood mission to settle the score with Lahluba the Pharisee.

But Sharshara is just another one-track-minded, simple thug. He is driven by blind revenge, the desire to restore his abject manhood and dignity, to kill Lahluba and get back his bride. He resembles neither Christ nor the vengeful St. George having a showdown with the dragon Lahluba. To impose Christian overtones on this character is to mock his private agony; and to turn his plight into kitsch by dispossessing him of his own ground. . . .

[When Sharshara] reaches his enemy's neighborhood he finds out that Lahluba has been dead for some years, and that his bride, Zainab, is now just a vendor of eggs at the souk. He sends off his gang to wait for him, and goes to see her. But it is over now. "All that's over and gone," Zainab tells him.

To get her back without a fight would mean getting her back with a loss of pride. Besides, her children are grown up now, and what's the point? The word *khala'* and its derivatives become more recurrent, until the final episode, when Sharshara has to make up his mind which road to take in order to meet again with his henchmen. Wishing to be left alone with his grief, he heads for the road—one would be tempted to say less traveled by, taking the empty path that passes through the vacant, open country. He does this, in the final sentence of the story, without the exhausted help of Christ or Robert Frost, and without knowing that a woman called Zainab had also been the heroine of the first Arabic novel, written in Paris the year Mahfouz was born:

> So there was the road to the wilderness; and that's
> the one he took, into the wilderness. . . .

The ellipsis, otherwise the most popular literary device among modern Arabic writers, including Mahfouz, is here contributed by the translator. It expands the limits of the wilderness, just in case there is not enough room for Sharshara's grief.

Averroës could not know what comedy and tragedy meant; and eight hundred years later the translators of Mahfouz, who could, made a Christian farce out of Muslim Sharshara's little tragedy. Another subject for Borges. (p. 21)

Anton Shammas, "The Shroud of Mahfouz," in The New York Review of Books, *Vol. XXXVI, No. 1, February 2, 1989, pp. 19-21.*

William (Morris) Meredith
Partial Accounts: New and Selected Poems
Pulitzer Prize: Poetry

American poet, critic, dramatist, and editor.

Partial Accounts: New and Selected Poems (1987) contains pieces from Meredith's seven previous volumes of poetry along with eleven new poems, providing an overview of the poet's career. Respected for his mastery of poetic forms, including the villanelle, sestina, ballad, and sonnet, Meredith writes controlled, well-crafted poems that incorporate his observations on such topics as nature, death, love, art, daily life, and the chaotic aspects of modern existence. Meredith's unobtrusive rhyme schemes and metrical patterns evoke a sense of serenity, gentle humor, and quiet contemplation. Edward Hirsch commented: "In one sense, all of [Meredith's] work constitutes a desire to recognize and then move beyond catastrophe and despair—whether personal, social or historical. Book by book, he has evolved into a poet by sly wit and quiet skill, working out a thoughtful esthetic of orderliness."

Meredith's first collection, *Love Letter from an Impossible Land* (1944), was chosen by Archibald MacLeish to be published in the Yale Series of Younger Poets. In many of his early poems, Meredith employs imagery and themes drawn from his experiences as a naval aviator during World War II and the Korean conflict. While also reflecting this background, his next three volumes, *Ships and Other Figures* (1948), *The Open Sea and Other Poems* (1958), and *The Wreck of the Thresher and Other Poems* (1964), evince his thematic interest in nature, art, and family life. In *Earth Walk: New and Selected Poems* (1970), *Hazard, the Painter* (1975), and *The Cheer* (1980), Meredith adopted a more colloquial and conversational tone in his observations on nature and personal experience. Among the eleven recent poems in *Partial Accounts*, several recall events Meredith witnessed in his travels. The title poem of this collection concerns the poet's heart surgery and convalescence, and "Talking Back (To W.H. Auden)" and "The American Living-Room: A Tract" reflect his continuing attention to art and ordinary life. In a review of *Partial Accounts*, Linda Gregerson stated: "Touched as they are by goodness, rich in craft and thoughtfulness, the poems collected here should find themselves well-treated by their readers."

(See also *CLC*, Vols. 4, 13, 22; *Contemporary Authors*, Vols. 9-12, rev. ed.; *Contemporary Authors New Revision Series*, Vol. 6; and *Dictionary of Literary Biography*, Vol. 5.)

be because of the unfashionably classical cast of his verse. His poems are exercises in discipline and craft—objective in the choice and handling of theme, clear and simple in style and restrained in tone. He is a master in the use of meter, rhyme and stanzaic structure, whose works fulfill William Carlos Williams's definition of the poem as "a small machine made of words." While his pose as the reasonable man—modest citizen, loving father, son and husband, discreet householder—seems out of step with an era whose finest poets celebrated personality and "confessionalism," the perfectly achieved formal aspects of Meredith's poetry mark him as a writer whose bedrock values transcend time and place. (p. 92)

A review of "Partial Accounts: New and Selected Poems," in Publishers Weekly, *Vol. 231, No. 14, April 10, 1987, pp. 90, 92.*

PUBLISHERS WEEKLY

If Meredith has enjoyed less recognition than contemporaries such as Lowell or Berryman, both of whom are lovingly eulogized [in *Partial Accounts: New and Selected Poems*], it may

MATTHEW FLAMM

Lying awake one night, far from home, the poet William Meredith thinks about his hands. Over the course of his life, he decides, they have traced "two shapes" that honor them. One, not surprisingly (the poem in which this meditation appears is called **"Five Accounts of a Monogamous Man"**), is his wife's body; the other is "The curve a plane rides out / As it leaves or takes a deck. . . ." Meredith, who was a naval aviator during World War II, mentions lovemaking and flying in the same breath not just because they've both brought pleasure. They are also acts that bridge civilization and nature. Connecting one with the other has been the continuing concern of his seven books of poems, which are polished and direct, formal and natural, in equal measure. For Meredith, it's only a fool who neither recognizes our dependence on nature nor takes pride in the human ability to build (marriages, societies, airplanes) and survive. These twin obligations form the foundation of **Partial Accounts,** the selected poems of someone who has been thinking for years about his place in the world, with no illusions of importance. Part of the book's charm, aside from its humor, craft, and civility, is that it's as modest as it is wise.

Meredith takes a broad look at whatever he encounters, his immediate, emotional response complicated by his impulse to understand. Poetry with him is a constant dig for the underlying patterns, though at times he also recognizes he can go only so far. "Some will has been done past our understanding," he eulogizes in **"The Wreck of the Thresher,"** a poem characteristically blending personal and public themes. The submarine crushed underwater is a monstrous tragedy; the poet recognizes that nature in its vastness can never accommodate grief. . . .

A generally benign poet, Meredith is nevertheless preoccupied with what he calls "the real aspect of things." From early in his career he was writing about the decline of civilizations, and by his forties he was a poet of middle age. He's a genial ascetic, favoring plain truths and winter landscapes, where, as he says, "the mind is in charge of things. . . ." He takes particular delight in clearing the air for others, even to the point of writing a letter-poem to President Nixon requesting that he make himself worthier of the White House. Meredith believes that the poet, in deciphering his own emotions, plays a public role. His benevolence is, also, as much the result of temperament as of a sense that kindness is a basic human element, one of the ingredients that have helped us survive. As he searches out his own suffering and fears, it's only the natural next step to sympathize with others. In [**"Partial Accounts"**], Meredith, recovering from heart surgery (the "account" is "partial" because his body's decline isn't over), remembers turning away from a woman having her tooth pulled in an open market. "Soon I will need to imagine again / what she was feeling. . . ." Pain makes them companions, which comforts the poet as he sorts out another of nature's impossible contradictions. . . .

Eloquent though he is, Meredith is far from being an ambitious, wide-ranging, or innovative poet. In a sense, his limitations are built in: concerned with common experience, he writes in accepted forms (traditional and otherwise); eccentric or really novel points of view are out of his reach— happily so, some might add. For while Meredith may be, as he calls himself, "a minor poet," he always knows who he is. His poetic urges are based in his wish to tell the truth, and he doesn't make any more of the job than that.

> Gnawed by a vision of rightness
> that no one else seems to see,

> what can a man do
> but bear witness?

Matthew Flamm, "Plain Songs," in The Village Voice, *Vol. XXXII, No. 33, August 18, 1987, p. 52.*

THE VIRGINIA QUARTERLY REVIEW

What first strikes me about [**Partial Accounts: New and Selected Poems**] is the variety of subjects Meredith has covered during his career: other poets, of course, but also wartime service, travel, bridges, crows, artists, nature. The second is the interesting variations in tone and voice that Meredith manages to capture in his always dignified meters and near-traditional forms: Meredith's poems are not restricted to the solemn tones that his style lends itself to, but are equally impressive when they are witty as when they voice protest or serenity or reserved contemplation. The volume's title hints at the modesty with which Meredith must view his distinguished career, a trait that is reflected in the quiet and restrained quality that readers have often found in his poems. The title is a beautiful summation of any honest poet's life; I hope that in this poet's case it also points toward more fine work to come.

A review of "Partial Accounts: New and Selected Poems," in The Virginia Quarterly Review, *Vol. 63, No. 4, Autumn, 1987, p. 138.*

An excerpt from "Five Accounts of a Monogamous Man"

iv. his hands, on a trip to Wisconsin

It is night. I am a thousand miles from home.
My hands lie awake and are aware of themselves,
One on my noisy chest, the other, the right one,
A matter of several pounds, oppressing my forehead.
It is a week since it fluted the air goodbye.
I think of the path in space the thing has made since then,
Veering and halting; of the shapes hands make
Washing a car, or in the uses of music.

Two shapes it has traced honor this right hand:
The curve that a plane rides out
As it leaves or takes a deck on the scalloped sea;
Handily, handily then this two-pound creature
Felt the wired air, let the two monsters kiss,
The shapes that it graphed then fairer
Than the hair of the clouds that watched
Or the sea's own scalloped hair.

And he and his gauche fellow, moving symmetrically,
Have described one body so well
They could dress that shape in air
As they long to do now though they lie
Laced hunks of flesh on my belly—
Ahead of them some years of roving
Before the white landscape of age checks them,
Your body's disaster, sure to be traced there,
Even so slight a change in a dear shape
Halting them, baffled, lascivious suddenly,
Or folded cold, or feeling your hands folded cold.

LINDA GREGERSON

Prominent among the pleasures [*Partial Accounts*] affords are those engendered by the suppleness and discretion and durability of its formal enterprise. [Meredith] is a poet who asks us seriously to consider the rhymed quatrain as a unit of perceptual pacing, the villanelle as the ambivalent and ritual simulation of fate, the sestina as a scaffolding for directed rumination, the sonnet as an instrument for testing the prodigious or the ineffable against the longing-for-shapeliness we know as "argument."

Time and again the most eloquent formal negotiations in this book are those of the sonnet. Meredith makes of the form a resource and receptacle for an exquisite poetic tact, a means by which the lyrist, for all his partialness and partiality, may make himself accountable, may address even the most intemperate calamity or immoderate joy without trivialization and without false puffing up. The calamity that formed the matrix for Meredith's first two books of poems was the Second World War, during which he served as an aviator in the United States Navy. Even—or most especially—for a readership brought up on other wars and other prosodic habits, the war sonnets **"Carrier"** and **"Transport"** constitute a remarkable lesson in the chastening power of decorum: it is we who are finally chastened, so safely away from the front. The war poems give way to love poems in Meredith's third book, but the sonnet takes up its familiar thematic burdens with the freshness of a reinvented form. **"Sonnet on Rare Animals"** addresses with sublime irreverence the very poet who made the sonnet English: the poem is at once a refutation and a reprise of Wyatt's "They Flee from Me," a sweet-and-scathing conversion of the older poet's spite into a fable of kindness-in-love, the sweeter and more scathing because Meredith lets drop no overt allusion to the predecessor whom he so outstrips in charity.

Meredith has a habit of talking back to his elders. He writes in alliterative tercets that hearken back to the very beginnings of poetry in English. He pursues in rhymed trimeter an Audenesque intractability . . . even more telling than the revisionary homage to "Musée des Beaux Arts" in **"Hazard's Optimism"** or the modest refutation in **"Talking Back (to W. H. Auden)."** He writes anatomies of trope and allusion: in a poem named for the **"Simile,"** Meredith gives us the venerable long-tailed figure run amok at last. The epic simile, the simile of Homer, the simile of digression-on-the-battlefield is here all vehicle, ungrounded and unretrieved by tenor. Here even the syntax is lost, all gone to subordinate clauses. . . . (pp. 423-24)

Among the previously uncollected poems in this volume is a sestina about **"The Jain Bird Hospital in Delhi,"** which describes the monks and nuns who tend sick birds and believe in the interconnectedness of human and animal life. Their gentle ministrations and gentler philosophy come to seem responsible for the filiations wrought by the sestina's six endwords in all their redundancy and overlay. As in any good sestina liberally construed, the modulations of the repeating words are themselves portentous. In the shelter of the Jain bird hospital, "prey" becomes "pray," though it cannot shake off "victims" and "quarry." Belief in the transmigration of souls makes for a fluid anthropology: "human beings" in this poem are interchangeably "men," "women," "laymen," "poultrymen," and "poor forked skyclad things." "Violence" divides its allotted appearances with its counterpart *"ahimsa"* or "non-violence," coming out just ahead at four

to three, which is about the best ratio we could hope for. Only "illusion" is constant.

Perhaps the best-known poem reprinted here ["**The Illiterate**"] is one that shares a strategy with **"Simile,"** in that it is all, or nearly all, poetic vehicle:

> Touching your goodness, I am like the man
> Who turns a letter over in his hand
> And you might think this was because the hand
> Was unfamiliar but, truth is, the man
> Has never had a letter from anyone;
> And now he is both afraid of what it means
> And ashamed because he has no other means
> To find out what it says than to ask someone.
> His uncle could have left the farm to him,
> Or his parents died before he sent them word,
> Or the dark girl changed and want him for beloved.
>
> Afraid and letter-proud, he keeps it with him.
> What would you call his feelings for the words
> That keep him rich and orphaned and beloved?

Rime riche and identical rhyme throughout, the word always and only equal to itself: these selfsame iterations insist upon the material, talismanic, iconic status of words, the status words must occupy for one to whom they do not habitually yield. The illiterate is of course a type of the poet: because he cannot or will not make words disappear into easy instrumentality, words do not lose their aura in his hands but gather into themselves a remarkable conjunction of powers and possibilities. And thus the conjunctions in the last line of Meredith's poem, not "or" but "and": the man is rich in reverence, orphaned or unsponsored by the common, disregardful pragmatism of language use, and beloved as only the last believer shall be beloved.

Socrates tells us that the written word is an orphaned word, and Chaucer sends his litel book into the world to make its way cut off from a father. The most mature of writers—and Meredith has been among this company even in his youth—consign their partial accounts to the public domain with some ruefulness, knowing full well that the health of their children must now depend upon the comprehending collaboration of strangers. Touched as they are by goodness, rich in craft and thoughtfulness, the poems collected here should find themselves well-treated by their readers . . . , having already made themselves beloved. (pp. 424-26)

Linda Gregerson, in a review of "Partial Accounts: New and Selected Poems," in Poetry, *Vol. CLI, No. 5, February, 1988, pp. 423-26.*

EDWARD HIRSCH

In one of the recent poems in *Partial Accounts,* William Meredith remembers older writers telling him to "look hard at the world." They also advised him to avoid "elevated / generics like *misery / wretchedness*" and to find "a like spectrum of exact / terms for joy, some of them / archaic, but all useful." Mr. Meredith took the advice, and for the past 45 years he has looked generously and hard at our common human world. He doesn't slight the disastrous, the "umpteen kinds of trouble" he has seen—accountability weighs heavily in his poems—but his work reverberates with old-fashioned terms such as fairness, morale, cheerfulness, joy and happiness. He is a master of the shivery anecdote, our "accidental and malicious violences," but more characteristically remembers "our sweet, deliberate lives." Mr. Meredith is a poet of such good sense and sanity that someone ought to appoint him—as he once wryly appointed his character Hazard, the painter—to be "in charge of morale in a morbid time."

Partial Accounts, his new and selected poems—which brought Mr. Meredith the 1988 Pulitzer Prize for Poetry—is a rigorous accounting of a life's work. In addition to 11 new poems, it contains 93 from seven books written over more than 40 years. Like Richard Wilbur, the poet he most closely resembles, early in his writing life Mr. Meredith wrote a number of war poems that revealed his strong inclination toward and gift for formalism. His first two books—*Love Letter From an Impossible Land* (1944) and *Ships and Other Figures* (1948)—are sparely represented in this collection (five poems from each), though wartime experiences inform much of his work. Thereafter he emphasized the need for a civilizing intelligence and humane values. In one sense, all of his work constitutes a desire to recognize and then move beyond catastrophe and despair—whether personal, social or historical. Book by book, he has evolved into a poet by sly wit and quiet skill, working out a thoughtful esthetic of orderliness.

Mr. Meredith's mature work is represented by three books: *The Open Sea* (1958), *The Wreck of the Thresher* (1964) and *Earth Walk* (1970). In these books he developed his own version of the elegant plain style, seeking a language of calm exactitude and modest formal transparency. He also developed a wry, somewhat Frostian way of attacking a subject at an angle. He relies on this process—not pointing directly but trying to catch something out of the corner of the eye—whether he is considering a view of the Brooklyn Bridge or Chartres Cathedral, a disaster like the wreck of the submarine Thresher or the image of a Korean woman seated by a wall, a botanical trope or a plaster cast of his own head. In considering his chosen subjects he seeks to penetrate appearances, to find the hidden necessity and the true consequence, the underlying code of fairness that governs things. His typical conclusions are that "it is no good trying to be what you are not" and that there is always another flowering: "there's a dark question answered yes."

Hazard, the Painter (1975) and *The Cheer* (1980) are Mr. Meredith's understated masterpieces. In these books, as well as in the new poems here, he develops and extends his running argument about the question of despair. We live in a culture "in late imperial decline," and yet he resolutely insists on facing the worst by focusing on "a few things made by men, / a galaxy made well." He disagrees with Simone de Beauvoir in her "civilized Gallic gloom" and sides with Yeats by calling for "hand-clapping lessons for the soul." He playfully sends Hazard out to found a sect for all those "who persist in being at home in the world." In the poem titled **"In Loving Memory of the Late Author of Dream Songs,"** he carries on a loving quarrel with John Berryman for "dread recidivism" and movingly argues with friends who are "making off ahead of time, / on their own." His own inclination is to look for things to praise on the river, to posit that "we are all relicts, of some great joy, wearing black." He consistently praises the universe for being random and lovely.

Partial Accounts counters a sense of large cultural disaster with a firm commitment to spiritual health. William Meredith's work suggests that we can recognize the hardest truths about ourselves and still live in the world. Over the years he has become one of our most encouraging poets of happiness and well-being. (p. 21)

Edward Hirsch, "Bleak Visions, Hand-Clapping Lessons," in The New York Times Book Review, *July 31, 1988, pp. 20-1.*

Toni Morrison
Beloved
Pulitzer Prize: Fiction

(Born Chloe Anthony Wofford) American novelist, editor, essayist, critic, and dramatist.

Morrison's widely acclaimed fifth novel, *Beloved* (1987), is set in the United States during the mid-nineteenth century. Through flashbacks to past tragedies and deeply symbolic delineations of continued emotional and psychological suffering, the novel explores the hardships endured by a former slave woman and her family during the Reconstruction era. Eliciting a variety of thematic interpretations, *Beloved* has been variously categorized as a Gothic romance, a ghost story, a holocaust novel, and a feminist doctrine, and critics extol Morrison's use of historical detail, startling imagery, and African-American colloquialisms in portraying the emotional aftermath of slavery in America. Discussing the scope of her novel, Morrison stated: "When I say that *Beloved* is not about slavery, I mean that the *story* is not about slavery. . . . I deal with five years of terror in a pathological society, living in a bedlam where nothing makes sense. . . . But these people are living in that situation and they survive it—and they are trying desperately to be parents, husbands and a mother with children."

A central incident in *Beloved* with great repercussions occurs when a fugitive slave murders her infant daughter to spare her a life in bondage. Morrison, a senior editor at the publishing firm of Random House, based this scenario on an article she read in a nineteenth-century magazine while editing a historical book. Like Sethe, the protagonist of *Beloved,* Margaret Garner was a runaway slave who was tracked by her owner to Cincinnati, where she sought refuge with her freed mother-in-law. Faced with imminent capture, Garner attempted to murder her four children, succeeding in killing one. "I just imagined the life of a dead girl which was the girl that Margaret Garner killed," Morrison stated. "And I call her Beloved so that I can filter all these confrontations and questions that she has . . . and then to extend her life . . . her search, her quest." In *Beloved,* Sethe's daughter returns from the grave after twenty years, seeking revenge for her death.

Beloved is set in a small Ohio town following the American Civil War. Sethe and Denver, her surviving daughter, are secluded in a house haunted by the ghost of Sethe's dead child. Their lives are dramatically changed when Paul D., who was a slave on the Kentucky plantation from which Sethe escaped, comes to live with them and exorcises the spirit from their home. The ghost returns in the form of a young woman who takes her name, "Beloved," from the gravestone of Sethe's dead baby. Through the use of flashbacks, fragmented narration, and multiple points of view, Morrison details the events that led to Sethe's crime and her refusal to seek expiation from the black community. Beloved eventually gains control of the household and attempts to destroy Sethe, but

is overcome by the same women who had ostracized her mother years before.

Charles Larson echoed the opinion of most commentators when he called *Beloved* Morrison's "darkest and most probing novel." While some critics contend that her depictions of violence and humiliation are sensational and melodramatic, many regard Morrison's rendition of slavery and its psychological manifestations as among the most affecting in contemporary American literature. Although Sethe physically survives, she remains emotionally subjugated, and her desire to give and receive love becomes a destructive force. Morrison also addresses the difficulties faced by former slaves in keeping the horrors of their pasts submerged within the subconscious. Ann Snitow observed: "[Morrison] twists and tortures and fractures events until they are little slivers that cut. She moves the lurid material of melodrama into the minds of her people, where it gets sifted and sorted, lived and relived, until it acquires the enlarging outlines of myth and trauma, dream and obsession."

Beloved became a source of controversy several months after publication. When the novel failed to win the 1987 National Book Award or the National Book Critics Circle Award, forty-eight prominent black writers and critics signed a tribute to Morrison's career, and the document was published in the January 24, 1988 edition of the *New York Times Book Review.* The tribute suggested that despite the international acclaim Morrison has garnered for her works, she has yet to receive sufficient national recognition. The writers' statement prompted heated debate within the New York literary community, and some critics charged Morrison's supporters with racist manipulation. Jonathan Yardley commented: "The sincerity of those who signed this statement is not open to question. . . . But however much we may sympathize with their feelings and their desire for recognition, we must not let this blind us to the rather less attractive implications of their protest." When *Beloved* was awarded the 1988 Pulitzer Prize for fiction, Robert Christopher, the secretary of the Pulitzer board, stated: "[It] would be unfortunate if anyone diluted the value of Toni Morrison's achievement by suggesting that her prize rested on anything but merit."

Prior to *Beloved,* Morrison published four novels. In her first book, *The Bluest Eye* (1969), she relates the story of a little black girl whose desire to change her brown eyes to blue in order to be accepted by whites results in tragic consequences. *Sula* (1973) involves two young black women who must confront the tensions of both racism and sexism in a small town. *Song of Solomon* (1977), which won the National Book Critics Circle Award for fiction, details a young man's mythic journey towards self-discovery, and *Tar Baby* (1981) is a highly symbolic tale of contemporary race relations. In addition to her novels, Morrison has also written a drama, *Dreaming Emmett* (1986).

(See also *CLC,* Vols. 4, 10, 22; *Contemporary Authors,* Vols. 29-32, rev. ed.; *Dictionary of Literary Biography,* Vols. 6, 33; and *Dictionary of Literary Biography Yearbook: 1981.*)

MERVYN ROTHSTEIN

In Toni Morrison's new novel, *Beloved,* a runaway slave, her capture imminent, slashes her infant daughter's throat rather than see the child in chains. "It was absolutely the right thing to do," Ms. Morrison said, "but she had no right to do it. I think if I had seen what she had seen, and knew what was in store, and I felt that there was an afterlife—or even if I felt that there wasn't—I think I would have done the same thing. But it's also the thing you have no right to do."

Ms. Morrison, the author of *Tar Baby* and of *Song of Solomon,* which won the National Book Critics Circle Award for fiction in 1978, said that she got the idea for *Beloved*—which has just arrived in the stores—while she was working on another book.

"I was amazed by this story I came across about a woman called Margaret Garner who had escaped from Kentucky, I think, into Cincinnati with four children. . . . And she was a kind of cause célèbre among abolitionists in 1855 or '56 because she tried to kill the children when she was caught. She killed one of them, just as in the novel. I found an article in a magazine of the period, and there was this young woman in her 20's, being interviewed—oh, a lot of people interviewed

her, mostly preachers and journalists, and she was very calm, she was very serene. They kept remarking on the fact that she was not frothing at the mouth, she was not a madwoman, and she kept saying, 'No, they're not going to live like that. They will not live the way I have lived.'"

"Now I didn't do any more research at all about that story," Ms. Morrison said. "I did a lot of research about everything else in the book—Cincinnati, and abolitionists, and the underground railroad—but I refused to find out anything else about Margaret Garner. I really wanted to invent her life.

"I had a few important things," she said. "The sex of the children, how many there were, and the fact that she succeeded in cutting the throat of one and that she was about to bash another one's head up against the wall when someone stopped her. The rest was novel writing. I don't know if that story came because I was considering certain aspects of self-sabotage, the ways in which the best things we do so often carry seeds of one's own destruction.

"One of the nice things that women do," she said, "is nurture and love something other than themselves—they do that rather nicely. Instinctively, perhaps, but they are certainly taught to do it, socialized to do it, or genetically predisposed to do it—whatever it is, it's something that I think the majority of women feel strongly about. But mother love is also a killer." . . .

In some ways, Ms. Morrison said, *Beloved* is a ghost story—a young woman suddenly appears 18 years after the child's death, and the characters believe she is the slain infant returned to earth. "I wanted it to be our past," she said, "which is haunting, and her past, which is haunting—the way memory never really leaves you unless you have gone through it and confronted it head on. But I wanted that haunting not to be really a suggestion of being bedeviled by the past, but to have it be incarnate, to have it actually happen that a person enters your world who is in fact—you believe, at any rate—the dead returned, and you get a second chance, a chance to do it right. Of course, you do it wrong again."

The novel is not, she said, about slavery. "Slavery is very predictable," she said. "There it is, and there's some stuff about how it is, and then you get out of it or you don't. It can't be driven by slavery. It has to be the interior life of some people, a small group of people, and everything that they do is impacted on by the horror of slavery, but they are also people."

Mervyn Rothstein, "Toni Morrison, in Her New Novel, Defends Women," in The New York Times, *August 26, 1987, p. C17.*

ANN SNITOW

The subject of Toni Morrison's new novel, *Beloved,* is slavery, and the book staggers under the terror of its material—as so much holocaust writing does and must. Morrison's other novels teem with people, but in *Beloved* half the important characters are dead in the novel's present, 1873. Though they appear in memory, they have no future. Slavery, says one character, "ain't a battle; it's a rout"—with hardly any of what one could confidently call survivors. The mood is woe, depression, horror, a sense of unbearable loss. Still, those who remain must exorcise the deadly past from their hearts or die themselves; *Beloved* is the tale of such an exorcism.

In complex narrative loops, *Beloved* circles around and hints at the different fates of a group of slaves who once lived on a plantation in Kentucky, "Sweet Home"—of course neither "sweet" nor "home": an old woman called Baby Suggs, her son Halle, Paul A, Paul D, Paul F, Sixo, and the one young woman among them, Sethe. (Here as everywhere in the novel names raise baleful questions. Slaves have a tragically tenuous hold on names, and it is only in their final destinies that the three Pauls are allowed separate lives.)

Halle strikes a bargain with his master to sell his few free hours and use the money to buy his mother's freedom. Baby Suggs wonders why he bothers. What can a crippled old woman do with freedom? But when she stands on the northern side of the Ohio River and walks through the streets of Cincinnati, "she could not believe that Halle knew what she didn't; that Halle, who had never drawn one free breath, knew that there was nothing like it in this world."

Back at Sweet Home the decent master dies. . . . The new boss, "schoolteacher," beats his slaves and measures them with rulers, keeping pseudo-scholarly lists of their "human and animal characteristics." He demonstrates that any time the whites want to, they can knock you into the middle of next week, or back into the dependency of childhood. But Sethe now has three babies by the generous-spirited Halle, and the idea that she might never see them grow (like Baby Suggs, who saw seven of her children sold), or that they will grow only into schoolteacher's eternal children, strengthens her resolve to join the Sweet Home slaves who plan to run, taking a "train" north. Paul F is long gone—sold, who knows where. During the escape, Paul A gets caught and hanged. Sixo gets caught and burned alive. Paul D gets caught and sold in chains with a bit in his mouth. Sethe manages to get her three children on the train, but is caught herself, assaulted, beaten. Halle fails to appear at their rendezvous—lost, mysteriously lost, and never to be found again. Sethe runs anyway, because she can't forget that hungry baby who's gone on ahead, and because a new one is waiting to be born.

Half dead, and saved only by the help of a young white girl, trash almost as exiled as herself, Sethe gives birth to her baby girl, Denver, on the banks of the Ohio and manages to get them both across and truly home, to Baby Sugg's door.

Told flat, the plot of *Beloved* is the stuff of melodrama, recalling *Uncle Tom's Cabin*. But Morrison doesn't really *tell* these incidents. Bits and pieces of them leak out between the closed eyelids of her characters, or between their clenched fingers. She twists and tortures and fractures events until they are little slivers that cut. She moves the lurid material of melodrama into the minds of her people, where it gets sifted and sorted, lived and relived, until it acquires the enlarging outlines of myth and trauma, dream and obsession.

In fact, the intense past hardly manages to emerge at all. It is repressed, just as the facts of slavery are. Instead, in the foreground of the novel, Morrison places a few lonely minds in torment: Sethe, Denver, Paul D. All the drama of past desire and escape has fled to the margins of their consciousness, while Morrison's survivors are living in one extended moment of grief. Slowly, painfully, we learn that in order to keep schoolteacher from recapturing her children, Sethe tried to kill them all, succeeding with the third, a baby girl Morrison leaves nameless. This act lies at the center of the book: incontrovertible, enormous. Sethe explains that she killed the baby

because "if I hadn't killed her she would have died." Morrison makes us believe in this logic down to the ground.

By 1873, 18 years after Sethe's fatal act of resistance, slavery is technically over, whether or not the former slaves feel finished with it. Sethe's eldest two boys have run off, perhaps overfull of the mother love that almost killed them as children. Baby Suggs's house has become the entire world to Sethe and Denver—now 18. They live there ostracized, proud, and alone—except for the active ghost of the murdered two-year-old.

This awkward spirit shakes the furniture, puts tiny handprints on the cakes, shatters mirrors, while Sethe and Denver live stolidly in the chaos, emotionally frozen. Into this landscape of regret walks Paul D, one of the dear lost comrades from Sweet Home. He has been tramping for these 18 years, and now comes to rest on Sethe's front porch. Innocent of the secret of the baby's death, he seems to exorcise her ghost with nothing much more than his warm presence. As it turns out, she is not that easy to dismiss. The bulk of the novel dwells on the ghost's desperate return as a grown woman who calls herself "Beloved," the one word she has found on her tombstone.

At first, Beloved seems benign in her new avatar, and Sethe is ecstatic to have her daughter back. But gradually the strange visitor in elegant clothes and mysteriously unscuffed shoes turns into a fearsome figure, seducing Paul D in order to drag him into the wrong and send him packing, eating all the best food until Sethe and Denver begin to starve, ruling the demented household. The whole center of the novel is a projection of Sethe's longing; Beloved is a snare to catch her anguished, hungry mother's heart and keep her in the prison of guilt forever. She is also memory, the return of the dreadful past. In her, the breathtaking horror of the breakup of Sweet Home lives, sucking up all the air.

And so Toni Morrison has written a novel that's airless. How could this happen to a writer this skillful, working with material this full and important? In the reading, the novel's accomplishments seem driven to the periphery by Morrison's key decision to be literal about her metaphor, to make the dead baby a character whose flesh-and-bone existence takes up a great deal of narrative space. Even Sethe and Denver complain at times about the irritating presence of their ghost. And when she returns as a woman, she is a zombie, animated by abstract ideas. Later those who loved her "realized they couldn't remember or repeat a single thing she said, and began to believe that, other than what they themselves were thinking, she hadn't said anything at all."

Symbolic thinking is one thing, magical thinking quite another. Morrison blurs the distinction in *Beloved,* stripping the real magic of its potency and the symbols of their poetry. Her undigested insistence on the magical keeps bringing this often beautiful novel to earth. Morrison's last two strange and original books, *Song of Solomon* and *Tar Baby,* had some of this unconvincing reliance on the supernatural, too. By contrast, *The Bluest Eye,* her first, was bitten and dry-eyed; the little girl in that novel who thinks she can get blue eyes by magic sinks into the psychosis of wishing. Morrison's best magic was in *Sula,* the novel where it is most elusive, making no more solid a claim for the Unseen than the human spiritual power to move mountains.

This isn't to say ghosts can't or shouldn't be the stuff of fiction. The present generation of South American gothicists often convince us of the living power of ghosts in the worlds they describe. And the literature of disaster is haunted by the noisy dead, clamoring to be remembered as active presences, not cut off from a continuing story. Morrison is working in these traditions when she tries to animate the resistant weight of the slave experience by pouring on magic, lurid visions, fantasies of reconciliation. And why not? In one way, she comes by her magic honestly: It is the lore of the folk she loves, a visionary inheritance that makes her people superior to those—black or white—who don't have any talent for noticing the unseen. She wants to show how the slave past lives on, raising havoc, and to give Sethe, her treasured heroine, a chance to fight it out with the demon of grief. If Beloved is a drag on the narrative, a sour mixed with a great deal of dross, well so be it, Morrison seems to say. When strong, loving women would rather kill their babies than see them hauled back into slavery, the damage to every black who inherits that moment is a literal damage and no metaphor. The novel is meant to give grief body, to make it palpable.

But I suspect Morrison knows she's in some trouble here, since she harps so on the presence of Beloved, sometimes neglecting the mental life of her other characters. Their vitality is sacrificed to the inert ghost until the very end—a structure that makes thematic sense but leaves the novel hollow in the middle. Beloved is, of course, what's heavy in all their hearts, but can the ghost of a tragically murdered two-year-old bear this weight of meaning? No matter how she kicks and squalls and screams, the ghost is too light to symbolize the static fact of her own death. She is a distraction from those in the flesh, who must bear the pain of a dead child's absence. She is dead, which is the only arresting thing about her, and Morrison's prose goes dead when it concerns her.

If **Beloved** fails in its ambitions, it is still a novel by Toni Morrison, still therefore full of beautiful prose, dialogue as rhythmically satisfying as music, delicious characters with names like Grandma Baby and Stamp Paid, and scenes so clearly etched they're like hallucinations. Morrison is one of the great, serious writers we have. Who else tries to do what Dickens did: create wild, flamboyant, abstractly symbolic characters who are at the same time not grotesques but sweetly alive, full of deep feeling? Usually in contemporary fiction, the grotesque is mixed with irony or zaniness, not with passion and romance. Morrison rejects irony, a choice that immediately sets her apart. Like Alice Walker (there are several small, friendly allusions to *The Color Purple* in **Beloved**), she wants to tend the imagination, search for an expansion of the possible, nurture a spiritual richness in the black tradition even after 300 years in the white desert. (pp. 25-6)

Even at her best, Morrison's techniques are risky, and sometimes, in **Beloved,** she loses her gamble. Slavery resists her impulse towards the grand summation of romance. The novel revolves and searches, searches and revolves, never getting any closer to these people numbed by their overwhelming grief. *Why* could they not save those they loved? Nothing moves here; everything is static and in pieces. The fragmentary, the unresolvable are in order in a story about slavery. When Morrison embraces this hideous fact, the book is dire and powerful: Halle is never found. Baby Suggs never reassembles her scattered children, whose names and faces are now those of strangers. Sethe has collapsed inside, unable to bear what has happened to them all.

Still, for Morrison, it is romance and not the fractured narrative of modernism that is the vehicle of her greatest feeling

for her people. Though in their sorrow they resist her, she keeps inviting them to rise up on wings. She can't bear for them to be lost, finished, routed. The romantic in her longs to fuse what's broken, to give us something framed, at least one polychromatic image from above. When this works, it's glorious. And even when it doesn't, it's a magnificent intention. But there are moments in Morrison's recent novels when the brilliant, rich, and evocative image seems a stylistic tic, a shortcut to intensity. Romance can be a temptation. At the end of **Beloved** Morrison joins Sethe and Paul D together for good. Their happy union is a device laid on them from without by a solicitous author. It *should* be possible—why should pain breed only more pain?—but Morrison doesn't manage to maintain a necessary tension between what she knows and what she desires. She wishes too hard. Something in the novel goes slack. . . .

It is a brave and radical project to center a novel on a dead child ignored by history, cruelly forgotten along with so much else that happened to black people in slavery. A slave baby murdered by its own mother is "not a story to pass on." Even the slaves who know Sethe's reasons find them hard to accept. Paul D is so horrified when he finally learns about her crime that he leaves her for a time, telling her she has two legs not four. It is beastly to kill a baby, and yet Sethe asks, who was the beast? To keep Beloved out of the hands of an owner who would see her only as an animal, Sethe would rather be wild herself, do her own subduing of the human spirit, if killed it must be. As always in the last pages of her novels, Morrison gathers herself together and sings, here of those who didn't even leave their names, who died before they had the chance to become the sort of people about whom you could tell real stories.

There are the novelists who try something new in each book (Doris Lessing, say, or Joanna Russ, Kurt Vonnegut, Alice Walker) and the novelists who keep on worrying the same material (Saul Bellow, Robert Stone, Philip Roth, and Morrison herself). The first group has all the advantage of surprise, offering the thrill of new territory. Some of these trips come out better than others, but the overall effect is of travel. The second group has a different task, to find the same small door into the same necessary world, to wander the same maze trying to find the way home. Each novel in this group says to its readers, here I am again; do you feel what I always feel—as fully as I want you to? Well, not this time. But Morrison is great even in pieces, and worth waiting for, however long it takes.

This novel deserves to be read as much for what it cannot say as for what it can. It is a book of revelations about slavery, and its seriousness insures that it is just a matter of time before Morrison shakes that brilliant kaleidoscope of hers again and the story of pain, endurance, poetry, and power she is born to tell comes out right. (p. 26)

> *Ann Snitow, "Death Duties: Toni Morrison Looks Back in Sorrow," in VLS, No. 58, September, 1987, pp. 25-6.*

MARGARET ATWOOD

Beloved is Toni Morrison's fifth novel, and another triumph. Indeed, Ms. Morrison's versatility and technical and emotional range appear to know no bounds. If there were any doubts about her stature as a pre-eminent American novelist, of her own or any other generation, *Beloved* will put them to rest. In three words or less, it's a hair-raiser. (p. 1)

The supernatural element is treated, not in an *Amityville Horror,* watch-me-make-your-flesh-creep mode, but with magnificent practicality, like the ghost of Catherine Earnshaw in *Wuthering Heights.* All the main characters in the book believe in ghosts, so it's merely natural for this one to be there. As Baby Suggs says, "Not a house in the country ain't packed to its rafters with some dead Negro's grief. We lucky this ghost is a baby. My husband's spirit was to come back in here? or yours? Don't talk to me. You lucky." In fact, Sethe would rather have the ghost there than not there. It is, after all, her adored child, and any sign of it is better, for her, than nothing. (p. 49)

Through the different voices and memories of the book, including that of Sethe's mother, a survivor of the infamous slave-ship crossing, we experience American slavery as it was lived by those who were its objects of exchange, both at its best—which wasn't very good—and at its worst, which was as bad as can be imagined. Above all, it is seen as one of the most viciously antifamily institutions human beings have ever devised. The slaves are motherless, fatherless, deprived of their mates, their children, their kin. It is a world in which people suddenly vanish and are never seen again, not through accident or covert operation or terrorism, but as a matter of everyday legal policy.

Slavery is also presented to us as a paradigm of how most people behave when they are given absolute power over other people. The first effect, of course, is that they start believing in their own superiority and justifying their actions by it. The second effect is that they make a cult of the inferiority of those they subjugate. It's no coincidence that the first of the deadly sins, from which all the others were supposed to stem, is Pride, a sin of which Sethe is, incidentally, also accused.

In a novel that abounds in black bodies—headless, hanging from trees, frying to a crisp, locked in woodsheds for purposes of rape, or floating downstream drowned—it isn't surprising that the "whitepeople," especially the men, don't come off too well. Horrified black children see whites as men "without skin." Sethe thinks of them as having "mossy teeth" and is ready, if necessary, to bite off their faces, and worse, to avoid further mossy-toothed outrages. There are a few whites who behave with something approaching decency. There's Amy, the young runaway indentured servant who helps Sethe in childbirth during her flight to freedom, and incidentally reminds the reader that the 19th century, with its child labor, wage slavery and widespread and accepted domestic violence, wasn't tough only for blacks, but for all but the most privileged whites as well. There are also the abolitionists who help Baby Suggs find a house and a job after she is freed. But even the decency of these "good" whitepeople has a grudging side to it, and even they have trouble seeing the people they are helping as full-fledged people, though to show them as totally free of their xenophobia and sense of superiority might well have been anachronistic.

Toni Morrison is careful not to make all the whites awful and all the blacks wonderful. Sethe's black neighbors, for instance, have their own envy and scapegoating tendencies to answer for, and Paul D., though much kinder than, for instance, the woman-bashers of Alice Walker's novel *The Color Purple,* has his own limitations and flaws. But then, considering what he's been through, it's a wonder he isn't a mass murderer. If anything, he's a little too huggable, under the circumstances.

Back in the present tense, in chapter one, Paul D. and Sethe make an attempt to establish a "real" family, whereupon the baby ghost, feeling excluded, goes berserk, but is driven out by Paul D's stronger will. So it appears. But then, along comes a strange, beautiful, real flesh-and-blood young woman, about 20 years old, who can't seem to remember where she comes from, who talks like a young child, who has an odd, raspy voice and no lines on her hands, who takes an intense, devouring interest in Sethe, and who says her name is Beloved.

Students of the supernatural will admire the way this twist is handled. Ms. Morrison blends a knowledge of folklore—for instance, in many traditions, the dead cannot return from the grave unless called, and it's the passions of the living that keep them alive—with a highly original treatment. The reader is kept guessing; there's a lot more to Beloved than any one character can see, and she manages to be many things to several people. She is a catalyst for revelations as well as self-revelations; through her we come to know not only how, but why, the original child Beloved was killed. And through her also Sethe achieves, finally, her own form of self-exorcism, her own self-accepting peace.

Beloved is written in an antiminimalist prose that is by turns rich, graceful, eccentric, rough, lyrical, sinuous, colloquial and very much to the point. Here, for instance, is Sethe remembering Sweet Home:

> . . . suddenly there was Sweet Home rolling, rolling, rolling out before her eyes, and although there was not a leaf on that farm that did not want to make her scream, it rolled itself out before her in shameless beauty. It never looked as terrible as it was and it made her wonder if hell was a pretty place too. Fire and brimstone all right, but hidden in lacy groves. Boys hanging from the most beautiful sycamores in the world. It shamed her— remembering the wonderful soughing trees rather than the boys. Try as she might to make it otherwise, the sycamores beat out the children every time and she could not forgive her memory for that.

In this book, the other world exists and magic works, and the prose is up to it. If you can believe page one—and Ms. Morrison's verbal authority compels belief—you're hooked on the rest of the book.

The epigraph to *Beloved* is from the Bible, Romans 9:25: "I will call them my people, which were not my people; and her beloved, which was not beloved." Taken by itself, this might seem to favor doubt about, for instance, the extent to which Beloved was really loved, or the extent to which Sethe herself was rejected by her own community. But there is more to it than that. The passage is from a chapter in which the Apostle Paul ponders, Job-like, the ways of God toward humanity, in particular the evils and inequities visible everywhere on the earth. Paul goes on to talk about the fact that the Gentiles, hitherto despised and outcast, have now been redefined as acceptable. The passage proclaims, not rejection, but reconciliation and hope. It continues: "And it shall come to pass, that in the place where it was said unto them, Ye are not my people; there shall they be called the children of the living God."

Toni Morrison is too smart, and too much of a writer, not to have intended this context. Here, if anywhere, is her own comment on the goings-on in her novel, her final response to the measuring and dividing and excluding "schoolteachers" of this world. An epigraph to a book is like a key signature in music, and *Beloved* is written in major. (pp. 49-50)

Margaret Atwood, "Haunted by Their Nightmares," in The New York Times Book Review, *September 13, 1987, pp. 1, 49-50.*

CAROL RUMENS

[*Beloved*], a vividly unconventional family saga, is set in Ohio in the mid-1880s. By that time, slavery had been shattered by the Civil War, the Emancipation Proclamation and the succeeding constitutional amendments, though daily reality for the freed slaves continued to be a matter of perpetual struggle, not only with segregation and its attendant insults, but the curse of memory. Morrison's heroine, Sethe, is literally haunted. . . .

Interwoven with this rather obviously symbolic story, and enriching it, is an account of the past lives of Sethe, Paul D., the anarchic Sixo and the other slaves who worked on the farm called "Sweet Home". Morrison increases our sense of the outrage of slavery by describing the system, initially, not at its most brutal but at its most enlightened. . . . Sethe has the astonishing luck of six years' married life with the father of her children, "a blessing she was reckless enough to take for granted, lean on, as though Sweet Home really was one". The false idyll ends decisively when [her master] dies. . . .

Toni Morrison can describe physical horror in an oddly delicate way that nevertheless makes the reader's nerve-endings jump; her metaphorical devices have an intensifying rather than distancing effect. Sethe, pregnant, is beaten with a cowhide; she escapes and while on the run is tended by a white girl, Amy, who describes the wound on her back as follows:

> It's a tree, Lu. A chokecherry tree. See, here's the trunk—it's red and split wide open, full of sap, and this here's the parting for the branches. You got a mighty lot of branches. Leaves too, look like, and dern if these ain't blossoms. Tiny little cherry blossoms, just as white. Your back got a whole tree on it. In bloom.

The well-worn metaphor of the tree-cross is thus brilliantly revitalized.

The story of the reincarnated Beloved takes up too much space in the narrative for it to be a mere symbolic embellishment: at times, and especially in the book's final pages, it seems that the girl speaks for all "the disremembered and unaccounted for". Yet, despite Morrison's descriptive verve and exactness, the travails of a ghost cannot be made to resonate in quite the same way as those of a living woman or child. In a bold but unsuccessful ploy, Morrison lets Beloved take over the narrative at one point; while there is horror in her description of her escape from the grave—the hold of a slave-ship seems fleetingly invoked—the detail remains too vague for it to have as powerful an effect as those harrowingly physical journeys undertaken by the flesh-and-blood characters elsewhere in the novel.

As a family saga, *Beloved* is somewhat lopsided and suffers from gaps. The reader is left with several unanswered questions: what has happened to Sethe's sons, Howard and Bugler, who, though frequently invoked, do not appear on stage? What will happen to Denver, whose new life is beginning as the novel ends? In a *Guardian* interview recently, Morrison spoke of her reluctance to end the story, and it certainly seems that there is more to be told. It may well be that Beloved's story will turn out to be the painful, moving but relatively minor part of a much larger narrative.

Carol Rumens, "Shades of the Prison-House," in The Times Literary Supplement, *No. 4411, October 16-22, 1987, p. 1135.*

An excerpt from *Beloved*

Sethe and Denver decided to end the persecution by calling forth the ghost that tried them so. Perhaps a conversation, they thought, an exchange of views or something would help. So they held hands and said, "Come on. Come on. You may as well just come on."

The sideboard took a step forward but nothing else did.

"Grandma Baby must be stopping it," said Denver. She was ten and still mad at Baby Suggs for dying.

Sethe opened her eyes. "I doubt that," she said.

"Then why don't it come?"

"You forgetting how little it is," said her mother. "She wasn't even two years old when she died. Too little to understand. Too little to talk much even."

"Maybe she don't want to understand," said Denver.

"Maybe. But if she'd only come, I could make it clear to her." Sethe released her daughter's hand and together they pushed the sideboard back against the wall. Outside a driver whipped his horse into the gallop local people felt necessary when they passed 124.

"For a baby she throws a powerful spell," said Denver.

"No more powerful than the way I loved her," Sethe answered and there it was again. The welcoming cool of unchiseled headstones; the one she selected to lean against on tiptoe, her knees wide open as any grave. Pink as a fingernail it was, and sprinkled with glittering chips. Ten minutes, he said. You got ten minutes I'll do it for free.

Ten minutes for seven letters. With another ten could she have gotten "Dearly" too? She had not thought to ask him and it bothered her still that it might have been possible—that for twenty minutes, a half hour, say, she could have had the whole thing, every word she heard the preacher say at the funeral (and all there was to say, surely) engraved on her baby's headstone: Dearly Beloved. But what she got, settled for, was the one word that mattered. She thought it would be enough, rutting among the headstones with the engraver, his young son looking on, the anger in his face so old; the appetite in it quite new. That should certainly be enough. Enough to answer one more preacher, one more abolitionist and a town full of disgust.

Counting on the stillness of her own soul, she had forgotten the other one: the soul of her baby girl.

Who would have thought that a little old baby could harbor so much rage? Rutting among the stones under the eyes of the engraver's son was not enough. Not only did she have to live out her years in a house palsied by the baby's fury at having its throat cut, but those ten minutes she spent pressed up against dawn-colored stone studded with star chips, her knees wide open as the grave, were longer than life, more alive, more pulsating than the baby blood that soaked her fingers like oil.

"We could move," she suggested once to her mother-in-law.

"What'd be the point?" asked Baby Suggs. "Not a house in the country ain't packed to its rafters with some dead Negro's grief. We lucky this ghost is a baby. My husband's spirit was to come back in here? or yours? Don't talk to me. You lucky. You got three left. Three pulling at your skirts and just one raising hell from the other side. Be thankful, why don't you? I had eight. Every one of them gone away from me. Four taken, four chased, and all, I expect, worrying somebody's house into evil." Baby Suggs rubbed her eyebrows. "My first-born. All I can remember of her is how she loved the burned bottom of bread. Can you beat that? Eight children and that's all I remember."

ROSELLEN BROWN

Beloved is an extraordinary novel. It has certain flaws that attach to its design and occasionally to its long reach for eloquence, and an ending that lacks the power of the tragedy it is meant to resolve. But its originality, the pleasure it takes in a language at the same time loose and tight, colloquial and elevated, is stunning. The rhythm of black speech in Morrison's control is complex and versatile, and with it she makes third person narrative sound as intimate as a back porch conversation, and confidences in the first person sound like a dream. . . .

[Beloved's] ghost is presented more matter-of-factly even than the flying off of Solomon and his African children in the final pages of *Song of Solomon,* or the plague of robins that accompanies Sula's return to the Bottom in the novel that bears her name. Haints and spirits routinely walk the roads of the black South; to explain would be to acknowledge that outsiders are listening. This is not exactly "magic realism," as some have called it, citing Gabriel García Márquez and I.B. Singer; that label makes an invented genre out of what is merely an extension of ubiquitous beliefs—if you talk to the right people. Morrison has comfortably walked right into the center of what we call from a distance "folk culture," and used it without so much as a raised eyebrow. (A certain number of exchanges in the early part of the book, however, have a quality of unintended absurdity, as when Paul D defends the angry Denver against her mother's impatience with all the deadpan aplomb of Dr. Joyce Brothers: "Leave off, Sethe. It's hard for a young girl living in a haunted house. That can't be easy.")

But fortunately it's not too many pages before Morrison settles fully into her subject. Just when Paul D seems to have cleared the air in Sethe's house and the three of them have joined hands to begin anew, a mysterious young woman emerges from the water of a stream, dressed, as it were, in

"new skin." Certain about some details of her history and of the world, yet strangely innocent of others, she enters their lives as an ordinary, if rather peculiar, visitor. She will not leave until an amazing upheaval and assertion of force and decisiveness on everybody's part drives her back. By this time we have grown to know her better than we'd have imagined possible.

The young woman is named Beloved and her astonishing presence is unlike that of any character in American fiction. Beloved is a ghost and yet she has a body; she has fears, which we see from within. But she also has needs too voracious to be borne: she is there to settle a score, and to do that she will suck the love and concern out of the others as if it were air, no matter how she may suffocate them in the act. In a scene of extraordinary, eerie poignancy, Beloved loses a tooth and suddenly thinks she could just as easily drop an arm, a hand, a toe, could find herself in pieces. This is a ghost who dreams: she is in terror of exploding or being swallowed. We feel about this vulnerable girl, at least at first, as we might about a benign extraterrestrial: in this scene, she sits "holding a small white tooth in the palm of her smooth smooth hand."

Meanwhile, in the course of re-establishing their friendship memory by memory, peeling time away like layers of live flesh, Sethe and Paul D re-experience their years in slavery. . . . (p. 418)

Others have written about slavery, from within and from without; what Morrison manages is a continual heaving up of images and specific memories like stones, only to have them disappear and resurface again and yet again, each time more deeply embedded in the jagged landscape of relationships. She uses these memories like the recurrent tolling of the end-words in the lines of a sestina, moving them, advancing them in their positions until the entire novel is like that most inventive and obsessive of poetic forms, a tight verbal net from which no feeling can escape unscrutinized. There are recurring, clarifying allusions to stories whose bits and pieces have gone before; there are cryptic images that solidify into circumstances whose very familiarity begins to attest to their truth. Morrison rarely mentions anything once: we seem to travel back and forth across an increasingly familiar psychological field until the whole deadly scene coheres. (pp. 418-19)

There is a memorable moment in Morrison's first novel, *The Bluest Eye,* in which she patiently anatomizes the hatred a poor man feels for a couch, still new but not yet paid for, which represents for him the sickening taste of his powerlessness. It is impossible to read this scene and fail to understand why so many fine schemes for social renewal and economic optimism are overthrown at the start. Some of Morrison's instances of slavery's annihilation of self and family have the same devastating power. Caught in the wheels of such a system, in which the terms are always someone else's, can parents protect their children from a world of pain? And if they can't? Do children have the right to punish their parents for their actions? "What's fair ain't necessarily right," says one of the community of women always portrayed by Morrison as a wise (though not necessarily kind) chorus. (p. 419)

Beloved may be the most "visualizable" of all Morrison's novels. There are consoling images—Sethe at prayer embraced by a white dress that kneels down beside her, its arm tenderly around her waist—and horrific ones—Paul D driven around Sweet Home like an animal, with a bit in his mouth.

Many of these moments are nothing less than overwhelming. But in the end, while this is *Beloved*'s satisfying strength, it is also its weakness. There is a slightly uneven, stepping-stone quality to *Beloved* that seems, at times, to take us from one ugly or poignant or reconciling scene to another, like an opera with a succession of great arias. In some profound way I believe in the beauty and horror of the individual instances more than I do in the story, in which a mother who has felt herself guilty of an atrocity for nearly two decades finally makes peace with herself and begins a "new" life with a man who has never stopped being good, no matter what has happened to undo him. The will to console, to make a positive myth out of unspeakable circumstances, seems to have moved Morrison to wrench her characters nearly free of their ghosts when we might imagine them fighting to a more complex or ambivalent conclusion. "It was not a story to pass on. . . . So [the community] forgot her. Like an unpleasant dream during a troubling sleep."

Of course they put Beloved aside because "remembering seemed unwise," and there is irony here. But while the novel's brilliance lies in its capacity to summon up guilt and anger no one could assuage in nine lifetimes, the burden of its resolution is simply "Accept yourself." This is not to dismiss the possibilities of healing, only to say that its details are skimped a bit. Nor is it to say that people foully wronged cannot find a way to go on loving their lives—obviously they do. But the psychological groundwork is not given amply enough here to convince us that once the ghost of a great wrong is felled, ordinary life, not madness, can resume.

Morrison has always had an exhaustive and generous understanding of the complexity of community, and the voices of the town are unfailingly heard and accounted for; many of her novels have begun and ended with them. They make a noisy chorus. Her folks drag one another down, hold one another up, betray and soothe and protect with a wholly realistic unpredictability and lack of hypocrisy. And, proof of the necessity of those others, the actions of her characters always have ramifications in the community: everyone is affected. (pp. 419-20)

In *Beloved,* Morrison is at pains to show us how much strength her people have summoned to get them through, to keep on keeping on in spite of every effort to lay them low. But the energy and audacity of her book is in its pain and in the ambivalence of its characters toward their memories, their forgetting. As in many folk and fairy tales, the witch-spirit is the one that prevails in memory and nightmare. No one who has not been haunted, Sethe thinks, knows "the downright pleasure of enchantment, of not suspecting but *knowing* the things behind things." In addition to its other surprises, *Beloved* brings us into the mind of the haunter as well as the haunted. That is an invitation no other American writer has offered, let alone fulfilled with such bravery and grace. (pp. 420-21)

Rosellen Brown, "The Pleasure of Enchantment," in The Nation, *New York, Vol. 245, No. 12, October 17, 1987, pp. 418-21.*

STANLEY CROUCH

[*Beloved*] explains black behavior in terms of social conditioning, as if listing atrocities solves the mystery of human motive and behavior. It is designed to placate sentimental feminist ideology, and to make sure that the vision of black woman as the most scorned and rebuked of the victims doesn't weaken. Yet perhaps it is best understood by its italicized inscription: "*Sixty Million and more.*" Morrison recently told *Newsweek* that the reference was to all the captured Africans who died coming across the Atlantic. But sixty is ten times six, of course. That is very important to remember. For *Beloved,* above all else, is a blackface holocaust novel. It seems to have been written in order to enter American slavery into the big-time martyr ratings contest, a contest usually won by references to, and works about, the experience of Jews at the hands of Nazis. As a holocaust novel, it includes disfranchisement, brutal transport, sadistic guards, failed and successful escapes, murder, liberals among the oppressors, a big war, underground cells, separation of family members, losses of loved ones to the violence of the mad order, and characters who, like the Jew in *The Pawnbroker,* have been made emotionally catatonic by the past.

That Morrison chose to set the Afro-American experience in the framework of collective tragedy is fine, of course. But she lacks a true sense of the tragic. Such a sense is stark, but it is never simpleminded. For all the memory within this book, including recollections of the trip across the Atlantic and the slave trading in the Caribbean, no one ever recalls how the Africans were captured. That would have complicated matters. It would have demanded that the Africans who raided the villages of their enemies to sell them for guns, drink, and trinkets be included in the equation of injustice, something far too many Afro-Americans are loath to do—including Toni Morrison. In *Beloved* Morrison only asks that her readers tally up the sins committed against the darker people and feel sorry for them, not experience the horrors of slavery as they do.

[Morrison] has real talent, an ability to organize her novel in a musical structure, deftly using images as motifs; but she perpetually interrupts her narrative with maudlin ideological commercials. Though there are a number of isolated passages of first-class writing, and though secondary characters such as Stamp Paid and Lady Jones are superbly drawn, Morrison rarely gives the impression that her people exist for any purpose other than to deliver a message. *Beloved* fails to rise to tragedy because it shows no sense of the timeless and unpredictable manifestations of evil that preceded and followed American slavery, of the gruesome ditches in the human spirit that prefigure all injustice. Instead, the novel is done in the pulp style that has dominated so many renditions of Afro-American life since *Native Son.*

As in all protest pulp fiction, everything is locked into its own time, and is ever the result of external social forces. We learn little about the souls of human beings, we are only told what will happen if they are treated very badly. The world exists in a purple haze of overstatement, of false voices, of strained homilies; nothing very subtle is ever really tried. *Beloved* reads largely like a melodrama lashed to the structural conceits of the miniseries. (pp. 40-1)

The book's beginning clanks out its themes. Aunt Medea's two sons have been scared off: there is the theme of black women facing the harsh world alone. Later on in the novel, Morrison stages the obligatory moment of transcendent female solidarity, featuring a runaway indentured white girl, Amy Denver, who aids pregnant Sethe in her time of need. . . . Woman to woman, out in nature, freed of patriarchal domination and economic exploitation, they deliver baby Denver. (Amy is also good for homilies. While massaging Sethe's feet, she says, "Anything dead coming back to life hurts." When Sethe quotes the girl as she tells Amy's namesake the story of her birth, Morrison writes, "A truth for all times, thought Denver." As if that weren't gooey enough, there's the fade-out: "Sethe felt herself falling into a sleep she knew would be deep. On the lip of it, just before going under, she thought, 'That's pretty. Denver. Real pretty.' ")

Then there is the sexual exploitation theme, introduced in a flashback in the opening pages: for ten minutes of sex, the impoverished Sethe gets the name "Beloved" put on the gravestone. This theme in particular is given many variations. One of the most clumsy comes in an amateurishly conceived flashback designed to reveal that even Sethe's mother had a touch of Medea:

> Nighttime. Nan holding her with her good arm, waving the stump of the other in the air. "Telling you. I am telling you, small girl Sethe," and she did that. She told Sethe that her mother and Nan were together from the sea. Both were taken up many times by the crew. "She threw them all away but you. The one from the crew she threw away on the island. The others from more whites she also threw away. Without names, she threw them. You she gave the name of the black man. She put her arms around him. The others she did not put her arms around. Never. Never. Telling you. I am telling you, small girl Sethe."

It doesn't get much worse, or the diction any more counterfeit. . . .

Morrison is best at clear, simple description, and occasionally she can give an account of the casualties of war and slavery that is free of false lyricism or stylized stoicism:

> Sethe took a little spit from the tip of her tongue with her forefinger. Quickly, lightly she touched the stove. Then she trailed her fingers through the flour, parting, separating small hills and ridges of it, looking for mites. Finding none, she poured soda and salt into the crease of her folded hand and tossed both into the flour. Then she reached into a can and scooped half a handful of lard. Deftly she squeezed the flour through it, then with her left hand sprinkling water, she formed the dough."

(p. 42)

But Morrison almost always loses control. She can't resist the temptation of the trite or the sentimental. There is the usual scene in which the black woman is assaulted by white men while her man looks on; Halle, Sethe's husband, goes mad at the sight. Sixo, a slave who is captured trying to escape, is burned alive but doesn't scream: he sings "Seven-o" over and over, because his woman has escaped and is pregnant. But nothing is more contrived than the figure of Beloved herself, who is the reincarnated force of the malevolent ghost that was chased from the house. Beloved's revenge—she takes over the house, turns her mother into a servant manipulated by guilt, and becomes more and more vicious—unfolds as portentous melodrama. When Beloved finally threatens to kill Sethe, 30 black women come to the rescue. At the fence of the haunted property, one of them shouts, and we are given this: "Instantly the kneelers and the standers joined her. They stopped praying and took a step back to the beginning. In the beginning there were no words. In the beginning was the sound, and they all knew what that sound sounded like."

Too many such attempts at biblical grandeur, run through by Negro folk rhythms, stymie a book that might have been important. Had Morrison higher intentions when she appropriated the conventions of a holocaust tale, *Beloved* might stand next to, or outdistance, Ernest Gaines's *The Autobiography of Miss Jane Pittman* and Charles Johnson's *Oxherding Tale*, neither of which submits to the contrived, post-Baldwin vision of Afro-American experience. Clearly the subject is far from exhausted, the epic intricacies apparently unlimited. Yet to render slavery with aesthetic authority demands not only talent, but the courage to face the ambiguities of the human soul, which transcend race. Had Toni Morrison that kind of courage, had she the passion necessary to liberate her work from the failure of feeling that is sentimentality, there is much that she could achieve. But why should she try to achieve anything? The position of literary conjure woman has paid off quite well. At last year's PEN Congress she announced that she had never considered herself American, but with *Beloved* she proves that she is as American as P. T. Barnum. (pp. 42-3)

Stanley Crouch, "Aunt Medea," in The New Republic, *Vol. 197, No. 16, October 19, 1987, pp. 38-43.*

JUDITH THURMAN

If you think about what's most frightening in a horror picture, what "gets" you, it isn't the images but the soundtrack. The reason, perhaps, is that human beings listen in the womb, and hearing is one of the first sensory experiences—one of trust and connection but also, later, of helpless vigilance. The ear listens for the heartbeat, and the footstep, and to the dark—and, in literature, for a certain unwilled cry, to be heard in works as different as the poetry of George Herbert and the stories of Kafka.

That cry resounds from the void in which an infant endures its anguish, rage, yearning, hunger, and worthlessness. A writer can't make a story of that experience, perhaps because language is a relation, and can only describe other relations. But a writer can make a story of the drama of that helplessness as it's played out in and perpetrated upon the world; and it is through that drama that the best fiction engages us in history.

Beloved, Toni Morrison's fifth novel, is such a piece of fiction. . . .

Despite the richness and authority of its detail, *Beloved* is not primarily a historical novel, and Morrison does not, for the most part, attempt to argue the immorality of slavery on rational grounds, or to make a dramatic case for her heroine's act of violence—the way, for example, Styron does in *The Confessions of Nat Turner*. She treats the past as if it were one of those luminous old scenes painted on dark glass—the scene of a disaster, like the burning of Parliament or the eruption of Krakatoa—and she breaks the glass, and recomposes it in a disjointed and puzzling modern form. As the reader struggles with its fragments and mysteries, he keeps being startled by flashes of his own reflection in them. (p. 175)

The scene in which the nephews force Sethe to suckle them is one of the most shocking in a novel stocked with savagery of every description, physical and verbal, and the point that it doesn't register as such for Paul D. is an important one. It is not because he lacks compassion—Morrison has endowed him with an almost mystical (perhaps even sentimental) tender-heartedness. But, as a man, his experience of slavery has been different from Sethe's, as a woman, and if his hardships have been more extreme they have also been less damaging to his pride. That pride has been invested in his own attributes: his strength, his mobility, his manhood, his ability to survive. Hers has been invested in her maternity and confused with her maternity, and until that confusion is resolved, which is the real business of the narrative, she is still, and in every sense, a slave/mother.

Sethe and her two daughters, one flesh and one spirit, are trapped in a void at the core of **Beloved,** trapped by a powerfully cohesive but potentially annihilating force—maternal love—that scatters and repels the male characters of the novel. Paul D. puts it one way when he tells Sethe, "Your love is too thick." Baby Suggs, Sethe's mother-in-law, describes it another way when she says, "A man ain't nothing but a man. But a son? Well now, that's *somebody*." What she also means, in the context of her own life, is "A woman ain't nothing but a woman. But a mother? Now, that's somebody."

Morrison goes on to amplify Baby's remark, and it is worth pausing at this passage—less for its own sake than because it suggests the kind of impassioned polemic that **Beloved** does not, ultimately, succumb to:

> It made sense for a lot of reasons because in all of Baby's life, as well as Sethe's own, men and women were moved around like checkers. Anybody Baby Suggs knew, let alone loved, who hadn't run off or been hanged, got rented out, loaned out, bought up, brought back, stored up, mortgaged, won, stolen or seized. So Baby's eight children had six fathers. What she called the nastiness of life was the shock that she received upon learning that nobody stopped playing checkers just because the pieces included her children. Halle she was able to keep the longest . . . Given to her, no doubt, to make up for *hearing* that her two girls . . . were sold and gone and she had not been able to wave goodbye.

This language is powerful but manipulative. It is meant to awe us, and it does—like the tiny human figure that a model-builder sets next to a pyramid. The abolitionist novels and tracts of the last century aimed for the same effect. They exposed the plight of the Negro as a slave, a victim, a hero, but not as an individual, not as a familiar. When Morrison sets Baby Suggs and all her griefs on one tray of the scale, she defies us to supply our own moral counterweight—and, of course, we fail.

The occasional excesses of rhetoric (and sentimentality) in **Beloved** may reflect an anxiety in Morrison that she attributes to her heroine: a need to overfeed and overprotect her children. Paul D. tries to warn Sethe about it, but she won't listen to him, asserting, grandiosely, that she will "protect [Denver] . . . while I'm live and . . . when I ain't." One of the ironies of the novel is, in fact, that its author hovers possessively around her own symbols and intentions, and so determines too much for the reader—flouting her own central moral principle and challenge. For throughout **Beloved** Morrison asks us to judge all her characters, black and white, according to the risks they take for their own autonomy and in honoring that of others.

Sethe, Paul D., and Denver are a fascinating family "unit" in part because they are so familiar: a middle-aged single mother, sexually out of practice, whose desire takes her by surprise; a middle-aged man ready to compromise with his own need to wander; and a lonely, "secretive" adolescent who strains their relationship. Denver is jealous and resentful of Paul D., particularly when he exorcises the ghost of her baby sister—her only companion. She comforts herself with carbohydrates and by daydreaming about the glorious adventure of her own birth, in a rowboat—she was dragged from her mother's womb, prematurely, by a young white girl. But Sethe has, in fact, never fully "delivered" Denver. Fat, dreamy, submissive, fearful of the world, and fixated on her moment of entry into it, Denver will be forced to complete the labor by herself.

Morrison makes this family romance just novelistically comfortable and promising enough so that one resents the apparition of a supernatural intruder. . . . She calls herself by the name of the dead baby—Beloved—so there isn't much suspense, either about her identity or about her reasons for coming back. But we are meant to feel, I think, that we are actually losing something to Beloved—losing a story, a family, just as they were becoming real. The family's members are seduced away by her, and forced to serve her, which they do in a trance; and the role of memory in the novel is, at least in part, to inflict enough vivid and specific pain to dispel the trance.

What is most physically striking about Beloved is her smoothness: she's the dark glass of the picture. What is most poignant about her is that, like any vindictive child but unlike most ghosts or vampires, she ("it") is "not evil, just sad." And you finally have to decide between your sympathy with her greed for love and your desire to see the others go on living—the same private choice, I suppose, that one has to make between the claims of past grief and potential happiness.

A number of critics, and Morrison herself, have described **Beloved** as a "ghost story," but that is a somewhat deceptive and sensational tag for it. The characters themselves take the same, almost casual attitude toward ghosts that they do toward violent death. . . . As a monster, a helpless but omnipotent "it," Beloved belongs to the family that Caliban and the monster in Mary Shelley's *Frankenstein* belong to. Freud, in an essay called "The Uncanny," suggests a way to understand them. "The uncanny," he writes, "is that class of the terrifying which leads back to something long known to us, once very familiar." The German word for uncanny is *unheimlich* (and a haunted house is an *unheimliches Haus*). But he interprets the prefix *un* not as a grammatical negation of what is "homelike" but as a "token of repression" for what is most secretly terrifying and desirable about home—what drives one away from it and compels one to resurrect it.

The slaves in **Beloved** recall their bondage to Sweet Home with the same mixture of homesick love and dread. . . . They were treated humanely there—insidiously so. Their master, Mr. Garner, was a man who encouraged them to "correct" and "even defy him. To invent ways of doing things . . . to buy [the freedom of] a mother, choose a horse or a wife, handle guns, even learn reading." But the illusion of autonomy, Morrison suggests, is more debilitating, and perhaps, in the long run, crueler, than a full consciousness of servility. The slaves discover when they are turned over to a fiend named Schoolteacher, Garner's heir, that they have been their master's creatures all along. "How 'bout that?" Paul D. reflects. "Everything rested on Garner being alive. Now ain't that slavery or what is it?"

It's important to the story that one of Paul D.'s first acts when he moves in with Sethe is to break her house up—smash her furniture and dishes—as a way of ridding her of the ghost. But he can't destroy her perverse attachment to the memory, to the idea of Sweet Home—in part because the roles of master and slave, mother and child, have been fused within her. This fusion is, I think, what we experience as most sinister, claustrophobic, and uncanny in the novel, and it's what drives home the meaning of slavery.

"I am Beloved and she is mine," the ghost daughter repeats, like a vow or a litany. She means that Sethe is hers—Sethe's body, her attention, her time—and she steals Sethe's "milk" more ruthlessly than the nephews did. "Beloved she my daughter. She mine," Sethe says, claiming a privilege that the law did not accord even the slave owner: he could breed or whip or starve or separate his slaves but not murder them. And in surrendering to each other, in claiming to own each other, Sethe and Beloved create a monster like slavery itself: a greedy infant with a parent's "supernatural" power.

Morrison has a dreamer's gift for choosing names and images, and for the ironic doubling of meanings which gives a dream its cohesiveness and makes it an experience of pure retrospect but pure present. Like a dream, however, the novel is vulnerable to the kind of morning-after synopsis that one critic gave it when, quoting coolly from its steamier passages, he labelled it a "soap opera."

It's worth considering the nature of the objections that people who don't like the better kind of Romantic opera make to those who do. The staging is contrived; the plot heaves; the passions are grandiose and the myths obsolete; no one has a sense of humor. "*Espressivo* at any price," Nietzsche says, scowling, "and music in the service, the slavery, of poses—*that is the end.*"

Morrison is essentially an operatic writer, and as a "production" **Beloved** has some of the excesses that Nietzsche objected to in Wagner. She doesn't eschew melodrama in her big, violent scenes, or weeping in her domestic ones. There is a chorus of stock characters—good neighbors, evil prison guards, a messenger of the gods called Stamp Paid, and even a tree named Brother. The prose is rife with motifs and images that the narration sometimes orchestrates too solemnly. Paul D.'s last speech to Sethe is not the only one that trembles on the edge of pathos: "Me and you, we got more yesterday than anybody. We need some kind of tomorrow."

But if you read **Beloved** with a vigilant eye, you should also listen to it with a vigilant ear. There's something great in it: a play of human voices, consciously exalted, perversely stressed, yet holding true. It gets you. (pp. 176-80)

> Judith Thurman, "A House Divided," in The New Yorker, Vol. LXIII, No. 37, November 2, 1987, pp. 175-80.

MICHIKO KAKUTANI

[*The following essay was excerpted and printed in a slightly different version in Larry Heinemann's entry in CLC, Vol. 50.*]

What happened? That was the question every one was asking last week, following the news that *Paco's Story* by Larry Heinemann had won the 1987 National Book Award for fiction. Members of the literary community had widely regarded Toni Morrison's novel **Beloved** as a virtual shoo-in for the prize. . . .

How good is *Paco's Story*? Is it truly the finest work of fiction published in America this year? Such assessments, like the jury's decision itself, are obviously subjective, though it might be interesting to compare it, say, with **Beloved.** Both novels deal with a huge, tragic fact of American history—Vietnam in one case, slavery in the other. Both reveal, through discontinuous narratives, the terrible consequences of those events—the ways in which they prevent ordinary people from living ordinary lives. And both are ghost stories of sorts, invoking the spirits of the dead to lend their narratives a heightened, even surreal dimension: *Paco's Story* is narrated by the hero's comrades in arms, who died during a devastating firefight; and the heroine of **Beloved** is confronted by the spirit of her baby daughter, whom she murdered under shocking circumstances many years before.

In the case of *Paco's Story* . . . , these narrative strategies provide Mr. Heinemann with ways of getting around some of the problems posed by this anomalous war. . . . By using the collective voice of Paco's dead buddies as his narrator, he's able to avoid having to delineate a whole cast of supporting characters. . . . And by making that voice a hip, cynical one, he's able to avoid dealing with many of the troubling political and moral ambiguities raised by the war. . . .

Beloved, on the other hand, remains a work of mature imagination—a magisterial and deeply moving meditation not only on the cruelties of a single institution, but on family, history and love. Instead of reconfirming our feelings about tragedies in our nation's past (war is hell, slavery is evil), the novel shakes up all our preconceptions, makes us grapple with the moral chiaroscuro that shades each of the characters' decisions. It does not merely give us a portrait of one individual's loss of innocence, but also reveals the myriad ways in which families and strangers can hurt and redeem one another.

It's unfair perhaps to compare a young author's second novel with one written by a highly experienced novelist, but then that's exactly what the judges on the fiction panel for the National Book Award did. The decision, said Hilma Wolmzer, chairman of the panel, came after "an agonizing down-to-the-wire deliberation."

Which reminds one of the speech that E. L. Doctorow made last year when he accepted the fiction award for *World's Fair.*

"I have ambivalent feelings about awards, he said, "because literature is not a horse race."

> Michiko Kakutani, "Did 'Paco's Story' Deserve Its Award?" in The New York Times, November 16, 1987, p. C15.

CAROL IANNONE

There are many compelling elements in **Beloved,** including the delineation of the psychological and emotional effects of being owned—of having no sense of self, of fearing to trust or to love when anything can be taken away at any time. The portrayal of the very limited consciousness of the slaves and ex-slaves, and of their painful slow growth toward damaged self-awareness, is also effective, although sometimes the halt and hesitant nature of their thoughts makes the novel almost catatonic. A couple of scenes in which Sethe begins to feel the rush of life are well and affectingly done.

But the book grows massive and heavy with cumulative and oft-repeated miseries, with new miseries and new dimensions of miseries added in each telling and retelling long after the point has been made and the reader has grown numb. The graphic descriptions of physical humiliation begin to grow sensationalistic, and the gradual unfolding of secret horror has an unmistakably Gothic dimension which soon comes to seem merely lurid, designed to arouse and entertain.

Still, while far from successful as a work of art, *Beloved* is fascinating to view in the progression of Toni Morrison's work, in which a tropism for simplistic plight-and-protest has done fitful battle with the more capacious demands of a functioning moral imagination. True, Miss Morrison does not display a really sure hand in her treatment of the moral dimensions of Sethe's initial act of child murder, yet unlike the almost offhand treatment of similar crimes in *Sula*, she does make the deed stand as a matter of great gravity and consequence. Sethe is defiant about what she has done, but then later on she must undergo the trial of Beloved's return and vengeance, must suffer the torment involved in confronting and overcoming the past, before she can be free to live. Interesting too is the way in which *Beloved* can almost be read as Miss Morrison's own effort to exorcise the burden of history, to be free in her work of what Howe called the "defining and crippling" violence that has been the subject of the black protest novel.

But Miss Morrison seems simply unsure how much she wants the past, which means both the immediate past and the historical past, to weigh in the lives and behavior of her characters. She cannot quite accept the standard of freedom held out by Ralph Ellison but neither is she satisfied with the determinism of a Richard Wright. And while she is caught between these two stools, the fantastical, sensational elements in her work often come to look like artistic evasions. (p. 63)

Carol Iannone, "Toni Morrison's Career," in Commentary, *Vol. 84, No. 6, December, 1987, pp. 59-63.*

MARTHA BAYLES

Eighteen years later, as he gazed out over the literary landscape, the swaggering, mustachioed Colombian called Gabriel García Márquez was to recall the remote afternoon when he slipped his magnum opus, *One Hundred Years of Solitude,* into the wax-cold, ink-smudged hands of a *New York Times* literary critic, . . . causing jewel-bright hardback copies, followed by glittering rows of paperbacks, to replicate like dragon's teeth on the shelves of a thousand bookstores, touching off aesthetic conflagrations in a million gringo skulls that had never, in their wildest fantasies of world domination through advanced technology, dreamed of an enchantment like the new Latin American novel.

Hey, this magic realism stuff is easy, once you get the hang of it.

Toni Morrison would never put it that way. But you can bet

she was impressed back in 1970, when her tentative but promising first novel, *The Bluest Eye,* was blown to obscurity by the firestorm of García Márquez. Almost immediately, she got the hang of magic realism. By 1981 she told *The New Republic* that "in general I think the South American novelists have the best of it now," and *The New Republic* credited her fiction with "a Latin American enchantment."

From the obscurity of 1970, Morrison has emerged as a literary heavyweight, teaching at prestigious colleges, exerting considerable influence over the direction of black writing as a senior editor at Random House, winning the 1978 National Book Critics Circle Award for her third novel, *Song of Solomon,* starring on the lecture circuit, and topping the bestseller list with each of her last three books. The critics, including Mrs. Leonard's son, have raved themselves hoarse over Morrison's homegrown version of Macondo, García Márquez's enchanted village where modernity has not yet demythologized the world. To my knowledge, no one has asked whether Morrison was wise in constructing such a place out of the materials of the black American experience.

Now there is a clamor of praise for Morrison's latest novel, *Beloved.* With the notable exception of Stanley Crouch in *The New Republic* [see excerpt above], the reviewers have reached new heights, or depths, of abject adoration. Thomas R. Edwards in *The New York Review of Books* proclaims Morrison to be "not just an important contemporary novelist but a major figure of our national literature." Margaret Atwood in *The New York Times* declares that *Beloved* assures Morrison's "stature as a pre-eminent American novelist, of her own or any other generation" [see Atwood's excerpt above]. Helen Dudar in *The Wall Street Journal* calls the novel "an amazing book, the best of [Morrison's] career." And Colin Walters in *The Washington Times* states, with a few qualifications, that "*Beloved* seems as successful as it is bold and pointed aesthetically toward the future."

In my heretical opinion, *Beloved* is a dreadful novel, final proof of Morrison's decline from high promise into fashionable mediocrity. This heresy can be defended, I believe, first by comparing *Beloved* with *The Bluest Eye,* and then by examining each of Morrison's intervening novels, so that we may understand how her embrace of magic realism has led her to neglect her strengths and indulge her weaknesses.

The Bluest Eye is a portrait of madness in Pecola Breedlove, the daughter of an impoverished, disintegrating black family living in a small city in Ohio. The book has flaws, but at its best it is an extraordinary fusion of poetic language and moral clarity. The descriptions range from simple precision (a child lying in a cold winter bed "generated a silhouette of warmth") to striking metaphor ("the tears rushed down his cheeks, to make a bouquet under his chin"). The story is told partly from the viewpoint of one of Pecola's tormentors, a classmate from a prouder, more stable black family who joins in ostracizing the Breedloves as "trifling." But it also delves into the hard lives of Pecola's parents, especially her father Cholly, himself the product of poverty, racism, and family breakup in the South.

Cholly Breedlove is an important character in Morrison's oeuvre, because she never created another like him. Abandoned in a ditch by his unmarried mother, he is retrieved by an elderly aunt who tries to raise him right. But her death leaves him unwanted, about to be farmed out to begrudging kinfolk. Sexually humiliated by local whites, and fearful that his relatives will reject him, Cholly runs away in quixotic search of the father he never knew. The pages describing this background, and Cholly's eventual meeting with his father—an angry-drunk stranger who hurls curses at Cholly before he can even state his business—are among the most austere and beautiful Morrison has ever written. Equally impressive is the scene in which the mature Cholly staggers home one Saturday afternoon, himself an angry-drunk stranger, to rape his eleven-year-old daughter on the kitchen floor.

Despite his wickedness, Cholly Breedlove should not be confused with a figure like "Mr.---," the incestuous rapist in *The Color Purple* who caused such a stir last year when Alice Walker's novel was confected into a movie by Steven Spielberg. Unlike the domineering males in Walker's "womanist" fiction, Cholly is not an ideologically conceived villain. He is an extraordinary sinner whom we are asked to love to the exact degree that we are asked to hate his sin. This equilibrium between condemnation and mercy must have cost Morrison a great deal of pain. The hard theme of *The Bluest Eye* is the degradation, and self-degradation, of desperate people perpetuating their own misery while being abandoned by the rest of society, including better-off blacks. Needless to say, the theme is even timelier today than it was eighteen years ago.

In the mid-1970s, Morrison helped edit a Random House publication called *The Black Book,* a black-history "scrapbook" which included a clipping from an 1856 issue of *The American Baptist* describing an incident in Cincinnati of a runaway slave who attempted to kill her own children rather than surrender them to slave-catchers. After striking two of the children with a shovel, the woman cut the throat of a third, and was in the act of assaulting a fourth when she was apprehended. All but one child survived, as did the woman, to be sent back to a fate she obviously considered worse than death. Morrison has said that this incident haunted her for years before she decided, in 1981, to make it the core of her first historical novel, a tale of slavery and its aftermath now published as *Beloved.*

We can see how the clear-eyed moralist who created Cholly Breedlove might be challenged by this similar, if more extreme, tale. Like Cholly, the slave woman ties a Gordian knot of good and evil when, victimized herself, she victimizes her own children. That moralist lives on in *Beloved* to the extent that its theme is the guilt of the slave woman, Sethe. Unlike her historical predecessor, Sethe does not get sold back down the river. Instead she remains in Cincinnati until 1873, when the events of the novel begin to unfold. Despite being free, Sethe and her youngest daughter live a wretched life, cut off from their fellow blacks in a house haunted by the ghost of Beloved, the baby Sethe killed. Their wretchedness seems to be ending when Paul D, another ex-slave, shows up and attempts to become their protector by banishing the ghost. Things go well until the ghost reappears as a grown-up zombie, a mysterious woman the same age Beloved would be if she had lived. Welcomed by her lonely, uncomprehending mother and sister, the reincarnated spirit first gets rid of Paul D, then starts extracting endless favors from Sethe.

Thus summarized, the plot sounds intriguing. But *Beloved* commits the imitative fallacy by extracting endless favors from its readers. We don't have to feed, bathe, or amuse Beloved, the way Sethe does. But we do have to plow through

two hundred and seventy-five pages of self-indulgent prose, like this account of Paul D's effect on women:

> Not even trying, he had become the kind of man who could walk into a house and make the women cry. Because with him, in his presence, they could. There was something blessed in his manner. Women saw him and wanted to weep—to tell him that their chest hurt and their knees did too. Strong women and wise saw him and told him things they only told each other: that way past the Change of Life, desire in them had suddenly become enormous, greedy, more savage than when they were fifteen, and that it embarrassed them and made them sad; that secretly they longed to die—to be quit of it—that sleep was more precious to them than any waking day . . . .

As much as this passage needs an editor's pencil, it might be acceptable if Paul D were convincing as a human being. But he's not. He's just a list of saintly traits, combined with a longer list of sufferings. Obviously, the clipping from *The American Baptist* was only one item in a bulging file of antebellum atrocities which Morrison decided to cram, willy-nilly, into this novel. Paul D, Sethe, and a few other slaves belonging to the same owner in Kentucky experience a complete catalogue of barbaric practices and ungodly perversions from all over the South, as well as from Brazil and the West Indies. For instance, they are forced to wear a type of iron headgear used to keep starving slaves on vast Caribbean plantations from eating the sugarcane they were cutting. Neither Morrison nor her conscience-stricken admirers bother to ask whether such a device would really have existed on a small farm in tobacco-growing Kentucky.

The denouement occurs when, one fine day, after Sethe has been worn to a husk catering to Beloved, whose true identity she has long since guessed, she sees a white man about to enter her yard. It's only a kindly old abolitionist on his way to fetch Sethe's daughter for a part-time job, but Sethe flashes back two decades to the day when the slave-catchers came. She seizes an ice pick, and for a moment we think she is once again going to attack her own children. But wait—she doesn't lunge at her daughter or Beloved, she lunges at the white man! She doesn't hurt him, though, because this also happens to be the same fine day when the neighbors, who have shunned Sethe for the last twenty years, decide to show up in her front yard. They rush forward to stop her, and when the dust settles, everyone gapes in astonishment because, lo and behold, Beloved has vanished!

Michiko Kakutani, lamenting in *The New York Times* that the 1987 National Book Award was not given to *Beloved,* calls the novel "a magisterial and deeply moving meditation not only on the cruelties of a single institution, but on family, history and love" [see excerpt above]. By "meditation" Miss Kakutani presumably means a series of ideas connected by logic. But what is the logic of this ending? Sethe's neighbors prevent a second murder, but it is not their action that exorcises the guilt-monster Beloved. Rather it is Sethe's decision, at long last, to attack the correct enemy. And that enemy is not slavery, as represented by slave-catchers, but the white race in general, as represented by an old man who happens to have spent his life opposing slavery. Critics made defensive by this novel's encyclopedia of horrors are so eager to find comfort in this portrait of a sympathetic white, they ignore the logic which discounts the man's goodness in favor of the symbolic evil of his whiteness. True, *Beloved* posits the Gordian knot of a greatly wronged woman who commits a great wrong. But rather than unravel the knot, it simply sunders it with the blade of reverse racism.

Now, what does all this have to do with magic realism? In the 1981 *New Republic* interview cited above, Morrison boasted of having created a black Macondo: "I write what I have recently begun to call village literature, fiction that is really for the village, for the tribe." This boast, with its cavalier inclusion of all black people into one "village," and its equally cavalier exclusion of all white readers from consideration, reflects Morrison's state of mind as she began ***Beloved.*** From bravely probing the consciences of even the most pitiable black characters, she had shifted to predictably blaming white racist oppression for every crime committed by the inhabitants of an enchanted village called blackness. The trouble is, there's an inherent contradiction between the theme of white racist oppression and the idea of blackness as an enchanted state.

García Márquez knew what he was doing when he hid Macondo deep in the Colombian interior. In terms of real time and space, Macondo seems to have been founded sometime in the nineteenth century by the adventurous Buendía family, descendants of sixteenth-century Spanish colonials who led a band of pioneers away from their safe coastal city over several impassable, cloud-covered mountain chains to the edge of an impenetrable swamp. In other words, Macondo is removed, by sheer force of will, from all those aspects of the modern world that literary people most love to hate. It represents pure romanticism, a flight into the wilderness by people who have experienced and rejected civilization. By dwelling there long enough—say, one hundred years—the inhabitants recapture the primal sense of wonder which used to animate the universe before science came along and reduced everything to a pile of unfriendly rubble.

Whatever the similarities between Macondo and Aracataca, García Márquez's actual birthplace, it is safe to say that neither resembles Lorain, Ohio, where Toni Morrison was born. In ***The Bluest Eye,*** Morrison makes fond use of the rich Southern folklore of Lorain's black migrants. But in those pre-García Márquez days, her fondness for folklore was balanced with humor and skepticism. When Cholly's aunt falls ill, her elderly friends' advice is "prolific, if contradictory." And when Pecola finally loses her sanity, it's because she visits a "conjure man" who pretends to grant her self-hating wish to have bright blue eyes. It's worth noting, in contrast with Morrison's later romanticization of magic, that this conjure man is both a phony and a pedophile.

Sula, Morrison's second (1973) novel about black life in Lorain, contains much of the precise language and striking metaphor of ***The Bluest Eye.*** But it also strains for the sonority of *One Hundred Years of Solitude,* only to end up sounding as if it, too, had been translated from the Spanish by Gregory Rabassa. Worse, it clouds the moral clarity of the first novel by clothing the bleaker aspects of ghetto life in the vivid garments of fantasy. Nowhere does this shift show up more clearly than in the contrast between Cholly and the "trifling" male character in ***Sula,*** a graceful panther named Ajax, who dreams of airplanes and releases butterflies—a shamelessly Márquezian touch—in the bedroom of the high-spirited Sula. At one point, while Sula and Ajax are making love, his face is described as having many layers: black on the surface, then gold leaf, then alabaster, then fertile loam. It almost seems stodgy, after admiring such a spellbinding love affair, to ask whether a guy with a goldleaf face will stick around and support a family.

At this point we can detect a deeper drawback of magic realism for Morrison. By embracing the genre, Morrison also embraces its willful romanticism, which, in the context of black America, leads to the corollary that the most marginal people are the least corrupted by the false values of the dominant white society. From now on, she assumes that the lower a character's social status, the higher his mythic consciousness. The shame, anguish, and pity of characters like Pecola and Cholly can be supplanted by the descendants of Sula and Ajax, proud owners of luxury condos in Macondo.

Morrison's next novel, the prizewinning ***Song of Solomon,*** works even harder at enchantment. Milkman Dead, the spoiled son of a black-bourgeois family in Michigan, flees his stifling home for the headier company of his eccentric Aunt Pilate, a penniless but bewitching matriarch who runs a bootlegging operation on the wrong side of town. Milkman starts out seeking a bag of gold which he thinks Pilate is hoarding, but before long he is seeking his family's roots in Virginia, where he discovers such marvels as a conversation between hunters and hounds, and a legendary great-grandfather named Solomon who "lifted his beautiful black ass up in the sky and flew on home."

Unfortunately, this attempt by Morrison to transform black folklore into painless enchantment comes dangerously close to reviving the spirit of antebellum nostalgia, updated as a Disney cartoon full of yarn-spinning "darkies" with droll names. Thus Morrison is at pains to re-introduce the grim facts of oppression via an ominous character named Guitar, a boyhood friend of Milkman's who belongs to a secret society practicing random violence against whites. Guitar spends a lot of time berating Milkman about the brutality being inflicted on the civil-rights movement. He does this, apparently, not because his message has direct bearing on Milkman's quest, but because ***Song of Solomon*** needs social and political ballast to keep it from floating up and turning into *Song of the South.*

In the end, Milkman attempts flight. Pursued by Guitar to the cliff called Solomon's Leap, he commits an act of faith by leaping off. But whether he soars or drops, we never learn, because the novel ends right there. It's almost as if Morrison contrived this ending in order to deal with the conflict between harsh racial reality, as embodied in Guitar, and blackness as enchantment, as embodied in Milkman—only to suspend the contradiction at the last moment because it cannot be resolved.

Morrison is not the first black writer to seek the down-home sources of a distinctive black literary style; such efforts date back to the Harlem Renaissance. But she may be the first to combine black folk culture with the romantic impulses of magic realism, thereby producing an admixture which, among other things, distorts the essence of the downhome tradition. Her fourth novel, ***Tar Baby,*** (1981), takes as its central metaphor the old animal fable about Fox setting a trap for Rabbit in the form of a statue of tar. Rabbit gets mad at the statue and tries to beat it up, only to get all four paws and his head stuck. Fox carries Rabbit off, saying "I don't know what hardly to do with you." Rabbit begs him to do anything he wants, only "please don't throw me there in them briars." Any red-blooded American, black or white, will recall the ending. Fox throws Rabbit in the briars, and Rabbit kicks up his heels: "Oh ho, here's where I want to be, here's where I was bred and bo'n anyhow."

Contemporary folklorists argue that these tales had a political subtext, with Rabbit the sly trickster as the slave, and Fox the gullible predator as the master. Accepting this, one might expect *Tar Baby* to apply the tale to a black-white interaction, especially since it is the first of Morrison's novels to include white characters. Set on a Caribbean island, *Tar Baby* concerns the Streets, a retired white couple from Philadelphia; Sydney and Ondine, their black servants, also from Philadelphia; Jadine, the servants' niece, who is educated by the Streets as their own; and finally Son, a low-down black sailor who jumps ship, breaks into the Streets' mansion, and seduces the high-toned Jadine. Son, as the free-spirited Rabbit figure, becomes . . . well, stuck on Jadine, a tempting creature sent out by the white liberal Streets to capture Son and lure him away from his true black identity. The difference with the fable is that Fox wanted to eat Rabbit, while the Streets just want to integrate blacks into their white world. To Son, however, firmly rooted in black mythic consciousness (he comes from a small town in Florida), integration is the same as being devoured. So he escapes into the forest, "lickety-split" (the novel's final word).

Because this is also magic realism, the white folks serve the added function of playing corrupt modernity to the blacks' pure Macondo. You see, the island is full of nature-spirits and departed souls susurrating miraculous messages into any ear capable of hearing. But the capability to hear does not depend on how long people have lived there, how removed they are from scientific consciousness, or any other philosophical consideration of the type found in García Márquez. No, for Morrison, enchantment is color-coded. Jadine, the fashion model with the Ph.D., can hear the murmurings of "the swamp women," and Son, the world-weary drifter, can join the ghostly march of a centuries-old slave insurrection, for the self-evident reason that both are black. Old Mr. Street just sits in his greenhouse listening to Bach, subjugated nature and recorded music being all the enchantment the white race can handle. And there's no magic at all for Mrs. Street, a typical white bitch who spends her early married life sticking pins and scissors into her infant son. I say "the white race" and "typical" because every character in this book speaks less as a quirky individual than as a looming racial archetype. The wry humor of the old fable is lost in a pretentious jumble of animation and animosity.

There is a folktale at the heart of *Beloved,* too. Whether or not the animal fables implicitly refer to relations between masters and slaves, another cycle of tales does so explicitly. Called the "Old Marster and John" tales, they were neglected by paternalistic nineteenth-century folklorists such as Joel Chandler Harris, who preferred the apparent harmlessness of Rabbit and his cronies. *Beloved* contains a particularly good example of these tales, sharp-edged as they frequently are. It's about a slave caught stealing meat, who defends himself by saying that he can't be stealing, since he himself belongs to the master. By eating good meat, he is only using one item of the master's property to improve another.

In *Beloved,* surprisingly, this well-known tale is not identified as a tale. Rather, Morrison presents it as part of her own narration, a scene occurring between a cruel master and a slave called Sixo. The tale's humor gets blunted when Morrison adds that Sixo's master "beat him anyway to show him that the definitions belong to the definers—not the defined." And

later, Sixo is burned to death for showing too much defiance. Obviously, Morrison is not interested in the tale's depiction of human give and take—the whole point being that the slave *does* define himself, as both cleverer and more righteous than the master. Clearly, human give and take has no place in Morrison's depiction of slavery as unrelieved genocide.

The main plot of *Beloved* can be seen as a variant on the same tale: a slave commits a crime, but it's not really a crime because it was committed by a slave. The system, and not the slave, stands unjustly condemned for a deed that would possess another meaning if committed in freedom. To some extent, a similar moral adjustment has to be made in judging the act of a woman in Sethe's position. But there has to be a qualitative difference. Instead of being a sardonic comment on property rights and responsibilities, the story of Sethe is a life-and-death catastrophe, as unlike the tale as one's own child is unlike a piece of meat. Yet by excusing Sethe from lasting blame, Morrison almost equates her infanticide with Sixo's pilfering. In Morrison's mind there seems to be only one crime, that of slavery itself, and no person who lives under it has to answer for anything. So intent is she on showing the inhumanity of the master, she dehumanizes the slave. From the subtle calibration of right and wrong which distinguishes the "Old Marster and John" tales we arrive at the collapse of all moral distinctions.

What Morrison seems to forget is that black American folklore, however intensely rich it may be, is also intensely entangled with white folklore. Indeed, many of the "Old Marster and John" stories have European precedents, just as many white tales have African roots. But that doesn't degrade either. In the case of black folklore, one of its admirable functions was to preserve a sense of dignity and identity among people forced to live in intimate proximity with another people who considered themselves superior. By insisting that her black village be as radically removed from the white world as Macondo is from modernity, Morrison deprives black folklore of one of its most vital functions. She also indulges in the worst kind of romanticism, the kind that would reconstruct people in the name of setting them free. (pp. 38-40)

Martha Bayles, "Special Effects, Special Pleading," in The New Criterion, *Vol. VI, No. 5, January, 1988, pp. 34-40.*

ROBERT ALLEN AND OTHERS

Despite the international stature of Toni Morrison, she has yet to receive the national recognition that her five major works of fiction entirely deserve: she has yet to receive the keystone honors of the National Book Award or the Pulitzer Prize. We, the undersigned black critics and black writers, here assert ourselves against such oversight and harmful whimsy.

The legitimate need for our own critical voice in relation to our own literature can no longer be denied. We, therefore, urgently affirm our rightful and positive authority in the realm of American letters and, in this prideful context, we do raise this tribute to the author of *The Bluest Eye, Sula, Song of Solomon, Tar Baby* and *Beloved.*

Alive, we write this testament of thanks to you, dear Toni: alive, beloved and persevering, magical. Among the fecund intimacies of our hidden past, and among the coming days of dream or nightmares that will follow from the bidden knowledge of our conscious heart, we find your life work ever building to a monument of vision and discovery and trust. You have never turned away the searching eye, the listening ear attuned to horror or to histories providing for our faith. And freely you have given to us every word that you have found important to the forward movement of our literature, our life. For all of America, for all of American letters, you have advanced the moral and artistic standards by which we must measure the daring and the love of our national imagination and our collective intelligence as a people.

Your gifts to us have changed and made more gentle our real time together. And so we write, here, hoping not to delay, not to arrive, in any way, late with this, our simple tribute to the seismic character and beauty of your writing. And, furthermore, in grateful wonder at the advent of *Beloved,* your most recent gift to our community, our country, our conscience, our courage flourishing as it grows, we here record our pride, our respect and our appreciation for the treasury of your findings and invention.

> Robert Allen and others, "Black Writers in Praise of Toni Morrison," in The New York Times Book Review, *January 24, 1988, p. 36.*

JUNE JORDAN AND HOUSTON A. BAKER, JR.

> I will call them my people
> which were not my people:
> and her beloved
> which was not beloved.
>
> —Romans 9:25

With this passage, Toni Morrison leads her readers into *Beloved,* a universe of complicated, sweetly desiring, fierce and deeply seductive human beings hitherto subsumed by, hitherto stifled by, that impenetrable nobody-noun: "the slave."

That same scripture might well stand as the cradling text or tight-lipped summary of the chaotic, chimerical and frightening task America imposes upon any one of us chosen to be or choosing to become a black artist in this freedom land.

For example, even as we mourn the passing of so legendary a writer as James Baldwin, and even as we may revel in the posthumous acclamations of his impact and his public glory, how shall we yet grieve, relieve or altogether satisfy? How shall we explain the exile of this man who wanted to be loved so much at home? . . .

Celebrity is not a serious embrace. It is a fact that James Baldwin, celebrated worldwide and posthumously designated as "immortal" and as "the conscience of his generation," it is a fact that Baldwin never received the honor of these keystones to the canon of American literature: the National Book Award and the Pulitzer Prize: never. . . .

We also grieve for every black artist who survives him in this freedom land. We grieve because we cannot yet assure that such shame, such national neglect will not occur again, and then again.

From that actual and emblematic death we turn, determined, to the living: 18 years ago the living black writer, Toni Morrison, demanded our collective and our private confrontation with the power of her work. Her first novel, *The Bluest Eye,* published in 1970, irreversibly abraded our responsible, unwilling consciousness with tragedies of absolute, interior dislocation: the unbearable self-loathing of one black child, Pecola Breedlove, who could not escape America. From that austere, that chiseled moment of publication here, among us, the written wizardry of Toni Morrison has earned her several books, best-seller popularity and a required reading presence on every respectable campus of the United States.

Throughout, she has persisted in the task of calling "her beloved / which was not beloved." She has insisted on the subjects of her sorrowing concern: "my people / which were not my people"—black children and women and men variously not themselves, variously not yet free from an inexplicable, mad, impinging hatred that would throttle or derange all village/family/sexual love. And devoutly, she has conjured up alternatives to such a destiny: political and skin-close means to a transcendent self-respect. Today, all the literate world knows Toni Morrison.

> June Jordan and Houston A. Baker, Jr., "Black Writers in Praise of Toni Morrison," in The New York Times Book Review, *January 24, 1988, p. 36.*

JONATHAN YARDLEY

The first question is: Inasmuch as the 1988 Pulitzer Prizes have yet to be awarded, why are four dozen Afro-American writers issuing a public complaint about Toni Morrison's failure to win one? The second: Are the prizes really so important—"keystones to the canon of American literature"—that it is necessary to make a scene over Morrison's alleged mistreatment at the hands of those who award them? The third: Since the suggestion has been made that Morrison has failed to win a major prize because she is black, are we now to understand that she should be given one . . . because she is black?

These and any number of other questions, few of them pleasant, are raised by the two documents published in yesterday's issue of *The New York Times Book Review* and widely discussed in various other publications and broadcasts last week. The first of the documents is a somewhat hysterical letter by poet June Jordan and University of Pennsylvania English professor Houston A. Baker Jr. lamenting the "shame" and "national neglect" suffered by Morrison and the late James Baldwin because of the failure of each to win either a Pulitzer or a National Book Award. The second is a "Statement" signed by these two writers and 46 others.

The sincerity of those who signed this statement is not open to question, nor is the dignity with which they, as black writers, "urgently affirm our rightful and positive authority in the realm of American letters"; their willingness to speak out as a group is heartening evidence of their self-esteem and the determination to be accepted, as well they should be, as legitimate and important contributors to American literature. But however much we may sympathize with their feelings and their desire for recognition, we must not let this blind us to the rather less attractive implications of their protest.

It comes 2½ months after the 1987 National Book Award for Fiction was presented not to Morrison's *Beloved,* one of the five finalists, but to Larry Heinemann's first novel, *Paco's Story* [see Heinemann's entry in *CLC,* Vol. 50]. The decision has been reached by a 2-to-1 vote of the jury, one member of which was the prominent Afro-American novelist Gloria Naylor, whose name was conspicuously absent among the signers of the current protest. According to a report last week on public radio, Morrison was "devastated" by this disappointment; the statement in *The New York Times Book Review,* with their deeply felt praise for Morrison, appear designed as much to ease this "devastation" as to protest the "neglect" she ostensibly has suffered.

But the truth is that it's a form of "neglect" virtually any other writer would kill for. Like all of Morrison's previous novels, **Beloved** was the recipient of extravagant, indeed excessive reviews, and it spent a number of weeks on the best-seller lists. It was a finalist for both the National Book Award and the National Book Critics Circle Award; it may well be among the three finalists recommended to the Pulitzer board by the fiction jury, though I have no inside knowledge to that effect. By any reasonable standard it has been a great success, one that Morrison and her claque should be applauding rather than bemoaning.

Yet here we have Morrison "devastated" at her failure to win an award and her admirers issuing a thinly veiled suggestion that this failure was due to racism on the part of the American literary community. Nothing could be further from the truth, and it is time to put the canard to rest once and for all. The plain fact is that over the years Morrison has if anything been the beneficiary of the literary community's good intentions. Literary people in the United States tend to be humane and liberal in outlook, if not always in practice, and to search out opportunities to express these sentiments. Morrison, who writes eloquently and powerfully about black life and history, has provided precisely such an opportunity; it has been seized over and again by publishers, reviewers, other writers and ordinary readers.

There are millions of black Americans with ample grievances about discrimination, but at least in literary terms Toni Morrison most emphatically is not among them; she is in fact among the privileged few, not merely as a nationally celebrated author but also as an editor at one of the country's most respected publishing firms, Random House. Nobody's out to "rob" Morrison of awards. She "lost" the National Book Award not for racial reasons but because one juror felt passionately about *Paco's Story* and managed to persuade another juror to that view; she "lost" the Book Critics Circle Award (which in fact she had won a decade earlier for **Song of Solomon**) because there was stronger support within the organization's board for Philip Roth's *The Counterlife.* . . . (p. 6)

The point is so basic that belaboring it is ridiculous, but here goes anyway: It is possible to make a literary judgment without making a racial judgment as well. It is possible that two groups of judges can meet, quite independently of each other, and decide that certain books by writers who happen to be white are "better" than a certain book by a writer who happens to be black—and that their decisions can have nothing, absolutely nothing, to do with race. It is even possible that when the Great Juror in the Sky comes to make the final decision, the one for all eternity, she will decide that **Beloved** is not as good a novel as *Passion Moon Rising* by Rebecca Brandewyne.

When it comes to judgments about books—or chocolate-chip cookies, or movies, or musical compositions—anything is possible; Toni Morrison is the victim, if that is how her admirers choose to see her, not of racism but of possibility. To suggest to the contrary is merely to muddy the waters, to raise an issue that is entirely irrelevant and to impugn the mo-

tives of honest people who tried, as best they could, to reach honest decisions under difficult circumstances.

To say this is not to deny that black writers have suffered discrimination or that some have been given insufficient recognition; certainly it is an oddity, and a literary if not racial injustice, that none of the country's most prestigious literary prizes managed to find its way to James Baldwin, though we do well to remember that in other ways he was much honored in his lifetime. But Scott Fitzgerald and Thomas Wolfe never won Pulitzers; neither did Flannery O'Connor nor John Dos Passos. The giving of awards, like life itself, is imperfect, and many deserving books have gone without honor; but race has nothing to do with it, and to suggest as much is nothing except dangerous self-delusion. (pp. 6-7)

> *Jonathan Yardley, "Toni Morrison and the Prize Fight," in* The Washington Post, *January 25, 1988.*

WALTER GOODMAN

The tribute to Toni Morrison by 48 black writers in last Sunday's, *New York Times Book Review* does not come right out and charge that Ms. Morrison has been denied a major literary prize because of her race, but the implication is inescapable. An accompanying letter by two of the signatories, June Jordan and Houston A. Baker Jr., dispels any doubt by reminding us that James Baldwin "never received the honor of these keystones to the canon of American literature: the National Book Award and the Pulitzer Prize: never."

Any hint of racism is too serious to be left dangling that way. Nothing that we know of the writers and critics who are chosen to be book judges supports it, and no evidence is offered in the letters. One notes that Gloria Naylor, a well-known black novelist, served as a member of the most recent National Book Award panel, and her name is missing from the tribute to Ms. Morrison.

Even if the imputation of racism is unmeant as well as unjustified, it will not go unnoticed by award givers. The group of 48 proclaims: "We, therefore, urgently affirm our rightful and positive authority in the realm of American letters and, in this prideful context, we do raise this tribute." The prose will win no prizes, but it cannot fail to be interpreted as a caution to future judges (on the very day, coincidentally, of the publication of the names of this year's Pulitzer Prize jury) that they had better do right or risk being stigmatized.

It is no comment on the accomplishments of Ms. Morrison to observe that such pressure is precisely what an honestly given honor is supposed to ignore. Yet the openness of this effort may prove salubrious if it draws attention to the nature of the awards themselves. Anybody who spends time in what passes as the literary community knows that lobbying is part of the awards game, and it would be healthy if the big prizes were not treated as though they sprang direct from the Muse.

Literary lobbying goes on all the time; the form it takes, perhaps just a friendly telephone call or some cocktail party chit-chat, is generally more discreet than a salvo in the *Times Book Review,* but the intent is the same. . . .

So, except for the unfortunate implication of racism and its boldness, Sunday's 48-gun salute was in accord with the system. It is a deplorable system—but there is as much hope of eliminating literary lobbying as there is of keeping defense contractors from buying dinners for Congressmen.

What's to be done about it? Probably nothing, short of tagging onto all prizes a statement on the order of the Surgeon General's warnings about cigarettes: "This award does not constitute God's will; it represents the fallible and temporary opinion of a few mortals and should not be swallowed whole." If the awards were kept in perspective, Ms. Morrison's admirers might not have felt impelled to go public in a way that can only be self-defeating—for if *Beloved* now receives the Pulitzer Prize, readers must wonder whether claque pressure had something to do with it.

As matters stand, prizes boost egos, sales and sometimes group spirits, so one can appreciate the disappointment of Ms. Morrison's friends and supporters. For what comfort it offers, she is not the first good writer not to get a Pulitzer (not yet, anyway) and her work has not exactly gone unremarked by critics of all races. In the long run—and literature is supposed to be a long-run endeavor—her books are what count, and they will be judged by readers at some distance from today's battles and rivalries who will not remember which awards she received or failed to receive. They may not even know her color.

Walter Goodman, "The Lobbying for Literary Prizes," in The New York Times, *January 28, 1988, p. C26.*

JOHN LEONARD

Forty-eight black writers and critics, all of whom think Toni Morrison has been so far stiffed in the dispensation of literary prizes, wrote a letter of collective protest that [was published] in the *Times Book Review,* and I wish they hadn't. . . .

In the preeminent bulletin of official literary culture, *Beloved* becomes a hot potato in race relations instead of a novel for everybody, a collectivized "cause" instead of a book of dreams, one more item in a black bill of indictment against the white power structure instead of a magical act of transcendence—as if the whole literary prize-giving business weren't so routinely insulting to every race, color, creed and sexual predisposition. And that includes the forthcoming Pulitzers, whose panelists will now be looking over their shoulders: Whether Morrison wins or loses the Pulitzer, we'll be arguing about everybody's politics instead of her novel. . . .

Prizes matter so much to writers, especially writers of fiction, because the habit of fiction-writing is itself so peculiar, almost unique in its disregard for the claims of sociability and order. Like a monk, a hermit, a yogi or a shaman, you disappear for years at a time behind closed doors to talk to the ghosts in your machine. It's a brave solitude, but also crazed with doubt. Your book takes longer than any baby to gestate, and it's delivered naked into the care of strangers. From these strangers you need not merely approval, but the assurance that your inwardness isn't diseased, that you aren't as sick as Narcissus, that you brought back something precious—mystical, revolutionary—from your dreamy desert.

Not many bring back a *Beloved.*

But a writer's solitude is experienced by the reader in a competing solitude. It's not communal. It's intimacy to intimacy, one on one, down there with the demons. In such solitudes, we also write book reviews, variously wet from their own

weathers. We sit in separate splendid singularities on prize-giving panels groping for a group-mind. And more often than not the winner is everybody's second-best, agreed upon in order to sacrifice the least of each panelist's embattled self-esteem. The systems stinks; and yet we will have prizes because we want that perfect love before we die.

Then a community—in this case, the community of the black intelligentsia, the liveliest talents, the brains and heart—stirs, surprised, angry, wounded, protective. So special is *Beloved* to this community's sense of itself in an endless Civil War that it perceives any neglect of the novel as an injury to the very texture of what it knows. Those of us outside this community are accused at the very least of bad faith. It doesn't do me any good to say that I am more a citizen of Morrison's novel than any other that I've read in years, by black or white or male or female, because talking about *Beloved* any more.

Finally, why Morrison hasn't won the prizes she deserves may be less important to know than the state of mind and the sense of community of the Morrison 48. We've seen this aggrieved behavior before, haven't we, this righteous agitation? And who were the aggrieved? Emigres, of course; the Jews, the Irish, the Italians, who proved their faith by works, and were nevertheless for so long discounted and despised. We are being told in the *Times* that even now, after *centuries,* in this country for which Martin Luther King Jr. died every bit as much as Abraham Lincoln, to be black is still to be an emigre. On this, they are the authorities. They've reviewed our book.

John Leonard, "In Person," in Newsday. *Reprinted in* The National Book Critics Circle Journal, *Vol. 14, No. 3, April 1, 1988, p. 7.*

DENNIS HEVESI

Beloved, a novel by Toni Morrison about the agonizing remembrances of a former slave in post-Civil War Ohio, was awarded the Pulitzer Prize for fiction [yesterday].

Ms. Morrison's work had been at the center of a controversy last fall when it failed to win the prestigious National Book Award, and 48 black writers wrote an open letter in January protesting that Ms. Morrison had never won that award or a Pulitzer. (p. 1)

In January, two months after *Beloved* failed to win the National Book Award, the 48 black writers and critics wrote the letter to The New York Times Book Review, attributing the failure to "oversight and harmful whimsy." Among the signers were Maya Angelou, Amiri Baraka, John Edgar Wideman, John A. Williams and Henry Louis Gates Jr. The authors of the statement said its purpose was not to influence the decision on the Pulitzer, but simply to praise a deserving writer.

Today, Robert Christopher, the secretary of the Pulitzer board, said: "Obviously the board was aware of the statement but, no, it didn't affect their decision. I think there was some feeling that it would be unfortunate if anyone diluted the value of Toni Morrison's achievement by suggesting that her prize rested on anything but merit." (p. 13)

Dennis Hevesi, "Toni Morrison's Novel 'Beloved'

Wins the Pulitzer Prize in Fiction," in The New York Times, *April 1, 1988, pp. 1, 13.*

HERBERT MITGANG

Responding to the first call . . . informing her that she had won the Pulitzer Prize for fiction, Toni Morrison caught her breath, asked for a few minutes to form her thoughts, then said:

"I think I know what I feel. It's true that I had no doubt about the value of the book and that it was really worth serious recognition. But I had some dark thoughts about whether the book's merits would be allowed to be the only consideration of the Pulitzer committee. The book had begun to take on a responsibility, an extra-literary responsibility that it was never designed for."

By "extra-literary responsibility," Ms. Morrison was referring to the controversy surrounding a statement on her behalf, signed by 48 black writers and published in *The New York Times Book Review* last January. . . . Some authors thought that this goodwill gesture might not have served her best interests; but the award today made that question moot.

Literary figures agreed today that *Beloved* had won the Pulitzer Prize on its own much-deserved merits as a novel. Ms. Morrison herself said she believed that the award was made despite "gossip and speculation."

"In the end I feel as though I have served the characters in the book well, and I have served the readers well, and I hope the Pulitzer people are as proud of me as I am of them," Ms. Morrison said. . . .

Asked about the statement the writers published in her behalf, Ms. Morrison said:

"That was a kind of blessing for me—to know that irrespective of the formal recognition that is available to a writer, that they appreciated the worth of my work to them. They redeemed me, but I am certain they played no significant role in the judgment. If anything, it was in the teeth of speculation and gossip that the Pulitzer committee was forced to operate. They apparently resisted it."

> *Herbert Mitgang, "For Morrison, Prize Silences Gossip," in* The New York Times, *April 1, 1988, p. 13.*

ELEANOR RANDOLPH

Toni Morrison was awarded the Pulitzer Prize for fiction yesterday for her novel *Beloved,* a complex fable about slavery and liberation of the slaves a century ago.

The Morrison prize followed protests from black writers and academics when the widely praised *Beloved* did not win either the National Book or the National Book Critics Circle awards this year. Pulitzer board members said they knew of the controversy, but that it did not affect their choice in that category. (p. A1)

Earlier this year Morrison was the subject of a letter to *The New York Times Book Review* signed by 48 black authors expressing outrage that the National Book Award and National Critics award had again been denied to a black. Writers June Jordan and Houston A. Baker wrote that James Baldwin,

"posthumously designated as 'immortal,' " had never received a Pulitzer or National Book Award.

Morrison told the Associated Press that joy was uppermost in her feelings because "I really was thinking dark and difficult thoughts about what was available to this book in terms of recognition."

Pulitzer board chairman Roger Wilkins, the first black to head the board, said that although the Pulitzer judges were aware of the letter, "It didn't affect our judgment."

Morrison was competing with two other women authors for the fiction prize. They were Diane Johnson for *Persian Nights* and Alice McDermott for *That Night.*

Asked whether getting the Pulitzer after the black protest would taint the prize, Wilkins said: "It's like the asterisk after Roger Maris' home-run record—61 home runs in a 162-game season. People will say that she won the Pulitzer Prize and in addition that year, she got an expression of enormous admiration and affection from some of the best black writers in the country.

"Not only could I live with that asterisk, I'd give my right arm for it," Wilkins said.

Henry Louis Gates, W.E.B. DuBois professor at Cornell and one of the signers of the letter protesting Morrison's lack of prizes, said yesterday that he and others had worried that the protest would insure that the Pulitzer board would deny the prize to Morrison.

"I'm ecstatic, I'm ecstatic," he said. "I decided it was more important to deny the evil, and I figured justice would out, and justice did." (p. A14)

> *Eleanor Randolph, "Morrison Novel 'Beloved' Wins Pulitzer Prize," in* The Washington Post, *April 1, 1988, pp. A1, A14.*

AMY E. SCHWARTZ

The progress of Toni Morrison's *Beloved* through bestsellerdom and controversy to the Pulitzer Prize has brought with it a kind of public, emotional sharing of the black experience of slavery in America, as much among white readers as black. Interestingly, the book's dedication page brings up echoes of another experience entirely: "Sixty Million, And More," it says. The echo has not gone unnoticed. Sixty million, Morrison says when asked—as she was repeatedly on her book tour—is the number of Africans who died on the way to slavery, on the slave ships which in *Beloved* become a hovering, nightmare background for every character's experience. It carries Morrison's clear intention to expand our understanding of the experience of slavery; to show that that unique horror was not only an enslavement but genocide as well.

The formulation caused some unease. One hostile book reviewer, Stanley Crouch, put it crudely in *The New Republic:* the book, he said, "seems to have been written in order to enter American slavery into the big-time martyr ratings contest, a contest usually won by references to, and works about, the experience of Jews at the hands of Nazis" [see excerpt above]. Most genocide scholars avoid this kind of debate over terms, precisely because of the unsavory who-suffered-more implications. After the infamous Louis Farrakhan outburst about "Don't shove your 6 million down our throats, we lost a hundred million in slavery," no rational discourse on the subject has seemed possible.

But, of course, it used to be that the "shared experience of oppression" between blacks and Jews was no danger zone but instead a source of kinship. In a civil rights context, it meant the parallel experiences of discrimination in America, but also something older: much of the imagery of gospel culture, from crossing the Jordan to milk and honey, comes from the Israel-in-Egypt story being commemorated this week by Passover. But the tensions between blacks and Jews in the political arena have diverted attention from matters of kinship. Of all these tensions the numbers game is the most destructive, but it seems that there is a chance of exorcising it.

That chance lies in **Beloved** and in the communal catharsis it seems to have produced in readers black and white alike. Its great bridging capacity is the way it opens up the imaginations of those who haven't lived it to the memory of slavery and the experience of carrying that memory in your past. In form and tone, and in the hugely appreciative, emotional response from the reading public, it resembles a perhaps less serious, certainly in retrospect less literary work of a generation ago: *Exodus,* Leon Uris' huge best seller about the founding of Israel. That book too was a sort of popularizing catharsis, a way to make one nation's torment accessible to a great many.

To this reader reared on *Exodus* from an early age, reading **Beloved** insistently called *Exodus* to mind: the sweeping historical plot, the many characters (some historical) with their differing experiences of the central horror; the way their imagined stories gave historical memory an anchor. Most strikingly similar are the points when the narrative halts momentarily for a cry of rage and suffering. In *Exodus* it's the cry of the Israeli commander Ari Ben Canaan at novel's end after yet another young friend is killed: "God! God! Why can't they let us alone? *Why can't they let us live?*" In **Beloved,** years after the Civil War is over, a character named Stamp Paid . . . sees a flicker of red in the water while mooring his boat and reaches down to get it. He thinks it's a cardinal feather, but what comes up in his hand is "a red ribbon

knotted around a curl of wet woolly hair, clinging still to its bit of scalp. . . . Before he took a step he turned to look back down the road he was traveling and said, to its frozen mud and the river beyond, 'What *are* these people? You tell me, Jesus. What *are* they?' " . . .

The nightmare-like memories of **Beloved,** the ghost daughter who returns to Sethe, are race memories of the crossing in slave ships; they are the most like camp narratives. Morrison told a *Newsweek* interviewer that half of all those on the slave ships died, but that in oral history there was only "a blank" about the ghastly experience; she felt she had to reclaim it for memory through imagination. This is a mental process somewhat akin to that described by the exemplar of those who reclaim the Holocaust to memory, Elie Wiesel.

Wiesel himself, like most Holocaust survivors and scholars, absolutely rejects comparisons of the Holocaust with any other experience, genocide or otherwise. He has said repeatedly, and rightly, that the uniqueness of that horror functions as a moral touchstone.

But why reach the question of who suffered more? What's important here is the bitter anger that Toni Morrison has been able to evoke without losing artistic control—the anger of a burden that cannot be put down or forgotten by its descendants; the resentment it creates against those who, not carrying that burden, *can't* imagine it, despite the greatest good intentions and sympathy.

And so we have two peoples still frequently at odds, each burdened with the trauma of a historical atrocity that was visited upon them as a people—and under the added bitterness of their certainty that no one else on Earth could possibly understand it. These are open wounds, and still so painful that each leaps away at the merest touch. But the anger is something they have in common. Wouldn't it help, just a little, to relax and pursue these themes to a partial understanding?

Amy E. Schwartz, " 'Beloved': It's Not a Question of Who Suffered More," in The Washington Post, *April 3, 1988, p. B7.*

(Ahmed) Salman Rushdie

The Satanic Verses

Whitbread Award: Fiction

Indian-born English novelist, critic, and nonfiction writer.

Written in the irreverent, self-reflexive, and fragmented style that characterizes all of Rushdie's work, *The Satanic Verses* (1988) explores themes relating to good and evil, religious faith and fanaticism, illusion versus reality, and the plight of Indians who have relocated to Great Britain. Utilizing the technique of magic realism to blur distinctions between reality and imagination, Rushdie blends evocations of present-day London with fantastic events, extended dream sequences, and lushly exotic settings. He creates several levels of symbolic and allegorical meaning through frequent use of puns, metaphors, similes, and myriad allusions to works of literature and film, popular culture, the folklore of India, and sacred beliefs of Islam. Rushdie's sportive examination and recreation of Islamic history was scorned by many devout Muslims and resulted in a far-ranging international controversy. Demonstrations and riots in protest of *The Satanic Verses* occurred in India, Pakistan, and South Africa soon after the book was first published, and several nations banned its importation. Numerous outraged religious and political leaders of the Muslim faith charged Rushdie with blasphemy towards both the founder of Islam, Mohammed, and the religion's sacred text, the Koran, culminating with a decree by Iranian leader Ayatollah Ruhollah Khomeini, head of the Shiite Muslim sect, that Rushdie and all those connected with publication of *The Satanic Verses* should be executed. Several Iranian clerics announced a bounty of up to $5 million for Rushdie's death. Khomeini's edict was widely condemned in the West, as several nations froze or broke off diplomatic relations with Iran. Some commentators believe the controversy illuminates fundamental differences between Western and Islamic cultural traditions, noting the former allows varying degrees of freedom of expression and artistic license to question accepted truths, while the latter upholds the Koran as divine and absolute. Others contend the outbursts of threats and violence are politically motivated by Muslim fundamentalists to increase their influence and power.

Muslims point to several elements in *The Satanic Verses* as defamations of their religion. The title of the book refers to a disputed episode that was first recorded by historians over a century after Mohammed's death. In this alleged incident, Mohammed, who had the verses of the Koran relayed to him by the archangel Gabriel, attempts to win favor for his monotheistic teachings in a region that recognizes hundreds of deities by granting semi-divine status to three local goddesses. According to some historians, Mohammed later recanted after realizing he had been inspired to make this decree by Satan, who mimicked the voice of Gabriel. While Rushdie presents these events ambiguously within a dream sequence, perturbed Muslims questioned the appropriateness of drawing upon an incident that many Islamic scholars and leaders have refuted. Muslims are also disturbed by Rushdie's use of

the name Mahound, a derisive epithet used in the West to degrade the prophet, for a character who strongly resembles Mohammed. In response, Rushdie notes that Mahound is a figure in another character's dream, and the author stated further that a passage in *The Satanic Verses* explains his use of the name: "His name: a dream-name, changed by the vision. . . . Here he is neither Mahomet nor MoeHammered; has adopted, instead, the demon-tag the farangis hung around his neck. To turn insults into strengths, whigs, tories, Blacks all chose to wear with pride the names they were given in scorn; likewise, our mountain-climbing, prophet-motivated solitary is to be the medieval baby-frightener, the Devil's synonym: Mahound."

Another point of contention concerns a scene where a group of courtesans adopt the names of Mohammed's wives, resulting in a sudden increase in business. Detractors of *The Satanic Verses* consider this scene a mockery of revered figures, while Rushdie's supporters note that the prostitutes are eventually punished for the transgression. Rushdie stated that his intention in this passage was to juxtapose the sacred and the profane. Many Muslims are also angered by a character in the book named Salman, a scribe who alters the verses dictated to him by Mohammed that will eventually form the Koran. Rushdie explains this as part of his self-conscious investigation into differences between religious and artistic revelation, while Muslims contend it serves to compromise the literal truth of the Koran. Finally, some Muslims claim that Rushdie violated taboos by making irreverential references to people, places, and objects sacred to Islam. Most Western commentators defend Rushdie's freedom of expression, pointing out that he explores the accepted truths of Islam in the tradition of metaphysical speculation, inviting the reader to ponder his observations and making insightful comments about the elusiveness of absolute truths. The differences of opinion led to unprecedented international tensions and debate over a work of fiction.

The phantasmagoric narrative of *The Satanic Verses* blends descriptions of events, landscapes, and characters with direct addresses to the reader in a playful format reminiscent of *The Thousand and One Nights*. Drawing upon a wide range of allusions, Rushdie explores the nature of fiction and reality, myth, religious faith, and contrasts between Indian and English society. In the beginning of the novel, two expatriate Indian men, Gibreel Farishta and Saladin Chamcha, miraculously survive a fall to Earth following an airplane explosion over England. These alter egos represent good and evil, but distinctions between them are frequently blurred as they undergo continual metamorphoses of body and personality. Gibreel, a movie star in the genre of Indian religious films, or "theologicals," experiences vivid dreams in which historical events surrounding the founding of Islam are depicted in epic detail similar to those found in theologicals. Saladin, who metamorphoses into a satanic figure, journeys to London and encounters police brutality, prejudice, and other seamy elements that reflect deep-rooted social problems. Saladin, who had disassociated himself from his Indian heritage, is forced to confront his past as part of Rushdie's extended examination of the various ways Indians have assimilated into British society. The narrative follows these characters through the intertwining of past and present, various locations, reality, dream, and films until their final confrontation on a movie set.

Critical reaction to *The Satanic Verses* was mixed. A. J. Mojtabai stated: "As a display of narrative energy and wealth of invention, *The Satanic Verses* is impressive. As a sustained exploration of the human condition, it flies apart into delirium. . . . Does it require so much fantasia and fanfare to remind us that good and evil are deeply, subtly intermixed in humankind?" Others praised Rushdie's exuberant narrative and his far ranging development of themes. Robert Irwin noted: "Once an image, pun, or reference has been brought into play, Rushdie gallops off with it in all directions. The reader may find himself exhausted, but he is never in danger of being bored. . . . [*The Satanic Verses*] is several of the best novels [Rushdie] has ever written."

Previous to *The Satanic Verses,* Rushdie won wide acclaim for his novels *Midnight's Children* (1981) and *Shame* (1983). *Midnight's Children* chronicles the recent history of India, beginning in 1947 when the subcontinent became independent from British rule. Saleem Sinai, the protagonist, is one of a thousand and one babies born during the first hour of India's independence. He is presented as a man in his early thirties who has aged prematurely and become impotent. The novel has been widely read as an allegory, with Saleem and the other thousand babies, many of whom died at birth, representing the hopes as well as the frustrating realities of independent India. *Midnight's Children* is rich in allusions to Indian history, literature, and mythology. *Shame* presents a fabulistic account of events in an unnamed country that strongly resembles Pakistan. Rushdie examines the related themes of honor and shame, shame and shamelessness, as cultural influences that affect the personalities and actions of individuals in Pakistan. A number of characters in this work embody various forms of disgrace and honor. Rushdie has also published the novel *Grimus* (1975) and *The Jaguar Smile: A Nicaraguan Journey* (1987), a look at contemporary social and political conditions in Nicaragua, based on his stay there in 1986.

(See also *CLC,* Vols. 23, 31 and *Contemporary Authors,* Vols. 108, 111.)

MADHU JAIN

The jinn is out of the lamp, once again. As ever, it is a journey without seat belts on a bumpy flight of the imagination. This time Salman Rushdie's magic carpet whisks the reader through turbulences in which the past and present keep bumping into each other. And far-flung countries go past as in a moviola.

The Satanic Verses opens with a bang: a hijacked Air-India jumbo: Bostan . . . 420 explodes over England. The only two survivors are India's matinee idol, Gibreel Farishta (he of the "low-slung eyelids" and star of countless "theologicals" who seems to be somewhere between Amitabh Bachchan and N. T. Rama Rao) and Saladin Chamcha, the expatriate "Brown Uncle Tom" who is more-loyal-than-the-queen.

Thus begins the Alice-in-Wonderland journey through narrow tunnels of history and religion. The protagonists keep metamorphosing into confused, haloed angels and foul-breathed, sulphurous devils. In other words, Archangel Gabriel and the man from down under. Characters keep popping up in the most unlikely places. Thatcher's apocalyptic England with gurgling rivers of blood at high tide; a prophet-expectant holy land of the sixth century; the Bombay *filmi duniya* (Pimple Billimoria and the twice-resurrected Farishta); the Bombay arty-tarty *duniya* with bearded Marxist film makers and uninhibited activists like Zeeny Baby.

This omnibus of a book dazzles like a kaleidoscope. It is studded with winged metaphors, parables, allegories, Hindi dialogues, sermons, smart one-liners of the advertising world and authorial interruptions. Hitchcock-like, with Rushdie in the guest role playing god with a small g. Like the kaleidoscope, each turn disorients. But taken together, the novel is, among several other themes, an uncompromising, unequivocal attack on religious fanaticism and fundamentalism, which in this book is largely Islamic. It makes V. S. Naipaul's *Among the Believers* seem like an OK certificate for Islamic fundamentalism.

The root idea of the novel is that there are no absolutes. Heaven and Hell have no boundaries. It's almost impossible to tell angel and devil apart: Mahound the prophet has a tough time telling the difference between the voice of the angel and the *shaitan* (devil) up there on Mount Coney. In the process, Rushdie takes a very irreverent look at Islamic folklore and fact.

Shuttling between the Koranic-Biblical past and present, the past is a searchlight for the absurdities of the present. Ayesha, the youngest and most desirable of Mahound's 12 wives, appears in the middle of the book "living chastely in the harem quarters of the great mosque at Yathrib". She re-surfaces several chapters and centuries later—clad only in butterflies—to lead an entire village, lemming-like, into the Arabian Sea. The sea is expected to part and the pilgrims to go straight to Mecca—which provokes the famous deflationary Rushdie punchline. The affluent man in a Mercedes who tries to stop his cancer-stricken wife from taking the fatal plunge says, "let me fly you to Mecca, pronto. . . . Why walk if you can go by Airbus?"

Angels and gods are dislodged from their heavens. (p. 98)

Pilgrim places get their mirror-image come-uppances. When Jahilia, the city of sand, begins to suffer after the camel trains start losing their business to the boats, the ruler Abu Simbel is convinced: "Only the pilgrimage stands between the city and its ruin." So the council searches the world for "statues of alien gods, to attract new pilgrims". But there is more competition. "Down in Sheba a great temple has been built, a shrine to rival the House of Black Stone." The rulers have no choice but to add "the tempting spices of profanity to their religious practices." (pp. 98-9)

Rushdie does not hesitate to name names, with the exception of the prophet. Here it is Mahound; but he has Hamza, Ayesha, and others straight from the Book. Moreover, the battles which the prophet had to win in order to convert people are very real. And characters like the idol goddesses Lat and Manat are part of Islamic folklore.

Migration is another major theme of this whirlpool of a book. The subcontinental migrants in England also undergo metamorphoses. Rushdie's contemporary mythic figures are not so different from the second generation British Asians finding their anthems in bhangra-discos—little islands within the larger islands of their homeward-looking parents and the Paki-bashing host community. . . .

The magic carpet does take us places but sometimes, in the many twists and turns into dreamscapes, readers may find themselves temporarily off-loaded. If not vertiginous. As for the sentinels of Islam, they will get off at the first stop. *The Satanic Verses* is bound to trigger an avalanche of protests from the ramparts. (p. 99)

> Madhu Jain, "An Irreverent Journey," in India Today, *Vol. XIII, No. 17, September 15, 1988, pp. 98-9.*

SALMAN RUSHDIE [INTERVIEW WITH MADHU JAIN]

[Jain]: *Do you see your new novel as the last in a trilogy after* **Midnight's Children** *and* **Shame**?

[Rushdie]: Yes. I didn't when I was writing it. But having finished the book, I have begun to see the novels as a body of work. I also see my first novel, *Grimus,* as part of this. Metaphysical concerns were present in a different way in the first novel. With the last one I have come to the end of the first

movement in my work and I feel I can do very different things now.

What are you doing now?

Being Zia's obituarist. [At the time of this interview, Rushdie was writing an article on President Zia-ul-Haq of Pakistan, who was killed in an explosion during an airplane flight.]

Your book begins with an exploding aeroplane too. Aren't there many coincidences between your work and events?

There have been unbelievable coincidences. In my novels there are five political figures. All have come to a violent end. Mujibur Rahman in Bangladesh, Indira Gandhi and Sanjay Gandhi in India, Bhutto and Zia in Pakistan. This whole generation either falls out of planes, or gets shot or hanged. None of these people has had a quiet end. (p. 98)

The novel appears to be quite a fierce critique of Islamic fanaticism. . . .

Actually, one of my major themes is religion and fanaticism. I have talked about the Islamic religion because that is what I know the most about. But the ideas about religious faith and the nature of religious experience and also the political implications of religious extremism are applicable with a few variations to just about any religion. In the beginning and the end of the novel there are other kinds of fundamentalism also. (pp. 98-9)

Some of the names you use are straight out of the Book, based on real characters in Islamic tradition; but others are made up. Why did you do that?

I have changed names. I have given the name of an Egyptian temple, Abu Simbel, to the leader of Mecca. I have not called the cities by their names. After all, this is a visionary thing; it happens in dreams. I wanted to distance events from historical events. Issues are being raised; it is not about whether they were historically true or not. The book is really about the fact that an idea or a new thing in the world must decide whether to compromise or not. Beyond that, the image out of which the book grew was of the prophet going to the mountain and not being able to tell the difference between the angel and the devil. The book is also about the wrestling match which takes place between the two.

Unlike your other novels, this one ends on some sort of an optimistic note.

Apart from this being my most serious book, it is also the most comic. I suddenly realised in the end of each of my books that the world disintegrates. But in this novel life goes on at the end of the story. No matter how terrible the events which have happened, at the end, it is not the end of the world. I do leave a few people standing at the end.

Do you fear a backlash from the mullahs?

Even *Shame* was attacked by fundamentalist Muslims. I cannot censor. I write whatever there is to write. (p. 99)

> Madhu Jain (Interview with Salman Rushdie) in India Today, *Vol. XIII, No. 17, September 15, 1988, pp. 98-9.*

HERMIONE LEE

'Here we come! Those bastards down there won't

know what hit them. Meteor or lightning or vengeance of God. Out of thin air, baby. Dharrraaammm! What an entrance, yaar. I swear: splat.'

What an entrance indeed; part cartoon film, part superhuman vision. . . .

Like his two great mythologisings of India and Pakistan, *Midnight's Children* and *Shame,* Salman Rushdie's new novel [*The Satanic Verses*] starts with an astounding image, hurtled vociferously at the readers ('those bastards down there'). But can *The Satanic Verses* stay airborne for 547 pages?

Our two free-fallers are *alter egos.* Coarse, bad-breathed, sensual, Gibreel Farishta, superstar of the Bombay 'theological' movies until his recent mysterious vanishing act, is an unlikely twin soul for Saladin Chamcha, this rational Anglophile. Chamcha's Naipaulian face ('handsome in a somewhat sour, patrician fashion, with long, thick, downturned lips like those of a disgusted turbot') is as carefully constructed as the protean accents he puts on for his parts in the bid to escape from his (superbly done) Bombay childhood and overbearing father.

Both actors are involved with English women. . . . Like their tiresomely meaningful names, [Alleluia Cone and Pamela Lovelace], these female characters fall flat (especially compared with their vengeful Indian rivals). In the end the narrator wipes them out, with unappetising ferocity: it is not a happy book for strong women. And though love as salvation, endangered by jealousy, is a main theme, this isn't Rushdie's forte: his linguistic panache seems to desert him here, as in 'That was the beginning of the sexual marathon that left them both sore, happy and exhausted when it finally ground to a halt.'

The real passion is in the politics and the theology. After their fall, both men are transformed. Gibreel becomes an Archangel from one of his own movies possessed with a fanatical mission to reform the 'tortured metropolis' he has landed in. Fastidious Saladin is turned into a hairy, fire-breathing monster with hoofs and horns. After all his efforts at assimilation, he is grotesquely reduced to the victim (and avatar) of 'Maggie Torture's' monstrously racist society. . . . The embattled London ghetto where Saladin is marooned—the Shaandaar cafe in 'Brickhall', with its philosophical Bangladeshi proprietor, his reactionary wife and tough, sexy, Anglicised daughters (all excellent)—makes a strong urban novel in itself, with immigration as transformation (those who are changed also making the changes) as its angry subject.

But though Rushdie transforms London all he can into a hallucinatory film, it doesn't give him the mythology or the panorama of his novels of India and Pakistan. For the book's *really* big subject, an inquiry into the Islamic belief in good and evil, he intercuts London with fabulous Oriental landscapes: Jahilia, a city made of sand; Peristan, an estate swarming with magical butterflies. These dream/film sequences, settings for holy wars between the followers and opponents of Islam, and for a pilgrimage into the Arabian Sea, are slow going. But they have a weird beauty: imagine the Koran rewritten as science fiction by Burroughs or Ballard. . . .

The avowed aim throughout is adulthood through disillusion. 'The world is real,' one of the 'real' characters says finely: 'We have to live in it; we have to live here, to live on.' The fanatic, hallucinating 'angel' Gibreel is destroyed, the devil-

ishly compromising Saladin survives (reconciled, in a moving ending, to his dying father). Yet the novel is split, like its split characters, its hybrid voices and its double narrative. Fanatical extremism—the kind of idea which gets smashed to bits but which 'the hundredth time, will change the world'— exerts a powerful fascination.

The teller of this amazingly tall tale appears to be the devil, subverting Holy Writ. The device points to the novel's impressive, but self-endangering hubris. Proud Satan as narrator-creator is a far cry from the amiably disaster-prone, snot-nosed Saleem of *Midnight's Children.* There is about this massive, wilful undertaking a *folie de grandeur* which sends its brilliant comic energy, its fierce satiric powers, and its unmatchable, demonic inventiveness plunging down, on melting wings, towards unreadability.

> Hermione Lee, "Falling towards England," in The Observer, *September 25, 1988, p. 43.*

PATRICK PARRINDER

[In *The Satanic Verses*] Rushdie's prose, by design and also (I suspect) by accident, tends to impede realistic recognition. His favourite mode is caricature. Here, a new character, Rosa Diamond, is introduced:

> I know what a ghost is, the old woman affirmed silently. Her name was Rosa Diamond; she was 88 years old; and she was squinting beakily through her salt-caked bedroom windows, watching the full moon's sea. And I know what it isn't, too, she nodded further, it isn't a scarification or a flapping sheet, so pooh and pish to all *that* bunkum. What's a ghost? Unfinished business, is what.

Without pausing over 'beakily' or the Masefieldian 'salt-caked', we can say that 'scarification' is a malapropism, and it is Rushdie's and not Rosa's, as we learn from other passages in the novel. Poor Rosa's idiom is idiosyncratic indeed if she gets 'pooh', 'pish' and 'bunkum' all into one sentence. Her notion that a ghost is unfinished business will be repeated almost verbatim by one of Rushdie's twin protagonists some hundreds of pages later: he, however, cannot have been privy to Rosa's thoughts. The other protagonist, the Indian filmstar Gibreel Farishta, finds on a visit to London that 'fictions were walking around wherever he went . . . fictions masquerading as real human beings.' In Rushdie's novels they aren't difficult to spot.

This hardly matters, I agree, since his novels have a Dickensian expansiveness and a driving narrative energy. Rushdie may produce baggy monsters, but he is one of the very few current writers whose works are attempts at the greater Bible, the 'bright book of life'. He tends to use a loosely Biblical structure, beginning with a Creation and a Fall and a miraculous birth—in *Midnight's Children* (1981) the build-up is so tremendous that the hero's birth does not happen until page 116—and leading towards some kind of apocalypse: the last section of *Shame* (1983) is entitled 'Judgment Day'. Rushdie's fictive repertoire has mostly been based on the archetypal male figures of the wanderer and the storyteller, and the women who surround them. The storyteller, obviously enough, is a surrogate for the author himself: in *Midnight's Children,* for example, he appears as a bumbling, mock-heroic first-person narrator. The wanderer is a more grandiose but equally self-projective figure.

In Rushdie's first novel, the ungainly *Grimus* (1975), the themes were there but they had not yet found an adequate vehicle. The hero, Flapping Eagle (get it?), is an Axona Indian exiled from the language and the ways of his ancestors. He falls through a 'gate' in space, landing on Thera, a satellite of the Star Nus in the Gorf Nirveesu. Here he is found washed up on the shore and is escorted on his subsequent journey by one Virgil Jones. Much else in this tedious fantasy seems to have been composed by the anagrammatic method or with the help of a mythological dictionary: the title *Grimus,* for example, alludes to the Sufi legend of the Simurg. Rushdie's reputation was made with *Midnight's Children* and *Shame,* which combined fantasy and fairy-tale with social satire and political allegory. Saleem Sinai in *Midnight's Children* is, like Flapping Eagle, gifted with miraculous powers; Flapping Eagle is an orphan, Saleem is a changeling, and Omar Khayyam Shakil in *Shame* has not one but three mothers. These protagonists all become exiles and wanderers, and *The Satanic Verses* reminds us that the archetypal wanderer is the Devil. But the wanderer is also the storyteller, or so the narrator of *Shame* insists: 'I too, like all migrants, am a fantasist. I build imaginary countries and try to impose them on the ones that exist.'

The wanderer-storyteller has invariably suffered a Fall. Like the Fall into the Quotidian which caused Saul Bellow's Herzog so much merriment, we may, if we wish, think of this as an event in the spiritual and political history of our century. Thus in *Midnight's Children* and *Shame* the Fall is the shock of independence, the birth of the new nations of India and Pakistan. In *The Satanic Verses* it is a more general disruption. 'Information got abolished sometime in the 20th-century . . . Since then we've been living in a fairy-story'—or so one of Rushdie's characters tells us. This hits off the carnivalesque note of these novels, but it does not mean that their author has failed to honour the poet's obligation, as stated in *The Satanic Verses* by the satirist Baal, to 'name the unnamable, to point out frauds, to take sides, to start arguments, shape the world and stop it from going to sleep'. The method of *Midnight's Children* and *Shame* may be fabulous rather than informative, but where it matters these novels are unflinchingly political. In *The Satanic Verses* Rushdie turns from the political development of India and Pakistan to the immigrant Asian communities in Britain, and, above all, to the global resurgence of Islamic fundamentalism.

The title refers to a much-disputed incident in the life of the Prophet. Mohammed used to meet and converse with the angel Gabriel on a mountain near Mecca, and the verses of the Koran were dictated to him on these occasions. But one day, as a ninth-century historian tells us, while Mohammed was negotiating with the rulers of Mecca, the Devil 'threw upon his tongue' verses conceding semi-divine status to three local pagan deities. Later Gabriel showed the Prophet his mistake, and the verses were changed to those that now appear in the scriptures. To Western scholars this account shows Mohammed making, and hurriedly correcting, a political blunder. But it also raises puzzling questions about the status of creative and prophetic inspiration, and of those near-neighbours to inspiration—improvisation and what we call forgery. From the standpoint of the faithful the Satanic verses are apocryphal and hence forged, but of course the majority of Western translations of the Islamic scriptures argue that the Koran as a whole is a forgery.

Gibreel Farishta in *The Satanic Verses* is a film-actor specialising in the popular Indian genre movies known as 'theologicals'. In the beginning he and another actor, Saladin Chamcha, fall together from a hijacked airliner which has been blown up over the English Channel at 29,000 feet. The Air India plane was named the *Bostan,* after one of the two gardens of paradise. Gibreel, by flapping his arms (compare Flapping Eagle), is able to slow down their descent so that they fall safely to earth, where they are miraculously 'born again', an angel and a devil respectively. The angel Gibreel spends much of his time dreaming, though in his waking life he begins to suffer from paranoid schizophrenia. His dreams are the source of several of Rushdie's multiply-embedded narratives, and in one of these, set in the Arabian city of Jahilia, the prophet Mahound comes to Gibreel for advice and then, in his next public appearance, speaks the Satanic verses. It is Gibreel this time who admits to a mistake, and who later corrects the prophet.

If Farishta now sports an undeserved halo, Saladin Chamcha sprouts cloven hoofs and a pair of horns. Once they have landed on the Sussex coast Gibreel treacherously disowns his companion, leaving him in the hands of the police, who promptly beat him up. Formerly a well-known London character-actor—he was the source of the outlandish voices on the TV *Aliens Show,* and in advertisements featuring talking crisp-packets and baked-bean cans—Saladin is now a suspected illegal immigrant and a virtual outlaw. Thrown out by his wife, he goes to ground in Brickhall, an Asian district of Inner London. Here racial tension mounts, as Saladin becomes a cult-hero while awaiting his opportunity for revenge on Gibreel. The two meet at last at a wild party in Shepperton Studios, on the set of *Our Mutual Friend;* soon after this Gibreel, further maddened by a spate of anonymous phone calls reflecting Saladin's gifts of tongues and voices, brings rioting and melodrama to the streets of Brickhall. Gibreel is now transformed into Azraeel, the fire-breathing Islamic angel of death. The multiple film-within-a-film effect is typical of Rushdie, whose whole novel could be regarded as a species of 'theological'. And there is more, much more, as (once again) he digs deep into the mythographical bran-tub. The story of Othello, Aladdin and his lamp, the Battle of Hastings, Beauty and the Beast, and the legends of Everest (29,000 feet and all that), all play a part. Fortunately, the limpidity of Rushdie's interpolated tales provides a crucial relief from the pandemonium of his main narrative.

In *Shame,* his most tightly-controlled and perhaps his best novel to date, the burgeoning multiple folk-tale plot was harnessed to a transparently allegorical account of Pakistan's political history. It was as if the *Decameron* or *Arabian Nights* had been yoked with the Sub-Continental equivalent of *Animal Farm. Shame* tells of the overthrow and execution of the former playboy and democratically-elected prime minister, Iskander Harappa, leaving his tough and beautiful daughter, the 'Virgin Ironpants', to become his political heir. Harappa is succeeded by his former army commander General 'Razor Guts' Hyder, a tyrant who undergoes a richly Dickensian process of moral disintegration through guilt before succumbing in his turn to a bloodthirsty, fairy-tale vengeance. How ironic that the real-life General Zia, like Gibreel and

Saladin but not like his counterpart in **Shame,** was to come to grief in a mid-air explosion.

In **Shame** Rushdie uses the novelist's privilege to exaggerate the dynastic nature of Pakistani politics. Almost everyone is related by birth or marriage to everyone else, and the novel begins with a genealogical table. Equally, the author is able to disclose the 'real' manner of Isky Harappa's death (the judicial hanging was solely for public consumption), and to predict his rival's downfall. **The Satanic Verses** looks, rather, at 'Mrs Torture's' England, endowing London with police violence, race-riots and (stretching credulity) with a tropical summer. The narrator's disclosures include the inside story of some brutal murders and the last fatal moments of a hijacking, but his most daring revelations are the theological ones.

Gibreel's dreams, in particular, 'name the unnamable' by portraying a bloodthirsty Imam's seizure of power, the tale of a pilgrimage of Indian villagers who end up drowning in the Arabian Sea, and some ungodly goings-on in Jahilia, the fictive equivalent of Mecca. As Mahound and his followers return from their flight to Yathrib to take over the city, we see two writers—the satirist Baal and his own Persian scribe Salman—becoming the prophet's mortal enemies. (Meanwhile, the inmates of the local brothel cheekily impersonate the prophet's 12 wives.) Salman finally admits to having changed the wording of some of Mahound's revelations, but saves his own skin by betraying Baal. Is there any way of escaping this fundamentalist universe—the universe as dreamed by Gibreel—or is a little verbal tinkering the best that can be done? Saladin Chamcha finally leaves behind his demonic powers, going off with a woman whose last words are 'Let's get the hell out of here.' Another woman, Gibreel's ex-lover Alleluia Cone, has turned herself into an intrepid mountaineer and Everest-explorer in order, as she hopes, to rise above good and evil: but she fails, so far as we can tell, since Gibreel in the end sends her prematurely to paradise. In a reversal of the story of *Paradise Lost,* it is Gibreel who gradually degenerates into a bringer of death, while Saladin finds some sort of redemption: but this, after all, is the Devil's version. It is all damnably entertaining, and fiendishly ingenious.

Rushdie wrote in **Shame** that 'every story one chooses to tell is a kind of censorship, it prevents the telling of other tales.' His own profuse and multiply-branching fictions do not give the impression that anything has been prevented from being told. (pp. 11-12)

Patrick Parrinder, "Let's Get the Hell Out of Here," in London Review of Books, *Vol. 10, No. 17, September 29, 1988, pp. 11-13.*

IAIN SINCLAIR

The Satanic Verses are obviously intended to hit the Booker scales with an irresistible thump: an offer that can't be refused . . . Big themes enacted on a global scale, the decaying fabric of society, good and evil . . . Magic! What we've got here isn't a mere novel . . . it's an investment. The arrival, the second coming, after all the teasings by supplement, the foreplay of retrospective interviews, the mugshots of Salman coyly hiding behind cheques, is inevitably something of a downer. No word-stud could live up to those promises—

even after five years hard labour and a text dredged from Rushdie's "entire sense of being in the world".

The hook, for anyone returning from a polar voyage, is a nice one and you'll be meeting it in all the reviews by hacks unethical enough to skim the stuff about visionary prophets, mad poets, desert sects and sand. A hijacked Air India continent-hopper disintegrates over the English Channel and the twinned saga-heroes, the Manichaean double-act, ungrateful as Laurel and Hardy, fall, locked together and chanting, unharmed onto a snowy beach. (p. 40)

The rebirth of these fabulous immigrants is achieved in a rapturous deluge of similes. The ex-jumbo, for example, is likened to a "seed-pod", an "egg", an "old cigar". So that the cumulative effect is to submerge the reader in oleaginous prose; an amniotic bath in which past and future slide over each other, textually replete, lush and sparkling, but almost impossible to bring into sharp focus.

The pair are soon separated: they slouch, angel and devil, down the *via dolorosa* of enterprise culture towards London, to be aborted rather than born. The mythic city they enter has been edited from newscasts and *Guardian* fillers: inner city riots, the Brick Lane Messiah—and plenty of conventional naughtiness from Special Branch. . . . Obedient stereotypes are drawn irresistibly through the mirror of their own narcissism. The authorial voice is so uniformly decent in its attitude towards the mean-spirited culture with which it seems forced to deal that one reader began to find himself guiltily longing to get back to the malign and centrifugal rhetoric of the old headbanger Céline.

London is reduced, finally, to no more than the film-set of another Dickens musical. . . . The myth of the "internationalisation" of British fiction began with **Midnight's Children:** this set might be a good place to bury it.

Rushdie's undoubted narrative skills, his good humour and boisterous characterisations, are overwhelmed by the crows perched on his shoulder, the agents and deal-makers who encourage him to invoke symbols of vastness and eternity . . . Go for it, Salman . . . Everest, ice-maidens, butterfly-shrouds, deserts, oceans. All the leaps and risks of his unfettered imagination are countered by a modest eschewal of originality in the basic armature, the imploding and exploding chain of serial fables.

He draws on well-worn dreams: David Niven floating down to the beach in Michael Powell's *A Matter of Life and Death:* Mervyn Peake's *Mr Pye,* with his horns and wings, his whimsical ways: Nathanael West's tinsel town apocalypse. Rushdie shares with Wim Wenders the knowledge that celestial messengers are among us. In the midnight terror of the rush towards the millennium our conditioned reflexes are inhibited. We are beginning to see the sights that the visionaries have always talked about.

But Salman Rushdie is not of that company. He is too civilised, too urbane, too self-consciously an artist. His hobby, we learn, is to pick imaginary football teams. With **The Satanic Verses** I hope he has not made the kind of Faustian deal that took Terry Venables to Tottenham. A collection of rented spare parts, however much they cost, will never be anything else without a living heart and soul. (pp. 40-1)

Iain Sinclair, "Imaginary Football Teams," in New

Statesman & Society, *Vol. 1, No. 17, September 30, 1988, pp. 40-1.*

ROBERT IRWIN

There is no evidence in Salman Rushdie's fourth novel of any flagging of the author's inventive powers; quite the contrary, an alarming increase. Rushdie is possessed by a storytelling demon. *The Satanic Verses* takes its title from a well-known incident in the life of the Prophet Muhammad. The Prophet came under pressure from the citizens of Mecca to moderate his unbending monotheism and to accommodate his new faith to the traditional polytheism, especially the cult of three local goddesses. Obligingly, he came up with the convenient verses, "Have ye considered al-Lat and al-Uzza, and Manat, the third, the other? These are the swans exalted, whose intercession is to be hoped for." The Meccans were naturally delighted, but very shortly afterwards Muhammad received a true Koranic revelation from the Archangel Gabriel. He then revoked the compromising verses, stigmatizing them as dictation from the Devil.

"There was. There was not", as Arab storytellers traditionally begin. Rushdie gives us a story not about Muhammad, but the Prophet Mahound, a story not about Mecca but the city of Jahilia ("paganism" or "ignorance" in Arabic), not about "Islam" but about the religion of "Submission", not about the Archangel Gabriel, but about a fretfully dreaming native of Bombay, Gibreel, who in his dreams finds himself forced to act as simultaneous Archangel and Devil to the demanding Mahound. . . . The tale is full of sentiment and colour, flashing eyes and waggling hips. Mahound is opposed by the witchy Hind, uncrowned queen of the aristocratic Shark tribe of Jahilia. Later, the opposition is joined by an erstwhile disciple, Salman the Persian, who has become disillusioned by the transformation of Mahound the Mystic into Mahound the Law Giver. At the centre of this strange fable about the incompatibility of poetic revelation and religious revelation stands the poet Baal. It is a superb story, a brilliant novella in its own right.

Just as events in long-ago Jahilia echo in distorted fashion the true story of the origins of Islam, so that story in turn has echoes and half-echoes in the later story of the Imam, a grim religious bigot in exile in London (who is and is not the Ayatollah Khomeini in exile in Paris) and his uncompromising struggle against the westernized Ayesha, Empress of contemporary Jahilia. Here Rushdie offers us a finely observed portrait of an exile whose vision is so blinkered, and so narrowly focused on the demands of religion and vengeance, that in a sense he does not inhabit London and has never left his homeland. It ends in apocalypse, one apocalypse among the many, great and small, that punctuate *The Satanic Verses*. Again, the story has been dreamed up by Gibreel.

A third tale unfolds in Gibreel's dreams. Set in contemporary India, it is the tale of the impact on a small community of a visionary butterfly-eating girl who summons the villagers to set out on pilgrimage for Mecca. If they will follow her, forsaking all that they have, then, when they arrive at the sea, the waves will part before them and dry-shod they will walk on towards Mecca. This mysterious Indo-Muslim version of the Children's Crusade completes Rushdie's trilogy on the theme of religion and its inexorable, unwelcome and dubious demands. One may guess that Rushdie sympathizes with the doubting Salman and the despairing Baal, but in another part of the novel he has one of his characters argue that "We can't deny the ubiquity of faith. If we write in such a way as to prejudge such belief as in some way deluded or false, then are we not guilty of élitism, of imposing our world-view on the masses?"

These enigmatic and engrossing parables, long short stories, are embedded in a frame story. . . . The frame story, concerning the intertwined destinies of Gibreel Farishta and Saladin Chamcha, is much longer and more complex than the stories it frames (and it feeds into and draws on the framed stories), and it is with their epic saga that the novel opens. . . . [In] some mysterious way they have been chosen, as rivals and friends, to incarnate the ambiguous forces of good and evil.

The story of the working out of the evil and good that they do defies sensible summary. . . . There are marvellous things in it, most notably another separately framed story concerning Gibreel's entrapment in an English widow's memories of her youth on the Argentinian pampas, an entrancing narrative of romance and flashing knives, equipped with multiple endings (shades of *The French Lieutenant's Woman*).

Rushdie is endlessly inventive. Yet somehow the frame story is less satisfying than the stories it frames. . . . Saladin Chamcha and Gibreel Farishta only seem to know who they are by seeing what they have done. So the chronicle of their adventures seems confusingly arbitrary in its development, and it poses problems for the reader which have nothing to do with metaphysics or ethics. There are perhaps praiseworthy reasons for the apparent lack of structure. Just as it is difficult for a writer to portray a dull dinner party interestingly, it may well be that an attempt to show how good and evil are confounded in people's acts and motives will be confusing in itself. Also, arbitrariness may come from Rushdie's stated aim (possibly disingenuous and surely impossible) to allow his protagonists freedom of will. This is a God-like decision on the part of the novelist and, as God, Rushdie inserts himself in his novel (shades of *The French Lieutenant's Woman* again).

In the absence of a more formal structure, the novel is held together by a bemusing cat's cradle of cross-referenced names and images. . . . Once an image, pun or reference has been brought into play, Rushdie gallops off with it in all directions. The reader may find himself exhausted, but he is never in danger of being bored. In *The Satanic Verses* Rushdie has created a fictional universe whose centre is everywhere and whose circumference is nowhere. It is several of the best novels he has ever written.

Robert Irwin, *"Original Parables," in* The Times Literary Supplement, *No. 4461, September 30-October 6, 1988, p. 1067.*

LEWIS JONES

A character in *The Satanic Verses* says "Columbus was right, maybe, the world's made up of Indies, East, West, North." Salman Rushdie's latest novel takes this rudimentary geographical notion, of a global, all-swallowing India, and carries it into the realms of psychology and poetry. His characters may travel as far as the fabled city of Ellowen Deeowen (our city, transformed by orthographic incantation: "l", "o", "n", "d", "o", "n"); but they arrive to find only a perplexing outpost of home.

In India, the narrator assures us, "the human population outnumbers the divine by less than three to one". The work of Gibreel Farishta, one of the story's two leading characters, is to impersonate the divine population for the delectation of the human: he is a film actor, a star of the "Bombay talkies". Specialising in "theologicals", Gibreel makes half a dozen feature films a week, playing innumerable deities and demons.

The other main character, Saladin Chamcha, is also an actor. Ardent anglophile and naturalised Brit, his bread and butter is voice-overs for advertisements. Superbly qualified for this task by the protective mimicry which has facilitated his assimilation into the English establishment, Saladin can speak in any register, any accent. Recently he has begun to enjoy greater success, as the star of a children's TV programme which sounds like a cross between *The Muppet Show* and *Max Headroom*. Caked in make-up and aided by state-of-the-art graphics, he plays the part of a comic alien.

Rushdie translates these two genres into literary terms. *The Satanic Verses* has all the characteristics of a hack Indian film: it is done in garishly artificial colour and with an insistently blaring soundtrack; it has a grotesquely implausible plot, energetically wooden performances and a frantically coy approach to sex. From time to time, though, the novelist gives us a nudge to show that he is, in the approved postmodern fashion, aware of the awfulness of his production—he invites us to share the joke.

This literary knowingness—"it was and it was not so"; "it happened and it never did"—turns the naive into the *faux naif* and raises the "tawdry shamming" of a low-budget film to the Parnassian heights of *The Muppet Show*. The author has, however, made a notable contribution to "magic realism", the sophisticated school of fiction pioneered by Emma Tennant, Fay Weldon and Angela Carter.

For those unfamiliar with the aesthetic tenets of this school, Rushdie obligingly has one of his characters offer an unusually frank explanation: "I am an intelligent female. I have read *Finnegans Wake* and am conversant with post-modernist critiques of the West, e.g. that we have here a society capable only of pastiche: a 'flattened' world . . . I am entering Flatland knowingly, understanding what I'm doing and why. Viz, I am earning cash." . . .

Rural India and post-Biblical Arabia serve as historic relief to the main story—the antics of G and S in London. When describing the city Rushdie achieves a standard of flatness which will reduce his rival magical realists to gasping admiration. The reader is arrested by such gems as "the cathedrals of the Industrial Revolution", and waits impatiently for the comparison to be made explicit: "the railway termini of north London"! Ah, the shock of the old!

The same admirable consistency is to be found in the jokes that litter this novel like so many elephant droppings. . . .

The trouble is that those cunningly posited alternatives—"it was and it was not so"; "it happened and it never did"—do not in fact arise. The reader has not one moment of doubt; it was not so; it never happened. If only it had never been written. . . .

Lewis Jones, "All the Magic of the Muppets," in The

Illustrated London News, *Vol. 276, No. 7083, October, 1988, p. 88.*

DAVID DEVADAS

BANNED. The word dropped like a bombshell last fortnight, sending shock waves pulsing through literary circles and the liberal world at large. Import [into India] of Salman Rushdie's latest novel *The Satanic Verses* had been banned. The Government had given in to pressure from Muslim leaders who argued that the book vilified their religion. Appalled, Rushdie said: "India is rapidly forfeiting its right to be called a democracy."

India has rarely banned books in the past, generally preferring to stall them with red tape at customs. (p. 72)

But things are obviously changing. While some of these books caused a rumpus in Parliament and others like *Lady Chatterley's Lover* were finally banned by courts, this time the Government pre-empted all discussion. . . . The book uses allegorical dreams and historical metaphor to examine the thin line between good and evil, dogmatism and distortions in perception.

The reaction was irate. Calling it "a deliberate insult to Islam and the holy prophet and an intentional device to outrage religious feelings", Janata MP Syed Shahabuddin held that it was "not an act of literary creativity". He said "you just have to read it" to know that, but added that he had not.

Not everyone was as unreasonable. There were those who argued cogently that the book acutely hurt their sensibilities. Congress(I) MP Khurshid Alam Khan meticulously marked objectionable parts. "I agree with freedom of expression but that does not mean that you hurt somebody's feelings," he said. In the tense communal mood prevailing, it could have ignited passions. Already, he noted, the Rashtriya Swayamsewak Sangh's *Organiser* had excerpted offensive portions and the Urdu daily *Nai Duniya* had responded angrily.

Though their reasons differed, a variety of Muslim leaders got together in late September to have the book banned. Visiting the Home Ministry every second day, the group met Home Minister Buta Singh and Minister of State for Home P. Chidambaram. Normally, such decisions take much longer but the ministry moved fast to placate these men. (pp. 72-3)

The delegation included a variety of Muslim politicians, ranging from the Indian Union Muslim League's Sulaiman Sait to the Congress(I)'s Khan.

If by placating them the ruling party shored up its electoral prospects, it lost points among the liberal intelligentsia in the bargain. Senior Advocate Soli Sorabjee called it "yet another surrender to forces of fundamentalism and intolerance". . . .

Veteran diplomat Badruddin Tyabji waxed eloquent. "It seems suspiciously like a *coup de theatre* in a comedy played by a group of deaf actors under the direction of a blind director. The blind have not read the script and the deaf only understand the sign language of the election-hustings." He added that the consequences were likely to be "exactly the contrary of what they proclaim". Clearly, pirated editions will flourish and many more will read it than would normally have. Already, the owner of a copy in Delhi was "getting five calls a day from people who want to read it".

The worst part of this prurient interest, as Tyabji points out, is that "the allegedly offending chapters in the book will be torn out of context and devoured by hordes of babu-English illiterates, who would otherwise have contentedly confined their reading to the daily newspaper headlines. And the less they are capable of understanding the purport and thrust of the whole book, the more agitated they will become". . . .

The Government is on slippery ground. This, after all, is a work of art which uses metaphors from Islamic lore to discuss larger themes. Nor is religion the only theme. Rushdie also felt the ire of English tabloids, incensed at his acid critique of racism in Thatcherite Britain. . . .

Not all supporters of free speech unequivocally opposed the ban though. The very real danger of riots weighed heavily with them. Cartoonist Abu Abraham . . . said: "We haven't reached a stage when people can take such things." Just two years ago, a mob attacked the Bangalore office of *The Deccan Herald* because a short story headline was considered offensive.

O. V. Vijayan, well-known Malayalam writer, shook his head sadly: "I would prefer the ban to the Bangalore type of riots. But that raises the question—aren't we a barbarian society still?" That question must surely agitate all Indians interested in the free flow of ideas as fundamentalism of various hues gets steadily stronger. (p. 73)

> David Devadas, "Salman Rushdie: Political Scapegoat," in India Today, Vol. XIII, No. 20, October 31, 1988, pp. 72-3.

JONATHAN C. RANDAL

LONDON, Jan. 17—Winner of Whitbread's $36,000 prize for 1988's best British novel—with 40,000 copies of [*The Satanic Verses*] sold in Britain alone—Salman Rushdie scarcely needed the publicity that has come his way in the past few days.

But the book's two allegedly blasphemous dream sequences and the 550-page novel's title proved enough to get *Satanic Verses* set alight in a ritual book burning in Bradford [England] last Saturday, at an angry demonstration organized by leaders of that West Yorkshire city's large Moslem population.

The book burning—and subsequent events—have focused Establishment attention on the more intolerant side of sections of Britain's 2 million-strong Moslem community, often praised for its hard work, close family ties and law-abiding nature. . . .

Prominently displayed photographs of the book in flames were part of extensive media coverage of the decision by W H Smith, Britain's biggest bookselling chain, to withdraw *Satanic Verses* from two Bradford shops on the advice of police who took threats to Smith's staff and property seriously.

Banned in Pakistan, Saudi Arabia and Rushdie's native India soon after it was published [in Great Britain] last September, *Satanic Verses* had prompted only limited attention among the general public despite earlier demonstrations organized

here by radical Islamic fundamentalist groups demanding its withdrawal. . . .

"People in the Islamic world will go to great lengths to prevent free expression and prefer burning books to reading them," Rushdie said in a telephone interview. "But the image of book-burning in Britain in 1989 horrified lots of people who are disturbed by this central iconic image of barbarism.

"Although the campaign had been going on for several months," he added, "this simple image of a burning book finally alerted people in this country to something extremely dangerous and ugly, even people who cannot stand me as a writer."

The controversial title and dream sequences turn on two verses that the prophet Mohammed is said to have removed from the Koran, believing they had been inspired by Satan masquerading as the angel Gabriel.

W H Smith's initial announcement that the book was being withdrawn from shops because of allegedly waning sales—rather than because of threats—only made matters worse.

Editorials in establishment newspapers castigated both religious intolerance and W H Smith's decisions. . . .

[Rushdie] charged that "a very carefully orchestrated campaign is being run by a number of extremists centered on the Regents Park mosque" in London thanks to "considerable Saudi and Iranian funding."

He said he and his American publisher, Viking, had received "fairly extreme threats" from people "who had not bothered to read the book." He expected similar pressures with publication now underway in the United States and said "Viking has taken precautions," which he declined to spell out.

Asked if he had expected the novel to provoke such turmoil, he said,

> "It is a fairly radical critique of Islam seen from a secular humanistic point of view.
>
> "I expected those with absolute literalist views would dissent strongly from what I had written. I was not writing to please the mullahs of Pakistan, Saudi Arabia, Iran, Britain or the U.S., and I knew I was breaking long-enshrined taboos.
>
> "But I did not anticipate the size, nature and ugliness of the protest."

He said that "rather sadly, the whole debate had centered on a very small part of the novel" whose main theme is the "migration from one culture to another and the metamorphoses and hybridization that result."

> Jonathan C. Randal, "Rushdie's Book Burned in Britain," in The Washington Post, January 18, 1989.

SALMAN RUSHDIE

Muhammad ibn Abdallah, one of the great geniuses of world history, a successful businessman, victorious general and sophisticated statesman as well as a prophet, insisted throughout his life on his simple humanity. There are no contemporary portraits of him because he feared that, if any were made, people would worship the portraits. He was only the messenger; it was the message that should be revered.

As to the revelation itself, it caused Muhammad considerable anguish. Sometimes he heard voices; sometimes he saw visions; sometimes, he said, the words were found in his inmost heart, and at such times their production caused him acute physical pain. When the revelations began he feared for his sanity and only after reassurances from his wife and friends did he accept that he was the recipient of the divine gift of the Word.

The religion which Muhammad established differs from Christianity in several important respects: the Prophet is not granted divine status, but the text is. It's worth pointing out, too, that Islam requires neither a collective act of worship nor an intercessionary caste of priests. The faithful communicate directly with their God.

Nowadays, however, a powerful tribe of clerics has taken over Islam. These are the contemporary Thought Police. They have turned Muhammad into a perfect being, his life into a perfect life, his revelation into the unambiguous, clear event it originally was not. Powerful taboos have been erected. One may not discuss Muhammad as if he were human, with human virtues and weaknesses. One may not discuss the growth of Islam as a historical phenomenon, as an ideology born out of its time. These are the taboos against which *The Satanic Verses* has transgressed (these and one other; I also tried to write about the place of women in Islamic society, and in the Koran). It is for this breach of taboo that the novel is being anathematised, fulminated against and set alight.

Dr Aadam Aziz, the patriarch in my novel *Midnight's Children,* loses his faith and is left with 'a hole inside him, a vacancy in a vital inner chamber'. I, too, possess the same God-shaped hole. Unable to accept the unarguable absolutes of religion, I have tried to fill up the hole with literature. The art of the novel is a thing I cherish as dearly as the bookburners of Bradford value their brand of militant Islam. Literature is where I go to explore the highest and lowest places in human society and in the human spirit, where I hope to find not absolute truth but the truth of the tale, of the imagination and of the heart. So the battle over *The Satanic Verses* is a clash of faiths, in a way. Or, more precisely, it's a clash of languages. As my fictional character 'Salman' says of my fictional prophet 'Mahound', 'It's his Word against mine.'

In this War of the Word, the guardians of religious truth have been telling their followers a number of lies. I am accused, for example, of calling Muhammad the devil. This is because I use the name Mahound which, long ago, was indeed used as a derogatory term. But my novel tries in all sorts of ways to reoccupy negative images, to repossess pejorative language, and on page 93 explains: 'To turn insults into strengths, whigs, tories, Blacks all chose to wear with pride the names they were given in scorn; likewise, our mountain-climbing, prophet-motivated solitary is to be . . . Mahound.'

Even the novel's title has been termed blasphemous; but the phrase is not mine. It comes from al-Tabari, one of the canonical Islamic sources. Tabari writes: 'When the Messenger of God saw his people draw away from him . . . he would gladly have seen those things that bore too harshly on them softened a little.'

Muhammad then received verses which accepted the three favourite Meccan goddesses as intercessionary agents. Mec-

cans were delighted. Later, the Archangel Gabriel told Muhammad that these had been 'Satanic verses', falsely inspired by the Devil in disguise and they were removed from the Koran. . . .

The Muslim world is full of censors these days, and many of its greatest writers have been forced into silence, exile or submission. (The Joycean option of cunning seems unavailable at present). To find Labour councillors in Bradford, and Labour MPs in Westminster joining forces with the mullahs is hugely depressing. . . .

The Satanic Verses is not, in my view, an anti-religious novel. It is, however, an attempt to write about migration, its stresses and transformations, from the point of view of migrants from the Indian subcontinent to Britain. This is, for me, the saddest irony of all; that after working for five years to give voice and fictional flesh to the immigrant culture of which I am myself a member, I should see my book burned, largely unread, by the people it's about, people who might find some pleasure and much recognition in its pages. I tried to write against stereotypes; the zealot protests serve to confirm, in the Western mind, all the worst stereotypes of the Muslim world.

How fragile civilisation is; how easily, how merrily a book burns! Inside my novel, its characters seek to become fully human by facing up to the great facts of love, death and (with or without God) the life of the soul. Outside it, the forces of inhumanity are on the march. 'Battle lines are being drawn up in India today,' one of my characters remarks. 'Secular versus religious, the light versus the dark. Better you choose which side you are on.' Now that the battle has spread to Britain, I can only hope it will not be lost by default. It is time for us to choose.

> Salman Rushdie, *"Choice between Light and Dark," in* The Observer, *January 22, 1989, p. 11.*

MICHIKO KAKUTANI

[*The Satanic Verses*] deals only incidentally with Islam. Indeed, the figure Mahound (who some critics say is a thinly and perversely disguised representation of the Prophet) turns out to be a character in the dream of another character, who may or may not be suffering from mental illness—a bit player in Mr. Rushdie's play within a play within a play. . . .

The Satanic Verses is less concerned with history than with the broader questions of good and evil, identity and metamorphosis, race and culture. As in [Rushdie's] earlier novels, allusions (to everything from *The Thousand and One Nights* to *Paradise Lost* to *Tristram Shandy*) proliferate throughout the text, while the tone of the novel veers daringly from the slapstick to the melodramatic.

The story begins simply enough with a miracle. A plane flying over England is exploded by a hijacker's bomb, and two men, amazingly, survive. The first is Gibreel Farishta, one of India's biggest movie stars, who has made a fortune playing the subcontinent's deities in the popular genre films known as theologicals. The second is Saladin Chamcha, a radio celebrity known as "the Man of a Thousand Voices and a Voice." They fall to earth, believing themselves dead, only to discover that they're very much alive—though in decidedly changed form. Gibreel has sprouted a halo, while Saladin has grown horns and a tail.

In the wake of the accident, Gibreel comes to believe that he is really the archangel Gabriel, a heavenly messenger sent by God to redeem the fallen city of London. He wanders the streets searching for lost souls, and he falls prey to strange dreams. One dream—and this is the one that has reportedly upset Muslim leaders—concerns Mahound, a businessman turned prophet, who preaches to Jahilia, a city built entirely of sand. A second dream features an orphan girl by the name of Ayesha who walks in a cloud of butterflies and leads the faithful on a difficult pilgrimage. Friends force Gibreel to accept the fact that he's mentally unbalanced, and they persuade him to return to work in the movies. This time he is to play the archangel himself, a role that enables Mr. Rushdie to build several additional halls of mirrors in his narrative.

Saladin, meanwhile, has been arrested as an illegal immigrant, then taken up as a kind of hero by a group of would-be devil worshipers. He discovers that his English wife, Pamela, has begun an affair with his best friend, that his father has remarried, that his whole life is not what it seems. What Saladin's unwanted rebirth as a devil has done is to force him to re-evaluate his entire existence, to re-examine the other changes he once willed in his life: his flight from Bombay and his family, his attempts to erase his Indian identity, his efforts to remake himself as the perfect English gentleman—with an expensive education, a proper accent and a pretty upper-class wife. . . .

There is something personal and touching about Saladin's search for his misplaced self. The scenes in which he visits a former Indian girlfriend and his dying father possess an immediacy and emotional power that's missing in the rest of this sprawling book; and his attempts to come to terms with the cultural and social dislocations wrought by his self-invention perfectly encapsulate the novel's central theme of metamorphosis. In fact, it often seems as though the bulk of *The Satanic Verses* is an elaborate work of decoration embroidered on top of Saladin's story—decoration that allows Mr. Rushdie to engage, rather self-indulgently, in all manner of narrative pyrotechnics.

To be sure, some of his conjuring tricks are magical: a couple of Gibreel's dreams have the inventiveness of the tales told by Scheherazade; and several of his and Saladin's adventures, as an angel and devil wandering the streets of London, have the comic brio of a 1940's movie. All in all, however, *The Satanic Verses* lacks the fierce visionary power that gave *Midnight's Children* such an organic, inclusive feel. As a result, the reader frequently suspects that in this volume, Mr. Rushdie is simply using the freedom conferred by magical realism as a license to avoid recounting a more straightforward tale.

There is a fine story somewhere in this volume—that of Saladin and his attempts to define a self that might embrace both the present and the past—but it doesn't take 500-plus pages to tell.

> *Michiko Kakutani, in a review of "The Satanic Verses," in* The New York Times, *January 27, 1989.*

JONATHAN YARDLEY

Salman Rushdie's [*The Satanic Verses*] has been banned in his native India as politically incendiary and honored in his adopted England as winner of the Whitbread Prize for 1988. Both actions prove nothing so much as the human capacity to overreact. The government of Rajiv Gandhi brings no honor to itself in proscribing *The Satanic Verses,* indeed if anything has assured Rushdie a larger readership than he might otherwise have received had the book been allowed to go without official notice. As for those who choose the Whitbread Prize, they seem to have been motivated more by sympathy for Rushdie's rights as a writer than by his actual accomplishment in this, his fourth novel; for the truth is that by comparison with its two immediate predecessors, *The Satanic Verses* is an odd, uninvolving book that shows only intermittent flashes of its author's considerable gifts.

The weird thing about India's suppression of *The Satanic Verses* is that, by comparison with *Midnight's Children* and *Shame,* it is a relatively nonpolitical book. It contains, to be sure, scenes of political conflict and a stinging depiction of Islamic fundamentalism—not to mention occasional outbursts of garden-variety anti-Americanism—but it is at heart a philosophical novel about the tangled relationship between good and evil, the angelic and the satanic, and it weighs that relationship more in human than in ideological terms. Whereas the central subject of *Midnight's Children* was the troubled birth of India, and that of *Shame* the betrayal by its leaders of a country much like Pakistan, *The Satanic Verses* reaches for vast, universal subjects and treats them for the most part in cosmic rather than localized terms.

As is so often true of fiction that aches with ambition, *The Satanic Verses* reaches for more than is within its grasp. It is smart, energetic, protean and clamorous, but its diverse elements never merge into a cohesive whole and it never engages the reader in the lives and hearts of its characters; for all the feeling that Rushdie expresses through these characters, the novel remains peculiarly cold and distant, more an exercise in pyrotechnical fiction than a recreation of human life in its individuality and community. . . .

What is angelic, and what satanic? Is Gibreel holy, and Saladin malign? Or are there both good and evil in each of them, in degrees the precise nature and manifestations of which can only be guessed at?

These are the central questions with which the novel struggles, though hardly the only ones, and Gibreel and Saladin are scarcely the sole figures through which Rushdie's imagination seeks expression. Each man dreams, fantasizes and hallucinates, and in these "night-sagas" much of the novel's action takes place: in a place called Jahilia, a city of sand, where a prophet named Mahound "is founding one of the world's great religions"; in London, where various antagonistic forces clash violently; in India itself, where the residents of a village are lured by a hypnotic woman to lemming-like self-destruction.

There is also, in the "real" world both men inhabit, a woman of astonishing beauty bearing the unlikely name of Allelulia Cone; she is "the golden girl from the roof of the world," a conqueror of Everest whose challenge to her lover Gibreel—"change your life, or did you get it back for nothing"—draws him under her eerie, chilly spell. Soon Saladin too is sucked in, and they become "a triangle of fictions" in which the line between reality and fantasy is so blurred as to be invisible, and thus in which reality and fantasy become one and the same.

The phrase for this, as all students of contemporary fiction well know, is "magical realism." Rushdie is an accomplished practitioner of the genre, and he hauls out all its tricks in **The Satanic Verses.** But apart from the peculiar bloodlessness of the novel, it suffers from a lack of real originality and an excess of transparency. On almost every page Rushdie's influences beg to be acknowledged—notable among them being Garcia Marquez, Borges and Pynchon—and everywhere the reader is too much aware of the author so busily at work: leaping back and forth between "real" worlds and dreams, moving his characters across the vast gameboard he has constructed, demanding that we gasp and applaud at his ability to shoot off firecrackers. In the end, though, what he produces is not astonishment but exhaustion.

> *Jonathan Yardley, "Wrestling with the Angel," in* Book World—The Washington Post, *January 29, 1989, p. 3.*

A. G. MOJTABAI

Salman Rushdie, author most famously of **Midnight's Children,** opens his fourth and latest novel, **Satanic Verses,** with a scene of human figures tumbling from the debris of a hijacked jumbo jetliner. The plane is named Bostan, which is both a Farsi word for garden and the title of the great didactic poem by the 13th-century Persian poet Sadi, proclaiming the virtues of justice, benevolence, self-restraint, gratitude, penitence and so on. This detail is not insignificant in Mr. Rushdie's work, where each act of naming is dense with implication. And the name "Bostan" might prompt us to ask, *isn't this* precisely what the fabled Oriental garden has become in our day—a terrorized, disintegrating jumbo jet?

Falling slowly over the English Channel, the sole survivors are a strange twosome: Gibreel Farishta and Saladin Chamcha. . . .

The two men are "conjoined opposites" in relation to one another and within themselves. Gibreel (Gabriel), who has a halo—an angelic countenance without, treachery and poisonous jealousy within—will do the work of Azraeel, the angel of death, as his radiance intensifies to consuming fire. Chamcha, a suffering mass of misunderstood, kindly intentions, will exact a terrible revenge before the end. Interestingly, it is only when Chamcha begins to vent his anger and rage that his satanic stigmata start to disappear.

The book moves with Gibreel and Chamcha from their past lives in Bombay to London, and back to Bombay again. For Gibreel, there is many an imaginary journey on the way—most notably to a city of sand called Jahilia (for ignorance), where a very decent, embattled businessman-turned-prophet by the name of Mahound is rising to prominence. . . .

Gibreel's adventures are more interior. He pursues his latest love (a beautiful mountain climber named Alleluia Cone), begins to stage a comeback as an actor, but mainly he broods and dreams. Gibreel's dreams, the nightmares that "leak into his waking life," form the spinoff narratives that keep the novel whirling.

One of the most vivid of these concerns an epileptic woman, a seer, who leads a pilgrimage to Mecca, a tale evoking the Sufi theme of the immolation of the moth, the Exodus account (with the promise of the Arabian Sea parting for the pilgrims), the Pied Piper, Jonestown and other more recent religio-political movements in which the faithful follow a charismatic leader into the depths of destruction. There are many magical embellishments: The pilgrims follow a cloud of butterflies by day; their leader is literally clothed in butterflies, and feeds upon them for her sustenance. Her name is Ayesha, which is—but only coincidentally here, I think—the name of the youngest and favorite wife of the prophet Mohammed.

Which brings us to the controversial part of the book—the tales of Mahound and Jahilia that embroider upon the life of Mohammed and the founding of Islam. Indeed, the title **The Satanic Verses** refers to an incident in the life of Mohammed, recorded by two early Arab historians (al-Waqidi, A.D. 747-823, and at-Tabari, A.D. c. 839-923), discredited by later commentators on the Koran, but taken up in Western accounts as the "lapse of Mohammed" or his "compromise with idolatry." (p. 3)

Mr. Rushdie's revival of this story, the duplicitous Gibreel/Satan agonizing over his role in the incident, compounded by the story of a scribe who deliberately placed erroneous words into his transcription of the Koran, was bound to touch an angry nerve in the world of Islam, where the Koran ("al-qu'ran" means "the recitation") is believed to be the word of God, transmitted without error.

And, to be sure, **The Satanic Verses** has sparked bitter controversy among Muslims in South Africa, where the author was prevented from appearing at a book fair by arson and death threats against all concerned with the event. Last fall the importation of the British edition of the book was banned in India as a precautionary measure against religious leaders using it to incite their followers to sectarian violence. Recently, the publisher's New York office has received several bomb threats and many angry letters.

As with Martin Scorsese's film *The Last Temptation of Christ,* much of the outrage has been fueled by hearsay. Some of the noisiest objections have been raised by people who have never read the book and have no intention of ever reading it. This opposition does little to educate a woefully ignorant and prejudiced Western public about the Islamic faith. Banning the book only increases its notoriety: it answers nothing. And there are, I think, real problems in the text that need to be addressed.

Let us consider two issues by way of example:

One of the furor-provoking episodes crops up in Gibreel's story "Return to Jahilia," where the women of a brothel called the Curtain decide to improve their trade by impersonating the wives of the Prophet. What the objectors have overlooked here is that the entire episode is one of Gibreel's dreams, a cinematic fantasy. Prior to his return to Jahilia, he signed a contract "for a series of films both historical and contemporary" based on his dreams. Granted, the brothel episode is rather too consciously elaborated to be convincingly dreamlike. As a cinematic fantasy based on a dream, however, it seems all too plausible. The script may strike the reader as tasteless, but this poor taste is an accurate satiric reflection of the state of much contemporary cinema.

Deeper ground for puzzlement, if not complaint, lies elsewhere—particularly in the choice of the name "Mahound" for Mohammed. In the medieval Christian mystery plays,

Mahound (spelled variously "Mahowne," "Mahon," "Mahum" or "Mahun") is sometimes the friend of Pontius Pilate or Caesar, sometimes the friend or cousin of Herod, but always a satanic figure. (The name "Mahound" seems to have been created by the conflation of "Mahomet" and "hound.") How are we to understand the adoption—by a writer born a Muslim—of so defamatory a name for the prophet of Islam? And how are we to account for Mr. Rushdie's incorporation of this name into the creed of Islam: "There is no God except Al-Lah, and Mahound is his Prophet"?

To understand the shock of this, Westerners might try a satanic substitution in the text of the Nicene Creed. Few orthodox Christians would find the alteration a laughing matter.

So why Mahound?

Again, it must be remembered that this is fiction. "It was so, it was not." . . . as the storytellers say. More precisely, this is a dream within a fiction — *twice* removed from the actual. Before his ill-fated flight, the dreamer, Gibreel, had a crisis in faith and did a lot of reading. And the insanity defense might be invoked, although it tends to explain away and diminish his visions. Gibreel is, we are told, in the grip of "paranoid schizophrenia."

Yet, clearly, something more programmatic is afoot here. In a direct aside to the reader, the author offers this by way of explanation:

> Here he [the prophet in Gibreel's dream] is neither Mahomet nor MoeHammered; has adopted, instead, the demon-tag the farangis [Europeans or foreigners] hung around his neck. To turn insults into strengths, whigs, tories, Blacks all choose to wear with pride the names they were given in scorn.

A sort of self-immunization, then? But it doesn't work like this, and who knows it better than Salman Rushdie? For much of the power of the novel lies in its ability to make clear the efficacy of our impersonations, of our monstrous descriptions of one another, to create monsters *in fact*.

It is all very puzzling. (pp. 3, 37)

It is Mr. Rushdie's wide-ranging power of assimilation and imaginative boldness that make his work so different from that of other well-known Indian novelists, such as R. K. Narayan, and the exuberance of his comic gift that distinguishes his writing from that of V. S. Naipaul. In Salman Rushdie's work, both India and England are repeopled and take on new shapes. For the Indian subcontinent there is a more commensurate bigness and teemingness, a registration of the pandemonium and sleaze of contemporary life. London neighborhoods suddenly leap to light as rich collages of transplanted Asian and African cultures. His fiction also takes on fashionable literary gestures—Joycean wordplay, magic realism and the hyperactivity, the "jouncing and bouncing" of the Coca-Cola ads that typify American culture to much of the world.

Talent? Not in question. Big talent. Ambition? Boundless ambition. Salman Rushdie is a storyteller of prodigious powers, able to conjure up whole geographies, causalities, climates, creatures, customs, out of thin air.

Yet, in the end, what have we?

As a display of narrative energy and wealth of invention, *The Satanic Verses* is impressive. As a sustained exploration of the human condition, it flies apart into delirium as "pilgrimage, prophet, adversary merge, fade into mists, emerge." Does it require so much fantasia and fanfare to remind us that good and evil are deeply, subtly intermixed in humankind? And why then trouble ourselves about it? In a world of mirages, of dreams within dreams, what is death and what is life, and why should it matter to choose between them?

For, often, the result of all this high-wire virtuosity is a dulling of affect, much like the blurring created by rapid hopping between channels on television: nothing seems quite real. Mr. Rushdie himself, an astute observer of the effects of fast-forwarding and remote-control devices on the way we perceive the world, takes careful note of the channel-hopping phenomenon, observing that "all the set's emissions, commercials, murders, game-shows, the thousand and one varying joys and terrors of the real and the imagined" begin to acquire "an equal weight."

But, of course, they aren't of equal weight, and after closing *The Satanic Verses* the real strengths of the book assert themselves. What finally lingers, what lives most vibrantly, for this reader, are the scenes that are grounded—the places where magic doesn't overwhelm the realism—the moments when Mr. Rushdie looks "history in the eye." They are scenes of expatriation, of political exile, and the story of Chamcha's patrimony—indeed, the whole, nearly complete novel-within-the-novel concerning Chamcha and his father.

But I suspect that Mr. Rushdie already knows this. His book is large enough to contain, implicitly, its own self-criticism and its own advice to the author. The words of advice come near the end of the novel. They are addressed to Chamcha. Zeeny Vakil, the first Indian woman Chamcha has ever loved, is letting him have it:

> "If you're serious about shaking off your foreignness, Salad baba, then don't fall into some kind of rootless limbo instead. Okay? We're all here. We're right in front of you. You should really try and make an adult acquaintance with this place, this time. Try and embrace this city, as it is, not some childhood memory that makes you both nostalgic and sick. Draw it close. The actually existing place."

(p. 37)

A. G. Mojtabai, "Magical Mystery Pilgrimage," in The New York Times Book Review, *January 29, 1989, pp. 3, 37.*

BARBARA CROSSETTE

ISLAMABAD, Pakistan, Feb. 12— Five people were killed and at least 50 were injured today as the center of Islamabad was turned into a battlefield when several thousand Muslims marched on the American cultural center, throwing stones and demanding the death of an author and the banning of a book.

The police, failing to disperse the crowd with tear gas, opened fire on the demonstrators, two of whom had climbed to the roof of the center and pulled down the American flag.

The violence was a startling reminder of the depth of radical Islamic fervor in a country that is trying to make a transition to democracy. It also was an indication of the difficulties Pakistan's Government confronts trying to steer a course between modernization and single-minded Islamic orthodoxy. . . .

The demonstration today, the culmination of protests all over Pakistan, was provoked by the publication in the United States of *The Satanic Verses* by Salman Rushdie. The book was banned here last year.

Last week, the Pakistani National Assembly voted unanimously to condemn the book and its author as "derogatory to the Holy Prophet and Islamic teaching."

Prime Minister Benazir Bhutto's Justice Minister supported the condemnation, which also called on the Government to urge Britain and the United States to stop publication of the work, a fantasy that involves characters identifiable from Muslim history. . . .

Opposition to the book is intense in Pakistan, even among people most Westerners would be inclined to describe as liberal until Islamic sensibilities come into the discussion. *The Satanic Verses* is almost universally regarded as objectionable here. . . .

By late afternoon today, a cloud of tear gas hung over the boulevard leading from Pakistan's Parliament to the commercial center of the city, where the American Express Bank and travel bureau were also attacked by stone-throwing demonstrators who broke into the travel bureau and set fire to furniture.

The demonstrators, many bused in from outlying areas, started their march in relatively good humor at an Islamabad mosque. Several mullahs, Islamic clergymen, rode at the head of the march in an open car.

After a procession through city streets, during which protesters—all men—carried placards attacking Zionism as well as the Rushdie book and its publisher, the crowd reached the American Center.

The center, more than a mile from the United States Embassy, contains a library and art gallery as well as offices of the United States Information Service. . . .

The demonstrators were allowed to gather around the building—they said they wanted to present a petition—without much interference from the police at first. But when hundreds of people began to surge toward the center, the police began firing tear gas and throwing stones back at the crowd.

Islamabad is a city built on dry, stony ground, and so both the police and demonstrators had ample supplies of stones. Some protestors also broke up street paving or brick walls to hurl at the building.

The police began firing rifles as the crowd seemed to grow and surge toward police lines, pushing back the officers, who had no masks and were also suffering the effects of tear gas. Until the firing began, many of the younger protesters appeared to be boys on a lark. Some were caught and beaten by the police.

> Barbara Crossette, *"5 Killed and 50 Hurt in Pakistan as Muslims Protest against Book," in* The New York Times, *February 13, 1989, p. A12.*

NIGHTLINE

JEFF GREENFIELD [Host] [*voice-over*]: Five people died here in Pakistan yesterday, another in India today. The cause? A book that some fundamentalist Muslims consider blasphemy. We'll talk with its author tonight.

[*on camera*] Good evening. I'm Jeff Greenfield, and this is *Nightline.*

MAN: The whole Muslim world's in an uproar about it. Because it's something that, like you said, it's completely blasphemous.

SALMAN RUSHDIE, Author, *The Satanic Verses:* I also have a right to say what I think, and my readers have a right to read what they want.

GREENFIELD [*voice-over*]: Among our guests, Salman Rushdie, author of the novel, *The Satanic Verses,* that has touched off an international wave of protest.

ANNOUNCER: This is *ABC News Nightline.* Substituting for Ted Koppel and reporting from Washington, Jeff Greenfield.

GREENFIELD: From the department of unlikely coincidences, this afternoon I began researching tonight's story by opening the Muslim bible, the Holy Koran, and found, quite by chance, this sentence: "Is there not in hell an abode for blasphemers?" Well, to those who have led the astonishing series of protests against the novel, *The Satanic Verses,* 41-year-old Indian-born, British-educated novelist Salman Rushdie is in for a decidedly unpleasant afterlife.

The novel, a dizzying mix of realism, fantasy, dreams, nightmares and magic, has been burned in the streets of London, banned officially or de facto in more than a dozen countries, and sparked rioting in Pakistan and India over the last two days that have left six dead and 180 injured.

To a westerner, raised to revere free speech and freedom of expression as perhaps the highest of political ideals, the specter of such bloodshed over a book seems utterly incomprehensible. But as ABC's Hilary Bowker reports from London, the protests stem from an utterly different premise: that some expression should not be permitted at all.

HILARY BOWKER, ABC News, [*voice-over*]: What is it about a work of fiction that has led to violent demonstrations killing five people in Pakistan yesterday and one in India today? Muslims around the world say Salman Rushdie's *Satanic Verses* is blasphemy, that it should be banned.

LEON WIESELTIER, Editor, *The New Republic:* You must understand one thing about believers. They are people without irony. They are not interested in art; they are interested in truth. And they believe they are in the possession exclusively of the truth. And they take what they believe in quite literally. For them, this is blasphemy, this is the opposite of the truth, this is pernicious falsehood and so on. (p. 2)

HESHEMOEL EL ESSAWY, Islamic Society: He describes the prophet and the faithful—the combining of the prophet, as bums and scums, and he describes them as living by lawlessness, like a bunch of criminals.

SALMAN RUSHDIE, Author, *The Satanic Verses:* Let's remember, we are talking here about a fiction. There's a fictional character going mad, suffering from paranoid schizophrenia, having had a crisis of religious belief, believing himself to be the archangel Gabriel, for God's sake.

BOWKER [*voice-over*]: Author Salman Rushdie has been the target of numerous death threats, as have the publishers and booksellers. . . . Now believers want it banned in Britain and in the United States. (pp. 2-3)

AMER HALEEM, Editor, *Islamic Horizon:* It's just a thinly veiled disguise for a frontal attack and distortion against Islam and against Muslims. And Salman Rushdie's responsible for that. He knew what he was doing when he wrote that book. It just didn't come on the spur of the moment.

Mr. RUSHDIE: It seems to me that the religious leaders in the Islamic world act increasingly like a form of thought police, and what they want to do is to be the only people who can orchestrate thought.

BOWKER [*voice-over*]: Rushdie says Muslims, who've never read the book, are being manipulated for political ends. After the violence yesterday in Pakistan, Prime Minister Benazir Bhutto accused Islamic fundamentalists of using the issue to topple her regime, but her government also said it would blacklist all books by the publishers of *Satanic Verses* unless they withdraw it from world sales and destroy all copies. (p. 3)

GREENFIELD: When we return, we'll be joined live by author Salman Rushdie, and by a leader of the Islamic community in North America, Ahmad Zaki Hammad, who describes Rushdie's book as offensive to all Muslims and to all religions. [*Commercial break*]

GREENFIELD: Novelist Salman Rushdie, who's with us now live in our London bureau, was born into a Muslim family in Bombay, India, although he's no longer a practicing Muslim. . . .

Dr. Ahmad Zaki Hammad, who's with us now in our Chicago bureau, is president of the Islamic Society of North America. That represents some 100,000 Muslims in the United States and Canada. Dr. Hammad, who is Egyptian by birth, has a doctorate in Islamic studies from the University of Chicago, and he is the author of several books on Islamic law.

Mr. Rushdie, in one sense, one of your critics who said in our piece by Hilary Bowker is right, isn't it? In taking some of the most revered lore in the whole Muslim religion and using it fictionally, you knew you were playing with dynamite, in one sense.

[*SALMAN RUSHDIE*]: Well, of course an artist knows what he is doing. I mean, the idea that I should not know would be—it would be very stupid of me not to know. The point is that what I've done is quite legitimate, it seems to me. I'm not denying the right of people who believe in religion to believe in religion. What I'm saying that there is also—it's also important and legitimate to take a skeptical look at it. The book does challenge preconceptions. It sets out to do so. It does so in a way which most critics and writers have found not insulting, which Muslim writers as well as non-Muslim writers have supported and liked, and which gets me letters every day from Muslim readers—as well as non-Muslim readers—saying that they've enjoyed it. So, you know, that's the truth of the matter, and what's happening is that one side is trying to prevent the other side from having anything to say about the subject.

GREENFIELD: Well, in that context and I realize that novelists do not expect unanimous reviews, there was a review in today's *Washington Times* by an American which concludes by saying, and I'll just read you one sentence, that "having discovered no literary reason why Mr. Rushdie chose to portray Mohammed's wives as prostitutes, the Koran as the work of Satan and the founders of the faith as roughnecks and cheats, I had to admit," says this reviewer, "a certain sympathy with the Islamic leaders' complaints that this book is not only—this is a nasty book." What do you think about that?

Mr. RUSHDIE: Well, I've not seen that review. But for that review there are 10 reviews which say exactly the opposite. The point is that nowhere in the book are the prophet's wives portrayed as prostitutes, and it's mischievous of the reviewer to say so. What happens in the novel at one point, in a dream sequence—and, at that, the dream sequence of a man who has not only lost his faith and is going crazy—is that I juxtaposed two opposites. One is the chaste and religious and puritan world of a prophet and his wives, and I set that against a degraded brothel in which a poet, a decrepit poet, hides out amongst prostitutes who take the names of the prophet's wives. The point about that is to make an opposition between the sacred and the profane world. Anybody who reads the novel will see what happens. The prostitutes all get executed, and come to extremely moral ends. They all get punished. Now, the idea that this is somehow an attack on the religion shows an absolute failure to understand what fiction is. Fiction is—

GREENFIELD: All right—now—I just want to, at this point, turn to Dr. Hammad and ask that precise question. Mr. Rushdie says that the protesters just don't understand what he is doing here, that you are taking this in the most literal, simplistic sense and ascribing to Mr. Rushdie beliefs of characters who he may not agree with at all.

AHMAD ZAKI HAMMAD, Islamic Society of North America: Jeff, in a world filled with tensions and conflicts, we in the Islamic Society of North America and American Muslims in general expect education, literature, politics, everything to bring people closer. Mr. Rushdie played the old Marxist line, but he knows very well that it will not sell either in the east or in the west if he speaks plainly as a leftist or a Marxist. So he masks himself by the veil of fiction, and goes and digs into the memories of hate and slanders the principal personalities, ideas and themes in Islam. In one of his chapters he calls the prophet of Islam, he uses the term "Mahound," which resembles the sound of Mohammed. Any dictionary will define "mahound" as the devil. Used for Mohammed, this term was used in the medieval literature by extremists and fanatics, and what Mr. Rushdie did, he digs into the memories of hate and attacks, slanders Islam, the principal figures—

GREENFIELD: But—

Dr. HAMMAD:—and principal ideas—

GREENFIELD:—Dr. Hammad—

Dr. HAMMAD:—yes.

GREENFIELD:—excuse me one second. Even assuming that your reading of this book is correct, which the author says is not, what you're saying here is that, as I understand it, it's not just that you object to this book, you don't want this book to be published in the United States.

Dr. HAMMAD: The—we want to protect the public from distortions and lying and misrepresentation about Islam and Muslims. Muslims or Islam is a hot topic now in the media, and we need, more than ever, to present it the way it is. I believe that Salman Rushdie's work contributes to foster hate, widens the gap between people, religions, and we want to protect the public from distorting Islam and misrepresenting Muslims.

GREENFIELD: But can you just say in plain words that you want the book not to be published? Isn't that the consequence of what you want? You just don't want the book to be read or published in the United States?

Dr. HAMMAD: The—this is not the question, Jeff, because the book is available in bookstores and it is available in the United States. We want the Islamic point of view to be heard, to know that Muslims are disturbed, are hurt, and the violence you have alluded to or stated clearly in the beginning of your piece has roots, and the roots of violence goes back to Mr. Rushdie and his work.

GREENFIELD: All right. We're going to take a break in just a second, but Mr. Rushdie, do you feel responsible for that violence in Pakistan and India?

Mr. RUSHDIE: I don't. I think it's very interesting that what happens here is I'm accused of simply, in a series of abuses, of things which are not intellectual arguments. I'm accused of Marxism. Before this other Islamic critics have accused me of being a product of the permissive society which created AIDS, and say that religious permissiveness will create a kind of religious AIDS. Some of the protesters in Pakistan have said this is somehow created by Jews in America, that Jews in America have put me up to this. So anti-Semitism is behind this as well. The point is that all they can do is hurl insults. The book doesn't hurl any insults, and frankly, I have not inflamed religious feelings. I didn't tell people to march against guns. The blood is on the hands of the people who inflamed feelings of people who've unfortunately, have not and cannot read the book, because the book is not available.

Dr. HAMMAD: I believe—

GREENFIELD: If I may, Dr. Hammad, we have to take a break, and we'll come back to both of you, but when we come back, we'll be joined by one of America's leading experts on the Muslim world, Professor Marvin Zonis of the University of Chicago. [*Commercial break*]

GREENFIELD: Professor Marvin Zonis of the University of Chicago is one of America's most knowledgeable scholars about the world of Islam, and particularly the history and impact of Islamic fundamentalism. He joins us now from our Chicago bureau.

Mr. Zonis, we've had movies ranging from *The Last Temptation of Christ,* which caused protests here, to Monty Python's *Life of Brian,* which was—to be charitable about it—a highly sacrilegious satirical look at some who consider the son of God. And yet there seems to be something about the portrayal of Mohammed that has sparked a level of violence that is almost incomprehensible to those of us in the west. Can you put it in a context for us? What's the source of this kind of fury and rage?

MARVIN ZONIS, University of Chicago: I think we really have to understand two separate issues which help explain why many Muslims are incensed, and particularly Muslims in the Middle East. The first is that in some very fundamental sense there is a competition between Islam and the west. The west has refused to recognize Islam, Christians have not accepted the final word of God, which is what Muslims believe Islam represents, and therefore there is a basic dynamic tension between Islam and Christianity, and the west is Christianity. The second point, however, is that Islamic fundamentalists in particular are not committed to pluralism. They are not committed to tolerance and democracy. They are committed to a set of values which all members of society must believe in order to further the goals of that Islamic society. That helps explain the passions.

GREENFIELD: But does the United States owe any obligation to compromise its tradition of pluralism, freedom of expression, in an effort to somehow pacify or ingratiate ourselves with the Islamic world? I mean, are there not our traditions of pluralism that we must hold to, no matter what?

Prof. ZONIS: Well, there's no question that for those governments which seek to subscribe to Islamic fundamentalism and impose a different set of values on their own people, it seems to me the United States has got to take the same kind of position that we take toward the Soviet Union, which is to say that we are for international human rights, irrespective of the nature of the social or political system which those countries hold to. And not—to the contrary, we should be celebrating our own values and continuing to internationalize human rights.

GREENFIELD: Yeah, I want to turn to Dr. Hammad about this. You have lived, Dr. Hammad, in the United States for, I believe, some 15 years. Surely you understand that we permit in the United States all kinds of sacrilegious, blasphemous, offensive publications that offend Jews, Christians, Muslims, every religion, every creed, because of that hierarchy of values in which we place freedom of expression highest. It seems to me that it comes a little odd for you to be not defending Mr. Rushdie's right to publish, and criticize him for what he said, rather than implicitly saying you don't think this book should be published at all.

Dr. HAMMAD: Jeff, I would like first of all to say that Muslims enjoy a tradition of forbidding what they think is right—of forbidding what they think is wrong and in joining what they think is right. Muslims deeply revere all the religious figures, and they stood when they felt that Jesus Christ was misrepresented from their point of view. And when Mr. Rushdie plans, God forbid, to write his next book about Christ and Mary and describe her as a prostitute, we will stand against this. Where Mr. Rushdie has the right to publish whatever he wants, provided that he does not deliberately trigger and instigate and foster hatred. He used the thin veil of fiction to cut right into the heart of Islamic values and principles, and to slander Islam and Muslims. We—Muslims in North America—want to inform the public that this is against, this is not the true Islam, this is a against Islam, and we would like to say that it serves no purpose, fosters hate. (pp. 3-6)

GREENFIELD: . . . [Mr. Rushdie,] I take it you have a different view.

Mr. RUSHDIE: Yes. I don't think that anybody who reads this book can seriously see it as an attempt to foster hate. I think one should point out, for example, that recently, a

Saudi Islamic group declared holy war, Jihad, on the entire movement known as modernism. That's an extraordinary fact. Sixty-six Arab intellectuals are blacklisted, many of whom now live in exile. This is a concerted attack on intellectuals, not just on me, but throughout the Muslim world, denying them the right to speak on issues which the controllers of thought, you know, seek to decide how they should be discussed. The idea, it seems to me, the center of modernism is uncertainty, is doubt. That's the place from which I write. It seems to me that is the center of the modern human condition. Even science these days contains a principle of uncertainty at the very center. I distrust people who claim to know the whole truth and to seek to orchestrate the world in line with that one true truth. I think that's a very dangerous position in the world. It needs to be challenged. It needs to be challenged by art, it needs to be challenged constantly in all sorts of ways, and that's what I tried to do. (p. 6)

GREENFIELD: Continuing our discussion with Salman Rushdie, Ahmad Zaki Hammad and Marvin Zonis. Professor Zonis, we've got a couple of minutes left, but give us your sense about whether these protests in Pakistan are really about the book, or whether they are about a broader political attack on the west.

Prof. ZONIS: I think, fundamentally, the riots in Pakistan, or the demonstrations in Pakistan, are not about the book. The book is a rationalization which provides an opportunity for Islamic fundamentalist groups—undoubtedly stimulated by outside interests—to attack the west. And what we are going to see, especially with the victory of the Afghan guerrillas against the Soviet Union, are renewed attacks against the west and against the Soviet Union throughout the Muslim world.

GREENFIELD: Dr. Hammad, I wonder, since the book was written by a British subject and published first in Britain, why the attacks on the American library in Islamabad? Why is America the bad guy in this?

Dr. HAMMAD: I don't think America is the bad guy. Every day may—Muslims, they know that the west, especially in Europe and America, is the largest market for this book. They would like to bring to the attention of the west that we are hurt, we are offended by the propagation of such slanderous attacks against the principal personalities and ideas of Islam. I don't think it is a step against the west. Muslims would like to express their outrage against this campaign of hate, again, and I do think that the roots of violence and confusion and conflict goes back to the—to Mr. Rushdie and his work.

GREENFIELD: Okay. Mr. Rushdie, as the author of the book, you might as well have the last as the first word. This controversy is going to sell a lot of copies of your book. Is there any satisfaction you can take out of that?

Dr. HAMMAD: That is why he wrote it.

Mr. RUSHDIE: There is very little, and I mean, here we are, this man is resorting to abuse again. To burn an American flag and then say you're not anti-America is very strange. To throw stones at a building and then say that I am the instigator of the violence is extremely strange. But it's the kind of doublespeak that's going on here. The point is that my book did—I mean, it's about many things, and the irony is that it's not really about this at all. It's about migration, and metamorphosis. But it does try to say that there is an old, old con-

flict between the secular view of the world and the religious view of the world, and particularly between texts which claim to be divinely inspired, and texts which are imaginatively inspired.

GREENFIELD: Excuse me, gentlemen.

Dr. HAMMAD: As it was stated yesterday—

Mr. RUSHDIE: Would you please be quiet, sir? That conflict is around the book.

GREENFIELD: Mr. Rushdie, I'm afraid that that's it because of the clock, which is the dominant figure in all our lives right now. That is our report for tonight. I'm Jeff Greenfield in Washington. For all of us here at *ABC News,* good night. (pp. 6-7)

"The 'Satanic Verses' Uproar," from a transcript of Nightline, *Show No. 2016, February 13, 1989, 7 p.*

PAUL GRAY

Occasionally, heartening evidence surfaces that some people still care about serious fiction after all. Here is a long, challenging novel [*The Satanic Verses*] by a highly praised writer, and it has spurred a frenzy of international attention. Headlines have bristled. Voices have been raised, although not exactly in unanimous praise. The book has been banned in a number of countries with substantial Muslim populations; its appearance in the West has been greeted with isolated public protests and telephoned bomb threats.

It must be added that few of those outraged by *The Satanic Verses* have ever seen it, much less opened it. Their fury, and the timorousness of government officials fearing violent uproars, has been prompted by one accusation: that the novel contains a blasphemous portrait of the Prophet Muhammad and thus amounts to a terrible insult to Islam. The plain, simple truth is that the novel does nothing of the sort, but only those who consent to read the thing will discover this for themselves.

If all the hubbub, with its attendant free publicity, increases the audience for *The Satanic Verses,* so much the better. The book is both an *Arabian Nights* narrative enchantment and a vast rumination on history, on the clash of cultures and individuals, and on the beliefs that people cherish for comfort and salvation. . . .

[The character] Gibreel develops a visible arc of light, a halo, around his head, and must cope with the awestruck reverence of perfect strangers. His new radiance aggravates an older problem, particularly puzzling in light of his newfound atheism: his vivid cinematic dreams, in which he is cast as the Archangel Gibreel, but without a script, and then asked by a series of petitioners to deliver Allah's word.

It is one of these—a businessman named Mahound—who has settled Rushdie's mulligatawny as far as Islamic fundamentalists are concerned. For the Gibreel-Mahound exchanges are based, in an obviously distorted and hallucinatory manner, on an episode in the life of Muhammad: the Prophet's early willingness to include in the Qur'an an acknowledgment of three female deities and his later repudiation of these verses as satanically inspired. If Muhammad himself was willing to admit that he had been deceived, it is difficult to see why a tangential, fictional version of this long-ago event should cause such contemporary furor.

For someone outside the faith to lecture Muslims on what they should or should not read would be impudent. But it must also be stated that there is no ridicule or harm in this novel, only an overwhelming sense of amazement and joy at the multifariousness of all Allah's children. As Gibreel and Saladin try to make their afflicted ways through contemporary London, a fascinating tapestry unfurls behind them. This backdrop contains vivid scenes—among them, the subjugation of an immense subcontinent and ancient cultures by an upstart island, and the upheavals that result when this thralldom is abruptly ended. But the history is parceled out in telling, individual details, people and places caught up in a grand design of which they are innocent and that, in the long run, may turn out to be simply chaos.

That possibility of meaninglessness tantalizes and bedevils throughout the novel. But Rushdie's furious, organizing energy seems to mark him as an angel of coherence. He has obviously read his García, Márquez, his Joyce, his Thomas Pynchon. He shares with those authors the desire to assemble everything he has known and seen and make it all fit together, beautifully. In his fourth novel, Rushdie has done just that.

Paul Gray, "An Explosive Reception," in Time, *New York, Vol. 133, No. 7, February 13, 1989, p. 82.*

BARBARA CROSSETTE

ISLAMABAD, Pakistan, Feb. 14—In a rising tide of religious fervor that might have been unimaginable only a week ago in Pakistan, Islamic leaders today called for nationwide protests on Friday, the Muslim Sabbath, against the wider publication in the West of the book *Satanic Verses.*

They also demanded the resignation of Interior Minister Aitzaz Ashan, a former civil rights lawyer whom the Muslim leaders accuse of ordering the police to suppress a march on the American cultural center here on Sunday. A judicial inquiry has been set up by the Government.

The campaign against the book, which Prime Minister Benazir Bhutto says is politically motivated, is nevertheless becoming a religious crusade. A prominent Muslim who led a protest march against the novel asserted today that emissaries were on their way to kill the author, Salman Rushdie.

"People have already gone to England to murder this man," said Kausar Niazi, the leader of the protest march to the American mission on Sunday, which resulted in an outbreak of violence and the deaths of five people, shot by the police.

"The people are after his blood," Mr. Niazi, former Religious Affairs Minister in the Government of Prime Minister Zulfikar Ali Bhutto, Ms. Bhutto's father, said in an interview at his home here. "My prediction is that he will be eliminated in the coming few months."

This chilling prediction was repeated matter-of-factly today in interviews with other Islamic leaders, some of them regarded as moderate or progressive in their social views.

All say that Westerners do not understand the depth of sentiment that this issue has stirred in Pakistan. They reject Ms. Bhutto's opinion that the agitation is the work of her political opponents, though they accept that her foes may try to benefit from it, even at the expense of civil peace.

Perhaps more difficult for Ms. Bhutto to deal with over the coming days, however, is the accusation that she is out of touch with Pakistani religiosity. . . .

Like some other Muslim clergymen and political analysts, Mr. Niazi says the Bhutto cabinet lacks a strong religious thinker with ties to the Muslim establishment.

Religious leaders say the issue is not anti-Americanism.

Mr. Niazi explained why the American center, which houses a library, art gallery and the offices of the United States Information Service, was the target of Sunday's march.

"No doubt the United States is a different society," he said. "But this book violates the fundamental rights of a community. American society is the most civilized society. They can't permit such attacks."

"Muslim organizations all over Europe, America and Canada had contacted me," Mr. Niazi said. "They said that Viking is now planning to publish this book in the United States. The publisher has announced it will be translated into eight languages, including Urdu, the language of Pakistan."

"We wanted to ask the American Government to convey our feelings to Washington and the publisher," Mr. Niazi said.

He said that as leader of the demonstration on Sunday, he had met in advance with American diplomats and together they had arranged for him to hand over a petition after several speeches outside the American center.

"We were astonished, when our procession began to reach the center, that there were barriers put up by the police," he said. "A thousand yards before the barriers, we stopped and asked the people to sit down while we went to give the memorandum."

"Without warning, the police made our jeep their target," Mr. Niazi said.

In the melee that followed, the American center was stoned, the flag pulled down and destroyed and the crowd fired on by the Pakistani police.

Mr. Niazi and other leaders of the next round of protests would like to present their undelivered statement to American diplomats on Friday, but so far negotiations with the United States Embassy on where and how to do this have been inconclusive.

Critics of Mr. Niazi, some of them religious leaders who asked not to be quoted by name because of the sensitivity of this issue, said they suspect he may have had other motives for raising the protest at this moment.

Mr. Niazi is widely regarded here as being close to Moscow, where he has made several trips. Last year he wrote a book praising the treatment of Muslims in the Soviet Union.

Mr. Niazi insists that the heart of the anti-Rushdie crusade is religious.

Barbara Crossette, "Irate Pakistani Muslim Calls for More Protests," in The New York Times, *February 15, 1989, p. A10.*

PATRICK E. TYLER

CAIRO, Feb. 14—Iranian leader Ayatollah Ruhollah Khomeini, in a decree that has whipped up new anti-American fervor in Iran, today exhorted Moslems to execute author Salman Rushdie and all those who helped publish or distribute his novel, *The Satanic Verses,* a work many Moslems consider blasphemous.

Pronouncing what amounted to a license to kill, Khomeini said in a statement broadcast by Tehran Radio this morning:

> "I inform the proud Moslem people of the world that the author of *The Satanic Verses* book, which is against Islam, the Prophet and the Koran, and all those involved in its publication who were aware of its contents, are sentenced to death.

> "I ask all Moslems to execute them quickly wherever they are found so that no others dare to do such a thing,"

Khomeini said, adding, "Whoever is killed doing this will be regarded as a martyr and will go directly to heaven."

Khomeini's declaration was the harshest expression of fundamentalist outrage thus far over the novel, which has inflamed Moslem communities around the world and sparked rioting in a number of cities because of its perceived defamatory treatment of the Prophet Mohammed.

Khomeini's edict, delivered under his religious authority as an Islamic jurist, shocked the literary world just as the novel is being readied for full-scale distribution in the United States.

Western analysts said it was the most explicit and most sweeping public execution order the 86-year-old spiritual leader has ever proclaimed.

Its focus on a foreign author—the Indian-born Rushdie resides in London—and hundreds of foreign publishing executives and employees, appeared to be a new and disturbing challenge by Iran to the West.

Western analysts said it reflects the still unstable political situation in Iran as pragmatic forces seek to calm the 10-year-old Islamic Revolution and open the country to the West while so-called radicals have focused on alleged conspiracies by western governments to exert new influence over the war-ravaged country.

Prime Minister Mir Hossein Mousavi, a leading Tehran radical, issued his own statement on the book emphasizing the American connection to the novel, which is being published in the United States by Viking-Penguin Inc. Mousavi described the publication as a "dirty and sinister conspiracy," and in an apparent call to violence, he exhorted pro-Iranian Hezbollah [Party of God] forces throughout the world to take necessary steps to neutralize the "plot."

On Tehran Radio, which broadcast "Death to America" chants as part of its programming today, Mousavi announced a national day of mourning in Iran "in protest against the newest conspiracy of the Great Satan [the United States] to publish poisonous and insulting subject matter concerning Islam, the Koran and the blessed Prophet."

Rushdie, 41, told news agencies that reached him at his London home today that he was horrified at Khomeini's reaction to his fictional work and that he and his publishers were taking the death threat seriously.

In a series of interviews on American television, Rushdie also expressed regret over Sunday's riots in Islamabad, Pakistan, where police fatally shot five people and wounded 80 others when a mob attacked a U.S. Information Service building there to protest U.S. publication of Rushdie's book. In a separate disturbance yesterday in the largely Moslem Indian state of Jammu-Kashmir, at least one person was killed when police clashed with demonstrators protesting the novel, which has been banned in India, Pakistan and Iran. . . .

Iranian officials and protesters have not cited specific passages in the book they find offensive, but Rushdie has discussed in interviews one scene in which a creature who could be construed as Mohammed is given a name for the devil. "The novel is about showing how devils are not always devilish," Rushdie told one American television interviewer.

Some protesters have singled out a dream sequence in the novel in which prostitutes use the names of Mohammed's wives. Rushdie pointed out today that his book contrasted the prostitutes with the purity of the Prophet and his wives and noted that in the novel the prostitutes were executed for their immorality. (pp. A1, A21)

> *Patrick E. Tyler, "Khomeini Says Writer Must Die," in* The Washington Post, *February 15, 1989, pp. A1, A21.*

YOUSSEF M. IBRAHIM

PARIS, Feb. 15—Ayatollah Ruhollah Khomeini's call for the execution of a writer he has accused of blasphemy appears to be largely a political maneuver by the Iranian leader to reassert his role as spokesman and protector of Islamic causes.

The Ayatollah, who is 88 years old, has a record of weighing his actions carefully. He may have seen in the protests over Salman Rushdie's novel, *The Satanic Verses,* an opportunity to bolster Iran's prestige among Muslims worldwide.

Ever since Iran accepted a cease-fire in the war with Iraq last summer and appeared to reverse fundamentalist Islamic policies of the last few years, its image as revolutionary model has slipped in much of the Islamic world.

An Iranian official who asked not to be identified said the Ayatollah might have seen an opportunity for one-upsmanship in the silence of other prominent Muslim leaders.

"The protests have been going on for weeks," the Iranian official said. "He has had plenty of time to think about it and many demands to act from inside and outside Iran."

But the Ayatollah's call for the execution of Mr. Rushdie, who was born a Kashmiri Muslim and lives in London, also carries risks for Iran.

It has already set back attempts to moderate its militant revolutionary image. And it may give an opening to those elements of the Iranian leadership that oppose the more pragmatic policies of the mainstream leaders in international and domestic politics. (p. A1)

In a view of several Iranian officials who asked not to be identified, Ayatollah Khomeini has made a practice of redressing the balance every time it tilts too much in one direction. Lately, events had been tilting toward pragmatists like the Speaker of Parliament, Hashemi Rafsanjani, and President Ali Khamenei. Some also put in this category the cleric chosen as the nation's future supreme religious leader, Ayatollah Hussein Ali Montazeri.

The pragmatists have been promoting the policies of liberalization to the detriment of more conservative leaders such as the Interior Minister and the Prime Minister. It was not too surprising, therefore, that Prime Minister Mir Hussein Moussavi jumped on the episode to declare a public day of mourning today in Iran, stirring up emotions. . . .

[These] events are bound, at the least, to freeze the improvement in Iran's relations with Western countries.

In addition, if Mr. Rushdie is harmed, the trend among Western countries toward restoring normal relations with Iran will almost certainly stop. . . .

[In] France, for instance, the newspaper *Le Monde* sharply denounced the Ayatollah's call for the killing of Mr. Rushdie, saying that "too many of the old Imam's opponents have already paid for his religious decrees with their lives." Imam is the title accorded to Ayatollah Khomeini in Iran as leader of the faithful.

France has been at the forefront of Western countries—along with West Germany, Italy and Spain—whose ranking diplomats visited Iran, advocating a reconciliation with Teheran after the end of the Persian Gulf war. . . .

Two other considerations may be behind the Ayatollah's move, however.

One is a real concern that Islamic leaders should unite in opposition to what he has always felt is a latent desire to undermine Islam in both the West and the East. The other is the fear that the controversy over the book is pitting Muslim against Muslim.

By focusing the anger on Britain and the United States for allowing such a book to be published, some experts say, the Ayatollah has deflected what threatened to become a fight between brethren in Pakistan, in Iran or elsewhere. (p. A6)

> *Youssef M. Ibrahim, "Khomeini's Judgment," in* The New York Times, *February 16, 1989, pp. A1, A6.*

SHEILA RULE

LONDON, Feb. 15—Thousands of people reportedly threw stones and waved pictures of Ayatollah Ruhollah Khomeini outside the British Embassy in Teheran today in protest against a book that has been deemed offensive to Islam.

The demonstration came as an aide to Ayatollah Khomeini, the Iranian revolutionary leader, was quoted as offering a $1 million reward to anyone who killed the book's author, Salman Rushdie. The reward was to be tripled if the killer was Iranian. . . .

The police today were guarding Mr. Rushdie's house in north London, as well as the offices of the book's publisher, Viking Penguin. Telephone calls to Mr. Rushdie's residence went unanswered, and the Press Association, Britain's domestic

news agency, said the author was believed to be in hiding with 24-hour armed police guards.

The official Iranian press agency quoted Fakhreddin Hejazi, a member of the Iranian Parliament, as telling demonstrators in Teheran that Britain was "the enemy of the Koran and Islam and the manifestation of all things evil." As the crowd broke into chants of "God is Great," he said that Iranians were disgusted at having relations with London. . . .

The [British] Foreign Secretary, Sir Geoffrey Howe, told the BBC today that Ayatollah Khomeini's declaration on Tuesday that Muslims should kill Mr. Rushdie and his publishers was a matter of "very grave concern" and that the Government was "looking into the background of it very carefully." He was quoted by the Press Association as saying the Ayatollah's statement seemed "strange" at a time when relations between Britain and Iran were improving. . . .

Sir Geoffrey told the BBC today that the Iranians' recent actions illustrated "the extreme difficulty of establishing the right kind of relationship with a manifestly revolutionary regime with ideas that are very much its own." But he told the Press Association that Britain would "try to serve the safety above all of the people of our country. One has to consider all these matters." . . .

A Reuters report from Nicosia, Cyprus, said the Iranian state television had broken into a news broadcast to report that Hassan Sanei, an aide to Ayatollah Khomeini, had offered a reward to "anyone who would punish this mercenary of colonialism for his shameful act." Mr. Sanei reportedly said his charity, the June Fifth Foundation, would pay a foreigner about $1 million in Iranian currency, or an Iranian $3 million, for what he termed a "holy crusade."

> *Sheila Rule, "Iranians Protest over Banned Book," in* The New York Times, *February 16, 1989, p. A6.*

THE NEW YORK TIMES

The passages in **The Satanic Verses** *that Muslim critics have condemned as blasphemous refer to a figure named Mahound, a figure whom they regard as a thinly and perversely disguised representation of the Prophet Mohammed. Mahound appears in the novel only as a character in another character's dreams. This character, Gibreel Farishta, suffers from the delusion that he is really the archangel Gabriel, and he later concedes that he is mentally ill. In Gibreel's dreams, Mahound is a businessman turned prophet, who is trying to preach to the city of Jahilia, a city "built entirely of sand."*

At the recommendation of Abu Simbel, the rulers of Jahilia have added to their religious practices the tempting spices of profanity. The city has become famous for its licentiousness, as a gambling den, a whorehouse, a place of bawdy songs and wild, loud music. . . . This is the world into which Mahound has brought his message: one one one. Amid such multiplicity it sounds like a dangerous word.

The title of Salman Rushdie's novel refers to an incident in Mohammed's life, recorded by early Arab historians, and discredited by later experts on the Koran. The incident involves Mohammed's acceptance of three pagan goddesses to aid his own cause, and his subsequent repudiation of this act as having been inspired by the Devil. In Gibreel's dream, the fictional prophet Mahound has a similar experience. After his "repudia-

tion of the Satanic verses," Mahound returns home to find his wife dead.

Mahound, alone and full of echoes in the house of his bereavement, gives his consent, and the faithful depart to make their plans. Khalid the water-carrier hangs back and the hollow-eyed Prophet waits for him to speak. Awkwardly, he says: "Messenger, I doubted you. But you were wiser than we knew. First we said, Mahound will never compromise, and you compromised. Then we said, Mahound has betrayed us, but you were bringing us a deeper truth. You brought us the Devil himself, so that we could witness the workings of the Evil One, and his overthrow by the Right. You have enriched our faith. I am sorry for what I thought."

Mahound moves away from the sunlight falling through the window. "Yes." Bitterness, cynicism. "It was a wonderful thing I did. Deeper truth. Bringing you the Devil. Yes, that sounds like me."

To believing Muslims, the Koran is accepted as the word of God. In contrast, Gibreel dreams that the prophet Mahound is victimized by an unfaithful scribe, a scribe (named Salman, just like Mr. Rushdie) who distorts the meaning of his words. In one passage Salman, the fictional scribe, recalls what he did.

"Little things at first. If Mahound recited a verse in which God was described as *all-hearing, all-knowing,* I would write, *all-knowing, all-wise.* Here's the point: Mahound did not notice the alterations. So there I was, actually writing the Book, or rewriting, anyway, polluting the word of God with my own profane language. But, good heavens, if my poor words could not be distinguished from the Revelation by God's own Messenger, then what did that mean? What did that say about the quality of the divine poetry? Look, I swear, I was shaken to my soul. It's one thing to be a smart bastard and have half-suspicions about funny business, but it's quite another thing to find out that you're right. Listen: I changed my life for that man. I left my country, crossed the world, settled among people who thought me a slimy foreign coward for saving their, who never appreciated what I, but never mind that. The truth is that what I expected when I made that first tiny change, *all-wise* instead of *all-hearing*—what I *wanted*— was to read it back to the Prophet, and he'd say, What's the matter with you, Salman, are you going deaf? And I'd say, Oops, O God, bit of a slip, how could I, and correct myself. But it didn't happen; and now I was writing the Revelation and nobody was noticing, and I didn't have the courage to own up. I was scared silly, I can tell you. Also: I was sadder than I have ever been. So I had to go on doing it. Maybe he'd just missed out once, I thought, anybody who can make a mistake. So the next time I changed a bigger thing. He said *Christian,* I wrote down *Jew.* He'd notice that, surely; how could he not? But when I read him the chapter he nodded and thanked me politely, and I went out of his tent with tears in my eyes. After that I knew my days in Yathrib were numbered; but I had to go on doing it. I had to. There is no bitterness like that of a man who finds out he has been believing in a ghost. I would fall, I knew, but he would fall with me. So I went on with my devilment, changing verses, until one day I read my lines to him and saw him frown and shake his head as if to clear his mind, and then nod his approval slowly, but with a little doubt. I knew I'd reached the edge, and that the next time I rewrote the Book he'd know everything."

Among the charges that Muslim critics have leveled against

Mr. Rushdie is that he has cast the Prophet's 12 wives as prostitutes in a brothel. The passage in question actually describes a group of whores, who have taken the names of Mahound's wives, as a kind of business ploy.

When the news got around Jahilia that the whores of The Curtain had each assumed the identity of one of Mahound's wives, the clandestine excitement of the city's males was intense; yet, so afraid were they of discovery, both because they would surely lose their lives if Mahound or his lieutenants ever found out that they had been involved in such irreverences, and because of their desire that the new service at The Curtain be maintained, that the secret was kept from the authorities.

"Passages Muslims Condemn from 'The Satanic Verses'," in The New York Times, *February 16, 1989, p. A6.*

JONATHAN C. RANDAL

LONDON, Feb. 16—Iranians today increased the reward for carrying out Ayatollah Ruhollah Khomeini's order to kill British novelist Salman Rushdie amid signs that Islamic hard-liners are using the crisis over alleged blasphemy to end Tehran's tentative opening to the West.

Only weeks after French hopes for improving links with Tehran foundered, Britain effectively froze relations with Iran today, charging that Khomeini's call to kill Rushdie and his publishers was "totally unacceptable."

As leading European politicians openly condemned the latest Iranian campaign, analysts noted the similarity with Tehran's self-imposed isolation of two years ago. They speculated that it might hurt the regime's efforts to rebuild the war-shattered country.

West European publishers, who yesterday seemed about to be stampeded into abandoning plans to print Rushdie's controversial novel *The Satanic Verses,* which many Moslems have condemned as blasphemous to the Prophet Mohammed, today appeared to be having second thoughts. . . .

In Iran, Mohammed Hashemian, a cleric in Kerman, a southeastern city, offered to match yesterday's pledge by a Tehran religious figure of between $1 million and $3 million to whoever assassinates Rushdie, according to Tehran Radio. Residents of Rafsanjan in southern Iran also pledged a sum worth $3 million at the inflated official exchange rate, the radio reported.

The radio also quoted fundamentalist clerics in Urumiyeh, in the northwest, as saying they had donned the white shrouds worn by suicide squads and "pledged to carry out" Khomeini's orders to kill Rushdie and his publishers.

In Rome, Salman Ghaffari, Iran's ambassador to the Vatican, urged Pope John Paul II to use his influence to stop publication of *The Satanic Verses* and said he was prepared to carry out Khomeini's sentence.

In Bombay, the Indian city where Rushdie was born a Moslem 41 years ago, a man claiming to represent Khomeini telephoned news media and threatened to blow up British Airways flights serving India until Rushdie "comes out of hiding."

Under police protection and reported severely shaken by the

threat to his life, Rushdie has made no public comment since going into seclusion in the English countryside less than 24 hours after Khomeini on Tuesday ordered his death on grounds of blasphemy. . . .

In Paris, Prime Minister Michel Rocard called on western leaders to "rise together and condemn" Khomeini's death order. The Dutch foreign minister canceled a visit to Tehran planned for later this year.

In Strasbourg, the European Parliament voted a resolution demanding that the European Community "make plain" to Iran that "severe sanctions will be taken against Iranian interests and force be used to bring the criminals accused to justice" if attempts are made to kill Rushdie and his publishers.

Here in London, the Foreign Office summoned Iran's lone diplomat, Charge d'Affaires Mohammed Basti, after Nicholas Browne, his British counterpart in Tehran, failed to receive a satisfactory explanation for what was called "incitement to violence" against Rushdie and his publishers.

A defiant Basti emerged from hearing Britain's "protest in the strongest possible terms" and told reporters that Khomeini's "decree or verdict" against Rushdie had been handed down "after careful consideration."

"It has nothing to do particularly with your country," he said, apparently indicating that Khomeini was not acting as head of state but as the leader of Iran's Moslems.

"We recognize that Moslems and others may have strong views about the contents of Mr. Rushdie's book," the Foreign Office statement said. "However no one has the right to incite people to violence on British soil or against British citizens."

Jonathan C. Randal, "Iranians Raise Reward for Killing Author," in The Washington Post, *February 17, 1989.*

MICHAEL HIRSLEY AND JOHN BLADES

Controversy over the novel **The Satanic Verses,** which spurred Moslem leaders abroad to call for author Salman Rushdie's execution, has disturbed Chicago's Islamic community and prompted a run that sold out the book by noon Thursday at the city's largest bookstores.

Available here since early January, the book had languished on shelves until this week, when the events surrounding it made it the fastest-moving book in the city. It has also been selling briskly elsewhere in the nation.

Reaction among Moslems here ranged from sympathy to embarrassment over the furor—which fanned this week from Pakistan, where six people were killed in a riot, to Iran, where Ayatollah Ruhollah Khomeini issued a public call for Rushdie's death, to London, where Rushdie went into hiding, and to the United States, where the author's book tour scheduled to begin Friday was canceled.

Chicago was to have been one stop on Rushdie's tour. An Islamic leader here said there are Moslems in Chicago "who would kill him" if he came.

Literary critics and historians could not recall a modern precedent for an author so blatantly being sentenced to death for his work.

"In the modern world, this is something unheard of," said

Nobel Prize-winning novelist Saul Bellow, who teaches at the University of Chicago. "When martyrs were burned at the stake, there was at least a semblance of a trial."

"This subject has been agitating our community for several weeks," said Atiqur Rahman, education chairman of Chicago's Muslim Community Center. "This book's malicious fabrications about the prophet Mohammed have hurt a billion followers around the world."

Rahman is a member of a coalition of area Islamic groups that tried unsuccessfully to persuade the book's publishers to halt its release.

"We were only met with indifference," he said.

Dr. Hussein Morsi of the Islamic Cultural Center of Chicago felt that his fellow Moslems' threatening reaction to the book "just gives us a bad image."

"As far as I'm concerned, it's a big commotion about absolutely nothing," he said. "The author has a right to express himself. Slander is his problem with God. These statements calling for the man's head are anti-Islamic. We don't go around calling for people's deaths."

Imam M. A. Rashid Yahya of the Ahmadiyya Movement in Islam center in suburban Glen Ellyn said that while he did not condone the bounty or death contract, "I understand it."

He said Moslems "have such great respect for Mohammed, peace and blessings of Allah be upon him, that they could sacrifice or slaughter their own children or family just to protect the honor of the prophet."

He said he had read excerpts of the book in which "the prophet's name has been used in a profane manner and his wives have been called whores."

Mohammed Kaiseruddin, president of the Muslim Community Center, also cited the excerpts. "The issue is not freedom of speech, but using it as a cloak for filth," he said. "Bookstores and libraries are full of books that misrepresent Islam. But to us, the prophet's wives are the mothers of all believers, and this book calls the prophet's wives whores.

"So it is calling my mother a whore."

Moslem leaders here estimate there are 200,000 Moslems in the [Chicago] metropolitan area. While Moslems don't want to take the law into their own hands, Yahya said, Rushdie's life would be in danger if he came here: "There are some, even here in Chicago, who would kill him, perish him." (pp. 1, 6)

While such writers as Dante, Zola, Voltaire and Osip Mandelstam (who died in a Soviet gulag) have been exiled or imprisoned for their writings, "there's never been an instance of a government ordering the death of the citizen of another country, as if bound by no law but its own, behaving with perfect autonomy," Bellow said.

Frederick Karl, literature professor at New York University, said the Rushdie situation goes beyond history's worst cases of censorship, even threats against writers and bookburnings in Hitler's Germany and Stalinist Russia: "Nobody ever talked about taking out a contract on an author's life. This is like a mob boss ordering a rubout. . . . This is a new and unbelievable form of insanity."

Criticism of the book focuses on a dream sequence that raises the question of humanity of a prophet named Mahound, a variation of Mohammed, in the face of temptation.

Noting similarities to American Christian fundamentalists' protests against the portrayal of Jesus Christ in last year's film *The Last Temptation of Christ,* Morsi, of the Islamic Cultural Center of Chicago, said: "We have some of the same problems with Moslem ministers that you have with Christian ministers. And we also have the same regrettable mixing of politics and religion." (p. 6)

> *Michael Hirsley and John Blades, "Moslem Death Threats Turn Novel into City's Best Seller," in* Chicago Tribune, *February 17, 1989, pp. 1, 6.*

EDWIN McDOWELL

Waldenbooks, the nation's largest bookseller, ordered that Salman Rushdie's novel *The Satanic Verses* be removed from the shelves of its 1,200 stores yesterday [Thursday, February 16], but said it had given store managers and employees the option of selling copies from the stockrooms.

The move, a Waldenbooks executive said last night, was carried out to protect the chain's 8,500 employees from terrorist acts in the wake threats by the Iranian leader, Ayatollah Ruhollah Khomeini, against the author and anyone involved in the publication of the novel.

"This is not a freedom of speech issue—the sole reason is the protection of our employees," Bonnie Predd, executive vice president of Waldenbooks, said last night. "We've fought long and hard against censorship. But when it comes to the safety of our employees, one sometimes has to compromise." (p. A1)

Telephone calls to 33 Waldenbooks stores in various cities late yesterday found employees at all but two saying they had no copies of the book; a few said no more would be ordered. Only one said he was selling copies, though all had been taken off the shelves.

Across the country, many outlets of the second-largest bookseller, B. Dalton, said they were sold out of the book. A spokesman at one B. Dalton outlet in San Francisco said no more copies were available from the distributors.

There were no reports of any violence at any bookstores. But one Waldenbooks executive said there had been anonymous threats: "We've already had two or three of our managers threatened because their stores carried the book. We just don't want to take any chance with our people until this blows over." (pp. A1, A12)

> *Edwin McDowell, " 'Satanic Verses' Is Both a Hot Seller and Too Sizzling to Keep in Stock," in* The New York Times, *February 17, 1989, pp. A1, A12.*

SHAUL BAKHASH

The "death sentence" pronounced by Iran's Ayatollah Khomeini on Salman Rushdie, the author of the novel *The Satanic Verses,* has as much to do with Khomeini's sense of his role in the larger Islamic community and factional infighting in Iran as with the contents of Rushdie's novel.

Khomeini could not remain quiet once the book, which contains passages on the Prophet and his wives offensive to Mus-

lims, achieved notoriety. He values his followers in India, Pakistan and elsewhere and aspires to the leadership of the Islamic world. He had reason to assume the lead in attacking the novel.

For those among Khomeini's lieutenants who enthusiastically seized on his declaration, however, Rushdie's novel is not the chief target. These men are intent, rather, on sabotaging recent moves by Iran to normalize economic and diplomatic relations with the West and to moderate the revolution itself. The furor over *The Satanic Verses* has played right into their hands.

The chief architect of Iran's middle-of-the-road policy is Speaker of Parliament Ali-Akbar Hashemi-Rafsanjani. With assistance from other senior officials and clerics, he persuaded Khomeini last July finally to agree to a cease-fire in the war with Iraq. He also secured his agreement for Iran to resume diplomatic relations with France, England and Canada, and to permit greater foreign and domestic private-sector participation in postwar economic reconstruction. . . .

Khomeini's successor-designate, Ayatollah Husain-Ali Montazeri, has been arguing for an end to executions, which resumed on a large scale last August, and a more open political environment. "People in the world," he said in a speech last week, "got the idea that our business in Iran is just murdering people."

But these developments have been galling to hard-liners like Prime Minister Mir-Husain Musavi and Interior Minister Ali-Akbar Mohtashami, who enjoy the support of Khomeini's son, Ahmad. For the hard-liners, the pursuit of the war was an article of faith and a token of Iran's determination to export the revolution and stand up to the "Great Satan" and the international community.

The prime minister and his Cabinet colleagues also oppose recourse to foreign firms, credits and technology. They fear a return of foreign firms means a reassertion of Western economic domination. They resent Rafsanjani's consolidation of power and have been working hard to undo his foreign and domestic policy initiatives.

British diplomats only recently returned to Tehran after a long absence. But last month, Interior Minister Mohtashami revived the specter of a trial and sentencing on spying charges for Roger Cooper, an Englishman who has long been in an Iranian prison. This and the stoning of the British Embassy in Tehran Wednesday by crowds protesting *The Satanic Verses* are clearly calculated to derail resumption of full diplomatic relations between Iran and England. . . .

By suggesting that the Rushdie book constitutes an American and CIA plot against a resurgent Islam, the hard-liners make much more difficult any attempts at an Iran-U.S. reconciliation. The cause of Iran's pragmatists has not been helped by Iran's inability to secure international support in its negotiations with Iraq, which six months after the cease-fire remains in occupation of Iranian territory. This leaves the pragmatists with little to show for their risky peace policy.

In light of Khomeini's declaration and aroused public opinion, the pragmatists, too, have dutifully fallen into line and are echoing Khomeini's sentiments on the Rushdie book. And the international reaction, as with the seizure of the

American Embassy in 1979, is bound to play into the hands of those eager to whip up public opinion in Iran.

However, although the offense to Muslim sentiments is deep and real, there is in Iran a makeshift air about the present crisis. Iran's increasingly frail leader appears to have grown more unpredictable and is perhaps more easily prevailed upon by advisers. Last month, he called for four officials of Iran radio to be imprisoned and flogged (and even threatened to have them executed) for remarks by an interviewee that he deemed disrespectful to the Prophet's daughter. (He later pardoned them, however.)

The cleric who offered a million-dollar bounty on Rushdie is a minor figure. And the mass of urban Iranians had hardly heard of Rushdie before last week. The policy carefully crafted by Rafsanjani and others has been steadily gaining ground over the past year. Unless the Rushdie affair spins out of control, it will probably mean a serious setback rather than a permanent derailment for this policy.

Shaul Bakhash, "What's Khomeini Up To?" in The Washington Post, *February 17, 1989.*

ALAN COWELL

CAIRO, Feb. 17—The winner of last year's Nobel Prize for Literature says Ayatollah Ruhollah Khomeini was guilty of "intellectual terrorism" in declaring that the author Salman Rushdie had been "sentenced to death" for a novel deemed offensive to Islam.

"The idea of killing someone because of what he wrote is rejected in principle," the Nobel laureate, Naguib Mahfouz of Egypt, said in an interview on Wednesday. "I consider it intellectual terrorism. The book, whatever its subject is and whatever its faults are, has to be discussed so the faults can be discussed in a democratic way."

Few Egyptians have read Mr. Rushdie's book, *The Satanic Verses,* which is banned here on the orders of the head of Al Azhar Mosque, the Sunni Muslim world's leading center of Islamic teaching and theology.

The novel has stirred widespread protest among Muslims in several countries who say they consider it profane. On Tuesday Ayatollah Khomeini, the Iranian revolutionary leader, urged the execution of Mr. Rushdie and his publishers. "I ask all Muslims to execute them wherever they find them," he said in a statement on the Teheran Radio.

But authoritative theological scholars from Al Azhar and elsewhere say the Ayatollah contravened Islamic law by calling for the death of the Indian-born Mr. Rushdie.

"In Islam there is no tradition of killing people without trying them," said a senior scholar at Al Azhar, who declined to be identified by name. Islamic law, he said, insisted that people accused of capital offenses like murder and heresy be tried and confess their guilt before execution.

"I do not approve the principle of murdering someone for writing something we did not like," said Sheik Abu el-Wafa, a leading Islamic scholar at Cairo University.

Like others, he suggested that Mr. Rushdie be tried, either in India or Britain, where he lives, to establish whether he is a true Muslim and whether he had committed heresy. "Kill-ing someone is not that easy," said a third Islamic scholar. "There are laws to be implemented."

The response among Egyptian religious authorities illuminated the centuries-old schism within Islam between the minority Shiite sect of Ayatollah Khomeini and the Sunni majority which predominates in Egypt and most other parts of the Muslim world. The Ayatollah's 10-year-old revolution has its roots in religious absolutism, but Egypt's response to the work is tempered by a secular political system that has sought to repress Islamic fanaticism in the name of democracy.

"It has to be fought by thought, not murder," Mr. Mahfouz said. One of his own works, the 1959 novel *Children of Our Alley,* is banned from serialization on the orders of Al Azhar. The book, which describes a family led by a strong father whose children rejected him, was seen by the Muslim clergy as an allegory for turning against Islam.

Mr. Mahfouz has said he concurs in the ban. "Not all countries are alike in cultural standards," he said Wednesday, referring to the outlawing of Mr. Rushdie's book in many parts of the Islamic world. "Some books could start unrest in some countries."

Senior Islamic scholars in Cairo said the banning of Mr. Rushdie's work was not based on a reading of *The Satanic Verses* in its entirety. "What we got was some excerpts from the book from the Foreign Ministry," said a high-ranking theologian, who requested anonymity. "The parts we received insulted Mohammed the prophet, the Koran and God."

On that basis, he said, the Grand Sheikh of Al Azhar, Gad el-Haq Ali Gad el-Haq, banned the book in Egypt and urged other Islamic countries to do the same.

Because of the ban, however, most Egyptians have no direct reading on which to base their views of it. "Even if Rushdie has written something that's against Islam," Mr. Mahfouz said, "this is his opinion and he is free to say it. He has to be debated and he has to make his point. That's the way to treat such things." He said he had not read the book himself.

Alan Cowell, "Clerics Challenge Rushdie 'Sentence'," in The New York Times, *February 18, 1989.*

JONATHAN C. RANDAL

LONDON, Feb. 17—In the first hint at Iranian conciliation since Ayatollah Ruhollah Khomeini ordered novelist Salman Rushdie killed for blaspheming Islam, Iranian President Ali Khamenei today offered a possible reprieve if the British author apologized for his book, *The Satanic Verses.*

In what struck western analysts as a carefully crafted government line designed to preserve Iran's tentative opening to the West, Khamenei told worshipers at Friday prayers at Tehran University: "This wretched man has no choice but to die because he has confronted a billion Moslems."

But, he added, "Of course, [Rushdie] may repent and say, 'I made a blunder,' and apologize to Moslems and the Iman," as Khomeini is known in Iran. "Then it is possible that the people may pardon him." . . .

Moslem sources speculated that an acceptable penance might also involve a ban on publication of the best-selling surrealistic novel, which many Moslems find blasphemous because of dream sequences involving the Prophet Mohammed.

Meanwhile, the Canadian government halted imports of the American edition of the novel acting on a complaint from a Moslem group that the book violates a law banning the dissemination of hate literature. . . .

In Iran, President Khamanei pointedly told Iranians to stay away from foreign embassies in Tehran, indicating the government's concern that extremists might seek to exploit the Rushdie furor for their own ends.

In contrast to 1979, when the fundamentalist clergy consolidated power after radical students seized the U.S. Embassy and held diplomats hostage for 444 days, Khamenei said, "I bear witness that such an action is absolutely, absolutely harmful to Iran and Moslems and detrimental to the Islamic Republic. Anyone who consciously does it is committing treason."

As anti-Rushdie demonstrations continued in India, Pakistan and Bangladesh, there were growing signs that West European government pressure was beginning to have a sobering effect on a government mindful of the need for outside assistance in rebuilding an economy shattered by the eight-year war with Iraq.

West Germany, which has maintained ties with Iran since the Islamic revolution triumphed a decade ago, recalled its charge d'affaires from Tehran for consultations. Iranian Ambassador Mehdi Ahary Mostafavi was summoned to the Foreign Ministry and told that Bonn "sharply condemns" the death threat to Rushdie which "burdens" bilateral relations.

British officials in London said they were encouraged after their charge d'affaires, Nicholas Browne, held a detailed, two-hour meeting in Tehran with Deputy Foreign Minister Javad Larijani. Britain Thursday stopped short of breaking diplomatic relations in favor of freezing them at their present low level.

The minister sought to portray Khomeini's death order—and the multimillion-dollar bounty for carrying it out—as a purely religious and not a bilateral political problem between Britain and Iran, a position interpreted here as seeking prudently to distance the government from the ayatollah's rhetoric.

Foreign Office sources were also encouraged by Larijani's assurances that despite recent Interior and Information ministry statements in Tehran, British businessman Roger Cooper, who has been detained without charges for the past three years, had neither been tried nor received a "heavy sentence" for espionage.

Officials in various European capitals expressed optimism that foreign ministers of the 12-nation European Community would take a united stand on the death threats when they meet Monday in Brussels.

Several West European publishers indicated during the last two days that they would go ahead with plans to publish Rushdie's book. In Milan today, members of the literary community applauded the decision by Italian publishing house Mondadori to distribute the novel, special correspondent Jennifer Parmelee reported from Rome.

The Iranian ambassador to the Vatican, meanwhile, defended the ayatollah's death order, citing a story from the Koran about a poet who, in the time of Mohammed, was condemned to death for insulting the Prophet.

"He who offends God must die," Ambassador Salman Ghaffari told *La Stampa* newspaper.

> *Jonathan C. Randal, "Iran Hints at Death Reprieve If 'Verses' Author Apologizes," in* The Washington Post, *February 18, 1989.*

THOMAS W. LIPPMAN

Salman Rushdie, born a Moslem, should have remembered the words of the Koran: "Who then doth more wrong than one who utters a lie concerning Allah and rejects the truth when it comes to him? Is there not in Hell an abode for blasphemers?"

And he should not be surprised that Moslems are outraged by his new book. He has denounced the "zealot protests" that greeted its publication, but he must know that seen through the prism of Islam, he is a blasphemer who merits dire punishment.

Whether that punishment should be murder, as prescribed this week by Iran's Ayatollah Ruhollah Khomeini, or damnation in the hereafter, as prescribed in the Koran, is a matter of intense disagreement among Moslems. Only Khomeini and a few of his fellow senior clerics in Iran's radical Shiite sect of Islam have gone so far as to say that Rushdie should be executed, but even to Moslems who reject Khomeini's extraordinary call for Rushdie's death, it is not lunatic. It is the logical culmination of months of growing protest against Rushdie and his novel *The Satanic Verses,* which in the eyes of Moslems parodies their faith, belittles the prophet Mohammed and violates taboos that have stood for more than a thousand years.

One of the most rigid of those taboos is the use of sacred symbols as metaphors. Rushdie's dream-sequence chapters abound in them. The prophet, the holy book, the sacred black stone shrine in Mecca known as the Kaaba, Mohammed's summons to prophecy from the archangel Gabriel, members of Mohammed's family—all are building blocks of Rushdie's baroque tale, recounted in cynical tones that must have been intended to shock.

Faced with this, what many Moslems see in Khomeini's proclamation is not a religious fanatic attacking cherished freedoms but a political leader endorsing a mass popular protest against an intolerable Western conspiracy to undermine their culture. Scholars at Cairo's Azhar university, the leading institution of mainstream Moslem thought for centuries, have condemned the book's "lies and figments of the imagination." India banned it. Moslems in Bradford, England, burned it in front of the town hall. And months before Khomeini called for the assassination of the India-born British novelist, Moslems from South Africa to Pakistan were marching in fury to protest Rushdie's slanders against their faith. These were not Shiites taking orders from the imams in Iran. These were Moslems of the mainstream Sunni branch, generally more restrained, less influenced by the religious hierarchy and less prone to religious excess, but still deeply offended by Rushdie's work.

The outrage grew as their protests went unheeded. *The Satanic Verses* became a bestseller in Britain. Rushdie was about to undertake a speaking tour in the United States. Reviews were copious and mostly flattering. In short, Rushdie—"he of the Oxbridge accent and American wife," as one scholar put it—was about to be lionized in a country that embodies the Western assault on Moslem culture. The anti-American violence that resulted in six deaths in Pakistan last weekend was probably inevitable.

"This is not just a Khomeini affair," says Shireen T. Hunter, an Iran specialist at the Center for Strategic and International Studies. "Khomeini is trying to capture the issue because he was in danger of losing his position as chief bully."

The campaign against Rushdie "didn't originate in Iran," says Hooshang Amirahmadi, executive secretary of the Center for Iranian Research and Analysis at Rutgers University. "For an Iranian religious leader to be silent about this would be strange. He was forced to take a stand. And Rushdie himself is a Muslim. Outsiders have always been hostile to Islam—they're used to that—but this comes from within. It's using a Moslem to destroy Islam."

Hamid Dabashi, a Harvard-based specialist in the religious aspect of Iranian ideology, said that the key to the timing of Khomeini's outburst was the publication of Rushdie's book in the United States. "What is the title of the book?" he said. "And what is Khomeini's name for the United States? The greatest assault on Islam has to come from the greatest power, the United States. The book is now in the United States, Rushdie was going to give readings—it's an assault on God Almighty."

According to Dabashi and others, publication of *The Satanic Verses* was bound to infuriate pious Moslems who resent the intrusion of Western ideas into their culture and feel themselves powerless to prevent it. "Remember that scene in *Raiders of the Lost Ark* where Harrison Ford blows away the Arab with the scimitar?" says Dabashi. "For Moslems, that's the most important scene. It's the humiliation. Everyone else has the atom bomb and not them. And Rushdie, living in England with his American wife [novelist Marianne Wiggins]—he is the symbol of this."

[In the March 2 issue of *The New York Review of Books,* which contains an essay first published in the *Observer* (January 29, 1989; see excerpt above),] Rushdie writes that he has "tried to give a secular, humanist version of the birth of a great world religion." But a "secular, humanist" vision is anathema to a culture based on religion. And Khomeini's response to it conforms to his well-known code of cultural extremism. Likening execution to amputation of a diseased limb, the ayatollah once wrote, "One who corrupts a country, or a group, and is incorrigible, he must be eliminated for the sake of purifying and protecting the society."

Two chapters of Rushdie's novel retell, in fictionalized form, the story of Mohammed and of the founding of Islam and the creation of the Koran. In his account, the prophet's name is "neither Mahomet nor MoeHammered" but "the Devil's synonym, Mahound," a name used in the past as a vulgar slur, and the entire sequence is written to blur the distinction between God and Satan—certainly a provocative notion among religious believers.

But Rushdie was on perilous ground with this literary notion even before he wrote a word. The life and sayings of the prophet Mohammed are second only to the Koran itself as a source of doctrine in Islam. To prevent the introduction of spurious stories into these "traditions," Moslem scholars

codified them in the 9th century. It has been impermissible ever since to invent new ones—in effect making any fiction about the prophet blasphemous by definition.

Production of a film about Mohammed touched off worldwide protests from Moslems in 1977, and most Moslem countries refused to permit its showing—even though the prophet was not actually depicted on the screen. Suppression of that film was among the demands of members of an American group, known as Hanafi Muslims, who invaded the District Building and other sites in Washington and held hostages in March 1977.

Moslems believe Mohammed was illiterate. When the words of the Koran were dictated to him by God, he did not write them down but relayed them to a scribe who recorded them. In *The Satanic Verses,* the scribe is "some sort of bum from Persia by the outlandish name of Salman," which is Rushdie's name, and this Salman takes liberties with the wording of the holy book.

"Little things at first," says the rascal Salman, recounting his work as the prophet's scribe.

> "If Mahound recited a verse in which God was described as all-hearing, all-knowing, I would write, all-knowing, all-wise. Here's the point: Mahound did not notice the alterations. So there I was, actually writing the Book, or rewriting, anyway, polluting the word of God with my own profane language. But, good heavens, if my poor words could not be distinguished from the Revelation by God's own Messenger, then what did that mean? What did that say about the quality of the divine poetry?"

To question the authenticity of the Koran, even in jest, is unacceptable to the vast majority of the world's 800 million Moslems. The Koran is the cornerstone not just of their religion but of their social structure, legal system and domestic arrangements. For centuries, the very purpose of literacy in Arabic was to master the Koran and scholars' commentaries on the text.

Only in the past 75 years or so have a few Arab authors produced plays and novels such as those that won the 1988 Nobel Prize for literature for Egyptian writer Naguib Mahfouz. Otherwise, the Moslem tradition of art on the printed page consists mostly of the elaborate illustrations and calligraphic flourishes that accompany religious texts—the illustrations are fanciful and creative but the text is not. Fanciful accounts of sacred events and the subordination of religion to art are unknown.

If an American were to write, say, a play in which four drug dealers were named Matthew, Mark, Luke and John, playgoers would note the symbolism and judge the drama on its merits. But similar use of names and places from the life of the prophet is anathema to Moslems.

Rushdie's book "is a parody of Islam," says Hunter. "The man wasn't even a little bit careful. Even if you write fiction, you should be a bit careful. This was a challenge, if you want to look at it that way."

The response to that challenge is a function of Moslems' traditional xenophobia and hostility toward alien value systems. "O ye who believe!" the Koran enjoins. "Take not into your intimacy those outside your ranks. They will not fail to corrupt you. They only desire your ruin." Ever since Napoleon invaded Egypt in 1798, Moslems from West Africa to Indonesia have struggled to maintain their traditions against the encroachment of Western ideas. And they have sought modernization without what they view as corruption.

Rushdie, then, is seen as the embodiment of a Moslem who has abandoned his heritage—thus the description of him as a "mercenary of colonialism" in an Iranian state television report that a senior religious scholar had offered a $1 million bounty to anyone who would kill him.

"Most Moslems live in Third World countries," Hunter says. "They can't understand the workings of the publishing and publicity system here. They don't understand why the government can't suppress something so insulting. When they see the book getting a lot of attention, many reviews, Rushdie being invited to speak, they naturally see it as a celebration of an anti-Islamic work by a hostile culture, part of a conspiracy. You can't explain it to them."

Indeed, Rushdie knows this. In his *New York Review* article, he said that Moslem "Thought Police . . . have turned Muhammad into a perfect being, his life into a perfect life, his revelations into the unambiguous, clear event it originally was not. Powerful taboos have been erected.

One may not discuss Muhammad as if he were human, with human virtues and weaknesses. One may not discuss the growth of Islam as a historical phenomenon, as an ideology born out of its time."

In the article, written before Khomeini's call for Rushdie's death, the novelist said he was sad "to see my book burned, largely unread, by the people it's about, people who might find some pleasure and much recognition in its pages." Apparently they have indeed found recognition, but it isn't giving them much pleasure.

> *Thomas W. Lippman, "The Islamic Taboos & Rushdie's Offense," in* The Washington Post, *February 18, 1989.*

SALMAN RUSHDIE

> As author of **The Satanic Verses** I recognize that Moslems in many parts of the world are genuinely distressed by the publication of my novel. I profoundly regret the distress that publication has occasioned to sincere followers of Islam. Living as we do in a world of many faiths this experience has served to remind us that we must all be conscious of the sensibilities of others.

> *Salman Rushdie, in an apology in* The Observer, *February 19, 1989, p. 1.*

ROBIN LUSTIG AND MARTIN BAILEY

British Islamic leaders yesterday broadly welcomed a statement of regret issued by author Salman Rushdie for the distress caused to Muslims by publication of his novel **The Satanic Verses.**

But first indications from Iran were that his carefully-worded statement would not be enough to have Ayatollah Khomeini's death threat lifted. Irna, the Iranian news agency, reported from London that the Indian-born author's

statement 'made no indication of his repentance or that his slanderous book would be withdrawn'.

Most British Muslim leaders, however, welcomed his statement. Mr Hashem El Essawy, chairman of the Islamic Society for the Promotion of Religious Tolerance, said: 'I regard it as an apology and it should pave the way out of this crisis. I now hope that it will resolve the problems between Iran and Britain.'

In Bradford, where a copy of the book was burned publicly last month, Mr Liaqat Hussain, general secretary of the city's Council for Mosques, said:

> 'I think the apology will calm down the situation, but it will not change the situation overall until the book is withdrawn from circulation.' . . .

> 'Our campaign will continue against the book itself and we are asking the publishers to withdraw and be sensible enough not to reprint it. That would be the sensible thing.'

Bradford's Council for Mosques, however, described the author's statement as 'not a sincere apology but a further insult to the Moslem community as a whole.'

The UK Action Committee on Islamic Affairs said that while it noted Mr Rushdie's statement, it reiterated its demand that the publishers should withdraw remaining copies of the book, undertake not to publish any further editions, tender an unqualified apology to all Muslims and pay damages to an agreed Muslim charity. . . .

The Islamic Society for the Promotion of Religious Tolerance issued a three-point 'peace formula' which it said could end the controversy. The society called on the book's publishers to insert a printed statement into all copies of the novel to tell Muslim readers that it should be regarded 'not as faction, but as fiction totally invented by Mr Rushdie's over-imaginative mind'. Non-Muslim readers should be warned that the book was 'not a source book for Islam'.

In addition, it called for all proceeds from sales of the book to be donated to charity since 'it is immoral to profit from libellous or scurrilous remarks that unjustly inflame people's feelings'.

> *Robin Lustig and Martin Bailey, "Iran Shuns Rushdie Apology," in* The Observer, *February 19, 1989, p. 1.*

BLAKE MORRISON

Somewhere in Salman Rushdie's abandoned North London home lies his review of Philip Roth's autobiography *The Facts*, which he was due to deliver to *The Observer* last Tuesday.

Literary editors can be hard taskmasters but Rushdie must have known that he had the strongest excuse in the history of literary journalism for missing his deadline. It's typical of his professionalism that he was on the phone before he took off into hiding to reassure us that, though he might be a little late, we'd be getting his piece in due course. Perhaps reading Roth, whose fiction also once brought down the wrath of his fathers, will afford him some kind of comfort. I hope so.

Rushdie is a brave man, not a quality much mentioned in the bitchy profiles of him that appeared at the time **The Satanic**

Verses was published. He has been articulate in his defence of his book, in these pages among others. If only the British Government had stuck up for him last week as forcefully as he has stuck up for himself.

His combativeness has been there from the beginning. He was labelled a 'magic realist', but the magic was chiefly in the eyes of British reviewers: in India and Pakistan they took him for a dirty realist. He announced his terms in an essay called **"Imaginary Homelands"** in 1982:

> The real risks for any artist are taken . . . in pushing the work to the limits of what is possible, in the attempt to increase the sum of what it is possible to think. Books become good when they go to this edge and risk falling over it—when they endanger the artist by reason of what he has, or has not, *artistically* dared.

The Satanic Verses has endangered Rushdie less because of particular passages about Muhammad's baldness or disputed parentage than through its essential nature: he has transgressed by treating the Holy Word as myth (up for grabs by a re-inventing novelist) not truth; by treating the Prophet as a fallible human rather than as a deity; and above all by bringing a sceptical, playful, punning intelligence to bear on a religion which, in these fundamentalist times, is not prepared to entertain doubts or jokes about itself.

For Muslims it is no argument to say that the book is a brilliant *tour de force* and a modernist work in the tradition of Joyce, to show that it is concerned with the plight of immigrants in Britain, or even to point out that it is intensely moving about at least one relationship sacred in most religions: that between father and son. All they understand, or have been made to understand, is its blasphemy.

Certainly Rushdie knew his book would provoke and offend but he could not have predicted an Ayatollah's death-call. Islam, after all, contains multitudes, as is clear from the Arab intellectuals who have written in support of Rushdie to papers both here and in New York. That support is worth remembering: Rushdie, who until this controversy was firmly identified (in the West at least) with the Third World and its aspirations, would deplore a racist backlash.

For his friends there is now a terrible sense of powerlessness. A writer going into hiding in his own country against the assassination squads of a foreign power: nothing quite like this has happened before, and we're not sure what to do. Salman Rushdie is gregarious, likes parties, likes talking, likes using the phone. Now there is only this unnerving silence.

I hope he will be able to break it, in his own good time. I hope he has a pen or typewriter in his refuge. I hope that his review will be on my desk on Tuesday.

> Blake Morrison, "The Hazards of Artistic Daring," in The Observer, *February 19, 1989, p. 15.*

THE NEW YORK TIMES

Ayatollah Ruhollah Khomeini of Iran . . . rejected a statement of regret by Salman Rushdie, the author of **The Satanic Verses,** and renewed his death threat against the novelist.

The Ayatollah, Iran's supreme leader, said it was every Muslim's duty to send Mr. Rushdie to hell even if he repented over the novel, which many Muslims condemn as sacrilegious.

"Even if Salman Rushdie repents and becomes the most pious man of time, it is incumbent on every Muslim to employ everything he's got, his life and wealth, to send him to hell," Ayatollah Khomeini said in a statement circulated by the official Iranian press agency.

There were reactions and other statements throughout the day from religious and secular leaders.

A spokesman for John Cardinal O'Connor said the New York Primate criticized both the novel and those who threaten its author, and he implied that Roman Catholics should avoid reading the novel.

An official of the British Foreign Office said in London that the Government viewed the Ayatollah's comments with "great concern" and that it "shall be considering carefully its implications." (p. A1)

Secretary of State James A. Baker 3d, in remarks on NBC's "Meet the Press" before the Ayatollah's latest statement, said that the death threat against Mr. Rushdie was "intolerable."

"If Iran wants to become a full member of the international community, this type of behavior won't lead there," he said, adding that he was not "passing judgment on the book" because he hadn't read it.

Ayatollah Khomeini's renewal of the death sentence he first pronounced last Tuesday followed a weekend of confusing signals from Teheran toward Mr. Rushdie, who with his American wife has gone into hiding under armed guard.

Earlier yesterday, British officials said, Deputy Foreign Minister Mohammad Javad Larijani told a British envoy that Teheran viewed as a positive step Mr. Rushdie's Saturday statement expressing regret over the distress that his novel caused Muslims.

"They do not talk with one voice," a British official said. "The whole point about Iran is the degree of dissent, division and confusion within their leadership. As we have already made clear, we regard any attempt to incite violence on British soil as totally unacceptable." (pp. A1, A6)

Early yesterday, the Iranian press agency quoted two Iranian newspapers as saying that the author's statement of regret was inadequate, although one said "the way was still open for real repentance and to reform the signs of this crime."

Ayatollah Khomeini's latest statement said the "imperialist mass media were falsely alleging that if the author repented, his execution order would be lifted."

"This is denied, 100 percent," the statement quoted the Ayatollah as saying.

The Iranian leader also confirmed that if a non-Muslim carried out the "death sentence" against Mr. Rushdie, he would qualify for a reward. In such a case "it is incumbent on Muslims to pay a reward or a fee in return for this action," the statement said.

At least three Iranian newspapers have criticized Iranian offers of a reward for the killing of Mr. Rushdie, saying they detract from the religious nature of Ayatollah Khomeini's judgment.

"Those tactics are exceptionally poor and ridiculous methods, and speak more of domestic political opportunism than a real desire to defend the faith," the English-language *Kayhan* newspaper said in an editorial. . . .

Iran's threats against Mr. Rushdie and his publishers have angered Western governments and put an abrupt brake on the recent improvement of their relations with the Teheran Government.

Britain has halted plans to increase its representation in the Iranian capital, just three months after the two countries agreed to restore ties after a yearlong rift.

The Foreign Office declined to comment on how Ayatollah Khomeini's latest comments would affect relations.

But a member of the opposition Labor Party called on the Government to again break off ties.

"The time has clearly come for diplomatic relations to be broken off," a member of Parliament, David Winnick, said. "No foreign government can remain in diplomatic relations with the United Kingdom when it threatens the life of a British citizen." (p. A6)

> *"Khomeini Spurns Rushdie Regrets and Reiterates Threat of Death," in* The New York Times, *February 20, 1989, pp. A1, A6.*

ERIC PACE

Muslim and Arab figures in the United States have expressed different views about the Salman Rushdie novel *The Satanic Verses* and the reaction to it in the Islamic world.

In interviews in recent days, some emphasized the role of tolerance in Islam. Others emphasized the importance of what they called responsibility in matters involving religion. Most of those interviewed were people who saw themselves as speaking from within the Muslim faith.

In the interviews, conducted by telephone, Muslims contended that the uproar over the book was a painful chapter in the wrenching history between Islam and the West.

Reached in Washington, Seyyed Hossein Nasr, a Shiite Muslim scholar, said he was angered by what he called Western critics' attacks on Islam. But he said he strove for serenity by recalling a verse from the Koran: "Say Allah and leave them to their vain play."

Speaking from Chicago, Hassan Abdallah, a Jordanian Sunni Muslim, said: "We are really outraged at the pronouncements of Khomeini and the fundamentalists because Islam is a religion of tolerance of opinion, of discussion, of dialogue. It's not really a closed religion."

And Clovis Maksoud, the Arab League observer at the United Nations, said from Washington that "the mainstream Muslim population is devout and not fanatic."

Born in Lebanon of Christian ancestry, Mr. Maksoud said mainstream Muslims around the world were "jolted by the threat to Salman Rushdie's life" as well as by parts of his book. He said the writer, a British subject, had become the focus of "a dimension of intolerance that is not tolerated by Islam itself." Mr. Rushdie, 41 years old, lives in London but has gone into hiding since the threat to his life.

Reached in New York, Zainab Istrabadi, who is on the staff of the English Department of Columbia University, said, "If you examine Muslim intellectual history" from its early years, "you will find diverse religious opinions and religious groups and religious debates being held at court, not only among various Muslim thinkers, but Christian and Jews."

Also arguing for tolerance, Ibrahim Abu Lughod, a Northwestern University political scientist and a Palestinian, said that as a Palestinian he strongly believed "that books ought not to be censored or banned" and that readers should be left to judge them and their authors for themselves.

A different view was voiced by Professor Nasr, a member of a family of Teheran intellectuals who teaches Islamic studies at George Washington University. He contended that "Islam envisages freedom of expression with responsibility as far as the well-being of human beings as religious beings is concerned."

"This goes a long way," he said, "to explain why people from all parts of the spectrum of Islamic thought and feeling, not only what the Western press calls fundamentalists but all Muslims, are hurt and offended by the contents of this book."

And Al-Amin Latif, spiritual leader of a Sunni Muslim mosque on Atlantic Avenue in Brooklyn, said of the Rushdie book, "To allow this type of blasphemy without any type of restriction shows a level of insensitivity from a Muslim perspective."

Mr. Latif, a black American who is a convert to Islam, said, "We are taught not to be disrespectful by violating other people's religious beliefs."

M. T. Mehdi, general secretary of the National Council on Islamic Affairs, an umbrella group of Islamic Organizations in the United States, said in a statement released Feb. 14 at his New York headquarters that Mr. Rushdie was "a frustrated, rootless individual."

Dr. Mehdi, who has a Ph.D. in political science, contended that Mr. Rushdie's "rootlessness must have made him bitter about himself and his background" and that the author was "now getting back at Islam by this obscene work."

In an interview after Mr. Rushdie's statement of regret, he added: "The bitterness will stay throughout the Muslim world until Rushdie apologizes without trying to rationalize and justify his work."

He said that if the writer apologized for "having insulted the Muslim people" that would "get him general approval throughout the Muslim world." Then, Dr. Mehdi said, Muslims would "overlook the insults."

But some other Muslims suggested that ill feelings would linger and contended that the affair was given undue emphasis in news reports in the United States and elsewhere in the West.

Ghassan Nakshbendi, a Syrian-born Sunni Muslim, speaking on behalf of the Islamic Science Foundation in Rye, N.Y., said the furor had brought "sad days for the relationship of America and the Muslim world."

A broader expression of regret came from Esin Atil, a Turkish-born scholar of Islamic art on the staff of the Smithsonian Institution. Reached at her Washington home, she said, "To me it is very unfortunate that this type of personal expression has turned into a blasphemy against a very large population who believe that they have been insulted."

Eric Pace, "Muslims in U.S. Embarrassed and Indignant," in The New York Times, *February 20, 1989, p. A6.*

YOUSSEF M. IBRAHIM

BRUSSELS, Feb. 20—The 12 European Community nations agreed today to recall their top diplomats from Teheran to protest Ayatollah Ruhollah Khomeini's death threats against Salman Rushdie, author of the novel *The Satanic Verses.*

The action, adopted at a meeting of Foreign Ministers, is to take effect immediately. The 12 countries also said they would suspend all high-level official visits to Iran, and consider restrictions on the movement of Iranian diplomats stationed in their own capitals.

Britain said it would go further, withdrawing all its staff from the British diplomatic mission in Teheran. The British Foreign Secretary, Sir Geoffrey Howe, also hinted that Iran's chargé d'affaires in London would be asked to leave.

The Community did not impose economic sanctions against Iran, meaning that it will not restrict the flow of Iranian oil to Europe or elsewhere. Oil is Iran's principal source of income.

But the statement said stronger measures, which were not specified, would be considered if any harm came to Mr. Rushdie. He reportedly remains in hiding in Britain under police protection. (p. A1)

The British Foreign Secretary said today that the Ayatollah's death edict for Mr. Rushdie, was "an affront to international standards of behavior," adding that "after quite serious attempts to establish a normal relationship with Iran, we see no point in maintaining any contact in the present circumstances." (pp. A1, A8)

The European Foreign Ministers who met here today said in their statement that while they favored normal relations with Iran, such relations would be impossible until the Teheran Government declared its "respect for international obligations and renounced the use or the threatened use of violence."

They said they condemned Ayatollah Khomeini's renewed call on Sunday for the death of Mr. Rushdie as "an unacceptable violation of the most elementary principles and obligations that govern relations among sovereign states."

The 12 countries of the European Community are Belgium, Britain, Denmark, France, Greece, Ireland, Italy, Luxembourg, the Netherlands, Spain, Portugal and West Germany. All have embassies in Teheran, although some are represented by a chargé d'affaires rather than an ambassador.

Speaking at a news conference, Sir Geoffrey said the Iranian threat amounted to interference in Britain's internal affairs and he warned that should any harm come to Mr. Rushdie, the Foreign Ministers of the European Community would impose much tougher sanctions. "A very grave situation would be transformed into a very serious matter," he told reporters.

The European action today seriously sets back Iran in its ef-

forts over the last seven months to normalize its diplomatic and political relations.

It may strengthen the hand of the so-called pragmatists in Iran, some diplomats here suggested, by showing that significant economic or diplomatic help will not be extended to Iran if it persists in taking extremist positions.

It was with this consideration in mind, several senior diplomats here said, that today's decision was not extended to include the present level of economic cooperation with Iran, including the purchase of Iranian oil. . . .

Several Iranian officials and diplomats, including President Ali Khameinei, were quoted late last week as saying that an apology from Mr. Rushdie might suffice to end the matter. But when Mr. Rushdie issued a statement on Saturday expressing "profound regret" for the distress his book had caused to "sincere followers of Islam," Ayatollah Khomeini rejected the gesture.

"It is incumbent on every Muslim to do everything possible to send him to hell," the Iranian press agency quoted the Ayatollah as saying Sunday. . . .

Close associates of Ayatollah Khomeini who are known for their opposition to pragmatic policies appear to be riding the wave of Muslim fury over the book. Their opposition is said to have been directed against the acceptance of a cease-fire in the war with Iraq last August, the resumption of diplomatic ties with France and Britain and the expansion of economic ties.

Mehdi Karoubi, a Khomeini aide who oversees pilgrimages to Mecca, today reiterated the call to kill Mr. Rushdie. He said in Teheran that all those who took part in the publication of the book, or who defended the right to publish it, are part of a plot against Islam. (p. A8)

Youssef M. Ibrahim, "Reply to Khomeini," in The New York Times, *February 21, 1989, pp. A1, A8.*

EUROPEAN COMMUNITY FOREIGN MINISTERS

[Reprinted below is the text of the declaration by the European Community Foreign Ministers on Ayatollah Ruhollah Khomeini's call for the death of Salman Rushdie. The statement was released in Brussels, Belgium on February 20, 1989.]

The Ministers of Foreign Affairs of the 12 member states of the European Community, meeting in Brussels on 20 February, discussed the Iranian threats and incitement to murder against novelist Salman Rushdie and his publishers, now repeated despite the apology made by the author on 18 February.

The Foreign Ministers view those threats with the gravest concern. They condemn this incitement to murder as an unacceptable violation of the most elementary principles and obligations that govern relations among sovereign states. They underline that such behavior is contrary to the Charter of the United Nations.

They believe that fundamental principles are at stake. They reaffirm that the 12 have the fullest respect for the religious feelings of all peoples. They remain fully committed to the principles of freedom of thought and expression within their territories. They will insure the protection of the life and properties of their citizens. In no case will they accept attempts to violate these basic rights.

The 12 express their continuing interest in developing normal constructive relations with the Islamic Republic of Iran, but if Iran shares this desire, it has to declare its respect for international obligations and renounce the use or threatened use of violence.

Meanwhile, the Foreign Ministers of the 12 decided to simultaneously recall their Heads of Mission in Teheran for consultations and to suspend exchanges of high-level official visits.

The Iranian authorities will be informed of the above in the hope that the universal values of tolerance, freedom and respect for international law will prevail. They look to the Iranian authorities to protect the life and safety of all Community citizens in their country.

> _European Community Foreign Ministers, "Text of European Statement," in_ The New York Times, _February 21, 1989, p. A8._

THOMAS L. FRIEDMAN

WASHINGTON, Feb. 22—President Bush today criticized Teheran's death decree against the novelist Salman Rushdie as "deeply offensive to the norms of civilized behavior" and warned that Iran would be "held accountable" for any violence against American interests.

The President's remarks were his first reaction to the international uproar over the call by Ayatollah Ruhollah Khomeini, Iran's supreme leader, for Muslims to seek out and kill Mr. Rushdie, the author of the novel _The Satanic Verses._

The remarks were also the strongest so far by anyone in the Administration about the affair, which has erupted at a delicate time in Iranian-American relations.

"I strongly support the E.C.-12 declaration in response to the Iranian threats against Rushdie," the President said, referring to a move by the 12 members of the European Community to remove their chief envoys from Teheran after the Iranian threats.

"However offensive that book may be," the President said, "inciting murder and offering rewards for its perpetration are deeply offensive to the norms of civilized behavior. And our position on terrorism is well known. In the light of Iran's incitement, should any action be taken against American interests, the Government of Iran can expect to be held accountable."

Asked whether he thought the West European allies should impose economic sanctions against Teheran, Mr. Bush said, "They will be discussing that, I'm sure, but I don't know where we go from there."

Today, Iran responded to the European action by recalling its own envoys from most of Western Europe. (p. A1)

Mr. Bush's reaction followed several days of restrained American response, beginning with Secretary of State James A. Baker 3d's comment last Thursday describing Ayatollah Khomeini's call for Mr. Rushdie's killing as "regrettable."

The President's comments came after several days of appeals and criticism by writers' groups, newspapers and civil liberties advocates, who felt that the Administration was too slow and reserved in its criticism. The 6,500-member Authors Guild and the American Civil Liberties Union, for example, had both written to the President urging a forceful statement.

While senior Administration officials would not say so explicitly, the statements by President Bush and Secretary of State Baker appear to have been calibrated to express Washington's condemnation of Iran in a low-key manner.

They contrast with the outspoken reaction of several European leaders, including Prime Minister Margaret Thatcher of Britain and Foreign Minister Hans-Dietrich Genscher of West Germany, who have condemned the Khomeini remarks.

The issue presents a quandary for the new Bush foreign policy team. On the one hand Mr. Baker and Mr. Bush are disturbed by the Iranian action and its implications for freedom of speech. But given the volatile nature of the Teheran Government, as well as that of the pro-Iranian elements in Lebanon assumed to be holding Americans hostage, they apparently want to proceed with caution.

The Administration's seemingly restrained response also appeared to reflect the analysis of Middle East experts in the State Department that the Ayatollah's threats have less to do with the substance of Mr. Rushdie's novel than with a power struggle in Teheran.

These analysts see a split between elements who want to draw closer to the West and those who want to go back to the days when Iran stood alone but indignant against the world.

A State Department official said that "fanning the flames" of the Rushdie controversy with excessive statements "would only serve the interests of those around Khomeini who are using the book affair as a way of bringing a halt to the trend in recent months of Iran improving relations with the West." (pp. A1, A7)

In Congress, Secretary of State Baker made his first appearance before the House Foreign Affairs Committee. He was asked by Representative Stephen J. Solarz, Democrat of Brooklyn, for his reaction to the Iranian threats. Mr. Solarz explained later that he posed his question in a way intended to elicit a strong statement by the Administration.

> "This constitutes an assault on our most cherished values of freedom of speech and freedom of the press," Mr. Solarz said to Mr. Baker. "It's an act of rhetorical terrorism, and quite possibly real terrorism, pure and simple. I'd like to ask you, Mr. Secretary, what we're planning to do about it? Have we consulted with our European allies? Are we considering the possibility of seeking a resolution in the United Nations condemning this? Are we taking any steps to protect those American citizens who might be vulnerable?"

Mr. Baker responded by saying,

> "I am not aware of any steps that we've taken in the United Nations, and I am not personally aware of consultations with our allies. We have made our views known, as have many of our allies. They have recently taken the step of pulling their ambassadors and their representatives out. We can't take that step because we don't have anybody there."

(p. A7)

Thomas L. Friedman, "Bush Finds Threat to Murder Author 'Deeply Offensive'," in The New York Times, *February 22, 1989, pp. A1, A7.*

YOUSSEF M. IBRAHIM

PARIS, Feb. 22—Ayatollah Ruhollah Khomeini, the Iranian revolutionary leader, said today that the dispute over the Salman Rushdie novel **The Satanic Verses** proved that it was pointless to pursue moderate policies in an attempt to win favor abroad.

In several references to what he described as "liberals," the Ayatollah strongly suggested such policies were doomed. He also reiterated his call for the death of Mr. Rushdie, whom he accused of slandering Islam.

The remarks were made in a speech to senior religious leaders that was carried by the Teheran radio and monitored in Nicosia, Cyprus. Excerpts were also provided by the official Iranian press agency. (p. 1)

The Ayatollah, the supreme religious authority in Iran, seemed to close the door on the recent moves to seek normal diplomatic, economic and political ties with the West and the Soviet bloc.

"When expressing our opinions and views, we should not act wrongly just to satisfy several sold-out liberals," the Ayatollah said. He said compromises on what he described as the firm principles of the Islamic Republic of Iran might lead true followers of Islam to "feel the Islamic Republic is retreating from its principal stands."

He indicated that the revolutionary aims that had guided Iran for the last decade remained its guidelines.

"The Iranian people succeeded in fulfilling most of their slogans," he said. "We shaped with our action the slogan of freedom and independence. We observed the slogan of 'Death to America' in the action of enthusiastic, heroic, and Muslim youths when capturing America's den of corruption and espionage." He was referring to the seizure of the United States Embassy in November 1979 and the taking of American diplomats as hostages for 444 days.

The Ayatollah seemed to reject criticism of those policies from Iranian leaders, including his heir apparent, Ayatollah Hossein Ali Montazeri, when he said it was categorically wrong for critics of Iran to assert that the country had failed in its policies and gained nothing from its militancy.

Ayatollah Montazeri, officially designated as the next supreme religious leader of Iran's revolution, said as recently as early February during Iran's celebrations of the first decade of its revolution that internal repression and radical international policies were "grave errors that ruined the image of Iran and frightened the world by making it believe that our only objective is to kill."

But Ayatollah Khomeini today, in what appeared to be a sweeping condemnation of all those who advocate a softening of Iran's militant policies, said the only mistake the Iranian revolution had made was to leave some room early on to "a group that did not have firm belief in genuine Islam or Prophet Mohammed. That, he said "was a mistake whose bitter consequences would not fade away so easily."

One Iranian official who asked not to be identified said in an interview tonight that the speech was "a most important development which sets things out for many years to come." He said it marks an end to what many in the West said they believed was a gradual abandonment by Iran of its "revolutionary principles."

Describing Mr. Rushdie, the Indian-born author who is at the center of a growing confrontation between Iran and the West as a "foreign mercenary," he said the action of members of the European Community to support Mr. Rushdie's right to publish the book and their opposition to the death sentence the Ayatollah pronounced on him were "desperate attempts" to defeat Islam.

He described those who defended Mr. Rushdie as "leaders of blasphemy" who are engaged in a conspiracy against Muslims and Islam. (pp. 1, A15)

In defending what he described as the accomplishments of Islamic revolution, Ayatollah Khomeini said foreign powers "today regard Islam as a boastful, dynamic and epic ideology, and are anxious over realizing that the room for their malice has been restricted and their mercenaries cannot write against Islamic sanctities so confidently as they did in the past."

He said the West's move against Iran in defense of Mr. Rushdie "is not to defend an individual, but to support an anti-Islamic current."

Iranian leaders who were seen as championing the policies of opening to the world appeared today to retreat from their previous positions. President Hojatolislam Ali Khamenei, who said in a speech on Friday that if Mr. Rushdie repented he might be forgiven, said tonight in a press conference in Yugoslavia that "there is no solution to the Rushdie affair."

The Iranian President said that Ayatollah Khomeini's death edict was irrevocable. "An arrow has been shot toward its target and it is now traveling towards its aim," Mr. Khamenei was quoted as saying by Reuters in Belgrade.

Mr. Khamenei asserted that it was hypocritical for the West to worry about freedom of speech for one person who insulted a billion muslims by his writing and ignore "an insult to the opinions of over one billion people."

The controversy seems to have exploded a latent struggle in Iran between various advocates of differing policies.

The struggle has been confused by the oversimplification implied in the use of terms such as "moderates" and "radicals" in describing the very complex mix of political and religious creed that characterizes Iranian leaders. (p. A15)

Youssef M. Ibrahim, "Khomeini Assails Western Response to Rushdie Affair," in The New York Times, *February 23, 1989, pp. 1, A15.*

YOUSSEF M. IBRAHIM

PARIS, Feb. 22—After a long official silence, the highest religious authority in Saudi Arabia is expected to recommend that Salman Rushdie, the British author of **The Satanic**

Verses, be put on trial in absentia in an Islamic country for heretic conduct.

In a front-page article today, a major Saudi daily, *Asharq Al-Awsat,* said that Sheik Abdelaziz Bin Abdallah Bin Baz, the most senior religious figure in Saudi Arabia, had reached this conclusion after days of deliberations with senior religious authorities from Egypt, Pakistan, India, Morocco and Jordan over the publication of the book.

Saudi officials said the move is in line with the general reaction among Sunni Muslim leaders who desire to register their objections to the book, but have been careful to place some distance between themselves and statements by the Shiite Muslim leader of Iran, Ayatollah Ruhollah Khomeini, who condemned Mr. Rushdie to death.

Asharq Al-Awsat reported that the recommendation will be issued by the Council of Islamic Jurisprudence, which has been meeting in Mecca to examine the issue in the past few days.

Arab diplomats here said the trial, if it takes place, is not likely to result in a pronouncement of a specific punishment for Mr. Rushdie. Rather it will turn on the judgment of his book to decide if it is indeed a blasphemy against Islam. There seemed little doubt that the book will be found blasphemous.

The Egyptian participant in the Mecca meeting, Sheik Gad Elhaq Ali Gad Elhap, the supreme religious authority of Egypt and head of the Al Azhar Mosque, said upon his return to Cairo on Tuesday that Islamic countries should answer Mr. Rushdie's book with another book that "refutes his lies."

The council, which includes senior religious figures from various Islamic countries, will also recommend that the Islamic Conference, the organization of 45 Muslim countries, sue Mr. Rushdie for slander against Islam in British courts, the Saudi daily said.

In most Sunni Muslim countries, many official government newspapers and semi-official media organs have limited their responses to the book to reports of the repercussions of the affair in Western Europe and Iran.

Unlike Ayatollah Khomeini, Arab leaders have avoided making any pronouncements on Mr. Rushdie or his book. Among religious Sunni Muslim authorities there appears to be a growing attempt to draw attention to a difference in approach between the two sects of Islam, by underlining the more legalistic approach in Sunni Islam. . . .

In Europe the repercussions of the Rushdie affair continued today. A spokesman for Brian Lenihan, the Irish Foreign Minister, said the minister's proposed visit to Iran has been "put on ice but not canceled."

In France, President François Mitterrand assailed the Iranian attempt to suppress Mr. Rushdie's book and threats against the author. A spokesman for the French President at the Elysée Palace said, "All dogmatism which through violence undermines freedom of thought and the right of free expression is, in my view, absolute evil."

> Youssef M. Ibrahim, "Saudi Muslim Weighs Rush-
> die Trial," in The New York Times, February 23,
> 1989, p. A15.

RICHARD BERNSTEIN

Faced with complaints from within their ranks that they have been slow to show support for the threatened writer Salman Rushdie, authors held readings from his work in New York and other cities yesterday [Wednesday, February 22, 1989] and called on each other to stand firm against attacks on freedom of speech.

The main event of the day was a meeting of 21 writers, including Norman Mailer, Joan Didion, E. L. Doctorow, Larry McMurtry, Diana Trilling and Susan Sontag, many of whom attacked the Iranian leader, Ayatollah Ruhollah Khomeini, as an international outlaw whose calls for Mr. Rushdie's assassination represent a direct threat to the freedom of every writer.

"We want to express our solidarity with Salman Rushdie, with his publisher, and with the independent booksellers who are continuing to sell his book," said Ms. Sontag, the president of PEN American Center and one of the organizers of the program.

"Most profoundly, we want to express a little civic fortitude in the face of this threat," she said. "We want to show our refusal to be intimidated."

Mr. Mailer declared, "If he is ever killed for a folly, we must be killed for the same folly."

Yesterday's activities in New York, echoed in rallies by writers' unions in Boston, Washington, Chicago, Minneapolis and San Francisco, were held to mark the official publication date of Mr. Rushdie's novel *The Satanic Verses* by Viking Penguin. The rallies demonstrated a surge in indignation that, after several days of uncertainty and hesitation, has built up in response to the Iranian leader's calls for Mr. Rushdie and his publishers to be killed.

Dozens of writers around the country called to support today's public meeting in New York, which was suggested by John R. MacArthur, the publisher of *Harper's* magazine, and jointly sponsored by American PEN, the Authors' Guild and Article 19, a recently created organization based in London that keeps track of censorship around the world. Those who took the rostrum were selected by one of the three organizations either to make statements or to read excerpts of Mr. Rushdie's novel, chosen by Gerald Marzorati, a *Harper's* senior editor.

Earlier in the morning, about 300 members of the National Writers Union, an organization made up mostly of freelance writers, demonstrated in front of the Iranian Mission to the United Nations, on Third Avenue between 40th and 41st Streets, where they heard Abbie Hoffman, the 1960's antiwar militant, say:

"I write controversial books. What publisher is now going to take chances with a controversial book?"

The group tried unsuccessfully to deliver a letter to the Iranian Mission that declared in part: "The attempt by Ayatollah Ruhollah Khomeini and others to force withdrawal of Rushdie's book is repugnant to Americans and, more important, in violation of our rights."

The program was intended to show support for Mr. Rushdie, who is living in hiding under British police protection, and to represent at least a symbolic sharing of the threat he is enduring. It took place under tight security in a white-painted loft-like floor of a downtown Manhattan building that is the home to several art galleries.

Outside, a crowd estimated by police as high as 3,000, umbrellas in hand, stood in a line that stretched up Broadway and around the block. Police officers, who used dogs to sweep the hall for bombs before the meeting began, had limited to 500 the total number of people who would be allowed inside, a move that turned the event into a kind of press conference rather than a public meeting.

Nonetheless, as each of the speakers pressed through the crowd to take the podium, there seemed to be a sense of portent—the feeling that the Iranian call for Mr. Rushdie and his publishers to be killed had awakened anew an awareness of principles often taken for granted.

Robert K. Massie, a biographer and president of the Authors' Guild, drew enthusiastic applause when he proposed that all of his organization's 6,000 members ask their publishers to withdraw their books from the chains—Waldenbooks, Barnes & Noble and B. Dalton—that stopped selling *The Satanic Verses* after the Iranian threats. Waldenbooks, B. Dalton and Barnes & Noble account for an estimated 20 to 30 percent of retail book sales in the United States.

Mr. Massie and the other speakers yesterday made their statements before the chain bookstores' announcement that they had decided to renew their displays and sales of Mr. Rushdie's novel.

"We have never taken the book off sales," Harry Hoffman, president of Waldenbooks, said last night. "We even have a reorder in, for when it's available again. But we decided not to display it because of safety considerations. We've had about 60 bomb threats, and people are painting our stores red. Some people don't believe we don't have the book now, because of all the adverse publicity."

Many speakers were also harshly critical of President Bush, whose statement Tuesday on the Rushdie affair was deemed a weak and uncertain defense of American constitutional rights. . . .

"What is the Government hoping for?" Mr. [Robert A.] Caro asked. "Compromise? On some issues there can be no compromise, and this is one of them."

During his presentation, a voice from the crowd, seeming to criticize his lack of a suggestion for a specific course of action that the Government might take, rang out: "What do want us to do? Bomb Teheran?"

If there was a unifying theme to the PEN-Authors' Guild program, it was that the battle for free speech and expression is everybody's battle, that if one person is threatened, then everybody is threatened.

"Rushdie the individual yields place to Rushdie the symbol of our freedom to write and to publish what we want," Diana Trilling said. . . .

Leon Wieseltier, an editor at *The New Republic,* said: "Europe, too, was once a theocratic society that burned books and people. We know all about the debt that democracy owes to heresy.

"Who is this man of God who has no mercy in his heart?" Mr. Wieseltier continued, referring to Ayatollah Khomeini. "In defense of our mind, let us show no mercy. Let us be dog-

matic about tolerance. It was blasphemy that made us free. Two cheers today for blasphemy."

Another speaker, Christopher Hitchens, a columnist for *The Nation,* received the loudest response of the two hour program, when he applied the poet Shelley's line about the aging King George III, an "old, mad, blind, despised and dying king," to the Ayatollah Khomeini. He also quoted Heine to the effect that "Where books are burned, men will be burned." Then he said:

> "Until the threat of murder by contract is lifted, all authors should declare themselves as co-conspirators. It is time for all of us to don the yellow star and end the hateful isolation of our colleague."

Mr. Mailer picked up this theme, declaring:

> "In this week of turmoil, we can now envision a fearful time in the future when fundamentalist groups in America, stealing their page from this international episode, will know how to apply the same methods to American writers and bookstores. If they ever succeed, it will be due to the fact that we never found an honest resistance to the terrorization of Salman Rushdie." . . .

Edward Said, a professor of English at Columbia University and a member of the Palestine National Council, said *The Satanic Verses* was "a deliberately transgressive work of nose-thumbing daring." He expressed dismay that the reaction to it by Ayatollah Khomeini had the effect, in non-Islamic eyes of reducing Islam to "terrorism and fundamentalism."

"We cannot accept," he said, "that democratic freedoms need to be abrogated to protect Islam."

Earlier, the British actress Claire Bloom, before reciting a passage from *The Satanic Verses,* read a statement from the novelist Philip Roth, who was unable to attend yesterday's meeting.

Mr. Roth declared his belief that he might on many questions disagree with Mr. Rushdie.

"We would want to challenge each other's points of view," he said, "but as to the right to challenge a point of view, we stand together."

> *Richard Bernstein, "Elegies for a Threatened Colleague: 21 Writers Speak Out for Rushdie," in* The New York Times, *February 23, 1989, p. A14.*

CRAIG R. WHITNEY

LONDON, Feb. 23—As the full implications of Ayatollah Ruhollah Khomeini's death sentence on the British author Salman Rushdie sink in, his friends here are saying that whatever happens to him in the future, he will never be able to go back to the highly active and visible life he was leading until last week.

His novel *The Satanic Verses,* denounced by the Ayatollah and by Muslims in India, Pakistan, Britain and elsewhere as a blasphemous insult to the Islamic faith and to the Prophet Mohammed, seems a fateful book to many of the author's friends. They find in it passages that seem to presage later tragedies, including the author's own, and irony that two British institutions harshly treated in the book—Prime Minister Margaret Thatcher and the London police—are now responsible for protecting his life. (p. 1)

"He is well," said one friend, the writer Tariq Ali. "He is bearing up well, he is in relatively good spirits, and is very gratified at all the support that he has received, and he is also very aware that there are many, many devout Muslims all over the world who do not agree with Khomeini."

Mr. Rushdie "does not feel under great strain or pressure," Mr. Ali said, "but it is going to be very difficult for him now. He will be constantly haunted by the spectre of death."

"The security is out of his hands, I think," Mr. Ali continued. "The people who are looking after him will have to decide how long he must remain under protection. My own feeling is that the stakes are constantly being upped, now that the clerics in Iran have united to call for his death." (pp.1, A8)

Mr. Rushdie mailed a review of Philip Roth's book *The Facts* that arrived at the offices of the Sunday newspaper *The Observer* today and called the journal's literary editor, Blake Morrison.

"He did not sound terminally depressed or anything," Mr. Morrison told Press Association, a British news agency. Mr. Rushdie told him the way Mr. Roth had coped with his own ordeal after *Portnoy's Complaint* aroused anger among Jews in the United States in 1967 had been a comfort to him, Mr. Morrison said.

But one of Mr. Rushdie's former publishers said:

> "It's an incredibly gloomy prospect for Salman. He was pretty defiant in the first days after the death sentence, but it must only be sinking in now. The general view in the publishing world here is that he is a marked man for life, and will need either protection or some form of complete seclusion or isolation. I suppose he could have plastic surgery and go live in Uruguay, but that for him would be the end of life as he knows it."

"But his life as he has known it is over," concluded this man, who asked that he and his publishing house not be identified, for fear of attracting the same kind of unwanted attention. . . .

A high-ranking aide to Mrs. Thatcher, whom Mr. Rushdie has repeatedly accused of repressing civil liberties and suppressing controversial books in the name of protecting official secrecy, said wryly, "The thought of Salman Rushdie, who accuses us of running a police state, being under police guard and our protection is a hard one for me to handle."

Mrs. Thatcher has denounced incitement to kill the author and on Monday ordered her Foreign Secretary, Sir Geoffrey Howe, to call back all five members of the British diplomatic mission in Teheran. But officials at 10 Downing Street said the police had made their own decision to take Mr. Rushdie under protection after the Ayatollah's call for his killing. "Their job is to protect British subjects," one of them said, "and Mr. Rushdie has done nothing wrong."

How long the British police will think it necessary to maintain extensive security arrangements for Mr. Rushdie, or whether he could afford to pay for private guards if the Government cuts them off or he decides to live in some other country, are unknown. . . .

James Adams, an expert on terrorism, said British intelli-

gence believed that the main danger—from a lone fanatic—would subside in intensity if Iranian leaders stopped repeating the call for Mr. Rushdie's death. "There is no evidence that Iranian death squads or terrorists are being sent from the Middle East to Britain, or of any extra activity by groups in this country," he said.

One of Mr. Rushdie's publishers noted that the London police and the British immigration authorities come in for a hard time in Mr. Rushdie's novel, which portrays them as heavy-handed and racist.

There are other eerie coincidences between fictional events in the book, published here last Sept. 26, and things that actually happened later. A character in the book named Salman, taking dictation of the Koran from the Prophet, deliberately changes some words, and Mahound pronounces a death sentence on him, saying: "Your blasphemy, Salman, can't be forgiven. Did you think I wouldn't work it out? To set your words against the Words of God."

The opening scene in the book finds the two principal characters, Gibreel and Saladin, tumbling through the sky over England after a terrorist explosion blows up their airliner in mid-air, as happened to Pan American World Airways flight 103 from London over the tiny Scottish town of Lockerbie on Dec. 21. In the book, Saladin drives through Lockerbie looking for Gibreel. The two of them survived their disaster; everyone on the Pan Am plane died.

"It does seem to be a fated book," one of Mr. Rushdie's friends said, noting hopefully that the Salman character in it is finally reprieved.

"Salman is clearly destined to outlive the Ayatollah," he said, "provided he can survive the next few years." (p. A8)

> *Craig R. Whitney, "Rushdie 'Bearing Up' under Life Transformed," in* The New York Times, *February 24, 1989, pp. 1, A8.*

SANJOY HAZARIKA

NEW DELHI, Feb. 24—At least 12 people were killed and 40 wounded today when the police fired at Muslims rioting in Bombay against Salman Rushdie's novel, **The Satanic Verses.**

News accounts of the violence in Bombay, Mr. Rushdie's birthplace, said the trouble began when Muslim demonstrators sought to move past police barricades set up to block their march on the British diplomatic mission in the city to protest British protection of the novelist. Mr. Rushdie, a British citizen, is in seclusion in England under police guard.

According to the Press Trust of India news agency, the police fired at the rioters in Bombay after people in the crowd opened fire on officers. The result was a three-hour battle, with rioters spilling across the crowded streets of South Bombay, burning cars, buses, motorcycles and even torching the small police station.

Reuters quoted a protest leader, Sharafat Khan, as saying organizers were pleading with the police to let a march proceed when the violence broke out. "It all happened so suddenly," he was quoted as saying. "The crowd surged forward, and the police hit them with clubs. There was stone throwing and then gunfire."

The news agency said the police had banned the march in anticipation of violence, detaining 500 people and arresting 800 others in the rioting itself. . . .

A leading Muslim figure in New Delhi, Syed Abdullah Bukhari, the chief cleric at the city's largest mosque, has endorsed Iran's condemnation of Mr. Rushdie and the calls for his killing.

The recent tension over Mr. Rushdie's book has aggravated existing sectarian problems, especially in northern India, officials say.

> *Sanjoy Hazarika, "12 Are Killed in New Delhi Protesting 'Satanic Verses',"* in *The New York Times, February 25, 1989, p. 3.*

RICHARD N. OSTLING

There is a character in *The Satanic Verses,* a scribe named Salman, who commits an unthinkable sin. His job is to write down the revelations of God as recited by Mahound, Rushdie's fictional prophet. But the mischievous scribe repeatedly changes Mahound's words. When the prophet finally realizes that Salman has corrupted the text of his holy book, he explodes, "Your blasphemy can't be forgiven." The proper punishment for Salman's crime is death, but Mahound is merciful and spares his life.

Rushdie, whose first name is also Salman, seems to share the character's skepticism about the authenticity of God's revealed word. But the real-life author will be lucky if he enjoys the same clemency as his fictional counterpart. His literary twisting of the Koran is the central transgression for which the Ayatollah Khomeini has condemned him to death. Explains Indian-born writer Mihir Bose: "Every Muslim, whether fundamentalist or liberal, believes the Koran is literally the very word of God, preserved in heaven and transmitted by the angel Gabriel through Muhammad." The Prophet himself, although not considered divine, is revered by Muslims as the model of sinless human perfection.

Though Rushdie denies that his convoluted novel is meant to be antireligious, its profane and satirical treatment of Islam's origins is guaranteed to offend any true Muslim. Rushdie points out that his work is fictional and the two most offensive chapters merely recount the demented dreams of one of its characters. But in the eyes of believers, both historical and religious truth have come under an unprecedented assault. Their reaction is especially harsh because Rushdie was raised a Muslim. Says Professor Georges Sabagh, director of the center for Near Eastern studies at UCLA: "He's engaged in the worst kind of blasphemy. He's a renegade, an apostate."

One of Rushdie's most bitterly disputed passages deals with the famous Satanic verses from which the novel takes its title. Here Mahound is tempted by Gibreel (obviously a reference to the angel Gabriel) to cut a deal with the enemies of his embryonic faith and tolerate worship of three of their goddesses alongside the one God. Gibreel later tells Mahound that the idea came from Satan, and the prophet orders acceptance of the rival deities to be stricken from his holy text.

Actually, this passage did not spring from Rushdie's imagi-

nation: similar accounts of Muhammad's temptation were recorded a millennium ago by Ibn Sa'd, al-Tabari and other authoritative Muslim historians. Today's Islamic scholars, however, do not consider the story authentic. Like the section dealing with the scribe Salman, this episode is seen by Rushdie's critics as a blatant attempt to undermine the Koran as the word of God.

What makes the story of the goddesses particularly offensive to Muslims is the fact that it was a standard argument hurled against Islam by 19th century Christian missionaries. Similarly, the name that Rushdie gives his prophet, Mahound, is one that Christians mockingly used in their medieval religious plays for a satanic version of Muhammad. (Rushdie's character explains that he has purposely adopted the name "to turn insults into strengths.") Some Muslims were similarly upset that Rushdie gave the holy city of Mecca the name Jahilia, meaning darkness, but the author seems to use the word to signify the spiritual ignorance that reigned there before the Koran was revealed to Muhammad. Believers are also angry because Rushdie ridicules various rules of daily life that the faith in fact never taught.

The most sensational episode of *Satanic Verses* takes place in a brothel and bestows on prostitutes the names of Muhammad's wives. This is outrageous to Muslims, since they revere the Prophet's spouses as the "mothers of all believers." Contrary to many press reports on the book, Rushdie does not present Mahound's wives as fallen women. Rather, the prostitutes borrow the names and then gradually take on the identities of the wives to mock Mahound. Nonetheless, Hasan Abdul-Hakim, a British Muslim convert, likens this episode to "presenting the Virgin Mary as a whore." Nor did Rushdie endear himself to Islamic readers by naming his brothel Hijab, the Arab term referring to the modest veiling of Muslim women.

Defenders of the book point out that, as in the brothel scene, scurrilous material is often not Rushdie's own characterization of Muhammad and his followers. Instead, it is the calumny of the idolaters whom the prophet was seeking to overthrow. The pagans, for example, call the prophet's companions "scum" and Ibrahim (Abraham) a "bastard."

Even if Muhammad had been portrayed with more respect, explains Amir Taheri, a Paris-based Iranian journalist, the mere fact of making him a fictional character would strike Muslims as a transgression against *hodud*—the limits of propriety. "Islam does not recognize unlimited freedom of expression," says Taheri. "Most Muslims are prepared to be broad-minded about most things but never about anything that even remotely touches on their faith." In ignoring that fact, Rushdie has made himself the bane of Islamic society— and the target of Khomeini's death squads. (pp. 30-1)

> *Richard N. Ostling, "Why Believers Are Outraged,"* in *Time, New York, Vol. 133, No. 9, February 27, 1989, pp. 30-1.*

CRAIG R. WHITNEY

LONDON, Feb. 28—Iran and Britain moved closer today to a break in diplomatic relations, as Iran threatened to sever ties unless the British Government withdrew its support in the next week for Salman Rushdie and his right to publish his novel *The Satanic Verses.*

Prime Minister Margaret Thatcher said nothing in reaction to the step today, but British officials said London remained firm in demanding the withdrawal of Ayatollah Ruhollah Khomeini's death sentence against the Bombay-born British writer, whose family is under armed British police protection at an undisclosed location.

Britain recalled all five members of its diplomatic mission to Teheran last Monday. The Iranian representative here, Mohammed M.A.Z. Basti, left London today, the telephone operator at the Iranian mission said.

In Moscow, the Foreign Ministry spokesman, Gennadi I. Gerasimov, said the Soviet leadership was "concerned" over the affair and believed that it could play a role in bringing about a solution—something British diplomats had asked the Soviets to do by bringing up the issue when Foreign Minister Eduard A. Shevardnadze visited Teheran last weekend.

In Iran, after a debate over demanding an immediate break in relations or asking a British apology or disavowal for the insults to Islam found by many Muslims in the book, Parliament passed a bill requiring its Foreign Ministry to sever all political links unless the British Government made a satisfactory declaration on the affair.

"If the British Government does not officially declare in a maximum period of one week its opposition to the unprincipled stands against the world of Islam, the Islamic Republic of Iran and the contents of the anti-Islamic book *The Satanic Verses,* the Foreign Ministry of the Islamic Republic of Iran is obliged to break all bilateral political ties," the bill said, according to an Iranian press agency radio report monitored and translated by the BBC.

The Iranian agency said that "nearly all" of the 201 members present in the 270-member Parliament stood, cheered and praised the prophet Mohammed in two separate votes, first on severing ties and then on giving Britain a week to revise its stance.

It also quoted the Iranian Foreign Minister, Ali Akbar Velayati, as saying, "In the future this will be our stand toward any country that attacks Islam and Islamic sanctities."

Britain's 11 European Community partners recalled their Ambassadors, but not their other diplomats in Teheran, for consultations last week in solidarity with the British position, and Austria, Finland, Norway, Canada and Sweden, which looks after British interests in Iran, have also recalled theirs.

"Clearly, the British position will not be altered by threats of that kind," said William Waldegrave, the British Foreign Office minister dealing with the Middle East. . . .

The British author Roald Dahl, in a letter to *The Times* of London dissenting from the support given the beleaguered author by most of his colleagues, denounced Mr. Rushdie today for ever writing *The Satanic Verses.*

Calling him "a dangerous opportunist," Mr. Dahl wrote:

> "Clearly he has profound knowledge of the Muslim religion and its people, and he must have been totally aware of the deep and violent feelings his book would stir up among devout Muslims. In other words he knew exactly what he was doing and he cannot plead otherwise. This kind of sensationalism does indeed get an indifferent book on to the

top of the best-seller list, but to my mind it is a cheap way of doing it."

"It's time somebody said it," Mr. Dahl said today, explaining why he had written the letter, which appeared with another one signed by 28 members of the British Society of Authors, to which Mr. Dahl belongs.

The signers of that letter, including Eric Ambler, Margaret Drabble, Antonia Fraser, William Golding, Roy Jenkins and Tom Stoppard, regretted the offense taken by many Muslims for *The Satanic Verses* but expressed support for strong measures taken by the British Government against Iran, and in protection of Mr. Rushdie.

> *Craig R. Whitney, "Iran and Britain Move Near Break," in* The New York Times, *March 1, 1989, p. A10.*

THOMAS D'EVELYN

With all that's happened—Muslim demonstrations, bannings and book burnings, a death-sentence from Ayatollah Khomeini—*The Satanic Verses* has begun to look prophetic. That's remarkable, if only because at first sight it's a savage satire of the very idea of prophecy, or the utterance, by man, of truth with a capital T.

The concept behind the book is simple: A plane from Bombay is blown up over the English Channel by terrorists. The only survivors are two media types from India, an actor and a voice-over artist.

The city they fall into, modern London, is the polyglot, multiracial sinkhole of the British Empire. The impact of their fall affects the two differently and even paradoxically. . . .

This concept controls with varying degrees of success an enormous amount of detail drawn from contemporary London and Islamic tradition.

The constantly shifting point of view rarely gets outside the alienated consciousness whose symbol and wand is the TV remote-control stick. The "tortured metropolis" of London is seen as a "composite video monster." The language of the characters and the book ranges from "smart-alec Bombay English" to parodies of the holy book of Islam, the *Koran.* This book about exile is drenched in fear and anxiety. "Paranoia," Rushdie writes, "for the exile, is the prerequisite of survival."

Words and images start from the page with unnatural lucidity. Rushdie's eclectic style, which gives voice to a multitude of brilliantly sketched characters—some only for a page or two—has a political and religious basis. The modern Indian culture, he says early on, can be seen as "based on the principle of borrowing whatever clothes seemed to fit, Aryan, Mughal, British, take-the-best-and-leave-the-rest." This style would replace the "authentic" Indian style.

But Rushdie's target is bigger than India, bigger than fundamentalist Islam. He seeks out, and often destroys, the "too many demons inside people claiming to believe in God." This has led to charges of arrogant, militant skepticism. Rather, this book is a kind of postmodern, speculative *Arabian Nights,* in which the fallen know-it-all gets his comeuppance and the tragedy of intellectual pride yields to the comedy of human love and enlightened political engagement.

The special tone of the book is not anger but an impish melancholy. Rushdie was meticulous in qualifying his criticisms of Islamic tradition by using literary fictions like the dream. Perhaps he's been too clever. . . .

Rushdie's vision is partly tragic. The idealism of love between the sexes seems out of place in the paranoid world of exile. In a book about the burden of inheritance, Henry James is quoted: "The natural inheritance of everyone who is capable of spiritual life is an unsubdued forest where the wolf howls and the obscene bird of night chatters."

"Take *that*, kids," adds the narrator, exhibiting once again his inability to keep a straight face. In its rhythms, this book brilliantly captures the surrealism of the media-mind, the monstrous product of openness and pluralism. Eventually, it may come to be seen as a dicey drama of monotheism in a pluralistic world. Against the vertiginous swirl of events, certain pieties, certain polarities, certain responsibilities, hold fast.

The book is serious about the spiritual equality of men and women. And this book is serious about the potential relationship between man and God. The dream that has so enraged some readers concludes with a remarkable passage in which the death of the messenger, the parody of Muhammad, is seen in the broader context of the inextinguishable life of God. . . .

As another Salman says in the book, "To dream of a thing is very different from being faced with the fact of it." Indeed, *The Satanic Verses* bears witness to multitudes of facts about modern life. Furthermore, it has engendered a host of new facts, facts that have been screaming from the headlines for weeks now.

The Satanic Verses can't be separated from those facts, any of them. Read carefully, it provides a map to a great deal of them. Which, at this moment, may be its most remarkable virtue.

> *Thomas D'Evelyn, "Arabian Nightmare," in* The Christian Science Monitor, *March 2, 1989, p. 13.*

D. J. ENRIGHT

Let us begin (although Salman Rushdie doesn't) with the affair of the Satanic verses, revealed in the second part of his new novel, *The Satanic Verses.* This second part is entitled "Mahound," a disrespectful name for Muhammad, found for example in Spenser to signify a heathen idol by whom wicked characters swear, and likewise, though perhaps also as a metrically convenient alternative to "Makomete," in Chaucer. *The Satanic Verses* has been banned in India on the grounds that it is offensive to Muslims, but in fact nobody in it is treated with very much respect; gods, angels, demons, prophets, they are all of them all too human, and most of the time unable to distinguish between good and evil. If they can't, how can we ordinary mortals be expected to?

The magical city of Jahilia is composed wholly of sand, together with its derivatives, glass and silicon, and the great enemy is consequently water. Mahound, "businessman-turned-prophet," is engaged in founding one of the world's greatest religions, in the face of the city's swarming gods, all

360 of them. He and his three followers are clearly troublemakers, if only because they are forever washing themselves with water. However, the Grandee of Jahilia, the head of the ruling council, offers Mahound a deal: if Mahound's Allah will receive a mere three of the local gods into his monopantheon, then the new religion will be recognized and Mahound given a seat on the council. The gods in question can be given the rank of archangels, since there are already two of these: Gibreel, the Voice of Allah, and Shaitan, the latter described in the Koran as a disobedient jinni who refused to bow down before Adam. Or better, since the gods happen to be goddesses, they can be styled the Daughters of Allah.

Mahound's followers protest that this cannot be, for the essence of their faith is that there is no god but Allah; but Mahound sees the arrangements as a useful maneuver, a small concession that will bring in large numbers of converts, and he climbs Cone Mountain to consult the archangel Gibreel, Angel of the Recitation.

The grandee's name is Abu Simbel. Is he, one wonders, a historical or legendary figure? Or can it be that Rushdie, having invented him, has named him after the village in Egypt that was flooded when the Aswan High Dam was created in the 1960s and its temples removed to higher ground? For we hear that the sea and maritime developments are robbing sand-based Jahilia with its camel-train economy of the city's old ascendancy. Questions of this kind raise their heads everywhere, and if the reader stops to puzzle out the answers he will never finish the book. (p. 25)

The novel itself begins in modern times and with a fall from the heavens, similar to other such falls, most recently the one with which Stefan Heym began his novel *The Wandering Jew,* but dissimilar in the outcome. A hijacked Air India jet is blown up over the English Channel and, "without benefit of parachutes or wings," two passengers tumble unharmed to earth. One is Gibreel Farishta, the other Saladin Chamcha, two real living men, we are told, though their downward progress is termed an "angelicdevilish fall."

Gibreel is a famous and flamboyant Bombay superstar who has specialized in "God stuff," portraying impartially such diverse deities of the Indian subcontinent as Krishna, Gautama Buddha, and Hanuman, in the popular genre known to the movie world as "theologicals." He is traveling to England in pursuit of the beautiful "ice queen," Alleluia Cone, climber of Everest. Saladin is returning, after an unhappy visit with his father, to London, where he lives, a self-made "goodand-proper Englishman," in love with "Bigben Nelsonscolumn Lordstavern Bloodytower Queen," with his English dreamland of equilibrium and moderation. He is an actor too, of the invisible kind, a voice, a thousand voices, much in demand on radio and in television commercials. He knows how a ketchup bottle should talk, or a packet of garlic-flavored potato crisps; "once, in a radio play for thirty-seven voices, he interpreted every single part under a variety of pseudonyms and nobody ever worked it out."

If, as seems likely at this stage, the angelicdevilish conglomeration is to be sorted out and divided between the two of them, then Gibreel, a violent character and unconscionable womanizer, is in the running for the role of devil, and Saladin, mild and worrying, for that of angel. Yet when they land on an English beach Saladin finds he has grown horns, cloven hooves, and a monstrous phallus, whereas Gibreel is now wearing a halo. Despite his bowler hat, Saladin is arrested as an illegal immigrant—which one might interpret as a sign of injured innocence—while Gibreel bedazzles the police, treacherously disowns his compatriot, and goes free. Messages must have got mixed up once again. Rather than cudgel one's brains over their theological status, it is wiser to think of Gibreel and Saladin as the bookends between which a series of hectic and mysteriously linked narratives is to be uneasily held.

Particularly striking is the two-fold story called "Ayesha," whose first and fearsome half concerns a "bearded and turbaned Imam" in exile from his homeland, called Desh, biding his time in infidel London, or Sodom as he sees it. He is "a massive stillness, an immobility. He is living stone." When the revolution begins in Desh, the overthrowing of the Westernized and hence corrupt Empress, Ayesha (that this was the name of Muhammad's favorite wife must be beside the point), the Imam flies there on Gibreel's back—the so-called archangel is, as ever, bemused, reluctant, put-upon, no matter that he may be dreaming it all—and we see the people being slaughtered as they march on the palace gates.

The revolution prevails, Ayesha turns into Al-Lat, one of the false daughters of Allah, and is destroyed in a combat involving thunderbolts and comets, and we see the people marching into the mouth of the Imam, grown monstrous, and being swallowed whole, just as earlier they had marched into the Empress's guns, martyrs still. The Imam's pronouncement becomes fact:

> After the revolution there will be no clocks; we'll smash the lot. The word *clock* will be expunged from our dictionaries. After the revolution there will be no birthdays. We shall all be born again, all of us the same unchanging age in the eye of Almighty God.

Gibreel has earlier mused on the curious circumstance that people who claim to believe in God should be possessed by demons. Yet later an Indian intellectual contends that we cannot "deny the ubiquity of faith" nor should we mock at the masses for what we see as their deludedness. Rushdie's book is copious in thesis and antithesis, but, not too surprisingly, synthesis hovers beyond it.

The second half begins charmingly, in a village where butterflies abound, and the landowner Mirza Saeed is devoted to his wife, Mishal. A young peasant girl appears, an epileptic, an eater of amenable butterflies, and to his horror he lusts after her. Mishal is found to have inoperable breast cancer, and Ayesha—for that is the peasant girl's name—declares that she is married to Gibreel and the archangel has told her that the village must go on a pilgrimage to Mecca, on foot, for the Arabian Sea will open to let them through. As did the Red Sea for Moses and the children of Israel in the Koran as well as the Bible. "Everything is required of us, and everything will be given." The sequel, recounted in a later chapter, is protracted, disjointed, and ambiguous: perhaps the pilgrims crossed the sea, perhaps the pilgrims drowned in the sea. In the ritual opening words of Arab storytellers, deployed repeatedly here, "It was so, it was not so."

"Ellowen Deeowen": as Mahound is to Muhammad, so is Babylon to Britain, whose capital city is Babylondon. The London scenes are both strong and weak, brilliant and muzzy, banal and inventive. Picked up as an illegal immigrant, though actually a British citizen (even a member of the Garrick Club), Saladin is beaten up nastily in the police van. While this looks like another instance of police brutality toward what are termed "ethnics," the fact that he sports horns, cloven hooves, and an immense erection, and moreover litters the van with soft pellets of excrement, hardly augurs well for an easy ride. The policemen gloat over the effects of feeding their horses richly on the eve of expected trouble: getting showered with shit provokes the demonstrators into violence, *"an' then we can really get amongst them, can't we just."*

This could be an attack on police methods; it could be a send-up of rightminded attacks on police methods. Blacks and browns, it begins to seem, are lovable rogues or displaced metaphysicians, and whites are racist yahoos or middle-class bigots, until they all dissolve into ultra-Dickensian phantasmagoria. The scene in the "ethnic" Club Hot Wax, where effigies of such villains as Enoch Powell and Margaret Thatcher ("Mrs. Torture") are melted down to cries of *"burn-burn-burn"* and "the fire this time," doesn't contribute to racial harmony; and yet it might be thought that the engagingly wild, Westernized daughters of Muhammad Sufyan, proprietor of the Shaandaar Café, hold out some hope for a racially integrated future, more or less, after all. . . . But Saladin is reckoned by some to be a "Brown Uncle Tom," more English than the British. Rushdie is having it both ways again—"What one hates in whites . . . one must also hate when it turns up, inverted, in black"—and it won't do to make heavy weather of light farce or break a hornet on a wheel. "I'm saying nothing," is the author's own message. "Don't ask me to clear things up one way or the other, the time of revelations is long gone." (pp. 25-6)

As we near the end of the novel we are bound to ask ourselves tougher questions about [the] two adversaries, or (it might be) two friends. In human form Gibreel is implicated in several deaths, but the most vicious, deliberate act of evil is that of Saladin, when he murders the love between Gibreel and Alleluia or Allie Cone—her name a conflation, for what that's worth, of the archangel's mountain and Al-Lat, the exalted bird, the desired—by whispering in Gibreel's ear, anonymously, over the phone, a second and suggestive set of Satanic verses:

> I like coffee, I like tea,
> I like things you do with me. . . .
>
> Violets are blue, roses are red,
> I've got her right here in my bed.

And yet Saladin is accorded the book's least fantasticated, most human and affecting chapter, when he goes home to his dying father, from whom he has been alienated since childhood. "To fall in love with one's father after the long angry decades was a serene and beautiful feeling; a renewing, life-giving thing, Saladin wanted to say, but did not, because it sounded vampirish." Death, he reflects, as friends and relatives gather around the sick man, brings out the best in people. Even, we could add, in writers.

Which of the two, Gibreel and Saladin, finally is good, which is evil? Computation won't come up with an answer. Both of them are both.

Rushdie incorporates a decade's headlines in his sprawling tapestry: the Union Carbide disaster in Bhopal, children massacred in Assam, the Falklands war, the Grosvenor Square demonstrations against American action in Vietnam, the yeti, drug addiction, the suspicious death of a black man in police custody, the fellow who conned wealthy women into giving him money to buy his soul back from the Devil, the recent phenomenon of multiple births, high-rise slums and the scandal of "temporary accommodation" in London. . . . He weaves in a plethora (some would say a plague) of jokes and allusions: the name "Othello" as a misspelling of "Attallah"; "kung-phooey" movies; "Whisky" Sisodia, a stutterer; the woman of property who owns a seacoast in Bohemia; the man (Saladin's father) who considers books pernicious and acquires thousands of them in order to let them rot, ignominiously, unread; the fallen arches that make Allie feel she is walking on broken glass (cf. Hans Andersen's humanized mermaid and the knife-pains she must suffer); a musical adaptation of *Our Mutual Friend* restyled *Friend!* (cf., rather obviously, Lionel Bart's *Oliver!*).

All this, plus the trickiness, the occasional *longueur*, the tedious international four-letter language (though Rushdie is a smart linguistic mimic), and the recurring motifs of uncertain significance, would sink a less vigorous and fleet-footed piece of writing for good. Rushdie's working motto could be Blake's hellish proverb, "The road of excess leads to the palace of wisdom," or the one alleging that crooked, unimproved roads, and not the straight or straitened, are roads of genius. As it happens, there is a description of the Koran, prefacing the first English translation (1649), which could be—which is and is not—an adverse account of *The Satanic Verses:* "Thou shalt find it of so rude, and incongruous a composure, so farced with contradictions, blasphemies, obscene speeches, and ridiculous fables," that it will surely "prove an Antidote," confirming the reader in "the health of Christianity." In the present case, confirming the reader of more conventional and temperate fiction in the healthiness of his literary tastes.

To put it another way, *The Satanic Verses* is a thousand and one nights crammed into a week of evenings, a fitting successor to *Midnight's Children* and *Shame* (novels whose feasible successors it was hard to imagine), a book that nobody else in Britain (at least) would have wanted to write, or could have written. Whatever the whole may amount to, the sum of the parts is a substantial one. There isn't so much to be said in the abstract about good and evil, except to acknowledge that they, or something very like them, do exist. "The world is incompatible, just never forget it: gaga," says Otto Cone, ex-Cohen, a Polish émigré and Allie's father. "Ghosts, Nazis, saints, all alive at the same time; in one spot, blissful happiness, while down the road, the inferno. You can't ask for a wilder place." Or a more Manichaean depiction of it.

Self-indulgent the author may be, but the reader is pleasured as well. The present reader is too old not to be grateful for that. No doubt rather more in the way of order and (what art can and ought to give us, although and because life doesn't) of clarity would have been appreciated too. It is written in the Koran that poets—and the Mighty One would surely be pleased to include novelists—rove aimlessly in every valley, preaching what they never practice, and followed by none save erring men. If doubts assail us, if all else fails us, we can still tell ourselves that we have been watching a prodigiously sophisticated yet action-packed mega-"theological." (p. 26)

D. J. Enright, "So, and Not So," in The New York Review of Books, *Vol. XXXVI, No. 3, March 2, 1989, pp. 25-6.*

MICHAEL WOOD

Contemporary fiction has several lookalike modes that are quite different beneath the narrative skin. Grass, Pynchon, Calvino, García Márquez, and Rushdie all deal in the extreme and the unlikely, but in each case the extremity and unlikeliness have accents of their own. In Grass, a crazy world is crazily pictured; in Pynchon, the craziness is questioned, becomes a chief topic; in Calvino, a fantastic secondary world is carefully elaborated; in García Márquez, the narrator doesn't notice anything untoward at all. Rushdie adopts all of these stances, in no particular order, and he is better at some than at others. But he also has a further specialty: the quick and crowded hallucination, the mind that is like a city, the mind that *is* a city, a population boom inside the head.

A good deal of what seems fantastic in *The Satanic Verses* is rooted in mental disorder or personal quirks within the story. A character dreams a whole series of legends, including a botched, erratic, but not unsympathetic history of the early years of Islam; dreams he is the Archangel Gabriel in person; sees the ghosts of someone else's past; waking, tries to play the archangel in modern London and discovers his fragile humanity by stepping into a stream of traffic along the Thames Embankment. The whimsical name Cone (belonging to a woman mountain-climber) turns out to be a version of the not so whimsical Cohen. The dream machinery seems clumsy to me, a rather weary narrative excuse. I think Rushdie could have done better. But the sense of breakdown in the archangel character is vividly evoked in all its pain and anguish; and Rushdie needs his rational, psychological grounding because it answers the sheer extravagance of the other elements of his plot, the craziness in the writing, so to speak, topping the craziness of the characters.

Two characters fall 29,000 feet from an exploding airplane and land unharmed on an English beach. Their descent occupies the whole brilliant first chapter of the novel. One of them turns into a hairy, horned devil complete with cloven hooves; even the archangel often has a halo that others can see. Rushdie's narrator intervenes periodically to remind us what a strange business this art of fiction is. "It was and it was not so," he likes to say, borrowing a traditional Arabic narrative formula, "it happened and it never did." "Let's face it," he remarks, "it was impossible." He means not the fortunate fall of the two characters, but their intricate antics as they drop. They can't have talked and sung in this elaborate and exhaustive way. Then the narrator adds: "But let's face this, too: they did." *They did* means that this is a novel and anything can happen; but it also hints, more subtly, that we have already believed stranger things outside of fiction. Novels are not the favorite haunt even of miracles.

Rushdie's two orders of fictional reality—the characters' delusions and the writer's inventions—come together to raise the question of belief. Rushdie wants us to understand what he at one point calls "the terrible power of metaphor," to remember that "fantasy can be stronger than fact." (Witness the exaggerations of Amerigo Vespucci, who "had continents named after him.") But mainly Rushdie is suggesting that such fictions are the closest a secular world can get to faith. Madness and literature are our substitutes for revelation, or at least our analogues. "We can't deny the ubiquity of faith," a non-religious Indian says in Bombay. One of the imaginary archangel's dreams concerns a pilgrimage toward Mecca that depends on the promised parting of the Arabian Sea before the travelers. Do the waters part? Well, the pilgrims seem to drown, and their swollen bodies float to shore; but almost all of the witnesses to the drowning *see* the waters part. We can worry, in other words, about faith and its fanaticisms—Rushdie's warmest admiration goes to a man he describes as a "godly and . . . unfanatic believer," as well as to several generous unbelievers—but we cannot doubt its power.

What we can doubt is its authority. This is where Rushdie's rather top-heavy narrative machinery begins to justify itself. A revelation requires first a revealer, a dictating archangel of God; then a listener, a messenger, an interpreter. If we believe in both parties, we are the faithful. But what if we believe in only one? The character who dreams that he is Gabriel illustrates precisely this question. On the one hand, he dreams languages he does not know, and so is, perhaps, authentically inspired, if only in dreams. On the other hand, he dictates, in his dreams, both the accepted verses of the Koran and the devious, accommodating verses said to have been delivered to Muhammed by Satan. "God knows whose postman I've been," he says breezily, but anxiously.

And again, of the time when the dream-Prophet acknowledges the previous dictation to have been that of the Adversary: "Gibreel . . . knows one small detail, just one tiny thing that's a bit of a problem here, namely *that it was me both times, baba, me first and second also me.*" There are other satanic verses in the novel, cruel jingles designed to drive a man—the same Gibreel, as it happens—mad with ordinary human jealousy; but the parody effect serves to enhance the point. If the other speaks, then, if the unknown makes itself known, the decision what to call it remains ours. God and the Devil, in this light, look less like antagonists and more like lurid options that we have invented for ourselves. The difference between good and evil is real enough, Rushdie suggests, but it is not as total as we think. That is not exactly a new lesson, but it is always worth offering, especially in harsh and schismatic times.

The most powerful moments in Rushdie's novel, though, have nothing to do with these high and difficult themes. A man returns to Bombay to see his father. He finds the old monster as crafty and aloof as ever, but turned religious, and morally slack into the bargain, seducing his servants from their former virtue. His house is a shoddy circus of imitations of the past. Son and father quarrel (again); much intervenes; the son returns as the father is dying, and finds the father he dreamed of but could never quite believe in. Too late, or not quite too late. "To fall in love with one's father after the long angry decades was an awesome and beautiful thing. . . ." A sentimental story? It would be one, if it were not realized with cool and telling detail. The son has come home without losing a jot of his sense of how complicated home is.

The Satanic Verses doesn't have the pace and the excitement of *Midnight's Children,* or the bitter concentration of *Shame.* There are moments when it threatens to disappear for good into one of its stately set pieces. The stories of the English lady's romance in Argentina, of Ms. Cone's climbing of Everest, of her sister's brief and glittering life, all have a strangely dutiful air, the feel of a writer trying to fill out a Big Book. But the pervading intelligence of the novel is so acute, the distress it explores so thoroughly understood, that the dullness doesn't settle, can't keep away the urgent questions and images that beset us.

This is Rushdie's most bewildered book, but it is also his most thoughtful. Its other great theme is dislocation and befuddled identity, its locus a Bombay and a London that have turned inside out and become each other. . . . What is telling about [the] fanciful and complex passage [which describes a "tropicalized" London] is its evocation not only of what immigrants to Britain must miss (and what they have escaped), but also of what they might bring to their adopted culture, if that culture were less scornful of them, less frightened of them.

One of the most haunting sequences in the novel evokes a ward in a London hospital full of freaks, humans half-turned into tigers, demons, snakes, wolves, water buffalo. How has this happened? "They describe us," one of the creatures whispers. "That's all. They have the power of description, and we succumb to the pictures they construct." *They* are the whites in Britain. This is how Britannia still nervously rules. Half of *The Satanic Verses* tells the terrible love story of Salahuddin Chamchawala, better known as Saladin Chamcha, an Indian Anglophile whose archaic and snobbish affection for Old England, anxiously sustained while the going was good, receives only shocks and insults when his carefully constructed Englishness comes apart.

All of these things—the tropics, the hospital ward, Chamcha's disarray—are mirrored and twisted in the scandal surrounding Rushdie's novel in England. . . . [*The Satanic Verses*] is said to blaspheme against Islam, and to insult the already much insulted Muslim community in Britain. But it can't blaspheme, because only believers can blaspheme, as Rushdie himself says in the novel, and this is a novel about doubt. (We may well wonder, as Rushdie did in an eloquent article in the *Observer* [see excerpt above], why a supposedly civilized and modern country is considering extending its blasphemy laws instead of abolishing them.) The book doesn't insult, either; but we are deep in the hospital ward here, and skins are understandably thin.

Yet the good liberal doctors who tell the patients that it's all right to be half-human may do more harm than the bigots who put the poor, colluding freaks in the ward in the first place. And the patients who don't collude, who don't feel themselves to be freaks, seem to think that they can keep their human dignity by being untouchable. Or, to put it differently, a great wave of fundamentalism, Christian, Muslim, Jewish, even secular, if we think of recurring appeals to "traditional values," is muddling issues all over the place.

The Satanic Verses is certainly irreverent; and it is not always funny enough to lift its irreverence into satire or speculation. But consider one of the most offending passages, the story of a brothel called The Curtain, the *Hijab,* in which the faithful can pretend to be the Prophet and sleep with courtesans who have taken the names and manners of the Prophet's 12 wives. It is brilliantly realized, a fine flight of comic, troubling, skeptical imagination, a moment worthy of Grass or García Márquez, or, to get a little closer to the source, of Genet. The story is surely in appalling taste. But that is its point. It casts no slur at all on religion. It comments wittily, instead, on the backsliding and the all too human material that religion has to work with.

Only edgy or beleaguered or tyrannical people take irreverence as insult. We should ask not what Rushdie has done to the Muslims in Britain. We should wonder, rather, what Britain has done to them, to make them so eager to turn their (admittedly mischievous) friend into their scapegoat. If they had read Rushdie's novel, they would have learned that the solemn religious respect that they want (and that he lacks) is the first step to the ghetto. Ghettos are made partly of unquestioned orthodoxies, partly of prejudice masked as tolerance. Tropical London is a lot more attractive than that. (pp. 28-30)

> Michael Wood, "The Prophet Motive," in The New Republic, *Vol. 200, No. 10, March 6, 1989, pp. 28-30.*

THE NEW YORK TIMES BOOK REVIEW

In a response to the crisis of Salman Rushdie, 28 distinguished writers born in 21 countries speak to him from their common land—the country of literature. For expressing their ideas publicly in the past many of these writers have suffered censorship, exile—forced or self-imposed—and imprisonment. Some have been politically active on behalf of the rights of writers under totalitarian regimes. Many are on the record here and in their own countries in support of Mr. Rushdie, the Indian-born British author of the novel **The Satanic Verses,** *who was still in hiding in England with a price on his head when* The Book Review *went to press. He has been accused by the Iranian revolutionary leader Ayatollah Ruhollah Khomeini of slandering Islam in his novel. The Ayatollah has called for his death.*

Mario Vargas Llosa
Peru.

I've been thinking about you very much and what has happened to you. I am in total solidarity with your book, and I would like to share with you this assault on rationalism, reason and freedom. Writers should unite forces in this most crucial moment in creative freedom. We thought this war was won a long time ago, but it wasn't. In the past, it was the Christian Inquisition, Fascism, Stalinism; now it's Muslim fundamentalism, and there will probably be others. The forces of fanaticism will always be there. The spirit of freedom will always be menaced by unrationality and intolerance, which are apparently deeply rooted in the human heart.

Nien Cheng
Born in China, lives in the United States.

You must be firm and be brave, because in some ways your position is worse than being in prison. You cannot identify your enemy. In Communist China during the Cultural Revolution many people who were not locked up suffered more than I did. They were beaten more frequently than I was. In prison you only have to contend with guards; hysterical mobs are worse. Death threats were only hinted at to me, but my daughter was beaten to death by a mob, though they did not intend to kill her. I hope you can resume normal life in the near future.

Chinua Achebe
Nigeria.

What does one say? I think probably all I can say is: Don't despair. The world has become a very dangerous place, but it is our responsibility to keep fighting for the freedom of the human spirit. It's not just for writers that we must do this, but for everyone. If we secure this freedom, the whole world benefits.

Joseph Brodsky
Born in Russia, lives in the United States.

I'm afraid the book itself asked for it. It was bound to create a stir among Muslims. Many professional writers count on a heightened reaction and there is nothing wrong with this calculation. But the volume, of course, could not have been foreseen. There is nothing surprising about the Ayatollah Khomeini, who is theoretically the top authority on Islam, commenting on the book. The death sentence he issued amounts as it were to a review of the book. As for Khomeini himself and what he has under his turban, I'm quite surprised that nobody thus far has put a price on that as well. It would be the only comparable response. If men of letters feel so indignant about the whole affair they should have pooled their resources and come up with the price. Mind you, it shouldn't be too big. On the whole this lifts the veil on Islamic fundamentalism. They execute people left and right and nobody gives a squeak.

Anita Desai
India.

Silence, exile and cunning, yes. And courage.

José Donoso
Chile.

The situation you are in is completely unfair, completely uncivilized. Stay in hiding until it blows over. This thing will blow over soon. After a while people will not remember the scandal, but if the book is good, they will remember the book. Let's hope all this is going to help writers band together against situations of this sort and reaffirm the fact that the word is more powerful than the sword.

Elie Wiesel
Born in Rumania, lives in the United States.

Any attack on you is directed at us all. Censorship in literature is the enemy of literature and death threats, addressed for whatever reason, if they succeed in silencing the author, would mean not only the end of literature but the end of civilization.

Iris Murdoch
Born in Ireland, lives in England.

Wars end. The night will end.

Amos Oz
Israel.

Written words still have the amazing power to bring out the best and the worst of human nature. We ought to treat words the way we treat nuclear energy or genetic engineering—with courage, caution, vision and precision. Those who vowed to kill you actually wish to kill our entire civilization. Take good care of yourself.

Nadine Gordimer
South Africa.

A writer has to have freedom. I cannot sufficiently express my horror at the threat and the consequences of that threat. There is no precedent for this at all; it is the ultimate, the very last measure, of dictatorship. I can understand that some people's sensibilities might be offended by the book, and even that Muslim countries might ban it, but they cannot tell the whole world what to do. I don't know what to tell you to do. I can only assure you of my horror and my full support.

Czeslaw Milosz
Born in Lithuania, lives in the United States.

I have particular reasons to defend your rights, Mr. Rushdie. My books have been forbidden in many countries or have had whole passages censored out. I'm grateful to people who stood then by the principle of free expression, and I back you now in my turn.

Umberto Eco
Italy.

Nobody can ignore your ordeal, for at least three reasons.

First (and once again), a man is being persecuted for having written a book.

Second, for the first time in the history of this century the death penalty is extended beyond the borders of a single country, in spite of the laws of other countries. Exile, the last resort of free men, does not work any longer.

Third, your potential killers are summoned through the media; ironically, any medium covering the event contributes to inform and mobilize new potential killers.

You deserve the full and passionate solidarity of any man of dignity, but I am afraid this is too little. This story of a man alone against worldwide intolerance, and of a book alone against the craziness of the media, can become the story of many others. The bell tolls for all of us.

Ralph Ellison
United States.

Keep to your convictions.

Try to protect yourself.

A death sentence is a rather harsh review.

Rumer Godden
Born in India, lives in Britain.

As someone who lived for so many years in India, I think you should have been more aware of what you were doing to offend Muslims, because they are exceedingly sensitive. Anything to do with their religion provokes a tremendous response, as it does with many committed Christians of the very orthodox type. Whatever you have done, probably you wrote it as a good story. I tremble for your safety.

Derek Walcott
Born in St. Lucia, lives in the United States.

It is regrettable that the phantasmagoric nature of your book has not been taken into consideration. Saints in the extremities of temptation are capable of nightmares beyond normal human fear. Literature is closest to religion when it tries to contain all human desperation. The madness in *The Satanic Verses* has been misread as yours and not that of your characters. All writers are endangered if they are to be judged by the characters they create: Shakespeare would be a racist, Dante a bigot.

Susan Sontag
United States.

I hope you are getting some exercise and listening to music, dear Salman. And writing. Write another book. And another.

David Grossman
Israel.

I know you feel lonely. Despite all the expressions of sympathy you are lonely and words from others will not comfort you. But even when you are surrounded by fear you still have something to defend yourself with. As a writer, a creator, you are used to being lonely at the most difficult struggles and you know how rich with nuances is your inner world and you know every human being is inhabited by countless characters—so you are not really alone. There are many people against you and they are motivated by hatred and fanaticism. To want to obliterate even one person they must first obliterate themselves. There are a lot of people in Israel who sympathize with your struggle against fanaticism. I wish you would use your light and write.

Heberto Padilla
Born in Cuba, lives in the United States.

This is terrorism indeed. It is like having the entire world intellectual community in a single hijacked airplane. You should remember, however, this is not the first time in history a writer has had to be in hiding; Fascism forced that on many in World War II, and there are other examples. You have uncovered the kind of oppression we are living under in our times; I myself have known some of that. You should accept this reality and keep on writing. The task now is to resist, to keep calm, to trust your friends all over the world, because this is not only the Rushdie battle but the battle of all free people, and free people will realize that. I think many people are still to be heard from; many in the Soviet Union will come to your defense, I think, many writers. People everywhere will do that.

Norman Mailer
United States.

"My country, right or wrong," Stephen Decatur said. That is faith. It seems all we writers who have no faith have been led back to one by your nightmare. The irony is that we have had it all along. We believe in freedom of expression as an absolute. How dangerous to use the word absolute, but you have pulled it forth from us—your health!

Adam Michnik
Poland.

I am deeply distressed that once again a time has returned when it's possible publicly to call for murder. My distress is all the greater because the designated victim of the murder is a writer. A world in which a fanatic governing Iran can rent paid murderers all over the globe is a world in which no one is safe. Salman Rushdie was condemned to death and that's why it's every person's duty to give him shelter. We need to be on the side of the writer and against those who want to murder him. I'd like Salman Rushdie to know that my house is his house.

Robertson Davies
Canada.

Your suffering shows the world, in an extreme form, what every serious writer must face. To write truly is not to deal in entrenched ideas but to give voice to whatever we can raise from the depths of the human spirit, which is where the future lies, waiting for the call. To raise the future inevitably provokes the malignity of the past. We are sorry for your distress but we would not wish unsaid what you have written, for the task of all of us is to say what entrenched opinion considers unspeakable.

Octavio Paz
Mexico.

We are seeing a disappearance of the modern values that came with the Enlightenment. These people who condemn you are living before the Enlightenment. We are facing a historical contradiction in our century.

I would say to you, remain firm. I defend the writer's right to be wrong.

Bharati Mukherjee
Born in India, lives in the United States.

I should like you, Salman, to know that we care more about your personal safety and about the preservation of your books and your message than we do about the chain bookstore owners' angst, which unfortunately has seized the media headlines. The religious establishment seems to have proved itself to be the source either of threat or of cowardice. I hope in spite of everything your next novel will be so scaldingly blasphemous that even liberals will cringe.

Josef Skvorecky
Born in Czechoslovakia, lives in Canada.

Meaning no harm, I, too, wrote a few sentences in my first novel that angered the mighty in my country. At that time, they only confiscated my book from bookstores and threatened my liberty, but although they did not threaten my life, perhaps I have at least some idea of what it is like. I pray that tolerance and respect for life prevail. I keep thinking of you.

Thomas Pynchon
United States.

Our thanks to you and to Marianne Wiggins, for recalling those of us who write to our duty as heretics, for reminding us again that power is as much our sworn enemy as unreason, for making us all look braver, wiser, more useful than we often think we are. We pray for your continuing good health, safety and lightness of spirit.

George Konrad
Hungary.

I will be speaking in Budapest on behalf of both you and Vaclav Havel [the dissident Czechoslovak playwright who was jailed in February for taking part in a protest in Prague]. I believe your causes are linked. It is absolutely irrelevant what is in your novel because a novel cannot be the object of any moral or legal judgment. It is an elementary question of the freedom of writing and I believe we writers have to share the responsibility you took, and we do support the publication of your work.

Thomas Keneally
Australia.

I remember the day you and Bruce Chatwin were setting off together from Adelaide to visit Alice Springs in central Australia. Now Bruce is dead and you are under a tyrant's sentence of death. All I can say is what I heard a number of authors crying in the streets of New York recently during a demonstration in favor of your right to free expression. "I am Rushdie." We all are.

Margaret Atwood
Canada.

You're the one in trouble; tell *us* what we can do to best support you. It's all too easy to pop off the handle and say what is on my mind without reflecting on your position. We feel deeply the horror of your position. And remember: You are worth a great deal more to the Ayatollah alive than dead, because dead you are no longer something to be waved around. (pp. 1, 28-9)

> *"Words for Salman Rushdie," in* The New York Times Book Review, *March 12, 1989, pp. 1, 28-9.*

THE EDITORS OF
THE NEW REPUBLIC

> For books are not absolutely dead things, but do contain a potency of life in them to be as active as the soul whose progeny they are. . . . [As] good almost kill a man as kill a good book: who kills a man kills a reasonable creature, God's image; but he who destroys a good book kills reason itself, kills the image of God, as it were, in the eye. . . . We should be wary, therefore, what persecution we raise against the living labors of public men, how we spill that seasoned life of man preserved and stored up in books; since we see a kind of homicide may be thus committed, sometimes a martyrdom . . .
>
> John Milton, *Areopagitica*

In the West, we read Milton and More and Galileo and Spinoza and Locke and Voltaire and Jefferson and Mill and Mann and Sakharov a little smugly, since they won. Glibly we attach a historical inevitability to the triumph of their spirit. We praise their courage, and flatter ourselves that we would have stood with them, that none of our loyalties to family, society, religion, and state would have interfered with our loyalty to freedom. After all, we know about the debt that democracy owes to heresy. The proper course of our thoughts and our actions would have been plain.

The persecution of Salman Rushdie and *The Satanic Verses* should dispel this triumphalism, and humble. It is, by the standards of our history, a classic affair: a man of the word against a man of the Word, the power of the word against the power of the powers. But look, Rushdie is more or less alone. He has only the resources of his soul and his wife and Scotland Yard to sustain him, while politicians, writers, publishers, and booksellers run for cover. By now many of the still, silent ones have been roused, or shamed, into finding their voice. But the complacence of the Western literary world the morning after the Ayatollah "sentenced" Rushdie to death, its overwhelming failure to treat Rushdie's enemy like the enemy of us all, continues to shock. In a moment of truth, we acted like heirs gone to seed.

It has been a long time, of course, since an Ayatollan darkness was a part of our experience. Even Rushdie seems to have forgotten, in the writing of his extraordinary book, the magnitude of an established faith's fury. "What the religious fundamentalists are saying," the stunned writer told a reporter before he was forced to flee, "is: 'God sent the Koran. Full stop. End of discussion.'" Well, yes. The zealot is a man without irony. He is not interested in wit. He detests doubt. He fears complexity. He consecrates violence. As the campaign against him escalated, Rushdie began to grasp that he was caught in a conflict between absolutes. "Frankly, I wish I'd written a more critical book," he bravely told British television. "I call upon the intellectual community in this country and abroad to stand up for freedom of the imagination, which is an issue much larger than my book or indeed my life." One day the Muslim world may remember that sentence gratefully, may look back fondly upon its late-20th-century Anglo-Indian Voltaire.

"It is not true," said Rushdie, "that this book is a blasphemy against Islam." But alas, it is true. It will profit nothing to teach the zealot about the techniques of magical realism, to plead that the prostitutes who are given the names of the Prophet's wives appear in a dream sequence, that the novel is a satire whose subject is madness, that art invents. The zealot is a man of literal meanings. More to the point, however, blasphemy is nothing to be ashamed about. It is a birthpang of democracy.

Remember that Europe was once a stifled, theocratic, feudal, crusading society, which was kept by a powerful church in what Milton called "a perpetual childhood of prescription"; and it was blasphemy that pushed open the shutters. The insult to the church served as an instrument of knowledge. Neither science nor art could proceed without offending. And as truth was added to, cruelty was subtracted from: tolerance for thoughts and thinkers that rebelled against the church and its compulsion became the very measure of justice. Two cheers for blasphemy, then; and for Rushdie's blasphemy, too.

We are hearing a lot about the hurt feelings of Muslims, particularly from the representatives of Muslim organizations on American television. But it is Rushdie, not Khomeini, who is running for his life. And it is *The Satanic Verses,* not the Koran, that is banned and burned. Do the people who put a match to Rushdie's book in England, who demand that it be withdrawn from bookstores in the United States, understand where they are living? If they cannot celebrate the pluralism of their adopted countries, they had better swallow it. In these countries we are dogmatic about tolerance. We hold communities high, but not at the cost of democracy. We hold that the right of the believer to protest against the blasphemer is precisely the right of the blasphemer to blaspheme.

For the believer, it is confusing, no doubt, to live in a society in which his truth counts only as an opinion. And it is doubly confusing for the immigrant believer, who wants liberty no less than authenticity, who carries his traditions willingly to a culture that puts them in peril, who wants to be a Muslim and a modern. Sometimes the pressures of freedom are fantastic, as the immigrant defends himself against the object of his own desire. It is easy to understand why immigrants feel threatened. It is less easy to understand why they make threats. And the bad joke is that few writers have written more obsessively than Rushdie about the contradictions of which he now is the victim.

We are also hearing a lot about Western ignorance of Islam,

about insulting stereotypes of Muslims in the media, and so on. There is no denying the coarseness of much that journalists say and write about the Muslim world. Nor should we, in the West, gloat. "The individual" was not "born" somewhere in Paris sometime around 1789; enlightenment in the West was an accomplishment of many centuries, during which many books and many people were immolated. But in the Rushdie affair the West has not a thing to apologize for. In truth, the West is the poor man's only hope. Let us call this the Islamabad irony. When the mobs in Islamabad marched against Rushdie's book before the American cultural center, many were baffled by the association. In fact, the association was beautifully appropriate. If you are for the banning and the burning of books, if you deny the right of a writer to write and the right of a publisher to publish, if you believe that an opinion may be refuted by a bullet, you are anti-American. The militant mullahs are right. Philosophically and historically, the United States is their enemy. The defender of *The Satanic Verses* is The Great Satan. For this we may be proud.

How to understand these convulsions in Iran, India, Pakistan, and throughout the Muslim world? We are given two kinds of explanations, political and cultural. The political explanation is too forgetting, the cultural explanation is too forgiving.

The political explanation, most clearly stated by Shaul Bakhash in the *Washington Post* [see excerpt above], teaches that "Rushdie's novel is not the chief target." Rushdie is trapped, rather, in a bitter fight between "hard-liners" and "pragmatists" over the future of Iran's relationship to the West. "By suggesting that the Rushdie book constitutes an American and CIA plot against an insurgent Islam," writes Bakhash, "the hard-liners make much more difficult any attempt at an Iran-U.S. reconciliation." Obviously there is some truth to this. (pp. 7-8)

The cultural explanation was exemplified by Edward Mortimer, in an astounding piece in the *Financial Times* of London. Rushdie "must have known, when he wrote *The Satanic Verses,* that many Muslims would be unable to take the novel in the playful, sardonic spirit in which it was apparently [!] meant. . . . By naming the book and the characters as he did, Mr. Rushdie clearly courted such a reaction." The point is not quite that the author is responsibile for his fate, but that the Muslim world is not quite responsible for its actions. For "many Muslims are very sensitive about attacks on their religion" (as, no doubt, many writers are very sensitive about attacks on their work). "They tend," you see, "to see themselves as a beleaguered community." "Does that mean" (this is the clincher) "that Ayatollah Khomeini is qualified to pass a death sentence in Islamic terms? Most Muslim authorities would say not, but in the eyes of his followers the Ayatollah has assumed a kind of leadership . . ." and so on.

Not an echo of horror here. Only the Orientalism, the patronizing pardon, of the apologist for Islam. Never mind that Islam does not require an apology; not even Khomeini can compromise his entire faith. Never mind that such apologetic sensitivity was precisely the reason for Rajiv Gandhi's banning of the book last fall. (South Africa, widely known for its sensitivity to the feelings of the many, banned the book for the same reasons. And Naguib Mahfouz, the Nobel laureate in literature, a secular man who casts a cold eye on clerics, whose own work is banned in his own country, boldly condemned the contract on Rushdie as "intellectual terrorism," and then concurred in the banning of the book in Egypt. Enlightenment works in mysterious ways.) The banning was supposed to prevent violence. Naturally, it had the opposite effect. The masses learned from the government only that they were correct in their judgment of the book. The subcontinent confirmed last week what Europeans can still remember: that the killing of books leads to the killing of people.

Rushdie has been writing for years precisely to banish this kind of condescension from the discussion of Muslim life. A student of Muslim history and a man of the left, he needs no lessons in the impact of imperialism upon Muslim society. He is alive to the fact that Muslims, especially immigrant Muslims, are "beleaguered." But still he holds them to the standard of truth. He studies their foibles, he burrows into their scars, he insists that they are accountable for the pain they make themselves. All of his novels are written in the confidence that Muslims will survive the mirror of art as well as anybody else. Beauty, of course, is not all that shows in Rushdie's glass. But the self-respect in the reflection is unmistakable.

The same cannot be said, alas, of the American literary community, or of the American political class. Jefferson ("Difference of opinion is advantageous in religion. . . . What has been the effect of coercion? To make one half the world fools, and the other half hypocrites.") would have been disgusted.

All the nations of the European Community have proudly withdrawn their diplomats from Tehran. Secretary of State James Baker, back from a trip to said community but immune to its influence, conceded on "Meet the Press" that Khomeini's contract on Rushdie is "basically intolerable," but added: "I haven't read the book. I haven't seen the book. I don't know what is said in there. I don't mean to be blessing the book." But he doesn't mean to be cursing its foes, either. (pp. 8-9)

Cardinal John O'Connor followed in the secretary's spirit. He, too, "denounced" the Ayatollah's edict. But the cardinal's heart was not in it. "We deplore seeing anyone's religion just treated with seeming contempt and ridicule or treated with anything less than great reverence. It's not for me to talk about what constitutes freedom of speech or what should or should not be censored." . . . A man not of the cloth nor the paperback.

Then there are the American writers, slow in the struggle for their ideal, unsteady in the service of their own. There were some—Susan Sontag, William Styron, John Updike, Frances Fitzgerald, Robert Coover, a few others—who threw caution to the winds, like writers. But it is fair to say that in the beginning American writers were almost nowhere to be found. Bookers for television and radio complained loudly that almost nobody would defend Rushdie on the air. The people whose hobby is protest in speech were speechless. Their humanities courses appear to have been wasted on them. "I'd have to be crazy not to have some apprehension," said Arthur Miller, the hero of the House Un-American Activities Committee. "Not going on television is not necessarily a sign of anything."

Norman Mailer announced that he would make his pronouncement in his own time. Rushdie would have to wait. Mailer, it appears, can live with writers endangering other people. It is when other people endanger writers that he

thinks twice. (Of course, the controversy about his procrastination was also nice.) And so it went. . . .

And finally there were the chains, or what Ted Solotaroff has called, in these pages, "the literary-industrial complex." If any proof is needed of the impact of the corporate mentality upon American publishing in recent years, Waldenbooks, B. Dalton, and Barnes & Noble have provided the proof. Even as Viking/Penguin, Rushdie's dauntless publisher, stood by the book, and independent bookstores nervously kept it on their shelves, it was announced that all these chain stores, 1,250 of them, almost a third of the book trade in the United States, will no longer sell it. These pin-striped booksellers seem to think that the book business is like the shoe business: merely a matter of commerce. They seem not to know that bookstores are one of the most significant institutions of a democracy; that they are vending the sacred objects of a free society; that the sale of a book is the endorsement of a principle; that there is high honor in their work. . . .

As we go to press, the Ayatollah is proclaiming that it is the duty of Muslims "to send [Rushdie] to hell." He is revolting, this man of God without mercy in his heart. Rushdie is underground, hunted, living a nightmare, looking for words that will restore the rest of his days to him without compromising him as a writer. And we, the lucky ones, have been taught, at this late date in the history of infamy, when we still needed the lesson, that democracy can have its martyrs, too. May Salman Rushdie not become one of them. (p. 9)

> *"Two Cheers for Blasphemy," in* The New Republic, *Vol. 200, No. 11, March 13, 1989, pp. 7-9.*

INDIA TODAY

The ironies piled up with the remorselessness of a magic realist's prose. That a book hardly read—or read and little understood—should have so jolted the world and created a literary maelstrom not seen many times since the last world war. That an author who was called impenetrable, convoluted if not confused and, in any case much too elitist to attract international popular attention should have caused such a storm in Khomeini's Iran. That a piece of fiction, dismissed by many reviewers as a complicated allegory which struggled to stay in the shelves of the western world's bookshops should have become an instant bestseller—one that book chains such as the venerable Waldenbooks of the US found too hot to stock and one that others sold under the counter. One that even Canada, Greece and France were afraid to publish.

Amazingly, before Iranian religious strongman Imam Ayatollah Ruhollah Khomeini's *fatwa* decreeing death for Salman Rushdie, the 41-year-old India-born author, hit the world in its face, not many knew what the controversy was all about. Some nations, including India, had banned the book. Yet even most reviewers were unsure if the book was talking about Islam. They sailed through the passages responsible for Rushdie's plight now. . . . Some thought the book was about evil; others about death; still others about Rushdie himself. (p. 14)

Now, the book is a collector's item, like a blue-chip share certificate to invest in. People are picking copies in bulk hoping that one day it will become a rare and valuable item.

The book is capacious—convoluted plot, array of outlandish characters—with the dazzling language and effects that are the hallmark of his fiction. It attempts to explore the questions of good and evil through the experiences of two Indian actors, Gibreel and Chamcha, who falling out of a plane into England, metamorphose into Archangel Gabriel and the Devil respectively. Gibreel's hallucinations call up the passages that have rocked the world. Rushdie weaves fantasies around traditional accounts of the Prophet's life and calls him Mahound—the Devil. In a chapter that is at the centre of the ruckus he has a dozen prostitutes assuming the names of the Prophet's wives. Rushdie's claim that he is trying to explore through fiction the issue of divine inspiration is not bought by many Muslims.

And therefore "that strange expatriate Indian novelist" who had made waves in New York, the publishing capital of the world, when he pocketed the *Verses* advance from Viking Penguin, was hiding in a London suburb with a price of nearly $6 million . . . on his head. Officers of Scotland Yard's Special Branch stood guard over Rushdie as an unprecedented international storm raged with the Ayatollah's death squads beginning the hunt and the entire western world embarking on a fresh isolation of Iran.

The storm raised by the book and the Ayatollah's decree that its author be killed had already left more than 20 persons dead and many more injured in India and Pakistan where it was banned anyway. The fury was in full evidence in Bombay last week as the crowd shouting "Rushdie Murdabad" gathered at the Zakaria Masjid near Crawford Market and went on a rampage when police stopped them from moving towards the British Council office. Later as the blazes turned into embers at least eight lay dead. Earlier, for three days the entire Kashmir valley was paralysed. Holding green Pakistani flags, rioting hordes shouted anti-India slogans and battled with the police.

"This is jihaad," declared writer Anthony Burgess. The *New York Times* thundered: "Firmness is required to counter this diabolical business." *Le Monde* chorussed: "The orders of the master of Teheran are a perversion of Islam, just as the inquisition was a perversion of Christianity."

While the world convulsed Rushdie attempted appeasement. "Living in a world of many faiths . . . we must be conscious of the sensibilities of others," he said in an apology that many thought was platitudinous and even allegorical in typical Rushdie style. Also, it was more condescending than remorseful. "Rushdie should do anything possible. I would grovel before the Ayatollah," suggested author Farrokh Dhondy. Rushdie's voice was lost in the din of the fractious post-war Iran's politics as IRNA, its official news agency, repeatedly contradicted itself, saying that the pardon had been denied, then granted and finally recanting again.

Meanwhile policemen were working overtime in cities as far apart as New Delhi, London, New York and Tokyo, handling bomb threats to shops that stocked the book and protecting its publishers. In Britain police jostled with rioters in the wool-town of Bradford. . . . (pp. 14-17)

In Rushdie's native city, Bombay, just one telephone call evoked at least a semblance of the fear he must have been living with. A man, speaking in broken English, claiming to represent the Islamic Revolutionary Guards, threatened to exterminate poet Dom Moraes, Shiv Sena supremo Bal Thackeray, Gandhian Usha Mehta, and Hindustani Andolan Convenor Madhu Mehta, for criticising Khomeini's death verdict on Rushdie. The police were investigating the antecedents of

Bombay's 9,000-strong Iranian community. Thackeray responded with characteristic bravado: he threatened the city's Iranians with retaliation. In Delhi's Jama Masjid Imam Abdullah Bukhari declared: "Whatever Khomeini has said should happen. It is very difficult for Rushdie to remain alive." . . .

Halfway round the globe, in New York, executives of Viking Penguin wore bullet-proof vests to work. A tell-tale tape recorder hung over the telephone switchboard to record incoming phone calls in case of bomb threats and FBI agents scoured the building, mocked by a copy of *Verses* displayed in a glass case in the lobby. "Terrorism has come to publishing," said Sonny Mehta, the president of the prestigious Alfred A. Knopf. "It is a grave concern when criticism is turned to mortal threats." In London publisher Andre Deutsch said: "I have been in publishing all my life and there has been nothing like this before."

Though Mehta described Rushdie as one of the five or six most important writers in the world and as "a stormraiser", the Satanic fury of the storm was not what Rushdie or his friends had bargained for.

Around the world indignation elbowed out reason. Iranian President Ali Khamenei announced that an "arrow had been aimed at the heart of Salman Rushdie, the blasphemous bastard". The usually soft-spoken US Secretary of State James Baker reacted in Oliver North-like fashion, declaring: "The action will block Iran's efforts to rejoin civilized society." Announcing the decision to withdraw their envoys from Teheran, the foreign ministers of the 12 EEC countries said in a joint statement that they condemned "this incitement to murder as an unacceptable violation of the most elementary principles and obligations that govern relations among sovereign states".

For Western Europe the crisis came at a most inopportune time, just when they were hoping to profit from Iran's post-war reconstruction. (p. 17)

As political rhetoric grew stronger the rag press merrily played the field. The British gutter press was full of insults against Khomeini calling him "Mad Imam" and Iran's envoy in London, Adhnuzade Basti, as "Nasty Basti". British media tycoon Robert Maxwell took the retaliatory lead offering £1 million to whoever "civilised Khomeini". Australian media marauder Rupert Murdoch warned the Muslims in Britain to behave. The announcement was front-paged in Persian script in *The News of the World*. In the streets of Teheran the madness was more than matched by demonstrators screaming "death to Rushdie".

If the controversy split the world, politically it served to coalesce the community of writers and artistes as nothing had ever done, not the annihilation of Jewish writers before the Second World War, nor the persecutions of Sakharov, Solzhenitsyn and Kundera. "The little enmities," as playwright Hanif Kureishi (*My Beautiful Laundrette, Sammy and Rosie Get Laid*) says, "have been forgotten".

Groups led by Harold Pinter and Lady Antonia Fraser gave letters to the House of Commons urging it to act. Even in the dog-eat-dog world of Asian writers and artistes there came an unprecedented identification with the new cause celebre. Said Kureishi: "I am shocked and ashamed by what my fellow Muslims are saying. We must urge Ayatollah Khomeini to withdraw the death threat." Author and TV producer

Tariq Ali didn't mince words either: "The spiritual leader of the Islamic Republic was speaking in the language of a mafia godfather."

At the prestigious PEN (Poets, Essayists, Novelists) Centre in Manhattan a bevy of American authors, led by Norman Mailer and E. L. Doctorow, read out of the "condemned" author's book. "If he is ever killed for a folly, we must be killed for the same folly, and we may need be," said Mailer, reasoning, "Since we will then vow to do our best to open all literary meetings with a reading of the critical passages of *The Satanic Verses*." Even more defiantly said Leon Wieseltier, the editor of *New Republic:* "Let us be dogmatic about tolerance. It was blasphemy that made us free. Two cheers today for blasphemy."

But it is the mere insinuation of blasphemy from inquisitors who, on their own admission, have not read the book, that has made Rushdie perhaps a prisoner for the rest of his life. And of course an inerasable part of literary history too.

Until now Rushdie and his *Verses* were the rarefied preserve of the pundits of literature. Today in Britain, Rushdie is a household name, a pop star of the literary world. Shop girls at lunch hour earnestly discuss the differences between Shias and Sunnis. Taxi drivers want to know if you are Muslim and what the book and fuss is all about. On television Rushdie's haunting face with the heavy-lidded eyes and unevenly folded lips dominate. State of art media brings images which are archaic, reminiscent of the battlefields of the Holy Wars; the smell of the smoke from the burning books is almost palpable; the angry eyes and raised fists of mobs in Bradford and Teheran electrify. (pp. 17-18)

One reason Rushdie did not foresee the threats from Islamic fundamentalists is that he was preoccupied and upset by the hostile reviews of his book in the British press. What had brought out the claws of some of the journalists was the unprecedented advance Rushdie had been paid. The literary world also resented the fact that Rushdie had changed his British agent and his publisher. Rushdie's new American agent, Andrew Wylie, had worked out the fabulous deal. Novelist and close friend Angela Carter believes the hostility goes even deeper: "There was a tone of contemptuous sneering. They had restrained envy and contempt for a long time. I think there is a very strong element of racism, this is very similar to the attitude towards the Jews." What the literary establishment could not accept, according to Carter, was Rushdie's new-found role as a public personality, and even a spokesman for the Third World.

Another bitter irony in the present situation stems from the fact that Rushdie, unlike many expatriate writers, did not distance himself from either the Asians in Britain or in the subcontinent. Unlike V.S. Naipaul, he did not go on and on about lavatories in Third World. He appeared time and again on television and with his aggressive articulation attacked racism in England and the Thatcher Government, making himself many enemies, even among the liberals. The hate mail had begun when he started appearing on television—he was even addressed as nigger-lover! It was a no-win situation. Rushdie's friends believe his frequent appearances on television were responsibile for alienating him even further. (p. 20)

Some of the reviews were truly vicious. Wrote Philip Howard in *The Times:* "In 1986 . . . Rushdie changed his wife, his publisher and his agent." Howard went on to write, somewhat prophetically: "As usual the book is very long, high-flown, mystical, clever and pretentious . . . but it is important as literature and a nuclear bomb politically." Mark Lawson in *The Independent* described Rushdie's divorce as "a classic post-fame alienation from the pre-fame partner."

So keyed up was Rushdie about these attacks that when he was asked about his reaction to the threats from the fundamentalists he said he might be "egocentric" but he was not an "ego maniac" and did not expect thousands to descend onto the streets against him. At that point he was ready to do battle with the British establishment.

The clergymen of Qom were a different matter. And now while he hides somewhere in the country, . . . it is ironically the very establishment which had turned against him that now supports him.

If the establishment quickly rallied to Rushdie's side his plight had brought opportunity for both left and ultra-right groups to rabble rouse. Labour Party leaders like Michael Foot and Tony Benn were firmly with Rushdie while MP Bernie Grant believed that people like Rushdie who want to change Islam ought to go back to Pakistan. Grant was actually present when the book was burnt at Bradford. The minorities are sensitive vote banks. The furore also was well-timed for the racist National Front which conjured up visions of little Ayatollahs growing up in their England. It was time for closet racists to hit the streets.

Later as US President George Bush himself came out strongly in Rushdie's defence there were indications that this could also provide a new war cry for the American Rambos itching for another showdown with Iran. Diplomatic sources in Washington emphatically say there are influential people in the State Department who think Rushdie could replace Ollie North as the hero of the large and vocal anti-Iran constituency.

Rushdie then may be getting reduced to a mere pawn, trapped in the pincer of global and religious politics. Nothing illustrated that better than the logical motive driving the Ayatollah's belated outburst, full five months after the publication of the book. After the indecisive, decade-long war of attrition with Iraq leaving over a million dead, Iran, in the 11th year after the Shah's overthrow, is facing the moment of truth: a shattered economy, ravaged cities, a divided clergy. Asks Bombay-based Islamic scholar Asghar Ali Engineer: "The book has been around for a long time. Why was he quiet? There was not a whimper of protest from the Ayatollah when India banned it."

It is also possible that Rushdie's virulent criticism of fundamentalism could have attracted the clergy's attention to his book. In an article in *The Observer* [see excerpt above] he wrote: "A powerful tribe of clerics have taken over Islam. These are the contemporary Thought Police. They have turned Mohammad into a perfect being, his life into a perfect life . . ." The "Thought Police" was now striking back.

The widespread demonstrations reassert the Ayatollah's authority, at a time when President Ali Khamenei and the Speaker of the Majlis, Hojatoleslam Ali Rafsanjani have been trying to build bridges with the West to refurbish the economy, and the Ayatollah's chosen successor, Ayatollah Hussain Ali Montazeri, has begun asking uncomfortable questions about the purposeless war with Iraq. Iran's oil revenues have fallen from $20 billion in 1983, when it defied OPEC and overproduced to finance the war, to about $8 billion this year.

With its image as the revolutionary model for the Islamic world slipping, Rushdie emerged as an Allah-sent devil-incarnate. The cost of such militancy—severed relations with the West—is not high for the Ayatollah, who had snubbed the US by holding 52 diplomats and other embassy personnel hostage for 444 days in end '70s.

Outside Iran the controversy highlighted the fissures in the Islamic world as none of the Arab nations came out in Khomeini's support though they had all banned the book. Even Saudi Arabia kept quiet and Iraq questioned the Ayatollah's motives. "Khomeini seems to think he has some kind of a hotline from above," said Nisar Hamdoon, Iraq's vice-foreign minister on a visit to India last fortnight. "He has always been issuing *fatwas* on our president, our army and our government. By making a fuss Khomeini seems to have served the cause of the book."

As a matter of fact the only countries where the hate-Rushdie campaign seemed to find support were in the subcontinent. That was, however, more because the controversy was well-timed from the viewpoint of the troublemakers' politics. Also, by some twisted logic, the campaign fed on the latent anti-Americanism in the region. In Pakistan, the opposition Islamic Democratic Alliance took to the streets leading up to the American Center in Islamabad just when Prime Minister Benazir Bhutto was on her first official visit to Beijing. The police firing left five people dead and immediately the Opposition set up a 13-member action committee to orchestrate the campaign against the "blasphemous book". (pp. 20-4)

In India too fundamentalists came to the fore. Even a moderate like Jammu and Kashmir Chief Minister Farooq Abdullah was forced into extreme postures: "The book is a product of the mischievous and lunatic brain of Rushdie. All its copies should be consigned to flames." With the sub-continent's history of sectarian violence the Rushdie affair could spark off yet another religious conflagration. Last week, addressing a large Friday prayer congregation, the Shahi Imam reiterated his support for Khomeini's death sentence against "Shaitan" Rushdie. "For the whole of humanity," he thundered, "this is a storm, an earthquake that will not end." Immediately after, the 2000-strong congregation marched through the streets of the capital and burnt effigies of Rushdie.

Elsewhere, though Indian Muslim leaders refrained from supporting Khomeini's threat, Rushdie was roundly condemned. "Without endorsing Khomeini's *fatwa,* I would add that the punishment for apostasy according to Islamic laws is death," said Janata Party's Syed Shahabuddin. Some counselled restraint. Said National Conference MP Saifuddin Soz: "If Khomeini was outraged at what he thinks is a bad pamphlet, he should have answered with another pamphlet."

There was also feverish debate on the religious justification behind the "punishment" and the *fatwa.* Asked noted Islamic scholar Rafiq Zakaria: "Here is a Prophet who moves a billion people in the world: can his character assassination be brushed aside?" Yet, Zakaria said the *fatwa* was "totally illegal" under Islamic law. Others too questioned the theory that

the punishment for apostasy was death. Significantly, the Al Azhar Seminary of Cairo has not passed any decree on the *Verses.*

On yet another plane the debate was ideological, as the Iranian supporters made it a West versus the Third World issue. Even Bani Sadr, the former Iranian prime minister now exiled in Paris told INDIA TODAY: "One has to be equally severe with Khomeini's fanaticism and the attitudes in the West. I did not hear one minister, apart from (French) Prime Minister Rocard, talk about the insults contained in Rushdie's book. This is also fanaticism."

Others termed the western outrage as hypocrisy. Javid Ghorbanoghli, the Iranian Charge d'Affaires in Delhi argued: "While the West is defending one individual, the Imam is defending the rights of one billion Muslims." Some in Pakistan asked why there was no uproar when in 1960 Israeli agents kidnapped Adolph Eichmann, a former Nazi "war criminal" living in Argentina and executed him. Or when the French sank the Rainbow Warrior, the peaceniks' ship interfering with their nuclear tests in the South Pacific. From a Muslim viewpoint, said an Islamabad scribe, Rushdie writing the *Verses* is like a Jew trying to justify the holocaust.

As the fortnight came to a close, there was no end to the Rushdie saga. Strange indeed that the man who stalked the subcontinent in his first two novels, *Midnight's Children* and *Shame,* to "reclaim" his heritage, as he so often used to say, should now have no place to go. (The reclamation of Bombay was the springboard for his rich metaphor.)

Rushdie and his wife, Marianne, are among the most heavily guarded people in London today. Their friends, however, fear that it will be a long time before they will be able to resurface. Some even feel that Rushdie ought to disappear. Tariq Ali suggested: "He should get plastic surgery done and disappear in Latin America."

For Rushdie, who is so gregarious and loves the social whirl of the literary world, life as a recluse or the assumption of another identity would be like death. Or at best imprisonment for life, possibly compounded by exile. In a message, his first since he went into hiding, to Blake Morrison, literary editor of *The Observer,* Rushdie said he was "holding up well, using Philip Roth's vilifications by angry Jews when he published *Portnoy's Complaint* to cope with my own persecution". Said Morrison: "He did not sound terminally depressed."

Khomeini's threat has assured Rushdie what his books might not have—a permanent place in literary history. And the threat grows more real and palpable as the fundamentalists retreat into themselves further and harden their position. Rushdie's words in *Midnight's Children* seem chillingly prophetic: "I had been mysteriously handcuffed in history." (p. 24)

"Salman Rushdie: Satanic Storm," in India Today, *Vol. XIV, No. 3, March 15, 1989, pp. 14-24.*

Alfred Uhry
Driving Miss Daisy
Pulitzer Prize: Drama

American dramatist and lyricist.

Set in Atlanta, Georgia and spanning twenty-five years, *Driving Miss Daisy* (1987) details the gradual development of understanding and affection between two elderly people separated by race, class, and religion. When Daisy Werther, a wealthy septuagenarian Jewish woman, wrecks her new car, her son hires Hoke Coleman, an illiterate, middle-aged black man, to be her chauffeur. Although she denies being racist, Miss Daisy is caustic toward Hoke, and he debates whether or not to remain in her service. As time passes, however, the two characters grudgingly begin to rely on each other for companionship and assistance. While the Civil Rights movement gains force during the 1960s, the characters acknowledge their encounters with discrimination and develop a stronger relationship. Peter Kemp described the play as being "perfectly pitched between comedy and pathos." John Simon added: "Even more than a delicate miniaturist's talent, [Uhry] exhibits tact: He milks neither the sentiment nor the humor of the situation, and also resists, without avoiding the issues of racism and anti-Semitism, giving us a social tract."

Uhry drew upon his family history in *Driving Miss Daisy,* as the two main characters are based upon his grandmother and her chauffeur. Previous to this play Uhry wrote lyrics for musicals, including *The Robber Bridegroom,* which was nominated for a Tony Award.

CLIVE BARNES

Since romantic love went out the window with monogamy, and tragedy was demoted to cinematic blood and TV thunder, one of the classic themes of contemporary drama has become the odd couple.

This is when two people of totally dissimilar tastes, backgrounds or personalities are chain-ganged together in a love-hate relationship devoid of sex.

Alfred Uhry's delightful new play, ***Driving Miss Daisy,*** . . . is a perfectly poised and shaped miniature on the odd-couple theme.

It starts in 1948 with a car crash, and it ends in 1973 with a slice of pumpkin pie. The place is Atlanta, Georgia.

Daisy Wertham, Uhry's eponymous heroine, is in 1948 a very rich 72-year-old widow, with a temperament so acidulated that vinegar wouldn't freeze in her mouth.

By confusing gears she manages—with a loud crash as the curtain rises—not only to total her brand-new Packard, but also to wipe out the garage and a neighboring outhouse. The

only thing left undamaged is Daisy—who hasn't even smashed her spectacles. . . .

Her son Boolie decides—against her wishes, as she regards servants as natural invaders of privacy and probably thieves—to engage a chauffeur.

He interviews and hires an unemployed black, Hoke Coleburn, who seems to be a peculiar mixture of independence and dependability. Hoke lives up to that "seems" to the hilt.

At first Daisy, with the niggardly thriftiness born of a poor childhood, spurns the new chauffeur. But gradually, over the years, the admirable Hoke makes himself indispensable.

In the play's tiny but heartfelt climax, Daisy is forced to recognize that Hoke indeed is her "best friend."

By setting the play in Atlanta, Uhry uses the delicate issues of the civil rights movement as the play's backdrop.

The relationship between the Jewish widow and her son on

264

the one hand and the non-militant but self-confident black on the other is subtle.

Note how the amiable and liberal Boolie has to explain to Daisy why it would not be expedient for him—a local businessman—to accompany her to a Martin Luther King testimonial dinner, and her maladroit attempt to persuade Hoke to go with her. . . .

What about the pumpkin pie at the end? Well, you'll just have to see the play for yourself to find out about that.

> *Clive Barnes, " 'Miss Daisy' Blooms," in* New York Post, *April 16, 1987.*

MEL GUSSOW

In ***Driving Miss Daisy,*** Alfred Uhry has taken familiar material—the growing friendship between a crotchety, aged Southern lady and her black chauffeur—and treated it with renewed sincerity. . . .

Driving Miss Daisy in no sense breaks new ground, and at times it seems more like an extended character sketch or family memoir than an actual drama, but it would be difficult to deny its homespun appeal. The play is sweet without being mawkish, ameliorative without being sanctimonious.

[Miss Daisy is] a formidable Atlanta woman who was fixed in her habits long before her husband died. Living on her own, she is not about to give up her independence, though as the play begins she reluctantly accepts the will of her son and allows him to hire a chauffeur for her. Daisy is 72 and we see her, closely and sympathetically, over the next 25 years, as she becomes increasingly dependent on her driver. . . .

Miss Daisy's crusty facade gradually crumbles as she comes to trust—and to cherish—[Hoke Coleman, her chauffeur], who is protective but never subservient. Though aware of the limits of his place in the woman's life, he is not about to sacrifice his dignity, even as he confesses to his inability to read. As a former schoolteacher, Miss Daisy immediately begins lessons.

While following a fairly predictable dramatic course, the author and his actors repeatedly embellish the story with strokes of humanity and humor, as the two people come to realize that they have far more in common than they can ever publicly admit. It is the chauffeur who opens the eyes of his employer; she enforces her stoical sense of position almost to the end.

Mr. Uhry, author and lyricist of ***The Robber Bridegroom,*** wisely refrains from melodramatic confrontation. The play remains quiet, and it becomes disarming, as it delineates the characters with almost offhanded glimpses. Driving Miss Daisy to visit relatives in Alabama, the chauffeur announces the limits of his travel. "The first time I left Georgia," he says, "was 25 minutes ago." . . .

It would be hard to diminish this man and impossible to subject him to ridicule. [Hoke Coleman] is marked by his gentility, though he is not without his wiles. When, at an advanced age, he finds himself with an alternative offer of employment, he cleverly manages to coax Miss Daisy's son into giving him a raise.

The son is the play's third character, a small, somewhat contrived intermediary. . . . There are also two unseen charac-

ters, the son's snobbish wife and Miss Daisy's housekeeper and the presence of both is felt. The play is almost a two-hander and . . . easily sustains our interest for its 90-minute duration.

Late in the evening, the author tries to superimpose social commentary, somewhat in the manner of, but without the naturalness of, Samm-Art Williams's *Home.* In this case, history remains background. The principal story is the personal relationship, the interdependence of the two irrevocably allied Southerners. . . .

> *Mel Gussow, in a review of "Driving Miss Daisy," in* The New York Times, *April 16, 1987, p. C22.*

JOHN SIMON

There is a kind of play as redolent of the good old days as 5-cent beer and about as likely to make a comeback. What a sweet surprise, then, to find ***Driving Miss Daisy,*** a two-and-a-half-character play by Alfred Uhry . . . ; it is full of an old-style unpretentiousness, coziness, and—despite genuine emotions—quietude. It concerns Miss Daisy Werthan, a crotchety, parsimonious, monumentally stubborn 72-year-old Atlanta widow, who, while insisting she can still drive, has to bow to the combined wills of her son, Boolie, and all the insurance companies in the land and accept a black chauffeur, Hoke, whom Boolie has hired for her.

Hoke is delighted that the Werthans are Jews, whom, in the past, he has found much easier to work for than Baptists. But he has never met the like of Miss Daisy for taciturn intractability, almost whimsical orneriness. He himself is a proud and determined man, respectful but never servile, possessed of amusingly ingenious ways to drive an iceberg as well as a car. The play covers, in bright but unflashy episodes, 25 years in these two lives, with Boolie providing an intermittent, droll or exasperated, obbligato to a duet that progresses from discord to close harmony in small, credible steps.

It is to Uhry's credit that there is no cheating. Miss Daisy, in her prosperity, never forgets her hard, impecunious childhood and struggling schoolteacher days; though she is not exactly a champion at the other virtues (except perhaps at propriety), in the generosity sweepstakes she was left at the starting gate. Her always-offstage maid, Idella, has come to terms with this; Boolie, who pays Hoke out of his pocket ("highway robbery," Daisy calls his modest salary), plays along with it; it is Hoke who, slowly, good-humoredly, dismantles Daisy's suspiciousness and isolation, even if he can never quite get her ungivingness to give.

Still, Daisy teaches Hoke to read and write even as he teaches her about human rights and wrongs, and a prickly (on her part) and wary (on his) affection develops between them, the limits of which she will not overstep even after she, well into her nineties and after many changes in cars and conditions, declares him her best friend. Even more than a delicate miniaturist's talent, the playwright exhibits tact: He milks neither the sentiment nor the humor of the situation, and also resists, without avoiding the issues of racism and anti-Semitism, giving us a social tract. Neither the bombing of the synagogue to which Hoke has been regularly driving her nor the testimonial dinner for Martin Luther King Jr. that, despite her son's cautious abstention, she insists on attending can induce Miss Daisy to accept Hoke as her equal in every way.

The dialogue is savory and spirited, and although not a moment of **Driving Miss Daisy** becomes momentous, not a minute of its 80 is boring. Even the predictable, in Uhry's hands, manages to be idiosyncratic enough to be palatable, and connoisseurs of filigree pleasures should feel snugly ensconced here. (p. 122)

John Simon, "Daisy and Miller," in New York Magazine, Vol. 20, No. 18, May 4, 1987, pp. 122, 124.

ROBERT BRUSTEIN

Alfred Uhry's **Driving Miss Daisy,** which might sound . . . unappealing in bare outline, proved to be an experience of considerable power and sensitivity.

It was also exquisitely acted and directed, one of those rare moments in theater when every aspect of production seems to be controlled by a single unifying imagination. **Driving Miss Daisy** plays for about 90 minutes without intermission, further documenting my only formula for popularity on the stage these days—that critics and audiences will embrace most warmly those productions that last an intermissionless hour and a half. . . .

Driving Miss Daisy has both appealing brevity and considerable quality. It is a first play by Uhry, who has hitherto been associated with musicals (he wrote book and lyrics for **The Robber Bridegroom**). If his talent holds against the inevitable pressures, we have another gifted playwright in our midst. Uhry comes from a German-Jewish family in Atlanta. His play is apparently autobiographical, a series of vignettes about the relationship between an aging Southern Jewish matriarch (presumably his grandmother) and her only slightly less venerable black chauffeur. . . . The play concerns the evolving intimacy between these two aged people, the gentle, bemused black man and the cranky Southern Jewess who resists his services—a kind of *I'm Not Rappaport* without the jokes. The old alliance between Jews and blacks is somewhat strained these days. It was already strained in the South during the period of the play, 1948 to 1973. Although "Miss Daisy" (as Hoke calls her, using the common form of subordinate Negro address) persists in believing that she feels no bigotry toward blacks, she is deeply opposed to Hoke's presence in her house, and not just because he reminds her of her helplessness. Daisy embodies all the racial prejudices of her class toward the "other" that Hoke represents.

Including an assumption about thieving black people. Daisy complains to her son that she is missing a can of salmon, having found the empty can under the coffee grounds. Hardly a generous spirit, she assumes that Hoke has stolen this 33-cent item and wants him dismissed. Hoke enters, offering her another can of salmon, to admit he helped himself because the pork chops she gave him were "stiff." . . .

They disagree about everything and Hoke spends his days moping in the kitchen, a talkative man deprived of conversation. Only when they drive to visit her husband's grave does some intimacy spring up between them. Unable to make out the writing on the gravestone, Hoke arouses Daisy's tutorial instincts by admitting he's illiterate. Before long she is teaching him to read phonetically, and later gives him a handwriting copy book as a gift.

Daisy denies this is a Christmas present. She disapproves deeply of Jews who observe that holiday, chief among them her daughter-in-law, Floreen, whose idea of heaven on earth, she says, is "socializing with Episcopalians." Floreen is an invisible character, deftly characterized by the playwright with simple strokes through Daisy's attitude toward her. Floreen puts reindeer in her trees, a Christmas wreath in every window. ("If I had [her] nose," snorts Daisy, "I wouldn't go around saying Merry Christmas to anyone.") Despite her nose, Floreen ends up as a Republican National Committeewoman, the type of woman who goes to New York to see *My Fair Lady* rather than attend the funeral of Daisy's brother in Mobile.

The trip to Mobile inspires tender and nostalgic memories in Daisy, who recalls tasting salt water on her face at her brother's wedding. As for Hoke, he admits to having never left Georgia before, and "Alabama ain't lookin' like much so far." Yet even this intimate journey inspires arguments. Hoke has to pass water; Daisy wants him to wait until they reach a Standard Oil gas station. But colored people aren't allowed to use white rest rooms and Hoke, shouting he will not be treated like a dog, stops the car and disappears into a bush. Her small piping "Hoke?" signifies a belated realization of just how much she needs him.

Going to the synagogue one morning, both of them see a big mess in the road. The temple has been bombed. By whom? "Always the same ones," says Hoke. Daisy is convinced the hoodlums meant to bomb the conservative synagogue, but as Hoke observes, "A Jew is a Jew—just as in the dark we're all the same nigger." This shared suffering moves Hoke to speak of a time when the father of his friend was lynched, his hands tied behind his back and flies all over his body. "Why did you tell me that story?" asks Daisy. "Stop talking to me."

By the time she's nearing 90, and extremely feeble, Daisy has developed enough social conscience to help organize a United Jewish Appeal banquet honoring Martin Luther King Jr. Now it is her son, a successful banker with business to conduct with a racist clientele, who is hesitant about public demonstration of Jewish-black friendship. But Daisy persists. "Isn't it wonderful the way things are changing?" she says to Hoke, who grumbles, "Things ain't changed that much." Daisy has waited until the very day of the King memorial to invite him to join her at the banquet—and with quiet pride he refuses.

Growing senile in her 90s, confused and rambling, convinced she's teaching school again, Daisy realizes, with a start, that Hoke, the black man, is her best friend. And when her son and Hoke come to visit her in the nursing home, it is Hoke she wishes to talk to. "How old are you?" he asks. "I'm doing the best I can." "Me too," he responds, ". . . that's all there is to it." In the final action of the play, a sweet, delicate moment, he feeds her two pieces of pie.

This odd love story, though it never underestimates the difficulty of intimacy between the races, could easily grow mawkish. It is a tribute to Uhry's discreet understatement that the sentiment does not grow into corn—or into *The Corn Is Green.* (pp. 28-9)

Driving Miss Daisy is all of a piece, combining elements of sense and sensibility, not to mention generous portions of pride and prejudice. It is the work of decent people, working against odds to show how humans still manage to reach out to each other in a divided world. (p. 30)

Robert Brustein, "Energy for Old Age," in The New Republic, *Vol. 197, No. 13, September 28, 1987, pp. 28-30.*

PETER KEMP

Driving Miss Daisy is a *tour de force*. Covering a quarter of a century, Alfred Uhry's streamlined play gives you vivid, passing glimpses of life in Atlanta, Georgia, from 1948 to 1973. . . .

When the play begins, Daisy Werthan, a wealthy Jewish widow in her early seventies, has just been stopped from driving after her latest mishap with her car. When it ends, she's a 97-year-old in a Zimmer frame, virtually unable to walk. In between, she has travelled a considerable distance—physically, psychologically and emotionally—with the Negro chauffeur, Hoke, her son has engaged for her. . . .

At first, you're most conscious of the gulfs—especially of race—between them. Though Daisy, once a schoolmistress, prides herself on being unprejudiced, bigotry still slips out. But by the time of the play's final scene—in which a now-shaky Hoke feeds a geriatric Daisy with forkfuls of Thanksgiving pie—you've become most conscious of the affinities between the two obstinate, touchy and blunt old folk. Even their backgrounds have something in common, you're reminded. The play's most dramatic scene has Daisy learning that the Temple she attends has been bombed by the Ku-Klux-Klan. This jolts Hoke into recollecting a lynching he witnessed as a child. Realistically, Uhry portrays Daisy as unable to grasp the offered camaraderie. To Hoke's "I know just how you feel, Miss Daisy", she responds with handkerchief-to-mouth near-terror and panicky distress.

Gradually, though, trust and friendship push through cultural barriers—and personal ones. . . . Daisy is as inhibited as she is outspoken: pernicketiness is one of the defence mechanisms set up by her clenched, brusque shyings away from emotion. . . .

What draws the couple together, you're shown, is partly shared dependence but also a shared journey into old age. Growing rapport is poignantly counterpointed by withering bodies. When she reminisces to Hoke about a girlhood trip to the coast in 1888, Daisy's old hands fidget movingly as she remembers first tasting salt water on her 12-year-old fingertips.

Through the conversations of his characters, Uhry gives you a sense of a whole community. Especially effective in keeping you aware of wider social dimensions is Daisy's natty, harrassed businessman son, Boolie. . . .

The result is 90 minutes of fine pleasure: a drama, perfectly pitched between comedy and pathos.

Peter Kemp, in a review of "Driving Miss Daisy," in The Independent, *June 10, 1988.*

CHRISTOPHER EDWARDS

Comfortable is one word for Alfred Uhry's Pulitzer Prize-winning play *Driving Miss Daisy.* Sentimental is another. What has become of this American award? I had just begun to think that if David Mamet could win it (for *Glengarry Glenn Ross*) then perhaps we could start taking it seriously again. Mamet was an original talent, without any doubt. This piece is an example of cosy American liberalism murmuring reassuring noises to itself. Purring is general, all over Broadway.

It is 1948. Rich, crusty old Atlanta Jewess is persuaded by long-suffering son Boolie to employ poor illiterate old black chauffeur Hoke. Daisy, in her seventies, is unfit to drive, but wishes to soldier independently on (hurray for indomitable old bats like Daisy). The last thing she wants is an old black in the house (boo, but we know she will learn), least of all one who might disturb her frank idea of the stereotype nigger ('they all take things'). But the author has a stereotype of his own in store. Enter Hoke, as honest as the day is long (hurray again), quietly dignified (goes without saying, but more cheers), loyal to his old charge and full of homely Deep South insight; oppression breeds wisdom in a black man's soul, yessir.

It is not the message that deprives the piece of bite so much as its user-friendly serrations; an autumnal glow just will bathe every prejudice in sight. And of course there is the utter predictability of the play's ending. (p. 38)

Christopher Edwards, "Southern Comfort," in The Spectator, *Vol. 260, No. 8345, June 18, 1988, pp. 38-9.*

Obituaries

Necrology

In addition to the authors included in the Obituary section, several other notable writers passed away during 1988:

John Clellon Holmes
March 12, 1926—March 30, 1988
American novelist, essayist, poet, and short story writer

Holmes is best-known for having chronicled the activities and concerns of the Beat Generation. His novel *Go* (1952) is acknowledged as the first fictional account of the Greenwich Village bohemian scene, and his essays on the Beat Generation are respected for their objectivity, lucidity, and insight.

Geoffrey (Edward West) Household
November 30, 1900—October 4, 1988
English novelist

As evidenced in *Rogue Male* and *Watcher in the Shadows,* Household created works that combined elements of mystery and the picaresque and examined themes relating to honor and courage.

Daniel (Lewis) James
1911—May 18, 1988
American screenwriter and novelist

James was blacklisted in 1951 by the House Un-American Activities Committee (HUAC) for his past association with the Communist party, effectively ending a screenwriting career that included his work on Charlie Chaplin's 1940 film *The Great Dictator.* James won acclaim in 1983 for *Famous All Over Town,* a novel he wrote under his pseudonym, Danny Santiago, which he adopted during the 1950s for fear that works under his own name would not be published. This novel, which is based upon his experiences as a volunteer social worker in an impoverished area of east Los Angeles, received awards from the American Academy and Institute of Arts and Letters and PEN, the international association of writers.

---

b(arrie) p(hillip) Nichol
September 30, 1944—September 25, 1988
Canadian poet

Nichol's experiments in "sound" and "concrete" poetry were an attempt to break "the artificial boundaries we have placed on the poem," as he stated in the introduction to his collection, *ABC. The Martyrology,* an ongoing poem that eventually encompassed seven volumes, is a self-reflexive work exploring the poetic process.

Francis (Jean Gaston Alfred) Ponge
March 27, 1899—August 6, 1988
French poet and educator

Ponge is best known for his "thing poetry," which consists of extended descriptions of an ordinary object, as in his long poem *Soap.* His interest in the varying associations inspired by simple objects led critics to categorize him as a surrealist. Jean-Paul Sartre once called Ponge's work "the most curious and perhaps the most important of the age."

Michael (Joseph) Shaara (Jr.)
June 23, 1929—May 5, 1988
American novelist and short story writer

Shaara won the Pulitzer Prize for fiction in 1975 for *The Killer Angels*. This historical novel, set at the Battle of Gettysburg during the American Civil War, was lauded for its vivid descriptions and factual detail.

Costas Taktis
October 8, 1927—August 25?, 1988
Greek novelist

Taktis won international acclaim in the late 1960s for *The Third Wedding Wreath*. This novel, which concerns a woman who survives World War II and the Greek Civil War through her wits, was praised for its colorful portrayal of life in Athens.

Raymond (Henry) Williams
August 31, 1921—January 26, 1988
Welsh educator, essayist, critic, and novelist

An author of numerous fiction and nonfiction works on society, culture, literature, education, and politics, Williams was a leading intellectual of the British left. Edward W. Said ranked Williams with "Saint-Beuve, Matthew Arnold, I. A. Richards, William Empson and a tiny number of other critics who by the range, power and sheer continuity and resourcefulness of their work were placed where literature and commentary approach each other most closely."

Raymond Carver

May 25, 1938 - August 2, 1988

American short story writer, poet, essayist, and scriptwriter.

For an overview of Carver's life and work see *CLC,* Vols. 22, 36, 53; *Contemporary Authors,* Vols. 33-36, rev. ed., 126 (obituary); *Contemporary Authors New Revision Series,* Vol. 17; and *Dictionary of Literary Biography Yearbook: 1984*)

RAYMOND CARVER (INTERVIEW WITH **WILLIAM L. STULL**)

[The interview excerpted below was conducted in November 1986.]

[The Bloomsbury Review:] *In a good many instances, you've approached what seems to be a single incident from two angles, treating it in both poetry and prose. Are there limits on a writer's experience?*

[Raymond Carver:] I don't feel I'm short on things to write about. But some things, I'm thinking of **"Distress Sale"** now, that poem, or the story **"Why Don't You Dance?"**—the yard sale situation—the idea, the image of the yard sale made such a strong impression on me that I dealt with it first in a poem and then in a story. The same thing is true with regard to the poem **"Late Night with Fog and Horses"** and the story **"Blackbird Pie."** In each instance I wrote the poem first and then wrote the story, I suppose, because I apparently felt a need to elaborate on the same theme.

Is narrative, the storytelling element, what links the genres for you?

Yes. And just as I'm more interested in representational art as opposed to abstract art, I'm more interested in poems with a narrative or story line to them than in free-associating poems that don't have any grounding in the real world. (pp. 14-15)

Your new poetry openly celebrates intimacy, and in some poems the walls between life and art seem very thin. Is there a risk of sentimentality or embarrassment in that?

Any right-thinking reader or writer abjures sentimentality. But there's a difference between sentiment and sentimentality. I'm all for sentiment. I'm interested in the personal, intimate relationships in life, so why not deal with these relationships in literature? What about intimate experiences like those recounted in **"A Haircut"** or **"The Gift"**? Why can't such experiences be turned into poetry? These little experiences are important underpinnings in our daily lives, and I don't see any problem in turning them into poems. They are,

after all, something that we all share—as readers, writers, and human beings.

You're not inclined to treat mundane matters ironically, then?

No. I can't imagine treating them ironically or denigrating them in any way. I don't think there should be any barriers, artificial or otherwise, between life as it's lived and life as it's written about. It's only natural to write about these things. The things that count are often intimate things. I'm embarrassed for the people who are embarrassed by the idea of someone writing about things such as haircuts and slippers and ashtrays and hominy and so on.

Still, for a long time, and even to an extent today, the facts of everyday living, things like getting haircuts and picking up the mail, were thought by some to be subjects beneath the poet's dignity.

But see where that's gotten us. So much of our poetry has become like something you see in a museum. You walk around and politely look at it and then go away and discuss it. It's been given over to teachers and students. And it also seems

273

to me that of all the art forms, poetry is probably the one with the worst press, if you know what I mean. It's got the largest number of hanging judges involved on the peripheries. So many people who don't even read poetry often make pronouncements about it. These people feel that standards have been thrown out the window, the barbarians are at the gate, and nothing is sacred any longer. I don't have sympathy for guardians, so-called, of sacred flames.

You don't hold with the modernist notion that poetry needs to be difficult?

Of course not. I'm saying just the opposite. My friend Richard Ford recently passed along a remark he'd heard from Joyce Carol Oates. She told him, "Ray's poems are arousing resentment in some quarters because he's writing poetry that people can understand." I take that as a compliment. I don't have a whole lot of patience with obscurity or rhetoric, in life or in literature.

Do you ever write poems and stories concurrently?

I never have, not yet, anyway. When I was writing poems, that's all I wrote. No fiction, anyway. The only thing I could do outside of writing poems, in the way of literary work, was, very rarely, an essay or book review. And I did that, wrote the prose, in the evenings after I had written poetry all day. I wrote the poems during the daylight hours. And now that I'm writing stories again, I'm only writing stories and nothing else. I'd be hard put right now to sit down and write a poem. (pp. 15-16)

You carried verbal economy to new extremes in revising the stories for **What We Talk About When We Talk About Love** *from their magazine versions. You told* The Paris Review *that you cut your work to the marrow, not just to the bone. Later, when you published alternate versions of the stories in* **Fires,** *you restored many of the excisions. What led you to perform such radical surgery in the first place?*

It had to do with the theory of omission. If you can take anything out, take it out, as doing so will make the work stronger. Pare, pare, and pare some more. Maybe it also had something to do with whatever I was reading during that period. But maybe not. It got to where I wanted to pare everything down and maybe pare too much. Then I guess I must have reacted against that. I didn't write anything for about six months. Then I wrote **"Cathedral"** and all the other stories in that book in a fairly concentrated period of time. I've said that if I had gone any further in the direction I was going, the direction of the earlier stories, I would have been writing stories that I wouldn't have wanted to read myself. . . .

Recently, Neo-Realist fiction, yours included, has been faulted from the left. Some critics urge a return to the literary experimentalism of the late sixties and early seventies. How do you react?

It's strange, because a number of right-wing neoconservative critics say I'm painting too dark a picture of American life. I'm not putting a happy face on America. That's the stick they swing at me. As for the experimental fiction of the sixties and seventies, much of that work I have a hard time with. I think that literary experiment failed. In trying out different ways of expressing themselves, the experimental writers failed to communicate in the most fundamental and essential way. They got farther and farther away from their audience. But maybe this is what they wanted. Still, I think when peo-

ple look back on that period fifty years from now it's going to be looked on as an odd time in the literary history of the country, an interruption, somehow. . . .

What makes your writing uniquely your own?

Well, certainly, the tone in the work, I suppose. Geoffrey Wolff said in a review of my first book of stories that he felt he could pick out a story of mine without seeing my name attached to it. I took that as a compliment. If you can find an author's fingerprints on the work, you can tell it's his and no other's.

Where do those fingerprints lie? In subject? In style?

Both. Subject and style, the two are pretty much inseparable, right? John Updike once said that when he thinks of writing a story only certain areas of writing and experience are open to him. Certain areas, and lives, are completely closed. So, the story chooses him. And I feel that's true of myself. Speaking as a poet and story writer, I think that my stories and poems have chosen me. I haven't had to go out looking for material. These things come. You're called to write them.

You're sometimes discussed as a social realist who focuses on the downside of working-class life. But, if your people are beat, they're seldom beaten. In fact, Kim Herzinger has suggested that your abiding subject is human endurance. Would you agree?

That's a preoccupation, yes, and a writer could do worse. I'm saying he could set his sights lower. Most things that we care for pass away or pass by in such a rush that we can scarcely get a fix on them. So it's really a question of enduring and abiding. (p. 16)

Endurance seemed about the most one could hope for in **What We Talk About When We Talk About Love.** *But in* **Cathedral** *things began to change. In that book some of your characters seemed to prosper in spirit, if not in hard cash.*

Yes, and as writer and a very interested bystander, I'm pleased to see this happening. A writer doesn't want to go on repeating himself, using the same characters in the same circumstances, time and again. It's not only desirable, it's healthy to move on. I'm not working any kind of conscious program in my stories, no, of course not. But it seems like every time I've finished a book there's been a clear line of demarcation. There's always been a time after I finished putting together a book manuscript when I haven't worked for a while on stories. After I finished **What We Talk About When We Talk About Love** I didn't write stories for a good long while. Six months or so. Then the first story that I wrote was **"Cathedral."** It happened again after **Cathedral.** I didn't write a story for nearly two years. It's true. I wrote poems. The first story that I wrote and published after **Cathedral** was **"Boxes,"** which appeared in *The New Yorker.* Then five or six stories came very close together. And I feel these new stories are different from the earlier ones in kind and degree. There's something about the voice, yes. Again, speaking just as an outsider or bystander, I'm glad to see these changes at work.

What common denominators do you see in the new stories?

Well, for one thing, they've all been written in the first person. It's nothing I planned on. It's just the voice I heard and began to go with.

Let's turn to your early work, the stories collected in **Will You**

Please Be Quiet, Please? and **Furious Seasons.** *Like your recent stories* **"Intimacy"** *and* **"Blackbird Pie,"** *the very first two stories you ever published seem stylistically at opposite poles. Your first,* **"The Furious Seasons"** *(1960), is a long, complex narrative told in flashbacks. Your next is your shortest story ever, a Kafkaesque vignette called* **"The Father"** *(1961).*

I'd be more likely to write something like **"The Father"** today than to write **"The Furious Seasons"** again. I haven't reread that story in years, but in retrospect it feels gothic to me. I have a profound lack of interest in that story now. When I'm writing a story, it's the most important thing in the world to me. When I'm through with it, and it's published, I have very little interest in it.

If every story is a fresh start, is a writer's development really cumulative?

I feel it's cumulative in that you know you have written other stories and poems. Work begins to accumulate. It gives you heart to go on. I couldn't be writing the stories I'm writing now if I hadn't written the ones I have written. But there's no way in the world I could go back now and write another **"Gazebo"** or another **"Where I'm Calling From"** or for that matter anything else I've written.

You wrote many of the stories in **Will You Please Be Quiet, Please?** *during 1970-1971, when you were on your first NEA Fellowship. What did you learn about writing during that year of concentrated work?*

Well, to put it simply, I discovered that I could do it. I had been doing it in such a hit-or-miss fashion for so long, since the early sixties. But I discovered that if I went to my desk every day and applied myself I could seriously and steadily write stories. That was probably the biggest discovery I made. Somehow, I suppose at some deeper level, I was tapping into some things that were important to me, things I'd wanted to write about and finally was able to, without a sense of grief or shame or confusion. I was able to confront some things in the work head on. Call it subject matter. And I suppose during that time I fastened on or discovered a way of writing about these things. Something happened during that time in the writing, *to* the writing. It went underground and then it came up again, and it was bathed in a new light for me. I was starting to chip away, down to the image, then the figure itself. And it happened during that period.

What's next for Raymond Carver, once the current hubbub dies down?

I have a contract for the new book of stories, and I'm in a story-writing mood. I can't wait until I can get back to my desk and stay there. I have a lot of stories I want to write. I'm wild to get settled in here and be still. (p. 17)

> William L. Stull, *"Matters of Life & Death: An Interview with Raymond Carver,"* in The Bloomsbury Review, *Vol. 8, No. 1, January-February, 1988, pp. 14-17.*

GREG KUZMA

Again and again in **Ultramarine** Carver produces poems both heavy with consequence, things taken head-on at full-force, and yet fragile, light, gentle in their modesty, their refusal to pretend or puff up or become self-important. It is as if he can be knowing and innocent at once. . . . (p. 355)

Carver's essential voice is understated and flat, and . . . his "pain" therefore becomes authenticated in the very bareness of the details and the sketching in. Coffee, cigarettes, insomnia, liquor, the typical traps and trappings, Hemingway's bare-bulb interiors and psychic leanness, a Proustian memory flooding profusion in the midst of emotional drought, the inexplicable yoked by force of fact or accident together with the happy contours of the known. Carver is authentic because he dares to or cannot help but be a type, to honor the old adages, to fight the same demons, to write, even, the bare-faced clichés of everyman: "losing her mind," thoughts that "began to wander," "the stuff he lives with," "to grow up," having one's breath taken away, a cry of relief, "an even keel," "the last thing on earth," and so on, sequenced to things never before given tongue—"The dying body is a clumsy partner"; "an infinite eight to nine hours of work"; "The lightning speed of the past." Carver's shopworn language is itself compelling. In Ashbery clichés seem part of some vast catalog and rescue operation, where language is examined, referred to, marvelled at, toyed with, forgiven in its faded glory, the heat now all but gone out of the once-lively phrases. But Carver speaks them as if they were still to be made to serve, filling them with his breath, old horses breathing in winter alive yet suspect, whose very limits are loved, the way we imagine our solicitous caring for the aged and dying, or ourselves so treated.

Carver's pilgrimage is necessarily toward truth by way of fact, circling in memory, remembering "humiliation" as he says in a poem about where his stories come from, haunted continually by death, the child that fears to smell the dirt of the fresh-turned fields; Frank's death that no CPR can bring life back to, "her lips / on Frank's icy lips. A dead man's lips. Black lips"; John Dugan, the carpenter **("Powder Monkey")** run smack into a truck; the father, "My dad / . . . Reduced to a cup of ashes, / and some tiny bones" **("The Meadow")**; the wife who "died in misery," the husband in "misery" who "took to his porch, where he watched / the sun set and the moon rise" **("The Lightning Speed of the Past").** And what Carver shores against these ruins: "It's good to live near the water"; "Delight, and a cry"; "the Bukowski line that flew / through his mind from time to time"; "all the milk I drank, cradled in her arms"; "the sound of meat / as it connects with hot grease in the pan. . . ." (p. 356)

Hemingway presides from the first, blessing the first poem in the book. It has snowed. Thoughts of duty, "tender memories, thoughts of death, how I should treat / with my former wife . . . / The stuff I live with every day." . . . There is artistry in fly fishing. There are pleasant distractions of travel, the coming upon unforgettable scenes in exotic settings. There is the raw mystery and power of nature, the wind of **"Wind,"** the arctic migration of animals through which Carver imagines and metaphors the dying of his dying friend **("Migration").** Bukowski is an influence, for how his casual asides to the reader on behalf of some invoked universal experience invite our complicity. Brautigan's inexplicable juxtapositions give soul to some of the poems, the outrageous and unlikely told in a flat tone, and Brautigan's gentleness. And all the while behind them ultimately Kafka's nightmare stories, utterly placid, utterly reasonable, utterly insufferable. (p. 359)

Carver's impulse is narrative. He is a short-story writer of large reputation. Narrative distinguishes these poems amidst most of what is published today where narrative is scarce. Refreshing too and distinctive is the use of third person rather than the first person that dominates our poetry. Even where Carver is clearly writing about things he himself has suffered (the insane mother is too-obsessively portrayed to be merely an invention) he uses third person. The distancing he achieves in the process gives breadth to the self—he is both I and he, a character in his own poems, someone witnessed, depicted, a point of view. What is learned thereby or concluded is offered as limited, the lessons partial, but the self is a double self. Even with this doubling or because of it the reader is not suffocated by the "I," but allowed to "read" the scenes and actions, to make them applicable to our own lives should we choose to or should they somehow fit. Carver himself seems to have taken the lead in this—he speaks in the poems as someone who, detached, cannot quite believe that this is in fact his life, and what he must do. (p. 361)

There is no way . . . to generalize the poems. In fact, what is most exciting about them is their capacity for being continually surprising. Going on from line to line in any one of them is sheer adventure. You always get in deeper than you can remember, the way back lost, the way ahead always a bit scary. But you can get the thrill of it right off at the beginning say of **"The Pen"**—"The pen that told the truth / went into the washing machine / for its trouble." And so on, though there is no way to read Carver's mind. A whole poem like **"The River"** keeps fighting between being a poem about the *exhilaration* of fishing in deep and dark water, or a poem about the *terror* of fishing in deep and dark water. Where king salmon watch from the current. Where something brushes your leg. Turning pages one achieves the same sorts of tension and delight, the thank-you note that turns into an apology for killing the "earwigs" that came with the rum cake, the speaker suddenly uncontrollable in his frenzy, "like an animal." There is an incredible poem about a phone booth, a couple taking turns at the news, and weeping, steaming the booth up. There is the poem about the girl minding the store with a piece of sinew caught in her teeth, watching a fisherman, who watches her. Here the title, **"Sinew,"** points up Carver's magnificent use of them. The title is an emblem, a symbol, a coded thing whose full significance will widen as our awareness grows, as we work the details over in our minds. The titles tend to be brief, usually one or two words, encapsulating the story, helping to foreshadow it, sometimes compromising it. Carver will allow the titles to be inadequate, because in effect he does not wish to claim a lot for the poems—his is a modest enterprise throughout, and because he appears not to know where any poem is going to until he goes there. So the poems seem to grow out of their titles, or grow back through them. Or they will far surpass them in import and consequence, to demonstrate how life continually exceeds our reach or expectation or fear.

If Carver has one driving concern it is to present through suitable example and to account for "conflicting feelings." His **"Earwigs"** begins as a friendly note to the baker of the cake but turns into a story of revulsion, violence, and finally humorous self-illumination. After reading the poem all these various things seem to co-exist, abide in it, comprise the experience. His fishing poems present both the excitement of the catch and the sense of diminishment the killing brings. A goose that calls the wild ones in to their deaths in the farmyard awakens a complex of responses in the poet. Sometimes an event promotes not just conflicting feelings but diametri-

cally opposed ones, as in **"Jean's TV"** where the speaker praises Jean for saving him even as he recounts his debasing of her. Some of Genet's sacred defilement of the other is involved in this, as well as the freedom truth brings even when one is confessing one's lies. Things in delicious conflict are perhaps best savored in **"The Autopsy Room,"** where the scenes are ghastly yet erotic. A woman's "pale and shapely leg . . . took my breath away," and later, the poet's wife has that same leg alive "ready to tremble / and raise slightly, at the slightest touch." The poem ends in a new place, as so many Carver poems do, somewhere entirely unforeseen, but which we feel we could only have discovered with him.

>   Nothing
> was happening. Everything was happening. Life
> was a stone, grinding and sharpening.

That's wonderful. Chilling. "Life was a stone, grinding and sharpening." It is altogether typical of this book, an intense moment of sudden clarity, where the world is understood as it *is*. One comes out of such poems changed, as if we have ourselves been there, seen, felt, and had such thoughts.

There are dozens of such poems here, a discovery in every one of them, a phrase turned slightly askew, or that turns itself, a question raised where none had ever been asked, a sudden burst of emotion, restraint where it is unexpected, self-control masterfully exhibited in the midst of exasperation, juxtaposition to show us the world as a new place, fertile, inexhaustible, and more strange than we ever knew or wanted it to be. Carver is a writer of immense consequence. The best of his poems become unforgettable even as one reads them for the first time. They are like traffic accidents, or miraculous escapes. We come away gasping, shaken, and in awe. (pp. 362-63)

> *Greg Kuzma, " 'Ultramarine': Poems That Almost Stop the Heart," in* Michigan Quarterly Review, *Vol. XXVII, No. 2, Spring, 1988, pp. 355-63.*

MARILYNNE ROBINSON

Of the 37 stories in Raymond Carver's new collection, **Where I'm Calling From,** 30 have been collected before in four earlier volumes—two of them, **"What We Talk About When We Talk About Love,"** and **"Cathedral,"** as title stories. I take this volume to invite a new look at Mr. Carver's career, a conviction encouraged in me by the fact that I would like to offer one. To be blunt, I propose to abduct Raymond Carver from the camp of the minimalists.

For 150 years or so, every kind of art whose style has caused it to be identified as "modern" has been interpreted in the same way—as a contemplation of, and protest against, a world leached of pleasure, voided of meaning, spiritually and culturally bankrupt, etc. This is supposedly the "modern condition," which we are schooled to accept as an objectively existing thing, like the Rock of Gibraltar. No matter that, by every measure, this teeming nation is, as it always has been, rapt as Byzantium, its man in the street entirely accustomed to viewing his life in cosmic terms. Such structuring and valuing habits of mind, we tell ourselves, are just what our age and culture lack, a deficiency our arts boldly mirror, being more or less helpless to do otherwise. The idea of "the modern" is now so very old it has had to be repackaged as "the post-modern" and covered with assurances that the new product is starker, more cynical, altogether more abysmal than the one we are accustomed to.

Assumptions about what writers must or should be doing tend to preclude curiosity about what they are doing in fact. Raymond Carver is generally taken to epitomize this arid tradition, to spearhead a new version of it called "minimalism."

Including him in this canon is intended as high praise, the assumption being commonplace that a serious writer cannot have any higher object than to make these bones walk yet again. So, on the basis of the strength students and critics sense in his work, Mr. Carver has been more or less dragooned. Then other critics berate in his person the hopeless and diminished landscape they find in contemporary fiction, seeing him through the eyes of his imitators and admirers.

In fact, Mr. Carver stands squarely in the line of descent of American realism. His weaknesses are for sentimentality and sensationalism. His great gift is for writing stories that create meaning through their form. Much attention has been paid to his prose, and to his preoccupation with very ordinary lives and with disruption, divorce, displacement, sadness, the thankless business of cadging income from small and unlikable jobs. He should be famous for the conceptual beauty of his best stories, and disburdened of his worst, which could then pass into relative neglect.

The narrative foreground in Mr. Carver's fiction is typically muted or flattened. The stories have in common a sort of bafflement, justified in the best ones by the fact that their burdens are truly mysterious. Anecdotes—for want of a better word—looming and untranslatable like remembered dreams (which they sometimes are) figure so largely in these stories as to suggest that they are analogues to fiction itself, and also to consciousness, specifically to consciousness as it is shared, collective or bonding. It has been usual for a long time to lament the absence of myth in modern life, as if intuitions of the primordial and essential were the products of culture and would be dispelled with the loss of certain images and illusions, as if the forces myth describes were not real or powerful enough to impose themselves on our attention all unbidden. The bafflement in the best of these stories does not render an absence of meaning but awkwardness in the face of meaning, a very different thing.

Mr. Carver uses his narrow world to generate suggestive configurations that could not occur in a wider one. His impulse to simplify is like an attempt to create a hush, not to hear less but to hear better. Nothing recurs so powerfully in these stories as the imagination of another life, always so like the narrator's or the protagonist's own that the imagination of it is an experience of the self, that fuddled wraith. It is as if the replication of the conditions of one's life in another's rescued one from the terrors of accident and randomness, as if the germ of myth or archetype were found at work in the tepid plasma of unstructured experience. This seems to me to express the rationale of Mr. Carver's own artistic practice.

In "Neighbors," a couple, the Millers, look after the apartment next to their own while the couple who live in it are away. The Millers are, in a way, seduced by the apartment, a perfectly ordinary place except for odds and ends brought back from the vacations that make their neighbors' life seem to the Millers "fuller and brighter" than their own. The unguarded intimacy of the closed apartment stimulates the attraction between the Millers, makes them feel amorous and happy. What they experience amounts to an objectification

of their own life, a little sweetened by reachable enhancements.

In "Why Don't You Dance?" a man whose marriage has collapsed puts his furniture up for sale in the front yard, where he has arranged it as it was inside his house, running out an extension cord so that the television and the record player work. A young couple come along and try out the furniture, stay for drinks and then, at the man's suggestion, dance together in the driveway. The intimacy of marriage is voided, exposed, reenacted and distanced, all at once. The moment may be said to suggest memory, art, the astonishing bond of intimacy among a world of strangers, the ghostliness of one's attachment to any place or relationship. (pp. 1, 35)

Marriage is the most characteristic and complex form of these imaginative extensions of the self that so preoccupy Mr. Carver.

To do justice to "What We Talk About When We Talk About Love" is not possible in a small space. It is an extraordinary example of the discovery of meaning in visually suggestive anecdotes—of a suicide with a bandaged head, knights encumbered in dying by the weight of armor, an old couple in bandages, casts and traction, and a beekeeper in helmet and gloves and padded clothes. This series of analogous images rises out of a conversation among two married couples drinking gin together at a kitchen table, who know from their combined experience that love is homicidal, self-destructive, symbiotic and (possibly) fugitive. When one of the men, at the end, imagines himself murdering his former wife, the implication is that he loves her still. Again, the fiction offers patterns, parables, which seem charged with suggestion, and which elude the powers of interpretation of those who recognize meaning in them. The story concludes: "I could hear my heart beating. I could hear everyone's heart. I could hear the human noise we sat there making, not one of us moving, not even when the room went dark." (p. 35)

The last seven stories here, previously uncollected, are more rueful and humorous, written in more elegant prose and more elegiac than the earlier ones. In "Boxes," the weakening of an old woman's ties with life manifests itself in her continually moving, never able to feel at home and at ease. "Whoever Was Using This Bed" is about a couple, awakened by a phone call, who talk through the night about the aches and anxieties that press at such times but are lost in the amnesia of daylight consciousness. Finally they come to the question of whether or not the plug should be pulled if one of them were hopelessly ill. It is a funny, very natural conversation. Their insomnia, and the rumpled bedclothes, bring to mind the extreme of intimacy their marriage implies, even to the point of one possibly choosing to end the other's life.

In the story called "Intimacy," a writer visits his former wife, a woman furious that her life with him has been cannibalized to make fiction and that he has become a success publishing the darkest passages of their marriage. She is aware of giving him new material, even in her wrath, and the story, with the writer as narrator, means she has done just that. But he falls to his knees in her living room and stays there immobilized until it occurs to her to say she forgives him. Then she can send him away. Divorce never really takes in Mr. Carver's stories. Marriage is, in essence, an innocent friendship, desperately vulnerable to derangement and bad luck, but always precious in itself, its lost pleasures always loyally remembered. As he leaves her house, he sees children tossing a football. "But," he says, "they aren't my kids, and they aren't her kids either."

"**Menudo**" is about a man caught miserably in an infidelity, on the point of losing his second wife when he has not really recovered from the loss of his first. "**Elephant**" is a wonderful little story that should put paid, if anything ever will, to a clamor in certain quarters for a Carver story about grace and transcendence. The narrator, a sort of suburban Père Goriot, is being bled of his substance by a former wife, a mother who is "poor and greedy," a shiftless son, a shiftless daughter with two children and a live-in good-for-nothing, and a brother who calls with hard-luck stories. The man is impoverished, exhausting his credit, working and worrying, trying to meet their endless demands. Then he dreams that his father is carrying him, as a child, on his shoulders. The image brings him a great release. He thinks of his daughter, "God love her and keep her," and hopes for the happiness of his son, and is glad that he still has his mother, and that his former wife, "the woman I used to love so much," is alive somewhere. Then perhaps he dies. He is carried past the place where he works at astonishing speed in a "big unpaid-for car." Whether it is death that has stopped for him, or an uncanny freedom, the exhilaration of the ending has a distinctly theological feel.

The last story, "**Errand,**" is about the death of Chekhov, a very formal piece in which that estimable man is shown to have brought credit to himself in the manner of his dying. A writer generally invokes another writer when he wishes to invite comparison. Mr. Carver, whose stories are merely narrative occasions within which some highly charged image floats like a holograph, reminds me of Chekhov scarcely at all, except in that Mr. Carver's work, like Chekhov's, creates the terms in which it should be interpreted.

Raymond Carver is not an easy writer to read. His narratives are often coarse. Sometimes he seems intent on proving that insensitive people have feelings, too. And while the impulse is generous, the experience of looking at the world through the eyes of a character as crude as the narrator of "**Cathedral,**" for example, is highly uncongenial.

In "**Feathers,**" a story centered on a fine moment in which an ugly baby and a bedraggled peacock frolic together under the dinner table, the reader's attention is drawn to an annoying plaster cast of terribly crooked teeth, displayed like a trophy in the living room of this strange household. In this story, as in "**Cathedral,**" characters are overcome by an esthetic experience or realization. *Mutatis mutandis,* it is Henry James—beauty is the mode of address of the world to the human soul.

But there is lump as well as leaven in Mr. Carver, and the lumpishness is more irksome because it feels intentional. The characters sometimes seem set up, or condescended to. It is this condition from which they are rescued in the course of the story. Mr. Carver is rather like the poet William Carlos Williams, who declared there were "no ideas but in things," and who turned banality's pockets out and found all their contents beautiful.

The process of Mr. Carver's fiction is to transform our perception. Perhaps what he does cannot be done in another way. And, viewed from sufficient distance, an interesting problem can take its place among the beautiful things. (p. 40)

Marilynne Robinson, "Marriage and Other Aston-

ishing Bonds," in The New York Times Book Review, *May 15, 1988, pp. 1, 35, 40.*

DAVID GATES

I always have the first line," says Raymond Carver, describing the initial stirrings of his stories. "And the first line is usually a line that never changes." It's his last lines, though, that seem graven in stone—those shapely blurtings that bring his shapely narratives to rest. One story ends as a drunk paws for aspirin: "I knocked down some more things. I didn't care. Things kept falling." Another man is last heard leaving his ex-wife's house: "I can't take a step without putting my shoe into some leaves. Somebody ought to make an effort here. Somebody ought to get a rake and take care of this." A waitress concludes her tale of serving a fat customer, and, later, being mounted by her lumpish husband: "It is August. My life is going to change. I feel it." To get every word right between the unwavering first line and the inevitable last may take 15 drafts; he's usually at his desk every morning. Routine, he says, is no ugly word to a writer.

Few American writers are more admired and imitated than 49-year-old Raymond Carver. His influence has been growing for two decades; as much as anyone, he may be responsible for so many of today's younger writers' abandoning the mirrored fun houses of Barth and Barthelme, the "metafictionists" fashionable in the '60s and '70s, in favor of an austere realism. His induction into the august American Academy and Institute of Arts and Letters is formal acknowledgment of his stature; it coincides with the publication of his new book, **Where I'm Calling From,** and he's come to New York from his home in Washington state for ceremonies and interviews. **Where I'm Calling From** assembles the stories Carver now believes he got right: 30 from as far back as the early '60s and seven new ones. The final story, "**Errand,**" a half-researched, half-imagined account of the death of Chekhov, gives the whole book the chilling cadence his last lines give individual stories. Chekhov, one of his acknowledged models, had tuberculosis; after writing the story, Carver was diagnosed with lung cancer. He had surgery last fall, relapsed and has now finished a course of seemingly successful radiation therapy.

Carver sees "**Errand**" as prophetic, all right—but of work to come. The stories for which he's known are set in his own backyard and among his own folk, the suburban and rural working class. "**Errand**" is a departure, he admits, "and I like that idea. The possibilities for writing stories are just endless." . . .

Simply getting the time and the place to write took years for the young man from small-town Washington. His earliest literary influence was his own father, who never got past sixth grade. "He used to tell me stories," says Carver. "Not really stories, I guess. More like anecdotes. Anecdotes of his great-grandfather killing a bear. With a hunting knife. Wounding the bear. Then tracking him. And I always found myself wanting to tell some of my own stories." He read haphazardly—historical novels, science fiction—and wished he weren't a misfit. "I wanted to be right in there with all the rest of the guys. But I also wanted to write. I was the nerd who always hung around the library, half ashamed to be seen carrying books home."

He married at 19, moved to California to find work and took

a writing class at a state college with John Gardner, not yet famous for such novels as *Grendel.* "I was like a sea creature washed up on the shore," says Carver. "I didn't know anything. But I *knew* I didn't know anything." Gardner introduced him to the masters of the conventional short story: Chekhov, Isaac Babel, Frank O'Connor, Hemingway. They made sense to him in a way the metafictionists did not. "The important things in my life," he says, "were to pay the rent, to get enough milk for the kids. So I had little patience with literature that had nothing to do with reality."

The extreme compression of some of his work and his characters' often bizarre behavior have given Carver himself an archmodernist reputation. In fact, his stories are rigorously classical. He is as knowing about "manners" as Jane Austen: when his people come to dinner, we learn what they bring, what they chat about and when the TV gets turned off. Their motivations are always legible, and there's always what Joyce called an "epiphany": a moment in which something is understood. Carver, often labeled a "minimalist," once revised by ruthless cutting. (**"Neighbors,"** one of his best-known stories, went from 30 pages to 10.) But today he adds as much as he cuts and regrets mutilating some early stories left out of the collection. "I used to revise even after a story was printed," he says. "I guess now I have a little more confidence."

Believers in a grim, minimalist Carver miss the fun of such comic figures as the fat restaurant customer who speaks in the royal "we," the blind, bearded house guest who calls people "Bub," his uncomfortable host ("A beard on a blind man! Too much, I say") and the old woman who natters on like a Beckett character about wanting a clock radio. Other readers see these people only as grotesques and miss their basic decency. The many failed marriages in Carver's stories always begin in love, and the partners take them seriously. In earlier stories, the great enemy of marriage is alcohol. No one has a better ear for drunken blather—"I don't have to be drunk to say what I think. I mean, we're all just talking, right?"—or a better eye for alcoholic dissociation. "He looks at his hand. It makes a fist as he watches." Since Carver himself stopped drinking a dozen years ago, he's found other emblems of the distance between his people.

Back in Washington, Carver's felt-tip pens and reams of unlined bond paper are waiting. (He always does his first drafts in longhand because he craves "physical contact with the page"; writing within ruled lines makes him feel constrained.) He's got these two stories which weren't quite ready for collection, and he's about to complete a new volume of poems—it will be his fifth. "I can just hardly wait to get back and get settled in," he says. "I'm glad to have that work to go to. And my strength is coming back now. I can feel it."

David Gates, "Carver: To Make a Long Story Short," in Newsweek, *Vol. CXI, No. 23, June 6, 1988, p. 70.*

STEWART KELLERMAN

Raymond Carver, a poet and short-story writer who chronicled the lives of America's working poor, died of lung cancer [August 2, 1988] at his home in Port Angeles, Wash. He was 50 years old.

Mr. Carver, who was married in Reno last June to the poet Tess Gallagher, died soon after finishing a book of poetry, *A New Path to the Waterfall.*

Ms. Gallagher said in a telephone interview from Port Angeles that they had decided not to tell anyone about his latest relapse, which was discovered in early June during a routine examination. "He wanted things to be calm so he could finish his book," she said. "He battled right up to the last minute."

Mr. Carver, a heavy cigarette smoker until he became ill, spent his last days sitting on the porch of his home, looking out at his rose garden. Hours before he died, Ms. Gallagher said, he spoke of how much he liked the stories of Chekhov. The last story in Mr. Carver's last book of stories was about the death of Chekhov.

Mr. Carver came from the hard-scrabble world of the down-and-out blue-collar characters in his stories. "I'm a paid-in-full member of the working poor," he said in one of two interviews with *The New York Times* last spring. "I have a great deal of sympathy with them. They're my people."

Mr. Carver published 10 books of prose and poetry in a career shadowed by alcoholism, poverty, a broken marriage and cancer.

In 1988 he collected what he considered the best of his stories in the book **Where I'm Calling From.** The novelist and critic Marilynne Robinson, reviewing it in *The New York Times Book Review,* said he "stands squarely in the line of descent of American realism" and "should be famous for the conceptual beauty of his best stories" [see excerpt above].

Mr. Carver was born on May 25, 1938, in Clatskanie, Ore., to Clevie Raymond Carver, a sawmill worker, and the former Ella Beatrice Casey, a waitress. He was brought up in a gray tract house in Yakima, Wash., a mile from Bachelor Creek, where he began a life-long love affair with fishing.

Frog, as he was nicknamed, used to sit at the foot of his parents' bed and listen to his father read from Zane Grey books or tell his own tales of hunting and fishing. He especially liked to hear stories about his great-grandfather's exploits in the Civil War—like the time he stole a hog for the hungry men in his regiment.

Before long, the boy was telling his own stories, amateurish efforts at escapism that drew groans from the grown-up Carver when he recalled them in the 1988 interviews. It was not until he went to Chico State College in California in 1958 and took John Gardner's creative writing course that he became serious about writing.

"He galvanized me," Mr. Carver said. "He told me who to read and helped me learn to write. He opened a door for me."

Mr. Carver graduated from Humboldt State College in California in 1963, then attended the Iowa Writers Workshop. He published his first story, **"Pastoral,"** and his first poem, **"The Brass Ring,"** in literary magazines while still at Humboldt.

But writing had to take second place to earning a living. Mr. Carver was married within a year of leaving high school and soon had a family to support. He returned to the West Coast with his wife, the former Maryann Burk, and their two children, Christine LaRae and Vance Lindsay. Like a displaced person, he knocked around California with his family, moving from one dead-end job to another in search of a better life.

"We were just looking for a place where I could write and my wife and the two children could be happy," he recalled. "It didn't seem like too much to ask for. But we never found it."

Mr. Carver was a janitor, a farm worker, a delivery boy. And in his spare time he wrote.

He began achieving recognition as a writer in 1967 when his story **"Will You Please Be Quiet, Please?"** was selected for the anthology "Best American Short Stories."

But that was also the year he began to drink heavily, torn between the demands of his family and those of his writing. He was in and out of alcohol rehabilitation centers in the 1970's as the drinking ruined his marriage and his health. He and his first wife were separated in 1977 and divorced five years later. In 1982, after being hospitalized for the fourth time, he turned to Alcoholics Anonymous and quit drinking.

Mr. Carver said in the 1988 interviews that he viewed his troubled life as an emotional reservoir to draw upon for his fiction. "Most of my stories, if not all of them, have some basis in real life," he said. "That's the kind of fiction I'm most interested in. I suppose that's one reason I don't have much respect for fiction that seems to be game playing."

Stewart Kellerman, "Raymond Carver, Writer and Poet of the Working Poor, Dies at 50," in The New York Times, August 3, 1988, p. B8.

RICHARD PEARSON

Raymond Carver, 50, a writer of poetry and fiction who fought to overcome poverty, alcoholism and family tribulations to become a recognized master of the short story, died of cancer Aug. 2 at his home in Port Angeles, Wash.

His most recent collection of short stories, recently published by Atlantic Monthly Press, was **Where I'm Calling From.** Shortly before his death, he finished work on a volume of poetry, **A New Path to the Waterfall.**

His 1976 short story collection **Will You Please Be Quiet, Please?** was nominated for a National Book Award. In 1984, his collection **Cathedral** was nominated for the National Book Critics Circle Award for fiction and the Pulitzer Prize for fiction. Other books included the collection **What We Talk About When We Talk About Love,** published in 1981, and **Fires,** a collection of essays, stories and poems that appeared in 1983.

He wrote in short declarative sentences, posing as a disinterested observer of events and reporting them to the reader in a deceptively simple and functional style. Although Mr. Carver came to intensely dislike the term, many critics point to his technique as an example of the "minimalist" school of writing.

Writer Joe David Bellamy once said of Mr. Carver's stories, "Beneath the surface conventionality of his salesmen, waitresses, bookkeepers, or hopeless middle-class 'occupants' lies a morass of inarticulated yearnings and unexamined horrors; repressed violence, the creeping certainty that nothing matters, perverse sexual wishes, the inadmissible evidence of inadequacy."

Mr. Carver wrote about the hard underside of life in the Pacific Northwest. Though his blue-collar characters live in a land of great physical beauty and glorious climate, money

and jobs can be scarce and help far away. His subjects suffer empty lives, have little hope and seem unable to explain their fears.

Mr. Carver said the critics had it all wrong, that his were not depressing stories about lives bereft of hope.

"Until I started reading these reviews of my work, praising me, I never felt the people I was writing about were so bad off. . . . The waitress, the bus driver, the mechanic, the hotel keeper. God, the country is filled with these people. They're good people. People doing the best they could."

Perhaps his stories were so effective because he was writing about lives he had lived and despair he had felt. He was born in the Oregon lumber town of Clatskanie, and grew up in Yakima, Wash.

Between drinking bouts, his father worked in lumber mills. His mother had worked as a waitress and clerk. In 1957, a year after graduating from high school, Mr. Carver had married a 16-year-old. By the time he was 20, he had fathered two children and had few marketable skills, no money and a burning desire to study and write. To feed his family, he picked tulips, pumped gas, worked as a hospital janitor and managed a small apartment complex. He wrote when he could.

In 1958, Mr. Carver and his family moved to California, where he took an introductory writing course at Chico State College in Paradise. It was taught by the late novelist John Gardner, who became a great influence on Mr. Carver, teaching him to write in simple language that he heard and understood every day. He also helped Mr. Carver get his first stories published and recommended that he pursue his studies at the University of Iowa's famous Writers Workshop.

After receiving a bachelor's degree at what is now California State University at Humboldt, he went to Iowa. After a year, he ran out of money, returned to California and worked as a hospital janitor.

In 1967, he got his first white-collar employment, as a textbook editor with Science Research Associates in Palo Alto. Later that year, his story **"Will You Please Be Quiet, Please?"** which had run in the Chicago literary journal *December,* was reprinted in the *Best American Short Stories,* an annual anthology.

Though his work was beginning to gain recognition, he could not seem to make money. He went through bankruptcy, began his struggle with alcohol and saw his first marriage ending. In the early 1970s, he was fired from his job with Science Research Associates, but after Esquire published his story **"Neighbors,"** his writing was increasingly recognized. His poems and stories appeared in mainstream and literary journals.

He tried alcohol treatment programs and was unable to hold a job. But in 1974, his first story collection, **Put Yourself in My Shoes,** appeared to favorable reviews. Living on severance pay and unemployment insurance, he found himself able to write full time. His collection **Will You Please Be Quiet, Please?** gained him a serious critical following.

By 1977, he was living alone, fighting his demons. In and out of hospitals, he managed to stop drinking after he became active in Alcoholics Anonymous. He and his first wife, Maryann Burk, divorced in 1982.

In 1983, his fifth, and perhaps best, story collection, **Cathe-**

dral, was published to almost universal acclaim. Many critics wrote that these stories were somehow less harsh and unforgiving than earlier ones and that their author had matured. It also was a commercial success, selling more than 20,000 copies in hard cover—an enormous number for a book of short stories.

> Richard Pearson, "Acclaimed Short-Story Writer Raymond Carver Dies at 50," in The Washington Post, August 4, 1988.

CHARLES JOHNSON

"Every day, every night of our lives, we're leaving little bits of ourselves, flakes of this and that, behind," says a vacuum cleaner salesman in Ray Carver's story, **"Collectors."** "Where do they go, these bits and pieces of ourselves? Right through the sheets and into the mattress, *that's* where! Pillows too. It's all the same."

Words like these, so ingenious in their co-mingling of common suffering and comic anguish, fill the pages of ***Will You Please Be Quiet Please?***—a story collection nominated for a 1977 National Book Award. Its author, who is to Northwest fiction what Theodore Roethke is to its poetry, left his signature on the American story. He did what O. Henry or Hemingway, with whom he is often compared, did for such obscure places as Yakima, Wash., and Joyce did for Dublin and Cheever for Westchester County. Yet Carver knew and told us in his interviews that "most of the stories, it seems to me, could take place anywhere." Thus, the distinct region on Earth called "Carver Country" is an emotional landscape where we find the most ordinary lives—waitresses, mill workers and postmen—made extraordinary. Your passport there is a knowledge of pain. And you cannot leave until you learn, as if for the first time, the anguish of the American underclass, the forgotten people who have fallen away from hope and, in some instances, entirely outside history.

The one time I met Raymond Carver—at a party after he read his story **"Cathedral"** to a packed audience at the University of Washington—he came across as a quiet, openhearted man with a sort of independent and practical outlook you see in so many Northwesterners. But, if you've lived here long enough, you know that the simplicity and dislike of frills is hard won and can't be romanticized, coming as it did in Carver's case from an early life of misfortune. Before he could vote, he was married and had two children, which led to a round of "crap jobs," as he called them, work so draining that it only left time for things he could "finish now, tonight, or at least tomorrow night, no later, after I got off work and before I lost interest," short bursts of brilliance he revised and pruned into prose where no word was unnecessary.

"For as long as I can remember," he explains in one of his essays, "since I was a teen-ager, the eminent removal of the chair from under me was a constant concern. For years and years my wife and I had no money, that is to say, marketable skills—nothing that we could do toward earning anything better than a get-by living."

He endured bouts of alcoholism, which he overcame, divorce, bankruptcy and died of lung cancer Aug. 2, but not before winning rewards as impressive as the stories he leaves behind: prestigious teaching posts; numerous honors, including a Mildred and Harold Strauss Living Award, providing $35,000 a year for five years; a legion of imitators (the University of Iowa once sponsored a Carver "write-alike contest"); the translation of his work into 23 languages; induction into the American Academy of the Institute of Arts and Letters this year; and a loving relationship to Tess Gallagher, one of this country's pre-eminent poets.

Strictly speaking, the most we shared in common was an apprenticeship to novelist John Gardner, who taught Carver at Chico State College in 1958. At first glance, no two writers could differ more in aesthetic vision and literary style. Gardner was contentious for short fiction, calling it a watercolor when compared to the mural-like range of the novel. But Carver distrusted novels, believing that to do one "the writer should be living their world to make sense, a world that will, for a time anyway, stay fixed in one place." In such a world, he had little faith because: "The time came and went when everything my wife and I held sacred, or considered worthy of respect, every spiritual value, crumbled away."

He also said, "At the first sign of a trick or a gimmick in a piece of fiction, a cheap trick or even an elaborate trick, I tend to look for cover." Yet it is precisely the pyrotechnical possibilities of language and literary form that so often fuel Gardner's stories. On one subject, however, they seemed in agreement, the moral priority of character in fiction.

For Carver in his early stories this is achieved, not by propositions or essayism, which often occur in Gardner's fiction, but rather by close attention to characters at the moment of heartbreak. The stories in his first collection, written over 12 years, with many first appearing in the *Little Magazine,* often began, "My marriage is falling apart. I couldn't find a job. I had another girl. But she wasn't in town." Or, my simpler, "I was out of work." The word "nothing," like a note, is heard again and again to describe spaces, faces, and the feeling of emptiness blimps peripherally at the edge of everyday experience.

"Carver Country," which seemed so compatible with the cruel penetrating light and loneliness of paintings by Edward Hooper, is inhabited by people like Earl Ober, an unemployed salesman who overhears two men in business suits make cruel sexual remarks about his fat wife Doreen, a waitress. His ego bruised, Earl urges her to go on a diet, then haunts the coffee shop, asking perfect strangers if they find Doreen desirable and special. In another story, **"Neighbors,"** Bill Miller, a bookkeeper and his wife Arlene, a secretary, are asked to watch the apartment of Harriet and Jim Stone, friends they envy who live a gayer life and are away for 10 days. Soon Bill finds himself slipping into their apartment to try on Jim's clothes, then Harriet's, and drink their liquor, all of which revitalizes his sex life with Arlene, a whole new world of possibilities opening to them until they accidentally leave the key inside and lock themselves out.

These stories, and those by writers like Ann Beattie, Bobbie Ann Mason and James Alan McPherson, are given credit for reviving American short fiction in the 1970s, although David Lehman, a *Newsweek* reviewer, said of the stories in Carver's fourth collection: "Fun to read they're not." True, much of Carver's fiction is bleak and his stories often seem anecdotal, but as the circumstances of his own life improved, his later work revealed a deepening of vision, a desire to draw connections between events, and tentative steps toward redemptions for his characters. In **"Cathedral,"** a husband must play host to Robert, a blind friend of his wife's, a man whose sightlessness is at first frightening (though still comic for Carver), then a challenge to the narrator when he is called upon to describe the beauty of cathedrals—and their homage to God—to Robert. To deliver cathedrals to a blind man is akin to describing religious faith to the husband who admits, "I guess I'm an agnostic or something." That is, in his own realm of darkness. Together, with Robert's hand on his own, the narrator draws spires and flying buttresses and finds himself unable to stop. Robert makes him close his eyes as he draws. At the story's end, the narrator is unsure of what's happened to him and concludes that "it's really something."

The great writer, said Carver, "has some special way of looking at things and gives expression to that way of looking: That writer may be around for a time." There can be no doubt that the work of Raymond Carver will be "around for a time" and that the renaissance of the American short story owes much to his contribution. (pp. 9, 11)

> *Charles Johnson, "Writing That Will Be 'Around for a Time'," in* Los Angeles Times Book Review, *August 21, 1988, pp. 9, 11.*

RAYMOND CARVER

"What The Doctor Said"

He said it doesn't look good
he said it looks bad in fact real bad
he said I counted thirty-two of them on one lung
    before
I quit counting them
I said I'm glad I wouldn't want to know
about any more being there than that
he said are you a religious man do you kneel down
in forest groves and let yourself ask for help
when you come to a waterfall
mist blowing against your face and arms
do you stop and ask for understanding at those mo-
    ments
I said not yet but I intend to start today
he said I'm real sorry he said
I wish I had some other kind of news to give you
I said Amen and he said something else
I didn't catch and not knowing what else to do
and not wanting him to have to repeat it
and me to have to fully digest it
I just looked at him
for a minute and he looked back it was then
I jumped up and shook hands with this man who'd
    just given me
something no one else on earth had ever given me
I may even have thanked him habit being so strong

> *Raymond Carver, " 'What the Doctor Said'," in* Granta, *Vol. 25, Autumn, 1988, p. 162.*

TESS GALLAGHER

Even though I don't choose to express the loss in this way, I understand Leonard Bernstein's having gone to bed and stayed there for six months after his wife died of cancer. But in my family no one would be so indulged. You have to get up, make an effort at normalcy, do your share, and how you feel doesn't come into it . . . part of the working-class ethic, I suppose. But that's where both Ray and I come from. Ray once said to me, speaking about the days before we met, 'I never had *time* to have a nervous breakdown.' The 'iron will' which he says in one of his poems is necessary for making art

must, I think, have been forged during just such times when there was 'no-choice-but-to-go-ahead'.

But Ray and I learned somehow to do more than just go ahead; we learned how to go ahead with hope. When we joined lives nearly eleven years ago in El Paso, Texas, we were both recovering from an erosion of trust and hope. Between us I think we'd left behind something like thirty years of failed marriage. We more than rebuilt trust. We got to a place where trust was second nature. But along the way, we had a saying that helped us. We used to say: 'Don't get weird on me, Babe. Don't get weird.' And believe me, by then we'd both lived enough to know what weird was.

You probably know the story. Ray'd been off alcohol about a year when we began to live together. He was shaky. He didn't know if he'd ever write again. He literally ran from the phone when it rang. He'd been bankrupt three times. I can still remember how his eyes lit up when he saw my VISA Card.

I think now we built and rebuilt on Ray's capacity for joy, which extended even to the ability to take immense pleasure in someone else's pleasure, and this capacity continued into his last days. But it hadn't always been this way. Since his death I've become the repository for many people's memories and stories about Ray. I've read in letters from friends he knew during what he called his 'Bad Raymond' days that he was, according to one writer, 'the most unhappy man I'd ever met.' Twenty years later the two met again and the friend was astonished at the transformation.

Theodore Roethke said, 'The right thing happens to the happy man,' and I was privileged to witness as Ray became that happy man. I'm often remembering how glad he was to be alive, and because he was happy to be alive Ray grieved to be leaving his life so early. I won't hide that from you. If will alone could have prevailed, he'd be alive today and with us.

Still, at each turn during his illness he asked: What can I do with the life that's left? He chose to work, to write his poems, in spite of the terror of a brain tumour and later, in June, of the recurrence of cancer in the lungs. His response to that blow was to think of something important to celebrate, and on 17 June we were married in Reno, Nevada. It was a very Carveresque affair, held in the little Heart of Reno Chapel across from the court-house. Afterwards we went gambling at Harrah's Club and with every turn of the wheel I won. I couldn't stop winning.

Near the end Ray knew, he was sure, that his stories were going to last: 'We're out there in history now, Babe,' he said, and he felt lucky to know it. He had a period of clear celebration when his book of stories, **Where I'm Calling From,** came out last spring. There was a brief interlude when we were free from the mental suffering that accompanied his disease and during which he accepted joyously and gratefully the wonderful reviews, induction into the American Academy of Arts & Letters, a Doctorate of Letters from the University of Hartford and the Brandeis Medal for Excellence.

I'm in mourning and celebration for the artist and the man, and also for that special entity which was our particular relationship which allowed such a beautiful alchemy in our lives, a kind of luminous reciprocity. We helped, nurtured and protected each other, and what's more, in the Rilkian sense, we guarded and respected each other's solitude. In our days we were always asking: *What really matters?*

Ray gave me encouragement to write stories and I gave him encouragement to write his stories and his poems, poems through which he out worked his own spiritual equanimity, for he was, I think, at his death, one of those rare, purified beings for whom, as Tolstoy says, the only response is love. He lived every day with the assurance and comfort that I cherished him. As Simone de Beauvoir said, when challenged by feminists for her devotion to Sartre and his work: 'But I *like* to work in the garden next to mine.' I'll miss working in that strange, real garden—Ray's garden. Everything I ever gave there I got back in his gifts of attention to my own work. It has sustained me since his death to be putting his last book in order. I'll miss his delight and laughter in the house and his unfailing kindness, for he was, before anything, my great friend.

All those qualities you sensed about Raymond Carver, that he was a man who would do the decent, the right and generous thing—that was how he was. I can tell you from inside the story. He was like that. And he managed this in a rather complicated life. For his hardships didn't all end back there in the bad old days, and the nature of those hardships is recorded in his stories and poems.

In the last book he completed, one of the epigraphs is a quote from Robert Lowell which reads: 'Yet why not tell it like it happened?' I see this as central to Ray's attitude towards his art and its relation to his life. He carried some burdens of guilt about 'what had happened', and he worked out his redemption and consequently some of ours in his art.

A few days after Ray's death I went into his study in Port Angeles. The study he'd always dreamed of, with a fireplace and a view of valley and mountain, then water beyond. I sat at the desk awhile. Just sat. Then I reached down and pulled open a drawer. Inside I found a dozen folders full of ideas for stories that would have carried him well into the year 2015. I'm sad we won't be reading those stories. But I can't stay in that sadness long. I keep feeling how much, in such a short time, how incredibly much he gave! We have to accept the blessing of that, and Ray believed that he had been graced and blessed and that he had done his utmost to return that blessing to the world. As he has.

I was standing with a friend at Ray's graveside overlooking the Strait of Juan de Fuca a week after his death, and the friend remembered a line from Rilke and said it aloud. It seemed to express the transformation Ray has come to now: 'And he was everywhere, like the evening hour.' To conclude I'd like to present the last poem in his new manuscript.

Late Fragment

And did you get what
you wanted from this life, even so?
I did.
And what did you want?
To call myself beloved, to feel myself
beloved on the earth.

(pp. 165-67)

Tess Gallagher, "Raymond Carver, 1938 to 1988," in Granta, *Vol. 25, Autumn, 1988, pp. 165-67.*

TED SOLOTAROFF

[A few weeks after Raymond Carver's death, Tess Gallagher] asked me to speak at the memorial for Ray in New York. This meant the writer as well as the man, so I stayed up one night reading his stories. The fact was that I hadn't read many of them until then. Except for **"Errand"** I had respected his fiction rather than cottoned to it. His typically small town isolates were of marginal interest to me; they didn't seem to see or feel or learn much beyond their insecurities, the bleakness of their prospects, the force of their streaks of envy, jealousy, cruelty, shame, dishonesty, or some other twisted energy that flared up like a chronic fever in a meager, congested life: the unemployed salesman who pressures his wife to lose weight so that he can watch men ogling her; the drinker and adulterer who drives himself to begin to put his family's life in order by secretly getting rid of their messy dog; the baker who torments the couple whose child has been run over about the birthday cake they had ordered. I admired the integrity of Carver's work—his firm grasp of damaged lives for which there was little help or hope and his bluff style that conceded nothing to literary entertainment. But his vision was too limiting, to my taste: the world seen from the barstool, the forsaken marriage bed, the car rubbernecking the traffic accident.

That was my superficial response. What I remembered best was his astonishing essay **"Fires,"** in which he said flat out that the main influence on his fiction had been his long subjection to the needs and caprices of his children. He and his wife had been teen-age parents, uneducated and unskilled, working at one "crap job" after another, subsisting, stretched thin, losing heart until " . . . everything my wife and I held sacred or considered worthy of respect, every spiritual value crumbled away. Something terrible had happened to us. . . . It was erosion and we couldn't stop it. Somehow, when we weren't looking, the children had got into the driver's seat. As crazy as it sounds now, they held the reins, and the whip." That kind of rockbottom honesty was electrifying: it generated the power and light of his stories. But it didn't make me a fan of the stories. It mostly made me wonder how the sweetness of the man had survived the bitter erosions and defeats the writer kept recounting and imagining.

That night and on into the early morning I read through most of **Where I'm Calling From,** his new and selected stories. I found myself giving up my dismissive respect or, rather, having it pushed aside by assent. At first it took a literary form, a fascination with the exactness of the writing—common language that "hit all the notes" as Carver put it, and with the subtle variations of the emotional burden that I'd read too glibly as an obsessive gray doom that fogged in his people's world. What I had taken to be a grim reductiveness was, when seen in the round, a finely calibrated ruefulness: a more tender and interesting and philosophical kind of understanding. As one of his characters, in the grip of an unwarranted but intractable jealousy, comes to see: "Yes, there was a great evil pushing at the world, . . . and it only needed a little slipway, a little opening."

Those rusted-out marriages and stalled affairs and misfiring bar seductions and sprung friendships: each testified in its own distinctive tone to the erosion at the heart of things that he spoke about in **"Fires."** I also began to see that his understanding of it had widened and become more nuanced: the blue-collar ruts of the earlier stories branched out, as it were, into the mazes of better-educated people, the undercurrent of menace or risk was giving way to more uncanny and strange threats, like the blind friend of the narrator's wife in **"Cathedral"** or the goodbye letter from the wife in **"Blackbird Pie"** that is not in her handwriting or style. But he still refused to brighten or soften the testimony of his narrators about their secret meannesses, screw-ups, losses, and the prose remained homely and unsparing, as though a naked lightbulb were burning in their minds. The ruefulness was built into the "unique and exact way of looking at things" he recommended, just as it was built into the lives he trained it upon, . . . just as it was built into my own. The pity was in the telling itself and it began to get to me, to chasten my way of reading him. (p. 47)

In his *Paris Review* interview Carver speaks of turning one's life's stories into fiction. "You have to be immensely daring, very skilled and imaginative and willing to tell everything on yourself. . . . What do you know better than your own secrets?" He's not saying that telling them guarantees anything, for fiction is more likely to fail from lack of skill and imagination than from evasiveness. What he is saying is that if you want the energy and authority that comes from telling your secrets, they had better be the real ones: the ones that make you go through their pain again. Otherwise the writing will be coming not from the secrets but from the defenses against them and the fiction will not be the bread of experience earned in the sweat of your brow but rather the cake of fantasies that you can have and eat too. . . .

As I read [Ray] now and write about him he has come to seem less like a dead friend than a vital ally. I imagine that when Chekhov died many Russians writers felt the same way: that his fiction was itself a friendship. What one wants most in a friend is both candor and empathy—qualities rarely found together. Chekhov's vision was less relentless than Carver's and he had more social range, but they started from and came back to the same ruefulness: a radical honesty and empathy about ordinary lives and how they go wrong.

Gorki wrote that in Chekhov's presence "everyone felt an involuntary desire to be simpler, more truthful, more oneself." This was also Ray Carver's gift as a person . . . and one that is literally conveyed by his stories and poems as it was by Chekhov's stories and plays. It explains, I think, much better than does the fashionable talk about "minimalism" and "rural chic" why Carver has been the most influential writer of his generation. He had the kind of gift that travels: the common touch raised to the next power, the power of art, that can be conveyed intact to his readers and brings out . . . the giftedness in them, the possibility of getting down to the charged and freighted roots of our lives. To God's honest truth, as he would have said, and as he did. (p. 49)

Ted Solotaroff, "Raymond Carver: Going through the Pain," in The American Poetry Review, *Vol. 18, No. 2, March-April, 1989, pp. 47-9.*

René (Emile) Char

June 14, 1907 - February 19, 1988

French poet and essayist.

For an overview of Char's life and work see *CLC,* Vols. 9, 11, 14 and *Contemporary Authors,* Vols. 13-16, rev. ed., Vol. 124 (obituary).

NANCY KLINE PIORE

The poems of René Char, whether they be fragmentary in form or structured as prose poems, strike us by the terseness of their beauty and by the wholly elusive presence of their maker, visible only in his invisibility. He resembles his trout, whose absence pervades the poem named for her, or his meteor, seen in its dying as a luminous line across the sky. On the page it is the poet's disappearance that illuminates . . . His characteristic gesture is departure, or in terms of writing, ellipsis—first, at the juncture between life and art (virtually every poem has a "story," Char says, but the reader is not privy to it, it gets left out, or transformed beyond recognition, although the poet frequently leaves in just enough autobiography to tantalize us . . .); second, at the level of language itself (he is the most elliptical of poets). This double ellipsis gives to everything he writes its distinctive and compelling mystery. His is hardly confessional poetry, yet like the spider to whom he compares himself, he spins from his own center and from the center of his life, and all his work glimmers with the tension between disclosure and concealment, what the poet shows and what he hides on the page. The reader feels, as Helen Vendler has remarked, that "he writes with absolute candor, but in a secret language." A language, it must be added, that can be learned. Surely this is central to the experience of reading René Char, this sense that one has come upon a poetic universe that is by turns transparent and completely opaque—of a beautiful opacity—but where at any given moment an illumination may occur, a connection be made, so that the mystery which was felt to be unsolvable but full of meaning yields its meaning to us, opens to us like a door, a book, a lover, and we are admitted into places where we could not go before, our pleasure, our delight akin to Char's, perhaps, in the moment when he forged the image. (pp. xv-xvi)

René Char was born in L'Isle-sur-Sorgue, in 1907. . . . [His] poetry takes its fragrance, its intense light, its creatures, from the Vaucluse, a water landscape ringed with mountains, and filtered on the page through the immense dark imagination of the poet. The early death of his father and the communal tragedies of this century cast deep shadows across his poetry, whose characteristic hour has always been the dawn, but a red dawn. (The color is not unambiguous. And then too, dawn is born of Night's blackness.) World War I occurred in the middle of Char's childhood; World War II in the mid-

dle of his manhood, and he was an active participant in the Resistance. The wreckage of the world, as he testifies with anguish, has continued ever since. But so, in counterpoint to it, has the poet's love of the earth and his attempt to salvage it, its beauty and fragility. And if certain themes such as warfare and eroticism have diminished in his later work, this theme—a passion for the planet and for the creatures who inhabit it—has only been strengthened, so that in 1975 he published a book called *Aromates chasseurs* (*Aromatic Hunters*), whose hero Orion leaves the sky to come back down among us, a human meteor who has the earth—no longer the moon—for honey.

In the figure of Orion and the voyage that he undertakes the two spheres of Char's poetic universe, the celestial and the terrestrial, are joined. Orion is a bridge-builder, as the poet suggests in texts like **"Pontonniers"** (**"Pontoniers"**) and **"Orion Iroquois."** But he is also a cluster of stars and a solitary, blinded hunter—which makes of him the quintessential Charian hero. For . . . the night sky, the Night itself, and the activity of hunting are among Char's recurrent leitmotifs; all are connected with love-making and with the making of poetry; and the hunter-lover-poet's power of sight (or lack of it) is crucial, as is the balance he chooses to strike between his solitude and his sense of community.

The tension between these last two—separateness and "common presence"—has been as great in the poet's personal life as in his work. He himself is a deeply private man, a man of silence, to use his own phrase, yet he participated actively in two of the most important communal efforts of the century, Surrealism and the Resistance, and both have marked his work.

He came to Surrealism late, in terms of the movement (1929-1930) and was a decade younger than his colleagues Eluard and Breton, with whom he collaborated on one book, *Ralentir travaux* (*Slacken Labors*). He was already published at that time, and it was when he sent his second book of poems to Eluard that the older poet came south to meet him. Char moved to Paris then, into the thick of things, returning to live in the Vaucluse only in 1934. In that same year he published *Le marteau sans maître* (*The Hammer with No Master*), his most important pre-World War II collection. In the following year he broke formally, though without venom, with the Surrealist movement.

There is some critical debate as to just how bona fide a Surrealist Char was. He never practiced automatic writing, and his poetry is characterized by quite the opposite of the verbal flux we associate with Breton. . . . Char's imagery has always been deeply reasoned, *wrought,* and his style always highly elliptical. Charian images do not float haphazardly into view, the poet goes after them with a pick and hammer; they are mined by him, underground. . . . If his raw materials come out of the unconscious, this alone does not validate them for Char. They must be shaped by the poet's consciousness. His discourse, like his serenity, is *clenched.*

What he does share with Surrealist doctrine is an emphasis on the marvelous in everyday life and an openness to those rare, privileged instants when all the disparate elements of reality come together in illuminative synthesis, "cet instant où la beauté, après s'être longtemps fait attendre surgit des choses communes, traverse notre champ radieux, lie tout ce qui peut être lié, allume tout ce qui doit être allumé de notre gerbe de ténèbres" ["that instant when beauty, so long awaited, rises out of common things, crosses our radiant field of vision, binds together all that can be bound, lights all that must be lit in our sheaf of shadows"]. His is a poetry of the sudden encounter—between lovers, adversaries, hunters and their prey, the poet and poetry, the reader and the poem; between words themselves within the text, within the image. And these encounters do not leave their participants unchanged. They are explosive fusions that destroy the elements fused to create new unities. . . . He is a poet who exalts life, communication, beauty, the world of nature. But he is also a Heraclitean poet, deeply pessimistic, who sees the universe in terms of opposites colliding, fire, constant flux, and violent metamorphosis.

Particularly as it applies to his conception of poetry, Char's passionate, combative stance constitutes another link between him and the Surrealists, with whom he shares a sense of poetry as rebellion, desperate, revolutionary, and fertile; and a belief that art, man's most precious radium and most effective weapon, can transform him and the quality of his life. Still, the creation of art, no matter how revolutionary,

how *committed,* requires an essential solitude: "La poésie est la solitude. . .qui a le moyen de se confier; on n'est, à l'aube, l'ennemi d'aucun, excepté des bourreaux" ["Poetry is solitude. . .which has found the way to be confiding; at dawn one isn't the enemy of anyone, except the hangman"]. The poet's withdrawal from the Surrealist community was inevitable. But their brief association had strengthened him and had served as a kind of basic training, or boot camp, for the Maquis. As Dominique Fourcade suggests, [in "Essai d'introduction," *L'Herne,* 1971], "the Surrealists must have confirmed in him the belief that there existed in life a small society of sensitive beings, totally isolated from society at large and in violent opposition to it; in the bosom of that small society, Char could go into action."[6]

Four years after his rift with Surrealism, war broke out. The poet was mobilized and sent to Alsace, where he saw France fall; he then returned to Provence to fight in the Resistance, his nom de guerre: le capitaine Alexandre.

His years in the Maquis left an indelible imprint on Char's poetry (not to say his life). . . . [The] war experience seems to have been anticipated, to a certain extent, by the Surrealist experience, its emphasis on community and revolt, violence and the unexpected. But the essence of art is play, if deeply serious play, and poems take place in the heart and on the page. This fact in no way diminishes their power. Quite the contrary:

> La poésie est à la fois parole et provocation silencieuse, désespérée de notre être-exigeant pour la venue d'une réalité qui sera sans concurrente. Imputrescible celle-là. Impérissable, non, car elle court les dangers de tous. Mais la seule qui visiblement triomphe de la mort matérielle. . . ." "Poetry is simultaneously word and silent desperate provocation on the part of our exacting-being, aimed at the coming of a peerless reality, incorruptible. Not imperishable, for it runs the same dangers as everyone. But the only reality that visibly triumphs over material death."

This empowers poetry—along—to "steal" the poet's death from him. However, he himself continues to exist in the flesh and in the world as well; and to write poetry, even if the poet calls it resistance, is a different endeavor from actively participating in the Resistance. During the war years, what had been metaphor became reality, both around the poet and within him.

After the war, in 1945, he wrote: . . .

> Toward what enraged sea, unknown even to poets, could this river, scarcely even perceived, have been flowing, around 1930, coursing through lands where the covenants of fertility were already expiring, where the allegory of horror was beginning to take on concrete existence—this radiant and enigmatic river baptized *The Hammer with No Master?* Toward the hallucinating experience of man riveted to evil, of man massacred and still victorious.

> The key of *The Hammer with No Master* turns in the reality of the years 1937-1944, foreshadowed. The first ray it gives forth hesitates between the imprecation of agony and a magnificent love.

It will be remembered that *Le marteau sans maître* was first published in 1934. In it, according to the poet, the war which did not erupt till five years later was already present. Certainly Char's own native violence, a violence pre-dating his association with Surrealism (the book he sent to Eluard in 1929 was entitled *Arsenal*), his thirst for justice, his anger and desire, his need to do battle for that which breaks easily, the very values and ways of thinking that drew him into the underground, had already begun to be articulated on the page. He had already spoken of poetry as warfare, as endless combat and voluntary death, within the context of a poem called **"Commune présence"** (**"Common Presence"**) which ended *Le marteau sans maître.* The Resistance made of the poet an actual guerrilla soldier, and validated the metaphor. I do not think the importance of this intersection between life and art can be too greatly stressed. (pp. xvi-xxi)

The war years seem to have influenced his work in at least two ways: on one level, by tempering his attitude toward human beings and the voice with which he speaks of them, so that his early anger and revolt are counterbalanced now with tenderness and deep fraternity; on another level, by reinforcing his conception of poetry as guerrilla warfare and his sense of himself as a *Résistant.*

After the war Char leaves the underground to move back out onto the page, but strengthened in the need to keep himself half-hidden in the very moment when he is most present. Ellipsis and fragmentation characterize his work. The poem is defined as veil and revelation, simultaneously: "Tu es reposoir d'obscurité sur ma face trop offerte, poème" ["You are, poem, a wayside altar of darkness on my too-exposed face"]. The poet has put aside his gun and taken up his words again as weapons, but since he is both hunted and hunter, and since in the poetic universe that he creates, as in the world of the Maquis, to be caught is to be killed, his words must also serve as shelter, as a hiding place. Were we to try to characterize the particular quality of Char's poetic voice and of his greatness, we would focus on this paradox: his is not simply lyric but also political poetry. It repeatedly addresses such questions as freedom versus oppression, truth versus lies; it is direct, directed to us; yet it eludes us at the same time. *Engagé* and *hermétique,* committed yet mysterious, Char's poetry—like the creatures it evokes—retains an essential distance. "Supprimer l'éloignement tue," he writes. "Les dieux ne meurent que d'être parmi nous" ["Doing away with distance kills. The gods die only from being amongst us"]. His poetic universe is permeated by violence and by enduring invisibility, and his lark and snake and swift reflect their maker and embody the ellipsis at the center of his work as they flash in and out of hiding on the page. The lightning bolt and meteor participate in Char's "guérilla sans reproche" ["blameless guerrilla warfare"] as does the rose, the lightning's earthly feminine counterpart, as ephemeral and as dazzling as itself: "Eclair et rose, en nous, dans leur fugacité, pour nous accomplir, s'ajoutent" ["Within us, lightning bolt and rose in their transience, to complete us, join"]. (pp. xxi-xxii)

Nancy Kline Piore, in her Lightning: The Poetry of René Char, *Northeastern University Press, 1981, 131 p.*

THE TIMES, London

René Char, French (Provencal) poet, dramatist, and Resistance hero, died in Paris on February 19. He was 80. His early *Marteau sans maître* (*The Masterless Hammer*) is famous as an epoch-making piece of music for contralto and orchestra set by his compatriot, Pierre Boulez.

Char's poetry is widely read outside his native France, and there are three substantial volumes in English translation: *Hypnos Waking* (1956), *Leaves of Hypnos* (1973) and *Poems of René Char* (1976).

He will always be associated with a group of painters who were his close friends ("substantial allies", he called them): Braque, Giacometti, Miró, Picasso and others illustrated beautiful limited editions of his poems.

Everything about Char was "mountainous"—writing, stature, character, "whether in generosity or anger". His is the most difficult poetry of undeniable quality since Mallarmé's, but only because he tried to make its language and rhythm match the humane experience behind it—not because he wished to express profound ideas; on the whole, it has not appealed to intellectuals. . . .

In 1929 he published *Arsenal* (his second book), a copy of which he sent to the surrealist poet Paul Éluard, who took him off to Paris, where he introduced him to the leader of the surrealists, André Breton.

Char's early poems were surrealist in style; but he soon cast off all but the appearance of surrealism in the interests of recapturing what he felt to be the essentials of life, especially, at that time, the struggle against fascism.

He maintained that his work of this period should be related to the "social strife" then going on in France, though the most impressive piece of these years **"Le visage nuptial"** (**"The Nuptial Countenance"**) is a long and resonant love poem. . . .

In 1939 he was called up, fought in Alsace, and on the defeat, was demobilized. The Vichy police investigated him, since anyone with surrealist connections was suspect as a communist. He escaped to the Alps, and became "Captain Alexandre", departmental commander of the parachute landing division of the second region of the Free French Forces.

He was wounded by Germans in 1944, and was cared for by *maquis* doctors; in the following month he was able to go to Algeria, whence he had been summoned by the North Africa Allied Council. He was parachuted back into France and participated in most of the battles which liberated Provence. He was demobilised in 1945.

With the publication of *Seuls demeurants* (*The Only Ones Left,* 1945) and *Feuillets d'Hypnos* (*Leaves of Hypnos,* 1946) he became famous. Accusations that he became increasingly grandiose were not entirely unfounded; but he refused to become embroiled in political squabbles.

His poetry and prose-poetry, collected in such volumes as *Commune présence* (*Common Presence*) and *La nuit talismanique* (*The Talismanic Night*) are highly regarded.

An obituary in The Times, *London, February 22, 1988.*

CHARLES GUENTHER

Critics admonish one another never to use superlatives, or else to use them sparingly. But René Char was a poet long accustomed to superlatives, especially in the decade after

World War II when his exploits as "Capitaine Alexandre," a leader of the Céreste maquis in the French resistance, grew from legend into fact. In his preface to Char in the *Poètes d'aujourd'hui* series (1951), Pierre Berger wrote of Char's wartime diary *Feuillets d'Hypnos* that, written in France's darkest hour, "it arose and awakened us, calling us to the reality of Revolt."

But others were more direct. Albert Camus called him "our greatest living poet . . . the poet for whom we have been waiting." Jean Paulhan saw him as "the light bearer." Louise Bogan and William Carlos Williams recognized him as the most important living French poet, and Williams added, "I don't know of a poet in my own language to equal him."

Yet poets and artists must live up to superlatives, and sometimes live them down. With Char it was rather different. He easily deserved the enthusiastic accolades for *Feuillets d'Hypnos (Leaves of Hypnos),* written in 1943-44 and dedicated to Camus, and for such earlier volumes as *Le Marteau sans maître* (1934) and *Moulin premier* (1936).

Born June 14, 1907, at L'Isle-sur-Sorgue in the Vaucluse, Char spent most of his life in his native Provence. He began writing poetry at seventeen, joined the Surrealists in 1929, with Reverdy, Eluard and others, but broke with the group in 1937. Only after the war, in which his feats as an officer in charge of a parachute reception unit became known, was his poetry well known also outside of France. . . .

In *Le Marteau sans maître,* containing all his poems up to 1934, he was just beginning to show the firm, aphoristic statement representing a departure from the diffuse, automatic writing of the Surrealists; from 1937 to 1939 he published four more volumes showing a further growth of his poetic identity. Whether Char's involvement with the Surrealists was more a liberating experience for him than one that shaped his direction in poetry is still debated among critics. It has long been recognized, however, that Char's three basic forms (prose poetry, free verse and the aphorism) were inherent in his work before he had aligned himself with the Surrealists.

After his wartime books, *Seuls demeurent* (1945), poems that survived the war period, and *Feuillets d'Hypnos* (1946), Char produced a steady stream of new poetry that continued to the 1980s. This work included *Les Matinaux* (1950), *La parole en archipel* (1962) and *Retour amont* (1966). This last book was reprinted in a further collection, *Le Nu perdu, 1964-1970,* published in 1971; and the next year *La nuit talismanique* . . . was first published by Skira (Geneva), and later (1978) republished by Gallimard (Paris). . . .

During the 1970s Gallimard also published three more significant collections of Char's poems written between 1972 and 1979: *Aromates chasseurs* (1975), *Chants de la Balandrane* (1977) and *Fenêtres dormantes et porte sur le toit* (1979). More recently, Gallimard produced a fine, 1,400-page volume of Char's complete works (*Oeuvres complètes*) . . . , and followed that with another volume, *Les voisinages de Van Gogh,* in 1985. . . .

Now, sixty years after Char's earliest work, we can discern how far he developed beyond his origins, and see how he remained faithful to them—to his obscurity, for example. His was not the narcissistic obscurity of a cult or a school, but rather the obscurity of a poet expressing complexities of the world around him, and its intensities of feeling. The war, of course, was the great maturing experience which catalyzed his writing from craft to social concern.

Despite (or perhaps because of) his aphoristic breadth, René Char cannot be pinned down in his evolving thought and philosophy, which leap out and spark again and again like high voltage wires downed by a storm. But surely among the many key aphorisms we may segregate in his work is the passage from *A une sérénité crispée (To a Tensed Serenity,* 1952), which opens with these thoughts:

> Produce (work) according to the laws of utility, but let that utility serve through everything but the medium of poetry. (Valuable to *one,* to *another,* and still another, and one *alone.* . . . Don't try to be *new* in it, or famous, but to retouch the same iron to insure yourself a healing aftergrowth.)

> (p. 23)

Charles Guenther, "René Char: Twelve Poems," in The American Poetry Review, *Vol. 17, No. 3, May-June, 1988, pp. 23-5.*

RENÉ CHAR

"Slow Pace Of The Future"

We must scale many dogmas and much ice to get lucky and wake up glowing red on the bed of rock.

Between them and me for a long time there was a kind of wild hedge whose flowering thorns we were allowed to gather and give each other. Never farther away than the hand and the arm. They loved me and I loved them. This obstacle *for the wind* where my full strength ran aground—what was it? A nightingale revealed it to me, and later a carcass.

Death in life is incompatible, it is repugnant; death with death is approachable, it is nothing, a fearful belly crawls there without trembling.

I've knocked down the last wall surrounding the nomads of the snow, and I see—oh my primeval parents—the summer of candle-making.

Our earthly form is only the second third of a continual pursuit, a point, upstream.

René Char, " 'Slow Pace of the Future'," *translated by Charles Guenther, in* The American Poetry Review, *Vol. 17, No. 3, May-June, 1988, p. 24.*

PAULÈNE ASPEL

The illustrations [by Alexandre Galpérine] are akin to [Char's poems in *Le gisant mis en lumière*]. They surround and penetrate them intimately. A feeling of serenity, which emanates from the poet's elegant handwriting, is enhanced by the painter's gouaches and delicate hues of sunset ochres, of gray and periwinkle blues. The recumbent figure of the title, hardly discernible, soon vanishes and turns into probable paths leading to the unknown; a candle at the opening of a quasi-grotto suggests a mysterious origin, that of poetry perhaps, or of beauty.

Char's beauty, as we have known for a long time . . . is *sans date.* "Dates have been erased" in **"The Noise of a Match,"** the candle poem where sparkles will shine beyond "nicks of future"; and if a dozen dates are given—1974, a first date followed by 1948 and 1949, for instance, or 1925 appearing between 1972 and 1982—it is no doubt because the poet of *ordre insurgé* invites the reader to ignore the chronological order. Annulling time is the intent. The fact that the book is not paginated confirms it.

Le gisant mis en lumière, however, offers much more than a Baudelairean program of luxury, calm, and perennial beauty. It offers an extraordinary microcosm of the whole Charian universe. All the poems, including the two new pieces, seem to have been selected for their faithful *mémoire amoureuse* to previous key texts and because together they bear the poet's main themes. Among them, the theme of poetry, its voyage to transcendence as well as the renewal it creates in us and our fellow men, is predominant. Starting with the second poem, after the poet's short, humble address to a "proximate earth," poetry is alluded to or invoked several times. Her names are the usual, tender ones of "Amie" and "source."

Water is the poet's dearest element. It is often placed in a typical *soleil des eaux* situation, a dialectic perspective with fire, the versatile fire that heats, lights, and enlightens. Water carries many of the metaphors pertaining to poetry. Reminding us of Char as a child "enshrined" by the Sorgue River, then of the young man dreaming **"Eauxmères"** in 1933, a great vivifying current pervades *Le gisant mis en lumière.* Torrents, rivers, springs, marshes, even the "vaste mer" are friends of the "green water hunter," whose desire is to moor and dwell on the bank of a brook, his old sorrows resting at the bottom like gravel. (pp. 433-34)

From the new poem **"Handwritten News,"** where a *fauvette* (warbler) trills, "l'eau des bêtes," a somewhat primal water drunk by animals in earthenware dishes, will lead to and climax in "l'élégante source séduite," the last three words of the volume. Following the sad love song of a bullfinch in the new, untitled, dateless text, poetry reaches its ultimate stage of transfiguration. A source became poetry, which, enraptured by light, has become light itself. Remarkably enough, the last page of each of Char's books of poems ends on a note of greenness, uplift, celebration, hope, thus constituting not a closure but rather an opening, a larger and higher vision. *Le gisant* is no exception.

A prophecy, we may recall, was made more than thirty years ago, in **"The Library Is on Fire":** "La finitude du poème est lumière"—"The end of the poem is light." *Le gisant mis en lumière* is the story of a prophecy fulfilled. (p. 434)

Paulène Aspel, in a review of "Le gisant mis en lumière," in World Literature Today, *Vol. 62, No. 3, Summer, 1988, pp. 433-34.*

EDOUARD GLISSANT

When poets die, some part of the illumination of the world dies with them; yet the reverberations of their works open up new horizons. Aloof from the fads and ephemeral triumphs of daily life, they bear witness to and, more often than not, are the dynamic source of those deeper currents that shape the course of the world.

René Char fashioned his writings from the French language with the silent concentration of a turner working at his lathe, inventing a form of expression which lies somewhere between that of the pastoral poem and the maxim. The phraseology is familiar and the formulation is enigmatic yet evocative; and this draws him close to the very source of the wisdom of the people, to the world of writings based on popular oral traditions in which the poet works the raw material of words with the same simplicity as a potter works his clay. Poetry of this kind thus stands at the interface of the spoken and the written word, even if it owes its permanence to the written dimension. To it could be applied the words that the poet Jean Grosjean used about the Gospels when he declared that ". . . they are manifestly spoken yet deliberately written".

This strange marriage of a diamond-hard economy of writing and the comfortably familiar grace of the voice is paralleled by the rapprochement that René Char made between justice and beauty. A militant who fought against the forces of darkness, he never resorted to simplistic anathematizing. In one of his finest and most profound books of poetry, **Feuillets d'Hypnos,** written at the time (1943-1944) that he was leading a resistance group in the Vaucluse against the Nazi occupying forces, he wrote: "We invite Liberty to sit down with us at all the meals we share. The seat remains empty but a place is always laid for her."

The source of the consistent quality of happiness and well-being that is to be found in René Char's writings is undoubtedly his passionate attachment to the Vaucluse, a region from which he never strayed. In this land of burning light, which gave him his love of painting and of certain artists such as Braque, Miró, Lam and Vieira da Silva, of intense silence, whose muffled echo can be heard in the aphorisms and philosophical notes of his **Recherche de la base et du sommet,** (1941-1965; **Search for the Base and the Summit**), of the benison of sunlit waters and the mute stirrings of olive trees, in this very special land René Char put down the roots of that unquenchable desire to create, to love, to go ever further, that makes him the contemporary of each and every inhabitant of this planet.

Edouard Glissant, "René Char: A Tribute," in The Courier, *Vol. 41, June, 1988, p. 33.*

Robert (Edward) Duncan

January 7, 1919 - February 3, 1988

(Born Edward Howard Duncan; has also written as Robert Edward Symmes) American poet, critic, essayist, dramatist, nonfiction writer, editor, and author of children's books.

For an overview of Duncan's life and work see *CLC,* Vols. 1, 2, 4, 7, 15, 41; *Contemporary Authors,* Vols. 9-12, rev. ed., and 124 (obituary); and *Dictionary of Literary Biography,* Vols. 5 and 16.

PAIDEUMA

The National Poetry Award began with some grumbling among poets. The occasion for the grumbling was the reception of Robert Duncan's *Ground Work: Before the War* when it was published from New Directions in 1984. The book marked the first national publication by Duncan in over fifteen years. He had deliberately chosen to publish segments of *Ground Work* in small editions from publishers in France, Australia, New York, and San Francisco, wanting in those crucial years to clarify and refine and extend the range and concerns of his work. (p. 471)

The book was reviewed widely and admiringly in various publications, but the larger national press managed to ignore it until a year after the publication of the book when, after much criticism, the *New York Times Book Review* finally published a review. When the main prizes for 1984 were announced, Duncan's *Ground Work* was not singled out. Carolyn Kizer, recipient of the Pulitzer Prize for her book of poems published in 1984, has said publicly on several occasions that if she had been the judge, she would have given the prize to Duncan. Her characteristically generous statement suggests why a large segment of the poetic community should have grumbled. It should also underline the fact that The National Poetry Award is in no way being given in any spirit of competition. The Award is not a reaction to any other award but a positive action affirming the admiration of the poetic community for the dedication and accomplishment of a grand poet.

Ground Work appeared in Duncan's 65th year. The book culminated a massive achievement and a lifetime of dedication to poetry. With this in mind, several poets established a Board to administer The National Poetry Award. The first step was to gather the members of the board and to phrase a statement which could be sent to members of the poetic community. Three hundred poets signed this statement: their names appear on the reproduction of the award certificate [included in *Paideuma,* Fall and Winter, 1985]. These poets were then invited to send in an expression of the poet's sense

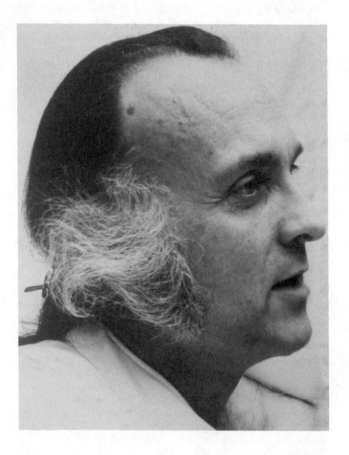

of the nature and importance of Duncan's poetry. (pp. 471-72)

All the respondents have published a substantial body of verse, and among them are many of the best known poets in the country. Their names have been placed on a special scroll which was presented to Duncan when the Award was officially given to him on August 28, 1985. . . .

In literary history, the National Poetry Award represents something very special. It is not the expression of conventional opinion announced by an established institution. It is an articulation of the community of poets, and its nature is best represented by the fact that the prize is a work of art given by artists to an artist. The award is neither official nor anti-official, and it is not intended in any way as a rebuke to any other award. The sense of the Board is that the Award supplements other awards, grants, and prizes by stressing achievement through a life of work as, for the moment, embodied in a magnificent book.

The members of the Board are united only by their common

admiration of Duncan's poetry. If one were to form an anthology from the works of the members of the board, the result would be a reasonable cross-section of the poetic art at present. And, in their several ways, they form a distinguished group.

The appended set of comments by poets on Duncan and his work testify to his technical powers, his largeness of grasp, and his extensive reach. They testify also to his involvement in the life of his time, his devotion to tradition, his openness to innovation, and his continuous growth.
—**Thomas Parkinson** (For the Board)

· · · · ·

Reading Duncan, I feel that he is *the* poet of ardor, encompassing the sheerest beauty, the widest myth, and the most exactly drawn intimacies. His is the poetry of a romantic metaphysician with a burning ear. To my mind, his work is a prime example of composition "by field," the graph of a passionate, historical mind, and the journals of a playful visionary, but there is more: his lifetime sense of what it means to compose restores continuously to us the ferocity of art, the *heart*, for which the word, as in his mouth and hands, becomes the circumstance.
—**Marvin Bell**

There is no living American poet whose work seems to me as central to our understanding of the art as Robert Duncan, and no recipient more worthy of the first National Poetry Award. From his earliest publications until his most recent volume, ***Ground Work: Before the War,*** Duncan's voice has enlarged our understanding of the possibilities—and responsibilities—of poetry with the authority of a master. The daring of his concerns as a writer, the fierceness of his integrity, and the brilliance of his technique have made Duncan the one indispensable contemporary source to whom we can keep returning, certain of finding there the quickening music upon which the life of the imagination depends.
—**Michael Andre Bernstein**

In the late summer of 1959, when I was living in Mill Valley, I had the good luck to offer a ride to Robert Duncan, who was hitchhiking from his home in Stinson Beach to San Francisco. After he got into my car, I recgonized him from some picture I had seen of him, confided that I was a poet too, and thereby became eligible to hear such talk about poetry as I had never heard before. I had already begun to read him, and I continued to do so. But in the meetings that followed that first one—there was some visiting back and forth between his household and mine—the talk continued too. I asked questions and listened, mainly listened, and Robert talked. I fell way short of understanding everything he said, for I was not well prepared to listen to him; my reading was much less than his, and also different. But the talk was generous, and extraordinary in both quantity and excellence. In it, he revealed unforgettably his dedication as a student, a poet, and a craftsman of verse. I was enormously grateful for it then, and I am still. I think I have remained under its influence.
—**Wendell Berry**

In Robert Duncan's best poems we feel an intelligence alert to every event he has lived mingle with subtle wavelike impulses far below the level of daylight apprehension in an amazing union supported and encouraged by music. It is a joy to honor such an intelligence and such a musician.
—**Robert Bly**

Robert Duncan's poetry is notable for a classic cast—which is modified by a subtle spice excitingly contemporary.
—**Gwendolyn Brooks**

I'm very moved, very honored, to be even a small contributor to the National Poetry Award's specific celebration of Robert Duncan. Would the whole world might share our pleasure! For myself, there is no world of poetry, or of the imagination, in which Robert is not in all senses a crucial presence. I think I have followed him all my determined life in this way, my literal hero of possibility. Again and again I have used Robert to define for me the commitment, the art, the imagination, the belief, and the transcendent pleasures of poetry—its veritable wonders, humanity, its isles of the blessed. So he is and will be always the *magister,* the singular Master of the Dance.
—**Robert Creeley**

Robert Duncan has led me to voices.

It was his voice, in his ***H. D. Book,*** that performed for me the dual functions, the double openings of knowledge of H.D. as a poet in the modernist context, and knowledge of the fluid and associative essay-voice which was one of H.D.'s—and Robert Duncan's—triumphs.

One of those openings has led me to a life's work of understanding women's contribution to modernism, the project of reading women.

The second led me to a style which I have too assumed for an exploration of the world.

And all this said, I have not even mentioned Robert's poetry, which was among the first of the new work which I read, moved and entranced, in the early '60s. An opening to vision and to pulse.

I can never thank Robert enough for his gifts, gifts from the gifted self which is always more than the self.

With admiration and affection, with love and thanks.
—**Rachel Blau DuPlessis**

Robert Duncan is one of my oldest friends, certainly my oldest fellow-poet friend. True, we have had many years of noncommunication, but always something brings us back into relationship again, usually some episode of literary significance rather than any exigence of personal relationship. Many of Robert's fellow-poet friendships were begun at least as erotic adventures, but that has never been a dimension of our association. And even our literary friendship lacks the intimacy of his other ones. It has been more a matter of aesthetic respect than aesthetic experimentation. In fact I most cheerfully concede that Robert understands more what I have done than I do what he has done, but I think I appreciate his more accessible poems quite as much as he appreciates mine. Mostly I cannot follow him through his program of experimentation. For him, experimentation can be an end in itself, is what poetry is all about, whereas for me its end is resolution. Not that Robert denies the uses of resolution; it's just that it is not the be all and end all that it is for me. I am a physical coward, timidity being endemic to my sensibility. But Robert is driven

to extremity by the pressure of painful fault-lines in the structure of his psyche as a result of his astounding infancy and early life. It will be interesting to see how we administer to these disparate needs in the few years remaining us, as we both suffer from severe physical disabilities from here on out.
—**William Everson**

The largeness of his achievement and the generosity of his example are equalled by no other living poet that I know of.
—**Thom Gunn**

In a narrow time, Robert Duncan has written with an almost-unequaled largeness of ambition and scope—historical, spiritual, and technical.
—**Donald Hall**

Glad to be associated with the recognition of a life dedicated so fully to poetry, suggesting what seems to me to be a main feature of Robert Duncan's career: the wide effective range of his energies; from the basic joint devotion to freedom and rigor, to the ability—at a crucial stage—to learn openly from the forms of Pound's *Cantos* and find the necessary personal resolution.
—**Thomas Kinsella**

I have been an admirer of Robert Duncan's work for many years. I was delighted that, when I was Director of Literary Programs for the N.E.A., Robert Duncan was one of the first recipients of a grant. And when I was recently awarded the Pulitzer Prize, I stated at the time that if I had been the jury, I would have given it to Robert Duncan, and I meant every word of it. I send him greetings, benisons, and unstinting praise.
—**Carolyn Kizer**

I have the highest regard for Robert Duncan. I especially treasure my recollection of a film of him, done by the National Endowment for the Arts, in which he read at some length, conducting the orchestration of his lines with very precise hand movements. It is fitting indeed that he receive the National Poetry Award.
—**Maxine Kumin**

He has created the most exciting poetic world since that of Ezra Pound.
—**James Laughlin**

Robert Duncan's work has for decades been a recurrent testimony and reminder that poetry has to do with music, with vision, with the life of the soul—not to the exclusion of all else, or indeed of anything, but on the contrary as ground and

environing air for whatever the range of experience may be.
—**Denise Levertov**

In the spirit of heroic struggle, of the prophet's passionate diagnosis, of the lover sacralized by his eroticism, Duncan writes. "I make poetry as other men make war or make states or revolution," he has said of his own work, that is, with the total commitment of a craftsman/priest who has heard a call. For Duncan, poetry is a vocation, not a career.
—**Ron Loewinsohn**

Since masters like MacDiarmid and David Jones died, Robert Duncan is the greatest living example of the full modern enterprise in poetry, an unashamed response to the living muse of Language.
—**John Montague**

Robert Duncan embodies the integrity of the poetic imagination. By that I mean a force of invention which is integral—whole—and one that is at no point less than true to a vision of created forms. He has taught two generations of poets that responsibility means "the ability to respond" to world and word. When I began to write, *The Opening of the Field* and works such as **"The Venice Poem"** represented commanding alternatives to currently fashionable practice. More recently I have turned repeatedly to Robert in his life and work for guidance through the difficulties of my own survival as an American poet. It feels a little silly to try to express thanks.
—**Michael Palmer**

It is appropriate that Duncan should be honored not by any official institution or establishment but by the one collective unit that has meaning for him, the community of poets. It is especially gratifying to witness their generous expression of admiration, respect, and indebtedness to a great working poet whose work shows forth the dignity of labor. Duncan has always been devoted to the highest possibilities of the art, through poverty and neglect, and he has earned the National Poetry Award. The laborer is worthy of his hire.
—**Thomas Parkinson**

Robert Duncan's poetry is beautifully crafted, moving, and intensely lyrical. He is a poet with a deep sense of the history of poetry and of the spoken word, a consciousness that reveals itself freshly again and again in his work.
—**Marge Piercy**

Unlike many modernist writers and critics, I never got the impression that Robert Duncan thought of himself as being superior to his fellow poets, and no matter how much prestige he has gained, he still spends his time with students and common people. He is no pompous know-it-all. I like him for that.
—**Ishmael Reed**

Robert Duncan is for me the finest poet now writing in the

United States—that is evident—but he is also a rare kind of poet, concerned with the soul's mysteries and the heart's affections, in a way that places him among those who have deepened our answer to the question "What is Man?" Rumi would surely have given his blessing to Robert who saw in him a master. We are proud to have published him in *Temenos;* and I to be able to call Robert a friend.
—Kathleen Raine

His lyrical genius has certainly touched my own imagination, as must happen whenever one poet is opened to the art of another who has crossed over beyond mere talent. What matter if his way may not be thy way or mine? It is nevertheless *our* way in its daring: its realizations of the beautiful and its distortions in search of new possibilities. He has written bravely as private man and citizen, as well as artist—a rare, visionary, pondering presence in our midst.
—M. L. Rosenthal

I have never believed in poetry awards until this one came along, but the difference here is obvious and telling.

Robert Duncan is not only a great poet; he is one who has confirmed for me—as only a few others have—that poetry can still be a noble, even a blessed calling.

There is no one else in fact about whom I can use words like those with such confidence that they will really stick.
—Jerome Rothenberg

Robert Duncan is one of the poets I admire most. I re-read him endlessly and I teach him, always. I think American poetry would be greatly different than it is if we had not had a Robert Duncan; he has combined deep feeling and deep intelligence in a new way. He has written great poems and deserves our praise.
—Gerald Stern

Duncan is the most original, most neglected American poet still working. My admiration for his poetry continues to grow.
—Mark Strand

What I like about Robert Duncan's work is its risky entanglement of the florid, the fresh, and sometimes the funny. He takes more chances with words than any other poet I know.
—John Unterecker

Duncan's work has always been a direct challenge to my own fondest notions about what is a poet, what is poetry. He has presented us with a universe that none of us could have imagined: a great and permanent achievement.
—Phil Whalen

Robert Duncan is extravagant, passionate, wise—a true poet.
—Reed Whittemore

I am more than happy to add my name to the list honoring Robert Duncan for his devotion to poetry. I certainly share with him his concern for cadence and the secret of the line and he has worked harder and more consistently than any to unlayer it. That he has not been given adequate credit for this has long been evident and offensive. I am glad to see it being corrected.
—Charles Wright

> *"The National Poetry Award,"* in Paideuma, *Vol. 14, Nos. 2 & 3, Fall & Winter, 1985, pp. 471-83.*

HERBERT MITGANG

Robert Duncan, a poet and author of a work on the Imagist poet H. D. (Hilda Doolittle), died yesterday at his home in San Francisco. He was 69 years old.

Mr. Duncan, who had suffered from kidney failure in the last few years, died of a heart attack, according to Peter Glassgold, his editor at New Directions.

Mr. Duncan once described the aim of his poetry this way:

> I work toward immediacy, and I do not aim at originality. The meanings in language are not original, any more than the sounds; they accrue from all the generations of human use. I am a traditionalist, a seeker after origins, not an original.

In an appearance in 1978 on a public television series called "The Originals," Mr. Duncan read some of his work and described himself as a "very bookish poet." Of his style, he said that he appreciated the "snakelike beauty in the living changes of syntax."

On the same program, he was candid about his homosexuality: "What is most interesting to me is that only in very recent years of gay liberation have I reflected upon the fact that I actually may have been determined all along by my repeated coming up against homosexuality."

Mr. Duncan's early books of poetry included **As Testimony, The Cat and the Blackbird, Medea at Kolchis** and **Of the War: Passages.** Later, he wrote **Roots and Branches, Bending the Bow, The Years as Catches, Opening of the Field, Ground Work: Before the War** and **Ground Work II: in the dark**. . . .

Mr. Duncan was born in Oakland, Calif., became a college dropout in the late 1930's and lived in New York during World War II, where he edited and wrote for *Experimental Review*. He returned to the University of California at Berkeley in 1947, where he studied medieval and renaissance history.

In recent years, Mr. Duncan was involved with the San Francisco poetry scene.

> *Herbert Mitgang, "Robert Duncan, Poet and Author of Works on the Creative Process," in* The New York Times, *February 4, 1988, p. B16.*

THE TIMES, LONDON

The prolific, eccentric, and, in some quarters, highly regarded American poet, playwright and teacher, Robert Duncan, has died in San Francisco, at the age of 69. . . .

He was raised in a Theosophist environment, and began writing poetry under the influence of a sympathetic schoolteacher, Edna Keough. He selected some of his juvenilia in a volume called *The Years as Catches: First Poems 1939-1946* (1966). They showed an astonishing range of influences, from Swinburne through Hopkins and Pound, to the English poet George Barker. . . .

Duncan wrote well over 35 collections of poetry (two generous volumes of selected poems, *The First Decade* and *Derivations* were published in London in 1968), and it widely regarded as work to be "read in its totality rather than in setpieces." It is, although influenced by Ezra Pound, mellifluous: Duncan, as is demonstrated by the many entertaining and intelligent interviews which he gave, was sometimes a little too much in love with his own voice.

Yet his work attracted considerable attention, especially in the 1960s, when the so-called "Black Mountain" school of American poetry came into prominence. . . . Duncan, Olson and Robert Creeley, were the most widely read representatives of this school. He taught briefly at Black Mountain College (North Carolina), in 1956.

Yet, although for a time influenced by their pragmatist theories, he was not really like any of the Black Mountain poets. He was concerned, as they were not, with poetry as what he called "manipulative magic", and a "magic ritual", and with the nature of what he thought of (in a markedly Freudian manner) as "human bisexuality."

He was famously learned in his craft, and largely deserved his reputation as a polymath. *The Truth and Life of Myth* (1968) is a fascinating "essential autobiography."

Duncan's tolerance of what many thought of as garish occultism, and his obsession with his sexuality, put some readers off; but his work was, as he was himself, "enormously engaging". He lived for the latter part of his life in San Francisco where he was a much sought after personality and a guru to younger poets.

An obituary in The Times, *London, February 11, 1988.*

THOM GUNN

When Elizabeth Bishop and Robert Duncan met in 1969, there was an immediate mutual attraction. They saw a lot of one another that year she lived in San Francisco, both being talkative people with a robust sense of humour and great personal warmth. But they were baffled by each other's poetry, as they continued to inform their friends. Though they exchanged books, they did not discuss either them or poetic theory.

After all, they had been pursuing their own projects for some time, and the poetics behind the two projects were fundamentally opposed in a way that their personalities were not. Bishop took the low road and Duncan took the high road, you might say, and the low road has proved to be a good deal more popular with readers and critics. . . . Duncan's attitude is both more private and more public, more oracular perhaps, whether from being experimental or visionary; you react often with admiration, sometimes with perplexity. Yet when he died early this year at the age of sixty-nine, just as his last book [*Ground Work II: In the dark*] was published, there were many who considered him the best poet we had. He was master of a twentieth-century grand style—but, more, he was admired for the range of the risks he took: so Robert Creeley described him as his "hero of possibility", and John Montague had spoken of him as "the greatest living example of the full modern enterprise in poetry, an unashamed response to the living muse of Language". Perhaps by unashamed he meant that Duncan disregarded just that literary decorum by which Bishop abided so admirably.

Duncan's writing may be found disconcerting in that very exploration of possibility Creeley mentioned: for there was a strong element of the unpredictable in Duncan—he was a daredevil rather as a cat is, jumping down into wells of obscurity or on to formidable spiked fences where no reasonable creature would have ventured. Moreover his ideas and practice, from the start, called into question the assumptions about style that dominated when he began to write in the 1940s and 50s. In one of the essays collected in *Fictive Certainties* (1985) he says provocatively, "I like rigor and even clarity as a quality of a work—that is, as I like muddle and floaty vagaries. It is the intensity of the conception that moves me." Not just toleration but *liking* for muddle would have been more than a little alarming to those educated on Brooks and Warren's *Understanding Poetry,* though current critical assumptions now would be more hospitable to such a statement.

Yet Montague is correct in referring to "the full modern enterprise", for if the New Critics had their reading of it, then Duncan had his, which was more expansive. On reading Browning in his teens, he had decided to be a poet, and from Browning to Pound had been an easy transition: his primary allegiance from that time on was certainly to Modernism, but it was not a Modernism at all like that of his contemporaries; it was a different mix. He was proud to proclaim himself a "derivative" poet, refusing to see the word as pejorative. We all derive, of course, we choose our own tradition, we have our influences—though it is as well to note, with Michael André Bernstein, that Duncan's influences are not of the *fathers* but rather of *allies*. He finds his allies up and down history (Dante is one, Rumi another), but what makes him unusual is the make-up of his particular home-circle of influences, which are picked equally from the Modernists and from the Romantics, so that Blake and Shelley and Whitman are found sitting around the same table as Pound and Stein and H. D. Duncan noticed the continuity between Modernist and Romantic long before most of the critics did: the specific life of his home-circle came from his connecting the Romantic admiration for impulse with the theory of "open form" that he, following Charles Olson, found suggested by the practice of Pound and the later W. C. Williams. Duncan praises that theory in the accents of the wilful Romantic as "proposing a primordial, titanic, unaccountable spirit in poetry, beyond measure", for which he aptly finds a source and antecedent in Emerson on Spontaneity.

The poem written in open form is meant to be viewed less as an artefact than as part of a *process* (a word Duncan uses repeatedly in his criticism), which may take directions unanticipated in the original conception. Duncan goes even further:

a true Freudian, he believes in the centrality of what we call accident or chance. By our inadvertence and error we find out what we really mean, beyond and beneath purpose. (Such is the gist of his magnificent long essay **"The Truth and Life of Myth"**, which opens *Fictive Certainties.*) Speaking as the Whitmanian poet, he says:

> Walk with me and you will begin to feel who I truly am, even as I find who I truly am as I come into my step fully; indeed, come into your stride with mine and you will begin to find yourself.

In practice, writing poetry like this should be subject to neither a fixed purpose before the composition is started nor revision once it is concluded. Everything depends on the energy of the present. Even a misspelling may be a legitimate part of the resulting poem: thus in Duncan's **"Styx"** (*Ground Work II*) the word "woundrous" occurs, describing the paths that water carves through rocks—wondrous wounds, in fact. The neologism is just as likely to be a misspelling preserved as a conscious intention embodied, and its suggestions are not therefore less integral to the poem.

Here it is necessary to recall Duncan's book of 1960, ***The Opening of the Field,*** not only because it remains the most accessible point of entry into his terrain, but because it is the true start of the project that was to occupy him for the rest of his life. It also embodies the only really influential new theory of poetry advanced in our lifetime.

It is conceived and written as a book, each poem linked to many of the others, elaborating on previous themes while proposing new ones. They are connected like "lamps strung among shadowy foliage". The foliage grows in the "field" of the title, which is conceived of as a field of energy, of activity, of the imagination. The image of the field is to be taken both in an abstract and in a physical, or pastoral, sense, then: a meadow, a pleasure ground, a pasture, the marsh covering the ruins of Sodom, or the middenheap that promotes fertility; it is all these and more in relationship. Tight-knit correspondences are found not only in the mastering image of the field but also in the detail of its contents. . . . His poetic allows for the inclusion of contradictions, just as his existence must be acknowledged to contain light and dark, good and evil, peace and war.

The recognition of an unresolvable internal conflict has important consequences in his poetic. For in the same way that Duncan sees his moral certainties compromised, he wishes to compromise, as he says, his own line of poetry. . . . It is this current that accounts for the most exciting, and the most exasperating, of Duncan's writing: for he trusts his spontaneity so completely that he encourages it to *trip up* his conscious intentions.

Yet there is room for both those intentions and the tripping up within the larger project, which started in the book of 1960 and was continued through ***Roots and Branches*** (1964), ***Bending the Bow*** (1968), ***Ground Work: Before the war*** (1984) and, now, ***Ground Work II: In the dark.*** The project might be characterized as an attempt to explore the entire field of a spontaneous imagination. His ambition, in fact, is fully as great as Whitman's or Pound's: he too wants to include everything he can in the great single poem of his collected work. The risk of inclusiveness is inflation, and he accepted that risk: certainly some of the poetry is inflated, as it is in Whitman and in Pound too, quite simply because, though you may want to include everything in your poem,

you cannot write with equal force about everything (unless you are Dante or Shakespeare). But the attempt is heroic, and for all that is inflated or occulted there still remains a large amount of poetry that is fully rewarding and that would not exist without the foolhardy heroism.

In 1972 Duncan announced that he did not intend to issue another collection of his work until fifteen years had passed since ***Bending the Bow.*** The fifteen years stretched into sixteen, and in February 1984 he suffered a complete kidney collapse. After this date he composed only one two-page poem, an eerie account of his illness, and lived his last four years essentially as a posthumous poet, still talking volubly and on occasion brilliantly (as is testified to by published interviews), but unable to concentrate long enough to read anything more demanding than the short stories of Kipling and the *Oz* books (he who had devoured books, as he once said, "gluttonously"), let alone write either poetry or prose. Later that year he published ***Ground Work: Before the war,*** which as one of his most accurate commentators, Ken Irby, has noted, consists of poetry written between 1968 and 1975. The succeeding collection, ***Ground Work II: In the dark,*** therefore consists of poems written in 1976-84 and, since two of those years were unexpectedly barren, is probably only half as long as he had hoped it would be. (pp. 1299-1300)

[His] health must have been secretly deteriorating during the years of composition, and there is far more about the subjects of death and disease in this collection than in any of the others. It is not for nothing that its subtitle is *In the dark,* for a major theme is the interpretation of life and death.

There are both serial groups and individual poems here which count among his best. Such a serial group, **"An Alternate Life"**, makes a fitting opening to the collection, for it exemplifies the peculiarities and strengths of Duncan in all their mutual involvement. Here we may appreciate the full adventure of entering the process of a Duncan composition, fifteen pages of it, energetic yet tentative, assertive yet self-revising, opportunistic yet receptive, taking place as it does in some area between directionless flux and rigid authorial control. It is about his having fallen in love during a visit to Australia and deals with his return to his household in San Francisco and his lover of many years. We may mark the fact that "household" is a word always associated in Duncan's work with his firmest values: it is not quite the same as "marriage", suggesting rather something "home-made", something built up bit by bit between the foundations and roof-beams of the physical house, individual, specific, improvised. These last three terms also apply to the whole work: Duncan follows the unpredictable currents of feeling, avoiding no awkwardness or inconsistency to make them seem smoother. He sees himself as ridiculous at one point ("An old man's hand fumbles at the young man's crotch"), but passes no judgment on the two others involved. And the poet of open form is also open in the sense of being frank—if this is about a form of adultery, it is not found with that hypocrisy which is adultery's customary companion.

Hypocrisy would give shape and order to this implied story of adultery; alibis, after all, tend to have classical and tightly knit plots. It is precisely the lack of such a plot that makes the work's overall structure obscure on early readings; nothing is closed off, nothing gets decided; there are no renunciations as there are no condemnations. Duncan moves, either physically or emotionally, between alternates, alternate *you*s, alternate *he*s, alternate hemispheres, alternate lives, alternate seasons. His problem, of course, is in fitting enough contents for two lives into "the one life I am leading". The situation is desperately commonplace, and one of its most commonplace features is that the influence is greatest of whatever place he is currently in: "O daily actual life", he says back home, "I am // deep in your thrall."

Commonplace language for a commonplace situation, the reader might remark of that last phrase. Duncan would say so too. "Deep in your thrall" exemplifies the kind of risk he is prepared to take, with language as with structure; it is lushly Romantic, certainly time-worn, if only from its endurance at least through the nineteenth century into the movies and songs of our own. Duncan both *means* it and is aware of its time-worneness, aware the emotion giving rise to it is both nineteenth-century Romantic and twentieth-century Hollywood. I insist on his disconcerting awareness, which is heightened by the variety of other modes of speech here, one of which is the self-scrutinizing language of wit, the cool perception of paradox. When "news comes from the South", he sees it as "gifts from another time I / most hold in losing". The letter from Australia in his hand, he holds that other life "in" losing it, that is, both *while* and *by* losing it. He almost relishes the neatness of the paradox, his tone is so far outside the conscious self-indulgence of the earlier phrase.

The "hero of possibility" necessarily takes such things as his subject-matter, but this is a book written "in the dark", and so we come to the magnificently eloquent poem **"Styx"**, and the river where the apparently endless mingling streams of human possibility come to stasis. **"Styx"** is organized as description; but every physical detail in it speaks to the death which will close off this collection:

> And a tenth part of bright clear Okeanos
>   his circulations—mists, rains, sheets, sheathes—
>   lies in poisonous depths, the black water.

"Circulations" is another loaded word for Duncan. It is in their circulation that not only ocean but blood and song remain vital: and the water of Styx is the *uncirculating* stillness that we originate from and also "thirst for" (as the last line tells us) "in dreams we dread". Once more the undeclared war, in which we thirst and dread at the same time, is brilliantly evoked. . . .

Most of us have in recent years taken a very low road indeed, finding our virtues in understatement and our safety in irony; we are tentative and evasive; we disown passion or we clothe it in indirection. Duncan by contrast makes claims for the importance of poetry that are both Poundian and Shelleyan (perhaps Dantean as well): in doing so he holds himself responsible for deep feeling, whether public or personal, without the qualification of irony, and adopts the voice of the seer or the bard even to the extent of giving an archaic cast to his speech. It is time to suggest, then, that we pay more attention to the work of a man whose aims and accomplishments have been larger than those of the run of contemporary poets, though assuredly the kind of ambition implied is not stylish on either side of the Atlantic. (p. 1300)

Thom Gunn, "Containing Multitudes," in The Times Literary Supplement, *No. 4469, November 25-December 1, 1988, pp. 1299-1300.*

MICHAEL DAVIDSON

I suspect that for many members of my generation the first image we had of a poet was a tweedy gentleman standing in front of a classroom discussing symbolism in Donne or Keats. Poetry was presented as serious business, not to be taken lightly. Levity was to be tempered with irony, passion with personae and intellect with discretion. What a revelation, then, to encounter Robert Duncan in person, a poet whose hypnotic, nonstop talk shattered all preconceptions of literary decorum.

The first time I saw Duncan read was in Buffalo, New York, at the height of the Vietnam War. He swept into the auditorium wearing a full-length cape, underneath which he wore a velvet jacket covered with elaborate embroidery. He wore his hair long, in the fashion of the day, and sported thick, fluffy sideburns that exploded on either side of his broad forehead. And when he began to talk, his voice seemed to explode as well. It was as though he had already been talking to us on the way to the podium so that when he reached it, he was already fully engaged.

And that conversation was really unbelievable—full of literary gossip, pronouncements on the escalating war, esoteric bits of information, catty asides and brilliant observations about literary figures. He seldom completed a thought but moved on to something else according to an associative logic of formidable complexity. One would "get" the point long after he had moved on to other subjects, so that listening became somewhat of a retrospective process. And when he finally read a poem, it appeared as a rhythmic and highly inflected lacuna in a much larger, oceanic discussion. He punctuated his pauses with his hand, as though conducting from a score, and his body swayed to cadences of Mahlerian grandeur. (p. 1)

I stress these impressions because they are among the most vivid images I have of Robert Duncan, but also because they are part of the participatory poetics that he encouraged. He wanted the audience to have as powerful a sense of his experience as he himself did—to take you up, as he said in one of his Dante sonnets, in a "sorcery" of excited talk and testimony. He willingly accepted the romantic projection of the poet as *vates,* as seer, as one who testifies to the aura surrounding natural phenomenon. At times this role conflicted with daily reality; he would lose his keys, misplace a book on the bus stop, forget someone's name, turn abruptly away from one conversation to begin another. But, in the poems, this distraction reflects his impatience to confront a dream

> in which all things are living
> I return to, leaving my self.
>
> I am beside myself with this
> thought of the One in the World-Egg

He often figured this dualism in terms of his eyesight: "Gladly the cross-eyed bear," a joke that he played against himself that he might become the witness of his own experience. He was unwilling to be Emerson's transparent eyeball, floating passively over a world of inert matter—he had more of Whitman's need to be in the crowd, moving in a phantasmagoria of sensations. That dazzling world was made out of words.

"I have more of being in the magic of the language and in the dreams of poets than I have in my personal existence." For a generation of poets fiercely attempting to reclaim the personal and confessional, such remarks must have seemed to avoid the hard reality of daily suffering. And for a generation of poets acutely aware of the social obligations of the poet in the wake of nuclear holocaust, such remarks might have seemed an elegant irrelevance. Yet Duncan was articulating in 1963 what we have come, painfully, to realize: that we live in and through an inherited language, that we do not make up our speech out of whole cloth, that we are spoken through. Duncan's rhetoric was much more vatic, perhaps, but he insisted on the life of and in the sign. Moreover, that sign never manifested itself as a transparent embodiment of some prior reality but brought with it a kind of semiotic surplus, a residue of its origins in human speech. The poet could attempt to expunge or efface that surplus in an ethos of the rhetorically balanced, well-made poem—or he could, as Duncan did, incorporate the unwanted, unexpected or otherwise "inappropriate" word into the ever-expanding structure. A slightly awkward figure, a childlike expostulation, a line by Pindar in a Victorian translation—those elements we were taught to eliminate from our verse—Duncan made the "lures," as he liked to say, for more intense feeling. Hence, in a paradox at the heart of his poetics, he made language his own by relinquishing control over it.

In memorial tributes of this sort, one must finally come to grips with what his loss will mean, and for me that loss involves the model of the poet for whom all of reality can enter the poem. Duncan's "permission" to exercise his faculties at large was not another word for supreme egoism but a challenge for all of us to live as though language mattered, as though speech were our last fatal pact with significant action. The end of such a stance is political, since it recognizes the relation between language and power—that if we don't treat words as the site of authority, someone else will speak for us, and we will truly become victims of the news instead of actors *within* it. (pp. 1, 19)

Michael Davidson, "A Variable Truth," in Poetry Flash, *No. 180, March 1988, pp. 1, 19.*

NORMAN FINKELSTEIN

Robert Duncan stands at the center of the so-called San Francisco Renaissance; and along with such firmly established figures as Charles Olson and Allen Ginsberg, he represents a deliberate return to the poet's vatic role, based on an unprecedented synthesis of Romantic and Modernist strategies. Duncan in particular has declared himself derivative in his craft, thus affording himself "permission" to create the frequently outrageous totalities that mark his poetry as one of the most ambitious bodies of work in our time. For Duncan's poetic is totalizing; to an even greater extent than Pound or Olson, he seeks to in-form the "orders" or "scales" of reality in an open-ended tapestry or collage of language. In this regard, he operates in exact antithesis to Ashbery and O'Hara: he seeks to establish, or rather, prove, that the interrelated networks of material, psychological, and spiritual realities are all coordinated hierarchies that function under the force of universal Law. Rather than level modes of perception, value systems and forms of knowledge, Duncan would place them all within their proper contexts, so that an awareness of overarching Form allows the reader to perceive a previously hidden totality. Poetry, of course, is the most significant medium for such a process; hence the poet holds a privileged place within the orders of language. Duncan's thought is transparently utopian in regard to matters of creativity and

tradition, as well as in relation to immediate political concerns; and while sometimes problematic in its applications, its inconsistence on infinite human potential within a communal identity is, as Oppen would say, "ennobling." As Duncan declares in **"Orders,"** *Passages 24:*

> There is no
> good a man has in his own things except
> it be in the community of every thing;
> no nature he has
> but in his nature hidden in the heart of the living
> in the great household.

Duncan's insistent metaphors are often so compelling that they seem to obviate criticism, and, therefore it is important to observe that at the same time Duncan's totalizing project is getting under way, a related but in some ways radically dissimilar poetic is being formulated by his old friend—and critic—Jack Spicer. Cranky, admonitory, haunted, Spicer's work presents as unified a poetic as Duncan's, but carefully avoids the sweeping gestures of order and coherence that have become the distinguishing mark of even the most open of Duncan's poetic fields. . . . For Duncan, Romantic mythmaking and theosophical doctrine combine with Modernist explorations of history, anthropology and phenomenology to confirm Yeats's old dictum that "The things below are as the things above." (pp. 62-3)

Because both poets pay great attention to "each word that is about to be mentioned," it can be said that the very notion of futurity in their work is closely related to the models of poetic inspiration to which they constantly refer. Spicer and Duncan are two of the leading practitioners among contemporary poets of poetry as poetics, which is to say that they attain that high level of self-consciousness necessary to relate their work as individuals to the ongoing activity of poetry as a historical continuum. (p. 64)

Spicer's vision of generations of poets is one of the most recent formulations of a venerable idea. Among poets writing in English, its spokesmen have included such major (and diverse) figures as Shelley, Yeats, Pound and Eliot, all of whom would agree that poets are always "writing the same poem," with invention always "the enemy of poetry."

Much the same is true for Duncan in *The Truth & Life of Myth:*

> Myth, for Dante, for Shakespeare, for Milton, was the poet-lore handed down in the tradition from poet to poet. It was the very matter of Poetry, the nature of the divine world as poets had testified to it; the poetic piety of each poet, his acknowledgement of what he had found true Poetry, worked to conserve that matter. And, for each, there was in the form of their work—the literary vision, the play of actors upon the stage, and the didactic epic—a kind of magic, for back of these forms we surmise distant origins in the rituals toward ecstasy of earliest Man.

Tradition here is a source of primal empowerment: it can provide the individual poet with a transpersonal, communal authority that will allow him to articulate his own contribution to the ongoing matter of the historical work. Duncan's open fields (*Passages, The Structure of Rime,* etc.) . . . [can] be seen as attempts to find contemporary correlatives to the historically appropriate forms of a Dante, a Shakespeare, a Milton. (p. 65)

In a revealing passage from *The Truth & Life of Myth,* Duncan explains one of his models for inspiration and composition:

> Speaking of a thing I call upon its name, and the Name takes over from me the story I would tell, if I let the dimmest realization of that power enter here. But the myth we are telling is the myth of the power of the Word. The Word, as we refer to It, undoes all the bounds of semantics we would draw in Its creative need to realize Its true Self. It takes over. Its desire would take over and seem to put out or to drown the individual reality—lonely invisible and consumed flame in the roaring light of the Sun—but Its creativity moves in all the realities and can only realize Itself in the Flesh, in the incarnation of concrete and mortal Form.

Significantly, Duncan *lets* the power enter and begin its work; mutuality and reciprocity are established between the individual and the Word. "Things," i.e., material reality, move the poet; such inspiration establishes the connection between consciousness and the otherwise distant sublime. The sense of continuity that Duncan is able to establish in his poetry, the totality of effort that encompasses even the most diverse content, may be traced back to his personal sense of confidence as expressed in this idea of inspiration. For Duncan, the world will respond to the responsive poet ("the Poet on Guard," as he calls him in an early poem); and even in the midst of the most severe personal or political crisis, apprehensions of universal order inevitably appear:

> I thought to come into an open room
> where in the south light of afternoon
> one I was improvised
> passages of changing dark and light
> a music dream and passion would have played
> to illustrate concords of order in order,
> a contrapuntal communion of all things
>
> (pp. 66-7)

Duncan's poems become increasingly more difficult to delimit as time goes on: not only do the ongoing *Passages* and *Structure of Rime* blur the textual borders between discrete volumes, but key themes and linguistic motifs appear with greater regularity in an ever expanding series of personal, literary and philosophical contexts. Furthermore, because of his stance as a derivative poet, Duncan deliberately blurs his own poetic ideas into those of his precursors and contemporaries, until a communal voice is heard, intoning a unified body of poetic revelation. One chooses a Duncan poem for an old-fashioned "close reading"—even when in search of new themes—at the risk of violating the very premises upon which *all* of the poetry is based. (p. 68)

[The] art of collage as practiced by Duncan and Spicer is most purely the art of the possible. Rather than consolidate temporal and spatial relations into self-sufficient worlds, they insist that the very notion of self-sufficiency is impossible, given the means by which their poetry comes into existence. No single meaning, however complex or ambiguous, can be sufficient; the text's polysemous nature not only summons other meanings, but other texts as well. . . .

Again and again in the reading of both poets, certain more or less discrete poems and fragments impose themselves upon the imagination: the work is not of a piece in its actual execution, and textual boundaries insist upon being drawn. (p. 70)

Consider Duncan's recent **"Circulation of the Song."** This magnificent poem, which appears at the end of *Ground Work,* is notable for its unusually self-sustained form, consistency of tone and voice, and completed (rather than fragmentary) syntax. It is built upon a clearly delineated stanza structure and makes use of a relatively limited and accessible set of literary allusions and references. It is a particularly striking contrast to the other major efforts in *Ground Work,* such as **"Poems from the Margins of Thom Gunn's *Moly,*" "A Seventeenth Century Suite"** and **"Dante Etudes,"** all of which are derivations and reworkings of freely acknowledged precursor texts; or the *Tribunals* sections of *Passages,* which, like earlier sections of that poem, make extensive use of quotation, allusion and spatialized fields of reference. The subtitle of **"Circulations of the Song"** is simply "After Jalai Al-Din Rumi," though Rumi's presence in the poem is totally subsumed by Duncan's own persistent, and by now easily identified tone. What's more, the poem is much less overtly self-reflexive than most of Duncan's mature work: although it does speak to questions of its own inspiration and composition, it is equally concerned with the connections between the poet's religious beliefs, his long-standing relationship to his lover, and his sense of himself as he grows old. Like the deeply moving **"My Mother Would Be A Falconress,"** its rich lyric diction may be correlated to a largely interior, subjective project which Duncan often calls "essential autobiography." In short, it is, at least on the surface, a far more conventional, "bounded" poem than Duncan is wont to write.

Yet **"Circulations of the Song"** confirms every important idea that Duncan has developed in regard to his poetic practice, and renews the utopian sense of openness and possibility that makes his best work so important:

> I am like a line cast out
>　　　into a melodic unfolding beyond itself
>　　　　　　　　　a mind hovering ecstatic
> above a mouth in which the heart rises
>　　　pouring itself into liquid and fiery speech
> for the sake of a rime not yet arrived
>　　　containing again and again resonant arrivals.

Here the poet is both a subjective force of ecstatic inspiration and an objective vehicle for that inspiration, whose words are perpetual preparations for "a rime not yet arrived," a poetry of pure futurity. But this ecstatic awareness is tempered by Duncan's increasing certainty of his own mortality. Thus the *He* of the poem, the dark homosexual Eros who consecrates the poet's marriage to his lover, is also a god of death; and the fulfillment of the sexual relationship is a premonition of that final fulfillment. . . . Physical beauty and the confidence of youth likewise pass into such knowledge. . . . Because of this, Duncan's relationship to his muse is all the more fierce and perilous;

> Again you have instructed me to let go,
> to hold to this falling,　　this
>　　　letting myself go.
> I will succumb entirely to your intention.
>
>　　　*Contend with me!*
> you demand. And I am surrounded by wingd
>　　　confusions. *He*
> is everywhere,　　nowhere
>　　　now where I am.
>
> In every irreality there is Promise.
>　　　But there

where I am not   *He*   really is.

> In Whose Presence
> it is as if I had a new name.

This passage is yet another restatement of one of Duncan's central myths, Jacob's wrestling with the angel, which permeates both his poetry *(The Opening of the Field)* and criticism *(The Truth & Life of Myth)*. This poetic fiction, or "irreality," is especially full of hope. The erotic physical contact with the divinely beautiful and the linguistic revelation that follows in Jacob's being renamed Israel have always attracted Duncan, but now the stakes are higher: as he ages he must give himself over more completely to struggle, confusion, and the intention of the Absolute. For Duncan such contention has always been equated with composition, and the shaping of the present poem comes to vindicate his faith. Yet this does not entail a merely personal expression of religious belief, or even the confirmation of the poet's metaphysical grounding of aesthetic doctrine. As Duncan concludes:

> In the Grand Assemblage of Lives,
> the Great Assembly-House,
> this Identity, this Ever-Presence,   arranged

rank for rank,   person for person,   each from
its own
sent out from what we were   to another place
now in the constant exchange

renderd true.

What begins as personal revelation is made into a concrete universal, not to be asserted in abstraction, but to be re-enacted in lived experience—including the encounter with linguistic form.

In composing a poem such as **"Circulations of the Song,"** a poem capable of demonstrating that "all of its parts are redeemed as meaning," Duncan implicitly transcends the open / closed dichtomy that can be found close to the heart of any discussion of his work. The totality that he would teach us to see, "the Grand Assemblage of Lives," emerges in an orderly and indeed, self-sufficient manner, without sacrificing, but rather heeding, the demands of perpetually unfolding events. (pp. 71-3)

Norman Finkelstein, "The New Arcady," in his The Utopian Moment in Contemporary American Poetry, *Bucknell University Press, 1988, pp. 62-95.*

Robert A(nson) Heinlein

July 7, 1907 - May 8, 1988

(Also wrote under pseudonyms Anson MacDonald, Lyle Monroe, John Riverside, Caleb Saunders, and Simea York.)

American novelist, short story writer, and nonfiction writer.

For an overview of Heinlein's life and work see *CLC*, Vols. 1, 3, 8, 14, 26; *Contemporary Authors*, Vols. 1-4, rev. ed., 125 (obituary); *Contemporary Authors New Revision Series*, Vols. 1 and 20; *Something about the Author*, Vol. 9; and *Dictionary of Literary Biography*, Vol. 8.

LOS ANGELES TIMES

Robert Anson Heinlein, considered by many to be the most influential author of science fiction since H. G. Wells, is dead at the age of 80. . . .

Heinlein was the winner of an unprecedented four Hugo awards, given by a popular vote of science fiction fans for best novel of the year. The four books are *Double Star* (1956), *Starship Troopers* (1959), *Stranger in a Strange Land* (1961) and *The Moon Is a Harsh Mistress* (1966). In 1975 Heinlein received the first Grand Master Nebula Award, given by the Science Fiction Writers of America for a lifelong contribution to the genre.

He was also guest commentator alongside CBS-TV's Walter Cronkite on the Apollo 11 space mission in 1969, when Neil A. Armstrong left the first footprints on the moon.

Fellow sci-fi author Ray Bradbury has called the prolific Heinlein "a popcorn machine," popping more ideas in half an hour than most people have in a year.

Christine Schilling, vice president and publisher of G. P. Putnam & Sons, one of Heinlein's publishers, remembered him as "one of the founders of what we know as science fiction today."

"He was a 50-year influence on the genre," she said. "He was one of the original writers who created from vision, what the future should be, what it might be." . . .

Stranger in a Strange Land was Heinlein's 1962 Hugo-winner and perhaps his most famous book. It is a tale of a Martian who establishes a religious movement on Earth . . . .

Stranger also added a new word to the language—"grok"—which dictionaries define as "to understand thoroughly because of having empathy" (with). It was a word that symbolized Valentine Smith, Heinlein's alien hero.

Heinlein . . . sold his first story in 1939. He was inspired to

write it by a $50 prize offered by *Thrilling Wonder Stories*. When Heinlein, born in Butler, Mo., finished the story, he decided it was too good for the contest and instead sent it to *Astounding Science Fiction*. The magazine's editor, John W. Campbell Jr., bought it for $70, then encouraged Heinlein to continue writing by buying one story after another for years.

That first story, **"Lifeline,"** tells of a man who invents a machine that can predict the moment of a person's death. It was the first in what came to be known as Heinlein's "Future History," a collection of stories with a common fictional background that extrapolates a possible future of the human race.

Science fact-and-fiction writer Isaac Asimov once said that between 1939 and 1942, Heinlein "single-handedly, under the aegis of John Campbell, lifted science fiction to a new pitch of quality." . . .

Through the late 1940s and the '50s, Heinlein wrote what many critics believe was his best work—the so-called "juveniles." Norman Spinrad, president of the Science Fiction Writers of America in 1980 said, "[They] were better than anybody else's. The only thing that made these different from his other science fiction was that the protagonists were teenagers. He didn't write down, he didn't patronize." . . .

Among the novels Heinlein wrote in that period are *Starman Jones, The Star Beast* and *Citizen of the Galaxy,* books that Peter Nicholls' prestigious *Science Fiction Encyclopedia* says "have strong appeal for adult readers as well as youngsters, and some critics consider them to be Heinlein's finest works."

David Gerrold, editor, novelist and television writer, said the main thing about a Heinlein novel is that "you could believe it."

This ability to write science fiction that was accessible to people not accustomed to reading it was one of the factors that allowed Heinlein, like Kurt Vonnegut, Harlan Ellison and a few others, to break the slick magazine barrier.

Traditionally, like most other writers of science fiction, he had been trapped in the pulp magazines. But his story **"The Green Hills of Earth"** about a blind poet, a Homeric figure who sang of the "spaceways," appeared in the Feb. 8, 1947, issue of the *Saturday Evening Post.* In subsequent years, his science fiction stories appeared in other such unlikely places as *Argosy, Town and Country, Blue Book* and *American Legion Magazine.* . . .

[Neither] Heinlein nor his fiction existed without controversy. Writer-editor Gerrold said, "Heinlein has been charged with being a racist and a fascist and a sexist and none of these charges are correct. The ignorant are reading their own prejudices into his stories."

Despite this, Heinlein, an advocate of free love and open marriage, found the outcry was sometimes so loud that he devoted a few paragraphs to self-defense in the book *Expanded Universe* (1981).

Heinlein's 1960 Hugo-winner, *Starship Troopers,* is about a soldier coming up through the ranks during a war of the far future. An overtone of fascism permeates the book. In *Expanded Universe,* Heinlein said it

> outraged 'em. I still can't see how that book got a Hugo. It continues to get lots of mail, not much of it favorable . . . but it sells and sells and sells and sells, in 11 languages. It doesn't slow down—four new contracts just this year (1981). And yet I almost never hear of it save when someone wants to chew me out over it. I don't understand it. . . .

In 1986, Heinlein's final work, *The Cat Who Walks Through Walls* was published. It was a tale of murder for hire and resurrected his longtime protagonist, the venerable Lazarus Long, who had walked through some of Heinlein's earlier books over a period of 10,000 space years. His final outing however, was dismissed in some reviews as a parody of the science fiction genre that Heinlein had made meaningful for so many.

In Part 2 of *The Road to Science Fiction,* there is this summing up of the Heinlein *oeuvre.*

> More than any other writer Heinlein had the ability to present carefully crafted backgrounds, including entire societies, in economical but convincing detail. This and at its best, his narrative drive and his spare, vigorous prose, provided science fiction with models for the authors who followed after.

"Robert A. Heinlein, Acclaimed Science Fiction Writer, Dies," in Los Angeles Times, *May 10, 1988.*

ERIC PACE

Robert A. Heinlein, a former aviation engineer whose clever interweaving of imagination and technical expertise helped make him one of the country's most successful writers of science fiction, died Sunday morning [May 8, 1988] at his home in Carmel, Calif. . . .

Mr. Heinlein's fictional writings repeatedly anticipated scientific and technical advances. He managed to write a story about an atomic power plant some years before the first atomic bomb was detonated. Over the years, he won an enormous and loyal public, and his dozens of books sold more than 40 million copies.

His writing won many science-fiction awards, and some of it was made into movies. He also wrote several screenplays, as well as some nonfiction books and articles on technical subjects.

Mr. Heinlein's eminence stemmed partly from the success among young people of *A Stranger in a Strange Land,* which was published in 1961. Its sardonic attitude toward modern mores proved popular in a decade that saw students challenge many established institutions.

Orville Prescott wrote in *The New York Times* that in the novel, Mr. Heinlein "expresses his sardonic opinions with violence and gusto." The reviewer also called an earlier Heinlein tale, **"The Green Hills of Earth,"** "a science-fiction classic."

Mr. Heinlein's writing style was generally simple, and so was his explanation of how he went about his writing.

"I start out with some characters and get them into trouble," he told one interviewer, "and when they get themselves out of trouble, the story's over."

Eric Pace, "Robert A. Heinlein Is Dead at 80: Renowned Science-Fiction Writer," in The New York Times, *May 10, 1988, p. 26.*

FRANK ROBINSON

Robert A. Heinlein, the most influential author in modern science fiction, died peacefully in his sleep Sunday morning, May 8, 1988. He was 80 years old. . . .

An enormously successful author, Heinlein had 44 of his 54 books in print at the time of his death, a record unmatched by any other writer—with sales over 40 million copies—Heinlein's impact on the world, however, extended far beyond that of an entertaining novelist. He was fascinated by how things worked and delighted in teaching others. As a result, his early novels and stories were didactic works in which he explained the intricacies of space travel, genetics, ballistics, and a dozen other sciences to a captivated readership.

It was this ability to entertain and teach that made Heinlein a formidable propagandist for space travel. In the late '40s he expanded the popularity of science fiction beyond the pulps with the sale of four short stories—all of them glamorizing space travel—to *The Saturday Evening Post.* A few years later, his juveniles were to sell space travel to a younger generation. One of them, *Space Cadet* (1948), was adapted as the popular television series *Tom Corbett, Space Cadet* (1951-1956), and another, *Rocket Ship Galileo* (1947), served as the springboard (along with his short story **"Requiem"**) for the film *Destination Moon* (1950), the first science fiction film to realistically portray a journey in outer space.

A generation later, with the formation of NASA and the landing of Neil Armstrong on the moon, it was hard to find a rocket scientist or an astronaut who had not been a fan of Heinlein when they were teenagers and entered the field of space travel because of his influence.

H. G. Wells tried to change the world through the advocacy of social revolution and largely failed. Heinlein tried to change it by influencing technological revolution and largely succeeded. . . .

He found his niche in life after being defeated for California State Assemblyman in 1939. Desperate for money, he tried his hand at writing a short story for *Thrilling Wonder Stories,* which had an ongoing "contest" open to amateur writers. (The prize was not $50, as Heinlein and others so often stated, but according to the contest entry blank, standard word rates.) Once the story was written, Heinlein changed his mind and tried for the big time by submitting it to *Colliers.* When they rejected it, he sent it on to *Astounding Science Fiction.*

The story was **"Lifeline"** and John W. Campbell, Jr., *Astounding*'s editor, paid Heinlein $70 for what amounted to less than a week's work. The story appeared in the August 1939 issue. With its publication, Campbell had found the writer who would spark the Golden Age of *Astounding* and Robert A. Heinlein had found a profession. In his own words, he would never again look for "honest work." (p. B)

Heinlein followed **"Lifeline"** with **"Misfit"** (in reality, that story was his first juvenile), which introduced Andrew Jackson Libby, better known as "Slipstick" Libby, who would be a recurring character in later Heinlein novels. His next story, **"Requiem"**, saw the first appearance of D. D. Harriman, "the man who sold the moon" and the prototype of Heinlein's wise-old-man-who-knows-how, best typified by Jubal Harshaw of *Stranger in a Strange Land* (1961).

His two-part serial **"If This Goes On—"** (*Astounding* 2-3/40), was to go a long way in establishing Heinlein's reputation. By now, it was apparent that no other writer in the history of science fiction had written about the future in such a way as to make it as believable as the present. Heinlein was prolific (his pennames included Anson MacDonald, Lyle Monroe, Caleb Saunders and John Riverside) and during the next two years wrote a series of stories that were to establish him as the leading author in the field and *Astounding Science Fiction* as the leading magazine.

Early stories included **"The Roads Must Roll"**, **"Blowups Happen"**, **"Logic of Empire"**, **"Waldo"**, **"Coventry"**, **"By His Bootstraps"**, and **"Solution Unsatisfactory"**. His output was so large it has been estimated he wrote close to 20 percent of the magazine's contents. He used Anson MacDonald as a penname not only for stories that didn't fit in his "future history" series but also because Campbell didn't want to use the Heinlein byline twice in the same issue.

The most significant story of the period was his novel *Methuselah's Children* (*Astounding* 7, 8, 9/41), which introduced the long-lived Howard Families and Heinlein's most charis-matic character of all, Lazarus Long. The Families and their various members, especially Lazarus, were to appear repeatedly in later novels. The themes of *Methuselah's Children* foreshadowed all his later philosophical novels. (pp. B, 78)

Heinlein was not above slyly mixing genres, especially after Campbell had laid down careful rules as to what constituted a science fiction story and what a fantasy. As one critic put it, **"Waldo"** was "a superficially science fiction story with a magical problem and solution," while **"Magic, Inc."** was "a fantasy story told as a logical science fiction narrative."

Heinlein has been given credit as the first truly professional science fiction writer, the first modern author to make a living by writing it and nothing else. He worked on a regular schedule, turning out four pages of copy a day come rain or come shine for four months at a crack, at the end of which he had a novel. He usually overwrote, then edited himself ruthlessly, often paring a novel by a third or more.

His assets as a writer were considerable. He had an engineering background, a thorough knowledge of the "hard" sciences as well as sociology and psychology, and a knack for blending technology and human characterization. Most of his early stories followed a rough "history of the future" which he kept on a large wall chart in his study. Campbell eventually published it, leading many readers to wonder about titles listed but never written ("Da Capo", "The Stone Pillow", "Fire Down Below", "The Sound of His Wings", etc.). The inspiration for the history, which Heinlein used to provide a consistent framework for his stories, he attributed to Sinclair Lewis, who used a variation of the same system to keep track of the citizens of his fictional city of Zenith. . . .

For most science fiction readers of the early '40s, the future had Heinlein's fingerprints all over it. It was Heinlein who took the science in science fiction out of the realm of fantasy and based his extrapolations on research then going on in the nation's laboratories. And it was Heinlein who decided that science fiction stories would be more believable if believable people did all those unbelievable things. He proved his point. Some critics later carped that his plots tended to be thin and that he sometimes had difficulty ending stories, but his readers seldom seemed to care. His influence on writers coming into the field was so strong that many of them patterned their stories and writing style after his. None of them were as successful. . . .

In 1947 he sold four stories to *The Saturday Evening Post* (he was the first genre writer to do so), including the classic **"The Green Hills of Earth"** (1947). He also sold to *Argosy* and *Blue Book, Boy's Life* and *The American Legion Magazine.* Of more significance was the sale of his first young adult novel, *Rocket Ship Galileo,* to Scribner's. Those that followed, at the rate of one a year—*Space Cadet* (1948), *Red Planet* (1949), *Farmer in the Sky* (1950), *Between Planets* (1951), *The Rolling Stones* (1952), *Starman Jones* (1953), *Tunnel in the Sky* (1955), *Time for the Stars* (1956), etc.—were to establish him as the world's most important writer of young adult science fiction. Their impact on the space program a generation later has already been noted.

He returned to the pulp magazines with his short novel **"Gulf"** (*Astounding,* 11/49), though now he was no longer an exclusive Campbell writer. One of the characters featured in **"Gulf"**, "Kettle Belly" Baldwin, would appear again, years later, as "Boss" in *Friday* (1982). . . .

His output in the '50s and early '60s was prodigious. *The Puppet Masters* (1951) appeared first in H. L. Gold's *Galaxy; Double Star* (1956) and *Citizen of the Galaxy* (1957) were serialized in *Astounding;* **"Star Lummox"** (1954, retitled *The Star Beast*), *The Door into Summer* (1957), *Have Space Suit—Will Travel* (1958), **"Starship Soldier"** (1959, retitled *Starship Troopers*), and *Glory Road* (1963) in *Fantasy and Science Fiction; Podkayne of Mars* (1962), *Farnham's Freehold* (1964), and *The Moon is a Harsh Mistress* (1966) in *Worlds of If.* Some of the novels were for young adults, but the line of demarcation between a Heinlein juvenile and a novel intended for adults had grown thinner with the years. The magazines didn't bill them as juveniles, and few readers knew or cared what audience they were meant for. (p. 78)

Heinlein published twelve young adult novels with Scribner's, but the thirteenth broke the contract. It was the book finally titled *Starship Troopers,* and his editor at Scribner's rejected it as too militaristic for the audience. (It was later published by G. P. Putnam's as a novel for adults.) The book won the Hugo but received a caustic reception from the critics, who complained of its militarism.

Heinlein's most successful and significant novel was not to be serialized at all. *Stranger in a Strange Land,* published by Putnam's in 1961, was the first science fiction novel ever to hit the *New York Times* bestseller list. Future Heinlein novels were to become a regular fixtures on the list. (pp. 78-9)

In *Stranger,* Valentine Michael Smith, a human being born on Mars, returns to Earth to bring mankind the benefits of "grokking" and "water-sharing."

Smith received a mixed reception from the fictional characters in the book but quickly became a cult figure to young, idealistic dropouts of the middle and late '60s. "Grokking" became a part of the language, and *Stranger in a Strange Land,* with its blend of free love and mysticism, became a multi-million-copy bestseller and a handbook for hippies. In Santa Cruz, a startled Heinlein was forced to build a fence around his home as protection against young, bearded enthusiasts who wanted to adopt him as their guru. . . .

The success of *Stranger in a Strange Land* in the middle '60s was a turning point for Heinlein, enabling him to exchange the narrow stage of science fiction for a world platform. However, he returned briefly to pure science fiction narration with *The Moon Is a Harsh Mistress* (1966), the story of a lunar revolt. The book won the Hugo in 1967, and some critics believe it to be his best book.

But the didactic novel with its traditional science fiction structure was now largely in Heinlein's past. For all of his skill and enthusiasm for teaching, one of his major incentives for writing had been a need to write for money. From the middle sixties on, that need was no longer uppermost in his mind. The truth was that he had transcended the field of science fiction as popularly conceived. From now on, it would be whatever he wanted it to be.

Heinlein now changed his style, story structure and, to a large extent, his audience. He went from writing science fiction books to writing mainstream novels. His later books were based on more philosophical themes, the major one of which one critic summarized as "You can conquer death through

love." He was now writing about the two themes most important to an adult audience: Love and Death. This is, perhaps, best illustrated by *Time Enough for Love* (1973), a novel which brought back Lazarus Long, the most outrageous and popular character in his earlier fiction. Long appeared in most of his novels that followed.

Standard science fiction elements no longer predominated in Heinlein's novels, but the central theme was strong enough so that it didn't matter. Heinlein was to comment later that the fans who now wrote him were sometimes unfamiliar with his earlier work but passionate in their praise of the new.

His books now invariably made the bestseller lists. Not quite as successful as most, however, was *I Will Fear No Evil* (1970), which dealt with an older, wealthy man who transfers his mind into the body of his beautiful young secretary. A gift book, *The Notebooks of Lazarus Long* (1978) was a collection of quotations from *Time Enough for Love. The Number of the Beast* (1980) was a book of anagrams and in-jokes paying homage to many of his literary heroes and mentioning a number of fellow writers and friends by name. . . .

Expanded Universe: The New Worlds of Robert A. Heinlein (1980) is an expanded version of *The Worlds of Robert A. Heinlein* adding previously uncollected stories and articles with commentaries on their genesis as Heinlein remembered it. At the age of 77, he once again made the *New York Times* bestseller list with *Job: A Comedy of Justice* (1984) and followed it with yet another bestseller, *The Cat Who Walks Through Walls* (1985).

Heinlein's last book was *To Sail Beyond the Sunset* (1987), published on his 80th birthday; it also made the *New York Times* bestseller list. The autobiography of Lazarus Long's mother, it was a mix of ideas about sex and politics and longevity, as well as a poignant reminiscence of growing up in the midwest at the turn of the century.

Praised in some quarters, damned in others (he was both booed and enthusiastically applauded when he took the stage at the World Science Fiction Convention in 1976), Heinlein was a writer whose career was unparalleled in science fiction. He won four Hugos—for *Double Star, Starship Troopers, Stranger in a Strange Land,* and *The Moon is a Harsh Mistress*—and in 1975 was given the Grand Master Nebula Award for lifetime achievement. It was the first such award, and there was never any doubt that he would get it. (p. 79)

As a writer, Heinlein never claimed to be a prophet, though his grasp of science and sociology made prediction inevitable. He described the waterbed so thoroughly in *Stranger in a Strange Land* that a latter-day entrepreneur could not patent it because Heinlein's description had put it in the public domain.

Heinlein predicted many of the fine details of space exploration, utilized his knowledge of atomic energy in the early '40s to write his prescient **"Solution Unsatisfactory"**, and is largely credited with predicting "waldoes," those remote-controlled servomechanisms frequently used in the handling of radioactives and other dangerous substances. Fictionally, they first appeared in Heinlein's **"Waldo"**, but he later disclaimed the mention as "prediction." He had read about the prototype in a 1918 copy of *Popular Mechanics* where a man afflicted with myasthenia gravis (much like the hero of his story) had developed a system of levers to help him with ordinary household tasks. Later, he was to become an industrial engineer specializing, logically, in how to achieve maximum results with minimum efforts. In *The Door into Summer,* Heinlein described the cleaning robot, a robot looking vaguely like a canister vacuum cleaner with tentacles designed for cleaning houses. Variations of it are now used in hospitals and office buildings.

Heinlein's "predictions" weren't restricted to the purely technological but included the sociological as well. **"The Year of the Jackpot"** (1952) was a frightening portrayal of "the crazy years" which might have served as a blueprint for the '60s, or the '70s or '80s for that matter. And the prophet Nehemiah Scudder of **"If This Goes On . . ."** was at least a kissing cousin of Jerry Falwell and Jimmy Swaggart. (pp. 79-80)

Heinlein's interest in science and science fiction led to a lifelong advocacy of space travel. One of the happiest and proudest days of his life was July 20, 1969, when he appeared as a guest commentator on CBS News with Walter Cronkite during the moon landing. For Heinlein, it was vindication for a lifetime devoted to prodding mankind to take that first small step into outer space. (p. 80)

Heinlein's impact on the field of science fiction is difficult to assess only because it was so enormous. His story-telling abilities were immense, his gift for character was well developed, his background in the sciences formidable. He had the patience and the energy to thoroughly research his work and the courage to venture beyond the safe and the familiar and the guaranteed-to-be-successful. He had his detractors, but the worst that could be said was that he was a man of strong beliefs whose literary reach sometimes exceeded his grasp.

Heinlein's world view, which provided the subtext for much of his work, was summarized early on in his story **"The Year of the Jackpot"**:

> What good is the race of man? Monkeys, he thought, monkeys with a touch of poetry in them, cluttering and wasting a second-string planet near a third-string star. But sometimes they finish in style.

Robert A. Heinlein was born in 1907 and died 80 years later. He was generous and learned, and believed in the virtues of freedom and the uniqueness of man. He lived a full life during which he wrote 54 books, many of them bestsellers. He largely created modern science fiction and in doing so changed the world as much as any politician or general.

He had no children, but his family of devoted readers numbered in the millions. (p. 81)

Frank Robinson, "Robert A. Heinlein Dies," in Locus, *Vol. 21, No. 6, June, 1988, pp. B, 78-81.*

ROBERT SILVERBERG

The tallest tree falls with the biggest crash. [Robert A. Heinlein's] death, unlike many of those that have afflicted the sf community in recent years, was neither a dismaying surprise nor a monstrous cruelty—he was old, he had been ill for years—nor can it be said that a great career had been cut off in mid-stride, not when he had nearly fifty years of production behind him. But still his passing hits with tremendous force and leaves an immense empty place where he had been. Like no one else but H. G. Wells, he gave science fiction its definition. He showed what it ought to be and what it *could*

be. His role in our field is equivalent to that of Hemingway's in general modern fiction: a tremendous technical innovator, a shaper and changer. No one who has written fiction since 1927 or so can fail to take into account Hemingway's theory and practice without seeming archaic or impossibly naive; no one since 1941 has written first-rate science fiction without a comprehension of the theoretical and practical example of Heinlein.

He believed that a science fiction story should make sense—that it should be rooted in the nuts-and-bolts reality of our world, and also of its own imagined world—and he argued that the invented reality should be allowed to emerge by example as the narrative proceeded, rather than being hurled at the reader in expository chunks. Those may seem like pretty elementary concepts now, but they were new ideas when—at the age of 32—he took up sf writing in 1939. In such works as **"If This Goes On—"**, **"Beyond This Horizon"**, **"The Roads Must Roll"**, **"Universe"**, **"Methusaleh's Children"**, and a dozen others, all within three phenomenal years, he utterly transformed our notions of how to tell a science fiction story, and the transformation has been a permanent and irreversible one.

Then came the hiatus of the war, and afterward he moved on into the *Saturday Evening Post* and other slick magazines—thereby pioneering the way for Bradbury, Vonnegut, and many others—and simultaneously launched a series of amiable adventure novels for young people that brought more new readers into science fiction than anybody since Jules Verne. By 1952 he had done a lifetime's solid work. But all the Hugo-winning novels were yet to come, among them the startling bestseller *Stranger in a Strange Land,* and much more for decades ahead. . . .

A great writer, an extraordinary man, a figure of high nobility: there was no one else remotely like him in our field. Within the science fiction world there were many who disagreed with him about many things, but there was no one who did not respect him, and there were a good many, myself included, who came close to revering him. His not being among us will take some getting used to.

Robert Silverberg, in an obituary, in Locus, *Vol. 21, No. 6, June, 1988, p. 82.*

FREDERIK POHL

It's easy to say that with Bob Heinlein's death science fiction has lost one of its greatest writers and the world has lost a bright, feisty human being, and of course that's all true. It just doesn't go far enough. Bob Heinlein wasn't just a Big Name SF Writer. For decades on end, he *defined* modern science fiction. Other people wrote other fine books, exploring styles and concepts Heinlein never touched, but all the while Robert A. Heinlein was firmly entrenched at home base.

As a human being, Bob was something special. I often disagreed with him. On most political questions I thought his attitudes were just as loopy as he thought mine were. As the editor who first published just about all the science fiction he wrote during the 1960s, I found the going in our author-editor relationship sometimes pretty thorny. None of that mattered, though. What I felt for Bob Heinlein wasn't simply liking, or admiration, or respect. The right word for it was "love." He gave me a lot of joy in my life, and for that I will always owe his memory.

Frederik Pohl, in an obituary, in Locus, *Vol. 21, No. 6, June, 1988, p. C.*

JAMES GUNN

A universe without Robert Heinlein is going to seem strange. Few of us have known that kind of reality, and it will take some getting used to. Every sf reader under the age of fifty discovered Heinlein in those wonderful Scribner's juveniles that were good enough to serialize in the adult magazines, and often were. Those of us who are older than that, who fell in love with sf in the magazines of the early 1930s or a few of us even in the 1920s, came upon the Heinlein who began writing in 1939 as the ideal form of sf that we had been looking for all this time.

The obituaries called Heinlein "the most influential sf writer since H. G. Wells," and that was accurate enough. He pioneered the techniques of modern sf writing, the matter-of-fact acceptance of change and the economical ways of evoking that change in his stories, and he pioneered new fields in which that sf could present itself: the slick magazine, books, the juvenile, film, and finally the bestseller. Like Moses he led sf into the promised land.

Their careers overlapped by nearly forty years (and one of Heinlein's proud possessions was a copy of *When the Sleeper Wakes* that Wells, on an American lecture tour, signed for Heinlein in 1935), so Heinlein could not have been a reincarnation of Wells, but perhaps he was the writer Wells might have been if he had been born in Butler, Missouri, in 1907. Certainly it is as impossible to imagine contemporary sf existing as it is without Heinlein as without Wells. He made a dif-ference—what that difference was and how he made it will take a long time for students and scholars to calculate.

It will make a difference that he is gone. That we know now.

James Gunn, in an obituary, in Locus, *Vol. 21, No. 7, July, 1988, p. 42.*

LOCUS

[On October 6, 1988, the National Aeronautics and Space Administration (NASA) awarded its highest civilian honor, the Distinguished Public Service Medal, posthumously to Robert A. Heinlein. Reprinted below is the citation which accompanied the Medal.]

The National Aeronautics and Space Administration Awards to ROBERT ANSON HEINLEIN the NASA DISTINGUISHED PUBLIC SERVICE MEDAL in recognition of his meritorious service to the Nation and mankind in advocating and promoting the exploration of space. Through dozens of superbly written novels and essays and his epoch-making movie ***Destination Moon,*** he helped inspire the Nation to take its first step into space and on to the moon. Even after his death, his books live on as testimony to a man of purpose and vision, a man dedicated to encouraging others to dream, explore, and achieve.

Signed and sealed at Washington D.C., this sixth day of October, Nineteen Hundred and Eighty-Eight. /s/James C. Fletcher Administrator, NASA.

A citation with the NASA Distinguished Public Service Medal, in Locus, *Vol. 21, No. 12, December, 1988, p. 36.*

Louis (Dearborn) L'Amour

1908 - June 10, 1988

American novelist, short story writer, and nonfiction writer.

For an overview of L'Amour's life and work see *CLC,* Vol. 25; *Contemporary Authors,* Vols. 1-4, rev. ed., 125 (obituary); *Contemporary Authors New Revision Series,* Vol. 3, 25; and *Dictionary of Literary Biography Yearbook : 1980.*

DONALD DALE JACKSON

L'Amour is a publishing phenomenon of colossal proportions. For more than 30 years, since **Hondo** in the early 1950s, he has been writing Western novels that sell with the volume and regularity of Scout handbooks. Presidents from Eisenhower to Reagan have delighted in his sagas of heroes and villains stalking each other across his authentically rendered landscapes of the American frontier. His stories, appearing first in now extinct pulp magazines, moved without breaking stride through the genre paperback category to movies (**The Burning Hills, Heller in Pink Tights**) and hardcover bestsellerdom (**Jubal Sackett, Last of the Breed**), a progression one editor compares to vaulting from the ghetto of publishing to a Fifth Avenue penthouse. In recent years honors and awards have been showered on him—a Congressional Gold Medal . . . , the Presidential Medal of Freedom, honorary degrees—and even critics, the last converts, have become semirespectful. Louis L'Amour has become part of our cultural consciousness. "He's the only movable piece of Mount Rushmore," said his old friend Saul David, once his editor and now a movie producer.

But there is another side to the man behind the monumental reputation that most of his ardently loyal fans know nothing about. In his own quiet and low-key way L'Amour has established himself recently as a cultural and literary philanthropist. A man who educated himself through a lifetime of omnivorous reading, he now helps encourage others to read as a member of the executive council of the Center for the Book in the Library of Congress. "In an electronic world there's a question whether people will still read," he says. "My education, from books, didn't depend on a power source." John Cole, who directs the Center for the Book, values L'Amour's participation "because he was in many ways shaped by the books he read, and he takes it farther in his feeling for books and his promotion of reading."

Another cherished L'Amour project is a "Library of Americana" he hopes to build (quite possibly on his ranch) in a part of the West he loves, the Four Corners region.

> The idea is to assemble local publications from all around America—memoirs, local histories, historical-society booklets, newspaper pamphlets—there

are thousands of them. It's history that the historians never see. I'd include the basic books on American history and the historical and genealogical manuscripts that readers send me.

He envisions an archive where scholars can study the story of America as recounted by ordinary Americans, and hopes that it will be in place within five years. He is also involved in an attempt to develop an authentic re-creation of a late 19th-century Western town, a privately financed "Western Williamsburg" that would be a living, functioning museum of the frontier, with stores and stage stations and a working ranch.

Though he recoils in protest when called philanthropic, L'Amour sponsors several outstanding high school students honored annually by the California-based American Academy of Achievement. The institution brings teenage high achievers to a three-day seminar where they meet with Nobel and Pulitzer Prize winners and other innovators. He has also supported and encouraged promising Navajo artist Clifford Brycelea, hosting an exhibition of his work. Brycelea's mystical paintings hang in his home and one is on the cover of L'Amour's most recent book, **The Haunted Mesa** (pp. 155-56)

L'Amour looks like he might once have been a tough hombre—he was a prizefighter and a seaman among other things as a young man—and he would be no pushover even now. Though he lives among the Hollywood glitterati, there is nothing Hollywood about him. (p. 156)

He has written 101 books, which probably equal the total lifetime output of any other 12 writers; more than 30 of his novels and stories have been sold to the movies; an estimated 182 million copies of his books are currently in print worldwide. L'Amour himself overcomes his antinumerical bias long enough to report that Bantam Books distributes more than ten million of his books in hard and soft covers each year. . . .

> Flying West to write this story, Don Jackson was seated beside a man reading a paperback—by L'Amour.
>
> (p. 158)

Donald Dale Jackson, "World's Fastest Literary Gun: Louis L'Amour," in Smithsonian, Vol. 18, No. 2, May, 1987, pp. 154-56, 158.

STARR JENKINS

In this novel of a great escape across Siberia [**Last of the Breed**], Louis L'Amour writes a fascinating page-turner that shows both his strengths and his weaknesses. His hero is Joe Makatozi, major in the U.S. Air Force, test pilot of some of our most advanced aircraft, and a Sioux Indian. Besides flying military aircraft, Joe is skilled in bow-hunting, arrowhead-making and trapping, and he is devoted to wilderness life. From the above description you can re-create the plot. Joe Mack, as his friends call him, is kidnapped to Siberia by the Soviet military to be grilled for information, but he promptly escapes. In the year that follows, all through the terrible sixty-below winter and many adventures, Joe is escaping, killing his pursuers, falling in love with beautiful Natalya, head of an outlaw band, and attempting to re-enact the Indian migrations across the Bering Strait.

L'Amour's great skill is his ability to create interesting plot, fast-moving action, many surprising twists and turns, short chapters with dramatic crises at the end of each, and a somewhat believable picture of Siberia today. The main problem with the novel in literary terms is that the hero, though he grows admirably in ability to physically survive, seems to learn nothing from all his suffering. If anything, he regresses to a lower, more savage level of understanding, which is perhaps L'Amour's basic point about tribal-warrior life. Or any kind of warrior life.

Yet the book does what many more literary works . . . fail to do: interest you immediately and hold you to the last page. (pp. 84-5)

Starr Jenkins, in a review of "Last of the Breed," in Western American Literature, Vol. XXIII, No. 1, May, 1988, pp. 84-5.

TRACY WILKINSON

Louis L'Amour, one of modern literature's most prolific novelists whose tales of man's conquest of the Old West enthralled millions of readers from truck drivers to President Reagan, has died of lung cancer. He was 80. . . .

A North Dakota native who dropped out of high school to wander the world, L'Amour started his career writing Western pulp magazine stories and Hopalong Cassidy novels in the '40s and '50s.

Finally, after many rejection slips, his first novel, **Hondo,** was published in 1953 and was made into a film starring John Wayne.

"He always said he was just a storyteller, in the ancient [folk] tradition of people sitting around the fire, just telling stories," said Joseph Wershba, a New York-based television news producer, who knew L'Amour for more than a decade.

Critics say that L'Amour took the distinctly American genre of the Western novel to an audience unprecedented in size. Vivid in detail, his works drew on a wealth of personal experience and indefatigable research.

"His readers felt he had walked the land his characters did," said Stuart Applebaum, L'Amour's publicist and his editor at Bantam Books. "His [stories] were as authentic as a text book, but a hell of a lot more entertaining to read. That combination of story-telling magic and unbeatable authenticity in background, place and time made his fans await eagerly each new book."

Once called the laureate of the lariat, L'Amour wrote of cowboys, gunfighters and lawmen, of history, of good versus evil, of man's relationship to nature, of survival.

"I go to an area I'm interested in and I try to find a guy who knows it better than anyone else. Usually it's some broken-down cowboy," L'Amour once said in an interview with the Associated Press.

> I'm actually writing history. It isn't what you'd call big history. I don't write about presidents and generals . . . I write about the man who was ranching, the man who was mining, the man who was opening up the country. . . .

L'Amour is the only novelist ever to be awarded the National Gold Medal, presented to him by Congress in 1983 for lifetime literary achievement, as well as the Medal of Freedom, bestowed on him by Reagan in 1984.

After leaving home at the age of 15, L'Amour embarked on a 20-year journey that could easily have been the stuff of his later novels. The odyssey found him working in the fish canneries of Alaska, jumping freight cars in New Orleans, writing for a newspaper in Oklahoma and handling circus elephants in Asia. He worked as a seaman, a lumberjack, a coal miner, a boxer, a farm hand, and served as an officer on a tank destroyer in World War II. . . .

Bantam publishes about three L'Amour novels a year. Ever-present in airport bookstores and at paperback counters, the books appeal to a wide range of readers. Reagan, according to Bantam, read one of L'Amour's novels, **Jubal Sackett,** during his recovery from cancer surgery in July, 1985.

Two books by L'Amour are scheduled to appear later this year: Lonigan, a short-story collection and The Sackett Com-

panion, a commentary to accompany the 17-novel series on the Sackett family.

"He worked seven days a week," Applebaum said. "The minute he finished one, he started on the next."

On the last afternoon of his life, he had been proofreading an autobiography that describes his self-education as a wandering youth, Applebaum said. . . .

Of 86 novels, 14 short story collections and one book of nonfiction, not all L'Amour's work dealt with the West. More recently he had expanded his literary range; in 1984, he read several thousand books on Medieval times before writing about a feudal warrior named Kerbouchard in the novel *The Walking Drum,* set in the Middle Ages.

> Tracy Wilkinson, "Louis L'Amour Dies; Prolific Western Writer," in Los Angeles Times, *June 13, 1988.*

JAMES BARRON

Louis L'Amour, who turned out novel after best-selling novel about plain-speaking, straight-shooting heroes of the old West, died Friday [June 10, 1988] at his home in Los Angeles. He was 80 years old.

Mr. L'Amour's editor at Bantam Books, Stuart S. Applebaum, said Mr. L'Amour, a nonsmoker, had died of lung cancer.

All 101 of Mr. L'Amour's books—86 novels, 14 short-story collections and one full-length work of nonfiction—are in print, and with almost 200 million copies in circulation, he was one of the world's most popular writers. Former President Jimmy Carter was reading *The Lonesome Gods* on an airplane trip last week, and President Reagan read *Jubal Sackett* while recovering from cancer surgery in 1985. . . .

On his way to the best-seller list, Mr. L'Amour worked at almost everything but writing. Before he handed in his first western—*Hondo,* in 1953—he had been a longshoreman, a lumberjack, an elephant handler, a fruit picker and an officer on a tank destroyer in World War II. He had also circled the world on a freighter, sailed a dhow on the Red Sea, been shipwrecked in the West Indies and been stranded in the Mojave Desert, and had won 51 of 59 fights as a professional boxer.

But he was certain that someday he would make his living as a writer. Since 1816, 33 members of his family had done so; and Mr. L'Amour, who had wanted to be a writer "almost from the time I could walk," was confident of his talent. "I could sit in the middle of Sunset Boulevard and write with my typewriter on my knees," he once said. "Temperamental I am not."

But at times he did seem annoyed that critics paid little attention to westerns. He attributed this to the literary world's "pure snobbishness."

"If you write a book about a bygone period that lies east of the Mississippi River, then it's a historical novel," he said in 1975. "If it's west of the Mississippi, it's a western, a different category. There's no sense to it."

For his part, Mr. L'Amour considered himself something of a latter-day Chaucer. "I don't travel and tell stories, because that's not the way these days," he said. "But I write my books to be read aloud and I think of myself in that oral tradition."

The result was a strong sense of time and place, the result of L'Amour's meticulous attention to details. When he wrote about mountains, he was geologically correct. When he wrote about guns, he wrote for the gun specialist. He checked what food people ate in a given time and place, he memorized architectural details and often took camping trips to familiarize himself with the landscapes he was writing about.

In the typical L'Amour book, law triumphs over lawlessness and order over chaos. But he was less concerned with stereotypes of good guys and bad guys than with his characters' spunkiness.

The typical L'Amour hero was a strapping young man in his late teens or early 20's, a resilient and somewhat romantic fighter bent on self-improvement. Tell Sackett carried law books in his saddlebags; Bendigo Shafter read Montaigne, Plutarch and Thoreau; and Drake Morrel, a one-time riverboat gambler, read Juvenal in the original Latin. . . .

A big man who came close to fitting the description of one of his heroes, Louis Dearborn L'Amour was born . . . in Jamestown, N.D. He was a son of a veterinarian who doubled as a farm-machinery salesman, grandson of a Civil War veteran and great-grandson of a settler who had been scalped by Sioux warriors. . . .

After World War II, he wrote under the name Tex Burns because, he insisted, "no editor believed that the name L'Amour could ever appear on a Western story." Only after *Hondo* had been published and made into a successful John Wayne movie did Mr. L'Amour write under his own name.

> James Barron, "Author Louis L'Amour Dies at 80; Chronicler of the American West," in The New York Times, *June 13, 1988, p. B12.*

RICHARD PEARSON

Louis L'Amour, 80, one of the world's best-selling novelists whose Homeric chronicles of the old West have sold more than 200 million books, died of cancer June 10 at his home in Los Angeles. . . .

His most recent novel was *The Haunted Mesa,* published in 1987. Other recent best-sellers included *Last of the Breed* (1986), *Jubal Sackett* (1985) and *The Walking Drum* (1984).

Shortly before his death, he had completed several as-yet-unpublished books, including *Lonigan,* a western short story collection, and *The Sackett Companion,* a nonfiction work about the research and facts of his popular series of 17 novels. That book series was made into a television miniseries "The Sacketts." . . .

More than 45 of his novels and short stories have been made into feature films and television movies. These included *Shalako,* . . . *The Burning Hills,* . . . and *Stranger on Horseback.* . . . Mr. L'Amour's novel *How the West Was Won,* was made into a 1962 film with a cast that included John Wayne, Jimmy Stewart and Gregory Peck.

In addition to novels, short story collections and works of nonfiction, Mr. L'Amour had published more than 400 magazine stories and articles. His work had appeared in such journals as *Collier's, The Saturday Evening Post,* and *Argosy.*

His work has been translated into 20 languages, including Serbo-Croatian and Chinese.

Mr. L'Amour was a recipient of the Congressional National Gold Medal for lifetime literary achievement, and in 1984 was presented with the nation's highest civilian award, the Medal of Freedom, by President Reagan. The president had once hailed Mr. L'Amour for "having brought the West to the people of the East and to people everywhere." . . .

The typical L'Amour western featured an all-American hero, though sometimes on the wrong side of the law, who sought to open the West. He came into conflict with both man and the elements. If the story featured gunplay, it was not often. Contrary to the traditional western, his Indians were as often heroes as villains.

Indeed, though Mr. L'Amour was often faulted by critics for cardboard, simplistic characters, his westerner heroes often fought an inner struggle against admiration for the Indian and his way of life on one hand and the need to advance "civilization" on the other. His were often stories of cultures in conflict.

In addition to carrying an encyclopedic knowledge of the Indian and his ways in their heads, his heroes also had saddlebags that bulged with the great works of civilization. These might include Blackstone's *Laws,* Montaigne's *Essays,* Plutarch's *Lives* or Juvenal's *Satires.*

If Mr. L'Amour's plots could be predictable and his narrative wooden, he had a story and could tell it. His plots spanned the continent, conveying an unyielding sense of optimism in the face of adversity. The books also were burnished with a wealth of historical research.

Among the myths he tried to shatter concerned those of townspeople fleeing from gunslingers. In fact, he pointed out, many settlers were Civil War veterans who were adept at using the rifles they were apt to own. He also pointed out that between 1800 and 1816, there were more gunfights in the U.S. Navy than along the American frontier.

Mr. L'Amour maintained a working library of more than 8,000 volumes of western history, as well as collections of frontier court records, old newspapers and letters. He also traveled to whatever part of the country he wrote about. If a bad guy met his fate after being cornered in a box canyon, Mr. L'Amour more than likely had scouted it.

He also conducted his own research and interviews. He once told the Associated Press:

> I go to an area I'm interested in and I try to find a guy who knows it better than anyone else. Usually it's some broken-down cowboy. I've known five men and two women who knew Billy the Kid well. I talked to the woman who prepared his body for burial. . . .

Despite his undeniable popularity, he never achieved critical acclaim. He blamed much of this on an East-West conflict in literature, in which the man of the West was critically shunned as throwing together mere genre fiction.

But Mr. L'Amour did not see it that way. He chose to write about what he called "hard-shelled men who built with nerve and hand that which the soft-bellied latecomers call the 'western myth.' "

Mr. L'Amour said, "I'm a storyteller in the old folk tradition, like the man on a corner in the marketplace."

He said his books were about the frontiersman's idea of freedom, the freedom to climb on a horse and move on. And, he added, everyone had dreams of that kind.

Richard Pearson, "Prolific Western Novelist Louis L'Amour, 80, Dies," in The Washington Post, *June 13, 1988.*

Alan (Stewart) Paton

January 11, 1903 - April 12, 1988

South African novelist, short story writer, dramatist, nonfiction writer, essayist, biographer, and autobiographer.

For an overview of Paton's life and work see *CLC*, Vols. 4, 10, 25; *Contemporary Authors*, Vols. 13-16, rev. ed., 125 (obituary); *Contemporary Authors New Revision Series*, Vol. 22; *Contemporary Authors Permanent Series*, Vol. 1; and *Something about the Author*, Vol. 11.

JOHN D. BATTERSBY

Alan Paton believes it is for others to judge whether *Cry, the Beloved Country,* his classic novel of racial hatred, despair and reconciliation, has stood the test of time.

"I had an eye on my fellow white South Africans and white Americans when I wrote the book," the 85-year old author said in a recent interview. "It wasn't a book written for the right or the middle or the left. I hoped to influence my fellow whites."

Mr. Paton's story about the trials of a Zulu priest seeking his fugitive son, a suspect in the murder of a white man in Johannesburg, was conceived in a cathedral in Norway 41 years ago.

The book has sold more than 15 million copies in 20 languages. . . .

Mr. Paton [recalled] the circumstances under which the book was written. As principal of the Diepkloof Reformatory for boys in Johannesburg, he went on a tour of reformatories and prisons in Europe and North America in 1946.

On a visit to Norway, Mr. Paton was taken by a friend to see the Trondheim Cathedral.

"We sat in the pews opposite the rose window, which is one of the most beautiful in the world," he said. "The light was shining behind it. I was very moved and felt very homesick." His friend took him back to the hotel, where he wrote the first chapter of *Cry, the Beloved Country* "with no idea," he said, "of what was to follow."

The rest of book was written at hotels in Sweden, Britain, on board the Queen Elizabeth and in New York, Atlanta and San Francisco.

Mr. Paton has stuck resolutely to his liberal convictions, but today is regarded as a conservative by anti-apartheid organizations because he is a vociferous opponent of disinvestment and sanctions on the ground that such actions would harm the very people they are supposed to help.

And the times have changed. Today Diepkloof Reformatory is the Doornkop military base from which white soldiers police black resistance to apartheid in the sprawling township complex of Soweto. . . .

Mr. Paton says he thinks the warring Zulu factions have moved beyond the control of their leaders. But despite the intensified problems in South Africa and the radicalization of opposition politics, he thinks the central message of *Cry, the Beloved Country* is still alive.

"I still believe there is hope," Mr. Paton said.

> John D. Battersby, "Reflections on 'Beloved Country'," in The New York Times, *April 2, 1988, p. 11.*

HERBERT MITGANG

Alan Paton, the South African author and political leader whose powerful 1948 novel *Cry, the Beloved Country* aroused many of his countrymen and much of the world against apartheid, died of throat cancer early Tuesday, [April

12], . . . at his home outside Durban, his wife Anne said. He was 85 years old.

Mr. Paton worked against the South African system of racial separation in his writings and by serving as head of the Liberal Party, which was eventually disbanded under South African legislation outlawing multi-racial parties (p. A1)

Cry, the Beloved Country tells the story of a Zulu minister, Stephen Kumalo, who is searching for his sister and for his son, who has murdered a white man; the father loses his faith and ultimately finds it again.

The novel, published without hoopla or book-club selection, received ecstatic reviews. Orville Prescott wrote in *The Times* that it was "a beautiful and profoundly moving story, a story steeped in sadness and grief but radiant with hope and compassion."

Mr. Paton had been an educator and a public official, but the success of *Cry, the Beloved Country* induced him to resign the directorship of a reformatory to devote his life to writing. Within weeks of his resignation, the election victory of the National Party, committed to apartheid for South Africa, "brought my intention to nothing," he wrote in 1980 in the first volume of his autobiography, "and condemned me to a struggle between literature and politics that has lasted until now."

He continued to write fiction and nonfiction, both successfully; he also worked unceasingly in behalf of his political views as a distinguished private citizen and, while it was still possible, as head of the Liberal Party.

"I could have made better use of my life," he wrote in an essay published in a collection entitled *The Long View,* "but I did try hard to do one thing. That was to persuade white South Africa to share its power, for reasons of justice and survival."

He conceded that he had met little success, but he wrote, "In a country like South Africa there are many things that must be undertaken without any hope that the ventures will be successful, and there are many ventures in which one must persevere in spite of this lack of success." . . .

Mr. Paton was born Jan. 11, 1913, in Pietermaritzburg, South Africa. He graduated from the University of Natal, became a teacher and in 1928 married Doris Francis Lusted, a widow.

In the late 1920's, Mr. Paton, a Methodist, became increasingly interested in and influenced by Anglicanism. He converted in 1930 and—partly through the growing importance of religion in his life—began to consider more and more seriously the nature of the society in which he lived.

He also became increasingly interested in working with delinquent youths, at about this time he met the politician Jan Hendrik Hofmeyr, whose biographer he was to become.

In 1935, Mr. Paton was made head of Diepkloof, a reformatory for black delinquents that became a model of penal reform. It was during a trip to Europe to observe prison reform that he wrote *Cry, the Beloved Country* . . .

In 1953, the Liberal Party was founded with Mr. Paton as its president. The party stood for a universal franchise and against violence. It had 3,000 members, with four seats in Parliament before black representation was eliminated; it was

disbanded in 1968, when the Government enacted legislation making interracial parties illegal.

Mr. Paton was undaunted. "Man was not created to go down on his belly before the state," he said at the party's last meeting. "We refuse to make a god of preservation of racial differences."

In 1960, the year his passport was withdrawn, he observed, "We are not a Nazi country, but we are not a bad imitation of one." He continued to speak hopefully of the prospects for nonviolent change in South Africa, but by 1977 he was saying that his hope had become very small. He feared that revolution was inevitable "because the Government is unwilling to make meaningful change."

In *Cry, the Beloved Country* he wrote of the fears of white South Africans: "We do not know, we do not know. We shall live from day to day, and put more locks on the doors, and get a fine fierce dog . . . and the beauty of the trees by night, and the raptures of lovers under the stars, these things we shall forgo."

And, in the sentence that gave the book its title, he wrote: "Cry, the beloved country, for the unborn child that is the inheritor of our fear." (p. D35)

Herbert Mitgang, "Alan Paton, Author and Apartheid Foe, Dies of Cancer at 85," in The New York Times, *April 12, 1988, pp. A1, D35.*

WILLIAM CLAIBORNE

Alan Paton, South Africa's best-known author and a tireless opponent of apartheid for more than four decades, died [on April 12] of cancer at his home outside Durban. He was 85.

Paton's most widely read novel was *Cry, The Beloved Country,* a compelling word picture of statutory racial separation drawn through the story of a simple Zulu parson's anguished search for his missing delinquent son in Johannesburg's teeming shanty towns.

It was published in 1948, the year that the National Party came to power, and later was dramatized and filmed, awakening the world to the conditions of the black majority in white-ruled South Africa. Over 100,000 copies are still sold annually.

Paton, who until his death remained a prolific—and controversial—political commentator in journals here and abroad, published half a dozen other acclaimed novels, the most recent of which was *Ah, But Your Land is Beautiful,* the first part of a planned trilogy published in 1981.

He also published an autobiography, *Toward the Mountain,* of which a sequel, *Journey Continued,* is scheduled to appear later this month.

Paton's life, however, was also characterized by political activism, particularly in support of mixed-race political parties.

He was a founder in 1954 and later president of the Liberal Party, which was disbanded in 1968 after interracial political parties were declared illegal under the Prohibition of Political Interference Act.

After the act was abolished in 1985, Paton campaigned against the continuation of whites-only opposition parties and only last month shared a platform in Durban with Indian politicians and leaders of the Progressive Federal Party (PFP), saying, "There is no room left for whites-only opposition parties to the left of the government."

While relentless in his criticism of the government's apartheid policies, Paton also was sharply critical of the radical left, and he often wrote and spoke on behalf of nonviolent strategies.

A critic of punitive sanctions and disinvestment, Paton generated anger among some white antiapartheid activists and militant black nationalists when, in 1984, he publicly questioned the "political morality" of Desmond Tutu, then Anglican bishop of Johannesburg, for supporting sanctions. Tutu went on to win the 1984 Nobel Peace Prize.

Some white liberals were pained by what they perceived to be a softening of Paton's political attitudes in his later years, particularly since his Liberal Party was, in its time, the only organized body then advocating universal suffrage and the complete removal of racial segregation.

However, Paton stuck by his moderate stance, advocating a cautious but steady course of change in South Africa, as opposed to the "quick-fix" solutions he believed would lead to the destruction of the country.

Paton's political commentaries were characteristic of his novels for their lack of bitterness and dogmatism and oversimplification, while still conveying forcefully the injustices of a system he deeply hated.

> *William Claiborne, "S. African Author Alan Paton Dies," in* The Washington Post, *April 12, 1988, p. A8.*

TOM McGURK

In 1948 two seemingly disparate events occurred in South Africa: Dr Malan's National Party took power and promptly circled the constitutional wagons on the veldt to hoist the flag of apartheid; while on a hill in Natal an obscure school teacher called Alan Paton published a novel *Cry, the Beloved Country.*

With the death of Alan Paton this week at the age of 85, the chasm between those two South African visions of life could hardly be wider and brings into perspective the extraordinary power that a single book can have. Perhaps more than anything else it succeeded in opening the first window on life in South Africa; since its publication it has been an international bestseller. Long before Sharpeville and Soweto and long before television, the enchanting power of Paton's tale gave generations a commitment towards justice in South Africa.

A few years before his death the authorities finally put the book on the school syllabus. One of his greatest pleasures, he told me, was to be invited to schools across South Africa to talk about it.

"I suppose that was when the book came to life again for me," he said. "It's strange how years after you have written something you almost feel it was written by someone else. At the end the greatest achievement for me was not its success or its critical acclaim but the fascination I discovered in the children as they read it and talked to me about it. At times I felt like an outsider looking in on all of this." (pp. 7-8)

In 1953 Paton abandoned writing for a period to devote him-

self to the then newly-formed Liberal Party. An organisation of blacks and whites, the party was attempting to challenge the Nationalist government at the onset of apartheid. With members drawn mainly from the English-speaking community, it was soon sidelined as the political scene developed into a struggle between the ANC and the National Party. After the treason trials, the banning of the ANC and the jailing of Mandela the crackdown was complete.

The Liberal Party disbanded in May 1968, while Paton was president. Following the Prohibition of Political Interference Bill which outlawed multiracial parties they had no choice but to close their doors.

It was the measure of what was to come in South Africa that 20 years ago there was nowhere in the political system for humanitarians like him. He abandoned active politics to write again and in recent years was a widely quoted and powerful critic of the Pretoria regime. But his outlook was complicated; for example, he totally opposed economic sanctions, pointing to the effect it would have on the thousands of Africans on the breadline; and in 1971 he had been lukewarm about the introduction of the homeland developments. He later admitted he had been totally wrong. . . .

Curiously for a country which boasts an extensive list of banned writers, he was never listed. No doubt his international reputation, established before the National Party was firmly in control, forestalled a ban.

Alan Paton lived just long enough to finally witness the end of all freedom of expression or of political organisation in South Africa. With a blanket press ban and the townships under military occupation, the Pretoria regime is struggling to survive the apartheid monster it itself created, which has now resurfaced in the guise of the Conservative Party.

Ironically, it has all come to pass as Paton warned it would. (p. 8)

> *Tom McGurk, "Paton's Nightmare Came True," in* New Statesman, *Vol. 115, No. 2977, April 15, 1988, pp. 7-8.*

SOUSA JAMBA

I read Alan Paton's *Cry, the Beloved Country* when I was 15. It was a riveting book. I kept re-reading the words at the beginning of the first chapter. They almost had a magical effect on me. The words described Ixopo, the protagonist's village. I was taken there myself and could see it with my own eyes.

My contemporaries did not think very much of African writers. It was said that they were boring. Who wanted to read about events in an African village? As for South Africa, we all knew that novels from that country would be dealing with apartheid in some way or the other. (p. 18)

I do remember my copy of *Cry, the Beloved Country.* It was decrepit and smelt of kerosene. Many people, I had concluded, must have stayed up late at night reading one of the best books that have come out of Africa. I never left it behind. I took it to the tavern to drink *chibuki* (maize beer) with my friends and however drunk I would get I would make sure that it was secure. I would get so completely carried away by it that I would forget the pot of beans that my sister had instructed me to tend. More than once, as I scraped the burnt beans from the bottom of the pot, she had threatened to throw the copy down the pit latrine. I later gave her the copy to read. She found it so interesting that she stayed in bed for two days, reading it.

As I began to read *Cry, the Beloved Country,* a strong suspicion began to mount in me. Alan Paton was white and I, like most of my contemporaries, was then very suspicious of white people. We believed that it was all very well to admire and emulate the white man's ways. But at the end of the day we were not the same. White people looked different; talked different; and smelt different. Would they be able to understand black people? I had thought it impossible.

I remember arguing on that basis with an Asian teacher of mine who had written about Africa. (At that time I was writing a story set in Washington, a place I had never been to.) We were often told that most of what white explorers such as David Livingstone had written about Africa was false. The time had come for us blacks to write the truth seen through African eyes.

It was at this time that I discovered negritude. My flimsy understanding of it was that Europeans had wiped out an African civilisation that had thriven in the past. I had also dipped into Walter Rodney's *How Europe Underdeveloped Africa.*

I had a bipolarised view of the world. I saw everything in terms of race. White men were there to defend the interests of the white and black men the interests of the blacks.

Why, then, was I going to believe what this white South African, Alan Paton, was going to say about black people? I thought the racial conflict in South Africa was a clear-cut one. On the one hand there were the blacks and on the other the whites. Alan Paton was white, *ergo* anti-black. If he was to treat his black characters with sympathy, then it was mere chicanery, which I then associated with whites.

As I read on, my suspicion waned. I forgot that what I was reading was written by a white man. I was momentarily transposed from the Lusaka shanty town where I lived to South Africa. What I was reading was simply written by an outstanding writer, a genius. He did not pontificate; neither did he reach out for the ready-made clichés as some public figures on our continent are wont to do.

The protagonist, who goes in search of his son in Johannesburg, is not only confronted with the racial problem but with the problem any African who moves from his rural village to an urban centre would face. The violence and the unpredictability of the city would have confounded a Zambian, a Tanzanian or a Nigerian.

Years later, I was to read Leo Tolstoy's short story "Alyosha the Pot". Whenever I thought about this masterpiece, Alan Paton's short story **"Ha'Penny"** came to mind. The clear language and the love which both writers had for their characters impressed me. All the suspicion with which I treated him in my teens has now been replaced by respect and admiration. (pp. 18-19)

Sousa Jamba, "Beloved Bookman," in The Spectator, *Vol. 260, No. 8336, April 16, 1988, pp. 18-19.*

COMMONWEAL

Alan Paton died April 12, 1988 at his home near Durban, South Africa. His novel, *Cry, the Beloved Country,* published in 1947 first revealed to many Americans the human costs of South Africa's policies of racial separation. The book's publication changed Paton's own life, enabling him to resign his post as principal of a reformatory, to write full-time, and, as he put it, "to do many things that brought in less money, or indeed no money at all." But the book did not change the face of apartheid. After winning the 1948 elections, the Afrikaner National Party enforced complete separation of the races.

Paton writes in his autobiography, *Towards the Mountain,* of his first encounter with this new policy during a farewell party given in his honor at the reformatory: "I was full of anger, and sick at heart. I drank my white tea and then went over to the black tables. . . . In my anger I could have spent the rest of the afternoon at the black tables, but I had white guests to consider, so I returned to them." These events, he says, "condemned me to a struggle between literature and politics. . . ." (pp. 292-93)

Paton's pleas for integration and reconciliation proved of little avail in South Africa and his moderate position ultimately excluded him from political life. Paton's first novel, with its simple language and pervasive religious sensibility, had a far greater impact on race relations in the United States. He wrote *Cry, the Beloved Country* while on an official trip to study prisons and reformatories in Europe and the United States. . . .

The journey through the United States, and especially the South, gave Paton a sense of black-white relations in this country which he compares and contrasts to those in South Africa in *Towards the Mountain.*

Nothing of this appears in *Cry, the Beloved Country.* Yet for millions of Americans the power of this simple tale has had an impact difficult to measure but real, that has helped bring us, if not yet to a satisfactory resolution of our race problem, at least to a better place than the poor sad land where "There is a lovely road that runs from Ixopo into the hills. These hills are grass-covered and rolling, and they are lovely beyond any singing of it." (p. 293)

"Alan Paton," in Commonweal, *Vol. CXV, No. 10, May 20, 1988, pp. 292-93.*

DAN JACOBSON

Forty-three years ago Alan Paton came to my home town, Kimberley, to make an oration and to give away the prizes at the annual speech-day of the school I attended, the Kimberley Boys' High School. This was well before he had become a household name in South Africa and a familiar one in many countries outside it. He was invited, as far as I can recall, because he had been an acquaintance of our headmaster's, when they had been students together at Rhodes University. All we were told about our guest's public life beforehand was that he was the principal of the reformatory for young black offenders at Diepkloof, near Johannesburg.

The ceremony took place not in the school itself, but amid the creaking floors, lofty windows, and forlornly distempered walls of Kimberley's old Town Hall. Alan Paton duly gave out the prizes; among many others, I had the privilege of going up to receive a book or two, a handshake, a rather stern glance, and a few muttered words of congratulation. Then, that part of the proceedings over, we settled down to listen to what I and my schoolfriends expected to be the usual speech-day affair: one which would be congratulatory, patronizing, full of references to the sterling work of our teachers and our own achievements on the sports field.

We did not get such a speech. We got instead an intense, almost angry-sounding lecture about the injustices of the social and racial conditions prevailing in South Africa and the dangers which confronted the country as a result—and about the ways in which we might try to meet those dangers. I can remember vividly how slight the speaker's figure appeared to be, in his double-breasted suit, and how earnest was his manner; how his brow gleamed under the lights on that warm Kimberley evening; and, above all, how unlike anything we had heard before at any school occasion was what he was saying to us. Whether our headmaster—not an enlightened man, in any sense—was pleased with his guest's performance, I cannot tell; some of the boys, I know, did not like it. But all of us were aware that every word addressed to us had been said out of conviction, out of a sense of imperative need.

That was to be my sole meeting with Alan Paton; the contact he and I were to have subsequently, decades later, was to be by correspondence only. *Cry the Beloved Country* came out just a few years after his visit to Kimberley, when I was a student at Witwatersrand University. Naturally, I felt a special interest in the book, because of my recollection of the occasion I have described; in any case novels about South Africa were much rarer then than they are now. I was moved by the book, and I heard clearly in it the fierce cadences of the voice that had addressed us that night in Kimberley. But I had literary and critical misgivings about the book too—about its homiletic tone, especially, and about the incorporation in it of relatively straightforward passages of contemporary history. So when I read, in a short-lived student publication, a review in which it was cuttingly described as "the South African *Uncle Tom's Cabin*", I at once recognized—or thought I recognized—what the writer meant. This was all the easier for me to do since at that time I had not actually read *Uncle Tom's Cabin*.

And today? The description still seems to me in some ways just; but it also seems to me a more honourable one than I would ever have supposed then. There are certain novels, of a relatively rare kind, which cannot be adequately assessed in literary terms—though they obviously use literary and imaginative means to achieve their effects. Nor can such novels be described solely in the language of politics—though their intentions are always and avowedly political. Nor is the power they have wholly to be identified with the fervour of the moral homilies they contain. Rather, precisely because they have no regard for the very distinctions I have just tried to make between the literary, the political, and the moral, such works sometimes acquire a life in the minds of readers that may best be described as *proverbial*. Even for non-readers, they become part of a common stock of reference and of modes of self-recognition. *Uncle Tom's Cabin* was such a book; so (to take a very different example) was Orwell's *Nineteen Eighty-four;* so too, for countless numbers of South Africans, and people elsewhere, was *Cry the Beloved Country.* Books like these endure long beyond the particular conditions that produce them; and they do so because they themselves have become one of the factors governing the self-consciousness of the communities to which they are addressed.

Dan Jacobson, "Nostalgia for the Future," in The

Times Literary Supplement, *No. 4452, July 29-August 4, 1988, p. 830.*

WILLIAM MINTER

For four decades, Alan Paton's novel *Cry, the Beloved Country* has given millions their first glimpses of the human tragedy of South African racism. Its simple eloquence leaves few unmoved. Appropriately, it forms the hinge between the two volumes of Paton's autobiography.

Towards the Mountain, which was published in 1980, recounted Paton's conversion from the white racist paternalism he had accepted until his mid-30's. Between 1941 and 1943 he sat on an Anglican commission on South African society that consisted of 31 whites and two blacks. From his fellow commissioners and others associated with the liberal Institute of Race Relations, Paton gained a vision. "I was no longer a white person but a member of the human race."

On leave from his position as director of a reformatory for African boys, Paton was inspired to write *Cry, the Beloved Country.* Its publication in 1948 transformed him overnight into South Africa's most celebrated writer. He was then 45 years old. *Journey Continued* takes up his story at this point, with his reactions to fame and to the election that year of the Afrikaner-based National Party, which advocated an intensification of the country's system of white racial dominance, using as a slogan, "apartheid" ("apartness").

Journey Continued maintains the clear writing style, the attention to detail and the candor of Paton's earlier works. It discusses South African politics, as well as his family, friends and life as a writer. Yet there is no strong theme comparable to the first volume's vision of a journey toward the holy mountain of justice.

Paton carries the narrative to 1968, with a brief epilogue on the two decades before his death on April 12 this year. One major topic is his leading role in the Liberal Party, which from 1953 to 1968 worked within the white electoral system for racial equality. . . .

Paton's participation in the Liberal Party, he makes clear, came from moral duty, not from any expectation that the majority of whites would respond. Duty also motivated his decision to testify for political prisoners in the 1950's, even though he rejected the politics of the African National Congress as too radical. He also never participated in the nonviolent resistance campaigns of the time. His vision of change was "to persuade white South Africa to share its power, for reasons of justice and survival."

His heroes were all white: men like Hofmeyr and Archbishop Geoffrey Clayton, whose biography Paton published in 1973. Like Paton, Clayton was eventually impelled to denounce racial injustice, but often seemed as disturbed by intemperate protest as by the system itself.

One of the most revealing passages in *Journey Continued* deals with the young members of the Liberal Party who, in the tumult of the 1960's, joined a clumsy sabotage campaign against the Government, causing the accidental death of a 77-year-old white woman. Paton's deep revulsion at this act contrasts strikingly with his description of the 1960 Sharpeville

An excerpt from *Journey Continued*

I hope our country will pull itself out of its present mess, and that the best and the wisest of our people will shape our new society. I take it for granted that our future has become the concern of many of the governments and the ordinary people of the world. They have every right to concern themselves and to bring pressure to bear upon us. I believe they are utterly mistaken to think that sanctions and disinvestment will bring beneficial change. You cannot change a society for the better by damaging or destroying its economy. Sanctions are intended to be punitive, and punishment is not the way to make people behave better. I learned that fifty-two years ago at Diepkloof Reformatory.

The events of the last forty years which I have described in this book could not have happened in the democracies of the West. That's not because the people of the West are better than we are. The most self-righteous of the Americans are not better than we are. I repeat that they should go down on their knees and thank God for their Constitution, their Bill of Rights, and their Supreme Court. We don't have any of these things, but I know many people who devote much of their lives to a struggle to create a more just society, and I thank God for them.

I shall not write anything more of any weight. I am grateful that life made it possible for me to pursue a writing career. I am now ready to go when I am called.

> *God bless Africa*
> *Guard her children*
> *Guide her rulers*
> *And give her peace*
> *Amen*

massacre, which verges on an apologia for the policemen who killed 69 black protesters.

Such glimpses make some sense of Paton's otherwise puzzling political stance of later years, when he found it easier to praise President P. W. Botha's willingness to reform than to accept Bishop Desmond Tutu's call for economic pressures against the apartheid regime. Although Paton refers several times to the mellowing of his outrage against apartheid, his political views probably changed little from his initial conversion in the 1940's.

In *Cry, the Beloved Country,* the black pastor expresses the fear that "when they turn to loving they will find we are turned to hating." Paton, it seems, found it impossible to listen with openness instead of fear to the new black voices of the 1960's, 70's or 80's. In the end, nevertheless, he will be remembered not for that fear, but for his cry for justice that continues to echo today.

> *William Minter, "Moderate to a Fault?" in* The New York Times Book Review, *November 20, 1988, p. 36.*

Miguel (Gomez) Piñero

December 19, 1946 - June 16, 1988

Puerto Rican-born American dramatist, novelist, poet, and editor.

For an overview of Pinero's life and work see *CLC,* Vol. 4 and *Contemporary Authors,* Vols. 61-64, 125 (obituary).

LOS ANGELES TIMES

Miguel Pinero, the one-time convict whose cell block experiences became the basis of the highly acclaimed play *Short Eyes* has died in a Manhattan hospital, the New York Public Theater announced Friday. He was 41.

Pinero died Thursday of cirrhosis of the liver, said Reva Cooper, a theater spokeswoman.

The first draft of *Short Eyes,* Pinero's most famous play, was written while the author was still in prison, Cooper said. It is set in the day room of a cell block and involves how other prisoners deal with a new inmate charged with the molestation of a young girl. He is the "short eyes" of the play who is eventually murdered.

The play opened in 1974 at the off-Broadway Riverside Theater as a part of the Third World Project, moved to the Public Theater and then to the Vivian Beaumont Theater in the Lincoln Center and won the coveted New York Drama Critics Award for best American play of the season.

At the time of his death, Pinero was writing another play for the Public Theater, *Every Form of Refuge Has Its Price,* Cooper said. The play takes place in the intensive-care unit of a Manhattan hospital, very similar to the one where he died, said Joseph Papp, head of the New York Public Theater.

"Pinero was the first major writer to come out of the large numbers of Puerto Ricans that came to New York in the '50s," Papp said.

In a reference to the violent, striking play that cemented Pinero's reputation, Papp said that Pinero "brought a hard-hitting realism to the stage that shook it up."

Pinero's other plays include *The Sun Always Shines for the Cool* and *Eulogy for a Small Time Thief.* Pinero also worked as an actor, playing God in *Steambath* in Philadelphia in 1975 and in such films as *The Jericho Mile* in 1979 and *Fort Apache the Bronx* in 1981.

"Miguel Pinero, 41; Ex-Convict and Playwright," in Los Angeles Times, *June 18, 1988.*

LESLIE BENNETTS

Miguel Pinero, who began his first play in prison and went on to be acclaimed as a major new voice in the theater 15 years ago, died of cirrhosis of the liver Friday morning [June 17, 1988] at Bellevue Hospital. He was 41 years old and lived in the Bronx.

Mr. Pinero, who was born in Puerto Rico and grew up on the Lower East Side, started to write for the theater while serving time at the Ossining Correctional Facility (Sing Sing) for armed robbery. The result was *Short Eyes,* a searing portrayal of violent prison life, which started at the Theater of the Riverside Church, was transferred to the Public Theater by Joseph Papp, and then ran at the Vivian Beaumont Theater in Lincoln Center. *Short Eyes,* which won an Obie Award and the New York Drama Critics Circle Award as best American play in 1974, was later made into a film with a screenplay by Mr. Pinero under the direction of Robert Young.

"Miguel Pinero was the first Puerto Rican to really break

through and be accepted as a major writer for the stage," Mr. Papp said yesterday.

> He was an extraordinarily original talent, and he became a mentor and a hero for people like Reinaldo Povod, who wrote *Cuba and His Teddy Bear*. The fact that Miguel was successful made it possible for Ray to write. All over the Lower East Side, Miguel was considered someone who had broken through. But in addition to being a symbol, he was a first-class playwright.

Mr. Pinero's other works for the theater included *Straight From the Ghetto, Eulogy for a Small-Time Thief, The Sun Always Shines for the Cool* and *A Midnight Moon at the Greasy Spoon.*

His themes revolved around life on the mean streets he knew best, populated by drug addicts and con men, pimps and prostitutes. Drugs and crime were a persistent theme as well in Mr. Pinero's own life; he was arrested several times on drug and robbery charges.

Mr. Pinero, who also began performing while in prison, played the role of a Spanish-speaking drug dealer in the film *Fort Apache, the Bronx,* and appeared in *Breathless, Alphabet City, Exposed, Deal of the Century, Times Square, Streets of L.A.* and *Pick-Up Artist,* among other movies. His television appearances included roles in "Baretta," "Kojak" and "Miami Vice."

A published poet, Mr. Pinero was one of the founders of the so-called Nuyorican movement, a group of Puerto Rican New York poets, and he edited an anthology of their work called *Nuyorican Poetry.* At the time of his death, he was working on a play for the Public Theater called *Every Form of Refuge Has Its Price,* which was set in the intensive-care unit of a hospital.

> Leslie Bennetts, "Miguel Pinero, Whose Plays Dealt with Life in Prison, Is Dead at 41," in The New York Times, *June 18, 1988, p. 32.*

THE TIMES, LONDON

Miguel Pinero, Puerto Rican dramatist who wrote his first play in Sing-Sing, and had it put on by an ex-convict cast, died of cirrhosis of the liver in New York on June 17. He was 41.

Short Eyes, which was first performed when Pinero came out of gaol fifteen years ago, suggested that its author might prove to be the first Puerto Rican playwright to emerge as a major voice in the theatre, and this promise was confirmed by his subsequent output. . . .

Miguel Pinero was born in Puerto Rico but brought to New York when he was only four. He was brought up in the racial melting pot of Manhattan's Lower East Side, which offered few of its denizens the opportunity of a life of honest toil.

Streetwise from a tender age, Pinero grew up hustling in pool halls and jemmying fruit machines. He soon developed drug addiction, and took to mugging and drug pushing to support the habit. Eventually he received a gaol term in Sing Sing for his part in an armed robbery.

He began writing for the theatre, and with the members of a theatre workshop, known as The Family, which began life in the men's division of the Bedford Hills Correctional Facility in Westchester County, New York, staged *Short Eyes,* when he emerged from gaol.

The freshness of The Family's acting, combined with Pinero's gritty—and often witty—dialogue, gave the play immediate impact. This marked the beginning of a success story for Pinero—*Short Eyes* became a movie scripted by himself, while he wrote other plays, among them *Straight from the Ghetto,* and *Eulogy for a Smalltime Thief.*

Yet Pinero never managed completely to extricate himself from the crime-ridden background which had nurtured him, and had several more brushes with the law, though none led to actual incarceration.

> "Miguel Pinero: Playwright of the Penitentiary," in The Times, *London, June 21, 1988.*

MEL GUSSOW

In 1972 I visited the Ossining correctional Facility (Sing Sing) in order to write about theater in prisons. While I was there, the inmates presented an anthology of their own short plays, monologues and poems. Twelve of the 20 pieces were written by—and some of them were performed by—one inmate, Miguel Piñero.

It was immediately evident that he had a striking, raw talent, as he demonstrated in a poem he entitled **"Gospel."** In it, he brought God down to earth, announcing, "In the beginning God created the ghettos and slums. And God saw this was good. So God said let there be more." By the seventh day, his God was so tired he "called in sick" and collected overtime. This and other pieces by Mr. Piñero were marked by a bitter humor and a lilting kind of street poetry.

After the show, I spoke with the author. He said that he had started stealing when he was 8 in order to provide food for his siblings, and that he had spent 7 of his 25 years in prison. Sentenced most recently on a charge of second-degree robbery, he had written poetry in his cell and kept his artistic interest to himself. Then he joined Clay Stevenson's prison workshop where he was encouraged by, among others, Marvin Felix Camillo, an actor and director with the workshop. Mr. Piñero said that when he was released, he planned to go into the theater rather than back on the street.

After reading my subsequent article, Arthur Bartow, director of the Theater at the Riverside Church, contacted Mr. Piñero in prison and asked him if he were writing a full-length play. This began a cycle of events that led after the inmate's release, to the Riverside production of his play, *Short Eyes,* as directed by Mr. Camillo. Wrenched from the author's own experience, *Short Eyes,* a harrowing slice of prison life, was like a message from a combat zone. In my initial review, I commented on Mr. Piñero's originality and suggested that we would be anticipating and witnessing his work for many years to come. . . .

In 1974, *Short Eyes* went from Riverside to the Public Theater to the Vivian Beaumont Theater in Lincoln Center, deservedly won the New York Drama Critics Circle prize as best American play of the year and was subsequently made into a film. The success of the play transformed the playwright's life. He became famous while never losing his air of notoriety. Miguel—or Mikey as he was known to his friends—seemed to cherish his role as an outcast, playing it in real life as well as in movies and on television. As an actor, he appeared on such shows as "Miami Vice," often cast as a drug addict or pusher.

Even as he continued to win acclaim for his plays and his performances, he still had trouble with the law. I was in court the day that a judge dropped a charge against him for using obscene language to a subway attendant. The judge suggested that if he were abusive he should apologize because, as an artist, "other avenues of expression" were open to him, and added, "We're proud of you. You're a talented man."

Outside the courthouse, the Transit Authority officer who had made the arrest shook his hand and praised *Short Eyes*—one of many favorable reviews he was to receive in his lifetime. In a further twist of irony, while Robert Young was directing the film of *Short Eyes* on location in the Tombs, the playwright was being indicted in that same building on charges of grand larceny and possession of heroin.

As Piñero increasingly became a public personality, he seemed to divert his energies further away from playwriting, spending much of his time helping younger writers. But periodically he returned to the theater. Though none of his other plays measured up to *Short Eyes,* several demonstrated the vibrancy of his talent. *Eulogy for a Small-Time Thief, The Sun Always Shines for the Cool, A Midnight Moon at the Greasy Spoon*—his titles as well as his plays were redolent with authenticity. The most provocative was *Midnight Moon,* which treated the author's favorite subject, the underclass, with a lingering sense of hopefulness.

His life and work were recently celebrated in a memorial at the Public Theater, with relatives and fellow actors and writers paying homage. Joseph Papp, who presented *Short Eyes* at two of his theaters, said that Piñero was a man of a thousand faces—and before he died, he was wearing his writing face. He was working on a new play called *Every Form of Refuge Has Its Price.* The producer added that Mr. Piñero's effect on other playwrights was not to be underestimated.

Short Eyes was a breakthrough, not only in personal terms, but as a harbinger of the art that is coming from the Hispanic-American community. In that sense, it served a purpose not unlike that of John Osborne's *Look Back in Anger,* challeng-

ing theatrical tradition and preconceptions. *Short Eyes* opened the door to urban reality, and among those who entered was Reinaldo Povod, one of a number of emerging young artists who studied with Mr. Piñero.

The playwright never made a secret about his own problems. As he freely confessed in a poem. "A thief, a junkie I've been committed every known sin." But that poem also demonstrated a lingering idealism. It began:

> Just once before I die
> I want to climb up on a tenement sky
> to dream my lungs out till
> I cry
> then scatter my ashes out thru
> the lower East Side

Sadly, Mr. Piñero's death comes soon after the death of Marvin Felix Camillo. If Mikey was, by his own admission, "bad" (in the Michael Jackson sense), "Pancho" Camillo was good, even saintly, a man whose theater group, The Family, is an invaluable resource as a human reclamation project. As playwright and as director, each man went his individual way. The partnership that produced *Short Eyes* was dissolved. But each remained active within the community and both were devoted to former inmates and potential offenders who found that, through theater, they could make a creative contribution to society.

Thinking about Mikey, I remember the enthusiasm with which he greeted my review of *Short Eyes.* It was the first indication that his voice was reaching the outside world, that his message was being received. He telephoned me and vowed an oath of eternal friendship. With the authority of someone who had grown up on the streets, he added that if I ever needed protection, he would see that it was provided. More compassionate words were never said to a critic.

Miguel Piñero's death cuts short what could have been—what should have been—a remarkable career.

Mel Gussow, "From the City Streets, a Poet of the Stage," in The New York Times, *July 3, 1988, p. 8.*

Clifford D(onald) Simak

August 3, 1904 - April 25, 1988

American novelist, short story writer, nonfiction writer, journalist, editor, and author of children's books.

For an overview of Simak's life and work see *CLC,* Vol. 1; *Contemporary Authors,* Vols. 1-4, rev. ed., 125 (obituary); *Contemporary Authors New Revision Series,* Vol. 1; and *Dictionary of Literary Biography,* Vol. 8.

JACK WILLIAMSON

[*The letter excerpted below was written by Williamson in 1977 to congratulate Simak for having won the Science Fiction Writers Association's Grand Master Award.*]

I'm completely delighted that you are getting the Grand Master Nebula. . . .

You have earned the Nebula well. Looking back across your career, I see more high points than I can mention. I recall *The Cosmic Engineers,* in which you turned John Campbell's sort of super-science space opera into something even more thrilling.

I recall the stories about the Webster family which you combined to make the *City* series—one of the most memorable and most moving of all visions of future history.

I recall the special spell of **"Time Quarry"**, a master work that helped Horace Gold lead science fiction in another exciting new direction.

I recall many fine novels since, all of them notable for character, for mood, for a glow of good feeling. Your great achievement, I think, is the humane emotion you put into your work. If literature really shows us better ways to feel about ourselves and our world, you have given us fine ways of feeling about our future and our universe. . . .

You have been one of the great makers of science fiction because you are what you are.

The man shines through. Keep shining!

Jack Williamson, in a letter to Clifford Simak, in Locus, *Vol. 21, No. 7, July, 1988, p. 45.*

THE NEW YORK TIMES

Mr. Simak wrote more than two dozen novels, several nonfiction science books and hundreds of short stories during a 37-year career as reporter, news editor and science editor for *The Minneapolis Star* and *The Minneapolis Tribune.*

Among his better-known titles are *City,* published in 1952;

Way Station (1963); *The Visitors* (1979) and *Skirmish: the Great Short Fiction of Clifford D. Simak,* comprising stories he published from 1944 to 1975.

He received three Hugo awards, regarded as the Oscar of science-fiction writing, and three Science Fiction Association of America Nebula Awards, including the Grand National in recognition of his entire collection of work. He was inducted into the Science Fiction Hall of Fame in 1973. . . .

Many science-fiction writers wrote of invincible supermen, but Mr. Simak wrote about common people who didn't always win.

"I have tried at times to place humans in perspective against the vastness of universal time and space," he once said. "I have been concerned with where we, as a race, may be going and what may be our purpose in the universal scheme—if we have a purpose.

"In general, I believe we do, and perhaps an important one."

"Clifford D. Simak, 83, Journalist and Science-

Fiction Writer, Dies," in The New York Times, *April 28, 1988, p. D27.*

THE TIMES, LONDON

Simak, whose work was translated into a dozen languages, will be principally remembered for the story sequence *The City* (1952) on which his reputation rests. A chronicle in which dogs and robots take over a world which has been abandoned by men, it preaches Simak's characteristic message, that urban humanity is not best fitted to carry the torch of civilization.

Much of Simak's work is informed by a pastoral nostalgia which his rural upbringing had implanted in him. . . .

[Simak maintained a long association with *The Minneapolis Star*], writing a weekly science column for the paper.

While there, Simak developed a science programme for schools, called the Science Reading Series, which won an award from the Westinghouse-American Association for the Advancement of Science.

H. G. Wells and Jules Verne were early influences, and Simak started to publish science fiction stories in 1931. All his output was science fiction, with the exception of two science books for teenagers—*Our New Front Yard,* a description of the Solar System, and *Trilobite, Dinosaur and Man,* a popular account of historical geology.

The City (1952) had first appeared as a series in the magazine *Astounding Stories* in the 1940s, and is now regarded as a science fiction classic. Simak's literate, but fast-moving style made it readable as well as metaphysical, and it was a bestseller.

Other books, such as *Ring Around the Sun,* and *A Choice of Gods,* echo Simak's perennial themes, his moral sense, his dislike of urban life and his upholding the rights of the individual—even individual robots. Simak described his task as a sci-fi writer as being that of placing human beings "in perspective against the vastness of universal time and space".

"Clifford D. Simak," in The Times, *London, April 29, 1988.*

DON D'AMMASSA

Clifford Donald Simak was born in Milville, Wisconsin in 1904, a rural community whose values and interests led to his continuing enjoyment of fishing, raising roses, playing chess, and collecting stamps. Educated at the University of Wisconsin, where he majored in journalism, Simak became a reporter, and by the 1960's, news editor and columnist for the *Minneapolis Star.* He married and raised two children, wrote nonfiction for juvenile readers, and produced during his lifetime 30 novels and over 100 short stories.

His first sale was **"World of the Red Sun",** published in *Wonder Stories* in 1931. Simak appears to have lost interest in writing during the next several years, but perhaps inspired by the innovative new policies at *Astounding* under John W. Campbell Jr., he began to write again in the late 1930's. His work during the 1940's and early 1950's established him as a major voice in the field, with such excellent novels as *Time and Again* and *Ring Around the Sun.* Most significant of all

was the series of stories he collected as the episodic novel *City,* which concerned itself with the end of urban life and the evolution of humanity into a higher form as it expanded into the universe.

His work during the ensuing years was to include such outstanding novels as *Time is the Simplest Thing,* 1961, *Waystation,* 1963, *Why Call Them Back from Heaven,* 1967, *Goblin Reservation,* 1969, and *A Heritage of Stars,* 1977. He was perhaps even better known as a short story writer. Stories such as **"Desertion", "The Big Front Yard", "Good Night Mr. James", "Neighbor"** and **"The World That Couldn't Be"** remain among the most familiar and frequently reprinted in the genre.

Simak won the International Fantasy Award in 1953 for *City,* the Hugo for **"The Big Front Yard"** in 1959, another Hugo in 1964 for *Waystation,* was Guest of Honor at the 1971 World SF Convention, was elected to the First Fandom Hall of Fame in 1973, became a Grand Master of the SFWA in 1977, and won the Jupiter Award for *A Heritage of Stars* in 1978. Earlier this year the Horror Writers of America named him recipient of one of the first three Life Achievement Awards.

There was an air to Simak's fiction which made it unique, a way of looking at the world and seeing the good in people, avoiding the emphasis on violent conflict that has been so pervasive in SF through the years. Most of his fiction is overtly pastoral, reflecting his own youth, perhaps most obvious in the *City* sequence, but present in all his other fiction as well. Simak was able to express reservations about technology and a preference for human values even in the formative years of the field when such a point of view from any other writer would have raised readers' hackles. His robotic characters are probably more familiar to most fans than any others except those of Isaac Asimov.

For more than 50 years, Clifford Simak contributed new material to the field. Now that he is gone, one of the greatest and most human voices has been taken from among us. Nevertheless, the body of work that he leaves behind will continue to be read and work its magic on generations of readers yet to come. (pp. 10, 12)

Don D'Ammassa, in an obituary in Science Fiction Chronicle, *Vol. 9, No. 9, June, 1988, pp. 10, 12.*

ISAAC ASIMOV

[Clifford Simak] first came into my purview toward the end of 1931, when I was about to turn twelve. His first science fiction story, **"The World of the Red Sun",** appeared in the December 1931 *Wonder Stories.* I read it and loved it. The name of the author meant nothing to me at the time and I didn't find out it had been Cliff's story till nearly twenty years later when the Donald Day index was published. The story was one of my all-time favorites, and I distinctly remember sitting on the curb outside the school at luncheon and telling the story (as best I could remember it) to a small crowd of spellbound schoolmates.

Cliff published a few more stories, then dropped out, till Campbell became editor of *Astounding Science Fiction* and he at last had the kind of magazine he wanted to write for. His first story for Campbell was **"Rule 18"**, which appeared in the July, 1938 issue. I read it, but this one I didn't like.

In those days I wrote letters to Campbell after every issue commenting on each story with lofty critiques, and I told him how I disliked **"Rule 18"**. (I hate kids like that, but at the time I didn't know how it felt from the other side.)

Cliff, however, was a most unusual fellow. I greet snot-nose kid-critics with a strained smile and a kind of wistful longing for a blackjack, but Cliff wrote me a letter which reached me on September 1, 1938. It was a very polite and kind letter, asking me please to answer with a more detailed critique so that he could perhaps improve. To this day I know of no other case in which a writer has accepted unwarranted criticism so graciously. Certainly I've never done it.

And it *was* unwarranted. Cliff's letter took me completely aback and I rushed to re-read the story so that I could reply intelligently. (A snot-nose kid I was, but even then I had this vague ambition to be intelligent.) On the *second* reading, a slow and thoughtful one, I realized that I had been *wrong*.

The story was very good. What had misled me was that it was told in discrete scenes with no effort to fill in the cracks with a "Then, on the next day . . ." or "After some time had passed during which he read a book. . . ." It had confused me because I had not encountered it before in quite so pronounced a form. Once I understood what Cliff was doing, I realized how quickly the story moved and how valuable it was to remove the dead weight.

I replied with a heartfelt explanation, and a correspondence began between us with no feeling at all that he was sixteen years older than I was. He always wrote to me as though I were an equal—no condescension. He told me his difficulties and I told him mine, and we consoled each other. In those days I was just in the stage of trying to sell my own stories and I cannot describe how comforting it was to be on good and friendly terms with a "real" writer.

The correspondence dwindled with time as both of us got busier, but it never stopped completely. . . .

It was not till October 20, 1961 that I met Cliff face to face. We had lunch together. It was a most unusual experience. We had been writing each other for nearly a quarter of a century. (He had impinged on me thirty years before if we count **"The World of the Red Sun"**.) We kept staring at each other without talking, as though each of us was finding it hard to believe the other was real.

By that time, we were both major science fiction writers, of course, but he was still my mentor. No one, except John Campbell, was more important to me. After the **"Rule 18"** affair, I read Cliff's stories with particular attention, and I couldn't help but notice the simplicity and directness of the writing—the utter clarity of it.

I made up my mind to imitate it, and I labored over the years to make my writing simpler, clearer, more uncluttered, to present my scenes on a bare stage. It was hard work—it's not so simple to be "simple" or, as I was once told, it takes a great deal of art to seem artless.

People may have noticed this. At least, when Sprague de Camp's *Science Fiction Handbook* was published in 1953, he said, in discussing Cliff: "Simak's stories may be compared with Asimov's." So they might, but it's more correct to put

it the other way around. "Asimov's stories may be compared with Simak's." I *hope*. It was my wish and ambition to be so compared.

When I met my dear wife Janet, one of the first things I found out about her was that she was a science fiction reader and that I was her second favorite writer (in more or less of a tie with Arthur C. Clarke). Her undisputed *favorite* was Cliff Simak. It stayed that way, too. She has all his books and continues to re-read them. It gave me a great opinion of her excellent taste. . . .

And now Cliff is gone. He died on April 25, 1988 at the age of 83. Four months later, I would have phoned him to celebrate the fiftieth anniversary of that first letter of his. I will celebrate it anyway on September 1, 1988, toasting his spirit and remembering the man who, in the kindliest way possible, revolutionized my life. (p. 77)

> *Isaac Asimov, in an obituary in* Locus, *Vol. 21, No. 6, June, 1988, pp. 76-7.*

JAMES GUNN

Clifford Simak was the least likely person to be picked out of a group as a science fiction writer: quiet, retiring, slow-moving, slow-speaking, gentle. And yet he was one of the best of his generation, and perhaps of any generation, sitting off in his Minnesota reservation turning out stories and novels of suprising originality and tone. Like himself, his work was compassionate. Without Simak, science fiction would have been without its most humane element, its most humane spokesman for the wisdom of the ordinary person and the value of life lived close to the land. . . .

Science fiction and everyone who knew him can count themselves fortunate for having had Cliff Simak for nearly 84 years, and the gentle man with the outsized talent, who shrank from hurting anyone by anything he did or failed to do, has broken many hearts in science fiction this year.

> *James Gunn, in an obituary in* Locus, *Vol. 21, No. 6, June, 1988, p. 77.*

FAREN MILLER

It has been said that the golden age of science fiction is twelve. The connection of sf with the feverish curiosity, energy, and power hunger of adolescence may have become less direct in recent decades. So perhaps it is a fitting time for the rediscovery of Clifford D. Simak, sf's odd man out—a proponent of the wisdom and tolerance of mature humans, aliens, and civilizations at a time when many of his fellow writers concentrated on space war and interstellar empires.

To Simak, violence was not a necessary survival trait but a potentially fatal flaw in humanity. Appalled by the forces unleashed in World War II, he began to write the stories later gathered in his first major book, *City,* a future history/fable with a bleak vision of man and his works—all but the robots and genetically engineered dogs who would inherit Earth from wayward mankind.

Although Simak was well versed in science, writing a column on the subject for years and developing an award-winning program for teaching it in the schools, his fiction generally eschews high-tech hardware and hard science in favor of more intangible qualities: spirit as well as flesh, a vast community of living beings, the potential of understanding and spiritual contact with the primal forces of life.

Like Olaf Stapledon and sf's later mystics, Simak could dream on a grand scale. But he had an equal love for things small, close, apparently commonplace, from ladyslippers to snails, squirrels, and 'coon hounds. Noted as a regionalist and writer of "pastoral" science fiction (along with such contemporaries as Edgar Pangborn and Zenna Henderson), Simak wrote his most passionate work using scenes from his childhood: rugged rural Wisconsin, a land where the virtues of community and "good neighbors" could nurture a paradoxical isolation like that of Enoch Wallace, the unaging Civil War veteran hero of **Way Station.** Wallace's contact with alien travelers from all over the galaxy is wondrous indeed, but it does not dim his appreciation for the land, down to its smallest details. Such things are best measured in solitude. Like the great 19th-century romantics, his direct predecessors, Simak prefered in his fiction to avoid humanity in the mass, dreaming of unpopulated alternate worlds, human-free pasts, and nearly-deserted future Earths. Thoreau or Wordsworth would feel at home in his isolated houses rooted in natural landscapes.

Was Simak, then, more a survivor from the past than a dreamer of the future? To some extent—in the characteristic trappings of his work, rural and unpretentious. But, like Enoch Wallace, he stood grounded in an earlier time, a changeless place, only to look outward to a vast universe, complex and stupendous in its variety. No hidebound parochial imagination could cope with such a thing. Simak prized mental flexibility, toleration, decency, and keen intelligence as the primary traits needed for survival amid a community of worlds. Such a vision cannot be dismissed as the nostalgic idealism of a pastoral conservative. Simak's work focuses on the best in Earth and mankind, and offers them up in the service of all the worlds and times still to come.

Faren Miller, in an obituary in Locus, *Vol. 21, No. 7, July, 1988, p. 45.*

Topics in Literature: 1988

The Controversy Surrounding
In Search of J. D. Salinger

After two extensive revisions and two years of litigation, Ian Hamilton, a respected English poet, editor, critic, and biographer, published his controversial biography *In Search of J. D. Salinger* (1988). Salinger, the reclusive author of the widely acclaimed novel *The Catcher in the Rye* (1951), blocked publication of earlier versions of the work, objecting to Hamilton's extensive quoting and paraphrasing of letters he had written in his youth. Salinger has shunned publicity since the early 1950s and has not published since 1965. When Hamilton informed Salinger of his projected biography and requested an interview, the author replied that he could not endure further instrusions on his privacy and refused to aid the biographer. Hamilton attempted to placate his resistant subject by restricting his inquiries to those years when Salinger published his work, but dismissed Salinger's fundamental objection to the project. Although Salinger won the court case and limited Hamilton's sources for information, his efforts to preserve his privacy have been thwarted, for, as Phoebe Hoban observed: "[In] the course of this well-documented lawsuit, the public is learning more about Salinger than it has at any time during the last 34 years."

In the first version of the biography, *J. D. Salinger: A Writing Life,* scheduled to be published in the fall of 1986, Hamilton documented his interpretation of his subject's life and work by quoting and paraphrasing Salinger's correspondence, which he discovered while conducting research at various libraries in the United States. Hamilton relied on the "fair use" clause within copyright law that allows writers to quote or paraphrase a reasonable percentage of an author's work without that author's consent. In May of 1986, Salinger's lawyers threatened to sue Hamilton and his publisher, Random House, Inc., contending that the percentage of quoted material from the letters exceeded the terms of fair use. At his publisher's request, Hamilton's second version of the biography paraphrased all but approximately three hundred words from the letters. In September of 1986, he submitted the revised manuscript to Salinger's lawyers who proceeded with litigation, claiming that Hamilton's paraphrases appropriated the "expressive heart" of Salinger's original prose. After a lower court ruled against Salinger, a federal court of appeals reversed the decision in January of 1987, and publication of *J. D. Salinger: A Writing Life* was barred, a ruling upheld by the United States Supreme Court. The final version of Hamilton's biography, *In Search of J. D. Salinger,* neither quotes nor paraphrases Salinger's personal correspondence.

A central issue of this controversy concerns the question of whether an individual's right to privacy should supercede freedom of expression. Members of the academic and publishing communities fear that Salinger's victory has broadened the copyright law to encompass privacy, setting a legal precedent that could hinder the work of biographers, journalists, historians, and others who utilize the fair use clause.

Critical response to *In Search of J. D. Salinger* was mixed. While many commentators sympathized with Hamilton's legal problems, they also noted that his inability to cite Salinger's letters in the final manuscript inhibits the reader's capacity to corroborate his judgement. Judy Warner stated: "If it were possible to hear Salinger speak, it would be easier to judge whether some of Hamilton's conclusions . . . are anything more than distaste born from bitter hindsight." In his preface to *In Search of J. D. Salinger,* however, Hamilton reveals that the final version realizes his original conception of the book: "It would be a biography, yes, but it would also be a semispoof in which the biographer would play a leading, sometimes comic, role." Although some critics objected to Hamilton's humorous style, particularly his projection of two opposing selves who debate the ethics of pursuing a reluctant subject, Robert Folkenflik added: "All the same, . . . Hamilton has produced as highly readable and as literate an account of Salinger's work as we are likely to receive."

MICHELE FIELD

Shrinking from the public gaze as completely as J. D. Salinger has is a kind of tease. Someone who would ordinarily sigh and say that a life as uneventful as Salinger's does not, unfortunately, lend itself to biography may find an incentive in the very inaccessibility of the subject.

Ian Hamilton, the Englishman who has written this biography, called *J. D. Salinger: A Writing Life . . .* , says that his first inclination was to write a book in the *Quest for Corvo* mode, the story of a biographer in search of his subject rather than a straight life.

"I began to think how there were two sorts of stories," Hamilton said recently. "One would be what happened when one set out to write a book about somebody who didn't want a book written about him, what the limits would be, how far it would be proper to go. There would be questions to do with fame, how some embrace it Mailer-style and some carry it to the other extreme. The general issues would be so interesting that even if one couldn't have a mountain of material, the book would still be interesting to write."

In fact, the book which emerged is not preoccupied with general issues. It fleshes out, as much as scanty facts can, the simple chronology of Salinger's career.

Hamilton admits that "at first I honestly thought Salinger might be lured out of his silence." His hopes were too high, but in 1983 Hamilton's editor, Jason Epstein at Random House, agreed to back him up to a point. "It was a very generous arrangement where I had nine months to find out how much could be done, and it would then be reviewed and we would decide whether we should proceed. I think they were prepared to write off the money if we had to decide that it couldn't be done." . . .

The biographical ball began rolling as Hamilton tried to find out what Salinger had done since he stopped publishing in 1965. "I tried to find out what extraordinarily little could be known about someone as famous as that, in America.

"Then I saw not only how little there was but also how such a large part of what was 'known' was contradictory. In Salinger's later comments (in the public record) there is almost a flirtatious tone, he seemed to be almost teasing. It didn't fit with the idea of somebody who wanted nothing to do with his audience."

Hamilton was hooked. "I began to wonder just how much one could find out about someone without actually interfering with their lives. He was in the army and so on, but nobody seemed to know what he did in the army. After all, there are ways of finding out."

Hamilton first wrote to Salinger asking for his cooperation and received no reply. "There was a period of about a month when I thought I wasn't going to do it. But my friends said, 'Oh, don't be silly. There must be a way of doing it that wouldn't make you feel bad about doing it.' So I decided then to write only about the years in which he was actually publishing, 1935 to 1965—the years when he was offering himself to the public." . . .

When Hamilton came up against the question of whether Salinger has a right to be left alone, the answer was, "Well, as long as he wasn't publishing and putting himself in the public arena, then yes, he did have that right." The biographer lowers his gaze, therefore, at the first 15 years of Jerry Salinger's life and the last 20—describing only 30 years out of 65. "I had to do something I'd be able to defend. I wrote to him again and said, 'Yes, I [am] going to do it, but I don't think you'll have reason to be upset when it's done.' I never got any reply to that." (p. 63)

The honorable constraints that Hamilton had imposed upon himself did not make his task easier. He was amazed that everyone he contacted wrote back saying they wouldn't talk. "Many had made an undertaking to Salinger years ago, even 25 years ago. I think it had been made clear that they would no longer be his friends if they talked." William Shawn and Peter De Vries are two men whom Hamilton believes are still in touch with Salinger—"but how much in touch, I don't know."

The friends, however, though their lips were sealed, were courteous and friendly to Hamilton. "I didn't get *from them* the impression that this biography was something they didn't wish me to attempt." Hamilton felt that Salinger's friends didn't seem to believe that the man had anything to hide. "But since they'd agreed, they'd agreed. And that was that."

Hamilton must have often wondered whether Salinger was protecting his privacy in a broad sense, or whether he was protecting himself from a painful public revelation of some kind. Several times in the biography, Hamilton makes the point that Salinger was a "terrific liar," but there is really very little in his life that calls for such camouflage and discretion.

"One doesn't know about his embarrassment level," Hamilton admits. "He had a first marriage which lasted only three or four months. He may have been in army intelligence, he probably had some sort of nervous breakdown, and then half in desperation he married this girl and flew her back to the States. When eventually he married for a second time, he said on his marriage certificate that he hadn't been married before."

Hamilton declares that nothing has been omitted from the book, however, for fear of a libel suit. The self-censorship which Hamilton exercised was only in respect to his sources. "There are one or two people who did talk to me in the condition of the greatest confidentiality. Particularly one girl who spoke to me, I had the feeling that the conversation was taking place with Salinger's approval. It wasn't a particularly revealing conversation but it was useful: I could ask, 'Is this true?' and get a yes or no answer, which meant I could check everything."

The book, says Hamilton, is "as austere as possible." There are no photographs because Hamilton anticipated that Salinger would object. "I tried as far as possible to play along with his wishes."

One great source of information for Hamilton was the *Time* magazine archive. In 1961, *Time* (to use Hamilton's expression) "really did a job" on Salinger. The reporters spoke to his sister and intruded in a way that Hamilton wouldn't permit himself to do. But the *Time* files were a great boon to the biographer. . . . "Seeing that file was the first moment I realized that I would be able to tell the actual story of his life instead of the story of not finding out about his life." . . .

Ian Hamilton's one previous biography, *Robert Lowell*, published in 1982, was a picture of a man in the center of the literary establishment, at the opposite pole of American letters from Salinger. . . . Salinger, even with his enormous success, was hungry for a kind of recognition that Lowell almost took for granted. "I don't think Salinger wanted to be a different writer than the one he was, but he wanted to be approved. English departments were very hostile to him because he had won the loyalty of their students in a way that they themselves never could. When the time came to jump on Salinger, which was 1962-1963, they really jumped very hard. It was quite unpleasant." . . .

J. D. Salinger: A Writing Life is sure to stir debate as to whether this picture of such a controversial and curious figure as Salinger is not itself perhaps too tame. The thread throughout is the idea that everything Salinger wrote contains little signals about his own life, so as a biography this is almost an introduction to the full autobiography that emerges from Salinger's collected and uncollected short stories. The biographical picture is incomplete, particularly where money and family are concerned, and there is intriguingly little about an early trip to Europe, possibly as an apprentice to Polish relatives.

The picture might be clearer if Salinger's unpublished work comes to light. There is, according to Hamilton, a body of this. "People *have* seen it, but they are not prepared to say whether they've read it."

Although it does not obtrude on the book, Hamilton confesses that as he followed the course of Salinger's career he felt a slight horror for the American way of celebrity, "especially at the point where it starts affecting the way one writes. . . . In Salinger's case, he was just writing less well than he used to. He was *not* writing badly, but I think it made him decide: not ever again." At one point, Hamilton says, Salinger expressed a wish to have lived in 19th century London "where nobody would take any notice of me."

Hamilton has sympathy for that point of view, despite his own difficulties writing the life of the man who holds it. He sees Salinger in a double-bind. "Somebody who knows him reasonably well said to me that sometimes he might have quite liked to come out of hiding, but it's too late now. Whatever he would publish now would be treated with hostility. Sometimes, in my more hopeful moments, I think that maybe this biography will soak up a lot of that hostility. The perfect time for him to publish a new novel would be three months after this book of mine appears." (p. 64)

> Michele Field, "In Pursuit of J. D. Salinger," in *Publishers Weekly, Vol. 229, No. 26, June 27, 1986, pp. 63-4.*

PHOEBE HOBAN

[*The first portion of the essay excerpted below reproduces J. D. Salinger's responses to the questions of Robert Callagy, lawyer for the defense in the case of* Jerome D. Salinger, a.k.a. J. D. Salinger v. Random House, Inc., and Ian Hamilton, *October 7, 1986.*]

Mr. Salinger, when was the last time that you wrote any work of fiction for publication?

[Salinger]: I'm not sure exactly.

At any time during the past 20 years, have you written a work of fiction for publication?

That has been published, you mean?

That has been published.

No. . . .

At any time during the past 20 years, have you written any fiction which has not been published?

Yes.

Could you describe for me what works of fiction you have written which have not been published? . . ."

It would be very difficult to do. . . .

Have you written any full-length works of fiction during the past 20 years which have not been published?

Could you frame that a different way? What do you mean by a full-length work? You mean ready for publication?

As opposed to a short story or a fictional piece or a magazine submission.

It's very difficult to answer. I don't write that way. I just start writing fiction and see what happens to it.

Maybe an easier way to approach this is, would you tell me what your literary efforts have been in the field of fiction within the last 20 years?

Could I tell you or would I tell you? . . . Just a work of fiction. That's all. That's the only description I can really give it. . . . It's almost impossible to define. I work with characters, and as they develop, I just go on from there.

—J. D. Salinger to Robert Callagy, the lawyer for the defense in *Jerome D. Salinger, a.k.a. J. D. Salinger* v. *Random House, Inc., and Ian Hamilton* (October 7, 1986).

• • • • •

J. D. Salinger is impatient. At one point, he turns to his lawyer, Marcia B. Paul. "Do I really have to answer all these questions?" he asks. Salinger doesn't like answering questions about himself or his work. To avoid talking to strangers about just these subjects, he has spent the last 34 years in Cornish, New Hampshire, a tiny town in the heart of New England, where his post-office box, unlisted phone number, and protective friends ensure that his famous silence will go uninterrupted.

Now he's delivering the punch line to the ultimate literary joke: The invisible man of letters is going public to protect his privacy. He is not only answering the kind of questions he's structured his entire life to avoid, he's doing it on the record. . . .

To prevent Random House from publishing Ian Hamilton's unauthorized biography, *J. D. Salinger: A Writing Life,* Salinger is suing for copyright infringement. The suit claims that Hamilton, a respected literary critic, unlawfully quoted and paraphrased letters that Salinger wrote to friends and editors, who donated them to libraries. (According to copyright law, the recipient owns the letter but the author owns the words.) As a result of the litigation, Salinger not only testified but also had to register all 79 disputed letters at the Copyright Office, where any person willing to pay $10 can peruse them. (Salinger, who often uses fictional letters—particularly old, lovingly preserved ones—in his stories, should appreciate the irony.) . . .

At issue is the biographer's right to make "fair use" of unpublished material. Until now, limited quotation was allowed, and paraphrasing was safe. But Hamilton's synonymous prose, said the Second Circuit Court judges, crossed the boundary between capturing simple fact and borrowing the author's idiosyncratic expression.

Here's Salinger writing to his editor Whit Burnett in March 1943: "I can see them home evenings. Chaplin squatting grey and nude, atop his chiffonier, swinging his thyroid around his head by his bamboo cane, like a dead rat. Oona in an aquamarine gown, applauding madly from the bathroom."

Here's Hamilton: "He provides a pen portrait of the Happy Hour Chez Chaplin: the comedian, ancient and unclothed, is brandishing his walking stick—attached to the stick, and horribly resembling a lifeless rodent, is one of Chaplin's vital organs. Oona claps her hands in appreciation."

Hamilton, says Salinger in his affidavit, is "chiseling away at my property, while professing not to steal it."

In the course of this well-documented lawsuit, the public is learning more about Salinger than it has at any time during the last 34 years. And if the precedent-setting case is finally decided in favor of Salinger, the elusive author's influence on future biography, journalism, and nonfiction could prove as indelible as his mark on modern fiction. (p. 37)

Salinger may be the most widely read, least prolific author ever. He is still living off the royalties of just four slim volumes. *The Catcher in the Rye* has sold as many as 400,000 copies in a year. His *Nine Stories,* published in 1953, is in its thirty-first printing. And the sagas of Salinger's other fictional kin, the Glass family, have acquired a cultlike following. The Glass siblings Seymour, Buddy, Franny, and Zooey became, like Holden, kindred spirits to a huge reading public. In 1961, when *Franny and Zooey* was published, *Time* put Salinger on the cover and *Life* proclaimed it the literary event of the year. His last published book, *Raise High the Roof Beam, Carpenters and Seymour—An Introduction,* came out in 1963.

Salinger's secluded way of life is as mythical as his work. Since 1953, he has lived on 99 acres at the top of a hill with a view of five states. Legions of literary pilgrims have trekked up the mountainside to visit the master; they find him entrenched behind a forbidding fence that shields a chalet-style house with a sun deck, connected by a tunnel to his cement-block, skylit writing room. Sometimes, persistent interlopers get a few grudging, heartfelt words and leave, feeling transcendent. Salinger's silence is contagious: The locals won't talk. . . .

Salinger is hardly a hermit: He sees a small, fiercely loyal circle of friends and doesn't lack for the company of women. He has published nothing since "Hapworth 16, 1924," a story in the form of a 50-page letter that appeared in *The New Yorker* in 1965, an issue that quickly became a collector's item. According to some sources, he has two manuscripts locked in a safe and has submitted at least one work to *The New Yorker* within the last six years. . . .

It's been 36 years since [the publisher] Little, Brown first printed Salinger's book-size picture on the back cover of *The*

Catcher in the Rye. Salinger later insisted that the photograph be removed. In those days, he looked like "a dark-eyed Jimmy Stewart," one former woman friend recalls. "He had these very paranoid eyes. He was very gawky, very thin."

Solitude seems to have agreed with him: The 68-year-old author is remarkably well preserved, though somewhat deaf. "Salinger stands very erect, about six feet tall," says Robert M. Callagy, a lawyer representing Random House. "He is graying, with stark features. He is well dressed, and appears quite athletic. He comes across more as a businessman than an author. He sort of objected to the fact that he had to be questioned at all." . . .

Salinger's obsession is to preserve his privacy at all costs. "It has always been a most terrible and almost unassimilable wonder to me that it is evidently quite lawful . . . to break into the privacy not only of a person not reasonably suspected of criminal activity but into the lives as well, however glancingly, of that person's relatives and friends," wrote Salinger to Ian Hamilton in 1983. "Speaking (as you may have gathered) from rather unspeakably bitter experience, I suppose I can't put you or Random House off . . . but I do feel I must tell you, for what very little it may be worth, that I think I've borne all the exploitation and loss of privacy I can possibly bear in a single lifetime."

Jason Epstein, Hamilton's editor at Random House, replied: "Though you have chosen to live obscurely, your works are widely known. One could argue in reply that a writer's life is his own business and has nothing to do with his books. . . . The fact is that literary biography is a legitimate pursuit for a writer and you are a legitimate subject."

Even before Salinger deposited his letters at the Copyright Office, an assiduous researcher could find an encyclopedic amount of written information. . . .

By sifting through this mass of Salingeriana, it is possible to draw a surprisingly detailed portrait of the artist as a young man. (p. 38)

[Up to 1940], Salinger's life is more or less neatly laid out in newsprint. But his letters provide insight into the life of the author from 1940 on. Many of the originals remain where Hamilton first scrutinized them, in permanent library collections. But five neat packets of photocopied letters are now on file at the Copyright Office on the fourth floor of the Madison Building of the Library of Congress, where I read them in March.

The letters cover the thirties to the sixties. Sometimes typewritten, sometimes penned in a neat, though urgent, hand, some on military stationery, some on postcards, they reveal a self-deprecatory, ambitious, droll, hypersensitive author. For a Salinger fan, reading them is almost as good as reading Seymour's diary.

They catalogue his writing—from his earliest stories to his first attempts at creating Holden to his deepening interest in Eastern religion. They chronicle his romances, his two marriages, the birth of his two children, and his increasing desire for privacy. Perhaps even more interesting, they parallel the lives and loves of the characters in his fiction, making a little more legible the line where Salinger leaves off and the Caulfields and Glasses begin.

From the outset, Salinger portrayed himself as a loner. In a letter dated November 21, 1939, to Whit Burnett, he admitted he had "complexes, inhibitions and yet strange egos." In an autobiographical note sent to *Story* magazine in January, he described himself as "alternately cynical and Polyanna-like, happy and morose, affectionate and indifferent."

His early letters sound like, well, Holden. He called himself a "kid," was "knocked out" by things or "crazy about" them. Romantic interests were "flashes" and "little numbers," and the magazines he sent his stories to were "slicks." The young author spent part of 1940 hanging out at his parents' Park Avenue apartment, playing records, drinking beer, going to plays, much like the young man in "Just Before the War With the Eskimos." But writing already dominated his life; his letters were mostly about the stories he was working on. (p. 39)

Ian Hamilton got the idea of writing a biography of Salinger in 1982. His credentials are impeccable. The founder of a literary magazine at Oxford, he was the poetry and fiction editor of *The Times Literary Supplement*. His most recent book is a highly acclaimed biography of the poet Robert Lowell. The Lowell book, however, had the family's approval. Nothing could have prepared Hamilton for the battle he would encounter with Salinger.

Hamilton, who got a $100,000 advance for the book, spent more than two years and $50,000 on research. He contacted about 60 people who knew Salinger. He visited Salinger's schools and wrote to his former classmates. He exhausted the *Time* archives. He even interviewed Salinger's agent, Dorothy Olding, unbeknownst to Salinger. But he didn't make much of a dent in the Salinger armor. Then he came across a reference book that identified collections of Salinger letters. Reading the letters was a little like talking to the young Salinger. Hamilton incorporated many of the more memorable quotations into his manuscript. By May 1986, Random House had sent about 60 copies of the uncorrected proofs to reviewers. Publication was set for August.

Olding got a copy of the proofs from a bookdealer named Bev Chaney and sent them to Salinger. On May 30, Salinger's lawyers sent a letter to Random House asserting that Hamilton's quotations exceeded "fair use." To avoid a lawsuit, Random House asked Hamilton to revise his biography, replacing the direct quotations with paraphrases. In September, Hamilton's revision was submitted to Salinger's lawyers, who said that Salinger would sue unless all references to the letters were deleted.

In his October affidavit, Salinger complained: "I refuse to believe that an author such as Hamilton, with a clever lawyer at his side, can rob me of [my] right by using the guts of what I wrote so many years ago, with a few cosmetic changes, to flesh out an otherwise lifeless and uninteresting biography." Salinger is suing for an injunction and monetary damages arising from copyright infringement, breach of contract as a third-party beneficiary (referring to Hamilton's agreements with the libraries that had the letters), and unfair competition.

The lawsuit has gone through nearly as many revisions as the sainthood of Seymour Glass. [In May, 1987], Judges Jon Newman and Roger J. Miner, of the U.S. Court of Appeals for the Second Circuit, reaffirmed their January ruling to enjoin the book because it infringes on Salinger's copyright. Salinger asserts that quotations and paraphrases from his letters made up more than 41 percent of the 190-page biography. Says Callagy, "If you take this opinion to an extreme, what it says is that you can't quote anything that has not been pub-

lished before, and if you attempt to paraphrase, you are at serious peril. Copyright law was created to protect an author in a property right, not to permit an author to obliterate the past." Random House claims that the biography contains only about 200 to 300 words drawn from the letters.

The publishing community is already reacting. One editor calls the ruling chilling: "We are in the process of doing two biographies. This decision is crippling." Harriette Dorsen, of Lankenau Kovner & Bickford, suggests an insidious scenario: A news reporter discovers Oliver North's private diary, but can neither quote nor paraphrase from it because it is unpublished.

Salinger is fighting for a right that many writers would rather not have—the right not to publish. And it looks as if he might have the last word. The situation has all the familiar elements of a Salinger short story. The saintlike writer, whose letters are sacramental, is finally pitted against his archenemy, the literary academic, the "section man" debunked in *Franny and Zooey*. "Phooey, I say, on all white-shoe college boys who edit their campus literary magazines," he wrote. "Give me an honest con man any day."

You'd think Salinger would understand the lure of letters. "Zooey" starts off with one from Buddy: "The letter itself was virtually endless in length, overwritten, teaching, repetitious, opinionated, remonstrative, condescending, embarrassing—and filled, to a surfeit, with affection. In short, it was exactly the kind of letter that a recipient, whether he wants to or not, carries around for some time in his hip pocket. And that professional writers of a type love to reproduce verbatim." (p. 42)

Phoebe Hoban, "The Salinger File," in New York Magazine, *Vol. 20, No. 24, June 15, 1987, pp. 36-42.*

DAVID MARGOLICK

In the past 20 years, J. D. Salinger has undoubtedly become the most famous—as well as the most read—recluse in the world. He has rarely been sighted in public, has not given an interview since 1953 and, although he continues to write fiction, hasn't published any of it since a short story appeared in *The New Yorker* in 1965. But even in his obsession with privacy, the author of *The Catcher in the Rye* continues to exert a profound influence on American letters. [In October, 1987] the Supreme Court upheld (by refusing to review) a Federal appeals court decision that barred the publication of an unauthorized biography of him. The appeals court had held that by quoting from, and paraphrasing, large portions of his unpublished letters the British literary critic Ian Hamilton had effectively appropriated Mr. Salinger's work.

It was an extraordinary decision, the first time in American memory that a book had been enjoined prior to publication, and it sent shock waves throughout the academic and publishing communities. When Mr. Hamilton and his publisher, Random House, appealed to the Supreme Court, they were joined by the Association of American Publishers, the Organization of American Historians and a group of authors that included John Hersey, A. E. Hotchner and Justin Kaplan.

Now Mr. Hamilton and his publisher must decide what to do about *J. D. Salinger: A Writing Life*—withdraw it, modify it (for a second time) or continue the fight to publish it as is. In the meantime, publishing industry officials, scholars and legal experts are trying to figure out precisely what the case means—and what chilling effect, if any, it will have on scholarly research and free expression.

Critics of the decision claim that Mr. Salinger is twisting the copyright law to protect his privacy—that by virtually eradicating the so-called fair use of unpublished materials, the case could inhibit historians and biographers from quoting primary sources. Simply as a matter of self-protection, some publishers' lawyers say they must now scrutinize manuscripts closely for anything that is arguably infringing on copyright, despite the fact that the language of the appeals court decision, particularly regarding what constitutes permissible paraphrasing, is, to them, alarmingly vague. (pp. 1, 44)

The spillover from the Salinger case, these critics say, can already be discerned in another ruling by Federal District Judge Pierre N. Leval, the man whose decision to permit publication of Mr. Hamilton's book was overruled by the appeals court. Three months ago, Judge Leval barred publication of a new biography of Igor Stravinsky by John Kobler on the ground that it relied too heavily on copyrighted materials by Stravinsky and Robert Craft, his collaborator and confidant. There are distinctions between the two cases. But coming so quickly on the heels of the Salinger decision, the Stravinsky injunction raised concerns that the ever-precarious balance between two fundamental and at times contradictory parts of the Constitution—the copyright clause and the First Amendment—may now be tipping against free speech.

Mr. Salinger's lawyers insist there is nothing ominous in the ruling. They maintain that an author, too, has First Amendment rights, including a right *not* to speak. "This decision is going to encourage people to write, knowing that they're going to be protected from having that writing wrested from them before they're ready or against their will," said Marcia B. Paul, one of Mr. Salinger's lawyers. "This is a case of plagiarism, and it isn't even a close case. Salinger created something, and now somebody else is taking his creation and profiting from it. That's not allowed."

The legal implications of the Salinger case constitute only one element of its newsworthiness. For in order to protect his privacy, Mr. Salinger necessarily had to sacrifice a small bit of it. A year ago, he slipped into New York to be questioned by lawyers for Random House and Mr. Hamilton—in a sense, the first real interview he'd granted since two high school students questioned him nearly 35 years ago for the local newspaper in Cornish, N.H., the town to which he repaired in the early 1950's and has only rarely left since. For six hours the attorneys interrogated him not only about his letters, but also his life.

At Mr. Salinger's insistence, large portions of the deposition remain under court seal. Indeed, when Judge Leval issued the initial decision in the case, the author tried to seal that too. But in the portion that was released, Mr. Salinger disclosed some information he has managed to withhold for 30 years. Among other things . . . , he explained what he thought he stood to gain were he to prevail in court. "I'll retain a very important sense of privacy, of property that I really believe is mine," he said. "Privacy is privacy. Letters were meant for a certain pair of eyes and those eyes alone."

Certain underlying issues in the Salinger case were never in dispute. Courts have long adhered to the somewhat curious notion that while the paper on which a letter is written belongs to the recipient, its content remains the property of the sender and can be copyrighted. Or, more accurately, certain parts of it can be copyrighted. The law states that only that material that reflects a writer's expression can be protected; ideas and facts cannot. The law also recognizes that there are more ways to misappropriate a writer's expression than by direct quotation; it can be done by paraphrasing, if the paraphrase tracks the original too slavishly. "The copyright covers not only the actual sequence of words used, but any equivalent expression which gives substantially the same impression to the mind as the author's words," according to a 1919 opinion by Judge Learned Hand, a man to whom, coincidentally, Mr. Salinger sent several of the letters at issue in this case. Moreover, even where material can be copyrighted, an additional safety valve is furnished by the concept of fair use, which permits a writer to use otherwise protected material in a reasonable manner without an author's consent.

But within these principles there is considerable ambiguity. How can one differentiate between facts and expression, particularly when one is contained in the other? How much expression must be leached from a phrase before it ceases to belong to a writer? Should the law protect the copyright of unpublished letters, which may never be printed, as scrupulously as it does manuscripts on the eve of their release? And what do the terms "unpublished" and "undisseminated" really mean and can they realistically be applied to letters available to scholars in university libraries and to anyone at all in the Library of Congress (where copies of Mr. Salinger's now copyrighted letters reside)?

Each of these questions had to be addressed in the Salinger case. Before issuing his opinion, Judge Leval read and color-coded Mr. Hamilton's book, marking quotations he deemed to infringe on Mr. Salinger's copyright in red, infringing paraphrases in yellow, noncopyrightable material in orange and facts and clichés, also noncopyrightable, in green and blue respectively. He concluded that the vast majority of what Mr. Hamilton used wasn't expression at all but information. Such information, he explained, "includes far more than the where, when and with whom." He continued: "Information as to the subject's thoughts and feelings is vital historical fact for the biographer and belongs in the unprotected categories, so long as the biographer does not overstep permissible limits by taking the author's craftsmanship."

Even unpublished materials, Judge Leval said, are subject to some fair use, and he went on to assess whether Mr. Hamilton's use was indeed fair. While admittedly a money-making venture, the judge wrote, the book was not merely "an act of commercial voyeurism or snooping into a private being's private life for commercial gain." Nor was this an instance where a "gun-jumping publication . . . pirated 'the heart' of the copyrighted work. . . . The wound [Mr. Salinger] has suffered is not from infringement of his copyright but from the publication of a biography that trespasses on his wish for privacy. The copyright law does not give him protection against that form of injury."

But in his 20-page opinion, Judge Jon O. Newman of the United States Court of Appeals for the Second Circuit saw things differently. Whether lifted verbatim or paraphrased, he wrote for himself and Judge Roger Miner, much of what Mr. Hamilton had used remained laden with Mr. Salinger's literary devices—to such an extent that they were in large part what made the book worth reading. Facts could be reported. "But Salinger," the judge wrote, "has a right to protect the expressive content of his unpublished writings."

Judge Newman rejected the notion that the letters had some-how ceased to be unpublished because they were available in libraries. And since they were unpublished, he ruled, there could be little question of fair use—a proposition established in the 1985 case that pitted Harper & Row against *The Nation* magazine.

In that case, the Supreme Court held that *The Nation* had violated Federal copyright laws by printing excerpts from former President Ford's soon-to-be-published memoirs. "Under ordinary circumstances," the Court ruled, "the author's right to control the first public appearance of his undisseminated expression will outweigh a claim of fair use." The publishing industry pressed for—and applauded—the decision against *The Nation.* Publishers saw it as a way to protect manuscripts from 11th-hour pirating. An irony of the Salinger decision is that the very precedent publishers sought in the *Nation* case became the linchpin of a ruling against them.

Publishing industry spokesmen are quick to point out the distinctions between the *Nation* case and Mr. Salinger's. The former, they note, concerned a purloined manuscript of an upcoming book; the latter involved letters already available to scholars, letters that Mr. Salinger, by his own admission, had no intention of publishing. (Indeed, his agent admitted destroying over 500 letters.) There are, nonetheless, those in the publishing community who feel some off-the-record sympathy for Mr. Salinger. Those who have read the few circulating galley proofs of Mr. Hamilton's biography note that portions of the book do indeed seem based on little else but Mr. Salinger's letters—a degree of dependence that, they argue, lawyers and editors at Random House surely should have spotted. They note, too, that in a less competitive era, an industry that depends ultimately on creative, if eccentric, personalities would have chosen to leave one of its own alone.

Indeed, to some, Mr. Salinger's uniqueness provides the greatest assurance that the impact of the case might be slight. "My best hope is that the case is distinguishable because of the plaintiff in the case—that because Salinger is such an important writer and his words have so high a potential cash value, the court has adopted a more limited reading of fair use," said Stanley Katz, a legal historian and president of the American Council of Learned Societies. "If the case is read in that way, it will have much less impact on scholarship. But that opinion can be read to cover a lot more than the recluses of the world, and if it is, it could badly inhibit the work of professional historians and other academic researchers." (pp. 44-5)

[Salinger's] letters were pithy and pungent, replete with reflections on World War II, women, politics, the literary scene and other topics. At least dimly aware of potential copyright concerns, Mr. Hamilton tried to limit the number of direct quotes he took and used no more than a third of any given letter. Nonetheless, the manuscript he submitted to Random House in late 1985 was heavily dependent on them. Indeed, so completely had Mr. Salinger papered over his past that entire chapters of the biography were based on nothing else. None of the required permissions had been obtained before the galley proofs were made, though Random House claims that this is not unusual.

In May 1986, Random House sent out review copies of the galleys of Mr. Hamilton's book. Aware that they were circulating, Dorothy Olding asked a well-connected book dealer friend to obtain a copy, which she promptly sent to Mr. Salin-

ger. Only then, apparently, did he realize that his old letters still existed. Quickly, his attorneys not only copyrighted 79 letters, but demanded that anything taken from them be deleted from Mr. Hamilton's book. Mr. Hamilton, intent on making the work more acceptable and fending off a lawsuit, reluctantly attempted to comply, boiling away Mr. Salinger's distinctive style and substituting his own more pallid, reconstituted alternatives.

Keeping the new version from becoming, as he put it, "pedestrian," was not always easy. "He is a very contagious writer," Mr. Hamilton later explained in a deposition. "His tone is infectious. His turns of phrase are memorable and hard to dislodge from the mind." Thus where Mr. Salinger wrote, "I suspect that money is a far greater distraction for the artist than hunger," Mr. Hamilton paraphrased: "Money, on the other hand, is a serious obstacle to creativity." Explaining why he used the initials J. D., Mr. Salinger wrote that Jerome "always sounds so much like Jerome." Mr. Hamilton reworked that tidbit as follows: "Jerome was such a dreadful name: however, you said it, Jerome always came out sounding like Jerome."

Mr. Salinger once complained about an editor who had rejected one of his stories but had called it a "competent handling." "Like saying, She's a beautiful girl, except for her face," Mr. Salinger wrote. Mr. Hamilton paraphrased him: "How would a girl feel if you told her she was stunning to look at but that facially there was something not quite right about her." And commenting on the warmth Parisians felt toward Americans after the liberation of Paris during World War II, Mr. Salinger wrote that they would have said, " 'What a charming custom!' " if "we had stood on top of the jeep and. . . ." In paraphrasing, Mr. Hamilton uses polite language: if "the conquerors had chosen to urinate from the roofs of their vehicles."

In the end, Mr. Hamilton reduced the direct quotations to roughly 200 words, or an average of just under 4 words from each of the some 70 letters he used. But the paraphrases did not mollify Mr. Salinger. Claiming that the book still contained extensive expressions of his "private opinions, philosophies, fantasies, criticisms and thought processes," he took Random House and Mr. Hamilton to court [in 1986]. Judge Leval barred release of the book, pending hearings. (p. 45)

David Margolick, "Whose Words Are They, Anyway?" in The New York Times Book Review, *November 1, 1987, pp. 1, 44-5.*

RHODA KOENIG

When Ian Hamilton, at seventeen, discovered *The Catcher in the Rye,* he was enthralled by the freshness, the honesty of it, the realization "that literature can speak *for* you, not just to you." As the reading public knows . . . , Hamilton has had reason to feel less than adoring about his former hero. His biography [*In Search of J. D. Salinger*], written without J. D. Salinger's cooperation and scheduled to appear nearly two years ago, has been not only delayed but severely altered as a result of the novelist's successful claim of copyright infringement. . . . (pp. 93-4)

Hamilton has tried to compensate for Salinger's evisceration of his work by casting himself as the schizophrenic hero of a quest: his own moral, scrupulous self and his alter ego, the relentless biographer. This is a dismal failure. The colloquies between these two, with Hamilton referring to "my companion" as frequently and archly as a restaurant reviewer (couldn't he at least have chatted with the herring maven or She Who Must Be Obeyed?), are just the sort of cutesy quaintness that Holden Caulfield despised.

In an orgy of self-dramatization, Hamilton says,

> Salinger had worked as a meat packer in Poland during the 1930s. Would it not make a readable adventure if some zealous biographer figure was to be seen trudging around the markets of Bydgoszcz 'making inquiries' about a sulky-looking young American who had worked there for a week or so some fifty years before? Although this particular sortie was not actually on my agenda, the book I had in mind would, I conjectured, be full of such delights.

I guess his friends chuckled when he tried it out on them.

The thin and fragmented story Hamilton tells is, not surprisingly, the less than compelling one of a man who never led an active life and has been a recluse for more than 30 years. For all his trouble, Hamilton is reduced to telling us that some of Salinger's classmates and Army buddies liked him, while others did not. A search through the *Time* archives reveals that his sister, Doris, when approached, said, "Why don't you leave us alone." A refusal of access to *The New Yorker*'s files means "we cannot know what was done" to his fiction. "We can guess. . . ."

From an account of a married woman who met Salinger at a party in 1952—he asked her to elope the same evening, then ranted for hours about the twelve stages of enlightenment—it is clear that the novelist could not cope with social life, certainly not the Manhattan variety. But he has had sufficient charm, or at least sincerity, to win the loyal silence of two ex-wives, as well as a band of neighbors, an impressive record in our slip-shod, chattering age. If he prefers a life of solitude, isn't he entitled to it? Hamilton's wispy book only convinces us even more that he does. (p. 94)

> *Rhoda Koenig, "Search and Destroy," in* New York Magazine, *Vol. 21, No. 21, May 23, 1988, pp. 93-4.*

MORDECAI RICHLER

Ian Hamilton's *In Search of J. D. Salinger* raises many questions larger than the legal tangle that delayed the book's publication for two years, about which more later.

For openers, beyond a taste for gossip (a taste I admittedly share), I fail to understand what I take to be a burgeoning curiosity about writers' lives. I find the biographies of politicians, tycoons and other con men great fun because their art *is* their lives, but with a few exceptions (most recently Richard Ellmann's *Oscar Wilde*) the lives of writers strike me as boring. This, of course, is just as it should be because it is their fiction that is charged with incident and invention while their lives, in the nature of things, tend to be uneventful. I wouldn't go quite so far as the publisher Colin Haycraft, who wrote in *The London Sunday Telegraph,* "The world is a peculiar place, but it has nothing on the world of books. This is largely a fantasy world, in which the pecking order goes as follows: if you can't cope with life, write about it; if you can't write, publish."

But the truth is that most novelists start out by retreating into

a cave with a ream of blank paper and when they totter out with a finished manuscript they are two, maybe three years older and have missed out on an awful lot. As a rule, embarrassingly little beyond the ordinary (marital messes, losing battles with booze and tobacco and the I.R.S., spats with other writers and publishers) has happened off the page. Take J. D. Salinger, for instance. According to a neighbor, he is said to rise at 5 or 6 A.M. in his home in Cornish, N.H., and then walk "down the hill to his studio, a tiny concrete shelter with a translucent plastic roof," and spend 15 or 16 hours at his typewriter. Later he may watch one of his vast collection of 1940's movies. Hardly the stuff of drama. . . .

In the opening pages of [*In Search of J. D. Salinger*], Ian Hamilton writes, "I had it in mind to attempt not a conventional biography—that would have been impossible—but a kind of *Quest for Corvo,* with Salinger as quarry." The analogy won't wash. A. J. A. Symons' book *The Quest for Corvo,* a fine and original work, happens to be about a literary scoundrel, Frederick Rolfe, a bizarre character whose squalid life was more fascinating than anything he wrote, while the obverse is true of J. D. Salinger, of whom Mr. Hamilton justifiably observes, "The action, for [him], was on the page."

There is another problem. Symons undertook his quest in 1925, 12 years after Rolfe's death, but Mr. Salinger, happily, is still among the quick. At the risk of sounding stuffy, I think it indecently hasty to undertake a biography-cum-critical study of a still working writer and in highly questionable taste to pronounce him a perfect subject because, in Mr. Hamilton's view, "he was, in any real-life sense, invisible, as good as dead." Invisible? Look here, we are talking about a writer whose only published novel, *The Catcher in the Rye,* which first appeared in 1951, was declared in 1968 to be one of America's 25 leading best sellers since the year 1895 and still sells something like a quarter of a million copies annually worldwide.

Ian Hamilton, to be fair, is not a vulgarian: he has good credentials as a biographer, poet and critic. In the first chapter of *In Search of J. D. Salinger,* he declares that he will confine himself to the years the author's life was in the public domain, that is to say, until 1965, when he last published. But Mr. Salinger, in a court deposition made in an attempt to restrain publication of Mr. Hamilton's book, revealed that he has been hard at it all these years, still writing, and so he is far from as good as dead. If and when he does publish again, he could astound us as he once did with *The Catcher in the Rye.*

Ian Hamilton first read *The Catcher in the Rye* when he was 17 years old. Discouraged from undertaking this biography by Mr. Salinger, Mr. Salinger's family and friends, he writes,

> when I really ask myself how this whole thing began, I have to confess that there was more to it than mere literary whimsy. There was more to it than mere scholarship. Although it will seem ludicrous, perhaps, to hear me say so now, I think the sharpest spur was an infatuation, an infatuation that bowled me over at the age of seventeen and which it seems I never properly outgrew. Well, I've outgrown it now.

Outgrown it, alas, by composing a biography that is at best unfriendly, at worst hostile. The 21-year-old Mr. Salinger's letters to Whit Burnett of *Story* magazine are described, for example, as "too garrulously self-promoting . . . mock-boastful, and, now and then, plain boastful." In January 1940, once Burnett had accepted the young writer's first story, we are told that for Mr. Salinger this was a way of showing Them. "To judge from his letters . . . he was fairly buzzing with self-admiration and not at all disposed to keep quiet about it." But an examination of these letters, as quoted in the original version of **Salinger** but excised from the published book, shows no such thing. They are, in fact, exuberant, self-deprecating and charged with hope.

After Burnett had accepted Mr. Salinger's first short story, we learn in these letters, he wrote to the editor:

> I'm twenty one. New York born, and I can draw a rejection slip with both hands tied behind me. Writing has been important to me since I was seventeen. I could show you a lot of nice faces I've stepped on to illustrate the point. Now that you've accepted the story I'll tell everyone to waste no pity on the unpublished short story writer, that his ego can cope with people and circumstance, that he is his own worst enemy. Oh, I'll be wisdom itself.
>
> (p. 7)

The letters are also, as Mr. Salinger noted with hindsight in court, occasionally gauche or effusive. "It's very difficult," he said. "I wish . . . you could read letters you wrote 46 years ago. It's very painful reading."

Yes, possibly. But Mr. Salinger would have been better served if he had allowed his letters to be quoted rather than described so vindictively. On the other hand, Mr. Hamilton's hostility is understandable. He has been through a good deal. The first judge to hear the case ruled in the biographer's favor:

> Hamilton's book cannot be dismissed as an act of commercial voyeurism or snooping into a private being's private life for commercial gain. It is a serious, well-researched history of a man who through his own literary accomplishments has become a figure of enormous public interest. This favors a finding of fair use.

But on Jan. 29, 1987, the United States Court of Appeals for the Second Circuit reversed the earlier judgment. Mr. Hamilton could not quote from the letters he had discovered in the Firestone Library at Princeton University and elsewhere. (pp. 7, 48-9)

In its present unfortunately truncated form, Ian Hamilton's biography does not turn up much that is new and does turn up a good deal that is neither here nor there. We are told, for instance, that the name Holden Caulfield probably came from joining the name of a boyhood friend called Holden to that of the movie actress Joan Caulfield, on whom Mr. Salinger once had a crush. J. D., we also learn, was bad at arithmetic. "A private for most of his time at Valley Forge [Military Academy]," Mr. Hamilton tells us, "he was promoted in time to appear as corporal in the yearbook. Academically, he did enough to graduate: 88 in English, 84 in German, 83 in French, and 79 in modern European history."

Mr. Hamilton's biography is tainted by a nastiness born of frustration perhaps, but hardly excused by it. Mr. Salinger is never given the benefit of a doubt. He is described as a "callow self-advancer." Aged 22, we are told, "the Salinger we were on the track of was surely getting less and less lovably Holdenish each day. So far, our eavesdropping had yielded

almost nothing in the way of human frailty or warmth. The first-person voice we'd been so pleased to come across had spent most of its time boasting or pushing its career."

This vengeful book is also marred by Mr. Hamilton's coy, tiresome device of splitting himself in two, as it were, referring to Mr. Salinger's biographer in the third person. ("I was already thinking of 'him' as somehow separate from 'me.' ") This, in turn, allows the use of the royal we, as in the opening of chapter three: "We traveled back from Valley Forge to New York feeling triumphant. Look at what had been amassed, so far: Salinger's school records, some telling items of juvenilia. . . . And, sure enough, my companion now had a smug, workmanlike look about him. . . . He'd done his job. He had his Chapter I." But when the first version of his book was completed in 1985 Mr. Hamilton already had doubts. It was, he writes, *all right,* but "whatever its merits, the book had by no means solved the mystery of Salinger." He tells friends, "It isn't much. Don't get the idea that it's a *biography,* because it isn't. But it's not too bad."

Starting out with his sleuthing other self, Mr. Hamilton set himself admirable ground rules. He would not attempt to seek out Mr. Salinger's ex-wife, his children, his sister, or surprise his friends on the telephone. In 1961, a less fastidious *Time* researcher waylaid Mr. Salinger's sister Doris at Bloomingdale's, where she worked. Ms. Salinger told him, "I wouldn't do anything in the world my brother didn't approve of. I don't want to be rude, but you put me in a very difficult position. Why don't you leave us alone? *Hundreds* of people want to write stories about him."

Anything I might add to this cry from the heart would obviously be redundant. (p. 49)

> Mordecai Richler, *"Rises at Dawn, Writes, Then Retires," in* The New York Times Book Review, *June 5, 1988, pp. 7, 48-9.*

JUDY WARNER

> If you really want to hear about it, the first thing you'll probably want to know is where I was born, and what my lousy childhood was like, and how my parents were occupied and all before they had me, and all that David Copperfield kind of crap, but I don't feel like going into it, if you want to know the truth. . . . I'm not going to tell you my whole goddam autobiography or anything.

Introducing himself as the narrator of *The Catcher in the Rye,* Holden Caulfield, J. D. Salinger's now-famous adolescent, commits a very adult act of irony: he simultaneously refuses to tell his life story, and embarks on a book-length self-description. At the beginning of Ian Hamilton's new biography, *In Search of J. D. Salinger,* Salinger begins his own life story in a similar way, but without the irony: he flatly says that he won't have anything to do with it, and he doesn't.

When Hamilton first approached Salinger in 1983 and proposed his idea for a literary life study, the author wrote back: "Speaking from rather unspeakably bitter experience . . . I do feel I must tell you, for what very little it may be worth, that I think I've borne all the exploitation and loss of privacy I can possibly bear in a single lifetime." . . .

Hamilton recalls this incident in his preface to this somewhat strange biography. "The signals," he writes, "were, well, shall we say, ill mannered, both hostile and provocative: 'You'll get nothing out of me.' " (p. 48)

Writing and publishing a biography of Salinger turned out to be a challenge of Sisyphean proportions. Hamilton's first attempt, an unauthorized study called *J. D. Salinger: A Writing Life,* which was scheduled to appear in 1986, died in bound galleys. This work drew heavily on unpublished letters Salinger had written to friends and editors between 1939 and 1961, and Salinger charged Hamilton with invasion of privacy and infringement of copyright. His lawyers argued, and in 1987 a federal appeals court ruled, that by quoting and paraphrasing large portions of these letters, Hamilton had exceeded the bounds of "fair use" and had effectively appropriated the "expressive heart" of Salinger's work. *J. D. Salinger: A Writing Life* became **In Search of J. D. Salinger** through two compulsory rewrites, which were purged the book of anything that might be construed as Salinger's "expressive heart." As a result, the story is frustrated, angry, stifled and stifling: a testimony to Salinger's silent will. (pp. 48-9)

Unfortunately, as Hamilton himself admits, the book's portrait of Salinger lacks "any vivid sense of presence"; what presence there is is the author's, and his prejudices form a dense screen. If it were possible to hear Salinger speak, it would be easier to judge whether some of Hamilton's conclusions ("We *wouldn't* have liked him much if we had known him then") are anything more than distaste born of bitter hindsight. Hamilton describes Salinger as "a cheeseman's son," calls his family "nouveau riche." He shows a predilection for quoting sources who disliked the young man, while giving little mention to those who might have found him a "regular guy" (as one is reported to have done). Salinger's letters are described as "tough, wise-cracking, mock-boastful, and, now and then, plain boastful," full of "cocksureness . . . wisecracks, [and] slick nightclubbing charm." Yet their omission makes it hard to trust such blanket statements.

Hamilton says he had planned his book as a "literary adventure story with the biographer as a leading character." . . . Hamilton does indeed appear in the book, and in a most unflattering light. Narrating in a pompous royal "we," he splits himself into a "good" biographer and a "bad" "sleuthing alter ego." He likens his detective triumphs to the work of "policemen" or "torturers."

Hamilton asserts that, by dropping out of the literary marketplace, Salinger committed a writer's suicide: "He was, in any real-life sense, invisible, as good as dead." And wish gives birth to fact: very little of Salinger lives and breathes in the pages of this book. (p. 49)

> *Judy Warner, "In Search of Ian Hamilton," in Na-*
> *tional Review, New York, Vol. XL, August 5, 1988,*
> *pp. 48-9.*

SANFORD PINSKER

Most biographers unroll their subjects' lives chronologically, starting, as Holden Caulfield once put it, with how their parents (and, often, their grandparents) were "occupied and all," and moving through the requisite stages of what he calls "that David Copperfield kind of crap." Other biographers prefer to begin their stories *in medias res,* at a point where, say, a Samuel Langhorne Clemens makes the fateful decision to transmogrify himself into Mark Twain, or a journalist

named Walter Whitman widens his vision to embrace epical poetry at the same moment he shortens his name to Walt. By contrast, Ian Hamilton opens his biographical tale where it began for *him:*

> Four years ago [i.e., in 1983], I wrote to the novelist J. D. Salinger, telling him that I proposed to write a study of his "life and work." Would he be prepared to answer a few questions? I could either visit him at his home in Cornish, New Hampshire, or I could put my really very elementary queries in the mail—which did he prefer? . . . I think I even gave him a couple of dates he could choose from for my visit.

One reads such lines with a mixture of fascination and dread. Did he really imagine that Salinger, a recluse of legendary proportions, would consent to an interview? Did he imagine him scurrying around his winterized cabin, vacuuming the carpet, emptying the ashtrays, and making sure that he had laid in enough cheese and crackers? How could Ian Hamilton—the same Ian Hamilton who brought such meticulous research and literary savvy to the making of *Robert Lowell: A Biography*—have been so naïve as to believe that his ploy would work?

On the other hand, suppose—just *suppose*—that it had, and that Hamilton had given us a book filled with insider information about one of contemporary American literature's most mysterious figures. Who among us would have cast the first theoretical stone, arguing that such a study constituted neither biography nor literary criticism, that it was merely gossip and therefore not worthy of serious attention? Short of Salinger signing with the William Morris agency for a college lecture tour, Hamilton's biography would have been *the* literary event of the decade.

As it turns out, of course, Hamilton knew full well that his letter was "entirely disingenuous," and furthermore, that Salinger would react to it with predictable dismay. Indeed, that was precisely Hamilton's complicated plan:

> . . . I had written just the sort of letter that Salinger—as I imagined him—would heartily despise. . . . According to my outline, the rebuffs I experienced would be as much part of the action as the triumphs—indeed, it would not matter much if there were no triumphs. The idea—or one of the ideas—was to see what would happen if orthodox biographical procedures were to be applied to a subject who actively set himself to resist, and even to forestall, them. . . . It would be a biography, yes, but it would also be a semispoof in which the biographer would play a leading, sometimes comic, role.

Those who make "orthodox" biography their business are not likely to be amused by Hamilton's loopy plan. Granted, something of the formula he describes—in which a buffoonish biographer appropriates the narrative space traditionally allotted to his subject—had been done in fictional works such as Vladimir Nabokov's *Pale Fire,* Bernard Malamud's *Dubin's Lives,* or Steven Millhauser's *Edwin Mulhouse.* But this, as they say, was different: despite the fact that Salinger had voluntarily withdrawn from public life on 19 June 1965 (the publication date of "Hapworth 16, 1924," his last *New Yorker* story), he was hardly the man Hamilton describes as "invisible, as good as dead." Indeed, as Hamilton came to discover, Salinger was very much alive—and very willing to play the role assigned to him as a biographical "subject" who preferred not to be subjected to biography.

Nor was Salinger the only stone wall Hamilton ran into. Those who could have talked his ear off about Salinger dummied up instead. *The New Yorker* crowd was especially given to closing ranks. Peter de Vries' terse comment that "If you asked me how to spell his name, I wouldn't be free to tell you" probably best sums up their magisterial aloofness and razor-edged wit. Faced with what can only be called a conspiracy of silence, even Hamilton had to admit that Salinger was going to be a stern biographical test:

> American intellectuals look with compassion on those Eastern bloc writers who have been silenced by the state, but here, in their own culture, a greatly loved author had elected to silence himself. He had freedom of speech, but what he had ended up wanting more than anything else, it seemed, was the freedom to be silent. And the power to silence anyone who wanted to find out why he had stopped speaking.

Vy, Hamilton kept wondering, did Salinger *vant to be alone?* At the same time, however, Hamilton kept making it clear—at least to himself—that he knew the difference between J. D. Salinger and Greta Garbo. True, this biographer intended to be resourceful and persistent, even something of a snoop, but he did not number himself among the *paparazzi,* nor was he writing about Salinger for *People* magazine. He was, after all, a professional, and more than that, one not adverse to setting up fair-minded ground rules. . . . But, alas, the Hamilton who likes to grapple with moral issues, and wake up victorious and cleansed, is accompanied by what he calls his "biographizing alter ego"—and for better or worse, both of them headed toward Manhattan, "eager to get on with the job."

What follows—in chapter after reflexive chapter—are accounts of where Hamilton's dual identities went, what they saw, and how they just missed conquering. Granted, some of the dead ends Hamilton wanders into make for interesting reading—he learns, for example, that Salinger's father worked for a cheese manufacturer once charged with selling products with "faked holes"—but the cheesemen Hamilton dutifully tracked down couldn't tell him much. "Let's just say I didn't ever see them [Sol Salinger and his son] together," one commented diplomatically. (pp. 609-11)

On the other hand, all the cheesemen agreed that "he and his mother were extremely close." At this point, Hamilton, playing the biographer who has done his homework, presses:

> I had read somewhere that Marie had been an actress, or had played in vaudeville (like Bessie in Salinger's Glass stories). There were reports too, on the "record," that when Salinger was a boy the Marx Brothers would often drop by the family apartment (and in an unpublished story of the 1940s, Holden Caulfield's mother is an actress called Mary Moriarity). I tried all this out on the Italians. "Yeah. She may have been. Why don't you ask the boy?"

Why not, indeed! Again and again, the man who could tell him wasn't talking. Nor did Hamilton have recourse to the usual materials that go into the making of a thickly documented biography: journals, notebooks, draft copies of stories and novels. But there were a few bare facts about Salinger's early schooling, and these were enough to send Hamilton scurrying, first to Manhattan's The McBurney School, and

then to the Valley Forge Military Academy. No academic grade or extracurricular activity is left unturned, as Hamilton tells us that Salinger was a dismal student, was something of an odd ball and a loner . . . , and had only one recorded interest: tropical fish. Hamilton even provides us with the full text of the song Salinger penned for the class of '36, one still being republished in the Valley Forge hymn book alongside the works of Martin Luther and John Wesley. Confronted with some twenty-four lines of treacle . . . , Hamilton nearly convinces us that he has thrown in the critical towel: probe as one might, he argues, there are simply no ironies at work here, no indicators that "the class song is other than what it seems." Hamilton, a poet with two collections under his belt, is probably correct; unfortunately, biographies, especially if they are semispoofs of the genre, could hardly be expected to let any matter stand at face value. There is always an "And yet . . ." hidden up the biographer's sleeve:

> And yet it is almost certainly a spoof—an act of mimicry so consummately straight-faced that no one could possibly see through it . . . The mode being what it is, fake sentiment is what the audience expects; so too is the mock-antique diction, the lachrymose team spirit. To achieve full, official piety, the hymn actually prefers a mimic author to a real one.

As Hamilton's split personality would have it, sometimes his biographer plays the earnest idealist, a Don Quixote who has tilted against the windmills of adversity, while his counterpart—a realist of the first water, plainer speaking and not afraid to play the heavy—pulls down the biographer's house of cards. For example, the third chapter opens on a note of triumph as the weary biographer settles back on the train from Valley Forge to New York City. After all, "Look at what had been amassed, so far: Salinger's school records, some telling items of juvenilia, frank testimony from contemporaries, some eyewitness location stuff from us, and so on. Material any biographer would have reason to be proud of." But a voice inside Hamilton keeps whispering otherwise, and Hamilton's alter ego is only too happy to sing out the reservations in full throat:

> But what . . . had we actually achieved? So Salinger was bad at arithmetic. All writers are bad at arithmetic. He was sardonic, moody, a bit of an outsider; again, what writer isn't all these things when young? . . . Did we think we now knew Salinger any better than before? And when we made connections between the "man of mystery" we're in pursuit of and the juvenile's love of playacting, were we not simply bending the material to suit our plot?

Good questions, every one, and I suspect that the "we" parading itself through the page as Hamilton knew their hard, unflattering answers. (pp. 611-13)

What, in fact, does *In Search of J. D. Salinger* tell us? Precious little. We learn, for example, that the hero of an uncollected short story entitled "Last Day of the Last Furlough" had the same army dog-tag number as Salinger himself (32325200); that Salinger probably suffered a mental breakdown sometime during July 1945, after his short marriage to a French woman dissolved; that the name Holden Caulfield derived, in part, from Salinger's longstanding affection for the movie actress, Joan Caulfield. There are, to be sure, other tidbits as well: Hamilton tells us a good deal about *The Gospel of Sri Ramakrishna* and why it appealed to Salinger; about the proprietary feelings Salinger develops for his characters and how this often borders on the sadistic; and perhaps most of all, about how a callow, ambitious youth grew up to become an unlovable adult.

None of this will matter, of course, to those who continue to read Salinger's fiction. Had Hamilton been able to tell us more about the two completed manuscripts rumored to be locked in Salinger's safe, now *that* would have been worth the price of admission. But like most of this "little biography that couldn't," he couldn't.

What Hamilton's exercise in padding and self-indulgence does manage to do, however, is raise serious questions about the nature of biographical inquiry itself. The complicated series of injunctions and appeals that Salinger's lawyers launched between October 1986 and October 1987 turned on matters of fair use, copyright protection, and something called "expressive content." Not surprisingly, journalists rushed in where lawyers cautiously tread. More than a hundred newspapers and magazines gleefully provided blow-by-blow accounts of the pitched battle between the rights of privacy and a desire for scholarly documentation. And if the niceties of legal distinction may have escaped them, the ironies of the case did not. As *New York* magazine pointed out, "In the course of this well-documented lawsuit, the public is learning more about Salinger than it has at any time during the last 34 years."

However, for Random House, and indeed for the entire community of critics and scholars, the issue was less the fate of a book entitled *J. D. Salinger: A Writing Life* than the numbing effect that a 29 January 1987 ruling of the United States Court of Appeals for the Second Circuit (reversing an earlier decision in Hamilton's favor and granting Salinger a preliminary injunction) might well have on future biographies. As Random House argued—unsuccessfully, as things turned out—in a petition to the Supreme Court, literary biographies are, by their very nature, "histories of the thoughts and ideas of writers, works on the process of imagination of writers. Such works would often be nearly pointless, not to say, superficial, if biographers were not permitted to make some fair, if modest, reference to the full range of published and unpublished writings that illuminated the creative process." Robert Callagy, the Random House lawyer who had the dubious honor of conducting the first-ever extensive interview with Salinger, characterized his publisher's defeat this way: "If you take this opinion [the appeals court judgment] to an extreme, what it says is that you can't quote anything that has not been published before, and if you attempt to paraphrase you are at serious peril."

The jury is still out on the full impact of Mr. Callagy's dire predictions, but two recent biographies—Scott Donaldson's *John Cheever* and Linda W. Wagner-Martin's *Sylvia Plath*—suggest that publishers are likely to be gun-shy indeed about what, and how much, an author quotes from a writer's letters, notebooks, diaries, or laundry lists. (pp. 614-15)

We have, in short, not seen the last of the legal department and its pronouncements, nor has the full chill of what this might bode for scholarship been felt. The ghost of Mr. Hamilton will, I'm afraid, be around to haunt us for some time to come. (p. 616)

Sanford Pinsker, "Biography as Comic Opera, as

Melodrama, as Legal Fiction," in The Georgia Review, *Vol. XLII, No. 3, Fall, 1988, pp. 609-16.*

ROBERT FOLKENFLIK

The reclusive J. D. Salinger is the subject of one of the literary world's most extraordinary photographic portraits. In it he has the expression of a man who is about to be hit by an automobile—and since the photo was snapped by paparazzi as they whizzed by, he is not far wrong. He seems to have responded in a similar manner to this first biography of him. It is a case of Johnson bites Boswell.

Ian Hamilton, who had already written an excellent biography of Robert Lowell, knew he was after a difficult quarry, and had even decided that [*In Search of J. D. Salinger*] would be in the same subgenre as Symons's *Quest for Corvo* ('a semispoof in which the biographer would play a leading, sometimes comic, role').

Hamilton seems not to have fully contemplated the implications of Salinger's unwillingness to sanction a biography, despite the fact that it was commissioned in large part because Salinger was so self-protective and mysterious. His first letter offered Salinger the choice of a meeting or of answering a list of 'really very elementary queries'. Salinger broke his silence only when Hamilton sent letters of inquiry to every Salinger in the New York City telephone book. His anguished request for privacy was interpreted by an unnamed friend of Hamilton's as ' "really a kind of come-on": "I can't stop you" to be translated as "Please go ahead." ' Hamilton himself found the letter 'touching but also just a shade repellent'; he fails to observe that the intention was to repel. In quoting such stuff, Hamilton is certainly playing the comic role he promised himself. He calls Salinger's letter of refusal 'dishonest or sentimental', phrases that might apply at times to the biographer. Yet Hamilton had the right to do the biography, and Salinger had the right to be uncooperative.

Early on, Hamilton develops an alter ego, The Biographer, who is a 'gumshoe' or 'low tec'. Hamilton himself remains the moral member of this duo, though the 'we' which allows for internal dialogues seems arch throughout. At the University of Texas he finds to his horror that a dozen of his own letters are on file along with those of Salinger that he had come to see. This irony is not lost upon him. Here the comic biographer is fine. (p. 23)

Hamilton holds off until the end facts that have been appearing for some time in the newspapers. The biography we are reading is not the one he wrote, for Salinger took him to court to prevent its publication after he had already rewritten it in response to Salinger's threat. . . . The major irony here is that advance copies of the original were quoted in the newspapers, so Hamilton is in the anomalous position of being forbidden to quote letters that have had very wide public dissemination. The ironies proliferate: Salinger himself had to submit a deposition in which he was extensively cross-questioned about his life and writings. . . .

For all his understandable regret at the lack of the letters he was denied, which would have been the heart of the book— the 'expressive heart', to use the term employed by Salinger's lawyers in arguing for their suppression—Hamilton does not make full enough use of the materials to which he had access. The book contains no photographs, not even one from an early dust wrapper of *Catcher* or others mentioned in the text.

We do not catch sight of Salinger in his 'Genghis Khan' beard and checked shirt.

The ironies of the book are mostly, as Hamilton is aware, at his own expense. Why has he written the book? The real subject is the disillusionment of the biographer. . . . All the same, despite the ploy of splitting himself in two for narrative purposes and his own modest judgment of even the unexpurgated version ('workmanlike', if we can take it straight), Hamilton has produced as highly readable and as literate an account of Salinger's work from a biographical perspective as we are likely to receive. He has ferreted out a number of letters to Salinger and other biographical information in addition to the unpublished Salinger letters, and the gloves-off animosity laced with the ability to be touched gives a certain tang and distinctiveness to the enterprise.

In Search of Salinger is, however, not a landmark in the history of biography but of copyright. (p. 24)

> *Robert Folkenflik, "Ferret in the Rye," in* The Listener, *Vol. 120, No. 3081, September 22, 1988, pp. 23-4.*

CAROLE ANGIER

[*In Search of J. D. Salinger*] is a muddle. I sympathise with Ian Hamilton, and with J. D. Salinger. But I could kick them both.

Salinger is one of the great literary recluses of our century. . . . [Through his choice of solitude], he's raised, in acute form, the moral question about biography (especially of living subjects): have we the right to invade someone's privacy, in the name of literature or history or anything else? Choosing Salinger meant choosing the deepest end of this problem, where the water was muddiest, the currents most treacherous. It has defeated Hamilton. The mud has closed over his head; the currents have borne him away.

That's not to say that this isn't the best biography of Salinger so far (there *is* one other). Hamilton is good at his job; despite everything we get a good sketch of Salinger's improbable education, traumatic war, absorption by eastern religion, influences (mostly the *New Yorker*) and style. Indeed we get a pretty good picture of the man—his Caulfieldish combination of the sardonic outsider and the boy who wants to be loved; his passion for literary professionalism, which later turned to loathing; his obsessive, possessive relationship to his characters.

But this is "despite everything"—that is, despite *them*. Not just despite Salinger, but despite Hamilton too. This is the third version of his book, because Salinger stopped the first two. (That's why he has my sympathy; it's hard enough to write a book *once*.) He says that the first version was "disabled by my anxiety to assure Salinger that I was not a rogue". Well, he's still doing it. However much this "legal" version is disabled by Salinger's censorship . . . , it's more disabled by Hamilton's own. (p. 33)

[Hamilton] drips with guilt for his profession; he calls biographers policemen and torturers, and pretends not to be one. He calls the biographer "my companion" and (like Moravia's penis) "him"; now "he" has all the nasty low ideas, so that "I", who constantly restrain him, can hold up my head for patting.

This is infuriatingly coy and dishonest. He's trying to have his cake and eat it, to write—and sell—literary biography while damning it. And it doesn't work. It produces a horrible tone, at the same time smug and mocking, ingratiating and aloof. It makes the book more about Hamilton and his fictional alter-egos than about Salinger and his. And it pulls the carpet out from under his contentions.

Thus, for example, he makes a large claim about Salinger's style: that the containment and ellipsis—in fact, the art—that entered it in the *New Yorker* stories of 1948 *came from the magazine's editors*. Without "breaking into" the *New Yorker* files, as Hamilton's "companion" puts it, this can only be a guess; still "they" suggest it, insinuatingly but firmly. Now this really isn't on. All the way through I felt like saying: is this a literary biography or isn't it? Do you *say* this (or do *you* say it) or don't you? But here it goes too far. You either do your research and make your claim, or neither.

That's part of my response to the moral dilemma: if biography is wrong you shouldn't do it, but if you do, then take the rap and do it properly. Poor Ian Hamilton has had—appropriate phrase!—the book thrown at him anyway; he might as well have written a better biography for it.

But there's more to my response. Of course biography isn't *wrong*, just like that, without distinction; nothing is except murder. We must distinguish between sensationalism and scholarship; we must settle individual issues about how far to go. But even if it is, sometimes, wrong, I don't think we can stop reading and writing biography.

It's like pursuing people we've fallen in love with. That's wrong often enough, God knows, but we can't help it. If you're in love with someone you want to *know* him, you want to hear every story about him since the day he was born. And that's just what we feel for our favourite writers. Salinger, of course, knows it. [He remarks in] *Catcher in the Rye:* "What really knocks me out is a book that, when you're all done reading it, you wish the author that wrote it was a terrific friend of yours and you could call him up on the phone whenever you felt like it." We want to call you up on the phone, Jerry. Well, okay, just *read* about you, then. *Please.* (pp. 33-4)

> *Carole Angier, "Shoot the Biographer," in* New Statesman & Society, *Vol. 1, No. 16, September 23, 1988, pp. 33-4.*

PATRICK SKENE CATLING

Once an author has published a book and the public have bought it the transaction is complete; he and his readers owe each other nothing. As Holden Caulfield, the defiant young anti-hero of *The Catcher in the Rye*, might have enquired, what's all this 'right to know' crap, for Chrissake?

Some biographers, if their subjects and everyone who ever knew them don't obediently open their hearts and minds, unlock every safe and reveal every diary, letter and laundry list, cry out in a tone of righteous indignation—Censorship! Kidnapping the truth! Call the culture cops! In the United States, where Ian Hamilton prepared the first and second (final) versions of [*In Search of J. D. Salinger*], . . . persons who withhold information about themselves from biographers are accused of defying the Freedom of Information Act and violating the First Amendment of the Constitution. Worse, such unco-operativeness may expose biographers to the risk of having to return their publishers' advances.

Though I sympathised with Mr Hamilton when J. D. Salinger refused to submit to interrogation, caused his past associates to refuse and legally prevented publication of his letters, thus making it impossible to write an intimate biography in the contemporary mode, I sympathised more with Mr Salinger. Even if his hermitic way of life in Cornish, New Hampshire, is a hollow charade, if he is not really engaged in a rigorous programme of literary endeavour and religious contemplation but spends his solitary days only counting his royalties and reading his fan-mail, playing impossible to get and increasing his fame by pretending flirtatiously to be indifferent to it, so what? Why shouldn't he?

Random House, the powerful New York publishing house, the sort of people whom Salinger in his reclusive years has regarded as the enemy, commissioned Mr Hamilton in 1984 to write a book to be called *J. D. Salinger: A Writing Life,* about his 'life and work', and advanced $100,000 for the project. The would-be biographer wrote Salinger a deferential letter requesting an audience to ask a few questions to help 'set the record straight'. Describing his plan, Mr Hamilton admits that his request was, 'of course, entirely disingenuous'. He says he knew the answer would be no. . . .

[However], if Salinger had surprised him by offering total co-operation, perhaps Mr Hamilton would have been willing to adjust his outline, even if doing so had meant sacrificing his preconceptions.

He protests too much. The confession of disingenuousness seems itself to be a disingenuous attempt to present himself as a decent, sensitive, respectful man who deplores the sneaky gumshoe tactics to which a persistent, hard-boiled biographer has to resort in order to disclose more than a reluctant subject could possibly want disclosed. Proclaiming his own ambivalence, Mr Hamilton presents himself as two, mutually contradictory selves, amateur biographer and professional, gentleman and player, who confuse their ethical standards and methods and even argue with each other throughout this puzzlingly schizoid enterprise.

If he had been able to grit his teeth and commit himself to integrated super-honesty, he would either have abandoned the book or, without complaining, done the best he could with whatever material he had gathered by any means. Here he tries to distance his virtuous self from the biographical rat-race by disparaging such rival intrusive investigators as the reporters for *Time, Life* and *Newsweek*—and then eagerly ransacks those magazines' archives and uses what he finds there. He says of biographies that 'unauthorised gives off a smell of sleaze', and then publishes an unauthorised, strenuously resisted biography which he evidently hopes, in vain, will smell of roses.

What Mr Hamilton has written, in effect, is the autobiography of a thwarted adoring fan—or, as he might say, having picked up the *New Yorker*'s hey-day camp tic of italics, the *autobiography.* I mean, that's really what it *is.* (p. 33)

Like a fan who stands in the rain outside a stage-door even though he knows his autograph book may never be signed, Mr Hamilton sometimes seems sulky, even vindictive, but his love endures. His analyses of Salinger's work, after it was accepted by the *New Yorker* and he was thus enabled to repudiate the glib formulas of the *Saturday Evening Post* and all, are percipient and deeply appreciative. He recognises "A Perfect Day for Bananafish", that most perfect Salinger short story (collected in *For Esmé—with Love and Squalor*), which introduced Seymour Glass at his most charming and elusively Salinger-like, as decisively pivotal.

Salinger's first story published in the *New Yorker,* "Bananafish", Mr Hamilton points out, is 'spare, teasingly mysterious, withheld. Salinger, it seems, had at last entered a world in which his own fastidiousness would be honoured, and perhaps surpassed, by that of his editorial attendants.' Mr Hamilton pays proper tribute to Harold Ross, the original editor of the magazine, his first successor, William Shawn, and one of their principal assistants, William Maxwell. Without them the Glass family might not have proliferated. (pp. 33-4)

Mr Hamilton records how some of America's influential writers predictably attacked Salinger when he had gained the status of a cult figure. There are quotations of characteristically snide comments by Norman Mailer ('I seem to be alone in finding him no more than the greatest mind to stay in prep school'), Leslie Fiedler ('Salinger of course speaks for the cleanest, politest, best-dressed, best-fed and best-read among the disaffected (and who is not disaffected?) young') and, 'most vitriolic of all', Mary McCarthy ('Salinger's world contains nothing but Salinger'). Is it possible that the adverse criticism created such an impenetrable writer's block that Salinger incommunicado with the world has written nothing at all? Non-writing would explain non-publishing. . . .

Like Mr Hamilton, we are two writers, a reasonable one who regrets Mr Hamilton's unnecessarily elaborate way of salvaging his 'project', and an emotional one who is bound to confess that he loved what finally emerged. I mean, *loved* it, really, every word, even the bits that the reviewer realised were bad. (p. 34)

Patrick Skene Catling, "People Who Live in Glass Houses May Remain Invisible," in The Spectator, *Vol. 261, No. 8360, October 1, 1988, pp. 33-4.*

JULIAN BARNES

Listen to Jeffrey Robinson, American biographer of figures such as Sheikh Yamani, describing how he goes to work:

> What I usually do is get two or three months' research under my belt before I go to see the guy. He may say: 'I don't want this biography.' I say to him: 'That is not one of your options. This book is going to be written, I have a publisher and I'm getting near being able to write something. Your two options are you co-operate with me or you don't.' The next thing is to make him see it's in his interest to co-operate.

Most of us will probably have no difficulty in finding this crude, pushy and—let's use the word for a change—wrong.

Now consider a more sophisticated version of the Robinson technique. Ian Hamilton, noted biographer of Robert Lowell, writes to J. D. Salinger and informs him that he has become Hamilton's latest subject: would the notoriously reclusive novelist mind answering some questions, could he take a visit? . . . Amazingly, and unhelpfully, Salinger replies. He recognises that he can't stop Hamilton, but asks him not to write the book as he can't endure any more intrusions on his privacy. Hamilton writes the book nonetheless.

We may not feel too strongly about Sheikh Yamani's right to privacy (though of course he does, and took Robinson to court), but what about the case of a writer nearing seventy who withdrew altogether from literary life nearly a quarter of a century ago? Before becoming mired in sentimentality and Zen, Salinger wrote the impeccable *Catcher in the Rye* and several excellent stories. Does our gratitude and pleasure mean that we should respect his desire to be left alone, or the exact opposite? Has Salinger forfeited his rights because the unpredicted success of *Catcher* brought him fame (which he shows no sign of enjoying) and money (which he shows no sign of wanting)? And if so, at what exact level of success are the biographers—like the VAT—men-allowed to become interested?

Hamilton argues his way round Salinger's letter with a sort of unedifying honesty. He shows it to 'one or two of my more sardonic literary friends', one of whom points out that 'I can't stop you' really means 'Please go ahead' (perhaps this particular friend missed a career as a rape-trial judge). What convinces him mostly, though, is the tone of the letter, 'touching in a way, but also a shade repellent'; it was 'somewhat too composed . . . for me to accept it as a direct cry from the heart'. This self-legitimising complaint sits rather oddly in Hamilton's mouth, since he admits that his own letter to Salinger had been 'completely disingenuous', and that he'd deliberately phrased it in a way which he imagined his subject would 'heartily despise'. Isn't there something 'a shade repellent' in this? And might not Salinger have spotted something less than 'a direct cry from the heart' in Hamilton's approach?

Having decided to go ahead, Hamilton establishes some ground rules designed 'to make myself sound decent—not just to Salinger, but to myself. . . . It is a very curious display of integrity, this. Salinger likens investigation into his life to burglary. Hamilton comes on as that rare thing, an ethically-aware thief (unsurprisingly rare, when you come to think about it), the sort who knocks at your door and says: 'Look, I think you ought to know I'm going to break into your house, but it's all right, because *I'm only going to steal the things you can see through the window.*' This is equally unsatisfactory for the householder, the burglar and those to whom he subsequently has to fence the swag.

And then after the book is written, more restrictive rules are imposed. Because, of course, 'I can't stop you' didn't mean 'Please go ahead.' Hamilton's main biographical finds in the course of his research were three caches of Salinger's letters—whose author naturally held their copyright. As a result of well-reported legal encounters, Hamilton was not permitted to quote, or paraphrase, or even steal 'the expressive heart' of these letters. This decision hurts the book deeply, and often renders it comically oblique. . . .

So what we have here is a bizarre item indeed: a literary biography whose writer hasn't talked to the subject, his wives, children or most of his friends; one where he won't permit himself to go within a hundred miles of the subject's house, and isn't allowed to represent more than distantly the breakthrough letters which are his main discovery. Sol Salinger, the writer's father, worked for a Chicago firm of cheese importers called J. S. Hoffman, 32 cases of whose Sliced Wisconsin were once seized by the FBI on the charge that they contained 'faked holes'. With Hamilton's biography, all the holes are genuine.

These enforced absences drive Hamilton into two technical procedures. The first is a reverse reductivism. Normally, the biographer establishes the course of a writer's life and then uses it to 'explain' the work. . . . With Salinger's life largely unavailable, or where available obscure, Hamilton finds himself doing the opposite: deducing the life from the work. The stories are trawled in the first instance for what they can tell us about the man who wrote them. Hamilton's extrapolations from the early, unreprinted stories are well done (if inevitably, and admittedly, hypothetical), but as with normally-directed reductivism, the effect is to diminish. Thus a piece of fairly autobiographical apprentice work will be scanned with greater zeal than a mature but opaque item. "A Perfect Day for Bananafish", one of Salinger's most elusive stories, is discussed in terms of a. Salinger's visit to a hotel at Daytona Beach; b. the history and genealogy of the Glass family; and c. the stylistic break it represents from "The Inverted Forest", published a month earlier. "Bananafish", Hamilton records in passing, is 'spare, teasingly mysterious, withheld'. Sure, but what's it, well, *about*? How does it work as a story, what do the bananafish signify, why the suicide? Hamilton merely notes that the ending was to prove 'a seminar talking point for years to come', as if the seminarists were wasting their time. He may argue that what he's writing is, after all, a biography, but since it's a determinedly abnormal one anyway, you frequently wish that Hamilton, one of our sharpest literary analysts, would play the straight critic more.

The second technique is for Hamilton himself to appear as a character in the unfolding story. With Salinger declining to shuffle on-stage, the biographer is impelled uneasily into the limelight. He solves the publicity problem by splitting himself into a comic double act. . . . This works quite well in a gagging sort of way, enabling Hamilton to disconcert traditional, supposedly objective biographical methods and frettingly cast doubt on the validity of what seems to have been discovered. But it's a self-consciousness without much self-revelation to it: often we want to know much more what Hamilton, there before us, is actually feeling about his frustrating quest, and instead get fobbed off with this double act. As a technique, moreover, it flirts with archness. When Hamilton is allowed to see the dossier *Time* Magazine assembled on Salinger for their 1961 cover story, the occasion naturally sets off reflection on the differing approaches of journalists and literary biographers:

> We weren't like them, because we didn't do what they did. We weren't like them because we had our precious ground rules, our taboos, and because our background and our ultimate intent were literary critical, not journalistic. We didn't speak up about closetsful of little girls, nor attempt crude life-art link-ups of the 'search for Sibyl' type. Even my companion shrank from being bracketed with *Time* and *Newsweek* and, you might have noticed, has made little or no effort to roughen the easy superiority of tone that comes naturally to me when I write about the methods of magazines like these.

That last sentence is so barnacled with irony that there seems no way of getting at what is underneath.

'Easy superiority of tone': of course, we're not meant to believe that he means it; or, if we *are* meant to believe it, we're also meant to see that Hamilton spots it more quickly than we do, that he calls in the style-police as soon as the typewriter bell rings for the end of the line, and that this makes it all right. Hamilton's robust unimpressibility has always been one of his strengths as a critic: here there are too many occasions when he yields not just to 'easy superiority of tone' but to a sourness, and a snootiness too. (p. 3)

Elsewhere, Hamilton is wryly urban when visiting backwoods Ursinus College in Collegeville, Pennsylvania, and pulls literary rank on the schemes of Whit Burnett, editor of *Story* magazine, for his cosy anthologising and promotional wheezes. One of these, he tells us, was 'a Factual Fiction series in which "the facts behind the story" would be printed alongside the author's "imaginative" text (he hoped to sell this gem to *Reader's Digest*).' At which point the reader can't help noting that Hamilton's book isn't that different from Burnett's 'wheeze', just classier.

Still, the main focus of Hamilton's disenchanted eye is Salinger himself, and those loyal to him. S. J. Perelman, we learn, was 'willing to talk unsolemnly about everything under the sun and yet able to fall obstinately silent when asked about J. D.'—obstinately silent, or just impressively loyal? Salinger's signals when seeking to deter Hamilton were, it seems, 'ill-mannered'—what of Hamilton's signals, with his 'entirely disingenuous' request? The trouble is compounded by the fact that Hamilton is unable to quote directly, which often drives him to summary judgment. Thus Salinger, as a college drop-out, is suddenly labelled 'surly' and 'boastful'—on secret evidence which the reader can't test. We are informed of the letter-writer's 'cocksureness' of tone and 'slick nightclubbing charm'; a letter about Chaplin's marriage to Oona (whom Salinger had been dating) makes 'nasty reading'; while another section of the correspondence yields to the 'eavesdropping' of the double act 'almost nothing in the way of human frailty or warmth'. (Is this, then, what he was looking for? Frailty and warmth? It is an uncommon moment of naivety in a narrative of domineering worldliness.)

The portrait of Salinger that emerges—and which largely convinces, even if we take much on trust—is of a touchy, arrogant, obsessive, even paranoid man, damaged by the war, ambitious for literary success and (like his editor) surprised by its sudden arrival; one unimpressed by journalists and publishers, answering to the higher principle, incapable of compromise, for whom No means Certainly Not, and whose final No was addressed to the outside world and the very act of publication. . . . (p. 4)

The first completed version of this book, Hamilton informs us towards the end, was 'too nervous and respectful'. There's no danger of anyone applying either of those adjectives to this third version, which is superior and disapproving. It's easy to forget that Salinger at his best is an extremely funny writer with a stupendous ear, and that *Catcher in the Rye* is a virtually perfect book, its tone a high-risk, high-triumph balancing-act. Hamilton agreed with this view at the age of 17, and one of the best, most straightforward passages in his book is an account of the effect *Catcher* had on him at that time ('It seemed to me "my book" '). So the reader waits for Hamilton to tell us what he thinks of it now. But no—another hole in the Sliced Wisconsin. The novel is discussed as a biographical and sociological event, then we jump-cut to a weary, post-battle conclusion. Perhaps the whole project, Hamilton reflects, began not in 'literary whimsy' or 'mere scholarship,' but in 'an infatuation that bowled me over at the age of 17

and which it seems I never properly outgrew. 'Well,' he concludes with a sigh, 'I've outgrown it now.'

It's probably possible to read Hamilton's book in a completely different way. If you think Salinger is on a par in terms of biographical rights with Sheikh Yamani, that his stuff is frankly a bit overrated, that his No means Yes, that money and fame cancel his right to privacy, if you enjoy being told that the chap may have talent (and money and fame) but that he isn't very nice and is frankly a bit potty—then you will respond differently.

What should Hamilton have done? Not started? Abandoned the project as soon as challenged? Written it off like a bad debt when Salinger took to the courts? This last is difficult on one count—the very stubbornness implicit in Hamilton's decision to begin isn't suddenly going to abandon him—and virtually impossible on another. He became caught in the terrible process whereby lawyers replace editors in a writer's life: he got turned into a test-case on the law of privacy. Money, of course, was also involved, and in this upfront biography which is pretty sardonic about Salinger's wealth ('He said he wanted neither fame nor money and by this means [silence] he'd contrived to get extra supplies of both'), we might expect the biographer's own financial arrangements to be more openly stated.

One ironic result of Hamilton's project is that Salinger's letters, whose every word and whose 'essential heart' the novelist was in court defending, are now available (by reason of copyright law) for anyone to read on payment of a ten dollar fee. The other result—not at all ironic, but sad and frightening—is a photograph which will undoubtedly become famous. (pp. 4-5)

It seems to have been taken from inside a car, and shows an elderly man being photographed against his will. He is a tall, white-haired, handsome man, whose mouth is open in protest, whose brow is furrowed in alarm, whose eyes are popping with fear. His right arm is held protectively across his body and the hand clenched into a feeble fist. He looks like a man warding off a burglar; he looks frail, alarmed, terrified. This, you think as you examine the photograph, this is what Hamilton—unintentionally, of course, perhaps even well-intentionedly—has done to Salinger: given him that hateful moment.

The burglar analogy is one close to Salinger's pen when trying to categorise biographical intrusion. Hamilton rejects it as excessive and substitutes gumshoe for burglar. . . . The metaphor begins in jokey self-consciousness and doesn't really run the distance; by the end of the book Hamilton appears neither burglar nor sleuth. Instead he seems like a man who's gone badger-hunting with an umbrella. The first time he pokes his weapon into the sett the badger chews off the ferrule. Undaunted—indeed, positively encouraged—by this, he thrusts the umbrella into the hole a second time. The badger, maddened, rips up the fabric, swipes away the spokes and snaps off the shaft. The hunter returns to town brandishing the stump of handle and proclaiming: 'Look how I licked that badger.' But there is a wry grin on his face, as if he isn't sure we're going to believe him, and isn't too convinced himself either. (p. 5)

Julian Barnes, "The Salinger Affair," in London Review of Books, *Vol. 10, No. 19, October 27, 1988, pp. 3-5.*

WILFRID SHEED

Sad things can happen when an author chooses the wrong subject: first the author suffers, then the reader, and finally the publisher, all together in a tiny whirlpool of pain. Ian Hamilton's book, *In Search of J. D. Salinger,* seems to have set in dolorous motion all of the above. The author's misunderstandings begin on page one, and his groans only a page or so later. And at the end Mr. Hamilton is still wearing his bitterness rather awkwardly on his sleeve, his publisher has become, as Hamilton puts it, "preoccupied," and the reader doesn't know which way to look.

The book's fate certainly has been an unusual one, of a kind that would have amused the Mikado. In the event you have been living in a cave, or conceivably, in New Hampshire, the story, plus commentary, goes roughly like this. Four years ago, Hamilton, a lifelong Holden Caulfield fan, wrote J. D. Salinger a *pro forma* letter announcing a plan to write a book about him. He didn't expect an answer, partly because everyone knows that Salinger despises literary biographies and publishers too (a position shared by an ample number of writers, though you wouldn't guess it from Hamilton, who treats Salinger throughout as a man without a species, unique unto himself) and partly because "he [J. D.] was, in any real-life sense, invisible, as good as dead" (joke). Incidentally, there are a lot of (jokes) in this book.

The small but crucial distinction between dead and invisible became sufficiently clear shortly after that when Salinger, who wasn't supposed to write one dead or alive, fired off a quite vigorous letter rounding on Hamilton for harassing his family (H. had written all the Salingers in the Manhattan phone book, and had winged a couple of relatives) "in the not particularly fair name of scholarship."

Writers, sad to say, often take this philistine view of "scholarship," feeling that they don't owe it anything except their published work: again Salinger was not alone. Hamilton, however, was quite nonplused by the letter as he would subsequently be by almost everything he learned about his subject—a signal, perhaps, that he didn't quite have a feel for this thing.

One of his friends told him the letter was really a " 'come-on': 'I can't stop you' to be translated as 'Please go ahead.' " (Remember when they used to say that about girls?) Hamilton, being of slightly finer stuff, isn't quite so sure—although he sounds pretty sure to me. . . .

[Viewing the letter] solely as a tactic, Hamilton was not altogether without respect for the privacy-for-profit angle. If playing hard to get enhances a girl's value, even the most lecherous of us can understand that. So, despite forebodings that do him credit, he essentially took his friend's view that the letter was a challenge; and right to the end he refused to believe that he just might not be Salinger's type, marketplace or no marketplace. . . . (p. 35)

Since Salinger's letter was so short, it's a pity that Hamilton didn't weigh each phrase more carefully and sense that that one about scholarship was the loaded one. Originally H. had hoped that by declaring himself a scholar instead of a news magazine, he would crack the case wide open. But as it turned out a news magazine could hardly have done worse. After all, from an author's point of view, a news magazine can only steal your clothes, while a scholar picks among your very bones, and lets the magic out of your plots, plastering the remains with names and dates like graffiti on a tombstone. So Salinger's hatred of academics may not, as they themselves prefer to believe, be based on graduate school envy at all, but on his own sense of Eros v. Thanatos, and thus a simple matter of life or death.

Hamilton's Salinger, on the other hand, just doesn't think like that, and so his creator plunged ahead with a high heart into a swampy area which, expressly because of him, will henceforth be carefully signposted against eager tourists: he appropriated some unpublished letters of J. D. that could be found in certain libraries, and printed them without a by-your-leave from either the libraries or Salinger (he must have thought that rare material was awfully easy to come by in the United States); wrote his book and duly sent it on to Salinger, still hoping, with a goofy ardor worthy of Freddy Hill in *Pygmalion,* that he would win the latter's heart, that *he* would prove the exception, the lucky lecher. Salinger promptly copyrighted the letters and obtained a writ delaying their (and the book's) publication. Hamilton just as promptly paraphrased the letters, quite excruciatingly (intentionally so, one hopes for his sake), and tried again. And this time Salinger took him to court. And goodness, was Hamilton nonplused.

By this time, Hamilton must have been practically certain he'd got the wrong man. When your subject turns around and bites you—and you don't expect it—you've probably missed a hint someplace. What's surprising in this instance is that Hamilton's Salinger, a biliously competitive careerist, sounds quite capable of taking his grandmother to court if necessary: and yet the biographer persisted in thinking the original was just kidding. [The assumption in Hamilton's corner was that Salinger would not reveal himself in New York long enough to give a deposition, a nasty piece of game playing to pull on one's old hero, but that's the law for you. Anyway, it backfired.] At any rate, the first legal proceeding (nobody just has one any more) went to Hamilton, on grounds of scholar's rights, but the appeal went to Salinger, largely on the grounds that the letters Hamilton had filched without permission had cash value, hence property value, which paraphrases would tend to diminish as much as quotes would, and that he had gone way beyond the "incidental" use of them allowed by law by citing them on 40 percent of his pages.

Journalism proceeded to have the last laugh over scholarship when several papers printed a legally "incidental" sampling of the forbidden letters, reminding one of their flavor—and reminding this particular reader, who had seen Hamilton's original manuscript, of how much the new book missed them. Hamilton, if anything, understates the matter when he says of the original that "it had (thanks to the letters) something of his tone, his presence." On the page at least, Salinger's tone *is* his presence to a unique extent, and a book that can't quote him verbatim might be about anybody.

In a human, as opposed to a legal, sense, it is obviously hard to pick any kind of fight with a man who has, after all, brought a good deal of pleasure at very little cost to anyone, and Hamilton feels quite queasy about it himself. But momentum now required him to proceed in a legal mode, and thus we find him, or at least his lawyers, comparing this superb writer with Howard Hughes, a fellow recluse who also happened to be a public figure. And an anonymous publisher weighs in with this thought: "What if 'a news reporter discovers Oliver North's private diary, but can neither quote nor paraphrase from it because it is unpublished'?"

This kind of thing may help to explain why, even in a case ostensibly concerning censorship, Hamilton seems to have so few creative writers in his corner right now (uncreative writers are another story). Whatever the law may have to say about it, this year or next, most writers stoutly refuse to consider themselves public figures in the same sense as Hughes or North, and in fact would probably prefer not to be seen in the same argument with either of them. So if a publisher, however anonymous, and an author can agree for even a moment in granting to a writer's personal papers the same status as those of a crazed manipulator or a government employee, then authors have no choice but to guard the door against publishers and scholars alike, and Salinger's alleged paranoia becomes a simple matter of professional necessity.

But in all this, Hamilton is probably just as much a victim of the law's clumsiness as Salinger. The cast of mind that can lump Oliver North in with J. D. Salinger can easily do the same for scholars and journalists, and thus Hamilton finds himself willy-nilly defending his scholarship with journalistic precedents, and making, or at least passing on, these embarrassing comparisons. . . . (pp. 35-6)

In real, nonlegal life, Hamilton has been a good deal more respectful of his subject's wishes than a journalist would dream of being, accepting, for instance, Salinger's implicit proposition that a writer who ceases to publish can, by so doing, cease to be a public figure upon the moment, and he has used no material dated after 1965—a condition that would make nonsense of any research relating to North or Hughes. But he has to insist for legal purposes that Salinger *was* "a public figure" once upon a time, and since the phrase still does not quite fit what scholars do, the old journalistic arguments have to be wheeled out, retroactively as it were, in all their awesome unsuitability, and we're back with North and Hughes again, for want of anything better.

The common-sense trouble with this is at least hinted at in the relevant statute when it lists, without insisting on it, unprofitability as a desideratum in a work of scholarship. But since the very word strikes at the core of what journalism is about, it follows that, at least to a degree, the very thing that still makes Salinger appealing to journalists (his publicness) makes him unready for scholars: if he sells newspapers, he sells books in a newspapery sort of way, even high-minded ones.

And finally, the public figure defense didn't even work on the law's own terms, perhaps because the statute doesn't really know what it is supposed to do about scholars, or indeed what they are doing in there in the first place. To put it too simply: a journalist leaking from North's diaries will presumably have to violate a trust somewhere along the line, as Hamilton did venially with the librarians (they *told* him he needed permission, but apparently let him be the judge of whether he had it—henceforth they won't be so nice), but the journalist can always justify it by invoking the Public Interest. But what precisely is the scholarly equivalent of the Public Interest?

The law, as now written, clearly hasn't the faintest idea, so herewith a few suggestions from the laity before it comes round again. If, in a case like this, one's justification is simply a generalized need-to-know where artistic creation comes from, then Hamilton's book passes cleanly, as indeed would any respectable piece of journalism that stressed the written record (Hamilton cites scraps of juvenilia, yearbook citations,

etc., spare but suggestive, like everything else about Salinger): journalism with a college degree, as Mark Twain might put it. But if the test is the better explication of texts—supposing that Salinger's texts *need* any explication that can't wait—well, the book would conceivably have passed again, as it appeared the first time round, if only as a skillfully annotated collection of letters, but might, by a paradox, have more trouble now, when it is legally in the clear. Because, in any but the most literal sense, Hamilton finds it even harder than it need be to link Salinger's life to his work; and this is where choosing the wrong subject comes in so painfully.

This, mind you, is the same Ian Hamilton who not so long ago wrote a masterly life of Robert Lowell which is so much the *right* subject for him that one might wish at this very moment to be reviewing that book instead of this one. His Lowell is as much a model of literary biography as this is not, and is, of course, the book that will be remembered.

So perhaps Hamilton's first mistake was in not realizing in time how much his subject had changed on him. Temperamentally, he seems to have understood Lowell (being English was no handicap in that case), and he knew the ingredients of an academic poet. But with Salinger he has his work cut out even placing him on a literary map.

Thus we find him noting, as if it were a major breakthrough, that "this rigorous, high-minded author had once tailored his prose to please the market." Well, yes. What might be news would be evidence that he'd ever stopped doing so. To a hardened reader of what Hamilton calls, without sufficient differentiation, "the slicks," it is immediately apparent that even in his best work Salinger was a recognizable graduate of commercial writing not art writing, a Billy Wilder not a Bresson, and that *The Catcher in the Rye* itself, which Hamilton says he so thrilled to, is in certain respects of tone and timing, a transcendent *Saturday Evening Post* story. (Very few classics are *that* easy to read, or that likable either.)

Hamilton seems to suggest that his late-blooming realization of this made him decide to roll up his sleeves and get to work, but it might have been a good moment to roll them down instead. Because the world of market writing may simply not be susceptible to his kind of scholarship, however hard he sweats it, or his sensibility either, which seems ineradicably disapproving, as if he is making a slight face as he writes; and there are signs in his slapdash treatment of Salinger's texts that his heart simply isn't in it. (p. 36)

Not only is the author . . . all at sea with his material, such as it is, but he doesn't seem to think it matters. The whole question of Salinger's humor, and where it came from, is skimmed over and around in a few cursory phrases ("hard-boiled urban wit" doesn't quite make it), although humor is absolutely crucial to all of Salinger's effects. . . . [One of the minor causes of Salinger's irritation with Hamilton's manuscript may have been its own lumbering stabs at humor, which have been sufficiently mocked by other reviewers. I would only add, vis-à-vis H.'s playful attempts to turn himself into two people the better to discuss his project, that this man was never meant to be playful, and that pitch-perfect humorists like Salinger tend to be screamingly intolerant of facetiousness in all forms.] . . .

So, in lieu of telling us one more time that Tolstoy has always been Salinger's favorite author, it might have been a good idea at some point for Hamilton to take a closer and more sympathetic look at Salinger's comic sources, whose influence on his work is somewhat more accessible than Tolstoy's, and in particular, to have asked himself whether there was ever anything about *The New Yorker* besides his own natural disadvantages that drew Salinger to the magazine in the first place. (p. 38)

Humor is notoriously resistant to criticism, and although Salinger is, of course, much else besides a humorist, he tends to write in the American humor language of the Twenties through Forties, which can make his work hard at times to analyze in a formal lit. crit. way. This is particularly true of his letters, which are shot through with variously successful attempts to be ironic. So it is particularly poignant that Hamilton should have made these his final trysting place. Because, lacking the right key, he seems to interpret every word of them quite literally, so that the stage boasts become real boasts and the whimsical self-deprecations turn too often into plain groveling. A man's ironic version of himself is a sorry sight whoever he is, but that is now the version we've got, because Salinger's own words, in his letters, are no longer around to temper it.

In retrospect, it should have been clear from Hamilton's own peculiar paraphrasing of the originals that the letters were written in a language quite foreign to him: but in any language he might have guessed that Salinger's self-advancement letters at least (and we all write them) could seldom have been less than somewhat charming, within the conventions of the situation, and however they read to him today. Surely no author who ever lived has known much more about how to ingratiate himself than the creator of Holden Caulfield, a character who could even reach across languages to Mr. Hamilton not so many years after the letters were written. So even as a callow youth buttering up prospective editors, chances are he knew pretty much what he was doing and did not unwittingly reveal all his character flaws for future biographers to seize on. . . .

Even in the taboo matter of Salinger's reclusiveness (and one writes about this man with care) there may be a few non-litigious things to say linking this most impressionable of writers with a tradition of some sort (although I'm not suggesting that Hamilton should have said them, only that he should have said *something*). Ever since Thoreau at the latest, many American writers besides Salinger have nurtured a generic (and very unEuropean) craving for solitude: naturally enough since that's what brought people here in the first place. (p. 40)

[The case of Thomas Merton] makes an instructive parallel in several respects. [Merton's] *Seven Storey Mountain* came out in 1948 and *Catcher in the Rye* in 1951, and both of them took off like thunder, against all conventional expectations. The generation they spoke to would later be referred to derisively as "silent," to which it might well have answered, out of the din of promotion that followed the war, that there was a lot to be silent about right then: Salinger called it "phoniness" and Merton called it "worldliness," but for most young readers there was only one enemy.

In fact, of course, there were at least two, but only one *Zeitgeist,* and both men were plugged into it all the way, quite sincerely and without calculation (you can't do it if you're not sincere). They were simply alive to their times at every moment with an agitated awareness that fairly screamed for es-

cape. And both, significantly, turned to Zen Buddhism among other things to soothe this torment of awareness.

So once again Salinger has company, and of a kind that should ensure respectability by association, but doesn't quite, because his sheer facility takes the grit out of the subject and makes it all go down too smoothly: a sort of "Zen Made Easy" effect. I believe the problem is one of technique rather than sincerity. Thomas Merton's very tone conveyed a spiritual and intellectual authority which made his divagations into Orientalism sound rock solid; but Salinger in those days was still obliged to work with the cap and bells of his profession—by which I don't mean that he was funny about his Eastern discoveries but that he was doomed to entertain whatever the subject. His story "Teddy" provides a far too slick introduction to Oriental wisdom (the magazines he trained under might have been okay at times for fiction, but they were death on wisdom). But when, in "Seymour: An Introduction," he attempts to reduce the slickness by stirring some seriousness into the entertainment, his message strains mightily against his style in all its too-perfect shapeliness, causing Buddy Glass to apologize more than once for his helpless wordiness.

So let us suppose the following: that Salinger swiftly became dissatisfied with this half-baked condition, half-slick and half-serious but really not enough of either, but yet was unwilling simply to retreat into his early triumphs, whose high polish might by now even have begun to strike him as a bit phony; so he simply decided to suspend publication then and there until such a time as he found a new style worthy of his subject. And if that should take forever, what is forever to a mystic?

It may not have happened quite like that, but the texts suggest it and the texts are, by agreement, our subject. In any event, a biographer with his eye on a breakthrough should probably try to make all he possibly can out of Salinger's religious conversion, suspending his skepticism at least long enough to imagine himself as far as his temperament permits into Salinger's position. Unfortunately, Hamilton seems congenitally unsympathetic to Salinger as such, and cannot or will not imagine himself into the man at any stage of his development, let alone this chic, apparently unearned one.

A similar refusal of imagination also keeps him from making much of anything out of Salinger's schooling, and the sundering alienation a Jewish New Yorker might be expected to feel in the rather cloddish Wasp schools that his father chose for him. Sol Salinger of Cleveland obviously saw no difficulty about getting his son assimilated overnight, it was just like taking out citizenship papers or getting vaccinated: you simply looked up a school in *The New York Times*—any school that advertised in that newspaper must be the best—and let the American dream do the rest. (pp. 40-1)

Such schools chosen in such a way can indeed create a conviction of intrinsic outsideness, both with one's family for letting it happen, but also with the outside world for presenting itself in such a strange way first time out. Hamilton describes young Salinger's persona at Valley Forge as being alternately aloof and eager to please: but having been in a similar situation twice myself, I would say that this is *exactly* how an outsider responds. Although there is no reason to be certain that the inmates at such a place even knew what a Jew was, it's clear from surviving testimony that they found him a prickly oddity, and this combined with the animal hostility small boys commonly feel at first toward their own species, must have presented an almost impenetrable surface of distrust, that one alternately dreams and despairs of cracking.

Hamilton's Salinger strikes me at various times as being at once too young and too old. For instance, a piece of early writing that seems to me quite advanced for its age will be dismissed as juvenile; yet when Jerry acts irritatingly superior, it seems to get forgotten that this is a fifteen-year-old boy we're talking about, in an alien world, and that sometimes burgeoning self-respect demands a show of tusks or answering display of menace. What seems to get overlooked when the words Salinger and prep school come to mind is that while Salinger would finally settle his own differences with a quite spectacular act of reconciliation, namely *The Catcher in the Rye,* his hero Holden Caulfield has to pay the price of going slightly insane—winningly so to be sure, and eager to please to the end, but nevertheless insane. (p. 41)

Although no one has ever called Salinger an angry young man, the figure Hamilton describes with presumable accuracy sounds made of anger. Grouchy in the army, splenetic at home, and given to tantrums at parties (my only reservation about this being that Hamilton seems to take anyone's word against Salinger, without ever questioning where, in the useful phrase, the witness is coming from), he seems at all times to be ticking with an explosive grievance over some wrong that has been done to him and that everything seems to remind him of—except, significantly, children, preferably small girls, who are preeminently people to whom things are done, reminders perhaps of himself before whatever it was happened.

Since every second adolescent in the world seems to tick with a nameless grievance, the only excuse for bringing it up now is that Salinger happens to write about youth, so if anything at all can be said about him and his texts, it has to be about that. In his stories any such grievance there might once have been is either coded out of sight (we don't really believe that Holden went crazy or Seymour killed himself) or sweetened to parody, so we only have a few odd things to go on, such as the fact that Caulfield (and it's safe to guess, the Glass family as well) cannot abide people who look as if they used to play football in college—in other words, precisely the type of All-American male that schools like Valley Forge delighted in; and that the authorial presence of Salinger has paid excruciating attention to the speech patterns of the kind of brassy rich WASP females that his family's upward mobility had thrust upon Salinger himself. It is almost as if he or the speaker had been used in some sociological experiment, the uptown equivalent of enforced busing, and something in him had rejected it. (pp. 41-2)

Hamilton notes the number of times young Salinger used the word "professional" about himself and his ambitions, which might seem puzzling on the face of it because he didn't need the money in any literal sense; but after Valley Forge and Ursinus and with a future in the sausage business looming, a man in his position might have felt he needed it all right, if only to avoid any more unpleasant surprises ever again.

Although one doesn't think of Salinger as a Depression writer, it was hard not to be at least a bit of one if you were born into the period. There were very very few safe fortunes back then, and even fewer that felt safe. And even though Sol's sausages were moving well, the Arthur Millers (and Sol must have known families just like them) had gone down with furs and the Irwin Shaws with real estate, and anyway his whole momentum, as he moved his brood downtown in forced marches, argued against taking time out to finance a writer. (On the other hand, he might have had a copy of *The New Yorker,* that Valley Forge Prep of magazines, on the coffee table: you might impress him by appearing in that.) . . .

But even subtracting the Depression, any writer anywhere who has ever heard some such phrase as "You'll never earn a living doing that stuff" will henceforth place an inordinate value on his royalty checks, which will look quite different from regular checks, and will fight for his copyright as for his honor. On the professional side of things Salinger has been unremittingly tough from the beginning, demanding all the control over production and promotion that a writer can conceivably be given, short of actually publishing the books himself, and hewing sternly to the professional writer's code which insists that there is no such thing as a free speech (or presumably letter).

The paradox of Salinger is that most of this toughness appears to have been strained out of his stories and only shows itself in the arduous, word-perfect phrasing (as the paraphrases suggest, Hamilton seems to have no ear at all for Salinger's prose, or interest in it—a desolate handicap in this particular case). The stories celebrate instead a sort of prelapsarian niceness, a willed return to some golden age of his own—what they call in sports a do-over, as if one could live one's whole life over again but with the curse taken off it. And perhaps the toughness is simply what stands guard over the playground. . . .

When and if Salinger releases from his care [his] long awaited manuscript-in-exile, he may very well wish that nobody remember anything about him at all, and that his artwork will not be disfigured by little tags of extraneous information: it's all any artist wishes. (p. 42)

Wilfrid Sheed, "The Exile," in The New York Review of Books, *Vol. XXXV, No. 16, October 27, 1988, pp. 35-6, 38, 40-2.*

T. S. Eliot Centenary

T(HOMAS) S(TEARNS) ELIOT

1888-1965

American-born English poet, critic, essayist, dramatist, and editor.

As an eminent poet and critic, in addition to his less celebrated position as playwright, Eliot has maintained an influence on literature that some critics claim is unequaled by any other writer of the twentieth century. His poetry and prose are frequently cited as having helped inaugurate the modern period in English and American letters. Eliot is best known for his distinctly erudite and innovative verse. Many of his poems combine classical references and concerns with elements drawn from contemporary culture in a format that often juxtaposes fragmentary, disjointed surfaces with underlying philosophical significance. Throughout his career, Eliot strongly advocated the development of a "historical sense," which, as he stated in his essay "Tradition and the Individual Talent," is "nearly indispensable to anyone who would continue to be a poet beyond his twenty-fifth year." Consequently, awareness of his literary and cultural heritage is one of the most prominent features of Eliot's criticism and poetry. Eliot's verse also incorporates experiments with form, phrasing, and tone, as evidenced in such seminal works as "The Love Song of J. Alfred Prufrock," *The Waste Land,* and *Four Quartets.* Concurrently, the astute observations, terms, and definitions introduced in his essays are significant contributions to literary analysis and stress the importance of tradition, religion, and morality in art and society. Northrop Frye observed: "A thorough knowledge of Eliot is compulsory for anyone interested in contemporary literature. Whether he is liked or disliked is of no importance, but he must be read."

Eliot's continuing significance in contemporary letters is reflected in the many activities, conferences, observances, and publications occasioned in 1988 by the centenary of his birth. Scholars and critics of Eliot's work gathered for conferences at Washington University in his native St. Louis, Missouri, at the University of Maine, at the Dali Museum and Poynter Institute in St. Petersburg, Florida, as well as in France and Japan. In England, where Eliot lived most of his life, the British Council organized an exhibition illustrating his career and the London Library created the T. S. Eliot Centenary Fund, which will allow students and scholars free access to library resources. The publications of *The Letters of T. S. Eliot: Volume One, 1898-1922,* edited by Valerie Eliot, the author's second wife, and Lyndall Gordon's biography, *Eliot's New Life,* a sequel to her previous work, *Eliot's Early Years,* prompted further critical commentary. Numerous tributes to Eliot and critical analyses of his writings were published in journals and books. In addition to these developments, a controversy arose concerning various anti-Semitic remarks attributed to Eliot during his life and career. Christopher Ricks's

study, *T. S. Eliot and Prejudice,* which examines prejudice in general as well as the motivations behind Eliot's remarks about Jews and other ethnic, social, racial, and religious groups, was one of several publications probing the extent of Eliot's alleged bias against Jews.

The Letters of T. S. Eliot: Volume One, 1898-1922 drew much attention, as critics perused the correspondences in hopes of finding references, notes, and reflections that would offer further insights into Eliot's writings. Although disappointed by Eliot's reticence toward discussing the ideas informing his work, critics generally agree the letters help illuminate the often tense and difficult life he led during the time he established his reputation and was composing *The Waste Land.* Soon after this poem was published, Eliot suffered a nervous breakdown. While reflecting his day-to-day concerns, the letters reveal Eliot's relationships with notable writers, including Ezra Pound and Conrad Aiken. Also evinced in the letters are the strains Eliot endured from overwork, an unhappy marriage, pressure from his family, the effects of World War I, his behind-the-scenes attempts to gain recognition for his writings, and the difficulties he encountered in founding and editing the *The Criterion,* a literary journal. Robert M. Adams echoed the general critical reception to *The Letters:* "Among literary letters not written deliberately for publication, the standard is set by those of Byron. . . . Eliot doesn't approach that class. . . ." Adams added: "Still, it's no use repining; the correspondence is what we now have and what we're going to get, and there are revelations in it that anyone who owes a debt to Eliot will treasure. (That includes anyone who's been interested in the development of English literature over the last seventy-five years)."

(For an overview of Eliot's life and work, see *CLC,* Vols. 1, 2, 3, 6, 9, 10, 13, 15, 24, 34, 41; *Contemporary Authors,* Vols. 5-8, rev. ed., Vols. 25-28, rev. ed. [obituary]; and *Dictionary of Literary Biography,* Vols. 7, 10, 45, 63.)

ROBERT CRAWFORD

The most striking aspect of the work of T. S. Eliot is its constancy. From his early years Eliot displayed a sensibility fascinated by the bringing together of apparent opposites. That sensibility flowered in the union of tradition and modernity, of Europe and America, of blasphemy and religion, of slapstick mischief and poker-faced enthronement. Most excitingly, and perhaps most revealingly, it flowered throughout his greatest work in the uniting of the world of the savage with the world of the city.

At the age of ten, Eliot celebrated twice in a childhood magazine the betrothal of Miss End and Mr Front; clearly he was amused by this meeting of opposites, and the change of name which would ensue. In **"Portrait of a Lady",** it is the lady, whose affected and empty refinement is mocked, who makes the aside

> (But our beginnings never know our ends!)

For Eliot, beginnings and ends were always closely bound together, though knowledge of their connecting pattern might emerge only much later. As he put it in **"Little Gidding",**

> What we call the beginning is often the end
> And to make an end is to make a beginning.

This preoccupation with bringing together apparent contraries lasted throughout Eliot's life. The *Fireside,* that little magazine which he edited in St Louis during early 1899, also records in its customary pencil the elopement of Mr Up and Miss Down. In 1912 at Harvard, James Woods would point Eliot to Diels's edition of Heraclitus whose philosophy saw the world as the result of contrary strains, and over twenty years after that, Eliot would select as an epigraph for his *Four Quartets* a fragment from his own copy of Diels's edition: . . . 'The way up and the way down are one.'

'When a poet's mind is perfectly equipped for its work,' Eliot wrote in **"The Metaphysical Poets"** (1921), 'it is constantly amalgamating disparate experience.' Clearly this concept was developed out of Eliot's enthusiasm for the *discordia concors* of Metaphysical poetry and the strange juxtapositions of later nineteenth-century French verse, but Eliot himself was attracted continually to setting explicit contraries together, Prufrocks against prophets. So, the repellently primitive confronts the brilliantly sophisticated when, in **"Burbank with a Baedeker: Bleistein with a Cigar",** a subhuman eye (or the eye of someone suffering from Graves' disease) confronts the sophisticated optics of a perspective of Canaletto. **"Gerontion"** sets withered inanity against full-blooded heroism. The placing of eastern beside western asceticism at the end of the third section of **The Waste Land,** Eliot wrote wryly in his notes, 'is not an accident'. With regard to **"Marina"**, he explained in a letter to Sir Michael Sadler, he intended a mixture of Seneca's Hercules awaking to discover that he has slaughtered his own children and Shakespeare's Pericles who, excitedly half-asleep, discovers his living lost daughter. Meetings of polar opposites are vital to the pattern of Eliot's work. One of the central interests of the **Four Quartets** concerns

> The point of intersection of the timeless
> With time . . .

"Little Gidding" ends with a resolution of themes developed in earlier movements, when 'the fire and the rose are one'. This last quartet concludes with a return to a struggled-for, childlike simplicity, pronouncing that

> the end of all our exploring
> Will be to arrive where we started
> And know the place for the first time.

The knot of ends and beginnings is once again being tied. (pp. 1-2)

[Eliot's] study of primitive societies went hand in hand with his study of decadent ones. This key preoccupation with savage and city emanates from his own childhood and is strengthened by his work at Harvard and in London, before it emerges as crucial to some of his greatest poetry in **The Waste Land,** **"The Hollow Men,"** and **Sweeney Agonistes.** The need to sharpen this theme continues in the later work. The **Quartets** modify the earlier treatment, yet continue to provide not only the urban world of London, but also

> the backward half-look
> Over the shoulder, towards the primitive terror.

Such a primitive terror had already been seen by the West End audiences of **The Family Reunion,** confronted by the Furies, while **The Cocktail Party** shocked its audiences with its sophisticated town gathering interrupted by news of a crucifixion among jungle tribesmen. . . . [The] combination of savage and city runs through Eliot's career. It is present in his scurrilous unpublished King Bolo poems, whose eponymous 'hero' is a savage in a bowler hat, as well as in Eliot's decidedly more sober social criticism where the legacy of earlier anthropologists moulds his view of modern society. The term 'savage' is employed here, because that is the term used by most of the anthropologists and anthropologically influenced scholars whose works Eliot read. Often he followed them in his use of the word. The 'city' is not simply London with its metropolitan sophisticate and its City financial district, but also the drab urban landscape which Eliot annexed as his poetic territory from his first book onwards. Eliot's urban landscape is a strange mixture of lived and literary experience. Often its nourishment came from unexpected ground. Eliot in 1932 wrote that 'some of Dickens' novels stand for London', and that he was particularly moved by 'the Chancery Prisoner in *Pickwick,* of whom is said finally, *He has got his discharge, by God'*. **The Waste Land** is certainly about prisoners, and involves 'different voices', but essentially the poem's city owes more to Kipling and Victorian poetry, both of which were childhood favourites. Similarly, an interest in the savage seems to date from Eliot's early childhood. Though the two elements were linked in the Victorian phrase

'city savage', Eliot's linking of them produced startling results. Understanding this peculiar combination in his work
makes possible a new interpretation of *The Waste Land* and
lets us see much more clearly what he was about in *Sweeney
Agonistes.* It helps restore to the reading of Eliot a sense of
the excitement, the openness and breadth of his art, an art
which drew on the *intichiuma* rites of the Australian aborigines as well as on the rites of the Christian Church; which
looked to jungles, jazz, and the Wild West as well as to the
tasks of bank clerk and churchwarden. Eliot's poetry is one
of struggle, longing, and mischief, as multifaceted as it is intense. The study of the savage and the city in his work opens
doors in his poetry which lead to predictable and less predictable destinations, including Mendelian heredity, evolution,
blood-and-thunder stories, Melanesia, and Lloyds Bank.
Most important is the realization that an understanding of
Eliot's continuing concerns with savage, city, and their connection helps us appreciate not only the ferocity and liveli-
ness of Old Possum, but also the way in which texts as diverse
as **"Growltiger's Last Stand"**, **"The Dry Salvages"**, and *The
Waste Land* emerge from the same temperament, showing
lighter and darker sides of an apocalyptic imagination. (pp.
2-4)

> *Robert Crawford, in his* The Savage and the City in
> the Works of T. S. Eliot, *Oxford at the Clarendon
> Press, 1987, 251 p.*

JOSEPH SCHWARTZ

[T. S. Eliot is the] greatest literary figure of the English-
speaking world in this century. Poetry and criticism were permanently changed and enriched by his work. He was himself
a living example of the powerful insight he offered us in **"Tradition and the Individual Talent."** No one added more substantially to tradition than he did in helping to shape it as it
had shaped him. He was always generous with the past,
knowing the debt he owed it, a debt we now owe to him. He
has joined that "dead master" and is no longer subject to "uncertain hours."

His poetry is of the highest quality. *Four Quartets* can be described only as magisterial. And yet it is never Olympian or
patronizing. *The Waste Land* remains (and probably will remain) the most famous poem of this century, so rich in its tension that it can still confuse the inattentive reader. . . . When
his poetry appeared it graciously gave its readers lines that
were "immemorial." He taught me, for instance, to listen to
the voices of the children in the apple tree, and I have been
blessedly lonely ever since.

Eliot's criticism makes us rank him with Dr. Samuel Johnson; it was a major force in shaping the critical enterprise—
"the common pursuit"—of this century. It helped to give its
true significance back to literature. He always welcomed new
insights and bold experiments; he paid his dues to the indispensable past. He was humble in front of the object upon
which criticism feeds for its life. He was courageous, unafraid
of stating his values, even though post-modernism attacked
them vigorously, and he was forthright in the carefully-
crafted judgments he made. As he found himself as a poet
over years of practice and contemplation, so, too, he was always a developing critic.

There are many of his readers who feel that his political and

cultural essays deserve as much attention as his literary
ones. . . .

When we think of Eliot now the great ones come to mind easily—Chaucer, Johnson, Goethe. He is of their company now,
as naturally as they were once his teachers. They share a vision together, a sense of the ultimate existence and supreme
value of deathless things in the very midst of the overwhelming reminders of the power of mutability.

> *Joseph Schwartz, in an editorial commentary in* Re-
> nascence, *Vol. XL, No. 3, Spring, 1988, p. 158.*

BERNARD WEINRAUB

LONDON, Aug. 8—A celebration honoring T. S. Eliot, one
of the most influential poets of the 20th century, has turned
into a dispute over accusations that the writer was anti-
Semitic.

At the center of the dispute is a plan by the London Library
to celebrate [September's] 100th anniversary of Eliot's birth
with the creation of a fund to help scholars and students. Several prominent Jews in Britain, including Lord Goodman, a
well-known lawyer who is powerful in the business and arts
communities, and Sir Isaiah Berlin, the philosopher and author, have joined the appeal to create the T. S. Eliot Centenary Fund.

But in recent days, questions have been raised about what
Eliot wrote about Jews, and some prominent Jews are questioning the involvement of others in the centenary fund.

Lewis Golden, treasurer of the London Library—of which
Eliot was chairman from 1952 to 1964—and one of the Jewish patrons of the appeal, said in an interview that Eliot, after
World War II, "mentions with great respect" such Jewish
writers as Karl Mannheim and Simone Weil, and that Eliot
wrote in 1948 of the "legacy of Greece, Rome and Israel."

Mr. Golden said that "although one cannot excuse it," the
anti-Semitic bias in Eliot's writing "has to be read in the context of the attitude prevalent in the 1920's and expressed in
some quarters in America and elsewhere long before the
dreadful consequences of the Nazis' frenzied use of anti-
Semitism."

But others insist that Eliot's writings remained highly offensive even after World War II.

Michael Hastings, who wrote the play *Tom and Viv,* about
Eliot's first marriage, said, "The letters he wrote and his silence postwar and the rather scurrilous and vitriolic racist
limericks he was still writing in the 50's show absolutely no
sense of apology."

"Privately, Eliot wrote hundreds of letters using words like
'kike' and 'nigger,' " Mr. Hastings said in an interview, "Like
Pound and Wyndham Lewis, Eliot's silence about the Holocaust cannot be dismissed as some kind of minor aberration.
The three of them were as seething and unpleasant a pile of
anti-Semites as you can find." . . .

The current dispute surfaced in *The Jewish Chronicle,* a British weekly, which quoted some derogatory references to Jews
from Eliot's poetry of the 1920's and questioned why some
prominent Jews were involved in celebrating his birth. . . .

Among the works most often cited was **"Burbank, With a**

Baedeker: Bleistein With a Cigar,"** which includes these lines:

> The rats are underneath the piles.
> The jew is underneath the lot.

Another poem, **"Gerontion,"** includes these lines:

> My house is a decayed house,
> And the jew squats on the window sill the owner,
> Spawned in some estaminet in Antwerp.

Emanuel Litvinoff, a poet now in his 70's who wrote a poem in 1951 that attacked Eliot as anti-Semitic, said over the telephone today:

> "I don't see any reason why there shouldn't be a centenary honoring T. S. Eliot. He was one of the great poets of the century. But he was also anti-Semitic. In 1948, after Auschwitz, after everything that had happened, he allowed his anti-Semitic poems to be published in a selected edition of his poems. It was grossly insensitive, really appalling. When he wrote about Jews he used a small j. It's an individual's choice to lend themselves to a fund-raising effort, but I wouldn't." . . .

Prof. John Carey, an English professor at Oxford who lectures on Eliot, said the work for which Eliot was being criticized was careless, commenting, "I do not think the word anti-Semitism is appropriate in Eliot's case."

He added: "What may seem to us in restrospect to be dangerous would have seemed relatively innocent in the 1920's and 1930's. It was impossible at the time to know what was going to happen in the 1940's."

But Mr. Hastings, the playwright, disagreed. "There is a grave problem with Eliot," he said. "All of his influences were frighteningly negative. In his personal life, he was an anti-Semite and a racist. You can't take the racism out of the man."

The appeal, which is being supported by Eliot's second wife, Valerie, is seeking about $170,000 to help scholars use the resources of the London Library.

> *Bernard Weinraub, "Anti-Semitism Issue Slows British Fund for Eliot," in* The New York Times, *August 9, 1988, p. C20.*

ANTHONY JULIUS

This centenary year of T. S. Eliot's birth has been scarred with controversy over his alleged anti-Semitism. The London Library is marking the event by fund-raising for young writers, which is appropriate because Eliot himself was once the subject of a private fund-raising effort by the poet Ezra Pound. A number of distinguished Jews, including Lord Goodman and Sir Isaiah Berlin, are among the patrons of the appeal. Their support is regarded by many as inappropriate: it is not right, it is said, to endorse the reputation of an anti-Semite.

There are two questions that call for answers. Was Eliot an anti-Semite? And if he was, does it matter? He did not make a career out of anti-Semitism. Unlike Pound, he was not a propagandist. His remarks about Jews are scattered through his work. They do not figure prominently in it. But they are

there, and their presence cannot be dismissed. Much of that material is dismaying.

Among the poems, there is **"Burbank with a Baedeker: Bleistein with a Cigar,"** a sardonic account of two tourists in Venice in which Bleistein is pilloried as "Chicago Semite Viennese". **"Gerontion"** is a despairing meditation by a narrator whose landlord, a "jew", "squats on the window sill". *Dirge,* a rejected part of **The Waste Land,** drowns Bleistein.

In each there is ample material to offend, and elsewhere, too. . . .

Late in the 1930s Eliot regarded reports of persecution of the Jews in Nazi Germany as greatly exaggerated. He dismissed Marx as a "Jewish economist" and Freud as an "adept" of the "parvenu science" of psycho-analysis. In a pre-war lecture he suggested that too many free-thinking Jews would be undesirable in an ideal, traditional society. After the war he wrote, in a footnote, that contact with such Jews led to the illusion that there could be culture without religion.

Whenever accused of anti-Semitism, Eliot denied it, protesting that as a Christian he could not be an anti-Semite, because it was a sin. Against this defence—which some in any event did not find plausible—his critics pointed to the notorious passages in his poetry. He told friends that the charge hurt him, but it pursued him throughout his life.

His comment about free-thinking Jews lost him the friendship of George Boas, one such free-thinker. He was threatened with a boycott at a poetry reading in New York and was ejected by a Jewish hostess when he admitted authorship of **"Burbank."** The Jewish poet Emanuel Litvinov wrote a poem attacking him (Eliot was in the audience when it was read). . . .

Eliot grappled with the charge in a variety of ways. In response to the New York boycott he wrote publicly, and in stirring terms, condemning anti-Semitism:

> "Any country which denies the rights of its own citizens or makes pariahs of any body of its own nationals—and most especially the Jews—will sooner or later have to pay the full price for so doing; and even the 'uninvolved' people whom it governs will have to expiate the crime of having allowed such a government to lead them."

In correspondence with Groucho Marx, he wrote of his admiration for the State of Israel. In a preface to a book by Simone Weil he criticized her for rejecting the Jewish origins of Christianity. He spoke admiringly of the Jewish philosopher Martin Buber. He suppressed the book which contained the reference to "free-thinking Jews". He rewrote his post-war footnote in 1963 to urge contact between "devout and practising" Christians and Jews.

Some of these expressions of opposition to anti-Semitism were in response to specific challenges. But there are others. For example, in his early religious drama, **The Rock,** he disparages fascist thugs chanting anti-Semitic abuse at workmen building a church. And in September 1941, when guest editor of *The Christian Newsletter,* he deplored the new anti-Semitic laws in Vichy France and hoped Christians would speak out against them.

But what he did not do was repudiate his poetry—the furthest he would go was print "jew" in the upper case in later editions. Nor did he concede that there was any anti-

Semitism in his work, or admit that Christian anti-Semitism was even possible. So the controversy was left unresolved, periodically to be revived. The present affair is simply the latest episode.

The Jewish response to Eliot is typically a combination of pain, perplexity and admiration. Eliot's poetry is difficult and its capacity to rebuff ordinary readers was a common early complaint of critics. But the offence that it gives to Jews is different. This is because it is a consequence not of any obscurity of meaning, but of its wounding simplicity. And it creates a problem. How does the Jewish reader respond to a text that insults him?

Litvinov made a poem out of this tension: "I am not one accepted in your parish. / Bleistein is my relative . . ." Instead of writing this, he could have turned his back on Eliot, but we would not then have his poem, and we would be the poorer for it. He created something out of a negation, which is not only an endorsement of Eliot (the poem is indebted to him) but also a critique of his limitations.

In their own modest way, the patrons of the London Library appeal are doing likewise. They are sponsoring a fund which can only do good. They should therefore not be criticized, but commended—and supported.

Anthony Julius, "The Mark against Eliot," in The Times, *London, August 9, 1988, p. 10.*

BERNARD LEVIN

The increasingly bizarre controversy over the T. S. Eliot Centenary Fund would hardly be complete without a contribution from me calculated to exacerbate feelings on all sides of the question. In case there is anyone who has not yet entered the maze, the few necessary facts can be quickly established. That indispensable institution the London Library is soliciting funds—a target of £100,000 has been mentioned—to set up a trust which would enable young or needy writers and researchers to make use of the library, because in the ordinary way there is a subscription which for some would be hard to meet. Because Eliot was the president of the London Library for 13 years, and himself instrumental in starting a similar fund, the present appeal bears his name.

It also bears, among the list of patrons of the appeal, the names of some very distinguished Jews, including Sir Isaiah Berlin and Lord Goodman, and shortly after it was launched mutterings were heard suggesting that it was inappropriate for such people to be associated with such a cause, because Eliot was anti-Semitic.

That was the first damned silly thing said on the subject (not the last, alas), since it implies that you have to be Jewish to deplore anti-Semitism. As soon as this idea was mooted, however, everybody forgot what the money was *for.* I would not be surprised to learn that some people are now convinced that it is to buy jackboots for retired SS officers of limited means.

The next slice of baloney consisted of a claim that Eliot was *not* anti-Semitic, and indeed that (ah, what scents not of lavender rise from the familiar old phrase, unheard now for decades!) some of Eliot's best friends were Jews. Well, anti-Semitic he was—not, of course, in the Mosley-rabble mode, though not in the robust Chesterton or slimy Belloc manner either; his anti-Semitism was what I would call the genteel-

demented. The anti-Semitic references in his work, which are sufficiently unambiguous to convict him of the charge, suggest that Jews are an alien, corrupt and debasing influence, a kind of impurity or bacillus in the blood of the body politic, allied with all those who in societies like ours, "worm-eaten with liberalism", cannot be trusted to uphold the ancient virtues. . . .

At this point, most sensible people will conclude that Eliot was anti-Semitic, but that the excellent cause to which his name has been attached by the London Library is in no way tainted by that fact. . . .

But I want to go somewhat further, since there is an aspect of this story which is rarely discussed, and which has bedevilled consideration of anti-Semitism for many years now. I think it was Maitland who said that one of the problems of establishing historical truth was that we forget that things now in the past were once in the future. If you put Eliot's anti-Semitism in its historical context, you are likely to get a surprise.

I take it that there will be no dissent from my view that anti-Semitism is wrong and vile. . . . Anti-Semitism, from the earliest ages till three quarters of the way through the 18th century, then again (at any rate in Russia) at the end of the 19th, and finally from the Nazis onward, is wholly inexcusable. The reason is that those who fanned the flames of *Judenhass* in those eras knew that the flames could and did destroy human beings, which of course was frequently the intention of the men who plied the bellows. . . .

Anyway, it gradually died out; the Enlightenment helped, and Napoleon still more—so much so that the horrors of late Tsarist Russia must have seemed a dreadful throwback to less civilized times. This is not to say that anti-Semitism had disappeared; only that massacre was no longer the inevitable result of it. Discrimination and hostility remained; but Jews in all civilized countries, and a surprisingly large number of uncivilized ones, no longer went in fear of their lives.

It was in the lull before the final, terrible storm that Eliot and his like were free to express what they felt about Jews, *with no social disapproval.* If you read at all widely in the literature of, say, the period from the end of the First World War to the beginning of the Second, you will find, frequently in the writings of the wisest and gentlest of men, let alone the less so, expressions and attitudes about Jews which would today rule out their authors from decent society. The point is that decent society, in those days, was filled with people who had forgotten what anti-Semitism *had* led to, and who could not guess what it *would* lead to.

Indeed, the situation was stranger still; the prevalence of casual anti-Semitism was such that its use became quite unconscious. . . .

In that atmosphere, anti-Semitic feelings could be expressed without embarrassment or guilt across almost any dinner table—even a table with Jews at it. . . .

For Eliot's generation the expression of anti-Semitic feelings was *safe;* therefore it was expressed. Now, we have no excuse; we know what it has led to, in the heart of Europe, in the lifetime of men and women not yet middle-aged. Those who strike matches today are playing with fire; yesterday, the world was non-flammable.

But I cannot find it in my heart to condemn Eliot and the others (Harold Nicolson was another) who thought that it was all right because they used only safety matches. There are, of course, no safety matches where anti-Semitism is concerned, but we must not judge the ignorant past by the knowing present.

Anti-Semitism is one of the oldest of the world's plagues; I doubt if it will ever be wholly eradicated. No two theories as to its cause are the same, and no lasting cure is in sight. But while the search for a vaccine is pursued, let not the London Library fund suffer for doing no more than attach T. S. Eliot's name to a most worthy project.

After all, perhaps one of those researchers who cannot afford the library's subscription, and whose work will be paid for by the fund, will there find the cure for anti-Semitism that has eluded mankind for so many centuries.

> Bernard Levin, "How Eliot Caught the Plague," in
> The Times, London, August 15, 1988, p. 10.

CRAIG RAINE

The task of the artist at any time is uncompromisingly simple—to discover what has not yet been done, and to do it. To do it, moreover, in a way which not only breaks with, but is also a logical extension of, the past. The late Hans Keller definitively observed that the greatest art is characterised by "unpredictable inevitability"—a quality which T. S. Eliot possessed in abundance. Extravagantly inventive yet fastidiously word perfect, stylistically prodigious yet always recognisably himself, Eliot is the century's greatest poet.

When **Poems**—1920 was reviewed by E. E. Cummings in the *Dial,* even while he deplored the obstinately unconventional modernism of others, Cummings noted Mr Eliot's "skilful and immediate violins." Of course, for a full description, one would now wish to add colours to Eliot's orchestra—a hint of crumhorn in the perfect pastiche of Prufrock's phrase "to swell a progress," however out of character it may seem for one of Prufrock's cultural anxiety; serialism for "Hysteria"; the thunder-sheet of Dayadhvam; the honky-tonk piano of **Sweeney Agonistes;** the organ fugue of **Ash-Wednesday;** the mixture of *sprechgesang* and *a cappella* of **"The Hollow Men."** None of these sounds was predictable, though all now strike us as inevitable.

Poetry lies at the centre of Eliot's achievement. But he was also a literary critic of originality and penetration, the influential editor of *The Criterion* from 1922 to 1939, a social critic, playwright, author of children's verse, the inspiration for a musical, a translator, a tireless lecturer, a quondam philosopher and a full-time publisher. To this one can add that he was a purveyor of titles, as demonstrated by Waugh's *A Handful of Dust* and F. R. Leavis's *The Common Pursuit,* as well as (with increasing licence) two recent films, one Irish, one Canadian—*Eat the Peach* and *I've Heard the Mermaids Singing.* He was, too, a supplier of tags and coiner of phrases: "I should be glad," he remarked, a little ruefully, in 1964, "to hear no more of a bang and a whimper." . . .

One might choose . . . to illustrate his unique temper by concentrating on a single essay, like that on Tennyson, replete as it is with Eliot's characteristic strengths—his grasp of detail and his gift for suggestive generalisations which frequently double as personal asides. Praising Tennyson's metrical virtuosity in "Mariana," Eliot reveals the subtle discrimina-

tions of which his own ear was capable: "*the blue fly sung in the pane* (the line would be ruined if you substituted *sang* for *sung*) is enough to tell us that something important has happened." The "something important" is the disruption of the metre in the middle of the line. Whether this is, as Eliot claims, "wholly new," is open to question. . . .

In his own poetry, Eliot's ear was both resourceful and almost completely reliable—the latter a much more rare quality than non-poets might suppose. Eliot's failures are not naked blunders, they are heavily camouflaged mistakes by a sophisticated ear. For example, "*This* is as I had reckoned" disguises, as best it can, that little pile-up of syllables at the beginning of the line. The italics Eliot so deplored in Arnold's poetry are here deployed to distract us from the initial stutter. The difference is enormous.

Eliot said that "to be able to quote as Arnold could do is the best evidence of taste." By this standard, Eliot has near perfect taste. Quoting "Tears, Idle Tears" from *The Princess,* Eliot omits the last line with its variant refrain, and greatly improves the poetry by this stroke of editing. Praising Tennyson as having the finest ear for vowel sounds of any English poet, Eliot silently emends Tennyson's weakness for repetition—an area where Tennyson is notably gifted but sometimes over-susceptible, and where Eliot's skills are unmatched. Has anyone dared to use the simple connective *and* as Eliot does in **"Prufrock"** so insistently, both for its ability to summon ironically the epic world of, say, Sohrab and Rustum, and for its surprisingly powerful music? Consider, too, the hypnotic Bolero-like development of this passage:

> And would it have been worth it, after all,
> Would it have been worth while,
> After the sunsets and the dooryards and the sprin-
>   kled streets,
> After the novels, after the teacups, after the skirts
>   that trail along the floor—
> And this, and so much more?
> It is impossible to say just what I mean!
> But as if a magic lantern threw the nerves in pat-
>   terns on a screen:
> Would it have been worth while
> If one, settling a pillow or throwing off a shawl,
> And turning toward the window should say:
> "That is not it at all,
> That is not what I meant at all."

The Tennyson essay is also remarkable for the thoroughness of Eliot's reading. Juvenilia which most of us would skip is cited instead as evidence, and convincing evidence, of Tennyson's aural inventiveness. Eliot's knowledge of the neglected, late dialect poems, like "Owd Roä," "The Village Wife" and "The Northern Cobbler," permits him to cite Tennyson as an influence on Kipling's "Barrack Room Ballads," thereby complicating our notion of Kipling as the artistic son and heir of Browning. Unlike many merely good writers, Eliot continued to read and to learn from his reading rather than be confirmed by it. This is one reason why he repeats himself less than any other modern writer—and why, for other poets, he has become a model for variousness.

Because Eliot was such a powerful exemplar, Lowell changed his style from the clotted theological intensities of "The Quaker Graveyard at Nantucket"—themselves closely modelled on **Four Quartets**—to the relatively relaxed simplicity of "Life Studies" and thereafter to the Marvellian formalism of "Near the Ocean." And if Seamus Heaney is currently purging his style in search of something more austere, a poetry of "the bare wire", Eliot is a presence in that process, too. Even Larkin's resolute refusal to develop as a poet was conditioned by Eliot's quick-change artistry.

Writing of Arnold—an irksomely important and therefore deeply resented intellectual father-figure—. . . Eliot brings in the eccentric verdict that "Arnold was not a man of vast or exact scholarship." Yet even while he criticises Arnold, he mimics his tone of lofty judiciousness: "there is petulance in such a judgment, arrogance and excess of heat."

Eliot is unjust, too, to Arnold's poetry. It is academic. Arnold, to have been a great poet, should have seen "the boredom, and the horror, and the glory"—and, according to Eliot, knew only "something of the boredom." There is some justice here, given the poems Eliot chooses to discuss—but he completely ignores "Dover Beach," a poem whose irregular rhymes, irregular line lengths, fluctuating stress-count provide the formal template for **"The Love Song of J. Alfred Prufrock,"** just as surely as Clough is godfather to its ironies and Browning to its way with the dramatic monologue. . . .

When Eliot writes, early in his career, that "the possessors of the inner voice ride 10 in a compartment to a football match at Swansea, listening to the inner voice, which breathes the eternal message of vanity, fear and lust"—when Eliot writes so, he takes his cue from Arnold, the greatest ironist in the English language. . . .

This major and influential critical injustice aside, Eliot's criticism is notable for its absence of showily perverse flourishes, as the essay on Tennyson shows. The swift and exact discriminations are as thrilling in their way as watching a Chinese chef wielding a cleaver with power and precision, as if he could never make a mistake. Eliot made very few. Of Wordsworth, whose "Tintern Abbey," "Ode: Intimations of Immortality" and much of the *Prelude* deal with the loss of vision, Eliot remarks somewhat mystifyingly: "His inspiration never having been of that sudden, fitful and terrifying kind that visited Coleridge, he was never, apparently, troubled by the consciousness of having lost it." His verdict on Maud is more typical: the meat, several distinguished lyrics, is set aside while the bones, Tennyson's incoherent and melodramatic plot, is put to one side for a nourishing soup—the reflection that Tennyson fails here is because he is undecided between lyric and dramatic expression. . . .

The great and persistent theme of Eliot's poetry, from first to last, can be summed up in the advice of Lambert Strether, the central protagonist of Henry James's *The Ambassadors,* to a young artist, little Bilham: "Live all you can. It's a mistake not to." For Eliot, the failure to live, the failure of emotion to find its proper expression, is an obsessive theme of his work. It begins with Prufrock's failure to ask the "overwhelming question," to make his feelings known in a proposal of marriage. He cannot pop the question and, instead, acknowledges: "I have measured out my life with coffee spoons." This line is generally, even universally, perceived as conceding the triviality of Prufrock's existence, but it should be read completely otherwise—as a tragic statement of repression and stoical suffering, like John Davidson's clerk in *Thirty Bob a Week* who sees his banal existence as "walking on a string across a gulf"—the unglamorous heroism of the almost poor. Life's sweetness, even as Prufrock loads his spoon with sugar, is accelerating to its vanishing point. And

he knows it, yet hasn't "the strength to force the moment to its crisis."

The pretentious anti-heroine of **"Portrait of a Lady"** finally claims our sympathy because her emotional desperation at last drives her to a directness that shames the narrator out of his cynically amused reserve. She can ask him "why we have not developed into friends?" He can respond only with the authentically modern poetic note of queasy emotional uncertainty—"not knowing what to feel . . ." Directly appealed to, the young man remains aridly self-possessed and unable to give himself.

In **"Rhapsody on a Windy Night,"** the idea of preparing for "life" is "the last twist of the knife" because the poem has shown us only a simulacrum of life, the form without the substance, or the substance without the soul. A rusty, inelastic spring; a child with nothing behind its eye; a crab with instincts to pinch: life, in this poem, is portrayed as nothing more than a series of physical reflexes. And it is no accident that the "automatic" hand of the child which pockets a toy should be echoed in *The Waste Land* by the typist who has stooped to folly with the "young man carbuncular" . . . Actions which once had consequence have now become weightless. The people in *The Waste Land,* like **"Gerontion,"** have lost their passion. Ariel's song in *The Tempest,* which leads Ferdinand to Miranda and the prospect of innocent love, is demoted by Eliot: the lyrical "Come unto these yellow sands, / And then take hands" becomes instead "On Margate Sands. / I can connect / Nothing with nothing."

"The Hollow Men" are hollow because they, too, are without substance. They are not "lost / Violent souls"—not real sinners who deserve hell and retribution, but people who have failed to live at all, failed even to sin, and have therefore been refused admission to Hell. They fetch up rather in limbo, where they ruminate on "death's other kingdom." They are not unlike Kipling's Tomlinson, who is rejected by heaven and hell alike. But the significant reference here is to Canto 3 of the *Inferno* (already alluded to in *The Waste Land* notes): Virgil indentifies the occupants of Hell's ante-room as "forlorn spirits," whose lives have been "without infamy and without praise," beside whom "the sinner would be proud." Eliot's attitude is summed up in his essay on Baudelaire: "so far as we do evil or good, we are human; and it is better, in a paradoxical way; to do evil than to do nothing; at least, we exist." Again: "the worst that can be said about most of our malefactors, from statesmen to thieves, is that they are not men enough to be damned."

In **Sweeney Agonistes,** published in *The Criterion* October 1926 and January 1927, the febrile socialising cannot hide the fundamental truth voiced by Sweeney. When asked by Doris what life is, he retorts that "Life is death." The (unfinished) piece closes with the lines, "And perhaps you're alive / And perhaps you're dead." As a result of Eliot's lowlife cast, the theme is coarsely articulated but still related to the spiritual diffidence and crippled sensibility of "Animula"—the "simple soul," "Fearing the warm reality, the offered good / Denying the importunity of the blood." And the doubtful nature of experience in *Sweeney Agonistes* where the man who has kept the murdered girl in a bath of lysol is uncertain whether "he was alive and the girl was dead"—anticipates *Burnt Norton,* whose speaker delineates an experience in all its vivid non-existence:

Footfalls echo in the memory
Down the passage which we did not take
Towards the door we never opened
Into the rose-garden.

Essentially, Eliot is conjuring an experience which has been tragically missed—something from the realm of might-have-been, a hypothesis of happiness. By the time of *Four Quartets,* he certainly knew it was a mistake not to live all you can.

> Craig Raine, "The Awful Daring of T. S. Eliot," in
> The Guardian, *August 19, 1988, p. 21.*

MICHAEL DIRDA

During his lifetime T. S. Eliot bestrode the literary world like a colossus. From the publication of *The Waste Land* in 1922 until his death in 1965 he was the chief cultural poohbah of England and America; in 1956 over 14,000 people jammed into a stadium in Minnesota to hear him—or, more accurately, simply to see him; literary histories spoke reverently of "The Age of Eliot."

After all, he was the author of the most admired poem of the century, generally regarded as the greatest literary critic in English, and hearkened to as a social visionary and religious prophet. He received the outward signs of success too: the Nobel Prize, the Order of Merit, and a hit on Broadway (his play *The Cocktail Party*).

Which just goes to show that nothing fails like success. During the past 20 years Eliot's reputation has taken a beating on all fronts. In terms of poetic influence Wallace Stevens and William Carlos Williams divide contemporary American poetry between them. Virtually all of Eliot's literary judgments have been seriously challenged or strongly qualified. Modern verse drama came and went. Critics talk of "The Pound Era."

There's always a swing downward in reputation after the death of a giant. But then matters even out as scholarship starts to strip away the veneer of the smiling—or in Eliot's case, sad-faced—public man. In his centennial year (he was born on September 26, 1888) Eliot is currently enjoying, some might say enduring, that process. Memoirs, biographies, the discovery and publication of the *Waste Land* manuscript, and now his letters are altering our image of the Anglo-Catholic royalist and classicist into something much richer and stranger. Those are pearls that were his eyes. (pp. 1, 10)

In her introduction [to *The Letters of T. S. Eliot: Volume One, 1898-1922*] Valerie Eliot, the poet's widow, mentions that she had originally intended the first volume to go up to the end of 1926, that is, up to the moment of Eliot's religious conversion. This would have allowed a neat continuity with Lyndall Gordon's superb *Eliot's New Life,* which focuses on the poet's spiritual biography from 1927 till his death. But the years between these two books are in fact their hidden focus: the dissolution of Eliot's marriage to his first wife, Vivienne, and the reblossoming of his love for the girl he left behind, Emily Hale. It is the revelation of this human drama that is largely responsible for the image of Eliot as a confessional poet, somewhere between Baudelaire and Robert Lowell.

Admittedly, it is sometimes hard to find the human being in Eliot's correspondence. . . . Eliot simply is not in the class of his poet-friends Conrad Aiken and Ezra Pound, who made their lively correspondence an extension of their personalities

and their poetic platforms. Happily, Valerie Eliot includes a few letters from these friends, as well as from Jean Verdenal, the mysterious dedicatee of *Prufrock and Other Observations,* who was killed in World War I. There was speculation at one time that he and Eliot were homosexual lovers; but Verdenal's letters are merely affectionate and nostalgic. However some of the correspondence with Aiken, Pound and other old friends displays a locker-room bawdiness: There are several excerpts from Eliot's obscene King Bolo poems, and lots of verbal towel-snapping about private parts and even more private acts.

Most of the time, though, these London letters show us Eliot the son (at times the mama's boy), the nurse-husband to neurotic wife Vivienne, and the ambitious young urban professional. In the early letters home Eliot stresses his accomplishments; only to his friends does he talk of emptiness and acedia, of the hollow man within: "In Oxford I have the feeling that I am not quite alive—that my body is walking about with a bit of my brain inside it, and nothing else."

This "aboulie," as Eliot calls it, may offer one reason why he suddenly and rashly married Vivienne Haigh-Wood—"the awful daring of a moment's surrender / Which an age of prudence can never retract." Emily Hale had not, apparently, made her feelings clear to Eliot before he left for England. Vivienne was vivacious, available; like characters in Henry James, they mistook each other's true selves. The result was a nightmare marriage. . . .

And yet, throughout this litany of woes, Eliot keeps saying things like "The present year has been, in some respects, the most awful nightmare of anxiety that the mind of man can conceive, but at least it is not dull . . ." One senses that the young Eliot's fear of the void within himself was so great that only by suffering and constant work could he keep it at bay. Eventually, I think, the ceaseless activity—both professional and social—became the workaholic's typical means of avoiding an impossible homelife.

Readers looking for Eliot the critic and poet in these pages will need to be highly imaginative. There are prefigurations of famous critical or poetic formulations—"I like to feel that a writer is perfectly cool and detached, regarding other people's feelings or his own, like a god who has got beyond them . . ."—but such tidbits are few and never developed. No one reading these pages would believe that their author was at work on the critical pieces that would make *The Sacred Wood* a touchstone in the history of literary theory.

What is true of the essays is even more true of the poems. Eliot never talks about **"The Love Song of J. Alfred Prufrock"** or **"Gerontion"** except as products—as poems to sell to *Poetry* or *The Dial.* . . .

Even though Eliot's letters give us no direct glimpse into his poetic workshop, they do relate some telling and touching moments. The pathos of Eliot writing his mother, when he learns of his father's death, that he wants to hear her "sing The Little Tailor to me." The probably unconscious double-entendre of a note to Bertrand Russell, who has taken Viv on a little vacation: "I am sure you have done everything possible and handled her in the very best way—better than I" (Russell almost certainly slept with her). The personal plea behind the letter to *The Athenaeum* urging that the British Museum library should stay open in the evenings for people who had jobs during the day.

There are, of course, occasional signs of the "bad" Eliot. He refers callously to "our servant" and almost never calls her by name; he mentions "Siegfried Sassoon (semitic)"; he cuts old friends, including "Conrad Aiken, stupider than ever." And all the while he is smiling at the right people, keeping his name in the news, managing his literary career with Rommel-like cunning.

These letters leave us at the end with Eliot on the verge of his greatest success. He has finished *The Waste Land* (while on leave from Lloyd's bank for nervous exhaustion) and has inaugurated *The Criterion*. He has every reason to be proud, perhaps a little too proud: "There is a small and select public which regards me as the best living critic, as well as the best living poet, in England . . . . I really think that I have far more influence on English letters than any other American has ever had, unless it be Henry James."

He was right, of course, despite the snotty tone. But Lyndall Gordon's *Eliot's New Life* shows in part how little that public success came to mean to him. By 1925 Vivienne Eliot's neurasthenia started to pass over into delusional madness. In 1928 Eliot converted to the Church of England, eventually going so far as to make a private vow of chastity. Soon thereafter he began to live apart from his wife, keeping his whereabouts secret, sneaking out of his office when she appeared, dodging her in public and private.

Lyndall Gordon's *Eliot's Early Years* (1977) tried to understand Eliot's treatment of Vivienne, often taking her part against received history. *Eliot's New Life* chronicles the poet's "search for salvation," but focuses closely on the place of women in that search: the gnawing guilt over leaving Vivienne, the promise of renewed happiness with Emily Hale. Eliot wrote over 1,000 letters to Hale—all of them locked up at Princeton until the year 2020—and spent many springs and summers in her company. She was simply a New England-born school teacher, with an interest in drama, but she represented for Eliot an ideal love, his own lost innocence and purity. Ultimately she served as Beatrice to his Dante—and then was cruelly cast aside. . . .

In her brilliant analysis of the *Quartets*—a companion piece to the "autobiographical" reading of *The Waste Land* in her earlier book—Gordon links Eliot's spiritual search with that of his puritan forebears. Building on the classic studies by F. O. Matthiessen and Helen Gardner, Gordon interprets the *Four Quartets* as a full-fledged spiritual autobiography—an attempt to understand how to live a religious life in a fallen world, how to achieve sanctity. These same highly personal themes recur in the plays of this era, not least in *The Cocktail Party* with its submerged homage to Emily Hale as Celia, whom the hero does not marry and instead sends to her martyrdom.

Which is what Eliot finally did. His family assumed that he and Emily would eventually wed; but when Vivienne died in 1947, after years in an asylum, Eliot looked within and found that all his desire for marriage had died too. He preferred his poetic dreams of the past and the lone path of the religious ordeal, divesting himself of everything in his quest to know God. . . .

In his later years Eliot slept on a simple bed under a heavy iron cross. He took the bus every day to church, recited his prayers quietly in the crowded tube. He expected to retire to an abbey. As a lecturer he had gradually become something of a spiritual authority, talking about life and society, religion

and literature with a voice beyond time, beyond place. And then, at age 68, he married his 30-year-old secretary, Valerie Fletcher.

This may seem almost a joke, the renunciation of a lifetime's habits. But this second marriage found Eliot surprised by joy, and his final years were, by all reports, extremely happy. He had journeyed from the inferno of his youth through the purgatory of his maturity to find an unexpected paradise in his last years.

For all his gifts and accomplishments, Eliot was for most of his life a haunted man, racked with a sense of sin, always yearning for "the peace that passeth understanding." In his self-obsession he sometimes treated others cruelly; he was often a holy prig; but knowing of his own purgatorial burning humanizes and transforms his poems, so perfectly beautiful, so terribly personal. Still, to read *The Waste Land* now is to hear the cries of Vivienne, as well as Philomel; and even though the end of "**Little Gidding**" may triumphantly unite the fire and the rose, it is hard to forget Emily Hale, ultimately left standing alone by the door that never opened. (p. 10)

> Michael Dirda, "The Love Song of T. S. Eliot," in Book World—The Washington Post, *September 25, 1988, pp. 1, 10.*

JONATHAN RABAN

'Poor Tom' is how he was tagged by Virginia Woolf, who revered Eliot's work but found the man often spineless and prudish, and its *poor Tom* who shows up in this handsome but joyless collection [*The Letters of T. S. Eliot: Volume One, 1898-1922*]. There is none of the pleasure in gaming with language that one meets in the correspondence of most writers; little humour, except of a forced and jocose kind; some whingeing and backbiting; much place-seeking; a few, very few, flashes of critical fire. Opened at almost any random page, the book gives off a boiled-cabbage smell of anxiety and fatigue, at the same time as it betrays a rankling self-regard and a notably cold-blooded, saurian intelligence. . . .

Candour came hard to him. His protean personality had a lighter-than-average specific gravity, and he instinctively moulded himself into the shape required by whoever was on the receiving end of a letter. He had a Garsington voice, a Lloyds Bank voice, a breezy-American-cousin voice. To Pound, he went in for Poundian capital letters, exclamations and abbreviations, along with some charmlessly Ezraic gibes against Jews. To his mother, he was *your devoted son Tom,* and it is this filial echo of his mother's voice that dominates the book in more than 90 letters home.

Charlotte Eliot had Great Expectations, and T. S. bore the mountainous responsibility of realising her dreams of literary and social success. For her, he moved in a world where Ottoline Morrell was always *Lady* Ottoline, where the doors of Society opened for him on oiled hinges and literary fame was conferred in the same hereditary manner as a dukedom. . . . Literary and social values were hopelessly tangled. When Arnold Bennett joined Eliot's circle at a Bloomsbury party, Eliot 'left for another part of the room' at the sound of Bennett's 'lower-middle-class Cockney accent'. Asking his brother Henry to wangle him an entree to the *Atlantic,* Eliot confided that 'Pound considers it important, wherever possible, to secure introductions to editors from people of better social position than themselves'.

Advising Scofield Thayer on picking English contributors to the *Dial,* he warned him off writers published by the *London Mercury* because the magazine was 'socially looked down upon'. . . .

In all of this, one hears Charlotte—her frigid snobbism, her obsession with respectability and 'eugenics'. Even with the Atlantic Ocean between them, Eliot was possessed by his mother. He found escape, of a sort, in the tremulous, milk-and-water bawdy of 'King Bolo and his Big Black Bastard Queen', with its daring talk of penises and sphincters—a continuing epic that appeared to excite him a good deal more than it amused his friends. He sent Conrad Aiken a draft of 'The Love Song of Saint Sebastian', a solemn, callow fantasy of sexual release achieved in martyrdom and murder. . . . It reads like an eerie prophecy. In June 1915—the same month that "**Prufrock**" came out—he married Vivien Haigh-Wood. Charlotte was grimly undeceived by that hyphen, and saw her dreams of social and artistic elevation vulgarly betrayed; T. S. had found his martyrdom.

Other people's marriages often look like gulags to outsiders, and one would have to be a Saint Sebastian to envy the home life of the Eliots; yet in the letters up to 1922 there is no hint of the breakdown that was eventually ratified 10 years later. Vivien and T. S. made each other ill; and sickness seems to have been as powerful, even as sensual, a conjugal bond between them as sex could ever be. Each dwelt fondly, fussily, on the other's complaints. By 30 they were a pair of crocks, regaling their friends by letter with their symptoms. . . .

Vivien took to her bed; Eliot exhausted himself to the point of nervous breakdown with work. . . . There is an element of flagellant satisfaction in the way Eliot writes from the torture chamber of 18 Crawford Mansions: 'One bleeds to death very slowly here', 'The present year has been, in some respects, the most awful nightmare of anxiety that the mind of man could conceive, but at least it is not dull, and it has its compensations.'

Vivien was his dependant, his first critic, his secretary, his cross and his closest colleague. She named the *Criterion* (after a favourite restaurant), wrote bits of his 'London Letters' for the *Dial,* worked with him on the manuscript of *The Waste Land.* . . .

At least Vivien, with her flightiness, her fits of nervous prostration, her chronically inflamed colon, was *real life.* If the Olympian ambition of *The Waste Land* echoed Charlotte's, much of its emotional directness sounds very like Vivien talking. . . . That animal immediacy, so foreign to Eliot's own temperament, is the great strength of the voices that cry out in the poem. Even so, the life revealed by the letters makes it even more bewildering that out of such drudgery, such greyness, such dislikeable jockeying for literary eminence, Eliot should have created the majestic despair of *The Waste Land.*

There are some troubling omissions from Valerie Eliot's seemingly encyclopaedic selection. Peter Ackroyd, in his fine biography of Eliot [*T. S. Eliot: A Life*], cites (but cannot quote) a letter written to Richard Aldington on 7 April 1921, in which 'he told Aldington that public events had provoked in him a mood of despair. . . Eliot despised democracy, he explained. . . and he described in vivid terms the feelings of loathing and repugnance which the contemporary situation induced in him.' This important letter is not here, and its absence leads one to suspect that there may be other equally serious exclusions.

Jonathan Raban, "Tom's a' Cold," in The Observer, *September 25, 1988, p. 44.*

PAUL GRAY

Thomas Stearns Eliot was born in St. Louis on Sept. 26, 1888. He died in London on Jan. 4, 1965. These dates and places bracket a life but are swamped by its reverberations. For Eliot, in transit, not only wrote *The Waste Land,* the single most influential poem in English of the 20th century. He also produced a body of work—poetry, criticism, plays—that permanently rearranged the cultural landscapes of his native and adopted lands.

Exactly how he created himself and his era remains something of a mystery, the topic of continuing debate. And this discussion is about to intensify nearly everywhere, thanks to the occasion provided by Eliot's centenary. For openers, a long awaited addition to the Eliot canon will be published next week on his 100th birthday: *The Letters of T. S. Eliot, 1898-1922,* the first of four volumes of Eliot's correspondence, edited by his second wife Valerie. Presses on both sides of the Atlantic are churning out new issues of Eliot's writing. The British Council has mounted an exhibition illustrating Eliot's life and work that will eventually travel to 70 countries. The U.S. observances will include a memorial lecture at the Library of Congress and a gathering of Eliot scholars and critics at Washington University in St. Louis. There will even be a conference in Japan.

And then there is *Cats,* Andrew Lloyd Webber's extravagant musical adaptation of Eliot's book of light verse, *Old Possum's Book of Practical Cats* (1939). The smash show has been seen by some 25 million people in 15 countries and contributed more than $2 million in royalties to the Eliot estate. Purists shudder at such commercial success and its spin-offs. Says Critic Hugh Kenner: "Eliot wanted to connect with a popular audience, but *Cats* wasn't what he had in mind."

But *Cats* and the hoopla still surrounding Eliot attest to the poet's surprising vitality. By many standards he should have been old news by now. He professed conservatism, elitism and sectarian Christianity at a time when the fashionable tides were running against all three. As a shy, uncertain young man, he was torn between the dictates of his proper upbringing and the tug of his emotions. He looked inward and saw himself coming apart; he looked outward and saw Western civilization dissolving into chaos. He tried to heal these rifts with words. . . . (p. 88)

He became famous by age 35 without growing satisfied with his accomplishments or happy with himself. Words were not enough. Behind the lectures and public appearances of the latter decades—the tall, stooped figure in the three-piece suits, issuing pronouncements—was concealed a soul in torment, trying to purge itself of sin and of the world that lavished so much praise on what he considered his unworthiness before God.

Much of this struggle remained hidden during his lifetime. As befitted a son of an old, distinguished American family, Eliot was fastidiously private about his inner life. Several important caches of the letters are still embargoed until the next century. But his spiritual autobiography, the only sort that mattered to him, is displayed throughout his poems. *The Waste Land,* it is now clear, is not simply an impersonal, jazz-age jeremiad. It is also a nerve-racking portrait of Eliot's emotional disintegration during his 20s: his emigration, against his family's wishes, from the U.S. to England and, once there, his disastrous marriage to Vivien Haigh-Wood, a vivacious but increasingly unstable partner whom Virginia Woolf once described as a "bag of ferrets" around Eliot's neck. To read *The Waste Land*'s overwhelming catalog of cultural decay is also to eavesdrop on a typical evening with Mr. and Mrs. Eliot. The wife is overheard: "My nerves are bad to-night. Yes, bad. Stay with me. / Speak to me. Why do you never speak. Speak."

The belated recognition of Eliot's intimate presence within his poetry has spurred some controversy. Two of his early poems, **"Gerontion"** and **"Burbank with a Baedeker: Bleistein with a Cigar,"** contain traces of anti-Semitism. (pp. 88, 90)

The answer must be sought in individual consciences. Eliot was guilty as charged, not so much in his poems, which mingle his thoughts with those of other, indeterminate voices, but in scattered remarks elsewhere: a few slurs in his letters, a stunning prescription in a 1933 lecture for the establishment of a "living tradition" in a society: "What is still more important is unity of religious background; and reasons of race and religion combine to make any large number of free-thinking Jews undesirable." Such an abominable opinion cannot be excused, yet Eliot has defenders who find the issue regrettable but overblown. British Poet D. J. Enright notes, "A friend of mine made the best observation: 'But good Lord, he did not like anybody.' " Critic Alfred Kazin seems inclined to set Eliot's lapses in a larger context: "As a writer of Jewish background, if I had to ignore all the great writers who made anti-Semitic comments, I'd have nothing to read."

Paradoxically, Eliot's failings are magnified by the enormous moral authority he acquired through his writing. He did not speak with the flamboyance of personality, that itch toward originality that distinguishes this blood-soaked century. Instead, he offered his words in the service of a long tradition, from Vergil to Dante to Donne to the Puritans among his ancestors. He saw himself, at times, as a modern Aeneas, compelled to struggle, suffer and carry old burdens to a new synthesis of civilization. He knew he was courting failure. He mocked his own earnestness in verse: "How unpleasant to meet Mr. Eliot! / With his features of clerical cut." (p. 90)

His claims were modest. He asked only for a hearing—say, between cleaning up after supper and getting ready for bed, a few moments' attention to a poet speaking as if speech could still alter society and the perception of hours. On his birthday, unbidden, hundreds and perhaps thousands will give him an audience. Nothing has changed for these solitary readers, who have been massing over the years and decades. Some, indeed, may not know that he is gone and that one of his more memorable lines has become self-descriptive: "The communication of the dead is tongued with fire beyond the language of the living." (p. 92)

Paul Gray, "A Long Way from St. Louis," in Time, *New York, Vol. 132, No. 13, September 26, 1988, pp. 88, 90, 92.*

MICHAEL HASTINGS

When Eliot died in 1965 he had been happily married for eight years to his former secretary Valerie. But the estate she inherited had a number of strings attached: Eliot insisted there was to be no official biography; he did not want the manuscript papers of *The Waste Land* published in any form; and he agreed to the sequestration of over one thousand of his letters until the year 2020. [*The Letters of T. S. Eliot: Volume One, 1898-1922*] is the first of a projected five-volume series of his letters, selected from what remained. His widow Valerie 'has spent twenty years preparing it'. Tom Eliot clearly intended to play 'Possum' with his widow and us for many years to come.

The editor has only been allowed to see about half of Eliot's letters. Eliot destroyed most of his correspondence with his mother, everything he exchanged with his first wife Vivienne Haigh Wood, and he ordered a friend to burn 30 years' worth of letters between himself and an old love, Emily Hale. Bearing all this in mind, one soon realises what a task Valerie Eliot has undertaken. Add to that the feuding and reticence from other quarters, and you have to say that this attempt to take the 'impersonal' out of Eliot is a brave but foolhardy one. It cannot be easy to prise material from the seedy mandarins of silence which surround Eliot (Sitwells, Mirlees, Morleys, Lucy/Scofield Thayers, Fabers, Hayward papers, Trevelyan papers, and the Hale family in Princeton). And it is not possible to simplify Eliot in death. The greatness of this poet does not lie in the absurdly swollen myth of the public artist; this theatrical dandy and his immortal lyric fragments remain inextricably linked with his own private world of grief.

There are gaping spaces in between the available letters. This first volume attempts a subtle and sensitive solution to this: the narrative is kept going by the incorporation of letters from various other people. We see many of Vivienne Haigh Wood's letters. And we glimpse something of a vindication of the claim that her existence and extraordinary energies did much to create the poet, no matter the racking pain of their life together. 'To her, the marriage brought no happiness,' confessed Eliot, 'to me, it brought the state of mind out of which came *The Waste Land.*'

To begin with, there isn't a single letter from 'Possum' in 1912. And we don't learn much from 1914 and 1915 about the making of *Prufrock.* What we get is a belated attempt to join the US Navy, bouts of neuralgia and influenza, and the daily grind of a job at Lloyds Bank. (p. 37)

Not even the insertion of other people's letters can explain the gaping spaces. What was the father's justification for cutting Tom Eliot out of the will? What was the true nature of Eliot's enthusiasm for the French bigot Maurras, in Paris? How did Eliot leap from family Unitarianism to a brief agnosticism? Alas, not a hint of this here. Just domestic trivia which becomes a coded cry for help. Eliot writes weekly letters to his lost love in America; Viv's menstrual cycle goes into turmoil. In a search for health, a raving quack puts her on a 48-hour starvation course, and daily cachets of boiled monkey glands laced with opium. (pp. 37, 39)

His mind still worked, even in this minefield of emotional fatigue. We glimpse his philosophy. He despised the emotional swill inside the writer's mind (ie Middleton Murry), he reacted violently against the emotional swill inside the work on the printed page (ie Edgar Lee Masters). He had begun to store his own fragments. The beauty and perfect pitch of his ear threw Swinburne in an ugly light.

Valerie Eliot comes into her own with the year 1921. Both Tom and Viv had nervous breakdowns. Viv's hand is all over the early draft of **The Waste Land** he sends to Ezra Pound. Viv provides him with the title of the poem. Tom persuades Lady Rothermere to finance a quarterly rag, and Viv finds it a title—*The Criterion.* . . .

There are more volumes of undecoded trivia to come. Valerie Eliot is wrong when she claims the Emily Hale letters stem from the Thirties. Tom indicates himself he is writing to Emily as early as 1915. Eliot referred to lavatory paper as 'bumwad', I don't know why the editor has turned this into 'bumwash'. Some things rankle—Tom and Viv were cheerful anti-Semites. Eliot cannot resist turning words like 'Jew' and 'semitic' into terms of abuse.

A note at the beginning of this book suggests that the editor and Fabers lay claim to the copyright of all Viv's papers. This is quite wrong. In her will, Viv specifically gave all her papers to the Bodleian Library. It is a sordid affair when these vested interests now try to claim Vivienne Haigh Wood. In her later years she was destroyed by a cabal of misogyny not unrelated to this publishing house. In more recent times she was virtually Stalinised out of existence by various mandarins of Eliotian silence. The Eliot industry has at last begun to concede the importance of Vivienne; indeed it appears urgently to need Viv's letters to explain the gaping spaces, but this does not give them the right to purloin copyright from the grave. Particularly Viv's grave, which remains still the barely acknowledged receptacle of Eliot's writhing grief and guilt. (p. 39)

> *Michael Hastings, "Playing Possum," in* The Listener, *Vol. 120, No. 3082, September 29, 1988, pp. 37, 39.*

FRANK KERMODE

'The idea that Eliot's poetry was rooted in private aspects of his life has now been accepted,' says Lyndall Gordon in the Foreword to [*Eliot's New Life,*] her second volume of biographical rooting among these aspects. This acceptance, which she evidently approves, has undoubtedly occurred, as a root through the enormous heap of books about the poet, now augmented by the centenary of his birth, will quickly demonstrate.

By the time of his death in 1965 people had long been curious about this very famous man. Collections such as the one made by Richard Marsh and Tambimuttu for his 60th birthday in 1948 contained much pleasant anecdote, and there were respectful reminiscences in Allen Tate's memorial volume of 1966. Meanwhile, off the page, there was some gossip about such matters as a putatively vast pornographic poem, and about Eliot's first marriage. I once heard J. B. Priestley explaining that the Eumenides in **The Family Reunion** were a direct representation of Vivien(ne), which I couldn't understand since in the play only Harry sees them ('*You* don't see them, but I see them,' he claims), whereas Priestley's point was that Vivien would storm unexpectedly and embarrassingly into parties where everybody could see her. As for the poem, it seems to have been a fitful series of mildly obscene

verses included in letters to such friends as Conrad Aiken. Gossips are not on oath.

While these oral versions of biography paid tribute to the celebrity of the poet, the poetry was usually treated as quite impersonal. It had come, in the post-war years, under heavy academic protection: this was a time when potent professors wanted to exclude biography from the institutional study of literature. Eliot's own doctrine of poetic impersonality had contributed to the formation of this austere doctrine, and though quite often subjected to more severe scrutiny than literary journalism normally attracts, the early essay **"Tradition and the Individual Talent"** remained influential, and suited the New Criticism well.

As Gordon suggests, we have moved on from there, not just because we like gossip better than professorial personality purges, but because many people have come to think that the impersonality business was nonsense anyway. (p. 3)

Eliot notoriously remarked that 'only those who have personality and emotions know what it means to want to escape from these things,' which implies a claim to poetic or spiritual election, and this is no doubt what gives rise to the notion that poetic impersonality has, in the long run, some nasty political implications. But one ought to reflect that among the poet's preferred models are Aristotle and Dante, Pascal and Baudelaire; impersonality and intelligence, as he understood them, are the achievement of heroic personalities, and it is hard to see that they *necessarily* imply political wickedness. What Eliot himself says about the topic in **"The Perfect Critic"** still seems innocuous: 'In an artist . . . suggestions made by a work of art, which are purely personal, become fused with a multitude of other suggestions from multitudinous experience, and result in the production of a new object, which is no longer purely personal.' Many artists—Milton and Picasso, to name two at random—might have subscribed to some form of this statement, without suspecting that to do so might, on such evidence alone, get them called fascists, or even Anglo-Catholic utopians.

Even in the years when the impersonality approach generally prevailed there were many books about the more polite and discussable aspects of Eliot as a person who had, for example, thought a bit and read a bit. Some writers tried, as Eliot himself never did, to work his critical observations up into a coherent theory; others, like Grover Smith, read what he had read, so far as this could be ascertained, and examined his sources with what looked like, but cannot quite have been, exhaustive care: for recently there has been a boom in such research. A procession of students combs the archives in New York, Cambridge and elsewhere. The poet's early philosophical studies and his work on F. H. Bradley have been very carefully examined; and those early slogans, Impersonality, Tradition, Dissociation of Sensibility, Objective Correlative, have been dissected again and again. One might even say that no other English critic except possibly Coleridge has had his ideas and his reading more intensely studied. The reason for all this activity isn't merely that there are so many more aspirants looking for something interesting to investigate, though that is not wholly irrelevant. It may be true that too much has been written and published about him, but it is also true that there is a lot to write about.

At the same time, however, the poet's life, and especially the first half of it, has been examined with a persistence that is beginning to seem prurient: it certainly goes well beyond what Eliot, or any other private and reserved person, would have thought tolerable. [*The Letters of T. S. Eliot: Volume One, 1898-1922*] offer several instances of his rage at intrusions into his privacy, and one remembers him forcing the withdrawal of John Peter's article from *Essays in Criticism* because it suggested a homosexual element in his relationship with Jean Verdenal. Lyndall Gordon reports a conversation with Mary Trevelyan which makes him seem mildly amused about this imputation, but his first reaction was quick and indignant. After his death the sanction of his disapproval no longer worked, and almost anything goes.

Now that so much has been said it seems impossible not to say more, and even Valerie Eliot is obliged to take part. The sufferings of both partners in the poet's first marriage have been amply described, sometimes, as by Peter Ackroyd [in *T. S. Eliot: A Life*], with reasonable delicacy, but research continues to discover more painful details. What will not be fully uncovered until 2019 (Gordon's date; Mrs Eliot says 2020) are the letters Eliot wrote to Emily Hale. He had known her since 1912, but most of the letters were written between 1927 (Gordon's date; 1932 according to Valerie Eliot) and 1947. We learn from Mrs Eliot that in the Sixties the poet, 'in a private paper' whose privacy has now gone the way of all privacy, said he had discovered, a year after his marriage to Vivien, that he was still in love with Miss Hale, though 'it may merely have been my reaction against my misery with Vivienne'—we are told that he gave her name the two extra letters when exasperated—'and desire to revert to an earlier situation.' He attributes the muddle to his timidity and immaturity, and to his worries about a choice of profession—for academic philosophy was still a possibility.

When she heard about Eliot's second marriage, Emily Hale presented his letters (numbering about a thousand, says Gordon) to Princeton University Library. He had wanted these letters preserved, but Mrs Eliot says he was irritated by Hale's act, calling it 'the *Aspern Papers* in reverse'; and when the Princeton Librarian informed him that they were to be sealed until fifty years after the death of the survivor he got somebody to burn all Hale's letters to him. There would appear to be an understandable difference in the attitudes of Mrs Eliot and Gordon to the Princeton letters. Gordon is far from wanting to minimise the importance of the triangular relation between the poet, his first wife and Emily Hale: indeed she makes it central to her account of Eliot's life. It was on Vivien's death in 1947 that he broke with Hale. It is true that at various times he abandoned other friends with equal abruptness (as, when he remarried, he dropped Mary Trevelyan, who had twice proposed to him), but it seems clear that Hale was not just another friend, and any doubt on the subject is likely to be dispelled by Gordon's researches. She is able to quote in full a letter of Hale's, written in 1947, which says she had understood that Eliot had intended to marry her if Vivien should die; during one of his visits to the United States, when they had actually discussed the prospect, he had spoken of a *mariage blanc*. And Gordon has seen, in another restricted Princeton archive, a copy of her sad last letter to Eliot, written as late as 1963.

Indefatigable and resourceful, Gordon has interviewed many witnesses, and had the cooperation of Maurice Haigh-Wood, Vivien's brother; she draws on Vivien's diaries in the Bodleian, the copyright of which, as we learn from the *Letters,* belongs to Eliot's widow. And, familiar with virtually all the archives, she has read a great many of the letters. Her acknowl-

edgments make interesting reading. Mrs Eliot, who helped with the earlier book, is absent from the list.

Emily Hale is Gordon's heroine. Her book has the pattern of a morality: Hale was 'the higher dream' and Vivien 'the sense of sin'. Out of the conflict between these forces come 'the great works of Eliot's maturity, as he converts life into meaning'. Vivien, we gather, 'was Eliot's muse only so long as he shared her hell', and Hale as heavenly muse took over the role in *Ash-Wednesday,* 'a dream of sexual purity to set against Vivien'. The *vita nuova* referred to in Gordon's title was announced in a vision inspired by Hale, and it involved a vow of celibacy.

It has long been known that it was with Emily Hale that Eliot visited Burnt Norton, probably in 1934. But Gordon adds much detail about their relationship, and about many other aspects of the long years between the poet's marriages. Even if we may doubt that Hale was his Urania or his Beatrice it seems clear that they were rather close. But I'm bound to say that there is something disturbing about Gordon's handling of all this. Her religiose attitude to the facts, a sort of muck-raking sublimity, affects her prose as well as her argument, and the whole pseudo-allegorical and hagiographical enterprise is vaguely disgusting, though I ought to add that it might seem just right to readers of different disposition.

Volume One of Mrs Eliot's edition of the letters takes us up to 1922, when the poet was 34 and had suffered seven years of marriage. It is not, on the whole, an enlivening collection. Quite a lot of it is familiar in one form or another from earlier books, and the depressing events, as well as the successes, of Eliot's first London decade are fairly well-known to all who have any interest in the subject, so there is sometimes a sense of *déjà lu*.

Mrs Eliot's brief and slightly odd Introduction, already mentioned in connection with Emily Hale, explains that she had persuaded Eliot to sanction such a publication. In the nature of the case, a lot of correspondence had been destroyed or lost, especially from the poet's schooldays; these lacunae are, as it were, filled by the inclusion of letters by other people, including Eliot's mother and Vivien, whose letters are very nervous and lively: she seems to have been a more vigorous and disconcerting correspondent than her husband. There is also a letter from Alain-Fournier, and a number from Jean Verdenal, the dedicatee of *Prufrock and Other Observations, 'mort aux Dardanelles'*. Their relationship wasn't of the kind improperly suggested, but it was close and involved some elegant youthful posing. *Ce n'est pas facile de se faire comprendre, et puis d'ailleurs ce n'est pas mon métier* is the kind of remark that would appeal to Eliot, who was fond of Byron's lines about not understanding his own meaning when he would be *very* fine: he quotes them in a letter, and again, a decade later, in *The Use of Poetry and the Use of Criticism.* Verdenal also complains about the way small artists form gangs for mutual support and start short-lived movements—a remark that might, at the time, have been less welcome. The mother's letters are eloquently maternal, calm but worried. Some are to schoolmasters; the boy wasn't robust and as the editor reminds us had to wear a truss, which can't have made things easier at school.

Some of the jollier letters are to a Boston cousin, Eleanor Hinkley, through whom he had met Hale. She had an interest in the theatre, and with her Eliot can go in for the sort of joshing he kept up in one way or another throughout his life.

More important, though in essence well-known, are the letters to Conrad Aiken, later dismissed by Eliot as stupid, but a principal confidant of the earlier years. The jesting is intermingled with worry about intellectual constipation, 'nervous sexual attacks', and fantasies about Saint Sebastian, including a version of the poem already known from Mrs Eliot's edition of the manuscripts the poet gave to his American patron John Quinn: though rejected, these verses bear his true voiceprint. It was to Aiken that he could speak of fantasies of flagellation and the murder of women. He also speculates, in what at least by hindsight we can call a characteristic manner, on the necessity of pain: 'what is necessary is a *certain kind* (could one but catch it) of *tranquillity* and *sometimes* pain does bring it.'

Aiken was also the recipient of this meditation: 'The idea of a submarine world of clear green light—one would be attached to a rock and swayed in two directions—would one be happiest or most wretched at the turn of the tide?' This fancy probably owes something to some strenuous lines in *Antony and Cleopatra:*

> This common body
> Like to a vagabond flag upon the stream,
> Goes to and back, lackeying the varying tide
> To rot itself with motion.

This is a good illustration of one of that 'multitude of other suggestions . . . which result in the production of a new object' without eliminating the personal: if you had to guess which distinguished poet wrote that little reverie you might well think first of Eliot. He also had a way of assimilating some particular line or passage that has provided him with what he calls 'a bewildering minute'. In *The Revenger's Tragedy* that expression refers with excitement and disgust to the sexual act: its transfer to the impact of poetry is presumably not insignificant. In the same way, the Shakespeare passage is the comment of chilly Octavius on the fickleness of a populace which switches support from him to the burnt-out lecher Antony. Lyndall Gordon rightly remarks on the psychological importance of these letters to Aiken, but they have interest, too, for students of poetry.

Mrs Eliot includes a series of letters from the young man to his Harvard professor J. H. Woods, which seem to have eluded Gordon. These have a certain dry interest. Eliot, at 26, was at Oxford, and engaged in the serious professional study of philosophy. He kept in touch with Woods, who had taught him some Indian philosophy at Harvard. At Oxford he was working through Aristotle's *Posterior Analytics* with Harold Joachim, reading the *Metaphysics* in Greek, and at the same time struggling with Husserl, whom he found 'terribly hard'. He offered to send Woods his notes on the *Posterior Analytics,* the *Ethics* and the *De Anima.* Although his 'fatal disposition to scepticism' interfered, he said, with his appreciation of Joachim, he was clearly working very seriously at philosophy. And it might be conjectured that the commentaries written since his thesis on Bradley turned up have not taken enough notice of his Aristotelian studies. They ought at least to be remembered when his famous dictum 'there is no method except to be very intelligent' is trotted out, for it occurs in a context extolling Aristotle, and specifically the *Posterior Analytics,* as a great example of what he means by intelligence.

Much has been written of late concerning Eliot's views on, and indebtedness, to F. H. Bradley. Richard Wollheim, an authority on Bradley, has argued that the famous quotation from *Appearance and Reality* in the note on 1.412 of **The**

Waste Land is misleading because out of context. Either Eliot is using it because its decontextualised sense fits his purpose, or because he had simply forgotten the context—in later years he professed not to understand his own book on Bradley. Wollheim detects a progressive loss of interest in philosophy. Eliot more than once spoke of his incapacity for abstruse thought (though this may not be wholly serious—the diligent young birdwatcher, possessor of Chapman's *Handbook of Birds of Eastern North America,* and closely acquainted with the water-dripping song of the hermit-thrush, tells Eleanor Hinkley that he is not sure whether some birds he sees are sparrows, for he knows nothing about ornithology).

He certainly had to decide between a steady job as an academic philosopher, probably at Harvard, and a rougher career in London, where he would have to support his poetry by lecturing, reviewing, and to the dismay of his mother, school-teaching, which she thought beneath him; in the end, it came to banking and publishing. But the philosophical years must surely have left some traces. It has been suggested that Josiah Royce, another Harvard philosopher, was more important than is usually realised, having a congenial theory of tradition and community; some think Russell, who was very close to Eliot in the early London years, cured him of Bradleyan idealism, so that Bradley's continuing influence depended finally on Eliot's admiration for his prose style. Not everybody agrees, and it can still be maintained, as by Lewis Freed in his book *The Critic as Philosopher* (1979), that Eliot's critical theories are Bradleyan almost through and through. Now, however, we have [Richard Shusterman's *T. S. Eliot and the Philosophy of Criticism*] with a new view of the whole matter. He believes that Eliot is much more interesting as a philosopher than even his supporters think, and that the easy dismissals on the part of such detractors as Terry Eagleton and Christopher Norris are founded on political prejudice and uninformed assumptions. Shusterman emphasises the Aristotelian studies, and the attack on Descartes in the unpublished Clark Lectures of 1926, which deplores that philosopher's upsetting of Aristotelianism. As to Bradley, he was thoroughly anti-empiricist, whereas Eliot was from the outset expressly not so: indeed he adopted, around 1916, the analytic empiricist realism of Russell, and did not abandon it till his conversion in 1927, when he moved to 'a nonrealist hermeneutical perspective'.

Shusterman's efforts to map Eliot's thought onto 20th-century philosophy may be too systematic, or too opportunist—he makes little allowance for accidental resemblances, claiming, for instance, that Eliot anticipated the thought of Gadamer. What Eliot calls 'the historical sense' is much the same as Gadamer's 'effective historical consciousness', and he is also said to share some of the later thinker's idea of aesthetic activity as a form of play. Moreover their ideas about tradition and community look rather alike. More interesting is the idea that his study of Aristotle's *phronesis* led the poet back towards a native American pragmatism, recalling William James at Harvard but also providing critical anticipations of Richard Rorty.

The truth is no doubt messier than these formulations suggest—say, that Eliot after a time was content to assimilate rather than extend his philosophical learning, but that the philosophical layer of his mind continued to influence an application to matters not manifestly philosophical. Shusterman's is an interesting book, but he seems to forget that even very intelligent people may have cluttered minds, and may be incapable of sustaining the kinds of prescient synthesis he discovers in Eliot's.

The decision to stop doing serious philosophy and take his chance in London was much influenced by Vivien and by Ezra Pound, who almost single-handed launched his protégé into the literary scene. Russell—despite his over-zealous and finally damaging interventions in Eliot's marriage—was probably the main influence on the social side, so important to Eliot. But the tale of Eliot's settling down [as reflected in **Letters**] is long and tortuous. (pp. 3-5)

[As] the war nears its end he can say that he gets on better with Englishmen than with Americans, who 'now impress me, almost invariably, as very immature'. Occasionally regretting his loss of contact with 'Americans and their ways', and also the 'spiritual decadence of England', he nevertheless urges his brother to come here and escape the appalling gregariousness of American life. . . .

Clive Bell found Eliot's 'studied primness' deliciously comic, and Virginia Woolf was a great tease. But this was his chosen milieu, and although Eliot could call himself 'Metoikos' (meaning exile) as late as 1945, he had obviously acquired the censorious Bloomsbury habit. Russell, he discovered, 'has a sensitive, but hardly a cultivated mind . . . in some ways an immature mind'. Lowes Dickinson is 'very common'. But Americans are of course far worse, witness Aiken and Max Bodenheim, an American Jew who made the mistake of supposing he could pick up a living in London as easily as he had done in America. 'He received his first blow,' Eliot contentedly tells his mother, 'when he found that no one had heard of him. I told him my history here, and left him to consider whether an American Jew, of only common school education and no university degree, with no money, no connections, and no social polish or experience, could make a living in London.'

His pride in his own achievement is understandable. It called for extraordinary industry as well as talent, and at the age of 31 it was with much satisfaction that he told his mother he had been asked to write for the *Times Literary Supplement*— 'the highest honour possible in the field of critical literature'. Yet despite such signal distinctions he continued to be poor. . . . At one rather amusing moment, near the end of the war, he says he would be willing to go into the (US) Army 'if I could have a rank high enough to support me financially'—an élite stipulation if ever there was one.

These embarrassments did not prevent the metoikos from quite quickly becoming an insider in the London literary world. . . .

There is a good account of his complex early relationships with London writers in Erik Svarny's *The Men of 1914*. One can hardly miss a certain ruthlessness, even some opportunism, in the Eliot of these years. For all his personal unhappiness he was remarkably successful; he knew how to make alliances and deal with misalliances, and how, amid all the bustle, to sustain his really important literary relationships, which were with Pound (sometimes sharply criticised) and Wyndham Lewis, for whom his admiration seems never to have flagged. He had other friendships—for example, with Brigid Patmore, Mary Hutchinson and Sydney Schiff, people less involved in the literary struggle, and perhaps for that reason recipients of some of his most interesting letters. All in

all, he seems to have made himself as much at home as it was in his nature to be.

Yet the letters testify, if we needed reminding, that these were also wretched years, plagued by overwork, illness and marital misery. (p. 5)

Apart from nursing Vivien, Eliot had to prepare lecture courses and to read, very quickly, writers he had no interest in, such as George Eliot. He knew he was writing too much for literary journals, but needed the money. In September 1922, the nervous collapse associated with **The Waste Land** only recently past, he told John Quinn that he found himself 'under the continuous strain of trying to suppress a vague but acutely intense horror and apprehension'. . . . He also had a sense of his own guilt to contend with, telling Pound, in 1922, that his mistakes were 'largely the cause' of Vivien's 'present catastrophic state of health'. And while there was all this to deal with there were also poems needing somehow to be written.

Such a man, in such a plight, could plausibly suppose himself different not only from the *Massenmenschen* but even from his gently bohemian, quite well-off writer friends: and so, after all, still metoikos, always an exile—not merely in the sense of being physically *dépaysé*, like Turgenev and James Joyce, but in the more general sense *dépaysé* anywhere, suffering an exile of the spirit right here in the London that so fascinated him, as the exile of one of his spiritual heroes, Baudelaire, was undergone in his native Paris. How much suffering, and how much guilt, is enough?

For all his social uncertainties and worries about money, Eliot seems to have been remarkably secure in his sense of class and calling. Yet it was still necessary to be separate. There was an apparently instinctive withdrawal from others, shown not only in the abrupt way he sometimes ended relationships, whether male friendships or *amitiés amoureuses,* but in a coldness which could affect even an obituary notice. He needed isolation, not as a *prince d'Aquitaine* pose, but because it was entailed both by his idea of poetry and his idea of intelligence. Some social success was obviously necessary, but so was a deep reserve and a deep self-esteem. He found Joyce to be 'a quiet but rather dogmatic man' who had '(as I am convinced most superior persons have) a sense of his own importance'. And Eliot was certainly a superior person.

It happens that the letters have little to say about Eliot's early life in St. Louis, a city which, if only because of its river, grew increasingly important to the poet in the second half of his life. The scholars have looked into his early background, and although Herbert Howarth wrote well about it in *Some Figures behind T. S. Eliot*, Robert Crawford has made a substantial addition [with *The Savage and the City in the Works of T. S. Eliot*]. His patient Oxford D.Phil. thesis is intended more generally to illustrate Eliot's preoccupation with the primitive and the city, but its opening chapters are about St Louis and the Mississippi. He illustrates them with gems from the *St Louis Globe-Democrat,* such as the daily advertisement of a Dr F. L. Sweaney, which promised relief to fatigued brains and bodies. The youthful poet carefully copied the drawing of the bearded doctor's face, together with the exhortation: 'When others fail consult . . .' Did the doctor form one of the multitude of suggestions incorporated in Sweeney? Does the young poet's interest indicate a consciousness or fear of debility? We must make up our own minds. And there may be an additional clue in an early story, printed in the school magazine, in which a man is almost eaten whole by vultures. Eliot, we may conjecture, was closing in on his subject.

Crawford also has a lot to say about Gloucester, Mass., another place of obvious importance to the poet. And as he goes he finds much to say about Eliot's reading in ethnology, even documenting his loss of interest in it, dated by an admission that he did not bother to read Malinowski. The book is a little dogged in manner, as the genre of dissertation requires, but it provides some hard information as well as many conjectures, which might be useful and can certainly do no harm. Stanley Sultan's book [*Eliot, Joyce and Company*] can be said to do likewise for the period of *Ulysses* and *The Waste Land.* [Martin] Scofield's [*T. S. Eliot: The Poems*] is for the most part a modest exercise in reading the poems. All such books, and there are lots of them, with the centenary likely to produce more, are bound to repeat much that is available already, but beginners will not suffer from using them.

Finally, it is curious that we seem to be keener than ever on centenaries. They are part of the *Aberglaube* of a secularised tradition, taking the place of religious feasts. Of course they are commercialised, but still fairly innocently so, and they serve to affirm, or on rarer occasions to disconfirm, canonical values: which of course makes it all the more apposite that we should celebrate Eliot on 26 September, continuing, if we choose, for the ensuing octave, in the manner prescribed by the best ecclesiastical authorities. (pp. 5-6)

Frank Kermode, "Feast of St. Thomas," in London Review of Books, *Vol. 10, No. 17, September 29, 1988, pp. 3-6.*

ROBERT GIROUX

[*The essay excerpted below was originally a talk given on September 30, 1988 at Washington University during the "T. S. Eliot Centennial Celebration."*]

I first met T. S. Eliot in the spring of 1946, when I was 32 and he was two years short of 60. The meeting took place in the offices of Harcourt, Brace and Company, where six years earlier I had been hired as an editor by Frank Morley, a friend and former colleague of Eliot's at Faber and Faber. The poet had debarked from the *Caronia* that morning, hoping to lunch with Morley, who was not free. Since I did not know this when Morley introduced us, I was dumbfounded when Eliot said, "May I take you to lunch, Mr. Giroux?" To me it was as unnerving as an invitation to dine with Don Giovanni's statue. But Eliot's manners were superb, and he could not have found a more effective way of putting me at ease. As we sat down in the restaurant he said, "As one editor to another, Giroux, tell me, do you have much *author trouble?*" I could not help laughing, he laughed in return, and that was the beginning of a friendship of almost 20 years.

Since he was both a writer and editor, I asked whether he agreed that most editors are failed writers. He did not answer at once, and then he slowly said, "Yes, I suppose most editors are failed writers—but so are most writers." Something in his manner made me realize he was thinking of himself in the failed company—in the sense that as a poet he had not accomplished all that he may have intended. It was an impressive moment, since he was at the height of his fame. (p. 1)

Beginning in 1949, when he was in New York Eliot stayed

at my apartment—at first in my walkup on East 92nd Street, where he met Robert Lowell for the first time one afternoon and John Berryman on another; and finally in my flat on East 66th Street, which he apparently enjoyed the most because, while I was at the office, he could lunch across the street at the Longchamps restaurant on the lower level of Manhattan House, which was rarely crowded and looked out onto trees and a lovely garden. Usually when I came home after work, I would find him reading a book or playing solitaire, but he would close his book or put the cards away, mix a drink before dinner, and become his convivial self. He rarely watched television after he discovered that we put more ingenuity and creativity into our commercials than into the regular programs. (pp. 1, 11)

Eliot once told me he admired the prose style of prize-fighter Joe Louis, and I thought he was kidding until he described Louis as "a master of succinctness," giving two examples. When Louis was to fight the German heavyweight champion Max Schmeling, he was warned that Schmeling was very fast on his feet. "Maybe he can run," said Louis, "but he can't hide." And his reply to the criticism that he should not have enlisted in our segregated wartime Army was: "There's nothing wrong with the U.S. that Hitler can cure." Eliot was once cornered at a cocktail party by a woman who said, "All my life I've wanted to meet T. S. Eliot and I can't believe you're here!" to which he said, "If that's how you feel, you're luckier than I am. All my life I've wanted to meet Joe Louis and I haven't."

Four Quartets, his last major poem, will doubtless stand as his greatest. The concluding section, **"Little Gidding,"** was his favorite. In New York he once told me he considered the long section of **"Little Gidding,"** which begins "In the uncertain hour before the morning," with its feminine rhymes in the Dantesque mode, the best of all his poems.

Eliot of course carried on publishing business while in New York, and I recall an interesting occasion when Ben Huebsch, the distinguished publisher of the Viking Press, came to my apartment to discuss a forthcoming James Joyce project with Eliot—it may have been Stanislaus Joyce's *My Brother's Keeper.* Eliot and Huebsch had jointly published *Finnegans Wake,* and years earlier Huebsch had launched Joyce in America, including the first edition anywhere of *Portrait of the Artist as a Young Man.* When we were drinking afterwards, Ben, a charming old gentleman, took the occasion to ask Eliot if Robert Graves' story about his role in publishing *The White Goddess* was true. Graves claimed that his book had the divine protection of the white goddess herself: the publisher to whom it was first sent in London declined it and died of heart failure within a month; the second, in New York, also declined it and soon afterwards hanged himself, dressed up in a woman's panties and bra, from a tree in his garden; the third publisher, who was Eliot, accepted the book and within the year was awarded the Order of Merit, the Nobel Prize, and had a hit on Broadway (**The Cocktail Party**). Eliot admitted that all the details were true, but insisted he was unaware of any influence the goddess may have had on his editorial report; he simply considered *The White Goddess* a remarkable book. . . .

Anyone close to Eliot soon found out that he was a deeply religious man and that he practiced what he believed. He was an Anglo-Catholic who used a rosary and who prayed for the reunion of Christendom. He said he wanted to accompany me to mass in New York, and did so at St. Vincent Ferrer's church and also at St. Ignatius Loyola's.

The Rev. William Turner Levy, whom Eliot always saw when he was in New York, published a memoir stating that he asked the poet about the charge that he was anti-Semitic. "I am grieved and sometimes angered by this matter," Eliot replied. "I am not an anti-Semite and never have been. It is a terrible slander on a man. And they do not know, as you and I do, that in the eyes of the church to be anti-Semitic is a sin." Levy asked him if he had ever been charged with being anti-Irish, in view of unflattering lines about the Irish in some early poems. "No," Eliot replied, "and I have two close friends whose names are Sweeney."

Elizabeth Bowen, the novelist, is one of the few persons I've encountered who actually knew Eliot's first wife, Vivienne. When I asked her what she remembered of those married years, she replied, "As Vivienne's illness worsened, his life was one of unrelieved horror." . . .

If, as some critics have maintained, his suffering made Eliot the great poet of *The Waste Land,* he felt he had paid too high a price to be a poet, that he had suffered too much. The words he wrote in his preface to Harold Munro's *Collected Poems* (1933) are apropos: "There is no way out. There never is. The compensations for being a poet are greatly exaggerated; and they dwindle as one becomes older, and the shadows lengthen and the solitude becomes harder to endure." But there was a way out: marriage to Valerie Fletcher in 1957.

"Radiant" is not a word one would ordinarily apply to T. S. Eliot, yet it is an accurate description of the last eight years of his life, during his second marriage. More than once in those years I heard him say, "I'm the luckiest man in the world." I remember Tom and Valerie's arrival at the pier in Nassau: they came down the gangplank holding hands and beaming.

In 1958 I accompanied them to the University of Texas and to Dallas, where Eliot was made an honorary sheriff and presented with a sheriff's badge and a Stetson hat, which he enjoyed wearing when he was with members of his family.

We celebrated New Year's eve in New York at the old Metropolitan Opera, where they performed *La Perichole,* which he and Valerie enjoyed. Afterwards we drank champagne and, with arms entwined, sang "Auld Lang Syne." A year later I called London on New Year's day. He could not come to the phone, but I clearly heard his cheerful greeting as he sat before the fireplace. Three days later, on January 4, 1965, he died. The memorial service was held at Westminster Abbey.

Eliot was buried at East Coker and the stone dedicated to him in the Poets Corner of the Abbey bears his words, "The communication of the dead is tongued with fire beyond the language of the living." (p. 11)

Robert Giroux, "Remembering T. S. Eliot: Poet, Editor and Friend," in Book World—The Washington Post, *December 18, 1988, pp. 1, 11.*

EDWIN M. YODER, JR.

By Shelley's test—that great romantic who boldly pronounced that poets are "the unacknowledged legislators of mankind"—T. S. Eliot, born a century ago this autumn, wielded more power than any other 20th century poet. Not over mankind, perhaps, but certainly over other writers.

When I studied Eliot in college 30 years ago an incense-burning cult swirled about his work and personality. And to tell the truth it was great fun. Somewhere, lost in a family storage room, is the deck of Tarot fortune-telling cards I bought in Lyman Cotten's modern poetry class. That was because Madame Sosostris, the "famous clairvoyante" in *The Waste Land,* uses the Tarot pack to tell the seeker's fortune.

Eliot inspired considerable foolishness of this sort—deliberately, I think. Like Faulkner and James, other heroes of mine, he was a great tease. There were, for instance, the esoteric footnotes he appended to *The Waste Land,* to help "any who think . . . elucidation of the poem worth the trouble." He actually wrote them to fill out the pages of the first edition; and their tone of mock erudition gives them away. Years later, he described this, the 20th century's most famous poem, as "rhythmical grumbling." But masked as it was with sly camouflage, a mare's nest for college sophomores, *The Waste Land* changed forever the tone and style of poetry.

Eliot's generation emerged from the trauma of World War I in a spiritual funk. As another writer put it, "the world broke in two in 1922 or thereabouts," dating this cosmic bisection in the year of *The Waste Land.*

That broken world was the world of Eliot's poetry. Recent biographers have chronicled his personal troubles. . . . But Eliot's subject was not himself; it was the state of culture. A glory had passed away from old Europe, and fine old passions were fading. Things were in a slide and heroism and religion were dispirited. This elusive mood was captured in rich, allusive and utterly unsentimental pictures—almost a poetic slide show.

Many who thought they knew what poetry ought to sound like were shocked. Eliot seemed never to say anything directly. His language was not "poetic." Indeed, it did not say; it showed and suggested. It did not maunder about the condition of the world. It borrowed a famous Shakespearean description of Cleopatra and flattened its grand and gorgeous imagery into a satirical portrait of a modern society woman. It did not declare that a generation had lost its nerve. It created J. Alfred Prufrock and provided his "love song" with magically wan, unenergetic lines:

I grow old . . . I grow old.
I shall wear the bottom of my trousers rolled.
Shall I part my hair behind? Do I dare to eat a
    peach?

This was poetry? Many thought not then. Many still think not. Certainly lines and images of this sort were very different from poetry as the Victorians and Edwardians had written it. Yet from Eliot's great deflation no poet of real consequence has yet found an escape. . . .

He has been dead for nearly 25 years, but his poetics are our poetics. It is impossible to write poetry today without hearing in some inner ear the echoes of those wonderfully dry, melancholy, cryptic, melodic and haunting poems—*The Waste Land,* "Prufrock," "The Hollow Men," The Four Quartets. If to be a poet-legislator for mankind is to outlaw certain indefinite and overinflated ways of writing, Eliot met Shelley's mark. He legislated with a chuckle, but the laws are still on the books.

Edwin M. Yoder, Jr., "Poet of Our Broken World,"
in The Washington Post, *October 8, 1988, p. A27.*

HUGH KENNER

The knowledge a poet draws on, T. S. Eliot once said, is not what is in his head but in his bones, and includes, so he remarked elsewhere, "the damage of a lifetime." By the end of the first volume of [*The Letters of T. S. Eliot: Volume One, 1898-1922*], Eliot is 34, and the accumulated damage is considerable. Expatriation, estrangement from his parents, a marriage that seemed doomed from its first weeks: these have taken their toll, and he has no fixed calling and is chronically short of money. On the other hand, he has just published *The Waste Land.*

Though the book abounds in sharp detail, it's not by our thirst for information that we're drawn to its 600-odd pages. It's by our fascination with the complex, introspective young man living through what Eliot lived through. Biographers have told much of the story before, but its impact alters when we overhear him tell it himself, like a character in an epistolary novel. Whole sequences of letters having long ago vanished for good, accident, not art, has arranged the narrative in intermittent vivid scenes.

On arriving in Gloucester, Mass., from St. Louis for summer vacation, 9-year-old Tom Eliot reported to his father: "I found the things in the upper tray of my trunk all knocked about. A microscope was broken and a box of butterflies and a spider." (A broken spider!) And the microscope and the butterflies, yes, those portend "And when I am formulated, sprawling on a pin, / When I am pinned and wriggling on the wall." Within a decade Tom would be writing those unforgettable lines. (pp. 1, 40).

[Eliot] tends to enter a new scene buoyantly, then afterward registers its downers. In Marburg, Germany he was very up on July 25, 1914; then by Sept. 8 he is recalling Marburg as "an intolerable bore." In Oxford (Oct. 14) he is entertaining "the highest respect for English methods of teaching" and wishing he had gone there before Harvard. But by Dec. 31: "In Oxford I have the feeling that I am not quite alive."

So when all gaiety suddenly vanishes from the letters, when, on June 26, 1915—thunderbolt!—Tom Eliot marries Vivienne Haigh-Wood at Hampstead Registry Office, careful readers will be braced for an impending reversal. What ensued was the longest downer of his life. Neither set of parents had had warning of this fateful step. The documents ascribe to Tom "no occupation." No. And his next move is very peculiar. Back in St. Louis, his father will be wondering how Tom plans to support a wife, and Tom's strategy is not to explain the possibilities to Henry Ware Eliot but to have his new friend Ezra Pound do that instead ("Dear Sir, Your son asked me to write this letter") Pound's communication is long and arresting, all about the advantages of London, where an astute gifted man can pick up cash. It did not likely impress Mr. Eliot Sr.

A month later, here's Tom writing to his father: "But now that we have been married a month, I am *convinced* that she has been the one person for me. She has everything to give that I want, and she gives it. I owe her everything. I have married her on nothing, and she knew it, and was willing, for my sake." That was a way of putting it. Here's another (to his cousin Eleanor, two months before that astonishing

move): "By being admitted to two dancing parties I have met several English girls, mostly about my own age, and especially two who are very good dancers. [They] have such amusing names—I have met two named 'Phyllis'—and one named 'Vivien.' " The latter seems to have been one of the two who "caught the American style very quickly"—"different from anything I have known at home or here." Dancing is a recurrent theme (compare from **"Portrait of a Lady"**: "Dance, dance / Like a dancing bear, /Cry like a parrot, chatter like an ape"). It is too easy, but tempting, to say that he danced himself into that union.

Vivienne (or Vivien: the shorter form became normal) dominated Eliot's existence for a decade and more. She could write, briskly; in his magazine, *The Criterion,* she is (several times) the pseudonymous "Fanny Marlowe." She haunts his poems too. In *The Waste Land* it is her nerves that are bad. In *Ash-Wednesday* she is the "Lady of silences," withdrawn "In a white gown, to contemplation / In a white Gown" (a hospital gown). In **"The Dry Salvages"** it is her mind, under ether, that "is conscious, but conscious of nothing" (Aldous Huxley would recall how in the 20's the Eliot flat always smelled of ether). Hers, in short, is the "condition of complete simplicity / Costing not less than everything." He never left off assaying her emotional distress.

Meanwhile, we are losing a thread. The single most arresting letter in this collection is the one of Jan. 6, 1915, to Norbert Wiener, the one with which Tom returns Wiener's paper on the rearrangement of integers. For there, as nowhere else, Eliot spells out his considered intellectual position. First, the only "universe" we can talk about coherently is that of physical science. Second, "all philosophising is a perversion of reality," a quick fix on complexity that ("cramming both feet into one shoe") grows preposterous "to everyone but its author." But people have always supposed philosophy existed, and meanwhile "There is art, and there is science. And there are works of art, and perhaps of science, which would never have occurred had not many people been under the impression that there was philosophy." So we can talk of science coherently, and we can make art, and that's it. A radical skeptic, that Possum.

None of this did he ever abandon, despite the transcendentals of his later Christian faith (which eludes "philosophy"). In short, art and science had a grip on something, whereas philosophy was but a partial though interesting game, for a poet sometimes to play with. So the art of *Four Quartets* does not versify philosophy but calmly discards it. Beware therefore of paraphrases. Surrender to "the stillness of the violin, while the note lasts." And "still" was a word that fluoresced for Eliot; if it means quiet, it also means being steadily there. The violin is, doctrine isn't.

Vivien was continually ill—influenza, "nerves," the catalogue exhausts—and so was Tom, though somehow he got (desperately) pages typed—reviews, even poems—and the 20th-century life of the mind went on. We see him in Lloyds Bank. . . . Or we see him fussing with Lady Rothermere about the review that became *The Criterion.* . . . Or he's writing Pound about placing *The Waste Land* ("Thayer [of The Dial] offered me $150, which did not strike me as good pay for a year's work"). There was never enough money, and Tom and Viv, albeit frugal, would have starved save for remittances from St. Louis. They would sit, evening after evening, exhausted till they fell asleep.

This volume ends with a letter to Eliot's brother Henry dated Dec. 31, 1922. He has received the Dial prize for **The Waste Land;** it "may . . . perhaps make my work of all kinds more sought after." But he has no time to do "work of all kinds." "I sometimes envy you for having an occasional evening in which you can sit down and read a book." Vivien's state was tearing him apart; she was oscillating, we may say at this distance, between quack and quack. About her condition nobody then understood anything, nor, it's safe to say, does anyone even now. Specialists babbled of "colitis" and "glands;" one man even ordered "two days of complete starvation" that might have killed a patient less tough. ("Physical exhaustion," she wrote to Pound, the trusty, implacable confidant of both Eliots. "Insomnia. . . . Migraines. I cannot think of anything else at the moment.") Once Vivien stayed with the Pounds in Paris while Tom was in Switzerland and Dorothy Pound once said that stay wore her and tough Ezra out.

All these decades later, we may look back and wonder that the life of the mind—*our* minds, that is—went on. *Our* minds. For in giving us words to remember and repeat in contexts of our own—lives measured out with coffee spoons, urban crowds amid which "I had not thought death had undone so many," a humankind that "cannot bear very much reality"—he brought the one gift a poet can offer: not "ideas" but assurance that the way we find ourselves living needn't leave us mute, can indeed be spoken about.

At what cost, though, he shaped the gift he brought us. The playful Tom who'd resurface in **Practical Cats** vanishes from the letters rather early. What's revealed in this book is an Eliot for many years trapped in something very bad: month after month of living day to day, confronting the task of the moment with the energies of the moment, willing off psychic disaster. He had, I once heard Pound say, "a great deal of what we used to call low vitality. If he'd been an antelope instead of a crocodile it would have killed him." "It?" That is what these letters document. And the low vitality (a crocodile's? a possum's?) guarded, we can see now, the core of incredible toughness where **The Waste Land** and **Ash-Wednesday** and **Four Quartets** were secreted. (pp. 40-1)

Hugh Kenner, "Old Possum's Postbag," in The New York Times Book Review, *October 16, 1988, pp. 1, 40-1.*

CHRISTOPHER RICKS

[*The excerpt below from* T. S. Eliot and Prejudice *first appeared in the* Times Literary Supplement *on November 4-10, 1988.*]

Lionel Trilling had a notable public exchange with T. S. Eliot on the matter of prejudice: specifically, on Rudyard Kipling and the Jews. Trilling had reviewed in *The Nation* Eliot's selection of Kipling's verse, and had discriminatingly deplored it: 'Mr. Eliot, it is true, would not descend to the snippy, *persecuted* anti-Semitism of ironic good manners which, in "The Waster", leads Kipling to write "etc." when the rhyme requires "Jew". Within his letter of reply (published 15 January 1944), Eliot demurred:

I would observe that in one stanza, at least, the rhyme required is not to *do* but to *done:* and the obvious rhyme for *done* is not *Jew* but *Hun.* Kipling made several opportunities for expressing his dislike of Germans; I am not aware that he cherished

any particularly anti-Semitic feelings. In any case, the interest of the poem lies rather in his criticism of the English than in any aversion to Jews, Germans, or Scotsmen that may be imputed to him.

The subjoined reply by Trilling was characteristic and exemplary. First, he apologized for having been in error: he had said, prejudicially, that Eliot 'must have been at some trouble to procure the poem for his selection, for it is not included in the Inclusive Edition'. Eliot's letter had shown that this was not so: the poem was readily accessible in the Definitive Edition. The apology was exemplary, first, because the honour of simple apology by a reviewer on a point of fact was not ordinary then and is not ordinary now. But what was no less fine in Trilling was his not being unnerved by having had to apologize; his not being deflected from engaging with Eliot's defence of Kipling and of the crucial rhymes; and his not being dissuaded from substantiating that Kipling could not be exculpated by Eliot's defence.

But I cannot admit Mr. Eliot's second objection. The gist of 'The Waster' is that the English, because of their public-school code, are always being beaten by certain unscrupulous racial groups. In the first and last stanzas they are beaten by the etc.-Jew because they believe that 'There are Things no Fellow can do'; in the second stanza they are beaten by the etc.-Hun because they think that there are 'Things that Are Never Done'; and in all three stanzas they are beaten by the Pict . . . It is of course true that the poem criticizes the English for being the victims of their own code; but the criticism, because of the nature of the comparisons by which it is made, is so ambiguous as to be almost a kind of praise.

Then, with a felicitous infusion of Eliot's own dryness of manner, Trilling ended:

As anti-Semitism goes these days, I suppose Kipling is not—to use Mr. Eliot's phrase—particularly anti-Semitic. I certainly should not think of isolating for discussion what anti-Semitism he has, but only of mentioning, as one aspect of a complex xenophobia, his queasy, resentful feelings about Jews.

Not particularly anti-Semitic: these were incautious words of Eliot's, not least in their measured air of caution; even Nicholas Mosley, in his very honourable life of his father Sir Oswald Mosley, lapses into the oblivious when he says of Mosley's fore-marchers, the British Fascisti, that they were 'not particularly anti-semitic'. It is not only that the phrase suggests an equanimity on the point of scarcely caring; it is also that there is a small crucial ambiguity in it. For 'not particularly' may mean either 'not very' or 'not specifically'. Eliot's use (as Trilling shrewdly intimates) hovers conveniently between the two, with the suggestion both that Kipling was not *very* anti-Semitic, and that he was not anti-Semitic *in particular* since he had harsh things to say here of Germans, too, and Picts, and even perhaps of the English. But Eliot should never have descended to these shifts on behalf of such a poem. 'The Waster' is not less appalling for being so dextrous.

As with Kipling, there can be no isolating for discussion what anti-Semitism Eliot had or did not have, though he, like Kipling, had his queasy resentful feelings about Jews. The question of anti-Semitism in Eliot is important exactly because it cannot be isolated for discussion; it entails the larger, though admittedly not more intense, question of prejudice in general.

George Steiner wrote a letter to the *Listener* [April 29, 1971], about, summarily, 'Eliot's anti-semitism':

> The obstinate puzzle is that Eliot's uglier touches tend to occur at the heart of very good poetry (which is *not* the case of Pound). One thinks of the notorious 'the Jew squats on the window-sill . . . Spawned in some estaminet of Antwerp' in **"Gerontion"**; of

> > The rats are underneath the piles.
> > The Jew is underneath the lot.

> in **"Burbank with a Baedeker: Bleistein with a Cigar"**; of

> > Rachel *née* Rabinovitch
> > Tears at the grapes with murderous paws

> in **"Sweeney among the Nightingales."**

Steiner shows courage in this insistence that the uglier touches are not only continuous with Eliot's greatness as a poet but are sometimes intimate with it, whereas if you dropped the anti-Semitic passages from Pound's *Cantos* you would lose no poetry for which Pound deserves gratitude. Yet Steiner's word 'puzzle'—'The obstinate puzzle . . .'—is not quite it, since this suggests the possibility of a solution.

Then again, the instances from Eliot's poems are much more diverse and elusive than Steiner's summary (in a letter only) could unfold. The consciousness in **"Gerontion"** after all is not offered as healthy, sane and wise; who would wish to be he, and what endorsement then is being asked for the thoughts of his dry brain in its dry season? Some of the queasy resentful feelings are bent upon a different Jew who may indeed be the owner, Christ.

> My house is a decayed house,
> And the Jew squats on the window sill, the owner,
> Spawned in some estaminet of Antwerp,
> Blistered in Brussels, patched and peeled in London.

It is like some appalling *curriculum vitae* and *cursus honorum*. But is this *curriculum mortis* and *cursus dishonorum* to be held against Gerontion or against **"Gerontion"**? Is it an earnest that the Jew is socially and spiritually rotten or that the dry brain which savours such sour gusto has rotted? Gabriel Pearson has written stirringly about these lines, exulting in their vituperative energy in a way which is then braced against his deploring their substance. . . . To Pearson's vivid exploration of the animus within the poem (not necessarily the same as the animus of the poem) should be added that the reader and the Jew do not exhaust the imaginable objects of attack: Gerontion, embittered and wily, is not immune from attack, ours or his. What his history gives may be 'What's not believed in'.

Nor will the instance from **"Sweeney among the Nightingales"** settle exactly where a confident repudiation would have it. The Jewish immigration into the United States brought many Jews who changed their names, and perhaps some, in changing their names, wished to conceal the Jewish name which might invite yet more prejudice. But the immigration also brought many who were simply allotted names upon entry, either as anglicizings of their foreign Jewish names or arbitrarily. And then there is the question, the one manifested in the form 'Rachel *née* Rabinovitch', of a change of name by marriage. Clearly this invites or incites the possibility of a prejudiced disapproval of such marriages as cross the Christian/Jewish divide—a disapproval that it would itself be an act of prejudice to suppose was limited to the Christian side of the divide. 'Rachel *née* Rabinovitch' invites the further suspicion that one devious motive for, or aspect of, such a marriage is that in changing one's name one will disguise one's Jewishness. Some such thoughts as these must swirl in with the line.

Yet any simple confidence that Eliot's line is merely riding upon the prejudice has to acknowledge that such confidence would itself prejudice the matter. For the line does not say that Rachel's married name is not Jewish; does not say that she has been metamorphosed into, for instance, Rachel Winthrop or Rachel Lowell or Rachel Eliot. 'Rachel *née* Rabinovitch': for all that the line explicitly vouchsafes, she might be Rachel Bleistein *née* Rabinovitch. This is not to deny that it is natural to suspect otherwise, or even that it is right to suspect otherwise; but it is wrong to put it to oneself that one knows rather than suspects, and this matters because of the relation of prejudice—of which Eliot stands accused—to suspicion. (pp. 26-31)

For the line 'Rachel *née* Rabinovitch', gets its especially disconcerting power from the fact that you can't in English say 'Rachel *née* Rabinovitch', and not just in the sense—relevant though this is too—that *née* is not an English word. It is odd to say '*née*' without supplying the name which has supplanted the maiden name; it is more than odd to supply the sequence of the first name and the maiden name, linked by *née*, while withholding the married name. The *Oxford English Dictionary* did not include *née*, though it could have done since the earliest citation (1758) now given in the Supplement so much antedates the *OED*; what the citations show is that if you use *née*, you give too the married name: 'The interview between Rebecca Crawley, *née* Sharp, and her Imperial Master' (*Vanity Fair*). But in Eliot's line the surname which is now Rachel's is remarkably—just because unremarkedly—withheld in a way that is sinisterly inconceivable in any world of social remark; what is sinister is such a dark way of speaking, much more than any darkness possessed by Rachel. The effect is dramatic, in both senses of dramatic, and the line—like so much else in **"Sweeney among the Nightingales"**—is beaded with the sweat of two equally horrible opposite fears: the fear that the terrors, here in this sleazy dive, may be paranoid, and the fear that they may not be. The line, the very notion—'Rachel *née* Rabinovitch'—is tense with a dramatized (terrorized) dementia unaware apparently that this is no way to speak. 'An idea which may appear to an outsider a pure imagination, possesses fatality for one crazed by fear or passion' [wrote Eliot in *Knowledge and Experience in the Philosophy of F. H. Bradley* (1964)]. The same goes for the imagination of a reader, who is both insider and outsider. Piers Gray has urged that 'the connotations of animality are suggested in the name Rachel: a "rache" is "A hunting-dog which pursues its prey by scent", *Shorter Oxford English Dictionary*'. But the nature of this unsettling poem is not such as to assure us whether, for instance, this suggestion is a warranted deducing or a pure imagination crazed by fear or passion.

A robustly demotic account of the dramatization of the narrator in **"Sweeney among the Nightingales"** has been given by Malcolm Pittock [in *Essays in Criticism*, Vol. XXX, 1980]: 'He does not know what the hell is going on: it is merely his prejudices (as in the case of "Rachel *née* Rabinovitch"), cultural associations, and the occasional prideful reaching after the illusion of omnipotence which allow him to bluff himself into thinking that he has everything taped.' But Pittock has no way of commenting on 'the evidence of unreasonable prejudice' without himself having recourse to a further prejudice, albeit a benignly credulous one: 'It is certain, however' (preemptively prejudicing any open consideration of the matter), 'It is certain, however, that Flora *née* Macdiarmid would not have done at all; for we have no prejudices against a woman merely because she is of Scottish origin, be she who she may, and wherever on the globe she is to be found.' Don't we, now? Has no one picked on the Picts? (pp. 31-2)

Granted, any instance of any effect at all in a great poet asks a more patient adherence and investigation than these caveats of mine about George Steiner's summary justice. But the prior point is that the instances themselves must be discriminated the one from the other. The more so, since Eliot himself, conscious of the intertwinings of these poems of 1918-19, did not—certainly at the time—estimate the difference between the dramatized hallucinatory clarity of **"Sweeney among the Nightingales"** and the melodramatized (that is, irresponsibly diffused) animus of **"Burbank with a Baedeker: Bleistein with a Cigar."** For that which can save melodrama from irresponsibility is just what is missing from the latter poem, being that which Eliot pinpointed in praise of a Wilkie Collins novella, *The Haunted Hotel:*

> Fatality in this story is no longer merely a wire jerking the figures. The principal characater, the fatal woman, is herself obsessed by the idea of fatality; her motives are melodramatic; she therefore compels the coincidences to occur, feeling that she is compelled to compel them. In this story, as the chief character is internally melodramatic, the story itself ceases to be merely melodramatic, and partakes of true drama.

For Eliot has so written **"Burbank with a Baedeker: Bleistein with a Cigar"** as to ensure that there can be no true drama, no drama available to scrutiny as truth and thereby 'placed', to apply James's word to a poem which alludes to James's writing. For there is no 'chief character' (this is one reason for insisting on the poem's full title, especially as the first draft had as title only 'Bleistein with a Cigar'), and so there is no position from which to gain purchase upon whether anyone is 'internally melodramatic', while at the same time there is an obdurate emphasis on fatality and on the fatal woman:

> Burbank crossed a little bridge
>   Descending at a small hotel;
> Princess Volupine arrived,
>   They were together, and he fell.

Tennyson's line exactly in his poem of revenge, 'The Sisters'—except of course for the switched pronoun: 'They were together, and she fell'. For Eliot's story is not of a man fatally and fatedly attractive (murdered by the sister of his victim) but of a *femme fatale*. Eliot's poem, like Collins's novella for Eliot, is 'obsessed by the idea of fatality'; is steeped in melodramatic motives; and is the work of a poet here compelling coincidences to occur. For the poem is compulsively allusive, itself an ostentatious coinciding, 'a wire jerking the figures' of Tennyson and Henry James and Shakespeare and Browning and and and; all this, with Eliot himself feeling that he is compelled to compel the coincidences, just as he compels

the coinciding of Burbank and the Princess. 'Descending at a small hotel': The Haunted Hotel.

For the subtitle of Collins's tale of fatality and murder exactly fits Eliot's Venetian poem: 'A Mystery of Modern Venice'. Collins's anguished *femme fatale* is the Countess Narona (kin to 'the countess' of Eliot's epigraph and to the poem's Princess Volupine); a cigar is bizarrely important to Collins's plot; so is the Countess's concealment as 'Mrs James' (the poem is a Jamesian story); and the central blackmail in the story is the threat by the Countess's brother to sell himself: ' "The woman who will buy me", he says, "is in the next room to us at this moment. She is the wealthy widow of a Jewish usurer." '

Collins mounts a plot which is no mystery once it is plumbed. Eliot thickens the plot of his poem to render it unplumbable. This is what makes the Jewish instance from **"Burbank with a Baedeker: Bleistein with a Cigar"** different in kind from that in **"Gerontion"** or from 'Rachel *née* Rabinovitch', quite differently objectionable. **"Burbank with a Baedeker: Bleistein with a Cigar"** is irresponsibly cunning in its combination of the overt and the covert. On the one hand, there is its flatly oppressive opprobrious parallelism:

> The rats are underneath the piles.
> The Jew is underneath the lot.

Yet even this does not come clean, since the effect of the article, 'The Jew', is to disparage all Jews ('The heathen Chinee is peculiar') while nevertheless leaving open a bolt-hole for the disingenuous reply that a particular Jew only is meant—some merchant of Venice. But then the indubitable parallelism of the rats and the Jew is masqued by the poem's being Eliot's most dubious, not only as to its worth but as to its deep obfuscation, at once obsessed and calculated. It is the only one of Eliot's collected poems penned with the ink of the cuttle-fish; it uses its energies of ink (its own, and those of the coinciding previous writers) at once to announce and to conceal its whereabouts. Of Grover Smith's remarking in an aside that the poem 'is in execrable taste', Gabriel Pearson observed:

> It is pointless merely to execrate because execration is precisely what the poem seeks to provoke. It is a hate poem, and when this is grasped its allusiveness—not to mention that of the epigraph whose six lines are made up of as many quotations—is understood as part of its central emotion, the wadding and buffering of raw places, disguises worn by the violence and despair enacted by stanza and syntax. This wadding becomes in turn an element of overcontrol or repression, which in turn generates further verbal violence.

This is the murky equivocal form of the concealing by exposure which deeply preoccupied Eliot. In this same year, 1919, Eliot found it estimable in Pound: 'He must hide to reveal himself' [*The Athenaeum,* October 24, 1919]. Later he was even to find a form of it unexpectedly estimable in G. K. Chesterton:

> Behind the Johnsonian fancy-dress, so reassuring to the British public, he concealed the most serious and revolutionary designs—concealing them by exposure, as his anarchist conspirators chose to hold their meetings on a balcony in Leicester Square.

And in 1920 (the year after publishing **"Burbank with a Bae-**

deker: Bleistein with a Cigar"), it was an application of the same thought, this time necessitating a condoling reservation about a fellow-writer, which animated Eliot's exploration of a particular congeries which is crucial to his understanding of prejudice. In pondering a verse-play by J. Middleton Murry, Eliot brought together the following considerations, all crucial to his art, to his imagination, and to the nature of prejudice. First, the needed predisposition of an audience, what he calls here 'a preparedness, a habit, on the part of the public, to respond in a predictable way, however crudely, to certain stimuli'. Second, a suspicion. Third, an instinct. Fourth, a protection. Fifth, prejudicial names. Sixth, language's aspiration, in the highest poetry, to silence. Seventh, a pressure. Eighth, the relation of poetry to drama. And ninth, the concealment which reveals, though in Murry's case not happily:

> Mr. Murry cannot escape an audience—comparatively small and comparatively cultivated—which has no dramatic habits, but desires to share, to destroy his solitude. We may suspect that Mr. Murry is aware of this audience, and that he instinctively protects himself from its intrusion by the titles which he gives his characters. . . . Why these grocery names? It is a movement of protection against the cultivated audience. Whoever is acutely sensitive of the pressure of this intruder will have his own grimace or buffoonery, to avoid sentiment or to decorate sentiment so that it will no longer appear personal, but at most—safely fashionable. This concealment is a 'give-away'; but we cannot say that Mr. Murry has given himself away either, for his 'close-knit intertexture' is a maze of such subtilized and elusive feelings as will hardly be threaded by any but those whom he would be willing to admit.

But **"Burbank with a Baedeker: Bleistein with a Cigar"**, too, has its protections, instincts, suspicions, and prejudicial names. It too becomes 'a maze of such subtilized and elusive feelings as will hardly be threaded by any but those whom he would be willing to admit'. This concealment is a give-away; but we cannot say that Mr Eliot has given himself away either.

The poem's multiplicity of partial dramatization furnishes a licence which Eliot seldom claimed and which is here licentious in allowing him to vent the pent without taking the rap. The poem permits Eliot too easy an application of his remark, not in itself unprincipled, that a poet's 'lines may be for him only a means of talking about himself without giving himself away'. For about this particular form of not giving himself away 'there hangs the shadow of the impure motive' (Eliot on Donne); hence the back-rush of aggressiveness. (pp. 33-8)

The ugliest touch of anti-Semitism in Eliot's poetry, in my judgement, is the **"Dirge"** (sibling to **"Burbank with a Baedeker: Bleistein with a Cigar"**) which was posthumously published with the manuscript of ***The Waste Land*** [in 1983]. The first of the two stanzas is this:

> Full fathom five your Bleistein lies
> Under the flatfish and the squids.
> Graves' Disease in a dead jew's eyes!
> When the crabs have eat the lids.
> Lower than the wharf rats dive
> Though he suffer a sea-change
> Still expensive rich and strange

Pound himself jotted on the manuscript: '?? doubtful'. Eliot wrote as the first draft 'dead jew's eyes'; he then added 'man's' above 'jew's', bracketing the two words; and in the fair copy he had 'dead jew's eyes'. Yet even here, in confronting what is probably the darkest variant reading in Eliot—a dead jew's eyes/a dead man's eyes—it is crucial that resistance to an injustice perpetrated by Eliot should not issue in an injustice to Eliot. It is all too easy to make disingenuous use of a convenient fact about manuscript material: that it may with equal plausibility, in principle though not in instance, be cited as evidence of what the writer really did or really did not think and feel. For any superseded words—say, Tennyson's cry to the spirit of Arthur Hallam, there in the manuscripts of *In Memoriam* XCIII, 'wed me'—may have been rescinded by the writer as false or may have been censored as too true. "Dirge" doubles the stakes, in that not only is there a variant reading added and then withdrawn, but the whole poem was written and then withdrawn, or rather never sent forth. The unavoidable doubleness of the principle lends itself to a critic's duplicity of *parti pris;* no critical insistence should be trusted which does not acknowledge the doubleness and say why on any particular occasion the pressure is running this way and not the opposite.

Eliot did not publish this "Dirge"; it does not become us to claim assuredly to know why not, especially as one thing at issue in questions of prejudice is the sufficiency of evidence. To determine that the poem was suppressed because Eliot so much believed it (not disbelieved it) is to succumb to just such a prompt prejudice as is reprehended in Eliot.

Moreover, Eliot—who believed in redemption and whose art is redemptive—came to contemplate the painful admission

> Of things ill done and done to others' harm
> —Which once you took for exercise of virtue.
>
>   **("Little Gidding")**

The unpublished "Dirge" about a drowned Jew might then be seen to count for less, even to matter exactly as the impulse triumphed over, an ugliness of spirit the contemplation of which could precipitate beauty and justice, crystallizing in the due limpid indifference within "Death by Water":

>   Gentile or Jew
> O you who turn the wheel and look to windward,
> Consider Phlebas, who was once handsome and tall
>   as you.
>
>   (pp. 38-40)

Christopher Ricks, "Uglier Touches," in his T. S. Eliot and Prejudice, *Faber & Faber, 1988, pp. 25-40.*

ROBERT M. ADAMS

"Last week I saw a woman flayed, and you will hardly believe how much it altered her person for the worse." The voice is that of the author of the "Digression on Madness" in Swift's *Tale of a Tub;* the application to literary biographies is all but universal. Writers are veil makers, illusion weavers; the most admiring of biographers cannot help exposing his author's artifice. A writer's outside—the face he prepares to face the faces of his public—is almost always more imposing and less nasty than the inside. Thomas Stearns Eliot forbade biographies.

Whether Eliot had anything to hide at all proportionate to

the many layers of mystery in which he sought to enfold it is an open question. Certainly the impulse to concealment and impersonation went very deep; he titled his first poetic efforts "Inventions of the March Hare," a pseudonym that, even as it blocks his real name, identifies him as a self-mocker. In the course of his life he picked up some dozen or so other pseudonyms in addition to the various characters he impersonated in his poems and plays, and the very different personae he assumed in social life. There hardly seems to have been a period when he was not playing possum—cultivating a mask, a façade, a polished and perceptibly alien surface. Some of this addiction to pose may have come from a youthful reading of Jules Laforgue, but he was cultivating a manner (some called it the "Harvard" manner) even before that.

As an American entering English society, he assumed the weighty, deliberate semblance of a polymath. Later, he confessed it was mostly bluff, but over the years it developed into a lofty, impersonal lecturer's demeanor, as of one delivering cosmic truths from on high. At a time when bohemianism was the order of the day, Eliot exaggerated his bank clerk's correctness—the bowler hat, the tightly rolled umbrella, the "four-piece suit" (as Virginia Woolf wickedly called it). At the same time, there was a larky side buried under the correct, urban manner. In his youth he exchanged obscene fantasies with Conrad Aiken, and visited the "vaudeville" houses of Boston—these were obviously burlesque shows. He made common cause with outspoken Ezra Pound, and took a lasting interest in the naughty-nice turns of the London music halls. Then there was his cat personality—not exactly Old Possum, who had many other uses, but a playful, Edward Lear identity—and there was the Good Old Boy of the predominantly Faber group that formed around him and John Hayward at the flat they shared on the Chelsea Embankment. Finally, there is the separate personality of Eliot the semi-mystical Christian ascetic, the reclusive penitent; was this after all the "real" Eliot, or just another façade? For a long time, that would have been an impertinent question, or worse; now, with the whole life gradually emerging from the shadows, it becomes an appropriate consideration.

Lyndall Gordon's account of Eliot's career, the second part of which [*Eliot's New Life*] has just been published eleven years after the first part, is not a proper biography (though it looks very much like one), but an imaginative analysis of Eliot's mind and its workings. *Eliot's Early Years* (1977) concerned itself with the first thirty-four years of Eliot's development, concluding with an account of the assembly and sifting processes that led in 1922 to the publication of **The Waste Land**. The second book, *Eliot's New Life,* with its not-so-covert allusion to Dante's narrative of his poetic and spiritual development, devotes its primary attention to the last forty-three years of Eliot's life. A curious reader will not fail to notice that Eliot's "new life" begins in middle age, after (rather than before) the creation of his epic or epyllion. He may also wonder who is going to be the Beatrice of this story.

It should be said at once that both volumes are copiously researched, making reference to an impressive selection of unpublished or uncollected materials, including poems, lectures, letters, reviews. There are caches of materials to which Mrs. Gordon did not have access, but nobody else will have access to them until the twenty-first century. In his review of *Eliot's Early Years* (*The New York Review,* February 9, 1978), Professor Irvin Ehrenpreis complained of inaccurate tran-

scriptions; I've not been in a position to check more than a few of Mrs. Gordon's citations, but unless some are much more serious than those Ehrenpreis discovered, the question of accuracy seems to me subordinate to the question of organization. Writing two books on Eliot's complex and inward mind, at a distance of eleven years from each other, has produced a good deal of churning over the same material. The temporal division between the two books is not sharp, nor was it meant to be; but the repetitions, not only from one book to the other but within each volume, are enough to afflict an attentive reader with *mal de mer*. (p. 3)

Her central argument twines together three main themes. Eliot is shown to have been a strongly, almost preeminently, American poet. This is not a novel insight, but it's a good one, and Mrs. Gordon brings it out convincingly in connection with certain particular landscapes on which Eliot hung important emotional associations. Cape Ann on the north shore of Massachusetts, Casco Bay in Maine, and the Mississippi River as it flows by St. Louis are among the most important of these landscapes. A second and closely allied theme, of which we have not heard so much, is the poet's longstanding friendship with Miss Emily Hale. About the basic facts there is not much question. Eliot got to know Miss Hale in 1911, perhaps as early as 1908; she was a friend of his first cousin, Eleanor Hinckley. For a while the acquaintance lay dormant; but about 1927 they began exchanging letters, and about 1930 they began meeting on both sides of the Atlantic—meeting quite openly and almost certainly (in the vulgar formula) platonically.

Mrs. Gordon makes a great deal of the relation with Emily Hale, and indeed there is apparently a great deal to be made; for Emily Hale was doubtless the accompanying female presence in **"Burnt Norton,"** she may well have provided a model for Celia in **The Cocktail Party,** and she haunted Eliot's imagination for many years, until—but that is part of a third story. Her importance to Eliot must have been, for a while, enormous; she must have been the woman with whom—so Eliot confessed, though very discreetly, to another person—he had been in love for years. She surely ties in closely with the idea of an essentially American Eliot. But the fact is that Mrs. Gordon cannot tell us much that is very specific about the relation because all Emily Hale's letters to Eliot were destroyed at his request, and his letters to her—numbering about a thousand—are sealed in the Princeton Library from public inspection until October 12, 2019. So this theme must be represented largely by Mrs. Gordon's apparently sensible and perfectly well-mannered speculation. It is just rather hazy stuff.

A third theme runs deeper in Eliot's life than the other two, is complexly entangled with both of them, and is a good deal harder for this reviewer to discuss or even describe: it is the matter of T. S. Eliot's religion. This was a formative factor of major importance in his life and thinking, and because it was deeply personal, his experiences can be placed in a particular space and time. It was in June 1910 when Eliot, walking through the slum streets of Boston, experienced an intimation about which he wrote (but did not publish) a poem called "Silence." Mrs. Gordon, who has seen it, says (*Eliot's Early Years,*) it is in Eliot's notebook and folder of miscellaneous manuscripts, in the Berg Collection, New York Public Library. But she does not describe either its dimensions, its form, or in any close way its content. Though she says "this is a paraphrase," what she is talking about could be no more than half a dozen words, and how much more there is to the poem a reader must guess for himself. Whatever it was, this brief, intense moment seems to have intimated to the twenty-one-year-old Eliot "that there was an area of experience just outside his grasp, which contemporary images of life could not compass." In Paris a year or two later, in the hyacinth garden of *The Waste Land,* and in the rose garden of **"Burnt Norton,"** he experienced partial adumbrations of the same vision.

Of course it is very hard to think of a topic defined only by the fact that contemporary (this seems to mean "everyday") images of life cannot compass it. Indescribable experiences are traditionally hard to describe, especially when all one has to go on is a partial paraphrase of a description of what may have been an access of emotion, an auditory experience, or a syncope. Still, we are probably not far wrong in thinking that "Silence" described a moment of surcease from the tumult and anxieties of the everyday world—and these for Eliot manifested themselves primarily in the squalid scrimmage of appetitive impulses characteristic of a commercial, mechanical society; and in the temptations and incitements of sex. (pp. 3-4)

[He] seems to have feared and hated [women] on principle, before he had any particular experience of them. In his later life he depended for support and sympathy on a long series of "exceptional" women whose immense value to him hardly disturbed at all the categorical contempt and dislike he expressed for the sex at large. What he shuddered to contemplate was the combination of physical intimacy with emotional entanglement; as a line canceled from *The Waste Land* manuscript put it, women are creatures of "unreal emotions and real appetite," predatory and degrading in both aspects.

His first wife, Vivienne Haigh-Wood, whom he married (in 1915) abruptly, impulsively, and without consulting either family or friends, fulfilled Eliot's worst nightmares. From the first, he was unable to satisfy her sexually. She suffered from an endless variety of symptoms and some chronic ailments; she was fretful, hysterical, self-pitying, and ferociously outspoken. At the same time, she was intelligent, witty, devoted, and dynamic. Vivienne supplied a great deal of the driving force (which Eliot lacked) that turned him away from an academic and toward a literary career. She harried him, she pushed him. Nobody has had a good word for Vivienne, but Eliot (as long as he could put up with her) profited from her instincts and energies. She made him an utterly miserable man, and, with the help of Ezra Pound, the greatest poet he was ever to be. The agonies she inflicted on him must have been cruelly bitter for Eliot. He suffered what he had long dreaded; he was trapped forever (neither partner could endure the thought of divorce); he never could explain his original impulse; and he had discarded a gentle, adoring woman (Emily Hale) with whom he would shortly be in love).

It is almost inescapable that Eliot's original deep sex-disgust ("bestial appetite" was his term for it) was at the root of his erotic troubles; and it was from this contamination primarily that the purity of the Silence offered relief. The path it proposed, if not that of sainthood (can one actually fix one's career goals on becoming a saint?), certainly pointed toward a contemplative, solitary life devoted to the intellectual, and exclusive, love of God. The second adjective is important. For reasons that can only be guessed, Eliot felt from the beginning that love of God did not include—in fact, somehow precluded—love of God's creatures, such as men and women.

It wouldn't be improper to speak of a Puritan or Calvinist strain in Eliot's religious constitution, except that Puritanism and Calvinism are not inherited characteristics. The impulse to a monastic existence was always before him; whether as a way to escape one sphere of being or to seek for another must have been—as it still is—inextricably unclear.

What seems certain is that the act of decision, to accept or reject the "temptations of this world," was almost always painful—abrupt, solitary, and (exceptionally so for this judicious, meditative man) impulsive. He did not notify his family before his first marriage, to a girl whom he had known only briefly; before his second marriage, he did not say a word to intimate friends of long standing. Both decisions apparently lay too deep for discussion, perhaps even for inner debate. And breaking ties was even harder; he did not always behave kindly in discarding people for whom he had no further use.

Though his first marriage must have been effectively over as early as 1928, when he took a vow of celibacy, Eliot allowed it to drag on until 1933, when, writing from America, he had his solicitor break to Vivienne the word of her dismissal. After that, he refused to have anything to do with her, resorting to office subterfuges and secret hideouts to keep out of her way. Then in 1938 he and her brother Maurice signed papers consigning the wretched, impossible woman to a mental institution. Eliot before her commitment and Maurice after it both expressed the view that she was quite sane; but in the asylum she remained, and Eliot never wrote to her or called on her. She made one desperate attempt to escape, but it failed, and she died in 1947, completely alone.

The dissolution of his relation with Emily Hale was more gradual but no less cold in the end. (p. 4)

It is well known from the literature that a visionary, seeking to soar into the highest levels of contemplative insight, must cut himself off from the things, and the people, of this everyday sensual world. But Eliot, when he took a turn *away* from his ascetic and contemplative ideal, did not seem to think he owed a word of thanks or even explanation to those who had devoted years of their own existence to supporting him. His decision to marry a second time brought eight years of gentle contentment at the end of his life; nobody aware of the hell he had passed through from 1915 to 1938 can think of begrudging him those moments of happiness. Yet surely the transition could have been managed with a bit more respect for the feelings of his closest friends, John Hayward and Mary Trevelyan. They had acted as his "Guardians"—appointed by him—for better than a decade. He knew how Mary felt about him; she had twice proposed. He cannot have been unaware of the degree to which Hayward, suffering from a terminal case of muscular dystrophy, depended on his friendship. They had—perhaps only with his tacit consent, but to his immense personal advantage—built a cocoon of comfort, reassurance, and protection around this curiously fearful man. He had used them for years. To disappear, then, without a word said, and communicate only by letter the news of his second marriage—to communicate only when his worried friend was on the point of calling the police to look for him—was not an act incident to a spiritual calling but that of a cold and unfeeling heart.

Lyndall Gordon very charitably steers away from this conclusion. She is glad that Eliot found happiness, if only at the age of sixty-eight; and so must every sympathetic reader be. But where does this conclusion to Eliot's new life leave the *via negativa,* the dark night of the soul, the agonizing search for atonement, the abatement of original sin, and all that? For some of us who are stuck in the mud and murk of this world it will seem that Eliot after 1957 had more need to atone for sins against his three friends, Emily, Mary, and John, than for anything he did in the long earlier period of his public penance. Had he decided that the message received from the Silence was a delusion after all? Did he think that with the final revelation so close, there was no need to seek a preliminary revelation in this life? If domestic bliss was the ultimate answer in 1957, why hadn't it been the answer in 1947? Was the ascetic contemplative Eliot only another mask to be dropped like the rest when no longer convenient? These are horrifying questions, and they will surely receive many different answers. But they are the questions with which this rendering of the life leaves us. Flaying Eliot, which is what a close search for the man behind the masks amounts to, alters his person radically for the worse. (p. 6)

Valerie Eliot, who did such an admirable job in preparing the facsimile drafts and annotations of *The Waste Land,* is responsible for [*The Letters of T. S. Eliot: Volume One, 1898-1922*]—a task in which she has her late husband's blessing. It will be no small task. According to word from the publisher, Eliot's correspondence may run to more than three thousand pages (five volumes of about six hundred pages per volume), and yet amount to only a selection—which is a word that sets scholars' teeth on edge.

For families and literary executors, who take a protective attitude toward the memory of a writer, have in fact been known to expunge unwelcome facets of their subject's character. I do not imply that Mrs. Eliot has done any such thing; but she does talk about "principles of selection," in which her husband evidently felt confidence, and she says remarkably little about what those principles are. It isn't just that one wants to know the last sordid tidbits about Eliot's life; one wants also to be able to say that they positively aren't true, if they aren't. At a Paris pension in 1910-1911 Eliot had a friend named Jean Verdenal; after a brief acquaintance, Eliot went back to America and Verdenal pursued his medical studies until he was killed at the Dardanelles in 1915. Speculation, rising to formal statement in a book (by James E. Miller, Jr., *T. S. Eliot's Personal Waste Land,* 1977) has hypothesized a homosexual relation and an expression of grief for Verdenal in the "Phlebas the Phoenician" section of *The Waste Land.* I'm no more persuaded by the second part of the argument than by the first and the chatty letters from Verdenal to Eliot now published give no support to either one; but if there were letters confirming either part, what assurance can we have that Mrs. Eliot would print them? She has not said explicitly what she would or wouldn't do.

Editorially, the new series of Eliot letters is being given a handsome treatment, with extensive footnotes, copious illustrations, a succinct biographical commentary containing much factual material not in the letters, and a thoroughly useful index. Where the letters happen not to deal with important events in Eliot's inner and outer lives, interpolated editorial comments eked out by the biographical commentary help to keep the story reasonably consecutive. Still, it's a jumpy procedure at best, and it will be an agile, determined, and very imaginative reader who is able to make of the letters a substitute for an insightful, full-length biography. For example, the three themes out of which Lyndall Gordon wove

her study of Eliot's mind hardly ever rise to articulate expression in the correspondence.

To turn to the letters themselves, while it is true that many of them, and not the least interesting, are off limits until the next century, plenty remain. . . . Very likely the letters of the present volume, covering the years of desperate struggle before recognition arrived, will prove to be the most revealing. Later on, as Eliot became a public figure, there is reason to think he became more guarded and impersonal in his private correspondence, as in his public statements. Even so, it must be confessed that among the present letters a good deal of inert material must be strained out in one's search for the vivid insight and keen judgment of a poet. Social engagements, money worries, flat rentals, family concerns, and personal gossip are, from a strictly literary point of view, inert material; and there's a lot of it. As Eliot settled into his double editorial roles at the *Criterion* and at Faber & Faber, he wrote thousands of marginal comments on manuscripts, notes to printers and authors, and letters to assorted people in the book business. These are by no means negligible documents; Eliot once said that most of his critical work had taken this form. But there's too much material to reproduce in full, and a lot of it depends on context; Mrs. Eliot will surely have to exclude most of it, and perhaps limit herself to a brief sample.

Reading over the present letters as brute chronology has arranged them, one is impressed by the way Eliot puts on different voices when writing to different correspondents. . . . [He] could even respond in kind to Ezra Pound's "Ole Ez" screeds—buffoonish as they were on the surface, but full of good sense, sharp poetic judgment, and a generosity of spirit for which Pound has only lately started to receive credit. The cut-and-paste process of piecing *The Waste Land* together from disparate fragments was well documented in Mrs. Eliot's 1971 facsimile and transcript of those prepublication materials. (Pound was at his absolute best in getting rid of Fresca the literary lady, an extended fishing expedition off the Grand Banks, and some types out of *Sweeney Agonistes,* while retaining Phlebas in the poem over Eliot's misgivings.) The present correspondence adds something to the story of that process, but nothing like what the 1971 publication adds to the letters.

Overall, the letters contain rather an oversupply of complaining and bewailing—too much to make agreeable reading. Some of these lamentations were surely justified; Eliot had every reason to feel exhausted when, after working all day in a bank six days a week, he returned home to nurse a perpetually ailing wife, to write reviews for money in his spare time, and to compose what poetry he could in odd minutes. But even when things were not as distressful as that, Eliot often fell into a querulous and plaintive tone. The man who later in life went to hospital for a case of athlete's foot was not one to underplay the minor discontents of existence.

Among literary letters not written deliberately for publication, the standard is set by those of Byron, which are as fresh and invigorating to read as the first cantos of *Don Juan.* Eliot doesn't approach that class, and now we have entered the age of the telephone and the FAX machine it doesn't seem that we will ever again have letter writers of such a free and spacious expressiveness. But this raises the perhaps ungrateful question whether his correspondence is really the most precious and urgent part of the surviving Eliot legacy. Mrs. Gordon, who seems to have spent much time among the manuscripts, reports several unpublished essays, such as one on the Bible (December 1932), two lectures on the development of Shakespeare's verse (1937 and 1941), a goodly number of obscure reviews, a radio interview of significance, a Paris lecture, and a 1939 article on the language of poetry—not to mention still unpublished poems like "Silence," "The Burnt Dancer," "The Love Song of Saint Sebastian," and "First Debate Between Body and Soul." There may be copyright or testamentary problems with this material; but it seems exasperating not to have readily available all the literary work of the major poet-critic of the twentieth century.

Still, it's no use repining; the correspondence is what we now have and what we're going to get, and there are revelations in it that anyone who owes a debt to Eliot will treasure. (That includes anyone who's been interested in the development of English literature over the last seventy-five years.) How gentle he was with Harold Peters, an old sailing companion who turned up in London at a time when Eliot was wild with other business! How human his discovery that his mother, visiting England at age seventy-seven, was not a sedentary old biddy at all, but could run him off his feet! There is a lovely letter describing the spider's nest of gossip, wounded feelings, backbiting, and preening that made up the London literary coterie involving Virginia Woolf, Mary Hutchinson, Clive Bell, and Ottoline Morrell. These are vignettes, hardly more. The best literary talk in the book is with Pound; reverberations from Eliot's deeper lives are few. But that, after all, is not what personal letters are for. It's been said that language was given to man to conceal his thoughts. One might write a curious study of Eliot, starting from there. (pp. 6, 8-9)

> *Robert M. Adams, "The Beast in the Jungle," in* The New York Review of Books, *Vol. XXXV, No. 17, November 10, 1988, pp. 3-4, 6, 8-9.*

JULIAN SYMONS

Sir,—Christopher Ricks's ingenious shadowboxing [see excerpt above] about Eliot's anti-Jewish verses is exactly that, a conflict with an opponent who is not in the ring. Or, to put it less in the manner of the Professor's fancy footwork, Eliot's evident intentions in the passages quoted do not match the possibilities Ricks suggests.

In relation to "Rachel *née* Rabinovitch / Tears at the grapes with murderous paws", Professor Ricks points out the omission of Rachel's surname, and says, in the course of a long paragraph about the meaning of this, that "You can't in English say 'Rachel *née* Rabinovitch'". True enough: but in the context of the poem the surname is irrelevant. Rachel can be a Jewish name, and by adding Rabinovitch Eliot is saying: it's a *Jewish* woman who behaves like this. And how does she behave? She tears at grapes with murderous paws. Ricks, curiously, in view of his elaborate analysis of "Rachel", does not comment on this obviously important line. Rachel's un-Wasp-like approach to the grapes is meant to show the uncivilized nature of this particular Jewish feline—she is, one might say, Old Possum's Jewish cat.

A similarly misplaced ingenuity is at work in the attempt to relate Wilkie Collins's novella to **"Burbank with a Baedeker".** It is said that his subtitle *A mystery of modern Venice* "exactly fits" the poem, and that Collins's Countess is "kin" to Eliot's Princess Volupine. But this is to import likenesses where none exists. The Countess is not in the least a mystery,

but an ironic comparison of past Venetian grandeur with the degradation represented by Babbittian Burbank and "Chicago Semite Viennese" Bleistein. The linking of past and present, of blue-nailed, phthisic-handed Princess Volupine with Sir Ferdinand Klein, is ingenious but not mysterious. And *pace* Ricks, nothing could be plainer than "The rats are underneath the piles. / The Jew is underneath the lot." Whether this is a particular Jew or not, the particular is in the poem made the general. Christopher Ricks adds his own small verbal bafflement here in saying that "the indubitable parallelism of the rats and the Jew is masqued by the poem's being Eliot's most dubious". Masqued? Masked? Neither a masque nor masking is apparent, and no dubiety exists.

The article as a whole is an elaborate evasion of what is perfectly plain: that Eliot at this period disliked Jews in general, and found unpleasant ways of saying so in poems. He said it also in letters to John Quinn, the genial Irish-American, Jew-hating patron of modern art and writing, expressing regret that his poems were in the hands of a "Jew publisher".

> *Julian Symons, in a letter to the editor of* The Times Literary Supplement, *No. 4468, November 18-24, 1988, p. 1279.*

A. C. GRAHAM

Sir,—Christopher Ricks writes of "Eliot's uglier touches" [see excerpt above] as though they were a simple matter of irrational prejudice. But Eliot's was a cultural antisemitism, of the same sort as the cultural anti-Americanism flourishing in England during the same period. He saw the rootless Jew who owns only what money can buy as a disintegrating and vulgarizing influence on the threatened Western and Christian tradition; and it is because the sense of a decaying civilization is at the vital centre of his imagination that, as Ricks notes, the jew squats on the window sill in his very best writing. It is right that since the Holocaust we should all be nervous of calling attention to the Jews as peculiar, whether in praise or disparaise. But the result has been a taboo on mentioning a plain sociological fact, that in struggling with the problems of emerging from the Ghetto into a suspicious and hostile world the Jews have made a contribution to modern sensibility, from high art and thought to low entertainment, which is out of all proportion to their numbers. Nowadays, we can be grateful for the richness of Jewish genius; being all more or less uprooted ourselves, we can recognize that the most uprooted of all have been doing us a service in finding directions ahead of the rest of us.

But for the same reason advocates of a cultural conservatism still tenable earlier in the century could hardly avoid seeing the people of Marx and Trotsky, Freud, Irving Berlin and Sam Goldwyn as uniquely placed to disrupt and debase their endangered values; and at a time when the Holocaust was not yet imaginable, why shouldn't they say so? Oddly enough, Eliot's antisemitism is the worse for the misplaced politeness which substituted a capital "J" in later editions. The animus in his early poetry is against jews, who would not all be Jews, and presumably include the "free-thinking Jews" he detested but not the Sephardic families he respected as having a tradition behind them. "Gentile or Jew" in *The Waste Land* always had the capital. The trouble with Bleistein in **"Burbank"** and the revolting passage dropped from *The Waste Land,* is not that he is a Jew but that he is an unholy mix belonging nowhere ("Chicago Semite Viennese"), a Semite with a capital but a jew without, evoking in Eliot a visceral loathing like the representatives of other tendencies in a rotting civilization, Sweeney and the small house-agent's clerk.

A. C. Graham, in a letter to the editor of The Times Literary Supplement, *No. 4468, November 18-24, 1988, p. 1279.*

DAN JACOBSEN

T. S. Eliot and Prejudice. Keats and Embarrassment. The parallel between the title of Christopher Ricks's new book [see excerpt above] and that of his earlier study of Keats is not accidental. In each case he takes a state of mind which is usually held to be disadvantageous, humanly and artistically speaking, and offers a critical reexamination of its presence in the work of his chosen author. One sees the polemical point clearly enough. Who would wish to read a book called *T. S. Eliot and Piety?* Or *Keats and Enthusiasm?*

Still, one might think 'prejudice' a hard case to plead—and especially so since the recent newspaper furore over the propriety or otherwise of eminent British Jews sponsoring a charitable appeal in the name of a poet who had written some deeply offensive lines about this or that 'jew' in one group of his poems; who had never repudiated these poems or the sentiments apparently expressed in them (except to the extent of granting the dignity of an upper-case 'J', in all printings of the poems after 1963, to the unfortunates involved); and who had also, at a time when the Jews of Europe were more seriously threatened than at any period in their long history, made a few unmistakably hostile remarks about them in his prose writings. Of course, Ricks could not have known while he was working on the book that this particular aspect of his subject would be quite as topical as it now appears to be. It is all the more to his credit, therefore, that a study which is in general so strongly admiring of Eliot should include a longish chapter which faces up to (almost) the worst that can be said about him in this regard—and in some others.

T. S. Eliot and Prejudice is a cunning and passionate book. One would not usually think of using such adjectives about a work of criticism, but this book earns them, not only because of the intensity of its engagement with the details of Eliot's verse (and much of his prose), but also because of the way its argument is put together. It is, in fact, unlike most works of criticism in having a discernible 'plot', or at least a quite elaborate narrative line. Ricks deals sequentially with the phases of Eliot's entire oeuvre: but the shape of the book derives more from his exploration of the term 'prejudice' than from mere chronology. For instance, the first chapter throws the light or darkness of that term into the reader's eyes, by showing how prejudiced, how quick to draw self-flattering conclusions, have been some interpretations by well-known critics of **"The Love Song of J. Alfred Prufrock."** The second chapter, labelled starkly enough 'Anti-Semitism', turns the argument back upon Eliot himself; and in so doing deals with the group of poems—**"Burbank with a Baedeker: Bleistein with a Cigar"**, **"Sweeney among the Nightingales"** and **"Gerontion"**—in which typified Jews are presented in repellent form. Only then does the author attempt to grapple abstractly or generally with his controlling concept, by examining the ways in which psychologists, sociologists and writers on politics have treated it. And indeed literary critics too, like Eliot himself.

It is at this stage that Ricks develops most fully his arguments for the defence: the defence, that is, not of T. S. Eliot's prejudices, but of 'prejudice'. Yes, he argues, racial and social and intellectual prejudices are malign in their effects both on those who are their victims and on those who cherish them. That is easy to see, and easy to say. What is more difficult is to detect the forms such prejudices can take within oneself rather than others. What is most difficult is to consider the relationship that exists or might exist between such prejudices and all the habits and unthinking responses, the myriad mental and physical prepossessions and preconceptions, without which our lives would literally be impossible to sustain. For without them we would be unable to see, to hear, to attend, to organise our experience, to recognise ourselves, to live together in families and communities. Ricks contends that Eliot's work reveals and embodies an ever-deepening concern with the tortuous relationship between these two kinds of judgment: between a maleficent prejudice, on the one hand, and an attentive prepossession on the other. We are to see his verse slowly purging itself of the energies released by the first, so that it might take greater advantage of the energies saved by the second. Indeed, each of these movements of mind and sensibility was a condition of the other; both depended on the capacity, which his art had had from the outset, 'to challenge itself'. . . .

As Ricks says, the 'uglier touches' are not merely continuous in their turn with the great poetry: they are 'intimate with it'. In effect, he attempts to establish a critical distinction between a poem like **"Burbank with a Baedeker: Bleistein with a Cigar"**, which is itself hysterical, and poems like **"Gerontion"** or **"Sweeney among the Nightingales"** which succeed in making of hysteria their subject. (To be fair to Ricks I should stress that that is my way of putting it, not his.) In the latter the poet is not speaking shiftily of others from whom he may easily distance himself (and the reader likewise): instead, he implicates himself and the rest of us in the experience—by dramatising it, by objectifying it, by giving it a frame, by finding a voice appropriate to the utterance of it. Thus, the Jew who 'squats' in toad-like fashion on Gerontion's windowsill is mediated to us by Gerontion, whose word we cannot accept at face-value, for he is himself a character, and a wretched, dried-out one too, in his own poem.

If I have reservations about this line of argument, it is not because I feel that Ricks is trying here to excuse the inexcusable. Nothing of the kind. I think he overlooks the likelihood that in poems as obscure as these a spasm of so 'traditional' and unmistakable a feeling as Jew-hatred might serve as a relatively fixed point of reference for the writer himself; and that it might perform something of the same function for the reader too. Even if I am wrong here, this does at least suggest the nature of the difference between us. When I say that—up to *Ash-Wednesday,* anyway—the poems seem to me more unstable than they do to him, I do not use the word with a derogatory intention. Instability can almost be called their aesthetic.

It is hardly an exaggeration to remark that there is no lyric impulse in them, no glimpse of transcendence, no capacity for sustained eloquence, which does not spring from an unusually intense exposure to feelings of degradation—at once suffered in the self and imposed on others. Gerontion may be supposed to be a little, dried-out old man, living in a decayed house, his senses gone: but notice the intellectual penetration he displays and listen to the wounded grandeur with which he speaks.

> After such knowledge, what forgiveness? Think
> now
> History has many cunning passages, contrived
> corridors
> And issues, deceives with whispering ambitions,
> Guides us by vanities. Think now
> She gives when our attention is distracted
> And what she gives, gives with such supple
> confusions
> That the giving famishes the craving . . .

And so on, to the end of the verse-paragraph and beyond it. In the poem devoted to them, Burbank, Princess Volupine and Bleistein ('Chicago Semite Viennese') conspire together to produce—what?

> The horses, under the axletree
> Beat up the dawn from Istria
> With even feet . . .

And when, after the contemplation of a few fragments of fragmented lives, a voice in *The Waste Land* asks,

> What are the roots that clutch, what branches
> grow
> Out of this stony rubbish?

I am tempted to answer: What grows out of it, and what could for you grow nowhere else, is the capacity to speak in just so masterful a fashion.

Neither the 'negative' nor the 'positive' element in the poems is there for the sake of the other; neither is subordinate to the other; the poem is their conjunction, the transformation of their incompatibility into a mutual dependence. That is the human possibility which it gives us to experience. Christopher Ricks writes of the earlier poetry deriving 'its animation from prejudicial animosity insistent and resisted'; and of the later poetry freeing itself 'from the stringencies of animosity . . . into the stringencies of loving-kindness'. Obviously the processes I am trying to describe are closely related to these: but they do not seem to me identical with them.

> *Dan Jacobsen, "Negative Capability," in* London Review of Books, *Vol. 10, No. 21, November 24, 1988, p. 26.*

LYNDALL GORDON

'Can a lifetime represent a single motive?' Eliot asked in a pencil note in 1941.

Only in his works did he give a full account of the inner drama that dominated his life, the search for saving grace, the agonizing over harm, and the long years of patient waiting as he prepared to meet a God whose attributes were 'unimaginable'.

To Eliot the 'life of a man of genius, viewed in relation to his writing, comes to take a pattern of inevitability, and even his disabilities will seem to have stood him in good stead'. If we apply this theory to his own life, its inner coherence is obvious. If we follow, say, his relations with women, it is curious to see how they were absorbed into what seems an almost predetermined pattern. Emily Hale prompted the sublime moments; Vivienne, the sense of sin, as well as providing, throughout the first marriage, the living martyrdom. Later,

sensible, efficient Mary Trevelyan served her long stint as support during the years of penitence. For her their friendship was a commitment, for Eliot quite peripheral. His passion for immortality was so commanding that it allowed him to reject each of these women with a firmness that shattered their lives.

The shape of Eliot's life is one of paring down, concentration. Much had to be discarded to make his life conform to the pattern of the pilgrim, and there is a constant tension between an idiosyncratic nature and an ideal biography. His early years turned on his acceptance of this pattern, his later years on the question of its fulfilment. Its drama lay in efforts to close the gap between nature and perfection at whatever personal cost, revelling to some degree in that cost, and inspecting his torment as the distinguishing brand of his election. To be chosen, he had to purify the very ambition that set him off. And so the moral drama of the later years, from *Murder in the Cathedral,* centres not on the earlier festering of primitive violence, epitomized by lust, but on the subtler taints of public dignitaries, epitomized by pride. Eliot always calls for judgment but, we can never forget, for divine not human judgement.

At best a life of Eliot can be but a complement to work which speaks for itself. The writer in Virginia Woolf's *The Waves* is intently aware of some future biographer dogging him. To forestall the predictable road-map from pedigree to grave, this writer speaks directly to a future reader: 'Take it. This is my life.' What he offers is an alternative to conventional biography which he calls 'a convenience, a lie.' All our stories of birth, school, marriage, and death, he argues, are not true, because lives turn on 'moments of humiliation and triumph' that happen now and then, but rarely at times of official crisis or celebration.

In Sweden in 1948 to receive the Nobel Prize, Eliot was shaving one morning when a procession of six girls, dressed (it seemed to him) in nightgowns and wearing crowns of lighted candles, marched into his room. Hastily wiping the suds from his face, he stretched an arm around the bathroom door for his overcoat which he put on over his underclothes, and then bowed to them as they sang. He shared publicity with the Harringay Rangers, a visiting hockey team composed mostly of Canadians who chewed highly scented mint gum. The celebrations of the Nobel Prize were peripheral to the moments on which his life turned, like the moment in 1926 when he fell on his knees before the *Pietà* in Rome. His first marriage was peripheral to 'the awful daring of a moment's surrender'. And his Harvard studies were peripheral to the Silence in the streets of Boston, that hour in June 1910 for which, already, he had waited, when life, he said, was justified. This vision that came to him at the age of 21 seemed to mark him for some exceptional destiny. His overriding desire was to meet this mystery.

Eliot tells us repeatedly that he was aware of feelings beyond the nameable, classifiable emotions of lives directed towards action. On 31 March 1933 he spoke of 'the deeper, unnamed feelings which form the substratum of our being, to which we rarely penetrate; for our lives are mostly a constant evasion of ourselves . . .'. Such feelings were the substance of that hidden life where words reach into silence. This might touch on the experience of the saints, though he was careful not to claim that. Yet to ignore the presence of this model, as it came to him initially through the poetry of his mother and then through his reading as a student, would be to miss a singleness of purpose to which life and art were both subordinate. With Eliot, writing was not an offshoot of the life; the life was an offshoot of writing. The work forecasts the life, even determines it, as, say, the dream of parting in *La Figlia che Piange* forecasts Eliot's actual parting with Emily Hale, or as the drafts of the last play spell his own discovery of human love. It is not enough to see, as Henry James put it, that art *makes* life, makes importance, for with Eliot it was an exemplary pattern which made the art that made the life. So the parting at the start of his career and the love that closed it were, in a sense, dictated by the religious pattern of renunciation and blessedness.

Eliot surrendered to a form of life that would fit an ideal order which we can never directly know, but may, at moments, apprehend. At such moments he burned with the nearness of the infinite 'thing', but it slipped away, and the rude clamour of the city returned to blunt his senses. Ground down amidst the worker-termites in post-war London, he remembered 'the heart of light, the silence'. The vision was linked with desire, the memory of light on a girl's hair. Trapped in a wretched marriage, he recalled a lost capacity for feeling. There followed years of savage deadness. But feeling did come back. Protected by a vow of celibacy, Eliot called to the 'Lady of silences', a chaste and hallowed presence in his imagination. After Eliot's reunion with Emily Hale in the early thirties, the moment came once more when they visited the rosegarden at Burnt Norton. And there, at last, he grasped 'reality'. He looked right into 'the heart of light' in a beating moment. 'Quick now, here, now . . .' It was gone. This time, though, he pursued the moment to its logical conclusion, 'Love', the 'unfamiliar Name'.

In setting out the formula for this pursuit, Eliot converts life into truth. This was his aim in the year of his conversion, when he spoke of the poet's gigantic attempt to 'metamorphose' private failures and disappointments into something universal and impersonal. Eliot's achievement was to redefine the exemplary life in the uncongenial conditions of the twentieth century, aware all the while that its marking points—moments of light and horror—were not the markers of his own life only, but those of many generations, past and future.

Eliot was only superficially a man of his time. His affinities were with the spokesmen for the exemplary life in other centuries, the Catholic mystics of the middle ages and the American Puritans of the seventeenth century. He said in 1954 that he combined 'a Catholic cast of mind, a Calvinistic heritage, and a Puritanical temperament'. This was not the cultural despair, the dead-end alienation of Modernity, but the purposeful withdrawal of one who passed through his age as a hermit, refusing its debasement. He accepted the solitude of a man of 'destiny', and for much of his life put love aside as a distraction. Denouncing the chaos of his century, he pointed to a vision that he was not himself to enjoy.

His move from America to Europe gave him a peculiar detachment from all environment, a universal foreignness which was the obverse to strong feeling for certain locales like Gloucester, Massachusetts. He remained somehow alien to Englishmen and the Anglican Church, from everything with which he identified himself. He devised an anti-self not, like Yeats, to extend the self, but to guard it: his jokey good fellowship was a cover for the solitary; his mild gentlemanliness a cover for the extremist; his impersonality a cover for confession; his acquired European tradition a cover for native roots.

Eliot cut from the draft of his last play two telling lines on the exile who must exchange

> The loneliness of home among foreign strange people
> For the loneliness of home which is only memories.

His youth was interred in another land, its shadow moving with the shades behind the grey rocks of the New England shore. Hope Mirrlees perceived something of this when she said categorically: 'He wasn't a bit like an Englishman', though he could feel 'most violently English' as when he sported his white rose on the anniversaries of the death of Richard III. 'I once said to him: "You know there is this indestructible American strain in you." And he was pleased. He said: "Oh yes, there is. I'm glad you realized it. There is." '

In his last years, he stressed his origins, and declared that his poetry, in its sources, its emotional springs, came from America and its past—not a specific past. His new life was rooted in the New World idea, in its invitation to formulate new modes of life. He revived two main modes which fused in his poetry. One was the pattern of spiritual pioneering, when Eliot said 'fare forward, voyagers', a continuation of Whitman's voyaging 'With questionings . . . / *Wherefore unsatisfied soul? and Whither O mocking life?*' The other mode of life was the set formula laid down in seventeenth-century New England. Eliot once said that he felt at home in America as it had been before about 1830. What that date meant to Eliot must be a guess. It was soon after that Eliot's grandfather left Boston for the frontier. It was also then that the civilized élite of the Eastern seaboard lost its power in the bitter election of 1828, when John Quincy Adams fell before the rude, uncultivated Andrew Jackson. Was Eliot still resisting the impact of Jacksonian democracy—more Western, more individualistic—a hundred years on? Or was it some more subtle change: the fading of the last traces of Calvinist piety before the cheery optimism of a new age of self-reliance? For Emerson, the very advocate of self-reliance, that old demanding piety remained a lingering force through his memory of his Calvinist aunt: 'What a debt is ours to that old religion which, in the childhood most of us, still dwelt like a sabbath morning in the country of New England, teaching privation, self-denial and sorrow!'

What distinguished the New England Puritans from their English brethren was their unique demand, in the words of Increase Mather, 'That persons should make a Relation of the work of Gods Spirit upon their hearts'. Eliot set down such a 'Relation' from **"The Hollow Men"** to the confession of the Elder Statesman. In the seventeenth century, public confession had been compelled by a church which saw itself as the farthest outpost of ecclesiastical holiness. It was quite beyond the requirements of entry into the mild Anglican church of which Eliot actually had little immediate knowledge at the time of his conversion. It was conversion itself that drew him, for, through that experience, he revived the strenuousness of the New England divines for whom it was not enough to profess faith. For Eliot too it was not enough to repeat 'For Thine is the Kingdom'. Those words must pierce the convert, must annihilate his rotten self. Whimpering, he must submit to the terror of God's hand. In New England, each person who would join the exclusive company of visible saints must experience and declare saving grace.

Grace, though, must come unsought to a soul wrestling with sin as Eliot wrestled with the devil of the stairs.

Eliot was an expert on election. Like the divines, his ancestors, no one knew better the stages and signs of salvation, but he had limited spiritual gifts. He had diagnostic self-insight, strength of will, endurance, and a readiness to recognize the reality of the unseen, but he had not much gift of vision. He craved a lifetime burning in every moment, but had to accept a lesser course of 'trying'. Yet it was this acceptance of the common lot that made his mature poetry more accessible than the merciless clairvoyance of the early verse. He strove to content himself with right action, and not to hope too hard that saving grace would come to fill the waiting vessel of perfected conduct. But Eliot's was a God of pain, whose punishment, until the last eight years, was almost the only sign of the absolute paternal care.

The irony of Eliot's life was that he was unsuited to the model life of saints. He was simply too self-conscious to be a saint. Yet his struggle to subdue intellectual pride, his almost savage intolerance, proved the fertile matter of his poetry. There remains the paradox of a man who wished to be saint above poet, but who became all the greater as poet for his failure to attain sainthood. He fell back on another goal, to be God's agent, and as public spokesman he achieved an extraordinary authority. His pronouncements are still repeated as truths from on high. The prophetic role, like the Puritan rigour of introspection, came most directly from America, as well as the challenge of a terrifying nature where man measures himself in the face of an immeasurable power that is and was from the beginning.

Eliot's career circled back so that the sources of his own life, the Mississippi and Cape Ann, became the source of all life. Despite his adaptation to England, his adoption of English religion, manners, and clothes, and despite his marriages to English women, his poetry led him back to 'the source of the longest river', and to the silence the child heard between two waves of the sea. (pp. 268-73)

Lyndall Gordon, in her Eliot's New Life, *Oxford University Press, Oxford, 1988, 356 p.*

MARTIN SCOFIELD

Eliot is first and foremost a great poet and after that a great critic, and he himself was fond of pointing out how closely (and perhaps indistinguishably) the 'creative' and the 'critical' interact. . . . In his time Eliot revolutionized readers' perceptions of Donne, Marvell, and the Metaphysical poets. That revolution has now long since been completed, but his criticism can still refresh, often unpredictably, our sense of poets as different as Johnson, Shelley, Tennyson and Kipling. He can challenge conventionally accepted valuations ('There is more essential poetry in Turgenev's "Sportsman's Sketches", even in translation, than in the whole of Thomas Browne or Walter Pater') or make us think again about writers we had perhaps not taken seriously enough (like Poe, more intelligent 'than Browne, than Pater, or even Ruskin'). . . . But the poetry itself has also, as well as its other powers and attractions, the power to make us re-read earlier poetry in a new way. The poetic style of the speech of the 'familiar compound ghost' in **"Little Gidding"** II with its powerful generalizations can, in conjunction with Eliot's essay on Johnson, give us an awareness of the possibilities of a Johnsonian poet-

ry; and the verse of **"Gerontion"**, as much as the critical essays, has enabled us to see the qualities of the verse of Middleton and Tourneur. (p. 5)

The complete poems . . . form a remarkably coherent whole. They have that 'continuous development from first to last' which Eliot found in Shakespeare, and are 'united by one significant, consistent and developing personality'. . . . They are bound together by recurring motifs and preoccupations, images that echo earlier images and in that echo achieve a resonance and significance they would not entirely have on their own. The poems, for example, begin and end with a journey. 'Let us go then, you and I', are the opening words of the first poem of Eliot's first volume, **"The Love Song of J. Alfred Prufrock"**; and the last of *Four Quartets* begins its closing verse-paragraph:

> We shall not cease from exploration
> And the end of all our exploring
> Will be to arrive where we started
> And know the place for the first time.

There is a sense in which those lines are true of a reading of Eliot's poems: the experiences which are the subject of **"Prufrock,"** **"Portrait of a Lady"** and other early poems are being continually revised in the later poems, and placed in a new perspective. The journey also proceeds through the intervening poems: from the walk in **"Rhapsody on a Windy Night"** and the 'old man driven by the Trades' in **"Gerontion"**, through the road to the chapel and the 'hordes swarming / Over the endless plains' in Part V of *The Waste Land,* to **"Journey of the Magi"**, the sea voyage in **"Marina"**, the return 'down the passage which we did not take / . . . Into the rose garden' in **"Burnt Norton"**, and the pilgrimage to Little Gidding. Ending as it does in 'the middle way' of **"East Coker"** and the pilgrimage, the ghostly 'patrol', and the continued 'exploration' in **"Little Gidding"**, it can not unjustly be compared (though there are no exact correspondences) with Dante's journey in *The Divine Comedy.* (p. 6)

Eliot can be seen as a 'compound ghost', a writer compounded out of many elements of the European tradition. But how far is he also, for us today, a 'master' as the ghost in **"Little Gidding"** was for him? He is no longer the great eminence, *the* predominant presence in English poetry and culture, that he was in the middle years of this century. His politics have been much attacked, his religious orthodoxy has not, it would seem, commanded any great following in the literary world. The influence of his poetry on other poets has always been rather elusive: after the first impact of his poetry in the twenties (when, it has been said, it was impossible to pick up a manuscript submitted by a young poet without finding the words 'dry', 'dust', 'desert' and the like on the first page) his deeper influence on outstanding poets is very often a matter of general professional example than of a direct stylistic kind. William Empson wrote [in "The Style of the Master"]: 'I do not know for certain how much of my own mind he invented, let alone how much of it is a reaction against him or indeed a consequence of misreading him. He has a very penetrating influence, perhaps not unlike an east wind.' And more recently Donald Davie [in "Eliot in One Poet's Life"] has written of the profound general influence of Eliot on his own literary life. Stylistically one can see traces in the early Auden, and most recently (and of a different kind) in Geoffrey Hill. But his poetic influence is more like Shakespeare's than Milton's, to the extent that his influence has been powerful but subter-

ranean: there is no tradition of Eliotic verse as there was a tradition of Miltonic verse in the eighteenth century.

Finally, does his poetry have—and was it ever its most important function to have—a moral message for modern civilization: is Eliot a master in that sense? Or should we (and can
we) detach Eliot's poetry from its 'philosophy' in the way
that Arnold detached Wordsworth's twenty-nine years after
the poet's death. The question of the part Eliot's beliefs play
in his poetry, and the question of how much our response to
his poetry depends on our response to his beliefs [is examined
in *T. S. Eliot: The Poems*]. But whatever our conclusions on
this question, it seems certain that Eliot will retain his place,
with W. B. Yeats, as one of the two greatest poets of the first
half of this century, because of both the quality of his art and
the predicament (and effort to overcome it) that his art presents. (pp. 7-8)

> *Martin Scofield, in his* T. S. Eliot: The Poems,
> *Cambridge University Press, 1988, 264 p.*

The Seventh Annual
Young Playwrights Festival

(The four dramatists honored during the Seventh Annual Young Playwrights Festival were, from left to right: **Kevin Corrigan, Jonathan Marc Sherman, Robert Kerr,** *and* **Eric Ziegenhagen.** *)*

Sponsored by the Foundation of the Dramatists Guild, the Young Playwrights Festival is an annual event open to American youths aged nineteen and under. Writers meeting this qualification are invited to submit their original plays to the Foundation of the Dramatists Guild following specific guidelines. All entrants receive a detailed evaluation of their work. A commitee chooses several plays each year for professional productions in New York City. The playwrights whose works are selected receive transportation, housing, royalties, as well as membership in the Dramatists Guild, Inc., and they are involved in all aspects of production. The plays are then presented during a monthlong run in a New York theater and are reviewed by noted drama critics. The Young Playwrights Festival was established in 1981 through the efforts of noted dramatist and lyricist Stephen Sondheim, Ruth Goetz, treasurer of the Dramatists Guild, and Gerald Chapman, who administered a similar festival in London during the mid-1970s. Mr. Sondheim stated: "The festival allows young people to use their creative imagination and to see their work done in collaboration with professionals. . . . But never are the playwrights treated as, quote, kids. Like all writers in the Dramatists Guild, they have total control over their material." Sondheim added: "These young playwrights are the theater's future."

Three plays were performed during the seventh Young Playwrights Festival in 1988, and a fourth, *Boiler Room,* by Kevin Corrigan, was presented as a staged reading. Jonathan Marc Sherman's *Women and Wallace* is composed of a series of brief scenes that follow the title character's life from age six, when his mother commits suicide, to eighteen. Focusing on Wallace's relationships with females, including his mother, grandmother, psychoanalyst, and young women with whom he shares friendship and romance, Sherman blends witty remarks, farcical incidents, and poignant moments of anguish as Wallace attempts to come to terms with his mother's death and his awkwardness, bitterness, and often self-defeating attitude. Robert Kerr's *And the Air Didn't Answer* concerns the crises of a young Catholic after he questions the depth of his religious faith and the existence of God. Feeling pressured by his mother, girlfriend, and priest after admitting his lapse, the young man attempts to resolve his dilemma. During a sleepless night in his room and while he is fatigued in class the next day, the young man experiences visions that underscore the questions perplexing him. Eric Ziegenhagen's *Seniority* involves two sisters, one of whom is free spirited while the other is passive, who are unwittingly interested in the same man. Conflict arises when the younger, more aggressive sister returns home following a date with the man.

For further information about the Young Playwrights Festival, including guidelines and helpful advice, please write to the following address:

> Young Playwrights Festival
> 234 West 44th Street
> New York, NY 10036

DAVID KAUFMAN

"The play has helped me understand who I am in relation to my mom's suicide, and how important that really was to me," said Jonathan Marc Sherman, an 18-year-old from Livingston, N.J. "I've come to terms with a lot of my feelings through writing it, and I think I've realized just how much it's affected my dealings with women. You know, you can rewrite things when you're writing, but you can't when you're living, which is a shame."

Jonathan Sherman's play, **Women and Wallace,** is one of four winners in the seventh annual Young Playwrights Festival, which this year elicited 612 entries from all over the country, written by young people ranging in age from 6 to 18. The festival was established by the Foundation of the Dramatists Guild to locate and nurture tomorrow's playwrights.

Two other winners, Robert Kerr's **And the Air Didn't Answer,** an autobiographical play that questions the existence of God, and Eric Ziegenhagen's **Seniority,** about two adolescent sisters in pursuit of the same boy, will be performed on the same program as **Women and Wallace.** . . . The fourth winner, Kevin Corrigan's full-length work **Boiler Room,** a coming-of-age story focusing on a father-son relationship, will be presented as a staged reading on three separate evenings during the festival's monthlong run.

Given the festival's professional production standards, it has quickly become the most important showcase for young playwrights, and has received predominantly favorable attention from the major New York critics.

"The festival allows young people to use their creative imagination and to see their work done in collaboration with professionals," said Stephen Sondheim, the composer and lyricist. Mr. Sondheim first conceived of the festival in the mid-70's when he saw advertisements for a similar program at the Royal Court Theater in London run by the director Gerald Chapman, who died last year. Along with Ruth Goetz, trea-

surer of the Dramatists Guild, Mr. Sondheim eventually persuaded Mr. Chapman to organize the Young Playwrights Festival in New York in 1981.

"The actors, directors and technical people are all professionals," said Mr. Sondheim. "But never are the playwrights treated as, quote, kids. Like all writers in the Dramatists Guild, they have total control over their material." . . .

"It's a little bit of giving youth its due," said Andre Bishop, a member of the committee responsible for selecting the plays to be presented. . . .

Since the festival began, it has received 5,465 plays, and 46 winners have had either full-scale productions or staged readings of their work presented before New York audiences. Every winner is assigned a director and an adviser (or dramaturg) to work with the author on casting and on developing the play through a thoroughly professional rehearsal process. Every entry receives a written critique.

So winning is not the only reason for entering the contest, as Mr. Kerr, 17, from Stillwater, Minn., confirmed. "When I found out I was a finalist I was stunned," he said. "Mostly I was going for the evaluation. Now I feel kind of vulnerable, because people I don't even know about are coming in contact with the script. But it's also a neat feeling, realizing you're reaching out this way."

One festival image that many are fond of recalling is of the youngest winner, Adam Berger—who was 8 when he wrote **It's Time for a Change**—sucking on a lollipop while watching his play in 1982. Now 15, Mr. Berger is in the 10th grade at Collegiate, a Manhattan private school, where two short musicals he's written since have been performed. . . .

"The goal," said Nancy Quinn, formerly coordinator of the O'Neill National Playwrights Conference and now the third producing director of the festival (after Chapman and Peggy Hanson), "is to encourage talented young writers. We don't want anyone bulldozed. One of the surprises for me is to hear over and over—from a Chris Durang, an Alfred Uhry, a Wendy Wasserstein, a Steve Sondheim, a Marsha Norman, an Albert Innaurato, a Charles Fuller, on and on—how much *they* get out of the process. You know, we all have a tendency to say, this is the way theater is done. Then suddenly you get young people saying why, why, why."

In response to the assumption that work by younger writers is bound to reflect naïve ideas, Mr. Bishop suggested, "Young people who have something to say and the guts to say it are totally worth listening to. Maybe it's their very lack of experience that makes them so bold. Maybe it's because their coming of age coincides with a growing ability to articulate."

> David Kaufman, "Heady Days for Junior Playwrights," in The New York Times, *Section II, September 11, 1988, p. 5.*

MEL GUSSOW

The plays presented in the annual Young Playwrights Festival have often dealt with young people going through rites of passage. In this season's festival there are indications that, at age 7, the series itself has reached its artistic maturity. Each of the three new playwrights whose works are produced demonstrates a definite theatrical talent, as well as an ability to treat perceptively such subjects as religion, sex and suicide.

Jonathan Marc Sherman's **Women and Wallace** is both the longest and the most venturesome of the trio, a dark comedy about the psychic effects of a mother's suicide on her adoring son. We see the title character from 6 to 18 years old, as he emerges from his embitterment to face the world—and the women who are irresistibly drawn to him.

In other hands, Wallace could have turned into a Norman Bates. . . . But the author is far more interested in the humorous absurdities of Wallace's sad story. He has a gift for acerbic, self-mocking dialogue, and sometimes he tries too hard to be clever. At the same time, he has a clear focus on the character's confusion of identity (mama's boy or ladies' man?).

Wallace is surrounded by women—the well-meaning [grandmother and psychiatrist] as well as a quintet of young ladies with whom he shares romantic encounters. Each represents a milestone in the education of Wallace, who, in [Josh] Hamilton's portrayal, emphasizes the charm behind the misanthropy. In one additional poignant note, while the young man is defeating himself at every opportunity, his mother remains on stage as a silent witness. . . .

Behind the scenes as playwright advisor (or dramaturg) is Albert Innaurato. One can feel the intuitive artistic bond between his work and that of the younger playwright. In both cases, there is laughter in the face of pain.

There would seem to be a similar connection between Robert Kerr, the author of **And the Air Didn't Answer,** and his director, Christopher Durang. This comedy about an adolescent's crisis of faith is in the *Sister Mary Ignatius* tradition, but with its own comic sensibility. The protagonist is a Catholic schoolboy who suddenly finds himself questioning the existence of God and, simultaneously, his girlfriend's piety.

Expanding his circle, he falls in with a free thinker, who describes herself as a nondenominational transcendentalist, but when he joins her in her rapturous meditations, he begins to laugh. During such moments of skepticism, he has outrageous dreams—acted out on stage—in which Crusaders and finally God himself walk the earth and talk like tuned-in teenagers.

The play is very funny up to a point, and then becomes unconvincingly sober at the ending. But the journey is a heartening one. . . .

In contrast to the daydreams and nightmares of the other two plays, Eric Ziegenhagen's **Seniority** is a straightforward slice of life—about the rivalry between two sisters. It is the younger, pretty high school freshman who indoctrinates her older, plain sibling in the ways of romance.

The relationship is keenly observed; love and envy pass back and forth in this late-night conversation. . . . The responsive direction is by Lisa Peterson. Alfred Uhry acted as playwright advisor, and, as with the other two plays, one can feel a kinship between an older writer and one embarking on his career.

Mel Gussow, "Writings of Passage," in The New York Times, September 23, 1988, p. C3.

JOHN SIMON

The seventh annual Young Playwrights Festival runs true to form: There is the good, the promising, the poor. But it's worth attending to for the rare chance to find out what the young make of the world. And what they may make it into.

And the Air Didn't Answer, by Robert Kerr (age seventeen when the play was submitted), is a Chris Durangish sort of work that was in fact directed by Durang. Let me hope that it was Durangish even before the director got to it. Its hero is Dan, a midwestern Catholic high-school student who loses his faith and goes looking for it everywhere, in the grips of cosmic-comic despair. He has trouble with his pious girlfriend, Jennifer, who leaves him; with his uncomprehending mother, who won't leave him alone (except in room arrest); and with all sorts of fantasy figures that hound him. Problems also with priests and teachers and scoutmasters—it seems not believing makes you lose credibility. Dan goes questing on, encouraged by a new girlfriend, Renee, a peacenik; though she cannot espouse atheism, she can go as far as Buddhism.

The play toys with daydreams and daymares, real-life and imagined absurdities, and lets them all commingle in a tasty but somewhat undercooked stew. The more daring the fantasies—say, about Abraham, Isaac, and God—the better; the tamer moments tend to go limp. . . .

Durang's staging is lively, and one must have some affection for a play in one of whose fantasy sequences Dan is sent to hell despite his good deeds because, he is told, "you did all this for your mother, not for the Almighty."

The second play, *Seniority,* by Eric Ziegenhagen (sixteen at the time of submission), is a slice of life crying out for butter, cheese, or meat. Debbie, a high-school senior, waits up for her freshman sister, Fiona, who, returning from a date with Ian, a senior, shocks Debbie by confessing to having had sex with him. Debbie, it appears, has had a crush on Ian all along. After Fiona retires, Ian arrives with the handbag she (deliberately) left in his car. He and Debbie start flirting, but Fiona comes down from her room to claim Ian and takes him back upstairs.

Nothing about the writing is noteworthy in the least, and the author's cause has not been served by having what were obviously meant to be white characters played by blacks, presumably to woo audiences on a forthcoming school tour for "differently abled" audiences, as the program barbarously puts it. If that subliterate euphemism refers to the mentally deprived, the play might just work; if to the economically underprivileged, the kids will rightly be nonplussed by the speech and behavior of these dillydallying Ians and Fionas trying to pass for them. (And as long as Ziegenhagen writes otherwise grammatical English, couldn't someone have corrected his ghastly "that big of an age difference" and "that deep of a person"?) (p. 78)

The third play, *Women and Wallace,* by Jonathan Marc Sherman (age eighteen), is accomplished and highly enjoyable but, at over an hour's duration, a trifle too long for what it has to say, even if, scene by scene, its constituent parts do not seem stretched out. It concerns Wallace, whose mother sends the second-grader off to school after packing a nice lunch for him, then calmly removes her turtleneck sweater (she always wears turtlenecks, because she doesn't like her neck) and proceeds to slit her throat (presumably not because she dislikes it). The play deliberately teeters between near-absurdist farce and wistful comedy with a darker strain or two, and it is to Sherman's not inconsiderable credit that he can carry off such a tricky mixture with such apple-cheeked aplomb.

The play progresses to Wallace's adolescence; his visits to a woman psychiatrist ("I've had my head measured by a close friend, and if you shrink it by so much as a millimeter, I'll take you to court!"); his relationship with his endearingly goofy, but also wise, grandmother, who likes to contemplate pictures of deceased relatives ("It was taken two minutes before he went"); his tussle with puberty ("I don't know what to do about all this . . . and it's my life"); his first kiss, in response to a cheeky tomboy's solicitation, which elicits a "You're too fast!" from the disgruntled girl; his deflowering in his freshman year by the high school's sexiest senior, whom he tells admiringly during their rapturous embrace, "You're *so* sweaty!" He insists that he was not a virgin, really, because during birth he was inside his mother's genitalia. Says the senior girl, "You're pretty weird, Wallace." "Thank you." "Well, did you ever have sex with anyone outside your immediate family?"

The seductress passes the initiated Wallace on to her younger sister. (I wonder whether all this sister stuff in two out of three plays is trying to tell us something?) Nina, the kid sister, is sweet, lovely, sagacious, and loving. Naturally, Wallace must immediately cheat on her. But she can handle that, too; find out the details for yourself. A fellow who can say "I've been having this dream for two months. Except sometimes it's in color and sometimes in black-and-white. And once the black-and-white was colorized" is no ordinary lad: Attention must be paid to a kid like this. It is too bad that the play cheats a little. For example, for the sake of keeping it about the eponymous Wallace and women, no other male is introduced, even though a six-year-old who finds his mother with her throat cut should be shown in at least one scene with his father.

Still, it is a real play, and Don Scardino has staged it exemplarily. Was it his idea, I wonder, to keep all the offstage women effectively onstage all the time, seated around the periphery and watching? Each playwright, by the way, had a senior-playwright adviser, and here it was Albert Innaurato. But no matter who helped and how, Sherman plainly has what it takes. (pp. 78-9)

John Simon, "Youth Wants to Know," in New York Magazine, Vol. 21, No. 39, October 3, 1988, pp. 78-9.

EDITH OLIVER

The annual Young Playwrights Festival is always a joyful occasion, and the seventh edition . . . is hands down the best. The three winners to be given full productions are comedies with an underlying seriousness, and are by writers who are still in their teens. Unlike a lot of what one sees in movies or on television, the plays, one-acters, seem to be based on first-hand observation or invention of people, not pictures of people. Here is no evening of "images;" the word is the thing, and the words are good. **And the Air Didn't Answer,** by Robert Kerr . . . is about a Catholic teen-ager, Dan Wilson, whom we first see standing at a lectern working on a speech about faith. His girlfriend, Jennifer, standing beside him, suggests that perhaps a bit more conviction or sincerity might bolster

his delivery, and he admits that he doesn't know what faith means, or even God, for that matter. At confession, the priest, to whom loss of faith is all in a day's work, puts the blame on lack of self-discipline, and tells him to forgo one dinner and one night's sleep. The night is sleepless but not dreamless, and a couple of crusaders appear to keep him company. They are the forerunners of many hallucinatory characters who intrude at intervals. Unable to keep awake at school the next day, he draws detention, and meets another detainee, Renee, a free spirit, open to every religious fad and sympathetic to his loss. The play is made up of many short episodes—with Dan's worried mother, who may have bought him the wrong Bible when he was a child, with pious Jennifer, with free-soul Renee, and with, among other revenants, Virgil, who conducts a guided tour through Dante's Inferno. All the episodes are funny, with a sharp satiric barb in many of them, and the ending, with God and faith as out of reach as ever, is neatly inconclusive. . . .

The brief, amusing *Seniority,* by Eric Ziegenhagen . . . , opens with a young girl, Debbie, sitting restlessly on a couch. The time is midnight, and she is waiting up for her sister Fiona, who is out on a date. Debbie is a high-school senior, Fiona a freshman, and when Fiona gets home the conversation is all about dating, with Debbie trying not to seem nosy and Fiona defensive. When Debbie eventually learns that the date was one Ian, a fellow-senior whom she is longing to go out with but far too timid to invite, she is both crushed and indignant. But Fiona is bold—"the only way," she asserts. She did the asking. After Fiona goes up to bed, Ian knocks at the door and comes in with Fiona's purse, which she left in his car. Debbie stops him (temporarily) on his way to Fiona's room, and in a short scene admits her own attraction. Ian handles this difficult situation with poise and tact and considerable sensitivity. . . .

At the beginning of **Women and Wallace,** by Jonathan Marc Sherman . . . , a handsome young man throws a tomato at a pretty young woman; it explodes all over her white dress. "I love you," he says. The young man is, of course, Wallace. We next see him at the edge of the stage. He tells the audience that he is six years old and he loves his mommy, who washes his clothes and makes sandwiches for his school lunch. As he speaks, his mother stands on a platform above him, knife in hand, spreading a sandwich; she then cuts her throat. The child finds her body on the kitchen floor. The play packs considerable substance, to say nothing of emotion and humor, into one act. The rest of the action is a series of encounters between Wallace, haunted by the suicide and unable to break the spell, and the various women he sees, in one capacity or another, through the years, until he turns eighteen. Mr. Sherman manages to make many of these scenes very funny (without breaking the spell); it is almost impossible to believe that he is a beginner. Two of the best scenes are with Wallace's grandmother but there are other good ones—with a little girl who swipes his sandwich, with his psychiatrist, and with a number of girls who become his friends.

Edith Oliver, "Winners," in The New Yorker, Vol. LXIV, No. 33, October 3, 1988, p. 91.

LAURIE STONE

[**Women and Wallace**] is schematic and too long, but it is unmistakably the work of a talented writer—examining his feelings, experimenting with language, making psychological pain play on stage. The 60-minute one-act, under Don Scardino's nimble, unobtrusive direction, moves back and forth in time, tracing the effects on Wallace of his mother's suicide. He is [six years old] when she hands him a peanut butter and banana sandwich, waits until he leaves for school, and slits her throat with a kitchen knife. From then on, all his attempts to connect with females end in misunderstandings and severings. The pattern is changed when, at college, he falls in love with a woman who leaves him but returns.

Wallace narrates in a voice that's alternately wry and anguished, one that happily escapes the pompous boy-chirp endemic to Neil Simon et al. Scenes are played on and around a sloped platform, lending the piece a dreaminess and rescuing it from stodgy naturalism. The other characters—all female—ring the platform, awaiting their times to enter the story. It's an Oedipal fantasy if ever there was one—the males absent, the women in readiness—but because Sherman is consciously exploring this terrain, he keeps it buoyant.

The dialogue is charged with arresting phrases and allusions. Wallace's mother's suicide note reads, "Cremate the parasite." When a girlfriend asks Wallace to describe his mother, he shoots, "She was like Sylvia Plath without the publishing contract." Later, he repeats the line with a variation, showing that bitterness rather than spontaneity fuels his wit. He can also be startlingly candid. He tells his analyst that, the day after his mother's funeral, his father made him a peanut butter and banana sandwich and he came home expecting to find another corpse in the kitchen. "I was disappointed when I saw he was alive and my system didn't work." (p. 110)

And the Air Didn't Answer . . . depicts another troubled boy surrounded by concerned dames. The lad's problem, losing his Catholic faith, isn't gripping, but fantasy sequences, playfully staged by Christopher Durang—who has Dante's Virgil do a turn as a used-car-salesman type—entertain. In *Seniority,* . . . a sexually adventurous sister and her older, frightened sibling argue predictably, but this play, too, is enlivened by surprising bits of business and by Bellina Logan's quiet assurance as the older girl. Anyway, who expects polish here? I was continually amazed by the writers' achievements and reminded of my own teenage self, who could barely keep her head above adolescence, much less conceive of completing a play. (pp. 110, 121)

Laurie Stone, "Well Aged," in The Village Voice, Vol. XXXIII, No. 40, October 4, 1988, pp. 110, 121.

JAN STUART

How did animals and kids ever get by without rights advocates? Spokespersons for each group are driven by the admirable if disturbingly new concept that the inability to articulate one's own suffering does not indicate an absence of pain. In the past seven years, the Young Playwrights Festival has provided lively evidence that, given the opportunity, one of those groups can speak for itself, thank you very much, and is possibly better served by its own voices.

The one-act plays in this marvelous annual event restore a sense of consequence to the conflicts of adolescence that adults are so expert at minimizing. It's agonizing to be old enough to comprehend one's problems but not old enough to work them through without a chaperone; adults add insult to injury by perpetuating a hierarchy of childhood vs. "Wait until you get out into . . ."), as if responsibility for the Con

Ed bill somehow made the burdens of the former less real, less urgent, less complex. The complexities of adolescence are glossed over by the adult writer who reduces its torments to bullies and detention hall; it is the young writer, with a direct line into his own alienation, who confronts the real demons.

The great irony of the Young Playwrights Festival is that many of the plays, because of their honesty, would be condemned by school communities as unacceptable to the very age group to whom they speak most directly. Consequently, teenagers who may be grappling with suicide, homosexuality, divorced parents, and religious/racial intolerance, which these plays address squarely, are still powdering their hair to play harmless, lovable old folks in *Harvey* or *Arsenic and Old Lace.*

Local church groups, the same ones that tried to halt professional productions of Christopher Durang's *Sister Mary Ignatius,* would hit the ceiling at a school staging of Robert Kerr's *And the Air Didn't Answer*. . . . Kerr's protagonist, Dan Wilson, is a young teenager who is beginning to question his faith, much to the alarm of his doctrinaire mother, his girlfriend, who heads the church youth group, and his priest, who prescribes privation.

What is startling is that Dan's soul-searching does not lead to a rosy reassertion of his faith, but rather an angry rejection of religious hypocrisy and a newfound conviction in atheism. Along the way, Kerr demonstrates a nice flair for theatrical flourishes, especially a fantasy tour through the ninth circle of Dante's *Inferno* and a game of *Jeopardy* in which contestants must reply to "Of all the world's religions, this is the one with all of the answers."

Too often ingenuity outpaces wit, however, and Kerr's play lumbers from the weight of cliche, such as a mom who harps on what the neighbors will think and Dan's new, vegetarian girlfriend, a textbook new-ager. Director Durang gets spirited performances from his actors. . . . In time, Kerr could learn from Durang the writer about the very thin lines that separate caricature from the real from the surreal.

Kerr's ambitions are at least those of one who is writing for the theater, which can't be said of Eric Ziegenhagen's *Seniority,* which would adapt with little adjustment into an after-school TV special. Ziegenhagen's risks are those of one attempting to inhabit characters of the opposite sex. . . .

Jonathan Marc Sherman's triumphant drama *Women and Wallace* . . . winds its way back around to its beginning, but by the time it does, the protagonist has gone through a wrenching process of maturation that almost leaves you gasping at the author's powers of observation. This would seem to be the work of a young man (18 when the play was submitted) who has done more than his share of time on the therapy couch and can barely contain the wealth of insight he has accrued. He doesn't. He puts it all out there: the primal shock, the therapy sessions, the dream analysis, the breakthrough, in fact virtually the whole life of 18-year-old Wallace, who came home from school one day at age 6 to find that his mother had slit her throat with a kitchen knife.

In *Women and Wallace,* Sherman, who endured this childhood trauma with his own mother (albeit with a different suicide weapon) works through the feelings of guilt and abandonment incurred by her death. In no less than 20 scenes, all honest to a fault, he charts how those feelings inform Wallace's encounters with the pivotal women in his life: his girlfriends, his therapist, and most centrally, his grandmother. . . . Particularly impressive is how Sherman achieves Wallace's catharsis with an open-ended awareness of the lessons yet to be learned. . . .

I particularly liked the empathic presence of Mary Joy seated in front as Wallace's mother, keeping loving watch on her son's progress. This silent eloquence, as much as any of Sherman's double-edged one-liners, confirms him as a theater writer of substance. ***Women and Wallace*** reaffirms the Young Playwrights Festival as a theater event with a capital E.

Jan Stuart, "Boy Bards," in 7 days, *October 5, 1988.*

The Wartime Journalism
of Paul de Man

On December 1, 1987, *The New York Times* reported the discovery of articles that Paul de Man (1919-1983), a leading literary theorist, wrote for collaborationist publications in his native Belgium between 1940 and 1942. While compiling a complete bibliography of this influential scholar, Ortwin de Graef, a Belgian graduate student, discovered de Man's byline on nearly two hundred articles appearing in the newspaper *Le Soir* and the journal *Het Vlaamsche Land.* In the most notorious of these pieces, "Les Juifs dans la littérature actuelle" (1941; "Jews in Contemporary Literature"), de Man employs organicist metaphors used by Nazis to unify the German people under the theory of racial purity. He defines the specific "genius" of several nationalities and examines the literature of these countries for contamination by "enjuivés" ("enjewished") influences. While it is impossible to ascertain the extent that the Nazis's ultimate plans for the Jewish population were known at the time de Man wrote this article, his reference to "the Jewish problem" and his dismissal of any "deplorable consequences" resulting from isolating the Jewish community are startling. Commentators debated whether de Man used these phrases naively or maliciously. De Man abruptly ceased contributing to collaborationist journals in 1942.

De Man emigrated to the United States in 1947 and began graduate studies at Harvard University in 1952. Over the next thirty years he became an influential teacher and literary scholar. De Man's first collection of essays, *Blindness and Insight* (1971), is a seminal reevaluation of the status and function of language. In *Allegories of Reading* (1979), his next collection, de Man established his own version of deconstruction. This philosophy of reading, invented by Jacques Derrida, argues that no text has a single, stable meaning and that language can never unequivocally convey its author's intended meanings. Jon Weiner summarized the opposition to this controversial theory: "The presuppositions of deconstruction—that literature is not part of the knowable social and political reality, that one must be resigned to the impossibility of truth—make it at worst nihilistic or implicitly authoritarian and at best an academic self-indulgence." Deborah Esch, representing the opposing view, argued that deconstruction is a powerful critique of authoritarianism: "De Man provided his students with a set of tools for reading, the most important function of which may be the unmasking of ideology. What we call ideology, he showed, entails taking a linguistic construct for a natural reality. This questioning of the authority of language yielded the most subversive pedagogy I know."

Although anti-Semitic remarks are absent from the majority of de Man's wartime articles, which are primarily concerned with cultural and literary events of the day, as well as from all his scholarly writings, reviewers debated how the existence of the journalism should affect the perception of his

later work and of deconstruction as a whole. Critics also speculated on why de Man failed to tell even his closest friends and colleagues about his wartime activities, and many attempted to find in his later work an exculpation, or, alternatively, a cryptic continuation of the anti-Semitic, authoritarian viewpoints found in some of these articles. While many critics expressed dismay toward the articles, it was noted that de Man was young and impressionable at the time he wrote these pieces and was possibly influenced by people and events surrounding him. David H. Hirsch summarized this view: "It is most probable that in 1941-42 de Man was acting not out of malice but out of opportunism."

In his complex and compelling essay, "Like the Sound of the Sea Deep within a Shell: Paul de Man's War" (*Critical Inquiry,* Spring 1988), Derrida proposes a binary interpretation of de Man's journalism: "*On the one hand,* the *massive, immediate, and dominant* effect of all these texts is that of a *relatively* coherent ideological ensemble which, *most often and in a preponderant fashion,* conforms to official rhetoric, that of the occupation forces or of the milieux that, in Belgium, had accepted the defeat and . . . the perspective of a European unity under German hegemony." Derrida then continues: "But *on the other hand* and within this frame, de Man's discourse is constantly split, disjointed, engaged in incessant conflicts. . . . [All] the propositions carry within themselves a counterproposition. . . . " He concludes: "To judge, to condemn the work or the man on the basis of what was a brief episode, to call for closing, that is to say, at least figuratively, for censuring or burning books is to reproduce the exterminating gesture which one accuses de Man of not having armed himself sooner with necessary vigilance. It is not even to draw a lesson that he, de Man, learned to draw from the war." Derrida also impugns the objectivity and perspicacity of the media's interpretation of deconstructionism and asserts that in order to comprehend the significance of the journalism it is necessary not only to read all of de Man's work but to be cognizant of the social, political, and historical context of their conception and reception. Derrida's exhaustive analysis of the controversy and, in particular, of "Jews in Contemporary Literature," is considered by many the definitive deconstructionist response to the questions posed by the discovery of these articles. These and other aspects of the controversy are discussed in the articles included in *Responses: On Paul de Man's Wartime Journalism* (1989), a collection of essays written by both proponents and detractors of deconstruction. All of de Man's wartime journalism, including pieces published in non-collaborationist periodicals, are reproduced in *Wartime Journalism, 1939-1943* (1988).

THE NEW YORK TIMES

In a finding that has stunned scholars, a Yale professor revered as one of the most brilliant intellectuals of his generation wrote for an anti-Semitic, pro-Nazi newspaper in Belgium during World War II, documents have disclosed.

The professor, Paul de Man, died at the age of 65 in December 1983 while Sterling Professor of the Humanities at Yale, a post reserved for the university's brightest luminaries. Venerated as a teacher and scholar, he was the originator of a controversial theory of language that some say may place him among the great thinkers of his age.

A researcher in Belgium has found at least 100 previously unknown articles Professor de Man wrote in 1941 and 1942 for *Le Soir,* a pro-Nazi newspaper. In one of the articles the young de Man addresses the question of whether Jews "pollute" modern fiction.

The findings about a man respected at Yale and elsewhere have shocked scholars. Several predicted the information will fan an intellectual debate already under way over the ethical implications of Professor de Man's theories and method, dubbed "deconstruction."

Deconstructionism views language as slippery and inherently false medium that always reflects the biases of its users. (p. B1)

"I was pained and saddened to learn of these writings." Neil Hertz, a close friend of Professor de Man's and a professor of humanities at Johns Hopkins University, said. "They seem so at odds with the sense of the person I knew later on," Dr. Hertz said.

Shochana Felman, a Yale professor of French and student of Dr. de Man, describes him as "almost entirely without prejudice" and says he "took an ethical stance in all his daily life."

The articles, uncovered by a Belgian graduate student, Ortwin de Graef, in libraries there this summer, show the Belgian-born de Man wrote nearly 100 book reviews, concert notes and essays under his own name for *Le Soir,* an anti-Semitic Belgian newspaper that collaborated with the Nazis.

At least one article by Professor de Man entitled "**The Jews and Contemporary Literature**" strikes researchers as anti-Semitic, appearing in a special supplement on Jews in the March 4, 1941, edition of the paper. Next to the essay is a caricature of Jews with horns and claws who, wearing prayer shawls, pray that "Jehovah will confound the gentiles."

"It shows the strength of our Western intellectuals that they could protect, from Jewish influence, a sphere as representative of the culture at large as literature," Professor de Man wrote. "Despite the lingering Semitism in all our civilization, literature showed that its essential nature was healthy."

Prof. Raoul Hilberg, a Holocaust historian at the University of Vermont, said almost all educated Belgians knew by 1941 or at the latest, 1942, that Jews were being sent eastward to be exterminated.

Some scholars said they detect anti-Nazi nuances in Professor de Man's favorable reviews of Jewish authors such as Kafka or the french historian Daniel Halevy. Others defended him as having been a young man, influenced perhaps by an uncle, Henri de Man, who was a minister in the collaborationist Belgian government, trying to protect Belgian autonomy against Nazi domination.

Mr. de Man quit writing for the newspaper in 1942, entering publishing until he left for the United States in 1947, where he worked at various publishing and bookselling jobs. He became a graduate student at Harvard in 1952. (pp. B1, B6)

Ironically enough, the articles appear to go to the heart of the ethical debates still raging over Dr. de Man's work at Yale, colleagues said.

Critics of Professor de Man have labeled deconstructionism a nihilistic philosophy that makes moral or political beliefs impossible.

Dr. Hertz, like other supporters of Dr. de Man, called the nihilism charge "foolish," and said it is based on an oversimplification of Mr. de Man's theories. As did other scholars, he predicted Dr. de Man's personal and intellectual reputation would emerge unscathed. (p. B6)

"Yale Scholar Wrote for Pro-Nazi Paper," in The New York Times, *December 1, 1987, pp. B1, B6.*

JON WIENER

A scandal has erupted in the powerful school of literary criticism known as deconstruction. Recent revelations that Paul de Man, the Yale professor who founded the school in America, wrote more than one hundred articles for anti-Semitic, pro-Nazi newspapers in Belgium during World War II, has generated a great deal of comment about both the author and the politics of deconstruction. De Man, who died in 1983 at age 65, had concealed his political past from colleagues and students, who were shocked and dismayed by the revelations. [Since] his past was brought to light de Man has become something of an academic Waldheim.

In one of the articles in question, **"Jews in Contemporary Literature,"** which appeared in March 1941, de Man examined the argument that "the Jews" had "polluted" modern literature. The article argued that "our civilization" had remained healthy by resisting "the Semitic infiltration of all aspects of European life." In another, he proposed that the Jews of Europe be sent to an island colony.

De Man's defenders acknowledge the seriousness of the revelations, but argue that the content of his collaborationist articles has been distorted. Neil Hertz, who teaches literature at Johns Hopkins University, points out that, of the ninety-two articles de Man is known to have published in the collaborationist Belgian newspaper *Le Soir,* only two were explicitly anti-Semitic. However, Jeffrey Mehlman of Boston University, a practitioner of deconstruction as well as the author of an influential book on anti-Semitism in French literature, explains that the rest included explicit calls for collaboration and numerous book reviews that "plugged the Nazi hit parade." An article of de Man's titled **"Testimony on the War in France,"** published in March 1941, concluded that "no abyss separates the two peoples [French and German]. When a common task is presented, their agreement has been perfect. That is the principal teaching to be drawn from this beautiful book." The author of the book in question, Benoist-Méchin, later proposed that the French take up arms against the British and Americans. De Man's other wartime articles included references to Hitler's war as "the current revolution" and a statement that "the necessity of immediate collaboration should be obvious to every objective mind."

De Man, who came to the United States in 1947, successfully concealed his pro-Nazi past except for one or two incidents. In 1953, when he was a member of the prestigious Society of Fellows at Harvard, he was denounced, anonymously, perhaps by his ex-wife, as a former collaborator; Harvard asked him for a response. De Man then told a few friends, and apparently Harvard as well, that the charge was false and that he had in fact been a member of the Belgian resistance. The friends, who have asked not to be identified, accepted his response; today at least one of them describes that response as "a lie." De Man clearly told other people different things about his past. Juliet MacCannell was a student of his at Cornell in the mid-1960s; she now teaches comparative literature at the University of California, Irvine: "I asked him what he did during the war. He said, 'I went to England and worked as a translator.' " There was also the matter of de Man's relationship to the German literary critic Hans Robert Jauss. He wrote about Jauss in **Blindness and Insight** and brought Jauss to Yale as a guest lecturer in the mid-1970s; Jauss is now known to have served in the S.S. (p. 22)

The debate over the collaborationist writings has become part of a wider questioning of the politics of deconstruction. J. Hillis Miller of the University of California, Irvine, the leading deconstructionist in the United States today and a friend of de Man, complains that journalists have defined deconstruction incorrectly, but he balks at providing a definition. He refers those who want to know what he thinks deconstruction is to his book, *The Ethics of Reading.* Edward Said, professor of English and comparative literature at Columbia University, author of *The World, the Text, and the Critic* and a critic of deconstruction, provided a definition:

> Deconstruction is a form of commentary that shows the connection between the stated content of a piece of writing and the rhetorical system which controls it. The connection establishes a discrepancy between the content and the rhetorical system. The deconstructive reading establishes the range of possible meanings that are thereby generated. In the range of decidable meanings, the deconstructed meaning locates itself.

"The deconstructionists won't accept that," he adds. "Their whole point is that their positions are not paraphrasable."

Deconstruction claims that not only are books "texts," but that everything is at some level a text and thus "undecidable." De Man wrote that this is true even of the texts that "masquerade in the guise of wars or revolutions." ("Tell that to the veterans of foreign texts," a Yale historian remarked.) Critics on the left have argued that the presuppositions of deconstruction—that literature is not part of a knowable social and political reality, that one must be resigned to the impossibility of truth—make it at worst nihilistic or implicitly authoritarian and at best an academic self-indulgence.

Whatever the current reservations about it, de Man's work had a tremendous appeal, especially for students in the 1960s and 1970s. Even more than the New Criticism had, [deconstruction] freed literature from context and history, opening it to complex new meanings in a way that was fertile, inventive and playful. [De Man's] work engaged the best of twentieth-century philosophy. At the same time he made criticism *the* creative activity of the period; the novel might have been dead, but criticism had become the inheritor of the ambitions of art. The critic could create meaning. And de Man's writing was brilliant.

Deborah Esch, who teaches English at the University of Toronto and was a student of de Man's from 1979 to 1983, said,

> de Man provided his students with a set of tools for reading, the most important function of which may be the unmasking of ideology. What we call ideology, he showed, entails taking a linguistic construct for a natural reality. This questioning of the authority of language yielded the most subversive pedagogy I know.

To those who would read de Man's mature work with an eye to his youthful publications, Hillis Miller responds, "I see no connection between de Man's collaborationist writings and deconstruction." But not everyone agrees. Mehlman points to de Man's chapter on Rousseau's *Confessions* in **Allegories of Reading.** There de Man writes that "it is always possible" to "excuse any guilt" because "the experience always exists simultaneously as fictional discourse and as empirical event and it is never possible to decide which one of the two possibilities is the right one. The indecision makes it possible to excuse the bleakest of crimes." Is it possible to read this now without thinking of de Man's collaboration?

De Man's discussion of forgetting in his classic essay **"Literary History and Literary Modernity"** from **Blindness and Insight** is full of references to a hidden past. He discusses Nietzsche's conception of "a past that . . . is so threatening that it has to be forgotten." He quotes Nietzsche's observation that we undertake "the destruction and dissolution of the past in order to be able to live," we "try to give ourselves a new past from which we should have liked to descend." But for Nietzsche, de Man writes, "the rejection of the past is not so much an act of forgetting as an act of critical judgment directed against himself." (pp. 22-3)

De Man's critique of history is also relevant. He goes beyond the useful post-structuralist point that facts about the past are structured like texts; [Frank] Lentricchia writes that de Man "is saying that history is an imitation of what he has defined as the literary," a "projection . . . of all those paralytic feelings of the literary onto the terrain of society and history." This argument leads to passivity, which, Lentricchia says, is "the most genuine meaning of political conservatism," and that is the message of de Manian deconstruction in the United States.

According to Anson Rabinbach, an intellectual historian at Cooper Union, the young de Man became a Fascist the way many intellectuals did in Europe in 1940: "They had a sense of malaise, of having been defeated by history." They turned to Fascism, hoping that it would provide a route to cultural renewal, but eventually abandoned it. The connection between de Man's early and mature writings, Rabinbach argues, "is not in their content, which is quite different; it is in the attitude of exhaustion in the face of politics, the feeling of despair at the possibilities that history offers."

However, Gerald Graff, of Northwestern University, author of *Literature Against Itself* and *Professing Literature,* is much more cautious in his approach to the connection between de Man's early writing and deconstruction. He observes that "people who adopt deconstructionist positions have various sorts of politics—including radical feminism and other progressive commitments—so an attempt to smear all de Manian deconstruction with de Man's past is unfair." But, Graff went on, "there is an irony here, since deconstructionists have a problem appealing to what politicians call 'deniability.' One of the themes of deconstruction is that the position you try to separate yourself from tends to reappear as a repressed motif in your own text." . . . Graff also thinks it important to emphasize that the overall effect of the current trend toward theory, including deconstruction, "has been an overwhelmingly democratic and progressive force which has raised central questions about the politics of language and culture which orthodox literary study still resists."

Whatever one makes of the politics of deconstruction, both followers and critics of Paul de Man will have to examine his past more thoroughly. In particular they will have to ask what de Man could have known about the fate of European Jews, and when could he have known it? De Man's collaborationist articles appeared in 1941 and 1942. Raoul Hilberg, a Holocaust historian at the University of Vermont, was quoted in *The New York Times* as saying that educated Belgians like de Man "knew by 1941 or at the latest, 1942, that Jews were being sent eastward to be exterminated" [see excerpt above]. That is wrong, says Arno Mayer, a Princeton historian and author of a forthcoming book on the "final solution." " 'Auschwitz' is not likely to have had any concrete meaning in Belgium in 1942. No one had a clear picture of the fate of even Poland's Jews before Germany's attack on Russia in June 1941." (p. 23)

The last of the de Man pieces which have been discovered is dated October 20, 1942. If he stopped his pro-Nazi writings at this point—which is not yet certain—his last collaborationist article appeared before he could have known of the ex-

termination of the Jews. Nevertheless, one can assume that the young journalist who urged isolating Europe's Jews on an island did not find the deportations of 1942 objectionable.

And there was plenty going on that de Man did know about: Belgium's first anti-Jewish law was passed in October 1940; it required that Jews register with the government and expelled them from the professions of law, teaching, journalism and government service. De Man's article on whether Jews "pollute" modern fiction appeared five months later. On May 31, 1941, Belgian Jews were forced to sell their businesses; in August 1941 they were restricted to four cities and subjected to a curfew. De Man certainly knew all that. Yet in December 1941, he published an article praising Drieu la Rochelle, a leading collaborator, for "the elan and conviction with which (he) has thrown himself into the creation of a radically new type of human being." As of June 1, 1942, Belgian Jews were required to wear the yellow star. . . . (pp. 23-4)

"Anyone who thinks that [de Man] left this all behind him, that it did not motivate the life and career that followed, is crazy," Lentricchia says.

> He came here in 1947 at age 28 with a Belgian wife and son; he divorced his wife when he got here, and didn't speak to his son ever again. The man tried very hard to separate himself from his Belgian collaborationist past, to cut that thing out of himself. I think he suffered, he wished he never did it. He didn't start graduate school until 1952, when he was 33. What was he doing before that? Working in a bookstore, working for a publisher—a brilliant man, prepared for a literary career, who does nothing for several years. Why?
>
> Then you come to deconstruction: a philosophy that says you can never trust language to anchor you into anything; that every linguistic act is duplicitous; that every insight you have is beset by blindness you can't predict. In an attempt to undercut politically engaged critics, de Man writes that whatever you thought about political events is not the case. His mature work is not just ahistorical; it is a principled, intentional, passionate antihistoricism. He didn't just say 'forget history'; he wanted to paralyze the move to history. And the work is beautifully rigorous. There's not a better example in the world.

Colleagues and students admired de Man not only for his scholarship but because he "was exemplary in his relations with people," Hertz says. "You used him as a standard for your own conduct. He was something special." Lentricchia disagrees: "The real problem of the de Manians is hero worship." . . .

De Man's defenders argue that they should get credit for making his pro-Nazi writings public. The collaborationist articles were discovered this past summer by a Belgian graduate student, Ortwin de Graef. In late October [1987], Jacques Derrida, the renowned French philosopher and literary theorist who founded deconstruction, brought copies to the United States to a meeting of deconstructionists. At this conference, held in Tuscaloosa, Alabama, . . . and attended by some twenty persons, they discussed how to handle the material. Critics of the school describe this meeting as an exercise in "damage control."

The deconstructionists decided to publish de Man's pro-Nazi articles in a special issue of the *Oxford Literary Review*. . . .

The dozen articles of de Man's originally published in Flemish will appear in English, but the ninety-two articles in French will not be translated. "We feel that anyone interested in these materials ought to read them in the original," Hertz said. In fact, that will discourage anyone but experts from examining the documents or taking part in the debate. De Man's defenders were surprised when *The New York Times* published an article on the controversy in early December [1987 (see excerpt above)], and have been angered by the press coverage, which they regard as premature, misleading and inaccurate. "I don't think this is a matter for journalists and newspapers," says Werner Hamacher of Johns Hopkins University, an organizer of the special issue. . . .

A reevaluation of the politics of deconstruction and the writings of de Man is now at the top of the agenda of both the deconstructionists and their critics. (p. 24)

> Jon Wiener, "Deconstructing de Man," in The Nation, New York, Vol. 246, No. 1, January 9, 1988, pp. 22-4.

CHRISTOPHER NORRIS

[*The essay excerpted below originally appeared in a slightly different form in* London Review of Books, *February 4, 1988.*]

On December 1st, 1987 the *New York Times* ran a piece under the title "Yale Scholar Wrote for Pro-Nazi Paper" [see excerpt above]. The scholar in question was Paul de Man, who had written these pieces during the early 1940s, before leaving Belgium for America. They were published in *Le Soir,* a newspaper of decidedly pro-Nazi sympathies, and contain many passages that can be read as endorsing what amounts to a collaborationist line. There is talk of the need to preserve national cultures against harmful cosmopolitan influences, and of German literature as a model for those other, less fortunate traditions that lack such an authentic national base. Their language often resorts to organicist metaphors, notions of cultural identity as rooted in the soil of a flourishing native literature. One could draw comparisons with a work like T. S. Eliot's *Notes Towards the Definition of Culture,* where it is likewise argued that the vitality of "satellite" traditions (for de Man most crucially the French, Dutch, and Belgian) must depend on the continuing existence of a strong hegemonic center. But of course de Man was writing at a time and in a political situation where thoughts of this kind carried a far more ominous charge. It is hard, if not impossible to redeem these texts by looking for some occasional sign that they are not to be taken at face value. They are utterly remote from de Man's more familiar writings, not only in their frequent naivety of utterance and sentiment, but also in the way that they uncritically endorse such mystified ideas as the organic relation between language, culture, and national destiny—ideas which he would later set out to deconstruct with such extreme sceptical rigor.

This is not to say that they can now be written off as mere youthful aberrations, texts for which he cannot fairly be held to account since they go so much against his subsequent thinking. Though their existence remained a secret all those years de Man would, I think, have acknowledged their discovery with the attitude "scripta manent"; that what is written is written and cannot be tactfully ignored, no matter how far his convictions had changed in the interim. But there are several points that need to be made before we can assess their

real significance. One is the fact that he wrote these pieces as a very young man under pressures of political and personal circumstances that may help to explain, if not to justify, their writing. . . . [His] uncle, Hendrik de Man, was a prominent Belgian socialist thinker during the 1920s and 1930s, a government minister whose two terms of office had been marked by numerous disappointments and policy setbacks. [Hendrik de Man's] response to the catastrophe of German occupation was to draw up a last-ditch tactical plan arguing that Nazism might, after all, evolve into something like a genuine National Socialism, and that therefore the only course open was to pin one's hope to that saving possibility and not hold out against the occupying forces. . . . [It] is fair to conjecture—on the basis of numerous passages in these articles—that [Paul de Man] thought the only prospect of survival for the Belgian people, languages, and culture lay in making terms (at least temporarily) with the fact of German occupation, and hoping that Nazism might indeed be "reinterpreted" in a more favorable light. Again, this is not to excuse those early writings, but to see how they might have been produced by a thinker whose subsequent reflections took such an utterly different path.

For this is what will strike any reader acquainted with the texts that de Man published after his passage to America. One could read this entire production as an attempt to exorcise the bad memory, to adopt a critical standpoint squarely opposed to that mystified philosophy of language, tradition, and organic national culture. Of course it is possible to argue the opposite case, to declare with the wisdom of hindsight that deconstruction was always a "nihilist" activity, that its politics were clearly reactionary, if not proto-fascist, and that therefore these latest revelations merely confirm what should have been evident from the start. Already the professors are lining up to make statements to this or similar effect. . . . Jeffrey Mehlman [quoted below in the essay by David Lehman] went so far as to surmise that deconstruction in America was really nothing more than an elaborate cover-up campaign, an "amnesty" organized by literary intellectuals who could find no other means to evade or excuse their burden of collective guilt. Such arguments, for all their patent absurdity, have found a ready platform in the American press and convinced many people that there must after all be something deeply suspect about the whole deconstructionist enterprise. Others—Frank Lentricchia among them—have fastened on passages from de Man's later work where he addresses the matter of guilt, responsibility, and self-exculpation in terms that can easily appear to invite a crypto-autobiographical reading. [Lentricchia is quoted above in the essay by Jon Wiener]. One such passage is the sentence on Rousseau from *Allegories* where he explains how any fault may be excused in confessional narrative since "the experience always exists simultaneously as fictional discourse and as empirical event and it is never possible to decide which one of the two possibilities is the right one. The indecision makes it possible to excuse the bleakest of crimes." As Lentricchia says, it is difficult to read such passages now without being put in mind of de Man's early writings and his burden of guilty memory.

The same applies to those middle-period essays (like "**Literary History and Literary Modernity**") where de Man takes a lead from Nietzsche's meditations on the dead weight of historical memory, its paralyzing effect on present thought and action, and the modernist desire to achieve a radical break with all such disabling legacies. Lentricchia once again has the relevant passages ready to hand, passages where de

Man writes of "a past that . . . is so threatening that it has to be forgotten," and of the way in which "we try to give ourselves a new past from which we should have liked to descend." There does seem reason to suppose de Man is here engaged in something more than a piece of purely diagnostic commentary; that his relentless pursuit of these Nietzschean aporias shows him in the grip of a compulsion to rehearse and yet somehow repress or sublimate the facts of his own past history. Such is at any rate a part of the significance these texts must bear for us now, whatever may have been de Man's conscious or unconscious intentions in the matter. But we should also bear in mind one further passage cited by Lentricchia, a sentence from the same essay [in **Blindness and Insight**] where de Man remarks of Nietzsche that "the rejection of the past is not so much an act of forgetting as an act of critical judgment directed against himself." The hostile commentators are united in supposing that de Man wished only to conceal the truth from himself and others; that his subsequent work was indeed nothing but a series of oblique strategies for pretending that it never happened, or at least that there existed no present responsibility for past thoughts and actions. I have argued, on the contrary, that de Man's later writings bear witness to a constant, often agonized attempt to explain the sources of that powerful "aesthetic ideology" which had played a prominent seductive role in his own youthful thinking. Of course there is still the question why he chose to pursue such a tortuously roundabout path of self-reckoning and didn't, so to speak, come clean by acknowledging what he had written in those early years. There is no way of answering this charge, save by pointing out that a public admission would almost certainly have meant a break with some of his closest, most valued colleagues, the loss of his academic livelihood (after ten years of wandering from one part-time job to another), and also of the one chance he now had for making some kind of intellectual reparation. In this respect at least I think there is room for a measure of charitable judgment.

The historian Jon Wiener, writing in *The Nation,* [see excerpt above], does at least make some effort to weigh up the evidence and establish just how much de Man could have known about the fate of Belgian Jews and the ultimate direction of Nazi policy. . . . [It] seems clear that, for whatever reason, de Man had severed his links with *Le Soir* before the time when any further involvement would have pointed to a knowing complicity with Nazi war crimes. This gesture might indeed have entailed some considerable risk, not only to his standing in Belgian cultural life but also to his safety under the new regime. All the same, as Wiener points out, he was still contributing articles during a period when various anti-Semitic laws were promulgated, when feeling against the Jews was being whipped up by successive propaganda campaigns, and when no Belgian citizen could possibly have failed to recognize the ominous turn of events.

Besides, there is an article by de Man—**"Jews in Contemporary Literature,"** published on March 1st, 1941—which shows all too clearly how willing he was to go along with at least certain currents of anti-Semitic prejudice. In it he rejects the idea that modern European culture has been "polluted" by Jewish influence, and asserts on the contrary that no Jewish artist or thinker has achieved such eminence as seriously to threaten the purity of the great national traditions. It could just conceivably be argued—putting the best case for de Man—that one effect of such statements might have been to head off "vulgar" anti-Jewish sentiment by persuading people

that no real "threat" existed, since the current campaign (as waged so zealously by other contributors to *Le Soir*) was based on a paranoid misperception of social and cultural realities. But in the end this defense won't do, any more than the idea that when de Man speaks of resettling large numbers of Jews in a separate "island colony," his suggestion might be read as prefiguring the establishment of Israel as an autonomous Jewish nation-state. On the evidence of this piece at least, one is obliged to accept Wiener's conclusion that de Man was at one stage willing to collaborate in anti-Semitic cultural propaganda. (pp. 177-81)

I have no wish either to minimize the disturbing force of de Man's contributions to *Le Soir* or to argue that they are simply unconnected with everything he went on to write. Nor can I speak with any first-hand knowledge of his personal qualities as teacher, colleague, and intellectual mentor, although a recent volume of tributes (*Yale French Studies,* 1985) bears eloquent witness in this regard. I want to suggest rather that opponents like Lentricchia have ignored one important aspect of the case; that deconstruction evolved, in de Man's work at least, as a form of ideological critique directed against precisely that seductive will to treat language and culture as organic, quasi-natural products rooted in the soil of some authentic native tradition. There is no question of excusing those early productions by showing just how far he went to disown and discredit their basic premises. They came to light . . . at a time when I had read only the handful of near-contemporaneous articles and reviews that de Man published in the journal *Het Vlaamsche Land*. These pieces . . . showed signs that his thinking was influenced at this stage by certain elements of National Socialist ideology. But they were mostly concerned with topics in the area of literary history and comparative criticism, topics which indeed had a bearing on current political events, but which none the less allowed de Man to conduct his arguments at a level quite remote from the sordid practicalities of day-to-day life in occupied Belgium. No such defense can be entered in the case of his writings for *Le Soir,* a national paper of wide circulation and known pro-German sympathies whose editorial policy was closely monitored.

That he agreed to write for such a paper, and under such circumstances, might seem to constitute evidence enough of strong collaborationist leanings on de Man's part. All the same it must be said that the pieces in question—169 in all, contributed over a two-year period—are many of them wholly innocuous, apart from the fact of their having appeared alongside material of a much worse character. There is a strong suggestion in the *Newsweek* [see excerpt below] and *New York Times* [see excerpt above] reports that everything he wrote at this time was either overtly anti-Semitic or designed to lend support to Nazi cultural propaganda. In fact very few of these pieces can honestly be said to serve such a purpose, and only one—his article on the Jewish influence in contemporary culture—to warrant the charge of downright racialist sentiment. Of those remaining, many are reviews of various cultural events—concert performances, chamber recitals, university seminars, poetry readings, and so forth—which occasionally touch on the question of national identity *vis-à-vis* the war and the current upheavals in European politics, but which cannot in all fairness be accused of exploiting those events for propaganda purposes. In what follows I shall look at some of the more substantial and revealing pieces in an attempt to explain what led de Man to identify—in however ambivalent a fashion—with the cultural policies adopted by *Le Soir.*

A large number of these articles appeared under the title "Notre Chronique Littéraire," a column devoted mainly to reviews of books that offered some pretext for generalized thoughts about the current state of European politics. One such piece (August 19, 1941) was de Man's fairly lengthy assessment of a work by Frédéric Grimm entitled *Le Testament Politique de Richelieu.* In it de Man reflects on the shifting balance of power within Europe over the past three centuries, from the high point of French cultural hegemony to the period of Bismarck, the growth of a unified German nation-state, and the triumph of National Socialism. De Man presents this history as a matter of accomplished fact, a product of inexorable forces which the French (and of course the Belgians) must accept without further pointless shows of resistance. In short, he adopts what looks very much like a collaborationist line, using the book as an object lesson in the destiny of nations and the need for adjustment to present political realities. (pp. 182-83)

The best that can be said for this piece and others like it is that de Man seems to treat European history on a vaguely cyclic model, such that the predominance of any one nation might always yield to yet another change of political fortunes. After all, this follows from the logic of his argument: that just as French supremacy declined partly through effects of internal "weakness and division," partly through the pressure of external events, so it might come about that the current ascendancy of German national culture would eventually suffer the same predestined fate. This may seem an overly generous reading, but it does find support elsewhere in his writings for *Le Soir.* On more than one occasion de Man plays down the significance of present events by suggesting that his readers shouldn't be misled into treating them as an endpoint or ultimate upheaval in the history of nations; that in fact the war is a passing episode which may turn out to have little effect on the long-term evolution of European history. Thus he writes ("Chronique Littéraire," September 30, 1941) that the Belgian public tends to overestimate the influence of current political events, but that really this has been confined to a "modification of tone, not in the work of [creative] writers themselves, but in the ideas and governing principles of criticism." And there are many other passages where de Man insists on this difference between art and the business of day-to-day intellectual life, the latter having to do with short-term adjustment to pressures of political circumstance, while the former transcends such interests by obeying its own mysterious laws of creative evolution. Thus "literature is an independent domain which has a life, laws, obligations that belong only to itself and don't depend in any way on those philosophical or ethical contingencies that exert their influence from its borders."

Now this could well be seen as just another piece of mystifying rhetoric on de Man's part, an attempt to disown any deep complicity by pretending that his kind of day-to-day cultural critique has no real impact in the long term. But I think there is a strong suggestion, in this and other articles, that de Man saw a hope for some future turn of events that would end the period of outright German hegemony and restore French cultural influence to its rightful place within the context of European history. In his column of April 28, 1942 de Man returns to this question by way of discussing "**Le Probleme Français**" and the question of Franco-German cultural relations.

There is, he writes, "a certain French form of reason that seeks above all to fix limits and impose measure . . .," which possesses "the virtues of clarity, logic, and harmony" that have always characterized "the great artistic and philosophical tradition of that country." But at present this tradition is up against a force of German nationalist sentiment to which it can offer no effective resistance. "We are entering a mystical era, a period of faith and belief, with all that this implies of suffering, exaltation, and rapture." Now there is not much that can be said in defense of this crudely stereotyped piece of collective pseudo-psychology. But it does suggest something of de Man's desire to imagine an alternative future, a Europe where these present conflicts would at length give way to a balanced, integrated form of supra-national coexistence. This is not to deny that, when faced with the choice, de Man comes out over and again in defense of German cultural values, German tradition, and the high destinies of German literature. He even states in one article (April 12, 1941) that the occupying forces have behaved with more generosity of spirit than the French showed toward the Germans at Versailles. And the practical upshot of de Man's arguments is always a counsel of non-resistance: that the ultimate lesson to be drawn from events in France is the pointlessness of presently standing in the way of German political and cultural supremacy. Nobody who reads these articles can remain in any doubt of his defeatist attitude. But I think that if we look more closely at some of them—especially those dealing with the topic of French-German cultural relations—there emerge at least the hints of a different reading, one that would show de Man striving to maintain some hope for better things to come.

One crucial piece here is an article on Belgian cultural politics published in *Le Soir* on April 22, 1941. It is concerned mainly with the question of how far Belgium can claim any kind of national identity, given its division into two distinct cultural and linguistic communities, the Flemish and the Walloon. . . . Long before World War II there had existed a strong current of feeling among some Flemish natives that Belgium ought to be divided on linguistic-cultural lines, with Flanders becoming an integral part of the German nation and Wallonia resuming its "original," authentically French identity. At the outbreak of hostilities this feeling was intensified in many quarters, and one finds distinct echoes of it in various of de Man's writings. But he also holds out, paradoxically, for the notion of a unified Belgium, a sense of national character transcending these short-term differences of interest. "It is false," he writes, "to believe that the Flemings and the Walloons have always considered each other enemies. . . . In those places where they have lived in close proximity they have endured the same sufferings, undergone the same wars and experienced the same joys. From this there has resulted a great sense of solidarity."

Again there is a crucial ambiguity here, depending on whether one takes it that de Man is advocating a unified Belgium modeled on the German-Flemish alliance, or that he rather envisages a genuine state of reciprocal interdependence where the different communities would exercise a degree of autonomy and self-determination. This doubt persists through many of the articles published in *Le Soir.* But one could also pick out numerous passages where he does quite explicitly state the need for recognition of the French and Walloon contributions to a diverse European culture, and therefore the requirement that these values be preserved in any future plan of postwar reconstruction. That is to say, he maintains a certain distance from the line of straightforwardly pro-German, Flemish nationalist sentiment that prevailed among many of his fellow contributors. And this goes along with de Man's argument—despite all his slighting references to French decadence, lack of "spirit," and disabling political divisions—that France still embodies certain values indispensable to European culture at large.

Those values were, I think, too closely bound up with de Man's own sense of intellectual identity for him to betray them entirely in the service of Nazi propaganda work. In the years immediately preceding the war he had been involved with a journal, *Les Cahiers du Libre Examen,* whose editorial policy was utterly opposed to the line later adopted in *Le Soir.* The proper business of criticism—so de Man and his colleagues affirmed—was *not* to give way to political interests or short-term values and imperatives, but to hold out for the freedom of disinterested judgment in preserving a space for enlightened intellectual debate. And furthermore, they pledged the journal to a continued defense of such values specifically against any violent imposition of dogmatic creeds and ideologies. *Les Cahiers* turned out to be a short-lived venture, since the Nazi occupation (just three years after its inaugural number) made it henceforth impossible for any publication openly to espouse such views. That de Man went on to write his pieces for *Le Soir* may seem all the more an opportunist and cynical act of self-betrayal. But I think those later articles do preserve at least a residual, intermittent sense of what is required in order to salvage any civilized values from the present grim state of Belgian national life. (pp. 184-86)

In Thomas Mann's novel *The Magic Mountain,* young Hans Castorp finds himself caught between two great opposing forces, personified in the figures of Naphta and Settembrini. On the one side German nationalism under its aspect of a dark, irrational, atavistic, and ultimately sinister force, yet possessing a power over Castorp's untutored mind that clearly captures something of Mann's ambivalent feelings. On the other Settembrini, apostle of enlightenment, freedom, democracy, and liberal reason, by far the more attractive figure yet always losing out in argument with Naphta and presented very often in a faintly ridiculous light. Of course *The Magic Mountain* was published in 1924 and treats of the situation in Europe during the years leading up to the First World War. But I think it is not unduly fanciful to see in Hans Castorp's situation something of the chronic confusions that assailed Paul de Man some two decades later. There is a piece on Charles Péguy (*Le Soir,* May 6, 1941) that offers perhaps the most pointed example of these tensions in de Man's thinking. Péguy was a young French socialist and Catholic intellectual who began writing in the mid-1890s, became passionately involved with political events (including the Dreyfus affair), and died in action during the Battle of the Marne. He was founder and editor-in-chief of *Les Cahiers de la Quinzaine,* a journal that pursued a fiercely independent line and attracted the hostility of right- and left-wing factions alike. De Man clearly admires this stance and regards Péguy as in some sense a model for the conduct of intellectual life under extreme pressures of political circumstance. In particular he praises Péguy's refusal to adopt any simplified party-line creed, his determination not to compromise in matters of religious or political faith. "Caught between these two hostilities [attacked, that is to say, both by right-wing Catholic and mainstream socialist intellectuals] he continued to hold his head high, defending his own work and bringing together, in

the *Cahiers,* the most remarkable French literary talents of the period."

Any mention of the Dreyfus affair must of course raise the question of anti-Semitism and the resistance to it mounted by writers like Péguy and, most famously, Zola. De Man is distinctly evasive here, commenting at one point that the affair played an "almost disproportionate" role in French intellectual life at this time, but then praising Péguy for having "remained a Dreyfusard to the end," one who impressed his comrades as a "passionate thinker, imbued with the ideas of socialism and egalitarian justice." No doubt it would be overgenerous to interpret these remarks as a covert profession of faith on de Man's part, signaling his continued allegiance to the ideals set forth in *Les Cahiers du Libre Examen.* But there is more than a hint that those ideas still exercised an influence on his thinking, especially when de Man makes a point of adverting to the title of Péguy's review and its connection with "ses cahiers d'école, si propres, si bien tenus." What he singles out for praise in Péguy's work is its spirit of liberal inquiry, a spirit that owed allegiance to no single party or faction, that allowed him to range freely over various questions and debates "without any governing interest or constraint." It is hard to believe that de Man could have written these words without reflecting ironically on the course of events in Belgium and his own conspicuous failure to uphold such standards. In his writings for *Le Soir* de Man continues to associate the French cultural tradition with these values of liberalism, rational inquiry, and open public debate.

This is not to deny that he often turns such arguments round against the French by attributing their defeat in war to the lack of any genuine spirit of national unity, a condition brought about by precisely that habit of detached, self-critical scrutiny. But these values are never entirely submerged in the strain of pro-German populist rhetoric that sometimes marks his writings for *Le Soir.* In fact there is evidence that de Man's sympathies were not only divided but complex to the point of downright political confusion. What is one to make of his article published in July 14, 1942—anniversary of the French Revolution—where de Man nominates the Surrealist movement, and particularly Paul Eluard, as the single most striking manifestation of French cultural vitality? It is all the more remarkable that he ventured this opinion while reviewing a journal (*Messages*) known for its links with the Resistance movement as well as with communist or left-leaning elements in the Surrealist group. One could interpret such passages as indicating either a weak grasp of political realities on de Man's part or perhaps—more generously—a will to keep the channels of communication open and to risk what must have been, by this date, the very real threat of reprisals from the German censor. The same might be said of his occasional admiring references to Kafka and other Jewish authors who had long since been condemned as decadent modernists by the Nazi cultural hacks. No matter how one reads them—as courageous or naive—these passages must at least complicate our sense of de Man's "collaborationist" activity. Furthermore, it now seems that he also wrote articles for the Resistance paper *Exercise du Silence,* a fact communicated to the present author by his son, Marc de Man. So I think there is good reason to reject the charge—taken up with such intemperate zeal in many quarters of the American and British press—that de Man was at any time wholly given over to the purposes of Nazi cultural propaganda.

There are three possible lines of response to the discovery of these wartime writings. The first—as argued by commentators like Wiener and Lentricchia—would take the worst possible view of their content, and would hold furthermore that everything de Man went on to write must (so to speak) carry guilt by association, and therefore be deeply suspect on ideological grounds. The second would hold, on the contrary, that de Man's later texts have absolutely nothing in common with his early writings, that in fact they exhibit an extreme resistance to precisely that form of dangerously mystified thinking, and should therefore be treated as belonging to a different order of discourse. The third—and this is basically the argument I have presented here—is that de Man's later work grew out of an agonized reflection on his wartime experience, and can best be read as a protracted attempt to make amends (albeit indirectly) in the form of an ideological autocritique. (pp. 187-90)

In the Introduction to his book *Frege: Philosophy of Language* Michael Dummett recalls having experienced something like the shock of belated discovery that has attended these recent revelations about de Man. Dummett had devoted many years to his study of Frege, thinking him the greatest of modern logicians and philosophers of language. . . . Subsequently he discovered that Frege had himself held views of an extreme right-wing character, that he had expressed overtly racist sentiments, and indeed gone along with the whole pernicious line of half-baked populist rhetoric that Dummett encountered in latter-day National Front propaganda. But in the end, as Dummett says, this discovery made no real difference to his estimate of Frege's contribution to the fields of logic and linguistic philosophy. That work belongs to such a specialized domain—so remote from Frege's individual psychopathology, or the content of his social and political beliefs—that Dummett was able to continue his project with a good (if sadly disillusioned) conscience. (pp. 190-91)

Now I don't think that this is a real option in de Man's case, despite the fact that so much of his later work is conducted in a style of austere, impersonal rigor that might seem to approximate "pure" philosophy of language. One could recall, in this connection, the passage from his essay on Benjamin's "The Task of the Translator" where de Man writes that "it is not *a priori* certain at all that the mode of meaning, the way in which I mean, is intentional in any way . . . [it] is dependent on linguistic properties that are not only not made by me, because I depend on the language as it exists for the devices which I will be using, it is as such not made by us as historical beings, it is perhaps not even made by humans at all." We cannot any longer read such passages as they ask to be read, that is to say, as referring purely to those questions in the province of language, translation, rhetoric, and the other topics that preoccupied de Man in his last years. From one point of view—that taken by the hostile commentators—they reveal the quite extraordinary lengths to which he went in order to repress, disguise, or evade the memory of those early journalistic writings. From another, they are the endpoint of a long and painful coming-to-terms with the fact of that guilt and the way that what is written possesses a starkly material force that can always return to haunt the writer. As [Geoffrey] Hartman points out [see excerpt below], there is something more than a circumstantial irony in the fact that de Man is here writing about Walter Benjamin, the German-Jewish critic who was driven to suicide while attempting to escape from the Nazi forces of occupation. I have spent a good part of this book [*Paul de Man: Deconstruction and the Critique of Aesthetic Ideology*] arguing the case for de Man's

work as a salutary warning against forms of aesthetic mystification which can have very real historical effects. Now, with the discovery of his articles in *Le Soir,* that lesson must be read as bearing directly on de Man's own burden of memory. But we shouldn't, for that reason, be tempted to conclude that the later work is *nothing more* than a species of obscure private atonement; that its claims to offer a rigorous reflection on the powers and the limits of language are simply a last-ditch strategy of evasion on de Man's part. (p. 191)

There can be no doubt that de Man had reasons enough—urgently personal reasons—for wanting to convince himself that language and history were utterly beyond the control or understanding of the situated individual subject. In this sense the whole of his later production could be read (as critics like Lentricchia read it) as one long attempt to disown responsibility for what he had once written. But this is to take those later pronouncements very much at face value, as if de Man had *really* succeeded in repressing all trace of such haunting memories. It is worth bearing in mind those remarks of Mizae Mizumura, herself hard put to account for the curious coexistence in de Man's work of an intense desire to renounce the pathos of subjective guilt and loss with an equally compulsive need to return to such themes and endlessly rehearse them in his writing. "The impression of deprivation comes closer, nonetheless, to grasping the quintessence of de Man than a placid acceptance of the extreme ascesis that reigns in his work. . . . The one who has not been tempted would not have spoken so often about the necessity (and the impossibility) of renunciation—and would not have done so with such authority," Mizumura was writing before the existence of those articles for *Le Soir* became public knowledge. But her comments take on an additional force when read—as one inevitably reads them now—in the context of de Man's wartime writings and his lifelong attempt to atone for past errors. The point is not just that his entire subsequent production must henceforth be seen as a species of cryptic autobiography, a confessional record that merely masquerades as textual exegesis, philosophy of language, or *Ideologiekritik.* Rather, it is the fact that de Man's own experience had left so deep and lasting an impression on his work that one simply cannot separate (in T. S. Eliot's phrase) the "man who suffers" from "the mind that creates," or the strain of anguished self-reckoning from the desire to put these lessons to work in a rigorously critical way. It is wrong to suppose that the two readings are wholly incompatible, or that somehow the presence of these sombre meditations counts against our accepting the validity and force of his arguments.

So we don't have the choice, like Dummett on Frege, of, so to speak, bracketing all questions of moral and political accountability, and reading de Man's later texts for what they are worth in terms of purely theoretical yield. But neither is it a case, as with Heidegger, of a thinker whose entire life's work is so deeply involved with a certain mystique of language, origins, and national destiny that it becomes impossible to disengage the one from the other. (pp. 192-93)

That de Man once fell under this same malignant spell cannot be doubted by anyone who has read his articles in *Le Soir* and *Het Vlaamsche Land.* But it is equally wrong to ignore the crucial difference between his and Heidegger's case, the fact . . . that de Man went on to devote the major part of his life's work to a critique of that same seductive mythology that had once so grievously misled his thinking. And we should also not forget that this episode belongs to de Man's early twenties, an age when very few people have yet had sufficient experience—or time for thought—to render them proof against dominant forms of political indoctrination. It seems to me quite appalling—in straightforward moral and human terms—that these texts should now be used as the basis of a wholesale media campaign to discredit the man and his work. In a passage from *Mémoires,* Derrida reflects on "what could be considered Paul de Man's relation to the 'political,' to what we tranquilly and commonly call politics, to his 'experience' of the thing." That experience, as we now know, was of a kind that Derrida could scarcely have guessed at when he wrote these words. But there is much in *Mémoires*—as indeed in *De l'esprit*—that does seem to bear a pointed, almost uncanny relevance to the issue of de Man's wartime journalism. These texts, along with Hartman's, do more for our understanding of the case than any of the hasty, ill-informed, and often vindicative polemics that have characterized the current media response. (pp. 197-98)

> *Christopher Norris, in his* Paul de Man: Deconstruction and the Critique of Aesthetic Ideology, *Routledge, 1988, 218 p.*

DAVID LEHMAN

During his 13 years at Yale, Paul de Man perfected the role of the influential literary critic. Until his death in 1983, he was the high priest of the arcane philosophy known as "deconstruction," a controversial analytic method which turns literature into a play of words, robbing it of any broader significance. Brilliant and rigorous, de Man attracted the finest graduate students; his piercing wit and demanding scholarship converted them into acolytes who have spread his message throughout American academia. But de Man's famed "intellectual honesty" had one blind spot: he never admitted that during the second world war he wrote anti-Semitic essays for a pro-Nazi newspaper in Belgium. Disclosures of his shameful past have been leaking slowly for months, forcing de Man's followers and his enemies to confront the painful issue of whether a thinker's odious political behavior discredits his theoretical or literary works.

The question applies with a vengeance to de Man, for critics have long seen deconstruction as hostile to the very principles of Western thought that make moral philosophy possible. A crucial tenet of any deconstruction program is that the relation between words and what they mean is sometimes arbitrary and always indeterminate. Deconstruction takes this linguistic notion, applies it to the full array of academic disciplines—from literature to history—and examines the fallout. More a method than a coherent body of knowledge, deconstruction likes putting ideas in question—things like cause and effect, right and wrong, the idea that a text expresses an author's intention. One forerunner of deconstruction is Humpty Dumpty, who declared that words mean what he wants them to mean. The deconstructionist view of the past was ably stated by automobile magnate Henry Ford: history is bunk.

It's history, of course, that is debunking de Man. . . . In short order, the de Man affair has become one of the most serious intellectual scandals of the decade—comparable in significance to the furies unleashed by Ezra Pound's pro-Mussolini broadcasts on Italian radio. By odd chance, it par-

allels a similar scandal now unfolding in France over the philosopher Martin Heidegger's Nazi ties.

In the articles he wrote through October of 1942, de Man voiced admiration for Germany, expressed a virulent strain of anti-Semitism and sounded a Wagnerian trumpet in airing other fascist themes. . . . "There's no doubt that de Man was a gung-ho collaborator," says Jeffrey Mehlman, a professor of French at Boston University. In Mehlman's view, there are even "grounds for viewing the whole of deconstruction as a vast amnesty project for the politics of collaboration during World War II."

De Man's disciples aren't so quick to rush to judgment. "It's a big question what relationship, if any at all, there is between those early writings, after which he fell silent for 10 years, and the writings he did over the last 30 years of his life," says Cynthia Chase, a Cornell University professor of English. But the moral implications of deconstruction were devastating all along. In ***Allegories of Reading,*** (1979), his most influential book, de Man asserted that one could "excuse any guilt" for the reason that "the experience always exists simultaneously as fictional discourse and as empirical event and it is never possible to decide which one of the two possibilities is the right one." The critic Denis Donoghue pointed out the moral idiocy of that position eight years ago. But a man who had something to hide might well be drawn to it. . . .

Opponents of deconstruction think the movement is finished. As one Ivy League professor gleefully exclaims, "deconstruction turned out to be the thousand-year Reich that lasted 12 years." What's next? Berkeley professor Frederick Crews sees the rise of "the new militant cultural materialism of the left." That school prescribes the study of books not because of their moral or esthetic value but because they permit the professor to advance a political, often Marxist agenda. Crews contends that there's more than a trace of deconstruction in "the new historicism"—which is one reason traditional humanists hope that it, too, will self-deconstruct in the wake of the de Man disgrace.

> *David Lehman, "Deconstructing de Man's Life: An Academic Idol Falls into Disgrace," in* Newsweek, *Vol. CXI, No. 7, February 15, 1988, p. 63.*

GEOFFREY HARTMAN

Last December it became known that a Belgian researcher, Ortwin de Graef, had discovered writings from the early career of Paul de Man, the seminal deconstructionist thinker who died in 1983. They were reviews of books, concerts, and conferences. Almost all of these writings date from after the fall of Belgium in May 1940. Except for a few articles in *Les Cahiers du Libre Examen* ("Notebooks of Free Inquiry"), a journal associated with the University of Brussels, and a few more in a Flemish language journal, *Het Vlaamsche Land* ("The Flemish Land"), the bulk of them (close to 170) were written for the important Belgian newspaper *Le Soir* ("The Evening"). During the period that de Man published in *Le Soir* and *Het Vlaamsche Land,* they were under some Nazi censorship. *Le Soir,* in particular, followed the Nazi line in many respects; after its takeover it received the nickname "Le Soir Volé" ("The Stolen Evening").

The shock of finding de Man's early articles in collaborationist journals was increased by the fact that one of them engaged explicitly with the ideology of anti-Semitism. Under the headline **"The Jews in Contemporary Literature,"** de Man argued that Jews do not have a significant influence on contemporary literature; that charges about this literature being judaized *(enjuivé)* serve merely to discredit that literature; that the Jews themselves helped to spread this myth of their influence; that the ability of Western intellectuals to safeguard so representative a cultural domain as literature from Jewish influence is comforting. De Man leaves it unclear whether it is comforting because Jewishness itself is unhealthy, or because *any* invasion of Western civilization by a foreign force, a *"force étrangère,"* would reflect badly on its vitality. . . .

This is not vulgar anti-Semitic writing, not by the terrible standards of the day. But the fact remains that, however polished de Man's formulations are, they show all the marks, and the dangerous implications, of identifying Jews as an alien and unhealthy presence in Western civilization. De Man's article, moreover, is framed on the page of the paper by a nasty cartoon, a caricature of two Jews in prayer shawls imploring God, which is captioned, "May Jehovah confound the Goy"; and by a quotation attributed to Benjamin Franklin: "A leopard can't change its spots. The Jews are Orientals *(Asiatiques);* they are a menace for the country that lets them in, and they should be excluded by the Constitution." (The source of these falsely attributed sentences was an American forgery, which originated in 1934 and was refuted by Charles Beard and others. It circulated widely among German and American Nazis.)

It is hardly necessary to point out that in March 1941, when this article appeared, Jews were still seeking refuge in unoccupied France, the United States, South America, Switzerland, and elsewhere. De Man was writing in a collaborationist paper, then, at a vulnerable period, when the "colony isolated from Europe" was turning into sealed ghettos and concentration camps, in part because this "foreign" element could not find a home elsewhere and was treated like a disease or a pollutant that had to be contained. In the light of history, de Man's article—and the cartoon and quotation that accompanied it (for which he may not have been responsible)—become more than a theoretical expression of anti-Semitism.

Again, de Man's infrequent remarks on the "Jewish problem," though ugly and prejudiced, are mild compared with the vicious anti-Semitic propaganda that flourished in Nazi-funded papers like *L'Ami du Peuple* ("Friend of the People"). What is especially grievous, however, is that de Man continued an association with overtly anti-Semitic and collaborationist newspapers to the end of 1942—well past the time when all but the deliberately ignorant would have known that the persecution of the Belgian Jews, begun before the end of 1940, had taken a drastic turn. . . .

It is hard to be dispassionate about de Man's conduct, given the anti-Semitic campaign in which *Le Soir* participated from the fall of 1940 on, and the tragic history of the persecution, and the final deportation, of Belgium's Jews. (They made up one percent of the country's population but accounted for a third of its civilian and military casualties.) It remains important, however, to place oneself into that era, into its motives and its attitudes. What role did anti-Semitism play in de Man's thought? His articles reveal a strong sympathy for the Flemish, who lost their independence in Napoleon's wars and their territorial integrity in 1830. A cultural nationalist, de Man believed in the "genius" or the "individual soul" of a people, in their "unanimity" as it was attested by a shared

language, a homeland, and an ancestral achievement. (These qualities somehow did not apply to the Jews; they were seen as a "ghostly anti-race," in J. L. Talmon's memorable phrase.) De Man's focus is on the "New Europe" under Nazi domination, a Europe that allowed this Flemish sympathizer to take his distance from French culture and turn toward the German sphere of influence.

Nothing in this common sort of nationalism had to result in anti-Semitism. Was it youthful inexperience, then, or a broader acceptance of fascist ideology that made de Man write an anti-Semitic piece? (p. 26)

In recent years the study of fascist thought has gradually come into its own. George Mosse and Zeev Sternhell in particular have made essential contributions. The appeal of a movement that drew significant authors into its ranks came in part from what Mosse calls its "open-endedness . . . its ideological fluidity under authoritarian leadership." Besides the sad and demented case of Ezra Pound, and the passing enthusiasm for Mussolini of such figures as W. B. Yeats and Emil Ludwig, there was a large group of fascist intellectuals active in France and Belgium. They were militant journalists and included some prestigious writers of very different character: Maurice Blanchot, Bertrand de Jouvenel, Céline, Thierry Maulnier (the proponent of "rational anti-Semitism"), Robert Brasillach, Drieu de la Rochelle (who became editor of the *Nouvelle Revue Française* during the Occupation), Robert Poulet, and Henri de Man (who was Paul de Man's uncle). . . .

[Paul de Man's] journalism stands out by its refusal to engage directly with political matters. But its sympathies are clearly with Germany, and its cultural politics must have furthered the cause of collaboration. Reporting in March 1941 on the first reactions of literary France to the defeat, de Man combines a dig at French intellectuals with a revealing comment about the laggard masses:

> The French are not yet used to the idea that the creation of a new world organization no longer depends on them. . . . The lucidity of some [French] writers when they condemn a nefarious regime, and their determination to launch themselves on new paths, is certainly a comforting symptom. But so long as this does not express itself unanimously in public opinion, it is at least premature to talk about a national revival.

Such "unanimity" between a nation and its leaders was stressed by fascist intellectuals. And in another article de Man moved closer to being explicitly collaborationist, when he claimed that Hitler brought about the "definite emancipation of a people called upon to exercise, in its turn, a hegemony in Europe."

De Man reviewed the work of several fascist thinkers, including Drieu, Brasillach, and Ernst Jünger. His relation to fascist ideology is not a simple matter. There is, clearly, an accommodation, but it remains very general, without recourse to the usual "virile" invective. To judge from his articles, de Man felt he was living in a revolutionary epoch, in which politics and a sense of collective action were an essential part of intellectual regeneration. Political militance was displacing the *douceur* of the arts—or rather, as Walter Benjamin (and not Paul de Man) saw so clearly, it was aestheticizing politics for the masses. Still, with respect to the arts an admirable inconsistency crops up: not only is de Man a supporter of modern literature (including Kafka), but he resists its political co-ordination. He praises Poulet for a novel that does not subordinate "artistic sincerity" to political imperatives. And in defense of the literary review *Messages* (which he may have helped to get published), de Man explicitly rejects any "brutal" targeting of art, "under the pretext that the present revolution is totalitarian . . . that it intends to modify all aspects of personal and collective existence." In most other respects, however, de Man's themes are conformist: the renewal of Europe, the worth and dignity of national cultures, the need for roots, the spiritual unity of state and individual, of collectivity and elite.

Whether de Man's anti-Semitic strain was conventional or an ideological reflex does not much matter. The argument he makes presupposes a claim that efforts to emancipate the Jews had only proved that they could not be assimilated. . . . This conviction could attach itself to a time-honored popular and Christian hatred that regarded the Jews as unspiritual (materialistic) enemies of the faith, as doomed and eternal outsiders. The Jewish intellectual in particular was regarded as free-floating, cynical, subversive. (p. 28)

I have found only one other prejudicial reference to Jews by de Man. It occurs in a discussion of Jünger and contemporary German fiction. De Man posits a proper tradition of German art, which is marked by "deep spiritual sincerity," and then a second strain, which abused the remarkable theses of German expressionism. It is not surprising, he writes, that those who went in the other direction, which he qualifies as "aberrant," and a "degeneration," "were mainly non-German, specifically Jews." Such a judgment about the degeneracy of expressionism, and about its link to the Jews, paralleled Nazi pronouncements. The bases of de Man's cultural anti-Semitism, however, are not all that different from T. S. Eliot's: the Jews do not fit into Christian culture (Eliot) or into the "content of the European idea" (de Man).

The destruction of European Jewry, abetted by such propaganda, is what de Man himself must have faced later, what every person with a past of this kind must face. It is also what a person like myself must face, for a different reason. Paul de Man and I were acquainted with each other since 1961, and became colleagues and friends in 1965. There was no trace of anti-Semitism in the de Man I knew. But I cannot ignore these expressions of anti-Jewish sentiment, even if they remained polite, even if they were limited to suave cultural essays and never spilled over into exhortatory rhetoric or demagoguery.

It is indeed hard to associate the young journalist (aged 21) with the distinguished theorist (aged 47) who wrote so critically, and so effectively, against Husserl's *The Crisis of European Humanity and Philosophy*. De Man accused Husserl of blindly privileging Western civilization ("European supremacy") at the very time (1935) that Europe "was about to destroy itself as center in the name of an unwarranted claim to be the center." But of de Man, too, it can now be said that "as a European it seems that [he] escaped from the necessary self-criticism that is prior to all philosophical truth about the self."

The discovery of these early articles must make a difference in the way we read the later de Man. The new disclosures imbed a biographical fact in our consciousness, a fact that tends to devour all other considerations; it does not spare the later achievement, whose intellectual power we continue to feel. One crucial and hurtful problem is that de Man did not address his past. We do not have his thoughts. Did he avoid confession (he was without a religious bone in his body, except for the subdued religious feelings that were still perceptible in his early enthusiastic emphasis on the *âme particulière* of nationalities), and instead work out his totalitarian temptation in a purely intellectual and impersonal manner?

One view of the impact of these disclosures on the reading of de Man has already surfaced. Those previously suspicious of deconstruction have seized on the revelations. Their sense of deconstruction as morally unsound and politically evasive seems to stand confirmed. They condemn it as untrustworthy because it seeks to avert the reality, and therefore the culpability, of error. That is how they interpret deconstruction's emphasis on the indeterminacy of meaning, and on the complexity of a medium that seems to "speak" us instead of submitting fully to our control.

Such a judgment is superficial, and divorces deconstruction from its context in the history of philosophy. We may argue about whether deconstruction yields a useful way of looking at the relation of language and meaning, but it takes up an age-old problem. Ernst Cassirer observed that while language wished to overcome "the curse of mediacy," it was itself part of the problem it tried to resolve. Our methods and our media of inquiry distance the truth we seek: we get trapped in epistemological, semantic, and interpretive hassles. And one result of this perplexing byproduct of our effort to clarify things has been that philosophy has often turned against slippery modes of expression in the name of scientific rigor. Blame is placed squarely on the figurative, or literary, uses of language. "No metaphor is good unless it is a dead metaphor."

Deconstruction is, in this respect, a defense of literature. It shows, by close reading, (1) that there are no dead metaphors, (2) that literature is often more self-aware than those who attack it, (3) that literary texts contain significant tensions that can be disclosed, but not resolved, by analysis. Any mode of analysis, therefore, that sees the text as an organic unity, or uses it for a totalizing purpose (as when the right or the left speaks for history), is blind, and the text itself will subvert or "deconstruct" such closures.

Within the history of thought, deconstruction is surely a significant critique of German idealism ("identity philosophy"), insofar as the latter resulted in various kinds of organicism, including fascism. De Man in particular moved away from such speculative politics. His position is the very opposite of an idealism that confuses intellect and action, ideology and political praxis. His emphasis, moreover, on the non-identity of these realms, on the asymmetry of the real and the ideal, does not result in a spiritualistic or nihilistic withdrawal, tempting to many whose God has failed. Deconstruction is neither nihilistic nor cynical when it questions whether there exists an arena for testing ideas other than the uncontrollable arena of activist politics; or when it demonstrates that philosophy and literature express the impasse from which ideas spring, as well as those ideas themselves.

The probity of the Paul de Man we knew, and his powerful analytic talent, must remain our focus. What is neglected by de Man's critics, who are in danger of reducing all to biography again, is the intellectual power in his later work, the sheer power of critique, whatever its source, that he deploys against the claims of philosophy and theory. (The only peculiar thing is that a philosophical mind of this caliber should turn against the pretensions of philosophy and toward literature.) What is harder to appreciate, however, is the standpoint from which de Man's critique was launched. In addition to the power of deconstructive reasoning, there is its purity: it does not reveal, not in de Man at least, its situatedness, its personal or ideological context. The method acts as if it had no relatives. To my mind, it is this purity of deconstructive thought, not its power, that can now be questioned.

Again, there is nothing of a confessional nature in de Man; but it may yet turn out that in the later essays we glimpse the fragments of a great confession. It is possible to link the intellectual strength of the later work to what is excluded by it, to what, in surging back, threatens to diminish its authority. Those who see a "flight from history" in de Man—and link it directly to what we know now of his early writing—are quite wrong. It is true that he does not place himself in historical context, and he should have done so. But the postwar writing may constitute an avowal of error, a kind of repudiation in its very methodology of a philosophy of reading.

De Man always asks us to look beyond natural experience or its mimesis to a specifically linguistic dilemma. He claims that the relation between meaning and language is not in our subjective control, perhaps not even human:

> The way in which I can try to mean is dependent on the linguistic properties that are not only not made by me, because I depend on the language as it exists for the devices which I will be using, it is as such not made by us as historical beings, it is perhaps not even made by humans at all. Benjamin says, from the beginning, that it is not at all certain that language is in any sense human.

This is interesting and scandalous, since by "not human" de Man (interpreting Benjamin, the German Jewish critic who committed suicide in 1940 while fleeing the Nazis) certainly does not mean divine, as if language were instituted by God. If language were God-given, there would surely be stability; but there is stability only insofar as language is purified of ordinary referential meaning and becomes pure speech, as in ritual or magic, or when we recite something by heart without attending to its meaning. According to de Man, we are always encountering epistemological or semantic instabilities, the incompatibility or disjunction between meaning and intent, or between what is stated and the rhetoric or mode of stating it.

De Man concludes that the language-meaning relationship is not a stable, mutual reflection or correspondence, as when sound reinforces sense, or when history seems to fall into a genealogical and progressive pattern. Oscar Wilde depreciated action in favor of imagination because action was "a thing incomplete in its essence, because limited by accident, and ignorant of its direction, being always at variance with its aim." But for de Man, this description of action is also a description of what cannot be overcome by art, even the most imaginative kind. There is no compensation for the failure of action in the perfection of art. The fields of critical philosophy, literary theory, and history have an interlinguistic, not an extralinguistic, correlative; they are secondary in relation to the original, which is itself a previous text. They reveal an essential failure or disarticulation, which was already there in the original. "They kill the original, by discovering that the original was already dead. They read the original from the per-

spective of pure language *(reine Sprache),* a language that would be entirely freed of the illusion of meaning."

This talk of killing the original, and of essential failure, is strong stuff. Knowing today about the writings of the young de Man, it is not possible to evade them as merely a biographical reference point: the early writing *is* an "original" to which the later writing reacts. De Man's method of reading implies that the relation between late and early is interlinguistic only, that the position he has abandoned, one that proved to be a failure and perhaps culpably blind, is not to be used to explain his eventual method; but the biographical disclosure may hurt de Man's intelligibility. Though his method insists on excluding the biographical ("extralinguistic") reference, I do not believe that we can read him without identifying the "original" in his case as the mediated and compromised idiom of his early, journalistic writings.

De Man's assertion, for example, that "What stands under indictment is language itself and not somebody's philosophical error" all of a sudden becomes a reflection by de Man on de Man. The earlier self is not off the hook, but the emphasis shifts to the way language operates. The later self acknowledges an error, yet it does not attribute it to an earlier self, to a self involved in ideas and responsible for the error, because that would perpetuate its blindness to the linguistic nature of the predicament. Such a view may have been self-serving. But according to de Man's analysis, enlightenment as such cannot resolve error, and even repeats it, if one is deluded into thinking that the new position stands in a progressive and sounder relation to language, that it has corrected a historical mistake once and for all. Even to say, quite simply, "I was young, I made a mistake, I've changed my mind" remains blind if it overlooks the narrative shape of this or any confession. (pp. 28-30)

We can accuse de Man of lacking foresight or civil courage, or of underestimating the ruthlessness of the Nazi regime. And we abhor the anti-Semitism, and any collaboration that occurred. Once again we feel betrayed by the intellectuals. The accusations we bring, however, are a warning to ourselves. They do not justify complacency or easy judgments about the relation of political ideas to moral conduct. Many on the left also welcomed what Kenneth Burke called "sinister unifying," and succumbed to xenophobic and anti-Jewish sentiment. De Man's "dirty secret" was the dirty secret of a good part of civilized Europe. In the light of what we now know, however, his work appears more and more as a deepening reflection on the rhetoric of totalitarianism. His turn from the politics of culture to the language of art was not an escape into, but an escape out of, aestheticism: a disenchantment with that fatal aestheticizing of politics, blatant in his own early articles, that gave fascism its false brilliance. De Man's critique of every tendency to totalize literature or language, to see unity where there is no unity, looks like a belated, but still powerful, act of conscience. (p. 31)

Geoffrey Hartman, "Blindness and Insight," in The New Republic, *Vol. 198, No. 10, March 7, 1988, pp. 26, 28-31.*

WOLFGANG HOLDHEIM

Christopher Norris's essay [see excerpt above] . . . deserves attention as an honest and generally lucid attempt by a sympathiser with de Man to come to terms with the recent revelations about that critic's wartime publications in collaborationist Belgian papers. I feel particularly qualified to comment, not only because I am de Man's successor at the Department of Comparative Literature in Cornell, but also because I myself spent the years of the German occupation in the Low Countries. . . .

[Norris] expatiates on de Man's demystification of Heidegger's view that the language of German poetry dwells in the immediate proximity of Being, and connects it with the Belgian critic's own rejection of his early infatuation with organicist metaphors that claimed to provide an immediate access to truth. Similarly, in exposing European preconceptions in the putatively universal viewpoint from which Husserl wanted to overcome the modern crisis, de Man remembers the fatal entanglements of his own crisis consciousness. Against all these totalising notions, fraught with 'blindness', de Man directs a ceaseless struggle for critical 'insight' based on close reading, on the continual exposure of language's mystificatory rhetorical strategies. I have little doubt that de Man saw things in this way, but I am from the outset struck by a colossal disproportion. 'Organicism' sounds respectable—but can we really say that about those columns in *Le Soir* and *Het Vlaamsche Land?* Mr Norris himself mentions their crudity. They are in fact common Nazi hack work, excruciatingly dull and totally unoriginal, embarrassing to read in their mediocrity; even as experiments in blindness, they have no common measure with Husserl's Eurocentrism or with Heidegger's oracular obscurantism.

The true problem, however, lies elsewhere. Actually we are dealing with a mere surface version of de Man's historical experience—its idealisation into near-abstractness, its dilution into the rarefied air of the 'history of ideas'. But the history that de Man lived, that we all lived, was pressing and concrete. Mr Norris's historical approach is not historical enough.

The later de Man is first and foremost a brilliant and sophisticated close reader of texts. But in the midst of his often dazzling performance, we are confronted with a small number of unproved and unproven philosophical assumptions that keep recurring with almost maniacal inevitability. There is a major discrepancy between the overall critical subtlety of the readings and the often simplistic nature of those presuppositions. This strange duality has remained hidden from true believers, who are never noted for watchfulness. They are to some degree excused by the fact that these invariable premises are cleverly smuggled into a highly subtle discourse in whose subtlety they can easily seem to share. De Man's texts tend to be virtuoso exercises in circularity where the presupposition is produced in the guise of a tortuously elaborated end-result. Nevertheless, the duality has long been clear to unmystified readers. I was one of them and was always sorely puzzled: now, having read the Belgian essays, I think I understand.

What helps me do so is my own historical experience, which was unfortunately quite concrete. How could one view the publication of articles such as de Man's, written by a Belgian, in occupied Belgium in 1941 and 1942? Only as an act of unspeakable moral shabbiness. And what must have been the status of such an author in 1945? Nothing less than that of a moral, political and probably social outcast. This may be hard to understand for a generation safely shielded from that period by temporal distance, and often by a chronic lack of historical insight. We can be certain, though, that it was fully

understood by de Man. In the light of the atrocious revelations that flooded us in 1945, he may even have reconsidered that praise of the Germans as exquisitely civilised occupiers which he had found it necessary to insert into a literary article at the time of his country's humiliation. He must have been permanently traumatised by events.

This I perceive to be the figure in the carpet, the ultimate historical and biographical ground of those stubborn presuppositions that pervade de Man's later work. Meaningfully coherent historical narratives are illusory; there is no subject, no real author—and if there seems to be, he knows not what he does. Texts are infinitely tricky, they never say what they seem to say, they always say the opposite, or both. The demystificatory uncovering of rhetorical subversions again and again escalates into a programmatic (and utterly simplistic) substitution of technical rhetorical categories for existential categories, until the latter cease to exist. Who can fail to detect a pattern of retreat from life, of denial of responsibility—an unending and tortuous process of disculpation and evasion? This is much more than the rejection of a silly blood-and-soil 'organicism': it is a deep-seated urge to dilute, to dissolve the weight of the past.

Wolfgang Holdheim, in a letter to the editor of London Review of Books, *Vol. 10, No. 6, March 17, 1988, p. 4.*

DAVID H. HIRSCH

The *New York Times* story [see excerpt above] reporting the discovery of Paul de Man's anti-Semitic writings for pro-Nazi newspapers stated: "The findings about a man respected at Yale and elsewhere have shocked scholars." One can understand the shock of de Man's friends and colleagues. All indications are that if de Man did have a Nazi past he had indeed put it behind him. It is most probable that in 1941-42 de Man was acting not out of malice but out of opportunism. But even if de Man was never a believing Nazi, the surprising news that he wrote for Nazi periodicals should not be taken lightly. We are reminded not only of de Man's buried personal past but of a European past that has been buried as effectively. One suspects that those same scholars who were shocked to learn about de Man's unsavory past would be equally surprised to learn about the existence of German death camps. . . . Anyone who derived his or her knowledge of literature and the world only from the journals de Man and his followers would be likely to publish in and read would probably live in blissful ignorance of the recent European past—and would never in the least suspect that the various literary and critical "postmodernisms" may directly result from the historical events of the thirties and forties.

For years I had been puzzled by this bizarre ignorance of this chapter in the recent past, but I thought it a mere coincidence—or perhaps a reflection of the "unworldliness" of literary critics who preferred fictional to real worlds. Now, in the light of the Waldheim affair, especially the indifference toward the past shown by the Austrian people in electing a former Nazi to high office; the insensitivity of Pope John Paul in conferring "respectability" on this same former Nazi; Claude Lanzmann's revealing documentary film *Shoah* and the ensuing denials and debate surrounding the film; the trauma and echoes of French collaboration surrounding the trial of Klaus Barbie; the Roques affair, in which a doctoral dissertation questioning the existence of Nazi death camps was accepted at a French university; the new German revisionist historians who complain of "a past that will not pass," and who instead of denying Nazi atrocities outright seek to mask the guilt of "civilized," systematic, and planned state-of-the-art genocide by submerging it beneath the current of general human cruelty and the mainstream violence of human history—in the light of all these developments, one can no longer ascribe the promotion of deconstructionist literary criticism, with its concomitant relegation of Holocaust literature to the garbage heap of literary history, to coincidence or daydreaming.

Once one ponders the audacity of the omission, and the immensity of the abyss this omission opens in western "literary history" as now conceived and written, then the connection between Paul de Man's deconstructive criticism and his Nazi past, far from being shocking, starts to make a great deal of sense. Despite the deconstructionist critics' insistent claims that they not only deconstruct texts but also probe into the deepest corners of their own consciousnesses, the deconstructionist de Man was apparently guarding a secret from himself as well as from his naive American graduate students and, as it turns out, equally naive academic peers, a secret that had to be kept by European intellectuals—the dark secret that European high culture in its most advanced phase not only was powerless to prevent the construction and implementation of the death camps, but actually provided the ideological base on which the death camps were built. (pp. 330-31)

As Leszek Kolakowski, among others, has pointed out, the Nazis did not keep their ideology or their evil intentions a secret. What lurks behind de Man's urbane, sophisticated, and obscurantist philosophical criticism, then, is the shame of the European intellectuals who participated in and profited from genocide, whether out of greed, or opportunism, or total commitment to Nazi racist ideology, or even out of sheer hatred. Nor is de Man the first European intellectual to hide behind self-deceiving distortions and obscurantism. (p. 331)

The convenient myth is that Nazism was a movement restricted to the uneducated masses, and that the killers were ignorant brutes recruited from the lumpenproletariat and the petit bourgeoisie. Inconvenient fact interferes with this comforting myth. We need but consider the career of none other than the Angel of Death of Auschwitz himself, Jozef Mengele. Dr. Mengele was the proud product of a European education. He considered himself a scientist and a man of culture. Victims testify that he was fond of quoting the poetry of Hölderlin. Of course Mengele was only one of many—more cruel perhaps, and certainly with a greater flair for the dramatic, than some of his peers. (pp. 331-32)

The information I have on de Man's life during the Nazi years is limited to the *New York Times* story, which tells us little about de Man's activities once he stopped worrying in print (if he did stop) about how the Jews were polluting European literature: "The young de Man quit the newspaper in 1942, entering publishing until he left for the United States in 1947." We do not know why de Man left Belgium, his native land; but many Nazi sympathizers left the place of their birth when the situation there started to become unpleasant for collaborators. Perhaps de Man was simply ashamed of his past, and wanted to eradicate it by starting life anew in a new country.

In any case what better way to conceal a shameful past, even from one's self, than by shifting attention away from the Nazi past and from the writings of poets, fiction writers, and essayists who might talk about the past honestly, and focusing instead on the question of how critics read. In the foreword to *Blindness and Insight* (1971), the book that vaulted him into academic prominence, de Man announces his intention to deal with criticism rather than primary creative works: "Because critics deal more or less openly with the problem of reading, it is a little easier to read a critical text *as text*—i.e., with an awareness of the reading process involved—than to read other literary works in this manner." De Man's purpose here as elsewhere in his writings seems to be to sow confusion. . . . (pp. 332-33)

In addition to deflecting literary criticism away from literature and its humanistic moral implications, de Man attacks the concept of "the past." Like many deconstructionists de Man has founded his poetics on a version of Saussurean linguistics. There is no need for me to repeat Saussure's definition of the "sign"; it is enough to point out here that what might make Saussure's linguistics so alluring to a critic trying to blot out the past is its synchronic tendencies.

This will to obliterate the past is evident in de Man's **"Literary History and Literary Modernity."** Most of the essay, which follows characteristic de Manian strategies of deception, recapitulates Nietzsche's "Of the Use and Misuse of History for Life" in such a way as to demonstrate Nietzsche's rejection of "history." In a typical turn, however, de Man finds that the seeming rejection of the past is actually, at a deeper level, a discovery of the impossibility of forgetting the past. In Nietzsche's "description of life," de Man writes, "it [i.e. life] is a temporal experience of human mutability, historical in the deepest sense of the term in that it implies the necessary experience of any present as a *passing* experience that makes the past irrevocable and unforgettable, because it is inseparable from any present or future." For an instant de Man seems to be saying that deeper than the urge to forget is the need to remember. But it is soon clear that "the past" that must be remembered has melted into an eternal present ("the past . . . is inseparable from any present or future"). I do not have the space here to enter into all the evasions and involutions of this labyrinthine exercise in obfuscation, but simply will quote the closing sentences to demonstrate that de Man's purpose in writing an essay on literary history is to destroy not only literary history but history itself:

> To become good literary historians, we must remember that what we usually call literary history has little or nothing to do with literature and that what we call literary interpretation—provided only it is good interpretation—is in fact literary history. If we extend this notion beyond literature, it merely confirms that the bases for historical knowledge are not empirical facts but written texts, even if these texts masquerade in the guise of wars or revolutions.

The bad faith in this passage is so clear and the indeterminate qualifiers and half-truths so obvious ("*good* literary historians," "*what we usually call* literary history," "provided only it is *good interpretation*," etc.) that I will only point out that the claims de Man makes in this passage rest on neither logic nor empirical evidence. To say that "what we call (good) literary interpretation" is "(*what we call?*) literary history" is merely to raise a series of questions, such as: What is literary interpretation? What is good, as distinguished (presumably) from bad, literary interpretation, and who is to decide what is good or bad? Who is the "we" that "call"? In what sense can a synchronic entity (interpretation) be equated to a diachronic entity (history)? But de Man thunders this highly questionable and actually nonsensical utterance as if it were a universally accepted absolute truth. He also slides from positing "literary history" as an indeterminate and possibly indeterminable entity to positing it as a clearly definable entity that can be pinned down (i.e., in the first instance, he talks about "what we usually call literary history" and in the next about something that "is in fact literary history"). Finally de Man's disingenuous claim that he has somehow confirmed "that the bases for historical knowledge are not empirical facts but written texts" is at best a half-truth. To a large extent "written texts" themselves become the "empirical facts," and a good historian tries to establish their accuracy. But written texts are not always the historian's only evidence. The assumption underlying this assertion, which de Man has stated explicitly in another essay, is that all written texts are merely components of a sign-system in which "the actual expression" never "coincides with what it signifies." If one accepts this assumption, then history itself, and with it de Man's own Nazi past, has been obliterated.

What is surprising is the eagerness with which de Manian deceptions have been taken up by younger American literary critics—and even by de Man's colleague Geoffrey H. Hartman [see excerpt above], who, having himself escaped the Nazis, should have known better. (pp. 333-34)

We should not be surprised to hear echoes of deconstructionist "historiography" in the German revisionist historian Ernst Nolte's infamous article, "The Past that will not Pass Away," which appeared in the *Frankfurter Allgemeine Zeitung* for June 6, 1986, " 'The past that will not pass,' " he writes, "can only mean the Nazi past of the Germans. The issue implies the thesis that every past passes away, and that this not-passing-away involves something very exceptional. On the other hand, the normal passing away of the past cannot be seen as a disappearance." In a penetrating commentary on the revisionists that appeared in the June 1987 issue of *Encounter* Josef Joffe has pointed out that "if the past could not be laid to rest, it had to be reconstructed. If images of cattle-cars and crematoria refused to subside, then the films must be taken in hand by the professionals for reediting and retouching. If the ancestral stain could not be scrubbed off, perhaps the crimes could be made to pale in the blinding light cast on those of others." I make two observations. One is that instead of the historian's "ancestral stain" de Man, we may infer, had a personal stain to scrub off. Second, while the historian must "reconstruct" the past to wash off the stain, the man of letters must "deconstruct" it, so that the past may be said never to have existed, or to exist only as a "supreme fiction" or a "rhetorical strategy"—which would then mean, of course, that the past could be "reconstructed" or "rerhetorized," as a film may be reedited and retouched, to eliminate the "images of cattle cars and crematoria."

With irony and dismay we perceive de Man's friends and colleagues beginning the process of reconstructing *him*. As the *Times* reporter puts it, "Some scholars said they detect anti-Nazi nuances in Professor de Man's favorable reviews of Jewish authors such as Kafka or the French historian Daniel Halevy" [see excerpt above]. It would certainly constitute a self-imposed blindness and would actually be unfair to de Man to let ourselves be taken in by such feeble rationalization; for as soon as we recognize de Man's dark past, his work starts to take on new meaning, and we can perceive a coherence and

cogency that were not previously there. To see this coherence we need only reexamine **"Criticism and Crisis"** (1967), which contains the donnée of his entire oeuvre.

De Man begins by announcing that "well established rules and conventions that governed the discipline of criticism and made it a cornerstone of the intellectual establishment have been so badly tampered with that the entire edifice threatens to collapse. One is tempted to speak of recent developments in continental criticism in terms of *crisis*." I pass over the accuracy of these assertions, which, despite the imperiousness with which they are stated, are highly questionable. (Were there ever "well established rules and conventions that governed the discipline of criticism," and, if there were, had they not been "badly tampered with" well before the 1960s—in fact at least as early as the eighteenth century?) Instead I call attention to de Man's strategy of deflection. A sheltered American critic, I believe, might be forgiven for being innocent enough to perceive a "crisis" in literary criticism as an apocalyptic event. But could de Man have been as naive as a sheltered American? Since he wrote for a pro-Nazi newspaper for more than a year, we must assume that he lived among and consorted with Nazis and that he must have been reading Nazi ideology and propaganda. In the *Times* story Raoul Hilberg, a historian of the Holocaust, is quoted as saying that "almost all educated Belgians knew by 1941 or at the latest, 1942, that Jews were being sent eastward to be exterminated." As late as the mid-sixties could de Man have failed to understand that the crisis in western culture was (and is) a crisis not of literary criticism, but of the ease with which Europe was Nazified, and that it was not the rules of criticism that had been tampered with but the rules of civilized human behavior? That is, "the edifice" of European culture "threatens to collapse" not because the rules of literary criticism have changed but because of Auschwitz.

What we now know of de Man's past may help to answer one of the enigmas of the essay: Why did de Man choose Husserl (a Jew) as his example of a philosopher whose "privileging" of "post-Hellenic European consciousness" blinded him to his own Eurocentrism and prevented him from doing justice to non-European cultures? Was Husserl the only Eurocentric philosopher? It is odd that de Man finds no Eurocentrism or blindness in Heidegger's exegesis of Hölderlin, and takes for granted the validity of Heidegger's "intention to collect and found Being by means of language," even though Heidegger never questioned his own belief that he could discover Being using only one European language. Knowing that de Man was concealing a dark past, perhaps even from himself, we must be struck by both the pathos and the irony of de Man's contention that it was Husserl who failed to live by one of the cornerstones of his own thinking: "Husserl conceived of philosophy primarily as a self-interpretation by means of which we eliminate what he calls *Selbstverhulltheit,* the tendency of the self to hide from the light it can cast on itself."

Paul de Man himself may have had most to fear from "the light . . . the self . . . can cast on itself." And perhaps that is why he had to conclude his **"Criticism and Crisis"** in a spurious nihilism:

> The 'virtual focus' [that is, Levi-Strauss's substitute for the subject] is, strictly speaking, a nothing, but its nothingness concerns us very little, since a mere act of reason suffices to give it a mode of being that leaves the rational order unchallenged. The same is true of the imaginary source of fiction. Here the

human self has experienced the void within itself and the invented fiction, far from filling the void, asserts itself as pure nothingness, our nothingness stated and restated by a subject that is the agent of its own instability.

What is at issue is not nihilism itself, but the insincerity of the nihilism expressed here, which is that of a clever child who has learned to play with words. This is not the kind of felt nihilism that a writer like Melville expresses with fear and trembling in "The Whiteness of the Whale." It is, once again, a nihilism conceived in bad faith.

Among the unidentified scholars cited in the *Times* story are some who "defended [de Man] as having been a young man, influenced perhaps by an uncle, Henri de Man, who was a minister in the collaborationist Belgian government." These defenders apparently ignored the fact that men much younger than de Man, and in many instances not so well educated, were able to tell right from wrong—and were willing to risk their lives fighting in the Resistance. (pp. 335-37)

> *David H. Hirsch, "Paul de Man and the Politics of Deconstruction," in* The Sewanee Review, *Vol. XCVI, No. 2, Spring, 1988, pp. 330-38.*

WALTER KENDRICK

"Yale Scholar Wrote for Pro-Nazi Newspaper," announced a headline in the December 1, 1987, *New York Times* [see excerpt above]; the next day in the *Providence Journal,* it got boiled down to "Yale Scholar Wrote for Nazis." Is there a difference? How about condensing it another step: "Yale Scholar *Was* Nazi"? The corridors of Academe have been abuzz ever since, and the furor shows no sign of fading. Those who abhorred Paul de Man while he lived have donned I-told-you-so smirks, those who flourished under his aegis are looking a bit queasy, and a few former acolytes have already jumped ship.

For 10 years or so, deconstruction was the enfant terrible of academic lit crit; according to the deconstructors, ignorance and hypocrisy had fought them at every step, but they'd risen to the top through sheer intellectual excellence and the irrefutable validity of their doctrines. Their self-righteousness made them obnoxious, and their ability to find an opponent behind every bush gave them, even in success, a rather paranoid air. Yet only six months ago, it seemed that history was on the deconstructors' side; nothing apparently could stop their march toward professional dominance, as their method and their lingo gradually swept the field. Now, all of a sudden, deconstructive paranoia has found a real enemy, within itself.

We owe this ironic development to Ortwin de Graef, a Belgian graduate student, who spent the summer of 1987 doing what grad students do best: grubbing about in archives. Most likely, nothing but hagiography was on his mind—the project of assembling a complete list of de Man's writings had been in the works for several years—but in the files of *Le Soir,* a venerable Brussels daily that's still going strong, de Graef found 169 articles (in French) with de Man's byline, dating from December 1940 through November 1942. Mostly book and music reviews, the articles would have been of strictly academic interest, except that Belgium was occupied by the

Nazis at the time, and *Le Soir* eagerly collaborated, especially when it came to anti-Semitism.

This was bad enough, but at least one of de Man's articles seemed to suggest that he'd gone beyond collaborating with the collaborators to embrace anti-Semitism himself. **"Jews in Today's Literature" ("Les Juifs dans la Littérature actuelle,"** March 4, 1941) appeared on a feature page headed "We and the Jews: Cultural Aspects," amid vile company: articles on "The Two Faces of Judaism" and "A Jewish Doctrine: Freudianism"; a cartoon showing a conspiratorial group of Jewish elders intoning "May Jehovah confound the goy!"; a spurious quotation from Benjamin Franklin: "A leopard cannot change its spots. Jews are Asiatics; they are a menace to the country that admits them, and they should be excluded by the Constitution."

Whatever de Man's private feelings may have been, the editors of *Le Soir* were unequivocal:

> At the head of this page devoted to studying some aspects of the Jewish question, it seems useful to underline the essential elements of our anti-Semitism.
> We do not think it sufficient to justify our position on social grounds. It goes without saying that the Jews have committed numerous social wrongs. With their trickery and tenacity, they have seized control of politics, the economy, and the Press; they have profited from their privileged situation, getting rich at the expense of the peoples who welcomed them and luring those peoples into catastrophic policies that could only result in war . . .
> Our anti-Semitism is of a racial order. In the mass of Jews, we see a vast community of individuals linked by a certain number of shared physical and moral characteristics.
> Roughly speaking, the Jews seem to us of a nature fundamentally foreign and radically opposed to our blood and our minds.
> We believe in the existence of a Jewish type, a Jewish genius. We are determined to forbid ourselves any cross-breeding with them and to liberate ourselves spiritually from their demoralizing influence in the realm of thought, literature, and the arts.

De Man didn't write this; the honor was claimed by a certain Léon van Buffel. But for nearly two years, de Man scribbled prolifically for a newspaper whose stated doctrine this was.

"Jews in Today's Literature" has nothing to say about cross-breeding, nor does it maintain that liberation is necessary. Instead, de Man proposes that the Jewish influence on contemporary literature has been "of remarkably little importance." Despite the "specific characteristics of the Jewish spirit," Jewish writers "have always remained second rate"— "comforting proof for occidental intellectuals that they have been able to preserve themselves from Jewish influence." As it has done in the past, "occidental" literature will continue to develop "according to its great evolutionary laws," because "foreign" Jewish culture is completely irrelevant to it.

The grounding of this repellent theory requires some fancy footwork: Stendhal's famous description of the novel as a mirror carried along a roadway, reflecting the world through which it passes, gets twisted, for the modern novel, into a purely psychological instrument focused on "the most secret recesses of the characters' souls." The great non-Jewish novelists of the day constitute an unlikely quartet: Gide, Hemingway, Lawrence, and—Kafka. All of them "seek to penetrate . . . the secrets of the interior life," a curious assessment of Hemingway, at least, almost as curious as the bestowal of *goyishkeit* on Kafka. On the whole, the essay is strained, pedestrian, and far less offensive than the company it kept. Except, that is, for its peroration: "A solution to the Jewish problem that aimed at the creation of a Jewish colony isolated from Europe would entail no deplorable consequences for the literary life of the Occident." A year and a half after this sinister fantasy was published, the first trainload of Belgian Jews set out for Auschwitz; de Man stayed at *Le Soir.*

None of his other wartime writings comes close to the anti-Semitism of **"Jews in Today's Literature,"** and even there it is anti-Semitism of a laissez-faire kind. De Man issued no call to action; he merely looked upon the status quo and found that, if he bent over backward to please the boss, he could make a living off it. De Man accommodated himself to a lethal regime; he accepted the timeworn, vulgarized oppositions *Occidental-Oriental* and *native-foreign* on which *Le Soir's* far more emphatic anti-Semitism was based, along with the notion that there were "specific characteristics" by which the "Jewish spirit" could be identified. None of this nonsense disfigured his American work, but a certain kind of literary separatism endured. Sealing literature in an independent realm, grounded in its own history and governed by its own rules, the de Man of 1941 sought to exempt poets and novelists from responsibility for the doings of the nonliterary world. By implication, the same immunity would apply to literary critics—de Man himself, for example. The de Man of the 1980s did exactly the same thing; if Yale had required its Jewish students to wear a yellow star, no doubt Professor de Man would have gone on writing his dense and difficult essays.

This interpretation needn't necessarily require the junking of de Manian deconstruction, though the deconstructors seem to fear that outcome. To forestall the discrediting of his (and their own) career, a self-appointed cadre of de Man's former colleagues, friends, and students has banded together in jittery solidarity. The roll call of defenders includes some of the best and brightest names among the academic lit-crit avant garde: Samuel Weber, Shoshana Felman, Cynthia Chase, Jonathan Culler, Andrzej Warminski, along with lesser lights on the order of Neil Hertz, Andrew Parker, and Tom Keenan, all presided over in appropriately shadowy fashion by Jacques Derrida.

After a brief lapse into panic when the news arrived, the pro-de Man forces devised a program that looks like a model of openness and fair play. The *Le Soir* articles were xeroxed in great numbers and shipped off to anyone who might care about the matter; the full French texts will be published in the *Oxford Literary Review,* to be followed by responses solicited from 50 interested parties, covering the range of relevant opinion. The problem, it appears, will receive the fullest possible airing, and after a while, the deconstructors hope, the dust will settle.

The unveiling of Nazi connections, no matter how tenuous, in an eminent figure's past leads automatically, in many minds, to discrediting him and everything he did. In *Newsweek* [see excerpt above], David Lehman has already pursued this route, invoking "moral idiocy," "terrible ironies," "the de Man disgrace," and lots of other overheated phrases—meanwhile demonstrating that he (like all their other attackers, according to the deconstructors) lacks even

a rudimentary understanding of deconstruction. In *The Nation,* [see excerpt above], Jon Wiener took a cooler tack but dropped dark hints about de Man's association with Hans Robert Jauss (former S.S. member and current leader of the German *Rezeptionsästhetik* school), along with suggestions that de Man's wartime anti-Semitism persisted until his death. There's no reason, though, to defend de Man against mudslingers like these; the popular press has been misreading deconstruction ever since word of it first leaked out of the ivory tower. The real threat comes from those within the profession who stand to gain from putting de Man down. Most of his defenders knew him intimately in one way or another, and of course they're eager to combat slurs against a beloved friend or mentor. But more than affectionate memory is at stake.

Bolting ahead of the pack, Geoffrey Hartman has already spoke out [see excerpt above], in a *New Republic* article that suggests the depth of the confusion now afflicting those numerous de Manians who are also Jews. Hartman veers repeatedly toward condemnation, then backs off: "It is hard to be dispassionate about de Man's conduct," he says, proving his point in the act of making it. De Man's "cultural politics must have furthered the cause of collaboration"; "I cannot ignore these expressions of anti-Jewish sentiment"; "these early articles must make a difference in the way we read the later de Man." Clearly, Hartman is hurt that he and de Man had been "colleagues and friends" for almost 20 years, during which de Man kept his secret. Hartman verges on condemning his false old friend, but when it comes to de Man's legacy, he plunges instead into rather desperate what-iffery.

"Did he avoid confession . . . and instead work out his totalitarian temptation in a purely intellectual and impersonal manner?" Evidently not, though Hartman never directly answers this provocative question. Instead, he summons up the de Manians' favorite straw men ("Those previously suspicious of deconstruction have seized on the revelation"), dishes out yet another capsule summary of the method ("It shows . . . that literary texts contain significant tensions that can be disclosed, but not resolved, by analysis"), and sidles his way toward a risky finale:

> In the light of what we now know, however, his work appears more and more as a deepening reflection on the rhetoric of totalitarianism. . . . De Man's critique of every tendency to totalize literature or language, to see unity where there is no unity, looks like a belated, but still powerful, act of conscience.

As a defense of de Man's silence, this is feeble; it also, perhaps unwittingly, plays into the anti-deconstructors' hands by proposing that de Man's late works, which have become the sacred texts of an academic sect, must now be read as a symptom of one man's neurosis.

Christopher Norris, a British deconstructor with impeccable credentials—including two handbooks, *Deconstruction* and *The Deconstructive Turn*—came to a similar conclusion in his *Paul de Man* [see excerpt above], without benefit of the notorious *Le Soir* articles. In some of the young de Man's other work, reviews for the Belgian journals *Les Cahiers du Libre Examen* (French) and *Het Vlaamsche Land* (Flemish), Norris noted a rhetoric that "strays more than once onto the dangerous ground of 'blood and soil,' of cultural identity as rooted in a sense of predestined (organic) development and growth which can only be asserted over and against all rival nationalist claims." This proto-Nazi rhetoric was common currency in its time, but as early as 1952, de Man had begun to repudiate it, and his last work purges it entirely. "In fact," says Norris, "one could read the entire course of his subsequent work as a single-minded effort to redeem or to exorcise the memory of those early reviews." (pp. 6-7)

Paul de Man is the first full-length study of de Man's work, and it's more than a simple guide or glorification. Norris is clearly a partisan, though more gracious than most; he admits that the essays of de Man's middle years tend to support the common charge (leveled most vehemently by Frank Lentricchia) that he cut literature off from politics, but Norris looks to the very last essays, most not yet published, for eventual proof that another career turn was on the way—toward the analysis of Marx, Althusser, and other overtly political writers. Norris's treatment is insightful and incisive throughout; he seeks, however, to detach de Man from the classic texts to which his work clung with the utmost closeness, to transform him into a literary-philosophical figure in his own right.

Reading de Man this way might help to salvage his personal reputation; it might even mystify his memory yet further by turning him into a modern-day Oedipus at New Haven. But you can't very well build a school on that foundation; in practical terms, it amounts to the same thing as dismissing de Manian deconstruction on account of Nazi taint. Either way, the deconstructors will have a hard time holding on to their claims of universal validity if their doctrines dwindle down to the traces of a dead leader's guilt. This is what they fear most, and correctly. Ten years of snowballing professional success have made the de Manians tempting targets, the air of Academe crackles with resentment, and it may have found its lightning rod. . . .

Now [the de Manians] have a nightmare to contend with: the shove of real history. It has propelled de Man out from the hush of the temple, where he died and where his epigones would like to enshrine his memory, into the clutches of those for whom dispassionate strength is not the primary virtue. It has placed him in the ill-assorted company of Kurt Waldheim and Martin Heidegger—an appropriately European crew, since a good deal of de Man's clout, both personal and professional, derived from his unassimilated Europeanness, despite his having made this country his residence for the last 30 years of his life. He played the bicontinental game with great skill, even better than Derrida does; belonging on neither side of the water, he effectively transcended, while he lived, the left-right politics at which his followers feel entitled to sneer.

De Man's formidable stature as a thinker is in large measure a product of the kowtowing Americans love to perform at the feet of Continental imports. That ritual is particularly prevalent in literary Academe, where the curriculum is mostly European and its peddlers suffer, with reason, from a chronic shortage of self-esteem. De Man could not have attained his odd eminence outside our manqué culture; foreignness, joined to an arcane vocabulary and a Germanic density of style, lent him and his work an aura beyond the powers of any native son. Yet there was more than a little obfuscation in it, not unlike the obscurity he allowed to envelop his early years—a moral shiftiness that may now be exacting its posthumous price. (p. 7)

De Man's beatification by American Academe seems to have taken him by surprise; it is a strange phenomenon, out of all apparent proportion to the work on which it rests. De Man published his first book, *Blindness and Insight,* in 1971, when he was over 50. His second, *Allegories of Reading,* came out in 1979, and there are two posthumous volumes, *The Rhetoric of Romanticism* (1984) and *The Resistance to Theory* (1986), with at least two more forthcoming. All are collections of essays, reprinted from journals and anthologies; only *Allegories* lays claim to book-length structure, but its unity derives more from a consistent method than from extended argument. By academic standards, which emphasize quantity of publication rather than quality, this is a flimsy foundation for stardom, and de Man was an extraordinarily late bloomer. But there were qualities in his work that made him an underground classic long before the outside world learned his name.

In the '70s, no aspiring academic critic could lay claim to credibility without having read *Blindness and Insight.* Its nine essays offered a radically new experience for inheritors of the Anglo-American critical tradition, which had amounted principally to private opinions tricked out with varying degrees of spleen. De Man practiced literary criticism as if it were an exercise of strength; he did his fellow critics the honor of assuming that they worked under the guidance of methods, just as scientists or philosophers would, then submitted their methods to sharp but courteous analysis. He proceeded as if literary criticism was a profession; following him, you no longer had to feel sheepish in the presence of your peers from law or medical school.

De Man never campaigned for the dignity and power of literary criticism; he merely acted on the assumption that it possessed these virtues as a matter of course. His stance was consistently sober and tough-minded, though he also attributed to literature a transcendent value that, phrased in hotter terms, might seem like moonshine:

> True understanding always implies a certain degree of totality; without it, no contact could be established with a foreknowledge that it can never reach, but of which it can be more or less lucidly aware. The fact that poetic language, unlike ordinary language, possesses what we call "form" indicates that it has reached this point. In interpreting poetic language, and especially in revealing its "form," the critic is therefore dealing with a privileged language: a language engaged in its highest intent and tending toward the fullest possible self-understanding.

This privilege, this height and fullness, naturally rub off on the critic:

> The relationship between author and critic does not designate a difference in the type of activity involved, since no fundamental discontinuity exists between two acts that both aim at full understanding; the difference is primarily temporal in kind. Poetry is the foreknowledge of criticism. Far from changing or distorting it, criticism merely discloses poetry for what it is.

De Man was a prominent advocate of the much-mocked claim that critics are equal or superior to "creative" artists. The assertion was neither as new nor as ridiculous as its mockers made out, but in any case de Man's appeal to the ambitious academic critic hardly depended on such extravagance. Trapped in a shrinking market, where the study of literature was coming to seem at best of decorative value, the grad students and professors of the '70s lusted after the solidity of professionalism, not the gaudiness of art. De Man provided what they sought, supplemented by the guaranteed cachet of a foreign accent and an easy familiarity with Heidegger and Blanchot. In his hands, the journal essay became a heady mix of the intensest close reading and vast generalizations like "Poetry is the foreknowledge of criticism." It seemed insignificant that the zone between the text and the universe—where, for example, society and history are found—remained a blank.

Blindness and Insight also marked de Man's first engagement with Derrida, an epoch-making event for both. **"The Rhetoric of Blindness"** tackled the discussion of Rousseau in *De la Grammatologie,* the founding text of deconstruction, and in effect deconstructed it. The "blindness" that Derrida pretended to find in Rousseau's *Essay on the Origin of Languages* turns out to be his own, because Rousseau's text, being "literary," already knows about the dead ends of thought that Derrida springs on it as a discovery. By a nice final twist, however, or perhaps an extremely rarefied joke, Derrida's text shares the "literary" prize: "What happens in Rousseau is exactly what happens in Derrida. . . . The pattern is too interesting not to be deliberate."

This was the birth of de Manian deconstruction—the oddest moment in an odd career, when de Man stamped with his own image a method that had been devised and named by another writer. De Man and Derrida continued to bow and scrape at each other—indeed, they became staunch allies—and after de Man's death, Derrida not only eulogized him but spun posthumous praise into yet another of his innumerable books, *Mémoires.* Amid much characteristic Derridian murk, one fairly clear fact stands out in this tribute: America has become the homeland of deconstruction. "It is that historical space which today, in all its dimensions and through all its power plays, reveals itself as being undeniably the most sensitive, receptive, or responsive space of all to the themes and effects of deconstruction." Far more than Derrida, de Man performed the transplant—reason enough for gratitude.

Unusually "text-productive," too, as the de Manians would say, because de Man's annexation of Derrida made deconstruction a perfect property for annexation by the American academy. In the decade after *Blindness and Insight,* de Man wrought a number of changes on the method, many of them with the effect, for his followers, of taming that possibly dangerous beast into a cuddly academic housepet. De Man domesticated deconstruction, importing it from metaphysics into literature and understanding literature in a thoroughly traditional, canonical way. Derrida rampaged around, spawning unreadable texts like *Glas* and in general behaving like an unusually cerebral performance artist. De Man lingered among the professors, sharpening his tools on familiar classics like Proust and especially Rousseau. Derrida struck sparks off Freud, but de Man kept a cool distance from psychoanalysis—that "Jewish doctrine," as one of his colleagues at *Le Soir* had called it.

De Manian deconstruction also normalized the deconstructor, transforming the activity from a sort of textual terrorism into just a classy version of business as usual on campus. True to the method of **"The Rhetoric of Blindness,"** de Man consistently attributed to literature a profounder self-awareness than any author or critic could hope to possess. Literature, he claimed, has always already deconstructed itself, and the

critic merely demonstrates this truth over and over again. Except for the austerity of his tone and the magnitude of his pretensions, little distinguishes the de Manian deconstructor from the traditional academic lit-critic, explicating the wisdom of the canon as it has been handed down. If deconstruction transcends vulgar politics—all that chatter about *left* and *right*—it does so by leaving the status quo alone and profiting from it when the chance comes along. For American professors leery of rocking the boat—or of being accused, as semioticians used to be, of seeing no difference between *Paradise Lost* and a Budweiser label—de Man's deconstruction offered the tempting prospect of avant-gardism without risk. (pp. 7-8)

Professionalism, self-importance, arcane wisdom, with a heavy douche of *lachrymae rerum,* all safely ensconced within an inviolate cannon, an unquestioned system. The combination was irresistible. And it emanated from a figure with considerable seductive power, a prime candidate for cult status. . . .

There's a dizzying discrepancy between the starry language of deconstruction and the mundane, even trivial nature of its practical goals. But that's Academe for you: In the end, for all their obnoxiousness, the deconstructors turn out no different from any other professional coterie.

De Man's work may or may not remain influential; in either case, the teapot tempest will probably amount to nothing more, since the de Manians never attempted to alter the world as they found it, merely to secure well-padded niches for themselves and their protégés. The worst crime they and their guru were guilty of is opportunism, which in America, deconstruction's destined home, hardly counts as a crime at all. (p. 8)

> *Walter Kendrick, "De Man That Got Away: Deconstructors on the Barricades," in VLS, No. 64, April, 1988, pp. 6-8.*

JONATHAN CULLER

Wolfgang Holdheim's response [see excerpt above] to Christopher Norris [see excerpt above] seeks to explain Paul de Man's views on language and meaning as a guilty reaction to his writing for collaborationist newspapers at the beginning of the Nazi occupation of Belgium. The views Holdheim mentions, however—the critique of the assumption that history is a coherent narrative, critique of the author or subject as the determining source of meaning, emphasis on the ambiguities of language and on the rhetorical subversion of existential claims and categories in texts—resemble conclusions reached independently by other thinkers whose historical experience was quite different from de Man's, such as Jacques Derrida, an Algerian Jew, and Roland Barthes, a Frenchman who spent the war undergoing treatment for tuberculosis in a sanatorium.

When one looks at what is distinctive in de Man's theorising, one finds, for instance, an account of the interdependency of blindness and insight: his book *Blindness and Insight* shows that for a range of thinkers from Husserl and Lukacs to Derrida, their best insights depend on assumptions that those insights disprove (and thus on their blindness). But far from excusing his own youthful blindness, de Man's account would rather indict it: in his wartime juvenilia, there is no insight made possible by blindness. One might say that his subsequent discovery of his blindness produced insight, but that is quite different, quite explicitly not the structure he discovers in other critics, where insights are made possible by a blindness that the insights expose.

The wartime writings, mostly book reviews produced by a young man of 21 and 22 with no formal literary training, are a very mixed bag. Highly evaluative, with the callowness of a youth enjoying the role of cultural arbiter, they combine a desire to map European literature, a conviction that one can grasp the inexorable laws of literary history, with diverse critical impulses that make him appear, not surprisingly, a young man experimenting with various *idées reçues.* . . .

However severely one may wish to condemn the act of collaboration itself, one must recognise that the reviews do not adhere to some party line. The most consistent note, as Christopher Norris had seen, is an organicist language: nations find or fail to find their identity; they have a destiny; literature develops according to its own strict evolutionary laws.

De Man ceased writing for *Le Soir* in the fall of 1942, when the Nazis extended censorship to the cultural section of the paper, and abandoned critical writing for a decade. For the remainder of the war he worked in publishing (among other things, he arranged for the publication of a volume of Resistance poetry, *Exercises du Silence,* edited by Georges Lambrichs, that could not be published in France). When he resumed writing about literature, as a graduate student at Harvard, it was to initiate the critique of organicist and narrative figures through which he had sought to master literature for journalistic purposes. Here, then, one can see de Man's work as in part a reaction against the assumptions of his wartime writing. The organicist figures used to describe language and literature are generated by a misreading of romanticism, whose greatest works, he came to argue, provide the instruments for their undoing. 'Pseudo-historical period terms such as "romanticism" or "classicism",' he later wrote, 'are always terms of resistance and nostalgia, at the furthest remove from the materiality of actual history.'

Another distinguishing feature of de Man's writing has been a critique of the aesthetic ideology and his linking of it to violence, as in his essays on Kleist and Schiller. Walter Benjamin called Fascism the introduction of aesthetics into politics, and de Man cites in a late essay, as an example of the most grievous misappropriation of the aesthetic ideology, the comparison, in a novel by Joseph Goebbels, of the Führer to an artist, who shapes the masses as a sculptor shapes stone. De Man's critique of the aesthetic ideology now resonates also as a critique of the fascist tendencies he had known and their deadly adoption of a language of unity, presence, and the elimination of difference.

The discovery of de Man's wartime writings will block an inclination to idealise the man and will prevent him from being cited simply as an authority but it also gives a new dimension to de Man's attempt—from his critiques of Heidegger in the Fifties to his critiques of phenomenality in the Seventies and Eighties—to undo totalising metaphors, myths of immediacy, organic unity, and presence, and combat their fascinations. His later writings offer some of the most powerful tools for combating the ideology with which he had earlier been complicitous.

Jonathan Culler, in a letter to the editor of London

Review of Books, *Vol. 10, No. 8, April 21, 1988, p. 4.*

J. HILLIS MILLER

> The new statement is always hated by the old, and, to those dwelling in the old, comes like an abyss of scepticism. But the eye soon gets wonted to it, for the eye and it are effects of one cause; then its innocency and benefit appear. . . . (Ralph Waldo Emerson, "Circles")

The violence of the reaction in the United States and in Europe to the discovery of Paul de Man's writings of 1941-42 marks a new moment in the collaboration between the university and the mass media. This is so at least in the United States, where literary theory and literary theorists have hardly been of much interest to the newspapers. It is an extremely instructive moment, one worth much sober reflection.

For the most part, so far at least, it has been a question of journalism all the way. It has also been a question of reading, a question of how one reads what de Man wrote both early and late, a question of what would constitute an accurate and adequate reading of the facts in the case. These facts are almost all written documents. The wartime writings of Paul de Man were published in a student journal, *Les Cahiers du libre examen,* and in two Belgian newspapers, *Het Vlaamsche Land* and *Le Soir.* The outpouring of denunciations of de Man and of so-called "deconstruction" has been, so far, primarily in newspapers. . . . Most, though not all, of these attacks have been written by academics who also write journalism. It is as though these professors had somewhat abruptly discovered the power of the press in this area, just as the young de Man discovered the power of the press in wartime Belgium, long before he began the advanced university study of literature as a Junior Fellow at Harvard in the mid-1950s.

Why was the finding of de Man's wartime writings so "newsworthy"? And why has the reporting of them in the mass media given rise to such extraordinary falsifications, misreadings, distortions and selective slanting of quotations, both of what de Man actually said in those writings and of "deconstruction", the mode of interpretation of philosophy, literature and culture with which he came to be associated thirty years later? And why have the falsehoods and distortions taken just the forms they have taken, with just the same errors being repeated from newspaper to newspaper? One of the most scandalous aspects of the whole affair, at least to an outsider to the way journalism apparently works, is that the same errors, the same quotations out of context, the same false characterizations of "deconstruction", are repeated from newspaper to newspaper in the United States, France, Germany and Great Britain, apparently without any attempt to verify the facts or to read de Man's writings, early or late. One would have thought that in a case of such gravity a little checking of facts and re-reading of the evidence would have been in order, especially on the part of those journalists who are also professors, professionally committed to a sober truth-telling. Liberal newspapers and conservative newspapers have rushed to condemn what they see as a common enemy and they have said almost the same things—the *Nation,* on the one hand, and *Newsweek* and the *Frankfurter Allgemeine Zeitung,* on the other?

No doubt the reasons for this are multiple. They include a suspicion of any new and difficult mode of thought, especially (in the United States) when imported from the Continent; a general hostility to critical theory (but that in itself takes some explaining); the fact that at this moment in history there is widespread concern to identify the last remnants of the Nazi regime and to purify ourselves of them, to cut ourselves off from that period of history and to deny that anything like that could happen again. (False analogies of de Man's "case" with those of Waldheim and Heidegger have of course been made.)

But the strongest motivation for the irresponsible errors and insinuations in these newspaper articles is clear enough. The real target is not de Man himself. He is dead, beyond the reach of attack. The real aim is to discredit that form of interpretation called "deconstruction", to obliterate it, as far as possible, from the curriculum, to dissuade students of literature, philosophy and culture from reading de Man's work or that of his associates, to put a stop to the "influence" of "deconstruction". Beyond that . . . the target is literary theory or critical theory generally, for example the so-called "new historicists", or feminist theorists, or students of popular culture, or practitioners of so-called "cultural criticism". The rapid widening of the targets of hostility has been a conspicuous fact.

The argument, implied or overt, goes as follows, in a crescendo of distortions. First error: it is asserted that de Man's wartime writings are facist, collaborationist, antisemitic through and through, and that he was himself a fascist, collaborator, and antisemite. Second error: de Man's later writings, after 1953, when he became a famous professor, theorist and teacher in the United States—at Cornell, Johns Hopkins and Yale—are asserted to be continuous with the early writings, whether by being a disguised autobiographical apology for them or by continuing to affirm in new and more sophisticated forms the same ideas and commitments. Third error: de Man was a "deconstructionist". All deconstruction must be all of a piece. De Man was a Fascist. Now we know what we have suspected all along: Deconstruction is Fascist. Therefore get rid of it.

All these propositions are false. The facts are otherwise. What is most terrifying in this argument is the way it repeats the well-known totalitarian procedures of vilification it pretends to deplore. It repeats the crime it would condemn.

I have said the facts are far otherwise. Let me try to state them as succinctly and exactly as possible, with a strong recommendation to all who read this and who interest themselves in the questions to read all of de Man's wartime writings . . . , to read de Man's later writings too and those of other "deconstructionists"—and then judge for yourselves. In this matter as in all such matters, there is no substitute for hard reading and for making up one's own mind. This is not a matter where you would want to let the newspapers do your reading and thinking for you.

First fact: de Man was by no means in these early writings totally fascist, antisemitic and collaborationist. The facts are much more complex. (p. 676)

Paul de Man wrote some 169 articles for *Le Soir* from December 1940 to November 1942, when he was twenty-one and twenty-two years old. . . . There is one inexcusable and unforgettable article, *"The Jews in Contemporary Literature,"* (*Le Soir*, March 4, 1941) written for a special antisemitic section of *Le Soir*, and there is one sentence echoing antisemitic rhetoric in one of the essays in Flemish (*Het Vlaam-*

sche Land, August 20, 1942). The essay in *Le Soir* uses the language of antisemitism to argue that the Jews have not corrupted modern European literature, but that European literature has remained fundamentally healthy. European literature, the essay argues, would hardly be weakened at all if all European Jews were put in a separate colony. This is an appalling idea, in itself and in view of what happened so soon thereafter, and it is an appalling untruth, but it must be recognized that this is not the same thing as saying that the Jews are a pollution to Western culture. This latter idea *is* expressed in the articles by other authors published adjacent to de Man's, and this idea is explicitly condemned by de Man as "vulgar antisemitism". "The reality", he says, is "different."

This is an example of a leitmotif of all de Man's essays for *Le Soir*, namely a putting in question of received ideas and opinions. Moreover, the same essay, strangely, mentions Kafka along with Hemingway and Lawrence as three great and exemplary modern authors. Other essays (in *Le Soir*, May 27, 1941, in *Het Vlaamsche Land*, May 17-18, 1942; and July 26-27, 1942) praise Proust as a major writer. Did de Man not know Kafka was a Jew, or could the mention of Kafka here be an example of the kind of double-talk one learns to practise under a totalitarian regime? In an essay written at the end of his life de Man, in one of the two references to Leo Strauss in his writings, praises Strauss for having understood "double-talk, the necessary obliqueness of any persecuted speech that cannot, at risk of survival, openly say what it means to say" (***The Resistance to Theory***). To suggest that this may explain the oddness of de Man's essay on the Jews in no way exonerates him from responsibility for whatever support his essay may have given to the then developing German policy that led seventeen months later to the first deportations of Jews from Belgium to the death camps. But it is important to note that the essay itself is by no means straight partyline antisemitism such as is represented in the attacks on Freud and Picasso in adjacent articles in the same issue of *Le Soir*.

Moreover, it is also important to put the now notorious article on the Jews in Western literature in the context of the other 168 articles in *Le Soir* and to recognize that antisemitism does not recur in them, nor does de Man, as has been asserted in the newspaper accounts, by any means consistently praise collaborationist authors or collaborationist ideas. One article on Charles Péguy, for example, (*Le Soir*, June 5, 1941), praises Péguy's support for the cause of Dreyfus. An antisemite would not have so unequivocally praised a Dreyfusard. Another article attacks with more than a little insolence as ignorant and mistaken a political book by the collaborationist writer Montherlant (*Le Soir*, November 11, 1941). Just because Montherlant is a polished writer, says de Man, does not mean he knows anything about politics or history. In fact, says de Man, his book is very bad. In another much later article (*Le Soir*, September 1, 1942), written after the deportations of Jews from Belgium had begun, de Man's discussion of a poem by Hubert Dubois called "Le Massacre des Innocents" seems a clear outcry against those deportations as evidence of "the guilt that has led humanity to the frightful state in which it finds itself at this moment".

These early writings must also be put in the context of the testimony of three people who knew de Man at the time, a colleague at *Les Cahiers du libre examen*, Charles Dosogne; a man linked to the Belgian resistance, Georges Goriély; and another man associated with the Resistance, George Lambrichs, later editor of *La Nouvelle nouvelle revue française*. All testify that Paul de Man was not antisemitic, that he was "anything but a collaborator", that he was neither fascist nor pro-Nazi. In the absence of personal testimony on the other side, from those who knew de Man in Belgium during the war, the assertions of these witnesses should carry much weight. I might add here my own testimony that in all the years I knew de Man (from 1966 until his death in 1983) I never heard him utter a single antisemitic word. The evidence suggests that he stupidly wrote the deplorable essay in order to please his employers and keep his job, putting in as much "double-talk" as he dared. . . .

Nevertheless, what *is* a crucial fact about the articles for *Le Soir* and *Het Vlaamsche Land*, taken as a whole, and with all proper recognition of their truly heterogeneous character, is the way they allow an understanding of the implicit connection between the article on the Jews and certain nationalist ideas about literature which are present there and which recur in many of the essays that are in no way antisemitic or even explicitly political, just book reviews or concert notes. These are ideas about the specificity of national character and of the literature of each nation, ideas about the power of literature to express directly transcendent truth, and, beyond that, certain ideas about the individual organic development of the literature of each country according to intrinsic laws of its own. The article on **"The Jews in Contemporary Literature"** depends on the absurd and extremely dangerous notion that there is a specific national and racial character in French literature, a different one in German literature, and that the Jews have yet another specific identity. These ideas about the specificity of the German, French, Spanish, Flemish, Walloon and Dutch national characters recur in essay after essay in which there is nothing at all anti-Semitic or even explicitly political, for example in reviews that praise now-forgotten Belgian novelists or composers for having roots in Belgian folklore or folk music and in the constant concern for the differences in culture between French-speaking and Flemish-speaking Belgium. (De Man himself came from a Flemish-speaking family.) . . .

[The] connection between all de Man's later work and his early wartime writings—for there is a connection, though it is not at all the one the journalists have attempted to find—can best be defined by saying that the special and most urgent targets of all his later work are just those ideas about national character, the independent and organic evolution of each national literature, and so on, that are presupposed in his writings for *Le Soir, Het Vlaamsche Land,* and even in what he wrote for *Les Cahiers du libre examen*. De Man later called this whole cluster of ideas "aesthetic ideology". It was the main object of his systematic attack in essay after essay of his writings after 1953, especially but by no means exclusively in the essays of his last years, for example in an important and as yet unpublished seminar on "Kant and Schiller" (1983). But already in 1955, for example, in an essay published in *Monde Nouveau* entitled **"Tentation de la permanence"**, de Man sharply criticizes the Heidegger of the later essays on Hölderlin for being tempted by the lure of an ahistorical permanence attained through poetic language.

What is significant and instructive about the presence of this "aesthetic ideology" in de Man's early writings is the confirmation it gives to one of his basic later insights about literature, namely his recognition of the potentially disastrous political implications of apparently innocuous and purely "aes-thetic" mistakes in assumptions about the nature of literature and of literary history. This may help to explain the urgency with which he always contested those ideas—in his writing, in his teaching and in his interventions in discussions of papers presented at conferences and symposia. The reading of the early writings *will* help to clarify the importance and the political import of de Man's writings after 1953.

As my account of his early writings has, I hope, made absolutely clear, the phrase "innocency and benefit" in my epigraph from Emerson is by no means meant to apply to de Man's early writings. Both the phrase and the whole citation from Emerson do describe, however, the indispensable usefulness of his later writings and of the work of "deconstruction" generally. For "aesthetic ideology" and the nationalism associated with it have by no means disappeared. They are extremely widespread and powerful in Europe and America today, for example in the xenophobia in the United States that resists literary theory because it is a foreign import. What de Man called "aesthetic ideology" forms an important part of the contemporary tissue of received opinion about literature, national identity and culture, both in the mass media and in the university. It was what I was taught at college and university, and it is what we are all likely to say or think on these topics if we are not vigilant. Which of us can say he or she is free of it? And yet de Man's work and his historical placement shows it is both false and can lead to hideous political and historical consequences.

What I have said about de Man's later work can also be said of "deconstruction" generally. Like his work, "deconstruction" is not one single thing. It is diverse and heterogeneous, with many active aspects, facets and functions, for example in religious studies, in architecture and in legal theory, as well as in philosophical and literary studies. Of "deconstruction" generally the same thing can be said that de Man said of his own work in the "Preface" to the posthumously published *The Rhetoric of Romanticism* (1984): it does not "evolve in a manner that easily allows for dialectical progression or, ultimately, for historical totalization". Nevertheless it can be said of "deconstruction", first, that the negative clichés that have been repeated over and over about it are false. "Deconstruction" is not nihilistic, nor anti-historical, nor mere play of language in the void, nor does it view literature or language generally as free play of language, nor is it committed to the notion that readers and critics are free to make texts mean anything they like. "Deconstruction", in all its diversity, *is* a certain kind of "critique of ideology", namely a kind that presupposes, as de Man put it in the interview with Rosso [in *The Resistance to Theory*], that "one could approach the problems of ideology and by extension the problems of politics only on the basis of critical-linguistic analysis, which had to be done in its own terms, in the medium of language." This approach goes by way of identifying the linguistic constructions that are the basis of ideologies. Ideology is defined by de Man as "the confusion of linguistic with natural reality." Of special importance are those linguistic constructions that depend on thinking in terms of oppositions, literal versus metaphorical language, man against woman, inside against outside, and so on. An example would be the way the nationalism that is so important a part of "aesthetic ideology" leads to defining one group in opposition to another. This can lead, as in the case of Nazi Germany, to the horror of the slaughter of the Jews in the attempt to create an Aryan nation purified of all "polluting" elements.

Far from being without an interest in history or being without political import, "deconstruction", as de Man said in a crucial late essay, **"The Resistance to Theory"**, is

> more than any other mode of inquiry, including economics . . . a powerful and indispensable tool in the unmasking of ideological aberrations, as well as a determining factor in accounting for their occurrence. Those who reproach literary theory for being oblivious to social and historical (that is to say ideological) reality are merely stating their fear at having their own ideological mystifications exposed by the tool the are trying to discredit.

It is fear of this power in "deconstruction" and in contemporary critical theory as a whole, in all its diversity, that accounts better than any other explanation for the unreasoning hostility, the abandoning of the canons of journalistic and academic responsibility, in the recent attacks on de Man, on "deconstruction" and on theory generally. (p. 685)

> *J. Hillis Miller, in an analysis of the de Man controversy in* The Times Literary Supplement, *No. 4446, June 17-23, 1988, pp. 676, 685.*

PATRICK PARRINDER

The real issue in this affair is no longer the early Paul de Man's collaboration with Nazism. It is, rather, the amount of disingenuousness in de Man's latest work (especially *The Resistance to Theory*) and in the outpourings of his current defenders. Who would have thought that the bold, bad deconstructionist Hillis Miller [see excerpt above] would so comprehensively fall back on the liberal-humanist arguments he has spent the past two decades trying to discredit? So we have the Distinguished Professor and *TLS* contributor whingeing at length about "academics who also write journalism" and the "collaboration between the university and the mass media". Miller finds that he doesn't like the "falsifications", "misreadings", "distortions", "selective slanting of quotations", "errors" and "false characterizations" perpetrated in newspaper articles about deconstruction. Has he forgotten that the customary oppositions of truth and error, of referentiality and nonreferentiality, of interpretation and misinterpretation and of fact and fiction have been constantly "called into question" (and as often as not declared illusory) in his own writings and those of his admirers? Proceeding to a bullying and simplistic lecture about "the facts" and the "need for hard evidence", Miller's rhetoric succeeds only in betraying his cause and insulting his readers' intelligence. . . .

De Man once said in a lecture that irony has its roots in the "covering up of the scandalous". Both Miller and Geoffrey Hartman have testified that he never made an antisemitic remark in their presence, as if this were "hard evidence" in his favour. But de Man was the dodger with something to hide, and they didn't notice.

> *Patrick Parrinder, in a letter to the editor of* The Times Literary Supplement, *No. 4447, June 24-30, 1988, p. 705.*

MARK EDMUNDSON

News of the Paul de Man scandal first reached me in London [in December, 1987] in a letter from a friend and competitor—every assistant professor of English being in a professional race with every other—who teaches at a small college in Pennsylvania and who frequently publishes literary journalism. The envelope contained a clipping from the *New York Times* [see excerpt above] and a note congratulating me on being a graduate of the newly renamed Albert Speer University, which would soon be offering degrees in anti-Semitic studies. Or so my friend interpreted the news that de Man—who'd been a teacher of mine in grad school at Yale and was, until his death in 1983, the major proponent in America of literary deconstruction—had written essays for a pro-Nazi newspaper in Belgium during the war.

No deconstructor myself, I have for some time sustained an admiring interest in de Man and other practitioners of the art, to the extent of conveying their techniques to students in my yearly seminar in literary theory at the University of Virginia. (p. 67)

My fairly slim association with the deconstructive menace brought two more copies of the *Times* article through the mail slot in the next week, as well as one overwrought letter on the subject. Another friend, a full-time literary journalist, suggested that the gang of neoconservatives at the *Times's* culture desk were probably whetting their blades. He didn't seem at all averse to watching another installment of the press's ritual abuse of literary theory. The feud between the academic critics and the journalists was about to flare up again. As it turns out, the debate over de Man's war record reveals some surprisingly large issues at stake in this feud, which is in fact a struggle for cultural authority.

My own initial reaction was confused. Nobody who has been subjected to a graduate education at Yale—where one of the chief lessons involves one's own spectacular nullity in comparison with the faculty, the undergrads, the departmental secretaries—can easily be made defensive about the place, or about the reputations of the chaired few, who draw large salaries and found modes of discourse. Yet in a few days' time I developed a (to me) persuasive story about how deconstruction actually demystifies totalitarian ideologies and how, arguably, de Man had devoted his intellectual life to redeeming . . . etc., etc. Press the button and you heard it.

Hitting the comparable button among the deconstructive elite, de Man's former colleagues and friends, brought forth some peculiar sounds indeed, and frequently no relevant noise at all. Although de Man's academic adversaries, some of whom preserve the clarity of their judgments on deconstructive theory by not bothering to read any of it, were quick to denounce him in the press, his allies seemed inclined to draw in the wagons and hold out. Some of the deconstructors would not speak publicly on the subject, at least until they'd taken it up in academic conferences and come to some consensus. It was eventually revealed that, at a conference held in Alabama in October [1987], Derrida and about twenty prominent deconstructors had reflected on the significance and potential repercussions of de Man's early articles without going public about their existence. In other words, a handful of distinguished scholars dedicated to promulgating "unsettling" and "subversive" truths had held on tightly to a rather important one; "damage control" was how one detractor characterized it. Some former associates of de Man did speak forthrightly to the press. One observed, "We are discussing the butchery of the Belgian Jewish community, down to the babies. To treat this as one more item about which to have a symposium is outrageous." Yet, surprisingly, this professor refused to be quoted by name. But perhaps the most peculiar response has come from the *Oxford Literary Review*. The *Review* is willing to reprint de Man's controversial articles . . . , but only in French—despite the fact that one of the *Review's* principal functions has been to make the work of French literary theorists available in translation.

The spectacle of persons who are put in a secure position in life so that they can speak their minds without fear of reprisal, who are supposed to keep the culture honest, going mute when they have what they presumably want most—the public's ear—is a dispiriting one. Writers associated with deconstruction did, in time, offer judicious accounts of the situation, but during the first weeks of the controversy the deconstructors seemed mainly to be taking the Fifth. Deconstructors did have some fairly difficult explaining ahead of them. But they were also silent because they were determined to avoid having their thoughts mediated by the cultural journalists. Given the way the critical establishment at the *New York Times, Newsweek,* and the *Washington Post,* among others, seems to feel about advanced literary theory, anyone from the deconstructors' camp who speaks to the press is likely to be portrayed as the collaborator's collaborator.

Evidence of journalistic hostility to literary theory isn't hard to find. One of the unspoken fears of everyone who gives a paper at the Modern Language Association Convention is that he or she will be one of the ones singled out for extended ridicule by a reporter on assignment from the *Nation* or the *New Republic*. Of course, one may be asking for it by participating in a panel discussion entitled "What Is a (Wo)Man Critic and What Does (S)He Want?" Still, the press's compulsion to print what is substantially the same debunking article every year suggests that editors may be administering more to their own anxieties than to the needs of their readers. (pp. 67-8)

Proponents of literary theory feared a fresh round of this sort of obloquy with the advent of the de Man scandal, and it quickly came. The first blow arrived from David Lehman of *Newsweek* [see excerpt above], in a piece entitled "Deconstructing de Man's Life." Lehman's article misconstrues deconstruction and misconstrues de Man, but the major injustice is one that owes to both Lehman and his editors. A photograph of de Man in the midst of the piece (not a wartime portrait, but the one on the jacket of *Allegories of Reading,* his 1979 book) is followed at the end by one, identical in size, of marching storm troopers beneath the caption "Anti-intellectuals: Nazis on the march." The graphic presentation of Lehman's story makes the claim that he himself never quite makes—for it is a claim that no one, no matter how free he might be with his interpretations, could justify—that de Manian literary theory, when submitted to a *Newsweek*-style "deconstruction," reveals itself as a fascist ideology.

But the journalists, for their part, have not been unprovoked. Literary theorists have taken few, if any, pains to make their work accessible to the educated public. There's little contemporary equivalent of the kind of pamphleteering that Freud or Marx, for example, did. Deconstructors seem to be unwilling, for the most part, to give up their exalted notions of their work, their sense that it is sublimely difficult, far beyond the general scope. (A strange idea, this one, considering that the people who the theorists seem to feel are irremediably ignorant were, in many cases, their students only a few years ago.) If there's a presiding taboo in academic writing today, it's against expressing oneself in accessible language. This reti-

cence, naturally, is good for business; the aura of miracle and mystery draws students to graduate school and gives professors some added social panache.

But not all of the invective and the perplexing rhetoric that has come out in the de Man affair derives from misunderstanding and malice, though neither is in short supply. There is actually a genuine conflict here, one that involves the social authority and power of the professors and the journalists. Journalists are in the process of consolidating and defending some recently won positions within the culture. The English professors, particularly the theorists, are driving to change their traditional roles, seeking a more radical, adversarial stance in society, something on the order of what French intellectuals have achieved. These simultaneous power plays have put the groups into rather direct conflict.

To understand the full dimension of this conflict, one has to back up somewhat, to the Fifties and Sixties. Most of the journalists influential today were themselves English majors in college, where they were educated according to the prevailing doctrines of the New Criticism. The journalists, by and large, still adhere to these teachings; many of today's English professors, on the other hand, are now engaged in deconstructing the beliefs and values that the New Critics taught.

The New Critics saw literary works as unified, autonomous, and coherent structures. The successful poem, to a New Critic like Cleanth Brooks, makes use of metaphor and irony to create a variety of connotations, but these connotations are always, in the last analysis, compatible with one another. Authentic poems exist as totalities, as "well-wrought urns" in Brooks's famous phrase. The poet exerts a shaping power over language, and this is possible because in the realm of art one can be completely free—from the quirks of one's own personality, from history, and from the pressures of everyday language. (pp. 68-9)

The well-wrought student of the New Critics would have a developed sense of his own individuality and autonomy, but would also be able to tolerate a certain amount of ambiguity in life, for great poets were connoisseurs of ambiguity, so long as it did not disturb the stability of the poem's overall meaning. By the examples of New Critical saints such as Donne, Dryden, Pope, and T. S. Eliot, the young students educated by Brooks and Co. were to become more self-reliant, autonomous, ironic, and—this term was perhaps the crucial one—"mature." (p. 69)

Modestly but earnestly, the New Critics took on the task of imparting moral education to America's best and brightest, which included the generation of English professors who took over from the New Critics, as well as many of today's most influential journalists.

The journalists for the most part have kept alive these values, which contribute to the assumptions underlying our political and cultural journalism. When a writer in the *New York Times Book Review* discusses, say, Saul Bellow, one of our standing literary institutions, he assumes that Bellow is an autonomous shaper of words, someone who masters language and the form of the novel, whose grand descriptions of Chicago and environs are triumphs of mirroring representation. Bellow gets it right because he's a genius, operating in the perfectly free space of art. And this art is potentially redemptive: it has the power to transform the reader and to some degree the world. Of course, the cultural critic's Bellow is doing on the Olympian scale exactly what the political reporters at the paper aspire to be doing themselves: using language masterfully to get at the truth, seeing things as they are, writing to influence the world for the better.

Such grand and energizing assumptions about language and the self have been, for at least the past fifteen years, under attack by the younger generation of English professors, influenced by writers like de Man and Derrida. This generation—for whom Vietnam and Watergate were decisive cultural experiences—no longer feels or for that matter wants the kind of continuous relationship to American culture that the New Critics developed. (pp. 69-70)

The deconstructors' target is the hubris of those "authors" and "authorities" who think that they can exert complete control over language and, by extension, over experience. . . . For the deconstructors, an excessive faith in the powers of the reasoning mind has become the prevailing superstition. Behind their subversive brand of criticism lies a strong suspicion of authority, and of every person and institution that pretends to offer the Truth in its ultimate form. (p. 70)

The coverage of the Vietnam War and Watergate conferred an unprecedented authority upon the journalists: having shown the government to be consistently mendacious, the press was able to present itself to the American public as the most reliable source of truth. It could thus finally lay claim to a status it had sought for some time, that of being an independent institution that stood above factions and saw things with genuine detachment. In other countries, and previously in America, the press had been unapologetically sectarian. Now, for the first time, the American press could present itself as a disinterested authority and could persuade a large segment of the public to accept its claim.

But it is precisely this sort of "disinterested authority" that the deconstructors, with their sense of the indeterminacy of every utterance, are out to challenge. Their methods attack the implicit claims to objectivity—embodied in the daily papers' omniscient third-person voice—that the press relies on to sustain its authority and prestige. In the *Times* article that broke the de Man story, for instance, deconstruction is described as a way of thinking that "views language as a slippery and inherently false medium that always reflects the biases of its users." If this passage is inconsistent with the subtle complexity of de Man's and Derrida's work, it is still not altogether inaccurate. For deconstruction constitutes a strong polemic against the possibility of a neutral or transparent language that gives perfect access to the world. Walter Cronkite's sign-off, "And that's the way it is," flaunted precisely the sort of hubris that deconstruction was conceived to combat. And surely the *Times* would have something to fear for its own future if the deconstructive view of language was broadly shared. For the language of the newspaper lays claim to a truth that is nearly transcendental and studiously hides its biases.

Even so, it often seems that the press is overreacting to the literary theorists. Is it possible that an obscure anti-philosophy of language espoused by an academic clerisy of modest size could unsettle lordly institutions like *Newsweek* and the *New York Times?* . . . For deconstruction does raise or endorse a number of unsettling possibilities about the press: that the requirements of comprehensiveness, finality, and assurance in the genre of newswriting determine the shape of the story more than the "facts" do (that is, journalists are in a sense "written by" their conventions); that the taboo against irony in reporting prevents journalists from acknowledging the boundaries of their knowledge and perceptions; that journalistic authority is based on generally shared but rather vulnerable myths about the power to achieve disinterest; that the press in fact has interests that tend to align it with the establishment it is supposed to be challenging; that journalists are makers of myth and not the authors of the first draft of a universal history. Such implications, naturally, contribute to the press's overarching fear that its recently won power may be disproportionate to its abilities and achievements, and that its current prestige derives from nothing so much as being the only contender left standing after its competitors for authority—the government, religion, and the professional communities—have fallen as a result of self-inflicted wounds.

The press, on the other hand, represents a major challenge to the deconstructors. Journalists can lay claim to real achievements over the past two or three decades in curbing arbitrary executive power. These achievements were won using old-fashionedly humanistic standards of writing and reporting, in full conformity with the values of New Criticism. "Advanced" literary critics, with their "radical" strategies of reading, can point to no comparable victories. . . . Young deconstructive critics like to think of themselves as embattled subversives, yet they have garnered a reputation for being the slickest, most ambitious people in the field. And the cultural press has taken no little delight in pointing out the rather congenial relationships that frequently obtain between the iconoclastic deconstructors and the traditional, elite schools in which they tend to thrive.

But perhaps the fear that buzzes most closely around every literary theorist is that he or she is a sort of self-deluding druid, absurdly deploying sequences of magic words that are both unilluminating and ineffectual. It's this fear that the journalists at their most aggressive can awaken. Thus the taboo among English professors against writing plainly, sounding like a journalist, and so proving that all the arcane terminology is superfluous. But the inhibitions are mutually enforced: a young *Times* writer who uses the term "logocentrism" without first applying a few swift rhetorical kicks to it is taking a step on the professional road back to the *El Paso Star.*

The winners in all this, I suppose, are those standing powers that find inertia to be in their best interests, because a fusion of journalistic urgency and acumen with academic speculation could probably still produce a potent cultural criticism. (pp. 70-1)

Mark Edmundson, "A Will to Cultural Power: Deconstructing the de Man Scandal," in Harper's, *Vol. 277, No. 1658, July, 1988, pp. 67-71.*

JONATHAN CULLER

The discovery that Paul de Man, who was a professor of comparative literature at Yale University and one of America's foremost literary critics, had in 1941-42 written for a collaborationist newspaper in Nazi-occupied Belgium has led to articles in the press that grossly misrepresent his activities. Their innuendoes have cast a shadow over his later work, as if the criticism de Man wrote in America from 1953 to his death in 1983 was somehow tainted. It is important to set the record straight. . . .

The *Le Soir* articles are the work of a young man enjoying his role as cultural arbiter: full of callow judgments about national traditions and the directions literature is taking. Those that touch on political matters show optimism, particularly in 1941, about the future of Europe in the new order established by what then seemed like a German victory, an interest in what "these revolutionary times" will bring to Europe. They occasionally praise the energy of the German "renewal" and the tradition of German culture, but not Hitler, not the Nazi party, not the German government or its policies. However dismaying their sentiments in the light of what later occurred, the articles are not pro-Nazi.

Many people in Belgium collaborated in some way, from editors of newspapers to the printers who produced them, from railway executives to the engineers and brakemen. After the war, Belgian commissions seeking out serious cases condemned many people—a higher percentage of the population than in any other country. In May 1945 de Man was interrogated by the *Auditeur general,* the military prosecutor's office, but not charged, although 24 of the editors and staff members of *Le Soir* were charged and tried. In general, the courts judged collaboration to be much less culpable if it had ceased, as de Man's had, by the end of 1942.

Was de Man's wartime writing anti-Semitic, as stories have claimed? There is one dismaying column. **"The Jews in Contemporary Literature,"** written in March 1941 for a special anti-Semitic section of *Le Soir.* In it, de Man adopted anti-Semitic language to argue that European literature had not been corrupted by the Jews but remained fundamentally healthy. The other articles for *Le Soir,* though written in a context that would have encouraged anti-Semitism, bear no traces of such views. . . .

Jewish friends of de Man who knew him in Belgium during the occupation suggest that the anti-Semitic column was an aberration, that the young man stupidly consented to write it to please his employers. Whatever the explanation, the article is deplorable. But it scarcely provides grounds for blanket condemnation of de Man's life and works.

Regardless of how severely one may judge his collaborationist journalism, one must recognize that it was not fascist propaganda. It also bears little resemblance either to the criticism focused on literary imagery that he developed in the 1950's, when he began to write about literature again, or to the style of analysis he developed in the 1970's when in contact with the French philosopher Jacques Derrida.

The literary criticism and theory that de Man produced in America must be debated and judged on its own merits. The discovery of his wartime juvenilia does, however, add a new dimension to his later writings. Walter Benjamin, a Jewish theoretician who did not escape the Nazis, called fascism the introduction of aesthetics into politics. De Man's critique in his later work of what he called "the aesthetic ideology" now resonates also, in the light of his early writings, as a critique of ideas and underlying fascism and their deadly quest for unity and the elimination of difference. Indeed, "deconstruction"—the term invented by Derrida in the 1960's to describe analysis showing that the major structures by which we organize our thoughts are *constructions,* not natural and inevitable—is especially relevant here. What makes Nazism the worst excess of Western civilization is the fact that it took to

an appalling extreme the process of constituting a group by opposing it to something else and attempting to exterminate what it falsely defined as a corrupting element. Nazism sought to construct a "pure" Aryan German nation by setting up Jews as its opposite and then slaughtering them. Never has there been so clear a case of how horrendously a culturally constructed opposition can function. Deconstruction seeks to undo (to deconstruct) oppositions that in the name of unity, purity, order, and hierarchy try to eliminate difference.

The anti-Semitic article and de Man's cooperation with the Nazi occupation are to be condemned. For literary studies, however, the important issue is the value of his subsequent critical work.

> *Jonathan Culler, "It's Time to Set the Record Straight About Paul de Man and His Wartime Articles for a Pro-Fascist Newspaper," in* The Chronicle of Higher Education, *Vol. XXXIV, No. 44, July 13, 1988, p. B1.*

STANLEY CORNGOLD

At least one contributor to the discussion of Paul de Man's wartime journalism—J. Hillis Miller—has tried to mitigate the degree of de Man's collaboration in order to separate his early from his later work [see excerpt above]. Other pieces critical of this separation have not yet attempted to show the kinds of continuity that may exist between the propaganda and the mature criticism.

Readers should consider from the start the marked degree of ideological commitment in many of the early essays. . . . In an article identified by Geoffrey Hartman [see excerpt above], de Man describes the "emancipation of a [German] people called upon to exercise, in its turn, a hegemony in Europe". Here, says Hartman, we see de Man moving "closer to being explicitly collaborationist." This could prompt one to ask what it would take to occupy an "explicitly" collaborationist position. . . .

De Man recommends an informed reading of Nazi political tracts to counterbalance French and English propaganda; discusses the "dignity, justice, and humanity" of the Nazi attitude towards France after its capitulation. (*Le Soir,* April 12-14, 1941), finds "a very beautiful and original poetry" flourishing "in the fascist climate" in Italy, in accord with the wishes of Mussolini (February 11, 1941, and February 18, 1941); and identifies the German soul with the "Hitlerian"; lest there be any doubt on this point:

> Germany is a *Volk* [*peuple*] . . . heavy with a host of aspirations, values, and claims coming to it from an ancestral culture and civilization. The War will only bring about a tighter union of these two things—the Hitlerian soul and the German soul which, from the start, were so close together—until they have been made one single and unique power. This is an important phenomenon, because it means that one cannot judge the fact of Hitler without judging at the same time the fact of Germany and that the future of Europe can be envisioned only in the frame of the needs and possibilities of the German spirit. . . .

For this "cause . . . an entire *Volk* [*peuple*] is sacrificing itself" (*Le Soir,* April 20, 1942). Preoccupations of such intensity are unlikely to be without lasting effect on de Man's later writings.

The late work is marked by a recurrent and major tone of arbitrary violence. De Man's essay on Rousseau's *Confessions* in *Allegories of Reading* (his wildest essay, and now we may be able to understand why) declares: "Writing always includes the moment of dispossession in favour of the arbitrary power play of the signifier; and from the point of view of the subject, this can only be experienced as a dismemberment, a beheading or a castration." This sentence is so much simply an instance of habit and preoccupation, of a subject-matter and an intellectual procedure, that I believe it represents a fascination or even complicity with violence. The passage on dismemberment, beheading and castration refers to texts of Rousseau, whose literary consciousness was perfect ("Rousseau's text has no blind spots; it accounts at all moments for its own rhetorical mode"). And it is to Rousseau's "curious brand of cunning and violence" that an appropriate criticism must respond. Indeed, wherever texts of a single author are inter-involved, "the power that takes one from one text to the other is not just a power of displacement . . . but . . . sheer blind violence."

Other aspects of this hermeneutic violence are more pointed. "With the threatening loss of control [of meaning], the possibility arises of the entirely gratuitous and irresponsible text, not just . . . as an intentional denial of paternity for the sake of self-protection, but as the radical annihilation of the metaphor of selfhood and of the will." This idea reappears in de Man's studies of Romantic poetry, which emphasize "defaced" and "decomposing" figures of selfhood and of the will. . . .

I stress that the persons whose real decomposition de Man's early hackwork may have helped bring about appear in his later writing as only the masks of a rigorous literary operation—objects of "coercive displacements" that occur, to be sure, only "tropologically." What Nazis and their collaborators once accomplished in fact, literature accomplishes only figuratively. But when "death", as de Man writes, becomes only "a displaced name for a linguistic predicament", it is clear that the textual world has begun to do more than "figure" as the factual world—it has begun actually to replace it. In *Blindness and Insight* de Man wrote, "The bases for historical knowledge are not empirical facts but written texts." But in *The Resistance to Theory*, textual events *are* the essential historical occurrences. "Things happen in the world . . . and they always happen in linguistic terms. . . . To account for them historically, *to account for them in any sense,* a certain initial discrepancy in language has to be examined" (my italics).

Unlike his wartime writing, what de Man went on to write about figures in *Allegories of Reading* did not make it easier for Nazis to torment their victims. And yet de Man consistently taught that the reality of persons is to be found in the "disarticulations" of rhetoric, stressing always the obligatory "dismemberment of the aesthetic whole into the unpredictable play of the literary letter." De Man's later theory submits so-called persons to the coercions of rhetoric with the same effect produced by his literary judgments when they smoothed out the moral obstacles in the way of eliminating Jewish personalities. Early and late, de Man has no stake whatsoever in the survival of persons—figurative or authori-

al. And the analogy is more than figurative when de Man literally displaces figures on to the world of real persons.

What is plain is that in neither case does his rhetoric encourage a grain of resistance to the coercions laid on individuals by the "hegemonic" violence of other peoples or texts. Such are the consequences of his steadfast belief in the need for a superself called "poetic consciousness" or "literary language" or "text" to evolve or "occur" according to its own great laws independent of its effect on the moral relations between persons and the lives of persons.

From this de Man emerges as a strong philosopher of the inhuman condition—a condition in which the important relations are necessarily inhuman. It is no individual poet but "poetic language" that engages "in its highest intent . . . tending toward the fullest possible self-understanding". "Poetic language names this void [of empirical reality] with ever-renewed understanding and . . . never tires of naming it again." Not the writer but "the text imposes its own understanding and shapes the reader's evasions." Not Shelley but *"The Triumph of Life"* warns us that nothing, whether deed, word, thought, or text, ever happens in relation, positive or negative, to anything that precedes, follows, or exists elsewhere, but only as a random event whose power, like the power of death, is due to the randomness of its occurrence." The viewpoint and rhetoric of both examples, meanwhile, are entirely in keeping with de Man's in 1942, when he wrote that "the development [of literary style] does not depend on arbitrary, personal decisions but is connected to forces which perform their relentless operations across the doings of individuals." . . .

When de Man in his late work gives texts the properties of persons who entrap, coerce, kill, disfigure and mutilate readers, he conjures a personality beyond Good and Evil of the type of Nietzsche's New Man as he was received in de Man's youth by George, by D'Annunzio, by Benn. . . . Though literature is supposed to arise from the non-empirical transcendental poetic consciousness (*Blindness and Insight*) and the non-empirical mechanisms of literary language (*Allegories of Reading*), it operates like a type of reckless person or implacable machine. Moreover, its attributes will be recognizable as those of the Nietzschean self of which, in his youth, de Man believed "the Hitlerian soul" and its collaborators to be the avatar.

I believe that de Man's critical work adheres to and reproduces, in literary theoretical masquerade, his experience as a collaborator. His later writings impose images, attitudes and ideas of the systematic and threatening application of excessive violence to persons; and this, not the "aestheticization of politics", defines the totalitarianism to whose empirical realization he once actually contributed.

Stanley Corngold, in a letter to the editor of The Times Literary Supplement, *No. 4456, August 26-September 1, 1988, p. 931.*

CAROL JACOBS

For many Americans who knew Paul de Man and his later writings well, nothing was more unimaginable than that signature closing a column of *Le Soir volé*, and this is because his later writings are an inexorable call to constant vigilance against the false assertion and misuse of authority. It is for this reason that I am so thoroughly puzzled by Stanley Corngold's mode of argumentation [see excerpt above].

Corngold's letter is not a call to reject all of de Man's work on the basis of his wartime writings. It is the far more universal claim that de Man's entire critical project was a continuation of the violent dehumanization begun in the concentration camps.

Corngold's argument about the late works is twofold. On the one hand he speaks of a "superself" of literary language in de Man's work. He seems to imply that this is the totalitarian authority that brings about the emptying or displacement of the empirical self. If one looks to such exemplary later texts of de Man as **"The Rhetoric of Temporality"** or the essay entitled **"Self"** (*Allegories of Reading*), however, we see it is never a scenario of a fixed "superself" of language denying life to an empirical world. In both these essays what takes place is a process which includes a questioning of the empirical as only one moment in a complex performance. Letters to the editor allow the space only for conclusions, not for lengthy readings. I can only note, then, however superficially, that de Man always insists on the self's quest for rigorous understanding, however disappointing it may turn out to be. That self is never annihilated but always renewed at greater if dizzier levels of interpretation. Moreover, de Man explicitly warns the reader against setting the deconstructive critic in the position of valid authority . . . from which the dehumanization Corngold describes would have to take place. He explicitly warns against the critical voice's potential as totalitarian. . . . De Man's work is a perpetual abdication of his own authority but at the same time an inexorable attempt at reflection and understanding.

The other thrust of Corngold's argument about the late work is to prove it "is marked by a recurrent and major tone of arbitrary violence". He attempts this by way of a long list of phrases which speak of a dispossession or violent displacement of "persons" through the agency of language. This is to show "de Man has no stake whatsoever in the survival of persons". Let us follow the logic of this mode of argumentation. If we are to reject those texts in which self-knowledge comes only at the price of a violence to the self, what are we to do with an entire tradition in literature since the myth of Narcissus, where Ovid tells us he came to know himself only on beholding his image and only at the price of death? Or with the myth of Oedipus who acquires self-knowledge only by way of patricide and incest, a self-knowledge that leads to the mutilation of his own eyes?

If the indictment of vicious dehumanization can be made on the basis of such phrases in de Man's texts, is there not an implicit call to exclude as violently fascist other writers in whom such decadent and degenerate tendencies are to be found, in whom there is an insistence, say, on the priority of language or on literary language replacing personal selves and lived lives? If so, we risk indicting much of modern literature where such insistence is quite explicit, at least since Rimbaud.

By the same logic shall we indict Roland Barthes, who writes, "Literature is . . . the very consciousness of the unreality of language: the truest literature is the one that knows itself as the most unreal" and "to write, far from referring to an 'expression' of subjectivity is . . . the very act which converts the indexical symbol into a pure sign"? (*Critical Essays*)

Shall we then censor the works of Walter Benjamin, who speaks (in *Trauerspiel*) of history "assuming the form of irre-

sistible decay" rather than eternal life, who speaks of criticism as erosion and the mortification of the works, as a process which renders the work a ruin, who speaks of significance as analogous to a "stern sultan in the harem of objects", like a "sadist" who "humiliates his object and . . . thereby satisfies it"? Shall we condemn Benjamin for writing that "no poem is intended for the reader, no picture for the beholder" ("The Task of the Translator"), for speaking of Proust's work as an act of forgetting rather than remembering life, as an "emptying the dummy, [Proust's] self . . . in order to keep garnering . . . the image"? . . .

Finally, shall we join Sigmund Freud's early readers and reject his works, as Corngold rejects de Man's, for speaking of castration and beheading?

Such attacks, such reduction of the rich context of these citations and their theoretical import would, of course, be absurdities. They would be the refusal to read, to think, to write. They would be the stuff of which propaganda is made.

> *Carol Jacobs, in letter to the editor of* The Times
> Literary Supplement, *No. 4460, September 23-29,*
> *1988, p. 1047.*

STANLEY CORNGOLD

Carol Jacobs is "puzzled" by my attempt to read Paul de Man's critical work as a continuation of his experience as a collaborator [see excerpt above]. That is not surprising, since she found it "unimaginable" that de Man wrote pro-Hitlerian, pro-fascist and antisemitic columns for *Le Soir*. Yet these facts could direct her to everything in de Man's work that contradicts the humanist's "call" to "life" and "self-renewal".

De Man's critical essays are based on a myth of universal disruption that can certainly have been projected from his experience as a collaborationist writer. The primary catastrophe of the Nazi invasion reappears as the violent origin of language or human society—a "power of death". Literary texts repeatedly "name" the catastrophe and otherwise convey its violence through a relentless, impersonal fragmentation of meaning. The critic collaborates with this ministry of death by repeating the truth of universal disruption. [De Man] encourages readers to abandon all recourse to their empirical experience (vulgarly, their "knowledge of life") for resistance, hope, or understanding, since experience is the merely naive form of ignorance and estrangement.

Pace Jacobs, de Man did not maintain that the profit of suffering is self-knowledge. His essay on Walter Benjamin [in ***The Resistance to Theory***] specifically denigrates the pathos of a self. If the self, according to Jacobs, "is always renewed at greater levels of interpretation", the form of its renewal is fatal. Typically, de Man reads Rousseau's *Pygmalion* as seeking to "undo selfhood as a tragic metaphor and replace it by the knowledge of its figural and epistemologically unreliable structure . . . . From the point of view of truth and falsehood, the self is not a privileged metaphor in Rousseau" (*Allegories of Reading*). Neither is the self a "privileged metaphor" for the tragic acquist of experience in *Oedipus Rex*. . . .

Jacobs wishes to identify de Man's statements about literary language with the impersonal poetics of other modern writers like Barthes, Benjamin, Celan and Freud. She evokes their canonical prestige (as well as their Jewish identity in three cases out of four) in order to rescue her teacher, the author of antisemitic articles, from "exclusion" and "condemnation". This plea to save de Man for future readers is unnecessary; her reasons for doing so, incoherent. I do not disagree when she reads my argument as "not a call to reject all of de Man's work on the basis of his wartime writings"; neither do I make "universal claims" about concentration camps and the poetics of dismemberment. What is at stake is the necessity of imagining the specific continuity of (1) de Man's experience as a collaborator and (2) de Man's work as a critic. Jacobs's *politique de l'autruiche* allows her to shun any knowledge she might have of de Man's empirical historical situation; hence she can conclude that his work should be saved on the strength of its resemblance to the work of other writers worth saving. But de Man's statements on violence and humiliation do not mean the same thing as Benjamin's or Celan's. . . .

Certainly, de Man's critical work makes good sense, once it has been identified as his carapace and portable house. But to continue to teach it while pretending to forget its beginnings in Nazi collaboration is to play out a masquerade—a life that is, then, precisely only a text.

> *Stanley Corngold, in a letter to the editor of* The Times Literary Supplement, *No. 4467, November 11-17, 1988, p. 1251.*

ZEEV STERNHELL

The great de Man debate that recently divided the American academic community has now led to the appearance of two large volumes, useful and well produced. The editors [Werner Hamacher, Neil Hertz, and Thomas Keenan] of Paul de Man's *Wartime Journalism, 1939-43* have gathered together, in facsimile, the whole of his journalistic production as far as it is known. The texts published in *Le Soir,* the great Belgian newspaper that, against the will of its owners, was placed at the service of German propaganda in occupied Belgium, are given in the original. The texts published in the Flemish journal *Het Vlaamsche Land* in 1942, far less numerous, are accompanied by an English translation. Thus the reader may judge, for the first time, from documentary evidence. The companion volume, *Responses on Paul de Man's Wartime Journalism,* brings together some new contributions to the debate, and several of these are excellent. . . .

There are some interesting documents in the companion volume, most notably the letter that Paul de Man wrote to the Society of Fellows at Harvard, to which he had been nominated, in January 1955. As a result of rumors about his past, de Man was forced to give an account, for the first and last time in public, of his activities during the war years. This tearful and undignified text is deserving of a real character study. It is extraordinary, because it is based on a brazen lie.

In order to move the Harvard authorities, who seem to have asked him for the moral equivalent of a sworn declaration, Paul de Man, 36 years old, presented himself as the son of Henri de Man. He claimed that the accusation against him was due to the hostility that the name of his "father"—whom he was careful to present only as a former minister and a political leader with a "controversial" past—still aroused in various Belgian circles. In truth, however, Henri de Man was not Paul de Man's father. He was his uncle and his godfather.

When a man claims another man for a father, he must feel, in some sense, like a son. . . . Paul de Man may indeed have felt a filial affinity for Henri de Man. His wartime journalism was conceived precisely in the spirit of the man he falsely called his father. It is very curious that this blatant lie passed unnoticed. "I am certainly in no position," he concluded in the letter, protesting that he was the innocent victim of slander, "to ask the Society of Fellows for anything but a chance to prove the truth of what I have stated in this letter." That should pose quite a challenge for de Man's unconditional defenders.

The outburst of feeling in American academic circles caused by the discovery of de Man's wartime writings reveals the magnitude of the emotional difficulties that result when the realities of the 1940s are confronted. The case of Paul de Man is important, in the end, because it is an example. De Man is an instructive illustration of a major phenomenon of European history during the interwar period: the rejection of the democratic order by a large part of the intellectual elite. This respected and admired individual, a major thinker and a charismatic scholar of great authority, participated during his youth in a great movement of revolt against the whole of the liberal, individualistic, and humanist political culture based on the theory of natural rights and the principles of the French Revolution. (p. 30)

For the historian, de Man's ideas and actions are interesting precisely for their ingenuousness. The ideas of this young journalist reflected something important: a confrontation between two rival political traditions that fought each other in the French intellectual sphere of influence throughout the period between the two world wars. At the end of the 19th century, a second tradition developed in France, which rebelled against the classical universalistic heritage, against rationalism, humanism, and liberalism. This second tradition, particularistic and organicist, was often characterized by a local variant of the biological and racial nationalism of *volkisch* Germany. Philosophically, it represented a total rejection of the vision of man and society developed from Hobbes to Kant, from the English revolutions of the 17th century to the time of the French Revolution. The attack on the philosophical foundations of liberal democracy extended to an attack on its institutions and structures, too. But liberalism was not all that was denounced: this was a revolt not only against all the "materialistic" foundations of the established order, but also against historical materialism, against the basic postulates of Marxist economics and the intellectual foundations of Marx's thought.

This alternative tradition was undeniably a minority tradition. But minorities also have influence: they pose questions, they raise problems, and they condition, no less than the majority, the intellectual climate of a period. Contrary to the conventional historical wisdom, this alternative tradition was far from being a marginal ideology in the culture of the French-speaking countries in the 20th century. Indeed, its influence on many modes of thought was considerable. It permeated society to a far greater extent than is generally admitted. More important, this minority knew how to await its hour. In France and in Belgium, but particularly in France, its hour came with the collapse in June 1940.

As long as conditions of peace and relative stability prevailed, this alternative tradition could not attempt to remold society. After the defeat in 1940, however, the ideology that had infiltrated society for half a century rose to the surface and assumed control. (pp. 31-2)

That is the context in which Paul de Man must be placed. He belonged to this milieu that had waited for years for the opportunity to overthrow democracy. These men were patriots, to be sure; and some of them sincerely regretted the defeat of their country. I say some, because for many the choice between a Franco-Belgian victory, which would represent the triumph of the detested liberal and bourgeois democracy, and a defeat of their country, which would mean the victory of a superior political culture, based on the primacy of the collectivity, on the sense of duty and sacrifice, on hierarchy and discipline—such a choice was difficult to make. The blitzkrieg of 1940, however, saved them from having to make it. The collapse of the regime was the chance to save a decadent civilization. . . .

This was the background to the intellectual formation of the young Paul de Man. For this extraordinarily talented student, moreover, the background took flesh and blood form in the person of his famous uncle. Derrida, in his painstaking effort to explain de Man's past, insists on the "powerful and no doubt decisive" influence that this "exceptional" figure must have exerted on his young nephew. And indeed, Henri de Man was not just anybody: vice president of the Socialist Party and its president since 1939, he was one of the greatest socialist theorists of the period, and perhaps the most controversial. Only Gramsci and Lukács, among his contemporaries, were intellectually superior to him; but they were, unlike him, Marxists. (p. 32)

More modestly, of course, the student Paul de Man set out on the same path [as his uncle]. The intellectual collaborator placed the written word at the service of the new order in the same way as the volunteer for the Russian front placed his strength and his physical courage. And there can be no doubt that the occupier needed intellectual collaboration no less than military or economic collaboration. Nazi Germany attached considerable importance to ideological warfare, to the indirect mobilization for the war effort.

This is generally not well understood. The propaganda services in Paris and Brussels did not encourage only vulgar collaboration, which called for people to leave for the eastern front, or to denounce acts of resistance, or to inform on Jews in hiding. The men in charge of German propaganda, such as Otto Abetz, Friedrich Grimm, or Karl Epting, had a wonderful knowledge of the mentality of the French-speaking intelligentsia. They grasped that a coarse, low-level anti-Semitism could be counterproductive, that they needed something subtle—something of the kind that one finds, say, in the writings of Henri de Man, who observed, in 1941, in his *Mémoires:*

> Convinced as I have been for a long time of the necessity of eliminating from our political organism the foreign body constituted by all the residues or embryos of the Ghetto, I am equally convinced that the problem of the protection of the race is only soluble in an orderly fashion and by means of international agreement.

At exactly the same time, Paul de Man expressed himself in a similar manner. He, too, protested against the Jewish invasion: "One cannot entertain much hope for the future of our

civilization if it has let itself be invaded without resistance by a foreign force." He, too, thought that the continent should be purged of the "Semitic interference" that was to be found "in all aspects of European life." The "Jewish spirit," according to him, was a virus that threatened European integrity; the deportation of the Jews outside Europe would be a natural and legitimate measure of protection. And Nazi propaganda required no more.

"The Jews in Contemporary Literature" is the only anti-Semitic article by Paul de Man so far known, and it does not really amount to much. The point, however, is that it was just one of a few dozen articles by de Man with which Nazi propaganda could not have failed to be pleased. (pp. 33-4)

The Germans did not demand that one servilely proclaim the cultural superiority of Germany, or of Nazism. It sufficed for them that one support European unity and analyze the reasons for the terrible defeat suffered by the oldest and greatest democracy of the European continent: that is, that one write critically of materialism, individualism, universal suffrage, political liberty, and the principles of 1789. The Germans wanted a credible propaganda. They wanted it known that the defeat of France and Belgium was not the fault of a badly commanded and ill-prepared army, or of an ineffective regime, but of a whole political culture.

This was the message of that enormous literature of the defeat that Paul de Man conscientiously reviewed, week after week, in *Le Soir* in 1941 and 1942 with a great deal of sympathy, often with admiration. These "Chroniques littéraires" were undoubtedly more moderate than many contributions to the collaborationist press, yet all the significant themes of the anti-democratic and anti-liberal revolt of the '30s were sounded in them. All the great names of the intellectual collaboration were praised: Brasillach, Drieu La Rochelle, Marc Augier, Chardonne, Jouhandeau, Alfred Fabre-Luce, Bertrand de Jouvenel, Jacques Bénoist-Méchin. All those who expatiated on the sickness of a civilization corrupted by the humanist tradition were carefully brought, in the columns of this young cultural journalist, to the notice of the educated public. . . .

Thus his readers were exposed, week after week, to all the works that the German propaganda services were trying to put before them. That was de Man's task: to put high culture at the service of a Nazi Europe. The reviewer's choice of writers alone indicated that one more young intellectual had committed himself to the great spiritual, moral, and national revolution that sought to rid Europe of its humanist tradition once and for all.

At the end of November 1942, Paul de Man's last "Chronique littéraire" appeared in *Le Soir,* and in May 1943 he ended his collaboration in *la Bibliographie Dechenne,* in which he had given eulogistic accounts of works by Fabre-Luce, Lucien Rebatet, and Pierre Daye. He retired to his paternal home (his real one) in Antwerp. In Brussels, the atmosphere had become somewhat hostile; de Man had been pilloried by students in the Resistance, who were formerly his friends.

Had his eyes been opened? Had the pressures of German censorship become intolerable, as he claimed? The credibility of Paul de Man, as we have seen, is hardly above suspicion. It is just as logical to suppose, therefore, that he simply understood that the fortunes of the war were changing. Montgomery was victorious at El-Alamein on November 3, 1942. The

German defeat at Stalingrad occurred on February 2, 1943. The brilliant young critic of *Le Soir* can hardly have failed to notice. (p. 34)

Zeev Sternhell, "The Making of a Propagandist," in The New Republic, *Vol. 200, March 6, 1989, pp. 30-4.*

FRANK KERMODE

As academic curricula vitae go, de Man's was certainly unusual, and an account of his publications might seem to make it more so, for his first book, ***Blindness and Insight,*** appeared only in 1971, when he was 51, and even then, it is said, he published only because Yale drew the line at bookless professors. There were to be only two more essay-collections before his death, but now we have two posthumous volumes [***Wartime Journalism, 1939-1943*** and ***Critical Writings, 1953-1978***] and there may be more to come. Considering the ever-increasing density and strangeness of his work, and its ever-increasing fame, it would take a very tough dean to say de Man had under-produced.

The corpus is now augmented by [***Wartime Journalism***], a volume he would not himself have wanted to see. This collection of his wartime writings looks like what it is, a heap of ephemera, ill-printed and hard to read in the photocopies. They testify to the exceptional industry and ability of the young literary journalist—he wrote a long succession of literary chronicles and reviewed large numbers of books in various languages—but it is unlikely that any degree of later eminence would have induced anybody to republish them had not their discovery caused such a tremendous bother. The editors, friends of de Man, decided, probably rightly, that in view of all that had been said and written about them on hearsay it would be as well to make them wholly accessible. (p. 3)

By now these wartime writings have been passionately scanned, especially by Jacques Derrida. Here there is room for only a few observations. First, there is certainly more than one anti-semitic piece. An article in Flemish (20 August 1942) about contemporary German fiction deplores the way some Expressionist writers came into conflict with 'the proper traditions of German art which had always before anything else clung to a deep spiritual sincerity. Small wonder, then, that it was mainly non-Germans, and specifically jews, who went in this direction.' Again, it is surely odd to find in a piece on Péguy (6 May 1941) a short, but not all that short, account of the Dreyfus affair which omits to mention that Dreyfus was a Jew; de Man is seemingly at a loss to understand why the straightforward case of an officer wrongly accused and reinstated by due course of law should have caused such a furor. He admires Péguy, a Dreyfusard, for quarrelling, at the cost of his job, with other liberal-socialist Dreyfusards. Christopher Norris [see excerpt above] remarks that 'any mention of the Dreyfus affair must of course raise the question of anti-semitism,' but fails to add that de Man's mention of it rather pointedly did not; Derrida likewise omits to notice the omission in his *Critical Inquiry* piece, also preferring to emphasise that de Man was here writing admiringly of a Dreyfusard. In fact, the drift of de Man's piece is best expressed in the words *au fond, il ne s'agit pas de grand-chose* [fundamentally, it's not about anything big].

Even if we recall that the affair lasted over a decade, that the

opponents of Dreyfus forged and suppressed evidence, and that the victim spent a long time in prison, it might still be maintained that the level of anti-semitism over all these articles is fairly low. But to confine attention to specific references is misleading, for a survey of the whole collection makes it apparent that anti-semitism was at least not entirely inconsistent with de Man's ideas about the national spirit and the need for cultural development to take place on national (and at any rate in some measure xenophobic) lines. Like his uncle, he was, it appears, ready to believe that the 'revolution' brought on by the *événements* of May 1940 had introduced a new and promising epoch of German hegemony in Europe. Flemish is a Germanic language, and it may have seemed opportune and possibly just, even for a writer of de Man's French formation, to score off France, the dominance of whose language and culture was inveterately resented in Flemish Belgium. Yet there is an obvious difference between the French and the Jews. Given a spell of German discipline, the French might yet pull themselves together: but what hope was there for the Jews with their non-European, 'foreign blood'? At the rather abstract level of discourse preferred by the young de Man, there was not much need to be as specific and insistent as some of his fellow contributors, either about Jews or about the flowering of the German spirit demonstrated in the conquests of 1940. Just as he refrains from further overt reflections on the Semite invasion, he silently declines to comment on the continuing progress of German arms, on the Italian alliance (though one article praises the successes of Italian nationalism), on the Russian campaign, the fighting in the Balkans and Africa, the entry of Japan and America into the war. Perhaps he regarded these matters as outside his cultural brief, though the fall of France had not quite been. Yet the military and political developments of 1941 and 1942 must have been of keen and at times disquieting interest to one who had taken the German victories of 1940 as final. For de Man had at first written, understandably, as if in 1940 the war was over, saying more than once that the difference between the two world wars was that the first was long and the second very brief, so that only in the first did people settle down to observable wartime behaviour. Since the Germans had won so completely, any future was going to be a German future, whether one liked the idea or not. But by the time he stopped writing for *Le Soir* the case was somewhat altered, with the Wehrmacht surrounded at Stalingrad, beaten in Egypt, and facing future battles in the west against forces enormously augmented since the American entry into the war. Meanwhile the Final Solution was well under way.

All these events, perhaps along with an increase of supervisory rigour in the office, may have been his inducement to leave *Le Soir,* but there seems to be no evidence for this except de Man's own remark quoted above. And he is said to have offered on occasion rather unreliable versions of his wartime career—for instance, that he worked in England.

In student articles, written during the phoney war or *drôle de guerre* period, de Man argued that the war had been inevitable, and that after the annexation of Czechoslovakia it could no longer be maintained that Hitler merely wished to correct the injustices of Versailles. As an anti-imperialist, he said, one must choose the less objectionable of two imperialisms—namely, the British. But when the war was won we would have to deal with all the problems left over from the Thirties—unemployment, for example; and that would require a vast reform of European (and imperial) politics generally. May 1940 changed his mind, and a year or so later we find him claiming that the invaders, far from being the barbarians of propaganda and of leaders in the pre-Occupation student paper, are highly civilised. He rejoices at reports that the French are working alongside their victors in a *solidarité purifiante.* Soon he is recommending some German handouts explaining National Socialism, and observing that the Germans have made much more generous armistice terms than the French had allowed at the end of the first war.

He sometimes speaks of the irresistible force of a nation's desire for unity, recommending Belgians to study the Italian example and commenting with severity on the record of the French. . . . Under Hitler, he contends, there flourished a pure literature, very different from recent French writing. The Germans would give the French, at this decisive moment in the history of their civilisation, what they now most needed: order and discipline, and presumably purity also. However, in April 1942 he complains that the French do not appear to be responding satisfactorily to 'the reforms at present in progress'.

Opinions of this sort surface from time to time in pieces of which the ostensible purpose is simply literary criticism, and the contention that in the mass these articles are just neutral accounts of books and concerts, leaving only one or two collaborationist obiter dicta to explain away, is simply absurd. Taken as literary criticism, they seem to offer few hints of the writer's future interests, though in saying so I find myself slightly, and unwillingly, at odds with both Lindsay Waters and Jacques Derrida. Some of de Man's judgments are routine—he thought very highly of Charles Morgan, for instance, as the French did in those days. He speaks well of Valéry, and that does remind us of the links between his later thought and his early interest in Symbolism. But his views on history, if he remembered them later, must have seemed embarrassingly undeManian. So with romanticism: an essay from the hand of the scholar of whom it is commonplace to maintain that he changed everybody's attitude to that subject says that romanticism was pretty feeble in France, but strong in Germany because deep in the German national spirit, indeed *la consécration définitive de la nature nationale* (21-22 November 1942)—a version of literary history which he was later to condemn.

Unlike some commentators, both friendly and hostile, I see nothing very reprehensible about his failure to talk about this body of work (as distinct from parts of the work itself). Generally speaking, few writers, of whatever kind, and even if conceited enough to think anybody else would be interested, would volunteer to bring their juvenilia to judgment, even if they didn't contain opinions later seen to be embarrassing or perverted. However, this writer's subsequent fame—and the continuing row between deconstructive admirers and more conservative academics—ensured that people *were* interested, some hoping to use the wartime pieces to discredit de Man and the movement associated with him, the rest needing to defend themselves and their hero. So the significance of these juvenilia is strenuously debated.

Few would deny that at least some of the wartime writing is odious, that of a clever young man corrupted by ideas, and corrupted by war (for in wartime the intellect grows as sordid as the conflict), or merely opportunist, or a mixture of all these. To work for *Le Soir* and *Het Vlaamsche Land* was manifestly to forego any right of dissent. To appear on that anti-semitic page was, as almost everybody would agree, an act amounting to full collaboration. The repeated triumphing

over the defeated French, having a possible origin in Belgian domestic conflicts, was presumably not done under direct external compulsion. And it is hard to find indications of concealed dissent in this collection, though some have tried to do so. The simplest explanations may be the least damaging in the end: the young man, on his return from attempted flight, found reasons for thinking it intellectually honest as well as expedient to collaborate with the victors. Others, especially in France, did likewise, until, their reasoning invalidated by events, they saw they must cease to do so; and it could be that de Man gave up his job for similar reasons. One wonders whether, had the Germans occupied Britain at the end of 1940, there would have been no clever young people willing to say in collaborationist newspapers (and wouldn't there have been collaborationist newspapers?) that this was at least not altogether a bad thing.

Lindsay Waters's long and interesting introduction to [de Man's] *Critical Writings 1953-78* amounts to an apologetic intellectual biography of de Man. He dwells on the forces—the failures of democracy, the desire for national redemption, the longing for action—which induced intelligent people in the pre-war period to succumb to 'the fascist temptation'. The comparison with Heidegger is here as elsewhere—and doubtless justly—used in de Man's favour. But the main argument is that in his earliest work de Man embraced an 'aesthetic ideology'—its political manifestation is a rather mystical nationalism—of just the kind he was later to attack with such contemptuous subtlety. This implies that the youthful errors were intellectual rather than ethical, though Waters is in no doubt that anti-semitism, a rather more than merely cerebral blunder, was an essential constituent of German nationalism, and he has no way of excusing de Man's endorsement of it. However, he finds in these 'marginal texts' the seeds of much later work: they display de Man's abiding interest in 'inwardness, interiority', so 'there is a fair degree of continuity.'

This connection seems rather tenuous, but Waters goes on to give a convincing account of the later career, from the early Sartrean phase through the decisive encounter at Harvard with American New Criticism, and the revisionary studies of romantic thought, to the decisive 'turn' to rhetoric and the concord with Derrida, which were the features of de Man's last and most influential phase. His rather exotic academic career in America was a genuine European intellectual adventure, typical of what the writer himself, in a letter of 1955, called 'the long and painful soul-searching of those who, like myself, come from the left and from the happy days of the Front Populaire'—which, though it takes us back to a date before there is any substantial record, is plausible enough, as is the highly metaphysical mode of the soul-search.

In support of his argument for continuity, Waters also supplies what many disciples have been demanding: a selection of uncollected essays from the years before the publication of *Blindness and Insight,* with one uncollected late piece at the end. Many of these items are reviews, some long celebrated, like that of Michael Hamburger's Hölderlin translations. Some—on Montaigne, Goethe and Mallarmé—were originally in French. All have that air of quiet, even tolerant authority which, despite occasional severities and bursts of ill temper, was of the essence of de Man's personality. In an essay called **"The Inward Generation"** he remarks of certain 'near-great' writers of the pre-war period—Malraux, Jünger, Pound and Hemingway—that they had all been 'forcefully committed politically, but their convictions proved so frail that they ended up by writing off this part of their lives altogether, as a momentary aberration, a step towards finding themselves.' The whole passage has concealed autobiographical interest. It attributes the course of such careers to the collapse of an aesthetic inherited from Symbolism, and used as a protection from real problems: but the war brought these into menacing actuality, and the political was now a matter of life and death. The political and aesthetic beliefs of such writers make them 'vulnerable targets for today's conservatism—more vulnerable, in fact, than they deserve to be, because their predicament was not an easy one'. Although he distances all this by talking about 'the political and aesthetic beliefs of the Twenties', it seems obvious enough that de Man here had himself in view: and in essence this is the best defence that could be offered. Reviewing books by Erich Heller and Ronald Gray, he remarks that both authors 'too readily call "German" a general feature of the romantic and post-romantic intellect', just as he had done himself.

The most intense of these speculations concern Mallarmé and Hölderlin, whose question *wozu Dichter in dürftiger Zeit?* seems to have haunted de Man: he quarrelled over it with the august interpretations of Heidegger. There is a measure of self-absorption about even the least of these pieces. They look forward as well as back, and one of their merits is that they often demonstrate how much can be said in a review or a relatively brief essay: which explains why de Man was so slow to publish a book, and why all his books are collections of essays. (pp. 3-6)

[Some] have declared that deconstruction is a means of destroying the value of any historical record, or at least blurring a past, as if de Man's work were 'nothing but a series of oblique strategies for pretending it never happened, or at least that there existed no present responsibility for past thoughts and actions'. This is Norris's account [see excerpt above] of a view that he of course rejects. It has been expressed with much indignation by Stanley Corngold and others—the holocaust, and de Man's own past, they say, conveniently vanish—but it is dismissed, in my view correctly, as founded on a false idea of the relation between deconstruction and history, admittedly a very dark topic. The alternative reading, vigorously expounded by Norris and more or less the same as that proposed by Waters, is that de Man's later life was dedicated to the purging of the false ideology that had once possessed him—in short, an aesthetic ideology, related to an organicism equally responsible for romantic error and for German nationalism with its attendant evils. Looking with 'principled scepticism' at these youthful beliefs, de Man perceived that they must all fall together, as romantic fallacies he had now seen through.

Some may think it strange to regard Nazism and anti-semitism largely as intellectual errors, corrigible by the mere taking of further thought. And although defences of de Man are decently animated by affection for a dead and admired friend, these attempts at biographical exculpation, these rakings through his evolving, exacting, rather melancholy writings, often seem to lack any serious understanding of how even people of high intelligence are sometimes induced to behave, especially when they may be under stress of a kind the exculpators have the good fortune to know nothing about. De Man himself has some tortuous but interesting observations on excuses in an essay on Rousseau's *Confessions* (in **Allegories of Reading,** 1979). For example, he distinguishes between confession and excuse. The former is 'governed by a principle of referential verification', whereas the latter lacks the possibility of verification—'its purpose is not to state but to convince': thus it is performative whereas confession is constative. He is interested in the curious interaction, in Rousseau, of the two rhetorical modes, but at the same time he is willing to say that Rousseau was clearly dissatisfied with his performance as judge of himself, and unable to get rid by excuses of a recurrent sense of shame. For the childish theft of a ribbon is only a beginning: it is followed by other faults that likewise call for excuses, such as the abandoning of one's children. (De Man, we are told by some of his accusers, abandoned his own wife and child, but I do not know whether the known facts really permit this inference.) The critic's interest is expressly not in any simple way biographical or ethical: it is firmly expressed as devoted to an entirely rhetorical problem. It nevertheless passes belief that anybody could write an essay such as this without reflecting on his or her own life, and it may surely be assumed that de Man did so.

It is true that such considerations are not strictly germane to rhetorical theory. Norris quotes an admiring judgment of Minae Mizimura: 'The shift from a concern with human errors to a concern with the problem inherent in language epitomises [de Man's] ultimate choice of language over man,' adding on his own account that it is here—'at the point of renouncing every tie between language and the will to make sense of language in acceptably human terms—that de Man leaves behind the existential pathos that persists in his early essays.' This apathetic purity is what his disciples admire and emulate, though the need to defend the master must sometimes hinder them from quite so scrupulous an avoidance of pathos: the enemy, after all, was representing him as a devious, opportunistic, dishonest human being. Furthermore, even if one breathes the air of pure theory, it must sometimes seem strained to argue that it is always impossible to say what one means, even if the statement you wish to make is that it is always impossible to make such a statement; or to combine this belief with the belief that one can and should intend to say, and say, what will make sense of de Man's life as a whole. (p. 6)

Norris speaks of the essential inhumanity of de Man's views on language, summarised in a neo-Nietzschean manner as 'a wholly impersonal network of tropological drives, substitutions and displacements'. 'To call de Man's position counter-intuitive,' he says, 'is a massive understatement.' Yet it is just this bleakness, this disclaimer of human authority over language, that attracts de Man's luxuriously ascetic followers. They mourn the man but rejoice in his 'inhuman' teachings.

The theory that theory is self-defeating, that it cannot possibly control or comprehend the workings of figural language, is part of the master's charm, but it is also a strange foundation for the ambitious institutional and political programmes now being quite stridently proposed by some—for instance, Jonathan Culler in his recent book *Framing the Sign.* Norris, no less committed but rather more critical, is less confident of the imperialist possibilities of theory, though he would like some sort of concordat with Marxism. De Man himself, with his 'extreme and principled scepticism', would possibly have thought this out of the question, as it must be if the inevitable terminus is that revolving door, where language moves in, impossibly, on an understanding of language, and is at once thrown out. The noble course is not to submit to the bewitchments of language, and to recoil from the Acrasian temptations of the aesthetic 'ideology'. But people outside the cult are probably less principled and more prone to mystification. Trilling's students, when he introduced them to the abyss of the Modern, gazed into it politely, said 'how interesting!' and passed by. Others may do the same to de Man's abyss, and carry on thematising and totalising because it is their pleasure to do so, even if it is shamefully human to do so; and they have a long history of resistance to puritanical imperatives. As a rule they will do so without reference to the youthful errors of Paul de Man, and the insiders should now be happy to stop worrying about them and get on with their necessary and impossible projects. (p. 7)

Frank Kermode, "Paul de Man's Abyss," in London Review of Books, *Vol. 11, No. 6, March 16, 1989, pp. 3-7.*

ELS DE BENS

If an assessment of the role that Paul de Man played is to be founded on a scientific basis, one will have to give an outline of the Belgian press during the German occupation. In consequence, the present paper will successively deal with the press regime imposed by the German occupiers, the way the censorship operated, the variety of Belgian papers, the varying degrees in which the different press organs collaborated with the Germans, and finally a detailed account will be given of the contribution that de Man made to two newspapers, *Le Soir* and *Het Vlaamsche Land*.

>   1. The German institutions involved in the "*Lenkung*" of the Belgian press

As soon as the Germans invaded Belgium, they sought to reorganize the news media as quickly as possible. Even before the capitulation of the Belgian army, two prewar newspapers received the Germans' backing to re-enter the market. Since Belgium had a military administration (*Militärverwaltung* or *MV*) until July 1944, the organization and control of the press was left to the *Wehrmacht,* not to the SS. Within the *Militärverwaltung,* it was the *Propaganda Abteilung* (PA) which controlled the media and the cultural sector. (p. 85)

[The] PA had three chief assignments: to organize information (daily and weekly papers, radio and film news), to design and implement an active propaganda strategy (brochures, leaflets, posters, etc.), and to redirect (*lenken*) cultural and social life as a whole, i.e. to sensitize public opinion to what the "new order" stood for.

In view of the subject of the present paper, it is mainly the PA's actions with regard to the daily and weekly press which are of primary importance. It was the PA which granted publication licenses, which set up the censorship system, which determined the distribution system, which allocated newsprint and which imposed sanctions on the "disobedient" press.

The media policy as adopted by the PA followed in the main the strategies laid down by [Joseph Goebbels, head of Nazi propaganda], . . . based on the concept of *Gleichschaltung*: the content of the media was to be made as uniform as possible in order to promulgate in all places and at all times one invariable message, that of national socialism. Goebbels thought, quite rightly, that "repetition" of the national socialist beliefs and slogans would have a cumulative effect in the long run. Of course, the concept of *Gleichschaltung* im-

plied that no media could function uncontrolled. Indeed, Hitler had stamped all forms of freedom of the press as *eine tödliche Gefahr für jeden Staat* (a mortal danger for any state). Every line in the newspaper, the political, business, cultural and regional news, the sports coverage, even the advertisements were to be imbued with the new teachings. Furthermore, the national socialists held firmly that the media should be keyed to the level of the masses, in other words that they should use black-and-white techniques and be brief, simple and emotional. . . .

The pursuit of *Gleichschaltung* and the attempt to convince public opinion meant that the censor's instructions were used to paint a rosy picture of events in the Third Reich. However, glossing over, and often hiding the truth, also resulted in the decreased credibility of the censored press, particularly in the occupied countries. There it was hard indeed to cut off the clandestine information flowing in from the allied camp. As a result the PA found it very difficult to achieve *Gleichschaltung* in Belgium.

The first important step was to issue a decree or *Verordnung* (14 June 1940) that all papers and periodicals were to apply for an official permission to be published. The purpose of this measure, according to the *Tätigkeitsbericht* of the MV, was "not to lose a comprehensive view" (*um den Überblick nicht zu verlieren*), and hence it was a convenient means for implementing a policy of *centralization*. (p. 86)

But *Gleichschaltung* was achieved much more efficiently by means of *censorship*.

Initially, the Germans had imposed a particularly rigid censorship system, notably *preventive censorship,* which implied that everything that was going to be published had to be submitted to the PA censors first. Such a system proved to be unworkable in the 20th century, because the censors were not able to check the huge mass of information in time. The passages deleted by them often could not be replaced with new copy, and blank spaces would constantly remind the reader of the presence of censorship. As early as 10 October, 1940, the Germans switched to a more practical formula: *a-posteriori censorship*. The editors were now snowed under with the German instructions coming from *Belgapress,* a news agency controlled by the occupying forces. In addition, the PA organized a weekly press conference, to which all the newspapers were required to send a representative and where the Germans made their wishes and demands clear to the assembled press. A journalist who went against the German instructions was punished with sanctions ranging from a mere warning to a fine, suspension from his work or imprisonment.

However it may be, the switchover to a-posteriori censorship entailed more freedom of action for the Belgian journalists. The press now presented a livelier picture, since more variation became possible. Some newspapers actually engaged in hot debates on delicate issues, such as the future destiny of Belgium, of Flanders and of Wallonia. These were precisely the subjects that the Germans had put under taboo, because Berlin had prohibited any discussion of what the future had in store for Belgium. In the end, the PA was forced to reintroduce preventive censorship on all matters relating to domestic affairs (August 1942). Journalists who contributed articles to the censored press after August 1942 must have realized that the Germans no longer allowed them any freedom of action. It is important, therefore, to note here that Paul de Man did not write any articles after the end of 1942! (p. 87)

As to the instructions that the PA transmitted via Belgapress, four groups can be distinguished:

—a request or an order for insertion or for comment;
—a ban on insertion or comment;
—a request to publish fully completed articles;
—extra-directives from the economic service.

Many of these directives were lost at the end of the occupation because the PA ordered everything to be burnt. Still, the remaining material does point out clearly that the PA sometimes went as far as to insist on even the slightest detail. Instructions were given, for example, on the place where a particular article was to be printed (page, title and typeface to be used, position of the picture, etc.), the descriptive words to be used, and so on. The negative result of this kind of *Gleichschaltung* is homogeneous and monotonous uniformity.

By and large, the journalists complied with these instructions (self-censorship!), for few sanctions had to be imposed. Such sanctions as were given were mainly confined to admonitions, fines and brief suspension from work; very rarely were journalists sent to prison.

Besides, the PA could also resort to *indirect pressure.* The allocation of newsprint, for example, was a very practical means for exercising pressure. Newspapers which did not prove to be very docile were put on a very meager ration of newsprint. Such a measure was not only disastrous from the editorial point of view, it also affected the paper's revenue from advertising.

The PA was also instrumental in restructuring the former *Algemene Belgische Persbond* (General Belgian Press League) into the *Vereniging van Belgische Journalisten* (Association of Belgian Journalists) in March 1942. The new Association's structure was copied from that of the *Reichsverband Deutscher Journalisten*. The publishers were obliged by the PA to employ as full-time journalists only those who were members of the Association.

At the ceremony marking the foundation of the Association, P. Colin made a speech to the journalists present, stating unambiguously that the new professional association backed the national socialist cause: "Vous êtes le Front de l'Intérieur, vous combattez comme nos frères qui combattent au Front de l'Est . . . (You constitute the Home Front, you fight the enemy just like our brothers who are fighting on the Eastern Front)." Being a casual contributor, Paul de Man was never a member of the Association.

In order to facilitate its control over the circulation, the sale and the distribution of the papers, the PA gave a distribution monopoly to the Dechenne agency, which was in charge of the distribution of newspapers throughout the occupation. The papers were forbidden to use their own channels of distribution. A letter from the PA to the distribution agency states in no uncertain terms that "the agency has a propagandist function . . . and the general management must look after the interest of the Third Reich." After discontinuing his journalistic activities Paul de Man worked in this distribution agency (see below).

2. Survey of the Belgian "collaborator press"

After issuing its *Verordnung* of 14 June 1940, the PA received many applications. As early as October 1940 24 dailies were on the market, i.e. about one third of the prewar number, but their overall circulation equalled that of before the war: in 1939 the overall number of copies stood at 1,560,000, and in November-December 1940 it was 1,472,290. Considering that the number of papers had been reduced to one third and that the overall circulation remained roughly the same as before the war, most newspaper publishers must have made a handsome profit during the war.

That the dailies could be published again so soon after the Germans had taken over, was largely due to the great willingness of Belgian journalists to contribute to the wartime press. There is a variety of motives which made the journalists "collaborate" with the occupying forces. The German victory of May 1940, the King's appeal for general resumption of work, and the fear of being out of a job were no doubt the major incentives for many journalists to return to their work.

Yet quite a number of them hesitated to do so and first sought the advice of eminent personalities from aristocratic, political, judicial and clerical circles. Among these dignitaries there were several who recommended a policy of attendance: they felt it was preferable to resume work as a journalist rather than leave the newspaper to extremists, who would then put it on the market as a "stolen" publication.

There were also opportunists among those who were willing to resume work, as well as confirmed advocates of the new order. But it is a fact that the phenomenon of collaborating with the enemy emerged in all ideological and political groups. Not only were collaborating journalists found in the prewar antiparliamentary movements such as VNV, Verdinaso, and Rex, but also the traditional catholic, liberal and socialist camps proved to have journalists who were willing to contribute to the censored press.

Because of his background (his studies at the Université Libre de Bruxelles and his relationship with his uncle Hendrik de Man) Paul de Man belonged to the socialist intellectual circles which were found to be ready to collaborate with the wartime press.

As a rule, the newspapers published in Belgium during the occupation are classified in three groups: old, new, and stolen papers. However, this classification is rather rudimentary. Indeed, the term "old" newspapers includes not only those papers which continued to be published on the grounds of their ideological convictions, being adherents of the new order . . . but also those papers which had adopted the policy of attendance. . . . This category therefore comprises two extremes, adherents of collaborating groups as well as those who did not want to have anything to do with collaboration with the enemy.

In the category of "new" newspapers we find, of course, a very clear situation: the papers founded during the occupation could only be published in close cooperation with the Germans [the newspaper *Het Vlaamsche Land* is an example].

"Stolen" newspapers, finally, refers to those newspapers which were published during the occupation against the wishes of their owners or managers. But again the situation is somewhat blurred: in the final analysis some of these "stolen" newspapers do turn out to have been published with the tacit or at least partial approval of their owners/managers. (pp. 87-89)

3.2 *Characterization of the "stolen" Le Soir*

Le Soir was the most widely read daily paper in occupied Belgium. . . .

The success of the "stolen" *Le Soir* was largely due to the use of the prewar title. Moreover, during the occupation there were 12 French-speaking dailies less in Brussels than before the war, which obviously greatly benefited the market position of the "stolen" *Le Soir.*

Actually, the "stolen" daily was a fine product, journalistically speaking. Also, it consistently took a belgicistic point of view. [German-appointed editor-in-chief] De Becker tried to find a new destiny for the country in the new Europe: "sauver de la Belgique tout ce qui peut être sauvé, construire une Belgique régénérée dans une Europe unifieé (save all that can be saved of Belgium, build a regenerated Belgium in a unified Europe)." He did state explicitly and repeatedly, however, that the destiny of the "new" Belgium was in the hands of the Germans. . . .

The relationship of *Le Soir* with the most important group of collaborators, Rex, was at first cautious and detached. But after the leader of Rex, L. Degrelle, had made his notorious speech of 17 January 1943, in which he called the Walloons a Germanic people, the relation cooled down completely. . . .

Paul de Man had contacts with the regular visitors to the "salon Didier" even before the war, and in all likelihood it is these relations that brought him to *Le Soir.* In prewar days, the salon of Mr. and Mrs. Didier was a fashionable meeting-place for intellectuals and artists. E. Didier was the founder of the club of "Jeune Europe" and the editor-in-chief of the periodical of the same name. In his salon eminent politicians, journalists and writers assembled. Hendrik de Man, Paul de Man's uncle, was one of the regular guests. (p. 90)

The salon Didier is often described as an embryonic pre-collaboration group. Though they were a politically very heterogeneous company, its frequenters shared an aversion to Belgium's "decadent" political establishment. They dreamt of a "new Europe", and for Belgium they claimed the status of a neutral country. It is obvious enough that some of the visitors to the salon Didier dabbled in fascism and national socialism. Indeed, Dr. M. Liebe and Dr. O. Abetz of the German embassy in Brussels were among the salon's habitués.

During the occupation the Didiers, together with R. de Becker and D. Daye, founded the publishing house of La Toison d'Or (March 1941). Actually, the firm was a subsidiary of the Mundus group, which was controlled by von Ribbentrop's services!

Paul de Man's introduction to *Le Soir* dates from the period when La Toison d'Or was founded. His uncle Hendrik de Man put him in touch with the group of intellectuals meeting at the Didiers'. He was recruited by R. de Becker to write a weekly "Chronique littéraire" and he was also to report various cultural activities (concerts, exhibitions, theatre, etc).

The reader of Paul de Man's weekly literary chronicle is struck by his focus on the publications of La Toison d'Or. This publishing house selected mainly authors whose work had much ground in common with the ideology of the new order. Examples are the works of Hendrik de Man (the founder of the united trade union), P. Colin (the founder of the daily *Le Nouveau Journal,* which sympathized with Rex), R. Poulet (the editor-in-chief of *Le Nouveau Journal*) and P. Daye (journalist of the same newspaper); all these authors were published by La Toison d'Or and consequently reviewed extensively by Paul de Man.

Foreign authors too, who sided with the new order, were published by La Toison d'Or: for example, R. Brasillach, J. Chardonne, Drieu la Rochelle, E. Jünger, H. Fallada.

Paul de Man's reviews and reports of cultural events will not be discussed in detail. . . . However, a number of topics will be dealt with in order to point out where de Man adheres to the ideas of the new order. The analysis is a qualitative one, and hence subjective. We feel that the traditional methods of content analysis are inadequate here because de Man's significant pronouncements are to be found in occasional subtle and carefully balanced passages.

A topic that recurs frequently in Paul de Man's articles is the concept of the *new Europe* which is being achieved. The precise content of the term remains vague, but it concerns a Europe which has shed off the old decadence and which promises a better world, with more solidarity, more real values, a greater sense of duty and greater soundness: ". . . et que la guerre présente est, en dehors d'une lutte économique et nationale, le début d'une révolution qui vise à organiser la société européenne d'une manière plus équitable . . . (the current war, apart from being an economic and national war, is the beginning of a revolution which seeks to reorganize European society in a more equitable fashion)."

Repeatedly, Paul de Man points to the *role of Germany* in the new Europe: "Il y a une raison pour laquelle le destin historique passé et futur de l'Allemagne ne peut nous laisser indifférents: c'est que nous en dépendons directement . . . En outre, parce que nul ne peut nier la signification fondamentale de l'Allemagne pour la vie de l'Occident tout entier (There is one good reason why Germany's past and future historical destiny should not leave us indifferent: we depend upon it directly. . . . Moreover, nobody can deny the fundamental significance of Germany for the West as a whole)."

His reviews often show up his admiration for the German victors and his contempt of the old Europe. . . . (pp. 90-1)

As a result of the year-long brainwashing by English and French propaganda, de Man writes, we neglected everything that Germany accomplished in the social and political fields.

Paul de Man sometimes displays a naive faith in the artistic freedom that fascism and national socialism grant artists. On the occasion of a lecture by Prof. Donini on Italian poetry, de Man writes that "le régime fasciste laisse entière liberté au poète pour chercher sa source d'inspiration où il veut (the fascist regime leaves the poet entirely free to find his inspiration wherever he wants to)." He concludes by pointing out that poetry "se développe en Italie et qui semble réaliser avec le plus grand bonheur, le souhait exprimé par Mussolini lorsqu'il déclara que c'est surtout dans les temps présents que la poésie est nécessaire à la vie des peuples (poetry is in full development in Italy; it appears to make come true to the full the wish expressed by Mussolini that particularly in these days poetry should be of the utmost importance in the life of the peoples)."

National socialism too extends the desired freedom of action to novelists, at least in de Man's opinion. . . . de Man contends that art must find an intermediate way in between individualism and commitment to solidarity. In a comment on *Das innere Reich,* the periodical edited by P. Alverdes, de Man argues that here this intermediate way has been found: no isolation in the ivory tower of poetry, away from what Germany has accomplished, but neither the uncritical and blind acceptance of German propaganda. . . . (pp. 91-2)

In Paul de Man's reviews of a number of French literary works, the following topic recurs frequently: France will have to understand that a new age has begun, and that it will have to side with the German victors in building up a new Europe. In reviewing Brasillach's *Notre Avant-Guerre,* de Man writes: "Je m'imagine que pour un Français cultivé *Notre avant-guerre* évoque encore un paradis perdu. Mais il faudra bien qu'il se résigne à parachever une révolution politique et sociale avant de pouvoir espérer retrouver un paradis semblable mais basé sur des fondements plus solides et, pourtant, moins éphémères (I can very well imagine that a cultivated Frenchman will find another paradise lost in *Notre avant-guerre.* But he will have to resign himself to the completion of a political and social revolution; only then will he find back a similar paradise, based on more solid foundations and therefore less ephemeral)."

In his discussion of J. Chardonne's *Voir la figure,* de Man has the comment that the individualism typical of the French will have to yield to duty, discipline and order. . . .

Quite often de Man criticized in his literary chronicle "le bavardage superficiel (the superficial tittle-tattle) of which he feels the French in particular are guilty. It comes as no surprise therefore that he praises Drieu la Rochelle's *Notes pour comprendre le siècle,* as this book seeks to create a new type of man: ". . . d'autant plus prometteur dans un pays qui était tombé si bas que la France (so very promising in a country that had fallen as low as France)."

It will be clear from the notes above that Paul de Man had, at least to some extent, taken to the ideology of the new order. One must bear in mind, however, that he was very young at the time, and that he must have been taken along by those he had met in the Didier circle and in particular by the fascinating personality of his uncle.

Paul de Man's main interests were art and literature; therefore the question arises if we ought not to characterize his "politically committed" views as merely political naivety. However, can one attribute his article **"Les Juifs dans la littérature actuelle"** (4 March 1941) to political naivete? The reader of the article has the uneasy feeling that Paul de Man shows a leaning towards the anti-semitic aspect of national socialism. (p. 92)

Although Paul de Man does not refer to the extermination camps, yet he does hint at the idea of isolating the Jews. He must have been aware of the anti-semitic witch hunt of the national socialists, and with the quotation above he appears to approve of their anti-semitic stand. We also feel that the antisemitic tones of the article are reinforced by the editorial layout, which inserts a vehement anti-Jewish quotation from Benjamin Franklin after de Man's text and name. Paul de

Man himself cannot have overlooked this; at the same time it is a blemish on the editorial policy adopted by *Le Soir.*

Before drawing a final conclusion, it is appropriate to have a brief look at Paul de Man's contributions to *Het Vlaamsche Land,* the second newspaper that he wrote for. (pp. 92-3)

4. *Het Vlaamsche Land*

Het Vlaamsche Land was founded during the occupation, which implies that it benefited from German financial assistance. It is often considered to have been the unofficial spokesman of Devlag, a politically active group collaborating with the Germans and among the most extreme groups in Flanders: it was backed by the ss, and its leader, Jef Van de Wiele, advocated the annexation of Flanders into the Third Reich. Indeed, the members of Devlag repeatedly took part in Gestapo raids against Jews and resistance fighters.

However, a content analysis of *Het Vlaamsche Land* shows that the newspaper did not put itself forward as the mouthpiece of Devlag. The newspaper owed this bad reputation to its so-called Reich edition, which was circulated among Flemish workers employed in Germany itself and which explicitly adhered to the Devlag principles. . . .

But the domestic, i.e. Belgian, edition of *Het Vlaamsche Land* shows hardly any traces of Devlag influence. Very exceptionally, an article by the Devlag leader Jef Van de Wiele was printed. Devlag had no great liking for *Het Vlaamsche Land,* which explains why a new Devlag paper was founded in 1943, *De Gazet.*

De Man wrote only ten articles for *Het Vlaamsche Land.* We have been unable to go through the Reich edition of the paper, but we are practically certain that his articles were printed in the Belgian edition alone. It is possible that Paul de Man was not aware of the link between the paper and Devlag. It has proved to be impossible to find out in what circumstances de Man began to contribute to this paper.

De Man's ten articles concern literary reviews and reports of cultural events. The topics that betray a certain affinity with the ideology of the new order are the same as in the *Le Soir* articles. (p. 93)

Towards the end of 1942 silence fell around de Man and his contributions to the daily press. His decision to stop writing for the dailies is probably due to a concurrence of circumstances: embittered, his uncle had renounced active collaboration as early as March 1942; the War was dragging on; and the climate of terror was growing worse. Of even greater importance is that, in August 1942, preventive censorship was imposed again on everything relating to domestic affairs. The journalists saw their freedom of action curtailed and the climate in which the press had to work was becoming increasingly rigid. Therefore Paul de Man's disappearance from the daily press at the end of 1942 is an important fact: during the postwar press trials those journalists who had gone on working after 1942 had severe charges pressed against them.

Paul de Man, looking for a livelihood, worked in the Dechenne agency until the middle of 1943. The agency, as pointed out above, had been granted by the Germans the monopoly of the distribution of dailies and weeklies. It was also producing a bibliography, and this is where de Man found work: he wrote seven essays and 93 bibliographic notes for this bibliography.

He must have known that the Dechenne agency was supervised by Lothar von Balluseck, who was working for the *Reichsverband Deutscher Zeitungsverleger,* the association of German newspaper publishers. Why de Man left the Dechenne agency, and where he went afterwards, are questions which we cannot answer.

To what extent are these war years significant for the status of Paul de Man as a scholar of literature? Are these years not to be considered a brief, isolated period of his life, one about which he himself was actually always anxious to keep silent? Perhaps his attitudes at the time can be explained as the ill-considered, youthful *Schwärmerei* or zealotry of a young man well-versed in cultural affairs but lacking in political insight. In any case, the links so far proposed between his wartime activities and his later career and theories remain rather vague and speculative. (pp. 93-4)

> Els de Bens, *"Paul de Man and the Collaborationist Press," in* Responses: On Paul de Man's Wartime Journalism, *Werner Hamacher, Neil Hertz and Thomas Keenan, eds., University of Nebraska Press, 1989, pp. 85-95.*

RODOLPHE GASCHÉ

Undoubtedly, the discovery of de Man's early journalistic writings represents a formidable legacy for his friends and foes alike. The bequest consists of coming to grips, in an intellectually and ethically responsible fashion, with the shocking fact that during a brief period, the young de Man wrote a literary chronicle for *Le Soir,* a newspaper whose political columns were at that time under strong German control. Responsible examination, however, requires detailed and in-depth documentation of the historical, cultural and political situation of Belgium between 1939 and 1942, so that the truly incriminating facts can be established with the necessary precision, and no confusion remains as to what under the given circumstances can and cannot be laid to de Man's charge. Responsible examination also requires that such inquiry be conducted in the spirit of respect that both friend and foe, as Others, demand. Yet, from the precipitation with which de Man's case has been taken up by the academic community and the newspapers, from the ludicrous and delirious charges leveled against him, as well as from the hatred that is evident in so many of the accounts, it is more than clear that the challenge of determining exactly what de Man's wartime activities amount to and what they mean has not been met. Or rather, since most of the discussions that have taken place have deliberately dismissed the most elementary rules of documentation (in this case, reading for instance, the incriminating material) as well as all other standards of philological honesty and integrity, not to mention the basic ethical guidelines for any debate, the minimal conditions for discussion have simply not been met. One cannot but be deeply terrified by the silliness, stupidity and maliciousness of the accounts in question, especially if one keeps in mind that the primary goal of the rage in question is a settling of accounts with "deconstruction." Indeed, one must assume that such trampling of all rules intellectual and ethical in the rampage against de Man and "deconstruction" is supposed to set future standards for the academic community. Disregard of history, disrespect for textual evidence, wild analogization, subjective elucubration, irrational outburst, are among the stupefying

exemplars raised to the status of precepts for the learning community.

If we are then to take account of de Man's war-time writings, and if we may, indeed, be compelled to consider them irresponsible and unpardonable, let us at least establish as precisely as possible what it is that we may have to judge as inadmissible. Intellectual probity and moral integrity require that we do so.

De Man's collaboration with a Nazi-controlled newspaper was obviously utterly irresponsible. But if this is not to be an abstract judgment (and thus a misjudgment) the irresponsibility has to be set into its proper context: the desire on the part of the young de Man to write on literature, perhaps at any price (a desire which becomes understandable if one recalls that his education did not permit him to study literature at any Belgian university), his economic situation, the publication opportunities in Belgium at that time, or the fact that he stopped writing for the literary column of *Le Soir* when that column was censured as well, etc. Fully irresponsible also is one article of the approximately 290 articles and reviews that he wrote between 1939 and 1943—**"Les Juifs dans la Littérature Actuelle"** (*Le Soir,* March 4, 1941)—that uses undeniably anti-Semitic language, and perhaps two others which are much more ambiguous, as we will see in a moment, and which, respectively, hold Jews responsible for decadence in art and seem to celebrate Hitlerianism as the essence of the German soul. But these two last essays—**"A View on Contemporary German Fiction"** (*Het Vlaamsche Land,* August 20, 1942) and *"Voir La Figure, de Jacques Chardonne"* (*Le Soir,* October 28, 1941)—definitely fall in a different category from the article on the Jews in literature. As I will argue, these two articles, in different ways, give in, more clearly than the others, to some Nazi stereotypes which they are naive enough to believe that they can circumvent and undo by textual maneuvers. To have given in to making use of these stereotypes, however ambiguously, to have perhaps believed that they could be subverted by other articles de Man wrote at that time, is perhaps a sign not necessarily of irresponsibility, but certainly of naiveté and confusion. But let me come back to **"Les Juifs dans la Littérature Actuelle."** It is the one truly incriminatory piece. Although the essay is undoubtedly rather complex, and is, as Derrida has pointed out—not in what Richard Bernstein calls "a bravura act of deconstruction," but merely in an act of attentive reading of what this text unmistakingly tells us—motivated by a desire to criticize vulgar anti-Semitism (and through it perhaps all anti-Semitism), it also speaks of Jews as foreign, or alien powers, of having meddled in all aspects of European life (except literature), and finally refers in a quite equivocal manner to the possibility of solving the Jewish problem by creating a Jewish colony isolated from Europe. Obviously, these statements are a far cry from the official anti-Semitism of the day, but they are nonetheless objectionable and unpardonable. If one can trust testimony by relatives and close friends (Jewish and non-Jewish) of the young Paul de Man, he had not the least strain of Anti-Semitism. But that in order to be able to write in these journals he gave in to the language of Nazi ideology, that he did not resist anti-Semitic stereotypes on several occasions, these are the facts with which we must charge de Man. They speak to his confusion at the time, to a certain blindness and opportunism on his part. These facts are bad enough, but, making due allowances, one must also admit that, however awful, they are rather harmless. The *Auditeur Général* who examined Paul de Man after the war decided not to pursue his case—in contrast to other journalists of *Le Soir*. This amounts to clearing de Man of the charge of collaboration and is thus evidence of the political and historical insignificance of his wrongdoings. In short, his wrongdoings must be seen in their proper perspective. To disregard the exact nature of his "crime," as it has been called, is to bear witness to an inexcusable injustice resulting either from stupidity or maliciousness. But it is not only an injustice regarding de Man himself—as when Jon Wiener calls him "something of an academic Waldheim" [see excerpt above]—it is also more importantly, more atrociously, an inexcuable injustice with respect to the Jewish people. To put Waldheim and de Man on the same plan is to show a staggering lack of historical discrimination which implies a shameless belittling of Nazi atrocities and the suffering of the Jewish people during World War II. Indeed, from many of the articles published on the de Man issue, it is rather obvious that their authors, or some of those quoted for statements, are less concerned with historical accuracy than with the attempt to settle accounts, even if this takes place at the price of all justice and decency. The de Man affair, although it has found its way into major newspapers, is a strictly academic affair. It makes sense only with respect to a debate that divides academics around something called "deconstruction." To score a hit against this spectre of perversion as its critics see it, they are willing, as one could witness over the last several months, to trash all standards of intellectual and ethical integrity. What is thus truly at stake in this debate is, as mentioned above, nothing less than the minimal criteria and rules of professional ethics and intellectual probity. (pp. 208-09)

If, consequently, one article which contains decidedly anti-Semitic statements, two that in spite of their ambiguity still seem to tilt in the direction of anti-Semitic ideology or of an uncritical acception of Hitlerianism, and finally the fact that most of these articles were written for a newspaper that followed (as far as its political content was concerned) a Nazi line, are the incriminating charges to be held against the young journalist as clearly disastrous evidence that allows for no attenuation, what then is the status of the remaining articles—288 to be precise? What happens if we read them?

To read, here, means to attentively seek to understand the sense of the writings in question which also implies situating them in their proper context, a skill normally to be expected from educated persons, but nowadays often associated with deconstruction, especially if the sense of the written does not fit preconceived notions. For anyone who is cognizant of the issues debated by both the left and the right between the wars, as well as of the style of those debates, these are not collaborationist or pro-Nazi writings as they have been labeled on numerous occasions. One cannot even say that they express a clear sympathy for German culture and literature. They certainly do not advocate any of the themes of German cultural politics. Still, since the bulk of these articles is far from being unambiguous, and I more often than not feel quite ill at ease with what I read in them, I choose to approach them through the two articles that I have singled out as being on the borderline between anti-Semitism and the inefficient subversion of its premises. Indeed, all the articles written during the occupation that are not just simple reviews have such a double face, owing to de Man's sometimes successful, sometimes unsuccessful, maneuvers between ideological positions. Sometimes the stakes are high as is the case with the two articles in question—**"A View on Contemporary German Fiction,"** and the Chardonne review—most of the time, the issues debated are of secondary interest. But from the start let us emphasize that such maneuvering is not characteristic of Nazi writings. Although one would have liked to see de Man opt unambiguously for one of the positions in question, and in spite of the fact that these articles convey at times a shocking violence, one must have the honesty to admit that in tone and style they are quite different from any of the collaborationist writings of the period. To show this, let me then focus, first on **"A View on Contemporary German Fiction."** In this article, de Man, seemingly in conformity with the Nazi defamatory evaluation of modern art, classifies expressionism as "aberrant" and "degenerate." In addition, he claims "that it was mainly non-Germans and specifically Jews that went in this direction." It is undoubtedly difficult to remain aloof when encountering such a statement, in particular, since it echoes the accusation made by the Nazis that this art is "subversive," and "un-German" (*undeutsch*). De Man, indeed, demarcates the "strongly cerebral disposition founded upon abstract principles and very remote from all naturalness" of the expressionist group, from another group at work in Germany that "remained true to the proper norms of the country." Nothing, ultimately, will make one's discomfort go away regarding these painful utterances by the young de Man. Yet, such distress does not exempt us from the obligation to examine these quotations in their proper context—the content of the article itself, as well as the whole production over the three years in question. . . . Intellectual probity requires that I acknowledge the following: First, expressionism as a whole is not condemned, but only a certain group that uses "the in themselves very remarkable theses of expressionism" in an aberrant fashion. In no way identical to the Nazi condemnation of expressionism which include those "very remarkable theses" as well, and which made no distinction between groups within this movement, de Man's elaborations are also extremely elusive as to the identity of the group he is talking about. Second, the "good" German literature pitted against this limited group of expressionist writers is not characterized in terms that would emphasize their Germanic qualities (*deutsch*, or *völkisch*) but in terms that stress this literature's "assimilation of foreign norms which are transformed and reduced to a number of specific and constant values in order to become the own spiritual property of the nation." . . . This characterization of "good" German literature is not in conformity with the premises of Nazi cultural politics geared toward the elimination of all literature not only of bolshevist but also of cosmopolitan signature. Third, the cerebral quality of expressionism, that sets it over and against the other type of German literature, is an attribute associated throughout all the articles not only with Jewish thinking but with French culture in particular. As we have seen, at least one group of the German writers that de Man celebrates in his essay is influenced by a cerebrality which in their case is even raised "to the realm of crystal clear beauty." And finally, the qualification 'degenerate' is, at least, complicated by the fact that de Man seeks to keep French artistic production clear from such accusations. Taken as a whole, French literature is said to be engaged in experiments that show "aberrations of such strength" that they cannot be classified. Yet, he goes on, it would be "a dangerous artificial simplification" to apply the criterion "degenerate" to French art. In an article from the same journal (dated May 17-18, 1942, entitled **"Contemporary Trends in French Literature"**) he notes that "monstrous hair-splitting" and a "style which has used up all of its vital force" (to be found on English and Dutch rather than on French soil) is not without "indisputable merit" if one thinks of Joyce, Woolf, or Vestdijk. As he points out here, "decadence and inferiority are not necessarily synonymous." Considering this positive valorization of the notion of decadence, a valorization based precisely on some of the dominant features of Nazi characterizations of decadence, one cannot but wonder what this notion can still mean when applied to a group of expressionist writers. The fact remains, of course, that de Man depicts this group as "decadent," and that he writes that "mainly non-Germans and specifically Jews" contributed to the production of the group in question. But after what we have seen, what precisely can the semantic value of the term "decadent" be? From the article, one gathers that this term designates cheap showmanship, artificiality, the "calculation of easy effects," "forced and caricatured representation of reality" (which, by the way, is not, as we will see later, the strength of German literary writing, according to de Man), "cheap success by using imported formulas." "Decadent" thus means nothing less and nothing more than lousy, artless art, perhaps also vulgar art in the sense that de Man gives this term on several occasions. "Decadent" also means the inability to assimilate foreign norms—apparently a strength of German literature—and thus the failure to mediate imported values and the spiritual values of a nation. Such failure turns the imported into cheap effects in art, into artless artifice. The article, as we have seen, associates "mainly non-Germans and specifically Jews" with this failure. It is difficult, if not impossible, to know whom de Man is particularly thinking of here, especially since not all of expressionism is included in this condemnation. Moreover, such characterization of the group in question does not match very well with its "apparently strong cerebral disposition." It harmonizes even less with the brilliant cerebral qualities of the Jewish mind, to which he refers in the article on **"Les Juifs dans la Littérature Actuelle."** In the same way that the pejorative use of "decadent" merely means "cheap" and "artless," the reference to the Germans, non-Germans, and Jews responsible for decadent art seems to boil down to a reference to third-rate artists. Kafka, undoubtedly, does not fall into this category. In short, then, the distressing fact remains that de Man draws on some themes of Nazi ideology, and that he gives in to the denunciatory gestures of pointing at alien forces and influences. This fact remains, and in all its bewildering force. But what a more careful reading of a text such as the one just analyzed shows is that the terms and the gestures referred to, when not simply hollowed out as is the case with the notion of "decadence," are complicated to the point of confusion. No deconstruction is necessary to see this, just a simple attentive reading. What such a reading brings to light is the true dimension of what we must continue to be upset about—namely to have given in to drawing on Nazi stereotypes and ideological themes, unaware of the danger that they represented, in the naive hope of containing them through textual manipulation. But once again, this sorry fact, for both historical as well as material reasons, is no excuse for calling de Man's early writings Nazi or collaborationist propaganda. Although the ambiguity of some of these texts remains intact, and although one's discomfort with some of their topics lingers on, one must also remain sensible to the strategies they display. One must, to do justice, patiently follow de Man's moves throughout these texts, in a war of displacements that could not be won. (pp. 209-11)

Although the bulk of the articles written for *Le Soir, Cahiers du Libre Examen,* and *Het Vlaamsche Land,* need a more careful and patient study than I can devote to them here, it can be said that with the German occupation of Belgium,

with the German hegemony in Europe having become an indisputable fact, de Man turns away from the internationalism of his writings in *Jeudi,* and takes recourse to the themes of nationalism and cultural patrimony in order to resist German rule. This issue which is a decisive thread throughout most of the articles—the concern with national personality and difference, patriotic feeling, the protection if not creative development of the national patrimony, the insistence on the independence of nationalities—is incongruous with the dominant Nazi ideology. (p. 211)

From the outset, let me say that not everything in these articles is entirely consistent. Especially when it comes to evaluating the role of Germany in Europe, what Germany's annexational politics and hegemony mean for Europe as a whole, de Man wavers. In March 1942 (**"A la recherche d'un nouveau mode d'expression"**), he writes: "For him who like me finds himself immersed in the hurly-burly of facts and actions, it is difficult to acquire a sufficiently synthetic overview of things in order to be able to grasp the meaning and the direction of the evolution that one is going through." Yet, in spite of all these doubts, uncertainties, and ambiguities whose effects (to the extent that they produce occasionally one-sided valorizations) are of course not negligible, a quite coherent picture arises if one reads the totality of the articles. This picture provides, indeed, an answer to the question of how de Man understood the German hegemony in Europe, and what the occasional reference to "immediate collaboration" in his articles could have meant. In a review from October, 1941 of Jacques Chardonne's book, *Voir La Figure*—that is, in the second borderline article—de Man explains that "the future of Europe can only be anticipated within the frame of the possibilities and the needs of the German genius." The war, he notes, is the result of "the definitive emancipation of a people that finds itself, in its turn, called upon to exercise a hegemony in Europe," of a people in which the "Hitlerian soul" fuses with the "German soul" for reasons that lie with "elementary givens, that is, with the historical constants that give the German people its unity and specific character." Now, what this means for de Man, and it is clearly spelled out, is that this war has a "national character." However deceptive this conclusion may seem (and we will come back to this issue later), one cannot overlook its rather unorthodox implication: if the war is a symptom of Germany's coming into its own proper national identity, then the hegemony that it is supposed to play in Europe must, obviously, come to a halt precisely at the borders of the other national blocks that make up Europe as a whole. As for many other thinkers during the years before the war (but afterward as well: E. R. Curtius, for instance), for de Man "Europe," and "Western culture and civilization," are politico-cultural categories in the name of which all events become evaluated. But what distinguishes de Man's concept of "Europe" from that of a Europe under German rule, or of a Europe as a spiritual unity beyond all nationalities (Curtius), is his insistence on the constituting role of the various nationalities that make up Europe as a geographical unit. De Man's emphasis on a "European thinking" in which "national sentiments can freely come to expression and . . . (in which) every nation is fully conscious of its own worth" (*Het Vlaamsche Land,* 29-30 March 1942), has the practical aim of defending "Western culture against a decomposition from the inside out or a surprise attack by neighboring civilizations." It goes without saying that this concern with warding off "the increasingly menacing interferences" that threaten the values of the West (*Le Soir,* March 12, 1942), can lend itself to all forms of xenophobia, anti-

Semitism first and foremost. **"Les Juifs dans la Littérature Actuelle"** is ample proof of this, as many of the present accounts of the de Man affair also exhibit a similar xenophobia of their own. Indeed, any discourse, then and now, that becomes set on defending a state of affairs, or values in the name of the proper, homogeneity, continuity, etc. *can* slip into fascist exorcism of the Other. The debate around the de Man affair and "deconstruction" is just another case in point. But, apart from some occasional ambiguities, de Man's insistence on a nationalism whose conception is "miles apart from sentimental patriotism" (*Het Vlaamsche Land,* March 29-30, 1942), serves to counter nationalistic isolation and hardening, and to keep interference by one nation in the affairs of another in check. Indeed, "the disappearance of one of those original centers [the individual nations], as a result of political arbitrariness or economic injustice," has to be avoided at all cost since it would mean "an impoverishment for the whole of Europe," de Man writes. Paradoxically, the idea of a "European parallelism", that is, of a nationalism that is "the exact opposite of being exclusive," is said to have been developed primarily in Germany (*Le Soir,* March 31, 1942), thus, by that nation which, at the time de Man is writing, has occupied most of Europe. Of this present nationalism, de Man says that it is "complementary. Its object is to discover the national virtues, to cultivate and to honor them, but also to adapt them to those of neighboring peoples in order to achieve through such summation of the particular gifts, a real unification of Western culture" (*Le Soir,* April 28, 1942). This is the point, then, where the references to the question of collaboration can be discussed. It is raised by de Man precisely in the *Le Soir* article on Chardonne (October 28, 1941) in which he argues that the German hegemony and the ensuing war are profoundly nationalistic in character. Yet he notes that the arguments that plead for immediate collaboration please only those who are already of such an opinion while they fail to convince anyone who is not. Similarly, in an article from October 14, 1941, after having claimed that the need for action under the form of immediate collaboration "is a compelling reality to any objective mind," he claims that it is too early to "become disheartened by the universal incomprehension [regarding this necessity] and to withdraw into one's ivory tower," because in any case such "activity cannot take on a direct and material form." The context for these statements is a review of Daniel Halévy's *Trois Epreuves* in which de Man insists that France can only be saved if it returns to its past in order to "discover among the laws, customs, and aspirations that constitute the patrimony of the nation, those that need to be eliminated or favored for the regeneration to take place." From this context, it becomes clear that "immediate collaboration," a necessity that arises from the need of a nation under German rule to choose between death and life, in no way means collaboration with the Nazi oppressor in the sense of denationalization and assimilation into the *Reich.* This is clearly spelled out in **"Le destin de la Flandre"** (*Le Soir,* September 1, 1941), where such temptation is called catastrophic. "Immediate collaboration" is said to be indirect and non-material because all it can consist of is a furthering of national identity and independence (thus exactly the opposite of what the Germans demanded of the subjected countries). It is thus not a collaboration with the occupier that de Man is advocating here, but collaboration at creating a Europe where "a free contact between peoples that know themselves as different and insist on difference, but also hold each other mutually in high esteem, secures political peace and stability" (*Le Soir,* August 28, 1942). It is a collab-

oration, thus, that seeks to contain the assimilation threat by working at creating a Europe in which each nation, although it tries at first to be itself, also respects the character of other nations, "and does not dream for one moment to impose its own views." The question that remains undecided is whether such European parallelism is to be achieved under German rule ("We can only be dignified members of a German state in so far as that state allows us to be dignified Dutchmen"), or in a Europe in which the German cultural bloc is contained by an equally powerful French cultural bloc (" 'To be dignified Dutchmen' amounts to maintaining between the two cultural blocs that are France and Germany that center [*noyau*] that was able to give humanity admirable products of an independent genius"). This uncertainty traverses all the articles, and in particular **"Le destin de la Flandre"** (September 1, 1941), from which I drew the preceding citations. Yet the sympathy of the young journalist is clearly with a Europe in which a confederation of nationalities evens out the strengths and weaknesses of any particular nation. This is manifest especially in the decisive role that de Man implores the French to play with respect to German culture within a unitary Europe. The fact that de Man is at times critical of French cerebrality, and has some good things to say about German novels, has led a number of hasty interpreters to conclude that his sympathies were unequivocally with German culture. Nothing could be more wrong, as a patient reading of the articles in their totality reveals. Indeed, de Man's pessimistic account of French thought between the wars, and above all since the armistice, has all the qualities of a call to action. In his eyes, only French genius can in the long run contain German mysticism and obscurantism. (pp. 212-13)

[It] should be evident that in spite of a variety of uncertainties and ambiguities that they contain, these articles cannot be called Nazi writings. They are not even sympathetic to the Nazi cause. They are, primarily, interested in protecting Flanders's independence. It must, however, be said that de Man's analytical vocabulary—his typology of nationalities and artforms, the binary oppositions of the aesthetic and the political, the abstract and the emotional, the spiritual and the social, the individual and the collective, rural and urban values, etc., as well as his emphasis on the spiritual unity of Europe (including Western civilization), and on what the individual nations are to contribute to it—has a strong traditionalist and conservative bent. Yet only someone who is ignorant of the intellectual climate between the wars, both on the left and the right, could mistake this analytical apparatus, and its use in de Man's journalistic writings, for rightist or collaborationist ideology. But to stress the traditionalist origin of de Man's categorial apparatus, as well as of his moves, is also to say that these articles are not very original and in themselves not especially interesting except perhaps for his emphasis on the specific character of the Flemish nation and the idiosyncratic implications of this valorization. Had he not become a well-known scholar at Yale, and were he not seen as a proponent of "deconstruction," these articles would have continued to go unnoticed. Although not particularly original, the articles are, however, intelligent, especially as far as their organization and their argumentative strategies are concerned. . . . Although de Man's categorial apparatus is very traditionalist, it is used with an analytical intent, and serves to get a hold on the events of the time by trying to circumscribe their meaning as precisely as possible. De Man's intellectual probity in the bulk of his journalistic writings—a probity, by contrast, blatantly absent from many of the recent articles published on his wartime productions—can be beheld in these essays' constant requestioning and delimiting of all the subjects broached. The typological vocabulary, as well as the set of binary oppositions, here serves to determine with as much accuracy as possible the contemporary situation, political and artistic, and not to polarize and to obscure it as would have been the case if the aim of the essays had been to commend Nazi ideology. This point being made, it must, however, also be acknowledged, that the essays of *Het Vlaamsche Land* and *Le Soir* do not show de Man to have sensed the catastrophic danger that Nazi Germany represented not only with respect to the Jewish people, but to the whole of Europe and the celebrated values of Western civilization as well. This is rather difficult to understand today, after the fact. But if de Man did not come to grips with the horror that was in the offering, it was *among other things* because his analytical apparatus did not provide the means to capture the viciousness and aberration of the Nazi endeavor *on all fronts*. Like so many other contemporary thinkers on the left and the right, the only categories that de Man had at his disposal to conceptualize his inevitable experience of the darker sides of Nazi ideology and the occupation, were those of obscurantism, historical and cultural regression, extremist polarization, etc. In spite of what I believe to have been a truly passionate attempt on de Man's part to understand as precisely as possible the reality he was facing, his intellectual instruments (like those of most of his contemporaries, and of many present intellectuals as well) prevented him from doing so. Faced with what was already visible in 1941 and 42, confronted with the implications of Nazi ideology, and in front of what was to come (the holocaust), humanistic language, traditional modes of thinking, and the type of understanding that it permits, had to fail miserably. It was left to the later de Man to systematically put into question all those blinding schemes, categories and concepts by means of which he had, in his journalistic writings, unsuccessfully tried to gain insight into the political situation in Belgium in the early forties. (p. 215)

Rodolphe Gasché, "Edges of Understanding," in Responses: On Paul de Man's Wartime Journalism, *Werner Hamacher, Neil Hertz and Thomas Keenan, eds., University of Nebraska Press, 1989, pp. 208-20.*

☐ Contemporary Literary Criticism
Indexes

Literary Criticism Series
  Cumulative Author Index
Cumulative Nationality Index
Title Index, Volume 55

This Index Includes References to Entries in These Gale Series

Contemporary Literary Criticism

Presents excerpts of criticism on the works of novelists, poets, dramatists, short story writers, scriptwriters, and other creative writers who are now living or who have died since 1960. Cumulative indexes to authors and nationalities are included, as well as an index to titles discussed in the individual volume. Volumes 1-55 are in print.

Twentieth-Century Literary Criticism

Contains critical excerpts by the most significant commentators on poets, novelists, short story writers, dramatists, and philosophers who died between 1900 and 1960. Cumulative indexes to authors, nationalities, and titles discussed are included in each new volume. Volumes 1-33 are in print.

Nineteenth-Century Literature Criticism

Offers significant passages from criticism on authors who died between 1800 and 1899. Cumulative indexes to authors, nationalities, and titles discussed are included in each new volume. Volumes 1-23 are in print.

Literature Criticism from 1400 to 1800

Compiles significant passages from the most noteworthy criticism on authors of the fifteenth through eighteenth centuries. Cumulative indexes to authors, nationalities, and titles discussed are included in each new volume. Volumes 1-11 are in print.

Classical and Medieval Literature Criticism

Offers excerpts of criticism on the works of world authors from classical antiquity through the fourteenth century. Cumulative indexes to authors, titles, and critics are included in each volume. Volumes 1-3 are in print.

Short Story Criticism

Compiles excerpts of criticism on short fiction by writers of all eras and nationalities. Cumulative indexes to authors, nationalities, and titles discussed are included in each new volume. Volumes 1-3 are in print.

Children's Literature Review

Includes excerpts from reviews, criticism, and commentary on works of authors and illustrators who create books for children. Cumulative indexes to authors, nationalities, and titles discussed are included in each new volume. Volumes 1-18 are in print.

Contemporary Authors Series

Encompasses five related series. *Contemporary Authors* provides biographical and bibliographical information on more than 92,000 writers of fiction, nonfiction, poetry, journalism, drama, motion pictures, and other fields. Each new volume contains sketches on authors not previously covered in the series. Volumes 1-127 are in print. *Contemporary Authors New Revision Series* provides completely updated information on active authors covered in previously published volumes of *CA*. Only entries requiring significant change are revised for *CA New Revision Series*. Volumes 1-27 are in print. *Contemporary Authors Permanent Series* consists of updated listings for deceased and inactive authors removed from the original volumes 9-36 when these volumes were revised. Volumes 1-2 are in print. *Contemporary Authors Autobiography Series* presents specially commissioned autobiographies by leading contemporary writers. Volumes 1-9 are in print. *Contemporary Authors Bibliographical Series* contains primary and secondary bibliographies as well as analytical bibliographical essays by authorities on major modern authors. Volumes 1-2 are in print.

Dictionary of Literary Biography

Encompasses three related series. *Dictionary of Literary Biography* furnishes illustrated overviews of authors' lives and works and places them in the larger perspective of literary history. Volumes 1-81 are in print. *Dictionary of Literary Biography Documentary Series* illuminates the careers of major figures through a selection of literary documents, including letters, notebook and diary entries, interviews, book reviews, and photographs. Volumes 1-6 are in print. *Dictionary of Literary Biography Yearbook* summarizes the past year's literary activity with articles on genres, major prizes, conferences, and other timely subjects and includes updated and new entries on individual authors. Yearbooks for 1980-1988 are in print. A cumulative index to authors and articles is included in each new volume.

Concise Dictionary of American Literary Biography

A six-volume series that collects revised and updated sketches on major American authors that were originally presented in *Dictionary of Literary Biography*. Volumes 1-3 are in print.

Something about the Author Series

Encompasses two related series. *Something about the Author* contains heavily illustrated biographical sketches on juvenile and young adult authors and illustrators from all eras. Volumes 1-54 are in print. *Something about the Author Autobiography Series* presents specially commissioned autobiographies by prominent authors and illustrators of books for children and young adults. Volumes 1-8 are in print.

Yesterday's Authors of Books for Children

Contains heavily illustrated entries on children's writers who died before 1961. Complete in two volumes. Volumes 1-2 are in print.

Literary Criticism Series
Cumulative Author Index

This index lists all author entries in the Gale Literary Criticism Series and includes cross-references to other Gale sources. References in the index are identified as follows:

AAYA: *Authors & Artists for Young Adults,* Volume 1
CAAS: *Contemporary Authors Autobiography Series,* Volumes 1-8
CA: *Contemporary Authors* (original series), Volumes 1-126
CABS: *Contemporary Authors Bibliographical Series,* Volumes 1-2
CANR: *Contemporary Authors New Revision Series,* Volumes 1-26
CAP: *Contemporary Authors Permanent Series,* Volumes 1-2
CA-R: *Contemporary Authors* (revised editions), Volumes 1-44
CDALB: *Concise Dictionary of American Literary Biography,* Volume 1-3
CLC: *Contemporary Literary Criticism,* Volumes 1-54
CLR: *Children's Literature Review,* Volumes 1-18
CMLC: *Classical and Medieval Literature Criticism,* Volumes 1-3
DLB: *Dictionary of Literary Biography,* Volumes 1-78
DLB-DS: *Dictionary of Literary Biography Documentary Series,* Volumes 1-6
DLB-Y: *Dictionary of Literary Biography Yearbook,* Volumes 1980-1988
LC: *Literature Criticism from 1400 to 1800,* Volumes 1-10
NCLC: *Nineteenth-Century Literature Criticism,* Volumes 1-22
SAAS: *Something about the Author Autobiography Series,* Volumes 1-7
SATA: *Something about the Author,* Volumes 1-54
SSC: *Short Story Criticism,* Volumes 1-2
TCLC: *Twentieth-Century Literary Criticism,* Volumes 1-33
YABC: *Yesterday's Authors of Books for Children,* Volumes 1-2

A. E. 1867-1935 . . . . TCLC 3, 10
See also Russell, George William
See also DLB 19

Abbey, Edward 1927- . . . . CLC 36
See also CANR 2; CA 45-48

Abbott, Lee K., Jr. 19??- . . . . CLC 48

Abe, Kobo 1924- . . . . CLC 8, 22
See also CA 65-68

Abell, Kjeld 1901-1961 . . . . CLC 15
See also obituary CA 111

Abish, Walter 1931- . . . . CLC 22
See also CA 101

Abrahams, Peter (Henry) 1919- . . . . . CLC 4
See also CA 57-60

Abrams, M(eyer) H(oward) 1912- . . . CLC 24
See also CANR 13; CA 57-60

Abse, Dannie 1923- . . . . CLC 7, 29
See also CAAS 1; CANR 4; CA 53-56;
DLB 27

Achebe, (Albert) Chinua(lumogu)
1930- . . . . CLC 1, 3, 5, 7, 11, 26, 51
See also CANR 6; CA 1-4R; SATA 38, 40

Acker, Kathy 1948- . . . . CLC 45
See also CA 117, 122

Ackroyd, Peter 1949- . . . . CLC 34

Acorn, Milton 1923- . . . . CLC 15
See also CA 103; DLB 53

Adamov, Arthur 1908-1970 . . . . . . CLC 4, 25
See also CAP 2; CA 17-18;
obituary CA 25-28R

Adams, Alice (Boyd) 1926- . . . CLC 6, 13, 46
See also CA 81-84; DLB-Y 86

Adams, Douglas (Noel) 1952- . . . . . . CLC 27
See also CA 106; DLB-Y 83

Adams, Henry (Brooks)
1838-1918 . . . . TCLC 4
See also CA 104; DLB 12, 47

Adams, Richard (George)
1920- . . . . CLC 4, 5, 18
See also CANR 3; CA 49-52; SATA 7

Adamson, Joy(-Friederike Victoria)
1910-1980 . . . . CLC 17
See also CANR 22; CA 69-72;
obituary CA 93-96; SATA 11;
obituary SATA 22

Adcock, (Kareen) Fleur 1934- . . . . . . CLC 41
See also CANR 11; CA 25-28R; DLB 40

Addams, Charles (Samuel)
1912-1988 . . . . CLC 30
See also CANR 12; CA 61-64

Adler, C(arole) S(chwerdtfeger)
1932- . . . . CLC 35
See also CANR 19; CA 89-92; SATA 26

Adler, Renata 1938- . . . . CLC 8, 31
See also CANR 5, 22; CA 49-52

Ady, Endre 1877-1919 . . . . TCLC 11
See also CA 107

Agee, James 1909-1955 . . . . TCLC 1, 19
See also CA 108; DLB 2, 26;
CDALB 1941-1968

Agnon, S(hmuel) Y(osef Halevi)
1888-1970 . . . . CLC 4, 8, 14
See also CAP 2; CA 17-18;
obituary CA 25-28R

Ai 1947- . . . . CLC 4, 14
See also CA 85-88

Aiken, Conrad (Potter)
1889-1973 . . . . CLC 1, 3, 5, 10
See also CANR 4; CA 5-8R;
obituary CA 45-48; SATA 3, 30; DLB 9,
45

Aiken, Joan (Delano) 1924- . . . . CLC 35
See also CLR 1; CANR 4; CA 9-12R;
SAAS 1; SATA 2, 30

Ainsworth, William Harrison
1805-1882 . . . . NCLC 13
See also SATA 24; DLB 21

Ajar, Emile 1914-1980
See Gary, Romain

Akhmatova, Anna 1888-1966 . . . . CLC 11, 25
See also CAP 1; CA 19-20;
obituary CA 25-28R

Aksakov, Sergei Timofeyvich
1791-1859 .... NCLC 2

Aksenov, Vassily (Pavlovich) 1932-
See Aksyonov, Vasily (Pavlovich)

Aksyonov, Vasily (Pavlovich)
1932- .... CLC 22, 37
See also CANR 12; CA 53-56

Akutagawa Ryunosuke
1892-1927 .... TCLC 16
See also CA 117

Alain-Fournier 1886-1914 .... TCLC 6
See also Fournier, Henri Alban

Alarcon, Pedro Antonio de
1833-1891 .... NCLC 1

Alas (y Urena), Leopoldo (Enrique Garcia)
1852-1901 .... TCLC 29
See also CA 113

Albee, Edward (Franklin III)
1928- ...... CLC 1, 2, 3, 5, 9, 11, 13, 25
See also CANR 8; CA 5-8R; DLB 7;
CDALB 1941-1968

Alberti, Rafael 1902- .... CLC 7
See also CA 85-88

Alcott, Amos Bronson 1799-1888 .. NCLC 1
See also DLB 1

Alcott, Louisa May 1832-1888 .... NCLC 6
See also CLR 1; YABC 1; DLB 1, 42;
CDALB 1865-1917

Aldanov, Mark 1887-1957 .... TCLC 23
See also CA 118

Aldington, Richard 1892-1962 ...... CLC 49
See also CA 85-88; DLB 20, 36

Aldiss, Brian W(ilson)
1925- .... CLC 5, 14, 40
See also CAAS 2; CANR 5; CA 5-8R;
SATA 34; DLB 14

Aleichem, Sholom 1859-1916 .... TCLC 1
See also Rabinovitch, Sholem

Aleixandre, Vicente 1898-1984 ... CLC 9, 36
See also CA 85-88; obituary CA 114

Alepoudelis, Odysseus 1911-
See Elytis, Odysseus

Aleshkovsky, Yuz 1929- .... CLC 44
See also CA 121

Alexander, Lloyd (Chudley) 1924- .. CLC 35
See also CLR 1, 5; CANR 1; CA 1-4R;
SATA 3, 49; DLB 52

Alger, Horatio, Jr. 1832-1899 ..... NCLC 8
See also SATA 16; DLB 42

Algren, Nelson 1909-1981 .... CLC 4, 10, 33
See also CANR 20; CA 13-16R;
obituary CA 103; DLB 9; DLB-Y 81, 82;
CDALB 1941-1968

Alighieri, Dante 1265-1321 .... CMLC 3

Allen, Heywood 1935-
See Allen, Woody
See also CA 33-36R

Allen, Roland 1939-
See Ayckbourn, Alan

Allen, Woody 1935- .... CLC 16
See also Allen, Heywood
See also DLB 44

Allende, Isabel 1942- .... CLC 39

Allingham, Margery (Louise)
1904-1966 .... CLC 19
See also CANR 4; CA 5-8R;
obituary CA 25-28R

Allston, Washington 1779-1843.... NCLC 2
See also DLB 1

Almedingen, E. M. 1898-1971 ...... CLC 12
See also Almedingen, Martha Edith von
See also SATA 3

Almedingen, Martha Edith von 1898-1971
See Almedingen, E. M.
See also CANR 1; CA 1-4R

Alonso, Damaso 1898- .... CLC 14
See also CA 110

Alta 1942- .... CLC 19
See also CA 57-60

Alter, Robert B(ernard) 1935- ...... CLC 34
See also CANR 1; CA 49-52

Alther, Lisa 1944- .... CLC 7, 41
See also CANR 12; CA 65-68

Altman, Robert 1925- .... CLC 16
See also CA 73-76

Alvarez, A(lfred) 1929- .... CLC 5, 13
See also CANR 3; CA 1-4R; DLB 14, 40

Alvarez, Alejandro Rodriguez 1903-1965
See Casona, Alejandro
See also obituary CA 93-96

Amado, Jorge 1912- .... CLC 13, 40
See also CA 77-80

Ambler, Eric 1909- .... CLC 4, 6, 9
See also CANR 7; CA 9-12R

Amichai, Yehuda 1924- .... CLC 9, 22
See also CA 85-88

Amiel, Henri Frederic 1821-1881 .. NCLC 4

Amis, Kingsley (William)
1922- ...... CLC 1, 2, 3, 5, 8, 13, 40, 44
See also CANR 8; CA 9-12R; DLB 15, 27

Amis, Martin 1949- .... CLC 4, 9, 38
See also CANR 8; CA 65-68; DLB 14

Ammons, A(rchie) R(andolph)
1926- .... CLC 2, 3, 5, 8, 9, 25
See also CANR 6; CA 9-12R; DLB 5

Anand, Mulk Raj 1905- .... CLC 23
See also CA 65-68

Anaya, Rudolfo A(lfonso) 1937- .... CLC 23
See also CAAS 4; CANR 1; CA 45-48

Andersen, Hans Christian
1805-1875 .... NCLC 7
See also CLR 6; YABC 1

Anderson, Jessica (Margaret Queale)
19??- .... CLC 37
See also CANR 4; CA 9-12R

Anderson, Jon (Victor) 1940- .... CLC 9
See also CANR 20; CA 25-28R

Anderson, Lindsay 1923- .... CLC 20

Anderson, Maxwell 1888-1959 ..... TCLC 2
See also CA 105; DLB 7

Anderson, Poul (William) 1926- .... CLC 15
See also CAAS 2; CANR 2, 15; CA 1-4R;
SATA 39; DLB 8

Anderson, Robert (Woodruff)
1917- .... CLC 23
See also CA 21-24R; DLB 7

Anderson, Roberta Joan 1943-
See Mitchell, Joni

Anderson, Sherwood
1876-1941 ...... TCLC 1, 10, 24; SSC 1
See also CAAS 3; CA 104, 121; DLB 4, 9;
DLB-DS 1

Andrade, Carlos Drummond de
1902- .... CLC 18

Andrewes, Lancelot 1555-1626 .... LC 5

Andrews, Cicily Fairfield 1892-1983
See West, Rebecca

Andreyev, Leonid (Nikolaevich)
1871-1919 .... TCLC 3
See also CA 104

Andrezel, Pierre 1885-1962
See Dinesen, Isak
See also Blixen, Karen (Christentze
Dinesen)

Andric, Ivo 1892-1975 .... CLC 8
See also CA 81-84; obituary CA 57-60

Angelique, Pierre 1897-1962
See Bataille, Georges

Angell, Roger 1920- .... CLC 26
See also CANR 13; CA 57-60

Angelou, Maya 1928- .... CLC 12, 35
See also CANR 19; CA 65-68; SATA 49;
DLB 38

Annensky, Innokenty 1856-1909 ... TCLC 14
See also CA 110

Anouilh, Jean (Marie Lucien Pierre)
1910-1987 ...... CLC 1, 3, 8, 13, 40, 50
See also CA 17-20R

Anthony, Florence 1947-
See Ai

Anthony (Jacob), Piers 1934- ...... CLC 35
See also Jacob, Piers A(nthony)
D(illingham)
See also DLB 8

Antoninus, Brother 1912-
See Everson, William (Oliver)

Antonioni, Michelangelo 1912- ..... CLC 20
See also CA 73-76

Antschel, Paul 1920-1970
See Celan, Paul
See also CA 85-88

Anwar, Chairil 1922-1949 .... TCLC 22
See also CA 121

Apollinaire, Guillaume
1880-1918 .... TCLC 3, 8
See also Kostrowitzki, Wilhelm Apollinaris
de

Appelfeld, Aharon 1932- .... CLC 23, 47
See also CA 112

Apple, Max (Isaac) 1941- .... CLC 9, 33
See also CANR 19; CA 81-84

Appleman, Philip (Dean) 1926- ..... CLC 51
See also CANR 6; CA 13-16R

Apuleius, (Lucius) (Madaurensis)
125?-175?................... CMLC 1

Aquin, Hubert 1929-1977.......... CLC 15
See also CA 105; DLB 53

Aragon, Louis 1897-1982........ CLC 3, 22
See also CA 69-72; obituary CA 108;
DLB 72

Arbuthnot, John   1667-1735 . . . . LC 1

Archer, Jeffrey (Howard)   1940- . . . . CLC 28
See also CANR 22; CA 77-80

Archer, Jules   1915- . . . . CLC 12
See also CANR 6; CA 9-12R; SATA 4

Arden, John   1930- . . . . CLC 6, 13, 15
See also CAAS 4; CA 13-16R; DLB 13

Arenas, Reinaldo   1943- . . . . CLC 41

Arguedas, Jose Maria
1911-1969 . . . . CLC 10, 18
See also CA 89-92

Argueta, Manlio   1936- . . . . CLC 31

Ariosto, Ludovico   1474-1533 . . . . LC 6

Arlt, Roberto   1900-1942 . . . . TCLC 29
See also CA 123

Armah, Ayi Kwei   1939- . . . . CLC 5, 33
See also CANR 21; CA 61-64

Armatrading, Joan   1950- . . . . CLC 17
See also CA 114

Arnim, Achim von (Ludwig Joachim von
Arnim)   1781-1831 . . . . NCLC 5

Arnold, Matthew   1822-1888 . . . . . . NCLC 6
See also DLB 32, 57

Arnold, Thomas   1795-1842 . . . . . . NCLC 18
See also DLB 55

Arnow, Harriette (Louisa Simpson)
1908-1986 . . . . CLC 2, 7, 18
See also CANR 14; CA 9-12R;
obituary CA 118; SATA 42, 47; DLB 6

Arp, Jean   1887-1966. . . . . CLC 5
See also CA 81-84; obituary CA 25-28R

Arquette, Lois S(teinmetz)   1934-
See Duncan (Steinmetz Arquette), Lois
See also SATA 1

Arrabal, Fernando   1932- . . . . . . CLC 2, 9, 18
See also CANR 15; CA 9-12R

Arrick, Fran   19??- . . . . CLC 30

Artaud, Antonin   1896-1948 . . . . TCLC 3
See also CA 104

Arthur, Ruth M(abel)   1905-1979. . . . CLC 12
See also CANR 4; CA 9-12R;
obituary CA 85-88; SATA 7;
obituary SATA 26

Artsybashev, Mikhail Petrarch
1878-1927 . . . . TCLC 31

Arundel, Honor (Morfydd)
1919-1973 . . . . CLC 17
See also CAP 2; CA 21-22;
obituary CA 41-44R; SATA 4;
obituary SATA 24

Asch, Sholem   1880-1957 . . . . TCLC 3
See also CA 105

Ashbery, John (Lawrence)
1927- . . . CLC 2, 3, 4, 6, 9, 13, 15, 25, 41
See also CANR 9; CA 5-8R; DLB 5;
DLB-Y 81

Ashton-Warner, Sylvia (Constance)
1908-1984 . . . . CLC 19
See also CA 69-72; obituary CA 112

Asimov, Isaac   1920- . . . . CLC 1, 3, 9, 19, 26
See also CLR 12; CANR 2, 19; CA 1-4R;
SATA 1, 26; DLB 8

Astley, Thea (Beatrice May)
1925- . . . . CLC 41
See also CANR 11; CA 65-68

Aston, James   1906-1964
See White, T(erence) H(anbury)

Asturias, Miguel Angel
1899-1974 . . . . CLC 3, 8, 13
See also CAP 2; CA 25-28;
obituary CA 49-52

Atheling, William, Jr.   1921-1975
See Blish, James (Benjamin)

Atherton, Gertrude (Franklin Horn)
1857-1948 . . . . TCLC 2
See also CA 104; DLB 9

Atwood, Margaret (Eleanor)
1939- . . . . CLC 2, 3, 4, 8, 13, 15, 25, 44;
SSC 2
See also CANR 3; CA 49-52; DLB 53

Aubin, Penelope   1685-1731? . . . . LC 9
See also DLB 39

Auchincloss, Louis (Stanton)
1917- . . . . CLC 4, 6, 9, 18, 45
See also CANR 6; CA 1-4R; DLB 2;
DLB-Y 80

Auden, W(ystan) H(ugh)
1907-1973 . . . . . CLC 1, 2, 3, 4, 6, 9, 11,
14, 43
See also CANR 5; CA 9-12R;
obituary CA 45-48; DLB 10, 20

Audiberti, Jacques   1899-1965 . . . . . . CLC 38
See also obituary CA 25-28R

Auel, Jean M(arie)   1936- . . . . CLC 31
See also CANR 21; CA 103

Austen, Jane   1775-1817 . . . . NCLC 1, 13, 19

Auster, Paul   1947- . . . . CLC 47
See also CA 69-72

Austin, Mary (Hunter)
1868-1934 . . . . TCLC 25
See also CA 109; DLB 9

Avison, Margaret   1918- . . . . CLC 2, 4
See also CA 17-20R; DLB 53

Ayckbourn, Alan   1939- . . . . CLC 5, 8, 18, 33
See also CA 21-24R; DLB 13

Ayme, Marcel (Andre)   1902-1967. . . CLC 11
See also CA 89-92; DLB 72

Ayrton, Michael   1921-1975 . . . . CLC 7
See also CANR 9, 21; CA 5-8R;
obituary CA 61-64

Azorin   1874-1967 . . . . CLC 11
See also Martinez Ruiz, Jose

Azuela, Mariano   1873-1952. . . . . . . TCLC 3
See also CA 104

"Bab"   1836-1911
See Gilbert, (Sir) W(illiam) S(chwenck)

Babel, Isaak (Emmanuilovich)
1894-1941 . . . . TCLC 2, 13
See also CA 104

Babits, Mihaly   1883-1941 . . . . TCLC 14
See also CA 114

Bacchelli, Riccardo   1891-1985 . . . . . CLC 19
See also CA 29-32R; obituary CA 117

Bach, Richard (David)   1936- . . . . CLC 14
See also CANR 18; CA 9-12R; SATA 13

Bachman, Richard   1947-
See King, Stephen (Edwin)

Bacovia, George   1881-1957 . . . . . . TCLC 24

Bagehot, Walter   1826-1877 . . . . . . NCLC 10
See also DLB 55

Bagnold, Enid   1889-1981. . . . . CLC 25
See also CANR 5; CA 5-8R;
obituary CA 103; SATA 1, 25; DLB 13

Bagryana, Elisaveta   1893- . . . . CLC 10

Bailey, Paul   1937- . . . . CLC 45
See also CANR 16; CA 21-24R; DLB 14

Baillie, Joanna   1762-1851 . . . . NCLC 2

Bainbridge, Beryl
1933- . . . . . CLC 4, 5, 8, 10, 14, 18, 22
See also CA 21-24R; DLB 14

Baker, Elliott   1922- . . . . CLC 8
See also CANR 2; CA 45-48

Baker, Russell (Wayne)   1925- . . . . . . CLC 31
See also CANR 11; CA 57-60

Bakshi, Ralph   1938- . . . . CLC 26
See also CA 112

Baldwin, James (Arthur)
1924-1987 . . . . . CLC 1, 2, 3, 4, 5, 8, 13,
15, 17, 42, 50
See also CANR 3; CA 1-4R; CABS 1;
SATA 9; DLB 2, 7, 33;
CDALB 1941-1968

Ballard, J(ames) G(raham)
1930- . . . . CLC 3, 6, 14, 36; SSC 1
See also CANR 15; CA 5-8R; DLB 14

Balmont, Konstantin Dmitriyevich
1867-1943 . . . . TCLC 11
See also CA 109

Balzac, Honore de   1799-1850 . . . . . NCLC 5

Bambara, Toni Cade   1939- . . . . CLC 19
See also CA 29-32R; DLB 38

Banim, John   1798-1842 and Banim, Michael
1796-1874 . . . . NCLC 13

Banim, John   1798-1842
See Banim, John and Banim, Michael

Banim, Michael   1796-1874
See Banim, John and Banim, Michael

Banim, Michael   1796-1874 and Banim, John
1798-1842
See Banim, John and Banim, Michael

Banks, Iain   1954- . . . . CLC 34

Banks, Lynne Reid   1929- . . . . CLC 23
See also Reid Banks, Lynne

Banks, Russell   1940- . . . . CLC 37
See also CANR 19; CA 65-68

Banville, John   1945- . . . . CLC 46
See also CA 117; DLB 14

Banville, Theodore (Faullain) de
1832-1891 . . . . NCLC 9

Baraka, Amiri
1934- . . . . CLC 1, 2, 3, 5, 10, 14, 33
See also Baraka, Imamu Amiri
See also Jones, (Everett) LeRoi; DLB 5, 7,
16, 38

Baraka, Imamu Amiri
1934- . . . . CLC 1, 2, 3, 5, 10, 14, 33
See also Baraka, Amiri
See also Jones, (Everett) LeRoi; DLB 5, 7,
16, 38; CDALB 1941-1968

Barbellion, W. N. P. 1889-1919 . . . **TCLC 24**

Barbera, Jack 1945- . . . . **CLC 44**
See also CA 110

Barbey d'Aurevilly, Jules Amedee
1808-1889 . . . . **NCLC 1**

Barbusse, Henri 1873-1935 . . . . **TCLC 5**
See also CA 105

Barea, Arturo 1897-1957 . . . . **TCLC 14**
See also CA 111

Barfoot, Joan 1946- . . . . **CLC 18**
See also CA 105

Baring, Maurice 1874-1945 . . . . **TCLC 8**
See also CA 105; DLB 34

Barker, George (Granville)
1913- . . . . **CLC 8, 48**
See also CANR 7; CA 9-12R; DLB 20

Barker, Howard 1946- . . . . **CLC 37**
See also CA 102; DLB 13

Barker, Pat 1943- . . . . **CLC 32**
See also CA 117, 122

Barlow, Joel 1754-1812 . . . . **NCLC 23**
See also DLB 37

Barnard, Mary (Ethel) 1909- . . . . . . **CLC 48**
See also CAP 2; CA 21-22

Barnes, Djuna (Chappell)
1892-1982 . . . **CLC 3, 4, 8, 11, 29; SSC 3**
See also CANR 16; CA 9-12R;
obituary CA 107; DLB 4, 9, 45

Barnes, Julian 1946- . . . . **CLC 42**
See also CANR 19; CA 102

Barnes, Peter 1931- . . . . **CLC 5**
See also CA 65-68; DLB 13

Baroja (y Nessi), Pio 1872-1956 . . . . **TCLC 8**
See also CA 104

Barondess, Sue K(aufman) 1926-1977
See Kaufman, Sue
See also CANR 1; CA 1-4R;
obituary CA 69-72

Barrett, (Roger) Syd 1946-
See Pink Floyd

Barrett, William (Christopher)
1913- . . . . **CLC 27**
See also CANR 11; CA 13-16R

Barrie, (Sir) J(ames) M(atthew)
1860-1937 . . . . **TCLC 2**
See also CLR 16; YABC 1; CA 104;
DLB 10

Barrol, Grady 1953-
See Bograd, Larry

Barry, Philip (James Quinn)
1896-1949 . . . . **TCLC 11**
See also CA 109; DLB 7

Barth, John (Simmons)
1930- . . . . . . **CLC 1, 2, 3, 5, 7, 9, 10, 14,
27, 51**
See also CANR 5, 23; CA 1-4R; CABS 1;
DLB 2

Barthelme, Donald
1931- . . . . . **CLC 1, 2, 3, 5, 6, 8, 13, 23,
46; SSC 2**
See also CANR 20; CA 21-24R; SATA 7;
DLB 2; DLB-Y 80

Barthelme, Frederick 1943- . . . . **CLC 36**
See also CA 114, 122; DLB-Y 85

Barthes, Roland 1915-1980 . . . . **CLC 24**
See also obituary CA 97-100

Barzun, Jacques (Martin) 1907- . . . . **CLC 51**
See also CANR 22; CA 61-64

Bassani, Giorgio 1916- . . . . **CLC 9**
See also CA 65-68

Bataille, Georges 1897-1962 . . . . **CLC 29**
See also CA 101; obituary CA 89-92

Bates, H(erbert) E(rnest)
1905-1974 . . . . **CLC 46**
See also CA 93-96; obituary CA 45-48

Baudelaire, Charles 1821-1867 . . . . **NCLC 6**

Baum, L(yman) Frank 1856-1919 . . . **TCLC 7**
See also CLR 15; CA 108; SATA 18;
DLB 22

Baumbach, Jonathan 1933- . . . . . . **CLC 6, 23**
See also CAAS 5; CANR 12; CA 13-16R;
DLB-Y 80

Bausch, Richard (Carl) 1945- . . . . . . **CLC 51**
See also CA 101

Baxter, Charles 1947- . . . . **CLC 45**
See also CA 57-60

Baxter, James K(eir) 1926-1972 . . . . **CLC 14**
See also CA 77-80

Bayer, Sylvia 1909-1981
See Glassco, John

Beagle, Peter S(oyer) 1939- . . . . **CLC 7**
See also CANR 4; CA 9-12R; DLB-Y 80

Beard, Charles A(ustin)
1874-1948 . . . . **TCLC 15**
See also CA 115; SATA 18; DLB 17

Beardsley, Aubrey 1872-1898 . . . . . **NCLC 6**

Beattie, Ann 1947- . . . . **CLC 8, 13, 18, 40**
See also CA 81-84; DLB-Y 82

**Beauvoir, Simone (Lucie Ernestine Marie
Bertrand) de**
1908-1986 . . . **CLC 1, 2, 4, 8, 14, 31, 44,
50**
See also CA 9-12R; obituary CA 118;
DLB 72; DLB-Y 86

Becker, Jurek 1937- . . . . **CLC 7, 19**
See also CA 85-88

Becker, Walter 1950- **and Fagen, Donald**
1948- . . . . **CLC 26**

Becker, Walter 1950-
See Becker, Walter and Fagen, Donald

Beckett, Samuel (Barclay)
1906- . . . . . . **CLC 1, 2, 3, 4, 6, 9, 10, 11,
14, 18, 29**
See also CA 5-8R; DLB 13, 15

Beckford, William 1760-1844 . . . . **NCLC 16**
See also DLB 39

Beckman, Gunnel 1910- . . . . **CLC 26**
See also CANR 15; CA 33-36R; SATA 6

Becque, Henri 1837-1899 . . . . **NCLC 3**

Beddoes, Thomas Lovell
1803-1849 . . . . **NCLC 3**

Beecher, John 1904-1980 . . . . **CLC 6**
See also CANR 8; CA 5-8R;
obituary CA 105

Beer, Johann 1655-1700 . . . . **LC 5**

Beerbohm, (Sir Henry) Max(imilian)
1872-1956 . . . . **TCLC 1, 24**
See also CA 104; DLB 34

Behan, Brendan
1923-1964 . . . . **CLC 1, 8, 11, 15**
See also CA 73-76; DLB 13

Behn, Aphra 1640?-1689 . . . . **LC 1**
See also DLB 39

Behrman, S(amuel) N(athaniel)
1893-1973 . . . . **CLC 40**
See also CAP 1; CA 15-16;
obituary CA 45-48; DLB 7, 44

Belasco, David 1853-1931 . . . . **TCLC 3**
See also CA 104; DLB 7

Belcheva, Elisaveta 1893-
See Bagryana, Elisaveta

Belinski, Vissarion Grigoryevich
1811-1848 . . . . **NCLC 5**

Belitt, Ben 1911- . . . . **CLC 22**
See also CAAS 4; CANR 7; CA 13-16R;
DLB 5

Bell, Acton 1820-1849
See Bronte, Anne

Bell, Currer 1816-1855
See Bronte, Charlotte

Bell, Madison Smartt 1957- . . . . **CLC 41**
See also CA 111

Bell, Marvin (Hartley) 1937- . . . . . **CLC 8, 31**
See also CA 21-24R; DLB 5

Bellamy, Edward 1850-1898 . . . . . . **NCLC 4**
See also DLB 12

**Belloc, (Joseph) Hilaire (Pierre Sebastien
Rene Swanton)**
1870-1953 . . . . **TCLC 7, 18**
See also YABC 1; CA 106; DLB 19

Bellow, Saul
1915- . . . . . **CLC 1, 2, 3, 6, 8, 10, 13, 15,
25, 33, 34**
See also CA 5-8R; CABS 1; DLB 2, 28;
DLB-Y 82; DLB-DS 3;
CDALB 1941-1968

Belser, Reimond Karel Maria de 1929-
See Ruyslinck, Ward

Bely, Andrey 1880-1934 . . . . **TCLC 7**
See also CA 104

Benary-Isbert, Margot 1889-1979 . . . **CLC 12**
See also CLR 12; CANR 4; CA 5-8R;
obituary CA 89-92; SATA 2;
obituary SATA 21

Benavente (y Martinez), Jacinto
1866-1954 . . . . **TCLC 3**
See also CA 106

Benchley, Peter (Bradford)
1940- . . . . **CLC 4, 8**
See also CANR 12; CA 17-20R; SATA 3

Benchley, Robert 1889-1945 . . . . **TCLC 1**
See also CA 105; DLB 11

Benedikt, Michael 1935- . . . . **CLC 4, 14**
See also CANR 7; CA 13-16R; DLB 5

Benet, Juan 1927- . . . . **CLC 28**

Benet, Stephen Vincent
1898-1943 . . . . **TCLC 7**
See also YABC 1; CA 104; DLB 4, 48

Benet, William Rose 1886-1950 . . . **TCLC 28**
See also CA 118; DLB 45

Benn, Gottfried 1886-1956 . . . . **TCLC 3**
See also CA 106; DLB 56

Bennett, Alan 1934- . . . . **CLC 45**
See also CA 103

Bennett, (Enoch) Arnold
1867-1931 . . . . **TCLC 5, 20**
See also CA 106; DLB 10, 34

Bennett, George Harold 1930-
See Bennett, Hal
See also CA 97-100

Bennett, Hal 1930- . . . . **CLC 5**
See also Bennett, George Harold
See also DLB 33

Bennett, Jay 1912- . . . . **CLC 35**
See also CANR 11; CA 69-72; SAAS 4;
SATA 27, 41

Bennett, Louise (Simone) 1919- . . . . **CLC 28**
See also Bennett-Coverly, Louise Simone

Bennett-Coverly, Louise Simone 1919-
See Bennett, Louise (Simone)
See also CA 97-100

Benson, E(dward) F(rederic)
1867-1940 . . . . **TCLC 27**
See also CA 114

Benson, Jackson J. 1930- . . . . **CLC 34**
See also CA 25-28R

Benson, Sally 1900-1972 . . . . **CLC 17**
See also CAP 1; CA 19-20;
obituary CA 37-40R; SATA 1, 35;
obituary SATA 27

Benson, Stella 1892-1933 . . . . **TCLC 17**
See also CA 117; DLB 36

Bentley, E(dmund) C(lerihew)
1875-1956 . . . . **TCLC 12**
See also CA 108; DLB 70

Bentley, Eric (Russell) 1916- . . . . **CLC 24**
See also CANR 6; CA 5-8R

Berger, John (Peter) 1926- . . . . . . **CLC 2, 19**
See also CA 81-84; DLB 14

Berger, Melvin (H.) 1927- . . . . **CLC 12**
See also CANR 4; CA 5-8R; SAAS 2;
SATA 5

Berger, Thomas (Louis)
1924- . . . . **CLC 3, 5, 8, 11, 18, 38**
See also CANR 5; CA 1-4R; DLB 2;
DLB-Y 80

Bergman, (Ernst) Ingmar 1918- . . . . . **CLC 16**
See also CA 81-84

Bergstein, Eleanor 1938- . . . . **CLC 4**
See also CANR 5; CA 53-56

Bermant, Chaim 1929- . . . . **CLC 40**
See also CANR 6; CA 57-60

Bernanos, (Paul Louis) Georges
1888-1948 . . . . **TCLC 3**
See also CA 104; DLB 72

Bernhard, Thomas 1931- . . . . **CLC 3, 32**
See also CA 85-88

Berriault, Gina 1926- . . . . **CLC 54**
See also CA 116

Berrigan, Daniel J. 1921- . . . . **CLC 4**
See also CAAS 1; CANR 11; CA 33-36R;
DLB 5

Berrigan, Edmund Joseph Michael, Jr.
1934-1983
See Berrigan, Ted
See also CANR 14; CA 61-64;
obituary CA 110

Berrigan, Ted 1934-1983 . . . . **CLC 37**
See also Berrigan, Edmund Joseph Michael,
Jr.
See also DLB 5

Berry, Chuck 1926- . . . . **CLC 17**

Berry, Wendell (Erdman)
1934- . . . . **CLC 4, 6, 8, 27, 46**
See also CA 73-76; DLB 5, 6

Berryman, Jerry 1914-1972
See also CDALB 1941-1968

Berryman, John
1914-1972 . . . . . **CLC 1, 2, 3, 4, 6, 8, 10,
13, 25**
See also CAP 1; CA 15-16;
obituary CA 33-36R; CABS 2; DLB 48;
CDALB 1941-1968

Bertolucci, Bernardo 1940- . . . . **CLC 16**
See also CA 106

Besant, Annie (Wood) 1847-1933 . . . **TCLC 9**
See also CA 105

Bessie, Alvah 1904-1985 . . . . **CLC 23**
See also CANR 2; CA 5-8R;
obituary CA 116; DLB 26

Beti, Mongo 1932- . . . . **CLC 27**
See also Beyidi, Alexandre

Betjeman, (Sir) John
1906-1984 . . . . **CLC 2, 6, 10, 34, 43**
See also CA 9-12R; obituary CA 112;
DLB 20; DLB-Y 84

Betti, Ugo 1892-1953 . . . . **TCLC 5**
See also CA 104

Betts, Doris (Waugh) 1932- . . . . **CLC 3, 6, 28**
See also CANR 9; CA 13-16R; DLB-Y 82

Bialik, Chaim Nachman
1873-1934 . . . . **TCLC 25**

Bidart, Frank 19??- . . . . **CLC 33**

Bienek, Horst 1930- . . . . **CLC 7, 11**
See also CA 73-76

Bierce, Ambrose (Gwinett)
1842-1914? . . . . **TCLC 1, 7**
See also CA 104; DLB 11, 12, 23, 71;
CDALB 1865-1917

Billington, Rachel 1942- . . . . **CLC 43**
See also CA 33-36R

Binyon, T(imothy) J(ohn) 1936- . . . . **CLC 34**
See also CA 111

Bioy Casares, Adolfo 1914- . . . . **CLC 4, 8, 13**
See also CANR 19; CA 29-32R

Bird, Robert Montgomery
1806-1854 . . . . **NCLC 1**

Birdwell, Cleo 1936-
See DeLillo, Don

Birney (Alfred) Earle
1904- . . . . **CLC 1, 4, 6, 11**
See also CANR 5, 20; CA 1-4R

Bishop, Elizabeth
1911-1979 . . . . . **CLC 1, 4, 9, 13, 15, 32**
See also CA 5-8R; obituary CA 89-92;
CABS 2; obituary SATA 24; DLB 5

Bishop, John 1935- . . . . **CLC 10**
See also CA 105

Bissett, Bill 1939- . . . . **CLC 18**
See also CANR 15; CA 69-72; DLB 53

Biyidi, Alexandre 1932-
See Beti, Mongo
See also CA 114

Bjornson, Bjornstjerne (Martinius)
1832-1910 . . . . **TCLC 7**
See also CA 104

Blackburn, Paul 1926-1971 . . . . . . **CLC 9, 43**
See also CA 81-84; obituary CA 33-36R;
DLB 16; DLB-Y 81

Black Elk 1863-1950 . . . . **TCLC 33**

Blackmore, R(ichard) D(oddridge)
1825-1900 . . . . **TCLC 27**
See also CA 120; DLB 18

Blackmur, R(ichard) P(almer)
1904-1965 . . . . **CLC 2, 24**
See also CAP 1; CA 11-12;
obituary CA 25-28R; DLB 63

Blackwood, Algernon (Henry)
1869-1951 . . . . **TCLC 5**
See also CA 105

Blackwood, Caroline 1931- . . . . **CLC 6, 9**
See also CA 85-88; DLB 14

Blair, Eric Arthur 1903-1950
See Orwell, George
See also CA 104; SATA 29

Blais, Marie-Claire
1939- . . . . **CLC 2, 4, 6, 13, 22**
See also CAAS 4; CA 21-24R; DLB 53

Blaise, Clark 1940- . . . . **CLC 29**
See also CAAS 3; CANR 5; CA 53-56R;
DLB 53

Blake, Nicholas 1904-1972
See Day Lewis, C(ecil)

Blake, William 1757-1827 . . . . **NCLC 13**
See also SATA 30

Blasco Ibanez, Vicente
1867-1928 . . . . **TCLC 12**
See also CA 110

Blatty, William Peter 1928- . . . . **CLC 2**
See also CANR 9; CA 5-8R

Blessing, Lee 1949- . . . . **CLC 54**

Blish, James (Benjamin)
1921-1975 . . . . **CLC 14**
See also CANR 3; CA 1-4R;
obituary CA 57-60; DLB 8

Blixen, Karen (Christentze Dinesen)
1885-1962
See Dinesen, Isak
See also CAP 2; CA 25-28; SATA 44

Bloch, Robert (Albert) 1917- . . . . **CLC 33**
See also CANR 5; CA 5-8R; SATA 12;
DLB 44

Blok, Aleksandr (Aleksandrovich)
1880-1921 . . . . **TCLC 5**
See also CA 104

Bloom, Harold 1930- . . . . **CLC 24**
See also CA 13-16R

Blount, Roy (Alton), Jr. 1941- . . . . . **CLC 38**
See also CANR 10; CA 53-56

Bloy, Leon 1846-1917........... **TCLC 22**
See also CA 121

Blume, Judy (Sussman Kitchens)
1938-................... **CLC 12, 30**
See also CLR 2, 15; CANR 13; CA 29-32R;
SATA 2, 31; DLB 52

Blunden, Edmund (Charles)
1896-1974................... **CLC 2**
See also CAP 2; CA 17-18;
obituary CA 45-48; DLB 20

Bly, Robert (Elwood)
1926-......... **CLC 1, 2, 5, 10, 15, 38**
See also CA 5-8R; DLB 5

Bochco, Steven 1944?- and **Kozoll, Michael**
1940?-.................... **CLC 35**

Bochco, Steven 1944?-
See Bochco, Steven and Kozoll, Michael

Bodker, Cecil 1927-............. **CLC 21**
See also CANR 13; CA 73-76; SATA 14

Boell, Heinrich (Theodor) 1917-1985
See Boll, Heinrich
See also CA 21-24R; obituary CA 116

Bogan, Louise 1897-1970..... **CLC 4, 39, 46**
See also CA 73-76; obituary CA 25-28R;
DLB 45

Bogarde, Dirk 1921-............. **CLC 19**
See also Van Den Bogarde, Derek (Jules
Gaspard Ulric) Niven
See also DLB 14

Bogosian, Eric 1953-............. **CLC 45**

Bograd, Larry 1953-............. **CLC 35**
See also CA 93-96; SATA 33

Bohl de Faber, Cecilia 1796-1877
See Caballero, Fernan

Boiardo, Matteo Maria 1441-1494.... **LC 6**

Boileau-Despreaux, Nicolas
1636-1711................... **LC 3**

Boland, Eavan (Aisling) 1944-...... **CLC 40**
See also DLB 40

Boll, Heinrich (Theodor)
1917-1985... **CLC 2, 3, 6, 9, 11, 15, 27,**
39
See also Boell, Heinrich (Theodor)
See also DLB 69; DLB-Y 85

Bolt, Robert (Oxton) 1924-........ **CLC 14**
See also CA 17-20R; DLB 13

Bond, Edward 1934-....... **CLC 4, 6, 13, 23**
See also CA 25-28R; DLB 13

Bonham, Frank 1914-............. **CLC 12**
See also CANR 4; CA 9-12R; SAAS 3;
SATA 1, 49

Bonnefoy, Yves 1923-........... **CLC 9, 15**
See also CA 85-88

Bontemps, Arna (Wendell)
1902-1973................. **CLC 1, 18**
See also CLR 6; CANR 4; CA 1-4R;
obituary CA 41-44R; SATA 2, 44;
obituary SATA 24; DLB 48, 51

Booth, Martin 1944-............. **CLC 13**
See also CAAS 2; CA 93-96

Booth, Philip 1925-............. **CLC 23**
See also CANR 5; CA 5-8R; DLB-Y 82

Booth, Wayne C(layson) 1921-...... **CLC 24**
See also CAAS 5; CANR 3; CA 1-4R

Borchert, Wolfgang 1921-1947..... **TCLC 5**
See also CA 104; DLB 69

Borges, Jorge Luis
1899-1986... **CLC 1, 2, 3, 4, 6, 8, 9, 10,**
13, 19, 44, 48
See also CANR 19; CA 21-24R; DLB-Y 86

Borowski, Tadeusz 1922-1951...... **TCLC 9**
See also CA 106

Borrow, George (Henry)
1803-1881................. **NCLC 9**
See also DLB 21, 55

Bosschere, Jean de 1878-1953..... **TCLC 19**
See also CA 115

Boswell, James 1740-1795.......... **LC 4**

Bourget, Paul (Charles Joseph)
1852-1935................. **TCLC 12**
See also CA 107

Bourjaily, Vance (Nye) 1922-....... **CLC 8**
See also CAAS 1; CANR 2; CA 1-4R;
DLB 2

Bourne, Randolph S(illiman)
1886-1918................. **TCLC 16**
See also CA 117; DLB 63

Bova, Ben(jamin William) 1932-.... **CLC 45**
See also CLR 3; CANR 11; CA 5-8R;
SATA 6; DLB-Y 81

Bowen, Elizabeth (Dorothea Cole)
1899-1973..... **CLC 1, 3, 6, 11, 15, 22;**
SSC 3
See also CAP 2; CA 17-18;
obituary CA 41-44R; DLB 15

Bowering, George 1935-........ **CLC 15, 47**
See also CANR 10; CA 21-24R; DLB 53

Bowering, Marilyn R(uthe) 1949-... **CLC 32**
See also CA 101

Bowers, Edgar 1924-............. **CLC 9**
See also CA 5-8R; DLB 5

Bowie, David 1947-............. **CLC 17**
See also Jones, David Robert

Bowles, Jane (Sydney) 1917-1973.... **CLC 3**
See also CAP 2; CA 19-20;
obituary CA 41-44R

Bowles, Paul (Frederick)
1910-........... **CLC 1, 2, 19; SSC 3**
See also CAAS 1; CANR 1, 19; CA 1-4R;
DLB 5, 6

Box, Edgar 1925-
See Vidal, Gore

Boyd, William 1952-........... **CLC 28**
See also CA 114, 120

Boyle, Kay 1903-........... **CLC 1, 5, 19**
See also CAAS 1; CA 13-16R; DLB 4, 9, 48

Boyle, Patrick 19??-............. **CLC 19**

Boyle, T. Coraghessan 1948-.... **CLC 36, 55**
See also CA 120; DLB-Y 86

Brackenridge, Hugh Henry
1748-1816................. **NCLC 7**
See also DLB 11, 37

Bradbury, Edward P. 1939-
See Moorcock, Michael

Bradbury, Malcolm (Stanley)
1932-..................... **CLC 32**
See also CANR 1; CA 1-4R; DLB 14

Bradbury, Ray(mond Douglas)
1920-............ **CLC 1, 3, 10, 15, 42**
See also CANR 2; CA 1-4R; SATA 11;
DLB 2, 8

Bradley, David (Henry), Jr. 1950-.. **CLC 23**
See also CA 104; DLB 33

Bradley, John Ed 1959-........... **CLC 55**

Bradley, Marion Zimmer 1930-..... **CLC 30**
See also CANR 7; CA 57-60; DLB 8

Bradstreet, Anne 1612-1672......... **LC 4**
See also DLB 24; CDALB 1640-1865

Bragg, Melvyn 1939-............. **CLC 10**
See also CANR 10; CA 57-60; DLB 14

Braine, John (Gerard)
1922-1986.............. **CLC 1, 3, 41**
See also CANR 1; CA 1-4R;
obituary CA 120; DLB 15; DLB-Y 86

Brammer, Billy Lee 1930?-1978
See Brammer, William

Brammer, William 1930?-1978..... **CLC 31**
See also obituary CA 77-80

Brancati, Vitaliano 1907-1954..... **TCLC 12**
See also CA 109

Brancato, Robin F(idler) 1936-..... **CLC 35**
See also CANR 11; CA 69-72; SATA 23

Brand, Millen 1906-1980.......... **CLC 7**
See also CA 21-24R; obituary CA 97-100

Branden, Barbara 19??-........... **CLC 44**

Brandes, Georg (Morris Cohen)
1842-1927............... **TCLC 10**
See also CA 105

Branley, Franklyn M(ansfield)
1915-..................... **CLC 21**
See also CANR 14; CA 33-36R; SATA 4

Brathwaite, Edward 1930-........ **CLC 11**
See also CANR 11; CA 25-28R; DLB 53

Brautigan, Richard (Gary)
1935-1984.... **CLC 1, 3, 5, 9, 12, 34, 42**
See also CA 53-56; obituary CA 113;
DLB 2, 5; DLB-Y 80, 84

Brecht, (Eugen) Bertolt (Friedrich)
1898-1956............. **TCLC 1, 6, 13**
See also CA 104; DLB 56

Bremer, Fredrika 1801-1865..... **NCLC 11**

Brennan, Christopher John
1870-1932................. **TCLC 17**
See also CA 117

Brennan, Maeve 1917-............. **CLC 5**
See also CA 81-84

Brentano, Clemens (Maria)
1778-1842................. **NCLC 1**

Brenton, Howard 1942-........... **CLC 31**
See also CA 69-72; DLB 13

Breslin, James 1930-
See Breslin, Jimmy
See also CA 73-76

Breslin, Jimmy 1930-.......... **CLC 4, 43**
See also Breslin, James

Bresson, Robert 1907-............. **CLC 16**
See also CA 110

Breton, Andre 1896-1966... **CLC 2, 9, 15, 54**
See also CAP 2; CA 19-20;
obituary CA 25-28R; DLB 65

Breytenbach, Breyten 1939-..... CLC 23, 37
See also CA 113

Bridgers, Sue Ellen 1942-......... CLC 26
See also CANR 11; CA 65-68; SAAS 1;
SATA 22; DLB 52

Bridges, Robert 1844-1930........ TCLC 1
See also CA 104; DLB 19

Bridie, James 1888-1951 .... TCLC 3
See also Mavor, Osborne Henry
See also DLB 10

Brin, David 1950-................ CLC 34
See also CA 102

Brink, Andre (Philippus)
1935-..................... CLC 18, 36
See also CA 104

Brinsmead, H(esba) F(ay) 1922-.... CLC 21
See also CANR 10; CA 21-24R; SATA 18

Brittain, Vera (Mary) 1893?-1970... CLC 23
See also CAP 1; CA 15-16;
obituary CA 25-28R

Broch, Hermann 1886-1951....... TCLC 20
See also CA 117

Brock, Rose 1923-
See Hansen, Joseph

Brodsky, Iosif Alexandrovich 1940-
See Brodsky, Joseph (Alexandrovich)
See also CA 41-44R

Brodsky, Joseph (Alexandrovich)
1940-........... CLC 4, 6, 13, 36, 50
See also Brodsky, Iosif Alexandrovich

Brodsky, Michael (Mark) 1948-.... CLC 19
See also CANR 18; CA 102

Bromell, Henry 1947-.............. CLC 5
See also CANR 9; CA 53-56

Bromfield, Louis (Brucker)
1896-1956.................. TCLC 11
See also CA 107; DLB 4, 9

Broner, E(sther) M(asserman)
1930-..................... CLC 19
See also CANR 8; CA 17-20R; DLB 28

Bronk, William 1918-............. CLC 10
See also CA 89-92

Bronte, Anne 1820-1849......... NCLC 4
See also DLB 21

Bronte, Charlotte 1816-1855 .... NCLC 3, 8
See also DLB 21

Bronte, (Jane) Emily 1818-1848 .. NCLC 16
See also DLB 21, 32

Brooke, Frances 1724-1789 .... LC 6
See also DLB 39

Brooke, Henry 1703?-1783 .... LC 1
See also DLB 39

Brooke, Rupert (Chawner)
1887-1915 .... TCLC 2, 7
See also CA 104; DLB 19

Brooke-Rose, Christine 1926-...... CLC 40
See also CA 13-16R; DLB 14

Brookner, Anita 1928-..... CLC 32, 34, 51
See also CA 114, 120; DLB-Y 87

Brooks, Cleanth 1906-............ CLC 24
See also CA 17-20R; DLB 63

Brooks, Gwendolyn
1917-.......... CLC 1, 2, 4, 5, 15, 49
See also CANR 1; CA 1-4R; SATA 6;
DLB 5; CDALB 1941-1968

Brooks, Mel 1926-............... CLC 12
See also Kaminsky, Melvin
See also CA 65-68; DLB 26

Brooks, Peter 1938-............... CLC 34
See also CANR 1; CA 45-48

Brooks, Van Wyck 1886-1963...... CLC 29
See also CANR 6; CA 1-4R; DLB 45, 63

Brophy, Brigid (Antonia)
1929-................... CLC 6, 11, 29
See also CAAS 4; CA 5-8R; DLB 14

Brosman, Catharine Savage 1934-.... CLC 9
See also CANR 21; CA 61-64

Broughton, T(homas) Alan 1936-... CLC 19
See also CANR 2; CA 45-48

Broumas, Olga 1949-............. CLC 10
See also CANR 20; CA 85-88

Brown, Claude 1937-............. CLC 30
See also CA 73-76

Brown, Dee (Alexander) 1908-.. CLC 18, 47
See also CAAS 6; CANR 11; CA 13-16R;
SATA 5; DLB-Y 80

Brown, George Douglas 1869-1902
See Douglas, George

Brown, George Mackay 1921-.... CLC 5, 28
See also CAAS 6; CANR 12; CA 21-24R;
SATA 35; DLB 14, 27

Brown, Rita Mae 1944-........ CLC 18, 43
See also CANR 2, 11; CA 45-48

Brown, Rosellen 1939-............ CLC 32
See also CANR 14; CA 77-80

Brown, Sterling A(llen) 1901-.... CLC 1, 23
See also CA 85-88; DLB 48, 51, 63

Brown, William Wells
1816?-1884................. NCLC 2
See also DLB 3, 50

Browne, Jackson 1950-........... CLC 21

Browning, Elizabeth Barrett
1806-1861 .... NCLC 1, 16
See also DLB 32

Browning, Robert 1812-1889 ..... NCLC 19
See also DLB 32

Browning, Tod 1882-1962 .... CLC 16
See also obituary CA 117

Bruccoli, Matthew J(oseph) 1931-.. CLC 34
See also CANR 7; CA 9-12R

Bruce, Lenny 1925-1966 .... CLC 21
See also Schneider, Leonard Alfred

Brunner, John (Kilian Houston)
1934-..................... CLC 8, 10
See also CANR 2; CA 1-4R

Brutus, Dennis 1924-............. CLC 43
See also CANR 2; CA 49-52

Bryan, C(ourtlandt) D(ixon) B(arnes)
1936-..................... CLC 29
See also CANR 13; CA 73-76

Bryant, William Cullen
1794-1878 .... NCLC 6
See also DLB 3, 43; CDALB 1640-1865

Bryusov, Valery (Yakovlevich)
1873-1924 .... TCLC 10
See also CA 107

Buchanan, George 1506-1582 .... LC 4

Buchheim, Lothar-Gunther 1918-.... CLC 6
See also CA 85-88

Buchwald, Art(hur) 1925-......... CLC 33
See also CANR 21; CA 5-8R; SATA 10

Buck, Pearl S(ydenstricker)
1892-1973 .... CLC 7, 11, 18
See also CANR 1; CA 1-4R;
obituary CA 41-44R; SATA 1, 25; DLB 9

Buckler, Ernest 1908-1984........ CLC 13
See also CAP 1; CA 11-12;
obituary CA 114; SATA 47

Buckley, William F(rank), Jr.
1925-................. CLC 7, 18, 37
See also CANR 1; CA 1-4R; DLB-Y 80

Buechner, (Carl) Frederick
1926-................ CLC 2, 4, 6, 9
See also CANR 11; CA 13-16R; DLB-Y 80

Buell, John (Edward) 1927-....... CLC 10
See also CA 1-4R; DLB 53

Buero Vallejo, Antonio 1916-... CLC 15, 46
See also CA 106

Bukowski, Charles 1920-.... CLC 2, 5, 9, 41
See also CA 17-20R; DLB 5

Bulgakov, Mikhail (Afanas'evich)
1891-1940 .... TCLC 2, 16
See also CA 105

Bullins, Ed 1935-............. CLC 1, 5, 7
See also CA 49-52; DLB 7, 38

Bulwer-Lytton, (Lord) Edward (George Earle
Lytton) 1803-1873 .... NCLC 1
See also Lytton, Edward Bulwer
See also DLB 21

Bunin, Ivan (Alexeyevich)
1870-1953 .... TCLC 6
See also CA 104

Bunting, Basil 1900-1985.... CLC 10, 39, 47
See also CANR 7; CA 53-56;
obituary CA 115; DLB 20

Bunuel, Luis 1900-1983 .... CLC 16
See also CA 101; obituary CA 110

Bunyan, John (1628-1688)........... LC 4
See also DLB 39

Burgess (Wilson, John) Anthony
1917-..... CLC 1, 2, 4, 5, 8, 10, 13, 15,
22, 40
See also Wilson, John (Anthony) Burgess
See also DLB 14

Burke, Edmund 1729-1797.......... LC 7

Burke, Kenneth (Duva) 1897-.... CLC 2, 24
See also CA 5-8R; DLB 45, 63

Burney, Fanny 1752-1840 .... NCLC 12
See also DLB 39

Burns, Robert 1759-1796........... LC 3

Burns, Tex 1908?-
See L'Amour, Louis (Dearborn)

Burnshaw, Stanley 1906-..... CLC 3, 13, 44
See also CA 9-12R; DLB 48

Burr, Anne 1937-................. CLC 6
See also CA 25-28R

Author Index

Burroughs, Edgar Rice   1875-1950. . . TCLC 2
See also CA 104; SATA 41; DLB 8

Burroughs, William S(eward)
1914- . . . . **CLC 1, 2, 5, 15, 22, 42**
See also CANR 20; CA 9-12R; DLB 2, 8,
16; DLB-Y 81

Busch, Frederick   1941- . . . **CLC 7, 10, 18, 47**
See also CAAS 1; CA 33-36R; DLB 6

Bush, Ronald   19??- . . . . CLC 34

Butler, Octavia E(stelle)   1947- . . . . . CLC 38
See also CANR 12; CA 73-76; DLB 33

Butler, Samuel   1835-1902 . . . . . . TCLC 1, 33
See also CA 104; DLB 18, 57

Butor, Michel (Marie Francois)
1926- . . . . **CLC 1, 3, 8, 11, 15**
See also CA 9-12R

Buzzati, Dino   1906-1972 . . . . CLC 36
See also obituary CA 33-36R

Byars, Betsy   1928- . . . . CLC 35
See also CLR 1, 16; CANR 18; CA 33-36R;
SAAS 1; SATA 4, 46; DLB 52

Byatt, A(ntonia) S(usan Drabble)
1936- . . . . CLC 19
See also CANR 13; CA 13-16R; DLB 14

Byrne, David   1953?- . . . . CLC 26

Byrne, John Keyes   1926-
See Leonard, Hugh
See also CA 102

Byron, George Gordon (Noel), Lord Byron
1788-1824 . . . . NCLC 2, 12

Caballero, Fernan   1796-1877. . . . . NCLC 10

Cabell, James Branch   1879-1958 . . . TCLC 6
See also CA 105; DLB 9

Cable, George Washington
1844-1925 . . . . TCLC 4
See also CA 104; DLB 12

Cabrera Infante, G(uillermo)
1929- . . . . CLC 5, 25, 45
See also CA 85-88

Cage, John (Milton, Jr.)   1912- . . . . . CLC 41
See also CANR 9; CA 13-16R

Cain, G.   1929-
See Cabrera Infante, G(uillermo)

Cain, James M(allahan)
1892-1977 . . . . CLC 3, 11, 28
See also CANR 8; CA 17-20R;
obituary CA 73-76

Caldwell, Erskine (Preston)
1903-1987 . . . . CLC 1, 8, 14, 50
See also CAAS 1; CANR 2; CA 1-4R;
obituary CA 121; DLB 9

Caldwell, (Janet Miriam) Taylor (Holland)
1900-1985 . . . . CLC 2, 28, 39
See also CANR 5; CA 5-8R;
obituary CA 116

Calhoun, John Caldwell
1782-1850 . . . . NCLC 15
See also DLB 3

Calisher, Hortense   1911- . . . . CLC 2, 4, 8, 38
See also CANR 1, 22; CA 1-4R; DLB 2

Callaghan, Morley (Edward)
1903- . . . . CLC 3, 14, 41
See also CA 9-12R

Calvino, Italo
1923-1985 . . . .   **CLC 5, 8, 11, 22, 33, 39;
SSC 3**
See also CANR 23; CA 85-88;
obituary CA 116

Cameron, Peter   1959- . . . . CLC 44

Campana, Dino   1885-1932 . . . . TCLC 20
See also CA 117

Campbell, John W(ood), Jr.
1910-1971 . . . . CLC 32
See also CAP 2; CA 21-22;
obituary CA 29-32R; DLB 8

Campbell, (John) Ramsey   1946- . . . . CLC 42
See also CANR 7; CA 57-60

Campbell, (Ignatius) Roy (Dunnachie)
1901-1957 . . . . TCLC 5
See also CA 104; DLB 20

Campbell, Thomas   1777-1844 . . . . NCLC 19

Campbell, (William) Wilfred
1861-1918 . . . . TCLC 9
See also CA 106

Camus, Albert
1913-1960 . . . . CLC 1, 2, 4, 9, 11, 14, 32
See also CA 89-92; DLB 72

Canby, Vincent   1924- . . . . CLC 13
See also CA 81-84

Canetti, Elias   1905- . . . . CLC 3, 14, 25
See also CA 21-24R

Canin, Ethan   1960- . . . . CLC 55

Cape, Judith   1916-
See Page, P(atricia) K(athleen)

Capek, Karel   1890-1938 . . . . TCLC 6
See also CA 104

Capote, Truman
1924-1984 . . . . .   **CLC 1, 3, 8, 13, 19, 34,
38; SSC 2**
See also CANR 18; CA 5-8R;
obituary CA 113; DLB 2; DLB-Y 80, 84;
CDALB 1941-1968

Capra, Frank   1897- . . . . CLC 16
See also CA 61-64

Caputo, Philip   1941- . . . . CLC 32
See also CA 73-76

Card, Orson Scott   1951- . . . . CLC 44, 47, 50
See also CA 102

Cardenal, Ernesto   1925- . . . . CLC 31
See also CANR 2; CA 49-52

Carey, Ernestine Gilbreth   1908-
See Gilbreth, Frank B(unker), Jr. and
Carey, Ernestine Gilbreth
See also CA 5-8R; SATA 2

Carey, Peter   1943- . . . . CLC 40, 55
See also CA 123, 127

Carleton, William   1794-1869 . . . . . . NCLC 3

Carlisle, Henry (Coffin)   1926- . . . . . . CLC 33
See also CANR 15; CA 13-16R

Carlson, Ron(ald F.)   1947- . . . . CLC 54
See also CA 105

Carman, (William) Bliss
1861-1929 . . . . TCLC 7
See also CA 104

Carpenter, Don(ald Richard)
1931- . . . . CLC 41
See also CANR 1; CA 45-48

Carpentier (y Valmont), Alejo
1904-1980 . . . . CLC 8, 11, 38
See also CANR 11; CA 65-68;
obituary CA 97-100

Carr, John Dickson   1906-1977 . . . . . . CLC 3
See also CANR 3; CA 49-52;
obituary CA 69-72

Carr, Virginia Spencer   1929- . . . . CLC 34
See also CA 61-64

Carrier, Roch   1937- . . . . CLC 13
See also DLB 53

Carroll, James (P.)   1943- . . . . CLC 38
See also CA 81-84

Carroll, Jim   1951- . . . . CLC 35
See also CA 45-48

Carroll, Lewis   1832-1898. . . . . NCLC 2
See also Dodgson, Charles Lutwidge
See also CLR 2; DLB 18

Carroll, Paul Vincent   1900-1968. . . . CLC 10
See also CA 9-12R; obituary CA 25-28R;
DLB 10

Carruth, Hayden   1921- . . . . CLC 4, 7, 10, 18
See also CANR 4; CA 9-12R; SATA 47;
DLB 5

Carter, Angela (Olive)   1940- . . . . . CLC 5, 41
See also CANR 12; CA 53-56; DLB 14

Carver, Raymond
1938-1988 . . . . CLC 22, 36, 55
See also CANR 17; CA 33-36R;
obituary CA 126; DLB-Y 84, 88

Cary, (Arthur) Joyce (Lunel)
1888-1957 . . . . TCLC 1, 29
See also CA 104; DLB 15

Casares, Adolfo Bioy   1914-
See Bioy Casares, Adolfo

Casely-Hayford, J(oseph) E(phraim)
1866-1930 . . . . TCLC 24

Casey, John   1880-1964
See O'Casey, Sean

Casey, Michael   1947- . . . . CLC 2
See also CA 65-68; DLB 5

Casey, Warren   1935-
See Jacobs, Jim and Casey, Warren
See also CA 101

Casona, Alejandro   1903-1965 . . . . . . CLC 49
See also Alvarez, Alejandro Rodriguez

Cassavetes, John   1929- . . . . CLC 20
See also CA 85-88

Cassill, R(onald) V(erlin)   1919- . . . CLC 4, 23
See also CAAS 1; CANR 7; CA 9-12R;
DLB 6

Cassity, (Allen) Turner   1929- . . . . CLC 6, 42
See also CANR 11; CA 17-20R

Castaneda, Carlos   1935?- . . . . CLC 12
See also CA 25-28R

Castro, Rosalia de   1837-1885 . . . . . NCLC 3

Cather, Willa (Sibert)
1873-1947 . . . . . . TCLC 1, 11, 31; SSC 2
See also CA 104; SATA 30; DLB 9, 54;
DLB-DS 1; CDALB 1865-1917

Catton, (Charles) Bruce
 1899-1978 . . . . **CLC 35**
 See also CANR 7; CA 5-8R;
  obituary CA 81-84; SATA 2;
  obituary SATA 24; DLB 17

Caunitz, William 1935- . . . . **CLC 34**

Causley, Charles (Stanley) 1917- . . . . . **CLC 7**
 See also CANR 5; CA 9-12R; SATA 3;
  DLB 27

Caute, (John) David 1936- . . . . **CLC 29**
 See also CAAS 4; CANR 1; CA 1-4R;
  DLB 14

Cavafy, C(onstantine) P(eter)
 1863-1933 . . . . **TCLC 2, 7**
 See also CA 104

Cavanna, Betty 1909- . . . . **CLC 12**
 See also CANR 6; CA 9-12R; SATA 1, 30

Cayrol, Jean 1911- . . . . **CLC 11**
 See also CA 89-92

Cela, Camilo Jose 1916- . . . . **CLC 4, 13**
 See also CANR 21; CA 21-24R

Celan, Paul 1920-1970 . . . . **CLC 10, 19**
 See also Antschel, Paul
 See also DLB 69

Celine, Louis-Ferdinand
 1894-1961 . . . . . **CLC 1, 3, 4, 7, 9, 15, 47**
 See also Destouches,
  Louis-Ferdinand-Auguste
 See also DLB 72

Cellini, Benvenuto 1500-1571 . . . . **LC 7**

Cendrars, Blaise 1887-1961 . . . . **CLC 18**
 See also Sauser-Hall, Frederic

Cernuda, Luis (y Bidon)
 1902-1963 . . . . **CLC 54**
 See also CA 89-92

Cervantes (Saavedra), Miguel de
 1547-1616 . . . . **LC 6**

Cesaire, Aime (Fernand) 1913- . . **CLC 19, 32**
 See also CA 65-68

Chabon, Michael 1965?- . . . . **CLC 55**

Chabrol, Claude 1930- . . . . **CLC 16**
 See also CA 110

Challans, Mary 1905-1983
 See Renault, Mary
 See also CA 81-84; obituary CA 111;
  SATA 23; obituary SATA 36

Chambers, Aidan 1934- . . . . **CLC 35**
 See also CANR 12; CA 25-28R; SATA 1

Chambers, James 1948-
 See Cliff, Jimmy

Chandler, Raymond 1888-1959 . . . **TCLC 1, 7**
 See also CA 104

Channing, William Ellery
 1780-1842 . . . . **NCLC 17**
 See also DLB 1, 59

Chaplin, Charles (Spencer)
 1889-1977 . . . . **CLC 16**
 See also CA 81-84; obituary CA 73-76;
  DLB 44

Chapman, Graham 1941?-
 See Monty Python
 See also CA 116

Chapman, John Jay 1862-1933 . . . . . **TCLC 7**
 See also CA 104

Chappell, Fred 1936- . . . . **CLC 40**
 See also CAAS 4; CANR 8; CA 5-8R;
  DLB 6

Char, Rene (Emile)
 1907-1988 . . . . **CLC 9, 11, 14, 55**
 See also CA 13-16R; obituary CA 124

Charyn, Jerome 1937- . . . . **CLC 5, 8, 18**
 See also CAAS 1; CANR 7; CA 5-8R;
  DLB-Y 83

Chase, Mary Ellen 1887-1973 . . . . . . **CLC 2**
 See also CAP 1; CA 15-16;
  obituary CA 41-44R; SATA 10

Chateaubriand, Francois Rene de
 1768-1848 . . . . **NCLC 3**

Chatterji, Bankim Chandra
 1838-1894 . . . . **NCLC 19**

Chatterji, Saratchandra
 1876-1938 . . . . **TCLC 13**
 See also CA 109

Chatterton, Thomas 1752-1770 . . . . . . **LC 3**

Chatwin, (Charles) Bruce 1940- . . . . . **CLC 28**
 See also CA 85-88

Chayefsky, Paddy 1923-1981 . . . . . . **CLC 23**
 See also CA 9-12R; obituary CA 104;
  DLB 7, 44; DLB-Y 81

Chayefsky, Sidney 1923-1981
 See Chayefsky, Paddy
 See also CANR 18

Chedid, Andree 1920- . . . . **CLC 47**

Cheever, John
 1912-1982 . . . . . **CLC 3, 7, 8, 11, 15, 25;**
                                          SSC 1
 See also CANR 5; CA 5-8R;
  obituary CA 106; CABS 1; DLB 2;
  DLB-Y 80, 82; CDALB 1941-1968

Cheever, Susan 1943- . . . . **CLC 18, 48**
 See also CA 103; DLB-Y 82

Chekhov, Anton (Pavlovich)
 1860-1904 . . . . . . **TCLC 3, 10, 31; SSC 2**
 See also CA 104, 124

Chernyshevsky, Nikolay Gavrilovich
 1828-1889 . . . . **NCLC 1**

Cherry, Caroline Janice 1942-
 See Cherryh, C. J.

Cherryh, C. J. 1942- . . . . **CLC 35**
 See also DLB-Y 80

Chesnutt, Charles Waddell
 1858-1932 . . . . **TCLC 5**
 See also CA 106; DLB 12, 50

Chester, Alfred 1929?-1971 . . . . **CLC 49**
 See also obituary CA 33-36R

Chesterton, G(ilbert) K(eith)
 1874-1936 . . . . **TCLC 1, 6; SSC 1**
 See also CA 104; SATA 27; DLB 10, 19,
  34, 70

Ch'ien Chung-shu 1910- . . . . **CLC 22**

Child, Lydia Maria 1802-1880 . . . . **NCLC 6**
 See also DLB 1

Child, Philip 1898-1978 . . . . **CLC 19**
 See also CAP 1; CA 13-14; SATA 47

Childress, Alice 1920- . . . . **CLC 12, 15**
 See also CLR 14; CANR 3; CA 45-48;
  SATA 7, 48; DLB 7, 38

Chislett, (Margaret) Anne 1943?- . . . **CLC 34**

Chitty, (Sir) Thomas Willes 1926-
 See Hinde, Thomas
 See also CA 5-8R

Chomette, Rene 1898-1981
 See Clair, Rene
 See also obituary CA 103

Chopin, Kate (O'Flaherty)
 1851-1904 . . . . **TCLC 5, 14**
 See also CA 104, 122; DLB 12;
  CDALB 1865-1917

Christie, (Dame) Agatha (Mary Clarissa)
 1890-1976 . . . . . . **CLC 1, 6, 8, 12, 39, 48**
 See also CANR 10; CA 17-20R;
  obituary CA 61-64; SATA 36; DLB 13

Christie, (Ann) Philippa 1920-
 See Pearce, (Ann) Philippa
 See also CANR 4

Christine de Pizan 1365?-1431? . . . . . . **LC 9**

Chulkov, Mikhail Dmitrievich
 1743-1792 . . . . **LC 2**

Churchill, Caryl 1938- . . . . **CLC 31, 55**
 See also CANR 22; CA 102; DLB 13

Churchill, Charles 1731?-1764 . . . . **LC 3**

Chute, Carolyn 1947- . . . . **CLC 39**

Ciardi, John (Anthony)
 1916-1986 . . . . **CLC 10, 40, 44**
 See also CAAS 2; CANR 5; CA 5-8R;
  obituary CA 118; SATA 1, 46; DLB 5;
  DLB-Y 86

Cicero, Marcus Tullius
 106 B.C.-43 B.C. . . . . **CMLC 3**

Cimino, Michael 1943?- . . . . **CLC 16**
 See also CA 105

Clair, Rene 1898-1981 . . . . **CLC 20**
 See also Chomette, Rene

Clampitt, Amy 19??- . . . . **CLC 32**
 See also CA 110

Clancy, Tom 1947- . . . . **CLC 45**

Clare, John 1793-1864 . . . . **NCLC 9**
 See also DLB 55

Clark, (Robert) Brian 1932- . . . . **CLC 29**
 See also CA 41-44R

Clark, Eleanor 1913- . . . . **CLC 5, 19**
 See also CA 9-12R; DLB 6

Clark, John Pepper 1935- . . . . **CLC 38**
 See also CANR 16; CA 65-68

Clark, Mavis Thorpe 1912?- . . . . **CLC 12**
 See also CANR 8; CA 57-60; SATA 8

Clark, Walter Van Tilburg
 1909-1971 . . . . **CLC 28**
 See also CA 9-12R; obituary CA 33-36R;
  SATA 8; DLB 9

Clarke, Arthur C(harles)
 1917- . . . . . . **CLC 1, 4, 13, 18, 35; SSC 3**
 See also CANR 2; CA 1-4R; SATA 13

Clarke, Austin 1896-1974 . . . . **CLC 6, 9**
 See also CANR 14; CAP 2; CA 29-32;
  obituary CA 49-52; DLB 10, 20, 53

Clarke, Austin C(hesterfield) 1934- . . . **CLC 8**
 See also CANR 14; CA 25-28R; DLB 53

Clarke, Marcus (Andrew Hislop)
 1846-1881 . . . . **NCLC 19**

Clarke, Shirley 1925- . . . . **CLC 16**

Clash, The .... CLC 30

Claudel, Paul (Louis Charles Marie)
    1868-1955 .... TCLC 2, 10
    See also CA 104

Clavell, James (duMaresq)
    1924- .... CLC 6, 25
    See also CA 25-28R

Cleaver, (Leroy) Eldridge 1935- .... CLC 30
    See also CANR 16; CA 21-24R

Cleese, John 1939-
    See Monty Python
    See also CA 112, 116

Cleland, John 1709-1789 .... LC 2
    See also DLB 39

Clemens, Samuel Langhorne 1835-1910
    See Twain, Mark
    See also YABC 2; CA 104; DLB 11, 12, 23,
    64; CDALB 1865-1917

Cliff, Jimmy 1948- .... CLC 21

Clifton, Lucille 1936- .... CLC 19
    See also CLR 5; CANR 2; CA 49-52;
    SATA 20; DLB 5, 41

Clutha, Janet Paterson Frame 1924-
    See Frame (Clutha), Janet (Paterson)
    See also CANR 2; CA 1-4R

Coburn, D(onald) L(ee) 1938- ...... CLC 10
    See also CA 89-92

Cocteau, Jean (Maurice Eugene Clement)
    1889-1963 .... CLC 1, 8, 15, 16, 43
    See also CAP 2; CA 25-28

Codrescu, Andrei 1946- .... CLC 46
    See also CANR 13; CA 33-36R

Coetzee, J(ohn) M. 1940- .... CLC 23, 33
    See also CA 77-80

Cohen, Arthur A(llen)
    1928-1986 .... CLC 7, 31
    See also CANR 1, 17; CA 1-4R;
    obituary CA 120; DLB 28

Cohen, Leonard (Norman)
    1934- .... CLC 3, 38
    See also CANR 14; CA 21-24R; DLB 53

Cohen, Matt 1942- .... CLC 19
    See also CA 61-64; DLB 53

Cohen-Solal, Annie 19??- .... CLC 50

Colegate, Isabel 1931- .... CLC 36
    See also CANR 8, 22; CA 17-20R; DLB 14

Coleridge, Samuel Taylor
    1772-1834 .... NCLC 9

Coles, Don 1928- .... CLC 46
    See also CA 115

Colette (Sidonie-Gabrielle)
    1873-1954 .... TCLC 1, 5, 16
    See also CA 104

Collier, Christopher 1930- and Collier, James
    L(incoln) 1928- .... CLC 30

Collier, Christopher 1930-
    See Collier, Christopher and Collier, James
    L(incoln)
    See also CANR 13; CA 33-36R; SATA 16

Collier, James L(incoln) 1928-
    See Collier, Christopher and Collier, James
    L(incoln)
    See also CLR 3; CANR 4; CA 9-12R;
    SATA 8

Collier, James L(incoln) 1928- and Collier,
    Christopher 1930-
    See Collier, Christopher and Collier, James
    L(incoln)

Collier, Jeremy 1650-1726 .... LC 6

Collins, Hunt 1926-
    See Hunter, Evan

Collins, Linda 19??- .... CLC 44

Collins, Tom 1843-1912
    See Furphy, Joseph

Collins, (William) Wilkie
    1824-1889 .... NCLC 1, 18
    See also DLB 18, 70

Collins, William 1721-1759 .... LC 4

Colman, George 1909-1981
    See Glassco, John

Colton, James 1923-
    See Hansen, Joseph

Colum, Padraic 1881-1972 .... CLC 28
    See also CA 73-76; obituary CA 33-36R;
    SATA 15; DLB 19

Colvin, James 1939-
    See Moorcock, Michael

Colwin, Laurie 1945- .... CLC 5, 13, 23
    See also CANR 20; CA 89-92; DLB-Y 80

Comfort, Alex(ander) 1920- .... CLC 7
    See also CANR 1; CA 1-4R

Compton-Burnett, Ivy
    1892-1969 .... CLC 1, 3, 10, 15, 34
    See also CANR 4; CA 1-4R;
    obituary CA 25-28R; DLB 36

Comstock, Anthony 1844-1915 .... TCLC 13
    See also CA 110

Condon, Richard (Thomas)
    1915- .... CLC 4, 6, 8, 10, 45
    See also CAAS 1; CANR 2; CA 1-4R

Congreve, William 1670-1729 .... LC 5
    See also DLB 39

Connell, Evan S(helby), Jr.
    1924- .... CLC 4, 6, 45
    See also CAAS 2; CANR 2; CA 1-4R;
    DLB 2; DLB-Y 81

Connelly, Marc(us Cook)
    1890-1980 .... CLC 7
    See also CA 85-88; obituary CA 102;
    obituary SATA 25; DLB 7; DLB-Y 80

Conner, Ralph 1860-1937 .... TCLC 31

Conrad, Joseph
    1857-1924 .... TCLC 1, 6, 13, 25
    See also CA 104; SATA 27; DLB 10, 34

Conroy, Pat 1945- .... CLC 30
    See also CA 85-88; DLB 6

Constant (de Rebecque), (Henri) Benjamin
    1767-1830 .... NCLC 6

Cook, Robin 1940- .... CLC 14
    See also CA 108, 111

Cooke, Elizabeth 1948- .... CLC 55

Cooke, John Esten 1830-1886 ..... NCLC 5
    See also DLB 3

Cooper, James Fenimore
    1789-1851 .... NCLC 1
    See also SATA 19; DLB 3;
    CDALB 1640-1865

Coover, Robert (Lowell)
    1932- .... CLC 3, 7, 15, 32, 46
    See also CANR 3; CA 45-48; DLB 2;
    DLB-Y 81

Copeland, Stewart (Armstrong) 1952-
    See The Police

Coppard, A(lfred) E(dgar)
    1878-1957 .... TCLC 5
    See also YABC 1; CA 114

Coppee, Francois 1842-1908 ...... TCLC 25

Coppola, Francis Ford 1939- .... CLC 16
    See also CA 77-80; DLB 44

Corcoran, Barbara 1911- .... CLC 17
    See also CAAS 2; CANR 11; CA 21-24R;
    SATA 3; DLB 52

Corman, Cid 1924- .... CLC 9
    See also Corman, Sidney
    See also CAAS 2; DLB 5

Corman, Sidney 1924-
    See Corman, Cid
    See also CA 85-88

Cormier, Robert (Edmund)
    1925- .... CLC 12, 30
    See also CLR 12; CANR 5; CA 1-4R;
    SATA 10, 45; DLB 52

Corn, Alfred (Dewitt III) 1943- ..... CLC 33
    See also CA 104; DLB-Y 80

Cornwell, David (John Moore) 1931-
    See le Carre, John
    See also CANR 13; CA 5-8R

Corso, (Nunzio) Gregory 1930- ... CLC 1, 11
    See also CA 5-8R; DLB 5, 16

Cortazar, Julio
    1914-1984 ..... CLC 2, 3, 5, 10, 13, 15,
                            33, 34
    See also CANR 12; CA 21-24R

Corvo, Baron 1860-1913
    See Rolfe, Frederick (William Serafino
    Austin Lewis Mary)

Cosic, Dobrica 1921- .... CLC 14
    See also CA 122

Costain, Thomas B(ertram)
    1885-1965 .... CLC 30
    See also CA 5-8R; obituary CA 25-28R;
    DLB 9

Costantini, Humberto 1924?-1987... CLC 49
    See also obituary CA 122

Costello, Elvis 1955- .... CLC 21

Cotter, Joseph Seamon, Sr.
    1861-1949 .... TCLC 28
    See also DLB 50

Couperus, Louis (Marie Anne)
    1863-1923 .... TCLC 15
    See also CA 115

Cousteau, Jacques-Yves 1910- ...... CLC 30
    See also CANR 15; CA 65-68; SATA 38

Coward, (Sir) Noel (Pierce)
    1899-1973 .... CLC 1, 9, 29, 51
    See also CAP 2; CA 17-18;
    obituary CA 41-44R; DLB 10

Cowley, Malcolm 1898- .... CLC 39
    See also CANR 3; CA 5-6R; DLB 4, 48;
    DLB-Y 81

Cowper, William 1731-1800 .... NCLC 8

Cox, William Trevor 1928-
See Trevor, William
See also CANR 4; CA 9-12R

Cozzens, James Gould
1903-1978 . . . . CLC 1, 4, 11
See also CANR 19; CA 9-12R;
obituary CA 81-84; DLB 9; DLB-Y 84;
DLB-DS 2; CDALB 1941-1968

Crane, (Harold) Hart
1899-1932 . . . . TCLC 2, 5
See also CA 104; DLB 4, 48

Crane, R(onald) S(almon)
1886-1967 . . . . CLC 27
See also CA 85-88; DLB 63

Crane, Stephen 1871-1900 . . . . . TCLC 11, 17
See also YABC 2; CA 109; DLB 12, 54;
CDALB 1865-1917

Craven, Margaret 1901-1980 . . . . CLC 17
See also CA 103

Crawford, F(rancis) Marion
1854-1909 . . . . TCLC 10
See also CA 107; DLB 71

Crawford, Isabella Valancy
1850-1887 . . . . NCLC 12

Crayencour, Marguerite de 1913-
See Yourcenar, Marguerite

Creasey, John 1908-1973 . . . . CLC 11
See also CANR 8; CA 5-8R;
obituary CA 41-44R

Crebillon, Claude Prosper Jolyot de (fils)
1707-1777 . . . . LC 1

Creeley, Robert (White)
1926- . . . . CLC 1, 2, 4, 8, 11, 15, 36
See also CA 1-4R; DLB 5, 16

Crews, Harry (Eugene)
1935- . . . . CLC 6, 23, 49
See also CANR 20; CA 25-28R; DLB 6

Crichton, (John) Michael
1942- . . . . CLC 2, 6, 54
See also CANR 13; CA 25-28R; SATA 9;
DLB-Y 81

Crispin, Edmund 1921-1978 . . . . CLC 22
See also Montgomery, Robert Bruce

Cristofer, Michael 1946- . . . . CLC 28
See also CA 110; DLB 7

Crockett, David (Davy)
1786-1836 . . . . NCLC 8
See also DLB 3, 11

Croker, John Wilson 1780-1857 . . NCLC 10

Cronin, A(rchibald) J(oseph)
1896-1981 . . . . CLC 32
See also CANR 5; CA 1-4R;
obituary CA 102; obituary SATA 25, 47

Cross, Amanda 1926-
See Heilbrun, Carolyn G(old)

Crothers, Rachel 1878-1953. . . . . . TCLC 19
See also CA 113; DLB 7

Crowley, Aleister 1875-1947 . . . . TCLC 7
See also CA 104

Crumb, Robert 1943- . . . . CLC 17
See also CA 106

Cryer, Gretchen 1936?- . . . . CLC 21
See also CA 114

Csath, Geza 1887-1919. . . . . TCLC 13
See also CA 111

Cudlip, David 1933- . . . . CLC 34

Cullen, Countee 1903-1946 . . . . TCLC 4
See also CA 108; SATA 18; DLB 4, 48, 51

Cummings, E(dward) E(stlin)
1894-1962 . . . . CLC 1, 3, 8, 12, 15
See also CA 73-76; DLB 4, 48

Cunha, Euclides (Rodrigues) da
1866-1909 . . . . TCLC 24

Cunningham, Julia (Woolfolk)
1916- . . . . CLC 12
See also CANR 4, 19; CA 9-12R; SAAS 2;
SATA 1, 26

Cunningham, J(ames) V(incent)
1911-1985 . . . . CLC 3, 31
See also CANR 1; CA 1-4R;
obituary CA 115; DLB 5

Cunningham, Michael 1952- . . . . CLC 34

Currie, Ellen 19??- . . . . CLC 44

Dabrowska, Maria (Szumska)
1889-1965 . . . . CLC 15
See also CA 106

Dabydeen, David 1956?- . . . . CLC 34

Dacey, Philip 1939- . . . . CLC 51
See also CANR 14; CA 37-40R

Dagerman, Stig (Halvard)
1923-1954 . . . . TCLC 17
See also CA 117

Dahl, Roald 1916- . . . . CLC 1, 6, 18
See also CLR 1, 7; CANR 6; CA 1-4R;
SATA 1, 26

Dahlberg, Edward 1900-1977 . . . CLC 1, 7, 14
See also CA 9-12R; obituary CA 69-72;
DLB 48

Daly, Maureen 1921- . . . . CLC 17
See also McGivern, Maureen Daly
See also SAAS 1; SATA 2

Daniken, Erich von 1935-
See Von Daniken, Erich

Dannay, Frederic 1905-1982
See Queen, Ellery
See also CANR 1; CA 1-4R;
obituary CA 107

D'Annunzio, Gabriele 1863-1938. . . . TCLC 6
See also CA 104

Danziger, Paula 1944- . . . . CLC 21
See also CA 112, 115; SATA 30, 36

Dario, Ruben 1867-1916 . . . . TCLC 4
See also Sarmiento, Felix Ruben Garcia
See also CA 104

Darley, George 1795-1846 . . . . NCLC 2

Daryush, Elizabeth 1887-1977. . . . CLC 6, 19
See also CANR 3; CA 49-52; DLB 20

Daudet, (Louis Marie) Alphonse
1840-1897 . . . . NCLC 1

Daumal, Rene 1908-1944 . . . . TCLC 14
See also CA 114

Davenport, Guy (Mattison, Jr.)
1927- . . . . CLC 6, 14, 38
See also CA 33-36R

Davidson, Donald (Grady)
1893-1968 . . . . CLC 2, 13, 19
See also CANR 4; CA 5-8R;
obituary CA 25-28R; DLB 45

Davidson, John 1857-1909 . . . . TCLC 24
See also CA 118; DLB 19

Davidson, Sara 1943- . . . . CLC 9
See also CA 81-84

Davie, Donald (Alfred)
1922- . . . . CLC 5, 8, 10, 31
See also CAAS 3; CANR 1; CA 1-4R;
DLB 27

Davies, Ray(mond Douglas) 1944- . . CLC 21
See also CA 116

Davies, Rhys 1903-1978 . . . . CLC 23
See also CANR 4; CA 9-12R;
obituary CA 81-84

Davies, (William) Robertson
1913- . . . . CLC 2, 7, 13, 25, 42
See also CANR 17; CA 33-36R

Davies, W(illiam) H(enry)
1871-1940 . . . . TCLC 5
See also CA 104; DLB 19

Davis, H(arold) L(enoir)
1896-1960 . . . . CLC 49
See also obituary CA 89-92; DLB 9

Davis, Rebecca (Blaine) Harding
1831-1910 . . . . TCLC 6
See also CA 104

Davis, Richard Harding
1864-1916 . . . . TCLC 24
See also CA 114; DLB 12, 23

Davison, Frank Dalby 1893-1970 . . . CLC 15
See also obituary CA 116

Davison, Peter 1928- . . . . CLC 28
See also CAAS 4; CANR 3; CA 9-12R;
DLB 5

Davys, Mary 1674-1732. . . . . LC 1
See also DLB 39

Dawson, Fielding 1930- . . . . CLC 6
See also CA 85-88

Day, Clarence (Shepard, Jr.)
1874-1935 . . . . TCLC 25
See also CA 108; DLB 11

Day, Thomas 1748-1789. . . . . LC 1
See also YABC 1; DLB 39

Day Lewis, C(ecil)
1904-1972 . . . . CLC 1, 6, 10
See also CAP 1; CA 15-16;
obituary CA 33-36R; DLB 15, 20

Dazai Osamu 1909-1948 . . . . TCLC 11
See also Tsushima Shuji

De Crayencour, Marguerite 1903-
See Yourcenar, Marguerite

Deer, Sandra 1940- . . . . CLC 45

Defoe, Daniel 1660?-1731 . . . . LC 1
See also SATA 22; DLB 39

De Hartog, Jan 1914- . . . . CLC 19
See also CANR 1; CA 1-4R

Deighton, Len 1929- . . . . . . CLC 4, 7, 22, 46
See also Deighton, Leonard Cyril

Deighton, Leonard Cyril 1929-
See Deighton, Len
See also CANR 19; CA 9-12R

De la Mare, Walter (John)
    1873-1956 .... **TCLC 4**
    See also CA 110; SATA 16; DLB 19

Delaney, Shelagh 1939- .... **CLC 29**
    See also CA 17-20R; DLB 13

Delany, Samuel R(ay, Jr.)
    1942- .... **CLC 8, 14, 38**
    See also CA 81-84; DLB 8, 33

De la Roche, Mazo 1885-1961 ..... **CLC 14**
    See also CA 85-88

Delbanco, Nicholas (Franklin)
    1942- .... **CLC 6, 13**
    See also CAAS 2; CA 17-20R; DLB 6

Del Castillo, Michel 1933- .... **CLC 38**
    See also CA 109

Deledda, Grazia 1875-1936 .... **TCLC 23**

Delibes (Setien), Miguel 1920- ... **CLC 8, 18**
    See also CANR 1; CA 45-48

DeLillo, Don
    1936- .... **CLC 8, 10, 13, 27, 39, 54**
    See also CANR 21; CA 81-84; DLB 6

De Lisser, H(erbert) G(eorge)
    1878-1944 .... **TCLC 12**
    See also CA 109

Deloria, Vine (Victor), Jr. 1933- .... **CLC 21**
    See also CANR 5, 20; CA 53-56; SATA 21

Del Vecchio, John M(ichael)
    1947- .... **CLC 29**
    See also CA 110

de Man, Paul 1919-1983 .... **CLC 55**
    See also obituary CA 111; DLB 67

De Marinis, Rick 1934- .... **CLC 54**
    See also CANR 9; CA 57-60

Denby, Edwin (Orr) 1903-1983 ..... **CLC 48**
    See also obituary CA 110

Dennis, John 1657-1734 .... **LC 11**

Dennis, Nigel (Forbes) 1912- .... **CLC 8**
    See also CA 25-28R; DLB 13, 15

De Palma, Brian 1940- .... **CLC 20**
    See also CA 109

De Quincey, Thomas 1785-1859 ... **NCLC 4**

Deren, Eleanora 1908-1961
    See Deren, Maya
    See also obituary CA 111

Deren, Maya 1908-1961 .... **CLC 16**
    See also Deren, Eleanora

Derleth, August (William)
    1909-1971 .... **CLC 31**
    See also CANR 4; CA 1-4R;
    obituary CA 29-32R; SATA 5; DLB 9

Derrida, Jacques 1930- .... **CLC 24**

Desai, Anita 1937- .... **CLC 19, 37**
    See also CA 81-84

De Saint-Luc, Jean 1909-1981
    See Glassco, John

De Sica, Vittorio 1902-1974 .... **CLC 20**
    See also obituary CA 117

Desnos, Robert 1900-1945 .... **TCLC 22**
    See also CA 121

Destouches, Louis-Ferdinand-Auguste
    1894-1961
    See Celine, Louis-Ferdinand
    See also CA 85-88

Deutsch, Babette 1895-1982 .... **CLC 18**
    See also CANR 4; CA 1-4R;
    obituary CA 108; SATA 1;
    obituary SATA 33; DLB 45

Devkota, Laxmiprasad
    1909-1959 .... **TCLC 23**

DeVoto, Bernard (Augustine)
    1897-1955 .... **TCLC 29**
    See also CA 113; DLB 9

De Vries, Peter
    1910- .... **CLC 1, 2, 3, 7, 10, 28, 46**
    See also CA 17-20R; DLB 6; DLB-Y 82

Dexter, Pete 1943- .... **CLC 34, 55**
    See also CA 127

Diamond, Neil (Leslie) 1941- .... **CLC 30**
    See also CA 108

Dick, Philip K(indred)
    1928-1982 .... **CLC 10, 30**
    See also CANR 2, 16; CA 49-52;
    obituary CA 106; DLB 8

Dickens, Charles
    1812-1870 .... **NCLC 3, 8, 18**
    See also SATA 15; DLB 21, 55, 70

Dickey, James (Lafayette)
    1923- .... **CLC 1, 2, 4, 7, 10, 15, 47**
    See also CANR 10; CA 9-12R; CABS 2;
    DLB 5; DLB-Y 82

Dickey, William 1928- .... **CLC 3, 28**
    See also CA 9-12R; DLB 5

Dickinson, Charles 1952- .... **CLC 49**

Dickinson, Peter (Malcolm de Brissac)
    1927- .... **CLC 12, 35**
    See also CA 41-44R; SATA 5

Didion, Joan 1934- ..... **CLC 1, 3, 8, 14, 32**
    See also CANR 14; CA 5-8R; DLB 2;
    DLB-Y 81, 86

Dillard, Annie 1945- .... **CLC 9**
    See also CANR 3; CA 49-52; SATA 10;
    DLB-Y 80

Dillard, R(ichard) H(enry) W(ilde)
    1937- .... **CLC 5**
    See also CAAS 7; CANR 10; CA 21-24R;
    DLB 5

Dillon, Eilis 1920- .... **CLC 17**
    See also CAAS 3; CANR 4; CA 9-12R;
    SATA 2

Dinesen, Isak 1885-1962 .... **CLC 10, 29**
    See also Blixen, Karen (Christentze
    Dinesen)
    See also CANR 22

Disch, Thomas M(ichael) 1940- ... **CLC 7, 36**
    See also CAAS 4; CANR 17; CA 21-24R;
    DLB 8

Disraeli, Benjamin 1804-1881 ..... **NCLC 2**
    See also DLB 21, 55

Dixon, Paige 1911-
    See Corcoran, Barbara

Doblin, Alfred 1878-1957 .... **TCLC 13**
    See also Doeblin, Alfred

Dobrolyubov, Nikolai Alexandrovich
    1836-1861 .... **NCLC 5**

Dobyns, Stephen 1941- .... **CLC 37**
    See also CANR 2, 18; CA 45-48

Doctorow, E(dgar) L(aurence)
    1931- .... **CLC 6, 11, 15, 18, 37, 44**
    See also CANR 2; CA 45-48; DLB 2, 28;
    DLB-Y 80

Dodgson, Charles Lutwidge 1832-1898
    See Carroll, Lewis
    See also YABC 2

Doeblin, Alfred 1878-1957 .... **TCLC 13**
    See also CA 110

Doerr, Harriet 1910- .... **CLC 34**
    See also CA 117, 122

Donaldson, Stephen R. 1947- ...... **CLC 46**
    See also CANR 13; CA 89-92

Donleavy, J(ames) P(atrick)
    1926- .... **CLC 1, 4, 6, 10, 45**
    See also CA 9-12R; DLB 6

Donnadieu, Marguerite 1914-
    See Duras, Marguerite

Donne, John 1572?-1631 .... **LC 10**

Donnell, David 1939?- .... **CLC 34**

Donoso, Jose 1924- .... **CLC 4, 8, 11, 32**
    See also CA 81-84

Donovan, John 1928- .... **CLC 35**
    See also CLR 3; CA 97-100; SATA 29

Doolittle, Hilda 1886-1961
    See H(ilda) D(oolittle)
    See also CA 97-100; DLB 4, 45

Dorfman, Ariel 1942- .... **CLC 48**

Dorn, Ed(ward Merton) 1929- ... **CLC 10, 18**
    See also CA 93-96; DLB 5

Dos Passos, John (Roderigo)
    1896-1970 ... **CLC 1, 4, 8, 11, 15, 25, 34**
    See also CANR 3; CA 1-4R;
    obituary CA 29-32R; DLB 4, 9;
    DLB-DS 1

Dostoevski, Fedor Mikhailovich
    1821-1881 .... **NCLC 2, 7; SSC 2**

Doughty, Charles (Montagu)
    1843-1926 .... **TCLC 27**
    See also CA 115; DLB 19, 57

Douglas, George 1869-1902 .... **TCLC 28**

Douglass, Frederick 1817-1895 .... **NCLC 7**
    See also SATA 29; DLB 1, 43, 50;
    CDALB 1640-1865

Dourado, (Waldomiro Freitas) Autran
    1926- .... **CLC 23**
    See also CA 25-28R

Dove, Rita 1952- .... **CLC 50**
    See also CA 109

Dowson, Ernest (Christopher)
    1867-1900 .... **TCLC 4**
    See also CA 105; DLB 19

Doyle, (Sir) Arthur Conan
    1859-1930 .... **TCLC 7, 26**
    See also CA 104, 122; SATA 24; DLB 18,
    70

Dr. A 1933-
    See Silverstein, Alvin and Virginia B(arbara
    Opshelor) Silverstein

Drabble, Margaret
    1939- .... **CLC 2, 3, 5, 8, 10, 22**
    See also CANR 18; CA 13-16R; SATA 48;
    DLB 14

Drayton, Michael 1563-1631 .... **LC 8**

Dreiser, Theodore (Herman Albert)
1871-1945 . . . . TCLC 10, 18
See also CA 106; SATA 48; DLB 9, 12;
DLB-DS 1; CDALB 1865-1917

Drexler, Rosalyn 1926- . . . . CLC 2, 6
See also CA 81-84

Dreyer, Carl Theodor 1889-1968. . . . CLC 16
See also obituary CA 116

Drieu La Rochelle, Pierre
1893-1945 . . . . TCLC 21
See also CA 117; DLB 72

Droste-Hulshoff, Annette Freiin von
1797-1848 . . . . NCLC 3

Drummond, William Henry
1854-1907 . . . . TCLC 25

Drummond de Andrade, Carlos 1902-
See Andrade, Carlos Drummond de

Drury, Allen (Stuart) 1918- . . . . CLC 37
See also CANR 18; CA 57-60

Dryden, John 1631-1700 . . . . LC 3

Duberman, Martin 1930- . . . . CLC 8
See also CANR 2; CA 1-4R

Dubie, Norman (Evans, Jr.) 1945- . . CLC 36
See also CANR 12; CA 69-72

Du Bois, W(illiam) E(dward) B(urghardt)
1868-1963 . . . . CLC 1, 2, 13
See also CA 85-88; SATA 42; DLB 47, 50;
CDALB 1865-1917

Dubus, Andre 1936- . . . . CLC 13, 36
See also CANR 17; CA 21-24R

Ducasse, Isidore Lucien 1846-1870
See Lautreamont, Comte de

Duclos, Charles Pinot 1704-1772 . . . . . LC 1

Dudek, Louis 1918- . . . . CLC 11, 19
See also CANR 1; CA 45-48

Dudevant, Amandine Aurore Lucile Dupin
1804-1876
See Sand, George

Duerrenmatt, Friedrich 1921-
See also CA 17-20R

Duffy, Bruce 19??- . . . . CLC 50

Duffy, Maureen 1933- . . . . CLC 37
See also CA 25-28R; DLB 14

Dugan, Alan 1923- . . . . CLC 2, 6
See also CA 81-84; DLB 5

Duhamel, Georges 1884-1966 . . . . CLC 8
See also CA 81-84; obituary CA 25-28R

Dujardin, Edouard (Emile Louis)
1861-1949 . . . . TCLC 13
See also CA 109

Duke, Raoul 1939-
See Thompson, Hunter S(tockton)

Dumas, Alexandre (Davy de la Pailleterie)
(pere) 1802-1870. . . . . NCLC 11
See also SATA 18

Dumas, Alexandre (fils)
1824-1895 . . . . NCLC 9

Dumas, Henry (L.) 1934-1968 . . . . CLC 6
See also CA 85-88; DLB 41

Du Maurier, Daphne 1907- . . . . . . CLC 6, 11
See also CANR 6; CA 5-8R; SATA 27

Dunbar, Paul Laurence
1872-1906 . . . . TCLC 2, 12
See also CA 104; SATA 34; DLB 50, 54;
CDALB 1865-1917

Duncan (Steinmetz Arquette), Lois
1934- . . . . CLC 26
See also Arquette, Lois S(teinmetz)
See also CANR 2; CA 1-4R; SAAS 2;
SATA 1, 36

Duncan, Robert (Edward)
1919-1988 . . . . CLC 1, 2, 4, 7, 15, 41, 55
See also CA 9-12R; obituary CA 124;
DLB 5, 16

Dunlap, William 1766-1839 . . . . NCLC 2
See also DLB 30, 37

Dunn, Douglas (Eaglesham)
1942- . . . . CLC 6, 40
See also CANR 2; CA 45-48; DLB 40

Dunn, Elsie 1893-1963
See Scott, Evelyn

Dunn, Stephen 1939- . . . . CLC 36
See also CANR 12; CA 33-36R

Dunne, Finley Peter 1867-1936. . . . TCLC 28
See also CA 108; DLB 11, 23

Dunne, John Gregory 1932-. . . . . . . CLC 28
See also CANR 14; CA 25-28R; DLB-Y 80

Dunsany, Lord (Edward John Moreton Drax
Plunkett) 1878-1957. . . . . TCLC 2
See also CA 104; DLB 10

Durang, Christopher (Ferdinand)
1949- . . . . CLC 27, 38
See also CA 105

Duras, Marguerite
1914- . . . . CLC 3, 6, 11, 20, 34, 40
See also CA 25-28R

Durban, Pam 1947-. . . . . CLC 39

Durcan, Paul 1944-. . . . . CLC 43

Durrell, Lawrence (George)
1912- . . . . CLC 1, 4, 6, 8, 13, 27, 41
See also CA 9-12R; DLB 15, 27

Durrenmatt, Friedrich
1921- . . . . CLC 1, 4, 8, 11, 15, 43
See also Duerrenmatt, Friedrich
See also DLB 69

Dwight, Timothy 1752-1817. . . . . . NCLC 13
See also DLB 37

Dworkin, Andrea 1946- . . . . CLC 43
See also CANR 16; CA 77-80

Dylan, Bob 1941-. . . . . CLC 3, 4, 6, 12
See also CA 41-44R; DLB 16

East, Michael 1916-
See West, Morris L.

Eastlake, William (Derry) 1917-. . . . . CLC 8
See also CAAS 1; CANR 5; CA 5-8R;
DLB 6

Eberhart, Richard 1904-. . . . . . CLC 3, 11, 19
See also CANR 2; CA 1-4R; DLB 48;
CDALB 1941-1968

Eberstadt, Fernanda 1960-. . . . . CLC 39

Echegaray (y Eizaguirre), Jose (Maria Waldo)
1832-1916 . . . . TCLC 4
See also CA 104

Echeverria, (Jose) Esteban (Antonino)
1805-1851 . . . . NCLC 18

Eckert, Allan W. 1931- . . . . CLC 17
See also CANR 14; CA 13-16R; SATA 27,
29

Eco, Umberto 1932-. . . . . CLC 28
See also CANR 12; CA 77-80

Eddison, E(ric) R(ucker)
1882-1945 . . . . TCLC 15
See also CA 109

Edel, Leon (Joseph) 1907-. . . . . . CLC 29, 34
See also CANR 1, 22; CA 1-4R

Eden, Emily 1797-1869 . . . . NCLC 10

Edgar, David 1948-. . . . . CLC 42
See also CANR 12; CA 57-60; DLB 13

Edgerton, Clyde 1944- . . . . CLC 39
See also CA 118

Edgeworth, Maria 1767-1849. . . . . . NCLC 1
See also SATA 21

Edmonds, Helen (Woods) 1904-1968
See Kavan, Anna
See also CA 5-8R; obituary CA 25-28R

Edmonds, Walter D(umaux) 1903- . . CLC 35
See also CANR 2; CA 5-8R; SAAS 4;
SATA 1, 27; DLB 9

Edson, Russell 1905- . . . . CLC 13
See also CA 33-36R

Edwards, G(erald) B(asil)
1899-1976 . . . . CLC 25
See also obituary CA 110

Edwards, Gus 1939-. . . . . CLC 43
See also CA 108

Edwards, Jonathan 1703-1758. . . . . . . LC 7
See also DLB 24

Ehle, John (Marsden, Jr.) 1925-. . . . CLC 27
See also CA 9-12R

Ehrenbourg, Ilya (Grigoryevich) 1891-1967
See Ehrenburg, Ilya (Grigoryevich)

Ehrenburg, Ilya (Grigoryevich)
1891-1967 . . . . CLC 18, 34
See also CA 102; obituary CA 25-28R

Eich, Guenter 1907-1971
See also CA 111; obituary CA 93-96

Eich, Gunter 1907-1971. . . . . CLC 15
See also Eich, Guenter
See also DLB 69

Eichendorff, Joseph Freiherr von
1788-1857 . . . . NCLC 8

Eigner, Larry 1927- . . . . CLC 9
See also Eigner, Laurence (Joel)
See also DLB 5

Eigner, Laurence (Joel) 1927-
See Eigner, Larry
See also CANR 6; CA 9-12R

Eiseley, Loren (Corey) 1907-1977. . . . CLC 7
See also CANR 6; CA 1-4R;
obituary CA 73-76

Eisenstadt, Jill 1963- . . . . CLC 50

Ekeloef, Gunnar (Bengt) 1907-1968
See Ekelof, Gunnar (Bengt)
See also obituary CA 25-28R

Ekelof, Gunnar (Bengt) 1907-1968 . . CLC 27
See also Ekeloef, Gunnar (Bengt)

Ekwensi, Cyprian (Odiatu Duaka)
1921- . . . . CLC 4
See also CANR 18; CA 29-32R

Eliade, Mircea 1907-1986 .... **CLC 19**
See also CA 65-68; obituary CA 119

Eliot, George 1819-1880.... **NCLC 4, 13, 23**
See also DLB 21, 35, 55

Eliot, John 1604-1690 .... **LC 5**
See also DLB 24

Eliot, T(homas) S(tearns)
1888-1965 .... **CLC 1, 2, 3, 6, 9, 10, 13, 15, 24, 34, 41, 55**
See also CA 5-8R; obituary CA 25-28R;
DLB 7, 10, 45, 63; DLB-Y 88

Elkin, Stanley (Lawrence)
1930- .... **CLC 4, 6, 9, 14, 27, 51**
See also CANR 8; CA 9-12R; DLB 2, 28;
DLB-Y 80

Elledge, Scott 19??- .... **CLC 34**

Elliott, George P(aul) 1918-1980..... **CLC 2**
See also CANR 2; CA 1-4R;
obituary CA 97-100

Elliott, Janice 1931-............. **CLC 47**
See also CANR 8; CA 13-16R; DLB 14

Elliott, Sumner Locke 1917-....... **CLC 38**
See also CANR 2, 21; CA 5-8R

Ellis, A. E. 19??-................. **CLC 7**

Ellis, Alice Thomas 19??-.......... **CLC 40**

Ellis, Bret Easton 1964-........... **CLC 39**
See also CA 118

Ellis, (Henry) Havelock
1859-1939 .... **TCLC 14**
See also CA 109

Ellis, Trey 1964-................. **CLC 55**

Ellison, Harlan (Jay) 1934-... **CLC 1, 13, 42**
See also CANR 5; CA 5-8R; DLB 8

Ellison, Ralph (Waldo)
1914-............... **CLC 1, 3, 11, 54**
See also CANR 24; CA 9-12R; DLB 2;
CDALB 1941-1968

Ellmann, Richard (David)
1918-1987 .... **CLC 50**
See also CANR 2; CA 1-4R;
obituary CA 122

Elman, Richard 1934-.............. **CLC 19**
See also CAAS 3; CA 17-20R

Eluard, Paul 1895-1952 .... **TCLC 7**
See also Grindel, Eugene

Elvin, Anne Katharine Stevenson 1933-
See Stevenson, Anne (Katharine)
See also CA 17-20R

Elyot, (Sir) James 1490?-1546....... **LC 11**

Elyot, (Sir) Thomas 1490?-1546 ..... **LC 11**

Elytis, Odysseus 1911-......... **CLC 15, 49**
See also CA 102

Emecheta, (Florence Onye) Buchi
1944- .... **CLC 14, 48**
See also CA 81-84

Emerson, Ralph Waldo
1803-1882 .... **NCLC 1**
See also DLB 1; CDALB 1640-1865

Empson, William
1906-1984 .... **CLC 3, 8, 19, 33, 34**
See also CA 17-20R; obituary CA 112;
DLB 20

Enchi, Fumiko (Veda) 1905-1986 ... **CLC 31**
See also obituary CA 121

Ende, Michael 1930-.............. **CLC 31**
See also CLR 14; CA 118; SATA 42

Endo, Shusaku 1923-..... **CLC 7, 14, 19, 54**
See also CANR 21; CA 29-32R

Engel, Marian 1933-1985.......... **CLC 36**
See also CANR 12; CA 25-28R; DLB 53

Engelhardt, Frederick 1911-1986
See Hubbard, L(afayette) Ron(ald)

Enright, D(ennis) J(oseph)
1920- .... **CLC 4, 8, 31**
See also CANR 1; CA 1-4R; SATA 25;
DLB 27

Enzensberger, Hans Magnus
1929- .... **CLC 43**
See also CA 116, 119

Ephron, Nora 1941- .... **CLC 17, 31**
See also CANR 12; CA 65-68

Epstein, Daniel Mark 1948- .... **CLC 7**
See also CANR 2; CA 49-52

Epstein, Jacob 1956- .... **CLC 19**
See also CA 114

Epstein, Joseph 1937-............. **CLC 39**
See also CA 112, 119

Epstein, Leslie 1938- .... **CLC 27**
See also CA 73-76

Erdman, Paul E(mil) 1932- .... **CLC 25**
See also CANR 13; CA 61-64

Erdrich, Louise 1954-......... **CLC 39, 54**
See also CA 114

Erenburg, Ilya (Grigoryevich) 1891-1967
See Ehrenburg, Ilya (Grigoryevich)

Eseki, Bruno 1919-
See Mphahlele, Ezekiel

Esenin, Sergei (Aleksandrovich)
1895-1925 .... **TCLC 4**
See also CA 104

Eshleman, Clayton 1935-........... **CLC 7**
See also CAAS 6; CA 33-36R; DLB 5

Espriu, Salvador 1913-1985......... **CLC 9**
See also obituary CA 115

Estleman, Loren D. 1952- .... **CLC 48**
See also CA 85-88

Evans, Marian 1819-1880
See Eliot, George

Evans, Mary Ann 1819-1880
See Eliot, George

Evarts, Esther 1900-1972
See Benson, Sally

Everson, Ronald G(ilmour) 1903- ... **CLC 27**
See also CA 17-20R

Everson, William (Oliver)
1912- .... **CLC 1, 5, 14**
See also CANR 20; CA 9-12R; DLB 5, 16

Evtushenko, Evgenii (Aleksandrovich) 1933-
See Yevtushenko, Yevgeny

Ewart, Gavin (Buchanan)
1916- .... **CLC 13, 46**
See also CANR 17; CA 89-92; DLB 40

Ewers, Hanns Heinz 1871-1943 ... **TCLC 12**
See also CA 109

Ewing, Frederick R. 1918-
See Sturgeon, Theodore (Hamilton)

Exley, Frederick (Earl) 1929-.... **CLC 6, 11**
See also CA 81-84; DLB-Y 81

Ezekiel, Tish O'Dowd 1943-....... **CLC 34**

Fagen, Donald 1948-
See Becker, Walter and Fagen, Donald

Fagen, Donald 1948- and **Becker, Walter**
1950-
See Becker, Walter and Fagen, Donald

Fair, Ronald L. 1932-............. **CLC 18**
See also CA 69-72; DLB 33

Fairbairns, Zoe (Ann) 1948- .... **CLC 32**
See also CANR 21; CA 103

Fairfield, Cicily Isabel 1892-1983
See West, Rebecca

Fallaci, Oriana 1930-............. **CLC 11**
See also CANR 15; CA 77-80

Faludy, George 1913-............. **CLC 42**
See also CA 21-24R

Fanshaw, Lady Anne 1625-1706 ..... **LC 11**

Fanshawe, Lady Ann 1625-1706 ..... **LC 11**

Fargue, Leon-Paul 1876-1947 ..... **TCLC 11**
See also CA 109

Farigoule, Louis 1885-1972
See Romains, Jules

Farina, Richard 1937?-1966........ **CLC 9**
See also CA 81-84; obituary CA 25-28R

Farley, Walter 1920- .... **CLC 17**
See also CANR 8; CA 17-20R; SATA 2, 43;
DLB 22

Farmer, Philip Jose 1918-....... **CLC 1, 19**
See also CANR 4; CA 1-4R; DLB 8

Farrell, James T(homas)
1904-1979 ....**CLC 1, 4, 8, 11**
See also CANR 9; CA 5-8R;
obituary CA 89-92; DLB 4, 9; DLB-DS 2

Farrell, J(ames) G(ordon)
1935-1979 .... **CLC 6**
See also CA 73-76; obituary CA 89-92;
DLB 14

Farrell, M. J. 1904-
See Keane, Molly

Fassbinder, Rainer Werner
1946-1982 .... **CLC 20**
See also CA 93-96; obituary CA 106

Fast, Howard (Melvin) 1914- ...... **CLC 23**
See also CANR 1; CA 1-4R; SATA 7;
DLB 9

Faulkner, William (Cuthbert)
1897-1962 .... **CLC 1, 3, 6, 8, 9, 11, 14, 18, 28; SSC 1**
See also CA 81-84; DLB 9, 11, 44;
DLB-Y 86; DLB-DS 2

Fauset, Jessie Redmon
1884?-1961................ **CLC 19, 54**
See also CA 109; DLB 51

Faust, Irvin 1924-................. **CLC 8**
See also CA 33-36R; DLB 2, 28; DLB-Y 80

Fearing, Kenneth (Flexner)
1902-1961 .... **CLC 51**
See also CA 93-96; DLB 9

Federman, Raymond 1928- ...... **CLC 6, 47**
See also CANR 10; CA 17-20R; DLB-Y 80

Federspiel, J(urg) F. 1931-........ **CLC 42**

Feiffer, Jules 1929-.............. CLC 2, 8
See also CA 17-20R; SATA 8; DLB 7, 44

Feinstein, Elaine 1930-.......... CLC 36
See also CAAS 1; CA 69-72; DLB 14, 40

Feldman, Irving (Mordecai) 1928-.... CLC 7
See also CANR 1; CA 1-4R

Fellini, Federico 1920-........... CLC 16
See also CA 65-68

Felsen, Gregor 1916-
See Felsen, Henry Gregor

Felsen, Henry Gregor 1916- .... CLC 17
See also CANR 1; CA 1-4R; SAAS 2;
SATA 1

Fenton, James (Martin) 1949-...... CLC 32
See also CA 102; DLB 40

Ferber, Edna 1887-1968........... CLC 18
See also CA 5-8R; obituary CA 25-28R;
SATA 7; DLB 9, 28

Ferlinghetti, Lawrence (Monsanto)
1919?- .... CLC 2, 6, 10, 27
See also CANR 3; CA 5-8R; DLB 5, 16;
CDALB 1941-1968

Ferrier, Susan (Edmonstone)
1782-1854 .... NCLC 8

Feuchtwanger, Lion 1884-1958 ..... TCLC 3
See also CA 104

Feydeau, Georges 1862-1921...... TCLC 22
See also CA 113

Fiedler, Leslie A(aron)
1917- .... CLC 4, 13, 24
See also CANR 7; CA 9-12R; DLB 28

Field, Andrew 1938-.............. CLC 44
See also CA 97-100

Field, Eugene 1850-1895 .... NCLC 3
See also SATA 16; DLB 21, 23, 42

Fielding, Henry 1707-1754 .... LC 1
See also DLB 39

Fielding, Sarah 1710-1768 .... LC 1
See also DLB 39

Fierstein, Harvey 1954-........... CLC 33

Figes, Eva 1932-................ CLC 31
See also CANR 4; CA 53-56; DLB 14

Finch, Robert (Duer Claydon)
1900- .... CLC 18
See also CANR 9; CA 57-60

Findley, Timothy 1930-........... CLC 27
See also CANR 12; CA 25-28R; DLB 53

Fink, Janis 1951-
See Ian, Janis

Firbank, Louis 1944-
See Reed, Lou

Firbank, (Arthur Annesley) Ronald
1886-1926 .... TCLC 1
See also CA 104; DLB 36

Fisher, Roy 1930-................ CLC 25
See also CANR 16; CA 81-84; DLB 40

Fisher, Rudolph 1897-1934 .... TCLC 11
See also CA 107; DLB 51

Fisher, Vardis (Alvero) 1895-1968.... CLC 7
See also CA 5-8R; obituary CA 25-28R;
DLB 9

FitzGerald, Edward 1809-1883 .... NCLC 9
See also DLB 32

Fitzgerald, F(rancis) Scott (Key)
1896-1940 .... TCLC 1, 6, 14, 28
See also CA 110; DLB 4, 9; DLB-Y 81;
DLB-DS 1

Fitzgerald, Penelope 1916-...... CLC 19, 51
See also CA 85-88; DLB 14

Fitzgerald, Robert (Stuart)
1910-1985 .... CLC 39
See also CANR 1; CA 2R;
obituary CA 114; DLB-Y 80

FitzGerald, Robert D(avid) 1902-.... CLC 19
See also CA 17-20R

Flanagan, Thomas (James Bonner)
1923- .... CLC 25
See also CA 108; DLB-Y 80

Flaubert, Gustave
1821-1880 .... NCLC 2, 10, 19

Fleming, Ian (Lancaster)
1908-1964 .... CLC 3, 30
See also CA 5-8R; SATA 9

Fleming, Thomas J(ames) 1927-.... CLC 37
See also CANR 10; CA 5-8R; SATA 8

Flieg, Hellmuth
See Heym, Stefan

Flying Officer X 1905-1974
See Bates, H(erbert) E(rnest)

Fo, Dario 1929-................. CLC 32
See also CA 116

Follett, Ken(neth Martin) 1949-.... CLC 18
See also CANR 13; CA 81-84; DLB-Y 81

Foote, Horton 1916-............. CLC 51
See also CA 73-76; DLB 26

Forbes, Esther 1891-1967......... CLC 12
See also CAP 1; CA 13-14;
obituary CA 25-28R; SATA 2; DLB 22

Forche, Carolyn 1950-........... CLC 25
See also CA 109, 117; DLB 5

Ford, Ford Madox 1873-1939 ... TCLC 1, 15
See also CA 104; DLB 34

Ford, John 1895-1973............. CLC 16
See also obituary CA 45-48

Ford, Richard 1944-............. CLC 46
See also CANR 11; CA 69-72

Foreman, Richard 1937-......... CLC 50
See also CA 65-68

Forester, C(ecil) S(cott)
1899-1966 .... CLC 35
See also CA 73-76; obituary CA 25-28R;
SATA 13

Forman, James D(ouglas) 1932-.... CLC 21
See also CANR 4, 19; CA 9-12R; SATA 8,
21

Fornes, Maria Irene 1930-........ CLC 39
See also CA 25-28R; DLB 7

Forrest, Leon 1937-.............. CLC 4
See also CAAS 7; CA 89-92; DLB 33

Forster, E(dward) M(organ)
1879-1970 .... CLC 1, 2, 3, 4, 9, 10, 13,
15, 22, 45
See also CAP 1; CA 13-14;
obituary CA 25-28R; DLB 34

Forster, John 1812-1876 .... NCLC 11

Forsyth, Frederick 1938-...... CLC 2, 5, 36
See also CA 85-88

Forten (Grimke), Charlotte L(ottie)
1837-1914 .... TCLC 16
See also Grimke, Charlotte L(ottie) Forten
See also DLB 50

Foscolo, Ugo 1778-1827.......... NCLC 8

Fosse, Bob 1925-................ CLC 20
See also Fosse, Robert Louis

Fosse, Robert Louis 1925-
See Bob Fosse
See also CA 110

Foucault, Michel 1926-1984 .... CLC 31, 34
See also CA 105; obituary CA 113

Fouque, Friedrich (Heinrich Karl) de La
Motte 1777-1843 .... NCLC 2

Fournier, Henri Alban 1886-1914
See Alain-Fournier
See also CA 104

Fournier, Pierre 1916-
See Gascar, Pierre
See also CANR 16; CA 89-92

Fowles, John (Robert)
1926- .... CLC 1, 2, 3, 4, 6, 9, 10, 15, 33
See also CA 5-8R; SATA 22; DLB 14

Fox, Paula 1923-................ CLC 2, 8
See also CLR 1; CANR 20; CA 73-76;
SATA 17; DLB 52

Fox, William Price (Jr.) 1926- ..... CLC 22
See also CANR 11; CA 17-20R; DLB 2;
DLB-Y 81

Frame (Clutha), Janet (Paterson)
1924- .... CLC 2, 3, 6, 22
See also Clutha, Janet Paterson Frame

France, Anatole 1844-1924 .... TCLC 9
See also Thibault, Jacques Anatole Francois

Francis, Claude 19??-............ CLC 50

Francis, Dick 1920- .... CLC 2, 22, 42
See also CANR 9; CA 5-8R

Francis, Robert (Churchill) 1901-... CLC 15
See also CANR 1; CA 1-4R

Frank, Anne 1929-1945 .... TCLC 17
See also CA 113; SATA 42

Frank, Elizabeth 1945-........... CLC 39
See also CA 121

Franklin, (Stella Maria Sarah) Miles
1879-1954 .... TCLC 7
See also CA 104

Fraser, Antonia (Pakenham)
1932- .... CLC 32
See also CA 85-88; SATA 32

Fraser, George MacDonald 1925-.... CLC 7
See also CANR 2; CA 45-48

Frayn, Michael 1933-...... CLC 3, 7, 31, 47
See also CA 5-8R; DLB 13, 14

Fraze, Candida 19??- .... CLC 50

Frazier, Ian 1951-................ CLC 46

Frederic, Harold 1856-1898...... NCLC 10
See also DLB 12, 23

Fredro, Aleksander 1793-1876..... NCLC 8

Freeling, Nicolas 1927- .... CLC 38
See also CANR 1, 17; CA 49-52

Freeman, Douglas Southall
1886-1953 .... TCLC 11
See also CA 109; DLB 17

Freeman, Judith 1946-............ CLC 55

Freeman, Mary (Eleanor) Wilkins
1852-1930 .... TCLC 9; SSC 1
See also CA 106; DLB 12

Freeman, R(ichard) Austin
1862-1943 .... TCLC 21
See also CA 113; DLB 70

French, Marilyn 1929-......... CLC 10, 18
See also CANR 3; CA 69-72

Freneau, Philip Morin 1752-1832 .. NCLC 1
See also DLB 37, 43

Friedman, B(ernard) H(arper)
1926- .... CLC 7
See also CANR 3; CA 1-4R

Friedman, Bruce Jay 1930-....... CLC 3, 5
See also CA 9-12R; DLB 2, 28

Friel, Brian 1929-.............. CLC 5, 42
See also CA 21-24R; DLB 13

Friis-Baastad, Babbis (Ellinor)
1921-1970 .... CLC 12
See also CA 17-20R; SATA 7

Frisch, Max (Rudolf)
1911- .... CLC 3, 9, 14, 18, 32, 44
See also CA 85-88; DLB 69

Fromentin, Eugene (Samuel Auguste)
1820-1876 .... NCLC 10

Frost, Robert (Lee)
1874-1963 ... CLC 1, 3, 4, 9, 10, 13, 15,
26, 34, 44
See also CA 89-92; SATA 14; DLB 54

Fry, Christopher 1907-....... CLC 2, 10, 14
See also CANR 9; CA 17-20R; DLB 13

Frye, (Herman) Northrop 1912- .... CLC 24
See also CANR 8; CA 5-8R

Fuchs, Daniel 1909-......... CLC 8, 22
See also CAAS 5; CA 81-84; DLB 9, 26, 28

Fuchs, Daniel 1934-............ CLC 34
See also CANR 14; CA 37-40R

Fuentes, Carlos
1928-......... CLC 3, 8, 10, 13, 22, 41
See also CANR 10; CA 69-72

Fugard, Athol 1932-... CLC 5, 9, 14, 25, 40
See also CA 85-88

Fugard, Sheila 1932- .... CLC 48

Fuller, Charles (H., Jr.) 1939-...... CLC 25
See also CA 108, 112; DLB 38

Fuller, (Sarah) Margaret
1810-1850 .... NCLC 5
See also Ossoli, Sarah Margaret (Fuller
marchesa d')
See also DLB 1; CDALB 1640-1865

Fuller, Roy (Broadbent) 1912-.... CLC 4, 28
See also CA 5-8R; DLB 15, 20

Furphy, Joseph 1843-1912........ TCLC 25

Futrelle, Jacques 1875-1912 ...... TCLC 19
See also CA 113

Gaboriau, Emile 1835-1873 ...... NCLC 14

Gadda, Carlo Emilio 1893-1973 .... CLC 11
See also CA 89-92

Gaddis, William
1922- .... CLC 1, 3, 6, 8, 10, 19, 43
See also CAAS 4; CANR 21; CA 17-20R;
DLB 2

Gaines, Ernest J. 1933-...... CLC 3, 11, 18
See also CANR 6; CA 9-12R; DLB 2, 33;
DLB-Y 80

Gale, Zona 1874-1938 .... TCLC 7
See also CA 105; DLB 9

Gallagher, Tess 1943-............ CLC 18
See also CA 106

Gallant, Mavis 1922- .... CLC 7, 18, 38
See also CA 69-72; DLB 53

Gallant, Roy A(rthur) 1924- .... CLC 17
See also CANR 4; CA 5-8R; SATA 4

Gallico, Paul (William) 1897-1976 ... CLC 2
See also CA 5-8R; obituary CA 69-72;
SATA 13; DLB 9

Galsworthy, John 1867-1933 ...... TCLC 1
See also CA 104; DLB 10, 34

Galt, John 1779-1839 .... NCLC 1

Galvin, James 1951-.............. CLC 38
See also CA 108

Gann, Ernest K(ellogg) 1910- ...... CLC 23
See also CANR 1; CA 1-4R

Garcia Lorca, Federico
1899-1936 .... TCLC 1, 7
See also CA 104

Garcia Marquez, Gabriel (Jose)
1928-.... CLC 2, 3, 8, 10, 15, 27, 47, 55
See also CANR 10; CA 33-36R

Gardam, Jane 1928-.............. CLC 43
See also CLR 12; CANR 2, 18; CA 49-52;
SATA 28, 39; DLB 14

Gardner, Herb 1934- .... CLC 44

Gardner, John (Champlin, Jr.)
1933-1982 .... CLC 2, 3, 5, 7, 8, 10, 18,
28, 34
See also CA 65-68; obituary CA 107;
obituary SATA 31, 40; DLB 2; DLB-Y 82

Gardner, John (Edmund) 1926-..... CLC 30
See also CANR 15; CA 103

Garfield, Leon 1921-.............. CLC 12
See also CA 17-20R; SATA 1, 32

Garland, (Hannibal) Hamlin
1860-1940 .... TCLC 3
See also CA 104; DLB 12, 71

Garneau, Hector (de) Saint Denys
1912-1943 .... TCLC 13
See also CA 111

Garner, Alan 1935-.............. CLC 17
See also CANR 15; CA 73-76; SATA 18

Garner, Hugh 1913-1979 .... CLC 13
See also CA 69-72

Garnett, David 1892-1981 .... CLC 3
See also CANR 17; CA 5-8R;
obituary CA 103; DLB 34

Garrett, George (Palmer, Jr.)
1929- .... CLC 3, 11, 51
See also CAAS 5; CANR 1; CA 1-4R;
DLB 2, 5; DLB-Y 83

Garrigue, Jean 1914-1972 .... CLC 2, 8
See also CA 5-8R; obituary CA 37-40R

Gary, Romain 1914-1980 .... CLC 25
See also Kacew, Romain

Gascar, Pierre 1916-.............. CLC 11
See also Fournier, Pierre

Gascoyne, David (Emery) 1916- .... CLC 45
See also CANR 10; CA 65-68; DLB 20

Gaskell, Elizabeth Cleghorn
1810-1865 .... NCLC 5
See also DLB 21

Gass, William H(oward)
1924- .... CLC 1, 2, 8, 11, 15, 39
See also CA 17-20R; DLB 2

Gautier, Theophile 1811-1872 ..... NCLC 1

Gaye, Marvin (Pentz) 1939-1984 ... CLC 26
See also obituary CA 112

Gebler, Carlo (Ernest) 1954-....... CLC 39
See also CA 119

Gee, Maurice (Gough) 1931-...... CLC 29
See also CA 97-100; SATA 46

Gelbart, Larry (Simon) 1923- ...... CLC 21
See also CA 73-76

Gelber, Jack 1932-........... CLC 1, 6, 14
See also CANR 2; CA 1-4R; DLB 7

Gellhorn, Martha (Ellis) 1908- ..... CLC 14
See also CA 77-80; DLB-Y 82

Genet, Jean
1910-1986 ... CLC 1, 2, 5, 10, 14, 44, 46
See also CANR 18; CA 13-16R; DLB 72;
DLB-Y 86

Gent, Peter 1942-................ CLC 29
See also CA 89-92; DLB 72; DLB-Y 82

George, Jean Craighead 1919-...... CLC 35
See also CLR 1; CA 5-8R; SATA 2;
DLB 52

George, Stefan (Anton)
1868-1933 .... TCLC 2, 14
See also CA 104

Gerhardi, William (Alexander) 1895-1977
See Gerhardie, William (Alexander)

Gerhardie, William (Alexander)
1895-1977 .... CLC 5
See also CANR 18; CA 25-28R;
obituary CA 73-76; DLB 36

Gertler, T(rudy) 1946?- .... CLC 34
See also CA 116

Gessner, Friedrike Victoria 1910-1980
See Adamson, Joy(-Friederike Victoria)

Ghelderode, Michel de
1898-1962 .... CLC 6, 11
See also CA 85-88

Ghiselin, Brewster 1903-.......... CLC 23
See also CANR 13; CA 13-16R

Ghose, Zulfikar 1935-............. CLC 42
See also CA 65-68

Ghosh, Amitav 1943- .... CLC 44

Giacosa, Giuseppe 1847-1906 ...... TCLC 7
See also CA 104

Gibbon, Lewis Grassic 1901-1935... TCLC 4
See also Mitchell, James Leslie

Gibbons, Kaye 1960- .... CLC 50

Gibran, (Gibran) Kahlil
1883-1931 .... TCLC 1, 9
See also CA 104

Gibson, William 1914-............ CLC 23
See also CANR 9; CA 9-12R; DLB 7

Gibson, William 1948-............ CLC 39

Gide, Andre (Paul Guillaume)
1869-1951 .... TCLC 5, 12
See also CA 104

Gifford, Barry (Colby) 1946-....... CLC 34
See also CANR 9; CA 65-68

Gilbert, (Sir) W(illiam) S(chwenck)
1836-1911 .... TCLC 3
See also CA 104; SATA 36

Gilbreth, Ernestine 1908-
See Carey, Ernestine Gilbreth

Gilbreth, Frank B(unker), Jr. 1911- and
Carey, Ernestine Gilbreth
1908- .... CLC 17

Gilbreth, Frank B(unker), Jr. 1911-
See Gilbreth, Frank B(unker), Jr. and
Carey, Ernestine Gilbreth
See also CA 9-12R; SATA 2

Gilchrist, Ellen 1935-......... CLC 34, 48
See also CA 113, 116

Giles, Molly 1942-............. CLC 39

Gilliam, Terry (Vance) 1940-
See Monty Python
See also CA 108, 113

Gilliatt, Penelope (Ann Douglass)
1932-.................. CLC 2, 10, 13
See also CA 13-16R; DLB 14

Gilman, Charlotte (Anna) Perkins (Stetson)
1860-1935 .... TCLC 9
See also CA 106

Gilmour, David 1944-
See Pink Floyd

Gilroy, Frank D(aniel) 1925-........ CLC 2
See also CA 81-84; DLB 7

Ginsberg, Allen
1926- .... CLC 1, 2, 3, 4, 6, 13, 36
See also CANR 2; CA 1-4R; DLB 5, 16;
CDALB 1941-1968

Ginzburg, Natalia 1916-...... CLC 5, 11, 54
See also CA 85-88

Giono, Jean 1895-1970......... CLC 4, 11
See also CANR 2; CA 45-48;
obituary CA 29-32R; DLB 72

Giovanni, Nikki 1943-.... CLC 2, 4, 19
See also CLR 6; CAAS 6; CANR 18;
CA 29-32R; SATA 24; DLB 5, 41

Giovene, Andrea 1904-............ CLC 7
See also CA 85-88

Gippius, Zinaida (Nikolayevna) 1869-1945
See Hippius, Zinaida
See also CA 106

Giraudoux, (Hippolyte) Jean
1882-1944 .... TCLC 2, 7
See also CA 104

Gironella, Jose Maria 1917-....... CLC 11
See also CA 101

Gissing, George (Robert)
1857-1903 .... TCLC 3, 24
See also CA 105; DLB 18

Gladkov, Fyodor (Vasilyevich)
1883-1958 .... TCLC 27

Glanville, Brian (Lester) 1931-...... CLC 6
See also CANR 3; CA 5-8R; SATA 42;
DLB 15

Glasgow, Ellen (Anderson Gholson)
1873?-1945................ TCLC 2, 7
See also CA 104; DLB 9, 12

Glassco, John 1909-1981 .... CLC 9
See also CANR 15; CA 13-16R;
obituary CA 102

Glasser, Ronald J. 1940?- .... CLC 37

Glendinning, Victoria 1937-....... CLC 50
See also CA 120

Glissant, Edouard 1928-.......... CLC 10

Gloag, Julian 1930- .... CLC 40
See also CANR 10; CA 65-68

Gluck, Louise (Elisabeth)
1943-................. CLC 7, 22, 44
See also CA 33-36R; DLB 5

Gobineau, Joseph Arthur (Comte) de
1816-1882 .... NCLC 17

Godard, Jean-Luc 1930-.......... CLC 20
See also CA 93-96

Godwin, Gail 1937-........ CLC 5, 8, 22, 31
See also CANR 15; CA 29-32R; DLB 6

Godwin, William 1756-1836...... NCLC 14
See also DLB 39

Goethe, Johann Wolfgang von
1749-1832 .... NCLC 4

Gogarty, Oliver St. John
1878-1957 .... TCLC 15
See also CA 109; DLB 15, 19

Gogol, Nikolai (Vasilyevich)
1809-1852 .... NCLC 5, 15
See also CAAS 1, 4

Gokceli, Yasar Kemal 1923-
See Kemal, Yashar

Gold, Herbert 1924-....... CLC 4, 7, 14, 42
See also CANR 17; CA 9-12R; DLB 2;
DLB-Y 81

Goldbarth, Albert 1948-......... CLC 5, 38
See also CANR 6; CA 53-56

Goldberg, Anatol 1910-1982 .... CLC 34
See also obituary CA 117

Golding, William (Gerald)
1911- .... CLC 1, 2, 3, 8, 10, 17, 27
See also CANR 13; CA 5-8R; DLB 15

Goldman, Emma 1869-1940...... TCLC 13
See also CA 110

Goldman, William (W.) 1931-.... CLC 1, 48
See also CA 9-12R; DLB 44

Goldmann, Lucien 1913-1970 ...... CLC 24
See also CAP 2; CA 25-28

Goldoni, Carlo 1707-1793 .... LC 4

Goldsberry, Steven 1949-......... CLC 34

Goldsmith, Oliver 1728?-1774........ LC 2
See also SATA 26; DLB 39

Gombrowicz, Witold
1904-1969 .... CLC 4, 7, 11, 49
See also CAP 2; CA 19-20;
obituary CA 25-28R

Gomez de la Serna, Ramon
1888-1963 .... CLC 9
See also obituary CA 116

Goncharov, Ivan Alexandrovich
1812-1891 .... NCLC 1

Goncourt, Edmond (Louis Antoine Huot) de
1822-1896 and **Goncourt, Jules (Alfred
Huot) de** 1830-1870........ NCLC 7

Goncourt, Edmond (Louis Antoine Huot) de
1822-1896
See Goncourt, Edmond (Louis Antoine
Huot) de and Goncourt, Jules (Alfred
Huot) de

Goncourt, Jules (Alfred Huot) de 1830-1870
See Goncourt, Edmond (Louis Antoine
Huot) de and Goncourt, Jules (Alfred
Huot) de

Goncourt, Jules (Alfred Huot) de 1830-1870
and **Goncourt, Edmond (Louis Antoine
Huot) de** 1822-1896
See Goncourt, Edmond (Louis Antoine
Huot) de and Goncourt, Jules (Alfred
Huot) de

Gontier, Fernande 19??-.......... CLC 50

Goodman, Paul 1911-1972.... CLC 1, 2, 4, 7
See also CAP 2; CA 19-20;
obituary CA 37-40R

Gorden, Charles William 1860-1937
See Conner, Ralph

Gordimer, Nadine
1923- .... CLC 3, 5, 7, 10, 18, 33, 51
See also CANR 3; CA 5-8R

Gordon, Caroline
1895-1981 .... CLC 6, 13, 29
See also CAP 1; CA 11-12;
obituary CA 103; DLB 4, 9; DLB-Y 81

Gordon, Mary (Catherine)
1949-................. CLC 13, 22
See also CA 102; DLB 6; DLB-Y 81

Gordon, Sol 1923-............... CLC 26
See also CANR 4; CA 53-56; SATA 11

Gordone, Charles 1925-......... CLC 1, 4
See also CA 93-96; DLB 7

Gorenko, Anna Andreyevna 1889?-1966
See Akhmatova, Anna

Gorky, Maxim 1868-1936 .... TCLC 8
See also Peshkov, Alexei Maximovich

Goryan, Sirak 1908-1981
See Saroyan, William

Gosse, Edmund (William)
1849-1928 .... TCLC 28
See also CA 117; DLB 57

Gotlieb, Phyllis (Fay Bloom)
1926-..................... CLC 18
See also CANR 7; CA 13-16R

Gould, Lois 1938?-............. CLC 4, 10
See also CA 77-80

Gourmont, Remy de 1858-1915.... TCLC 17
See also CA 109

Govier, Katherine 1948-.......... CLC 51
See also CANR 18; CA 101

Goyen, (Charles) William
1915-1983 .... CLC 5, 8, 14, 40
See also CANR 6; CA 5-8R;
obituary CA 110; DLB 2; DLB-Y 83

Goytisolo, Juan 1931- .... CLC 5, 10, 23
See also CA 85-88

Gozzi, (Conte) Carlo 1720-1806 .. NCLC 23

Grabbe, Christian Dietrich
1801-1836 .... NCLC 2

Gracq, Julien 1910- .... CLC 11, 48
See also Poirier, Louis

Grade, Chaim 1910-1982 .... CLC 10
See also CA 93-96; obituary CA 107

Graham, Jorie 1951- .... CLC 48
See also CA 111

Graham, R(obert) B(ontine) Cunninghame
1852-1936 .... TCLC 19

Graham, Winston (Mawdsley)
1910- .... CLC 23
See also CANR 2; CA 49-52;
obituary CA 118

Graham, W(illiam) S(ydney)
1918-1986 .... CLC 29
See also CA 73-76; obituary CA 118;
DLB 20

Granville-Barker, Harley
1877-1946 .... TCLC 2
See also CA 104

Grass, Gunter (Wilhelm)
1927- .. CLC 1, 2, 4, 6, 11, 15, 22, 32, 49
See also CANR 20; CA 13-16R

Grau, Shirley Ann 1929- .... CLC 4, 9
See also CANR 22; CA 89-92; DLB 2

Graves, Richard Perceval 1945- .... CLC 44
See also CANR 9; CA 65-68

Graves, Robert (von Ranke)
1895-1985 ... CLC 1, 2, 6, 11, 39, 44, 45
See also CANR 5; CA 5-8R;
obituary CA 117; SATA 45; DLB 20;
DLB-Y 85

Gray, Alasdair 1934- .... CLC 41

Gray, Amlin 1946- .... CLC 29

Gray, Francine du Plessix 1930-.... CLC 22
See also CAAS 2; CANR 11; CA 61-64

Gray, John (Henry) 1866-1934 .... TCLC 19
See also CA 119

Gray, Simon (James Holliday)
1936- .... CLC 9, 14, 36
See also CAAS 3; CA 21-24R; DLB 13

Gray, Spalding 1941- .... CLC 49

Gray, Thomas 1716-1771 .... LC 4

Grayson, Richard (A.) 1951- .... CLC 38
See also CANR 14; CA 85-88

Greeley, Andrew M(oran) 1928-.... CLC 28
See also CAAS 7; CANR 7; CA 5-8R

Green, Hannah 1932-......... CLC 3, 7, 30
See also Greenberg, Joanne
See also CA 73-76

Green, Henry 1905-1974 .... CLC 2, 13
See also Yorke, Henry Vincent
See also DLB 15

Green, Julien (Hartridge) 1900- .. CLC 3, 11
See also CA 21-24R; DLB 4, 72

Green, Paul (Eliot) 1894-1981...... CLC 25
See also CANR 3; CA 5-8R;
obituary CA 103; DLB 7, 9; DLB-Y 81

Greenberg, Ivan 1908-1973
See Rahv, Philip
See also CA 85-88

Greenberg, Joanne (Goldenberg)
1932- .... CLC 3, 7, 30
See also Green, Hannah
See also CANR 14; CA 5-8R; SATA 25

Greene, Bette 1934- .... CLC 30
See also CLR 2; CANR 4; CA 53-56;
SATA 8

Greene, Gael 19??- .... CLC 8
See also CANR 10; CA 13-16R

Greene, Graham (Henry)
1904- ..... CLC 1, 3, 6, 9, 14, 18, 27, 37
See also CA 13-16R; SATA 20; DLB 13, 15;
DLB-Y 85

Gregor, Arthur 1923- .... CLC 9
See also CANR 11; CA 25-28R; SATA 36

Gregory, Lady (Isabella Augusta Persse)
1852-1932 .... TCLC 1
See also CA 104; DLB 10

Grendon, Stephen 1909-1971
See Derleth, August (William)

Greve, Felix Paul Berthold Friedrich
1879-1948
See Grove, Frederick Philip
See also CA 104

Grey, (Pearl) Zane 1872?-1939 ..... TCLC 6
See also CA 104; DLB 9

Grieg, (Johan) Nordahl (Brun)
1902-1943 .... TCLC 10
See also CA 107

Grieve, C(hristopher) M(urray) 1892-1978
See MacDiarmid, Hugh
See also CA 5-8R; obituary CA 85-88

Griffin, Gerald 1803-1840 .... NCLC 7

Griffin, Peter 1942- .... CLC 39

Griffiths, Trevor 1935- .... CLC 13
See also CA 97-100; DLB 13

Grigson, Geoffrey (Edward Harvey)
1905-1985 .... CLC 7, 39
See also CANR 20; CA 25-28R;
obituary CA 118; DLB 27

Grillparzer, Franz 1791-1872...... NCLC 1

Grimke, Charlotte L(ottie) Forten 1837-1914
See Forten (Grimke), Charlotte L(ottie)
See also CA 117

Grimm, Jakob (Ludwig) Karl 1785-1863 and
Grimm, Wilhelm Karl
1786-1859 .... NCLC 3
See also SATA 22

Grimm, Jakob (Ludwig) Karl 1785-1863
See Grimm, Jakob (Ludwig) Karl and
Grimm, Wilhelm Karl

Grimm, Wilhelm Karl 1786-1859
See Grimm, Jakob (Ludwig) Karl and
Grimm, Wilhelm Karl

Grimm, Wilhelm Karl 1786-1859 and **Grimm,
Jakob (Ludwig) Karl** 1785-1863
See Grimm, Jakob (Ludwig) Karl and
Grimm, Wilhelm Karl

**Grimmelshausen, Johann Jakob Christoffel
von** 1621-1676 .... LC 6

Grindel, Eugene 1895-1952
See also CA 104

Grossman, Vasily (Semenovich)
1905-1964 .... CLC 41

Grove, Frederick Philip
1879-1948 .... TCLC 4
See also Greve, Felix Paul Berthold
Friedrich

Grumbach, Doris (Isaac)
1918- .... CLC 13, 22
See also CAAS 2; CANR 9; CA 5-8R

Grundtvig, Nicolai Frederik Severin
1783-1872 .... NCLC 1

Grunwald, Lisa 1959-............. CLC 44
See also CA 120

Guare, John 1938- .... CLC 8, 14, 29
See also CANR 21; CA 73-76; DLB 7

Gudjonsson, Halldor Kiljan 1902-
See Laxness, Halldor (Kiljan)
See also CA 103

Guest, Barbara 1920-............. CLC 34
See also CANR 11; CA 25-28R; DLB 5

Guest, Judith (Ann) 1936-....... CLC 8, 30
See also CANR 15; CA 77-80

Guild, Nicholas M. 1944-......... CLC 33
See also CA 93-96

Guillen, Jorge 1893-1984.......... CLC 11
See also CA 89-92; obituary CA 112

Guillen, Nicolas 1902-............. CLC 48
See also CA 116

Guillevic, (Eugene) 1907-.......... CLC 33
See also CA 93-96

Gunn, Bill 1934-................. CLC 5
See also Gunn, William Harrison
See also DLB 38

Gunn, Thom(son William)
1929- .... CLC 3, 6, 18, 32
See also CANR 9; CA 17-20R; DLB 27

Gunn, William Harrison 1934-
See Gunn, Bill
See also CANR 12; CA 13-16R

Gurney, A(lbert) R(amsdell), Jr.
1930- .... CLC 32, 50, 54
See also CA 77-80

Gurney, Ivor (Bertie) 1890-1937... TCLC 33

Gustafson, Ralph (Barker) 1909-.... CLC 36
See also CANR 8; CA 21-24R

Guthrie, A(lfred) B(ertram), Jr.
1901- .... CLC 23
See also CA 57-60; DLB 6

Guthrie, Woodrow Wilson 1912-1967
See Guthrie, Woody
See also CA 113; obituary CA 93-96

Guthrie, Woody 1912-1967 .... CLC 35
See also Guthrie, Woodrow Wilson

Guy, Rosa (Cuthbert) 1928-........ CLC 26
See also CANR 14; CA 17-20R; SATA 14;
DLB 33

Haavikko, Paavo (Juhani)
1931- .... CLC 18, 34
See also CA 106

Hacker, Marilyn 1942- .... CLC 5, 9, 23
See also CA 77-80

Haggard, (Sir) H(enry) Rider
1856-1925 .... TCLC 11
See also CA 108; SATA 16; DLB 70

Haig-Brown, Roderick L(angmere)
1908-1976 .... CLC 21
See also CANR 4; CA 5-8R;
obituary CA 69-72; SATA 12

Hailey, Arthur 1920- .... CLC 5
See also CANR 2; CA 1-4R; DLB-Y 82

Hailey, Elizabeth Forsythe   1938-... **CLC 40**
See also CAAS 1; CANR 15; CA 93-96

Haley, Alex (Palmer)   1921-...... **CLC 8, 12**
See also CA 77-80; DLB 38

Haliburton, Thomas Chandler
1796-1865 .... **NCLC 15**
See also DLB 11

Hall, Donald (Andrew, Jr.)
1928- .... **CLC 1, 13, 37**
See also CAAS 7; CANR 2; CA 5-8R;
SATA 23; DLB 5

Hall, James Norman   1887-1951 ... **TCLC 23**
See also SATA 21

Hall, (Marguerite) Radclyffe
1886-1943 .... **TCLC 12**
See also CA 110

Hall, Rodney   1935- .... **CLC 51**
See also CA 109

Halpern, Daniel   1945- .... **CLC 14**
See also CA 33-36R

Hamburger, Michael (Peter Leopold)
1924- .... **CLC 5, 14**
See also CAAS 4; CANR 2; CA 5-8R;
DLB 27

Hamill, Pete   1935-.............. **CLC 10**
See also CANR 18; CA 25-28R

Hamilton, Edmond   1904-1977...... **CLC 1**
See also CANR 3; CA 1-4R; DLB 8

Hamilton, Gail   1911-
See Corcoran, Barbara

Hamilton, Ian   1938-............. **CLC 55**
See also CA 106; DLB 40

Hamilton, Mollie   1909?-
See Kaye, M(ary) M(argaret)

Hamilton, (Anthony Walter) Patrick
1904-1962 .... **CLC 51**
See also obituary CA 113; DLB 10

Hamilton, Virginia (Esther)   1936-... **CLC 26**
See also CLR 1, 11; CANR 20; CA 25-28R;
SATA 4; DLB 33, 52

Hammett, (Samuel) Dashiell
1894-1961 .... **CLC 3, 5, 10, 19, 47**
See also CA 81-84

Hammon, Jupiter   1711?-1800? .... **NCLC 5**
See also DLB 31, 50

Hamner, Earl (Henry), Jr.   1923- ... **CLC 12**
See also CA 73-76; DLB 6

Hampton, Christopher (James)
1946- .... **CLC 4**
See also CA 25-28R; DLB 13

Hamsun, Knut   1859-1952...... **TCLC 2, 14**
See also Pedersen, Knut

Handke, Peter   1942- .. **CLC 5, 8, 10, 15, 38**
See also CA 77-80

Hanley, James   1901-1985 ... **CLC 3, 5, 8, 13**
See also CA 73-76; obituary CA 117

Hannah, Barry   1942- .... **CLC 23, 38**
See also CA 108, 110; DLB 6

Hansberry, Lorraine (Vivian)
1930-1965 .... **CLC 17**
See also CA 109; obituary CA 25-28R;
DLB 7, 38; CDALB 1941-1968

Hansen, Joseph   1923-............ **CLC 38**
See also CANR 16; CA 29-32R

Hanson, Kenneth O(stlin)   1922-.... **CLC 13**
See also CANR 7; CA 53-56

Hardenberg, Friedrich (Leopold Freiherr) von
1772-1801
See Novalis

Hardwick, Elizabeth   1916- .... **CLC 13**
See also CANR 3; CA 5-8R; DLB 6

Hardy, Thomas
1840-1928 ...... **TCLC 4, 10, 18; SSC 2**
See also CA 104; SATA 25; DLB 18, 19

Hare, David   1947- .... **CLC 29**
See also CA 97-100; DLB 13

Harlan, Louis R(udolph)   1922-..... **CLC 34**
See also CA 21-24R

Harmon, William (Ruth)   1938-..... **CLC 38**
See also CANR 14; CA 33-36R

Harper, Frances Ellen Watkins
1825-1911 .... **TCLC 14**
See also CA 111; DLB 50

Harper, Michael S(teven)   1938- .. **CLC 7, 22**
See also CA 33-36R; DLB 41

Harris, Christie (Lucy Irwin)
1907- .... **CLC 12**
See also CANR 6; CA 5-8R; SATA 6

Harris, Frank   1856-1931........ **TCLC 24**
See also CAAS 1; CA 109

Harris, George Washington
1814-1869 .... **NCLC 23**
See also DLB 3

Harris, Joel Chandler   1848-1908 ... **TCLC 2**
See also YABC 1; CA 104; DLB 11, 23, 42

Harris, John (Wyndham Parkes Lucas)
Beynon   1903-1969
See Wyndham, John
See also CA 102; obituary CA 89-92

Harris, MacDonald   1921- .... **CLC 9**
See also Heiney, Donald (William)

Harris, Mark   1922- .... **CLC 19**
See also CAAS 3; CANR 2; CA 5-8R;
DLB 2; DLB-Y 80

Harris, (Theodore) Wilson   1921-.... **CLC 25**
See also CANR 11; CA 65-68

Harrison, Harry (Max)   1925-...... **CLC 42**
See also CANR 5, 21; CA 1-4R; SATA 4;
DLB 8

Harrison, James (Thomas)   1937-
See Harrison, Jim
See also CANR 8; CA 13-16R

Harrison, Jim   1937-......... **CLC 6, 14, 33**
See also Harrison, James (Thomas)
See also DLB-Y 82

Harrison, Tony   1937-............. **CLC 43**
See also CA 65-68; DLB 40

Harriss, Will(ard Irvin)   1922-...... **CLC 34**
See also CA 111

Harte, (Francis) Bret(t)
1836?-1902................. **TCLC 1, 25**
See also CA 104; SATA 26; DLB 12, 64;
CDALB 1865-1917

Hartley, L(eslie) P(oles)
1895-1972 .... **CLC 2, 22**
See also CA 45-48; obituary CA 37-40R;
DLB 15

Hartman, Geoffrey H.   1929-....... **CLC 27**
See also CA 117

Haruf, Kent   19??-................ **CLC 34**

Harwood, Ronald   1934-........... **CLC 32**
See also CANR 4; CA 1-4R; DLB 13

Hasek, Jaroslav (Matej Frantisek)
1883-1923 .... **TCLC 4**
See also CA 104

Hass, Robert   1941-............ **CLC 18, 39**
See also CA 111

Hastings, Selina   19??- .... **CLC 44**

Hauptmann, Gerhart (Johann Robert)
1862-1946 .... **TCLC 4**
See also CA 104

Havel, Vaclav   1936-.............. **CLC 25**
See also CA 104

Haviaras, Stratis   1935- .... **CLC 33**
See also CA 105

Hawkes, John (Clendennin Burne, Jr.)
1925-...... **CLC 1, 2, 3, 4, 7, 9, 14, 15,
27, 49**
See also CANR 2; CA 1-4R; DLB 2, 7;
DLB-Y 80

Hawthorne, Julian   1846-1934 ..... **TCLC 25**

Hawthorne, Nathaniel
1804-1864 ... **NCLC 2, 10, 17, 23; SSC 3**
See also YABC 2; DLB 1, 74;
CDALB 1640-1865

Hayashi, Fumiko   1904-1951 ...... **TCLC 27**

Haycraft, Anna   19??-
See Ellis, Alice Thomas

Hayden, Robert (Earl)
1913-1980 .... **CLC 5, 9, 14, 37**
See also CA 69-72; obituary CA 97-100;
CABS 2; SATA 19; obituary SATA 26;
DLB 5; CDALB 1941-1968

Hayman, Ronald   1932-........... **CLC 44**
See also CANR 18; CA 25-28R

Haywood, Eliza (Fowler)   1693?-1756.. **LC 1**
See also DLB 39

Hazzard, Shirley   1931- .... **CLC 18**
See also CANR 4; CA 9-12R; DLB-Y 82

H(ilda) D(oolittle)
1886-1961 .... **CLC 3, 8, 14, 31, 34**
See also Doolittle, Hilda

Head, Bessie   1937-1986........... **CLC 25**
See also CA 29-32R; obituary CA 109

Headon, (Nicky) Topper   1956?-
See The Clash

Heaney, Seamus (Justin)
1939- .... **CLC 5, 7, 14, 25, 37**
See also CA 85-88; DLB 40

Hearn, (Patricio) Lafcadio (Tessima Carlos)
1850-1904 .... **TCLC 9**
See also CA 105; DLB 12

Heat Moon, William Least   1939-... **CLC 29**

Hebert, Anne   1916- .... **CLC 4, 13, 29**
See also CA 85-88

Hecht, Anthony (Evan)
1923- .... **CLC 8, 13, 19**
See also CANR 6; CA 9-12R; DLB 5

Hecht, Ben   1894-1964 .... **CLC 8**
See also CA 85-88; DLB 7, 9, 25, 26, 28

Hedayat, Sadeq 1903-1951....... **TCLC 21**
See also CA 120

Heidegger, Martin 1889-1976 ...... **CLC 24**
See also CA 81-84; obituary CA 65-68

Heidenstam, (Karl Gustaf) Verner von
1859-1940 .... **TCLC 5**
See also CA 104

Heifner, Jack 1946- .... **CLC 11**
See also CA 105

Heijermans, Herman 1864-1924 ... **TCLC 24**

Heilbrun, Carolyn G(old) 1926-..... **CLC 25**
See also CANR 1; CA 45-48

Heine, Harry 1797-1856
See Heine, Heinrich

Heine, Heinrich 1797-1856 .... **NCLC 4**

Heinemann, Larry C(urtiss) 1944- .. **CLC 50**
See also CA 110

Heiney, Donald (William) 1921-
See Harris, MacDonald
See also CANR 3; CA 1-4R

Heinlein, Robert A(nson)
1907-1988 ...... **CLC 1, 3, 8, 14, 26, 55**
See also CANR 1, 20; CA 1-4R;
obituary CA 125; SATA 9; DLB 8

Heller, Joseph
1923- .... **CLC 1, 3, 5, 8, 11, 36**
See also CANR 8; CA 5-8R; CABS 1;
DLB 2, 28; DLB-Y 80

Hellman, Lillian (Florence)
1905?-1984... **CLC 2, 4, 8, 14, 18, 34, 44**
See also CA 13-16R; obituary CA 112;
DLB 7; DLB-Y 84

Helprin, Mark 1947- ..... **CLC 7, 10, 22, 32**
See also CA 81-84; DLB-Y 85

Hemingway, Ernest (Miller)
1899-1961 ... **CLC 1, 3, 6, 8, 10, 13, 19,**
30, 34, 39, 41, 44, 50; SSC 1
See also CA 77-80; DLB 4, 9; DLB-Y 81;
DLB-DS 1

Hempel, Amy 1951- .... **CLC 39**
See also CA 118

Henley, Beth 1952-.............. **CLC 23**
See also Henley, Elizabeth Becker
See also DLB-Y 86

Henley, Elizabeth Becker 1952-
See Henley, Beth
See also CA 107

Henley, William Ernest
1849-1903 .... **TCLC 8**
See also CA 105; DLB 19

Hennissart, Martha
See Lathen, Emma
See also CA 85-88

Henry 1491-1547 .... **LC 10**

Henry, O. 1862-1910 .... **TCLC 1, 19**
See also Porter, William Sydney

Hentoff, Nat(han Irving) 1925- ..... **CLC 26**
See also CLR 1; CAAS 6; CANR 5;
CA 1-4R; SATA 27, 42

Heppenstall, (John) Rayner
1911-1981 .... **CLC 10**
See also CA 1-4R; obituary CA 103

Herbert, Frank (Patrick)
1920-1986 .... **CLC 12, 23, 35, 44**
See also CANR 5; CA 53-56;
obituary CA 118; SATA 9, 37, 47; DLB 8

Herbert, Zbigniew 1924- .... **CLC 9, 43**
See also CA 89-92

Herbst, Josephine 1897-1969...... **CLC 34**
See also CA 5-8R; obituary CA 25-28R;
DLB 9

Herder, Johann Gottfried von
1744-1803 .... **NCLC 8**

Hergesheimer, Joseph
1880-1954 .... **TCLC 11**
See also CA 109; DLB 9

Herlagnez, Pablo de 1844-1896
See Verlaine, Paul (Marie)

Herlihy, James Leo 1927- .... **CLC 6**
See also CANR 2; CA 1-4R

Hernandez, Jose 1834-1886...... **NCLC 17**

Herriot, James 1916- .... **CLC 12**
See also Wight, James Alfred

Herrmann, Dorothy 1941- .... **CLC 44**
See also CA 107

Hersey, John (Richard)
1914-................ **CLC 1, 2, 7, 9, 40**
See also CA 17-20R; SATA 25; DLB 6

Herzen, Aleksandr Ivanovich
1812-1870 .... **NCLC 10**

Herzog, Werner 1942- .... **CLC 16**
See also CA 89-92

Hesse, Hermann
1877-1962 .... **CLC 1, 2, 3, 6, 11, 17, 25**
See also CAP 2; CA 17-18

Heyen, William 1940- .... **CLC 13, 18**
See also CA 33-36R; DLB 5

Heyerdahl, Thor 1914-............ **CLC 26**
See also CANR 5, 22; CA 5-8R; SATA 2,
52

Heym, Georg (Theodor Franz Arthur)
1887-1912 .... **TCLC 9**
See also CA 106

Heym, Stefan 1913-.............. **CLC 41**
See also CANR 4; CA 9-12R; DLB 69

Heyse, Paul (Johann Ludwig von)
1830-1914 .... **TCLC 8**
See also CA 104

Hibbert, Eleanor (Burford) 1906-.... **CLC 7**
See also CANR 9; CA 17-20R; SATA 2

Higgins, George V(incent)
1939-.............**CLC 4, 7, 10, 18**
See also CAAS 5; CANR 17; CA 77-80;
DLB 2; DLB-Y 81

Highsmith, (Mary) Patricia
1921-.............**CLC 2, 4, 14, 42**
See also CANR 1, 20; CA 1-4R

Highwater, Jamake 1942- .... **CLC 12**
See also CAAS 7; CANR 10; CA 65-68;
SATA 30, 32; DLB 52; DLB-Y 85

Hikmet (Ran), Nazim 1902-1963.... **CLC 40**
See also obituary CA 93-96

Hildesheimer, Wolfgang 1916- ..... **CLC 49**
See also CA 101; DLB 69

Hill, Geoffrey (William)
1932-................ **CLC 5, 8, 18, 45**
See also CANR 21; CA 81-84; DLB 40

Hill, George Roy 1922-........... **CLC 26**
See also CA 110

Hill, Susan B. 1942-.............. **CLC 4**
See also CA 33-36R; DLB 14

Hilliard, Noel (Harvey) 1929-...... **CLC 15**
See also CANR 7; CA 9-12R

Hilton, James 1900-1954......... **TCLC 21**
See also CA 108; SATA 34; DLB 34

Himes, Chester (Bomar)
1909-1984 .... **CLC 2, 4, 7, 18**
See also CANR 22; CA 25-28R;
obituary CA 114; DLB 2

Hinde, Thomas 1926-........... **CLC 6, 11**
See also Chitty, (Sir) Thomas Willes

Hine, (William) Daryl 1936-....... **CLC 15**
See also CANR 1, 20; CA 1-4R; DLB 60

Hinton, S(usan) E(loise) 1950- ..... **CLC 30**
See also CLR 3; CA 81-84; SATA 19

Hippius (Merezhkovsky), Zinaida
(Nikolayevna) 1869-1945...... **TCLC 9**
See also Gippius, Zinaida (Nikolayevna)

Hiraoka, Kimitake 1925-1970
See Mishima, Yukio
See also CA 97-100; obituary CA 29-32R

Hirsch, Edward (Mark) 1950-... **CLC 31, 50**
See also CANR 20; CA 104

Hitchcock, (Sir) Alfred (Joseph)
1899-1980 .... **CLC 16**
See also obituary CA 97-100; SATA 27;
obituary SATA 24

Hoagland, Edward 1932- .... **CLC 28**
See also CANR 2; CA 1-4R; SATA 51;
DLB 6

Hoban, Russell C(onwell) 1925-.. **CLC 7, 25**
See also CLR 3; CA 5-8R; SATA 1, 40;
DLB 52

Hobson, Laura Z(ametkin)
1900-1986 .... **CLC 7, 25**
See also CA 17-20R; obituary CA 118;
SATA 52; DLB 28

Hochhuth, Rolf 1931-........ **CLC 4, 11, 18**
See also CA 5-8R

Hochman, Sandra 1936-.......... **CLC 3, 8**
See also CA 5-8R; DLB 5

Hochwalder, Fritz 1911-1986 ...... **CLC 36**
See also CA 29-32R; obituary CA 120

Hocking, Mary (Eunice) 1921-..... **CLC 13**
See also CANR 18; CA 101

Hodgins, Jack 1938-............. **CLC 23**
See also CA 93-96; DLB 60

Hodgson, William Hope
1877-1918 .... **TCLC 13**
See also CA 111; DLB 70

Hoffman, Alice 1952-............ **CLC 51**
See also CA 77-80

Hoffman, Daniel (Gerard)
1923-.................. **CLC 6, 13, 23**
See also CANR 4; CA 1-4R; DLB 5

Hoffman, Stanley 1944-........... **CLC 5**
See also CA 77-80

Hoffman, William M(oses) 1939- ... **CLC 40**
See also CANR 11; CA 57-60

Hoffmann, Ernst Theodor Amadeus
1776-1822 .... **NCLC 2**
See also SATA 27

Hoffmann, Gert 1932- .... **CLC 54**

**Hofmannsthal, Hugo (Laurenz August
Hofmann Edler) von**
1874-1929 .... **TCLC 11**
See also CA 106

Hogg, James 1770-1835 .... **NCLC 4**

Holberg, Ludvig 1684-1754 .... **LC 6**

Holden, Ursula 1921- .... **CLC 18**
See also CANR 22; CA 101

Holderlin, (Johann Christian) Friedrich
1770-1843 .... **NCLC 16**

Holdstock, Robert (P.) 1948- ...... **CLC 39**

Holland, Isabelle 1920- .... **CLC 21**
See also CANR 10; CA 21-24R; SATA 8

Holland, Marcus 1900-1985
See Caldwell, (Janet Miriam) Taylor
(Holland)

Hollander, John 1929- ...... **CLC 2, 5, 8, 14**
See also CANR 1; CA 1-4R; SATA 13;
DLB 5

Holleran, Andrew 1943?- .... **CLC 38**

Hollinghurst, Alan 1954- .... **CLC 55**
See also CA 114

Hollis, Jim 1916-
See Summers, Hollis (Spurgeon, Jr.)

Holmes, Oliver Wendell
1809-1894 .... **NCLC 14**
See also SATA 34; DLB 1;
CDALB 1640-1865

Holt, Victoria 1906-
See Hibbert, Eleanor (Burford)

Holub, Miroslav 1923- .... **CLC 4**
See also CANR 10; CA 21-24R

Homer c. 8th century B.C.- .... **CMLC 1**

Honig, Edwin 1919- .... **CLC 33**
See also CANR 4; CA 5-8R; DLB 5

Hood, Hugh (John Blagdon)
1928- .... **CLC 15, 28**
See also CANR 1; CA 49-52; DLB 53

Hood, Thomas 1799-1845 .... **NCLC 16**

Hooker, (Peter) Jeremy 1941- ...... **CLC 43**
See also CANR 22; CA 77-80; DLB 40

Hope, A(lec) D(erwent) 1907- .... **CLC 3, 51**
See also CA 21-24R

Hopkins, Gerard Manley
1844-1889 .... **NCLC 17**
See also DLB 35, 57

Hopkins, John (Richard) 1931- ...... **CLC 4**
See also CA 85-88

Hopkins, Pauline Elizabeth
1859-1930 .... **TCLC 28**
See also DLB 50

Horgan, Paul 1903- .... **CLC 9**
See also CANR 9; CA 13-16R; SATA 13;
DLB-Y 85

Horwitz, Julius 1920-1986 .... **CLC 14**
See also CANR 12; CA 9-12R;
obituary CA 119

Hospital, Janette Turner 1942- ..... **CLC 42**
See also CA 108

Hostos (y Bonilla), Eugenio Maria de
1893-1903 .... **TCLC 24**

Hougan, Carolyn 19??- .... **CLC 34**

Household, Geoffrey (Edward West)
1900- .... **CLC 11**
See also CA 77-80; SATA 14

Housman, A(lfred) E(dward)
1859-1936 .... **TCLC 1, 10**
See also CA 104; DLB 19

Housman, Laurence 1865-1959 ..... **TCLC 7**
See also CA 106; SATA 25; DLB 10

Howard, Elizabeth Jane 1923- ... **CLC 7, 29**
See also CANR 8; CA 5-8R

Howard, Maureen 1930- ..... **CLC 5, 14, 46**
See also CA 53-56; DLB-Y 83

Howard, Richard 1929- ...... **CLC 7, 10, 47**
See also CA 85-88; DLB 5

Howard, Robert E(rvin)
1906-1936 .... **TCLC 8**
See also CA 105

Howe, Fanny 1940- .... **CLC 47**
See also CA 117; SATA 52

Howe, Julia Ward 1819-1910 ..... **TCLC 21**
See also CA 117; DLB 1

Howe, Tina 1937- .... **CLC 48**
See also CA 109

Howells, William Dean
1837-1920 .... **TCLC 7, 17**
See also CA 104; DLB 12, 64;
CDALB 1865-1917

Howes, Barbara 1914- .... **CLC 15**
See also CAAS 3; CA 9-12R; SATA 5

Hrabal, Bohumil 1914- .... **CLC 13**
See also CA 106

Hubbard, L(afayette) Ron(ald)
1911-1986 .... **CLC 43**
See also CANR 22; CA 77-80;
obituary CA 118

Huch, Ricarda (Octavia)
1864-1947 .... **TCLC 13**
See also CA 111

Huddle, David 1942- .... **CLC 49**
See also CA 57-60

Hudson, W(illiam) H(enry)
1841-1922 .... **TCLC 29**
See also CA 115; SATA 35

Hueffer, Ford Madox 1873-1939
See Ford, Ford Madox

Hughart, Barry 1934- .... **CLC 39**

Hughes, David (John) 1930- .... **CLC 48**
See also CA 116; DLB 14

Hughes, Edward James 1930-
See Hughes, Ted

Hughes, (James) Langston
1902-1967 ..... **CLC 1, 5, 10, 15, 35, 44**
See also CANR 1; CA 1-4R;
obituary CA 25-28R; SATA 4, 33;
DLB 4, 7, 48, 51

Hughes, Richard (Arthur Warren)
1900-1976 .... **CLC 1, 11**
See also CANR 4; CA 5-8R;
obituary CA 65-68; SATA 8;
obituary SATA 25; DLB 15

Hughes, Ted 1930- ..... **CLC 2, 4, 9, 14, 37**
See also CLR 3; CANR 1; CA 1-4R;
SATA 27, 49; DLB 40

Hugo, Richard F(ranklin)
1923-1982 .... **CLC 6, 18, 32**
See also CANR 3; CA 49-52;
obituary CA 108; DLB 5

Hugo, Victor Marie
1802-1885 .... **NCLC 3, 10**
See also SATA 47

Huidobro, Vicente 1893-1948 ..... **TCLC 31**

Hulme, Keri 1947- .... **CLC 39**

Hulme, T(homas) E(rnest)
1883-1917 .... **TCLC 21**
See also CA 117; DLB 19

Hume, David 1711-1776 .... **LC 7**

Humphrey, William 1924- .... **CLC 45**
See also CA 77-80; DLB 6

Humphreys, Emyr (Owen) 1919- .... **CLC 47**
See also CANR 3; CA 5-8R; DLB 15

Humphreys, Josephine 1945- .... **CLC 34**
See also CA 121

Hunt, E(verette) Howard (Jr.)
1918- .... **CLC 3**
See also CANR 2; CA 45-48

Hunt, (James Henry) Leigh
1784-1859 .... **NCLC 1**

Hunter, Evan 1926- .... **CLC 11, 31.**
See also CANR 5; CA 5-8R; SATA 25;
DLB-Y 82

Hunter, Kristin (Eggleston) 1931- ... **CLC 35**
See also CLR 3; CANR 13; CA 13-16R;
SATA 12; DLB 33

Hunter, Mollie (Maureen McIlwraith)
1922- .... **CLC 21**
See also McIlwraith, Maureen Mollie
Hunter

Hunter, Robert (d.?1734- .... **LC 7**

Hurston, Zora Neale
1891-1960 .... **CLC 7, 30**
See also CA 85-88; DLB 51

Huston, John (Marcellus) 1906- .... **CLC 20**
See also CA 73-76; DLB 26

Huxley, Aldous (Leonard)
1894-1963 .. **CLC 1, 3, 4, 5, 8, 11, 18, 35**
See also CA 85-88; DLB 36

Huysmans, Charles Marie Georges
1848-1907
See Huysmans, Joris-Karl
See also CA 104

Huysmans, Joris-Karl 1848-1907 .. **NCLC 7**
See also Huysmans, Charles Marie Georges

Hwang, David Henry 1957- .... **CLC 55**
See also CA 127

Hyde, Anthony 1946?- .... **CLC 42**

Hyde, Margaret O(ldroyd) 1917- ... **CLC 21**
See also CANR 1; CA 1-4R; SATA 1, 42

Ian, Janis 1951- .... **CLC 21**
See also CA 105

Ibarguengoitia, Jorge 1928-1983 .... **CLC 37**
See also obituary CA 113

Ibsen, Henrik (Johan)
1828-1906 .... **TCLC 2, 8, 16**
See also CA 104

Ibuse, Masuji 1898- .... **CLC 22**

Ichikawa, Kon 1915-.............. **CLC 20**
See also CA 121

Idle, Eric 1943-
See Monty Python
See also CA 116

Ignatow, David 1914-...... **CLC 4, 7, 14, 40**
See also CAAS 3; CA 9-12R; DLB 5

Ihimaera, Witi (Tame) 1944-....... **CLC 46**
See also CA 77-80

Ilf, Ilya 1897-1937 and **Petrov, Evgeny**
1902-1942 .... **TCLC 21**

Immermann, Karl (Lebrecht)
1796-1840 .... **NCLC 4**

Ingalls, Rachel 19??-.............. **CLC 42**

Inge, William (Motter)
1913-1973 .... **CLC 1, 8, 19**
See also CA 9-12R; DLB 7;
CDALB 1941-1968

Innaurato, Albert 1948-........... **CLC 21**
See also CA 115, 122

Innes, Michael 1906-
See Stewart, J(ohn) I(nnes) M(ackintosh)

Ionesco, Eugene
1912- .... **CLC 1, 4, 6, 9, 11, 15, 41**
See also CA 9-12R; SATA 7

Iqbal, Muhammad 1877-1938 ..... **TCLC 28**

Irving, John (Winslow)
1942- .... **CLC 13, 23, 38**
See also CA 25-28R; DLB 6; DLB-Y 82

Irving, Washington
1783-1859 .... **NCLC 2, 19; SSC 2**
See also YABC 2; DLB 3, 11, 30;
CDALB 1640-1865

Isaacs, Susan 1943- .... **CLC 32**
See also CANR 20; CA 89-92

Isherwood, Christopher (William Bradshaw)
1904-1986 .... **CLC 1, 9, 11, 14, 44**
See also CA 13-16R; obituary CA 117;
DLB 15; DLB-Y 86

Ishiguro, Kazuo 1954?-............ **CLC 27**
See also CA 120

Ishikawa Takuboku 1885-1912 .... **TCLC 15**
See also CA 113

Iskander, Fazil (Abdulovich)
1929- .... **CLC 47**
See also CA 102

Ivanov, Vyacheslav (Ivanovich)
1866-1949 .... **TCLC 33**
See also CA 122

Ivask, Ivar (Vidrik) 1927- .... **CLC 14**
See also CA 37-40R

Jackson, Jesse 1908-1983 .... **CLC 12**
See also CA 25-28R; obituary CA 109;
SATA 2, 29, 48

Jackson, Laura (Riding) 1901-
See Riding, Laura
See also CA 65-68; DLB 48

Jackson, Shirley 1919-1965........ **CLC 11**
See also CANR 4; CA 1-4R;
obituary CA 25-28R; SATA 2; DLB 6;
CDALB 1941-1968

Jacob, (Cyprien) Max 1876-1944 ... **TCLC 6**
See also CA 104

Jacob, Piers A(nthony) D(illingham) 1934-
See Anthony (Jacob), Piers
See also CA 21-24R

Jacobs, Jim 1942- and **Casey, Warren**
1935- .... **CLC 12**

Jacobs, Jim 1942-
See Jacobs, Jim and Casey, Warren
See also CA 97-100

Jacobs, W(illiam) W(ymark)
1863-1943 .... **TCLC 22**
See also CA 121

Jacobsen, Josephine 1908-........ **CLC 48**
See also CA 33-36R

Jacobson, Dan 1929- .... **CLC 4, 14**
See also CANR 2; CA 1-4R; DLB 14

Jagger, Mick 1944- and **Richard, Keith**
1943- .... **CLC 17**

Jagger, Mick 1944-
See Jagger, Mick and Richard, Keith

Jakes, John (William) 1932-....... **CLC 29**
See also CANR 10; CA 57-60; DLB-Y 83

James, C(yril) L(ionel) R(obert)
1901- .... **CLC 33**
See also CA 117

James, Daniel 1911-
See Santiago, Danny

James, Henry (Jr.)
1843-1916 .... **TCLC 2, 11, 24**
See also CA 104; DLB 12, 71;
CDALB 1865-1917

James, M(ontague) R(hodes)
1862-1936 .... **TCLC 6**
See also CA 104

James, P(hyllis) D(orothy)
1920- .... **CLC 18, 46**
See also CANR 17; CA 21-24R

James, William 1842-1910....... **TCLC 15**
See also CA 109

Jami, Nur al-Din 'Abd al-Rahman
1414-1492 .... **LC 9**

Jandl, Ernst 1925- .... **CLC 34**

Janowitz, Tama 1957- .... **CLC 43**
See also CA 106

Jarrell, Randall
1914-1965 .... **CLC 1, 2, 6, 9, 13, 49**
See also CLR 6; CANR 6; CA 5-8R;
obituary CA 25-28R; CABS 2; SATA 7;
DLB 48, 52; CDALB 1941-1968

Jarry, Alfred 1873-1907........ **TCLC 2, 14**
See also CA 104

Jean Paul 1763-1825 .... **NCLC 7**

Jeffers, (John) Robinson
1887-1962 .... **CLC 2, 3, 11, 15, 54**
See also CA 85-88; DLB 45

Jefferson, Thomas 1743-1826 .... **NCLC 11**
See also DLB 31; CDALB 1640-1865

Jellicoe, (Patricia) Ann 1927- ...... **CLC 27**
See also CA 85-88; DLB 13

Jennings, Elizabeth (Joan)
1926- .... **CLC 5, 14**
See also CAAS 5; CANR 8; CA 61-64;
DLB 27

Jennings, Waylon 1937-.......... **CLC 21**

Jensen, Laura (Linnea) 1948- ...... **CLC 37**
See also CA 103

Jerome, Jerome K. 1859-1927..... **TCLC 23**
See also CA 119; DLB 10, 34

Jerrold, Douglas William
1803-1857 .... **NCLC 2**

Jewett, (Theodora) Sarah Orne
1849-1909 .... **TCLC 1, 22**
See also CA 108; SATA 15; DLB 12

Jhabvala, Ruth Prawer
1927- .... **CLC 4, 8, 29**
See also CANR 2; CA 1-4R

Jiles, Paulette 1943-.............. **CLC 13**
See also CA 101

Jimenez (Mantecon), Juan Ramon
1881-1958 .... **TCLC 4**
See also CA 104

Joel, Billy 1949-................. **CLC 26**
See also Joel, William Martin

Joel, William Martin 1949-
See Joel, Billy
See also CA 108

Johnson, B(ryan) S(tanley William)
1933-1973 .... **CLC 6, 9**
See also CANR 9; CA 9-12R;
obituary CA 53-56; DLB 14, 40

Johnson, Charles (Richard)
1948- .... **CLC 7, 51**
See also CA 116; DLB 33

Johnson, Diane 1934-........ **CLC 5, 13, 48**
See also CANR 17; CA 41-44R; DLB-Y 80

Johnson, Eyvind (Olof Verner)
1900-1976 .... **CLC 14**
See also CA 73-76; obituary CA 69-72

Johnson, James Weldon
1871-1938 .... **TCLC 3, 19**
See also Johnson, James William
See also CA 104; DLB 51

Johnson, James William 1871-1938
See Johnson, James Weldon
See also SATA 31

Johnson, Lionel (Pigot)
1867-1902 .... **TCLC 19**
See also CA 117; DLB 19

Johnson, Marguerita 1928-
See Angelou, Maya

Johnson, Pamela Hansford
1912-1981 .... **CLC 1, 7, 27**
See also CANR 2; CA 1-4R;
obituary CA 104; DLB 15

Johnson, Uwe
1934-1984 .... **CLC 5, 10, 15, 40**
See also CANR 1; CA 1-4R;
obituary CA 112

Johnston, George (Benson) 1913- ... **CLC 51**
See also CANR 5, 20; CA 1-4R

Johnston, Jennifer 1930-........... **CLC 7**
See also CA 85-88; DLB 14

Jolley, Elizabeth 1923-............ **CLC 46**

Jones, David
　　1895-1974 . . . . **CLC 2, 4, 7, 13, 42**
　　See also CA 9-12R; obituary CA 53-56;
　　DLB 20

Jones, David Robert　1947-
　　See Bowie, David
　　See also CA 103

Jones, D(ouglas) G(ordon)　1929- . . . . **CLC 10**
　　See also CANR 13; CA 113; DLB 53

Jones, Diana Wynne　1934- . . . . **CLC 26**
　　See also CANR 4; CA 49-52; SATA 9

Jones, Gayl　1949- . . . . **CLC 6, 9**
　　See also CA 77-80; DLB 33

Jones, James　1921-1977 . . . . **CLC 1, 3, 10, 39**
　　See also CANR 6; CA 1-4R;
　　obituary CA 69-72; DLB 2

Jones, (Everett) LeRoi
　　1934- . . . . **CLC 1, 2, 3, 5, 10, 14, 33**
　　See also Baraka, Amiri
　　See also Baraka, Imamu Amiri; CA 21-24R

Jones, Madison (Percy, Jr.)　1925- . . . **CLC 4**
　　See also CANR 7; CA 13-16R

Jones, Mervyn　1922- . . . . **CLC 10**
　　See also CAAS 5; CANR 1; CA 45-48

Jones, Mick　1956?-
　　See The Clash

Jones, Nettie　19??- . . . . **CLC 34**

Jones, Preston　1936-1979 . . . . **CLC 10**
　　See also CA 73-76; obituary CA 89-92;
　　DLB 7

Jones, Robert F(rancis)　1934- . . . . . . **CLC 7**
　　See also CANR 2; CA 49-52

Jones, Rod　1953- . . . . **CLC 50**

Jones, Terry　1942?-
　　See Monty Python
　　See also CA 112, 116; SATA 51

Jong, Erica　1942- . . . . **CLC 4, 6, 8, 18**
　　See also CA 73-76; DLB 2, 5, 28

Jonson, Ben(jamin)　1572-1637 . . . . **LC 6**
　　See also DLB 62

Jordan, June　1936- . . . . **CLC 5, 11, 23**
　　See also CLR 10; CA 33-36R; SATA 4;
　　DLB 38

Jordan, Pat(rick M.)　1941- . . . . **CLC 37**
　　See also CA 33-36R

Josipovici, Gabriel (David)
　　1940- . . . . **CLC 6, 43**
　　See also CA 37-40R; DLB 14

Joubert, Joseph　1754-1824 . . . . **NCLC 9**

Jouve, Pierre Jean　1887-1976 . . . . . . **CLC 47**
　　See also obituary CA 65-68

Joyce, James (Augustine Aloysius)
　　1882-1941 . . . . **TCLC 3, 8, 16, 26; SSC 3**
　　See also CA 104, 126; DLB 10, 19, 36

Jozsef, Attila　1905-1937 . . . . **TCLC 22**
　　See also CA 116

Juana Ines de la Cruz　1651?-1695 . . . . **LC 5**

Julian of Norwich　1342?-1416? . . . . **LC 6**

Just, Ward S(wift)　1935- . . . . **CLC 4, 27**
　　See also CA 25-28R

Justice, Donald (Rodney)　1925- . . **CLC 6, 19**
　　See also CA 5-8R; DLB-Y 83

Kacew, Romain　1914-1980
　　See Gary, Romain
　　See also CA 108; obituary CA 102

Kacewgary, Romain　1914-1980
　　See Gary, Romain

Kafka, Franz
　　1883-1924 . . . . **TCLC 2, 6, 13, 29**
　　See also CA 105

Kahn, Roger　1927- . . . . **CLC 30**
　　See also CA 25-28R; SATA 37

Kaiser, (Friedrich Karl) Georg
　　1878-1945 . . . . **TCLC 9**
　　See also CA 106

Kaletski, Alexander　1946- . . . . **CLC 39**
　　See also CA 118

Kallman, Chester (Simon)
　　1921-1975 . . . . **CLC 2**
　　See also CANR 3; CA 45-48;
　　obituary CA 53-56

Kaminsky, Melvin　1926-
　　See Brooks, Mel
　　See also CANR 16

Kane, Paul　1941-
　　See Simon, Paul

Kanin, Garson　1912- . . . . **CLC 22**
　　See also CANR 7; CA 5-8R; DLB 7

Kaniuk, Yoram　1930- . . . . **CLC 19**

Kantor, MacKinlay　1904-1977 . . . . . . **CLC 7**
　　See also CA 61-64; obituary CA 73-76;
　　DLB 9

Kaplan, David Michael　1946- . . . . . . **CLC 50**

Karamzin, Nikolai Mikhailovich
　　1766-1826 . . . . **NCLC 3**

Karapanou, Margarita　1946- . . . . **CLC 13**
　　See also CA 101

Karl, Frederick R(obert)　1927- . . . . . **CLC 34**
　　See also CANR 3; CA 5-8R

Kassef, Romain　1914-1980
　　See Gary, Romain

Katz, Steve　1935- . . . . **CLC 47**
　　See also CANR 12; CA 25-28R; DLB-Y 83

Kauffman, Janet　1945- . . . . **CLC 42**
　　See also CA 117; DLB-Y 86

Kaufman, Bob (Garnell)
　　1925-1986 . . . . **CLC 49**
　　See also CANR 22; CA 41-44R;
　　obituary CA 118; DLB 16, 41

Kaufman, George S(imon)
　　1889-1961 . . . . **CLC 38**
　　See also CA 108; obituary CA 93-96; DLB 7

Kaufman, Sue　1926-1977 . . . . **CLC 3, 8**
　　See also Barondess, Sue K(aufman)

Kavan, Anna　1904-1968 . . . . **CLC 5, 13**
　　See also Edmonds, Helen (Woods)
　　See also CANR 6; CA 5-8R

Kavanagh, Patrick (Joseph Gregory)
　　1905-1967 . . . . **CLC 22**
　　See also obituary CA 25-28R; DLB 15, 20

Kawabata, Yasunari
　　1899-1972 . . . . **CLC 2, 5, 9, 18**
　　See also CA 93-96; obituary CA 33-36R

Kaye, M(ary) M(argaret)　1909?- . . . . **CLC 28**
　　See also CA 89-92

Kaye, Mollie　1909?-
　　See Kaye, M(ary) M(argaret)

Kaye-Smith, Sheila　1887-1956 . . . . . **TCLC 20**
　　See also CA 118; DLB 36

Kazan, Elia　1909- . . . . **CLC 6, 16**
　　See also CA 21-24R

Kazantzakis, Nikos
　　1885?-1957 . . . . **TCLC 2, 5, 33**
　　See also CA 105

Kazin, Alfred　1915- . . . . **CLC 34, 38**
　　See also CAAS 7; CANR 1; CA 1-4R

Keane, Mary Nesta (Skrine)　1904-
　　See Keane, Molly
　　See also CA 108, 114

Keane, Molly　1904- . . . . **CLC 31**
　　See also Keane, Mary Nesta (Skrine)

Keates, Jonathan　19??- . . . . **CLC 34**

Keaton, Buster　1895-1966 . . . . **CLC 20**

Keaton, Joseph Francis　1895-1966
　　See Keaton, Buster

Keats, John　1795-1821 . . . . **NCLC 8**

Keene, Donald　1922- . . . . **CLC 34**
　　See also CANR 5; CA 1-4R

Keillor, Garrison　1942- . . . . **CLC 40**
　　See also Keillor, Gary (Edward)
　　See also CA 111

Keillor, Gary (Edward)
　　See Keillor, Garrison
　　See also CA 117

Kell, Joseph　1917-
　　See Burgess (Wilson, John) Anthony

Keller, Gottfried　1819-1890 . . . . **NCLC 2**

Kellerman, Jonathan (S.)　1949- . . . . . **CLC 44**
　　See also CA 106

Kelley, William Melvin　1937- . . . . . . **CLC 22**
　　See also CA 77-80; DLB 33

Kellogg, Marjorie　1922- . . . . **CLC 2**
　　See also CA 81-84

Kelly, M. T.　1947- . . . . **CLC 55**
　　See also CANR 19; CA 97-100

Kemal, Yashar　1922- . . . . **CLC 14, 29**
　　See also CA 89-92

Kemble, Fanny　1809-1893 . . . . **NCLC 18**
　　See also DLB 32

Kemelman, Harry　1908- . . . . **CLC 2**
　　See also CANR 6; CA 9-12R; DLB 28

Kempe, Margery　1373?-1440? . . . . **LC 6**

Kempis, Thomas á　1380-1471 . . . . **LC 11**

Kendall, Henry　1839-1882 . . . . **NCLC 12**

Keneally, Thomas (Michael)
　　1935- . . . . . . **CLC 5, 8, 10, 14, 19, 27, 43**
　　See also CANR 10; CA 85-88

Kennedy, John Pendleton
　　1795-1870 . . . . **NCLC 2**
　　See also DLB 3

Kennedy, Joseph Charles　1929-
　　See Kennedy, X. J.
　　See also CANR 4; CA 1-4R; SATA 14

Kennedy, William　1928- . . . . . . **CLC 6, 28, 34**
　　See also CANR 14; CA 85-88; DLB-Y 85

Kennedy, X. J. 1929- . . . . CLC **8, 42**
See also Kennedy, Joseph Charles
See also DLB 5

Kerouac, Jack
1922-1969 . . . . . . CLC **1, 2, 3, 5, 14, 29**
See also Kerouac, Jean-Louis Lebrid de
See also DLB 2, 16; DLB-DS 3;
CDALB 1941-1968

Kerouac, Jean-Louis Lebrid de 1922-1969
See Kerouac, Jack
See also CA 5-8R; obituary CA 25-28R;
CDALB 1941-1968

Kerr, Jean 1923- . . . . CLC **22**
See also CANR 7; CA 5-8R

Kerr, M. E. 1927- . . . . CLC **12, 35**
See also Meaker, Marijane
See also SAAS 1

Kerr, Robert 1970?- . . . . CLC **55**

Kerrigan, (Thomas) Anthony
1918- . . . . CLC **4, 6**
See also CANR 4; CA 49-52

Kesey, Ken (Elton)
1935- . . . . CLC **1, 3, 6, 11, 46**
See also CANR 22; CA 1-4R; DLB 2, 16

Kesselring, Joseph (Otto)
1902-1967 . . . . CLC **45**

Kessler, Jascha (Frederick) 1929- . . . . CLC **4**
See also CANR 8; CA 17-20R

Kettelkamp, Larry 1933- . . . . CLC **12**
See also CANR 16; CA 29-32R; SAAS 3;
SATA 2

Kherdian, David 1931- . . . . CLC **6, 9**
See also CAAS 2; CA 21-24R; SATA 16

Khlebnikov, Velimir (Vladimirovich)
1885-1922 . . . . TCLC **20**
See also CA 117

Khodasevich, Vladislav (Felitsianovich)
1886-1939 . . . . TCLC **15**
See also CA 115

Kielland, Alexander (Lange)
1849-1906 . . . . TCLC **5**
See also CA 104

Kiely, Benedict 1919- . . . . CLC **23, 43**
See also CANR 2; CA 1-4R; DLB 15

Kienzle, William X(avier) 1928- . . . . CLC **25**
See also CAAS 1; CANR 9; CA 93-96

Killens, John Oliver 1916- . . . . CLC **10**
See also CAAS 2; CA 77-80; DLB 33

Killigrew, Anne 1660-1685 . . . . LC **4**

Kincaid, Jamaica 1949?- . . . . CLC **43**

King, Francis (Henry) 1923- . . . . CLC **8**
See also CANR 1; CA 1-4R; DLB 15

King, Stephen (Edwin)
1947- . . . . CLC **12, 26, 37**
See also CANR 1; CA 61-64; SATA 9;
DLB-Y 80

Kingman, (Mary) Lee 1919- . . . . CLC **17**
See also Natti, (Mary) Lee
See also CA 5-8R; SATA 1

Kingsley, Sidney 1906- . . . . CLC **44**
See also CA 85-88; DLB 7

Kingsolver, Barbara 1955- . . . . CLC **55**

Kingston, Maxine Hong 1940- . . CLC **12, 19**
See also CANR 13; CA 69-72; SATA 53;
DLB-Y 80

Kinnell, Galway
1927- . . . . CLC **1, 2, 3, 5, 13, 29**
See also CANR 10; CA 9-12R; DLB 5

Kinsella, Thomas 1928- . . . . . . CLC **4, 19, 43**
See also CANR 15; CA 17-20R; DLB 27

Kinsella, W(illiam) P(atrick)
1935- . . . . CLC **27, 43**
See also CAAS 7; CANR 21; CA 97-100

Kipling, (Joseph) Rudyard
1865-1936 . . . . TCLC **8, 17**
See also YABC 2; CA 20, 105; DLB 19, 34

Kirkup, James 1918- . . . . CLC **1**
See also CAAS 4; CANR 2; CA 1-4R;
SATA 12; DLB 27

Kirkwood, James 1930- . . . . CLC **9**
See also CANR 6; CA 1-4R

Kizer, Carolyn (Ashley) 1925- . . . CLC **15, 39**
See also CAAS 5; CA 65-68; DLB 5

Klausner, Amos 1939-
See Oz, Amos

Klein, A(braham) M(oses)
1909-1972 . . . . CLC **19**
See also CA 101; obituary CA 37-40R

Klein, Norma 1938- . . . . CLC **30**
See also CLR 2; CANR 15; CA 41-44R;
SAAS 1; SATA 7

Klein, T.E.D. 19??- . . . . CLC **34**
See also CA 119

Kleist, Heinrich von 1777-1811 . . . . NCLC **2**

Klimentev, Andrei Platonovich 1899-1951
See Platonov, Andrei (Platonovich)
See also CA 108

Klinger, Friedrich Maximilian von
1752-1831 . . . . NCLC **1**

Klopstock, Friedrich Gottlieb
1724-1803 . . . . NCLC **11**

Knebel, Fletcher 1911- . . . . CLC **14**
See also CAAS 3; CANR 1; CA 1-4R;
SATA 36

Knight, Etheridge 1931- . . . . CLC **40**
See also CA 21-24R; DLB 41

Knight, Sarah Kemble 1666-1727 . . . . . LC **7**
See also DLB 24

Knowles, John 1926- . . . . . . CLC **1, 4, 10, 26**
See also CA 17-20R; SATA 8; DLB 6

Koch, C(hristopher) J(ohn) 1932- . . . CLC **42**

Koch, Kenneth 1925- . . . . CLC **5, 8, 44**
See also CANR 6; CA 1-4R; DLB 5

Kochanowski, Jan 1530-1584 . . . . LC **10**

Kock, Charles Paul de
1794-1871 . . . . NCLC **16**

Koestler, Arthur
1905-1983 . . . . CLC **1, 3, 6, 8, 15, 33**
See also CANR 1; CA 1-4R;
obituary CA 109; DLB-Y 83

Kohout, Pavel 1928- . . . . CLC **13**
See also CANR 3; CA 45-48

Konrad, Gyorgy 1933- . . . . CLC **4, 10**
See also CA 85-88

Konwicki, Tadeusz 1926- . . . . . CLC **8, 28, 54**
See also CA 101

Kopit, Arthur (Lee) 1937- . . . . CLC **1, 18, 33**
See also CA 81-84; DLB 7

Kops, Bernard 1926- . . . . CLC **4**
See also CA 5-8R; DLB 13

Kornbluth, C(yril) M. 1923-1958. . . . TCLC **8**
See also CA 105; DLB 8

Korolenko, Vladimir (Galaktionovich)
1853-1921 . . . . TCLC **22**
See also CA 121

Kosinski, Jerzy (Nikodem)
1933- . . . . CLC **1, 2, 3, 6, 10, 15**
See also CANR 9; CA 17-20R; DLB 2;
DLB-Y 82

Kostelanetz, Richard (Cory) 1940- . . CLC **28**
See also CA 13-16R

Kostrowitzki, Wilhelm Apollinaris de
1880-1918
See Apollinaire, Guillaume
See also CA 104

Kotlowitz, Robert 1924- . . . . CLC **4**
See also CA 33-36R

Kotzwinkle, William 1938- . . . CLC **5, 14, 35**
See also CLR 6; CANR 3; CA 45-48;
SATA 24

Kozol, Jonathan 1936- . . . . CLC **17**
See also CANR 16; CA 61-64

Kozoll, Michael 1940?-
See Bochco, Steven and Kozoll, Michael

Kramer, Kathryn 19??- . . . . CLC **34**

Kramer, Larry 1935- . . . . CLC **42**

Krasicki, Ignacy 1735-1801 . . . . NCLC **8**

Krasinski, Zygmunt 1812-1859 . . . . NCLC **4**

Kraus, Karl 1874-1936 . . . . TCLC **5**
See also CA 104

Kreve, Vincas 1882-1959 . . . . TCLC **27**

Kristofferson, Kris 1936- . . . . CLC **26**
See also CA 104

Krleza, Miroslav 1893-1981. . . . . CLC **8**
See also CA 97-100; obituary CA 105

Kroetsch, Robert 1927- . . . . CLC **5, 23**
See also CANR 8; CA 17-20R; DLB 53

Kroetz, Franz Xaver 1946- . . . . CLC **41**

Krotkov, Yuri 1917- . . . . CLC **19**
See also CA 102

Krumgold, Joseph (Quincy)
1908-1980 . . . . CLC **12**
See also CANR 7; CA 9-12R;
obituary CA 101; SATA 48;
obituary SATA 23

Krutch, Joseph Wood 1893-1970. . . . CLC **24**
See also CANR 4; CA 1-4R;
obituary CA 25-28R; DLB 63

Krylov, Ivan Andreevich
1768?-1844. . . . . NCLC **1**

Kubin, Alfred 1877-1959 . . . . TCLC **23**
See also CA 112

Kubrick, Stanley 1928- . . . . CLC **16**
See also CA 81-84; DLB 26

Kumin, Maxine (Winokur)
  1925- .... **CLC 5, 13, 28**
  See also CANR 1, 21; CA 1-4R; SATA 12;
  DLB 5

Kundera, Milan 1929- ..... **CLC 4, 9, 19, 32**
  See also CANR 19; CA 85-88

Kunitz, Stanley J(asspon)
  1905- .... **CLC 6, 11, 14**
  See also CA 41-44R; DLB 48

Kunze, Reiner 1933- .... **CLC 10**
  See also CA 93-96

Kuprin, Aleksandr (Ivanovich)
  1870-1938 .... **TCLC 5**
  See also CA 104

Kurosawa, Akira 1910-........... **CLC 16**
  See also CA 101

Kuttner, Henry 1915-1958........ **TCLC 10**
  See also CA 107; DLB 8

Kuzma, Greg 1944-............... **CLC 7**
  See also CA 33-36R

Labrunie, Gerard 1808-1855
  See Nerval, Gerard de

**Laclos, Pierre Ambroise Francois Choderlos
  de** 1741-1803 .... **NCLC 4**

**La Fayette, Marie (Madelaine Pioche de la
  Vergne, Comtesse) de**
  1634-1693 .... **LC 2**

Lafayette, Rene
  See Hubbard, L(afayette) Ron(ald)

Laforgue, Jules 1860-1887........ **NCLC 5**

Lagerkvist, Par (Fabian)
  1891-1974 .... **CLC 7, 10, 13, 54**
  See also CA 85-88; obituary CA 49-52

Lagerlof, Selma (Ottiliana Lovisa)
  1858-1940 .... **TCLC 4**
  See also CLR 7; CA 108; SATA 15

La Guma, (Justin) Alex(ander)
  1925-1985 .... **CLC 19**
  See also CA 49-52; obituary CA 118

Lamartine, Alphonse (Marie Louis Prat) de
  1790-1869 .... **NCLC 11**

Lamb, Charles 1775-1834........ **NCLC 10**
  See also SATA 17

Lamming, George (William)
  1927- .... **CLC 2, 4**
  See also CA 85-88

LaMoore, Louis Dearborn 1908?-
  See L'Amour, Louis (Dearborn)

L'Amour, Louis (Dearborn)
  1908-1988 .... **CLC 25, 55**
  See also CANR 3; CA 1-4R;
  obituary CA 125; DLB-Y 80

**Lampedusa, (Prince) Giuseppe (Maria
  Fabrizio) Tomasi di**
  1896-1957 .... **TCLC 13**
  See also CA 111

Lancaster, Bruce 1896-1963........ **CLC 36**
  See also CAP 1; CA 9-12; SATA 9

Landis, John (David) 1950-........ **CLC 26**
  See also CA 112

Landolfi, Tommaso 1908-1979... **CLC 11, 49**
  See also obituary CA 117

Landon, Letitia Elizabeth
  1802-1838 .... **NCLC 15**

Landor, Walter Savage
  1775-1864 .... **NCLC 14**

Landwirth, Heinz 1927-
  See Lind, Jakov
  See also CANR 7; CA 11-12R

Lane, Patrick 1939-.............. **CLC 25**
  See also CA 97-100; DLB 53

Lang, Andrew 1844-1912........ **TCLC 16**
  See also CA 114; SATA 16

Lang, Fritz 1890-1976 .... **CLC 20**
  See also CA 77-80; obituary CA 69-72

Langer, Elinor 1939- .... **CLC 34**

Lanier, Sidney 1842-1881 .... **NCLC 6**
  See also SATA 18; DLB 64

Lanyer, Aemilia 1569-1645 .... **LC 10**

Lapine, James 1949-............. **CLC 39**

Larbaud, Valery 1881-1957....... **TCLC 9**
  See also CA 106

Lardner, Ring(gold Wilmer)
  1885-1933 .... **TCLC 2, 14**
  See also CA 104; DLB 11, 25

Larkin, Philip (Arthur)
  1922-1985 ... **CLC 3, 5, 8, 9, 13, 18, 33,
                                            39**
  See also CA 5-8R; obituary CA 117;
  DLB 27

Larra (y Sanchez de Castro), Mariano Jose de
  1809-1837 .... **NCLC 17**

Larsen, Eric 1941- .... **CLC 55**

Larsen, Nella 1893-1964 .... **CLC 37**

Larson, Charles R(aymond) 1938-... **CLC 31**
  See also CANR 4; CA 53-56

Latham, Jean Lee 1902-.......... **CLC 12**
  See also CANR 7; CA 5-8R; SATA 2

Lathen, Emma.................... **CLC 2
  See also Hennissart, Martha
  See also Latsis, Mary J(ane)

Latsis, Mary J(ane)
  See Lathen, Emma
  See also CA 85-88

Lattimore, Richmond (Alexander)
  1906-1984 .... **CLC 3**
  See also CANR 1; CA 1-4R;
  obituary CA 112

Laughlin, James 1914-........... **CLC 49**
  See also CANR 9; CA 21-24R; DLB 48

Laurence, (Jean) Margaret (Wemyss)
  1926-1987 .... **CLC 3, 6, 13, 50**
  See also CA 5-8R; obituary CA 121;
  DLB 53

Laurent, Antoine 1952- .... **CLC 50**

Lautreamont, Comte de
  1846-1870 .... **NCLC 12**

Lavin, Mary 1912-............. **CLC 4, 18**
  See also CA 9-12R; DLB 15

Lawrence, D(avid) H(erbert)
  1885-1930 .... **TCLC 2, 9, 16, 33**
  See also CA 104, 121; DLB 10, 19, 36

Lawrence, T(homas) E(dward)
  1888-1935 .... **TCLC 18**
  See also CA 115

Lawson, Henry (Archibald Hertzberg)
  1867-1922 .... **TCLC 27**
  See also CA 120

Laxness, Halldor (Kiljan) 1902- .... **CLC 25**
  See also Gudjonsson, Halldor Kiljan

Laye, Camara 1928-1980........ **CLC 4, 38**
  See also CA 85-88; obituary CA 97-100

Layton, Irving (Peter) 1912-..... **CLC 2, 15**
  See also CANR 2; CA 1-4R

Lazarus, Emma 1849-1887........ **NCLC 8**

Leacock, Stephen (Butler)
  1869-1944 .... **TCLC 2**
  See also CA 104

Lear, Edward 1812-1888 .... **NCLC 3**
  See also CLR 1; SATA 18; DLB 32

Lear, Norman (Milton) 1922- ...... **CLC 12**
  See also CA 73-76

Leavis, F(rank) R(aymond)
  1895-1978 .... **CLC 24**
  See also CA 21-24R; obituary CA 77-80

Leavitt, David 1961?-............. **CLC 34**
  See also CA 116, 122

Lebowitz, Fran(ces Ann)
  1951?- .... **CLC 11, 36**
  See also CANR 14; CA 81-84

Le Carre, John 1931-... **CLC 3, 5, 9, 15, 28**
  See also Cornwell, David (John Moore)

Le Clezio, J(ean) M(arie) G(ustave)
  1940- .... **CLC 31**
  See also CA 116

Leduc, Violette 1907-1972........ **CLC 22**
  See also CAP 1; CA 13-14;
  obituary CA 33-36R

Ledwidge, Francis 1887-1917...... **TCLC 23**
  See also DLB 20

Lee, Andrea 1953- .... **CLC 36**

Lee, Andrew 1917-
  See Auchincloss, Louis (Stanton)

Lee, Don L. 1942-................. **CLC 2**
  See also Madhubuti, Haki R.
  See also CA 73-76

Lee, (Nelle) Harper 1926-........ **CLC 12**
  See also CA 13-16R; SATA 11; DLB 6;
  CDALB 1941-1968

Lee, Lawrence 1903- .... **CLC 34**
  See also CA 25-28R

Lee, Manfred B(ennington) 1905-1971
  See Queen, Ellery
  See also CANR 2; CA 1-4R;
  obituary CA 29-32R

Lee, Stan 1922-................... **CLC 17**
  See also CA 108, 111

Lee, Tanith 1947-................ **CLC 46**
  See also CA 37-40R; SATA 8

Lee, Vernon 1856-1935 .... **TCLC 5**
  See also Paget, Violet
  See also DLB 57

Lee-Hamilton, Eugene (Jacob)
  1845-1907 .... **TCLC 22**

Leet, Judith 1935- .... **CLC 11**

Le Fanu, Joseph Sheridan
  1814-1873 .... **NCLC 9**
  See also DLB 21, 70

Author Index

Leffland, Ella 1931- .... CLC 19
See also CA 29-32R; DLB-Y 84

Leger, (Marie-Rene) Alexis Saint-Leger
1887-1975
See Perse, St.-John
See also CA 13-16R; obituary CA 61-64

Le Guin, Ursula K(roeber)
1929- ....CLC 8, 13, 22, 45
See also CLR 3; CANR 9; CA 21-24R;
SATA 4, 52; DLB 8, 52

Lehmann, Rosamond (Nina) 1901- ... CLC 5
See also CANR 8; CA 77-80; DLB 15

Leiber, Fritz (Reuter, Jr.) 1910- ... CLC 25
See also CANR 2; CA 45-48; SATA 45;
DLB 8

Leino, Eino 1878-1926........... TCLC 24

Leithauser, Brad 1953-............ CLC 27
See also CA 107

Lelchuk, Alan 1938-.............. CLC 5
See also CANR 1; CA 45-48

Lem, Stanislaw 1921-........ CLC 8, 15, 40
See also CAAS 1; CA 105

Lemann, Nancy 1956-............. CLC 39
See also CA 118

Lemonnier, (Antoine Louis) Camille
1844-1913 .... TCLC 22

Lenau, Nikolaus 1802-1850...... NCLC 16

L'Engle, Madeleine 1918- .... CLC 12
See also CLR 1, 14; CANR 3, 21; CA 1-4R;
SATA 1, 27; DLB 52

Lengyel, Jozsef 1896-1975......... CLC 7
See also CA 85-88; obituary CA 57-60

Lennon, John (Ono) 1940-1980 and
McCartney, Paul 1942-....... CLC 12

Lennon, John (Ono) 1940-1980..... CLC 35
See also Lennon, John (Ono) and
McCartney, Paul
See also CA 102

Lennon, John Winston 1940-1980
See Lennon, John (Ono)

Lennox, Charlotte Ramsay 1729 or
1730-1804 .... NCLC 23
See also DLB 39, 39

Lennox, Charlotte Ramsay
1729?-1804................. NCLC 23
See also DLB 39

Lentricchia, Frank (Jr.) 1940-...... CLC 34
See also CA 25-28R

Lenz, Siegfried 1926-............ CLC 27
See also CA 89-92

Leonard, Elmore 1925-......... CLC 28, 34
See also CANR 12; CA 81-84

Leonard, Hugh 1926-............. CLC 19
See also Byrne, John Keyes
See also DLB 13

Lerman, Eleanor 1952-............ CLC 9
See also CA 85-88

Lermontov, Mikhail Yuryevich
1814-1841 .... NCLC 5

Leroux, Gaston 1868-1927....... TCLC 25
See also CA 108

Lesage, Alain-Rene 1668-1747....... LC 2

Lessing, Doris (May)
1919- ..... CLC 1, 2, 3, 6, 10, 15, 22, 40
See also CA 9-12R; DLB 15; DLB-Y 85

Lessing, Gotthold Ephraim
1729-1781 .... LC 8

Lester, Richard 1932-........... CLC 20

Lever, Charles (James)
1806-1872 .... NCLC 23
See also DLB 21

Leverson, Ada 1865-1936........ TCLC 18
See also CA 117

Levertov, Denise
1923- .... CLC 1, 2, 3, 5, 8, 15, 28
See also CANR 3; CA 1-4R; DLB 5

Levi, Peter (Chad Tiger) 1931-..... CLC 41
See also CA 5-8R; DLB 40

Levi, Primo 1919-1987........ CLC 37, 50
See also CANR 12; CA 13-16R;
obituary CA 122

Levin, Ira 1929- .... CLC 3, 6
See also CANR 17; CA 21-24R

Levin, Meyer 1905-1981 .... CLC 7
See also CANR 15; CA 9-12R;
obituary CA 104; SATA 21;
obituary SATA 27; DLB 9, 28; DLB-Y 81

Levine, Norman 1924-............ CLC 54
See also CANR 14; CA 73-76

Levine, Philip 1928-.. CLC 2, 4, 5, 9, 14, 33
See also CANR 9; CA 9-12R; DLB 5

Levinson, Deirdre 1931-.......... CLC 49
See also CA 73-76

Levi-Strauss, Claude 1908- .... CLC 38
See also CANR 6; CA 1-4R

Levitin, Sonia 1934-............. CLC 17
See also CANR 14; CA 29-32R; SAAS 2;
SATA 4

Levr, Charles James 1806-1872... NCLC 23
See also DLB 21

Lewis, Alun 1915-1944........... TCLC 3
See also CA 104; DLB 20

Lewis, C(ecil) Day 1904-1972
See Day Lewis, C(ecil)

Lewis, C(live) S(taples)
1898-1963 .... CLC 1, 3, 6, 14, 27
See also CLR 3; CA 81-84; SATA 13;
DLB 15

Lewis (Winters), Janet 1899-....... CLC 41
See also Winters, Janet Lewis

Lewis, Matthew Gregory
1775-1818 .... NCLC 11
See also DLB 39

Lewis, (Harry) Sinclair
1885-1951 .... TCLC 4, 13, 23
See also CA 104; DLB 9; DLB-DS 1

Lewis, (Percy) Wyndham
1882?-1957.............TCLC 2, 9
See also CA 104; DLB 15

Lewisohn, Ludwig 1883-1955...... TCLC 19
See also CA 73-76; obituary CA 29-32R

Lieber, Stanley Martin 1922-
See Lee, Stan

Lieberman, Laurence (James)
1935- .... CLC 4, 36
See also CANR 8; CA 17-20R

Li Fei-kan 1904-
See Pa Chin
See also CA 105

Lightfoot, Gordon (Meredith)
1938-....................... CLC 26
See also CA 109

Ligotti, Thomas 1953-............ CLC 44

Liliencron, Detlev von
1844-1909 .... TCLC 18
See also CA 117

Lima, Jose Lezama 1910-1976
See Lezama Lima, Jose

Lima Barreto, (Alfonso Henriques de)
1881-1922 .... TCLC 23
See also CA 117

Lincoln, Abraham 1809-1865..... NCLC 18

Lind, Jakov 1927-.......... CLC 1, 2, 4, 27
See also Landwirth, Heinz
See also CAAS 4; CA 9-12R

Lindsay, David 1876-1945....... TCLC 15
See also CA 113

Lindsay, (Nicholas) Vachel
1879-1931 .... TCLC 17
See also CA 114; SATA 40; DLB 54;
CDALB 1865-1917

Linney, Romulus 1930- .... CLC 51
See also CA 1-4R

Li Po 701-763.................. CMLC 2

Lipsyte, Robert (Michael) 1938-.... CLC 21
See also CANR 8; CA 17-20R; SATA 5

Lish, Gordon (Jay) 1934-......... CLC 45
See also CA 113, 117

Lispector, Clarice 1925-1977....... CLC 43
See also obituary CA 116

Littell, Robert 1935?-............ CLC 42
See also CA 109, 112

Liu E 1857-1909................ TCLC 15
See also CA 115

Lively, Penelope 1933-......... CLC 32, 50
See also CLR 7; CA 41-44R; SATA 7;
DLB 14

Livesay, Dorothy 1909-......... CLC 4, 15
See also CA 25-28R

Llewellyn, Richard 1906-1983....... CLC 7
See also Llewellyn Lloyd, Richard (Dafydd
Vyvyan)
See also DLB 15

Llewellyn Lloyd, Richard (Dafydd Vyvyan)
1906-1983
See Llewellyn, Richard
See also CANR 7; CA 53-56;
obituary CA 111; SATA 11, 37

Llosa, Mario Vargas 1936-
See Vargas Llosa, Mario

Lloyd, Richard Llewellyn 1906-
See Llewellyn, Richard

Locke, John 1632-1704 .... LC 7
See also DLB 31

Lockhart, John Gibson
1794-1854 .... NCLC 6

Lodge, David (John) 1935-........ CLC 36
See also CANR 19; CA 17-20R; DLB 14

Logan, John 1923-................ CLC 5
See also CA 77-80; DLB 5

Lombino, S. A. 1926-
See Hunter, Evan

London, Jack 1876-1916 ...... **TCLC 9, 15**
See also London, John Griffith
See also SATA 18; DLB 8, 12;
CDALB 1865-1917

London, John Griffith 1876-1916
See London, Jack
See also CA 110, 119

Long, Emmett 1925-
See Leonard, Elmore

Longbaugh, Harry 1931-
See Goldman, William (W.)

Longfellow, Henry Wadsworth
1807-1882 .... **NCLC 2**
See also SATA 19; DLB 1;
CDALB 1640-1865

Longley, Michael 1939- .... **CLC 29**
See also CA 102; DLB 40

Lopate, Phillip 1943- .... **CLC 29**
See also CA 97-100; DLB-Y 80

Lopez Portillo (y Pacheco), Jose
1920- .... **CLC 46**

Lopez y Fuentes, Gregorio
1897-1966 .... **CLC 32**

Lord, Bette Bao 1938- .... **CLC 23**
See also CA 107

Lorde, Audre (Geraldine) 1934- ..... **CLC 18**
See also CANR 16; CA 25-28R; DLB 41

Loti, Pierre 1850-1923 .... **TCLC 11**
See also Viaud, (Louis Marie) Julien

Lovecraft, H(oward) P(hillips)
1890-1937 .... **TCLC 4, 22; SSC 3**
See also CA 104

Lovelace, Earl 1935- .... **CLC 51**
See also CA 77-80

Lowell, Amy 1874-1925 .... **TCLC 1, 8**
See also CA 104; DLB 54

Lowell, James Russell 1819-1891 .. **NCLC 2**
See also DLB 1, 11, 64; CDALB 1640-1865

Lowell, Robert (Traill Spence, Jr.)
1917-1977 ... **CLC 1, 2, 3, 4, 5, 8, 9, 11, 15, 37**
See also CA 9-12R; obituary CA 73-76;
CABS 2; DLB 5

Lowndes, Marie (Adelaide) Belloc
1868-1947 .... **TCLC 12**
See also CA 107; DLB 70

Lowry, (Clarence) Malcolm
1909-1957 .... **TCLC 6**
See also CA 105; DLB 15

Loy, Mina 1882-1966 .... **CLC 28**
See also CA 113; DLB 4, 54

Lucas, George 1944- .... **CLC 16**
See also CA 77-80

Lucas, Victoria 1932-1963
See Plath, Sylvia

Ludlam, Charles 1943-1987 ..... **CLC 46, 50**
See also CA 85-88; obituary CA 122

Ludlum, Robert 1927- .... **CLC 22, 43**
See also CA 33-36R; DLB-Y 82

Ludwig, Otto 1813-1865 .... **NCLC 4**

Lugones, Leopoldo 1874-1938 ..... **TCLC 15**
See also CA 116

Lu Hsun 1881-1936 .... **TCLC 3**

Lukacs, Georg 1885-1971 .... **CLC 24**
See also Lukacs, Gyorgy

Lukacs, Gyorgy 1885-1971
See Lukacs, Georg
See also CA 101; obituary CA 29-32R

Luke, Peter (Ambrose Cyprian)
1919- .... **CLC 38**
See also CA 81-84; DLB 13

Lurie (Bishop), Alison
1926- .... **CLC 4, 5, 18, 39**
See also CANR 2, 17; CA 1-4R; SATA 46;
DLB 2

Luther, Martin 1483-1546 .... **LC 9**

Luzi, Mario 1914- .... **CLC 13**
See also CANR 9; CA 61-64

Lynn, Kenneth S(chuyler) 1923- .... **CLC 50**
See also CANR 3; CA 1-4R

Lytle, Andrew (Nelson) 1902- ...... **CLC 22**
See also CA 9-12R; DLB 6

Lyttelton, George 1709-1773 .... **LC 10**

Lytton, Edward Bulwer 1803-1873
See Bulwer-Lytton, (Lord) Edward (George
Earle Lytton)
See also SATA 23

Maas, Peter 1929- .... **CLC 29**
See also CA 93-96

Macaulay, (Dame Emile) Rose
1881-1958 .... **TCLC 7**
See also CA 104; DLB 36

MacBeth, George (Mann)
1932- .... **CLC 2, 5, 9**
See also CA 25-28R; SATA 4; DLB 40

MacCaig, Norman (Alexander)
1910- .... **CLC 36**
See also CANR 3; CA 9-12R; DLB 27

MacDermot, Thomas H. 1870-1933
See Redcam, Tom

MacDiarmid, Hugh
1892-1978 .... **CLC 2, 4, 11, 19**
See also Grieve, C(hristopher) M(urray)
See also DLB 20

Macdonald, Cynthia 1928- ...... **CLC 13, 19**
See also CANR 4; CA 49-52

MacDonald, George 1824-1905 ..... **TCLC 9**
See also CA 106; SATA 33; DLB 18

MacDonald, John D(ann)
1916-1986 .... **CLC 3, 27, 44**
See also CANR 1, 19; CA 1-4R;
obituary CA 121; DLB 8; DLB-Y 86

Macdonald, (John) Ross
1915-1983 .... **CLC 1, 2, 3, 14, 34, 41**
See also Millar, Kenneth

MacEwen, Gwendolyn (Margaret)
1941-1987 .... **CLC 13, 55**
See also CANR 7, 22; CA 9-12R;
obituary CA 124; SATA 50; DLB 53

Machado (y Ruiz), Antonio
1875-1939 .... **TCLC 3**
See also CA 104

Machado de Assis, (Joaquim Maria)
1839-1908 .... **TCLC 10**
See also CA 107

Machen, Arthur (Llewelyn Jones)
1863-1947 .... **TCLC 4**
See also CA 104; DLB 36

Machiavelli, Niccolo 1469-1527 ...... **LC 8**

MacInnes, Colin 1914-1976 ..... **CLC 4, 23**
See also CA 69-72; obituary CA 65-68;
DLB 14

MacInnes, Helen (Clark)
1907-1985 .... **CLC 27, 39**
See also CANR 1; CA 1-4R;
obituary CA 65-68, 117; SATA 22, 44

Macintosh, Elizabeth 1897-1952
See Tey, Josephine
See also CA 110

Mackenzie, (Edward Montague) Compton
1883-1972 .... **CLC 18**
See also CAP 2; CA 21-22;
obituary CA 37-40R; DLB 34

Mac Laverty, Bernard 1942- .... **CLC 31**
See also CA 116, 118

MacLean, Alistair (Stuart)
1922-1987 .... **CLC 3, 13, 50**
See also CA 57-60; obituary CA 121;
SATA 23

MacLeish, Archibald
1892-1982 .... **CLC 3, 8, 14**
See also CA 9-12R; obituary CA 106;
DLB 4, 7, 45; DLB-Y 82

MacLennan, (John) Hugh
1907- .... **CLC 2, 14**
See also CA 5-8R

MacNeice, (Frederick) Louis
1907-1963 .... **CLC 1, 4, 10**
See also CA 85-88; DLB 10, 20

Macpherson, (Jean) Jay 1931- ...... **CLC 14**
See also CA 5-8R; DLB 53

MacShane, Frank 1927- .... **CLC 39**
See also CANR 3; CA 11-12R

Macumber, Mari 1896-1966
See Sandoz, Mari (Susette)

Madach, Imre 1823-1864 .... **NCLC 19**

Madden, (Jerry) David 1933- .... **CLC 5, 15**
See also CAAS 3; CANR 4; CA 1-4R;
DLB 6

Madhubuti, Haki R. 1942- .... **CLC 6**
See also Lee, Don L.
See also DLB 5, 41

Maeterlinck, Maurice 1862-1949 ... **TCLC 3**
See also CA 104

Mafouz, Naguib 1912- .... **CLC 55**
See also DLB-Y 88

Maginn, William 1794-1842 .... **NCLC 8**

Mahapatra, Jayanta 1928- .... **CLC 33**
See also CANR 15; CA 73-76

Mahon, Derek 1941- .... **CLC 27**
See also CA 113; DLB 40

Mailer, Norman
1923- ...... **CLC 1, 2, 3, 4, 5, 8, 11, 14, 28, 39**
See also CA 9-12R; CABS 1; DLB 2, 16,
28; DLB-Y 80, 83; DLB-DS 3

Maillet, Antonine 1929- .... **CLC 54**
See also CA 115, 120; DLB 60

Mais, Roger 1905-1955 . . . . TCLC 8
See also CA 105

Maitland, Sara (Louise) 1950- . . . . . . CLC 49
See also CANR 13; CA 69-72

Major, Clarence 1936- . . . . CLC 3, 19, 48
See also CAAS 6; CANR 13; CA 21-24R;
DLB 33

Major, Kevin 1949- . . . . CLC 26
See also CLR 11; CANR 21; CA 97-100;
SATA 32; DLB 60

Malamud, Bernard
1914-1986 . . . . . CLC 1, 2, 3, 5, 8, 9, 11,
18, 27, 44
See also CA 5-8R; obituary CA 118;
CABS 1; DLB 2, 28; DLB-Y 80, 86;
CDALB 1941-1968

Malherbe, Francois de 1555-1628 . . . . . LC 5

Mallarme, Stephane 1842-1898 . . . . NCLC 4

Mallet-Joris, Francoise 1930- . . . . . . CLC 11
See also CANR 17; CA 65-68

Maloff, Saul 1922- . . . . CLC 5
See also CA 33-36R

Malone, Michael (Christopher)
1942- . . . . CLC 43
See also CANR 14; CA 77-80

Malory, (Sir) Thomas ?-1471 . . . . LC 11
See also SATA 33

Malouf, David 1934- . . . . CLC 28

Malraux, (Georges-) Andre
1901-1976 . . . . CLC 1, 4, 9, 13, 15
See also CAP 2; CA 21-24;
obituary CA 69-72; DLB 72

Malzberg, Barry N. 1939- . . . . CLC 7
See also CAAS 4; CANR 16; CA 61-64;
DLB 8

Mamet, David (Alan)
1947- . . . . CLC 9, 15, 34, 46
See also CANR 15; CA 81-84; DLB 7

Mamoulian, Rouben 1898- . . . . CLC 16
See also CA 25-28R

Mandelstam, Osip (Emilievich)
1891?-1938? . . . . TCLC 2, 6
See also CA 104

Mander, Jane 1877-1949 . . . . TCLC 31

Mandiargues, Andre Pieyre de
1909- . . . . CLC 41
See also CA 103

Manley, (Mary) Delariviere
1672?-1724. . . . . LC 1
See also DLB 39

Mann, (Luiz) Heinrich 1871-1950. . . TCLC 9
See also CA 106

Mann, Thomas
1875-1955 . . . . TCLC 2, 8, 14, 21
See also CA 104

Manning, Frederic 1882-1935 . . . . . TCLC 25

Manning, Olivia 1915-1980 . . . . . . CLC 5, 19
See also CA 5-8R; obituary CA 101

Mano, D. Keith 1942- . . . . CLC 2, 10
See also CAAS 6; CA 25-28R; DLB 6

Mansfield, Katherine
1888-1923 . . . . TCLC 2, 8
See also CA 104

Manso, Peter 1940- . . . . CLC 39
See also CA 29-32R

Mapu, Abraham (ben Jekutiel)
1808-1867 . . . . NCLC 18

Marat, Jean Paul 1743-1793 . . . . LC 10

Marcel, Gabriel (Honore)
1889-1973 . . . . CLC 15
See also CA 102; obituary CA 45-48

Marchbanks, Samuel 1913-
See Davies, (William) Robertson

Marie de l'Incarnation 1599-1672. . . . LC 10

Marinetti, F(ilippo) T(ommaso)
1876-1944 . . . . TCLC 10
See also CA 107

Marivaux, Pierre Carlet de Chamblain de
(1688-1763) . . . . LC 4

Markandaya, Kamala 1924- . . . . . . CLC 8, 38
See also Taylor, Kamala (Purnaiya)

Markfield, Wallace (Arthur) 1926- . . . CLC 8
See also CAAS 3; CA 69-72; DLB 2, 28

Markham, Robert 1922-
See Amis, Kingsley (William)

Marks, J. 1942-
See Highwater, Jamake

Marley, Bob 1945-1981 . . . . CLC 17
See also Marley, Robert Nesta

Marley, Robert Nesta 1945-1981
See Marley, Bob
See also CA 107; obituary CA 103

Marmontel, Jean-Francois
1723-1799 . . . . LC 2

Marquand, John P(hillips)
1893-1960 . . . . CLC 2, 10
See also CA 85-88; DLB 9

Marquez, Gabriel Garcia 1928-
See Garcia Marquez, Gabriel

Marquis, Don(ald Robert Perry)
1878-1937 . . . . TCLC 7
See also CA 104; DLB 11, 25

Marryat, Frederick 1792-1848 . . . . NCLC 3
See also DLB 21

Marsh, (Edith) Ngaio 1899-1982 . . . . . CLC 7
See also CANR 6; CA 9-12R

Marshall, Garry 1935?- . . . . CLC 17
See also CA 111

Marshall, Paule 1929- . . . . . CLC 27; SSC 3
See also CANR 25; CA 77-80; DLB 33

Marsten, Richard 1926-
See Hunter, Evan

Martin, Steve 1945?- . . . . CLC 30
See also CA 97-100

Martin du Gard, Roger
1881-1958 . . . . TCLC 24
See also CA 118

Martinez Ruiz, Jose 1874-1967
See Azorin
See also CA 93-96

Martinez Sierra, Gregorio 1881-1947 and
Martinez Sierra, Maria (de la
O'LeJarraga) 1880?-197 . . . . . . TCLC 6

Martinez Sierra, Gregorio 1881-1947
See Martinez Sierra, Gregorio and Martinez
Sierra, Maria (de la O'LeJarraga)
See also CA 104, 115

Martinez Sierra, Maria (de la O'LeJarraga)
1880?-1974
See Martinez Sierra, Gregorio and Martinez
Sierra, Maria (de la O'LeJarraga)
See also obituary CA 115

Martinez Sierra, Maria (de la O'LeJarraga)
1880?-1974 and **Martinez Sierra,**
Gregorio 1881-194
See Martinez Sierra, Gregorio and Martinez
Sierra, Maria (de la O'LeJarraga)

Martinson, Harry (Edmund)
1904-1978 . . . . CLC 14
See also CA 77-80

Marvell, Andrew 1621-1678. . . . . LC 4

Marx, Karl (Heinrich)
1818-1883 . . . . NCLC 17

Masaoka Shiki 1867-1902 . . . . TCLC 18

Masefield, John (Edward)
1878-1967 . . . . CLC 11, 47
See also CAP 2; CA 19-20;
obituary CA 25-28R; SATA 19; DLB 10,
19

Maso, Carole 19??- . . . . CLC 44

Mason, Bobbie Ann 1940- . . . . . . CLC 28, 43
See also CANR 11; CA 53-56; SAAS 1

Mason, Nick 1945-
See Pink Floyd

Mason, Tally 1909-1971
See Derleth, August (William)

Masters, Edgar Lee
1868?-1950. . . . . TCLC 2, 25
See also CA 104; DLB 54;
CDALB 1865-1917

Masters, Hilary 1928- . . . . CLC 48
See also CANR 13; CA 25-28R

Mastrosimone, William 19??- . . . . . . CLC 36

Matheson, Richard (Burton)
1926- . . . . CLC 37
See also CA 97-100; DLB 8, 44

Mathews, Harry 1930- . . . . CLC 6
See also CAAS 6; CANR 18; CA 21-24R

Mathias, Roland (Glyn) 1915- . . . . . . CLC 45
See also CANR 19; CA 97-100; DLB 27

Matthews, Greg 1949- . . . . CLC 45

Matthews, William 1942- . . . . CLC 40
See also CANR 12; CA 29-32R; DLB 5

Matthias, John (Edward) 1941- . . . . . . CLC 9
See also CA 33-36R

Matthiessen, Peter 1927- . . . CLC 5, 7, 11, 32
See also CANR 21; CA 9-12R; SATA 27;
DLB 6

Maturin, Charles Robert
1780?-1824. . . . . NCLC 6

Matute, Ana Maria 1925- . . . . CLC 11
See also CA 89-92

Maugham, W(illiam) Somerset
1874-1965 . . . . CLC 1, 11, 15
See also CA 5-8R; obituary CA 25-28R;
DLB 10, 36

Maupassant, (Henri Rene Albert) Guy de
    1850-1893 . . . . NCLC 1; SSC 1

Mauriac, Claude 1914- . . . . CLC 9
    See also CA 89-92

Mauriac, Francois (Charles)
    1885-1970 . . . . CLC 4, 9
    See also CAP 2; CA 25-28

Mavor, Osborne Henry   1888-1951
    See Bridie, James
    See also CA 104

Maxwell, William (Keepers, Jr.)
    1908- . . . . CLC 19
    See also CA 93-96; DLB-Y 80

May, Elaine 1932- . . . . CLC 16
    See also DLB 44

Mayakovsky, Vladimir (Vladimirovich)
    1893-1930 . . . . TCLC 4, 18
    See also CA 104

Maynard, Joyce 1953- . . . . CLC 23
    See also CA 111

Mayne, William (James Carter)
    1928- . . . . CLC 12
    See also CA 9-12R; SATA 6

Mayo, Jim 1908?-
    See L'Amour, Louis (Dearborn)

Maysles, Albert 1926- and Maysles, David
    1932- . . . . CLC 16

Maysles, Albert 1926-
    See Maysles, Albert and Maysles, David
    See also CA 29-32R

Maysles, David 1932-
    See Maysles, Albert and Maysles, David

Mazer, Norma Fox 1931- . . . . CLC 26
    See also CANR 12; CA 69-72; SAAS 1;
    SATA 24

McAuley, James (Phillip)
    1917-1976 . . . . CLC 45
    See also CA 97-100

McBain, Ed 1926-
    See Hunter, Evan

McBrien, William 1930- . . . . CLC 44
    See also CA 107

McCaffrey, Anne 1926- . . . . CLC 17
    See also CANR 15; CA 25-28R; SATA 8;
    DLB 8

McCarthy, Cormac 1933- . . . . CLC 4
    See also CANR 10; CA 13-16R; DLB 6

McCarthy, Mary (Therese)
    1912- . . . . CLC 1, 3, 5, 14, 24, 39
    See also CANR 16; CA 5-8R; DLB 2;
    DLB-Y 81

McCartney, (James) Paul 1942- . . . . CLC 35
    See also Lennon, John (Ono) and
    McCartney, Paul

McCauley, Stephen 19??- . . . . CLC 50

McClure, Michael 1932- . . . . CLC 6, 10
    See also CANR 17; CA 21-24R; DLB 16

McCorkle, Jill (Collins) 1958- . . . . . . CLC 51
    See also CA 121; DLB-Y 87

McCourt, James 1941- . . . . CLC 5
    See also CA 57-60

McCoy, Horace 1897-1955 . . . . . . TCLC 28
    See also CA 108; DLB 9

McCrae, John 1872-1918 . . . . TCLC 12
    See also CA 109

McCullers, (Lula) Carson (Smith)
    1917-1967 . . . . CLC 1, 4, 10, 12, 48
    See also CANR 18; CA 5-8R;
    obituary CA 25-28R; CABS 1; SATA 27;
    DLB 2, 7; CDALB 1941-1968

McCullough, Colleen 1938?- . . . . CLC 27
    See also CANR 17; CA 81-84

McElroy, Joseph (Prince)
    1930- . . . . CLC 5, 47
    See also CA 17-20R

McEwan, Ian (Russell) 1948- . . . . . . CLC 13
    See also CANR 14; CA 61-64; DLB 14

McFadden, David 1940- . . . . CLC 48
    See also CA 104; DLB 60

McGahern, John 1934- . . . . . . CLC 5, 9, 48
    See also CA 17-20R; DLB 14

McGinley, Patrick 1937- . . . . CLC 41
    See also CA 120

McGinley, Phyllis 1905-1978 . . . . . . CLC 14
    See also CANR 19; CA 9-12R;
    obituary CA 77-80; SATA 2, 44;
    obituary SATA 24; DLB 11, 48

McGinniss, Joe 1942- . . . . CLC 32
    See also CA 25-28R

McGivern, Maureen Daly 1921-
    See Daly, Maureen
    See also CA 9-12R

McGrath, Patrick 1950- . . . . CLC 55

McGrath, Thomas 1916- . . . . CLC 28
    See also CANR 6; CA 9-12R; SATA 41

McGuane, Thomas (Francis III)
    1939- . . . . CLC 3, 7, 18
    See also CANR 5; CA 49-52; DLB 2;
    DLB-Y 80

McGuckian, Medbh 1950- . . . . CLC 48
    See also DLB 40

McHale, Tom 1941-1982 . . . . CLC 3, 5
    See also CA 77-80; obituary CA 106

McIlvanney, William 1936- . . . . CLC 42
    See also CA 25-28R; DLB 14

McIlwraith, Maureen Mollie Hunter 1922-
    See Hunter, Mollie
    See also CA 29-32R; SATA 2

McInerney, Jay 1955- . . . . CLC 34
    See also CA 116

McIntyre, Vonda N(eel) 1948- . . . . . CLC 18
    See also CANR 17; CA 81-84

McKay, Claude 1890-1948 . . . . TCLC 7
    See also CA 104; DLB 4, 45

McKuen, Rod 1933- . . . . CLC 1, 3
    See also CA 41-44R

McLuhan, (Herbert) Marshall
    1911-1980 . . . . CLC 37
    See also CANR 12; CA 9-12R;
    obituary CA 102

McManus, Declan Patrick 1955-
    See Costello, Elvis

McMillan, Terry 19??- . . . . CLC 50

McMurtry, Larry (Jeff)
    1936- . . . . CLC 2, 3, 7, 11, 27, 44
    See also CANR 19; CA 5-8R; DLB 2;
    DLB-Y 80

McNally, Terrence 1939- . . . . . . CLC 4, 7, 41
    See also CANR 2; CA 45-48; DLB 7

McPhee, John 1931- . . . . CLC 36
    See also CANR 20; CA 65-68

McPherson, James Alan 1943- . . . . . CLC 19
    See also CA 25-28R; DLB 38

McPherson, William 1939- . . . . CLC 34
    See also CA 57-60

McSweeney, Kerry 19??- . . . . CLC 34

Mead, Margaret 1901-1978 . . . . CLC 37
    See also CANR 4; CA 1-4R;
    obituary CA 81-84; SATA 20

Meaker, M. J. 1927-
    See Kerr, M. E.
    See also Meaker, Marijane

Meaker, Marijane 1927-
    See Kerr, M. E.
    See also CA 107; SATA 20

Medoff, Mark (Howard) 1940- . . . CLC 6, 23
    See also CANR 5; CA 53-56; DLB 7

Megged, Aharon 1920- . . . . CLC 9
    See also CANR 1; CA 49-52

Mehta, Ved (Parkash) 1934- . . . . CLC 37
    See also CANR 2; CA 1-4R

Mellor, John 1953?-
    See The Clash

Meltzer, Milton 1915- . . . . CLC 26
    See also CA 13-16R; SAAS 1; SATA 1;
    DLB 61

Melville, Herman
    1819-1891 . . . . NCLC 3, 12; SSC 1
    See also DLB 3; CDALB 1640-1865

Mencken, H(enry) L(ouis)
    1880-1956 . . . . TCLC 13
    See also CA 105; DLB 11, 29, 63

Mercer, David 1928-1980 . . . . CLC 5
    See also CA 9-12R; obituary CA 102;
    DLB 13

Meredith, George 1828-1909 . . . . . . TCLC 17
    See also CA 117; DLB 18, 35, 57

Meredith, William (Morris)
    1919- . . . . CLC 4, 13, 22, 55
    See also CANR 6; CA 9-12R; DLB 5

Merezhkovsky, Dmitri
    1865-1941 . . . . TCLC 29

Merimee, Prosper 1803-1870 . . . . . . NCLC 6

Merkin, Daphne 1954- . . . . CLC 44

Merrill, James (Ingram)
    1926- . . . . CLC 2, 3, 6, 8, 13, 18, 34
    See also CANR 10; CA 13-16R; DLB 5;
    DLB-Y 85

Merton, Thomas (James)
    1915-1968 . . . . CLC 1, 3, 11, 34
    See also CANR 22; CA 5-8R;
    obituary CA 25-28R; DLB 48; DLB-Y 81

Merwin, W(illiam) S(tanley)
    1927- . . . . . . CLC 1, 2, 3, 5, 8, 13, 18, 45
    See also CANR 15; CA 13-16R; DLB 5

Metcalf, John 1938- . . . . CLC 37
    See also CA 113; DLB 60

Mew, Charlotte (Mary)
    1870-1928 . . . . TCLC 8
    See also CA 105; DLB 19

Mewshaw, Michael 1943-.......... **CLC 9**
See also CANR 7; CA 53-56; DLB-Y 80

Meyer-Meyrink, Gustav 1868-1932
See Meyrink, Gustav
See also CA 117

Meyers, Jeffrey 1939-........... **CLC 39**
See also CA 73-76

**Meynell, Alice (Christiana Gertrude
Thompson)** 1847-1922 .... **TCLC 6**
See also CA 104; DLB 19

Meyrink, Gustav 1868-1932...... **TCLC 21**
See also Meyer-Meyrink, Gustav

Michaels, Leonard 1933-........ **CLC 6, 25**
See also CANR 21; CA 61-64

Michaux, Henri 1899-1984 ..... **CLC 8, 19**
See also CA 85-88; obituary CA 114

Michener, James A(lbert)
1907-................ **CLC 1, 5, 11, 29**
See also CANR 21; CA 5-8R; DLB 6

Mickiewicz, Adam 1798-1855 ..... **NCLC 3**

Middleton, Christopher 1926-...... **CLC 13**
See also CA 13-16R; DLB 40

Middleton, Stanley 1919-........ **CLC 7, 38**
See also CANR 21; CA 25-28R; DLB 14

Migueis, Jose Rodrigues 1901-..... **CLC 10**

Mikszath, Kalman 1847-1910 ..... **TCLC 31**

Miles, Josephine (Louise)
1911-1985 .... **CLC 1, 2, 14, 34, 39**
See also CANR 2; CA 1-4R;
obituary CA 116; DLB 48

Mill, John Stuart 1806-1873 ..... **NCLC 11**

Millar, Kenneth 1915-1983
See Macdonald, Ross
See also CANR 16; CA 9-12R;
obituary CA 110; DLB 2; DLB-Y 83

Millay, Edna St. Vincent
1892-1950 .... **TCLC 4**
See also CA 104; DLB 45

Miller, Arthur
1915-...... **CLC 1, 2, 6, 10, 15, 26, 47**
See also CANR 2; CA 1-4R; DLB 7;
CDALB 1941-1968

Miller, Henry (Valentine)
1891-1980 .... **CLC 1, 2, 4, 9, 14, 43**
See also CA 9-12R; obituary CA 97-100;
DLB 4, 9; DLB-Y 80

Miller, Jason 1939?-.............. **CLC 2**
See also CA 73-76; DLB 7

Miller, Sue 19??-................. **CLC 44**

Miller, Walter M(ichael), Jr.
1923-.................... **CLC 4, 30**
See also CA 85-88; DLB 8

Millhauser, Steven 1943-....... **CLC 21, 54**
See also CA 108, 110, 111; DLB 2

Millin, Sarah Gertrude 1889-1968 .. **CLC 49**
See also CA 102; obituary CA 93-96

Milne, A(lan) A(lexander)
1882-1956 .... **TCLC 6**
See also CLR 1; YABC 1; CA 104; DLB 10

Milosz, Czeslaw 1911-.... **CLC 5, 11, 22, 31**
See also CA 81-84

Milton, John 1608-1674............ **LC 9**

Miner, Valerie (Jane) 1947-....... **CLC 40**
See also CA 97-100

Minot, Susan 1956- .... **CLC 44**

Minus, Ed 1938-................. **CLC 39**

Miro (Ferrer), Gabriel (Francisco Victor)
1879-1930 .... **TCLC 5**
See also CA 104

Mishima, Yukio
1925-1970 .... **CLC 2, 4, 6, 9, 27**
See also Hiraoka, Kimitake

Mistral, Gabriela 1889-1957 .... **TCLC 2**
See also CA 104

Mitchell, James Leslie 1901-1935
See Gibbon, Lewis Grassic
See also CA 104; DLB 15

Mitchell, Joni 1943-.............. **CLC 12**
See also CA 112

Mitchell (Marsh), Margaret (Munnerlyn)
1900-1949 .... **TCLC 11**
See also CA 109; DLB 9

Mitchell, W(illiam) O(rmond)
1914-..................... **CLC 25**
See also CANR 15; CA 77-80

Mitford, Mary Russell 1787-1855.. **NCLC 4**

Mitford, Nancy 1904-1973........ **CLC 44**
See also CA 9-12R

Mo, Timothy 1950-.............. **CLC 46**
See also CA 117

Modarressi, Taghi 1931- .... **CLC 44**
See also CA 121

Modiano, Patrick (Jean) 1945-..... **CLC 18**
See also CANR 17; CA 85-88

Mofolo, Thomas (Mokopu)
1876-1948 .... **TCLC 22**
See also CA 121

Mohr, Nicholasa 1935-............ **CLC 12**
See also CANR 1; CA 49-52; SATA 8

Mojtabai, A(nn) G(race)
1938-................ **CLC 5, 9, 15, 29**
See also CA 85-88

Moliere 1622-1673 .... **LC 10**

Molnar, Ferenc 1878-1952....... **TCLC 20**
See also CA 109

Momaday, N(avarre) Scott
1934-..................... **CLC 2, 19**
See also CANR 14; CA 25-28R; SATA 30,
48

Monroe, Harriet 1860-1936...... **TCLC 12**
See also CA 109; DLB 54

Montagu, Elizabeth 1720-1800 .... **NCLC 7**

Montagu, Lady Mary (Pierrepont) Wortley
1689-1762 .... **LC 9**

Montague, John (Patrick)
1929-.................... **CLC 13, 46**
See also CANR 9; CA 9-12R; DLB 40

Montaigne, Michel (Eyquem) de
1533-1592 .... **LC 8**

Montale, Eugenio 1896-1981... **CLC 7, 9, 18**
See also CA 17-20R; obituary CA 104

Montgomery, Marion (H., Jr.)
1925- .... **CLC 7**
See also CANR 3; CA 1-4R; DLB 6

Montgomery, Robert Bruce 1921-1978
See Crispin, Edmund
See also CA 104

Montherlant, Henri (Milon) de
1896-1972 .... **CLC 8, 19**
See also CA 85-88; obituary CA 37-40R;
DLB 72

Montisquieu, Charles-Louis de Secondat
1689-1755 .... **LC 7**

Monty Python................... **CLC 21**
See also Cleese, John
See also Gilliam, Terry (Vance); Idle, Eric;
Jones, Terry; Palin, Michael

Moodie, Susanna (Strickland)
1803-1885 .... **NCLC 14**

Mooney, Ted 1951-.............. **CLC 25**

Moorcock, Michael (John)
1939-..................... **CLC 5, 27**
See also CAAS 5; CANR 2, 17; CA 45-48;
DLB 14

Moore, Brian
1921-........ **CLC 1, 3, 5, 7, 8, 19, 32**
See also CANR 1; CA 1-4R

Moore, George (Augustus)
1852-1933 .... **TCLC 7**
See also CA 104; DLB 10, 18, 57

Moore, Lorrie 1957-.......... **CLC 39, 45**
See also Moore, Marie Lorena

Moore, Marianne (Craig)
1887-1972 ... **CLC 1, 2, 4, 8, 10, 13, 19,
47**
See also CANR 3; CA 1-4R;
obituary CA 33-36R; SATA 20; DLB 45

Moore, Marie Lorena 1957-
See Moore, Lorrie
See also CA 116

Moore, Thomas 1779-1852....... **NCLC 6**

Morand, Paul 1888-1976 .... **CLC 41**
See also obituary CA 69-72

Morante, Elsa 1918-1985....... **CLC 8, 47**
See also CA 85-88; obituary CA 117

Moravia, Alberto
1907-........ **CLC 2, 7, 11, 18, 27, 46**
See also Pincherle, Alberto

More, Henry 1614-1687............ **LC 9**

More, Thomas 1478-1573.......... **LC 10**

Moreas, Jean 1856-1910 .... **TCLC 18**

Morgan, Berry 1919-.............. **CLC 6**
See also CA 49-52; DLB 6

Morgan, Edwin (George) 1920-..... **CLC 31**
See also CANR 3; CA 7-8R; DLB 27

Morgan, (George) Frederick
1922-..................... **CLC 23**
See also CANR 21; CA 17-20R

Morgan, Janet 1945- .... **CLC 39**
See also CA 65-68

Morgan, Robin 1941-.............. **CLC 2**
See also CA 69-72

Morgenstern, Christian (Otto Josef Wolfgang)
1871-1914 .... **TCLC 8**
See also CA 105

Moricz, Zsigmond 1879-1942 ..... **TCLC 33**

Morike, Eduard (Friedrich)
1804-1875 .... **NCLC 10**

Mori Ogai 1862-1922............ **TCLC 14**
See also Mori Rintaro

Mori Rintaro 1862-1922
See Mori Ogai
See also CA 110

Moritz, Karl Philipp 1756-1793 ...... **LC 2**

Morris, Julian 1916-
See West, Morris L.

Morris, Steveland Judkins 1950-
See Wonder, Stevie
See also CA 111

Morris, William 1834-1896 .... **NCLC 4**
See also DLB 18, 35, 57

Morris, Wright (Marion)
1910- .... **CLC 1, 3, 7, 18, 37**
See also CA 9-12R; DLB 2; DLB-Y 81

Morrison, James Douglas 1943-1971
See Morrison, Jim
See also CA 73-76

Morrison, Jim 1943-1971......... **CLC 17**
See also Morrison, James Douglas

Morrison, Toni 1931-..... **CLC 4, 10, 22, 55**
See also CA 29-32R; DLB 6, 33; DLB-Y 81;
AAYA 1

Morrison, Van 1945- .... **CLC 21**
See also CA 116

Mortimer, John (Clifford)
1923- .... **CLC 28, 43**
See also CANR 21; CA 13-16R; DLB 13

Mortimer, Penelope (Ruth) 1918-.... **CLC 5**
See also CA 57-60

Mosley, Nicholas 1923-........... **CLC 43**
See also CA 69-72; DLB 14

Moss, Howard
1922-1987 .... **CLC 7, 14, 45, 50**
See also CANR 1; CA 1-4R; DLB 5

Motion, Andrew (Peter) 1952-...... **CLC 47**
See also DLB 40

Motley, Willard (Francis)
1912-1965 .... **CLC 18**
See also CA 117; obituary CA 106

Mott, Michael (Charles Alston)
1930- .... **CLC 15, 34**
See also CAAS 7; CANR 7; CA 5-8R

Mowat, Farley (McGill) 1921- ..... **CLC 26**
See also CANR 4; CA 1-4R; SATA 3

Mphahlele, Es'kia 1919-
See Mphahlele, Ezekiel

Mphahlele, Ezekiel 1919-......... **CLC 25**
See also CA 81-84

Mqhayi, S(amuel) E(dward) K(rune Loliwe)
1875-1945 .... **TCLC 25**

Mrozek, Slawomir 1930-........ **CLC 3, 13**
See also CA 13-16R

Mtwa, Percy 19??-............... **CLC 47**

Mueller, Lisel 1924-........... **CLC 13, 51**
See also CA 93-96

Muir, Edwin 1887-1959 .... **TCLC 2**
See also CA 104; DLB 20

Muir, John 1838-1914 .... **TCLC 28**

Mujica Lainez, Manuel
1910-1984 .... **CLC 31**
See also CA 81-84; obituary CA 112

Muldoon, Paul 1951-............. **CLC 32**
See also CA 113; DLB 40

Mulisch, Harry (Kurt Victor)
1927-...................... **CLC 42**
See also CANR 6; CA 9-12R

Mull, Martin 1943-.............. **CLC 17**
See also CA 105

Munford, Robert 1737?-1783........ **LC 5**
See also DLB 31

Munro, Alice (Laidlaw)
1931- .... **CLC 6, 10, 19, 50; SSC 3**
See also CA 33-36R; SATA 29; DLB 53

Munro, H(ector) H(ugh) 1870-1916
See Saki
See also CA 104; DLB 34

Murasaki, Lady c. 11th century-... **CMLC 1**

Murdoch, (Jean) Iris
1919- ...... **CLC 1, 2, 3, 4, 6, 8, 11, 15,
22, 31, 51**
See also CANR 8; CA 13-16R; DLB 14

Murphy, Richard 1927-........... **CLC 41**
See also CA 29-32R; DLB 40

Murphy, Sylvia 19??-............. **CLC 34**

Murphy, Thomas (Bernard) 1935-... **CLC 51**
See also CA 101

Murray, Les(lie) A(llan) 1938- ..... **CLC 40**
See also CANR 11; CA 21-24R

Murry, John Middleton
1889-1957 .... **TCLC 16**
See also CA 118

Musgrave, Susan 1951- .... **CLC 13, 54**
See also CA 69-72

Musil, Robert (Edler von)
1880-1942 .... **TCLC 12**
See also CA 109

Musset, (Louis Charles) Alfred de
1810-1857 .... **NCLC 7**

Myers, Walter Dean 1937- .... **CLC 35**
See also CLR 4, 16; CANR 20; CA 33-36R;
SAAS 2; SATA 27, 41; DLB 33

Nabokov, Vladimir (Vladimirovich)
1899-1977 .... **CLC 1, 2, 3, 6, 8, 11, 15,
23, 44, 46**
See also CANR 20; CA 5-8R;
obituary CA 69-72; DLB 2; DLB-Y 80;
DLB-DS 3; CDALB 1941-1968

Nagy, Laszlo 1925-1978........... **CLC 7**
See also obituary CA 112

Naipaul, Shiva(dhar Srinivasa)
1945-1985 .... **CLC 32, 39**
See also CA 110, 112; obituary CA 116;
DLB-Y 85

Naipaul, V(idiadhar) S(urajprasad)
1932- .... **CLC 4, 7, 9, 13, 18, 37**
See also CANR 1; CA 1-4R; DLB-Y 85

Nakos, Ioulia 1899?-
See Nakos, Lilika

Nakos, Lilika 1899?- .... **CLC 29**

Nakou, Lilika 1899?-
See Nakos, Lilika

Narayan, R(asipuram) K(rishnaswami)
1906- .... **CLC 7, 28, 47**
See also CA 81-84

Nash, (Frediric) Ogden 1902-1971 .. **CLC 23**
See also CAP 1; CA 13-14;
obituary CA 29-32R; SATA 2, 46;
DLB 11

Nathan, George Jean 1882-1958 ... **TCLC 18**
See also CA 114

Natsume, Kinnosuke 1867-1916
See Natsume, Soseki
See also CA 104

Natsume, Soseki 1867-1916..... **TCLC 2, 10**
See also Natsume, Kinnosuke

Natti, (Mary) Lee 1919-
See Kingman, (Mary) Lee
See also CANR 2; CA 7-8R

Naylor, Gloria 1950- .... **CLC 28**
See also CA 107

Neihardt, John G(neisenau)
1881-1973 .... **CLC 32**
See also CAP 1; CA 13-14; DLB 9

Nekrasov, Nikolai Alekseevich
1821-1878 .... **NCLC 11**

Nelligan, Emile 1879-1941....... **TCLC 14**
See also CA 114

Nelson, Willie 1933-............. **CLC 17**
See also CA 107

Nemerov, Howard 1920- .... **CLC 2, 6, 9, 36**
See also CANR 1; CA 1-4R; CABS 2;
DLB 5, 6; DLB-Y 83

Neruda, Pablo
1904-1973 .... **CLC 1, 2, 5, 7, 9, 28**
See also CAP 2; CA 19-20;
obituary CA 45-48

Nerval, Gerard de 1808-1855...... **NCLC 1**

Nervo, (Jose) Amado (Ruiz de)
1870-1919 .... **TCLC 11**
See also CA 109

Neufeld, John (Arthur) 1938- ...... **CLC 17**
See also CANR 11; CA 25-28R; SAAS 3;
SATA 6

Neville, Emily Cheney 1919-....... **CLC 12**
See also CANR 3; CA 5-8R; SAAS 2;
SATA 1

Newbound, Bernard Slade 1930-
See Slade, Bernard
See also CA 81-84

Newby, P(ercy) H(oward)
1918-.................... **CLC 2, 13**
See also CA 5-8R; DLB 15

Newlove, Donald 1928- .... **CLC 6**
See also CA 29-32R

Newlove, John (Herbert) 1938-..... **CLC 14**
See also CANR 9; CA 21-24R

Newman, Charles 1938-.......... **CLC 2, 8**
See also CA 21-24R

Newman, Edwin (Harold) 1919- .... **CLC 14**
See also CANR 5; CA 69-72

Newton, Suzanne 1936-.......... **CLC 35**
See also CANR 14; CA 41-44R; SATA 5

Ngugi, James (Thiong'o)
1938-................. **CLC 3, 7, 13, 36**
See also Ngugi wa Thiong'o
See also Wa Thiong'o, Ngugi; CA 81-84

Ngugi wa Thiong'o 1938-... CLC **3, 7, 13, 36**
See also Ngugi, James (Thiong'o)
See also Wa Thiong'o, Ngugi

Nichol, B(arrie) P(hillip) 1944-..... CLC **18**
See also CA 53-56; DLB 53

Nichols, John (Treadwell) 1940-.... CLC **38**
See also CAAS 2; CANR 6; CA 9-12R;
DLB-Y 82

Nichols, Peter (Richard) 1927-... CLC **5, 36**
See also CA 104; DLB 13

Nicolas, F.R.E. 1927-
See Freeling, Nicolas

Niedecker, Lorine 1903-1970.... CLC **10, 42**
See also CAP 2; CA 25-28; DLB 48

Nietzsche, Friedrich (Wilhelm)
1844-1900 .... TCLC **10, 18**
See also CA 107

Nightingale, Anne Redmon 1943-
See Redmon (Nightingale), Anne
See also CA 103

Nin, Anais 1903-1977... CLC **1, 4, 8, 11, 14**
See also CANR 22; CA 13-16R;
obituary CA 69-72; DLB 2, 4

Nissenson, Hugh 1933-.......... CLC **4, 9**
See also CA 17-20R; DLB 28

Niven, Larry 1938-............... CLC **8**
See also Niven, Laurence Van Cott
See also DLB 8

Niven, Laurence Van Cott 1938-
See Niven, Larry
See also CANR 14; CA 21-24R

Nixon, Agnes Eckhardt 1927-...... CLC **21**
See also CA 110

Nkosi, Lewis 1936-............... CLC **45**
See also CA 65-68

Nodier, (Jean) Charles (Emmanuel)
1780-1844 .... NCLC **19**

Nordhoff, Charles 1887-1947..... TCLC **23**
See also CA 108; SATA 23; DLB 9

Norman, Marsha 1947- .... CLC **28**
See also CA 105; DLB-Y 84

Norris, (Benjamin) Frank(lin)
1870-1902 .... TCLC **24**
See also CA 110; DLB 12, 71;
CDALB 1865-1917

Norris, Leslie 1921-.............. CLC **14**
See also CANR 14; CAP 1; CA 11-12;
DLB 27

North, Andrew 1912-
See Norton, Andre

North, Christopher 1785-1854
See Wilson, John

Norton, Alice Mary 1912-
See Norton, Andre
See also CANR 2; CA 1-4R; SATA 1, 43

Norton, Andre 1912- .... CLC **12**
See also Norton, Mary Alice
See also DLB 8, 52

Norway, Nevil Shute 1899-1960
See Shute (Norway), Nevil
See also CA 102; obituary CA 93-96

Norwid, Cyprian Kamil
1821-1883 .... NCLC **17**

Nossack, Hans Erich 1901-1978 ..... CLC **6**
See also CA 93-96; obituary CA 85-88;
DLB 69

Nova, Craig 1945-.............. CLC **7, 31**
See also CANR 2; CA 45-48

Novalis 1772-1801 .... NCLC **13**

Nowlan, Alden (Albert) 1933-...... CLC **15**
See also CANR 5; CA 9-12R; DLB 53

Noyes, Alfred 1880-1958 .... TCLC **7**
See also CA 104; DLB 20

Nunn, Kem 19??-................. CLC **34**

Nye, Robert 1939- .... CLC **13, 42**
See also CA 33-36R; SATA 6; DLB 14

Nyro, Laura 1947- .... CLC **17**

Oates, Joyce Carol
1938- ... CLC **1, 2, 3, 6, 9, 11, 15, 19, 33**
See also CA 5-8R; DLB 2, 5; DLB-Y 81

O'Brien, Darcy 1939-............. CLC **11**
See also CANR 8; CA 21-24R

O'Brien, Edna 1932-.... CLC **3, 5, 8, 13, 36**
See also CANR 6; CA 1-4R; DLB 14

O'Brien, Flann
1911-1966 .... CLC **1, 4, 5, 7, 10, 47**
See also O Nuallain, Brian

O'Brien, Richard 19??-............ CLC **17**

O'Brien, (William) Tim(othy)
1946- .... CLC **7, 19, 40**
See also CA 85-88; DLB-Y 80

Obstfelder, Sigbjorn 1866-1900.... TCLC **23**

O'Casey, Sean
1880-1964 .... CLC **1, 5, 9, 11, 15**
See also CA 89-92; DLB 10

Ochs, Phil 1940-1976............. CLC **17**
See also obituary CA 65-68

O'Connor, Edwin (Greene)
1918-1968 .... CLC **14**
See also CA 93-96; obituary CA 25-28R

O'Connor, (Mary) Flannery
1925-1964 ... CLC **1, 2, 3, 6, 10, 13, 15,
21; SSC 1**
See also CANR 3; CA 1-4R; DLB 2;
DLB-Y 80; CDALB 1941-1968

O'Connor, Frank 1903-1966 .... CLC **14, 23**
See also O'Donovan, Michael (John)

O'Dell, Scott 1903-............... CLC **30**
See also CLR 1, 16; CANR 12; CA 61-64;
SATA 12; DLB 52

Odets, Clifford 1906-1963 .... CLC **2, 28**
See also CA 85-88; DLB 7, 26

O'Donovan, Michael (John) 1903-1966
See O'Connor, Frank
See also CA 93-96

Oe, Kenzaburo 1935- .... CLC **10, 36**
See also CA 97-100

O'Faolain, Julia 1932-....... CLC **6, 19, 47**
See also CAAS 2; CANR 12; CA 81-84;
DLB 14

O'Faolain, Sean 1900- ..... CLC **1, 7, 14, 32**
See also CANR 12; CA 61-64; DLB 15

O'Flaherty, Liam 1896-1984 ..... CLC **5, 34**
See also CA 101; obituary CA 113; DLB 36;
DLB-Y 84

O'Grady, Standish (James)
1846-1928 .... TCLC **5**
See also CA 104

O'Hara, Frank 1926-1966 ..... CLC **2, 5, 13**
See also CA 9-12R; obituary CA 25-28R;
DLB 5, 16

O'Hara, John (Henry)
1905-1970 .... CLC **1, 2, 3, 6, 11, 42**
See also CA 5-8R; obituary CA 25-28R;
DLB 9; DLB-DS 2

O'Hara Family
See Banim, John and Banim, Michael

O'Hehir, Diana 1922-............. CLC **41**
See also CA 93-96

Okigbo, Christopher (Ifenayichukwu)
1932-1967 .... CLC **25**
See also CA 77-80

Olds, Sharon 1942-............ CLC **32, 39**
See also CANR 18; CA 101

Olesha, Yuri (Karlovich)
1899-1960 .... CLC **8**
See also CA 85-88

Oliphant, Margaret (Oliphant Wilson)
1828-1897 .... NCLC **11**
See also DLB 18

Oliver, Mary 1935-............ CLC **19, 34**
See also CANR 9; CA 21-24R; DLB 5

Olivier, (Baron) Laurence (Kerr)
1907- .... CLC **20**
See also CA 111

Olsen, Tillie 1913- .... CLC **4, 13**
See also CANR 1; CA 1-4R; DLB 28;
DLB-Y 80

Olson, Charles (John)
1910-1970 ..... CLC **1, 2, 5, 6, 9, 11, 29**
See also CAP 1; CA 15-16;
obituary CA 25-28R; CABS 2; DLB 5, 16

Olson, Theodore 1937-
See Olson, Toby

Olson, Toby 1937- .... CLC **28**
See also CANR 9; CA 65-68

Ondaatje, (Philip) Michael
1943- .... CLC **14, 29, 51**
See also CA 77-80; DLB 60

Oneal, Elizabeth 1934-
See Oneal, Zibby
See also CA 106; SATA 30

Oneal, Zibby 1934-............... CLC **30**
See also Oneal, Elizabeth

O'Neill, Eugene (Gladstone)
1888-1953 .... TCLC **1, 6, 27**
See also CA 110; DLB 7

Onetti, Juan Carlos 1909-....... CLC **7, 10**
See also CA 85-88

O'Nolan, Brian 1911-1966
See O'Brien, Flann

O Nuallain, Brian 1911-1966
See O'Brien, Flann
See also CAP 2; CA 21-22;
obituary CA 25-28R

Oppen, George 1908-1984 ... CLC **7, 13, 34**
See also CANR 8; CA 13-16R;
obituary CA 113; DLB 5

Orlovitz, Gil 1918-1973 . . . . **CLC 22**
See also CA 77-80; obituary CA 45-48;
DLB 2, 5

Ortega y Gasset, Jose 1883-1955 . . . **TCLC 9**
See also CA 106

Ortiz, Simon J. 1941- . . . . **CLC 45**

Orton, Joe 1933?-1967 . . . . . . **CLC 4, 13, 43**
See also Orton, John Kingsley
See also DLB 13

Orton, John Kingsley 1933?-1967
See Orton, Joe
See also CA 85-88

Orwell, George
1903-1950 . . . . **TCLC 2, 6, 15, 31**
See also Blair, Eric Arthur
See also DLB 15

Osborne, John (James)
1929- . . . . **CLC 1, 2, 5, 11, 45**
See also CANR 21; CA 13-16R; DLB 13

Osborne, Lawrence 1958- . . . . **CLC 50**

Osceola 1885-1962
See Dinesen, Isak
See also Blixen, Karen (Christentze
Dinesen)

Oshima, Nagisa 1932- . . . . **CLC 20**
See also CA 116

Ossoli, Sarah Margaret (Fuller marchesa d')
1810-1850
See Fuller, (Sarah) Margaret
See also SATA 25

Otero, Blas de 1916- . . . . **CLC 11**
See also CA 89-92

Owen, Wilfred (Edward Salter)
1893-1918 . . . . **TCLC 5, 27**
See also CA 104; DLB 20

Owens, Rochelle 1936- . . . . **CLC 8**
See also CAAS 2; CA 17-20R

Owl, Sebastian 1939-
See Thompson, Hunter S(tockton)

Oz, Amos 1939- . . . **CLC 5, 8, 11, 27, 33, 54**
See also CA 53-56

Ozick, Cynthia 1928- . . . . **CLC 3, 7, 28**
See also CA 17-20R; DLB 28; DLB-Y 82

Ozu, Yasujiro 1903-1963 . . . . **CLC 16**
See also CA 112

Pa Chin 1904- . . . . **CLC 18**
See also Li Fei-kan

Pack, Robert 1929- . . . . **CLC 13**
See also CANR 3; CA 1-4R; DLB 5

Padgett, Lewis 1915-1958
See Kuttner, Henry

Padilla, Heberto 1932- . . . . **CLC 38**

Page, Jimmy 1944- and **Plant, Robert**
1948- . . . . **CLC 12**

Page, Jimmy 1944-
See Page, Jimmy and Plant, Robert

Page, Louise 1955- . . . . **CLC 40**

Page, P(atricia) K(athleen)
1916- . . . . **CLC 7, 18**
See also CANR 4; CA 53-56

Paget, Violet 1856-1935
See Lee, Vernon
See also CA 104

Palamas, Kostes 1859-1943 . . . . **TCLC 5**
See also CA 105

Palazzeschi, Aldo 1885-1974 . . . . **CLC 11**
See also CA 89-92; obituary CA 53-56

Paley, Grace 1922- . . . . **CLC 4, 6, 37**
See also CANR 13; CA 25-28R; DLB 28

Palin, Michael 1943-
See Monty Python
See also CA 107

Palma, Ricardo 1833-1919 . . . . **TCLC 29**

Pancake, Breece Dexter 1952-1979
See Pancake, Breece D'J

Pancake, Breece D'J 1952-1979 . . . . **CLC 29**
See also obituary CA 109

Papadiamantis, Alexandros
1851-1911 . . . . **TCLC 29**

Papini, Giovanni 1881-1956 . . . . . . **TCLC 22**
See also CA 121

Parini, Jay (Lee) 1948- . . . . **CLC 54**
See also CA 97-100

Parker, Dorothy (Rothschild)
1893-1967 . . . . **CLC 15; SSC 2**
See also CAP 2; CA 19-20;
obituary CA 25-28R; DLB 11, 45

Parker, Robert B(rown) 1932- . . . . . . **CLC 27**
See also CANR 1; CA 49-52

Parkin, Frank 1940- . . . . **CLC 43**

Parkman, Francis 1823-1893 . . . . . **NCLC 12**
See also DLB 1, 30

Parks, Gordon (Alexander Buchanan)
1912- . . . . **CLC 1, 16**
See also CA 41-44R; SATA 8; DLB 33

Parnell, Thomas 1679-1718 . . . . **LC 3**

Parra, Nicanor 1914- . . . . **CLC 2**
See also CA 85-88

Pasolini, Pier Paolo
1922-1975 . . . . **CLC 20, 37**
See also CA 93-96; obituary CA 61-64

Pastan, Linda (Olenik) 1932- . . . . . . **CLC 27**
See also CANR 18; CA 61-64; DLB 5

Pasternak, Boris 1890-1960 . . . **CLC 7, 10, 18**
See also obituary CA 116

Patchen, Kenneth 1911-1972 . . . **CLC 1, 2, 18**
See also CANR 3; CA 1-4R;
obituary CA 33-36R; DLB 16, 48

Pater, Walter (Horatio)
1839-1894 . . . . **NCLC 7**
See also DLB 57

Paterson, Katherine (Womeldorf)
1932- . . . . **CLC 12, 30**
See also CLR 7; CA 21-24R; SATA 13, 53;
DLB 52

Patmore, Coventry Kersey Dighton
1823-1896 . . . . **NCLC 9**
See also DLB 35

Paton, Alan (Stewart)
1903-1988 . . . . **CLC 4, 10, 25, 55**
See also CANR 22; CAP 1; CA 15-16;
obituary CA 125; SATA 11

Paulding, James Kirke 1778-1860 . . **NCLC 2**
See also DLB 3

Paulin, Tom 1949- . . . . **CLC 37**
See also DLB 40

Paustovsky, Konstantin (Georgievich)
1892-1968 . . . . **CLC 40**
See also CA 93-96; obituary CA 25-28R

Paustowsky, Konstantin (Georgievich)
1892-1968
See Paustovsky, Konstantin (Georgievich)

Pavese, Cesare 1908-1950 . . . . **TCLC 3**
See also CA 104

Payne, Alan 1932-
See Jakes, John (William)

Paz, Octavio 1914- . . **CLC 3, 4, 6, 10, 19, 51**
See also CA 73-76

Peake, Mervyn 1911-1968 . . . . **CLC 7, 54**
See also CANR 3; CA 5-8R;
obituary CA 25-28R; SATA 23; DLB 15

Pearce, (Ann) Philippa 1920- . . . . **CLC 21**
See also Christie, (Ann) Philippa
See also CA 5-8R; SATA 1

Pearl, Eric 1934-
See Elman, Richard

Pearson, T(homas) R(eid) 1956- . . . . **CLC 39**
See also CA 120

Peck, John 1941- . . . . **CLC 3**
See also CANR 3; CA 49-52

Peck, Richard 1934- . . . . **CLC 21**
See also CLR 15; CANR 19; CA 85-88;
SAAS 2; SATA 18

Peck, Robert Newton 1928- . . . . **CLC 17**
See also CA 81-84; SAAS 1; SATA 21

Peckinpah, (David) Sam(uel)
1925-1984 . . . . **CLC 20**
See also CA 109; obituary CA 114

Pedersen, Knut 1859-1952
See Hamsun, Knut
See also CA 104

Peguy, Charles (Pierre)
1873-1914 . . . . **TCLC 10**
See also CA 107

Pepys, Samuel 1633-1703 . . . . **LC 11**

Percy, Walker
1916- . . . . . . **CLC 2, 3, 6, 8, 14, 18, 47**
See also CANR 1; CA 1-4R; DLB 2;
DLB-Y 80

Pereda, Jose Maria de
1833-1906 . . . . **TCLC 16**

Perelman, S(idney) J(oseph)
1904-1979 . . . **CLC 3, 5, 9, 15, 23, 44, 49**
See also CANR 18; CA 73-76;
obituary CA 89-92; DLB 11, 44

Peret, Benjamin 1899-1959 . . . . **TCLC 20**
See also CA 117

Peretz, Isaac Leib 1852?-1915 . . . . . **TCLC 16**
See also CA 109

Perez, Galdos Benito 1853-1920 . . . **TCLC 27**

Perrault, Charles 1628-1703 . . . . **LC 2**
See also SATA 25

Perse, St.-John 1887-1975 . . . . **CLC 4, 11, 46**
See also Leger, (Marie-Rene) Alexis
Saint-Leger

Pesetsky, Bette 1932- . . . . **CLC 28**

Peshkov, Alexei Maximovich 1868-1936
See Gorky, Maxim
See also CA 105

Pessoa, Fernando (Antonio Nogueira)
1888-1935 .... TCLC 27

Peterkin, Julia (Mood) 1880-1961... CLC 31
See also CA 102; DLB 9

Peters, Joan K. 1945-............ CLC 39

Peters, Robert L(ouis) 1924-........ CLC 7
See also CA 13-16R

Petrakis, Harry Mark 1923-........ CLC 3
See also CANR 4; CA 9-12R

Petrov, Evgeny 1902-1942 and Ilf, Ilya
1897-1937
See Ilf, Ilya 1897-1937 and Petrov, Evgeny
1902-1942

Petry, Ann (Lane) 1908- ...... CLC 1, 7, 18
See also CLR 12; CAAS 6; CANR 4;
CA 5-8R; SATA 5

Petursson, Halligrimur 1614-1674 .... LC 8

Phillips, Jayne Anne 1952- ..... CLC 15, 33
See also CA 101; DLB-Y 80

Phillips, Robert (Schaeffer) 1938-... CLC 28
See also CANR 8; CA 17-20R

Pica, Peter 1925-
See Aldiss, Brian W(ilson)

Piccolo, Lucio 1901-1969.......... CLC 13
See also CA 97-100

Pickthall, Marjorie (Lowry Christie)
1883-1922 .... TCLC 21
See also CA 107

Piercy, Marge 1936-... CLC 3, 6, 14, 18, 27
See also CAAS 1; CANR 13; CA 21-24R

Pilnyak, Boris 1894-1937?....... TCLC 23

Pincherle, Alberto 1907-
See Moravia, Alberto
See also CA 25-28R

Pineda, Cecile 1942-............. CLC 39
See also CA 118

Pinero, Miguel (Gomez)
1946-1988 .... CLC 4, 55
See also CA 61-64; obituary CA 125

Pinget, Robert 1919- .... CLC 7, 13, 37
See also CA 85-88

Pink Floyd............... CLC 35

Pinkwater, D(aniel) M(anus)
1941-.................... CLC 35
See also Pinkwater, Manus
See also CLR 4; CANR 12; CA 29-32R;
SAAS 3; SATA 46

Pinkwater, Manus 1941-
See Pinkwater, D(aniel) M(anus)
See also SATA 8

Pinsky, Robert 1940-........ CLC 9, 19, 38
See also CAAS 4; CA 29-32R; DLB-Y 82

Pinter, Harold
1930- .... CLC 1, 3, 6, 9, 11, 15, 27
See also CA 5-8R; DLB 13

Pirandello, Luigi 1867-1936..... TCLC 4, 29
See also CA 104

Pirsig, Robert M(aynard) 1928- ... CLC 4, 6
See also CA 53-56; SATA 39

Pix, Mary (Griffith) 1666-1709 ...... LC 8

Plaidy, Jean 1906-
See Hibbert, Eleanor (Burford)

Plant, Robert 1948-
See Page, Jimmy and Plant, Robert

Plante, David (Robert)
1940- .... CLC 7, 23, 38
See also CANR 12; CA 37-40R; DLB-Y 83

Plath, Sylvia
1932-1963 .... CLC 1, 2, 3, 5, 9, 11, 14,
17, 50, 51
See also CAP 2; CA 19-20; DLB 5, 6;
CDALB 1941-1968

Platonov, Andrei (Platonovich)
1899-1951 .... TCLC 14
See also Klimentov, Andrei Platonovich

Platt, Kin 1911- .... CLC 26
See also CANR 11; CA 17-20R; SATA 21

Plimpton, George (Ames) 1927-..... CLC 36
See also CA 21-24R; SATA 10

Plomer, William (Charles Franklin)
1903-1973 .... CLC 4, 8
See also CAP 2; CA 21-22; SATA 24;
DLB 20

Plumly, Stanley (Ross) 1939- ...... CLC 33
See also CA 108, 110; DLB 5

Poe, Edgar Allan
1809-1849 .... NCLC 1, 16; SSC 1
See also SATA 23; DLB 3;
CDALB 1640-1865

Pohl, Frederik 1919- .... CLC 18
See also CAAS 1; CANR 11; CA 61-64;
SATA 24; DLB 8

Poirier, Louis 1910-
See Gracq, Julien
See also CA 122

Poitier, Sidney 1924?- .... CLC 26
See also CA 117

Polanski, Roman 1933- .... CLC 16
See also CA 77-80

Poliakoff, Stephen 1952- .... CLC 38
See also CA 106; DLB 13

Police, The.................... CLC 26

Pollitt, Katha 1949- .... CLC 28
See also CA 120, 122

Pollock, Sharon 19??-............. CLC 50

Pomerance, Bernard 1940-........ CLC 13
See also CA 101

Ponge, Francis (Jean Gaston Alfred)
1899-.................... CLC 6, 18
See also CA 85-88

Pontoppidan, Henrik 1857-1943 ... TCLC 29

Poole, Josephine 1933-............ CLC 17
See also CANR 10; CA 21-24R; SAAS 2;
SATA 5

Popa, Vasko 1922-............... CLC 19
See also CA 112

Pope, Alexander 1688-1744......... LC 3

Porter, Gene (va Grace) Stratton
1863-1924 .... TCLC 21
See also CA 112

Porter, Katherine Anne
1890-1980 ... CLC 1, 3, 7, 10, 13, 15, 27
See also CANR 1; CA 1-4R;
obituary CA 101; obituary SATA 23, 39;
DLB 4, 9; DLB-Y 80

Porter, Peter (Neville Frederick)
1929-................. CLC 5, 13, 33
See also CA 85-88; DLB 40

Porter, William Sydney 1862-1910
See Henry, O.
See also YABC 2; CA 104; DLB 12;
CDALB 1865-1917

Potok, Chaim 1929-....... CLC 2, 7, 14, 26
See also CANR 19; CA 17-20R; SATA 33;
DLB 28

Pound, Ezra (Loomis)
1885-1972 ..... CLC 1, 2, 3, 4, 5, 7, 10,
13, 18, 34, 48, 50
See also CA 5-8R; obituary CA 37-40R;
DLB 4, 45, 63

Povod, Reinaldo 1959-............ CLC 44

Powell, Anthony (Dymoke)
1905-.......... CLC 1, 3, 7, 9, 10, 31
See also CANR 1; CA 1-4R; DLB 15

Powell, Padgett 1952-............. CLC 34

Powers, J(ames) F(arl) 1917-.... CLC 1, 4, 8
See also CANR 2; CA 1-4R

Pownall, David 1938-............. CLC 10
See also CA 89-92; DLB 14

Powys, John Cowper
1872-1963 .... CLC 7, 9, 15, 46
See also CA 85-88; DLB 15

Powys, T(heodore) F(rancis)
1875-1953 .... TCLC 9
See also CA 106; DLB 36

Pratt, E(dwin) J(ohn) 1883-1964.... CLC 19
See also obituary CA 93-96

Premchand 1880-1936 .... TCLC 21

Preussler, Otfried 1923-........... CLC 17
See also CA 77-80; SATA 24

Prevert, Jacques (Henri Marie)
1900-1977 .... CLC 15
See also CA 77-80; obituary CA 69-72;
obituary SATA 30

Prevost, Abbe (Antoine Francois)
1697-1763 .... LC 1

Price, (Edward) Reynolds
1933- .... CLC 3, 6, 13, 43, 50
See also CANR 1; CA 1-4R; DLB 2

Price, Richard 1949- .... CLC 6, 12
See also CANR 3; CA 49-52; DLB-Y 81

Prichard, Katharine Susannah
1883-1969 .... CLC 46
See also CAP 1; CA 11-12

Priestley, J(ohn) B(oynton)
1894-1984.......... CLC 2, 5, 9, 34
See also CA 9-12R; obituary CA 113;
DLB 10, 34; DLB-Y 84

Prince (Rogers Nelson) 1958?- ..... CLC 35

Prince, F(rank) T(empleton) 1912-.. CLC 22
See also CA 101; DLB 20

Prior, Matthew 1664-1721.......... LC 4

Pritchard, William H(arrison)
1932-..................... CLC 34
See also CA 65-68

Pritchett, V(ictor) S(awdon)
1900-............... CLC 5, 13, 15, 41
See also CA 61-64; DLB 15

Procaccino, Michael   1946-
See Cristofer, Michael

Prokosch, Frederic   1908-........ **CLC 4, 48**
See also CA 73-76; DLB 48

Prose, Francine   1947-............ **CLC 45**
See also CA 109, 112

Proust, Marcel   1871-1922 .. **TCLC 7, 13, 33**
See also CA 104, 120; DLB 65

Pryor, Richard   1940-........ **CLC 26**

Puig, Manuel   1932- .... **CLC 3, 5, 10, 28**
See also CANR 2; CA 45-48

Purdy, A(lfred) W(ellington)
1918- .... **CLC 3, 6, 14, 50**
See also CA 81-84

Purdy, James (Amos)
1923- .... **CLC 2, 4, 10, 28**
See also CAAS 1; CANR 19; CA 33-36R;
DLB 2

Pushkin, Alexander (Sergeyevich)
1799-1837 .... **NCLC 3**

P'u Sung-ling   1640-1715 .... **LC 3**

Puzo, Mario   1920-......... **CLC 1, 2, 6, 36**
See also CANR 4; CA 65-68; DLB 6

Pym, Barbara (Mary Crampton)
1913-1980 .... **CLC 13, 19, 37**
See also CANR 13; CAP 1; CA 13-14;
obituary CA 97-100; DLB 14

Pynchon, Thomas (Ruggles, Jr.)
1937- .... **CLC 2, 3, 6, 9, 11, 18, 33**
See also CANR 22; CA 17-20R; DLB 2

Quasimodo, Salvatore   1901-1968 ... **CLC 10**
See also CAP 1; CA 15-16;
obituary CA 25-28R

Queen, Ellery   1905-1982 .... **CLC 3, 11**
See also Dannay, Frederic
See also Lee, Manfred B(ennington)

Queneau, Raymond
1903-1976 .... **CLC 2, 5, 10, 42**
See also CA 77-80; obituary CA 69-72;
DLB 72

Quin, Ann (Marie)   1936-1973 .... **CLC 6**
See also CA 9-12R; obituary CA 45-48;
DLB 14

Quinn, Simon   1942-
See Smith, Martin Cruz

Quiroga, Horacio (Sylvestre)
1878-1937 .... **TCLC 20**
See also CA 117

Quoirez, Francoise   1935-
See Sagan, Francoise
See also CANR 6; CA 49-52

Rabe, David (William)   1940-... **CLC 4, 8, 33**
See also CA 85-88; DLB 7

Rabelais, Francois   1494?-1553........ **LC 5**

Rabinovitch, Sholem   1859-1916
See Aleichem, Sholom
See also CA 104

Rachen, Kurt von   1911-1986
See Hubbard, L(afayette) Ron(ald)

Radcliffe, Ann (Ward)   1764-1823 .. **NCLC 6**
See also DLB 39

Radiguet, Raymond   1903-1923 .... **TCLC 29**

Radnoti, Miklos   1909-1944 .... **TCLC 16**
See also CA 118

Rado, James   1939-
See Ragni, Gerome and Rado, James
See also CA 105

Radomski, James   1932-
See Rado, James

Radvanyi, Netty Reiling   1900-1983
See Seghers, Anna
See also CA 85-88; obituary CA 110

Raeburn, John   1941- .... **CLC 34**
See also CA 57-60

Ragni, Gerome   1942- and **Rado, James**
1939- .... **CLC 17**

Ragni, Gerome   1942-
See Ragni, Gerome and Rado, James
See also CA 105

Rahv, Philip   1908-1973 .... **CLC 24**
See also Greenberg, Ivan

Raine, Craig   1944-................ **CLC 32**
See also CA 108; DLB 40

Raine, Kathleen (Jessie)   1908- ... **CLC 7, 45**
See also CA 85-88; DLB 20

Rainis, Janis   1865-1929......... **TCLC 29**

Rakosi, Carl   1903- .... **CLC 47**
See also Rawley, Callman
See also CAAS 5

Rampersad, Arnold   19??-.......... **CLC 44**

Ramuz, Charles-Ferdinand
1878-1947 .... **TCLC 33**

Rand, Ayn   1905-1982........ **CLC 3, 30, 44**
See also CA 13-16R; obituary CA 105

Randall, Dudley (Felker)   1914-...... **CLC 1**
See also CA 25-28R; DLB 41

Ransom, John Crowe
1888-1974 .... **CLC 2, 4, 5, 11, 24**
See also CANR 6; CA 5-8R;
obituary CA 49-52; DLB 45, 63

Rao, Raja   1909- .... **CLC 25**
See also CA 73-76

Raphael, Frederic (Michael)
1931- .... **CLC 2, 14**
See also CANR 1; CA 1-4R; DLB 14

Rathbone, Julian   1935- .... **CLC 41**
See also CA 101

Rattigan, Terence (Mervyn)
1911-1977 .... **CLC 7**
See also CA 85-88; obituary CA 73-76;
DLB 13

Ratushinskaya, Irina   1954- .... **CLC 54**

Raven, Simon (Arthur Noel)
1927- .... **CLC 14**
See also CA 81-84

Rawley, Callman   1903-
See Rakosi, Carl
See also CANR 12; CA 21-24R

Rawlings, Marjorie Kinnan
1896-1953 .... **TCLC 4**
See also YABC 1; CA 104; DLB 9, 22

Ray, Satyajit   1921-............... **CLC 16**
See also CA 114

Read, Herbert (Edward)   1893-1968 .. **CLC 4**
See also CA 85-88; obituary CA 25-28R;
DLB 20

Read, Piers Paul   1941- ...... **CLC 4, 10, 25**
See also CA 21-24R; SATA 21; DLB 14

Reade, Charles   1814-1884 .... **NCLC 2**
See also DLB 21

Reade, Hamish   1936-
See Gray, Simon (James Holliday)

Reading, Peter   1946- .... **CLC 47**
See also CA 103; DLB 40

Reaney, James   1926- .... **CLC 13**
See also CA 41-44R; SATA 43

Rebreanu, Liviu   1885-1944 .... **TCLC 28**

Rechy, John (Francisco)
1934-................. **CLC 1, 7, 14, 18**
See also CAAS 4; CANR 6; CA 5-8R;
DLB-Y 82

Redcam, Tom   1870-1933 .... **TCLC 25**

Redgrove, Peter (William)
1932- .... **CLC 6, 41**
See also CANR 3; CA 1-4R; DLB 40

Redmon (Nightingale), Anne
1943- .... **CLC 22**
See also Nightingale, Anne Redmon
See also DLB-Y 86

Reed, Ishmael   1938-.. **CLC 2, 3, 5, 6, 13, 32**
See also CA 21-24R; DLB 2, 5, 33

Reed, John (Silas)   1887-1920 ...... **TCLC 9**
See also CA 106

Reed, Lou   1944-................. **CLC 21**

Reeve, Clara   1729-1807 .... **NCLC 19**
See also DLB 39

Reid, Christopher   1949-........... **CLC 33**
See also DLB 40

Reid Banks, Lynne   1929-
See Banks, Lynne Reid
See also CANR 6, 22; CA 1-4R; SATA 22

Reiner, Max   1900-
See Caldwell, (Janet Miriam) Taylor
(Holland)

Reizenstein, Elmer Leopold   1892-1967
See Rice, Elmer

Remark, Erich Paul   1898-1970
See Remarque, Erich Maria

Remarque, Erich Maria
1898-1970 .... **CLC 21**
See also CA 77-80; obituary CA 29-32R

Remizov, Alexey (Mikhailovich)
1877-1957 .... **TCLC 27**

Renard, Jules   1864-1910 .... **TCLC 17**
See also CA 117

Renault, Mary   1905-1983 .... **CLC 3, 11, 17**
See also Challans, Mary
See also DLB-Y 83

Rendell, Ruth   1930-........... **CLC 28, 48**
See also Vine, Barbara
See also CA 109

Renoir, Jean   1894-1979 .... **CLC 20**
See also obituary CA 85-88

Resnais, Alain   1922-.............. **CLC 16**

Rexroth, Kenneth
1905-1982 ...... **CLC 1, 2, 6, 11, 22, 49**
See also CANR 14; CA 5-8R;
obituary CA 107; DLB 16, 48; DLB-Y 82;
CDALB 1941-1968

Reyes, Alfonso   1889-1959 .... **TCLC 33**

Reyes y Basoalto, Ricardo Eliecer Neftali
  1904-1973
  See Neruda, Pablo

Reymont, Wladyslaw Stanislaw
  1867-1925 .... TCLC 5
  See also CA 104

Reynolds, Jonathan 1942?- ...... CLC 6, 38
  See also CA 65-68

Reynolds, Michael (Shane) 1937- ... CLC 44
  See also CANR 9; CA 65-68

Reznikoff, Charles 1894-1976 .... CLC 9
  See also CAP 2; CA 33-36;
    obituary CA 61-64; DLB 28, 45

Rezzori, Gregor von 1914- .... CLC 25

Rhys, Jean
  1890-1979 ...... CLC 2, 4, 6, 14, 19, 51
  See also CA 25-28R; obituary CA 85-88;
    DLB 36

Ribeiro, Darcy 1922- .... CLC 34
  See also CA 33-36R

Ribeiro, Joao Ubaldo (Osorio Pimentel)
  1941- .... CLC 10
  See also CA 81-84

Ribman, Ronald (Burt) 1932- .... CLC 7
  See also CA 21-24R

Rice, Anne 1941- .... CLC 41
  See also CANR 12; CA 65-68

Rice, Elmer 1892-1967 .... CLC 7, 49
  See also CAP 2; CA 21-22;
    obituary CA 25-28R; DLB 4, 7

Rice, Tim 1944- and **Webber, Andrew Lloyd**
  1948- .... CLC 21

Rice, Tim 1944-
  See Rice, Tim and Webber, Andrew Lloyd
  See also CA 103

Rich, Adrienne (Cecile)
  1929- .... CLC 3, 6, 7, 11, 18, 36
  See also CANR 20; CA 9-12R; DLB 5

Richard, Keith 1943-
  See Jagger, Mick and Richard, Keith

Richards, I(vor) A(rmstrong)
  1893-1979 .... CLC 14, 24
  See also CA 41-44R; obituary CA 89-92;
    DLB 27

Richards, Keith 1943-
  See Richard, Keith
  See also CA 107

Richardson, Dorothy (Miller)
  1873-1957 .... TCLC 3
  See also CA 104; DLB 36

Richardson, Ethel 1870-1946
  See Richardson, Henry Handel
  See also CA 105

Richardson, Henry Handel
  1870-1946 .... TCLC 4
  See also Richardson, Ethel

Richardson, Samuel 1689-1761 .... LC 1
  See also DLB 39

Richler, Mordecai
  1931- .... CLC 3, 5, 9, 13, 18, 46
  See also CA 65-68; SATA 27, 44; DLB 53

Richter, Conrad (Michael)
  1890-1968 .... CLC 30
  See also CA 5-8R; obituary CA 25-28R;
    SATA 3; DLB 9

Richter, Johann Paul Friedrich 1763-1825
  See Jean Paul

Riding, Laura 1901- .... CLC 3, 7
  See also Jackson, Laura (Riding)

Riefenstahl, Berta Helene Amalia 1902-
  See Riefenstahl, Leni
  See also CA 108

Riefenstahl, Leni 1902- .... CLC 16
  See also Riefenstahl, Berta Helene Amalia

Rilke, Rainer Maria
  1875-1926 .... TCLC 1, 6, 19
  See also CA 104

Rimbaud, (Jean Nicolas) Arthur
  1854-1891 .... NCLC 4

Ringwood, Gwen(dolyn Margaret) Pharis
  1910-1984 .... CLC 48
  See also obituary CA 112

Rio, Michel 19??- .... CLC 43

Ritsos, Yannis 1909- .... CLC 6, 13, 31
  See also CA 77-80

Rivers, Conrad Kent 1933-1968 ...... CLC 1
  See also CA 85-88; DLB 41

Roa Bastos, Augusto 1917- .... CLC 45

Robbe-Grillet, Alain
  1922- ...... CLC 1, 2, 4, 6, 8, 10, 14, 43
  See also CA 9-12R

Robbins, Harold 1916- .... CLC 5
  See also CA 73-76

Robbins, Thomas Eugene 1936-
  See Robbins, Tom
  See also CA 81-84

Robbins, Tom 1936- .... CLC 9, 32
  See also Robbins, Thomas Eugene
  See also DLB-Y 80

Robbins, Trina 1938- .... CLC 21

Roberts, (Sir) Charles G(eorge) D(ouglas)
  1860-1943 .... TCLC 8
  See also CA 105; SATA 29

Roberts, Kate 1891-1985 .... CLC 15
  See also CA 107; obituary CA 116

Roberts, Keith (John Kingston)
  1935- .... CLC 14
  See also CA 25-28R

Roberts, Kenneth 1885-1957 ...... TCLC 23
  See also CA 109; DLB 9

Roberts, Michele (B.) 1949- .... CLC 48
  See also CA 115

Robinson, Edwin Arlington
  1869-1935 .... TCLC 5
  See also CA 104; DLB 54;
    CDALB 1865-1917

Robinson, Henry Crabb
  1775-1867 .... NCLC 15

Robinson, Jill 1936- .... CLC 10
  See also CA 102

Robinson, Kim Stanley 19??- .... CLC 34

Robinson, Marilynne 1944- .... CLC 25
  See also CA 116

Robinson, Smokey 1940- .... CLC 21

Robinson, William 1940-
  See Robinson, Smokey
  See also CA 116

Robison, Mary 1949- .... CLC 42
  See also CA 113, 116

Roddenberry, Gene 1921- .... CLC 17

Rodgers, Mary 1931- .... CLC 12
  See also CANR 8; CA 49-52; SATA 8

Rodgers, W(illiam) R(obert)
  1909-1969 .... CLC 7
  See also CA 85-88; DLB 20

Rodriguez, Claudio 1934- .... CLC 10

Roethke, Theodore (Huebner)
  1908-1963 ...... CLC 1, 3, 8, 11, 19, 46
  See also CA 81-84; CABS 2; SAAS 1;
    DLB 5; CDALB 1941-1968

Rogers, Sam 1943-
  See Shepard, Sam

Rogers, Will(iam Penn Adair)
  1879-1935 .... TCLC 8
  See also CA 105; DLB 11

Rogin, Gilbert 1929- .... CLC 18
  See also CANR 15; CA 65-68

Rohan, Koda 1867-1947 .... TCLC 22

Rohmer, Eric 1920- .... CLC 16
  See also Scherer, Jean-Marie Maurice

Rohmer, Sax 1883-1959 .... TCLC 28
  See also Ward, Arthur Henry Sarsfield
  See also DLB 70

Roiphe, Anne (Richardson)
  1935- .... CLC 3, 9
  See also CA 89-92; DLB-Y 80

**Rolfe, Frederick (William Serafino Austin
    Lewis Mary)** 1860-1913 ...... TCLC 12
  See also CA 107; DLB 34

Rolland, Romain 1866-1944 .... TCLC 23
  See also CA 118

Rolvaag, O(le) E(dvart)
  1876-1931 .... TCLC 17
  See also CA 117; DLB 9

Romains, Jules 1885-1972 .... CLC 7
  See also CA 85-88

Romero, Jose Ruben 1890-1952 ... TCLC 14
  See also CA 114

Ronsard, Pierre de 1524-1585 .... LC 6

Rooke, Leon 1934- .... CLC 25, 34
  See also CA 25-28R

Roper, William 1498-1578 .... LC 10

Rosa, Joao Guimaraes 1908-1967 ... CLC 23
  See also obituary CA 89-92

Rosen, Richard (Dean) 1949- .... CLC 39
  See also CA 77-80

Rosenberg, Isaac 1890-1918 ...... TCLC 12
  See also CA 107; DLB 20

Rosenblatt, Joe 1933- .... CLC 15
  See also Rosenblatt, Joseph

Rosenblatt, Joseph 1933-
  See Rosenblatt, Joe
  See also CA 89-92

Rosenfeld, Samuel 1896-1963
  See Tzara, Tristan
  See also obituary CA 89-92

Rosenthal, M(acha) L(ouis) 1917- ... CLC 28
  See also CAAS 6; CANR 4; CA 1-4R;
    DLB 5

Ross, (James) Sinclair 1908- .... **CLC 13**
See also CA 73-76

Rossetti, Christina Georgina
1830-1894 .... **NCLC 2**
See also SATA 20; DLB 35

Rossetti, Dante Gabriel
1828-1882 .... **NCLC 4**
See also DLB 35

Rossetti, Gabriel Charles Dante 1828-1882
See Rossetti, Dante Gabriel

Rossner, Judith (Perelman)
1935- .... **CLC 6, 9, 29**
See also CANR 18; CA 17-20R; DLB 6

Rostand, Edmond (Eugene Alexis)
1868-1918 .... **TCLC 6**
See also CA 104

Roth, Henry 1906- .... **CLC 2, 6, 11**
See also CAP 1; CA 11-12; DLB 28

Roth, Joseph 1894-1939 .... **TCLC 33**

Roth, Philip (Milton)
1933- ...... **CLC 1, 2, 3, 4, 6, 9, 15, 22,
31, 47**
See also CANR 1, 22; CA 1-4R; DLB 2, 28;
DLB-Y 82

Rothenberg, Jerome 1931- .... **CLC 6**
See also CANR 1; CA 45-48; DLB 5

Roumain, Jacques 1907-1944 ..... **TCLC 19**
See also CA 117

Rourke, Constance (Mayfield)
1885-1941 .... **TCLC 12**
See also YABC 1; CA 107

Rousseau, Jean-Baptiste 1671-1741 ... **LC 9**

Roussel, Raymond 1877-1933 ..... **TCLC 20**
See also CA 117

Rovit, Earl (Herbert) 1927- .... **CLC 7**
See also CANR 12; CA 5-8R

Rowe, Nicholas 1674-1718 .... **LC 8**

Rowson, Susanna Haswell
1762-1824 .... **NCLC 5**
See also DLB 37

Roy, Gabrielle 1909-1983 ...... **CLC 10, 14**
See also CANR 5; CA 53-56;
obituary CA 110

Rozewicz, Tadeusz 1921- .... **CLC 9, 23**
See also CA 108

Ruark, Gibbons 1941- .... **CLC 3**
See also CANR 14; CA 33-36R

Rubens, Bernice 192?- .... **CLC 19, 31**
See also CA 25-28R; DLB 14

Rudkin, (James) David 1936- ...... **CLC 14**
See also CA 89-92; DLB 13

Rudnik, Raphael 1933- .... **CLC 7**
See also CA 29-32R

Ruiz, Jose Martinez 1874-1967
See Azorin

Rukeyser, Muriel
1913-1980 .... **CLC 6, 10, 15, 27**
See also CA 5-8R; obituary CA 93-96;
obituary SATA 22; DLB 48

Rule, Jane (Vance) 1931- .... **CLC 27**
See also CANR 12; CA 25-28R; DLB 60

Rulfo, Juan 1918-1986 .... **CLC 8**
See also CA 85-88; obituary CA 118

Runyon, (Alfred) Damon
1880-1946 .... **TCLC 10**
See also CA 107; DLB 11

Rush, Norman 1933- .... **CLC 44**
See also CA 121

Rushdie, (Ahmed) Salman
1947- .... **CLC 23, 31, 55**
See also CA 108, 111

Rushforth, Peter (Scott) 1945- ..... **CLC 19**
See also CA 101

Ruskin, John 1819-1900 .... **TCLC 20**
See also CA 114; SATA 24; DLB 55

Russ, Joanna 1937- .... **CLC 15**
See also CANR 11; CA 25-28R; DLB 8

Russell, George William 1867-1935
See A. E.
See also CA 104

Russell, (Henry) Ken(neth Alfred)
1927- .... **CLC 16**
See also CA 105

Rutherford, Mark 1831-1913 ..... **TCLC 25**
See also DLB 18

Ruyslinck, Ward 1929- .... **CLC 14**

Ryan, Cornelius (John) 1920-1974 ... **CLC 7**
See also CA 69-72; obituary CA 53-56

Rybakov, Anatoli 1911?- .... **CLC 23**

Ryder, Jonathan 1927-
See Ludlum, Robert

Ryga, George 1932- .... **CLC 14**
See also CA 101; DLB 60

**Sévigné, Marquise de Marie de
Rabutin-Chantal** 1626-1696 ..... **LC 11**

Saba, Umberto 1883-1957 .... **TCLC 33**

Sabato, Ernesto 1911- .... **CLC 10, 23**
See also CA 97-100

Sachs, Marilyn (Stickle) 1927- ..... **CLC 35**
See also CLR 2; CANR 13; CA 17-20R;
SAAS 2; SATA 3, 52

Sachs, Nelly 1891-1970 .... **CLC 14**
See also CAP 2; CA 17-18;
obituary CA 25-28R

Sackler, Howard (Oliver)
1929-1982 .... **CLC 14**
See also CA 61-64; obituary CA 108; DLB 7

Sade, Donatien Alphonse Francois, Comte de
1740-1814 .... **NCLC 3**

Sadoff, Ira 1945- .... **CLC 9**
See also CANR 5, 21; CA 53-56

Safire, William 1929- .... **CLC 10**
See also CA 17-20R

Sagan, Carl (Edward) 1934- .... **CLC 30**
See also CANR 11; CA 25-28R

Sagan, Francoise
1935- .... **CLC 3, 6, 9, 17, 36**
See also Quoirez, Francoise

Sahgal, Nayantara (Pandit) 1927- ... **CLC 41**
See also CANR 11; CA 9-12R

Saint, H(arry) F. 1941- .... **CLC 50**

Sainte-Beuve, Charles Augustin
1804-1869 .... **NCLC 5**

Sainte-Marie, Beverly 1941-
See Sainte-Marie, Buffy
See also CA 107

Sainte-Marie, Buffy 1941- .... **CLC 17**
See also Sainte-Marie, Beverly

**Saint-Exupery, Antoine (Jean Baptiste Marie
Roger) de** 1900-1944 ..... **TCLC 2**
See also CLR 10; CA 108; SATA 20;
DLB 72

Saintsbury, George 1845-1933 ..... **TCLC 31**

Sait Faik (Abasiyanik)
1906-1954 .... **TCLC 23**

Saki 1870-1916 .... **TCLC 3**
See also Munro, H(ector) H(ugh)

Salama, Hannu 1936- .... **CLC 18**

Salamanca, J(ack) R(ichard)
1922- .... **CLC 4, 15**
See also CA 25-28R

Salinas, Pedro 1891-1951 .... **TCLC 17**
See also CA 117

Salinger, J(erome) D(avid)
1919- .... **CLC 1, 3, 8, 12; SSC 2**
See also CA 5-8R; DLB 2;
CDALB 1941-1968

Salter, James 1925- .... **CLC 7**
See also CA 73-76

Saltus, Edgar (Evertson)
1855-1921 .... **TCLC 8**
See also CA 105

Saltykov, Mikhail Evgrafovich
1826-1889 .... **NCLC 16**

Samarakis, Antonis 1919- .... **CLC 5**
See also CA 25-28R

Sanchez, Luis Rafael 1936- .... **CLC 23**

Sanchez, Sonia 1934- .... **CLC 5**
See also CA 33-36R; SATA 22; DLB 41

Sand, George 1804-1876 .... **NCLC 2**

Sandburg, Carl (August)
1878-1967 .... **CLC 1, 4, 10, 15, 35**
See also CA 5-8R; obituary CA 25-28R;
SATA 8; DLB 17, 54; CDALB 1865-1917

Sandburg, Charles August 1878-1967
See Sandburg, Carl (August)

Sanders, Lawrence 1920- .... **CLC 41**
See also CA 81-84

Sandoz, Mari (Susette) 1896-1966 .. **CLC 28**
See also CANR 17; CA 1-4R;
obituary CA 25-28R; SATA 5; DLB 9

Saner, Reg(inald Anthony) 1931- .... **CLC 9**
See also CA 65-68

Sannazaro, Jacopo 1456?-1530 .... **LC 8**

Sansom, William 1912-1976 .... **CLC 2, 6**
See also CA 5-8R; obituary CA 65-68

Santiago, Danny 1911- .... **CLC 33**

Santmyer, Helen Hooven
1895-1986 .... **CLC 33**
See also CANR 15; CA 1-4R;
obituary CA 118; DLB-Y 84

Santos, Bienvenido N(uqui) 1911- ... **CLC 22**
See also CANR 19; CA 101

Sappho c. 6th-century B.C.- .... **CMLC 3**

Sarduy, Severo 1937- .... **CLC 6**
See also CA 89-92

Sargeson, Frank 1903-1982 .... **CLC 31**
See also CA 106

Sarmiento, Felix Ruben Garcia 1867-1916
    See also CA 104

Saroyan, William
    1908-1981 . . . . **CLC 1, 8, 10, 29, 34**
    See also CA 5-8R; obituary CA 103;
    SATA 23; obituary SATA 24; DLB 7, 9;
    DLB-Y 81

Sarraute, Nathalie
    1902- . . . . **CLC 1, 2, 4, 8, 10, 31**
    See also CA 9-12R

Sarton, Eleanore Marie 1912-
    See Sarton, (Eleanor) May

Sarton, (Eleanor) May
    1912- . . . . **CLC 4, 14, 49**
    See also CANR 1; CA 1-4R; SATA 36;
    DLB 48; DLB-Y 81

Sartre, Jean-Paul
    1905-1980 . . . **CLC 1, 4, 7, 9, 13, 18, 24,**
                                                44, 50
    See also CANR 21; CA 9-12R;
    obituary CA 97-100; DLB 72

Sassoon, Siegfried (Lorraine)
    1886-1967 . . . . **CLC 36**
    See also CA 104; obituary CA 25-28R;
    DLB 20

Saul, John (W. III) 1942- . . . . . . **CLC 46**
    See also CANR 16; CA 81-84

Saura, Carlos 1932- . . . . **CLC 20**
    See also CA 114

Sauser-Hall, Frederic-Louis 1887-1961
    See Cendrars, Blaise
    See also CA 102; obituary CA 93-96

Savage, Thomas 1915- . . . . **CLC 40**

Savan, Glenn 19??- . . . . **CLC 50**

Sayers, Dorothy L(eigh)
    1893-1957 . . . . **TCLC 2, 15**
    See also CA 104, 119; DLB 10, 36

Sayers, Valerie 19??- . . . . **CLC 50**

Sayles, John (Thomas)
    1950- . . . . **CLC 7, 10, 14**
    See also CA 57-60; DLB 44

Scammell, Michael 19??- . . . . **CLC 34**

Scannell, Vernon 1922- . . . . **CLC 49**
    See also CANR 8; CA 5-8R; DLB 27

Schaeffer, Susan Fromberg
    1941- . . . . **CLC 6, 11, 22**
    See also CANR 18; CA 49-52; SATA 22;
    DLB 28

Schell, Jonathan 1943- . . . . **CLC 35**
    See also CANR 12; CA 73-76

Scherer, Jean-Marie Maurice 1920-
    See Rohmer, Eric
    See also CA 110

Schevill, James (Erwin) 1920- . . . . . . **CLC 7**
    See also CA 5-8R

Schisgal, Murray (Joseph) 1926- . . . . . **CLC 6**
    See also CA 21-24R

Schlee, Ann 1934- . . . . **CLC 35**
    See also CA 101; SATA 36, 44

Schlegel, August Wilhelm von
    1767-1845 . . . . **NCLC 15**

Schlegel, Johann Elias (von)
    1719?-1749 . . . . **LC 5**

Schmitz, Ettore 1861-1928
    See Svevo, Italo
    See also CA 104

Schnackenberg, Gjertrud 1953- . . . . . **CLC 40**
    See also CA 116

Schneider, Leonard Alfred 1925-1966
    See Bruce, Lenny
    See also CA 89-92

Schnitzler, Arthur 1862-1931 . . . . . . **TCLC 4**
    See also CA 104

Schorer, Mark 1908-1977 . . . . **CLC 9**
    See also CANR 7; CA 5-8R;
    obituary CA 73-76

Schrader, Paul (Joseph) 1946- . . . . . . **CLC 26**
    See also CA 37-40R; DLB 44

**Schreiner (Cronwright), Olive (Emilie
    Albertina)** 1855-1920 . . . . **TCLC 9**
    See also CA 105; DLB 18

Schulberg, Budd (Wilson)
    1914- . . . . **CLC 7, 48**
    See also CANR 19; CA 25-28R; DLB 6, 26,
    28; DLB-Y 81

Schulz, Bruno 1892-1942 . . . . **TCLC 5**
    See also CA 115

Schulz, Charles M(onroe) 1922- . . . . **CLC 12**
    See also CANR 6; CA 9-12R; SATA 10

Schuyler, James (Marcus)
    1923- . . . . **CLC 5, 23**
    See also CA 101; DLB 5

Schwartz, Delmore
    1913-1966 . . . . **CLC 2, 4, 10, 45**
    See also CAP 2; CA 17-18;
    obituary CA 25-28R; DLB 28, 48

Schwartz, Lynne Sharon 1939- . . . . . **CLC 31**
    See also CA 103

Schwarz-Bart, Andre 1928- . . . . **CLC 2, 4**
    See also CA 89-92

Schwarz-Bart, Simone 1938- . . . . **CLC 7**
    See also CA 97-100

Schwob, (Mayer Andre) Marcel
    1867-1905 . . . . **TCLC 20**
    See also CA 117

Sciascia, Leonardo 1921- . . . . . . **CLC 8, 9, 41**
    See also CA 85-88

Scoppettone, Sandra 1936- . . . . **CLC 26**
    See also CA 5-8R; SATA 9

Scorsese, Martin 1942- . . . . **CLC 20**
    See also CA 110, 114

Scotland, Jay 1932-
    See Jakes, John (William)

Scott, Duncan Campbell
    1862-1947 . . . . **TCLC 6**
    See also CA 104

Scott, Evelyn 1893-1963 . . . . **CLC 43**
    See also CA 104; obituary CA 112; DLB 9,
    48

Scott, F(rancis) R(eginald)
    1899-1985 . . . . **CLC 22**
    See also CA 101; obituary CA 114

Scott, Joanna 19??- . . . . **CLC 50**

Scott, Paul (Mark) 1920-1978 . . . . . . **CLC 9**
    See also CA 81-84; obituary CA 77-80;
    DLB 14

Scott, Sir Walter 1771-1832 . . . . . **NCLC 15**
    See also YABC 2

Scribe, (Augustin) Eugene
    1791-1861 . . . . **NCLC 16**

Scudery, Madeleine de 1607-1701 . . . . . **LC 2**

Sealy, I. Allan 1951- . . . . **CLC 55**

Seare, Nicholas 1925-
    See Trevanian
    See also Whitaker, Rodney

Sebestyen, Igen 1924-
    See Sebestyen, Ouida

Sebestyen, Ouida 1924- . . . . **CLC 30**
    See also CA 107; SATA 39

Sedgwick, Catharine Maria
    1789-1867 . . . . **NCLC 19**
    See also DLB 1

Seelye, John 1931- . . . . **CLC 7**
    See also CA 97-100

Seferiades, Giorgos Stylianou 1900-1971
    See Seferis, George
    See also CANR 5; CA 5-8R;
    obituary CA 33-36R

Seferis, George 1900-1971 . . . . **CLC 5, 11**
    See also Seferiades, Giorgos Stylianou

Segal, Erich (Wolf) 1937- . . . . **CLC 3, 10**
    See also CANR 20; CA 25-28R; DLB-Y 86

Seger, Bob 1945- . . . . **CLC 35**

Seger, Robert Clark 1945-
    See Seger, Bob

Seghers, Anna 1900-1983 . . . . **CLC 7**
    See also Radvanyi, Netty Reiling
    See also DLB 69

Seidel, Frederick (Lewis) 1936- . . . . . **CLC 18**
    See also CANR 8; CA 13-16R; DLB-Y 84

Seifert, Jaroslav 1901-1986 . . . . . **CLC 34, 44**

Selby, Hubert, Jr. 1928- . . . . . **CLC 1, 2, 4, 8**
    See also CA 13-16R; DLB 2

Senacour, Etienne Pivert de
    1770-1846 . . . . **NCLC 16**

Sender, Ramon (Jose) 1902-1982 . . . . **CLC 8**
    See also CANR 8; CA 5-8R;
    obituary CA 105

Senghor, Léopold Sédar 1906- . . . . . . **CLC 54**
    See also CA 116

Serling, (Edward) Rod(man)
    1924-1975 . . . . **CLC 30**
    See also CA 65-68; obituary CA 57-60;
    DLB 26

Serpieres 1907-
    See Guillevic, (Eugene)

Service, Robert W(illiam)
    1874-1958 . . . . **TCLC 15**
    See also CA 115; SATA 20

Seth, Vikram 1952- . . . . **CLC 43**

Seton, Cynthia Propper
    1926-1982 . . . . **CLC 27**
    See also CANR 7; CA 5-8R;
    obituary CA 108

Seton, Ernest (Evan) Thompson
    1860-1946 . . . . **TCLC 31**
    See also CA 109; SATA 18

Settle, Mary Lee 1918- . . . . **CLC 19**
    See also CAAS 1; CA 89-92; DLB 6

Sévigné, Marquise de Marie de
 Rabutin-Chantal 1626-1696..... LC 11

Sexton, Anne (Harvey)
 1928-1974 ...... CLC 2, 4, 6, 8, 10, 15
 See also CANR 3; CA 1-4R;
  obituary CA 53-56; CABS 2; SATA 10;
 DLB 5; CDALB 1941-1968

Shaara, Michael (Joseph) 1929- .... CLC 15
 See also CA 102; DLB-Y 83

Shackleton, C. C. 1925-
 See Aldiss, Brian W(ilson)

Shacochis, Bob 1951-............. CLC 39
 See also CA 119

Shaffer, Anthony 1926- .... CLC 19
 See also CA 116; DLB 13

Shaffer, Peter (Levin)
 1926-.............. CLC 5, 14, 18, 37
 See also CA 25-28R; DLB 13

Shalamov, Varlam (Tikhonovich)
 1907?-1982.................. CLC 18
 See also obituary CA 105

Shamlu, Ahmad 1925- .... CLC 10

Shammas, Anton 1951-........... CLC 55

Shange, Ntozake 1948-....... CLC 8, 25, 38
 See also CA 85-88; DLB 38

Shapcott, Thomas W(illiam) 1935- .. CLC 38
 See also CA 69-72

Shapiro, Karl (Jay) 1913- ..... CLC 4, 8, 15
 See also CAAS 6; CANR 1; CA 1-4R;
 DLB 48

Sharpe, Tom 1928-.............. CLC 36
 See also CA 114; DLB 14

Shaw, (George) Bernard
 1856-1950 .... TCLC 3, 9, 21
 See also CA 104, 109; DLB 10, 57

Shaw, Henry Wheeler
 1818-1885 .... NCLC 15
 See also DLB 11

Shaw, Irwin 1913-1984....... CLC 7, 23, 34
 See also CANR 21; CA 13-16R;
  obituary CA 112; DLB 6; DLB-Y 84;
 CDALB 1941-1968

Shaw, Robert 1927-1978 .... CLC 5
 See also CANR 4; CA 1-4R;
  obituary CA 81-84; DLB 13, 14

Shawn, Wallace 1943- .... CLC 41
 See also CA 112

Sheed, Wilfrid (John Joseph)
 1930-............. CLC 2, 4, 10
 See also CA 65-68; DLB 6

Sheffey, Asa 1913-1980
 See Hayden, Robert (Earl)

Sheldon, Alice (Hastings) B(radley)
 1915-1987
 See Tiptree, James, Jr.
 See also CA 108; obituary CA 122

Shelley, Mary Wollstonecraft Godwin
 1797-1851 .... NCLC 14
 See also SATA 29

Shelley, Percy Bysshe
 1792-1822 .... NCLC 18

Shepard, Jim 19??-.............. CLC 36

Shepard, Lucius 19??-............. CLC 34

Shepard, Sam
 1943- .... CLC 4, 6, 17, 34, 41, 44
 See also CANR 22; CA 69-72; DLB 7

Shepherd, Michael 1927-
 See Ludlum, Robert

Sherburne, Zoa (Morin) 1912-...... CLC 30
 See also CANR 3; CA 1-4R; SATA 3

Sheridan, Frances 1724-1766........ LC 7
 See also DLB 39

Sheridan, Richard Brinsley
 1751-1816 .... NCLC 5

Sherman, Jonathan Marc 1970?-.... CLC 55

Sherman, Martin 19??-............ CLC 19
 See also CA 116

Sherwin, Judith Johnson 1936-... CLC 7, 15
 See also CA 25-28R

Sherwood, Robert E(mmet)
 1896-1955 .... TCLC 3
 See also CA 104; DLB 7, 26

Shiel, M(atthew) P(hipps)
 1865-1947 .... TCLC 8
 See also CA 106

Shiga, Naoya 1883-1971........... CLC 33
 See also CA 101; obituary CA 33-36R

Shimazaki, Haruki 1872-1943
 See Shimazaki, Toson
 See also CA 105

Shimazaki, Toson 1872-1943...... TCLC 5
 See also Shimazaki, Haruki

Sholokhov, Mikhail (Aleksandrovich)
 1905-1984 .... CLC 7, 15
 See also CA 101; obituary CA 112;
 SATA 36

Shreve, Susan Richards 1939-...... CLC 23
 See also CAAS 5; CANR 5; CA 49-52;
 SATA 41, 46

Shulman, Alix Kates 1932- ...... CLC 2, 10
 See also CA 29-32R; SATA 7

Shuster, Joe 1914-
 See Siegel, Jerome and Shuster, Joe

Shute (Norway), Nevil 1899-1960... CLC 30
 See also Norway, Nevil Shute

Shuttle, Penelope (Diane) 1947- ..... CLC 7
 See also CA 93-96; DLB 14, 40

Siegel, Jerome 1914- and Shuster, Joe
 1914- .... CLC 21

Siegel, Jerome 1914-
 See Siegel, Jerome and Shuster, Joe
 See also CA 116

Sienkiewicz, Henryk (Adam Aleksander Pius)
 1846-1916 .... TCLC 3
 See also CA 104

Sigal, Clancy 1926-................ CLC 7
 See also CA 1-4R

Siguenza y Gongora, Carlos de
 1645-1700 .... LC 8

Sigurjonsson, Johann 1880-1919... TCLC 27

Silkin, Jon 1930- .... CLC 2, 6, 43
 See also CAAS 5; CA 5-8R; DLB 27

Silko, Leslie Marmon 1948- .... CLC 23
 See also CA 115, 122

Sillanpaa, Franz Eemil 1888-1964... CLC 19
 See also obituary CA 93-96

Sillitoe, Alan 1928-..... CLC 1, 3, 6, 10, 19
 See also CAAS 2; CANR 8; CA 9-12R;
 DLB 14

Silone, Ignazio 1900-1978 .... CLC 4
 See also CAP 2; CA 25-28;
  obituary CA 81-84

Silver, Joan Micklin 1935- .... CLC 20
 See also CA 114

Silverberg, Robert 1935- .... CLC 7
 See also CAAS 3; CANR 1, 20; CA 1-4R;
 SATA 13; DLB 8

Silverstein, Alvin 1933- and Silverstein,
 Virginia B(arbara Opshelor)
 1937-..................... CLC 17

Silverstein, Alvin 1933-
 See Silverstein, Alvinand Silverstein,
 Virginia B(arbara Opshelor)
 See also CANR 2; CA 49-52; SATA 8

Silverstein, Virginia B(arbara Opshelor)
 1937-
 See Silverstein, Alvin and Silverstein,
 Virginia B(arbara Opshelor)
 See also CANR 2; CA 49-52; SATA 8

Simak, Clifford D(onald)
 1904-1988 .... CLC 1, 55
 See also CANR 1; CA 1-4R;
  obituary CA 125; DLB 8

Simenon, Georges (Jacques Christian)
 1903- .... CLC 1, 2, 3, 8, 18, 47
 See also CA 85-88; DLB 72

Simenon, Paul 1956?-
 See The Clash

Simic, Charles 1938-....... CLC 6, 9, 22, 49
 See also CAAS 4; CANR 12; CA 29-32R

Simmons, Dan 1948-............. CLC 44

Simmons, James (Stewart Alexander)
 1933-..................... CLC 43
 See also CA 105; DLB 40

Simms, William Gilmore
 1806-1870 .... NCLC 3
 See also DLB 3, 30

Simon, Carly 1945-............... CLC 26
 See also CA 105

Simon, Claude (Henri Eugene)
 1913-................ CLC 4, 9, 15, 39
 See also CA 89-92

Simon, (Marvin) Neil
 1927-.............. CLC 6, 11, 31, 39
 See also CA 21-24R; DLB 7

Simon, Paul 1941- .... CLC 17
 See also CA 116

Simonon, Paul 1956?-
 See The Clash

Simpson, Louis (Aston Marantz)
 1923-...........CLC 4, 7, 9, 32
 See also CAAS 4; CANR 1; CA 1-4R;
 DLB 5

Simpson, Mona (Elizabeth) 1957-... CLC 44

Simpson, N(orman) F(rederick)
 1919- .... CLC 29
 See also CA 11-14R; DLB 13

Sinclair, Andrew (Annandale)
 1935-..................... CLC 2, 14
 See also CAAS 5; CANR 14; CA 9-12R;
 DLB 14

Sinclair, Mary Amelia St. Clair 1865?-1946
See Sinclair, May
See also CA 104

Sinclair, May 1865?-1946 ...... TCLC 3, 11
See also Sinclair, Mary Amelia St. Clair
See also DLB 36

Sinclair, Upton (Beall)
1878-1968 .... CLC 1, 11, 15
See also CANR 7; CA 5-8R;
obituary CA 25-28R; SATA 9; DLB 9

Singer, Isaac Bashevis
1904- .... CLC 1, 3, 6, 9, 11, 15, 23, 38;
SSC 3
See also CLR 1; CANR 1; CA 1-4R;
SATA 3, 27; DLB 6, 28, 52;
CDALB 1941-1968

Singer, Israel Joshua 1893-1944 ... TCLC 33

Singh, Khushwant 1915- .... CLC 11
See also CANR 6; CA 9-12R

Sinyavsky, Andrei (Donatevich)
1925- .... CLC 8
See also CA 85-88

Sirin, V.
See Nabokov, Vladimir (Vladimirovich)

Sissman, L(ouis) E(dward)
1928-1976 .... CLC 9, 18
See also CANR 13; CA 21-24R;
obituary CA 65-68; DLB 5

Sisson, C(harles) H(ubert) 1914- ..... CLC 8
See also CAAS 3; CANR 3; CA 1-4R;
DLB 27

Sitwell, (Dame) Edith 1887-1964 ... CLC 2, 9
See also CA 9-12R; DLB 20

Sjoewall, Maj 1935-
See Wahloo, Per
See also CA 65-68

Sjowall, Maj 1935-
See Wahloo, Per

Skelton, Robin 1925- .... CLC 13
See also CAAS 5; CA 5-8R; DLB 27, 53

Skolimowski, Jerzy 1938- .... CLC 20

Skolimowski, Yurek 1938-
See Skolimowski, Jerzy

Skram, Amalie (Bertha)
1847-1905 .... TCLC 25

Skrine, Mary Nesta 1904-
See Keane, Molly

Skvorecky, Josef (Vaclav)
1924- .... CLC 15, 39
See also CAAS 1; CANR 10; CA 61-64

Slade, Bernard 1930- .... CLC 11, 46
See also Newbound, Bernard Slade
See also DLB 53

Slaughter, Frank G(ill) 1908- ...... CLC 29
See also CANR 5; CA 5-8R

Slavitt, David (R.) 1935- .... CLC 5, 14
See also CAAS 3; CA 21-24R; DLB 5, 6

Slesinger, Tess 1905-1945 .... TCLC 10
See also CA 107

Slessor, Kenneth 1901-1971 .... CLC 14
See also CA 102; obituary CA 89-92

Slowacki, Juliusz 1809-1849 ..... NCLC 15

Smart, Christopher 1722-1771 .... LC 3

Smart, Elizabeth 1913-1986 .... CLC 54
See also CA 81-84; obituary CA 118

Smith, A(rthur) J(ames) M(arshall)
1902-1980 .... CLC 15
See also CANR 4; CA 1-4R;
obituary CA 102

Smith, Betty (Wehner) 1896-1972 ... CLC 19
See also CA 5-8R; obituary CA 33-36R;
SATA 6; DLB-Y 82

Smith, Cecil Lewis Troughton 1899-1966
See Forester, C(ecil) S(cott)

Smith, Charlotte (Turner)
1749-1806 .... NCLC 23
See also DLB 39

Smith, Clark Ashton 1893-1961 .... CLC 43

Smith, Dave 1942- .... CLC 22, 42
See also Smith, David (Jeddie)
See also CAAS 7; DLB 5

Smith, David (Jeddie) 1942-
See Smith, Dave
See also CANR 1; CA 49-52

Smith, Florence Margaret 1902-1971
See Smith, Stevie
See also CAP 2; CA 17-18;
obituary CA 29-32R

Smith, John 1580?-1631 .... LC 9
See also DLB 24, 30

Smith, Lee 1944- .... CLC 25
See also CA 114, 119; DLB-Y 83

Smith, Martin Cruz 1942- .... CLC 25
See also CANR 6; CA 85-88

Smith, Martin William 1942-
See Smith, Martin Cruz

Smith, Mary-Ann Tirone 1944- ..... CLC 39
See also CA 118

Smith, Patti 1946- .... CLC 12
See also CA 93-96

Smith, Pauline (Urmson)
1882-1959 .... TCLC 25
See also CA 29-32R; SATA 27

Smith, Sara Mahala Redway 1900-1972
See Benson, Sally

Smith, Stevie 1902-1971 .... CLC 3, 8, 25, 44
See also Smith, Florence Margaret
See also DLB 20

Smith, Wilbur (Addison) 1933- ..... CLC 33
See also CANR 7; CA 13-16R

Smith, William Jay 1918- .... CLC 6
See also CA 5-8R; SATA 2; DLB 5

Smollett, Tobias (George) 1721-1771 .. LC 2
See also DLB 39

Snodgrass, W(illiam) D(e Witt)
1926- .... CLC 2, 6, 10, 18
See also CANR 6; CA 1-4R; DLB 5

Snow, C(harles) P(ercy)
1905-1980 .... CLC 1, 4, 6, 9, 13, 19
See also CA 5-8R; obituary CA 101;
DLB 15

Snyder, Gary (Sherman)
1930- .... CLC 1, 2, 5, 9, 32
See also CA 17-20R; DLB 5, 16

Snyder, Zilpha Keatley 1927- ...... CLC 17
See also CA 9-12R; SAAS 2; SATA 1, 28

Sodergran, Edith 1892-1923 .... TCLC 31

Sokolov, Raymond 1941- .... CLC 7
See also CA 85-88

Sologub, Fyodor 1863-1927 .... TCLC 9
See also Teternikov, Fyodor Kuzmich

Solomos, Dionysios 1798-1857 ... NCLC 15

Solwoska, Mara 1929-
See French, Marilyn

Solzhenitsyn, Aleksandr I(sayevich)
1918- ... CLC 1, 2, 4, 7, 9, 10, 18, 26, 34
See also CA 69-72

Somers, Jane 1919-
See Lessing, Doris (May)

Sommer, Scott 1951- .... CLC 25
See also CA 106

Sondheim, Stephen (Joshua)
1930- .... CLC 30, 39
See also CA 103

Sontag, Susan 1933- ... CLC 1, 2, 10, 13, 31
See also CA 17-20R; DLB 2

Sophocles c. 496?-c. 406? .... CMLC 2

Sorrentino, Gilbert
1929- .... CLC 3, 7, 14, 22, 40
See also CANR 14; CA 77-80; DLB 5;
DLB-Y 80

Soto, Gary 1952- .... CLC 32
See also CA 119

Souster, (Holmes) Raymond
1921- .... CLC 5, 14
See also CANR 13; CA 13-16R

Southern, Terry 1926- .... CLC 7
See also CANR 1; CA 1-4R; DLB 2

Southey, Robert 1774-1843 .... NCLC 8

Soyinka, Akinwande Oluwole 1934-
See Soyinka, Wole

Soyinka, Wole 1934- .. CLC 3, 5, 14, 36, 44
See also CA 13-16R; DLB-Y 86

Spackman, W(illiam) M(ode)
1905- .... CLC 46
See also CA 81-84

Spacks, Barry 1931- .... CLC 14
See also CA 29-32R

Spanidou, Irini 1946- .... CLC 44

Spark, Muriel (Sarah)
1918- .... CLC 2, 3, 5, 8, 13, 18, 40
See also CANR 12; CA 5-8R; DLB 15

Spencer, Elizabeth 1921- .... CLC 22
See also CA 13-16R; SATA 14; DLB 6

Spencer, Scott 1945- .... CLC 30
See also CA 113; DLB-Y 86

Spender, Stephen (Harold)
1909- .... CLC 1, 2, 5, 10, 41
See also CA 9-12R; DLB 20

Spengler, Oswald 1880-1936 ...... TCLC 25
See also CA 118

Spenser, Edmund 1552?-1599 .... LC 5

Spicer, Jack 1925-1965 .... CLC 8, 18
See also CA 85-88; DLB 5, 16

Spielberg, Peter 1929- .... CLC 6
See also CANR 4; CA 5-8R; DLB-Y 81

Spielberg, Steven 1947- .... CLC 20
See also CA 77-80; SATA 32

Spillane, Frank Morrison   1918-
    See Spillane, Mickey
    See also CA 25-28R

Spillane, Mickey   1918- .... **CLC 3, 13**
    See also Spillane, Frank Morrison

Spinoza, Benedictus de   1632-1677 .... **LC 9**

Spinrad, Norman (Richard)   1940-... **CLC 46**
    See also CANR 20; CA 37-40R; DLB 8

Spitteler, Carl (Friedrich Georg)
    1845-1924 .... **TCLC 12**
    See also CA 109

Spivack, Kathleen (Romola Drucker)
    1938- .... **CLC 6**
    See also CA 49-52

Spoto, Donald   1941-.............. **CLC 39**
    See also CANR 11; CA 65-68

Springsteen, Bruce   1949-......... **CLC 17**
    See also CA 111

Spurling, Hilary   1940-............ **CLC 34**
    See also CA 104

Squires, (James) Radcliffe   1917-.... **CLC 51**
    See also CANR 6, 21; CA 1-4R

Stael-Holstein, Anne Louise Germaine Necker,
    Baronne de   1766-1817 .... **NCLC 3**

Stafford, Jean   1915-1979 ..... **CLC 4, 7, 19**
    See also CANR 3; CA 1-4R;
    obituary CA 85-88; obituary SATA 22;
    DLB 2

Stafford, William (Edgar)
    1914- .... **CLC 4, 7, 29**
    See also CAAS 3; CANR 5, 22; CA 5-8R;
    DLB 5

Stannard, Martin   1947-.......... **CLC 44**

Stanton, Maura   1946- .... **CLC 9**
    See also CANR 15; CA 89-92

Stapledon, (William) Olaf
    1886-1950 .... **TCLC 22**
    See also CA 111; DLB 15

Stark, Richard   1933-
    See Westlake, Donald E(dwin)

Stead, Christina (Ellen)
    1902-1983 .... **CLC 2, 5, 8, 32**
    See also CA 13-16R; obituary CA 109

Steele, Timothy (Reid)   1948-....... **CLC 45**
    See also CANR 16; CA 93-96

Steffens, (Joseph) Lincoln
    1866-1936 .... **TCLC 20**
    See also CA 117; SAAS 1

Stegner, Wallace (Earle)   1909-... **CLC 9, 49**
    See also CANR 1, 21; CA 1-4R; DLB 9

Stein, Gertrude   1874-1946... **TCLC 1, 6, 28**
    See also CA 104; DLB 4, 54

Steinbeck, John (Ernst)
    1902-1968 ... **CLC 1, 5, 9, 13, 21, 34, 45**
    See also CANR 1; CA 1-4R;
    obituary CA 25-28R; SATA 9; DLB 7, 9;
    DLB-DS 2

Steiner, George   1929-............ **CLC 24**
    See also CA 73-76

Steiner, Rudolf(us Josephus Laurentius)
    1861-1925 .... **TCLC 13**
    See also CA 107

Stendhal   1783-1842............ **NCLC 23**

Stephen, Leslie   1832-1904 .... **TCLC 23**
    See also CANR 9; CA 21-24R; DLB 57

Stephens, James   1882?-1950 .... **TCLC 4**
    See also CA 104; DLB 19

Stephens, Reed
    See Donaldson, Stephen R.

Steptoe, Lydia   1892-1982
    See Barnes, Djuna

Sterling, George   1869-1926 ...... **TCLC 20**
    See also CA 117; DLB 54

Stern, Gerald   1925- .... **CLC 40**
    See also CA 81-84

Stern, Richard G(ustave)   1928-... **CLC 4, 39**
    See also CANR 1; CA 1-4R

Sternberg, Jonas   1894-1969
    See Sternberg, Josef von

Sternberg, Josef von   1894-1969..... **CLC 20**
    See also CA 81-84

Sterne, Laurence   1713-1768.......... **LC 2**
    See also DLB 39

Sternheim, (William Adolf) Carl
    1878-1942 .... **TCLC 8**
    See also CA 105

Stevens, Mark   19??-.............. **CLC 34**

Stevens, Wallace   1879-1955..... **TCLC 3, 12**
    See also CA 104; DLB 54

Stevenson, Anne (Katharine)
    1933- .... **CLC 7, 33**
    See also Elvin, Anne Katharine Stevenson
    See also CANR 9; CA 17-18R; DLB 40

Stevenson, Robert Louis
    1850-1894 .... **NCLC 5, 14**
    See also CLR 10, 11; YABC 2; DLB 18, 57

Stewart, J(ohn) I(nnes) M(ackintosh)
    1906- .... **CLC 7, 14, 32**
    See also CAAS 3; CA 85-88

Stewart, Mary (Florence Elinor)
    1916- .... **CLC 7, 35**
    See also CANR 1; CA 1-4R; SATA 12

Stewart, Will   1908-
    See Williamson, Jack

Still, James   1906-............... **CLC 49**
    See also CANR 10; CA 65-68; SATA 29;
    DLB 9

Sting   1951-
    See The Police

Stitt, Milan   1941-............... **CLC 29**
    See also CA 69-72

Stoker, Abraham
    See Stoker, Bram
    See also CA 105

Stoker, Bram   1847-1912 .... **TCLC 8**
    See also Stoker, Abraham
    See also SATA 29; DLB 36, 70

Stolz, Mary (Slattery)   1920-....... **CLC 12**
    See also CANR 13; CA 5-8R; SAAS 3;
    SATA 10

Stone, Irving   1903-................ **CLC 7**
    See also CAAS 3; CANR 1; CA 1-4R;
    SATA 3

Stone, Robert (Anthony)
    1937?- .... **CLC 5, 23, 42**
    See also CA 85-88

Stoppard, Tom
    1937- ...... **CLC 1, 3, 4, 5, 8, 15, 29, 34**
    See also CA 81-84; DLB 13; DLB-Y 85

Storey, David (Malcolm)
    1933- ....**CLC 2, 4, 5, 8**
    See also CA 81-84; DLB 13, 14

Storm, Hyemeyohsts   1935- .... **CLC 3**
    See also CA 81-84

Storm, (Hans) Theodor (Woldsen)
    1817-1888 .... **NCLC 1**

Storni, Alfonsina   1892-1938 .... **TCLC 5**
    See also CA 104

Stout, Rex (Todhunter)   1886-1975 ... **CLC 3**
    See also CA 61-64

Stow, (Julian) Randolph   1935- .. **CLC 23, 48**
    See also CA 13-16R

Stowe, Harriet (Elizabeth) Beecher
    1811-1896 .... **NCLC 3**
    See also YABC 1; DLB 1, 12, 42;
    CDALB 1865-1917

Strachey, (Giles) Lytton
    1880-1932 .... **TCLC 12**
    See also CA 110

Strand, Mark   1934-......... **CLC 6, 18, 41**
    See also CA 21-24R; SATA 41; DLB 5

Straub, Peter (Francis)   1943-...... **CLC 28**
    See also CA 85-88; DLB-Y 84

Strauss, Botho   1944- .... **CLC 22**

Straussler, Tomas   1937-
    See Stoppard, Tom

Streatfeild, (Mary) Noel   1897- ..... **CLC 21**
    See also CA 81-84; obituary CA 120;
    SATA 20, 48

Stribling, T(homas) S(igismund)
    1881-1965 .... **CLC 23**
    See also obituary CA 107; DLB 9

Strindberg, (Johan) August
    1849-1912 .... **TCLC 1, 8, 21**
    See also CA 104

Strugatskii, Arkadii (Natanovich)   1925- and
    Strugatskii, Boris(Natanovich)
    1933- .... **CLC 27**

Strugatskii, Arkadii (Natanovich)   1925-
    See Strugatskii, Arkadii (Natanovich) and
        Strugatskii, Boris (Natanovich)
    See also CA 106

Strugatskii, Boris (Natanovich)   1933-
    See Strugatskii, Arkadii (Natanovich) and
        Strugatskii, Boris (Natanovich)
    See also CA 106

Strugatskii, Boris (Natanovich)   1933- and
    Strugatskii, Arkadii (Natanovich)   1925-
    See Strugatskii, Arkadii (Natanovich) and
        Strugatskii, Boris (Natanovich)

Strummer, Joe   1953?-
    See The Clash

Stuart, (Hilton) Jesse
    1906-1984 .... **CLC 1, 8, 11, 14, 34**
    See also CA 5-8R; obituary CA 112;
    SATA 2; obituary SATA 36; DLB 9, 48;
    DLB-Y 84

Sturgeon, Theodore (Hamilton)
    1918-1985 .... **CLC 22, 39**
    See also CA 81-84; obituary CA 116;
    DLB 8; DLB-Y 85

Styron, William 1925- .. **CLC 1, 3, 5, 11, 15**
See also CANR 6; CA 5-8R; DLB 2;
DLB-Y 80

Sudermann, Hermann 1857-1928 .. **TCLC 15**
See also CA 107

Sue, Eugene 1804-1857 .... **NCLC 1**

Sukenick, Ronald 1932-..... **CLC 3, 4, 6, 48**
See also CA 25-28R; DLB-Y 81

Suknaski, Andrew 1942- .... **CLC 19**
See also CA 101; DLB 53

Sully-Prudhomme, Rene
1839-1907 .... **TCLC 31**

Su Man-shu 1884-1918........... **TCLC 24**

Summers, Andrew James 1942-
See The Police

Summers, Andy 1942-
See The Police

Summers, Hollis (Spurgeon, Jr.)
1916- .... **CLC 10**
See also CANR 3; CA 5-8R; DLB 6

Summers, (Alphonsus Joseph-Mary Augustus)
Montague 1880-1948 .... **TCLC 16**

Sumner, Gordon Matthew 1951-
See The Police

Surtees, Robert Smith
1805-1864 .... **NCLC 14**
See also DLB 21

Susann, Jacqueline 1921-1974....... **CLC 3**
See also CA 65-68; obituary CA 53-56

Suskind, Patrick 1949-............ **CLC 44**

Sutcliff, Rosemary 1920- .... **CLC 26**
See also CLR 1; CA 5-8R; SATA 6, 44

Sutro, Alfred 1863-1933........... **TCLC 6**
See also CA 105; DLB 10

Sutton, Henry 1935-
See Slavitt, David (R.)

Svevo, Italo 1861-1928............ **TCLC 2**
See also Schmitz, Ettore

Swados, Elizabeth 1951- .... **CLC 12**
See also CA 97-100

Swados, Harvey 1920-1972 .... **CLC 5**
See also CANR 6; CA 5-8R;
obituary CA 37-40R; DLB 2

Swarthout, Glendon (Fred) 1918- ... **CLC 35**
See also CANR 1; CA 1-4R; SATA 26

Swenson, May 1919- .... **CLC 4, 14**
See also CA 5-8R; SATA 15; DLB 5

Swift, Graham 1949- .... **CLC 41**
See also CA 117

Swift, Jonathan 1667-1745........... **LC 1**
See also SATA 19; DLB 39

Swinburne, Algernon Charles
1837-1909 .... **TCLC 8**
See also CA 105; DLB 35, 57

Swinfen, Ann 19??-............. **CLC 34**

Swinnerton, Frank (Arthur)
1884-1982 .... **CLC 31**
See also obituary CA 108; DLB 34

Symons, Arthur (William)
1865-1945 .... **TCLC 11**
See also CA 107; DLB 19, 57

Symons, Julian (Gustave)
1912- .... **CLC 2, 14, 32**
See also CAAS 3; CANR 3; CA 49-52

Synge, (Edmund) John Millington
1871-1909 .... **TCLC 6**
See also CA 104; DLB 10, 19

Syruc, J. 1911-
See Milosz, Czeslaw

Szirtes, George 1948-............. **CLC 46**
See also CA 109

Tabori, George 1914-............. **CLC 19**
See also CANR 4; CA 49-52

Tagore, (Sir) Rabindranath
1861-1941 .... **TCLC 3**
See also Thakura, Ravindranatha

Taine, Hippolyte Adolphe
1828-1893 .... **NCLC 15**

Talese, Gaetano 1932-
See Talese, Gay

Talese, Gay 1932-................ **CLC 37**
See also CANR 9; CA 1-4R

Tallent, Elizabeth (Ann) 1954- ..... **CLC 45**
See also CA 117

Tally, Ted 1952-.................. **CLC 42**
See also CA 120

Tamayo y Baus, Manuel
1829-1898 .... **NCLC 1**

Tammsaare, A(nton) H(ansen)
1878-1940 .... **TCLC 27**

Tanizaki, Jun'ichiro
1886-1965 .... **CLC 8, 14, 28**
See also CA 93-96; obituary CA 25-28R

Tarkington, (Newton) Booth
1869-1946 .... **TCLC 9**
See also CA 110; SATA 17; DLB 9

Tasso, Torquato 1544-1595 .... **LC 5**

Tate, (John Orley) Allen
1899-1979 .... **CLC 2, 4, 6, 9, 11, 14, 24**
See also CA 5-8R; obituary CA 85-88;
DLB 4, 45, 63

Tate, James 1943-........... **CLC 2, 6, 25**
See also CA 21-24R; DLB 5

Tavel, Ronald 1940-.............. **CLC 6**
See also CA 21-24R

Taylor, C(ecil) P(hillip) 1929-1981 .. **CLC 27**
See also CA 25-28R; obituary CA 105

Taylor, Edward 1644?-1729........ **LC 11**
See also DLB 24

Taylor, Eleanor Ross 1920-........ **CLC 5**
See also CA 81-84

Taylor, Elizabeth 1912-1975 ... **CLC 2, 4, 29**
See also CANR 9; CA 13-16R; SATA 13

Taylor, Henry (Splawn) 1917-...... **CLC 44**

Taylor, Kamala (Purnaiya) 1924-
See Markandaya, Kamala
See also CA 77-80

Taylor, Mildred D(elois) 1943- ..... **CLC 21**
See also CLR 9; CA 85-88; SATA 15;
DLB 52

Taylor, Peter (Hillsman)
1917- .... **CLC 1, 4, 18, 37, 44, 50**
See also CANR 9; CA 13-16R; DLB-Y 81

Taylor, Robert Lewis 1912-........ **CLC 14**
See also CANR 3; CA 1-4R; SATA 10

Teasdale, Sara 1884-1933......... **TCLC 4**
See also CA 104; SATA 32; DLB 45

Tegner, Esaias 1782-1846.......... **NCLC 2**

Teilhard de Chardin, (Marie Joseph) Pierre
1881-1955 .... **TCLC 9**
See also CA 105

Tennant, Emma 1937-............. **CLC 13**
See also CANR 10; CA 65-68; DLB 14

Teran, Lisa St. Aubin de 19??- ..... **CLC 36**

Terkel, Louis 1912-
See Terkel, Studs
See also CANR 18; CA 57-60

Terkel, Studs 1912- .... **CLC 38**
See also Terkel, Louis

Terry, Megan 1932-.............. **CLC 19**
See also CA 77-80; DLB 7

Tertz, Abram 1925-
See Sinyavsky, Andrei (Donatevich)

Tesich, Steve 1943?-............. **CLC 40**
See also CA 105; DLB-Y 83

Tesich, Stoyan 1943?-
See Tesich, Steve

Teternikov, Fyodor Kuzmich 1863-1927
See Sologub, Fyodor
See also CA 104

Tevis, Walter 1928-1984 .... **CLC 42**
See also CA 113

Tey, Josephine 1897-1952 .... **TCLC 14**
See also Mackintosh, Elizabeth

Thackeray, William Makepeace
1811-1863 .... **NCLC 5, 14**
See also SATA 23; DLB 21, 55

Thakura, Ravindranatha 1861-1941
See Tagore, (Sir) Rabindranath
See also CA 104

Thelwell, Michael (Miles) 1939-.... **CLC 22**
See also CA 101

Theroux, Alexander (Louis)
1939- .... **CLC 2, 25**
See also CANR 20; CA 85-88

Theroux, Paul
1941- .... **CLC 5, 8, 11, 15, 28, 46**
See also CANR 20; CA 33-36R; SATA 44;
DLB 2

Thibault, Jacques Anatole Francois
1844-1924
See France, Anatole
See also CA 106

Thiele, Colin (Milton) 1920- .... **CLC 17**
See also CANR 12; CA 29-32R; SAAS 2;
SATA 14

Thomas, Audrey (Grace)
1935- .... **CLC 7, 13, 37**
See also CA 21-24R; DLB 60

Thomas, D(onald) M(ichael)
1935- .... **CLC 13, 22, 31**
See also CANR 17; CA 61-64; DLB 40

Thomas, Dylan (Marlais)
1914-1953 .... **TCLC 1, 8; SSC 3**
See also CA 104, 120; DLB 13, 20

Thomas, Edward (Philip)
 1878-1917 . . . . TCLC **10**
 See also CA 106; DLB 19

Thomas, John Peter 1928-
 See Thomas, Piri

Thomas, Joyce Carol 1938- . . . . CLC **35**
 See also CA 113, 116; SATA 40; DLB 33

Thomas, Lewis 1913- . . . . CLC **35**
 See also CA 85-88

Thomas, Piri 1928- . . . . CLC **17**
 See also CA 73-76

Thomas, Ross (Elmore) 1926- . . . . . . CLC **39**
 See also CANR 22; CA 33-36R

Thomas, R(onald) S(tuart)
 1913- . . . . CLC **6, 13, 48**
 See also CAAS 4; CA 89-92; DLB 27

Thompson, Ernest 1860-1946
 See Seton, Ernest (Evan) Thompson

Thompson, Francis (Joseph)
 1859-1907 . . . . TCLC **4**
 See also CA 104; DLB 19

Thompson, Hunter S(tockton)
 1939- . . . . CLC **9, 17, 40**
 See also CA 17-20R

Thompson, Judith 1954- . . . . CLC **39**

Thomson, James 1834-1882 . . . . . . NCLC **18**
 See also DLB 35

Thoreau, Henry David 1817-1862 . . NCLC **7**
 See also DLB 1; CDALB 1640-1865

Thurber, James (Grover)
 1894-1961 . . . . CLC **5, 11, 25;** SSC **1**
 See also CANR 17; CA 73-76; SATA 13;
 DLB 4, 11, 22

Thurman, Wallace 1902-1934 . . . . . . TCLC **6**
 See also CA 104; DLB 51

Tieck, (Johann) Ludwig
 1773-1853 . . . . NCLC **5**

Tillinghast, Richard 1940- . . . . CLC **29**
 See also CA 29-32R

Tindall, Gillian 1938- . . . . CLC **7**
 See also CANR 11; CA 21-24R

Tiptree, James, Jr. 1915-1987 . . . CLC **48, 50**
 See also Sheldon, Alice (Hastings) B(radley)
 See also DLB 8

**Tocqueville, Alexis (Charles Henri Maurice
 Clerel, Comte) de** 1805-1859 . . NCLC **7**

Tolkien, J(ohn) R(onald) R(euel)
 1892-1973 . . . . CLC **1, 2, 3, 8, 12, 38**
 See also CAP 2; CA 17-18;
 obituary CA 45-48; SATA 2, 32;
 obituary SATA 24; DLB 15

Toller, Ernst 1893-1939 . . . . TCLC **10**
 See also CA 107

Tolson, Melvin B(eaunorus)
 1900?-1966 . . . . CLC **36**
 See also obituary CA 89-92; DLB 48

Tolstoy, (Count) Alexey Nikolayevich
 1883-1945 . . . . TCLC **18**
 See also CA 107

Tolstoy, (Count) Leo (Lev Nikolaevich)
 1828-1910 . . . . TCLC **4, 11, 17, 28**
 See also CA 104; SATA 26

Tomlin, Lily 1939- . . . . CLC **17**

Tomlin, Mary Jean 1939-
 See Tomlin, Lily

Tomlinson, (Alfred) Charles
 1927- . . . . CLC **2, 4, 6, 13, 45**
 See also CA 5-8R; DLB 40

Toole, John Kennedy 1937-1969 . . . . CLC **19**
 See also CA 104; DLB-Y 81

Toomer, Jean
 1894-1967 . . . . . CLC **1, 4, 13, 22;** SSC **1**
 See also CA 85-88; DLB 45, 51

Torrey, E. Fuller 19??- . . . . CLC **34**

Tournier, Michel 1924- . . . . . . CLC **6, 23, 36**
 See also CANR 3; CA 49-52; SATA 23

Townshend, Peter (Dennis Blandford)
 1945- . . . . CLC **17, 42**
 See also CA 107

Tozzi, Federigo 1883-1920 . . . . TCLC **31**

Trakl, Georg 1887-1914 . . . . TCLC **5**
 See also CA 104

Traven, B. 1890-1969 . . . . CLC **8, 11**
 See also CAP 2; CA 19-20;
 obituary CA 25-28R; DLB 9, 56

Tremain, Rose 1943- . . . . CLC **42**
 See also CA 97-100; DLB 14

Tremblay, Michel 1942- . . . . CLC **29**
 See also CA 116; DLB 60

Trevanian 1925- . . . . CLC **29**
 See also CA 108

Trevor, William 1928- . . . . . CLC **7, 9, 14, 25**
 See also Cox, William Trevor
 See also DLB 14

Trifonov, Yuri (Valentinovich)
 1925-1981 . . . . CLC **45**
 See also obituary CA 103

Trilling, Lionel 1905-1975 . . . . CLC **9, 11, 24**
 See also CANR 10; CA 9-12R;
 obituary CA 61-64; DLB 28, 63

Trogdon, William 1939-
 See Heat Moon, William Least
 See also CA 115

Trollope, Anthony 1815-1882 . . . . . NCLC **6**
 See also SATA 22; DLB 21, 57

Trotsky, Leon (Davidovich)
 1879-1940 . . . . TCLC **22**
 See also CA 118

Trotter (Cockburn), Catharine
 1679-1749 . . . . LC **8**

Troyat, Henri 1911- . . . . CLC **23**
 See also CANR 2; CA 45-48

Trudeau, Garry 1948- . . . . CLC **12**
 See also Trudeau, G(arretson) B(eekman)

Trudeau, G(arretson) B(eekman) 1948-
 See Trudeau, Garry
 See also CA 81-84; SATA 35

Truffaut, Francois 1932-1984 . . . . . . CLC **20**
 See also CA 81-84; obituary CA 113

Trumbo, Dalton 1905-1976 . . . . CLC **19**
 See also CANR 10; CA 21-24R;
 obituary CA 69-72; DLB 26

Tryon, Thomas 1926- . . . . CLC **3, 11**
 See also CA 29-32R

Ts'ao Hsueh-ch'in 1715?-1763 . . . . LC **1**

Tsushima Shuji 1909-1948
 See Dazai Osamu
 See also CA 107

Tsvetaeva (Efron), Marina (Ivanovna)
 1892-1941 . . . . TCLC **7**
 See also CA 104

Tunis, John R(oberts) 1889-1975 . . . CLC **12**
 See also CA 61-64; SATA 30, 37; DLB 22

Tuohy, Frank 1925- . . . . CLC **37**
 See also DLB 14

Tuohy, John Francis 1925-
 See Tuohy, Frank
 See also CANR 3; CA 5-8R

Turco, Lewis (Putnam) 1934- . . . . . . CLC **11**
 See also CA 13-16R; DLB-Y 84

Turner, Frederick 1943- . . . . CLC **48**
 See also CANR 12; CA 73-76; DLB 40

Tutuola, Amos 1920- . . . . CLC **5, 14, 29**
 See also CA 9-12R

Twain, Mark 1835-1910 . . . . TCLC **6, 12, 19**
 See also Clemens, Samuel Langhorne
 See also DLB 11, 12, 23

Tyler, Anne 1941- . . . . CLC **7, 11, 18, 28, 44**
 See also CANR 11; CA 9-12R; SATA 7;
 DLB 6; DLB-Y 82

Tyler, Royall 1757-1826 . . . . NCLC **3**
 See also DLB 37

Tynan (Hinkson), Katharine
 1861-1931 . . . . TCLC **3**
 See also CA 104

Tytell, John 1939- . . . . CLC **50**
 See also CA 29-32R

Tzara, Tristan 1896-1963 . . . . CLC **47**
 See also Rosenfeld, Samuel

Uhry, Alfred 1947?- . . . . CLC **55**
 See also CA 127

Unamuno (y Jugo), Miguel de
 1864-1936 . . . . TCLC **2, 9**
 See also CA 104

Underwood, Miles 1909-1981
 See Glassco, John

Undset, Sigrid 1882-1949 . . . . TCLC **3**
 See also CA 104

Ungaretti, Giuseppe
 1888-1970 . . . . CLC **7, 11, 15**
 See also CAP 2; CA 19-20;
 obituary CA 25-28R

Unger, Douglas 1952- . . . . CLC **34**

Unger, Eva 1932-
 See Figes, Eva

Updike, John (Hoyer)
 1932- . . . . . . CLC **1, 2, 3, 5, 7, 9, 13, 15,**
                                             23, 34, 43
 See also CANR 4; CA 1-4R; CABS 2;
 DLB 2, 5; DLB-Y 80, 82; DLB-DS 3

Urdang, Constance (Henriette)
 1922- . . . . CLC **47**
 See also CANR 9; CA 21-24R

Uris, Leon (Marcus) 1924- . . . . CLC **7, 32**
 See also CANR 1; CA 1-4R; SATA 49

Ustinov, Peter (Alexander) 1921- . . . . CLC **1**
 See also CA 13-16R; DLB 13

Vaculik, Ludvik 1926- . . . . CLC **7**
 See also CA 53-56

Valenzuela, Luisa 1938-........... **CLC 31**
See also CA 101

Valera (y Acala-Galiano), Juan
1824-1905 .... **TCLC 10**
See also CA 106

Valery, Paul (Ambroise Toussaint Jules)
1871-1945 .... **TCLC 4, 15**
See also CA 104, 122

Valle-Inclan (y Montenegro), Ramon (Maria)
del 1866-1936.............. **TCLC 5**
See also CA 106

Vallejo, Cesar (Abraham)
1892-1938 .... **TCLC 3**
See also CA 105

Van Ash, Cay 1918-.............. **CLC 34**

Vance, Jack 1916?-.............. **CLC 35**
See also DLB 8

Vance, John Holbrook 1916?-
See Vance, Jack
See also CANR 17; CA 29-32R

Van Den Bogarde, Derek (Jules Gaspard
Ulric) Niven 1921-
See Bogarde, Dirk
See also CA 77-80

Vanderhaeghe, Guy 1951- .... **CLC 41**
See also CA 113

Van der Post, Laurens (Jan) 1906-... **CLC 5**
See also CA 5-8R

Van de Wetering, Janwillem
1931-...................... **CLC 47**
See also CANR 4; CA 49-52

Van Dine, S. S. 1888-1939....... **TCLC 23**

Van Doren, Carl (Clinton)
1885-1950 .... **TCLC 18**
See also CA 111

Van Doren, Mark 1894-1972..... **CLC 6, 10**
See also CANR 3; CA 1-4R;
obituary CA 37-40R; DLB 45

Van Druten, John (William)
1901-1957 .... **TCLC 2**
See also CA 104; DLB 10

Van Duyn, Mona 1921-.......... **CLC 3, 7**
See also CANR 7; CA 9-12R; DLB 5

Van Itallie, Jean-Claude 1936-.... **CLC 3**
See also CAAS 2; CANR 1; CA 45-48;
DLB 7

Van Ostaijen, Paul 1896-1928..... **TCLC 33**

Van Peebles, Melvin 1932- ...... **CLC 2, 20**
See also CA 85-88

Vansittart, Peter 1920-........... **CLC 42**
See also CANR 3; CA 1-4R

Van Vechten, Carl 1880-1964 ...... **CLC 33**
See also obituary CA 89-92; DLB 4, 9, 51

Van Vogt, A(lfred) E(lton) 1912-..... **CLC 1**
See also CA 21-24R; SATA 14; DLB 8

Varda, Agnes 1928-.............. **CLC 16**
See also CA 116

Vargas Llosa, (Jorge) Mario (Pedro)
1936-....... **CLC 3, 6, 9, 10, 15, 31, 42**
See also CANR 18; CA 73-76

Vassilikos, Vassilis 1933-......... **CLC 4, 8**
See also CA 81-84

Vazov, Ivan 1850-1921........... **TCLC 25**
See also CA 121

Veblen, Thorstein Bunde
1857-1929 .... **TCLC 31**
See also CA 115

Verga, Giovanni 1840-1922 .... **TCLC 3**
See also CA 104

Verhaeren, Emile (Adolphe Gustave)
1855-1916 .... **TCLC 12**
See also CA 109

Verlaine, Paul (Marie) 1844-1896.. **NCLC 2**

Verne, Jules (Gabriel) 1828-1905 ... **TCLC 6**
See also CA 110; SATA 21

Very, Jones 1813-1880........... **NCLC 9**
See also DLB 1

Vesaas, Tarjei 1897-1970........ **CLC 48**
See also obituary CA 29-32R

Vian, Boris 1920-1959 .... **TCLC 9**
See also CA 106; DLB 72

Viaud, (Louis Marie) Julien 1850-1923
See Loti, Pierre
See also CA 107

Vicker, Angus 1916-
See Felsen, Henry Gregor

Vidal, Eugene Luther, Jr. 1925-
See Vidal, Gore

Vidal, Gore
1925-........ **CLC 2, 4, 6, 8, 10, 22, 33**
See also CANR 13; CA 5-8R; DLB 6

Viereck, Peter (Robert Edwin)
1916-...................... **CLC 4**
See also CANR 1; CA 1-4R; DLB 5

Vigny, Alfred (Victor) de
1797-1863 .... **NCLC 7**

Villiers de l'Isle Adam, Jean Marie Mathias
Philippe Auguste, Comte de,
1838-1889 .... **NCLC 3**

Vine, Barbara 1930-.............. **CLC 50**
See also Rendell, Ruth

Vinge, Joan (Carol) D(ennison)
1948-...................... **CLC 30**
See also CA 93-96; SATA 36

Visconti, Luchino 1906-1976....... **CLC 16**
See also CA 81-84; obituary CA 65-68

Vittorini, Elio 1908-1966...... **CLC 6, 9, 14**
See also obituary CA 25-28R

Vizinczey, Stephen 1933-.......... **CLC 40**

Vliet, R(ussell) G(ordon)
1929-1984 .... **CLC 22**
See also CANR 18; CA 37-40R;
obituary CA 112

Voight, Ellen Bryant 1943-........ **CLC 54**
See also CANR 11; CA 69-72

Voigt, Cynthia 1942-............. **CLC 30**
See also CANR 18; CA 106; SATA 33, 48

Voinovich, Vladimir (Nikolaevich)
1932-.................... **CLC 10, 49**
See also CA 81-84

Von Daeniken, Erich 1935-
See Von Daniken, Erich
See also CANR 17; CA 37-40R

Von Daniken, Erich 1935-........ **CLC 30**
See also Von Daeniken, Erich

Vonnegut, Kurt, Jr.
1922-.... **CLC 1, 2, 3, 4, 5, 8, 12, 22, 40**
See also CANR 1; CA 1-4R; DLB 2, 8;
DLB-Y 80; DLB-DS 3

Vorster, Gordon 1924-............ **CLC 34**

Voznesensky, Andrei 1933-...... **CLC 1, 15**
See also CA 89-92

Waddington, Miriam 1917-........ **CLC 28**
See also CANR 12; CA 21-24R

Wagman, Fredrica 1937-.......... **CLC 7**
See also CA 97-100

Wagner, Richard 1813-1883...... **NCLC 9**

Wagner-Martin, Linda 1936-....... **CLC 50**

Wagoner, David (Russell)
1926-.................. **CLC 3, 5, 15**
See also CAAS 3; CANR 2; CA 1-4R;
SATA 14; DLB 5

Wah, Fred(erick James) 1939-...... **CLC 44**
See also CA 107; DLB 60

Wahloo, Per 1926-1975 .... **CLC 7**
See also CA 61-64

Wahloo, Peter 1926-1975
See Wahloo, Per

Wain, John (Barrington)
1925-................ **CLC 2, 11, 15, 46**
See also CAAS 4; CA 5-8R; DLB 15, 27

Wajda, Andrzej 1926-............. **CLC 16**
See also CA 102

Wakefield, Dan 1932-............. **CLC 7**
See also CAAS 7; CA 21-24R

Wakoski, Diane
1937-.......... **CLC 2, 4, 7, 9, 11, 40**
See also CAAS 1; CANR 9; CA 13-16R;
DLB 5

Walcott, Derek (Alton)
1930-.......... **CLC 2, 4, 9, 14, 25, 42**
See also CA 89-92; DLB-Y 81

Waldman, Anne 1945-............. **CLC 7**
See also CA 37-40R; DLB 16

Waldo, Edward Hamilton 1918-
See Sturgeon, Theodore (Hamilton)

Walker, Alice
1944-.......... **CLC 5, 6, 9, 19, 27, 46**
See also CANR 9; CA 37-40R; SATA 31;
DLB 6, 33

Walker, David Harry 1911-........ **CLC 14**
See also CANR 1; CA 1-4R; SATA 8

Walker, Edward Joseph 1934-
See Walker, Ted
See also CANR 12; CA 21-24R

Walker, George F. 1947-.......... **CLC 44**
See also CANR 21; CA 103; DLB 60

Walker, Joseph A. 1935-.......... **CLC 19**
See also CA 89-92; DLB 38

Walker, Margaret (Abigail)
1915-.................... **CLC 1, 6**
See also CA 73-76

Walker, Ted 1934-............... **CLC 13**
See also Walker, Edward Joseph
See also DLB 40

Wallace, David Foster 1962-....... **CLC 50**

Wallace, Irving 1916-............ **CLC 7, 13**
See also CAAS 1; CANR 1; CA 1-4R

Wallant, Edward Lewis
1926-1962 .... CLC **5, 10**
See also CANR 22; CA 1-4R; DLB 2, 28

Walpole, Horace   1717-1797......... LC **2**
See also DLB 39

Walpole, (Sir) Hugh (Seymour)
1884-1941 .... TCLC **5**
See also CA 104; DLB 34

Walser, Martin   1927-............ CLC **27**
See also CANR 8; CA 57-60

Walser, Robert   1878-1956 .... TCLC **18**
See also CA 118

Walsh, Gillian Paton   1939-
See Walsh, Jill Paton
See also CA 37-40R; SATA 4

Walsh, Jill Paton   1939-........... CLC **35**
See also CLR 2; SAAS 3

Wambaugh, Joseph (Aloysius, Jr.)
1937- .... CLC **3, 18**
See also CA 33-36R; DLB 6; DLB-Y 83

Ward, Arthur Henry Sarsfield   1883-1959
See Rohmer, Sax
See also CA 108

Ward, Douglas Turner   1930-....... CLC **19**
See also CA 81-84; DLB 7, 38

Warhol, Andy   1928-1987.......... CLC **20**
See also CA 89-92; obituary CA 121

Warner, Francis (Robert le Plastrier)
1937- .... CLC **14**
See also CANR 11; CA 53-56

Warner, Rex (Ernest)   1905-1986.... CLC **45**
See also CA 89-92; obituary CA 119;
DLB 15

Warner, Sylvia Townsend
1893-1978 .... CLC **7, 19**
See also CANR 16; CA 61-64;
obituary CA 77-80; DLB 34

Warren, Mercy Otis   1728-1814... NCLC **13**
See also DLB 31

Warren, Robert Penn
1905- ..... CLC **1, 4, 6, 8, 10, 13, 18, 39**
See also CANR 10; CA 13-16R; SATA 46;
DLB 2, 48; DLB-Y 80

Washington, Booker T(aliaferro)
1856-1915 .... CLC **34**
See also CA 114; SATA 28

Wassermann, Jakob   1873-1934 ..... TCLC **6**
See also CA 104

Wasserstein, Wendy   1950-........ CLC **32**
See also CA 121

Waterhouse, Keith (Spencer)
1929- .... CLC **47**
See also CA 5-8R; DLB 13, 15

Waters, Roger   1944-
See Pink Floyd

Wa Thiong'o, Ngugi
1938- .... CLC **3, 7, 13, 36**
See also Ngugi, James (Thiong'o)
See also Ngugi wa Thiong'o

Watkins, Paul   1964?-............. CLC **55**

Watkins, Vernon (Phillips)
1906-1967 .... CLC **43**
See also CAP 1; CA 9-10;
obituary CA 25-28R; DLB 20

Waugh, Auberon (Alexander)   1939-.. CLC **7**
See also CANR 6, 22; CA 45-48; DLB 14

Waugh, Evelyn (Arthur St. John)
1903-1966 ... CLC **1, 3, 8, 13, 19, 27, 44**
See also CANR 22; CA 85-88;
obituary CA 25-28R; DLB 15

Waugh, Harriet   1944- .... CLC **6**
See also CANR 22; CA 85-88

Webb, Beatrice (Potter)   1858-1943 and
Webb, Sidney (James)
1859-1947 .... TCLC **22**

Webb, Beatrice (Potter)   1858-1943
See Webb, Beatrice (Potter) and Webb,
Sidney (James)
See also CA 117

Webb, Charles (Richard)   1939-...... CLC **7**
See also CA 25-28R

Webb, James H(enry), Jr.   1946-.... CLC **22**
See also CA 81-84

Webb, Mary (Gladys Meredith)
1881-1927 .... TCLC **24**
See also DLB 34

Webb, Phyllis   1927-............. CLC **18**
See also CA 104; DLB 53

Webb, Sidney (James)   1859-1947
See Webb, Beatrice (Potter) and Webb,
Sidney (James)
See also CA 117

Webb, Sidney (James)   1859-1947 and **Webb,
Beatrice (Potter)**   1858-1943
See Webb, Beatrice (Potter) and Webb,
Sidney (James)

Webber, Andrew Lloyd   1948-
See Rice, Tim and Webber, Andrew Lloyd

Weber, Lenora Mattingly
1895-1971 .... CLC **12**
See also CAP 1; CA 19-20;
obituary CA 29-32R; SATA 2;
obituary SATA 26

Wedekind, (Benjamin) Frank(lin)
1864-1918 .... TCLC **7**
See also CA 104

Weidman, Jerome   1913-............ CLC **7**
See also CANR 1; CA 1-4R; DLB 28

Weil, Simone   1909-1943.......... TCLC **23**
See also CA 117

Weinstein, Nathan Wallenstein   1903?-1940
See West, Nathanael
See also CA 104

Weir, Peter   1944-................ CLC **20**
See also CA 113

Weiss, Peter (Ulrich)
1916-1982 .... CLC **3, 15, 51**
See also CANR 3; CA 45-48;
obituary CA 106; DLB 69

Weiss, Theodore (Russell)
1916- .... CLC **3, 8, 14**
See also CAAS 2; CA 9-12R; DLB 5

Welch, (Maurice) Denton
1915-1948 .... TCLC **22**
See also CA 121

Welch, James   1940-............ CLC **6, 14**
See also CA 85-88

Weldon, Fay   1933-.... CLC **6, 9, 11, 19, 36**
See also CANR 16; CA 21-24R; DLB 14

Wellek, Rene   1903- .... CLC **28**
See also CAAS 7; CANR 8; CA 5-8R;
DLB 63

Weller, Michael   1942-............ CLC **10**
See also CA 85-88

Weller, Paul   1958-............... CLC **26**

Wellershoff, Dieter   1925-.......... CLC **46**
See also CANR 16; CA 89-92

Welles, (George) Orson
1915-1985 .... CLC **20**
See also CA 93-96; obituary CA 117

Wellman, Manly Wade   1903-1986 .. CLC **49**
See also CANR 6, 16; CA 1-4R;
obituary CA 118; SATA 6, 47

Wells, H(erbert) G(eorge)
1866-1946 .... TCLC **6, 12, 19**
See also CA 110; SATA 20; DLB 34, 70

Wells, Rosemary   1943-............ CLC **12**
See also CLR 16; CA 85-88; SAAS 1;
SATA 18

Welty, Eudora (Alice)
1909- .... CLC **1, 2, 5, 14, 22, 33;** SSC **1**
See also CA 9-12R; CABS 1; DLB 2;
CDALB 1941-1968

Wen I-to   1899-1946 .... TCLC **28**

Werfel, Franz (V.)   1890-1945 ...... TCLC **8**
See also CA 104

Wergeland, Henrik Arnold
1808-1845 .... NCLC **5**

Wersba, Barbara   1932-............ CLC **30**
See also CLR 3; CANR 16; CA 29-32R;
SAAS 2; SATA 1; DLB 52

Wertmuller, Lina   1928- .... CLC **16**
See also CA 97-100

Wescott, Glenway   1901-1987....... CLC **13**
See also CA 13-16R; obituary CA 121;
DLB 4, 9

Wesker, Arnold   1932- .... CLC **3, 5, 42**
See also CAAS 7; CANR 1; CA 1-4R;
DLB 13

Wesley, Richard (Errol)   1945-....... CLC **7**
See also CA 57-60; DLB 38

Wessel, Johan Herman   1742-1785 .... LC **7**

West, Anthony (Panther)
1914-1987 .... CLC **50**
See also CANR 3, 19; CA 45-48; DLB 15

West, Jessamyn   1907-1984 ...... CLC **7, 17**
See also CA 9-12R; obituary CA 112;
obituary SATA 37; DLB 6; DLB-Y 84

West, Morris L(anglo)   1916-..... CLC **6, 33**
See also CA 5-8R

West, Nathanael   1903?-1940 .... TCLC **1, 14**
See also Weinstein, Nathan Wallenstein
See also DLB 4, 9, 28

West, Paul   1930- .... CLC **7, 14**
See also CAAS 7; CANR 22; CA 13-16R;
DLB 14

West, Rebecca   1892-1983 .. CLC **7, 9, 31, 50**
See also CA 5-8R; obituary CA 109;
DLB 36; DLB-Y 83

Westall, Robert (Atkinson)   1929- ... CLC **17**
See also CANR 18; CA 69-72; SAAS 2;
SATA 23

Westlake, Donald E(dwin)
1933- .... CLC 7, 33
See also CANR 16; CA 17-20R

Westmacott, Mary 1890-1976
See Christie, (Dame) Agatha (Mary Clarissa)

Whalen, Philip 1923- .... CLC 6, 29
See also CANR 5; CA 9-12R; DLB 16

Wharton, Edith (Newbold Jones)
1862-1937 .... TCLC 3, 9, 27
See also CA 104; DLB 4, 9, 12;
CDALB 1865-1917

Wharton, William 1925-........ CLC 18, 37
See also CA 93-96; DLB-Y 80

Wheatley (Peters), Phillis
1753?-1784..................... LC 3
See also DLB 31, 50; CDALB 1640-1865

Wheelock, John Hall 1886-1978.... CLC 14
See also CANR 14; CA 13-16R;
obituary CA 77-80; DLB 45

Whelan, John 1900-
See O'Faolain, Sean

Whitaker, Rodney 1925-
See Trevanian

White, E(lwyn) B(rooks)
1899-1985 .... CLC 10, 34, 39
See also CLR 1; CANR 16; CA 13-16R;
obituary CA 116; SATA 2, 29;
obituary SATA 44; DLB 11, 22

White, Edmund III 1940-......... CLC 27
See also CANR 3, 19; CA 45-48

White, Patrick (Victor Martindale)
1912- .... CLC 3, 4, 5, 7, 9, 18
See also CA 81-84

White, Terence de Vere 1912-...... CLC 49
See also CANR 3; CA 49-52

White, T(erence) H(anbury)
1906-1964 .... CLC 30
See also CA 73-76; SATA 12

White, Walter (Francis)
1893-1955 .... TCLC 15
See also CA 115; DLB 51

White, William Hale 1831-1913
See Rutherford, Mark

Whitehead, E(dward) A(nthony)
1933- .... CLC 5
See also CA 65-68

Whitemore, Hugh 1936-........... CLC 37

Whitman, Sarah Helen
1803-1878 .... NCLC 19
See also DLB 1

Whitman, Walt 1819-1892........ NCLC 4
See also SATA 20; DLB 3, 64;
CDALB 1640-1865

Whitney, Phyllis A(yame) 1903-.... CLC 42
See also CANR 3; CA 1-4R; SATA 1, 30

Whittemore, (Edward) Reed (Jr.)
1919- .... CLC 4
See also CANR 4; CA 9-12R; DLB 5

Whittier, John Greenleaf
1807-1892 .... NCLC 8
See also DLB 1; CDALB 1640-1865

Wicker, Thomas Grey 1926-
See Wicker, Tom
See also CANR 21; CA 65-68

Wicker, Tom 1926-................ CLC 7
See also Wicker, Thomas Grey

Wideman, John Edgar
1941-.................. CLC 5, 34, 36
See also CANR 14; CA 85-88; DLB 33

Wiebe, Rudy (H.) 1934-...... CLC 6, 11, 14
See also CA 37-40R; DLB 60

Wieland, Christoph Martin
1733-1813 .... NCLC 17

Wieners, John 1934-.............. CLC 7
See also CA 13-16R; DLB 16

Wiesel, Elie(zer) 1928-..... CLC 3, 5, 11, 37
See also CAAS 4; CANR 8; CA 5-8R;
DLB-Y 1986

Wight, James Alfred 1916-
See Herriot, James
See also CA 77-80; SATA 44

Wilbur, Richard (Purdy)
1921-.................. CLC 3, 6, 9, 14
See also CANR 2; CA 1-4R; CABS 2;
SATA 9; DLB 5

Wild, Peter 1940-................ CLC 14
See also CA 37-40R; DLB 5

Wilde, Oscar (Fingal O'Flahertie Wills)
1854-1900 .... TCLC 1, 8, 23
See also CA 104; SATA 24; DLB 10, 19,
34, 57

Wilder, Billy 1906-.............. CLC 20
See also Wilder, Samuel
See also DLB 26

Wilder, Samuel 1906-
See Wilder, Billy
See also CA 89-92

Wilder, Thornton (Niven)
1897-1975 ...... CLC 1, 5, 6, 10, 15, 35
See also CA 13-16R; obituary CA 61-64;
DLB 4, 7, 9

Wiley, Richard 1944-............. CLC 44
See also CA 121

Wilhelm, Kate 1928-.............. CLC 7
See also CAAS 5; CANR 17; CA 37-40R;
DLB 8

Willard, Nancy 1936-........... CLC 7, 37
See also CLR 5; CANR 10; CA 89-92;
SATA 30, 37; DLB 5, 52

Williams, Charles (Walter Stansby)
1886-1945 .... TCLC 1, 11
See also CA 104

Williams, C(harles) K(enneth)
1936- .... CLC 33
See also CA 37-40R; DLB 5

Williams, Ella Gwendolen Rees 1890-1979
See Rhys, Jean

Williams, (George) Emlyn 1905-.... CLC 15
See also CA 104; DLB 10

Williams, Hugo 1942-............. CLC 42
See also CA 17-20R; DLB 40

Williams, John A(lfred) 1925-.... CLC 5, 13
See also CAAS 3; CANR 6; CA 53-56;
DLB 2, 33

Williams, Jonathan (Chamberlain)
1929- .... CLC 13
See also CANR 8; CA 9-12R; DLB 5

Williams, Joy 1944-............. CLC 31
See also CANR 22; CA 41-44R

Williams, Norman 1952- .... CLC 39
See also CA 118

Williams, Paulette 1948-
See Shange, Ntozake

Williams, Tennessee
1911-1983 .... CLC 1, 2, 5, 7, 8, 11, 15,
19, 30, 39, 45
See also CA 5-8R; obituary CA 108; DLB 7;
DLB-Y 83; DLB-DS 4;
CDALB 1941-1968

Williams, Thomas (Alonzo) 1926-... CLC 14
See also CANR 2; CA 1-4R

Williams, Thomas Lanier 1911-1983
See Williams, Tennessee

Williams, William Carlos
1883-1963 .... CLC 1, 2, 5, 9, 13, 22, 42
See also CA 89-92; DLB 4, 16, 54

Williamson, Jack 1908- .... CLC 29
See also Williamson, John Stewart
See also DLB 8

Williamson, John Stewart 1908-
See Williamson, Jack
See also CA 17-20R

Willingham, Calder (Baynard, Jr.)
1922- .... CLC 5, 51
See also CANR 3; CA 5-8R; DLB 2, 44

Wilson, A(ndrew) N(orman) 1950- .. CLC 33
See also CA 112; DLB 14

Wilson, Andrew 1948-
See Wilson, Snoo

Wilson, Angus (Frank Johnstone)
1913- .... CLC 2, 3, 5, 25, 34
See also CA 5-8R; DLB 15

Wilson, August 1945-.......... CLC 39, 50
See also CA 115, 122

Wilson, Brian 1942-.............. CLC 12

Wilson, Colin 1931- .... CLC 3, 14
See also CAAS 5; CANR 1; CA 1-4R;
DLB 14

Wilson, Edmund
1895-1972 .... CLC 1, 2, 3, 8, 24
See also CANR 1; CA 1-4R;
obituary CA 37-40R; DLB 63

Wilson, Ethel Davis (Bryant)
1888-1980 .... CLC 13
See also CA 102

Wilson, John 1785-1854.......... NCLC 5

Wilson, John (Anthony) Burgess 1917-
See Burgess, Anthony
See also CANR 2; CA 1-4R

Wilson, Lanford 1937-....... CLC 7, 14, 36
See also CA 17-20R; DLB 7

Wilson, Robert (M.) 1944-....... CLC 7, 9
See also CANR 2; CA 49-52

Wilson, Sloan 1920-............. CLC 32
See also CANR 1; CA 1-4R

Wilson, Snoo 1948-.............. CLC 33
See also CA 69-72

Wilson, William S(mith) 1932- ..... CLC 49
See also CA 81-84

Winchilsea, Anne (Kingsmill) Finch, Countess
of 1661-1720.................. LC 3

Winters, Janet Lewis 1899-
See Lewis (Winters), Janet
See also CAP 1; CA 9-10

Winters, (Arthur) Yvor
1900-1968 . . . . **CLC 4, 8, 32**
See also CAP 1; CA 11-12;
obituary CA 25-28R; DLB 48

Wiseman, Frederick 1930- . . . . **CLC 20**

Wister, Owen 1860-1938 . . . . **TCLC 21**
See also CA 108; DLB 9

Witkiewicz, Stanislaw Ignacy
1885-1939 . . . . **TCLC 8**
See also CA 105

Wittig, Monique 1935?- . . . . **CLC 22**
See also CA 116

Wittlin, Joseph 1896-1976 . . . . **CLC 25**
See also Wittlin, Jozef

Wittlin, Jozef 1896-1976
See Wittlin, Joseph
See also CANR 3; CA 49-52;
obituary CA 65-68

Wodehouse, (Sir) P(elham) G(renville)
1881-1975 . . . **CLC 1, 2, 5, 10, 22; SSC 2**
See also CANR 3; CA 45-48;
obituary CA 57-60; SATA 22; DLB 34

Woiwode, Larry (Alfred) 1941- . . . **CLC 6, 10**
See also CANR 16; CA 73-76; DLB 6

Wojciechowska, Maia (Teresa)
1927- . . . . **CLC 26**
See also CLR 1; CANR 4; CA 9-12R;
SAAS 1; SATA 1, 28

Wolf, Christa 1929- . . . . **CLC 14, 29**
See also CA 85-88

Wolfe, Gene (Rodman) 1931- . . . . **CLC 25**
See also CANR 6; CA 57-60; DLB 8

Wolfe, George C. 1954- . . . . **CLC 49**

Wolfe, Thomas (Clayton)
1900-1938 . . . . **TCLC 4, 13, 29**
See also CA 104; DLB 9; DLB-Y 85;
DLB-DS 2

Wolfe, Thomas Kennerly, Jr. 1931-
See Wolfe, Tom
See also CANR 9; CA 13-16R

Wolfe, Tom 1931- . . . **CLC 1, 2, 9, 15, 35, 51**
See also Wolfe, Thomas Kennerly, Jr.

Wolff, Geoffrey (Ansell) 1937- . . . . . **CLC 41**
See also CA 29-32R

Wolff, Tobias (Jonathan Ansell)
1945- . . . . **CLC 39**
See also CA 114, 117

Wolitzer, Hilma 1930- . . . . **CLC 17**
See also CANR 18; CA 65-68; SATA 31

Wollstonecraft (Godwin), Mary
1759-1797 . . . . **LC 5**
See also DLB 39

Wonder, Stevie 1950- . . . . **CLC 12**
See also Morris, Steveland Judkins

Wong, Jade Snow 1922- . . . . **CLC 17**
See also CA 109

Woodcott, Keith 1934-
See Brunner, John (Kilian Houston)

Woolf, (Adeline) Virginia
1882-1941 . . . . **TCLC 1, 5, 20**
See also CA 104; DLB 36

Woollcott, Alexander (Humphreys)
1887-1943 . . . . **TCLC 5**
See also CA 105; DLB 29

Wordsworth, William 1770-1850 . . **NCLC 12**

Wouk, Herman 1915- . . . . **CLC 1, 9, 38**
See also CANR 6; CA 5-8R; DLB-Y 82

Wright, Charles 1935- . . . . **CLC 6, 13, 28**
See also CAAS 7; CA 29-32R; DLB-Y 82

Wright, Charles (Stevenson) 1932- . . **CLC 49**
See also CA 9-12R; DLB 33

Wright, James (Arlington)
1927-1980 . . . . **CLC 3, 5, 10, 28**
See also CANR 4; CA 49-52;
obituary CA 97-100; DLB 5

Wright, Judith 1915- . . . . **CLC 11**
See also CA 13-16R; SATA 14

Wright, L(aurali) R. 1939- . . . . **CLC 44**

Wright, Richard (Nathaniel)
1908-1960 . . . **CLC 1, 3, 4, 9, 14, 21, 48;
SSC 2**
See also CA 108; DLB-DS 2

Wright, Richard B(ruce) 1937- . . . . . . **CLC 6**
See also CA 85-88; DLB 53

Wright, Rick 1945-
See Pink Floyd

Wright, Stephen 1946- . . . . **CLC 33**

Wright, Willard Huntington 1888-1939
See Van Dine, S. S.
See also CA 115

Wright, William 1930- . . . . **CLC 44**
See also CANR 7; CA 53-56

Wu Ch'eng-en 1500?-1582? . . . . **LC 7**

Wu Ching-tzu 1701-1754 . . . . **LC 2**

Wurlitzer, Rudolph 1938?- . . . . . **CLC 2, 4, 15**
See also CA 85-88

Wycherley, William 1640?-1716 . . . . . . **LC 8**

Wylie (Benet), Elinor (Morton Hoyt)
1885-1928 . . . . **TCLC 8**
See also CA 105; DLB 9, 45

Wylie, Philip (Gordon) 1902-1971 . . . **CLC 43**
See also CAP 2; CA 21-22;
obituary CA 33-36R; DLB 9

Wyndham, John 1903-1969 . . . . **CLC 19**
See also Harris, John (Wyndham Parkes
Lucas) Beynon

Wyss, Johann David 1743-1818 . . **NCLC 10**
See also SATA 27, 29

Yanovsky, Vassily S(emenovich)
1906- . . . . **CLC 2, 18**
See also CA 97-100

Yates, Richard 1926- . . . . **CLC 7, 8, 23**
See also CANR 10; CA 5-8R; DLB 2;
DLB-Y 81

Yeats, William Butler
1865-1939 . . . . **TCLC 1, 11, 18, 31**
See also CANR 10; CA 104; DLB 10, 19

Yehoshua, A(braham) B.
1936- . . . . **CLC 13, 31**
See also CA 33-36R

Yep, Laurence (Michael) 1948- . . . . . **CLC 35**
See also CLR 3; CANR 1; CA 49-52;
SATA 7; DLB 52

Yerby, Frank G(arvin) 1916- . . . **CLC 1, 7, 22**
See also CANR 16; CA 9-12R

Yevtushenko, Yevgeny (Alexandrovich)
1933- . . . . **CLC 1, 3, 13, 26, 51**
See also CA 81-84

Yezierska, Anzia 1885?-1970 . . . . **CLC 46**
See also obituary CA 89-92; DLB 28

Yglesias, Helen 1915- . . . . **CLC 7, 22**
See also CANR 15; CA 37-40R

Yorke, Henry Vincent 1905-1974
See Green, Henry
See also CA 85-88; obituary CA 49-52

Young, Al 1939- . . . . **CLC 19**
See also CA 29-32R; DLB 33

Young, Andrew 1885-1971 . . . . **CLC 5**
See also CANR 7; CA 5-8R

Young, Edward 1683-1765 . . . . **LC 3**

Young, Neil 1945- . . . . **CLC 17**
See also CA 110

Yourcenar, Marguerite
1903-1987 . . . . **CLC 19, 38, 50**
See also CA 69-72; DLB 72

Yurick, Sol 1925- . . . . **CLC 6**
See also CA 13-16R

Zamyatin, Yevgeny Ivanovich
1884-1937 . . . . **TCLC 8**
See also CA 105

Zangwill, Israel 1864-1926 . . . . **TCLC 16**
See also CA 109; DLB 10

Zappa, Francis Vincent, Jr. 1940-
See Zappa, Frank
See also CA 108

Zappa, Frank 1940- . . . . **CLC 17**
See also Zappa, Francis Vincent, Jr.

Zaturenska, Marya 1902-1982 . . . . **CLC 6, 11**
See also CA 13-16R; obituary CA 105

Zelazny, Roger 1937- . . . . **CLC 21**
See also CA 21-24R; SATA 39; DLB 8

Zhdanov, Andrei A(lexandrovich)
1896-1948 . . . . **TCLC 18**
See also CA 117

Ziegenhagen, Eric 1970- . . . . **CLC 55**

Ziegenhagen, Eric 1970?- . . . . **CLC 55**

Zimmerman, Robert 1941-
See Dylan, Bob

Zindel, Paul 1936- . . . . **CLC 6, 26**
See also CLR 3; CA 73-76; SATA 16;
DLB 7, 52

Zinoviev, Alexander 1922- . . . . **CLC 19**
See also CA 116

Zola, Emile 1840-1902 . . . . . . **TCLC 1, 6, 21**
See also CA 104

Zorrilla y Moral, Jose 1817-1893 . . **NCLC 6**

Zoshchenko, Mikhail (Mikhailovich)
1895-1958 . . . . **TCLC 15**
See also CA 115

Zuckmayer, Carl 1896-1977 . . . . **CLC 18**
See also CA 69-72; DLB 56

Zukofsky, Louis
1904-1978 . . . . **CLC 1, 2, 4, 7, 11, 18**
See also CA 9-12R; obituary CA 77-80;
DLB 5

Zweig, Paul 1935-1984......... **CLC 34, 42**
  See also CA 85-88; obituary CA 113

Zweig, Stefan 1881-1942 .... **TCLC 17**
  See also CA 112

CLC Cumulative Nationality Index

ALBANIAN
Kadare, Ismail **52**

ALGERIAN
Camus, Albert **1, 2, 4, 9, 11, 14, 32**
Cohen-Solal, Annie **50**

ALSATIAN
Arp, Jean **5**

AMERICAN
Abbey, Edward **36**
Abbott, Lee K., Jr. **48**
Abish, Walter **22**
Abrahams, Peter **4**
Abrams, M. H. **24**
Acker, Kathy **45**
Adams, Alice **6, 13, 46**
Addams, Charles **30**
Adler, C. S. **35**
Adler, Renata **8, 31**
Ai **4, 14**
Aiken, Conrad **1, 3, 5, 10, 52**
Albee, Edward **1, 2, 3, 5, 9, 11, 13, 25, 53**
Alexander, Lloyd **35**
Algren, Nelson **4, 10, 33**
Allen, Woody **16, 52**
Alta **19**
Alter, Robert B. **34**
Alther, Lisa **7, 41**
Altman, Robert **16**
Ammons, A. R. **2, 3, 5, 8, 9, 25**
Anaya, Rudolfo A. **23**
Anderson, Jon **9**
Anderson, Poul **15**
Anderson, Robert **23**
Angell, Roger **26**
Angelou, Maya **12, 35**
Anthony Piers **35**

Apple, Max **9, 33**
Appleman, Philip **51**
Archer, Jules **12**
Arnow, Harriette **2, 7, 18**
Arrick, Fran **30**
Ashbery, John **2, 3, 4, 6, 9, 13, 15, 25, 41**
Asimov, Isaac **1, 3, 9, 19, 26**
Auchincloss, Louis **4, 6, 9, 18, 45**
Auden, W. H. **1, 2, 3, 4, 6, 9, 11, 14, 43**
Auel, Jean M. **31**
Auster, Paul **47**
Bach, Richard **14**
Baker, Elliott **8**
Baker, Russell **31**
Bakshi, Ralph **26**
Baldwin, James **1, 2, 3, 4, 5, 8, 13, 15, 17, 42, 50**
Bambara, Toni Cade **19**
Banks, Russell **37**
Baraka, Imamu Amiri **1, 2, 3, 5, 10, 14, 33**
Barbera, Jack **44**
Barnard, Mary **48**
Barnes, Djuna **3, 4, 8, 11, 29**
Barrett, William **27**
Barth, John **1, 2, 3, 5, 7, 9, 10, 14, 27, 51**
Barthelme, Donald **1, 2, 3, 5, 6, 8, 13, 23, 46**
Barthelme, Frederick **36**
Barzun, Jacques **51**
Baumbach, Jonathan **6, 23**
Bausch, Richard **51**
Baxter, Charles **45**
Beagle, Peter S. **7**
Beattie, Ann **8, 13, 18, 40**
Becker, Walter **26**
Beecher, John **6**
Behrman, S. N. **40**
Belitt, Ben **22**
Bell, Madison Smartt **41**

Bell, Marvin **8, 31**
Bellow, Saul **1, 2, 3, 6, 8, 10, 13, 15, 25, 33, 34**
Benary-Isbert, Margot **12**
Benchley, Peter **4, 8**
Benedikt, Michael **4, 14**
Benford, Gregory **52**
Bennett, Hal **5**
Bennett, Jay **35**
Benson, Jackson J. **34**
Benson, Sally **17**
Bentley, Eric **24**
Berger, Melvin **12**
Berger, Thomas **3, 5, 8, 11, 18, 38**
Bergstein, Eleanor **4**
Berriault, Gina **54**
Berrigan, Daniel J. **4**
Berrigan, Ted **37**
Berry, Chuck **17**
Berry, Wendell **4, 6, 8, 27, 46**
Berryman, John **1, 2, 3, 4, 6, 8, 10, 13, 25**
Bessie, Alvah **23**
Betts, Doris **3, 6, 28**
Bidart, Frank **33**
Bishop, Elizabeth **1, 4, 9, 13, 15, 32**
Bishop, John **10**
Blackburn, Paul **9, 43**
Blackmur, R. P. **2, 24**
Blaise, Clark **29**
Blatty, William Peter **2**
Blessing, Lee **54**
Blish, James **14**
Bloch, Robert **33**
Bloom, Harold **24**
Blount, Roy, Jr. **38**
Blume, Judy **12, 30**
Bly, Robert **1, 2, 5, 10, 15, 38**
Bochco, Steven **35**
Bogan, Louise **4, 39, 46**

Bogosian, Eric 45
Bograd, Larry 35
Bonham, Frank 12
Bontemps, Arna 1, 18
Booth, Philip 23
Booth, Wayne C. 24
Bottoms, David 53
Bourjaily, Vance 8
Bova, Ben 45
Bowers, Edgar 9
Bowles, Jane 3
Bowles, Paul 1, 2, 19, 53
Boyle, Kay 1, 5, 19
Boyle, T. Coraghessan 36, 55
Bradbury, Ray 1, 3, 10, 15, 42
Bradley, David, Jr. 23
Bradley, John Ed 55
Bradley, Marion Zimmer 30
Brammer, William 31
Brancato, Robin F. 35
Brand, Millen 7
Branden, Barbara 44
Branley, Franklyn M. 21
Brautigan, Richard 1, 3, 5, 9, 12, 34, 42
Brennan, Maeve 5
Breslin, Jimmy 4, 43
Bridgers, Sue Ellen 26
Brin, David 34
Brodsky, Joseph 4, 6, 13, 36, 50
Brodsky, Michael 19
Bromell, Henry 5
Broner, E. M. 19
Bronk, William 10
Brooks, Cleanth 24
Brooks, Gwendolyn 1, 2, 4, 5, 15, 49
Brooks, Mel 12
Brooks, Peter 34
Brooks, Van Wyck 29
Brosman, Catharine Savage 9
Broughton, T. Alan 19
Broumas, Olga 10
Brown, Claude 30
Brown, Dee 18, 47
Brown, Rita Mae 18, 43
Brown, Rosellen 32
Brown, Sterling A. 1, 23
Browne, Jackson 21
Browning, Tod 16
Bruccoli, Matthew J. 34
Bruce, Lenny 21
Bryan, C. D. B. 29
Buchwald, Art 33
Buck, Pearl S. 7, 11, 18
Buckley, William F., Jr. 7, 18, 37
Buechner, Frederick 2, 4, 6, 9
Bukowski, Charles 2, 5, 9, 41
Bullins, Ed 1, 5, 7
Burke, Kenneth 2, 24
Burnshaw, Stanley 3, 13, 44
Burr, Anne 6
Burroughs, William S. 1, 2, 5, 15, 22, 42
Busch, Frederick 7, 10, 18, 47
Bush, Ronald 34
Butler, Octavia E. 38
Byars, Betsy 35
Byrne, David 26
Cage, John 41
Cain, James M. 3, 11, 28
Caldwell, Erskine 1, 8, 14, 50
Caldwell, Taylor 2, 28, 39
Calisher, Hortense 2, 4, 8, 38
Cameron, Peter 44

Campbell, John W., Jr. 32
Canby, Vincent 13
Canin, Ethan 55
Capote, Truman 1, 3, 8, 13, 19, 34, 38
Capra, Frank 16
Caputo, Philip 32
Card, Orson Scott 44, 47, 50
Carey, Ernestine Gilbreth 17
Carlisle, Henry 33
Carlson, Ron 54
Carpenter, Don 41
Carr, John Dickson 3
Carr, Virginia Spencer 34
Carroll, James 38
Carroll, Jim 35
Carruth, Hayden 4, 7, 10, 18
Carver, Raymond 22, 36, 53, 55
Casey, Michael 2
Casey, Warren 12
Cassavetes, John 20
Cassill, R. V. 4, 23
Cassity, Turner 6, 42
Castenada, Carlos 12
Catton, Bruce 35
Caunitz, William 34
Cavanna, Betty 12
Chabon, Michael 55
Chappell, Fred 40
Charyn, Jerome 5, 8, 18
Chase, Mary Ellen 2
Chayefsky, Paddy 23
Cheever, John 3, 7, 8, 11, 15, 25
Cheever, Susan 18, 48
Cherryh, C. J. 35
Chester, Alfred 49
Childress, Alice 12, 15
Chute, Carolyn 39
Ciardi, John 10, 40, 44
Cimino, Michael 16
Clampitt, Amy 32
Clancy, Tom 45
Clark, Eleanor 5, 19
Clark, Walter Van Tilburg 28
Clarke, Shirley 16
Clavell, James 6, 25
Cleaver, Eldridge 30
Clifton, Lucille 19
Coburn, D. L. 10
Codrescu, Andrei 46
Cohen, Arthur A. 7, 31
Collier, Christopher 30
Collier, James L. 30
Collins, Linda 44
Colum, Padraic 28
Colwin, Laurie 5, 13, 23
Condon, Richard 4, 6, 8, 10, 45
Connell, Evan S., Jr. 4, 6, 45
Connelly, Marc 7
Conroy, Pat 30
Cook, Robin 14
Cooke, Elizabeth 55
Coover, Robert 3, 7, 15, 32, 46
Coppola, Francis Ford 16
Corcoran, Barbara 17
Corman, Cid 9
Cormier, Robert 12, 30
Corn, Alfred 33
Corso, Gregory 1, 11
Costain, Thomas B. 30
Cowley, Malcolm 39
Cozzens, James Gould 1, 4, 11
Crane, R. S. 27

Creeley, Robert 1, 2, 4, 8, 11, 15, 36
Crews, Harry 6, 23, 49
Crichton, Michael 2, 6, 54
Cristofer, Michael 28
Crumb, Robert 17
Cryer, Gretchen 21
Cudlip, David 34
Cummings, E. E. 1, 3, 8, 12, 15
Cunningham, J. V. 3, 31
Cunningham, Julia 12
Cunningham, Michael 34
Currie, Ellen 44
Dacey, Philip 51
Dahlberg, Edward 1, 7, 14
Daly, Elizabeth 52
Daly, Maureen 17
Danziger, Paula 21
Davenport, Guy 6, 14, 38
Davidson, Donald 2, 13, 19
Davidson, Sara 9
Davis, H. L. 49
Davison, Peter 28
Dawson, Fielding 6
De Man, Paul 55
De Palma, Brian 20
De Vries, Peter 1, 2, 3, 7, 10, 28, 46
Deer, Sandra 45
Del Vecchio, John M. 29
Delany, Samuel R. 8, 14, 38
Delbanco, Nicholas 6, 13
DeLillo, Don 8, 10, 13, 27, 39, 54
Deloria, Vine, Jr. 21
DeMarinis, Rick 54
Demby, William 53
Denby, Edwin 48
Deren, Maya 16
Derleth, August 31
Deutsch, Babette 18
Dexter, Pete 34, 55
Diamond, Neil 30
Dick, Philip K. 10, 30
Dickey, James 1, 2, 4, 7, 10, 15, 47
Dickey, William 3, 28
Dickinson, Charles 49
Didion, Joan 1, 3, 8, 14, 32
Dillard, Annie 9
Dillard, R. H. W. 5
Disch, Thomas M. 7, 36
Dixon, Stephen 52
Dobyns, Stephen 37
Doctorow, E. L. 6, 11, 15, 18, 37, 44
Doerr, Harriet 34
Donaldson, Stephen R. 46
Donleavy, J. P. 1, 4, 6, 10, 45
Donovan, John 35
Dorn, Ed 10, 18
Dos Passos, John 1, 4, 8, 11, 15, 25, 34
Dove, Rita 50
Drexler, Rosalyn 2, 6
Drury, Allen 37
Du Bois, W. E. B. 1, 2, 13
Duberman, Martin 8
Dubie, Norman 36
Dubus, André 13, 36
Duffy, Bruce 50
Dugan, Alan 2, 6
Dumas, Henry 6
Duncan, Robert 1, 2, 4, 7, 15, 41, 55
Duncan Lois 26
Dunn, Stephen 36
Dunne, John Gregory 28
Durang, Christopher 27, 38

Durban, Pam 39
Dworkin, Andrea 43
Dylan, Bob 3, 4, 6, 12
Eastlake, William 8
Eberhart, Richard 3, 11, 19
Eberstadt, Fernanda 39
Eckert, Allan W. 17
Edel, Leon 29, 34
Edgerton, Clyde 39
Edmonds, Walter D. 35
Edson, Russell 13
Edwards, Gus 43
Ehle, John 27
Eigner, Larry 9
Eiseley, Loren 7
Eisenstadt, Jill 50
Eliade, Mircea 19
Eliot, T. S. 1, 2, 3, 6, 9, 10, 13, 15, 24, 34, 41, 55
Elkin, Stanley 4, 6, 9, 14, 27, 51
Elledge, Scott 34
Elliott, George P. 2
Ellis, Bret Easton 39
Ellis, Trey 55
Ellison, Harlan 1, 13, 42
Ellison, Ralph 1, 3, 11, 54
Ellmann, Richard 50
Elman, Richard 19
Ephron, Nora 17, 31
Epstein, Daniel Mark 7
Epstein, Jacob 19
Epstein, Joseph 39
Epstein, Leslie 27
Erdman, Paul E. 25
Erdrich, Louise 39, 54
Eshleman, Clayton 7
Estleman, Loren D. 48
Everson, William 1, 5, 14
Exley, Frederick 6, 11
Ezekiel, Tish O'Dowd 34
Fagen, Donald 26
Fair, Ronald L. 18
Fariña, Richard 9
Farley, Walter 17
Farmer, Philip José 1, 19
Farrell, James T. 1, 4, 8, 11
Fast, Howard 23
Faulkner, William 1, 3, 6, 8, 9, 11, 14, 18, 28, 52
Fauset, Jessie Redmon 19, 54
Faust, Irvin 8
Fearing, Kenneth 51
Federman, Raymond 6, 47
Feiffer, Jules 2, 8
Feldman, Irving 7
Felsen, Henry Gregor 17
Ferber, Edna 18
Ferlinghetti, Lawrence 2, 6, 10, 27
Fiedler, Leslie A. 4, 13, 24
Field, Andrew 44
Fierstein, Harvey 33
Fisher, Vardis 7
Fitzgerald, Robert 39
Flanagan, Thomas 25, 52
Fleming, Thomas J. 37
Foote, Horton 51
Forbes, Esther 12
Forché, Carolyn 25
Ford, John 16
Ford, Richard 46
Foreman, Richard 50
Forman, James D. 21

Fornes, Maria Irene 39
Forrest, Leon 4
Fosse, Bob 20
Fox, Paula 2, 8
Fox, William Price 22
Francis, Robert 15
Frank, Elizabeth 39
Fraze, Candida 50
Frazier, Ian 46
Freeman, Judith 55
French, Marilyn 10, 18
Friedman, B. H. 7
Friedman, Bruce Jay 3, 5
Frost, Robert 1, 3, 4, 9, 10, 13, 15, 26, 34, 44
Fuchs, Daniel (1909-) 8, 22
Fuchs, Daniel (1934-) 34
Fuller, Charles 25
Fulton, Alice 52
Gaddis, William 1, 3, 6, 8, 10, 19, 43
Gaines, Ernest J. 3, 11, 18
Gallagher, Tess 18
Gallant, Roy A. 17
Gallico, Paul 2
Galvin, James 38
Gann, Ernest K. 23
Gardner, Herb 44
Gardner, John (Champlin, Jr.) 2, 3, 5, 7, 8, 10, 18, 28, 34
Garrett, George 3, 11, 51
Garrigue, Jean 2, 8
Gass, William H. 1, 2, 8, 11, 15, 39
Gaye, Marvin 26
Gelbart, Larry 21
Gelber, Jack 1, 6, 14
Gellhorn, Martha 14
Gent, Peter 29
George, Jean Craighead 35
Gertler, T. 34
Ghiselin, Brewster 23
Gibbons, Kaye 50
Gibson, William (1948-) 39
Gibson, William (1914-) 23
Gifford, Barry 34
Gilbreth, Frank B., Jr. 17
Gilchrist, Ellen 34, 48
Giles, Molly 39
Gilroy, Frank D. 2
Ginsberg, Allen 1, 2, 3, 4, 6, 13, 36
Giovanni, Nikki 2, 4, 19
Glasser, Ronald J. 37
Glück, Louise 7, 22, 44
Godwin, Gail 5, 8, 22, 31
Gold, Herbert 4, 7, 14, 42
Goldbarth, Albert 5, 38
Goldman, William 1, 48
Goldsberry, Steven 34
Goodman, Paul 1, 2, 4, 7
Gordon, Caroline 6, 13, 29
Gordon, Mary 13, 22
Gordon, Sol 26
Gordone, Charles 1, 4
Gould, Lois 4, 10
Goyen, William 5, 8, 14, 40
Graham, Jorie 48
Grau, Shirley Ann 4, 9
Gray, Amlin 29
Gray, Francine du Plessix 22
Gray, Spalding 49
Grayson, Richard 38
Greeley, Andrew M. 28
Green, Paul 25

Greenberg, Joanne 3, 7, 30
Greene, Bette 30
Greene, Gael 8
Gregor, Arthur 9
Griffin, Peter 39
Grumbach, Doris 13, 22
Grunwald, Lisa 44
Guare, John 8, 14, 29
Guest, Barbara 34
Guest, Judith 8, 30
Guild, Nicholas M. 33
Gunn, Bill 5
Gurney, A. R., Jr. 32, 50, 54
Guthrie, A. B., Jr. 23
Guthrie, Woody 35
Guy, Rosa 26
H. D. 3, 8, 14, 31, 34
Hacker, Marilyn 5, 9, 23
Hailey, Elizabeth Forsythe 40
Haley, Alex 8, 12
Hall, Donald 1, 13, 37
Halpern, Daniel 14
Hamill, Pete 10
Hamilton, Edmond 1
Hamilton, Ian 55
Hamilton, Virginia 26
Hammett, Dashiell 3, 5, 10, 19, 47
Hamner, Earl, Jr. 12
Hannah, Barry 23, 38
Hansberry, Lorraine 17
Hansen, Joseph 38
Hanson, Kenneth O. 13
Hardwick, Elizabeth 13
Harlan, Louis R. 34
Harling, Robert 53
Harmon, William 38
Harper, Michael S. 7, 22
Harris, MacDonald 9
Harris, Mark 19
Harrison, Harry 42
Harrison, Jim 6, 14, 33
Harriss, Will 34
Hartman, Geoffrey H. 27
Haruf, Kent 34
Hass, Robert 18, 39
Haviaras, Stratis 33
Hawkes, John 1, 2, 3, 4, 7, 9, 14, 15, 27, 49
Hayden, Robert 5, 9, 14, 37
Hayman, Ronald 44
Heat Moon, William Least 29
Hecht, Anthony 8, 13, 19
Hecht, Ben 8
Heifner, Jack 11
Heilbrun, Carolyn G. 25
Heinemann, Larry 50
Heinlein, Robert A. 1, 3, 8, 14, 26, 55
Heller, Joseph 1, 3, 5, 8, 11, 36
Hellman, Lillian 2, 4, 8, 14, 18, 34, 44, 52
Helprin, Mark 7, 10, 22, 32
Hemingway, Ernest 1, 3, 6, 8, 10, 13, 19, 30, 34, 39, 41, 44, 50
Hempel, Amy 39
Henley, Beth 23
Hentoff, Nat 26
Herbert, Frank 12, 23, 35, 44
Herbst, Josephine 34
Herlihy, James Leo 6
Herrmann, Dorothy 44
Hersey, John 1, 2, 7, 9, 40
Heyen, William 13, 18
Higgins, George V. 4, 7, 10, 18

Highsmith, Patricia **2, 4, 14, 42**
Highwater, Jamake 12
Hill, George Roy 26
Himes, Chester **2, 4, 7, 18**
Hinton, S. E. 30
Hirsch, Edward **31, 50**
Hoagland, Edward 28
Hoban, Russell C. **7, 25**
Hobson, Laura Z. **7, 25**
Hochman, Sandra **3, 8**
Hoffman, Alice 51
Hoffman, Daniel **6, 13, 23**
Hoffman, Stanley 5
Hoffman, William M. 40
Holland, Isabelle 21
Hollander, John **2, 5, 8, 14**
Holleran, Andrew 38
Honig, Edwin 33
Horgan, Paul **9, 53**
Horwitz, Julius 14
Hougan, Carolyn 34
Howard, Maureen **5, 14, 46**
Howard, Richard **7, 10, 47**
Howe, Fanny 47
Howe, Tina 48
Howes, Barbara 15
Hubbard, L. Ron 43
Huddle, David 49
Hughart, Barry 39
Hughes, Langston **1, 5, 10, 15, 35, 44**
Hugo, Richard F. **6, 18, 32**
Humphrey, William 45
Humphreys, Josephine 34
Hunt, E. Howard 3
Hunter, Evan **11, 31**
Hunter, Kristin 35
Hurston, Zora Neale **7, 30**
Huston, John 20
Huxley, Aldous **1, 3, 4, 5, 8, 11, 18, 35**
Hwang, David Henry 55
Hyde, Margaret O. 21
Ian, Janis 21
Ignatow, David **4, 7, 14, 40**
Ingalls, Rachel 42
Inge, William **1, 8, 19**
Innaurato, Albert 21
Irving, John **13, 23, 38**
Isaacs, Susan 32
Ivask, Ivar 14
Jackson, Jesse 12
Jackson, Shirley 11
Jacobs, Jim 12
Jacobsen, Josephine 48
Jakes, John 29
Janowitz, Tama 43
Jarrell, Randall **1, 2, 6, 9, 13, 49**
Jeffers, Robinson **2, 3, 11, 15, 54**
Jennings, Waylon 21
Jensen, Laura 37
Jiles, Paulette 13
Joel, Billy 26
Johnson, Charles **7, 51**
Johnson, Denis 52
Johnson, Diane **5, 13, 48**
Jones, Gayl **6, 9**
Jones, James **1, 3, 10, 39**
Jones, Madison 4
Jones, Nettie 34
Jones, Preston 10
Jones, Robert F. 7
Jong, Erica **4, 6, 8, 18**
Jordan, June **5, 11, 23**

Jordan, Pat 37
Just, Ward S. **4, 27**
Justice, Donald **6, 19**
Kahn, Roger 30
Kaletski, Alexander 39
Kallman, Chester 2
Kanin, Garson 22
Kantor, MacKinlay 7
Kaplan, David Michael 50
Karl, Frederick R. 34
Katz, Steve 47
Kauffman, Janet 42
Kaufman, Bob 49
Kaufman, George S. 38
Kaufman, Sue **3, 8**
Kazan, Elia **6, 16**
Kazin, Alfred **34, 38**
Keaton, Buster 20
Keene, Donald 34
Keillor, Garrison 40
Kellerman, Jonathan 44
Kelley, William Melvin 22
Kellogg, Marjorie 2
Kemelman, Harry 2
Kennedy, William **6, 28, 34, 53**
Kennedy, X. J. **8, 42**
Kerouac, Jack **1, 2, 3, 5, 14, 29**
Kerr, Jean 22
Kerr, M. E. **12, 35**
Kerr, Robert 55
Kerrigan, Anthony **4, 6**
Kesey, Ken **1, 3, 6, 11, 46**
Kesselring, Joseph 45
Kessler, Jascha 4
Kettelkamp, Larry 12
Kherdian, David **6, 9**
Kienzle, William X. 25
Killens, John Oliver 10
Kincaid, Jamaica 43
King, Stephen **12, 26, 37**
Kingman, Lee 17
Kingsley, Sidney 44
Kingsolver, Barbara 55
Kingston, Maxine Hong **12, 19**
Kinnell, Galway **1, 2, 3, 5, 13, 29**
Kirkwood, James 9
Kizer, Carolyn **15, 39**
Klein, Norma 30
Klein, T. E. D. 34
Knebel, Fletcher 14
Knight, Etheridge 40
Knowles, John **1, 4, 10, 26**
Koch, Kenneth **5, 8, 44**
Kopit, Arthur **1, 18, 33**
Kosinski, Jerzy **1, 2, 3, 6, 10, 15, 53**
Kostelanetz, Richard 28
Kotlowitz, Robert 4
Kotzwinkle, William **5, 14, 35**
Kozol, Jonathan 17
Kozoll, Michael 35
Kramer, Kathryn 34
Kramer, Larry 42
Kristofferson, Kris 26
Krumgold, Joseph 12
Krutch, Joseph Wood 24
Kubrick, Stanley 16
Kumin, Maxine **5, 13, 28**
Kunitz, Stanley J. **6, 11, 14**
Kuzma, Greg 7
L'Amour, Louis **25, 55**
Lancaster, Bruce 36
Landis, John 26

Langer, Elinor 34
Lapine, James 39
Larsen, Eric 55
Larsen, Nella 37
Larson, Charles R. 31
Latham, Jean Lee 12
Lattimore, Richmond 3
Laughlin, James 49
Le Guin, Ursula K. **8, 13, 22, 45**
Lear, Norman 12
Leavitt, David 34
Lebowitz, Fran **11, 36**
Lee, Andrea 36
Lee, Don L. 2
Lee, George Washington 52
Lee, Harper 12
Lee, Lawrence 34
Lee, Stan 17
Leet, Judith 11
Leffland, Ella 19
Leiber, Fritz 25
Leithauser, Brad 27
Lelchuk, Alan 5
Lemann, Nancy 39
L'Engle, Madeleine 12
Lentricchia, Frank 34
Leonard, Elmore **28, 34**
Lerman, Eleanor 9
Lester, Richard 20
Levertov, Denise **1, 2, 3, 5, 8, 15, 28**
Levin, Ira **3, 6**
Levin, Meyer 7
Levine, Philip **2, 4, 5, 9, 14, 33**
Levinson, Deirdre 49
Levitin, Sonia 17
Lewis, Janet 41
L'Heureux, John 52
Lieber, Joel 6
Lieberman, Laurence **4, 36**
Ligotti, Thomas 44
Linney, Romulus 51
Lipsyte, Robert 21
Lish, Gordon 45
Littell, Robert 42
Loewinsohn, Ron 52
Logan, John 5
Lopate, Phillip 29
Lord, Bette Bao 23
Lorde, Audre 18
Lowell, Robert **1, 2, 3, 4, 5, 8, 9, 11, 15, 37**
Loy, Mina 28
Lucas, George 16
Ludlam, Charles **46, 50**
Ludlum, Robert **22, 43**
Lurie, Alison **4, 5, 18, 39**
Lynn, Kenneth S. 50
Lytle, Andrew 22
Maas, Peter 29
Macdonald, Cynthia **13, 19**
MacDonald, John D. **3, 27, 44**
Macdonald, Ross **1, 2, 3, 14, 34, 41**
MacInnes, Helen **27, 39**
MacLeish, Archibald **3, 8, 14**
MacShane, Frank 39
Madden, David **5, 15**
Madhubuti, Haki R. 6
Mailer, Norman **1, 2, 3, 4, 5, 8, 11, 14, 28, 39**
Major, Clarence **3, 19, 48**
Malamud, Bernard **1, 2, 3, 5, 8, 9, 11, 18, 27, 44**
Maloff, Saul 5

Malone, Michael **43**
Malzberg, Barry N. **7**
Mamet, David **9, 15, 34, 46**
Mamoulian, Rouben **16**
Mano, D. Keith **2, 10**
Manso, Peter **39**
Markfield, Wallace **8**
Marquand, John P. **2, 10**
Marshall, Garry **17**
Marshall, Paule **27**
Martin, Steve **30**
Maso, Carole **44**
Mason, Bobbie Ann **28, 43**
Masters, Hilary **48**
Mastrosimone, William **36**
Matheson, Richard **37**
Mathews, Harry **6, 52**
Matthews, William **40**
Matthias, John **9**
Matthiessen, Peter **5, 7, 11, 32**
Maxwell, William **19**
May, Elaine **16**
Maynard, Joyce **23**
Maysles, Albert **16**
Maysles, David **16**
Mazer, Norma Fox **26**
McBrien, William **44**
McCaffrey, Anne **17**
McCarthy, Cormac **4**
McCarthy, Mary **1, 3, 5, 14, 24, 39**
McCauley, Stephen **50**
McClure, Michael **6, 10**
McCorkle, Jill **51**
McCourt, James **5**
McCullers, Carson **1, 4, 10, 12, 48**
McElroy, Joseph **5, 47**
McGinley, Phyllis **14**
McGinniss, Joe **32**
McGrath, Thomas **28**
McGuane, Thomas **3, 7, 18, 45**
McHale, Tom **3, 5**
McInerney, Jay **34**
McIntyre, Vonda N. **18**
McKuen, Rod **1, 3**
McMillan, Terry **50**
McMurtry, Larry **2, 3, 7, 11, 27, 44**
McNally, Terrence **4, 7, 41**
McPhee, John **36**
McPherson, James Alan **19**
McPherson, William **34**
Mead, Margaret **37**
Medoff, Mark **6, 23**
Mehta, Ved **37**
Meltzer, Milton **26**
Meredith, William **4, 13, 22, 55**
Merkin, Daphne **44**
Merrill, James **2, 3, 6, 8, 13, 18, 34**
Merton, Thomas **1, 3, 11, 34**
Merwin, W. S. **1, 2, 3, 5, 8, 13, 18, 45**
Mewshaw, Michael **9**
Meyers, Jeffrey **39**
Michaels, Leonard **6, 25**
Michener, James A. **1, 5, 11, 29**
Miles, Josephine **1, 2, 14, 34, 39**
Miller, Arthur **1, 2, 6, 10, 15, 26, 47**
Miller, Henry **1, 2, 4, 9, 14, 43**
Miller, Jason **2**
Miller, Sue **44**
Miller, Walter M., Jr. **4, 30**
Millhauser, Steven **21, 54**
Miner, Valerie **40**
Minot, Susan **44**

Minus, Ed **39**
Modarressi, Taghi **44**
Mohr, Nicholasa **12**
Mojtabai, A. G. **5, 9, 15, 29**
Momaday, N. Scott **2, 19**
Montague, John **46**
Montgomery, Marion **7**
Mooney, Ted **25**
Moore, Lorrie **39, 45**
Moore, Marianne **1, 2, 4, 8, 10, 13, 19, 47**
Morgan, Berry **6**
Morgan, Frederick **23**
Morgan, Robin **2**
Morris, Wright **1, 3, 7, 18, 37**
Morrison, Jim **17**
Morrison, Toni **4, 10, 22, 55**
Moss, Howard **7, 14, 45, 50**
Motley, Willard **18**
Mueller, Lisel **13, 51**
Mukherjee, Bharati **53**
Mull, Martin **17**
Murphy, Sylvia **34**
Myers, Walter Dean **35**
Nabokov, Vladimir **1, 2, 3, 6, 8, 11, 15, 23, 44, 46**
Nash, Ogden **23**
Naylor, Gloria **28, 52**
Neihardt, John G. **32**
Nelson, Willie **17**
Nemerov, Howard **2, 6, 9, 36**
Neufeld, John **17**
Neville, Emily Cheney **12**
Newlove, Donald **6**
Newman, Charles **2, 8**
Newman, Edwin **14**
Newton, Suzanne **35**
Nichols, John **38**
Niedecker, Lorine **10, 42**
Nin, Anaïs **1, 4, 8, 11, 14**
Nissenson, Hugh **4, 9**
Niven, Larry **8**
Nixon, Agnes Eckhardt **21**
Norman, Marsha **28**
Norton, Andre **12**
Nova, Craig **7, 31**
Nunn, Kem **34**
Nyro, Laura **17**
Oates, Joyce Carol **1, 2, 3, 6, 9, 11, 15, 19, 33, 52**
O'Brien, Darcy **11**
O'Brien, Tim **7, 19, 40**
Ochs, Phil **17**
O'Connor, Edwin **14**
O'Connor, Flannery **1, 2, 3, 6, 10, 13, 15, 21**
O'Dell, Scott **30**
Odets, Clifford **2, 28**
O'Hara, Frank **2, 5, 13**
O'Hara, John **1, 2, 3, 6, 11, 42**
O'Hehir, Diana **41**
Olds, Sharon **32, 39**
Oliver, Mary **19, 34**
Olsen, Tillie **4, 13**
Olson, Charles **1, 2, 5, 6, 9, 11, 29**
Olson, Toby **28**
Oneal, Zibby **30**
Oppen, George **7, 13, 34**
Orlovitz, Gil **22**
Ortiz, Simon J. **45**
Owens, Rochelle **8**
Ozick, Cynthia **3, 7, 28**
Pack, Robert **13**

Paley, Grace **4, 6, 37**
Pancake, Breece D'J **29**
Parini, Jay **54**
Parker, Dorothy **15**
Parker, Robert B. **27**
Parks, Gordon **1, 16**
Pastan, Linda **27**
Patchen, Kenneth **1, 2, 18**
Paterson, Katherine **12, 30**
Pearson, T. R. **39**
Peck, John **3**
Peck, Richard **21**
Peck, Robert Newton **17**
Peckinpah, Sam **20**
Percy, Walker **2, 3, 6, 8, 14, 18, 47**
Perelman, S. J. **3, 5, 9, 15, 23, 44, 49**
Pesetsky, Bette **28**
Peterkin, Julia **31**
Peters, Joan K. **39**
Peters, Robert L. **7**
Petrakis, Harry Mark **3**
Petry, Ann **1, 7, 18**
Philipson, Morris **53**
Phillips, Jayne Anne **15, 33**
Phillips, Robert **28**
Piercy, Marge **3, 6, 14, 18, 27**
Pineda, Cecile **39**
Pinkwater, D. M. **35**
Pinsky, Robert **9, 19, 38**
Pirsig, Robert M. **4, 6**
Plante, David **7, 23, 38**
Plath, Sylvia **1, 2, 3, 5, 9, 11, 14, 17, 50, 51**
Platt, Kin **26**
Plimpton, George **36**
Plumly, Stanley **33**
Pohl, Frederik **18**
Poitier, Sidney **26**
Pollitt, Katha **28**
Pomerance, Bernard **13**
Porter, Katherine Anne **1, 3, 7, 10, 13, 15, 27**
Potok, Chaim **2, 7, 14, 26**
Pound, Ezra **1, 2, 3, 4, 5, 7, 10, 13, 18, 34, 50**
Povod, Reinaldo **44**
Powell, Padgett **34**
Powers, J. F. **1, 4, 8**
Price, Reynolds **3, 6, 13, 43, 50**
Price, Richard **6, 12**
Prince **35**
Pritchard, William H. **34**
Prokosch, Frederic **4, 48**
Prose, Francine **45**
Pryor, Richard **26**
Purdy, James **2, 4, 10, 28, 52**
Puzo, Mario **1, 2, 6, 36**
Pynchon, Thomas **2, 3, 6, 9, 11, 18, 33**
Queen, Ellery **3, 11**
Rabe, David **4, 8, 33**
Rado, James **17**
Raeburn, John **34**
Ragni, Gerome **17**
Rahv, Philip **24**
Rakosi, Carl **47**
Rampersad, Arnold **44**
Rand, Ayn **3, 30, 44**
Randall, Dudley **1**
Ransom, John Crowe **2, 4, 5, 11, 24**
Raphael, Frederic **2, 14**
Rechy, John **1, 7, 14, 18**
Redmon, Anne **22**
Reed, Ishmael **2, 3, 5, 6, 13, 32**

Reed, Lou 21
Remarque, Erich Maria 21
Rexroth, Kenneth 1, 2, 6, 11, 22, 49
Reynolds, Jonathan 6, 38
Reynolds, Michael 44
Reznikoff, Charles 9
Ribman, Ronald 7
Rice, Anne 41
Rice, Elmer 7, 49
Rich, Adrienne 3, 6, 7, 11, 18, 36
Richter, Conrad 30
Riding, Laura 3, 7
Ringwood, Gwen Pharis 48
Robbins, Harold 5
Robbins, Tom 9, 32
Robbins, Trina 21
Robinson, Jill 10
Robinson, Kim Stanley 34
Robinson, Marilynne 25
Robinson, Smokey 21
Robison, Mary 42
Roddenberry, Gene 17
Rodgers, Mary 12
Roethke, Theodore 1, 3, 8, 11, 19, 46
Rogin, Gilbert 18
Roiphe, Anne 3, 9
Rooke, Leon 25, 34
Rosen, Richard 39
Rosenthal, M. L. 28
Rossner, Judith 6, 9, 29
Roth, Henry 2, 6, 11
Roth, Philip 1, 2, 3, 4, 6, 9, 15, 22, 31, 47
Rothenberg, Jerome 6
Rovit, Earl 7
Ruark, Gibbons 3
Rudnik, Raphael 7
Rukeyser, Muriel 6, 10, 15, 27
Rule, Jane 27
Rush, Norman 44
Russ, Joanna 15
Ryan, Cornelius 7
Sachs, Marilyn 35
Sackler, Howard 14
Sadoff, Ira 9
Safire, William 10
Sagan, Carl 30
Saint, H. F. 50
Sainte-Marie, Buffy 17
Salamanca, J. R. 4, 15
Salinger, J. D. 1, 3, 8, 12
Salter, James 7, 52
Sandburg, Carl 1, 4, 10, 15, 35
Sanders, Ed 53
Sanders, Lawrence 41
Sandoz, Mari 28
Saner, Reg 9
Santiago, Danny 33
Santmyer, Helen Hooven 33
Santos, Bienvenido N. 22
Saroyan, William 1, 8, 10, 29, 34
Sarton, May 4, 14, 49
Saul, John 46
Savage, Thomas 40
Savan, Glenn 50
Sayers, Valerie 50
Sayles, John 7, 10, 14
Schaeffer, Susan Fromberg 6, 11, 22
Schell, Jonathan 35
Schevill, James 7
Schisgal, Murray 6
Schnackenberg, Gjertrud 40
Schorer, Mark 9

Schrader, Paul 26
Schulberg, Budd 7, 48
Schulz, Charles M. 12
Schuyler, James 5, 23
Schwartz, Delmore 2, 4, 10, 45
Schwartz, Lynne Sharon 31
Scoppettone, Sandra 26
Scorsese, Martin 20
Scott, Evelyn 43
Scott, Joanna 50
Sebestyen, Ouida 30
Seelye, John 7
Segal, Erich 3, 10
Seger, Bob 35
Seidel, Frederick 18
Selby, Hubert, Jr. 1, 2, 4, 8
Serling, Rod 30
Seton, Cynthia Propper 27
Settle, Mary Lee 19
Sexton, Anne 2, 4, 6, 8, 10, 15, 53
Shaara, Michael 15
Shacochis, Bob 39
Shange, Ntozake 8, 25, 38
Shapiro, Karl 4, 8, 15, 53
Shaw, Irwin 7, 23, 34
Shawn, Wallace 41
Sheed, Wilfrid 2, 4, 10, 53
Shepard, Jim 36
Shepard, Lucius 34
Shepard, Sam 4, 6, 17, 34, 41, 44
Sherburne, Zoa 30
Sherman, Jonathan Marc 55
Sherman, Martin 19
Sherwin, Judith Johnson 7, 15
Shreve, Susan Richards 23
Shue, Larry 52
Shulman, Alix Kates 2, 10
Shuster, Joe 21
Siegel, Jerome 21
Sigal, Clancy 7
Silko, Leslie Marmon 23
Silver, Joan Micklin 20
Silverberg, Robert 7
Silverstein, Alvin 17
Silverstein, Virginia B. 17
Simak, Clifford 55
Simic, Charles 6, 9, 22, 49
Simmons, Dan 44
Simon, Carly 26
Simon, Neil 6, 11, 31, 39
Simon, Paul 17
Simpson, Louis 4, 7, 9, 32
Simpson, Mona 44
Sinclair, Upton 1, 11, 15
Singer, Isaac Bashevis 1, 3, 6, 9, 11, 15, 23, 38
Sissman, L. E. 9, 18
Slade, Bernard 11, 46
Slaughter, Frank G. 29
Slavitt, David 5, 14
Smiley, Jane 53
Smith, Betty 19
Smith, Clark Ashton 43
Smith, Dave 22, 42
Smith, Lee 25
Smith, Martin Cruz 25
Smith, Mary-Ann Tirone 39
Smith, Patti 12
Smith, William Jay 6
Snodgrass, W. D. 2, 6, 10, 18
Snyder, Gary 1, 2, 5, 9, 32
Snyder, Zilpha Keatley 17

Sokolov, Raymond 7
Sommer, Scott 25
Sondheim, Stephen 30, 39
Sontag, Susan 1, 2, 10, 13, 31
Sorrentino, Gilbert 3, 7, 14, 22, 40
Soto, Gary 32
Southern, Terry 7
Spackman, W. M. 46
Spacks, Barry 14
Spanidou, Irini 44
Spencer, Elizabeth 22
Spencer, Scott 30
Spicer, Jack 8, 18
Spielberg, Peter 6
Spielberg, Steven 20
Spillane, Mickey 3, 13
Spinrad, Norman 46
Spivack, Kathleen 6
Spoto, Donald 39
Springsteen, Bruce 17
Squires, Radcliffe 51
Stafford, Jean 4, 7, 19
Stafford, William 4, 7, 29
Stanton, Maura 9
Starbuck, George 53
Steele, Timothy 45
Stegner, Wallace 9, 49
Steinbeck, John 1, 5, 9, 13, 21, 34, 45
Steiner, George 24
Stern, Gerald 40
Stern, Richard G. 4, 39
Sternberg, Josef von 20
Stevens, Mark 34
Stevenson, Anne 7, 33
Still, James 49
Stitt, Milan 29
Stolz, Mary 12
Stone, Irving 7
Stone, Robert 5, 23, 42
Storm, Hyemeyohsts 3
Stout, Rex 3
Strand, Mark 6, 18, 41
Straub, Peter 28
Stribling, T. S. 23
Stuart, Jesse 1, 8, 11, 14, 34
Sturgeon, Theodore 22, 39
Styron, William 1, 3, 5, 11, 15
Sukenick, Ronald 3, 4, 6, 48
Summers, Hollis 10
Susann, Jacqueline 3
Swados, Elizabeth 12
Swados, Harvey 5
Swarthout, Glendon 35
Swenson, May 4, 14
Talese, Gay 37
Tallent, Elizabeth 45
Tally, Ted 42
Tate, Allen 2, 4, 6, 9, 11, 14, 24
Tate, James 2, 6, 25
Tavel, Ronald 6
Taylor, Eleanor Ross 5
Taylor, Henry 44
Taylor, Mildred D. 21
Taylor, Peter 1, 4, 18, 37, 44, 50
Taylor, Robert Lewis 14
Terkel, Studs 38
Terry, Megan 19
Tesich, Steve 40
Tevis, Walter 42
Theroux, Alexander 2, 25
Theroux, Paul 5, 8, 11, 15, 28, 46
Thomas, Audrey 7, 13, 37

Thomas, Joyce Carol 35
Thomas, Lewis 35
Thomas, Piri 17
Thomas, Ross 39
Thompson, Hunter S. 9, 17, 40
Thurber, James 5, 11, 25
Tillinghast, Richard 29
Tiptree, James, Jr. 48, 50
Tolson, Melvin B. 36
Tomlin, Lily 17
Toole, John Kennedy 19
Toomer, Jean 1, 4, 13, 22
Torrey, E. Fuller 34
Traven, B. 8, 11
Trevanian 29
Trilling, Lionel 9, 11, 24
Trow, George W. S. 52
Trudeau, Garry 12
Trumbo, Dalton 19
Tryon, Thomas 3, 11
Tunis, John R. 12
Turco, Lewis 11
Tyler, Anne 7, 11, 18, 28, 44
Tytell, John 50
Uhry, Alfred 55
Unger, Douglas 34
Updike, John 1, 2, 3, 5, 7, 9, 13, 15, 23, 34, 43
Urdang, Constance 47
Uris, Leon 7, 32
Van Ash, Cay 34
Van Doren, Mark 6, 10
Van Duyn, Mona 3, 7
Van Peebles, Melvin 2, 20
Van Vechten, Carl 33
Vance, Jack 35
Vidal, Gore 2, 4, 6, 8, 10, 22, 33
Viereck, Peter 4
Vinge, Joan D. 30
Vliet, R. G. 22
Voigt, Cynthia 30
Voigt, Ellen Bryant 54
Vonnegut, Kurt, Jr. 1, 2, 3, 4, 5, 8, 12, 22, 40
Wagman, Frederica 7
Wagner-Martin, Linda 50
Wagoner, David 3, 5, 15
Wakefield, Dan 7
Wakoski, Diane 2, 4, 7, 9, 11, 40
Waldman, Anne 7
Walker, Alice 5, 6, 9, 19, 27, 46
Walker, Joseph A. 19
Walker, Margaret 1, 6
Wallace, David Foster 50
Wallace, Irving 7, 13
Wallant, Edward Lewis 5, 10
Wambaugh, Joseph 3, 18
Ward, Douglas Turner 19
Warhol, Andy 20
Warren, Robert Penn 1, 4, 6, 8, 10, 13, 18, 39, 53
Wasserstein, Wendy 32
Watkins, Paul 55
Webb, Charles 7
Webb, James H., Jr. 22
Weber, Lenora Mattingly 12
Weidman, Jerome 7
Weiss, Theodore 3, 8, 14
Welch, James 6, 14, 52
Wellek, René 28
Weller, Michael 10, 53
Welles, Orson 20

Wellman, Manly Wade 49
Wells, Rosemary 12
Welty, Eudora 1, 2, 5, 14, 22, 33
Wersba, Barbara 30
Wescott, Glenway 13
Wesley, Richard 7
West, Jessamyn 7, 17
West, Paul 7, 14
Westlake, Donald E. 7, 33
Whalen, Philip 6, 29
Wharton, William 18, 37
Wheelock, John Hall 14
White, E. B. 10, 34, 39
White, Edmund III 27
Whitney, Phyllis A. 42
Whittemore, Reed 4
Wicker, Tom 7
Wideman, John Edgar 5, 34, 36
Wieners, John 7
Wiesel, Elie 3, 5, 11, 37
Wilbur, Richard 3, 6, 9, 14, 53
Wild, Peter 14
Wilder, Billy 20
Wilder, Thornton 1, 5, 6, 10, 15, 35
Wiley, Richard 44
Wilhelm, Kate 7
Willard, Nancy 7, 37
Williams, C. K. 33
Williams, John A. 5, 13
Williams, Jonathan 13
Williams, Joy 31
Williams, Norman 39
Williams, Tennessee 1, 2, 5, 7, 8, 11, 15, 19, 30, 39, 45
Williams, Thomas 14
Williams, William Carlos 1, 2, 5, 9, 13, 22, 42
Williamson, Jack 29
Willingham, Calder 5, 51
Wilson, August 39, 50
Wilson, Brian 12
Wilson, Edmund 1, 2, 3, 8, 24
Wilson, Lanford 7, 14, 36
Wilson, Robert 7, 9
Wilson, Sloan 32
Wilson, William S. 49
Winters, Yvor 4, 8, 32
Wiseman, Frederick 20
Wodehouse, P. G. 1, 2, 5, 10, 22
Woiwode, Larry 6, 10
Wojciechowska, Maia 26
Wolfe, Gene 25
Wolfe, George C. 49
Wolfe, Tom 1, 2, 9, 15, 35, 51
Wolff, Geoffrey 41
Wolff, Tobias 39
Wolitzer, Hilma 17
Wonder, Stevie 12
Wong, Jade Snow 17
Wouk, Herman 1, 9, 38
Wright, Charles 6, 13, 28
Wright, Charles (Stevenson) 49
Wright, James 3, 5, 10, 28
Wright, Richard 1, 3, 4, 9, 14, 21, 48
Wright, Stephen 33
Wright, William 44
Wurlitzer, Rudolph 2, 4, 15
Wylie, Philip 43
Yates, Richard 7, 8, 23
Yep, Laurence 35
Yerby, Frank G. 1, 7, 22
Yglesias, Helen 7, 22

Young, Al 19
Yurick, Sol 6
Zappa, Frank 17
Zaturenska, Marya 6, 11
Zelazny, Roger 21
Ziegenhagen, Eric 55
Zindel, Paul 6, 26
Zukofsky, Louis 1, 2, 4, 7, 11, 18
Zweig, Paul 34, 42

ARAB
Shamas, Anton 55

ARGENTINIAN
Bioy Casares, Adolfo 4, 8, 13
Borges, Jorge Luis 1, 2, 3, 4, 6, 8, 9, 10, 13, 19, 44, 48
Cortázar, Julio 2, 3, 5, 10, 13, 15, 33, 34
Costantini, Humberto 49
Mujica Láinez, Manuel 31
Puig, Manuel 3, 5, 10, 28
Sabato, Ernesto 10, 23
Valenzuela, Luisa 31

ARMENIAN
Mamoulian, Rouben 16

AUSTRALIAN
Anderson, Jessica 37
Astley, Thea 41
Brinsmead, H. F. 21
Carey, Peter 40, 55
Clark, Mavis Thorpe 12
Davison, Frank Dalby 15
Elliott, Sumner Locke 38
FitzGerald, Robert D. 19
Hall, Rodney 51
Hazzard, Shirley 18
Hope, A. D. 3, 51
Hospital, Janette Turner 42
Jolley, Elizabeth 46
Jones, Rod 50
Keneally, Thomas 5, 8, 10, 14, 19, 27, 43
Koch, C. J. 42
Malouf, David 28
Matthews, Greg 45
McAuley, James 45
McCullough, Colleen 27
Murray, Les A. 40
Porter, Peter 5, 13, 33
Prichard, Katharine Susannah 46
Shapcott, Thomas W. 38
Slessor, Kenneth 14
Stead, Christina 2, 5, 8, 32
Stow, Randolph 23, 48
Thiele, Colin 17
Weir, Peter 20
West, Morris L. 6, 33
White, Patrick 3, 4, 5, 7, 9, 18
Wright, Judith 11, 53

AUSTRIAN
Adamson, Joy 17
Bernhard, Thomas 3, 32
Canetti, Elias 3, 14, 25
Gregor, Arthur 9
Handke, Peter 5, 8, 10, 15, 38
Hochwälder, Fritz 36
Jandl, Ernst 34
Lang, Fritz 20
Lind, Jakov 1, 2, 4, 27
Sternberg, Josef von 20

Nationality Index

Wellek, René   28
Wilder, Billy   20

BARBADIAN
Brathwaite, Edward   11
Clarke, Austin C.   8, 53
Lamming, George   2, 4

BELGIAN
Ghelderode, Michel de   6, 11
Lévi-Strauss, Claude   38
Mallet-Joris, Françoise   11
Michaux, Henri   8, 19
Sarton, May   4, 14, 49
Simenon, Georges   1, 2, 3, 8, 18, 47
Tytell, John   50
Van Itallie, Jean-Claude   3
Yourcenar, Marguerite   19, 38, 50

BRAZILIAN
Amado, Jorge   13, 40
Andrade, Carlos Drummond de   18
Dourado, Autran   23
Lispector, Clarice   43
Ribeiro, Darcy   34
Ribeiro, João Ubaldo   10
Rosa, João Guimarães   23

BULGARIAN
Bagryana, Elisaveta   10

CAMEROONIAN
Beti, Mongo   27

CANADIAN
Acorn, Milton   15
Aquin, Hubert   15
Atwood, Margaret   2, 3, 4, 8, 13, 15, 25, 44
Avison, Margaret   2, 4
Barfoot, Joan   18
Bellow, Saul   1, 2, 3, 6, 8, 10, 13, 15, 25, 33, 34
Birney, Earle   1, 4, 6, 11
Bissett, Bill   18
Blais, Marie-Claire   2, 4, 6, 13, 22
Blaise, Clark   29
Bowering, George   15, 47
Bowering, Marilyn R.   32
Buckler, Ernest   13
Buell, John   10
Callaghan, Morley   3, 14, 41
Carrier, Roch   13
Child, Philip   19
Chislett, Anne   34
Cohen, Leonard   3, 38
Cohen, Matt   19
Coles, Don   46
Craven, Margaret   17
Davies, Robertson   2, 7, 13, 25, 42
De la Roche, Mazo   14
Donnell, David   34
Dudek, Louis   11, 19
Engel, Marian   36
Everson, Ronald G.   27
Faludy, George   42
Finch, Robert   18
Findley, Timothy   27
Frye, Northrop   24
Gallant, Mavis   7, 18, 38
Garner, Hugh   13
Glassco, John   9
Gotlieb, Phyllis   18

Govier, Katherine   51
Gustafson, Ralph   36
Haig-Brown, Roderick L.   21
Hailey, Arthur   5
Harris, Christie   12
Hébert, Anne   4, 13, 29
Hine, Daryl   15
Hodgins, Jack   23
Hood, Hugh   15, 28
Hospital, Janette Turner   42
Hyde, Anthony   42
Jacobsen, Josephine   48
Jiles, Paulette   13
Johnston, George   51
Jones, D. G.   10
Kelly, M. T.   55
Kinsella, W. P.   27, 43
Klein, A. M.   19
Kroetsch, Robert   5, 23
Lane, Patrick   25
Laurence, Margaret   3, 6, 13, 50
Layton, Irving   2, 15
Levine, Norman   54
Lightfoot, Gordon   26
Livesay, Dorothy   4, 15
MacEwen, Gwendolyn   13, 55
MacLennan, Hugh   2, 14
Macpherson, Jay   14
Maillet, Antonine   54
Major, Kevin   26
McFadden, David   48
McLuhan, Marshall   37
Metcalf, John   37
Mitchell, Joni   12
Mitchell, W. O.   25
Moore, Brian   1, 3, 5, 7, 8, 19, 32
Morgan, Janet   39
Mowat, Farley   26
Munro, Alice   6, 10, 19, 50
Musgrave, Susan   13, 54
Newlove, John   14
Nichol, B. P.   18
Nowlan, Alden   15
Ondaatje, Michael   14, 29, 51
Page, P. K.   7, 18
Pollack, Sharon   50
Pratt, E. J.   19
Purdy, A. W.   3, 6, 14, 50
Reaney, James   13
Richler, Mordecai   3, 5, 9, 13, 18, 46
Ringwood, Gwen Pharis   48
Ritter, Erika   52
Rooke, Leon   25, 34
Rosenblatt, Joe   15
Ross, Sinclair   13
Roy, Gabrielle   10, 14
Rule, Jane   27
Ryga, George   14
Scott, F. R.   22
Skelton, Robin   13
Slade, Bernard   11, 46
Smart, Elizabeth   54
Smith, A. J. M.   15
Souster, Raymond   5, 14
Suknaski, Andrew   19
Thomas, Audrey   7, 13, 37
Thompson, Judith   39
Tremblay, Michel   29
Vanderhaeghe, Guy   41
Vizinczey, Stephen   40
Waddington, Miriam   28
Wah, Fred   44

Walker, David Harry   14
Walker, George F.   44
Webb, Phyllis   18
Wiebe, Rudy   6, 11, 14
Wilson, Ethel Davis   13
Wright, L. R.   44
Wright, Richard B.   6
Young, Neil   17

CHILEAN
Allende, Isabel   39
Donoso, José   4, 8, 11, 32
Dorfman, Ariel   48
Neruda, Pablo   1, 2, 5, 7, 9, 28
Parra, Nicanor   2

CHINESE
Ch'ien Chung-shu   22
Kingston, Maxine Hong   12, 19
Lord, Bette Bao   23
Mo, Timothy   46
Pa Chin   18
Peake, Mervyn   7
Wong, Jade Snow   17

COLOMBIAN
García Márquez, Gabriel   2, 3, 8, 10, 15, 27, 47, 55

CUBAN
Arenas, Reinaldo   41
Cabrera Infante, G.   5, 25, 45
Carpentier, Alejo   8, 11, 38
Fornes, Maria Irene   39
Guillén, Nicolás   48
Lezama Lima, José   4, 10
Padilla, Heberto   38
Sarduy, Severo   6

CZECHOSLOVAKIAN
Havel, Václav   25
Hrabal, Bohumil   13
Kohout, Pavel   13
Kundera, Milan   4, 9, 19, 32
Seifert, Jaroslav   34, 44
Škvorecký, Josef   15, 39
Stoppard, Tom   1, 3, 4, 5, 8, 15, 29, 34
Vaculík, Ludvík   7

DANISH
Abell, Kjeld   15
Bødker, Cecil   21
Dinesen, Isak   10, 29
Dreyer, Carl Theodor   16

DUTCH
Bernhard, Thomas   3, 32
De Hartog, Jan   19
Mulisch, Harry   42
Ruyslinck, Ward   14
Van de Wetering, Janwillem   47

EGYPTIAN
Chedid, Andrée   47
Mahfūz, Najīb   52, 55

ENGLISH
Ackroyd, Peter   34, 52
Adams, Douglas   27
Adams, Richard   4, 5, 18
Adcock, Fleur   41
Aiken, Joan   35

Aldington, Richard 49
Aldiss, Brian W. 5, 14, 40
Allingham, Margery 19
Almedingen, E. M. 12
Alvarez, A. 5, 13
Ambler, Eric 4, 6, 9
Amis, Kingsley 1, 2, 3, 5, 8, 13, 40, 44
Amis, Martin 4, 9, 38
Anderson, Lindsay 20
Anthony, Piers 35
Archer, Jeffrey 28
Arden, John 6, 13, 15
Armatrading, Joan 17
Arthur, Ruth M. 12
Arundel, Honor 17
Auden, W. H. 1, 2, 3, 4, 6, 9, 11, 14, 43
Ayckbourn, Alan 5, 8, 18, 33
Ayrton, Michael 7
Bagnold, Enid 25
Bailey, Paul 45
Bainbridge, Beryl 4, 5, 8, 10, 14, 18, 22
Ballard, J. G. 3, 6, 14, 36
Banks, Lynne Reid 23
Barker, Clive 52
Barker, George 8, 48
Barker, Howard 37
Barker, Pat 32
Barnes, Julian 42
Barnes, Peter 5
Bates, H. E. 46
Bennett, Alan 45
Berger, John 2, 19
Bermant, Chaim 40
Betjeman, John 2, 6, 10, 34, 43
Billington, Rachel 43
Binyon, T. J. 34
Blunden, Edmund 2
Bogarde, Dirk 19
Bolt, Robert 14
Bond, Edward 4, 6, 13, 23
Booth, Martin 13
Bowen, Elizabeth 1, 3, 6, 11, 15, 22
Bowie, David 17
Boyd, William 28, 53
Bradbury, Malcolm 32
Bragg, Melvyn 10
Braine, John 1, 3, 41
Brenton, Howard 31
Brittain, Vera 23
Brooke-Rose, Christine 40
Brookner, Anita 32, 34, 51
Brophy, Brigid 6, 11, 29
Brunner, John 8, 10
Bunting, Basil 10, 39, 47
Burgess, Anthony 1, 2, 4, 5, 8, 10, 13, 15, 22, 40
Byatt, A. S. 19
Caldwell, Taylor 2, 28, 39
Campbell, Ramsey 42
Carter, Angela 5, 41
Causley, Charles 7
Caute, David 29
Chambers, Aidan 35
Chaplin, Charles 16
Chatwin, Bruce 28
Christie, Agatha 1, 6, 8, 12, 39, 48
Churchill, Caryl 31, 55
Clark, Brian 29
Clarke, Arthur C. 1, 4, 13, 18, 35
Clash, The 30
Clavell, James 6, 25
Colegate, Isabel 36

Comfort, Alex 7
Compton-Burnett, Ivy 1, 3, 10, 15, 34
Costello, Elvis 21
Coward, Noël 1, 9, 29, 51
Creasey, John 11
Crispin, Edmund 22
Dahl, Roald 1, 6, 18
Daryush, Elizabeth 6, 19
Davie, Donald 5, 8, 10, 31
Davies, Ray 21
Davies, Rhys 23
Day Lewis, C. 1, 6, 10
Deighton, Len 4, 7, 22, 46
Delaney, Shelagh 29
Dennis, Nigel 8
Dickinson, Peter 12, 35
Drabble, Margaret 2, 3, 5, 8, 10, 22, 53
Du Maurier, Daphne 6, 11
Duffy, Maureen 37
Durrell, Lawrence 1, 4, 6, 8, 13, 27, 41
Edgar, David 42
Edwards, G. B. 25
Eliot, T. S. 1, 2, 3, 6, 9, 10, 13, 15, 24, 34, 41, 55
Elliott, Janice 47
Ellis, A. E. 7
Ellis, Alice Thomas 40
Empson, William 3, 8, 19, 33, 34
Enright, D. J. 4, 8, 31
Ewart, Gavin 13, 46
Fairbairns, Zoë 32
Farrell, J. G. 6
Feinstein, Elaine 36
Fenton, James 32
Figes, Eva 31
Fisher, Roy 25
Fitzgerald, Penelope 19, 51
Fleming, Ian 3, 30
Follett, Ken 18
Forester, C. S. 35
Forster, E. M. 1, 2, 3, 4, 9, 10, 13, 15, 22, 45
Forsyth, Frederick 2, 5, 36
Fowles, John 1, 2, 3, 4, 6, 9, 10, 15, 33
Francis, Dick 2, 22, 42
Fraser, Antonia 32
Fraser, George MacDonald 7
Frayn, Michael 3, 7, 31, 47
Freeling, Nicolas 38
Fry, Christopher 2, 10, 14
Fugard, Sheila 48
Fuller, Roy 4, 28
Gardam, Jane 43
Gardner, John (Edmund) 30
Garfield, Leon 12
Garner, Alan 17
Garnett, David 3
Gascoyne, David 45
Gerhardie, William 5
Gilliatt, Penelope 2, 10, 13, 53
Glanville, Brian 6
Glendinning, Victoria 50
Gloag, Julian 40
Godden, Rumer 53
Golding, William 1, 2, 3, 8, 10, 17, 27
Graham, Winston 23
Graves, Richard P. 44
Graves, Robert 1, 2, 6, 11, 39, 44, 45
Gray, Simon 9, 14, 36
Green, Henry 2, 13
Greene, Graham 1, 3, 6, 9, 14, 18, 27, 37
Griffiths, Trevor 13, 52

Grigson, Geoffrey 7, 39
Gunn, Thom 3, 6, 18, 32
Haig-Brown, Roderick L. 21
Hailey, Arthur 5
Hall, Rodney 51
Hamburger, Michael 5, 14
Hamilton, Patrick 51
Hampton, Christopher 4
Hare, David 29
Harrison, Tony 43
Hartley, L. P. 2, 22
Harwood, Ronald 32
Hastings, Selina 44
Heppenstall, Rayner 10
Herriot, James 12
Hibbert, Eleanor 7
Hill, Geoffrey 5, 8, 18, 45
Hill, Susan B. 4
Hinde, Thomas 6, 11
Hitchcock, Alfred 16
Hocking, Mary 13
Holden, Ursula 18
Holdstock, Robert 39
Hollinghurst, Alan 55
Hooker, Jeremy 43
Hopkins, John 4
Household, Geoffrey 11
Howard, Elizabeth Jane 7, 29
Hughes, Richard 1, 11
Hughes, Ted 2, 4, 9, 14, 37
Huxley, Aldous 1, 3, 4, 5, 8, 11, 18, 35
Ingalls, Rachel 42
Isherwood, Christopher 1, 9, 11, 14, 44
Jacobson, Dan 4, 14
Jagger, Mick 17
James, P. D. 18, 46
Jellicoe, Ann 27
Jennings, Elizabeth 5, 14
Jhabvala, Ruth Prawer 4, 8, 29
Johnson, B. S. 6, 9
Johnson, Pamela Hansford 1, 7, 27
Jolley, Elizabeth 46
Jones, David 2, 4, 7, 13, 42
Jones, Diana Wynne 26
Jones, Mervyn 10, 52
Josipovici, Gabriel 6, 43
Kavan, Anna 5, 13
Kaye, M. M. 28
Keates, Jonathan 34
King, Francis 8, 53
Koestler, Arthur 1, 3, 6, 8, 15, 33
Kops, Bernard 4
Larkin, Philip 3, 5, 8, 9, 13, 18, 33, 39
Le Carré, John 3, 5, 9, 15, 28
Leavis, F. R. 24
Lee, Tanith 46
Lehmann, Rosamond 5
Lennon, John 12, 35
Lessing, Doris 1, 2, 3, 6, 10, 15, 22, 40
Levertov, Denise 1, 2, 3, 5, 8, 15, 28
Levi, Peter 41
Lewis, C. S. 1, 3, 6, 14, 27
Lively, Penelope 32, 50
Lodge, David 36
Loy, Mina 28
Luke, Peter 38
MacInnes, Colin 4, 23
Mackenzie, Compton 18
MacNeice, Louis 1, 4, 10, 53
Macpherson, Jay 14
Maitland, Sara 49
Manning, Olivia 5, 19

Markandaya, Kamala **8, 38**
Masefield, John **11, 47**
Maugham, W. Somerset **1, 11, 15**
Mayne, William **12**
McCartney, Paul **12, 35**
McEwan, Ian **13**
McGrath, Patrick **55**
Mercer, David **5**
Metcalf, John **37**
Middleton, Christopher **13**
Middleton, Stanley **7, 38**
Mitford, Nancy **44**
Mo, Timothy **46**
Monty Python **21**
Moorcock, Michael **5, 27**
Mortimer, John **28, 43**
Mortimer, Penelope **5**
Mosley, Nicholas **43**
Motion, Andrew **47**
Mott, Michael **15, 34**
Murdoch, Iris **1, 2, 3, 4, 6, 8, 11, 15, 22, 31, 51**
Naipaul, V. S. **4, 7, 9, 13, 18, 37**
Newby, P. H. **2, 13**
Nichols, Peter **5, 36**
Nye, Robert **13, 42**
O'Brien, Richard **17**
O'Faolain, Julia **6, 19, 47**
Olivier, Laurence **20**
Orton, Joe **4, 13, 43**
Osborne, John **1, 2, 5, 11, 45**
Osborne, Lawrence **50**
Page, Jimmy **12**
Page, Louise **40**
Parkin, Frank **43**
Paulin, Tom **37**
Peake, Mervyn **7, 54**
Pearce, Philippa **21**
Pink Floyd **35**
Pinter, Harold **1, 3, 6, 9, 11, 15, 27**
Plant, Robert **12**
Poliakoff, Stephen **38**
Police, The **26**
Poole, Josephine **17**
Powell, Anthony **1, 3, 7, 9, 10, 31**
Pownall, David **10**
Powys, John Cowper **7, 9, 15, 46**
Priestley, J. B. **2, 5, 9, 34**
Prince, F. T. **22**
Pritchett, V. S. **5, 13, 15, 41**
Pym, Barbara **13, 19, 37**
Quin, Ann **6**
Raine, Craig **32**
Raine, Kathleen **7, 45**
Rathbone, Julian **41**
Rattigan, Terence **7**
Raven, Simon **14**
Read, Herbert **4**
Read, Piers Paul **4, 10, 25**
Reading, Peter **47**
Redgrove, Peter **6, 41**
Reid, Christopher **33**
Renault, Mary **3, 11, 17**
Rendell, Ruth **28, 48, 50**
Rhys, Jean **2, 4, 6, 14, 19, 51**
Rice, Tim **21**
Richard, Keith **17**
Richards, I. A. **14, 24**
Roberts, Keith **14**
Roberts, Michèle **48**
Rudkin, David **14**
Rushforth, Peter **19**

Russell, Ken **16**
Sansom, William **2, 6**
Sassoon, Siegfried **36**
Scammell, Michael **34**
Scannell, Vernon **49**
Schlee, Ann **35**
Scott, Paul **9**
Shaffer, Anthony **19**
Shaffer, Peter **5, 14, 18, 37**
Sharpe, Tom **36**
Shaw, Robert **5**
Sheed, Wilfrid **2, 4, 10, 53**
Shute, Nevil **30**
Shuttle, Penelope **7**
Silkin, Jon **2, 6, 43**
Sillitoe, Alan **1, 3, 6, 10, 19**
Simpson, N. F. **29**
Sinclair, Andrew **2, 14**
Sisson, C. H. **8**
Sitwell, Edith **2, 9**
Smith, Stevie **3, 8, 25, 44**
Snow, C. P. **1, 4, 6, 9, 13, 19**
Spender, Stephen **1, 2, 5, 10, 41**
Spurling, Hilary **34**
Stannard, Martin **44**
Stewart, J. I. M. **7, 14, 32**
Stewart, Mary **7, 35**
Stoppard, Tom **1, 3, 4, 5, 8, 15, 29, 34**
Storey, David **2, 4, 5, 8**
Streatfeild, Noel **21**
Sutcliff, Rosemary **26**
Swift, Graham **41**
Swinfen, Ann **34**
Swinnerton, Frank **31**
Symons, Julian **2, 14, 32**
Szirtes, George **46**
Taylor, Elizabeth **2, 4, 29**
Tennant, Emma **13, 52**
Teran, Lisa St. Aubin de **36**
Thomas, D. M. **13, 22, 31**
Tindall, Gillian **7**
Tolkien, J. R. R. **1, 2, 3, 8, 12, 38**
Tomlinson, Charles **2, 4, 6, 13, 45**
Townshend, Peter **17, 42**
Tremain, Rose **42**
Tuohy, Frank **37**
Ustinov, Peter **1**
Vansittart, Peter **42**
Wain, John **2, 11, 15, 46**
Walker, Ted **13**
Walsh, Jill Paton **35**
Warner, Francis **14**
Warner, Rex **45**
Warner, Sylvia Townsend **7, 19**
Waterhouse, Keith **47**
Waugh, Auberon **7**
Waugh, Evelyn **1, 3, 8, 13, 19, 27, 44**
Waugh, Harriet **6**
Webber, Andrew Lloyd **21**
Weldon, Fay **6, 9, 11, 19, 36**
Weller, Paul **26**
Wesker, Arnold **3, 5, 42**
West, Anthony **50**
West, Paul **7, 14**
West, Rebecca **7, 9, 31, 50**
Westall, Robert **17**
White, Patrick **3, 4, 5, 7, 9, 18**
White, T. H. **30**
Whitehead, E. A. **5**
Whitemore, Hugh **37**
Williams, Hugo **42**
Wilson, A. N. **33**

Wilson, Angus **2, 3, 5, 25, 34**
Wilson, Colin **3, 14**
Wilson, Snoo **33**
Wodehouse, P. G. **1, 2, 5, 10, 22**
Wyndham, John **19**
Young, Andrew **5**

FIJIAN
Prichard, Katharine Susannah **46**

FINNISH
Haavikko, Paavo **18, 34**
Salama, Hannu **18**
Sillanpää, Franz Eemil **19**

FRENCH
Adamov, Arthur **4, 25**
Anouilh, Jean **1, 3, 8, 13, 40, 50**
Aragon, Louis **3, 22**
Arrabal, Fernando **2, 9, 18**
Audiberti, Jacques **38**
Aymé, Marcel **11**
Barthes, Roland **24**
Barzun, Jacques **51**
Bataille, Georges **29**
Beauvoir, Simone de **1, 2, 4, 8, 14, 31, 44, 50**
Beckett, Samuel **1, 2, 3, 4, 6, 9, 10, 11, 14, 18, 29**
Bonnefoy, Yves **9, 15**
Bresson, Robert **16**
Breton, André **2, 9, 15, 54**
Butor, Michel **1, 3, 8, 11, 15**
Cayrol, Jean **11**
Céline, Louis-Ferdinand **1, 3, 4, 7, 9, 15, 47**
Cendrars, Blaise **18**
Chabrol, Claude **16**
Char, René **9, 11, 14, 55**
Chedid, Andrée **47**
Clair, René **20**
Cocteau, Jean **1, 8, 15, 16, 43**
Cousteau, Jacques-Yves **30**
Del Castillo, Michel **38**
Derrida, Jacques **24**
Duhamel, Georges **8**
Duras, Marguerite **3, 6, 11, 20, 34, 40**
Federman, Raymond **6, 47**
Foucault, Michel **31, 34**
Francis, Claude **50**
Gary, Romain **25**
Gascar, Pierre **11**
Genet, Jean **1, 2, 5, 10, 14, 44, 46**
Giono, Jean **4, 11**
Godard, Jean-Luc **20**
Goldmann, Lucien **24**
Gontier, Fernande **50**
Gracq, Julien **11, 48**
Gray, Francine du Plessix **22**
Green, Julien **3, 11**
Guillevic **33**
Ionesco, Eugène **1, 4, 6, 9, 11, 15, 41**
Jouve, Pierre Jean **47**
Laurent, Antoine **50**
Le Clézio, J. M. G. **31**
Leduc, Violette **22**
Lévi-Strauss, Claude **38**
Mallet-Joris, Françoise **11**
Malraux, André **1, 4, 9, 13, 15**
Mandiargues, André Pieyre de **41**
Marcel, Gabriel **15**
Mauriac, Claude **9**

Mauriac, François **4, 9**
Merton, Thomas **1, 3, 11, 34**
Modiano, Patrick **18**
Montherlant, Henri de **8, 19**
Morand, Paul **41**
Perse, St.-John **4, 11, 46**
Pinget, Robert **7, 13, 37**
Ponge, Francis **6, 18**
Prévert, Jacques **15**
Queneau, Raymond **2, 5, 10, 42**
Renoir, Jean **20**
Resnais, Alain **16**
Reverdy, Pierre **53**
Rio, Michel **43**
Robbe-Grillet, Alain **1, 2, 4, 6, 8, 10, 14, 43**
Rohmer, Eric **16**
Romains, Jules **7**
Sagan, Françoise **3, 6, 9, 17, 36**
Sarduy, Severo **6**
Sarraute, Nathalie **1, 2, 4, 8, 10, 31**
Sartre, Jean-Paul **1, 4, 7, 9, 13, 18, 24, 44, 50, 52**
Schwarz-Bart, André **2, 4**
Schwarz-Bart, Simone **7**
Simenon, Georges **1, 2, 3, 8, 18, 47**
Simon, Claude **4, 9, 15, 39**
Steiner, George **24**
Tournier, Michel **6, 23, 36**
Troyat, Henri **23**
Truffaut, François **20**
Tzara, Tristan **47**
Varda, Agnès **16**
Wittig, Monique **22**
Yourcenar, Marguerite **19, 38, 50**

GERMAN
Amichai, Yehuda **9, 22**
Becker, Jurek **7, 19**
Benary-Isbert, Margot **12**
Bienek, Horst **7, 11**
Böll, Heinrich **2, 3, 6, 9, 11, 15, 27, 39**
Buchheim, Lothar-Günther **6**
Bukowski, Charles **2, 5, 9, 41**
Dürrenmatt, Friedrich **1, 4, 8, 11, 15, 43**
Eich, Günter **15**
Ende, Michael **31**
Enzensberger, Hans Magnus **43**
Fassbinder, Rainer Werner **20**
Figes, Eva **31**
Grass, Günter **1, 2, 4, 6, 11, 15, 22, 32, 49**
Hamburger, Michael **5, 14**
Heidegger, Martin **24**
Herzog, Werner **16**
Hesse, Hermann **1, 2, 3, 6, 11, 17, 25**
Heym, Stefan **41**
Hildesheimer, Wolfgang **49**
Hochhuth, Rolf **4, 11, 18**
Hofmann, Gert **54**
Johnson, Uwe **5, 10, 15, 40**
Kroetz, Franz Xaver **41**
Kunze, Reiner **10**
Lenz, Siegfried **27**
Levitin, Sonia **17**
Mueller, Lisel **13, 51**
Nossack, Hans Erich **6**
Preussler, Otfried **17**
Remarque, Erich Maria **21**
Riefenstahl, Leni **16**
Sachs, Nelly **14**
Seghers, Anna **7**
Strauss, Botho **22**

Süskind, Patrick **44**
Walser, Martin **27**
Weiss, Peter **3, 15, 51**
Wellershoff, Dieter **46**
Wolf, Christa **14, 29**
Zuckmayer, Carl **18**

GHANAIAN
Armah, Ayi Kwei **5, 33**

GREEK
Broumas, Olga **10**
Elytis, Odysseus **15, 49**
Haviaras, Stratis **33**
Karapánou, Margaríta **13**
Nakos, Lilika **29**
Ritsos, Yannis **6, 13, 31**
Samarakis, Antonis **5**
Seferis, George **5, 11**
Spanidou, Irini **44**
Vassilikos, Vassilis **4, 8**

GUADELOUPEAN
Condé, Maryse **52**
Schwarz-Bart, Simone **7**

GUATEMALAN
Asturias, Miguel Ángel **3, 8, 13**

GUINEAN
Laye, Camara **4, 38**

GUYANESE
Harris, Wilson **25**

HUNGARIAN
Faludy, George **42**
Koestler, Arthur **1, 3, 6, 8, 15, 33**
Konrád, György **4, 10**
Lengyel, József **7**
Lukács, Georg **24**
Nagy, László **7**
Szirtes, George **46**
Tabori, George **19**
Vizinczey, Stephen **40**
Wiesel, Elie **3, 5, 11, 37**

ICELANDIC
Laxness, Halldór **25**

INDIAN
Anand, Mulk Raj **23**
Desai, Anita **19, 37**
Ghosh, Amitav **44**
Mahapatra, Jayanta **33**
Markandaya, Kamala **8, 38**
Mehta, Ved **37**
Mukherjee, Bharati **53**
Narayan, R. K. **7, 28, 47**
Rao, Raja **25**
Ray, Satyajit **16**
Rushdie, Salman **23, 31, 55**
Sahgal, Nayantara **41**
Sealy, I. Allan **55**
Seth, Vikram **43**
Singh, Khushwant **11**

IRANIAN
Modarressi, Taghi **44**
Shamlu, Ahmad **10**

IRISH
Banville, John **46**
Beckett, Samuel **1, 2, 3, 4, 6, 9, 10, 11, 14, 18, 29**
Behan, Brendan **1, 8, 11, 15**
Blackwood, Caroline **6, 9**
Boland, Eavan **40**
Bowen, Elizabeth **1, 3, 6, 11, 15, 22**
Boyle, Patrick **19**
Brennan, Maeve **5**
Carroll, Paul Vincent **10**
Clarke, Austin **6, 9**
Dillon, Eilís **17**
Donleavy, J. P. **1, 4, 6, 10, 45**
Durcan, Paul **43**
Gébler, Carlo **39**
Friel, Brian **5, 42**
Hanley, James **3, 5, 8, 13**
Heaney, Seamus **5, 7, 14, 25, 37**
Johnston, Jennifer **7**
Kavanagh, Patrick **22**
Keane, Molly **31**
Kiely, Benedict **23, 43**
Kinsella, Thomas **4, 19**
Lavin, Mary **4, 18**
Leonard, Hugh **19**
Longley, Michael **29**
Mac Laverty, Bernard **31**
MacNeice, Louis **1, 4, 10, 53**
Mahon, Derek **27**
McGahern, John **5, 9**
McGinley, Patrick **41**
McGuckian, Medbh **48**
Montague, John **13, 46**
Moore, Brian **1, 3, 5, 7, 8, 19, 32**
Morrison, Van **21**
Muldoon, Paul **32**
Murphy, Richard **41**
Murphy, Thomas **51**
O'Brien, Edna **3, 5, 8, 13, 36**
O'Brien, Flann **1, 4, 5, 7, 10, 47**
O'Casey, Sean **1, 5, 9, 11, 15**
O'Connor, Frank **14, 23**
O'Faolain, Julia **6, 19, 47**
O'Faoláin, Seán **1, 7, 14, 32**
O'Flaherty, Liam **5, 34**
Paulin, Tom **37**
Rodgers, W. R. **7**
Simmons, James **43**
Trevor, William **7, 9, 14, 25,**
White, Terence de Vere **49**

ISRAELI
Agnon, S. Y. **4, 8, 14**
Amichai, Yehuda **9, 22**
Appelfeld, Aharon **23, 47**
Kaniuk, Yoram **19**
Levin, Meyer **7**
Megged, Aharon **9**
Oz, Amos **5, 8, 11, 27, 33, 54**
Shamas, Anton **55**
Yehoshua, A. B. **13, 31**

ITALIAN
Antonioni, Michelangelo **20**
Bacchelli, Riccardo **19**
Bassani, Giorgio **9**
Bertolucci, Bernardo **16**
Buzzati, Dino **36**
Calvino, Italo **5, 8, 11, 22, 33, 39**
De Sica, Vittorio **20**
Eco, Umberto **28**

Nationality Index

Fallaci, Oriana **11**
Fellini, Federico **16**
Fo, Dario **32**
Gadda, Carlo Emilio **11**
Ginzburg, Natalia **5, 11, 54**
Giovene, Andrea **7**
Landolfi, Tommaso **11, 49**
Levi, Primo **37, 50**
Luzi, Mario **13**
Montale, Eugenio **7, 9, 18**
Morante, Elsa **8, 47**
Moravia, Alberto **2, 7, 11, 18, 27, 46**
Palazzeschi, Aldo **11**
Pasolini, Pier Paolo **20, 37**
Piccolo, Lucio **13**
Quasimodo, Salvatore **10**
Silone, Ignazio **4**
Ungaretti, Giuseppe **7, 11, 15**
Visconti, Luchino **16**
Vittorini, Elio **6, 9, 14**
Wertmüller, Lina **16**

JAMAICAN
Bennett, Louise **28**
Cliff, Jimmy **21**
Marley, Bob **17**
Thelwell, Michael **22**

JAPANESE
Abé, Kōbō **8, 22, 53**
Enchi, Fumiko **31**
Endo, Shusaku **7, 14, 19, 54**
Ibuse, Masuji **22**
Ichikawa, Kon **20**
Ishiguro, Kazuo **27**
Kawabata, Yasunari **2, 5, 9, 18**
Kurosawa, Akira **16**
Mishima, Yukio **2, 4, 6, 9, 27**
Ōe, Kenzaburō **10, 36**
Oshima, Nagisa **20**
Ozu, Yasujiro **16**
Shiga, Naoya **33**
Tanizaki, Jun'ichirō **8, 14, 28**

KENYAN
Ngugi wa Thiong'o **3, 7, 13, 36**

MEXICAN
Fuentes, Carlos **3, 8, 10, 13, 22, 41**
Ibargüengoitia, Jorge **37**
López Portillo, José **46**
López y Fuentes, Gregorio **32**
Paz, Octavio **3, 4, 6, 10, 19, 51**
Rulfo, Juan **8**

MOROCCAN
Arrabal, Fernando **2, 9, 18**

NEW ZEALAND
Adcock, Fleur **41**
Ashton-Warner, Sylvia **19**
Baxter, James K. **14**
Frame, Janet **2, 3, 6, 22**
Gee, Maurice **29**
Hilliard, Noel **15**
Hulme, Keri **39**
Ihimaera, Witi **46**
Marsh, Ngaio **7, 53**
Sargeson, Frank **31**

NICARAGUAN
Cardenal, Ernesto **31**

NIGERIAN
Achebe, Chinua **1, 3, 5, 7, 11, 26, 51**
Clark, John Pepper **38**
Ekwensi, Cyprian **4**
Emecheta, Buchi **14, 48**
Okigbo, Christopher **25**
Soyinka, Wole **3, 5, 14, 36, 44**
Tutuola, Amos **5, 14, 29**

NORWEGIAN
Friis-Baastad, Babbis **12**
Heyerdahl, Thor **26**

PAKISTANI
Ghose, Zulfikar **42**

PALESTINIAN
Bakshi, Ralph **26**

PARAGUAYAN
Roa Bastos, Augusto **45**

PERUVIAN
Arguedas, José María **10, 18**
Goldemberg, Isaac **52**
Vargas Llosa, Mario **3, 6, 9, 10, 15, 31, 42**

POLISH
Agnon, S. Y. **4, 8, 14**
Becker, Jurek **7, 19**
Bermant, Chaim **40**
Bienek, Horst **7, 11**
Dąbrowska, Maria **15**
Gombrowicz, Witold **4, 7, 11, 49**
Herbert, Zbigniew **9, 43**
Konwicki, Tadeusz **8, 28, 54**
Kosinski, Jerzy **1, 2, 3, 6, 10, 15, 53**
Lem, Stanislaw **8, 15, 40**
Miłosz, Czesław **5, 11, 22, 31**
Mrozek, Sławomir **3, 13**
Polanski, Roman **16**
Różewicz, Tadeusz **9, 23**
Singer, Isaac Bashevis **1, 3, 6, 9, 11, 15, 23, 38**
Skolimowski, Jerzy **20**
Wajda, Andrzej **16**
Wittlin, Joseph **25**
Wojciechowska, Maia **26**

PORTUGUESE
Miguéis, José Rodrigues **10**

PUERTO RICAN
Piñero, Miguel **4, 55**
Sánchez, Luis Rafael **23**

RUMANIAN
Appelfeld, Aharon **23, 47**
Celan, Paul **10, 19, 53**
Codrescu, Andrei **46**
Ionesco, Eugène **1, 4, 6, 9, 11, 15, 41**
Rezzori, Gregor von **25**
Tzara, Tristan **47**

RUSSIAN
Akhmadulina, Bella **53**
Akhmatova, Anna **11, 25**
Aksyonov, Vasily **22, 37**
Aleshkovsky, Yuz **44**
Almedingen, E. M. **12**
Brodsky, Joseph **4, 6, 13, 36, 50**
Ehrenburg, Ilya **18, 34**

Eliade, Mircea **19**
Gary, Romain **25**
Goldberg, Anatol **34**
Grade, Chaim **10**
Grossman, Vasily **41**
Iskander, Fazil **47**
Ivask, Ivar **14**
Kaletski, Alexander **39**
Krotkov, Yuri **19**
Nabokov, Vladimir **1, 2, 3, 6, 8, 11, 15, 23, 44, 46**
Olesha, Yuri **8**
Pasternak, Boris **7, 10, 18**
Paustovsky, Konstantin **40**
Rahv, Philip **24**
Rand, Ayn **3, 30, 44**
Ratushinskaya, Irina **54**
Rybakov, Anatoli **23, 53**
Shalamov, Varlam **18**
Sholokhov, Mikhail **7, 15**
Sinyavsky, Andrei **8**
Solzhenitsyn, Aleksandr I. **1, 2, 4, 7, 9, 10, 18, 24, 26, 34**
Strugatskii, Arkadii **27**
Strugatskii, Boris **27**
Trifonov, Yuri **45**
Troyat, Henri **23**
Voinovich, Vladimir **10, 49**
Voznesensky, Andrei **1, 15**
Yanovsky, Vassily S. **2, 18**
Yevtushenko, Yevgeny **1, 3, 13, 26, 51**
Yezierska, Anzia **46**
Zaturenska, Marya **6, 11**
Zinoviev, Alexander **19**

SALVADORAN
Argueta, Manlio **31**

SCOTTISH
Banks, Iain **34**
Brown, George Mackay **5, 48**
Cronin, A. J. **32**
Dunn, Douglas **6, 40**
Graham, W. S. **29**
Gray, Alasdair **41**
Hunter, Mollie **21**
Jenkins, Robin **52**
MacBeth, George **2, 5, 9**
MacCaig, Norman **36**
MacDiarmid, Hugh **2, 4, 11, 19**
MacInnes, Helen **27, 39**
MacLean, Alistair **3, 13, 50**
McIlvanney, William **42**
Morgan, Edwin **31**
Spark, Muriel **2, 3, 5, 8, 13, 18, 40**
Taylor, C. P. **27**
Walker, David Harry **14**
Young, Andrew **5**

SENGALESE
Senghor, Léopold Sédar **54**

SICILIAN
Sciascia, Leonardo **8, 9, 41**

SOMALIAN
Farah, Nuruddin **53**

SOUTH AFRICAN
Breytenbach, Breyten **23, 37**
Brink, André **18, 36**
Brutus, Dennis **43**

Coetzee, J. M.   23, 33
Fugard, Athol   5, 9, 14, 25, 40
Fugard, Sheila   48
Gordimer, Nadine   3, 5, 7, 10, 18, 33, 51
Harwood, Ronald   32
Head, Bessie   25
Hope, Christopher   52
La Guma, Alex   19
Millin, Sarah Gertrude   49
Mphahlele, Ezekiel   25
Mtwa, Percy   47
Nkosi, Lewis   45
Paton, Alan   4, 10, 25, 55
Plomer, William   4, 8
Prince, F. T.   22
Smith, Wilbur   33
Tolkien, J. R. R.   1, 2, 3, 8, 12, 38
Van der Post, Laurens   5
Vorster, Gordon   34

SPANISH
Alberti, Rafael   7
Aleixandre, Vicente   9, 36
Alonso, Dámaso   14
Azorín   11
Benet, Juan   28
Buero Vallejo, Antonio   15, 46
Buñuel, Luis   16
Casona, Alejandro   49
Cela, Camilo José   4, 13
Cernuda, Luis   54
Del Castillo, Michel   38
Delibes, Miguel   8, 18
Donoso, José   4, 8, 11, 32
Espriu, Salvador   9
Gironella, José María   11
Gómez de la Serna, Ramón   9
Goytisolo, Juan   5, 10, 23
Guillén, Jorge   11
Matute, Ana María   11
Otero, Blas de   11
Rodríguez, Claudio   10
Saura, Carlos   20
Sender, Ramón   8

SWEDISH
Beckman, Gunnel   26
Bergman, Ingmar   16
Ekelöf, Gunnar   27
Johnson, Eyvind   14
Lagerkvist, Pär   7, 10, 13, 54
Martinson, Harry   14
Tranströmer, Tomas   52
Wahlöö, Per   7
Weiss, Peter   3, 15, 51

SWISS
Cendrars, Blaise   18
Dürrenmatt, Friedrich   1, 4, 8, 11, 15, 43
Federspiel, J. F.   42
Frisch, Max   3, 9, 14, 18, 32, 44
Hesse, Hermann   1, 2, 3, 6, 11, 17, 25
Pinget, Robert   7, 13, 37
Von Däniken, Erich   30

TRINIDADIAN
Lovelace, Earl   51
Naipaul, Shiva   32, 39
Naipaul, V. S.   4, 7, 9, 13, 18, 37

TURKISH
Hikmet, Nâzim   40

Kemal, Yashar   14, 29

URUGUAYAN
Onetti, Juan Carlos   7, 10

WELSH
Abse, Dannie   7, 29
Dahl, Roald   1, 6, 18
Davies, Rhys   23
Francis, Dick   2, 22, 42
Hughes, Richard   1, 11
Humphreys, Emyr   47
Jones, David   2, 4, 7, 13, 42
Levinson, Deirdre   49
Llewellyn, Richard   7
Mathias, Roland   45
Norris, Leslie   14
Roberts, Kate   15
Rubens, Bernice   19, 31
Thomas, R. S.   6, 13, 48
Watkins, Vernon   43
Williams, Emlyn   15

WEST INDIAN
Armatrading, Joan   17
Césaire, Aimé   19, 32
Dabydeen, David   34
Edwards, Gus   43
Glissant, Édouard   10
Guy, Rosa   26
James, C. L. R.   33
Kincaid, Jamaica   43
Rhys, Jean   2, 4, 6, 14, 19, 51
Walcott, Derek   2, 4, 9, 14, 25, 42

YUGOSLAVIAN
Andrić, Ivo   8
Ćosić, Dobrica   14
Krleža, Miroslav   8
Popa, Vasko   19
Simic, Charles   6, 9, 22, 49
Tesich, Steve   40

Nationality Index

"A la recherche d'un nouveau mode d'expression" (de Man) **55**:422

A une sérénité crispée (To a Tensed Serenity) (Char) **55**:288

"Absences" (MacEwen) **55**:168

"Afterimages" (MacEwen) **55**:163-64, 169

"After-Thoughts" (MacEwen) **55**:163-64, 167, 169

Afterworlds (MacEwen) **55**:163-69

Ah, but Your Land Is Beautiful (Paton) **55**:311

"al Khala" ("The Wilderness") (Mahfūz) **55**:188

Allegories of Reading (de Man) **55**:384, 386, 391, 400, 406, 409-10, 415

al-Liss wa'l-kilāb (The Thief and the Dogs) (Mahfūz) **55**:174, 181, 183

"al-Majnūna" ("The Mad One") (Mahfūz) **55**:176

al-Qāhira al-jadīda (Mahfūz) **55**:176

al-Sukkariyya (Mahfūz) **55**:171-72, 175-76

al-Tarīq (The Search; The Way) (Mahfūz) **55**:174, 181-82

An Alternate Life (Duncan) **55**:295

al-Thulatthiyya (The Trilogy; The Cairo Trilogy) (Mahfūz) **55**:171, 174, 181-85, 187-88

"al-Wahj al-ākhar" ("The Other Face") (Mahfūz) **55**:172-74

"Ambrose Syme" (McGrath) **55**:74, 76

"American Beauty" (Canin) **55**:36, 38-9

An American Memory (Larsen) **55**:69-72

"Anarchy" (MacEwen) **55**:163, 168

"Ancient Slang" (MacEwen) **55**:163, 167

And the Air Didn't Answer (Kerr) **55**:377-80

"The Angel" (McGrath) **55**:73-75

"The Anonymous Telephone Caller" (MacEwen) **55**:168

"Apocalypse" (MacEwen) **55**:163-64, 167-69

Arabeskot (Arabesques) (Shammas) **55**:85-91

Arabesques
See *Arabeskot*

The Armies of the Moon (MacEwen) **55**:163, 166

"The Arnold Crombeck Story" (McGrath) **55**:76

Aromates chasseurs (Aromatic Hunters) (Char) **55**:285, 288

Aromatic Hunters
See *Aromates chasseurs*

Arsenal (Char) **55**:287

As Testimony (Duncan) **55**:293

Ash-Wednesday (Eliot) **55**:350, 362, 371

"The Autopsy Room" (Carver) **55**:276

The Autumn of the Patriarch (García Márquez) **55**:139, 144-47

Autumn Quail (Mahfūz) **55**:181

"Avatars" (MacEwen) **55**:163-64, 167, 169

"The Awakening of the Mummy"
See "Yaqzat al mūmyā"

Awlād hāretnā (The Children of Gabalawi; Children of Our Neighborhood) (Mahfūz) **55**:171-76, 178, 183, 185

Bayna 'l-qasrayn (Mahfūz) **55**:171

The Bean Trees (Kingsolver) **55**:64-8

The Beggar (Mahfūz) **55**:181

The Beginning and the End
See *Bidāya wa-nihāya*

Beloved (Morrison) **55**:195-213

Bending the Bow (Duncan) **55**:293, 295

Between Planets (Heinlein) **55**:302

"Beyond This Horizon" (Heinlein) **55**:304

Bidāya wa-nihāya (The Beginning and the End) (Mahfūz) **55**:173-74, 181-82

"The Big Front Yard" (Simak) **55**:320

"Big Mama's Funeral" (García Márquez) **55**:146

The Black Cat Tavern
See *Khammārat al-qitt al-aswad*

"The Black Hand of the Raj" (McGrath) **55**:73

"Blackbird Pie" (Carver) **55**:273, 275, 284

Blindness and Insight (de Man) **55**:384, 386, 396, 400-01, 409, 413-14

Bliss (Carey) **55**:114, 117

"Blood and Water" (McGrath) **55**:73-4, 76

Blood and Water and Other Tales (McGrath) **55**:73-7

"Blood Disease" (McGrath) **55**:73, 75

"Blowups Happen" (Heinlein) **55**:302

The Bluest Eye (Morrison) **55**:196, 200, 205, 207-09

Boiler Room (Corrigan) **55**:377

"The Boot's Tale" (McGrath) **55**:74

"The Botanic Gardens" (Freeman) **55**:55, 57

"Boxes" (Carver) **55**:274, 277

"The Brass Ring" (Carver) **55**:279

Budding Prospects: A Pastoral (Boyle) **55**:106, 111

"Burbank with a Baedeker: Bleistein with a Cigar" (Eliot) **55**:346-48, 355, 364-66, 370-71

The Burning Hills (L'Amour) **55**:306, 308

"Burnt Norton" (Eliot) **55**:367-68, 374

"But" (MacEwen) **55**:164-66

"By His Bootstraps" (Heinlein) **55**:302

The Cairo Trilogy
See *al-Thulatthiyya*

"Camp Rose" (Freeman) **55**:56-7

"The Carnival Dog, the Buyer of Diamonds" (Canin) **55**:36

"Carrier" (Meredith) **55**:192

The Cat and the Blackbird (Duncan) **55**:293

The Cat Who Walks Through Walls (Heinlein) **55**:301, 303

"Cathedral" (Carver) **55**:274, 276, 278, 281-82

"The Chance" (Carey) **55**:114

Chants de la Balandrane (Char) **55**:288

Chatting on the Nile (Mahfūz) **55**:183

The Cheer (Meredith) **55**:193

The Children of Gabalawi
See *Awlād hāretnā*

Children of Our Neighborhood
See *Awlād hāretnā*

A Choice of Gods (Simak) **55**:320

Chronicle of a Death Foretold (García Márquez) **55**:134

Cien años de soledad (*One Hundred Years of Solitude*) (García Márquez) **55**:134, 136, 138-39, 144-47

"Circulation of the Song" (Duncan) **55**:298-99

"Citizen of the Galaxy" (Heinlein) **55**:301

City (Simak) **55**:319-21

"Clearfield" (Freeman) **55**:57-8

Cloud Nine (Churchill) **55**:122

The Cocktail Party (Eliot) **55**:346, 352-53, 360, 367

"A Coin for the Ferryman" (MacEwen) **55**:169

"Collectors" (Carver) **55**:281

Common Presence
See *Commune présence*

Complicity (Cooke) **55**:46-8

"Contemporary Trends in French Literature" (de Man) **55**:421

The Cosmic Engineers (Simak) **55**:319

Country You Can't Walk In (Kelly) **55**:159

"Coventry" (Heinlein) **55**:302

Critical Writings, 1953-1978 (de Man) **55**:413-14

"Criticism and Crisis" (de Man) **55**:397

Cry, the Beloved Country (Paton) **55**:310-14

The Dance and the Railroad (Hwang) **55**:151-52

"Dante Etudes" (Duncan) **55**:298

"Daynights" (MacEwen) **55**:164

"The Death of a Mormon Elder" (Freeman) **55**:57-8

Derivations (Duncan) **55**:294

"Desertion" (Simak) **55**:320

"Le destin de la Flandre" (de Man) **55**:423

Destination Moon (Heinlein) **55**:304

"Dirge" (Eliot) **55**:366

"Distress Sale" (Carver) **55**:273

"The Door into Summer" (Heinlein) **55**:304

Double Star (Heinlein) **55**:300, 303

A Dream Like Mine (Kelly) **55**:156-61

Driving Miss Daisy (Uhry) **55**:264-67

"The Dry Salvages" (Eliot) **55**:347, 362

Earth Walk (Meredith) **55**:193

Earthlight (MacEwen) **55**:163

"Earwigs" (Carver) **55**:276

"East Coker" (Eliot) **55**:374

"Eaux-meres" (Char) **55**:289

"The E(rot)ic Potato" (McGrath) **55**:73-4

"Elephant" (Carver) **55**:278

"Emperor of the Air" (Canin) **55**:35-6, 38

"Errand" (Carver) **55**:278, 283

Eulogy for a Small Time Thief (Piñero) **55**:316-18

Every Form of Refuge Has Its Price (Piñero) **55**:316-18

Expanded Universe: The New Worlds of Robert A. Heinlein (Heinlein) **55**:301, 303

"Family Attractions" (Freeman) **55**:55

Family Devotions (Hwang) **55**:151-52

The Family Reunion (Eliot) **55**:346, 356

Farmer in the Sky (Heinlein) **55**:302

Farnham's Freehold (Heinlein) **55**:303

"The Father" (Carver) **55**:275

"Feathers" (Carver) **55**:278

Fen (Churchill) **55**:126

Fenêtres dormantes et porte sur la toit (Char) **55**:288

Feuillets d'Hypnos (*Leaves of Hypnos*) (Char) **55**:287-89

Fictive Certainties (Duncan) **55**:294-95

The Fire-Eaters (MacEwen) **55**:164

"Fires" (Carver) **55**:283

The First Decade (Duncan) **55**:294

"Five Accounts of a Monogamous Man" (Meredith) **55**:191

FOB (Hwang) **55**:152

Four Quartets (Eliot) **55**:346, 350, 353, 360, 362, 374

Friday (Heinlein) **55**:303

"The Furious Seasons" (Carver) **55**:275

Furious Seasons (Carver) **55**:275

"Gazebo" (Carver) **55**:275

"Genesis 2" (MacEwen) **55**:167

"Gerontion" (Eliot) **55**:346, 348, 351-52, 355, 364-65, 371, 374

"The Gift" (Carver) **55**:273

Le gisant mis en lumiere (Char) **55**:288-89

Glory Road (Heinlein) **55**:303

Goblin Reservation (Simak) **55**:320

God's World (Mahfūz) **55**:183, 188

"Going Out to Sea" (Freeman) **55**:55, 58

"Good Night Mr. James" (Simak) **55**:320

"Gospel" (Piñero) **55**:317

"The Grand Dance" (MacEwen) **55**:165

"The Green Hills of Earth" (Heinlein) **55**:301-02

Grimus (Rushdie) **55**:216, 218

Ground Work: Before the War (Duncan) **55**:290-91, 293, 295, 298

Ground Work II: In the Dark (Duncan) **55**:293-95

"Growltiger's Last Stand" (Eliot) **55**:347

"Gulf" (Heinlein) **55**:302-03

H.D. Book (Duncan) **55**:291

"Ha' Penny" (Paton) **55**:313

"A Haircut" (Carver) **55**:273

The Hammer with No Master
See *Le marteau sans maître*

Hams al-junūn (*The Whisper of Madness*) (Mahfūz) **55**:174, 176

"Hand of a Wanker" (McGrath) **55**:73, 75

"Handwritten News" (Char) **55**:289

Hardcover (Shammas) **55**:86

The Haunted Mesa (L'Amour) **55**:307-08

Hazard, the Painter (Meredith) **55**:193

"Hazard's Optimism" (Meredith) **55**:192

Heller in Pink Tights (L'Amour) **55**:306

A Heritage of Stars (Simak) **55**:320

"The Hollow Men" (Eliot) **55**:346, 350-51, 373

Hondo (L'Amour) **55**:306-08

How the West Was Won (L'Amour) **55**:308

Hypnos Walking (Char) **55**:287

I Do Remember the Fall (Kelly) **55**:159

I Will Fear No Evil (Heinlein) **55**:303

"If This Goes On" (Heinlein) **55**:302, 304

"The Illiterate" (Meredith) **55**:192

Illywhacker (Carey) **55**:112-18

"Imaginary Homelands" (Rushdie) **55**:241

"In Loving Memory of the Late Author of Dream Songs" (Meredith) **55**:193

In Search of J. D. Salinger (Hamilton) **55**:334-37, 341

"Intimacy" (Carver) **55**:275, 277

"The Inward Generation" (de Man) **55**:414

"It Sure Is Cold Here at Night" (Freeman) **55**:57

"The Jain Bird Hospital in Delhi" (Meredith) **55**:192

"Jean's TV" (Carver) **55**:276

"The Jews and Contemporary Literature"
See "Les Juifs dans la littérature actuelle"

"Jews in Contemporary Literature"
See "Les Juifs dans la littérature actuelle"

"Jews in Present-Day Literature"
See "Les Juifs dans la littérature actuelle"

"Jews in Today's Literature"
See "Les Juifs dans la littérature actuelle"

Job: A Comedy of Justice (Heinlein) **55**:303

Journey Continued (Paton) **55**:311, 314

"Journey of the Magi" (Eliot) **55**:374

Jubal Sackett (L'Amour. Louis) **55**:306-08

"Les Juifs dans la littérature actuelle" ("The Jews and Contemporary Literature"; "Jews in Contemporary Literature"; "Jews in Present-Day Literature"; "Jews in Today's Literature") (de Man) **55**:383-84, 386, 398, 403-04, 408, 412, 419-20, 422

Khammārat al-qitt al-aswad (*The Black Cat Tavern*) (Mahfūz) **55**:174, 176, 188

Knowledge and Experience in the Philosophy of F. H. Bradley (Eliot) **55**:364

Last of the Breed (L'Amour) **55**:306-07

"Late Night with Fog and Horses" (Carver) **55**:273

Leafstorm (García Márquez) **55**:138

Leaves of Hypnos
See *Feuillets d'Hypnos*

"Let Me Make This Perfectly Clear" (MacEwen) **55**:166-67

"The Letter" (MacEwen) **55**:168

The Letters of T. S. Eliot: Volume One, 1898-1922 (Eliot) **55**:352-55, 359, 362, 369

"Letters to Josef in Jerusalem" (MacEwen) **55**:163-65, 167-69

"The Library Is on Fire" (Char) **55**:289

"Lies" (Canin) **55**:39

"Lifeline" (Heinlein) **55**:300, 302

"The Lightning Speed of the Past" (Carver) **55**:275

"Literary History and Literary Modernity" (de Man) **55**:384, 386, 396

"Little Gidding" (Eliot) **55**:346, 353, 360, 366, 374

"Logic of Empire" (Heinlein) **55**:302

The Lonesome Gods (L'Amour) **55**:308

"The Lost Explorer" (McGrath) **55**:73

Love in the Time of Cholera (García Márquez) **55**:134-40, 142-48

Love Letter from an Impossible Land (Meredith) **55**:193

"The Love Song of J. Alfred Prufrock" (Eliot) **55**:351-52, 371, 374

"Lush Triumphant" (McGrath) **55**:75

M. Butterfly (Hwang) **55**:150-55

"The Mad One"
See "al-Majnūna"

"Magic, Inc." (Heinlein) **55**:302

"The Man with Three Violins" (MacEwen) **55**:164

"Marina" (Eliot) **55**:346, 374

"Marmilion" (McGrath) **55**:74, 76

Le marteau sans maître (*The Hammer with No Master*; *The Masterless Hammer*) (Char) **55**:287-88
The Masterless Hammer
See *Le marteau sans maître*
Les Matinaux (Char) **55**:288
"Me and the Runner" (MacEwen) **55**:164
"The Meadow" (Carver) **55**:275
Medea at Kolchis (Duncan) **55**:293
"Menudo" (Carver) **55**:278
"The Metaphysical Poets" (Eliot) **55**:346
Methuselah's Children (Heinlein) **55**:302, 304
Midaq Alley
See *Zuqaq al-Midaqq*
The Middle of the Night
See *Qalb al-layl*
A Midnight Moon at the Greasy Spoon (Piñero) **55**:317-18
Midnight's Children (Rushdie) **55**:216-19, 223-25, 253-54, 263
"Migration" (Carver) **55**:275
Miramar (Mahfūz) **55**:177-79, 181, 183, 185
"Misfit" (Heinlein) **55**:302
The Moon Is a Harsh Mistress (Heinlein) **55**:300, 303
Moulin premier (Char) **55**:288
Murder in the Cathedral (Eliot) **55**:372
"My Mother Would Be a Falconress" (Duncan) **55**:298
The Mysteries of Pittsburgh (Chabon) **55**:41-5
"Neighbor" (Simak) **55**:320
"Neighbors" (Carver) **55**:277, 279-81
A New Path to the Waterfall (Carver) **55**:279-80
"Niagara Daredevil, 37, Buried near the Falls" (MacEwen) **55**:168
Night over Day over Night (Watkins) **55**:92-5
No Man's Land (Shammas) **55**:86
No One Writes to the Colonel (García Márquez) **55**:140
"The Noise of a Match" (Char) **55**:288
The Notebooks of Lazarus Long (Heinlein) **55**:303
Le nu perdu, 1964-1970 (Char) **55**:288
La nuit talismanique (*Talismanic Night*) (Char) **55**:287-88
The Number of the Beast (Heinlein) **55**:303
"The Nuptial Countenance"
See "Le visage nuptial"
Oeuvres complètes (Char) **55**:288
Of the War: Passages (Duncan) **55**:293
Old Possum's Book of Practical Cats (Eliot) **55**:354
"One Arab Flute" (MacEwen) **55**:163
One Hundred Years of Solitude
See *Cien años de soledad*
"1958" (MacEwen) **55**:167
The Only Ones Left
See *Seuls demeurants*
The Open Sea (Meredith) **55**:193
The Opening of the Field (Duncan) **55**:292-93, 295, 299
"Orders" (Duncan) **55**:297
"Orion Iroquois" (Char) **55**:285
Oscar and Lucinda (Carey) **55**:112-19
"The Other Face"
See "al-Wahj al-ākhar"
Our New Front Yard (Simak) **55**:320
Owners (Churchill) **55**:126
Paris Trout (Dexter) **55**:129-32
La parole en archipel (Char) **55**:288
"Partial Accounts" (Meredith) **55**:191

Partial Accounts: New and Selected Poems (Meredith) **55**:190-93
Passages 24 (Duncan) **55**:297-98
"Pastoral" (Carver) **55**:279
"The Pen" (Carver) **55**:276
"The Perfect Critic" (Eliot) **55**:356
"Pitch Memory" (Canin) **55**:37-8
Platitudes (Ellis) **55**:50-4
Podkayne of Mars (Heinlein) **55**:303
Poems (Eliot) **55**:350
"Poems from the Margins of Thom Gunn's *Moly*" (Duncan) **55**:298
Poems of René Char (Char) **55**:287
"Polaris, or Gulag Nightscapes" (MacEwen) **55**:164-65
"Pontoniers"
See "Pontonniers"
"Portrait of a Lady" (Eliot) **55**:346, 362, 374
"Powder Monkey" (Carver) **55**:275
"Pretend We're French" (Freeman) **55**:57
Prufrock and Other Observations (Eliot) **55**:350, 352, 354-55, 374
The Puppet Masters (Heinlein) **55**:303
Put Yourself in My Shoes (Carver) **55**:280
Qalb al-layl (*The Middle of the Night*) (Mahfūz) **55**:175
Qasr al-shawq (Mahfūz) **55**:171, 174
Ralentir travaux (*Slacken Labors*) (Char) **55**:286
Recherche de la base et du sommet (*Search for the Base and the Summit*) (Char) **55**:289
Red Planet (Heinlein) **55**:302
"Requiem" (Heinlein) **55**:302
The Resistance to Theory (de Man) **55**:403-05, 409-10
Retour amont (Char) **55**:288
"Rhapsody on a Windy Night" (Eliot) **55**:350, 374
"The Rhetoric of Blindness" (de Man) **55**:401
The Rhetoric of Romanticism (de Man) **55**:400, 404
"The Rhetoric of Temporality" (de Man) **55**:410
Ring around the Sun (Simak) **55**:320
"The River" (Carver) **55**:276
"The Roads Must Roll" (Heinlein) **55**:302, 304
The Robber Bridegroom (Uhry) **55**:265-66
The Rock (Eliot) **55**:348
Rocket Ship Galileo (Heinlein) **55**:302
The Rolling Stones (Heinlein) **55**:302
Roots and Branches (Duncan) **55**:293, 295
"Rule 18" (Simak) **55**:321
The Sacred Wood (Eliot) **55**:352
The Satanic Verses (Rushdie) **55**:215-28, 230-51, 253-56, 258-59, 261-63
The Search
See *al-Tarīq*
Search for the Base and the Summit
See *Recherche de la base et du sommet*
"Self" (de Man) **55**:410
Seniority (Ziegenhagen) **55**:377-80
Serious Money (Churchill) **55**:121-27
Seuls demeurants (*The Only Ones Left*) (Char) **55**:287-88
"A Seventeenth Century Suite" (Duncan) **55**:298
The Shadow-Maker (MacEwen) **55**:163, 165
Shalako (L'Amour) **55**:308
Shame (Rushdie) **55**:216-19, 224, 253, 263
Ships and Other Figures (Meredith) **55**:193
Short Eyes (Piñero) **55**:316-18

"Simile" (Meredith) **55**:192
"Sinew" (Carver) **55**:276
"The Skewer" (McGrath) **55**:73, 75-6
Skirmish: The Great Short Fiction of Clifford D. Simak (Simak) **55**:319
Slacken Labors
See *Ralentir travaux*
"Slow Pace of the Future" (Char) **55**:288
"Solution Unsatisfactory" (Heinlein) **55**:302-03
Song of Solomon (Morrison) **55**:195-96, 200, 205, 207-08, 210
"Sonnet on Rare Animals" (Meredith) **55**:192
Space Cadet (Heinlein) **55**:302
"The Star Beast" (Heinlein) **55**:301, 303
"Star Food" (Canin) **55**:36-8
"Star Lummox" (Heinlein) **55**:303
Starman Jones (Heinlein) **55**:301-02
Starship Troopers (Heinlein) **55**:303
"Stones and Angels" (MacEwen) **55**:165
Straight from the Ghetto (Piñero) **55**:317
Stranger in a Strange Land (Heinlein) **55**:300-04
Stranger on Horseback (L'Amour) **55**:308
The Structure of Rime (Duncan) **55**:297-98
"Styx" (Duncan) **55**:295-96
Sula (Morrison) **55**:196, 205, 207-08
The Sun Always Shines for the Cool (Piñero) **55**:316-18
Sweeney Agonistes (Eliot) **55**:346-47, 350-51, 369, 371
"Sweeney among the Nightingales" (Eliot) **55**:364-65
The Swimming-Pool Library (Hollinghurst) **55**:55-63
The T. E. Lawrence Poems (MacEwen) **55**:163
Taht al-mizalla (Mahfūz) **55**:172
Talismanic Night
See *La nuit talismanique*
"Talking Back (to W. H. Auden)" (Meredith) **55**:192
Tar Baby (Morrison) **55**:195-96, 207-08
"Tentation de la permanence" (de Man) **55**:404
"Terror and Erebus" (MacEwen) **55**:163-64, 166, 169
"Testimony on the War in France" (de Man) **55**:384
The Thief and the Dogs
See *al-Liss wa'l-kilāb*
Time and Again (Simak) **55**:320
Time Enough for Love (Heinlein) **55**:303
Time for the Stars (Heinlein) **55**:302
Time Is the Simplest Thing (Simak) **55**:320
"Time Quarry" (Simak) **55**:319
To a Tensed Serenity
See *A une sérénité crispée*
To Sail beyond the Sunset (Heinlein) **55**:303
Top Girls (Churchill) **55**:122, 126-27
Towards the Mountain (Paton) **55**:311, 313-14
"Tradition and the Individual Talent" (Eliot) **55**:347, 356
"Transport" (Meredith) **55**:192
Trilobite, Dinosaur and Man (Simak) **55**:320
The Trilogy
See *al-Thulatthiyya*
The Trotter-Nama (Sealy) **55**:78-83
"The Truth and Life of Myth" (Duncan) **55**:295, 298
"Tuesday Siesta" (García Márquez) **55**:148
Tunnel in the Sky (Heinlein) **55**:302

Tupelo Nights (Bradley)   **55**:31-4
Ultramarine (Carver)   **55**:275
"Universe" (Heinlein)   **55**:304
"Vacuum Genesis" (MacEwen)   **55**:163
"The Venice Poem" (Duncan)   **55**:292
"A View on Contemporary German Fiction"
   (de Man)   **55**:420-21
"Le visage nuptial" ("The Nuptial
   Countenance") (Char)   **55**:287
The Visitors (Simak)   **55**:319
"Voir la figure, de Jacques Chardonne"
(de Man)   **55**:420
Les voisinages de Van Gogh (Char)   **55**:288
"Waldo" (Heinlein)   **55**:302-03
The Walking Drum (L'Amour)   **55**:308
Wartime Journalism, 1939-1943 (de Man)
   55:411, 413
The Waste Land (Eliot)   **55**:346-48, 351-56,
   358-60, 362, 366-70, 372, 374
The Way
   See *al-Tarīq*
The Waystation (Simak)   **55**:319-20, 322
"We Are the Nighttime Travelers" (Canin)
   55:35-6, 38-9
"What Is This Movie?" (Freeman)   **55**:57
"What the Doctor Said" (Carver)   **55**:282
"What We Talk About When We Talk About
   Love" (Carver)   **55**:276-77
"Where Are We Now" (Canin)   **55**:38-9
"Where I'm Calling From" (Carver)   **55**:275
The Whisper of Madness
   See *Hams al-junūn*
"The Whisper of Madness"
   See "Hams al-junūn"
"The White Horse" (MacEwen)   **55**:167
"Whoever Was Using This Bed" (Carver)
   55:277
Why Call Them Back from Heaven (Simak)
   55:320
"Why Don't You Dance" (Carver)   **55**:273,
   277
"The Wilderness"
   See "al Khala"
"Will You Please Be Quiet, Please?" (Carver)
   55:280
"Wind" (Carver)   **55**:275
Women and Wallace (Sherman)   **55**:377-80
"World of the Red Sun" (Simak)   **55**:320-21
"The World That Couldn't Be" (Simak)
   55:320
World's End (Boyle)   **55**:106-11
The Worlds of Robert A. Heinlein (Heinlein)
   55:303
"The Wreck of the Thresher" (Meredith)
   55:191
"Yaqzat al mūmyā'" ("The Awakening of the
   Mummy") (Mahfūz)   **55**:174
"The Year of Getting to Know Us" (Canin)
   55:36, 38-9
"The Year of the Jackpot" (Heinlein)   **55**:304
The Years as Catches: First Poems, 1939-1946
   (Duncan)   **55**:293-94
"Yeletov" (Shammas)   **55**:86
"The Yellow House" (MacEwen)   **55**:169
"You Know Me" (MacEwen)   **55**:168
Zuqaq al-Midaqq (*Midaq Alley*) (Mahfūz)
   55:181, 185, 188